Solutions Manual for Physical Chemistry

Solutions Manual for Physical Chemistry

THIRD EDITION

P.W. Atkins

with solutions to introductory problems by
J. Charles Morrow

W. H. Freeman and Company
New York

Printed in the United States of America

ISBN 0-7167-1774-3

3 4 5 6 7 8 9 VB 5 4 3 2 1 0 8 9 8

Preface

The following pages give detailed solutions to almost all the approximately 1400 end-of-chapter Problems in the main text, the exceptions being Problems that ask for a computer program. The solutions to the 300 *Introductory Problems* (designated A here and in the text) have been supplied by Professor Morrow.

All the solutions have been reworked during the preparation of this edition, and all my solutions to the new main problems have been checked by Professor Morrow. Moreover, *all* the solutions have been scrutinized for logic, presentation, and numerical accuracy by Michael Golde of the University of Pittsburgh and Juvencio Robles of the University of North Carolina, Chapel Hill, and their suggestions have also resulted in a reformulation and clarification of some of the questions. I am most grateful to them for the huge amount of valuable work they have done, as users of the *Manual* will be too, I am sure.

The format is as follows. Equations in the main text are referred to as [10.2.6.], etc. Illustrations in the main text are referred to as 'of the text'. All references relate to the third edition of the text. Although BASIC interprets expressions like $a/b \times c$ as $(a/b) \times c$, the convention here is that $a/b \times c = a/(b \times c)$. All graphs have been plotted with dimensionless coordinates by plotting, for example, the dimensionless quantity p/kPa. As in the main text, in this edition I adopt 1 M = 1 mol dm^{-3} for, even though M is outside SI, its use greatly simplifies the appearance of expressions. As explained in the text, the standard pressure adopted is $p^{\ominus} = 1$ bar $= 10^5$ N m^{-2} exactly. The symbol $\mathcal{T}$ stands for 298.15 K exactly.

I am grateful to everyone who has contributed helpful comments, and would like to single out for thanks Professor L. Epstein of the University of Pittsburgh who made very extensive, detailed, and useful comments. I would also like to record a special word of thanks to the typesetters, who had to cope with an extraordinarily difficult manuscript.

Oxford
1985

P. W. A.

Contents

PART 1: EQUILIBRIUM

1. The properties of gases

A1.1 $p_i = p_f V_f / V_i$ [1.1.3]

(a) $p_i = (3.78 \times 10^3\,\text{Torr})\,(4.65\,\text{dm}^3)/(4.65\,\text{dm}^3 + 2.20\,\text{dm}^3) = \underline{2.57 \times 10^3\,\text{Torr.}}$

(b) $p_i = 2.57 \times 10^3\,\text{Torr}/(760\,\text{Torr/atm}) = \underline{3.38\,\text{atm.}}$

A1.2 $T_f = T_i(V_f/V_i)$ [1.1.5]

$= (340\,\text{K})\,(1.18/1) = \underline{401\,\text{K.}}$

A1.3 $p = nRT/V$ [1.1.1]

$= [(0.255/20.2)\text{mol}]\,[8.31\,\text{J K}^{-1}\,\text{mol}^{-1}]\,[122\,\text{K}]\ (3.00 \times 10^{-3}\,\text{m}^3)^{-1}$

$= 4.27 \times 10^3\,\text{Pa, or } \underline{4.27\,\text{kPa.}}$

A1.4 (a) $V = n_J RT/p_J$ [1.2.3]

$= [(0.225/20.2)\text{mol}]\ [8.31\,\text{J K}^{-1}\,\text{mol}^{-1}]\,[300\,\text{K}]/[(66.5\,\text{Torr})$

$\times (133\,\text{Pa/Torr})] = 3.14 \times 10^{-3}\,\text{m}^3, \text{ or } \underline{3.14\,\text{dm}^3.}$

(b) $p_J = n_J RT/V$ [1.2.3]

$= [(0.175/40.0)\text{mol}]\,[8.31\,\text{J K}^{-1}\,\text{mol}^{-1}]\,[300\,\text{K}]/(3.14 \times 10^{-3}\,\text{m}^3)$

$= 3.47 \times 10^3\,\text{Pa, or } \underline{3.47\,\text{kPa.}}$

(c) $p = (n_A + n_B + n_C)RT/V$ [1.2.1]

$= [(0.320/16.0)\text{mol} + (0.175/40.0)\text{mol} + (0.225/20.2)\text{mol}]$

$\times\ [8.31\,\text{J K}^{-1}\,\text{mol}^{-1}]\ [300\,\text{K}]/(3.14 \times 10^{-3}\,\text{m}^3) = \underline{2.83 \times 10^4\,\text{Pa.}}$

A1.5 $n = pV/RT = (150\,\text{Torr})(133\,\text{Pa/Torr})(10^{-3}\,\text{m}^3)(8.31\,\text{J K}^{-1}\,\text{mol}^{-1})^{-1}$

$\times\ (330\,\text{K})^{-1} = 7.27 \times 10^{-3}\,\text{mol,}$ [1.1.1]

$\text{RMM} = 1.23(7.27 \times 10^{-3})^{-1} = \underline{169.}$

A1.6 (a) $V_m(\text{perfect}) = RT/p$ [1.1.1]

$Z = pV_m/RT = [p/RT]\,[0.88(RT/p)] = \underline{0.88.}$ [Section 1.3(a)]

(b) $V_m = 0.88(RT/p) = (0.88)(8.3\,\text{J K}^{-1}\,\text{mol}^{-1})(250\,\text{K})(15 \times 1.0 \times 10^5\,\text{Pa})^{-1}$

$= 1.2 \times 10^{-3}\,\text{m}^3$ or $\underline{1.2\,\text{dm}^3}$. Attractive forces dominate.

A1.7 $Z = pV_m/RT = 0.86$

$V_m = 0.86(RT/p) = (0.86)(8.3\,\text{J K}^{-1}\,\text{mol}^{-1})(300\,\text{K})(20 \times 1.0 \times 10^5\,\text{Pa})^{-1}$

$= 1.1 \times 10^{-3}\,\text{m}^3\,\text{mol}^{-1}$, or $\underline{1.1\,\text{dm}^3\,\text{mol}^{-1}}$.

(a) $V = (1.1\,\text{dm}^3\,\text{mol}^{-1})(8.2 \times 10^{-3}\,\text{mol}) = 9.0 \times 10^{-3}\,\text{dm}^3$, or $\underline{9.0\,\text{cm}^3}$.

(b) $B = V_m[(pV_m/RT) - 1] = V_m[Z - 1] = (1.1\,\text{dm}^3\,\text{mol}^{-1})(0.86 - 1.00)$

$= \underline{-0.15\,\text{dm}^3\,\text{mol}^{-1}}$. [1.3.2]

A1.8 $T_c = (2/3)(2a/3bR)^{\frac{1}{2}} = (2/3)[12p_c(b/R)] = (2/3)(12p_c)(V_{m,c}/3R)$

$= (2/3)(12)(40.0 \times 1.0 \times 10^5\,\text{Pa})(160 \times 10^{-6}\,\text{m}^3\,\text{mol}^{-1})$

$\times [(3)(8.3\,\text{J K}^{-1}\,\text{mol}^{-1})]^{-1}$

$= \underline{206\,\text{K}}$.

$4\pi r^3/3 = (1/3)(V_{m,c})/N_A$ [1.4.3]

$r = [(4 \times 3.14)^{-1}(160 \times 10^{-6}\,\text{m}^3\,\text{mol}^{-1})(6.02 \times 10^{23}\,\text{mol}^{-1})^{-1}]^{1/3} = \underline{2.77 \times 10^{-10}\,\text{m}}$.

A1.9 (a) $V_m = RT/p = (8.31\,\text{J K}^{-1}\,\text{mol}^{-1})(350\,\text{K})(2.30 \times 1.01 \times 10^5\,\text{Pa})^{-1}$

$= 1.25 \times 10^{-2}\,\text{m}^3\,\text{mol}^{-1}$, or $\underline{12.5\,\text{dm}^3\,\text{mol}^{-1}}$.

(b) $V_m = RT(p + a/V_m^2)^{-1} + b$ [1.4.2] $= (8.31\,\text{J K}^{-1}\,\text{mol}^{-1})(350\,\text{K})$

$\times [2.30\,\text{atm} + (6.49\,\text{atm dm}^6\,\text{mol}^{-2})(12.5\,\text{dm}^3\,\text{mol}^{-1})^{-2}]^{-1}$

$\times [1.01 \times 10^5\,\text{Pa/atm}]^{-1}[10^3\,\text{dm}^3/\text{m}^3] + (5.62 \times 10^{-2}\,\text{dm}^3\,\text{mol}^{-1})$

$= 12.4\,\text{dm}^3\,\text{mol}^{-1}$. Use of $12.4\,\text{dm}^3\,\text{mol}^{-1}$ in the attractive term produces:

$V_m = \underline{12.4\,\text{dm}^3\,\text{mol}^{-1}}$, and the iteration is stopped. [Table 1.3]

A1.10 (a) $T_B = a/bR = (6.493\,\text{dm}^6\,\text{atm mol}^{-2})(5.622 \times 10^{-2}\,\text{dm}^3\,\text{mol}^{-1})^{-1}$

$\times (10^{-3}\,\text{m}^3/\text{dm}^3)(1.013 \times 10^5\,\text{Pa/atm})(8.314\,\text{J K}^{-1}\,\text{mol}^{-1})^{-1}$

$= \underline{1.407 \times 10^3\,\text{K}}$. [1.4.5, Table 1.3]

(b) $4\pi r^3/3 = b/N_A$ [1.4.3, Table 1.3]

$r = [(4 \times 3.14)^{-1}(3)(5.62 \times 10^{-2}\,\text{dm}^3\,\text{mol}^{-1})(10^{-3}\,\text{m}^3/\text{dm}^3)(6.02 \times 10^{23}\,\text{mol}^{-1})^{-1}]^{1/3}$

$= 2.81 \times 10^{-10}\,\text{m}$, or $\underline{0.281\,\text{nm}}$.

1.1 $p_f = (V_i/V_f)p_i$ [1.1.3].

$V_i = 1\ dm^3 = 1000\ cm^3$, $V_f = 100\ cm^3$, $p_i = 1\ atm$.

$p_f = (1000\ cm^3/100\ cm^3) \times (1\ atm) = 10 \times 1\ atm = \underline{10\ atm.}$

1.2 $V_f = (p_i/p_f)V_i$ [1.1.3].

$V_i = 2\ m^3$, $p_i = 755\ Torr$, $p_f =$ (a) 100 Torr, (b) 10 Torr.

(a) $V_f = (755\ Torr/100\ Torr) \times (2\ m^3) = \underline{15\ m^3}$.

(b) $V_f = (755\ Torr/10\ Torr) \times (2\ m^3) = \underline{150\ m^3}$.

1.3 $V_f = (p_i/p_f)V_i$ [1.1.3]; $p_f = \rho g h$ [hydrostatics] + 1 atm.

$V_i = 3\ m^3$, $p_i = 1\ atm$, $\rho = 1.025\ g\ cm^{-3}$, $g = 9.81\ m\ s^{-2}$, $h = 50\ m$.

$p_f = (1.025\ g\ cm^{-3}) \times (9.81\ m\ s^{-2}) \times (50\ m) + 1\ atm = 5.03 \times 10^5\ kg\ m^{-1}\ s^{-2} + 1\ atm$

$= 5.03 \times 10^5\ N\ m^{-2} + 1\ atm = 4.96\ atm + 1\ atm$ [end-paper 1] $\approx 6\ atm$.

$V_f = (1\ atm/6\ atm) \times (3\ m^3) = (1/6) \times 3\ m^3 = \underline{0.5\ m^3}$.

1.4 External pressure: p_i. Pressure at foot of column: $p_f + \rho g h$.

At equilibrium $p_i = p_f + \rho g h$, or $p_f = p_i - \rho g h$.

$\Delta V/V = (V_f - V_i)/V_i = [(p_i/p_f)V_i - V_i]/V_i = (p_i/p_f) - 1$

$= (p_i - p_f)/p_f = \rho g h/p_f \approx \rho g h/p_i$ [$\rho g h \ll p_i$].

$\rho g h = (1.0\ g\ cm^{-3}) \times (9.81\ m\ s^{-2}) \times (15\ cm)$

$= (1.0 \times 10^3\ g\ m^{-3}) \times (9.81\ m\ s^{-2}) \times (0.15\ m) = 1.47 \times 10^3\ N\ m^{-2}$.

$\Delta V/V = (1.47 \times 10^3\ N\ m^{-2})/(1.013 \times 10^5\ N\ m^{-2}) = \underline{0.0145, \text{ or } 1.5 \text{ per cent.}}$

1.5 $T_f = (V_f/V_i)T_i$ [1.1.5].

$V_i = 1\ dm^3$, $V_f = 100\ cm^3 = 0.1\ dm^3$, $T_i = 298\ K$.

$T_f = (0.1\ dm^3/1.0\ dm^3) \times (298\ K) = 0.1 \times (298\ K) \approx \underline{30\ K.}$

1.6 $p_f = (T_f/T_i)p_i$ [1.1.6].

Internal pressure = (quoted pressure) + (atmospheric pressure) [$14.7\ lb\ in^{-2}$].

$p_i = (24\ lb\ in^{-2}) + (14.7\ lb\ in^{-2}) = 39\ lb\ in^{-2}$.

$T_i \mathrel{\hat{=}} -5\ °C$, or 268 K; $T_f \mathrel{\hat{=}} 35\ °C$, or 308 K.

$p_f = (308\ K/268\ K) \times (38\ lb\ in^{-2}) = 43.7\ lb\ in^{-2}$.

$p_f(\text{internal}) = (43.7 - 14.7)\ \text{lb in}^{-2} = \underline{29\ \text{lb in}^{-2}}.$

1.7 Disregard the elasticity of the envelope. $p_i V_i = nRT_i, p_f V_f = nRT_f$ [1.1.1]

$p_i V_i / nRT_i = p_f V_f / nRT_f$, or $p_f = (V_i/V_f)(T_f/T_i)p_i$

$V_f = (4/3)\pi R_f^3,\ V_i = (4/3)\pi R_i^3,\ p_f = (R_i/R_f)^3(T_f/T_i)p_i.$

$R = 1\ \text{m}, R_f = 3\ \text{m}, T_i = 298\ \text{K}, T_f \mathrel{\hat{=}} -20\ °\text{C}$, or $253\ \text{K}, p_i = 1\ \text{atm}.$

$p_f = (1\ \text{m}/3\ \text{m})^3 \times (253\ \text{K}/298\ \text{K}) \times (1\ \text{atm}) = (\tfrac{1}{3})^3 \times (0.849) \times (1\ \text{atm}) = \underline{0.03\ \text{atm.}}$

1.8 $n = M/M_m$ [Box 0.1]; $n/V = M/M_m V = \rho/M_m$ $[\rho = M/V]$.

For a perfect gas, $p = nRT/V = \underline{\rho RT/M_m}$.

For a real gas,

$$p = (nRT/V)\{1 + B'p + \ldots\} = (\rho RT/M_m)\{1 + B'p + \ldots\}$$

$$p/\rho = (RT/M_m) + B'(RT/M_m)p + \ldots$$

Therefore, plot p/ρ against p and expect a straight line with intercept RT/M_m at $p = 0$. Convert p to N m^{-2} using 1 Torr $\hat{=}$ 133.3 N m^{-2} [end-paper 1].

p/Torr	91.74	188.93	277.3	452.8	639.3	760.0
$p/10^5\ \text{Pa}$	0.1223	0.2518	0.3696	0.6036	0.8522	1.0131
$\rho/\text{kg m}^{-3}$	0.225	0.456	0.664	1.062	1.468	1.734
$(p/\rho)/10^5\ \text{m}^2\,\text{s}^{-2}$	0.544	0.552	0.557	0.568	0.581	0.584

These points are plotted in Fig. 1.1, and the limiting behavior is confirmed.

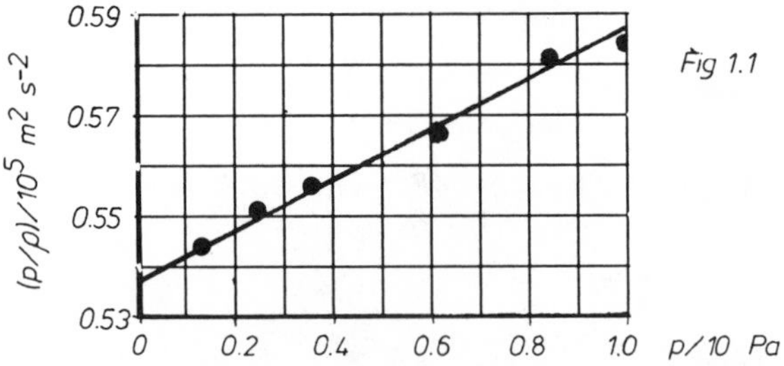

Fig 1.1

The intercept at $p = 0$ is at $(p/\rho)/10^5\ \text{m}^2\,\text{s}^{-2} = 0.540$. Therefore,

$$RT/M_m = 0.540 \times 10^5\ \text{m}^2\,\text{s}^{-2}, \text{ or } M_m = RT/(0.540 \times 10^5\ \text{m}^2\,\text{s}^{-2}).$$

$$M_m = \frac{(8.3144\,\text{J K}^{-1}\,\text{mol}^{-1}) \times (298.15\,\text{K})}{0.540 \times 10^5\,\text{m}^2\,\text{s}^{-2}} = 4.59 \times 10^{-2}\,\text{kg mol}^{-1}\ [\text{J} = \text{kg m}^2\,\text{s}^{-2}]$$

$$= 45.9\,\text{g mol}^{-1};\ \underline{M_r = 45.9.}$$

1.9 $n = pV/RT$ [1.1.1], $V = (4/3)\pi R^3$,

$p = 1\,\text{atm} = 1.013 \times 10^5\,\text{N m}^{-2}$, $T = 298\,\text{K}$, $R = 3\,\text{m}$,

$V = (4/3)\pi(3.0\,\text{m})^3 = 113.1\,\text{m}^3$, $RT = 2.479\,\text{kJ mol}^{-1}$ [end-paper 1].

$$n = \frac{1.013 \times 10^5 \times 113.1}{2.479 \times 10^3} \cdot \frac{\text{N m}^{-2}\,\text{m}^3}{\text{J mol}^{-1}} = \underline{4622\,\text{mol}}\quad [\text{J} = \text{N m}]$$

$M = nM_r\,\text{g mol}^{-1}$ [M = mass of sample] $= (4622\,\text{mol}) \times (2\,\text{g mol}^{-1}) = 9244\,\text{g} = 9.2\,\text{kg}$.

Mass of displaced air $= (113.1\,\text{m}^3) \times (1.22\,\text{kg m}^{-3}) = 138\,\text{kg}$.

Therefore, payload $= 138\,\text{kg} - 9.2\,\text{kg} = \underline{129\,\text{kg}}$.

For helium, $M = 4622\,\text{mol} \times (4.0\,\text{g mol}^{-1})$ [end-paper 4] $= 18.5\,\text{kg}$.

Therefore, payload $= 138\,\text{kg} - 18.5\,\text{kg} = \underline{120\,\text{kg}}$.

At 30,000 ft, 4.6×10^3 mol of gas occupies a volume

$$V = (nRT/p)\ [1.1.1] = \frac{(4.6 \times 10^3\,\text{mol}) \times (8.31\,\text{J K}^{-1}\,\text{mol}^{-1}) \times (230\,\text{K})}{0.28 \times (1.013 \times 10^5\,\text{N m}^{-2})} = 310\,\text{m}^3.$$

Therefore, the mass of displaced air is

$$M_{air} = (310\,\text{m}^3) \times (0.43\,\text{kg m}^{-3}) = 133\,\text{kg}$$

and the payload is $133\,\text{kg} - 9\,\text{kg} = \underline{124\,\text{kg}}$ (hydrogen)

or $133\,\text{kg} - 18\,\text{kg} = \underline{155\,\text{kg}}$ (helium).

Whether or not you and your companion can reach that height depends on your combined mass. The combined mass of two 140 lb people is 127 kg. Don't forget to include the mass of the gondola, envelope, sandwiches, etc. Choose an emaciated companion.

In order to inflate the balloon further you would carry extra hydrogen. Suppose, for simplicity, you carried a further 9.2 kg in a compressed state in the same cylinder as before. The payload would then be 120 kg at sea level. If you got to 30,000 ft, and injected the extra 9.2 kg (4.6×10^3 mol) into the indefinitely extensible envelope, you would stretch it to $2 \times 310\,\text{m}^3$, and so displace 266 kg of air, leaving a payload of 248 kg. You will go up. The same conclusion applies to smaller injections of gas.

1.10 $p = \rho RT/M_m$ [Problem 1.8]; $m = M_m/N_A$ [Box 0.1].

$\rho = M/V = (33.5 \times 10^{-6}\,\text{kg})/(250 \times 10^{-6}\,\text{m}^3) = 0.134\,\text{kg m}^{-3}$.

$p = 152 \times (133.22\,\mathrm{N\,m^{-2}})$ [end-paper 1] $= 2.026 \times 10^4\,\mathrm{N\,m^{-2}}$.

$$M_m = \rho RT/p = \frac{(0.134\,\mathrm{kg\,m^{-3}}) \times (8.3144\,\mathrm{J\,K^{-1}\,mol^{-1}}) \times (298.15\,\mathrm{K})}{(2.026 \times 10^4\,\mathrm{N\,m^{-2}})}$$

$$= 1.64 \times 10^{-2}\,\mathrm{kg\,J\,mol^{-1}/N\,m} = 1.64 \times 10^{-2}\,\mathrm{kg\,mol^{-1}}\ [\mathrm{J} = \mathrm{N\,m}]$$

$$= 16.4\,\mathrm{g\,mol^{-1}};\ \underline{M_r = 16.4.}$$

$m = M_m/N_A = (1.64 \times 10^{-2}\,\mathrm{kg\,mol^{-1}})/(6.022 \times 10^{23}\,\mathrm{mol^{-1}}) = \underline{2.7 \times 10^{-26}\,\mathrm{kg}.}$

1.11 The mass of displaced gas is $V\rho$, where V is the volume of the bulb and ρ the gas density. The balance condition for two gases is $m(\text{bulb}) = V(\text{bulb})\,\rho(1)$, $m(\text{bulb}) = V(\text{bulb})\rho(2)$ and so $\rho(1) = \rho(2)$. But $\rho(X) = M_m(X)p(X)/kT$ [Problem 1.8], $X = 1, 2$ and so the balance condition is $M_m(1)p(1) = M_m(2)p(2)$, or $M_r(1)p(1) = M_r(2)p(2)$. Therefore, $M_r(2) = M_r(1)[p(1)/p(2)]$. This is valid in the limit of vanishing pressures. In experiment 1, $p(1) = 423.22$ Torr, $p(2) = 327.10$ Torr and so $M_r(2) = 70.014 \times (423.22\,\mathrm{Torr}/327.10\,\mathrm{Torr}) = 90.59$. In experiment 2, $p(1) = 427.22$ Torr, $p(2) = 293.22$ Torr and so $M_r = 70.014 \times (427.22\,\mathrm{Torr}/293.22\,\mathrm{Torr}) = 102.0$. In a proper series of experiments one should reduce the pressure (e.g. by adjusting the balanced weight). Experiment 2 is closer to zero pressure than Experiment 1, and so we take $\underline{M_r = 102.}$ The molecule CH_2FCF_3 has $M_r = 102$ [end-paper 4].

1.12 $pV = nRT$ [1.1.1], $V =$ constant.

At $T = T_3^*$ $(= 273.16\,\mathrm{K})$, $p = p_3$ $(= 50.2\,\mathrm{Torr})$.

At a general temperature T, $p(T) = p_3(T/T_3^*)$ [1.1.6]. Therefore,

$$p(274.16\,\mathrm{K}) - p(273.16\,\mathrm{K}) = p_3\left(\frac{274.16\,\mathrm{K} - 273.16\,\mathrm{K}}{273.16\,\mathrm{K}}\right)$$

$$= p_3/273.16 = (50.2\,\mathrm{Torr})/273.16 = \underline{0.184\,\mathrm{Torr}.}$$

For 100 °C:

$$p(373.15\,\mathrm{K}) = (50.2\,\mathrm{Torr}) \times (373.15\,\mathrm{K}/273.16\,\mathrm{K})$$

$$= 1.366 \times 50.2\,\mathrm{Torr} = \underline{68.6\,\mathrm{Torr}.}$$

At 100 °C $p(374.15\,\mathrm{K}) - p(373.15\,\mathrm{K}) = p_3/273.16 = \underline{0.184\,\mathrm{Torr}.}$

1.13 $n = n(H_2) + n(N_2) = 2.0\,\mathrm{mol} + 1.0\,\mathrm{mol} = 3.0\,\mathrm{mol}$.

$x(H_2) = n(H_2)/n$ [Section 1.2(a)] $= (2.0\,\mathrm{mol})/(3.0\,\mathrm{mol}) = \underline{0.67.}$

$x(N_2) = n(N_2)/n = (1.0\,\mathrm{mol})/(3.0\,\mathrm{mol}) = \underline{0.33.}$

$$p = nRT/V = (3.0\,\mathrm{mol}) \times (8.3144\,\mathrm{J\,K^{-1}\,mol^{-1}}) \times (273.15\,\mathrm{K})/(22.4\,\mathrm{dm^3})$$

$$= 3.0 \times 10^5\,\mathrm{N\,m^{-2}} \mathrel{\hat{=}} \underline{3.0\,\mathrm{atm}}\ [\text{end-paper 1}].$$

$p(H_2) = x(H_2)p$ [1.2.4] $= 0.67 \times (3.0\,\text{atm}) = \underline{2.0\,\text{atm}}.$

$p(N_2) = x(N_2)p = 0.33 \times (3.0\,\text{atm}) = \underline{1.0\,\text{atm}}.$

1.14 Draw up the following table based on $H_2 + \frac{1}{3}N_2 \rightarrow \frac{2}{3}NH_3$.

	H_2	N_2	NH_3	
Initially	n_1	n_2	0	
Finally	0	$n_2 - \frac{1}{3}n_1$	$\frac{2}{3}n_1$	
or:	0	0.33 mol	1.33 mol	$[n_1 = 2.0\,\text{mol}, n_2 = 1.0\,\text{mol}]$
Mole fraction:	0	0.20	0.80	[total $n = 1.66$ mol]

$$p = nRT/V = (1.66\,\text{mol}) \times \left\{\frac{(8.3144\,\text{J K}^{-1}\,\text{mol}^{-1}) \times (273.15\,\text{K})}{22.4\,\text{dm}^3}\right\} = 1.66\,\text{atm}.$$

$p(H_2) = x(H_2)p = \underline{0}.$

$p(N_2) = x(N_2)p = 0.20 \times (1.66\,\text{atm}) = \underline{0.33\,\text{atm}}.$

$p(NH_3) = x(NH_3)p = 0.80 \times (1.66\,\text{atm}) = \underline{1.33\,\text{atm}}.$

1.15 Find what pressure a perfect gas exerts from $p = nRT/V$.

$n = 131\,\text{g}/(131\,\text{g mol}^{-1})$ [end-paper 4] $= 1.00$ mol.

$R = 0.0821\,\text{dm}^3\,\text{atm K}^{-1}\,\text{mol}^{-1}$ [end-paper 2].

$$p = \frac{(1.00\,\text{mol}) \times (0.0821\,\text{dm}^3\,\text{atm K}^{-1}\,\text{mol}^{-1}) \times (298.15\,\text{K})}{(1.0\,\text{dm}^3)} = 24\,\text{atm}.$$

Therefore, the sample would exert 24 atm, not 20 atm.

1.16 $p = nRT/(V - nb) - an^2/V^2$ [1.4.1a],

$a = 4.194\,\text{dm}^6\,\text{atm mol}^{-2}, b = 5.105 \times 10^{-2}\,\text{dm}^3\,\text{mol}^{-1}$ [Table 1.3],

$n = 1.00$ mol [Problem 1.15], $V = 1.0\,\text{dm}^3$.

$$nRT/(V - nb) = \frac{(1.00\,\text{mol}) \times (0.0821\,\text{dm}^3\,\text{atm K}^{-1}\,\text{mol}^{-1}) \times (298.15\,\text{K})}{(1.0\,\text{dm}^3) - (1.00\,\text{mol}) \times (5.105 \times 10^{-2}\,\text{dm}^3\,\text{mol}^{-1})}$$

$$= \frac{0.0821 \times 298.15\,\text{dm}^3\,\text{atm}}{(1.0 - 0.05)\,\text{dm}^3} = \frac{24.5\,\text{atm}}{0.95} = 26\,\text{atm}.$$

$an^2/V^2 = (4.194\ \mathrm{dm^6\,atm\,mol^{-2}}) \times (1.00\ \mathrm{mol})^2/(1.0\ \mathrm{dm^3})^6 = 4.2\ \mathrm{atm}.$

Therefore $p = 26\ \mathrm{atm} - 4.2\ \mathrm{atm} = \underline{22\ \mathrm{atm}.}$

1.17 (a) $p = nRT/V$ [1.1.1], (b) $p = nRT/(V - nb) - an^2/V^2$ [1.4.1a].

$a = 4.471\ \mathrm{dm^6\,atm\,mol^{-2}}$, $b = 5.714 \times 10^{-2}\ \mathrm{dm^3\,mol^{-1}} = 57.14\ \mathrm{cm^3\,mol^{-1}}$ [Table 1.3].

$RT/V = 1.00\ \mathrm{atm\,mol^{-1}}$ at 273.15 K and 22.414 dm^3.

(a(i)) $p = (1.00\ \mathrm{mol}) \times (1.00\ \mathrm{atm\,mol^{-1}}) = \underline{1.00\ \mathrm{atm}.}$

$$\text{(a(ii))}\,p = \frac{(1.00\ \mathrm{mol}) \times (0.0821\ \mathrm{dm^3\,atm\,K^{-1}\,mol^{-1}}) \times (1000\ \mathrm{K})}{(0.100\ \mathrm{dm^3})} = \underline{821\ \mathrm{atm}.}$$

$$\text{(b(i))}\,nRT/(V - nb) = \frac{(1.00\ \mathrm{mol}) \times (22.414\ \mathrm{dm^3\,atm\,mol^{-1}})}{(22.414\ \mathrm{dm^3}) - (5.714 \times 10^{-2}\ \mathrm{dm^3})} = 1.003\ \mathrm{atm}.$$

$$an^2/V^2 = \frac{(4.471\ \mathrm{dm^6\,atm\,mol^{-2}}) \times (1.00\ \mathrm{mol})^2}{(22.414\ \mathrm{dm^3})^2} = 0.009\ \mathrm{atm}.$$

$p = (1.003 - 0.009)\ \mathrm{atm} = \underline{0.994\ \mathrm{atm}.}$

$$\text{(b(ii))}\,nRT/(V - nb) = \frac{(1.00\ \mathrm{mol}) \times (82.06\ \mathrm{dm^3\,atm\,mol^{-1}})}{(0.100\ \mathrm{dm^3}) - (1.00\ \mathrm{mol}) \times (5.714 \times 10^{-2}\ \mathrm{dm^3\,mol^{-1}})}$$

$$= 1915\ \mathrm{atm}.$$

$$an^2/V^2 = \frac{(4.471\ \mathrm{dm^6\,atm\,mol^{-2}}) \times (1.00\ \mathrm{mol})^2}{(0.100\ \mathrm{dm^3})^2} = 447\ \mathrm{atm}.$$

$p = 1915\ \mathrm{atm} - 447\ \mathrm{atm} = \underline{1468\ \mathrm{atm}.}$

1.18 At 25 °C and 1 atm the reduced temperature and pressure of hydrogen are

$T_r = (298.15\ \mathrm{K})/(33.23\ \mathrm{K})$ [Table 1.2, and eqn. (1.4.6)] $= 8.97$,

$p_r = (1\ \mathrm{atm})/(12.8\ \mathrm{atm}) = 0.0781$.

Ammonia, xenon, and helium are in corresponding states when their reduced pressures and temperatures have these values. Hence use $p = p_r p_c$ and $T = T_r T_c$ with $p_r = 0.0781$. $T_r = 8.97$, and the appropriate values (Table 1.2) of p_c and T_c.

(a) Ammonia; $p_c = 111.3\ \mathrm{atm}$, $T_c = 405.5\ \mathrm{K}$

hence $\underline{p = 8.69\ \mathrm{atm},\ T = 3640\ \mathrm{K}.}$

(b) Xenon; $p_c = 58.0\ \mathrm{atm}$, $T_c = 289.8\ \mathrm{K}$

hence $\underline{p = 4.53\ \mathrm{atm},\ T = 2600\ \mathrm{K}.}$

(c) Helium; $p_c = 2.26$ atm, $T_c = 5.21$ K
hence $\underline{p = 0.177 \text{ atm}, T = 46.7 \text{ K}}$.

1.19 From [1.4.3] $V_{m,c} = 3b = 3 \times (0.0226 \text{ dm}^3 \text{ mol}^{-1}) = \underline{67.8 \text{ cm}^3 \text{ mol}^{-1}}$

$$p_c = a/27b^2 = \frac{0.751 \text{ atm dm}^6 \text{ mol}^{-2}}{27 \times (0.0226 \text{ dm}^3 \text{ mol}^{-1})^2} = \underline{54.5 \text{ atm.}}$$

$$T_c = 8a/27Rb = \frac{8 \times (0.751 \text{ atm dm}^6 \text{ mol}^{-2})}{27 \times (0.08206 \text{ dm}^3 \text{ atm K}^{-1} \text{ mol}^{-1}) \times (0.0226 \text{ dm}^3 \text{ mol}^{-1})}$$
$$= 120/\text{K}^{-1} = \underline{120 \text{ K}}.$$

1.20 $b = V_{m,c}/3$ [1.4.3], $a = 3p_c V_{m,c}^2$ [1.4.3]
$V_{m,c} = 98.7 \text{ cm}^3 \text{ mol}^{-1} = 0.0987 \text{ dm}^3 \text{ mol}^{-1}, p_c = 45.6$ atm
$b = \frac{1}{3} \times (0.0987 \text{ dm}^3 \text{ mol}^{-1}) = \underline{0.0329 \text{ dm}^3 \text{ mol}^{-1}}$.
$a = 3 \times (45.6 \text{ atm}) \times (0.0987 \text{ dm}^3 \text{ mol}^{-1})^2 = \underline{1.333 \text{ atm dm}^6 \text{ mol}^{-2}}$.
$v_{mol} \approx b/N_A$ [Section 1.4(a)] $= (0.0329 \times 10^{-3} \text{ m}^3 \text{ mol}^{-1})/(6.022 \times 10^{23} \text{ mol}^{-1})$
$= \underline{5.5 \times 10^{-29} \text{ m}^3 (0.055 \text{ nm}^3)}$.
$v_{mol} \approx \frac{4}{3}\pi r^3$,

$$\text{whence } r = \left[\frac{3}{4\pi} \times (5.5 \times 10^{-29} \text{ m}^3)\right]^{1/3} = 2.4 \times 10^{-10} \text{ m or } \underline{r \approx 0.24 \text{ nm}}.$$

1.21 $V_{m,c} = 2b$ [Box 1.1], $b \approx (4/3)\pi r^3 N_A$ so that $r \approx [(3/8\pi)(V_{m,c}/N_A)]^{1/3}$.
From Table 1.2, $V_{m,c}(\text{He}) = 57.8 \text{ cm}^3 \text{ mol}^{-1} = 57.8 \times 10^{-6} \text{ m}^3 \text{ mol}^{-1}$.
$V_{m,c}/N_A = (57.8 \times 10^{-6} \text{ m}^3 \text{ mol}^{-1})/(6.022 \times 10^{23} \text{ mol}^{-1})$
$= 9.60 \times 10^{-29} \text{ m}^3$.
Then $r \approx [(3/8\pi) \times (9.60 \times 10^{-29} \text{ m}^3)]^{1/3} = \underline{2.26 \times 10^{-10} \text{ m} = 226 \text{ pm}}$.
Similarly, $V_{m,c}(\text{Ne}) = 41.7 \text{ cm}^3 \text{ mol}^{-1}$ gives $\underline{r(\text{Ne}) \approx 202 \text{ pm}}$.
$V_{m,c}(\text{Ar}) = 75.3 \text{ cm}^3 \text{ mol}^{-1}$ gives $\underline{r(\text{Ar}) \approx 246 \text{ pm}}$.
$V_{m,c}(\text{Xe}) = 118.8 \text{ cm}^3 \text{ mol}^{-1}$ gives $\underline{r(\text{Xe}) \approx 287 \text{ pm}}$.

1.22 $V_{m,c} = 2b$, $T_c = a/4bR$ [Box 1.1]. Hence $b = \frac{1}{2}V_{m,c}$, $a = 4RT_c b = 2RT_c V_{m,c}$.
$V_{m,c} = 118.8 \text{ cm}^3 \text{ mol}^{-1}$; $\underline{b = 59.4 \text{ cm}^3 \text{ mol}^{-1}}$. $T_c = 289.75$ K;
$a = 2 \times (0.08206 \text{ dm}^3 \text{ atm K}^{-1} \text{ mol}^{-1}) \times (289.75 \text{ K}) \times (0.1188 \text{ dm}^3 \text{ mol}^{-1})$
$= \underline{5.65 \text{ dm}^6 \text{ atm mol}^{-2}}$; hence $p = 20.6$ atm [Dieterici equation, Box 1.1].

1.23 $p = RT/(V_m - b) - a/V_m^2$ [Box 1.1] $= (RT/V_m)\left\{\dfrac{1}{1-(b/V_m)}\right\} - a/V_m^2$.

Use $\dfrac{1}{1-x} = 1 + x + x^2 + \ldots$ with $x = b/V_m$.

Then $p = (RT/V_m)\{1 + (b/V_m) + (b/V_m)^2 + \ldots\} - a/V_m^2$

$= (RT/V_m)\{1 + [b - (a/RT)]/V_m + (b/V_m)^2 + \ldots\}$.

Compare with

$p = (RT/V_m)\{1 + B/V_m + C/V_m^2 + \ldots\}$ [Box 1.1].

Then $\underline{B = b - a/RT, C = b^2}$.

1.24 $p = \{RT/(V_m - b)\}\exp(-a/RTV_m)$ [Box 1.1].

Use $1/(1-x) = 1 + x + x^2 + \ldots$, $e^y = 1 + y + \dfrac{1}{2!}y^2 + \ldots$ and then collect co-efficients of powers of $1/V_m$.

$$p = (RT/V_m)\left[\frac{1}{1-(b/V_m)}\right]\exp(-a/RTV_m)$$

$= (RT/V_m)\{1 + (b/V_m) + (b/V_m)^2 + \ldots\}\{1 - (a/RTV_m) + \tfrac{1}{2}(a/RTV_m)^2 + \ldots\}$

$= (RT/V_m)\{1 + [b - (a/RT)](1/V_m) + [b^2 - (ab/RT) +$

$+ (a^2/2R^2T^2)](1/V_m)^2 + \ldots\}$.

Compare with $p = (RT/V_m)\{1 + B(T)/V_m + C(T)/V_m^2 + \ldots\}$.

Then $\underline{B(T) = b - a/RT, C(T) = b^2 - (ab/RT) + (a^2/2R^2T^2)}$.

1.25 For a van der Waals gas $B = b - a/RT$, $C = b^2$ [Problem 1.23], hence $b = \sqrt{C}$, $a = (b - B)RT$. Then use $p_c = a/27b^2$, $V_{m,c} = 3b$, $T_c = 8a/27Rb$.

$B(T) = -21.7\ \text{cm}^3\,\text{mol}^{-1}$, $C(T) = 1200\ \text{cm}^6\,\text{mol}^{-2}$.

Therefore $b = 34.6\ \text{cm}^3\,\text{mol}^{-1}$,

$a = \{34.6\ \text{cm}^3\,\text{mol}^{-1} - (-21.7\ \text{cm}^3\,\text{mol}^{-1})\}\{(0.0821\ \text{dm}^3\,\text{atm}\,\text{K}^{-1}\,\text{mol}^{-1}) \times (273\ \text{K})\}$

$= (56.3\ \text{cm}^3\,\text{mol}^{-1}) \times (22.4\ \text{dm}^3\,\text{atm}\,\text{mol}^{-1})$

$= 1260\ \text{cm}^3\,\text{dm}^3\,\text{atm}\,\text{mol}^{-2} = 1.26\ \text{dm}^6\,\text{atm}\,\text{mol}^{-2}$.

Then $p_c = (1.26\ \text{dm}^6\,\text{atm}\,\text{mol}^{-2})/27(34.6 \times 10^{-3}\ \text{dm}^3\,\text{mol}^{-1})^2 = \underline{39.0\ \text{atm}}$.

$V_{m,c} = 3 \times (34.6\ \text{cm}^3\,\text{mol}^{-1}) = \underline{104\ \text{cm}^3\,\text{mol}^{-1}}$.

$$T_c = \frac{8 \times (1.26\ \text{dm}^6\,\text{atm}\,\text{mol}^{-2})}{27 \times (0.0821\ \text{dm}^3\,\text{atm}\,\text{K}^{-1}\,\text{mol}^{-1}) \times (34.6 \times 10^{-3}\ \text{dm}^3\,\text{mol}^{-1})} = \underline{131\ \text{K}}.$$

For a Dieterici gas, $B = b - a/RT$, $C = b^2 - (ab/RT) + (a^2/2R^2T^2)$ [Problem 1.24].

Hence $C - \frac{1}{2}B^2 = \frac{1}{2}b^2$, so that $b = \sqrt{(2C - B^2)}$ and $a = (b - B)RT$. Then use

$p_c = a/4e^2b^2$, $V_{m,c} = 2b$, $T_c = a/4bR$.

$b = \sqrt{\{2400\ \text{cm}^6\ \text{mol}^{-2} - (-21.7\ \text{cm}^3\ \text{mol}^{-1})^2\}} = \underline{43.9\ \text{cm}^3\ \text{mol}^{-1}}$.

$a = \{43.9\ \text{cm}^3\ \text{mol}^{-1} - (-21.7\ \text{cm}^3\ \text{mol}^{-1})\} \times \{22.4\ \text{dm}^3\ \text{atm}\ \text{mol}^{-1}\}$

$= 1470\ \text{cm}^3\ \text{dm}^3\ \text{mol}^{-2}\ \text{atm} = 1.47\ \text{dm}^3\ \text{atm}\ \text{mol}^{-2}$.

$p_c = (1.47\ \text{dm}^3\ \text{atm}\ \text{mol}^{-2})/4e^2(43.9 \times 10^{-3}\ \text{dm}^3\ \text{mol}^{-1})^2 = \underline{25.8\ \text{atm}}$.

$V_{m,c} = 2 \times (43.9\ \text{cm}^3\ \text{mol}^{-1}) = \underline{87.8\ \text{cm}^3\ \text{mol}^{-1}}$.

$T_c = (1.47\ \text{dm}^3\ \text{atm}\ \text{mol}^{-2})/4 \times (43.9 \times 10^{-3}\ \text{dm}^3\ \text{atm}\ \text{mol}^{-1})$

$\times (0.0821\ \text{dm}^3\ \text{atm}\ \text{K}^{-1}\ \text{mol}^{-1}) = \underline{102\ \text{K}}$.

1.26 For critical behavior, show that there is a point of inflection with zero slope [Section 1.4(b)] and find the critical constants.

$$p = RT/V_m - B/V_m^2 + C/V_m^3$$

$$\left.\begin{aligned} dp/dV_m &= -RT/V_m^2 + 2B/V_m^3 - 3C/V_m^4 = 0 \\ d^2p/dV_m^2 &= 2RT/V_m^3 - 6B/V_m^4 + 12C/V_m^5 = 0 \end{aligned}\right\} \text{at } p_c, V_{m,c}, T_c.$$

$$\left.\begin{aligned} -RT_cV_{m,c}^2 + 2BV_{m,c} - 3C &= 0 \\ RT_cV_{m,c}^2 - 3BV_{m,c} + 6C &= 0 \end{aligned}\right\}$$

which solve to $\underline{V_{m,c} = 3C/B,\ T_c = B^2/3RC}$.

Use the equation of state to find p_c:

$p_c = RT_c/V_{m,c} - B/V_{m,c}^2 + C/V_{m,c}^3$

$= R(B^2/3RC)/(3C/B) - B/(3C/B)^2 + C/(3C/B)^3 = \underline{B^3/27C^2}$.

$Z_c = p_cV_{m,c}/RT_c = (B^3/27C^2)(3C/B)/R(B^2/3RC) = \underline{\tfrac{1}{3}}$.

1.27 $pV_m/RT = 1 + B'p + C'p^2 + \ldots$ [1.3.1]

$pV_m/RT = 1 + B/V_m + C/V_m^2 + \ldots$ [1.3.2].

Equating the two expressions for pV_m/RT gives

$B'p + C'p^2 + \ldots = B/V_m + C/V_m^2 + \ldots$

Therefore $B'pV_m + C'pV_m^2 + \ldots = B + C/V_m \ldots$

Replace pV_m by $RT\{1 + (B/V_m) + \ldots\}$ and equate coefficients of powers of $1/V_m$.

$B'RT\{1 + (B/V_m) + \ldots\} + (C'/V_m)(RT)^2\{1 + (B/V_m) + \ldots\}^2 = B + C/V_m + \ldots$

or $B'RT + (BB'RT + C'R^2T^2)/V_m + \ldots = B + C/V_m + \ldots$

Therefore $B'RT = B$, implying $\underline{B' = B/RT}$.

Also $BB'RT + C'R^2T^2 = C$, or $B^2 + C'R^2T^2 = C$, implying $\underline{C' = (C - B^2)/R^2T^2}$.

1.28 At $T = T_B, B' = 0$ [Section 1.3(b)]. $B' = B/RT$ [Problem 1.27] $= (b - a/RT)/RT$ [Problem 1.23]. Therefore, $b - a/RT_B = 0$, or $T_B = a/Rb$.

At $T = T_B, Z = pV/RT_B = (1/RT_B)RT_B\{1 + B'(T_B)p + C'(T_B)p^2 + \dots\}$
$$= 1 + C'(T_B)p^2 + \dots \approx 1 \text{ if } C'p^2 \ll 1.$$

Therefore, xenon has $Z \approx 1$ at $T \approx T_B \approx a/Rb$.

$$T_B(\mathrm{Xe}) \approx \frac{4.194\ \mathrm{dm^6\,atm\,mol^{-2}}}{(0.08206\ \mathrm{dm^3\,atm\,K^{-1}\,mol^{-1}}) \times (0.05105\ \mathrm{dm^3\,mol^{-1}})} = \underline{1000\ \mathrm{K}}.$$

1.29 (a) $T_B = a/Rb$ [Problem 1.28]; $T_c = 8a/27Rb$ [Table 1.4].

$T_{B,r} = T_B/T_c = (a/Rb)/(8a/27Rb) = 27/8 = \underline{3.375}$.

(b) For a Dieterici gas, $B = b - a/RT$ [Problem 1.24], hence $B' = (b - a/RT)/RT$ [Problem 1.27] $= 0$ when $b = a/RT$. Therefore, $T_B = a/Rb$. Since $T_c = a/4bR$ [Table 1.4],

$T_{B,r} = (a/Rb)/(a/4bR) = \underline{4}$.

1.30 $p/\rho = (RT/M_m) + (B'RT/M_m)p + \dots$ [Problem 1.8]. A plot of p/ρ against p therefore has a limiting slope $B'RT/M_m$. Write $(p/\rho)/(10^5\ \mathrm{m^2\,s^{-2}}) = (RT/M_m)/(10^5\ \mathrm{m^2\,s^{-2}}) + \{(B'RT/M_m)/(10^5\ \mathrm{m^2\,s^{-2}})\}\,(p/10^5\ \mathrm{N\,m^{-2}})\,(10^5\ \mathrm{N\,m^{-2}})$ and so a plot of $(p/\rho)/(10^5\ \mathrm{m^2\,s^{-2}})$ against $(p/10^5\ \mathrm{N\,m^{-2}})$, as in Fig. 1.1, has a (dimensionless) slope equal to $\{(B'RT/M_m)/(10^5\ \mathrm{m^2\,s^{-2}})\} \times (10^5\ \mathrm{N\,m^{-2}}) = (B'RT/M_m)\ \mathrm{N\,m^{-4}\,s^2}$.

From Fig. 1.1, limiting slope $\approx \dfrac{0.584 - 0.544}{1.0131 - 0.1223} = 4.5 \times 10^{-2}$.

Therefore $(B'RT/M_m)\ \mathrm{N\,m^{-4}\,s^2} = 4.5 \times 10^{-2}$, $RT/M_m = 0.540 \times 10^5\ \mathrm{m^2\,s^{-2}}$

$$B' = \frac{5.50 \times 10^{-2}}{(RT/M_m)\ \mathrm{N\,m^{-4}\,s^2}} = \frac{4.5 \times 10^{-2}}{0.540 \times 10^5\ \mathrm{m^{-2}\,N}} = \underline{8.3 \times 10^{-7}\ \mathrm{Pa^{-1}}}.$$

$$B = B'RT \text{ [Problem 1.27]} = (8.3 \times 10^{-7}\ \mathrm{N^{-1}\,m^2}) \times (8.3144\ \mathrm{J\,K^{-1}\,mol^{-1}}) \times (298.15\ \mathrm{K})$$
$$= 2.07 \times 10^{-3}\ \mathrm{J\,N^{-1}\,m^2\,mol^{-1}} = 2.07 \times 10^{-3}\ \mathrm{m^3\,mol^{-1}} = \underline{2.07\ \mathrm{dm^3\,mol^{-1}}}.$$

1.31 Consider a slab of fluid of area A, thickness $\mathrm{d}h$, density ρ. Its mass is $\rho A\mathrm{d}h$. The force downwards is $\rho Ag\mathrm{d}h$. The force per unit area is $\rho Ag\mathrm{d}h/A = \rho g\mathrm{d}h$. This is the difference of the pressures at the bottom and top of the slab. Therefore, if h is measured vertically, $\mathrm{d}p = -\rho g\mathrm{d}h$ ($\mathrm{d}p/\mathrm{d}h$ is negative: pressure decreases as height increases). For a perfect gas $\rho = (M_m/RT)p$ [Problem 1.8]; Therefore $\mathrm{d}p = -(M_m/RT)\,gp\mathrm{d}h$ or $\mathrm{d}p/p = -(M_m/RT)\,g\mathrm{d}h$. If $p = p_0$ at $h = 0$ and $p = p(h)$ at a height h, this integrates to $\ln\,[p(h)/p_0] = -(M_m g/RT)h$ or $\underline{p(h) = p_0 \exp\{(-M_m g/RT)h\}}$.

1.32 $p_0 = 1$ atm, $M_m \approx 30\,\text{g mol}^{-1}$.

$$M_m g/RT = \frac{(30\,\text{g mol}^{-1}) \times (9.81\,\text{m s}^{-2})}{(2.48 \times 10^3\,\text{J mol}^{-1})} = 1.19 \times 10^{-4}\,\text{m}^{-1}.$$

(a) $h = 15$ cm $= 0.15$ m

$$p = p_0 \exp(-0.15 \times 1.19 \times 10^{-4}) = \underline{0.999\,98\,p_0}.$$

(b) $h = 1350$ ft $\triangleq$ 411 m

$$p(411\,\text{m}) = p_0 \exp(-411 \times 1.19 \times 10^{-4}) = 0.952\,p_0.$$

Therefore, if $p_0 = 1.0$ atm, $p(411\,\text{m}) = \underline{0.95\text{ atm}}$.

1.33 Each component of a perfect gas behaves independently, and so for the component J of molar mass $M_{J,m}$

$$p_J(h) = p_{0J}\exp\{-M_{J,m}g/RT)h\}.$$

From *Example* 1.3, partial pressures at sea level ($p = 1$ atm) are $p_0(N_2) = 0.782$ atm, $p_0(O_2) = 0.208$, $p_0(Ar) = 0.009$ atm, $p_0(CO_2) = 0.003$ atm; use $M_r(N_2) = 28$, $M_r(O_2) = 32$, $M_r(Ar) = 40$, $M_r(CO_2) = 44$.

$$M_{J,m}g/RT = (M_{J,r}\,\text{g mol}^{-1}) \times (9.81\,\text{m s}^{-2})/(2.437 \times 10^3\,\text{J mol}^{-1})$$
$$= 4.02 \times 10^{-6} M_{J,r}\,\text{m}^{-1}.$$

Hence, draw up the following table using the appropriate values of M_r and h.

$h =$		1350 ft	29000 ft	100 km
$\triangleq$		411 m	8840 m	10^5 m
$p_J(h)/\text{atm} =$	N_2	0.747	0.289	1.01×10^5
$[x_J(h)] =$		[0.781]	[0.807]	[0.949]
	O_2	0.198	0.067	5.39×10^{-7}
		[0.208]	[0.187]	[0.051]
	Ar	0.008	0.002	9.3×10^{-10}
		[0.008]	[0.006]	[8.7×10^{-5}]
	CO_2	0.003	0.001	6.2×10^{-11}
		[0.003]	[0.003]	[5.8×10^{-6}].

Mole fractions were computed from $x_J = p_J/p$, $p = p(N_2) + p(O_2) + \ldots$

1.34 $N \propto \exp(-m'gh/kT)$, $m' = v(\rho_{\text{solute}} - \rho_{\text{solvent}})$, [$v$: specific volume].

$\ln N = \text{const.} - (m'g/kT)h$. Hence, plot $\ln N$ against h; the slope is $-m'g/kT$. Draw up the following Table:

h/mm	0	0.05	0.07	0.09	0.10	0.15	0.20
$\ln N$	6.91	5.99	5.63	5.25	5.08	4.09	3.22

The points are plotted in Fig. 1.2. The slope is -18.4, which should be identified with the slope of the line $\ln N = \text{const.} - (m'g/kT)(h/\text{mm})\,\text{mm}$, or $(-m'g/kT)\,\text{mm}$. Hence $m'g/kT = 18.4/\text{mm} = 18.4 \times 10^3\,\text{m}^{-1}$.

$$m' = \tfrac{4}{3}\pi R^3(\rho_{\text{solute}} - \rho_{\text{solvent}}) = \tfrac{4}{3}\pi \times (2.12 \times 10^{-7}\,\text{m})^3 \times (1.2049 - 0.9982)\,\text{g cm}^{-3}$$
$$= 8.25 \times 10^{-18}\,\text{kg}.$$

Therefore $k = (m'g/T)/(18.4 \times 10^3\,\text{m}^{-1}) = \dfrac{(8.25 \times 10^{-18}\,\text{kg}) \times (9.81\,\text{m s}^{-2})}{(293.15\,\text{K}) \times (18.4 \times 10^3\,\text{m}^{-1})}$

$$= \underline{1.50 \times 10^{-23}\,\text{J K}^{-1}}.$$

Since $N_A = R/k$ and $R = 8.3144\,\text{J K}^{-1}\,\text{mol}^{-1}$,

$$N_A = (8.3144\,\text{J K}^{-1}\,\text{mol}^{-1})/(1.50 \times 10^{-23}\,\text{J K}^{-1}) = \underline{5.5 \times 10^{23}\,\text{mol}^{-1}}.$$

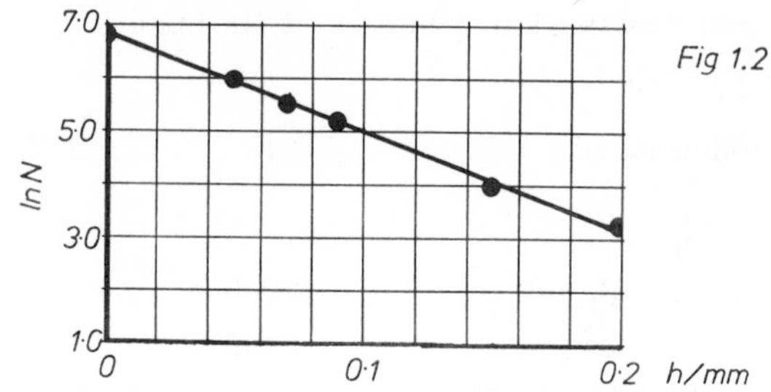

Fig 1.2

2. The First Law: the concepts

A2.1 $w = -nRT \ln(V_f/V_i)$ [2.2.11b]

$= -(52.0 \times 10^{-3}\,\text{mol})(8.31\,\text{J K}^{-1}\,\text{mol}^{-1})(260\,\text{K}) \ln(1/3)$

$= \underline{1.23 \times 10^2\,\text{J}}.$

$w' = -w = \underline{-1.23 \times 10^2\,\text{J}}.$ [2.2.11a]

$q = \Delta U - w = 0 - w = \underline{-1.23 \times 10^2\,\text{J}}.$ [Section 2.1(b)]

A2.2 $w = -p_{ex}\Delta V = -(200\,\text{Torr})(133\,\text{Pa/Torr})(3.30 \times 10^{-3}\,\text{m}^3)$

$= \underline{-87.8\,\text{J}}.$ [2.2.7b]

$q = \Delta U - w = 0 - w = \underline{87.8\,\text{J}}.$ [Section 2.1(b)]

$\Delta U = 0$ [isothermal process, perfect gas].

$w_{rev} = -nRT \ln(V_f/V_i)$ [2.2.11b]

$= -[(4.50/16.0)\text{mol}]\,(8.31\,\text{J K}^{-1}\,\text{mol}^{-1})\,(310\,\text{K}) \ln(16.0\,\text{dm}^3/12.7\,\text{dm}^3)$

$= \underline{-167\,\text{J}}.$

$q_{rev} = \Delta U - w_{rev} = 0 - w_{rev} = \underline{167\,\text{J}}.$

$\Delta U = \underline{0}$ [isothermal process, perfect gas].

A2.3 $w = -p_{ex}\Delta V$ [2.2.7b]

$= -(95\,\text{atm})(1.0 \times 10^5\,\text{Pa/atm})(-0.67 \times 10^{-2} \times 0.450 \times 10^{-3}\,\text{m}^3) = \underline{28.6\,\text{J}}.$

A2.4 $q = C_p\Delta T = (3.00\,\text{mol})(29.4\,\text{J K}^{-1}\,\text{mol}^{-1})(285\,\text{K} - 260\,\text{K}) = \underline{2.20\,\text{kJ}}.$
[Table 2.1, 2.3.1]

$\Delta H = q = \underline{2.20\,\text{kJ}}.$ [2.3.6]

$\Delta U = \Delta H - nR\Delta T = 2.20\,\text{kJ} - (3.00\,\text{mol})(8.31\,\text{J K}^{-1}\,\text{mol}^{-1})(285\,\text{K} - 260\,\text{K})$

$= \underline{1.58\,\text{kJ}}.$ [Section 2.3(c)]

A2.5 $\Delta T = q/C_p = (4.89 \times 10^3\,\text{J})(35.6\,\text{J K}^{-1}\,\text{mol}^{-1})^{-1}(5.00\,\text{mol})^{-1} = 27.5\,\text{K}$

$T_f = 375\,\text{K} + 28\,\text{K} = \underline{403\,\text{K}}.$ [2.3.1]

A2.6 $C_{p,m} = (q/\Delta T)/n$ [2.3.1]

$= (229\,\text{J})(2.55\,\text{K})^{-1}(3.00)^{-1} = \underline{29.9\,\text{J K}^{-1}\,\text{mol}^{-1}}.$

$C_{V,m} = C_{p,m} - R = 29.9\,\text{J K}^{-1}\,\text{mol}^{-1} - 8.3\,\text{J K}^{-1}\,\text{mol}^{-1}$ [2.3.9]

$= \underline{21.6\,\text{J K}^{-1}\,\text{mol}^{-1}}.$

A2.7 $w = -\int_{V_i}^{V_f} p\mathrm{d}V = -n\int_{V_{i,m}}^{V_{f,m}} (RT/V_m)(1 + B/V_m)\mathrm{d}V_m$ [2.2.9, 1.3.2]

$= -nRT[\ln(V_f/V_i) - B(V_{m,f}^{-1} - V_{m,i}^{-1})]$

$= -(0.0700\ \mathrm{mol})(8.31\ \mathrm{J\,K^{-1}\,mol^{-1}})(373\ \mathrm{K})$

$\times \{\ln(6.79\ \mathrm{cm^3}/5.25\ \mathrm{cm^3}) - (-28.7\ \mathrm{cm^3\,mol^{-1}})(0.0700\ \mathrm{mol})$

$\times [(6.79\ \mathrm{cm^3})^{-1} - (5.25\ \mathrm{cm^3})^{-1}]\} = \underline{-37.0\ \mathrm{J}}.$

$q = \Delta U - w = 83.5\ \mathrm{J} + 37.0\ \mathrm{J} = \underline{1.20 \times 10^2\ \mathrm{J}}.$ [Section 2.1(b)]

$\Delta H = \Delta U + \Delta(pV) = \Delta U + nRTB(V_{f,m}^{-1} - V_{i,m}^{-1})$

$= 83.5\ \mathrm{J} + (0.0700\ \mathrm{mol})(8.31\ \mathrm{J\,K^{-1}\,mol^{-1}})(373\ \mathrm{K})(-28.7\ \mathrm{cm^3\,mol^{-1}})$

$\times [(6.79\ \mathrm{cm})^{-1} - (5.25\ \mathrm{cm^3})^{-1}] = \underline{353\ \mathrm{J}}.$

A2.8 $w = \underline{0}$ since the volume is fixed. [2.2.5(b)]

$\Delta U = q + 0 = \underline{2.35\ \mathrm{kJ}}.$ [2.1.2]

$\Delta H = \Delta U + \Delta(pV) = \Delta U + V\Delta p$

$\Delta p = \Delta[RT/(V_m - b) - a/V_m^2] = [R/(V_m - b)]\Delta T$

$\Delta H = \Delta U + V[R/(V_m - b)]\ [T_f - T_i]$

$V_m = 15.0 \times 10^{-3}\ \mathrm{m^3}/2.00\ \mathrm{mol} = 7.50 \times 10^{-3}\ \mathrm{m^3\,mol^{-1}}$

$\Delta H = 2.35 \times 10^3\ \mathrm{J} + (15.0 \times 10^{-3}\ \mathrm{m^3})\ [(8.31\ \mathrm{J\,K^{-1}\,mol^{-1}})(7.50 \times 10^{-3}\ \mathrm{m^3\,mol^{-1}}$

$- 4.27 \times 10^{-5}\ \mathrm{m^3\,mol^{-1}})^{-1}]\ [341\ \mathrm{K} - 300\ \mathrm{K}] = 3.04 \times 10^3\ \mathrm{J}$, or $\underline{3.04\ \mathrm{kJ}}.$

[Table 1.3, Section 2.3(b)]

A2.9 $q = \underline{-1200\ \mathrm{J}}.$

$\Delta H = q_p = \underline{-1200\ \mathrm{J}}.$ [Section 2.3(b)]

$C_p \approx \Delta H/\Delta T = (-1200\ \mathrm{J})(275\ \mathrm{K} - 290\ \mathrm{K})^{-1} = \underline{80\ \mathrm{J\,K^{-1}}}.$

A2.10 $q = (0.500\ \mathrm{mol})(26.0\ \mathrm{kJ\,mol^{-1}}) = 13.0\ \mathrm{kJ}$

$w = -p_{ex}\Delta V \approx -p_{ex}V_{gas} = -nRT$ [2.2.7b]

$= -(0.500\ \mathrm{mol})(8.31\ \mathrm{J\,K^{-1}\,mol^{-1}})(250\ \mathrm{K}) = -1.04 \times 10^3\ \mathrm{J}$, or $-\underline{1.04\ \mathrm{kJ}}.$

$\Delta H = q_p = \underline{13.0\ \mathrm{kJ}}.$ [Section 2.3(b)]

$\Delta U = q + w = 13.0\ \mathrm{kJ} - 1.0\ \mathrm{kJ} = \underline{12.0\ \mathrm{kJ}}.$ [Section 2.1(b)]

2.1 $w = mgh$ [*Example* 2.1];

$m = 1.0\ \mathrm{kg}$, $h = 1.0\ \mathrm{m}$, $g =$ (a) $9.8\ \mathrm{m\,s^{-2}}$, (b) $1.6\ \mathrm{m\,s^{-2}}$.

(a) $w = (1.0\ \mathrm{kg}) \times (9.8\ \mathrm{m\,s^{-2}}) \times (1.0\ \mathrm{m}) = 9.8\ \mathrm{kg\,m^2\,s^{-2}} = \underline{9.8\ \mathrm{J}}.$

(b) $w = (1.0\,\text{kg}) \times (1.6\,\text{m}\,\text{s}^{-2}) \times (1.0\,\text{m}) = 1.6\,\text{kg}\,\text{m}^2\,\text{s}^{-2} = \underline{1.6\,\text{J}}.$

2.2 $w = mgh$ [*Example* 2.1];

$m = 150\,\text{lbs} \mathrel{\hat{=}} 68\,\text{kg}, h = 10\,\text{ft} \mathrel{\hat{=}} 3.0\,\text{m}, g = 9.8\,\text{m}\,\text{s}^{-2}.$

$w = (68\,\text{kg}) \times (9.8\,\text{m}\,\text{s}^{-2}) \times (3.0\,\text{m}) = 2000\,\text{kg}\,\text{m}^2\,\text{s}^{-2} = \underline{2.0\,\text{kJ}}.$

2.3 $w = \int_{z_\text{i}}^{z_\text{f}} F(z)\text{d}z$ [2.2.4], $F(z) = -kz$ [restoring force $\propto$ displacement].

Therefore $w = k \int_{z_\text{i}}^{z_\text{f}} z\text{d}z = \frac{1}{2}k(z_\text{f}^2 - z_\text{i}^2).$

Initially the displacement is zero; hence $z_\text{i} = 0$; therefore $w = \frac{1}{2}kz_\text{f}^2$.

$k = 2.0 \times 10^5\,\text{N}\,\text{m}^{-1}, z_\text{f} = -1.0\,\text{cm}.$

$w = \frac{1}{2} \times (2.0 \times 10^5\,\text{N}\,\text{m}^{-1}) \times (1.0 \times 10^{-2}\,\text{m})^2 = 10\,\text{N}\,\text{m} = \underline{10\,\text{J}}.$

2.4 $w = \frac{1}{2}kz^2$ [Problem 2.3].

$k = 2.0 \times 10^6\,\text{N}\,\text{m}^{-1}, z = \pm 1.0\,\text{cm};$

$w = \frac{1}{2} \times (2.0 \times 10^6\,\text{N}\,\text{m}^{-1}) \times (1.0 \times 10^{-2}\,\text{m})^2 = 100\,\text{N}\,\text{m} = 100\,\text{J}.$

The work done per cycle (one compression, one extension) is therefore 200 J; the work required for 1000 cycles is therefore $\underline{200\,\text{kJ}}$. If this work is to be expended in 1000 s, the power required is $(200\,\text{kJ})/(1000\,\text{s}) = 200\,\text{J}\,\text{s}^{-1} = \underline{200\,\text{W}}$ [as $1\,\text{W} = 1\,\text{J}\,\text{s}^{-1}$, W = watt]. If 200 kJ of energy is dispersed as heat, the rise in temperature of an object of heat capacity $C = 4.2\,\text{kJ}\,\text{K}^{-1}$ is

$\Delta T = q/C$ [2.3.1] $= (200\,\text{kJ})/(4.2\,\text{kJ}\,\text{K}^{-1}) = 48\,\text{K}.$

The final temperature will therefore be $\underline{68\,^\circ\text{C}}$.

2.5 $w = -\int_0^{x_\text{f}} F(x)\text{d}x$ [2.2.4], $F(x) = -F\sin(\pi x/a);$

$x_\text{f} =$ (a) a, (b) $2a$,

(a) $w = F\int_0^a \sin(\pi x/a)\text{d}x = -(Fa/\pi)\,[\cos(\pi x/a)]\Big|_0^a = \underline{2Fa/\pi}.$

(b) The force *opposes* extension only up to $x = a$, and no work needs to be done for the extension from $x = a$ to $x = 2a$. Hence the work is also $2Fa/\pi$. If, however, the external force in balanced against the internal (so that the overall extension is reversible), then the system *does* work in the $x = a$ to $2a$ region, and overall the path from 0 to $2a$ results in $\underline{w \mp 0}$.

2.6 $w' = p_\text{ex}\Delta V$ [2.2.7a].

$p_{ex} = 1.0\,\text{atm} = 1.0 \times 10^5\,\text{N m}^{-2}$,

$\Delta V = (100\,\text{cm}^2) \times (10\,\text{cm}) = 1000\,\text{cm}^3 = 10^{-3}\,\text{m}^3$.

$w = (1.0 \times 10^5\,\text{N m}^{-2}) \times (10^{-3}\,\text{m}^3) = 1.0 \times 10^2\,\text{N m}$

$\quad = \underline{100\,\text{J}}$.

2.7 $w' = mgh$

$m = 5.0\,\text{kg}, g = 9.81\,\text{m s}^{-2}, h = 10\,\text{cm} = 0.10\,\text{m}$

$w' = (5.0\,\text{kg}) \times (9.81\,\text{m s}^{-2}) \times (0.10\,\text{m}) = 4.9\,\text{kg m}^2\,\text{s}^{-2} = \underline{4.9\,\text{J}}$.

The area of the piston is irrelevant, and so 4.9 J of work is done in both cases.

2.8 A mass of 5.0 kg falls through 10 cm in the outside world, and so 4.9 J of work capability is destroyed. The amount of work done *on* the system is 4.9 J [See the discussion in Section 2.2(b)].

2.9 (a) $w = -p_{ex}\Delta V$ [2.2.7]; (b) $w = -nRT\ln(V_f/V_i)$ [2.2.11].

$V_i = 100\,\text{cm}^3 = 1.00 \times 10^{-4}\,\text{m}^3, T = 298\,\text{K}, p_{ex} = 1.0\,\text{atm} = 1.0 \times 10^5\,\text{N m}^{-2}$.

$n = (5.0\,\text{g})/(44\,\text{g mol}^{-1}) = 0.114\,\text{mol}$.

$V_f = nRT/p_f = (0.114\,\text{mol}) \times (0.0821\,\text{dm}^3\,\text{atm K}^{-1}\,\text{mol}^{-1}) \times (298\,\text{K})/(1.0\,\text{atm})$

$\quad = 2.8\,\text{dm}^3 = 2.8 \times 10^{-3}\,\text{m}^3$.

$\Delta V = V_f - V_i = 28 \times 10^{-4}\,\text{m}^3 - 1.00 \times 10^{-4}\,\text{m}^3 = 27 \times 10^{-4}\,\text{m}^3$.

(a) $w = -(1.01 \times 10^5\,\text{N m}^{-2}) \times (27 \times 10^{-4}\,\text{m}^3) = -270\,\text{N m}$

$\quad = \underline{-0.27\,\text{kJ}}$.

(b) $w = -(0.114\,\text{mol}) \times (2.48\,\text{kJ mol}^{-1}) \times \ln(2.8 \times 10^{-3}/1.00 \times 10^{-4})$

$\quad = -(283\,\text{J}) \times \ln 28 = \underline{-0.94\,\text{kJ}}$.

2.10 $w = -p_{ex}\Delta V$ [2.2.7]

$V_i = 0, V_f = nRT/p_f$

$n = 1.0\,\text{mol}, T = 700\,°\text{C} \mathrel{\hat=} 973\,\text{K}, p_f = p_{ex} = 1.0\,\text{atm} = 1.01 \times 10^5\,\text{N m}^{-2}$.

$V_f = (1.0\,\text{mol}) \times (0.0821\,\text{dm}^3\,\text{atm K}^{-1}\,\text{mol}^{-1}) \times (973\,\text{K})/(1.0\,\text{atm})$

$\quad = 80\,\text{dm}^3 = 80 \times 10^{-3}\,\text{m}^3$.

$w = -(1.01 \times 10^5\,\text{N m}^{-2}) \times (80 \times 10^{-3}\,\text{m}^3 - 0)$

$\quad = -8.1 \times 10^3\,\text{N m} = \underline{-8.1\,\text{kJ}}$.

2.11 The gas also drives back the atmosphere even though there is no material piston between gas and air. Hence the same amount of work is done: $\underline{w = -8.1\,\text{kJ}}$.

2.12 $w = -p_{ex}\Delta V$ [Problem 2.11].

$Mg(s) + 2HCl(aq) \rightarrow H_2(g) + MgCl_2(aq)$; $M_r(Mg) = 24.3$ [end-paper 4],

$V_i = 0$, $V_f = nRT/p_f$, $p_f = p_{ex} = 1.0\,\text{atm} = 1.01 \times 10^5\,\text{N m}^{-2}$,

$n = (15\,\text{g})/(24.3\,\text{g mol}^{-1}) = 0.62\,\text{mol}$, $\Delta V = V_f - V_i = nRT/p_f$.

$w = -p_{ex}(nRT/p_f) = -nRT = -(0.62\,\text{mol}) \times (2.48\,\text{kJ mol}^{-1})$

$= \underline{-1.53\,\text{kJ}}.$

2.13 $w = -\int_{V_i}^{V_f} p_{in}\,dV$ [2.2.9]

$p_{in} = RT[(1/V_m) + (B/V_m^2) + (C/V_m^3) + \ldots] = nRT[(1/V) + (nB/V^2)$
$+ (n^2C/V^3) + \ldots]$ as $nV_m = V$.

$$\text{Therefore, } w = -nRT\left[\int_{V_i}^{V_f}(1/V)\,dV + nB\int_{V_i}^{V_f}(1/V^2)\,dV + n^2C\int_{V_i}^{V_f}(1/V^3)\,dV + \ldots\right]$$

$$= \underline{-nRT[\ln(V_f/V_i) - nB\left(\frac{1}{V_f} - \frac{1}{V_i}\right) - n^2C\left(\frac{1}{V_f^2} - \frac{1}{V_i^2}\right) + \ldots].}$$

2.14 (a) w is given in Problem 2.13, (b) $w = -p_{ex}\Delta V$,

(c) $w = -nRT\ln(V_f/V_i)$ for ideal, reversible expansion [2.2.11].

$n = 1.0\,\text{mol}$, $V_i = 500\,\text{cm}^3$, $V_f = 1000\,\text{cm}^3$, $T = 273\,\text{K}$

$B = -21.7\,\text{cm}^3\,\text{mol}^{-1}$, $C = 1200\,\text{cm}^6\,\text{mol}^{-2}$.

$$\text{(a) } w = -(2.27\,\text{kJ}) \times \left[\ln(1000\,\text{cm}^3/500\,\text{cm}^3) - (1\,\text{mol}) \times (-21.7\,\text{cm}^3\,\text{mol}^{-1}) \times \left(\frac{1}{1000\,\text{cm}^3} - \frac{1}{500\,\text{cm}^3}\right) - (1\,\text{mol})^2 \times (1200\,\text{cm}^6\,\text{mol}^{-2}) \times \left(\frac{1}{(1000\,\text{cm}^3)^2} - \frac{1}{(500\,\text{cm}^3)^2}\right)\right]$$

$$= -(2.27\,\text{kJ}) \times \left[\ln 2 + 21.7 \times \left(\frac{1}{1000} - \frac{1}{500}\right) - 1200\left(\frac{1}{1000^2} - \frac{1}{500^2}\right)\right]$$

$= \underline{-1.53\,\text{kJ}}.$

(b) $w = -p_{ex}\Delta V = -(1.013 \times 10^5\,\mathrm{N\,m^{-2}}) \times (1000\,\mathrm{cm^3} - 500\,\mathrm{cm^3})$

$= -(1.013 \times 10^5\,\mathrm{N\,m^{-2}}) \times (500 \times 10^{-6}\,\mathrm{m^3}) = -51\,\mathrm{N\,m} = \underline{-51\,\mathrm{J}}.$

(c) $w = -nRT\ln(V_f/V_i) = -(2.27\,\mathrm{kJ})\ln(1000\,\mathrm{cm^3}/500\,\mathrm{cm^3})$

$= -(2.27\,\mathrm{kJ})\ln 2 = \underline{-1.57\,\mathrm{kJ}}.$

2.15 $w = -\int_{V_i}^{V_f} p_{in}\,\mathrm{d}V$ [2.2.9]; $p_{in} = nRT/(V-nb) - n^2a/V^2$ [Box 1.1].

$$w = -nRT\int_{V_i}^{V_f}\left(\frac{\mathrm{d}V}{V-nb}\right) + n^2a\int_{V_i}^{V_f}\left(\frac{\mathrm{d}V}{V^2}\right)$$

$$= -nRT\ln\left(\frac{V_f - nb}{V_i - nb}\right) - n^2a\left(\frac{1}{V_f} - \frac{1}{V_i}\right)$$

$$= \underline{-nRT\ln\left(\frac{V_f - nb}{V_i - nb}\right) + n^2a\left(\frac{V_f - V_i}{V_fV_i}\right).}$$

Suppose $nb \ll V_i, V_f$; then $\ln(V - nb) = \ln V + \ln(1 - nb/V) \approx \ln V - nb/V$; so that

$$w \approx -nRT\ln(V_f/V_i) - n^2bRT\left(\frac{1}{V_i} - \frac{1}{V_f}\right) + n^2a\left(\frac{V_f - V_i}{V_fV_i}\right)$$

$$\approx w^o + n^2\left(\frac{V_f - V_i}{V_iV_f}\right)(a - bRT),$$

where w^o is the work done on the basis of perfect gas behavior. In a reversible compression $V_f - V_i < 0$, and so $w < w^o$ if $bRT < a$, but $w > w^o$ if $bRT > a$. If attractions dominate repulsions ($bRT < a$) we should expect less work to be involved in compression and so expect $w < w^o$, as found.

2.16 Plot p against V [Section 2.2(d)] using

(a) $p = nRT/V$.

(b) $p = nRT/V - n^2a/V^2$, $a = 4.2\,\mathrm{dm^6\,atm\,mol^{-2}}$.

(c) $p = nRT/(V - nb)$, $b = 5.1 \times 10^{-2}\,\mathrm{dm^3\,mol^{-1}}$.

At $T = 298\,\mathrm{K}$, $RT = 24.5\,\mathrm{dm^3\,atm\,mol^{-1}}$; then $nRT/V_i = 24.5\,\mathrm{atm}$. Write $V = cV_i$, and let c increase from 1 to 10.

(a) $p = (24.5\,\mathrm{atm})/c$, or $p/\mathrm{atm} = 24.5/c$.

(b) $p = (24.5\,\mathrm{atm})/c - (4.2\,\mathrm{atm})/c^2$, or $p/\mathrm{atm} = 24.5/c - 4.2/c^2$.

(c) $p = (24.5\,\mathrm{atm})/(c - 0.051)$, or $p/\mathrm{atm} = 24.5/(c - 0.051)$.

Draw up the following Table:

	$c=$	1	2	3	4	5	6	7	8	9	10
p/atm	(a)	24.5	12.3	8.17	6.13	4.90	4.08	3.50	3.06	2.72	2.45
	(b)	20.3	11.2	7.70	5.86	4.73	3.97	3.41	3.00	2.67	2.41
	(c)	25.8	12.6	8.31	6.20	4.95	4.12	3.53	3.08	2.74	2.46

Plot the points as in Fig. 2.1.

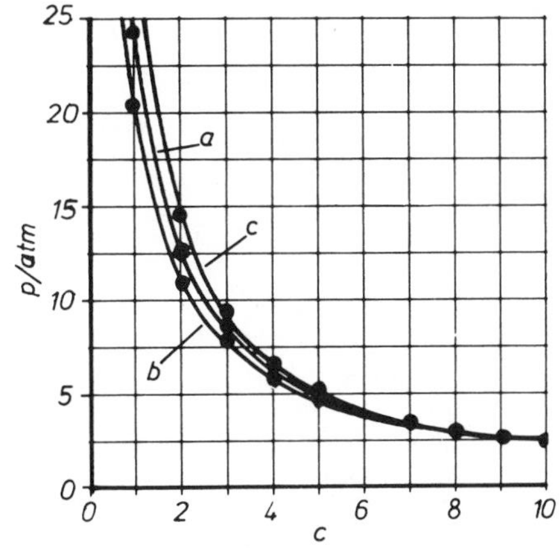

Fig 2·1

2.17

$$w = -nRT\ln\left\{\frac{V_f - nb}{V_i - nb}\right\} + n^2a\left\{\frac{V_f - V_i}{V_fV_i}\right\} \quad \text{[Problem 2.15]}$$

$$= -nR(T/T_c)T_c\ln\left\{\frac{(V_f/V_c) - n(b/V_c)}{(V_i/V_c) - n(b/V_c)}\right\} + \frac{n^2a}{V_c}\left\{\frac{(V_f/V_c) - (V_i/V_c)}{(V_f/V_c)(V_i/V_c)}\right\}.$$

$T/T_c = T_r$, $V/V_c = V_r$ [1.4.6]; $T_c = 8a/27Rb$, $V_c = nV_{c,m} = 3nb$ [Box 1.1].

$$w = -(8na/27b)T_r\ln\left\{\frac{V_{r,f} - \frac{1}{3}}{V_{r,i} - \frac{1}{3}}\right\} + (na/3b)\left\{\frac{V_{r,f} - V_{r,i}}{V_{r,f}V_{r,i}}\right\}.$$

$$w_r = 3bw/a$$

$$= -(\tfrac{8}{9})nT_r\ln\left\{\frac{3V_{r,f} - 1}{3V_{r,i} - 1}\right\} + n\left\{\frac{V_{r,f} - V_{r,i}}{V_{r,f}V_{r,i}}\right\}.$$

2.18 (a) $p = nRT/V$

$(\partial p/\partial T)_V = [(\partial/\partial T)(nRT/V)]_V = nR/V = \underline{p/T}$

$(\partial p/\partial V)_T = [(\partial/\partial V)(nRT/V)]_T = -nRT/V^2 = \underline{-p/V}$

$$\partial^2 p/\partial V\partial T = [(\partial/\partial V)(\partial p/\partial T)_V]_T = [(\partial/\partial V)(nR/V)]_T = -nR/V^2$$

$$\partial^2 p/\partial T\partial V = [(\partial/\partial T)(\partial p/\partial V)_T]_V = [(\partial/\partial T)(-nRT/V^2)]_V = -nR/V^2$$

(b) $p = [RT/(V_m - b)]\exp(-a/RTV_m)$ [Box 1.1]

$$= [nRT/(V-nb)]\exp(-na/RTV)$$

$$(\partial p/\partial T)_V = \left(\frac{nR}{V-nb}\right)\exp(-na/RTV) + \left(\frac{na}{RT^2V}\right)\left(\frac{nRT}{V-nb}\right)\times\exp(-na/RTV)$$

$$= \left(\frac{nR}{V-nb}\right)\left(1+\frac{na}{RTV}\right)\exp(-na/RTV) = \underline{\left(1+\frac{na}{RTV}\right)\left(\frac{p}{T}\right)}.$$

$$(\partial p/\partial V)_T = -[nRT/(V-nb)^2]\exp(-na/RTV)$$

$$+\left(\frac{na}{RTV^2}\right)\left(\frac{nRT}{V-nb}\right)\exp(-na/RTV)$$

$$= \left(\frac{nRT}{V-nb}\right)\left(\frac{na}{RTV^2}-\frac{1}{V-nb}\right)\exp(-na/RTV)$$

$$= \left(\frac{na}{RTV}-\frac{V}{V-nb}\right)\left(\frac{p}{V}\right).$$

$$\partial^2 p/\partial V\partial T = [(\partial/\partial V)(\partial p/\partial T)_V]_T = \left[(\partial/\partial V)\left(1+\frac{na}{RTV}\right)\left(\frac{p}{T}\right)\right]_T$$

$$= [(\partial/\partial V)(p/T)]_T + [(\partial/\partial V)(na/RTV)(p/T)]_T$$

$$= (1/T)(\partial p/\partial V)_T - (na/RT)(1/V^2)(p/T) + (na/RT^2V)(\partial p/\partial V)_T$$

$$= \left(\frac{n^2a^2p}{R^2T^3V^3}\right) - \left(\frac{p}{T(V-nb)}\right) - \left(\frac{nap}{RT^2V(V-nb)}\right).$$

$$\partial^2 p/\partial T\partial V = [(\partial/\partial T)(\partial p/\partial V)_T]_V = \left[(\partial/\partial T)\left(\frac{nap}{RTV^2}-\frac{p}{V-nb}\right)\right]_V$$

$$= \left(\frac{na}{RTV^2}\right)\left(\frac{\partial p}{\partial T}\right)_V - \frac{nap}{RT^2V^2} - \left(\frac{1}{V-nb}\right)\left(\frac{\partial p}{\partial T}\right)_V$$

$$= \left(\frac{n^2a^2p}{R^2T^3V^3}\right) - \left(\frac{p}{T(V-nb)}\right) - \left(\frac{nap}{RT^2V(V-nb)}\right);$$

hence $\partial^2 p/\partial V\partial T = \partial^2 p/\partial T\partial V$.

2.19 (a) $\delta p \approx (\partial p/\partial T)_V\delta T = p\delta T/T$ [Problem 2.18a].

Therefore $\delta p/p \approx \delta T/T$, and if $\delta T/T \approx 1$ percent, $\underline{\delta p/p \approx 1 \text{ percent.}}$

(b) $\delta p \approx (\partial p/\partial V)_T \delta V = -(p/V)\delta V$ [Problem 2.18a].

Therefore $\delta p/p \approx -\delta V/V$, and if $|\delta V/V| \approx 2$ percent, $\underline{\delta p/p \approx 2 \text{ percent.}}$

(c) $\delta p = (\partial p/\partial T)_V \delta T + (\partial p/\partial V)_T \delta V = p\delta T/T - p\delta V/V$.

Therefore, the maximum range of uncertainty in δp is the range from ($\delta T > 0, \delta V < 0$) to ($\delta T < 0, \delta V > 0$), or $\delta p/p \approx 1$ percent + 2 percent = $\underline{3 \text{ percent.}}$

2.20 $C_V = (\partial U/\partial T)_V$ [2.3.3], $U = \frac{3}{2}nRT$ [given].

(a) $C_V = [(\partial/\partial T)(\frac{3}{2}nRT)]_V = \underline{\frac{3}{2}nR}$.

(b) For translation $U = \frac{3}{2}nRT$.

For rotation $U = \frac{3}{2}nRT$ [Section 0.1(f), 3 axes of rotation].

For vibration $U = 0$ [Section 0.1(f), vibrations not excited].

Total mean internal energy, $U = 3nRT$.

Therefore, $C_V = (\partial U/\partial T)_V = \underline{3nR.}$

2.21 $C_p = (\partial H/\partial T)_p \approx (\delta q)_p/\delta T$

$= (1 \text{ calorie})/(1 \text{ K}) = 1 \text{ cal K}^{-1}$.

1 g water corresponds to $(1 \text{ g})/(18.02 \text{ g mol}^{-1}) = 0.0555$ mol; therefore the molar heat capacity is $C_{p,\text{m}} = (1 \text{ cal K}^{-1})/(0.0555 \text{ mol}) = \underline{18.02 \text{ cal K}^{-1} \text{ mol}^{-1}}$. As 1 cal $\widehat{=}$ 4.184 J [endpaper 1], or cal/J = 4.184, it follows that

$$C_{p,\text{m}} = 18.02 \text{ J(cal/J) K}^{-1} \text{ mol}^{-1} = 18.02 \times 4.184 \text{ J K}^{-1} \text{ mol}^{-1}$$
$$= \underline{75.4 \text{ J K}^{-1} \text{ mol}^{-1}}.$$

2.22 (a) $q = C_V \delta T$ [Section 2.3(a)]; (b) $q = C_p \delta T$ [Section 2.3(b)]; $C_V = C_p - nR$ [2.3.9].

$n = 1.0$ mol, $C_{p,\text{m}} = 20.79 \text{ J K}^{-1} \text{ mol}^{-1}$, $\delta T = 10$ K.

(a) $C_V = (1.0 \text{ mol}) \times C_{V,\text{m}}$;

$C_{V,\text{m}} = C_{p,\text{m}} - R = 20.79 \text{ J K}^{-1} \text{ mol}^{-1} - 8.31 \text{ J K}^{-1} \text{ mol}^{-1} = 12.48 \text{ J K}^{-1} \text{ mol}^{-1}$;

$C_V = 12 \text{ J K}^{-1}$.

$q = (12 \text{ J K}^{-1}) \times (10 \text{ K}) = \underline{0.12 \text{ kJ.}}$

(b) $C_p = (1.0 \text{ mol}) \times C_{p,\text{m}} = 21 \text{ J K}^{-1}$.

$q = (21 \text{ J K}^{-1}) \times (10 \text{ K}) = \underline{0.21 \text{ kJ.}}$

For the work done, use $w = -p_{\text{ex}}\Delta V$ [2.2.7], $p_{\text{ex}} = 10$ atm.

(a) $\Delta V = 0$, hence $w = 0$

(b) $V_\text{i} = nRT_\text{i}/p_\text{i} = (1.0 \text{ mol}) \times (0.0821 \text{ dm}^3 \text{ atm K}^{-1} \text{ mol}^{-1}) (298 \text{ K})/(10 \text{ atm})$

$= 2.4 \text{ dm}^3$.

$$V_f = nRT_f/p_i = (1.0\,\text{mol}) \times (0.0821\,\text{dm}^3\,\text{atm}\,\text{K}^{-1}\,\text{mol}^{-1})\,(308\,\text{K})/(10\,\text{atm})$$
$$= 2.5\,\text{dm}^3.$$

Therefore, $w = -(10 \times 1.013 \times 10^5\,\text{N}\,\text{m}^{-2}) \times (2.5 \times 10^{-3}\,\text{m}^3 - 2.4 \times 10^{-3}\,\text{m}^3)$
$$= -80\,\text{N}\,\text{m} = \underline{-80\,\text{J}}.$$

2.23 $q \approx C_p\delta T; C_p = nC_{p,\text{m}}$.

$C_{p,\text{m}} = 21\,\text{J}\,\text{K}^{-1}\,\text{mol}^{-1}, \delta T = 10\,\text{K}, M_r(\text{air}) \approx 29, \rho(\text{air}) \approx 1.22\,\text{kg}\,\text{m}^{-3}$ [Problem 1.9].

$n = \rho(\text{air})\,V(\text{room})/M_\text{m}(\text{air}) = (1.22 \times 10^3\,\text{g}\,\text{m}^{-3}) \times (75\,\text{m}^3)/(29\,\text{g}\,\text{mol}^{-1}) = 3.2 \times 10^3\,\text{mol}.$

$q \approx (3.2 \times 10^3\,\text{mol}) \times (21\,\text{J}\,\text{K}^{-1}\text{mol}^{-1}) \times (10\,\text{K}) = \underline{6.7 \times 10^2\,\text{kJ}}.$

A 1kW heater generates 1 kJ each second; therefore, in order to provide 670 kJ it must operate for 670 s (11 minutes). In practice, the walls and furniture of a room are also heated.

2.24 $q \approx C_p\delta T$ [2.3.2].

$C_{p,\text{m}} \approx 75.4\,\text{J}\,\text{K}^{-1}\,\text{mol}^{-1}, \delta T = 75\,\text{K}, n = (1.0\,\text{kg})/(18.02\,\text{g}\,\text{mol}^{-1}) = 56\,\text{mol}.$

$q \approx (56\,\text{mol}) \times (75.4\,\text{J}\,\text{K}^{-1}\,\text{mol}^{-1}) \times (75\,\text{K}) = \underline{320\,\text{kJ}}.$

A 1 kW heater can provide this amount of heat in 320 s (just over 5 min).

2.25 (a) $w = -p_\text{ex}\Delta V$.

$n = 56\,\text{mol}$ [Problem 2.24], $p_\text{ex} = 1\,\text{atm}, \Delta V = V_f - V_i \approx V_f = nRT/p_\text{ex}, T = 373\,\text{K}.$

(a) $w \approx p_\text{ex}V_f = nRT = -(56\,\text{mol}) \times (8.314\,\text{J}\,\text{K}^{-1}\,\text{mol}^{-1}) \times (373\,\text{K}) = \underline{-170\,\text{kJ}}.$

(b) $q_p = n\Delta H_{\text{vap,m}} = (56\,\text{mol}) \times (40.6\,\text{kJ}\,\text{mol}^{-1})$
$$= \underline{2.3 \times 10^3\,\text{kJ}}.$$

(c) $\Delta U = q_p + w$ [2.1.1] $= 2.3 \times 10^3\,\text{kJ} - 0.17 \times 10^3\,\text{kJ}$
$$= \underline{2.1 \times 10^3\,\text{kJ}}.$$

(d) $\Delta H = q_p$ [2.3.6] $= \underline{2.3 \times 10^3\,\text{kJ}}.$

2.26 (a) $w = -nRT$ [Problem 2.25a] $= -(56\,\text{mol}) \times (8.314\,\text{J}\,\text{K}^{-1}\,\text{mol}^{-1})$
$$\times (319\,\text{K}) = \underline{-0.15 \times 10^3\,\text{kJ}}$$

(b) $q_p = n\Delta H_{\text{vap,m}} = (56\,\text{mol}) \times (44\,\text{kJ}\,\text{mol}^{-1}) = \underline{2.5 \times 10^3\,\text{kJ}}.$

(c) $\Delta U = q_p + w = 2.5 \times 10^3\,\text{kJ} - 0.15 \times 10^3\,\text{kJ} = \underline{2.3 \times 10^3\,\text{kJ}}.$

(c) $\Delta H = q_p = \underline{2.5 \times 10^3\,\text{kJ}}.$

2.27 $q = 2.3 \times 10^3\,\text{kJ}$ can be supplied in 10 min (600 s) by a heater rated at $(2.3 \times 10^3 \times 10^3\,\text{J})/(600\,\text{s}) = 3.8 \times 10^3\,\text{J}\,\text{s}^{-1} = \underline{3.8\,\text{kW}}.$ Likewise, $q = 2.5 \times 10^3$ kJ can be supplied in 10 min by a heater rated at $(2.5 \times 10^3 \times 10^3\,\text{J})/(600\,\text{s}) = 4.2 \times 10^3\,\text{J}\,\text{s}^{-1} = \underline{4.2\,\text{kW}}.$ For the height h through which a mass $m = 10\,\text{kg}$ must be dropped, solve $mgh = q$, with $g = 9.81\,\text{m}\,\text{s}^{-2}$.

(a) $h \approx (2.3 \times 10^6\,\text{J})/(10\,\text{kg}) \times (9.8\,\text{m}\,\text{s}^{-2}) = \underline{24\,\text{km}}.$

(b) $h \approx (2.5 \times 10^6\,\text{J})/(10\,\text{kg}) \times (9.8\,\text{m}\,\text{s}^{-2}) = \underline{26\,\text{km}}.$

In terms of hydroelectric power generated at a 300 ft high dam, the energy requirements correspond to falls of 230 kg and 250 kg of water respectively.

2.28 $q \approx nC_{p,\text{m}}\delta T.$

$C_{p,\text{m}} = 75.48\,\text{J}\,\text{K}^{-1}\,\text{mol}^{-1}, n = 56\,\text{mol}, \delta T = 75\,\text{K}.$

$q \approx \underline{0.32\,\text{MJ}}.$

2.29 $q = n_{\text{vap}}\Delta H_{\text{vap,m}}$ hence $\Delta H_{\text{vap,m}} = q/n_{\text{vap}}$

$\Delta H_{\text{vap}} = q = \underline{22.2\,\text{kJ}}.$

$n_{\text{vap}} = (10\,\text{g})/(18.02\,\text{g}\,\text{mol}^{-1}) = 0.56\,\text{mol}, q = 22.2\,\text{kJ}$

$\Delta H_{\text{vap.m}} = (22.2\,\text{kJ})/(0.56\,\text{mol}) = \underline{40\,\text{kJ}\,\text{mol}^{-1}}.$

$\Delta U_{\text{vap}} = \Delta(H_{\text{vap}} - pV) = \Delta H_{\text{vap}} - p\Delta V$ [from $H = U + pV$, $p = \text{const}$].

$p\Delta V = p(V_\text{f} - V_\text{i}) \approx pV_\text{f} = n_{\text{vap}}RT, T = 373\,\text{K}.$

Therefore $\Delta U_{\text{vap}} \approx \Delta H_{\text{vap}} - n_{\text{vap}}RT.$

$n_{\text{vap}}RT = (0.56\,\text{mol}) \times (8.314\,\text{J}\,\text{K}^{-1}\,\text{mol}^{-1}) \times (373\,\text{K}) = 1.7\,\text{kJ}$

$\Delta U_{\text{vap}} = 22.2\,\text{kJ} - 1.7\,\text{kJ} = \underline{20.5\,\text{kJ}}.$

$w_{\text{rev}} = q - \Delta U$ [from $\Delta U = q + w$] $= 22.2\,\text{kJ} - 20.5\,\text{kJ} = \underline{1.7\,\text{kJ}}$.

2.30 Follow *Example* 1.6.

$$q_{\text{vap}} = ItV = (0.232\,\text{A}) \times (650\,\text{s}) \times (12.0\,\text{V}) = 1810\,\text{V}\,\text{A}\,\text{s} = 1.81\,\text{kJ}.$$

$$\Delta H_{\text{vap}} = q_{\text{vap}} = 1.81\,\text{kJ}.$$

$$n_{\text{vap}} = m_{\text{vap}}/M_\text{m} = (1.871\,\text{g})/(102\,\text{g}\,\text{mol}^{-1}) = 0.0183\,\text{mol}$$

$$\Delta H_{\text{vap,m}} = \Delta H_{\text{vap}}/n_{\text{vap}} = (1.81\,\text{kJ})/(0.0183\,\text{mol}) = \underline{98.9\,\text{kJ}\,\text{mol}^{-1}}.$$

$$\begin{aligned}\Delta U_{\text{vap}} &= \Delta H_{\text{vap}} - p\Delta V_{\text{vap}} \approx \Delta H_{\text{vap}} - n_{\text{vap}}RT\ [T = 351\,\text{K}]\\ &= 1.81\,\text{kJ} - (0.0183\,\text{mol}) \times (8.314\,\text{J}\,\text{K}^{-1}\,\text{mol}^{-1}) \times (351\,\text{K})\\ &= 1.81\,\text{kJ} - 53.4\,\text{J} = 1.76\,\text{kJ}.\end{aligned}$$

$$\Delta U_{\text{vap,m}} = \Delta U_{\text{vap}}/n_{\text{vap}} = (1.76\,\text{kJ})/(0.0183\,\text{mol}) = \underline{96.2\,\text{kJ}\,\text{mol}^{-1}}.$$

3. The First Law: the machinery

A3.1 (a) $\partial(\partial f/\partial x)/\partial y = \partial(2xy)/\partial y = 2x$ [Box 3.1].
$\partial(\partial f/\partial y)/\partial x = \partial(x^2 + 6y)/\partial x = 2x$.
(b) $\partial(\partial f/\partial x)/\partial y = \partial\,[\cos(xy) - (xy)\sin(xy)]\,/\partial y$

$$= -(x)\sin(xy) - (x)\sin(xy) - (xy)(x)\cos(xy)$$

$$= -2(x)\sin(xy) - (x^2y)\cos(xy),$$

$\partial(\partial f/\partial y)/\partial x = \partial\,[-x^2\sin(xy)]\,/\partial x = -2(x)\sin(xy) - (x^2y)\cos(xy)$.
(c) $\partial(\partial f/\partial t)/\partial s = \partial(2t + e^s)/\partial s = e^s$,
$\partial(\partial f/\partial s)/\partial t = \partial(te^s + 25)/\partial t = e^s$.

A3.2 $(\partial C_V/\partial V)_T = [\partial(\partial U/\partial T)_V/\partial V]_T = [\partial(\partial U/\partial V)_T/\partial T]_V$.
Since $(\partial U/\partial V)_T = 0$ for perfect gases, [Section 3.2(a)] $(\partial C_V/\partial V)_T = 0$ also.

A3.3 $H = U + pV$ [3.2.4]
$(\partial H/\partial U)_p = 1 + p(\partial V/\partial U)_p$.
$(\partial H/\partial U)_p = (\partial H/\partial V)_p/(\partial U/\partial V)_p = (\partial V/\partial U)_p\,[\partial(U + pV)/\partial V]_p$

$$= (\partial V/\partial U)_p\,[(\partial U/\partial V)_p + p] = \underline{1 + p(\partial V/\partial U)_p}.$$

A3.4 $dV = (\partial V/\partial p)_T dp + (\partial V/\partial T)_p dT$
$d(\ln V) = V^{-1}dV = V^{-1}(\partial V/\partial p)_T dp + V^{-1}(\partial V/\partial T)_p dT$.
$\alpha = V^{-1}(\partial V/\partial T)_p$ [3.2.9]; $\kappa = -V^{-1}(\partial V/\partial p)_T$ [3.2.11]
$d(\ln V) = -\kappa dp + \alpha dT$.

A3.5 $\alpha = V^{-1}(\partial V/\partial T)_p$ [3.2.9]
$V_{320} = V_{300}[0.75 + (3.9 \times 10^{-4})(320) + (1.48 \times 10^{-6})(320)^2] = (1.03)V_{300}$
$V_{320}^{-1} = 0.97V_{300}^{-1}$; $(\partial V/\partial T)_p = V_{300}(3.9 \times 10^{-4} + 2.96 \times 10^{-6}\,T/\mathrm{K})$
$[(\partial V/\partial T)_p]_{320} = V_{300}[3.9 \times 10^{-4} + (2.96 \times 10^{-6})(320)] = (1.3 \times 10^{-3}\,\mathrm{K}^{-1})V_{300}$
$\alpha_{320} = V_{320}^{-1}[(\partial V/\partial T)_p]_{320} = (0.97V_{300}^{-1})(1.3 \times 10^{-3}\,\mathrm{K}^{-1})V_{300}$

$$= (0.97)(1.3 \times 10^{-3}\,\mathrm{K}^{-1}) = \underline{1.3 \times 10^{-3}\,\mathrm{K}^{-1}}.$$

A3.6 $\kappa = -V^{-1}(\partial V/\partial p)_T = -[\partial(\ln V)/\partial p]_T$ [3.2.11].
$\Delta p = -\Delta(\ln V)/\kappa$; $V = m/\rho$; $-\Delta(\ln V) = \Delta(\ln\rho) \approx \rho^{-1}\Delta\rho = 0.0800 \times 10^{-2}$.
$\Delta p = (0.0800 \times 10^{-2})(7.35 \times 10^{-7}\,\mathrm{atm}^{-1})^{-1} = \underline{1.09 \times 10^3\,\mathrm{atm}}$.

A3.7 $(\partial H/\partial p)_T = -\mu_{JT}C_p = -(0.25\ \mathrm{K\ atm^{-1}})(29\ \mathrm{J\ K^{-1}\ mol^{-1}}) = \underline{-7.2\ \mathrm{J\ atm^{-1}\ mol^{-1}}}$ [Table 2.1, 3.2.15]

$q = -(\partial H/\partial p)_T(\Delta p) = (7.2\ \mathrm{J\ atm^{-1}\ mol^{-1}})(15\ \mathrm{mol})(75\ \mathrm{atm}) = \underline{8.1 \times 10^3\ \mathrm{J}}.$

A3.8 $q = \underline{0}$ [adiabatic process];

$w = -p_{ex}\Delta V = -(600\ \mathrm{Torr})(133\ \mathrm{Pa/Torr}) \times (40.0 \times 10^{-3}\ \mathrm{m^3}) = \underline{-3.19 \times 10^3\ \mathrm{J}}.$ [2.2.7b]

$\Delta T = -p_{ex}\Delta V/C_V$ [3.3.2] $= (-3.19 \times 10^3\ \mathrm{J})(21.1\ \mathrm{J\ K^{-1}\ mol^{-1}})^{-1}(4.00\ \mathrm{mol})^{-1}$
$= \underline{-37.8\ \mathrm{K}}.$

$\Delta U = q + w = 0 - 3.19\ \mathrm{kJ} = \underline{-3.19\ \mathrm{kJ}}.$

$\Delta H = \Delta U + nR\Delta T = -3.19 \times 10^3\ \mathrm{J} + (4.00\ \mathrm{mol})(8.31\ \mathrm{J\ K^{-1}\ mol^{-1}})(-37.8\ \mathrm{K})$
$= \underline{-4.45 \times 10^3\ \mathrm{J}}.$ [Section 2.3(c)]

A3.9 $q = \underline{0}$ [adiabatic process].

$\Delta U = C_V\Delta T = (3.00\ \mathrm{mol})(27.5\ \mathrm{J\ K^{-1}\ mol^{-1}})(50\ \mathrm{K}) = \underline{4.12 \times 10^3\ \mathrm{J}}.$

$w = \Delta U - q = 4.12 \times 10^3\ \mathrm{J} - 0 = \underline{4.12 \times 10^3\ \mathrm{J}}.$ [2.1.2]

$\Delta H = \Delta U + nR\Delta T = 4.12 \times 10^3\ \mathrm{J} + (3\ \mathrm{mol})(8.31\ \mathrm{J\ K^{-1}\ mol^{-1}})(50\ \mathrm{K}) = \underline{5.37 \times 10^3\ \mathrm{J}}.$

$V_i = nRT_i/p_i = (3.00\ \mathrm{mol})(8.31\ \mathrm{J\ K^{-1}\ mol^{-1}})(200\ \mathrm{K})(2.00\ \mathrm{atm})^{-1}(1.01 \times 10^5\ \mathrm{Pa/atm})^{-1}$
$= 2.47 \times 10^{-2}\ \mathrm{m^3}$, or $\underline{24.7\ \mathrm{cm^3}}.$ [1.1.1]

$c = C_{V,m}/R = 27.5\ \mathrm{J\ K^{-1}\ mol^{-1}}/8.31\ \mathrm{J\ K^{-1}\ mol^{-1}} = \underline{3.31}.$

$V_f = V_i(T_i/T_f)^c$ [3.3.3] $= (24.7\ \mathrm{dm^3})(200\ \mathrm{K}/250\ \mathrm{K})^{3.31} = \underline{11.8\ \mathrm{dm^3}}.$

$p_f = nRT_f/V_f = (3.00\ \mathrm{mol})(8.31\ \mathrm{J\ K^{-1}\ mol^{-1}})(250\ \mathrm{K})(11.8 \times 10^{-3}\ \mathrm{m^3})^{-1}$
$= \underline{5.28 \times 10^5\ \mathrm{Pa}}.$ [1.1.1]

A3.10 $V_i = nRT_i/p_i$ [1.1.1] $= (1.00\ \mathrm{mol})(8.31\ \mathrm{J\ K^{-1}\ mol^{-1}})(310\ \mathrm{K})(3.25\ \mathrm{atm})^{-1} \times$
$\times (1.01 \times 10^5\ \mathrm{Pa/atm})^{-1} = 7.85 \times 10^{-3}\ \mathrm{m^3}$,
or $\underline{7.85\ \mathrm{dm^3}}.$

$\gamma = C_{p,m}/C_{V,m}$ [3.3.6] $= (20.8\ \mathrm{J\ K^{-1}\ mol^{-1}} + 8.3\ \mathrm{J\ K^{-1}\ mol^{-1}})/(20.8\ \mathrm{J\ K^{-1}\ mol^{-1}})$
$= 1.40;\ 1/\gamma = 0.714.$

$V_f = V_i(p_i/p_f)^{1/\gamma}$ [3.3.8] $= (7.85\ \mathrm{dm^3})(3.25\ \mathrm{atm}/2.50\ \mathrm{atm})^{0.714} = \underline{9.47\ \mathrm{dm^3}}.$

$T_f = p_fV_f/nR$ [1.1.1] $= (2.50\ \mathrm{atm})(1.01 \times 10^5\ \mathrm{Pa/atm})(9.47 \times 10^{-3}\ \mathrm{m^3})(1.00\ \mathrm{mol})^{-1}$
$\times (8.31\ \mathrm{J\ K^{-1}\ mol^{-1}})^{-1} = \underline{288\ \mathrm{K}}.$

$w = C_V(T_f - T_i)$ [3.3.5] $= (20.8\ \mathrm{J\ K^{-1}})(288\ \mathrm{K} - 310\ \mathrm{K}) = \underline{-4.58 \times 10^2\ \mathrm{J}}.$

3.1 $\rho = M/V$; M is extensive, so is V; hence ρ is intensive.

p is independent of the amount of material; hence p is intensive.

M depends on amount of material; hence M is extensive.

T is independent of the amount of material; hence T is intensive.

H depends on the amount of material; hence H is extensive.

n_r (refractive index) is independent of the amount of material; hence n_r is intensive.

C depends on amount of material; hence C is extensive.

C_m is the ratio of two extensive properties, and so is intensive.

3.2 $(\partial U/\partial V)_T = [(\partial/\partial V)(\frac{3}{2}nRT)]_T = \underline{0}$.

$H = U + pV$ [3.2.4] $= U + nRT$ [$pV = nRT$]

$(\partial H/\partial V)_T = (\partial U/\partial V)_T + (\partial nRT/\partial V)_T = 0 + 0 = \underline{0}$.

3.3 $\kappa = 2.3 \times 10^{-6}\,\text{atm}^{-1} = 2.3 \times 10^{-6}(\text{N m}^{-2}/\text{atm})(\text{N m}^{-2})^{-1}$

$= 2.3 \times 10^{-6}(\text{N m}^{-2}/1.013 \times 10^{5}\,\text{N m}^{-2})\,\text{N}^{-1}\,\text{m}^{2}$ [endpaper 1]

$= \underline{2.3 \times 10^{-11}\,\text{N}^{-1}\,\text{m}^{2}}$.

$\delta V \approx (\partial V/\partial p)_T \delta p = -\kappa V \delta p$ [3.2.11]; $\delta p \approx \rho g h$ [hydrostatics].

$\rho = 1.03\,\text{g cm}^{-3} = 1.03 \times 10^{3}\,\text{kg m}^{-3}$, $g = 9.81\,\text{m s}^{-2}$,

$V = 1.0 \times 10^{3}\,\text{cm}^{3} = 1.0 \times 10^{-3}\,\text{m}^{3}$.

$\delta V = -(2.3 \times 10^{-11}\,\text{N}^{-1}\,\text{m}^{2}) \times (1.0 \times 10^{-3}\,\text{m}^{3}) \times (1.03 \times 10^{3}\,\text{kg m}^{-3})$

$\times (9.81\,\text{m s}^{-2}) \times h = -(2.3 \times 10^{-10}\,\text{m}^{2})h$.

(a) $h = 100\,\text{ft} \mathrel{\hat{=}} 30.5\,\text{m}$, $\delta V = -7.0 \times 10^{-9}\,\text{m}^{3} = \underline{-7.0\,\text{mm}^{3}}$.

(b) $h = 5000\,\text{fathoms} \mathrel{\hat{=}} 30\,000\,\text{ft} \mathrel{\hat{=}} 9144\,\text{m}$,

$\delta V = -2.1 \times 10^{-6}\,\text{m}^{3} = \underline{-2.1\,\text{cm}^{3}}$.

3.4 $\alpha = (1/V)(\partial V/\partial T)_p$ [3.2.9] $= 8.61 \times 10^{-5}\,\text{K}^{-1}$.

$\delta V \approx (\partial V/\partial T)_p \delta T = \alpha V \delta T$.

$V = 10^{-3}\,\text{m}^{3}$, $\delta T \mathrel{\hat{=}} (-5\,°\text{C}) - (25\,°\text{C}) = -30\,°\text{C}$, or $-30\,\text{K}$.

$\delta V = (8.61 \times 10^{-5}\,\text{K}^{-1}) \times (1.0 \times 10^{-3}\,\text{m}^{3}) \times (-30\,\text{K}) = -2.6 \times 10^{-6}\,\text{m}^{3}$

$= \underline{-2.6\,\text{cm}^{3}}$.

The combined effect is the sum of the δV for the pressure and temperature effects. Therefore (a) $\delta V \approx -2.6\,\text{cm}^{3}$ (δT effect dominating); (b) $\delta V \approx -4.7\,\text{cm}^{3}$ (approximately equal effects).

3.5 If $p = p(V,T)$, then $dp = (\partial p/\partial V)_T dV + (\partial p/\partial T)_V dT$.

As V, T depend on the time t, divide by $\mathrm{d}t$ and obtain

$\mathrm{d}p/\mathrm{d}t = (\partial p/\partial V)_T(\mathrm{d}V/\mathrm{d}t) + (\partial p/\partial T)_V(\mathrm{d}T/\mathrm{d}t)$.

For a perfect gas $(\partial p/\partial V)_T = -p/V$, $(\partial p/\partial T)_V = p/T$ [Problem 2.18a]; therefore

$$\mathrm{d}p/\mathrm{d}t = -(p/V)(\mathrm{d}V/\mathrm{d}t) + (p/T)(\mathrm{d}T/\mathrm{d}t)$$

or $\underline{\mathrm{d}\ln p/\mathrm{d}t = -\mathrm{d}\ln V/\mathrm{d}t + \mathrm{d}\ln T/\mathrm{d}t}$.

3.6 For Newtonian cooling towards absolute zero $T = T_\mathrm{i}\exp(-t/\tau_T)$,

and so $\mathrm{d}\ln T/\mathrm{d}t = (1/T)\mathrm{d}T/\mathrm{d}t = (1/T)(-T_\mathrm{i}/\tau_T)\exp(-t/\tau_T) = -1/\tau_T$.

For exponential compression, $V = V_\mathrm{i}\exp(-t/\tau_V)$, and so $\mathrm{d}\ln V/\mathrm{d}t = -1/\tau_V$.

Therefore, from Problem 3.5, $\mathrm{d}\ln p/\mathrm{d}t = 1/\tau_V - 1/\tau_T$ which integrates to

$$\ln p = t\left(\frac{1}{\tau_V} - \frac{1}{\tau_T}\right) + \text{constant}.$$

Consequently $\underline{p = p_\mathrm{i}\,\mathrm{e}^{-t/\tau_T}\,\mathrm{e}^{t/\tau_V}}$. When $\tau_T = \tau_V$, $p = p_\mathrm{i}$, independent of time.

3.7 $\mathrm{d}p = (\partial p/\partial V)_T\mathrm{d}V + (\partial p/\partial T)_V\mathrm{d}T$ [Problem 3.5].

$p = nRT/(V - nb) - n^2a/V^2$ [Box 1.1].

$$(\partial p/\partial V)_T = -nRT/(V - nb)^2 + 2n^2a/V^3 = -p/(V - nb) + (n^2a/V^3)\left(\frac{V - 2nb}{V - nb}\right).$$

$(\partial p/\partial T)_V = nR/(V - nb) = p/T + n^2a/TV^2$.

Therefore

$$\mathrm{d}p = -p\left(\frac{\mathrm{d}V}{V - nb}\right) + \left(\frac{n^2a}{V^3}\right)(V - 2nb)\left(\frac{\mathrm{d}V}{V - nb}\right) + p\left(\frac{\mathrm{d}T}{T}\right) + \frac{n^2a}{V^2}\left(\frac{\mathrm{d}T}{T}\right).$$

$$\text{or } \mathrm{d}\ln p = -\mathrm{d}\ln(V - nb) + \mathrm{d}\ln T + \left(\frac{n^2a}{pV^2}\right)\left[\left(1 - \frac{2nb}{V}\right)\mathrm{d}\ln(V - nb) + \mathrm{d}\ln T\right].$$

The modification should be to let V compress to nb as its limiting value.

3.8 $p = nRT/(V - nb) - n^2a/V^2$ [Box 1.1].

Therefore $T = (p/nR)(V - nb) + (na/RV^2)(V - nb)$.

$(\partial T/\partial p)_V = (V - nb)/nR = 1/(\partial p/\partial T)_V$ [Problem 3.7].

For Euler's chain relation [Box 3.1] we need to show that

$(\partial T/\partial p)_V(\partial p/\partial V)_T(\partial V/\partial T)_p = -1$.

Hence, in addition to $(\partial T/\partial p)_V$ [above] and $(\partial p/\partial V)_T$ [Problem 3.7], we require

$(\partial V/\partial T)_p = 1/(\partial T/\partial V)_p$ [Relation 2, Box 3.1]

$$\begin{aligned}(\partial T/\partial V)_p &= (p/nR) + (na/RV^2) - (2na/RV^3)(V - nb)\\ &= T/(V - nb) - (2an/RV^3)(V - nb).\end{aligned}$$

Therefore, $(\partial T/\partial p)_V(\partial p/\partial V)_T(\partial V/\partial T)_p = (\partial T/\partial p)_V(\partial p/\partial V)_T/(\partial T/\partial V)_p$

$$= \left\{\frac{\left(\dfrac{V-nb}{nR}\right)\left[\dfrac{-nRT}{(V-nb)^2}+\dfrac{2n^2a}{V^3}\right]}{\left[\left(\dfrac{T}{V-nb}\right)-\left(\dfrac{2an}{RV^3}\right)(V-nb)\right]}\right\} = \left\{\frac{\left(\dfrac{-T}{V-nb}\right)+\left(\dfrac{2na}{RV^3}\right)(V-nb)}{\left(\dfrac{T}{V-nb}\right)-\left(\dfrac{2na}{RV^3}\right)(V-nb)}\right\} = -1.$$

3.9 $\alpha = (1/V)(\partial V/\partial T)_p = (1/V)/(\partial T/\partial V)_p$ [Relation 2]

$$= \left(\frac{1}{V}\right)\left\{\frac{1}{T/(V-nb)-(2na/RV^3)(V-nb)}\right\} \text{ [Problem 3.8]}$$

$$= \frac{RV^2(V-nb)}{RTV^3-2na(V-nb)^2}.$$

$\kappa = -(1/V)(\partial V/\partial p)_T = -(1/V)/(\partial p/\partial V)_T$ [Relation 2]

$$= -\left(\frac{1}{V}\right)\left\{\frac{1}{-nRT/(V-nb)^2+2n^2a/V^3}\right\} \text{ [Problem 3.7]}$$

$$= \frac{V^2(V-nb)^2}{nRTV^3-2n^2a(V-nb)^2}.$$

Then $\kappa/\alpha = (V-nb)/Rn$, so that $nR\kappa = \alpha(V-nb)$, or $R\kappa = \alpha(V_m - b)$.

Using the chain relation [Box 3.1]:

$\kappa/\alpha = -(\partial V/\partial p)_T/(\partial V/\partial T)_p$ [Definition]

$= -1/(\partial p/\partial V)_T(\partial V/\partial T)_p$ [Relation 2]

$= (\partial T/\partial p)_V$ [Chain relation, Problem 3.8]

$= (V-nb)/nR$ [Problem 3.8].

Hence $\underline{\kappa R = \alpha(V_m - b)}$.

For the introduction of reduced variables [21.4.6]; define

$\kappa_r \equiv -(1/V_r)(\partial V_r/\partial p_r)_T = -(1/V)(\partial V/\partial p)p_c = \kappa p_c$

$\alpha_r \equiv (1/V_r)(\partial V_r/\partial T_r)_p = (1/V)(\partial V/\partial T)T_c = \alpha T_c$

Therefore $R\kappa = \alpha(V_m - b)$ becomes $R\kappa_r/p_c = (\alpha_r/T_c)(V_m - b)$,

or $\kappa_r = \alpha_r(V_r - b/V_c)(V_c p_c/RT_c)$. But $p_c V_c/RT_c = \frac{3}{8}$, $b/V_c = \frac{1}{3}$ [Box 1.1].

Therefore, $\underline{8\kappa_r = \alpha_r(3V_r - 1)}$.

3.10 $\mu_{JT}C_p = T(\partial V/\partial T)_p - V = [T/(\partial T/\partial V)_p] - V$ [Relation 2]

$$(\partial T/\partial V)_p = \left(\frac{T}{V-nb}\right) - \left(\frac{2an}{RV^3}\right)(V-nb) \text{ [Problem 3.8]}.$$

Therefore $\mu_{JT} C_p = -\left[\frac{nbRTV^2 - 2an(V-nb)^2}{RTV^3 - 2an(V-nb)^2}\right] V.$

The appearance of this may be simplified by writing

$\zeta = RTV^3/2an(V-nb)^2$,

for then $\mu_{JT}C_p = -\left(\frac{\zeta(nb/V) - 1}{\zeta - 1}\right) V.$

For xenon, take $n = 1$ mol, $V = 24.6\ \text{dm}^3$, $T = 298$ K

$a = 4.194\ \text{dm}^6\ \text{atm mol}^{-2}$, $b = 5.105 \times 10^{-2}\ \text{dm}^3\ \text{mol}^{-1}$.

$nb/V = (1\ \text{mol}) \times (5.105 \times 10^{-2}\ \text{dm}^3\ \text{mol}^{-1})/(24.6\ \text{dm}^3)$

$\quad = 2.1 \times 10^{-3}$; $V - nb = 24.6\ \text{dm}^3$.

$$\zeta = \frac{(0.0821\ \text{dm}^3\ \text{atm K}^{-1}\ \text{mol}^{-1}) \times (298\ \text{K}) \times (24.6\ \text{dm}^3)^3}{2 \times (1\ \text{mol}) \times (4.194\ \text{dm}^6\ \text{atm mol}^{-2}) \times (24.6\ \text{dm}^3)^2} = 71.8.$$

$$\mu_{JT}C_p = -\left(\frac{71.8 \times 2.1 \times 10^{-3} - 1}{71.8 - 1}\right) \times (24.6\ \text{dm}^3) = 0.295\ \text{dm}^3.$$

$C_p = nC_{p,m} = (1\ \text{mol}) \times (20.79\ \text{J K}^{-1}\ \text{mol}^{-1})$ [Table 2.1, or from $C_p - C_V = nR$ and equipartition].

Therefore $\mu_{JT} = (0.295 \times 10^{-3}\ \text{m}^3)/(20.79\ \text{J K}^{-1}) = 1.42 \times 10^{-5}\ \text{K m}^3\ \text{J}^{-1}$.

Consider $\text{J m}^{-3} = \text{N m m}^{-3} = \text{N m}^{-2} = (\text{atm}) \times (\text{N m}^{-2}/\text{atm})$

$\quad = \text{atm} \times (1/1.013 \times 10^5)$.

Therefore $\mu_{JT} = 1.42 \times 10^{-5} \times 1.013 \times 10^5\ \text{K atm}^{-1} = \underline{1.44\ \text{K atm}^{-1}}.$

3.11 μ_{JT} changes sign when the numerator in the expression for $\mu_{JT}C_p$ [Problem 3.10] changes sign (the denominator is positive). This occurs at $T = T_I$, where $nbRT_IV^2 = 2an(V-nb)^2$ or $T_I = \underline{2(a/bR)(1 - nb/V)^2}$.

For reduced variables define $T_{I,r} \equiv T_I/T_c$; then $T_{I,r} = 2(a/bRT_c)(1 - nb/V_rV_c)^2$

$= 2(a/bR)(27Rb/8a)(1 - b/3bV_r)^2$ [$T_c = 8a/27Rb$, $V_{c,m} = 3b$]

$= \underline{(27/4)(1 - 1/3V_r)^2}$.

Regard H_2 and CO_2 as van der Waals gases and assume $nb/V \ll 1$. Then $T_I \approx 2a/bR$. From Table 1.3:

(a) H_2 $a = 0.244\ \text{dm}^6\ \text{atm mol}^{-2}$, $b = 2.661 \times 10^{-2}\ \text{dm}^3\ \text{mol}^{-1}$

(b) CO_2 $a = 3.592\ \text{dm}^6\ \text{atm mol}^{-2}$, $b = 4.267 \times 10^{-2}\ \text{dm}^3\ \text{mol}^{-1}$.

Therefore, $T_I(H_2) = 223\,K$, $T_I(CO_2) = 2050\,K$.

Alternatively, from the reduced temperature expression with $3V_r \gg 1$, $T_I = T_{I,r}T_c \approx 27T_c/4$.

From Table 1.2, $T_c(H_2) = 33.2$, hence $T_I(H_2) = \underline{224\,K}$;

$T_c(CO_2) = 304.2$, hence $T_I(CO_2) = \underline{2053\,K}$.

3.12 $\mu_{JT} = (\partial T/\partial p)_H$ [3.2.14], and so $\delta T \approx (\partial T/\partial p)_H \delta p = \mu_{JT}\delta p$.

$\mu_{JT} = 1.2\,K\,atm^{-1}$, $\delta T = -5\,K$.

$\delta p = \delta T/\mu_{JT} = (-5\,K)/(1.2\,K\,atm^{-1}) = \underline{-4.2\,atm.}$

3.13 $\mu_{JT} = (\partial T/\partial p)_H = \lim_{\delta p \to 0} (\delta T/\partial p)_H$.

Draw up the following Table of $(\partial T/\partial p)$ for various δp:

p/atm	32	24	18	11	8	5
$-\delta p$/atm	31	23	17	10	7	4
$-\delta T$/K	22	18	15	10	7.4	4.6
$(\delta T/\delta p)/(K\,atm^{-1})$	0.71	0.78	0.88	1.00	1.06	1.15

Plot $(\delta T/\delta p)$ against δp, and extrapolate to $\delta p = 0$, Fig. 3.1. Hence find $\underline{\mu_{JT} = 1.3\,K\,atm^{-1}}$. That is, a smaller pressure difference is required than in the case of freon (Problem 3.12) to bring about the same temperature drop. In practice, take into account flammability, availability, toxicity, cost.

3.14 $(\partial H/\partial p)_T = (\partial H/\partial V)_T(\partial V/\partial p)_T$ [change of variable]

$= [(\partial/\partial V)(U + pV)]_T (\partial V/\partial p)_T$ [definition of H]

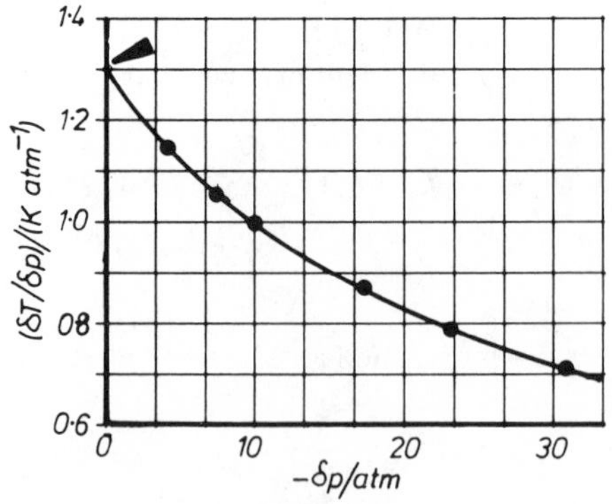

Fig 3·1

$$= \left(\frac{\partial U}{\partial V}\right)_T \left(\frac{\partial V}{\partial p}\right)_T + \left(\frac{\partial pV}{\partial V}\right)_T \left(\frac{\partial V}{\partial p}\right)_T$$

$$= \left\{T\left(\frac{\partial p}{\partial T}\right)_V - p\right\}\left(\frac{\partial V}{\partial p}\right)_T + \left(\frac{\partial pV}{\partial p}\right)_T \left[\text{equation for } \left(\frac{\partial U}{\partial V}\right)_T\right]$$

$$= T\left(\frac{\partial p}{\partial T}\right)_V \left(\frac{\partial V}{\partial p}\right)_T - p\left(\frac{\partial V}{\partial p}\right)_T + V + p\left(\frac{\partial V}{\partial p}\right)_T = T\left(\frac{\partial p}{\partial T}\right)_V \left(\frac{\partial V}{\partial p}\right)_T + V$$

$= -T/(\partial T/\partial V)_p + V$ [chain relation] $= -T(\partial V/\partial T)_p + V$ [Relation 2].

3.15 $\mu_{JT} = (\partial T/\partial p)_H$

$(\partial p/\partial T)_H(\partial H/\partial p)_T(\partial T/\partial H)_p = -1$ [chain relation]

$\quad\|\qquad\qquad\qquad\quad\|$

$1/\mu_{JT} \qquad\qquad\quad 1/C_p$

Therefore, $\mu_{JT}C_p = -(\partial H/\partial p)_T = T(\partial V/\partial T)_p - V$ [Problem 3.14]

$$= T^2\left(\frac{\partial(V/T)}{\partial T}\right)_p.$$

The equation of state $pV/nRT = 1 + nB/V$ [$V = nV_m$] converts to $(p/nRT)V^2 - V - nB = 0$. Therefore $V = (nRT/2p)\{1 + \sqrt{(1 + 4pB/RT)}\}$.

Write $\xi = \sqrt{(1 + 4pB/RT)}$, then $V/T = (nR/2p)(1 + \xi)$.

Therefore $[(\partial/\partial T)(V/T)]_p = (nR/2p)(\partial\xi/\partial T)_p$

$= (nR/2p)(4p/R)(1/2\xi)[(\partial/\partial T)(B/T)]_p = (n/\xi)[(\partial/\partial T)(B/T)]_p.$

Therefore $\mu_{JT}C_p = n(T^2/\xi)[(\partial/\partial T)(B/T)]_p$.

If $4pB/RT \ll 1$, $\xi \approx 1$. Then $\mu_{JT} \approx (T^2/C_{p,m})\left[\frac{\partial}{\partial T}\left(\frac{B}{T}\right)\right]_p$.

For argon at room temperature

$$\left[\frac{\partial}{\partial T}\left(\frac{B}{T}\right)\right]_p \approx \left(\frac{B(373\,\mathrm{K})}{373\,\mathrm{K}} - \frac{B(273\,\mathrm{K})}{273\,\mathrm{K}}\right)\Big/(373\,\mathrm{K} - 273\,\mathrm{K})$$

$$= \left\{\left(\frac{-4.2\,\mathrm{cm^3\,mol^{-1}}}{373\,\mathrm{K}}\right) - \left(\frac{-21.7\,\mathrm{cm^3\,mol^{-1}}}{273\,\mathrm{K}}\right)\right\}\Big/(100\,\mathrm{K}) \text{ [Table 1.1]}$$

$= 6.8 \times 10^{-4}\,\mathrm{cm^3\,K^{-2}\,mol^{-1}}$.

$p = 1$ atm, $T = 298$ K, $B(298\,\mathrm{K}) \approx -4.4\,\mathrm{cm^3\,mol^{-1}}$ [interpolation].

$$4pB/RT = \frac{4 \times (1\,\text{atm}) \times (-4.4 \times 10^{-3}\,\text{dm}^3\,\text{mol}^{-1})}{(0.0821\,\text{dm}^3\,\text{atm}\,\text{K}^{-1}\,\text{mol}^{-1}) \times (298\,\text{K})} = 7.2 \times 10^{-4} \ll 1.$$

$C_{p,\text{m}} = 20.78\,\text{J}\,\text{K}^{-1}\,\text{mol}^{-1}$ [Table 2.1]. Therefore,

$$\mu_{JT} \approx \frac{(298\,\text{K})^2 \times (6.8 \times 10^{-4} \times 10^{-6}\,\text{m}^3\,\text{K}^{-2}\,\text{mol}^{-1})}{20.78\,\text{J}\,\text{K}^{-1}\,\text{mol}^{-1}}$$

$$= 2.9 \times 10^{-6}\,\text{K}\,\text{m}^3\,\text{J}^{-1} = 2.9 \times 10^{-6}\,\text{K}(\text{N}\,\text{m}^{-2})^{-1}$$

$$= 2.9 \times 10^{-6}\,\text{K}\,\text{atm}^{-1}(\text{atm}/\text{N}\,\text{m}^{-2})$$

$$= (2.9 \times 10^{-6}\,\text{K}\,\text{atm}^{-1}) \times (1.013 \times 10^5) = \underline{0.29\,\text{K}\,\text{atm}^{-1}}.$$

3.16 $\delta V \approx (\partial V/\partial T)_p \delta T = \alpha V \delta T$ [3.2.9]

(a) Mercury: $\alpha = 1.82 \times 10^{-4}\,\text{K}^{-1}$;

(b) Diamond: $\alpha = 0.03 \times 10^{-4}\,\text{K}^{-1}$; $V = 1\,\text{cm}^3$, $\delta T = 5\,\text{K}$.

(a) $\delta V \approx (1.82 \times 10^{-4}\,\text{K}^{-1}) \times (1\,\text{cm}^3) \times (5\,\text{K}) = 9.1 \times 10^{-4}\,\text{cm}^3 = \underline{0.9\,\text{mm}^3}$

(b) $\delta V \approx (3.0 \times 10^{-6}\,\text{K}^{-1}) \times (1\,\text{cm}^3) \times (5\,\text{K}) = 15 \times 10^{-6}\,\text{cm}^3 = \underline{0.02\,\text{mm}^3}$.

3.17 $C_p - C_V = (\alpha^2/\kappa)TV$ [3.2.18] $= \alpha TV(\partial p/\partial T)_V$ [line above]

$(\partial p/\partial T)_V = nR/(V - nb)$ [Problem 3.8]; $\alpha V = (\partial V/\partial T)_p = 1/(\partial T/\partial V)_p$.

$(\partial T/\partial V)_p = T/(V - nb) - (2an/RV^3)(V - nb)$ [Problem 3.8]

$$C_p - C_V = T(\partial p/\partial T)_V/(\partial T/\partial V)_p = \frac{nRT/(V - nb)}{T/(V - nb) - (2an/RV^3)(V - nb)} = n\lambda R,$$

$$1/\lambda = 1 - \left\{\frac{2na(V - nb)^2}{RTV^3}\right\}.$$

Introduce reduced variables $T = T_r T_c$, $V = nV_r V_{\text{m,c}}$ and use $T_c = 8a/27Rb$, $V_{\text{m,c}} = 3b$ [Box 1.1]:

$$1/\lambda = 1 - \left\{\frac{2na(nV_r V_{\text{m,c}} - nb)^2}{RT_r T_c n^3 V_{\text{m,c}}^3 V_r^3}\right\} = 1 - \left\{\frac{2a(V_r - b/V_{\text{m,c}})^2}{RT_r T_c V_r^3 V_{\text{m,c}}}\right\}$$

$$= 1 - \left\{\frac{9(V_r - \frac{1}{3})^2}{4T_r V_r^3}\right\} \text{ [Box 1.1]} = 1 - \left\{\frac{(3V_r - 1)^2}{4T_r V_r^3}\right\}.$$

For xenon $V_\text{m} \approx 2.46\,\text{dm}^3\,\text{mol}^{-1}$, $V_{\text{m,c}} = 118.8\,\text{cm}^3\,\text{mol}^{-1}$, $T_c = 289.8\,\text{K}$ [Table 1.2]. $V_r \approx (2.46\,\text{dm}^3)/(119\,\text{cm}^3\,\text{mol}^{-1}) = 20.7$; $T_r \approx (298.2\,\text{K})/(289.7\,\text{K}) = 1.03$.

$$\text{Therefore } 1/\lambda \approx 1 - \left\{\frac{(62.1 - 1)^2}{4 \times 1.03 \times (20.7)^3}\right\} = 0.90,\ \lambda = 1.11;$$

so that $C_{p,\text{m}} - C_{V,\text{m}} \approx 1.11\,R = \underline{9.2\ \text{J K}^{-1}\,\text{mol}^{-1}}$.

3.18 $C_{p,\text{m}} - C_{V,\text{m}} = (\alpha^2/\kappa)TV_\text{m}$ [3.2.18].

(a) Copper: $\alpha = 0.501 \times 10^{-4}\,\text{K}^{-1}$, $\kappa = 0.735 \times 10^{-6}\,\text{atm}^{-1}$,

$V_\text{m} = (63.6\ \text{g mol}^{-1})/(8.97\ \text{g cm}^{-3}) = 7.09\ \text{cm}^3\,\text{mol}^{-1} = 7.09 \times 10^{-6}\,\text{m}^3\,\text{mol}^{-1}$.

$$C_{p,\text{m}} - C_{V,\text{m}} = \frac{(0.501 \times 10^{-4}\,\text{K}^{-1})^2 \times (289.15\ \text{K}) \times (7.09 \times 10^{-6}\,\text{m}^3\,\text{mol}^{-1})}{0.735 \times 10^{-6}\,\text{atm}^{-1}}$$

$$= 7.22 \times 10^{-6}\,\text{atm m}^3\,\text{K}^{-1}\,\text{mol}^{-1}$$

$$= 7.22 \times 10^{-6}\,\text{N m}^{-2} \times (\text{atm}/\text{N m}^{-2})\ \text{m}^3\,\text{K}^{-1}\,\text{mol}^{-1}$$

$$= 7.22 \times 10^{-6} \times 1.0133 \times 10^5\,\text{N m K}^{-1}\,\text{mol}^{-1} = \underline{0.731\ \text{J K}^{-1}\,\text{mol}^{-1}}.$$

(b) Benzene: $\alpha = 12.4 \times 10^{-4}\,\text{K}^{-1}$, $\kappa = 92.1 \times 10^{-6}\,\text{atm}^{-1}$,

$V_\text{m} = (78.1\ \text{g mol}^{-1})/(0.99\ \text{g cm}^{-3}) = 78.9\ \text{cm}^3\,\text{mol}^{-1}$.

$$C_{p,\text{m}} - C_{V,\text{m}} = \frac{(12.4 \times 10^{-4}\,\text{K}^{-1})^2 \times (298.15\ \text{K}) \times (78.9 \times 10^{-6}\,\text{m}^3\,\text{mol}^{-1})}{92.1 \times 10^{-6}\,\text{atm}^{-1}}$$

$$= 3.93 \times 10^{-4}\,\text{atm m}^3\,\text{K}^{-1}\,\text{mol}^{-1} = \underline{39.8\ \text{J K}^{-1}\,\text{mol}^{-1}}.$$

500 g of each represent $(500\ \text{g}/63.6\ \text{g mol}^{-1}) = 7.86$ mol Cu or $(500\ \text{g}/78.1\ \text{g mol}^{-1}) = 6.40$ mol C_6H_6. The differences $C_p - C_V$ are therefore

copper: $C_p - C_V = (7.86\ \text{mol}) \times (0.731\ \text{J K}^{-1}\,\text{mol}^{-1}) = 5.75\ \text{J K}^{-1}$

benzene: $C_p - C_V = (6.40\ \text{mol}) \times (39.8\ \text{J K}^{-1}\,\text{mol}^{-1}) = 255\ \text{J K}^{-1}$.

Since $\delta q \approx C\delta T$, the differences in the quantities of heat required for a 50 K temperature rise are

(a) copper: $\Delta(\delta q) = \delta q_p - \delta q_V = \underline{(5.75\ \text{J K}^{-1}) \times (50\ \text{K}) = 0.29\ \text{kJ}}$.

(b) benzene: $\Delta(\delta q) = \delta q_p - \delta q_V = \underline{(255\ \text{J K}^{-1}) \times (50\ \text{K}) = 12.7\ \text{kJ}}$.

3.19 $C_p - C_V = \alpha V\{p + (\partial U/\partial V)_T\}$ [3.2.17]

$(\partial U/\partial V)_T = \{(C_{p,\text{m}} - C_{V,\text{m}})/\alpha V_\text{m}\} - p$.

(a) Copper: $C_{p,\text{m}} - C_{V,\text{m}} = 0.731\ \text{J K}^{-1}\,\text{mol}^{-1}$, $V_\text{m} = 7.1 \times 10^{-6}\,\text{m}^3\,\text{mol}^{-1}$,

$\alpha = 0.501 \times 10^{-4}\,\text{K}^{-1}$, $p = 1\ \text{atm} = 1.013 \times 10^5\,\text{N m}^{-2}$.

$$(\partial U/\partial V)_T = \frac{0.731\ \text{J K}^{-1}\,\text{mol}^{-1}}{(0.501 \times 10^{-4}\,\text{K}^{-1}) \times (7.1 \times 10^{-6}\,\text{m}^3\,\text{mol}^{-1})} - 1.013 \times 10^5\,\text{N m}^{-2}$$

$$= 2.06 \times 10^9\,\text{J m}^{-3} - 1.013 \times 10^5\,\text{J m}^{-3} = \underline{2.06 \times 10^9\,\text{J m}^{-3}}$$

(b) Benzene:

$$(\partial U/\partial V)_T = \frac{39.8\ \text{J K}^{-1}\,\text{mol}^{-1}}{(12.4 \times 10^{-4}\,\text{K}^{-1}) \times (78.9 \times 10^{-6}\,\text{m}^3\,\text{mol}^{-1})} - 1.013 \times 10^5\,\text{J m}^{-3}$$

$= 4.07 \times 10^8\,\text{J m}^{-3} - 1.013 \times 10^5\,\text{J m}^{-3} = \underline{4.07 \times 10^8\,\text{J m}^{-3}}.$

3.20 (a) $\delta U \approx (\partial U/\partial T)_p \delta T$; $(\partial U/\partial T)_p = C_V + \alpha V(\partial U/\partial V)_T$ [3.2.10].

$(\partial U/\partial V)_T = \{(C_{p,\text{m}} - C_{V,\text{m}})/\alpha V_\text{m}\} - p$ [Problem 3.19]

$(\partial U/\partial T)_p = C_V + \{\alpha V(C_{p,\text{m}} - C_{V,\text{m}})/\alpha V_\text{m}\} - \alpha p V$

$= C_V + n(C_{p,\text{m}} - C_{V,\text{m}}) - \alpha p V = C_p - \alpha p V.$

$C_{p,\text{m}} = 75.3\,\text{J K}^{-1}\,\text{mol}^{-1}$ [Table 2.1], $\alpha = 2.1 \times 10^{-4}\,\text{K}^{-1}$ [Table 3.1]

$p = 1\,\text{atm} = 1.013 \times 10^5\,\text{N m}^{-2}$, $V_\text{m} = 18.07 \times 10^{-6}\,\text{m}^3\,\text{mol}^{-1}$,

$n = 1\,\text{mol}$.

$(\partial U/\partial T)_p = (75.3\,\text{J K}^{-1}) - (2.1 \times 10^{-4}\,\text{K}^{-1}) \times (1.013 \times 10^5\,\text{N m}^{-2}) \times (18.07 \times 10^{-6}\,\text{m}^3)$

$= 75.3\,\text{J K}^{-1} - 3.8 \times 10^{-4}\,\text{N m K}^{-1} = 75.3\,\text{J K}^{-1}.$

Therefore, $\delta U \approx (74.3\,\text{J K}^{-1}) \times (10\,\text{K}) = \underline{0.75\,\text{kJ}}.$

(b) $\delta H \approx (\delta H/\partial T)_p \delta T = C_p \delta T$ [3.2.8] $\approx (75.3\,\text{J K}^{-1}) \times (10\,\text{K}) = \underline{0.75\,\text{kJ}}.$

3.21 $w = -p_\text{ex}\Delta V$ [2.2.7]

$p_\text{ex} = 1.0\,\text{atm} = 1.01 \times 10^5\,\text{N m}^{-2}$; $\Delta V = 20\,\text{cm} \times 10\,\text{cm}^2 = 200\,\text{cm}^3 = 2.0 \times 10^{-4}\,\text{m}^3$.

$w = -(1.01 \times 10^5\,\text{N m}^{-2}) \times (2 \times 10^{-4}\,\text{m}^3) = -2.0 \times 10\,\text{N m} = \underline{-20\,\text{J}}.$

$\underline{q = 0}$ [adiabatic].

$\Delta U = q + w = w$ [adiabatic] $= \underline{-20\,\text{J}}.$

$\Delta H = \Delta U + \Delta(pV)$ [definition, $H = U + pV$] $\approx \Delta U + nR\Delta T$ [perfect gas].

$\Delta T = -p_\text{ex}\Delta V/C_V$ [3.3.2]

$C_{V,\text{m}} = 28.5\,\text{J K}^{-1}\,\text{mol}^{-1}$ [Table 2.1], $\Delta V = 2.0 \times 10^{-4}\,\text{m}^3$ [above]

$n = 2.0\,\text{mol}$, $C_V = (2\,\text{mol}) \times (28.5\,\text{J K}^{-1}\,\text{mol}^{-1}) = 57.0\,\text{J K}^{-1}$

$\Delta T = -(1.01 \times 10^5\,\text{N m}^{-2}) \times (2.0 \times 10^{-4}\,\text{m}^3)/(57.0\,\text{J K}^{-1}) = \underline{-0.35\,\text{K}}$ [J = N m].

$\Delta H = -20\,\text{J} + (2\,\text{mol}) \times (8.31\,\text{J K}^{-1}\,\text{mol}^{-1}) \times (-0.35\,\text{K}) = \underline{-26\,\text{J}}.$

3.22 (a) $T_\text{f} = (V_\text{i}/V_\text{f})^{1/c}\,T_\text{i}$ [3.3.4], $p_\text{f} = (V_\text{i}/V_\text{f})^\gamma p_\text{i}$ [3.3.8], or

$(V_\text{i}/V_\text{f}) = (p_\text{f}/p_\text{i})^{1/\gamma}.$

Therefore $T_\text{f} = (p_\text{f}/p_\text{i})^{1/c\gamma}T_\text{i}$, $c\gamma = (C_{V,\text{m}}/R)(C_{p,\text{m}}/C_{V,\text{m}}) = C_{p,\text{m}}/R$.

$p_\text{i} = 2.0\,\text{atm}$, $p_\text{f} = 1.0\,\text{atm}$, $T_\text{i} = 298\,\text{K}$.

$C_{p,\text{m}} = 20.79\,\text{J K}^{-1}\,\text{mol}^{-1}$ [Table 2.1], $c\gamma = 2.5$.

$T_\text{f} = (1.0\,\text{atm}/2.0\,\text{atm})^{1/2.5} \times (298\,\text{K}) = 0.76 \times (298\,\text{K}) = \underline{226\,\text{K}}.$

(b) $\Delta T = -p_\text{ex}\Delta V/C_V$ [3.3.2].

$C_V = (0.50\,\text{mol}) \times (12.5\,\text{J K}^{-1}\,\text{mol}^{-1}) = 6.7\,\text{J K}^{-1}.$

$$V_i \approx \frac{(0.50\,\text{mol}) \times (0.0821\,\text{dm}^3\,\text{atm K}^{-1}\,\text{mol}^{-1}) \times (298\,\text{K})}{2.0\,\text{atm}} = 6.1\,\text{dm}^3.$$

$V_f \approx nRT_f/p_f, p_f = p_{ex} = 1.0\,\text{atm}.$

$\Delta T = T_f - T_i = -p_{ex}(V_f - V_i)/C_V = -(p_{ex}/C_V)(nRT_f/p_f - V_i)$, so that

$T_f(1 + nR/C_V) = T_i + p_{ex}V_i/C_V$, or

$T_f = (T_i + p_{ex}V_i/C_V)/(1 + R/C_{V,m})$

$$= \frac{(298\,\text{K}) + (1.013 \times 10^5\,\text{N m}^{-2}) \times (6.1 \times 10^{-3}\,\text{m}^3)/(6.25\,\text{J K}^{-1})}{1 + (8.314\,\text{J K}^{-1}\,\text{mol}^{-1})/(12.5\,\text{J K}^{-1}\,\text{mol}^{-1})} = \underline{238\,\text{K}}.$$

3.23 $T_f = (V_i/V_f)^{1/c}\,T_i$ [3.3.4, $c = C_{V,m}/R$], or $\ln(T_f/T_i) = (1/c)\ln(V_i/V_f)$.

Therefore $c = \dfrac{\ln(V_i/V_f)}{\ln(T_f/T_i)}$; then $C_{V,m} = Rc$.

$V_i/V_f = 1/2,\ T_f/T_i = 248.44/298.15 = 0.833.$

$C_{V,m} = (8.314\,\text{J K}^{-1}\,\text{mol}^{-1}) \times \{\ln(0.5)/\ln(0.833)\}$

$\quad = (8.314\,\text{J K}^{-1}\,\text{mol}^{-1}) \times 3.80 = \underline{31.6\,\text{J K}^{-1}\,\text{mol}^{-1}}.$

A perfect gas is not necessarily a structureless gas. This figure suggests that there are internal mode contributions (e.g. vibrations) which increase $C_{V,m}$ from its translational and rotational value of $3R = 24.9\,\text{J K}^{-1}\,\text{mol}^{-1}$.

3.24 $T_f = (p_f/p_i)^{1/c\gamma}T_i$ [Problem 3.22], $c\gamma = C_{p,m}/R$,

$$C_{p,m} = R\left\{\frac{\ln(p_f/p_i)}{\ln(T_f/T_i)}\right\}$$

$p_f/p_i = (613.85\,\text{mmHg})/(1522.2\,\text{mmHg}) = 0.403.$

$$C_{p,m} = (8.314\,\text{J K}^{-1}\,\text{mol}^{-1})\left(\frac{\ln 0.403}{\ln 0.833}\right) = \underline{41.3\,\text{J K}^{-1}\,\text{mol}^{-1}}.$$

$\gamma = C_{p,m}/C_{V,m}$ [3.2.31] $= (41.3\,\text{J K}^{-1}\,\text{mol}^{-1})/(31.6\,\text{J K}^{-1}\,\text{mol}^{-1}) = \underline{1.31}.$

3.25 $\Delta U = w + q = w\,[q = 0$, adiabatic$]$

$w = C_V\Delta T$ [3.3.1] $= nC_{V,m}(T_f - T_i).$

$C_{V,m} = 31.6\,\text{J K}^{-1}\,\text{mol}^{-1},\ T_f - T_i = -49.71\,\text{K}.$

$\Delta U = w = (31.6\,\text{J K}^{-1}\,\text{mol}^{-1}) \times (-49.71\,\text{K}) = \underline{-1.57\,\text{kJ mol}^{-1}}.$

$\Delta H = \Delta U + \Delta pV = \Delta U + n\Delta RT = \Delta U + nR\Delta T$

$= -1.57\,\text{kJ mol}^{-1} + (8.314\,\text{J K}^{-1}\,\text{mol}^{-1}) \times (-49.71\,\text{K})$

$= -1.57\,\text{kJ} - 0.41\,\text{kJ} = \underline{-1.98\,\text{kJ mol}^{-1}}.$

3.26 $\mathrm{d}H = V\mathrm{d}p, \Delta H = \int_{p_\mathrm{i}}^{p_\mathrm{f}} V(p)\,\mathrm{d}p.$

$pV^\gamma = \text{constant [3.3.9]} \overset{\text{def}}{=} A^\gamma$, or $V = A/p^{1/\gamma}$.

$$\Delta H = A\int_{p_\mathrm{i}}^{p_\mathrm{f}} \frac{\mathrm{d}p}{p^{1/\gamma}} = \left(\frac{A}{1-\frac{1}{\gamma}}\right)\left(\frac{1}{p^{1/(\gamma-1)}}\right)\Bigg|_{p_\mathrm{i}}^{p_\mathrm{f}} = \left(\frac{\gamma A}{\gamma-1}\right)\left(\frac{1}{p_\mathrm{f}^{1/(\gamma-1)}} - \frac{1}{p_\mathrm{i}^{1/(\gamma-1)}}\right)$$

$$= \left(\frac{\gamma A}{\gamma-1}\right)\left(\frac{p_\mathrm{f}}{p_\mathrm{f}^{1/\gamma}} - \frac{p_\mathrm{i}}{p_\mathrm{i}^{1/\gamma}}\right) = \left(\frac{\gamma}{\gamma-1}\right)(p_\mathrm{f}V_\mathrm{f} - p_\mathrm{i}V_\mathrm{i})$$

$$= \left(\frac{nR\gamma}{\gamma-1}\right)(T_\mathrm{f} - T_\mathrm{i})\ [pV = nRT].$$

$$\gamma/(\gamma-1) = (C_{p,\mathrm{m}}/C_{V,\mathrm{m}})/\left(\frac{C_{p,\mathrm{m}}}{C_{V,\mathrm{m}}} - 1\right) = (C_{p,\mathrm{m}}/C_{V,\mathrm{m}})C_{V,\mathrm{m}}/(C_{p,\mathrm{m}} - C_{V,\mathrm{m}})$$

$$= C_{p,\mathrm{m}}/(C_{p,\mathrm{m}} - C_{V,\mathrm{m}}) = C_{p,\mathrm{m}}/R.$$

$\Delta H = (nRC_{p,\mathrm{m}}/R)(T_\mathrm{f} - T_\mathrm{i}) = \underline{C_p(T_\mathrm{f} - T_\mathrm{i})}.$

3.27 $C_{V,\mathrm{m}} = \frac{3}{2}R$ [translation].

$C_{p,\mathrm{m}} = C_{V,\mathrm{m}} + R\ [3.2.18] = \frac{3}{2}R + R = \frac{5}{2}R,$

Therefore $\gamma = C_{p,\mathrm{m}}/C_{V,\mathrm{m}} = \frac{5}{2}R/\frac{3}{2}R = \underline{\frac{5}{3}}.$

For a translating, rotating non-linear molecule,

$C_{V,\mathrm{m}} = \frac{3}{2}R + \frac{3}{2}R = 3R$ [Problem 2.20], $C_{p,\mathrm{m}} = C_{V,\mathrm{m}} + R = 4R.$

Therefore $\gamma = C_{p,\mathrm{m}}/C_{V,\mathrm{m}} = 4R/3R = \underline{4/3}.$

3.28 $C_{p,\mathrm{m}} - C_{V,\mathrm{m}} = \lambda R$, $1/\lambda = 1 - (3V_\mathrm{r} - 1)^2/4T_\mathrm{r}V_\mathrm{r}^3$ [Problem 3.17]

(a) $C_{V,\mathrm{m}} = \frac{3}{2}R$, $C_{p,\mathrm{m}} = \frac{3}{2}R + \lambda R$

$\gamma = C_{p,\mathrm{m}}/C_{V,\mathrm{m}} = \underline{1 + 2\lambda/3}.$

(b) $C_{V,\mathrm{m}} = 3R$ [Problem 2.20], $C_{p,\mathrm{m}} = 3R + \lambda R,$

$\gamma = C_{p,\mathrm{m}}/C_{V,\mathrm{m}} = \underline{1 + \lambda/3}.$

3.29 $T = 373\,\text{K}, p = 1\,\text{atm}, V_\mathrm{m} \approx 30.6\,\text{dm}^3\,\text{mol}^{-1}$ [from $V_\mathrm{m} \approx RT/p$].

(a) Xenon $V_{\mathrm{m,c}} = 118.8\,\text{cm}^3\,\text{mol}^{-1}$, $T_\mathrm{c} = 289.8\,\text{K}$ [Table 1.2].

$V_\mathrm{r} = (30.6 \times 10^3\,\text{cm}^3\,\text{mol}^{-1})/(118.8\,\text{cm}^3\,\text{mol}^{-1}) = 258.$

$T_r = (373\,\text{K})/(289.8\,\text{K}) = 1.29.$

$1/\lambda = 1 - (3 \times 258 - 1)^2/4 \times 1.29 \times 258^3 = 0.9932,\ \lambda = 1.0069.$

$\gamma = 1 + 2\lambda/3$ [Problem 3.28] $= \underline{1.671.}$

(b) Water vapour $V_{c,m} = 55.3\,\text{cm}^3\,\text{mol}^{-1}$, $T_c = 647.4\,\text{K}$ [Table 1.2].

$V_r = (30.6 \times 10^3\,\text{mol}^{-1})/(55.3\,\text{cm}^3\,\text{mol}^{-1}) = 553.$

$T_r = (373\,\text{K})/(647.4\,\text{K}) = 0.576.$

$1/\lambda = 1 - (3 \times 553 - 1)^2/(4 \times 0.576 \times 553^3) = 0.9929,\ \lambda = 1.0071.$

$\gamma = 1 + \lambda/3$ [Problem 3.28] $= \underline{1.336.}$

3.30 $c_s = \sqrt{(RT\gamma/M_m)}; p = \rho(RT/M_m)$ [Problem 1.8], $M_m = M_r\,\text{g}\,\text{mol}^{-1}$

$\underline{c_s = \sqrt{(p\gamma/\rho)}.}$

(a) $T = 298.15\,\text{K}$, $\gamma(\text{He}) = 5/3$ [Problem 3.27], $M_m(\text{He}) = 4.0 \times 10^{-3}\,\text{kg}\,\text{mol}^{-1}$.

$$c_s = \sqrt{\left\{\frac{(8.314\,\text{J}\,\text{K}^{-1}\,\text{mol}^{-1}) \times (298.15\,\text{K}) \times 5}{3 \times (4.0 \times 10^{-3}\,\text{kg}\,\text{mol}^{-1})}\right\}} = \sqrt{(1.03 \times 10^6\,\text{m}^2\,\text{s}^{-2})}$$
$$= \underline{1.02\,\text{km}\,\text{s}^{-1}}.$$

(b) $T = 298.15\,\text{K}$, $\gamma(\text{Air}) = 7/5$ [$C_{V,m}^{\text{diatomic}} = 5R/2$], $M_r(\text{Air}) \approx 29$

$$c_s = \sqrt{\left\{\frac{(2.48 \times 10^3\,\text{J}\,\text{mol}^{-1}) \times 7}{5 \times (29 \times 10^{-3}\,\text{kg}\,\text{mol}^{-1})}\right\}} = \sqrt{(1.20 \times 10^5\,\text{m}^2\,\text{s}^{-2})} = \underline{346\,\text{m}\,\text{s}^{-1}}.$$

3.31 $c_s = \sqrt{(RT\gamma/M_m)}$ [Problem 3.30], or $\gamma = M_m c_s^2/RT$

$M_r(\text{ethene}) = 28.1$ [end-paper 4], $c_s = 317\,\text{m}\,\text{s}^{-1}$, $T = 273\,\text{K}$.

$$\gamma = \frac{(28.1 \times 10^{-3}\,\text{kg}\,\text{mol}^{-1}) \times (317\,\text{m}\,\text{s}^{-1})^2}{(8.314\,\text{J}\,\text{K}^{-1}\,\text{mol}^{-1}) \times (273\,\text{K})} = \underline{1.24.}$$

$C_{p,m}/C_{V,m} = \gamma = 1.24;\ C_{p,m} - C_{V,m} = R.$

$C_{V,m} = R/(\gamma - 1) = R/0.24 = (8.314\,\text{J}\,\text{K}^{-1}\,\text{mol}^{-1})/0.24$

$= \underline{34.6\,\text{J}\,\text{K}^{-1}\,\text{mol}^{-1}}.$

3.32 $\nu = Kc_s$ [given], $c_s = \sqrt{(RT\gamma/M_m)}$ [Problem 3.30]

$$\frac{\nu(CO_2)}{\nu(\text{air})} = \frac{c_s(CO_2)}{c_s(\text{air})} = \sqrt{\left(\frac{\gamma(CO_2)}{\gamma(\text{air})}\,\frac{M_r(\text{air})}{M_r(CO_2)}\right)}.$$

$\gamma(CO_2) \approx 7/5$ [$C_{V,m}^{\text{linear}} = 5R/2$]; $\gamma(\text{air}) \approx 7/5$ [$C_{V,m}^{\text{diatomic}} = 5R/2$].

$M_r(\text{air}) \approx 29,\ M_r(CO_2) \approx 44.$

$\nu(CO_2) \approx \sqrt{(29/44)}\,\nu(\text{air}) = 0.81 \times (440\,\text{Hz}) = \underline{357\,\text{Hz}.}$

357 Hz is the F above middle C.

4. The First Law in action: thermochemistry

A4.1 $\Delta_f H^\ominus(T)$ $[KClO_3(s)]$ $= \Delta_f H^\ominus(T)$ $[KCl(s)] - (0.500)(-89.4\ kJ)$ [Table 4.1]

$= -436.8\ kJ\ mol^{-1} + 44.7\ kJ\ mol^{-1} = \underline{-392.1\ kJ\ mol^{-1}}.$

$\Delta_f H^\ominus(T)$ $[NaHCO_3(s)] = \Delta_f H^\ominus(T)$ $[NaOH(s)] + \Delta_f H^\ominus(T)$ $[CO_2(g)] + (-127.5\ kJ)$

$= -425.6\ kJ\ mol^{-1} - 393.5\ kJ\ mol^{-1} - 127.5\ kJ\ mol^{-1} = \underline{-946.6\ kJ\ mol^{-1}}.$

$\Delta_f H^\ominus(T)$ $[NOCl(g)] = \Delta_f H^\ominus(T)$ $[NO(g)] - (0.500)(+75.5\ kJ)$

$= +90.2\ kJ\ mol^{-1} - 37.8\ kJ\ mol^{-1} = \underline{+52.4\ kJ\ mol^{-1}}.$

A4.2 $C_8H_{10}(l) + (21/2)O_2(g) \rightarrow 8CO_2(g) + 5H_2O(l)$

$\Delta_r H^\ominus(T) = 8\Delta_f H^\ominus(T)$ $[CO_2(g)] + 5\Delta_f H^\ominus(T)$ $[H_2O(l)] - \Delta_f H^\ominus(T)$ $[C_8H_{10}(l)]$

$= 8(-393.5\ kJ\ mol^{-1}) + 5(-285.8\ kJ\ mol^{-1}) - (-12.5\ kJ\ mol^{-1})$

$= \underline{-4.564 \times 10^3\ kJ\ mol^{-1}}.$ [Table 4.1, 4.1.4]

A4.3 (a) $C_6H_{12}(l) + 9O_2(g) \rightarrow 6CO_2(g) + 6H_2O(l)$

(b) $6CO_2(g) + 7H_2O(l) \rightarrow C_6H_{14}(l) + (19/2)O_2(g)$

(c) $H_2(g) + (1/2)O_2(g) \rightarrow H_2O(l)$

(d) $C_6H_{12}(l) + H_2(g) \rightarrow C_6H_{14}(l)$

$\Delta_r H^\ominus(T)\ (d) = \Delta_r H^\ominus(T)\ (a) + \Delta_r H^\ominus(T)\ (b) + \Delta_f H^\ominus(T, H_2O(l))$

$= (-4003\ kJ\ mol^{-1}) - (-4163\ kJ\ mol^{-1}) + (-286\ kJ\ mol^{-1})$

$= \underline{-126\ kJ\ mol^{-1}}.$ [Tables 4.1, 4.2]

A4.4 $3C(s) + 3H_2(g) + O_2(g) \rightarrow C_3H_6O_2(l)$

$\Delta U = \Delta H - \Delta\nu_{gas}RT$, [4.1.11]

$\Delta\nu_{gas}RT = (-4.00\ mol)(8.31\ J\ K^{-1}\ mol^{-1})(298.15\ K) = -9.91 \times 10^3\ J$,

$\Delta_f U^\ominus(T) = -442\ kJ\ mol^{-1} - (-10\ kJ\ mol^{-1}) = \underline{-432\ kJ\ mol^{-1}}.$

A4.5 $2C(s) + 3H_2(g) \rightarrow C_2H_6(g)$

$$\Delta_f H^\ominus(350\ K) = \Delta_f H^\ominus(T) + \int_{298}^{350} \Delta_f C_p^\ominus\ dT \quad [4.1.6]$$

$C_p^\ominus[C_2H_6(g)] = [14.73 + 0.1272(T/K)]\ J\ K^{-1}\ mol^{-1}$

$C_p^\ominus[C(s)] = [16.86 + 4.77 \times 10^{-3}(T/K) - 8.54 \times 10^5\ (T/K)^{-2}]\ J\ K^{-1}\ mol^{-1}$

$C_p^{\ominus}$ [H_2(g)] $= [27.28 + 3.26 \times 10^{-3}\,(T/\mathrm{K}) + 0.50 \times 10^5\,(T/\mathrm{K})^{-2}]\ \mathrm{J\,K^{-1}\,mol^{-1}}$
[Table 4.3]

$$\Delta_f C_p^{\ominus} = [14.73 - 2(16.86) - 3(27.28) + 0.1272(T/\mathrm{K}) - 2(4.77 \times 10^{-3})\,(T/\mathrm{K}) - 3(3.26 \times 10^{-3})(T/\mathrm{K}) - 2(-8.54 \times 10^5)\,(T/\mathrm{K})^{-2} - 3(0.50 \times 10^5)\,(T/\mathrm{K})^{-2}]\ \mathrm{J\,K^{-1}\,mol^{-1}}$$

$$= [-100.83 + 0.1079(T/\mathrm{K}) + 15.58 \times 10^5 (T/\mathrm{K})^{-2}]\ \mathrm{J\,K^{-1}\,mol^{-1}}.$$

$$\int_{298}^{350} \Delta_f C_p^{\ominus}\, \mathrm{d}(T/\mathrm{K}) = [(-100.83)\,(350 - 298) + (1/2)\,(0.1079)\,(350^2 - 298^2) - (15.58 \times 10^5)\,(350^{-1} - 298^{-1})]\ \mathrm{J\,mol^{-1}} = -2.65 \times 10^3\ \mathrm{J\,mol^{-1}}$$

$\Delta_f H^{\ominus}(350\ \mathrm{K}) = -84.64\ \mathrm{kJ\,mol^{-1}} - 2.65\ \mathrm{kJ\,mol^{-1}} = \underline{-87.29\ \mathrm{kJ\,mol^{-1}}}.$

A4.6 $C_{10}H_8(s) + 12O_2(g) \rightarrow 10CO_2(g) + 4H_2O(l)$

$\Delta \nu_{\mathrm{gas}} = -2$ mol;

$\Delta \nu_{\mathrm{gas}} RT = (-2.00\ \mathrm{mol})(8.31\ \mathrm{J\,K^{-1}\,mol^{-1}})(298\ \mathrm{K}) = -4.95 \times 10^3\ \mathrm{J}$

$\Delta_r U = \Delta_r H - \Delta \nu_{\mathrm{gas}} RT$ [4.1.11] $= -5157\ \mathrm{kJ\,mol^{-1}} - (-5\mathrm{kJ\,mol^{-1}}) = \underline{-5152\ \mathrm{kJ\,mol^{-1}}}.$

$q_V = [(120 \times 10^{-3}/128)\ \mathrm{mol}]\ [-5152\ \mathrm{kJ\,mol^{-1}}] = \underline{-4.83\ \mathrm{kJ}.}$ [4.1.1]

$C = |q|\,(\Delta T)^{-1} = (4.83\ \mathrm{kJ})\,(3.05\ \mathrm{K})^{-1} = \underline{1.58\ \mathrm{kJ\,K^{-1}}}.$

$C_6H_5OH(s) + 7O_2(g) \rightarrow 6CO_2(g) + 3H_2O(l)$; $\Delta \nu_{\mathrm{gas}} = -1$ mol

$\Delta \nu_{\mathrm{gas}} RT = (-1.00\ \mathrm{mol})\,(8.31\ \mathrm{J\,K^{-1}\,mol^{-1}})\,(298\ \mathrm{K}) = -2.48 \times 10^3\ \mathrm{J}$

$\Delta_r U = \Delta_r H - \Delta \nu_{\mathrm{gas}} RT$ [4.1.11] $= -3054\ \mathrm{kJ\,mol^{-1}} - (-2\ \mathrm{kJ\,mol^{-1}})$
$= \underline{-3052\ \mathrm{kJ\,mol^{-1}}}.$

$q_V = [(100 \times 10^{-3}/94.1)\ \mathrm{mol}]\ [-3052\ \mathrm{kJ\,mol^{-1}}] = \underline{-3.24\ \mathrm{kJ}.}$ [4.1.1]

$\Delta T = |q|\,C^{-1} = (3.24\ \mathrm{kJ})(1.58\ \mathrm{kJ\,K^{-1}})^{-1} = \underline{2.05\ \mathrm{K}.}$ [Table 4.2]

A4.7 Enthalpy of fusion $= (2.60\ \mathrm{kJ\,mol^{-1}})[(750 \times 10^3/23.0)\ \mathrm{mol}] = \underline{8.48 \times 10^4\ \mathrm{kJ}.}$
[Table 4.7]

A4.8 $n(CH_4) = (32.5\ \mathrm{kJ})(8.18\ \mathrm{kJ\,mol^{-1}})^{-1} = 3.97$ mol [Table 4.7]

$V = nRT/p$ [1.1.1] $= (3.97\ \mathrm{mol})(8.31\ \mathrm{J\,K^{-1}\,mol^{-1}})(112\ \mathrm{K})(1.00\ \mathrm{atm})^{-1} \times$
$\times\,(1.01 \times 10^5\ \mathrm{Pa/atm})^{-1} = \underline{3.66 \times 10^{-2}\ \mathrm{m^3}}.$

A4.9 $\Delta_r H^{\ominus}(T) = \Delta_f H^{\ominus}(T)(Cu^{2+}) - 2\,[\Delta_f H^{\ominus}(T)(Ag^+)]$ [4.1.4]
$= 64.8\ \mathrm{kJ} - 2(105.6\ \mathrm{kJ}) = \underline{-1.46 \times 10^2\ \mathrm{kJ}.}$ [Table 4.8]

A4.10 $AgCl(s) \rightarrow Ag^+(aq) + Cl^-(aq)$

$$\Delta_r H^\ominus(T) = -\Delta_f H^\ominus(T)\,[AgCl(s)] + \Delta_f H^\ominus(T)\,[Ag^+(aq)] + \Delta_f H^\ominus(T)[Cl^-(aq)] \quad [4.1.4]$$
$$= 127.0\,kJ\,mol^{-1} + 105.6\,kJ\,mol^{-1} + (-167.2\,kJ\,mol^{-1})$$
$$= \underline{65.4\,kJ\,mol^{-1}}. \quad [Table\ 4.8]$$

4.1 $\Delta H > 0$ is diagnostic of an endothermic reaction (and $\Delta H < 0$ of an exothermic reaction). Hence, (a) is exothermic; (b), (c) are endothermic.

4.2 (a) $0 = CO_2 + 2H_2O - CH_4 - 2O_2$,
$\nu(CO_2) = 1, \nu(H_2O) = 2, \nu(CH_4) = -1, \nu(O_2) = -2.$
(b) $0 = C_2H_2 - 2C - H_2$,
$\nu(C_2H_2) = 1, \nu(C) = -2, \nu(H_2) = -1.$
(c) $0 = NaCl(aq) - NaCl(s)$,
$\nu(NaCl, aq) = 1, \nu(NaCl, s) = -1.$

4.3 $\Delta_r H^\ominus = \Delta_f H^\ominus(N_2O_4,g) - 2\Delta_f H^\ominus(NO_2,g)$
$= 9.16\,kJ\,mol^{-1} - 2(33.18\,kJ\,mol^{-1}) = \underline{-57.20\,kJ\,mol^{-1}}.$
(b) $\Delta_r H^\ominus = \Delta_f H^\ominus(NH_4Cl,s) - \Delta_f H^\ominus(NH_3,g) - \Delta_f H^\ominus(HCl,g)$
$= (-314.43\,kJ\,mol^{-1}) - (-46.11\,kJ\,mol^{-1}) - (-92.31\,kJ\,mol^{-1})$
$= \underline{-176.01\,kJ\,mol^{-1}}.$
(c) $\Delta_r H^\ominus = \Delta_f H^\ominus(propene,g) - \Delta_f H^\ominus(cyclopropane,g)$
$= 20.42\,kJ\,mol^{-1} - 53.30\,kJ\,mol^{-1} = \underline{-32.88\,kJ\,mol^{-1}}.$
(d) Since the reaction is also
$H^+(aq) + Cl^-(aq) + Na^+(aq) + OH^-(aq) \rightarrow Na^+(aq) + Cl^-(aq) + H_2O(l)$,
or $H^+(aq) + OH^-(aq) \rightarrow H_2O(l)$, it follows that
$\Delta_r H^\ominus = \Delta_f H^\ominus(H_2O,l) - \Delta_f H^\ominus(H^+,aq) - \Delta_f H^\ominus(OH^-,aq)$
$= (-285.83\,kJ\,mol^{-1}) - (0) - (-229.99\,kJ\,mol^{-1}) = \underline{-55.84\,kJ\,mol^{-1}}.$

4.4 $C \approx q/\delta T$ [2.3.1], $q = ItV$ [*Example* 1.6],
$I = 3.200$ A, $t = 27.0$ s, $V = 12.0$ V, $\delta T = 1.617$ K.
$C = (3.200\,A) \times (27.0\,s) \times (12.0\,V)/(1.617\,K) = 641\,A\,V\,s\,K^{-1}$
$= \underline{641\,J\,K^{-1}}$ [A V s = J].

4.5 $q = C\delta T$, $\Delta U = q_V$ [4.1.1]
$C = 641\,J\,K^{-1}$ [Problem 4.3], $\delta T = 7.793$ K.
$M = 0.3212$ g, $M_r = 180.16$;

$n = (0.3212\ \text{g})/(180.16\ \text{g mol}^{-1}) = 1.78 \times 10^{-3}\ \text{mol}$.

(b) $\Delta_r U = -(641\ \text{J K}^{-1}) \times (7.793\ \text{K})/(1.783 \times 10^{-3}\ \text{mol})$

$= \underline{-2800\ \text{kJ mol}^{-1}}$.

(a) $\Delta H = \Delta U + \Delta\nu_{\text{gas}} RT$ [4.1.11], $\Delta\nu_{\text{gas}} = 0$,

$\Delta_r H = \Delta_r U = \underline{-2800\ \text{kJ mol}^{-1}}$.

(c) Since $6CO_2(g) + 6H_2O(l) \rightarrow 6O_2(g) + \text{glucose(s)}$.

$\Delta_r H^\ominus = +2800\ \text{kJ mol}^{-1}$.

$C(s) + O_2(g)$; $\Delta_r H^\ominus = -393.51\ \text{kJ mol}^{-1}$ [Table 4.1].

$H_2(g) + \frac{1}{2}O_2(g) \rightarrow H_2O(l)$, $\Delta_r H^\ominus = -285.83\ \text{kJ mol}^{-1}$ [Table 4.1].

$\Delta_f H^\ominus(\text{glucose}) = (2800\ \text{kJ mol}^{-1}) + 6(-393.51\ \text{kJ mol}^{-1})$

$+ 6(-285.83\ \text{kJ mol}^{-1}) = \underline{-1270\ \text{kJ mol}^{-1}}$.

4.6 $Cr(C_6H_6)_2(c) \rightarrow Cr(c) + 2C_6H_6(g)$, $\Delta\nu_{\text{gas}} = 2$

$\Delta_r H = \Delta_r U + \Delta\nu_{\text{gas}} RT$ [4.1.11]

$= (8.0\ \text{kJ mol}^{-1}) + 2 \times (8.314\ \text{J K}^{-1}\text{mol}^{-1}) \times (583\ \text{K})$

$= (8.0\ \text{kJ mol}^{-1}) + (9.7\ \text{kJ mol}^{-1}) = \underline{17.7\ \text{kJ mol}^{-1}}$.

$\Delta_f H^\ominus = 2\Delta_f H(C_6H_6, g, 583\ \text{K}) - 17.7\ \text{kJ mol}^{-1}$.

$\Delta_f H^\ominus(C_6H_6, g, 583\ \text{K}) = \Delta_f H^\ominus(C_6H_6, l, 298\ \text{K}) + (T_b - 298\ \text{K})C_{p,m}(l)$

$$+ \Delta H^\ominus_{\text{vap,m}} + (583\ \text{K} - T_b)C_{p,m}(g) - 6\int_{298\ \text{k}}^{583\ \text{k}} C_{p,m}\ [C(gr)]\, dT$$

$$-3\int_{298\ \text{K}}^{583\ \text{K}} C_{p,m}\ [H_2(g)]\, dT \quad [4.1.6]$$

$C_{p,m}\ [C(gr)] = 16.86 + 4.77 \times 10^{-3}\, T - 8.54 \times 10^5/T^2$ [Table 4.3]

$C_{p,m}\ [H_2(g)] = 27.28 + 3.26 \times 10^{-3}\, T + 0.50 \times 10^5/T^2$ [Table 4.3].

$$\int_{298\ \text{K}}^{583\ \text{K}} \{6C_{p,m}(C) + 3C_{p,m}(H_2)\}dT = \int_{298\ \text{K}}^{583\ \text{K}} \{183.0 + 3.84 \times 10^{-2}\, T - 4.97 \times 10^6/T^2\}dT$$

$$= \left\{183.0(583 - 298) + 1.92 \times 10^{-2}(583^2 - 298^2) + 4.97 \times 10^6 \left(\frac{1}{583} - \frac{1}{298}\right)\right\} \text{J}$$

$= 48.8\ \text{kJ mol}^{-1}$.

$\Delta_f H^\ominus(C_6H_6, l, 298\ \text{K}) = 49.0\ \text{kJ mol}^{-1}$, $\Delta H^\ominus_{\text{vap,m}} = 30.8\ \text{kJ mol}^{-1}$,

$$T_b = 353.2\,\mathrm{K}\ [\text{Table 4.7}].$$

$\Delta_f H^\ominus(C_6H_6, g, 583\,K) = \{49.0 + (55 \times 0.140) + 30.8 + (0.230 \times 28) - 48.8\}\,\mathrm{kJ\,mol^{-1}}$

$= (93.9 - 48.8)\,\mathrm{kJ\,mol^{-1}} = \underline{45.1\,\mathrm{kJ\,mol^{-1}}}.$

$\Delta_f H^\ominus(Cr(C_6H_6)_2(c), 583\,K) = (90.2 - 17.7)\,\mathrm{kJ\,mol^{-1}} = \underline{72.5\,\mathrm{kJ\,mol^{-1}}}.$

4.7 $C_5H_{10}O_5(s) + 5O_2(g) \rightarrow 5CO_2(g) + 5H_2O(l),\ \Delta\nu_g = 0$

$C_6H_5CO_2H(s) + \frac{15}{2}O_2(g) \rightarrow 7CO_2(g) + 3H_2O(l),\ \Delta\nu_g = -\frac{1}{2}$

ribose: $M_r = 150.13,\ n = (0.727\,\mathrm{g}/150.13\,\mathrm{g\,mol^{-1}}) = 4.84 \times 10^{-3}\,\mathrm{mol}$

benzoic acid: $M_r = 122.12$,

$n = (0.825\,\mathrm{g}/122.12\,\mathrm{g\,mol^{-1}}) = 6.76 \times 10^{-3}\,\mathrm{mol}.$

From the benzoic acid data,

$\Delta U = -(3251\,\mathrm{kJ\,mol^{-1}}) \times (6.76 \times 10^{-3}\,\mathrm{mol}) = -22.0\,\mathrm{kJ} = -C\delta T.$

Since $\delta T = 1.940\,\mathrm{K}$, $C = (22.0\,\mathrm{kJ})/(1.940\,\mathrm{K}) = 11.3\,\mathrm{kJ\,K^{-1}}$

For the D-ribose, $\Delta U = -C\delta T = -(11.3\,\mathrm{kJ\,K^{-1}}) \times (0.910\,\mathrm{K}) = -10.3\,\mathrm{kJ}.$

Therefore $\Delta_r U = (-10.3\,\mathrm{kJ})/(4.84 \times 10^{-3}\,\mathrm{mol}) = \underline{-2130\,\mathrm{kJ\,mol^{-1}}}.$

$\Delta_r H = \Delta_r U\,[\Delta\nu_{gas} = 0] = \underline{-2130\,\mathrm{kJ\,mol^{-1}}}.$

The standard molar enthalpy of formation is

$\Delta_f H^\ominus = 2130\,\mathrm{kJ\,mol^{-1}} + 5\Delta H_f^\ominus(H_2O) + 5\Delta H_f^\ominus(CO_2)$

$= 2130\,\mathrm{kJ\,mol^{-1}} + 5(-285.8\,\mathrm{kJ\,mol^{-1}}) + 5(-393.5\,\mathrm{kJ\,mol^{-1}})$

$= \underline{-1270\,\mathrm{kJ\,mol^{-1}}}.$

4.8 $C_{10}H_8(s) + 12O_2(g) = 10CO_2(g) + 4H_2O(l);\ \Delta_r H^\ominus = -5157\,\mathrm{kJ\,mol^{-1}}.$

Therefore $10CO_2(g) + 4H_2O(l) \rightarrow C_{10}H_8(s) + 12O_2(g);\ \Delta_r H^\ominus = +5157\,\mathrm{kJ\,mol^{-1}}.$

Consequently,

$\Delta_f H^\ominus = (5157\,\mathrm{kJ\,mol^{-1}}) + 10\Delta_f H^\ominus(CO_2) + 4\Delta_f H^\ominus(H_2O)$

$= (5157\,\mathrm{kJ\,mol^{-1}}) + 10(-393.51\,\mathrm{kJ\,mol^{-1}}) + 4(-285.83\,\mathrm{kJ\,mol^{-1}})$

$= \underline{78.6\,\mathrm{kJ\,mol^{-1}}}.$

4.9 $NH_3SO_2 \rightarrow NH_3 + SO_2,\ \Delta_r H^\ominus = +40\,\mathrm{kJ\,mol^{-1}}.$

$NH_3 + SO_2 \rightarrow NH_3SO_2,\ \Delta_r H^\ominus = -40\,\mathrm{kJ\,mol^{-1}}.$

$\Delta_f H^\ominus = \Delta_f H^\ominus(NH_3) + \Delta_f H^\ominus(SO_2) + (-40\,\mathrm{kJ\,mol^{-1}})$

$= (-46.1\,\mathrm{kJ\,mol^{-1}}) + (-296.8\,\mathrm{kJ\,mol^{-1}}) + (-40\,\mathrm{kJ\,mol^{-1}})$

$= \underline{-383\,\mathrm{kJ\,mol^{-1}}}.$

4.10 $(C_6H_5)_2 + (29/2)\ O_2(g) \rightarrow 12CO_2(g) + 5H_2O(x)$

x = liquid at 25 °C, 99 °C; $\Delta\nu_{gas} = 12 - 29/2 = -5/2$,

x = gas at 101 °C; $\Delta\nu_{gas} = 17 - 29/2 = +5/2$.

$RT = 2.48\ \text{kJ mol}^{-1}$ at 25 °C $[R = 8.314\ \text{J K}^{-1}\ \text{mol}^{-1}]$.

$3.09\ \text{kJ mol}^{-1}$ at 99 °C,

$3.11\ \text{kJ mol}^{-1}$ at 101 °C.

(a) $\Delta_r H^\ominus - \Delta_r U^\ominus = (-5/2) \times 2.48\ \text{kJ mol}^{-1} = \underline{-6.20\ \text{kJ mol}^{-1}}$,

(b) $\Delta_r H^\ominus - \Delta_r U^\ominus = (-5/2) \times 3.09\ \text{kJ mol}^{-1} = \underline{-7.73\ \text{kJ mol}^{-1}}$,

(c) $\Delta_r H^\ominus - \Delta_r U^\ominus = (+5/2) \times 3.11\ \text{kJ mol}^{-1} = \underline{+7.78\ \text{kJ mol}^{-1}}$.

4.11 $\Delta H_m - \Delta U_m = \Delta p V_m$ [4.1.9] $= p\Delta V_m$

$V_m(\text{graphite}) = (12.01\ \text{g mol}^{-1})/(2.27\ \text{g cm}^{-3}) = 5.29\ \text{cm}^3\ \text{mol}^{-1}$.

$V_m(\text{diamond}) = (12.01\ \text{g mol}^{-1})/(3.52\ \text{g cm}^{-3}) = 3.41\ \text{cm}^3\ \text{mol}^{-1}$.

$\Delta V_m = V_m(\text{diamond}) - V_m(\text{graphite}) = -1.88\ \text{cm}^3\ \text{mol}^{-1}$

$$\Delta H_m - \Delta U_m = (500\ \text{kbar}) \times (-1.88\ \text{cm}^3\ \text{mol}^{-1})$$
$$= (500 \times 10^3) \times (1.013 \times 10^5\ \text{N m}^{-2}) \times (-1.88 \times 10^{-6}\ \text{m}^3\ \text{mol}^{-1})$$
$$= \underline{-95.2\ \text{kJ mol}^{-1}}.$$

4.12 $\Delta H_c^\ominus(C_4H_{10}) = -2877\ \text{kJ mol}^{-1}, M_r = 58.12$.

q_p evolved per mole $= 2877\ \text{kJ mol}^{-1}$,

q_p evolved per gram $= (2877\ \text{kJ mol}^{-1})/(58.12\ \text{g mol}^{-1}) = 49.50\ \text{kJ g}^{-1}$.

$\Delta H_c^\ominus(\text{pentane}) = -3536\ \text{kJ mol}^{-1}, M_r = 72.15$

q_p evolved per mole $= 3536\ \text{kJ mol}^{-1}$,

q_p evolved per gram $= (3536\ \text{kJ mol}^{-1})/(72.15\ \text{g mol}^{-1}) = \underline{49.01\ \text{kJ g}^{-1}}$.

$\Delta H_c^\ominus(\text{octane}) = -5471\ \text{kJ mol}^{-1}, M_r = 114.2$.

q_p evolved per mole $= 5471\ \text{kJ mol}^{-1}$,

q_p evolved per gram $= (5471\ \text{kJ mol}^{-1})/(114.2\ \text{g mol}^{-1}) = \underline{47.91\ \text{kJ g}^{-1}}$.

4.13 (a) $C_4H_{10} + \frac{13}{2}O_2 \rightarrow 4CO_2 + 5H_2O(l)$; $\Delta\nu_g = 4 - \frac{13}{2} = -\frac{5}{2}$.

$q_V = \Delta U_c^\ominus = \Delta H_c^\ominus - \Delta\nu_g RT = -2877\ \text{kJ mol}^{-1} - (-5/2) \times (2.48\ \text{kJ mol}^{-1})$

$= -2871\ \text{kJ mol}^{-1} \triangleq -49.40\ \text{kJ g}^{-1}$.

(b) $C_5H_{12} + 8O_2 \rightarrow 5CO_2 + 6H_2O$, $\Delta\nu_g = 5 - 8 = -3$.

$q_V = -3536\ \text{kJ mol}^{-1} - (-3) \times (2.48\ \text{kJ mol}^{-1})$

$= -3529\ \text{kJ mol}^{-1} \triangleq \underline{-48.91\ \text{kJ g}^{-1}}$.

(c) $C_8H_{18} + \frac{25}{2}O_2 \rightarrow 8CO_2 + 9H_2O$, $\Delta\nu_g = 8 - \frac{25}{2} = -\frac{9}{2}$

$q_V = -5512\,\text{kJ mol}^{-1} - (-9/2) \times (2.48\,\text{kJ mol}^{-1})$

$= -5501\,\text{kJ mol}^{-1} \mathrel{\hat{=}} \underline{-48.17\,\text{kJ g}^{-1}}$.

4.14 $w = mgh$ [*Example* 2.1], M_r(glucose) = 180.2.

$m \approx 140\,\text{lb} \mathrel{\hat{=}} 63\,\text{kg}$, $g = 9.81\,\text{m s}^{-2}$, h = (a) 3m, (b) 3000 m.

(a) $w = (63\,\text{kg}) \times (9.81\,\text{m s}^{-2}) \times (3\,\text{m}) = 1852\,\text{J}$

$|\Delta H_c| = 2808\,\text{kJ mol}^{-1} \mathrel{\hat{=}} 15.58\,\text{kJ g}^{-1}$. At 25 per cent efficiency,

$|\Delta H_c|_{\text{effective}} \approx 3.90\,\text{kJ g}^{-1}$. For 1.85 kJ, the required consumption is

$(1.85\,\text{kJ})/(3.90\,\text{kJ g}^{-1}) = \underline{0.47\,\text{g}}$.

(b) $w = (63\,\text{kg}) \times (9.81\,\text{m s}^{-2}) \times (3000\,\text{m}) = 1852\,\text{kJ}$.

Required consumption is 0.47 g × 1000 = $\underline{0.47\,\text{kg}}$.

4.15 $N_2 + \frac{5}{2}O_2 \rightarrow N_2O_5$; $\Delta_f H^\ominus$.

$N_2 + \frac{5}{2}O_2 \xrightarrow{a} 2NO + \frac{3}{2}O_2 \xrightarrow{b} 2NO_2 + \frac{1}{2}O_2 \xrightarrow{c} N_2O_5$.

$\Delta_f H^\ominus = a + b + c$

$= \{(+180.5) + (-114.1) + \frac{1}{2}(-110.2)\}\,\text{kJ mol}^{-1} = \underline{11.3\,\text{kJ mol}^{-1}}$.

4.16 $C(gr) + O_2 \rightarrow CO_2$; $\Delta_r H^\ominus = -393.51\,\text{kJ mol}^{-1}$

$C(d) + O_2 \rightarrow CO_2$; $\Delta_r H^\ominus = -395.41\,\text{kJ mol}^{-1}$

$CO_2 \rightarrow C(d) + O_2$; $\Delta_r H^\ominus = +395.41\,\text{kJ mol}^{-1}$

$C(gr) + O_2 \rightarrow C(d) + O_2$; $\Delta_r H^\ominus = -393.51\,\text{kJ mol}^{-1} + 395.41\,\text{kJ mol}^{-1} = 1.90\,\text{kJ mol}^{-1}$.

$C(gr) \rightarrow C(d)$; $\Delta H_m^\ominus = \underline{1.90\,\text{kJ mol}^{-1}}$.

4.17 $\Delta H(373\,\text{K}) = \Delta H(T) + (373\,\text{K} - 298\,\text{K}) \times \Delta C_p$

$= \Delta H(T) + 75\,\text{K} \times \Delta C_p$

$\Delta C_p = C_{p,m}(N_2O_4) - 2C_{p,m}(NO_2)$

$= (77.28 - 2 \times 37.20)\,\text{J K}^{-1}\,\text{mol}^{-1} = 2.88\,\text{J K}^{-1}\,\text{mol}^{-1}$

$\Delta H(373\,\text{K}) = -57.20\,\text{kJ mol}^{-1} + (75\,\text{K}) \times (2.88\,\text{J K}^{-1}\,\text{mol}^{-1})$

$= -57.20\,\text{kJ mol}^{-1} + 0.22\,\text{kJ mol}^{-1} = \underline{-56.98\,\text{kJ mol}^{-1}}$.

4.18 $\Delta H(T_2) = \Delta H(T_2) + \int_{T_1}^{T_2} \Delta C_p(T)\,dT$ [4.1.6]

$C_p(T) = a + bT + c/T^2$;

$\Delta C_p(T) = \Delta a + \Delta bT + \Delta c/T^2$

where $\Delta a = \sum_{J} \nu_J a_J$, etc.

$$\Delta H(T_2) = \Delta H(T_1) + \int_{T_1}^{T_2} (\Delta a + \Delta bT + \Delta c/T^2)\,\mathrm{d}T$$

$$= \Delta H(T_1) + \Delta a(T_2 - T_1) + \tfrac{1}{2}\Delta b(T_2^2 - T_1^2) - \Delta c\left(\frac{1}{T_2} - \frac{1}{T_1}\right).$$

4.19 $a(H_2O) = 75.48\ \mathrm{J\,K^{-1}\,mol^{-1}}$, $b = 0$, $c = 0$.

$a(H_2) = 27.28\ \mathrm{J\,K^{-1}\,mol^{-1}}$, $b = 3.26 \times 10^{-3}\ \mathrm{J\,K^{-2}\,mol^{-1}}$, $c = 0.50 \times 10^5\ \mathrm{J\,K\,mol^{-1}}$.

$a(O_2) = 29.96\ \mathrm{J\,K^{-1}\,mol^{-1}}$, $b = 4.18 \times 10^{-3}\ \mathrm{J\,K^{-2}\,mol^{-1}}$, $c = -1.67 \times 10^5\ \mathrm{J\,K\,mol^{-1}}$.

$H_2(g) + \tfrac{1}{2}O_2(g) \rightarrow H_2O(l)$; $\Delta_f H^\ominus(\mathcal{T}) = -285.83\ \mathrm{kJ\,mol^{-1}}$.

$\Delta a = (75.48 - 27.28 - \tfrac{1}{2}29.96)\ \mathrm{J\,K^{-1}\,mol^{-1}} = 33.22\ \mathrm{J\,K^{-1}\,mol^{-1}}$.

$\Delta b = (0 - 3.26 \times 10^{-3} - \tfrac{1}{2}4.18 \times 10^{-3})\ \mathrm{J\,K^{-2}\,mol^{-1}} = -5.35 \times 10^{-3}\ \mathrm{J\,K^{-2}\,mol^{-1}}$.

$\Delta c = (0 - 0.50 \times 10^5 + \tfrac{1}{2}1.67 \times 10^5)\ \mathrm{J\,K\,mol^{-1}} = 0.34 \times 10^5\ \mathrm{J\,K\,mol^{-1}}$.

(a) $\Delta_f H(273.15\ \mathrm{K}) = \Delta H_f(\mathcal{T}) + \Delta a(273.15\ \mathrm{K} - 298.15\ \mathrm{K})$

$$+ \tfrac{1}{2}\Delta b[(273.15\ \mathrm{K})^2 - (298.15\ \mathrm{K})^2] - \Delta c\left(\frac{1}{273.15\ \mathrm{K}} - \frac{1}{298.15\ \mathrm{K}}\right) \quad \text{[Problem 4.18]}$$

$$= -285.83\ \mathrm{kJ\,mol^{-1}} + (33.22\ \mathrm{J\,K^{-1}\,mol^{-1}}) \times (-25\ \mathrm{K})$$
$$+ \tfrac{1}{2} \times (-5.35 \times 10^{-3}\ \mathrm{J\,K^{-2}\,mol^{-1}}) \times (-14.3 \times 10^3\ \mathrm{K^2})$$
$$-(0.34 \times 10^5\ \mathrm{J\,K\,mol^{-1}}) \times (3.1 \times 10^{-4}\ \mathrm{K^{-1}})$$
$$= -286.6\ \mathrm{kJ\,mol^{-1}}.$$

$\Delta_f H^\ominus(-0.1\ ^\circ\mathrm{C}) \approx \Delta_f H^\ominus(273.15\ \mathrm{K}) - \Delta H^\ominus_{\mathrm{m,fus}}$

$= -286.6\ \mathrm{kJ\,mol^{-1}} - 6.01\ \mathrm{kJ\,mol^{-1}}$ [Table 4.5]

$= \underline{-292.6\ \mathrm{kJ\,mol^{-1}}}$.

(b) $\Delta_f H(373.15\ \mathrm{K}) = \Delta H_f(\mathcal{T}) + \Delta a(373.15\ \mathrm{K} - 298.15\ \mathrm{K})$

$$+ \tfrac{1}{2}\Delta b[(373.15\ \mathrm{K})^2 - (298.15\ \mathrm{K})^2] - \Delta c\left(\frac{1}{373.15\ \mathrm{K}} - \frac{1}{298.15\ \mathrm{K}}\right)$$

$$= -285.8\ \mathrm{kJ\,mol^{-1}} + (33.22\ \mathrm{J\,K^{-1}\,mol^{-1}}) \times (75\ \mathrm{K})$$
$$+ \tfrac{1}{2} \times (-5.35 \times 10^{-3}\ \mathrm{J\,K^{-2}\,mol^{-1}}) \times (50.3 \times 10^3\ \mathrm{K^2})$$
$$-(0.34 \times 10^5\ \mathrm{J\,K\,mol^{-1}}) \times (-6.75 \times 10^{-4}\ \mathrm{K^{-1}})$$
$$= -283.4\ \mathrm{kJ\,mol^{-1}}.$$

$\Delta_f H^\ominus(100.1\ ^\circ\mathrm{C}) = \Delta_f H^\ominus(373.15\ \mathrm{K}) + \Delta H^\ominus_{\mathrm{vap,m}}$

$= -283.4\ \mathrm{kJ\,mol^{-1}} + 40.7\ \mathrm{kJ\,mol^{-1}}$ [Table 4.7] $= \underline{-242.7\ \mathrm{kJ\,mol^{-1}}}$.

4.20 $\Delta_f H^\ominus(99\ °C) = \Delta_f H(T) + \Delta a(372.15\ K - 298.15\ K)$

$$+\tfrac{1}{2}\Delta b[(372.15\ K)^2 - (298.15\ K)^2] - \Delta c\left(\frac{1}{372.15\ K} - \frac{1}{298.15\ K}\right) \quad \text{[Problem 4.18]}$$

$= \underline{-283.2\ kJ\ mol^{-1}}$.

$C_{p,m}(H_2, T) = 75.29\ J\ K^{-1}\ mol^{-1}$ [Table 4.1]

$C_{p,m}(H_2, T) = 28.82\ J\ K^{-1}\ mol^{-1}$.

$C_{p,m}(O_2, T) = 29.36\ J\ K^{-1}\ mol^{-1}$.

$\Delta C_{p,m} = (75.29 - 28.82 - \tfrac{1}{2} \times 29.36)\ J\ K^{-1}\ mol^{-1} = 31.79\ J\ K^{-1}\ mol^{-1}$.

$\Delta_f H(99\ °C) \approx \Delta_f H(T) + (31.79\ J\ K^{-1}\ mol^{-1}) \times (372.15\ K - 298.15\ K)$

$\approx (-285.83\ kJ\ mol^{-1}) + (31.79\ J\ K^{-1}\ mol^{-1}) \times (74.0\ K) \approx \underline{-283.5\ kJ\ mol^{-1}}$.

4.21 $dU = C_V dT$ [3.2.7]; $U(T_2) - U(T_1) = \int_{T_1}^{T_2} C_V(T) dT$;

$$\Delta U(T_2) = \Delta U(T_1) + \int_{T_1}^{T_2} \Delta C_V(T) dT.$$

4.22 $n(\text{arabinose}) = (88 \times 10^{-3}\ g)/(150.1\ g\ mol^{-1}) = 5.86 \times 10^{-4}\ mol$.

$n(\text{glucose}) = (102 \times 10^{-3}\ g)/(180.2\ g\ mol^{-1}) = 5.66 \times 10^{-4}\ mol$.

$C\delta T(\text{arabinose}) = -q(\text{arabinose})$, $\delta T(\text{arabinose}) = 0.761\ K$.

$C\delta T(\text{glucose}) = -\delta T(\text{glucose})$, $\delta T(\text{glucose}) = 0.881\ K$.

$q(\text{glucose}) = \Delta H^\ominus_{m,c}(\text{glucose}) n(\text{glucose})$,

$q(\text{arabinose}) = \Delta H^\ominus_{m,c}(\text{arabinose}) n(\text{arabinose})$.

$\Delta H_{m,c}(\text{glucose}) = -2802\ kJ\ mol^{-1}$ [Table 4.2, or from ΔH_f].

$$\Delta H_{m,c}(\text{arabinose}) = \left(\frac{\delta T(a)}{\delta T(g)}\right)\left(\frac{n(g)}{n(a)}\right)\Delta H_{c,m}(g)$$

$$= \left(\frac{0.761\ K}{0.881\ K}\right)\left(\frac{5.66 \times 10^{-4}\ mol}{5.86 \times 10^{-4}\ mol}\right) \times (-2802\ kJ\ mol^{-1})$$

$= \underline{-2340\ kJ\ mol^{-1}}$.

$C_6H_{10}O_5 + 5O_2 \rightarrow 5CO_2 + 5H_2O$; $\Delta_r H^\ominus = -2340\ kJ\ mol^{-1}$ [above].

$5CO_2 + 5H_2O \rightarrow C_6H_{10}O_5 + 5O_2$; $\Delta_r H^\ominus = 2340\ kJ\ mol^{-1}$.

$\Delta_f H^\ominus = (2340\ kJ\ mol^{-1}) + 5\Delta_f H^\ominus(CO_2) + 5\Delta_f H^\ominus(H_2O)$

$= 2340\ kJ\ mol^{-1} + 5(-393.51\ kJ\ mol^{-1}) + 5(-285.83\ kJ\ mol^{-1})$

$= \underline{-1060\ kJ\ mol^{-1}}$.

4.23 $C_{12}H_{22}O_{11} + H_2O \rightarrow 4CH_3CH(OH)CO_2H$ (lactic acid).

$\Delta_r H^\ominus = 4\Delta_f H^\ominus(\text{lactic acid}) - \Delta_f H^\ominus(\text{sucrose}) - \Delta_f H^\ominus(\text{water})$

$= 4 \times (-694.0\,\text{kJ mol}^{-1}) - (-2222\,\text{kJ mol}^{-1}) - (-285.8\,\text{kJ mol}^{-1})$

$= \underline{-268\,\text{kJ mol}^{-1}}.$

$C_{12}H_{22}O_{11} + 12O_2 \rightarrow 12CO_2 + 11H_2O, \Delta_r H^\ominus = -5645\,\text{kJ mol}^{-1}$.

Therefore $\Delta_r H(\text{aerobic}) - \Delta_r H(\text{anaerobic}) = (-5645\,\text{kJ mol}^{-1}) - (-268\,\text{kJ mol}^{-1})$

$= \underline{-5376\,\text{kJ mol}^{-1}}.$

This answer is also obtained from $4\Delta H_c$ (lactic acid).

4.24 $n = (1.5\,\text{g})/(342.3\,\text{g mol}^{-1}) = 4.4 \times 10^{-3}\,\text{mol}$.

$\Delta H_c^\ominus = n\Delta H_{c,m}^\ominus = (4.4 \times 10^{-3}\,\text{mol}) \times (-5645\,\text{kJ mol}^{-1}) = -25\,\text{kJ}$.

$(\Delta H_c^\ominus)_{\text{effective}} \approx \frac{1}{4}(-25\,\text{kJ}) = -6.2\,\text{kJ}$.

$h = w/mg \approx (6.2\,\text{kJ})/(63\,\text{kg}) \times (9.81\,\text{m s}^{-2}) = \underline{10\,\text{m}}.$

4.25 $\Delta H_{\text{vap,m}}^\ominus = 44\,\text{kJ mol}^{-1}, n = (1\,\text{kg})/(18.01\,\text{g mol}^{-1}) = 56\,\text{mol}$.

$q = (44\,\text{kJ mol}^{-1}) \times (56\,\text{mol}) = \underline{2.5 \times 10^3\,\text{kJ}}.$

$\Delta H_c^\ominus(\text{glucose}) = -2808\,\text{kJ mol}^{-1}$.

$2.5 \times 10^3\,\text{kJ}$ heat can be provided by $(2.5 \times 10^3\,\text{kJ})/(2.8 \times 10^3\,\text{kJ mol}^{-1})$

$= 0.89$ mol glucose, or $\underline{160\,\text{g}}.$

$\delta T = q/C; C = (75.5\,\text{J K}^{-1}\text{mol}^{-1}) \times [(63\,\text{kg})/(18.0\,\text{g mol}^{-1})] = 264\,\text{kJ K}^{-1}$.

$\delta T = -(2.5 \times 10^3\,\text{kJ})/(264\,\text{kJ K}^{-1}) = -9.5\,\text{K}\ (-17\,^\circ\text{F})$.

Therefore, $\underline{T_f = 81\,^\circ\text{F}}$ for $T_i = 98.4\,^\circ\text{F}$.

4.26 $C_3H_8(l) + 5O_2 \xrightarrow{\Delta H_{\text{vap,m}}^\ominus} C_3H_8(g) + 5O_2 \xrightarrow{\Delta H_c^\ominus} 3CO_2 + 4H_2O(l)$.

$\Delta H_{\text{vap,m}}^\ominus = 15\,\text{kJ mol}^{-1}, \Delta H_c^\ominus = -2220\,\text{kJ mol}^{-1}$.

$\Delta H_c(\text{liq}) = (15\,\text{kJ mol}^{-1}) + (-2220\,\text{kJ mol}^{-1}) = \underline{-2205\,\text{kJ mol}^{-1}}.$

$\Delta\nu_{\text{gas}} = 3 - 5 = -2, \Delta U_c(\text{liq}) = -2205\,\text{kJ mol}^{-1} - (-2)RT = \underline{-2200\,\text{kJ mol}^{-1}}.$

4.27 $\Delta H_c^\ominus(308\,\text{K}) = \Delta H_c^\ominus(298\,\text{K}) + \Delta C_p \delta T$ [4.1.5].

$= (-2205\,\text{kJ mol}^{-1}) + [(3 \times 37.1 + 4 \times 75.5 - 39.0 - 5 \times 29.3)\,\text{J K}^{-1}\text{mol}^{-1}] \times (10\,\text{K})$

$= \underline{-2203\,\text{kJ mol}^{-1}}.$

$\Delta U_c^\ominus(308\,\text{K}) = \Delta U_c^\ominus(298\,\text{K}) + \Delta C_V \delta T$ [Problem 4.21]

For liquids $C_p \approx C_V$; for gases $C_{p,\text{m}} - C_{V,\text{m}} = R$.

Therefore $C_{V,\text{m}}(\text{liquid propane}) \approx 39.0\,\text{J K}^{-1}\,\text{mol}^{-1}$, $C_{V,\text{m}}(\text{liquid water})$

$\approx 75.5\,\mathrm{J\,K^{-1}\,mol^{-1}}$.

$C_{V,\mathrm{m}}(\mathrm{O_2}) \approx 29.3\,\mathrm{J\,K^{-1}\,mol^{-1}} - 8.3\,\mathrm{J\,K^{-1}\,mol^{-1}} = 21.0\,\mathrm{J\,K^{-1}\,mol^{-1}}$.

$C_{V,\mathrm{m}}(\mathrm{CO_2}) \approx 37.1\,\mathrm{J\,K^{-1}\,mol^{-1}} - 8.3\,\mathrm{J\,K^{-1}\,mol^{-1}} = 28.8\,\mathrm{J\,K^{-1}\,mol^{-1}}$.

$\Delta U_\mathrm{c}^\ominus(308\,\mathrm{K}) = (-2200\,\mathrm{kJ\,mol^{-1}}) + [(3 \times 28.8 + 4 \times 75.5$
$-39.0 - 5 \times 21.0)\,\mathrm{J\,K^{-1}\,mol^{-1}}] \times (10\,\mathrm{K}) = \underline{-2198\,\mathrm{kJ\,mol^{-1}}}$.

4.28 $E_\mathrm{Res} = \Delta H_\mathrm{m}^\ominus(\text{benzene}) - 3\Delta H_\mathrm{m}^\ominus(\text{ethane})$ [Section 4.2(a)]
$= (-246\,\mathrm{kJ\,mol^{-1}}) - 3(-132\,\mathrm{kJ\,mol^{-1}}) = \underline{150\,\mathrm{kJ\,mol^{-1}}}$.

4.29 $q = -\Delta T C,\ \Delta H_\mathrm{m} = q/n$

(a) KF, $C = 4.168\,\mathrm{kJ\,mol^{-1}}$.

molality/(mol KF/kg AcOH)	0.194	0.590	0.821	1.208
$\Delta T/\mathrm{K}$	1.592	4.501	5.909	8.115
$q = -\Delta T C/\mathrm{kJ}$	−6.635	−18.76	−24.63	−33.82
$\Delta H_\mathrm{m}/\mathrm{kJ\,mol^{-1}}$	−34.2	−31.8	−30.0	−28.0

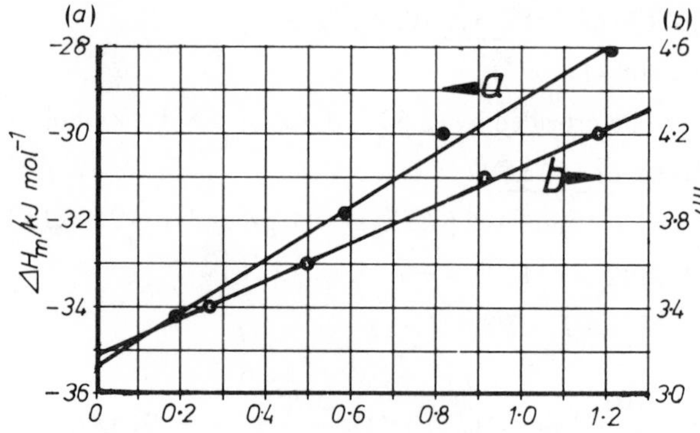

Fig 4·1

Plot ΔH_m against m (Fig. 4.1(a)) and find best straight line; or else do a least squares fit (Appendix):

$\underline{\Delta H_\mathrm{m}/\mathrm{kJ\,mol^{-1}} = -35.4 + 6.2\,m/(\mathrm{mol\,KF/kg\,AcOH})}$;

$\underline{\Delta H_\mathrm{m}(\text{inf. diln.}) = -35.4\,\mathrm{kJ\,mol^{-1}}}$.

(b) KF.AcOH, $C = 4.203\,\mathrm{kJ\,K^{-1}}$.

molality/(mol KF/kg AcOH)	0.280	0.504	0.910	1.190
$\Delta T/\mathrm{K}$	−0.227	−0.432	−0.866	−1.189
$q = -\Delta T C/\mathrm{kJ}$	+0.954	1.816	3.64	5.00
$\Delta H_\mathrm{m}/\mathrm{kJ\,mol^{-1}}$	+3.4	+3.6	+4.0	+4.2

Plot ΔH_m against m(Fig. 4.1(b)), or use least squares fit.

$\Delta H_m/\text{kJ mol}^{-1} = 3.15 + 0.9\,m/(\text{mol KF/kg AcOH})$;

$\Delta H_m(\text{inf. diln.}) = 3.15\ \text{kJ mol}^{-1}$.

See *J. Chem. Soc.*, 1971, 2702 for discussion.

4.30 $\frac{3}{2}H_2(g) + \frac{1}{2}N_2(g) \rightarrow NH_3(g);\ \Delta_f H^\ominus = -46.11\ \text{kJ mol}^{-1}$ [Table 4.1].

$NH_3(g) \rightarrow \frac{3}{2}H_2(g) + \frac{1}{2}N_2(g);\ \Delta_r H^\ominus = 46.11\ \text{kJ mol}^{-1}$.

$$\left.\begin{array}{l} H_2(g) \rightarrow 2H(g);\ \Delta H_m = 436\ \text{kJ mol}^{-1} \\ N_2(g) \rightarrow 2N(g);\ \Delta H_m = 945\ \text{kJ mol}^{-1} \end{array}\right\}\ \text{[given]}.$$

Therefore $NH_3(g) \rightarrow 3H(g) + N(g)$, $\Delta H_m = (46.1 + \frac{3}{2} \times 436 + \frac{1}{2} \times 945)\ \text{kJ mol}^{-1}$

$= 1173\ \text{kJ mol}^{-1}$.

4.31 Express the data as follows (enthalpies in kJ mol^{-1})

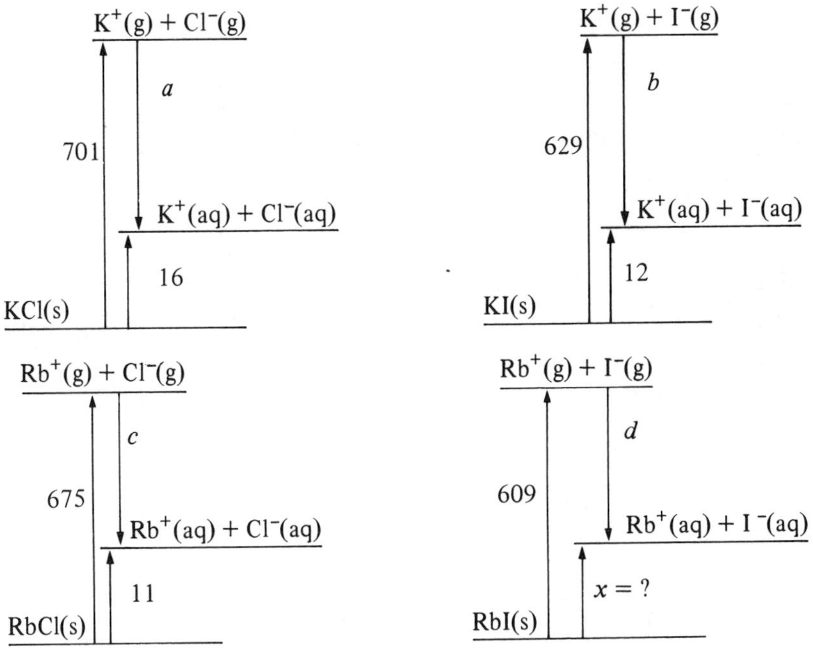

Then $a = 685\ \text{kJ mol}^{-1}$, $b = 617\ \text{kJ mol}^{-1}$,

$c = 664\ \text{kJ mol}^{-1}$, $d = (609 - x)\ \text{kJ mol}^{-1}$,

$\Delta H(Cl^-) - \Delta H(I^-) = a - b = 68\ \text{kJ mol}^{-1} = c - d$.

$d = c - 68\ \text{kJ mol}^{-1} = 596\ \text{kJ mol}^{-1}$.

Therefore, x = 13 kJ mol^{-1}.

4.32 Draw the following Born-Haber cycle, using 1 eV ≙ 96.485 kJ mol^{-1} [end-paper 1]

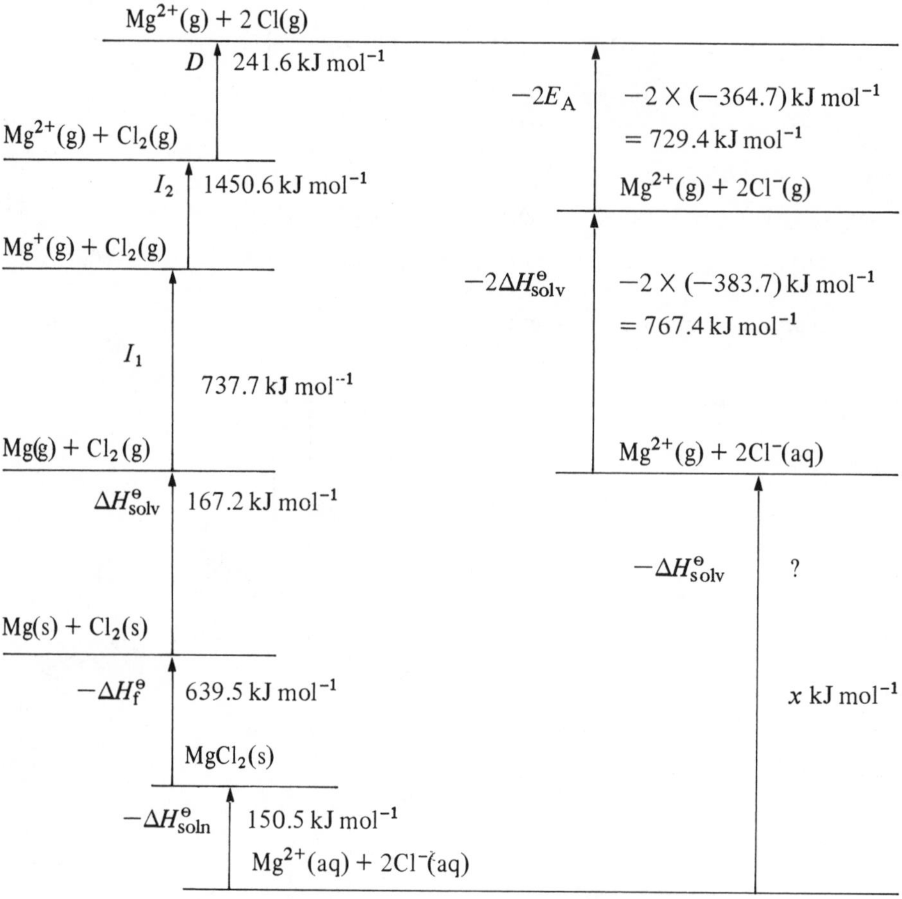

From the diagram, 150.5 + 639.5 + 167.2 + 737.7 + 1450.6 + 241.6]
= x + 729.4 + 767.4 [distance up on left = distance up on right].
Hence, x = 1890.3 and so $\Delta H^{\ominus}_{solv,m} = -1890.3$ kJ mol^{-1}.

4.33 Draw up the following Born-Haber cycle:

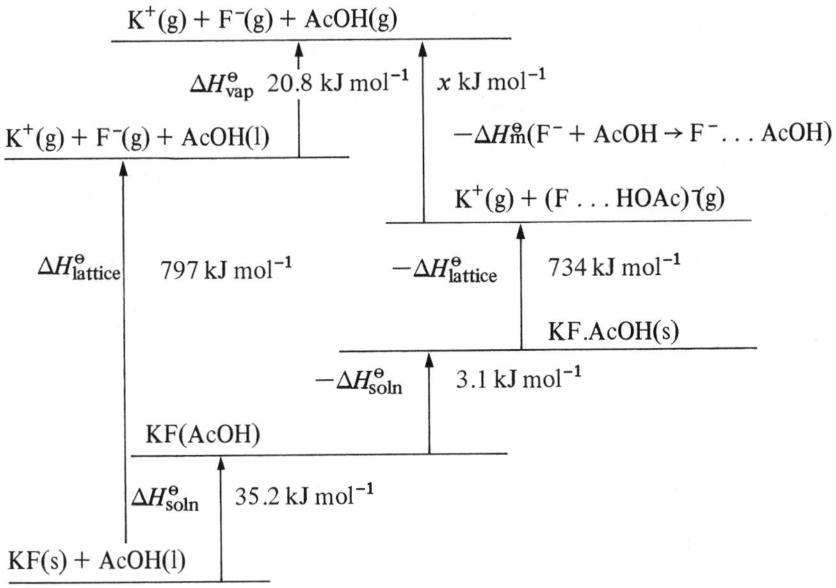

$797 + 20.8 = x + 734 + 3.1 + 35.2$ [distance up on left = distance up on right]; $x = 46$. Therefore $\Delta H_m^{\ominus} = \underline{-46 \text{ kJ mol}^{-1}}$.

5. The Second Law: the concepts

A5.1 Heat extracted $= \int_{265}^{300} C_p \mathrm{d}(T/\mathrm{K}) = \int_{265}^{300} [(1.75 \times 10^3/27.0)\mathrm{mol}]$

$\times\ [20.67 + 0.01238(T/\mathrm{K})]\ [\mathrm{J\,K^{-1}\,mol^{-1}}]\,\mathrm{d}(T/\mathrm{K})$

$= [64.8\ \mathrm{mol}]\ [(20.67)(300 - 265) + (1/2)(0.01238)(300^2 - 265^2)]\ \mathrm{J\,mol^{-1}}$

$= 5.48 \times 10^4\ \mathrm{J}$ [Table 4.3].

$\Delta S = \int_{300}^{265} C_p(T/\mathrm{K})^{-1}\,\mathrm{d}(T/\mathrm{K}) = [64.8\ \mathrm{mol}] \int_{300}^{265} [20.67(T/\mathrm{K})^{-1} + 0.012\,38]$

$\times\ [\mathrm{J\,K^{-1}\,mol^{-1}}]\,\mathrm{d}(T/\mathrm{K})$

$= [64.8\ \mathrm{mol}]\ [20.67 \ln(265/300) + 0.012\,38(265 - 300)]\ [\mathrm{J\,K^{-1}\,mol^{-1}}]$

$= \underline{-194\ \mathrm{J\,K^{-1}}}.$ [5.2.1]

A5.2 $\Delta S = nR \ln(V_\mathrm{f}/V_\mathrm{i})$ [5.1.4]

$= nR \ln(p_\mathrm{i}/p_\mathrm{f})$ [1.1.1]

$= [(25.0/16.0)\mathrm{mol}]\ [8.31\ \mathrm{J\,K^{-1}\,mol^{-1}}]\ [\ln(18.5/2.5)] = \underline{26.0\ \mathrm{J\,K^{-1}}}.$

A5.3 $n = p_\mathrm{i}V_\mathrm{i}/RT_\mathrm{i}$ [1.1.1] $= (1.01 \times 10^5\ \mathrm{Pa})(15.0 \times 10^{-3}\ \mathrm{m^3})(8.31\ \mathrm{J\,K^{-1}\,mol^{-1}})^{-1}$

$\times\ (250\ \mathrm{K})^{-1}$

$= 7.29 \times 10^{-1}\ \mathrm{mol}.$

$\Delta S = nR \ln(V_\mathrm{f}/V_\mathrm{i});\ V_\mathrm{f} = V_\mathrm{i}\exp(\Delta S/nR)$ [5.1.4].

$\Delta S/nR = (-5.00\ \mathrm{J\,K^{-1}})(7.29 \times 10^{-1}\ \mathrm{mol})^{-1}(8.31\ \mathrm{J\,K^{-1}\,mol^{-1}})^{-1} = -0.825.$

$V_\mathrm{f} = (15.0\ \mathrm{dm^3})\exp(-0.825) = \underline{6.57\ \mathrm{dm^3}}.$

A5.4 $\Delta S_\mathrm{m} = \Delta H_\mathrm{vap,m}/T_\mathrm{b} = (29.4 \times 10^3\ \mathrm{J\,mol^{-1}})/335\ \mathrm{K} = \underline{87.8\ \mathrm{J\,K^{-1}\,mol^{-1}}}.$ [5.2.4].

A5.5 $\Delta S(\mathrm{CHCl_3}) = \int_{275}^{300} C_p(T/\mathrm{K})^{-1}\,\mathrm{d}(T/\mathrm{K})$ [5.2.1]

$= \int_{275}^{300} [1.00\ \mathrm{mol}]\ [91.47(T/\mathrm{K})^{-1} + 0.075]\ [\mathrm{J\,K^{-1}\,mol^{-1}}]\,\mathrm{d}(T/\mathrm{K})$

$= [91.47 \ln(300/275) + 0.075(300 - 275)]\ [\mathrm{J\,K^{-1}}] = \underline{9.83\ \mathrm{J\,K^{-1}}}.$

$q = \int_{275}^{300} [1.00\ \mathrm{mol}]\ [91.47 + 0.075(T/\mathrm{K})]\ [\mathrm{J\,mol^{-1}}]\,\mathrm{d}(T/\mathrm{K})$

$= [91.47(300 - 275) + (1/2)(0.075)(300^2 - 275^2)]\ \mathrm{J} = \underline{2.83 \times 10^3\ \mathrm{J}}.$

$\Delta S(\text{solid}) = (-q)/T = (-2.83 \times 10^3\ \mathrm{J})/300\ \mathrm{K} = -9.43\ \mathrm{J\,K^{-1}}$ [5.1.1]

$\Delta S(\text{total}) = 9.83\ \mathrm{J\,K^{-1}} - 9.43\ \mathrm{J\,K^{-1}} = 0.40\ \mathrm{J\,K^{-1}} > 0.$

A5.6 (a) $\Delta_r S^\ominus(T) = 2S_m^\ominus(T)[CH_3COOH(l)] - 2S_m^\ominus(T)[CH_3CHO(g)] - S_m^\ominus(T)[O_2(g)]$

$= [2(159.8) - 2(250.2) - 205.0]\ \mathrm{J\,K^{-1}} = -385.8\ \mathrm{J\,K^{-1}}$ [Table 4.1a, 5.4.3].

(b) $\Delta_r S^\ominus(T) = 2S_m^\ominus(T)[AgBr(s)] + S_m^\ominus(T)[Cl_2(g)] - 2S_m^\ominus(T)[AgCl(s)] - S_m^\ominus(T)[Br_2(l)]$

$= [2(107.1) + 223.0 - 2(96.2) - 152.2]\ \mathrm{J\,K^{-1}} = \underline{92.6\ \mathrm{J\,K^{-1}}}.$

A5.7 $\Delta_r G^\ominus(T) = 2\Delta_f G^\ominus(T)[H_2O(l)] + 2\Delta_f G^\ominus(T)[SO_2(g)] - 2\Delta_f G^\ominus(T)[H_2S(g)]$

$= 2[(-237.1) + (-300.2) - (-33.6)]\ \mathrm{kJ} = \underline{-1007\ \mathrm{kJ}}$ [Table 4.1] [5.4.4].

A5.8 $C(s) + (1/2)O_2(g) + 2H_2(g) \rightarrow CH_3OH(l);\ \Delta n_{gas} = -2.5\ \mathrm{mol}.$

$\Delta(pV)(T) \approx \Delta n_{gas}RT$ [1.1.1] $= (-2.5\ \mathrm{mol})(8.31\ \mathrm{J\,K^{-1}\,mol^{-1}})(298\ \mathrm{K}) = -6.19 \times 10^3\ \mathrm{J},$

$\Delta_f A^\ominus(T) = \Delta_f G^\ominus(T) - \Delta(pV)(T)$ [5.3.6] $= [(-166.4) - (-6.2)]\ \mathrm{kJ\,mol^{-1}}$

$= \underline{-160.2\ \mathrm{kJ\,mol^{-1}}}.$

A5.9 (a) $\Delta_r G^\ominus(T) = 2\Delta_f G^\ominus(T)[NO(g)] - 2\Delta_f G^\ominus(T)[NO_2(g)]$ [5.4.4]

$= 2[+86.6 - 51.3]\ \mathrm{kJ} = 70.6\ \mathrm{kJ} > 0;$ <u>nonspontaneous.</u>

(b) $\Delta_r G^\ominus(T) = \Delta_f G^\ominus(T)[C_2H_6(g)] - \Delta_f G^\ominus(T)[C_2H_4(g)]$

$= [(-32.8) - (68.2)]\ \mathrm{kJ} = -101.0\ \mathrm{kJ} < 0;$ <u>spontaneous.</u>

(c) $\Delta_r G^\ominus(T) = 2\Delta_f G^\ominus(T)[NO_2(g)] - \Delta_f G^\ominus(T)[N_2O_4(g)] = [2(51.3) - (97.9)]\ \mathrm{kJ}$

$= +4.7\ \mathrm{kJ} > 0;$ <u>nonspontaneous.</u> [Table 4.1, Table 4.1a]

A5.10 $6C(s) + 3H_2(g) + (1/2)O_2(g) \rightarrow C_6H_5OH(s)$

$\Delta_r S^\ominus(T) = S^\ominus(T)[C_6H_5OH(s)] - 6S^\ominus(T)[C(s)] - 3S^\ominus(T)[H_2(g)] - (1/2)S^\ominus(T)[O_2(g)]$

$= [144.0 - 6(5.7) - 3(130.7) - (1/2)(205)]\ \mathrm{J\,K^{-1}} = \underline{-384.8\ \mathrm{J\,K^{-1}}}$ [5.4.3].

$C_6H_5OH(s) + 7O_2(g) \rightarrow 6CO_2(g) + 3H_2O(l).$

$\Delta_r H^\ominus(T) = 3\Delta_f H^\ominus(T)[H_2O(l)] + 6\Delta_f H^\ominus(T)[CO_2(g)] - \Delta_f H^\ominus(T)[C_6H_5OH(s)]$ [4.1.4]

$\Delta_f H^\ominus(T)\ [C_6H_5OH(s)] = [3(-285.8) + 6(-393.5) - (-3054)]\ \mathrm{kJ\,mol^{-1}}$

$= \underline{-164.4\ \mathrm{kJ\,mol^{-1}}}.$

$\Delta_f G^\ominus(T) = \Delta_f H^\ominus(T) - T\Delta_r S^\ominus(T) = [-164.4 - (298.2)(-0.3848)]\ \mathrm{kJ\,mol^{-1}}$

$= \underline{-49.7\ \mathrm{kJ\,mol^{-1}}}.$ [Tables 4.1, 4.1a]

5.1 $\Delta S = q_{\text{rev}}/T$ [5.1.3].

(a) $\Delta S = (25 \times 10^3\,\text{J})/(273.15\,\text{K}) = \underline{92\,\text{J}\,\text{K}^{-1}}$.

(b) $\Delta S = (25 \times 10^3\,\text{J})/(373.15\,\text{K}) = \underline{67\,\text{J}\,\text{K}^{-1}}$.

5.2 Since ΔS depends only on initial and final states, $\Delta S = C_p \ln(T_\text{f}/T_\text{i})$ [5.2.1a].
$T_\text{f} = T_\text{i} + q/C_p = T_\text{i} + I^2Rt/C_p$ [$q = ItV = I^2Rt$].
$\Delta S = C_p \ln[1 + (I^2RT/C_pT_\text{i})]$; $n = 500\,\text{g}/63.6\,\text{g}\,\text{mol}^{-1} = 7.86\,\text{mol}$.

$$\Delta S = (7.86\,\text{mol}) \times (24.4\,\text{J}\,\text{K}^{-1}\,\text{mol}^{-1}) \times \ln\left(1 + \frac{(1.00\,\text{A})^2 \times (1000\,\Omega) \times (15.0\,\text{s})}{(7.86 \times 24.4\,\text{J}\,\text{K}^{-1}) \times (293\,\text{K})}\right)$$

$$= (192\,\text{J}\,\text{K}^{-1}) \times \ln 1.27 = \underline{45.4\,\text{J}\,\text{K}^{-1}}.$$

5.3 $\text{d}q_{\text{rev}}(\text{net}) = 0$; therefore $\text{d}S = 0$; therefore $\underline{\Delta S = 0}$.

$$\Delta S_{\text{water}} = \int \text{d}q_{\text{rev}}/T = q_{\text{rev}}/T,\ T = 293\,\text{K}.$$

$$\Delta S_{\text{water}} = I^2Rt/T = (1.00\,\text{A})^2 \times (1000\,\Omega) \times (15.0\,\text{s})/(293\,\text{K})$$
$$= \underline{51.2\,\text{J}\,\text{K}^{-1}}\ [1\,\text{J} = 1\,\text{A}\,\text{V}\,\text{s} = 1\,\text{A}^2\,\Omega\,\text{s}].$$

5.4 At constant volume $\text{d}q = \text{d}U$; $\text{d}U = C_V\text{d}T$ [2.3.3].
$\Delta S = C_V \ln(T_2/T_1)$ [5.2.1b].
$C_{V,\text{m}} = 12.49\,\text{J}\,\text{K}^{-1}\,\text{mol}^{-1}$ [Table 2.1], $T_2 = 500\,\text{K}$, $T_1 = 298\,\text{K}$.
$$S_\text{m}(500\,\text{K}) = 146.22\,\text{J}\,\text{K}^{-1}\,\text{mol}^{-1} + (12.49\,\text{J}\,\text{K}^{-1}\,\text{mol}^{-1}) \times \ln(500/298)$$
$$= (146.22 + 6.46)\,\text{J}\,\text{K}^{-1}\,\text{mol}^{-1} = \underline{152.68\,\text{J}\,\text{K}^{-1}\,\text{mol}^{-1}}.$$

5.5 $$S^\ominus_\text{m}(T_2) = S^\ominus_\text{m}(T_1) + \int_{T_1}^{T_2} (C_{p,\text{m}}/T)\text{d}T\ [5.2.1\text{a}],$$

$$= S^\ominus_\text{m}(T_1) + \int_{T_1}^{T_2} \left(\frac{a}{T} + b + \frac{c}{T^3}\right) \text{d}T\ [\text{as } C_{p,\text{m}} = a + bT + cT^{-2}]$$

$$= S^\ominus_\text{m}(T_1) + a\ln(T_2/T_1) + b(T_2 - T_1) - \tfrac{1}{2}c\left(\frac{1}{T_2^2} - \frac{1}{T_1^2}\right).$$

$S^\ominus_\text{m}(298\,\text{K}) = 192.4\,\text{J}\,\text{K}^{-1}\,\text{mol}^{-1}$, $a = 29.75\,\text{J}\,\text{K}^{-1}\,\text{mol}^{-1}$,
$b = 25.10 \times 10^{-3}\,\text{J}\,\text{K}^{-2}\,\text{mol}^{-1}$, $c = -1.55 \times 10^5\,\text{J}\,\text{K}\,\text{mol}^{-1}$.

(a) $$S^\ominus_\text{m}(373\,\text{K}) = (192.4\,\text{J}\,\text{K}^{-1}\,\text{mol}^{-1}) + (29.75\,\text{J}\,\text{K}^{-1}\,\text{mol}^{-1}) \ln(373\,\text{K}/T)$$
$$+ (25.10 \times 10^{-3}\,\text{J}\,\text{K}^{-2}\,\text{mol}^{-1}) \times (75\,\text{K})$$

$$-\tfrac{1}{2}(-1.55 \times 10^5\,\mathrm{J\,K\,mol^{-1}}) \times \left(\frac{1}{(373\,\mathrm{K})^2} - \frac{1}{(298\,\mathrm{K})^2}\right)$$

$$= (192.4 + 6.68 + 1.88 - 0.32)\,\mathrm{J\,K^{-1}\,mol^{-1}} = \underline{200.6\,\mathrm{J\,K^{-1}\,mol^{-1}}}.$$

(b) $S_m^\ominus(773\,\mathrm{K}) = (192.4\,\mathrm{J\,K^{-1}\,mol^{-1}}) + (29.75\,\mathrm{J\,K^{-1}\,mol^{-1}}) \times \ln(773/298\,\mathrm{K})$

$$+ (25.10 \times 10^{-3}\,\mathrm{J\,K^{-2}\,mol^{-1}}) \times (475\,\mathrm{K})$$

$$-\tfrac{1}{2}(-1.55 \times 10^5\,\mathrm{J\,K\,mol^{-1}}) \times \left(\frac{1}{(773\,\mathrm{K})^2} - \frac{1}{(298\,\mathrm{K})^2}\right)$$

$$= (192.4 + 28.36 + 11.92 - 0.74)\,\mathrm{J\,K^{-1}\,mol^{-1}} = \underline{231.9\,\mathrm{J\,K^{-1}\,mol^{-1}}}.$$

5.6 $q(1) = -q(2)$ [heat lost by sample 1 (mass 50 g) is gained by sample 2 (mass 100 g)].

Therefore $C_p(1)\,(T_f - T_{i1}) = -C_p(2)\,(T_f - T_{i2})$ [$T_{f1} = T_{f2}$, common final temperature],

$$\text{hence } T_f = \frac{C_p(1)T_{i1} + C_p(2)T_{i2}}{C_p(1) + C_p(2)} = \frac{n(1)T_{i1} + n(2)T_{i2}}{n(1) + n(2)}.$$

$n(1)/n(2) = 1/2$, $T_{i1} = 353\,\mathrm{K}$, $T_{i2} = 283\,\mathrm{K}$.

Therefore $T_f = \tfrac{1}{3}(353\,\mathrm{K} + 2 \times 283\,\mathrm{K}) = 306\,\mathrm{K}$.

$\Delta S = \Delta S(1) + \Delta S(2) = C_p(1)\ln(T_f/T_{i1}) + C_p(2)\ln(T_f/T_{i2})$.

$n(1) = (50\,\mathrm{g}/18\,\mathrm{g\,mol^{-1}}) = 2.8\,\mathrm{mol}$, $n(2) = 5.6\,\mathrm{mol}$.

Therefore $\Delta S = (2.8\,\mathrm{mol}) \times (75.5\,\mathrm{J\,K^{-1}\,mol^{-1}})\ln(306/353)$

$$+ (5.6\,\mathrm{mol}) \times (75.5\,\mathrm{J\,K^{-1}\,mol^{-1}})\ln(306/283)$$

$$= -30.21\,\mathrm{J\,K^{-1}} + 33.0\,\mathrm{J\,K^{-1}} = \underline{2.83\,\mathrm{J\,K^{-1}}}.$$

5.7 $T_f = \dfrac{n(1)T_{i1} + n(2)T_{i2}}{n(1) + n(2)} = \tfrac{1}{2}(T_{i1} + T_{i2})\ [n(1) = n(2)] = 318\,\mathrm{K}$.

$$\Delta S = C_p(1)\ln(T_f/T_{i1}) + C_p(2)\ln(T_f/T_{i2})$$

$$= C_p\ln(T_f^2/T_{i1}T_{i2})\ [C_p(1) = C_p(2) \text{ as } n(1) = n(2)]$$

$$= [(200\,\mathrm{g})/(18.0\,\mathrm{g\,mol^{-1}})] \times (75.5\,\mathrm{J\,K^{-1}\,mol^{-1}}) \times \ln(318^2/273 \times 363)$$

$$= \underline{17.0\,\mathrm{J\,K^{-1}}}.$$

5.8 Heat required for melting

$$= n\Delta H_{m,fus} = \underbrace{(200\,\mathrm{g}/18.0\,\mathrm{g\,mol^{-1}})}_{11.1\,\mathrm{mol}} \times \underbrace{(6.01\,\mathrm{kJ\,mol^{-1}})}_{[\text{Table 4.7}]}$$

$= 66.8\,\mathrm{kJ}$.

Temperature drop in hot water required to bring about melting

$= (66.8\,\text{kJ})/(75.5\,\text{J K}^{-1}\,\text{mol}^{-1}) \times (11.1\,\text{mol})$

$= 79.6\,\text{K}.$

At this stage there is 200 g water at 0 °C and 200 g water at 90 °C − 79.6 °C = 10 °C (283 K).

Entropy change so far:

$$\Delta S = \frac{n\Delta H_{\text{m,fus}}}{T_{\text{fus}}}\ [5.2.4] + nC_{p,\text{m}} \ln\left(\frac{283\,\text{K}}{363\,\text{K}}\right)\ [5.2.2]$$

$$= \left(\frac{(11.1\,\text{mol}) \times (6.01\,\text{kJ mol}^{-1})}{273\,\text{K}}\right) + (11.1 \times 75.5\,\text{J K}^{-1}) \times \ln\left(\frac{283}{363}\right)$$

$$= 244\,\text{J K}^{-1} - 208.6\,\text{J K}^{-1} = 35.7\,\text{J K}^{-1}.$$

Final temperature $T_f = \frac{1}{2}(273\,\text{K} + 283\,\text{K})$ [Problem 5.7] $= 278\,\text{K}$.

Entropy change in this step $\Delta S = C_p \ln(T_f^2/T_{i1}T_{i2})$ [Problem 5.7]

$= (11.1 \times 75.5\,\text{J K}^{-1}) \times \ln(278^2/(273 \times 283)) = 0.27\,\text{J K}^{-1}.$

Total entropy change $\Delta S = 35.7\,\text{J K}^{-1} + 0.27\,\text{J K}^{-1} = \underline{36.0\,\text{J K}^{-1}}.$

5.9 (a) $\Delta S(\text{gas}) = nR\ln(V_f/V_i)$ [5.1.4].

$n = (14\,\text{g}/28\,\text{g mol}^{-1}) = 0.50\,\text{mol}.$

$\Delta S = (0.50\,\text{mol}) \times (8.314\,\text{J K}^{-1}\,\text{mol}^{-1})\ln 2 = \underline{2.88\,\text{J K}^{-1}}.$

$\Delta S(\text{surroundings}) = -2.88\,\text{J K}^{-1}$ [5.2.3].

$\Delta S(\text{universe}) = \Delta S(\text{gas}) + \Delta S(\text{surr}) = \underline{0}.$

(b) $\Delta S(\text{gas}) = 2.88\,\text{J K}^{-1}$ [S a state function].

$\Delta S(\text{surr}) = \underline{0}$ [Section 5.2(d)].

$\Delta S(\text{universe}) = \Delta S(\text{gas}) + \Delta S(\text{surr}) = \underline{2.88\,\text{J K}^{-1}}.$

(c) $dq_{\text{rev}} = 0$, hence $\Delta S(\text{sys}) = 0$, $\Delta S(\text{surr}) = 0$, $\Delta S(\text{universe}) = \underline{0}.$

5.10 (a) $\Delta S_{\text{m}}(\text{l} \to \text{s}, T) = \Delta S_{\text{m}}(\text{l} \to \text{s}, T_f) - \Delta C_{p,\text{m}}\ln(T/T_f)$ [5.2.2, $\Delta C = C(\text{l}) - C(\text{s})$]

$= \Delta H_{\text{m}}(\text{l} \to \text{s}, T_f)/T_f - \Delta C_{p,\text{m}}\ln(T/T_f)$ [5.2.5]

$= -\Delta H_{\text{melt,m}}(T_f)/T_f - \Delta C_{p,\text{m}}\ln(T/T_f).$

$\Delta H_{\text{melt,m}}(T_f) = 6.01\,\text{kJ mol}^{-1}$, $\Delta C_{p,\text{m}} = +37.3\,\text{J K}^{-1}\,\text{mol}^{-1}.$

$\Delta S_{\text{m}}(\text{l} \to \text{s}, 268\,\text{K}) = \{(-6.01\,\text{kJ mol}^{-1})/(273\,\text{K})\} - (+37.3\,\text{J K}^{-1}\,\text{mol}^{-1})$

$\times \ln(268/273) = \underline{-21.3\,\text{J K}^{-1}\,\text{mol}^{-1}}.$

$\Delta S_m(\text{surr}) = -\Delta H_m(1 \to s, T)/T = \Delta H_{fus,m}(T)/T = \Delta H_{fus,m}(T_f)/T + \Delta C_{p,m}(T - T_f)/T$
$= \{(6.01\ \text{kJ mol}^{-1})/(268\ \text{K})\} + \{(37.3\ \text{J K}^{-1}\,\text{mol}^{-1}) \times (268 - 273)/268\}$
$= \underline{21.7\ \text{J K}^{-1}\,\text{mol}^{-1}}.$

$\Delta S_m(\text{univ.}) = \{(-21.3) + (21.7)\}\text{J K}^{-1}\,\text{mol}^{-1} = \underline{+0.4\ \text{J K}^{-1}\,\text{mol}^{-1}}.$

Since $\Delta S(\text{univ}) > 0$, the transition $1 \to s$ is spontaneous at $-5\ ^\circ\text{C}$.

(b) $\Delta S_m(1 \to g, T) = \Delta S_m(1 \to g, T_b) + \Delta C_{p,m} \ln(T/T_b)$ [5.2.2, $\Delta C = C(g) - C(1)$]
$= \Delta H_m(1 \to g, T_b)/T_b + \Delta C_{p,m} \ln(T/T_b)$ [5.2.5]
$= \Delta H_{vap,m}(T_b)/T_b + \Delta C_{p,m} \ln(T/T_b).$

$\Delta H_{vap,m}(T_b) = 40.7\ \text{kJ mol}^{-1}$, $\Delta C_{p,m} = -41.9\ \text{J K}^{-1}\,\text{mol}^{-1}$.

$\Delta S_m(1 \to g, 368\ \text{K}) = (40.7\ \text{kJ mol}^{-1})/(373\ \text{K}) + (-41.9\ \text{J K}^{-1}\,\text{mol}^{-1})\ln(368/373)$
$= \underline{109.7\ \text{J K}^{-1}\,\text{mol}^{-1}}.$

$\Delta S_m(\text{surr}) = -\Delta H_m(1 \to g, T)/T = -\Delta H_{vap,m}(T)/T$
$= -\Delta H_{vap,m}(T_b)/T - \Delta C_{p,m}(T - T_b)/T.$
$= -(40.7\ \text{kJ mol}^{-1})/(368\ \text{K}) - (-41.9\ \text{J K}^{-1}\,\text{mol}^{-1}) \times (368 - 373)/368$
$= -111.17\ \text{J K}^{-1}\,\text{mol}^{-1}.$

$\Delta S_m(\text{univ}) = \underline{-1.5\ \text{J K}^{-1}\,\text{mol}^{-1}}.$

Since $\Delta S_m(\text{univ}) < 0$, the reverse transition, $g \to 1$, is spontaneous at $95\ ^\circ\text{C}$.

5.11 $G = H - TS$ [5.3.6]

(a) $\Delta G_m(1 \to s, T) = \Delta H_m(1 \to s, T) - T\Delta S_m(1 \to s, T)$
$= \Delta H_m(1 \to s, T_f) - \Delta C_{p,m}(T - T_f) - T\{\Delta S_m(1 \to s, T_f) - \Delta C_{p,m} \ln(T/T_f)\}$
[4.1.6, 5.2.2]
$= \Delta H_m(1 \to s, T_f) - (T/T_f)\Delta H_m(1 \to s, T_f) - \Delta C_{p,m}\{T - T_f - T\ln(T/T_f)\}$ [5.2.5]
$= \{(T/T_f) - 1\}\Delta H_{fus,m}(T_f) - \Delta C_{p,m}\{T - T_f - T\ln(T/T_f)\}.$

$T = 268\ \text{K}$, $T_f = 273\ \text{K}$, $\Delta H_{fus,m}(T_f) = 6.01\ \text{kJ mol}^{-1}$;

$\Delta C_{p,m} = C_p(1) - C_p(s) = 37.3\ \text{J K}^{-1}\,\text{mol}^{-1}.$

$\Delta G_m(1 \to s, 268\ \text{K}) = (268/273 - 1) \times (6.01\ \text{kJ mol}^{-1}) - (37.3\ \text{J mol}^{-1})$
$\times \{268 - 273 - 286\ln(268/273)\}$
$= \underline{-0.11\ \text{kJ mol}^{-1}}.$

Since $\Delta G < 0$, the transition $1 \to s$ is spontaneous at $-5\ ^\circ\text{C}$. Note that $\Delta G_m = -T\Delta S_m(\text{univ})$ as calculated in the last problem.

(b) $\Delta G_m(1 \to g, T) = \Delta H_m(1 \to g, T) - T\Delta S_m(1 \to g, T) + (T - T_b)\Delta C_{p,m}$

$= \Delta H_{vap,m}(T_b) + (T - T_b)\Delta C_{p,m} - T\{\Delta S_{vap,m}(T_b) + [C_{p,m}(g) - C_{p,m}(l)] \times \ln(T/T_b)\}$ [4.1.6, 5.2.2]

$= \Delta H_{vap,m}(T_b)\{1 - (T/T_b)\} + \Delta C_{p,m}\{T - T_b - T\ln(T/T_b)\}$.

$T = 368\text{ K}$, $T_b = 373\text{ K}$, $\Delta H_{vap,m}(T_b) = 40.7\text{ kJ mol}^{-1}$, $\Delta C_{p,m} = -41.9\text{ J K}^{-1}\text{ mol}^{-1}$.

$\Delta G_m(l \to g, 368\text{ K}) = (40.7\text{ kJ mol}^{-1}) \times \{1 - (368/373)\} + (-41.9\text{ J mol}^{-1}) \times \{368 - 373 - 368\ln(368/373)\} = \underline{+0.55\text{ kJ mol}^{-1}}.$

Since $\Delta G_m > 0$, the reverse process, $g \to l$, is spontaneous at 95 °C. Note that $\Delta G_m = -T\Delta S_m(\text{univ})$ as calculated in the last problem.

5.12 $\Delta S_m^{sys} = \Delta H_{m,vap}/T_b$ [5.2.4], $\Delta S_m^{surr} = -\Delta S_m^{sys}$, $\Delta S_m^{univ} = 0$ [Section 5.2(c)].

(a) water: $\Delta H_{m,vap} = 40.7\text{ kJ mol}^{-1}$, $T_b = 373\text{ K}$.

(i) $\Delta S_m^{sys} = (40.7 \times 10^3\text{ J mol}^{-1})/(373\text{ K}) = \underline{109\text{ J K}^{-1}\text{ mol}^{-1};}$

(ii) $\Delta S_m^{surr} = \underline{-109\text{ J K}^{-1}\text{ mol}^{-1};}$

(iii) $\Delta S_m^{univ} = \underline{0.}$

(b) benzene: $\Delta H_{m,vap} = 30.8\text{ kJ mol}^{-1}$, $T_b = 353\text{ K}$.

(i) $\Delta S_m^{sys} = (30.8 \times 10^3\text{ J mol}^{-1})/(353\text{ K}) = \underline{87.3\text{ J K}^{-1}\text{ mol}^{-1};}$

(ii) $\Delta S_m^{surr} = \underline{-87.3\text{ J K}^{-1}\text{ mol}^{-1};}$

(iii) $\Delta S_m^{univ} = \underline{0}.$

5.13 $\Delta S_m = R\ln(V_f/V_i) + C_{V,m}\ln(T_f/T_i)$ [5.1.4 + 5.2.1].

(a) water: $\Delta S_m = (8.314\text{ J K}^{-1}\text{ mol}^{-1})\ln\frac{1}{2} + (25.3\text{ J K}^{-1}\text{ mol}^{-1})\ln 2$

$= -5.76\text{ J K}^{-1}\text{ mol}^{-1} + 17.5\text{ J K}^{-1}\text{ mol}^{-1} = \underline{11.8\text{ J K}^{-1}\text{ mol}^{-1}}.$

(b) benzene: $\Delta S_m = (8.314\text{ J K}^{-1}\text{ mol}^{-1})\ln\frac{1}{2} + (130\text{ J K}^{-1}\text{ mol}^{-1})\ln 2$

$= -5.76\text{ J K}^{-1}\text{ mol}^{-1} + 90.1\text{ J K}^{-1}\text{ mol}^{-1} = \underline{84.4\text{ J K}^{-1}\text{ mol}^{-1}}.$

5.14 $w'_{rev} = -\Delta A$ [5.3.9], $w'_{e,max} = -\Delta G$ [5.3.11]

$\Delta A = \Delta U - T\Delta S$ [5.3.6]. $\Delta G = \Delta H - T\Delta S$ [5.3.6].

$\Delta G_m(l \to s, 268\text{ K}) = -0.11\text{ kJ mol}^{-1}$ [Problem 5.11a];

$w'_{e,max} = \underline{0.11\text{ kJ mol}^{-1}}.$

$\Delta A = \Delta G - \Delta pV$ [as $H = U + pV$] $= \Delta G - p\Delta V$

$\Delta V_m = V_m(s) - V_m(l) = [(18.01\text{ g mol}^{-1})/(0.917\text{ g cm}^{-3})] - (18.01\text{ g mol}^{-1})/(0.999\text{ g cm}^{-3})]$

$= 1.612\text{ cm}^3\text{ mol}^{-1} = 1.612 \times 10^{-6}\text{ m}^3\text{ mol}^{-1}$

$\Delta A_m = -0.11\,\text{kJ mol}^{-1} - (1.013 \times 10^5\,\text{N m}^{-2}) \times (1.612 \times 10^{-6}\,\text{m}^3\,\text{mol}^{-1})$

$\quad = -0.11\,\text{kJ mol}^{-1}$;

$w'_{max} = 0.11\,\text{kJ mol}^{-1}$.

5.15 $CH_4(g) + 2O_2(g) \rightarrow CO_2(g) + 2H_2O(l)$; $\Delta G_m^\ominus = -802.8\,\text{kJ mol}^{-1}$.

$w'_{e,max} = -\Delta G_m$ [5.3.11] $= 802.8\,\text{kJ mol}^{-1}$.

$w'_{max} = -\Delta A_m$ [5.3.9], $\Delta A_m = \Delta G_m - \Delta p V_m \approx \Delta G_m - \Delta\nu_{gas}RT$

$\Delta\nu_{gas} = 1 - 2 - 1 = -2$; $\Delta A_m = -802.8\,\text{kJ mol}^{-1} - (-2) \times (2.48\,\text{kJ mol}^{-1})$

$\quad = -798\,\text{kJ mol}^{-1}$; $w'_{max} = 798\,\text{kJ mol}^{-1}$.

Therefore a maximum of 798 kJ mol^{-1} of work, or 803 kJ mol^{-1} of non-pV work (e.g. electrical work) may be extracted from the process.

5.16 $S_m(T) = S_m(0) + \int_0^T (C_{p,m}/T)\mathrm{d}T$ [5.2.1].

From the data draw up the following Table.

T/K	10	15	20	25	30	50
$C_{p,m}$/J K^{-1} mol^{-1}	2.8	7.0	10.8	14.1	16.5	21.4
$(C_{p,m}/T)$/J K^{-2} mol^{-1}	0.284	0.47	0.540	0.564	0.550	0.428

T/K	70	100	150	200	250	298
$C_{p,m}$/J K^{-1} mol^{-1}	23.3	24.5	25.3	25.8	26.2	26.6
$(C_{p,m}/T)$/J K^{-2} mol^{-1}	0.333	0.245	0.169	0.129	0.105	0.089

Plot $(C_{p,m}/T)$ against T, Fig. 5.1. This has been done on two scales. The region 0–10 K has been constructed using $C_{p,m} = aT^3$ [Section 5.4] fitted to the point ($T = 10$ K, $C_{p,m} = 2.8\,\text{J K}^{-1}\,\text{mol}^{-1}$), from which $a = 2.8 \times 10^{-3}\,\text{J K}^{-4}\,\text{mol}^{-1}$. Determine the areas by counting squares. Area $A = 38.28\,\text{J K}^{-1}\,\text{mol}^{-1}$, area B (up to 0 °C) = 25.60 J K^{-1} mol^{-1}, B (up to 25 °C) = 27.80 J K^{-1} mol^{-1}.

$S_m^\ominus(273\,\text{K}) = S_m^\ominus(0) + 63.88\,\text{J K}^{-1}\,\text{mol}^{-1}$.

$S_m^\ominus(298\,\text{K}) = S_m^\ominus(0) + 66.08\,\text{J K}^{-1}\,\text{mol}^{-1}$.

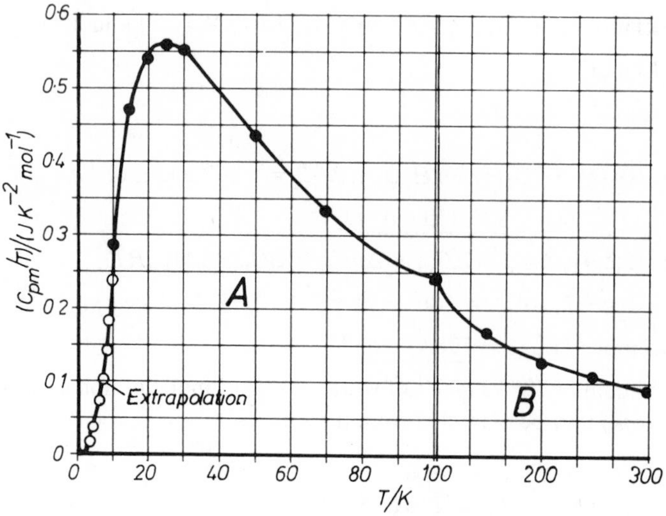

Fig 5·1

5.17 $S^\ominus_m(\mathrm{g}, 77\,\mathrm{K}) = S^\ominus_m(0) + \int_0^{T_t} (C_{p,m}/T)\mathrm{d}T + \Delta H_{m,t}/T_t$

$$+\int_{T_t}^{T_f} (C_{p,m}/T)\mathrm{d}T + \Delta H^\ominus_{m,fus}/T_f + \int_{T_f}^{T_b} (C_{p,m}/T)\mathrm{d}T + \Delta H^\ominus_{m,vap}/T_b \text{ [Example 5.9]}$$

$= S^\ominus_m(0) + (27.2\,\mathrm{J\,K^{-1}\,mol^{-1}})$
$+ (0.229 \times 10^3\,\mathrm{J\,K^{-1}\,mol^{-1}})/(35.61\,\mathrm{K}) + (23.4\,\mathrm{J\,K^{-1}\,mol^{-1}})$
$+ (0.721 \times 10^3\,\mathrm{J\,mol^{-1}})/(63.14\,\mathrm{K}) + (11.4\,\mathrm{J\,K^{-1}\,mol^{-1}}) + (5.58 \times 10^3\,\mathrm{J\,mol^{-1}})/(77.32\,\mathrm{K})$
$= S^\ominus_m(0) + (27.2 + 6.4 + 23.4 + 11.4 + 11.4 + 72.2)\,\mathrm{J\,K^{-1}\,mol^{-1}}$
$= S^\ominus_m(0) + \underline{152.0\,\mathrm{J\,K^{-1}\,mol^{-1}}}.$

5.18 We have to show that $\oint \mathrm{d}q/T < 0$ [5.1.7] when the cycle contains an irreversible step.

Step 1 $w(1) = -p_{ex}(V_B - V_A)$ [Box 3.1], $q(1) = p_{ex}(V_B - V_A)$.

$$\Delta U(1) = 0, \int \mathrm{d}q(1)/T = q(1)/T_h = p_{ex}(V_B - V_A)/T_h.$$

Steps 2, 3, 4 are given in the text, Fig. 5.5.
$\Delta U(\text{cycle}) = 0, \oint \mathrm{d}q/T = p_{ex}(V_B - V_A)/T_h + nRT_c\ln(V_D/V_C)$.
But $p_{ex}(V_B - V_A) < nRT_h\ln(V_B/V_A)$ because $|w_{irrev}| < |w_{rev}|$.

Therefore $\oint \mathrm{d}q/T < nR\ln(V_B/V_A) + nR\ln(V_D/V_C) = \Delta S(\text{cycle}) = 0;$

hence $\oint \mathrm{d}q/T < 0.$

5.19 Consider Step 1: $\Delta S(1) = nR\ln(V_B/V_A)$ [S a state function].

$\int_1 \mathrm{d}q/T = q(1)/T_h = p_{ex}(V_B - V_A)/T_h$ [Problem 5.18].

But $p_{ex}(V_B - V_A) < nRT_h\ln(V_B/V_A)$ because $|w_{irrev}| < |w_{rev}|$.
Therefore $p_{ex}(V_B - V_A)/T_h < nR\ln(V_B/V_A) = \Delta S(1)$, and so

$$\Delta S(1) > p_{ex}(V_B - V_A)/T_h = \int_1 \mathrm{d}q/T.$$

Consequently $\Delta S(1) > \int_1 \mathrm{d}q/T$

for this irreversible step, in accord with the Clausius inequality, eqn [5.1.5].

5.20 (a) $c_o = (373\,\mathrm{K} - 333\,\mathrm{K})/(373\,\mathrm{K}) = \underline{0.11}$ (11 percent efficient).
(b) $c_o = (573\,\mathrm{K} - 353\,\mathrm{K})/(573\,\mathrm{K}) = \underline{0.38}$ (38 percent efficient).

5.21 $w' = mgh$ [*Example* 2.1] $= (1000\,\mathrm{kg}) \times (9.81\,\mathrm{m\,s^{-2}}) \times (50\,\mathrm{m}) = 490\,\mathrm{kJ}$.
$q(\text{required}) = w(\max)/c_o$.
(a) $c_o = 0.11$; $q(\text{required}) = (490\,\mathrm{kJ})/(0.11) = 4450\,\mathrm{kJ}$;
mass fuel $= (4450\,\mathrm{kJ})/(4.3 \times 10^4\,\mathrm{kJ\,kg^{-1}}) = \underline{0.10\,\mathrm{kg}}$.
(b) $c_o = 0.38$; $q(\text{required}) = (490\,\mathrm{kJ})/(0.38) = 1290\,\mathrm{kJ}$;
mass fuel $= (1290\,\mathrm{kJ})/(4.3 \times 10^4\,\mathrm{kJ\,kg^{-1}}) = \underline{0.03\,\mathrm{kg}}$.

5.22 $$c_o = \frac{T_h - T_c}{T_h} = \frac{1200\,\mathrm{K}}{2273\,\mathrm{K}} = 0.53.$$

$w'_{max} = mgh_{max}$, $w'_{max} = c_o q$; $h_{max} = c_o q/mg$.
$c_o = 0.53$, $m = 2500\,\mathrm{lb} \mathrel{\widehat{=}} 1134\,\mathrm{kg}$, $g = 9.81\,\mathrm{m\,s^{-2}}$, $M_r = 114.2$.
$q = (5512\,\mathrm{kJ\,mol^{-1}}) \times (3.03 \times 10^3\,\mathrm{g})/(114.2\,\mathrm{g\,mol^{-1}}) = 146 \times 10^3\,\mathrm{kJ}$.

Therefore $$h_{max} = \frac{0.53 \times (146 \times 10^3 \times 10^3\,\mathrm{J})}{(1.134 \times 10^3\,\mathrm{kg}) \times (9.81\,\mathrm{m\,s^{-2}})} = \underline{6.9\,\mathrm{km}}.$$

5.23 The isotherms correspond to T = constant, and the reversibly traversed adiabats correspond to S = constant. This lets us draw the diagram as in Fig. 5.2.

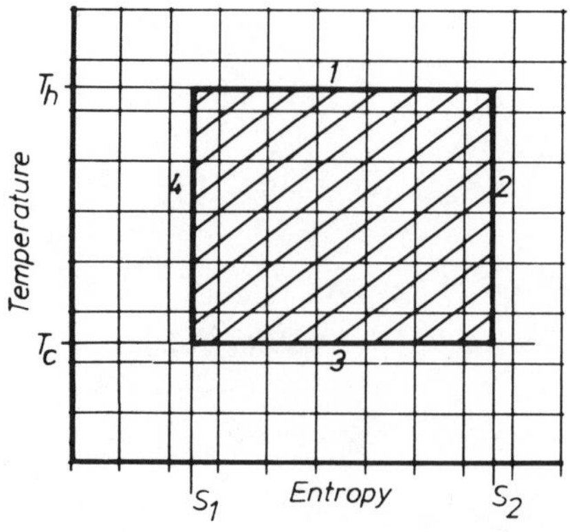

Fig 5.2

$$\text{Area} = \int_{\text{cycle}} T\text{d}S = (T_\text{h} - T_\text{c}) \times (S_2 - S_1) = (T_\text{h} - T_\text{c})\Delta S(1)$$

$$= (T_\text{h} - T_\text{c})nR\ln(V_\text{B}/V_\text{A}).$$

But $w'(\text{cycle}) = qc_\text{o} = nR(T_\text{h} - T_\text{c})\ln(V_\text{B}/V_\text{A})$ [Section 5.2(e)].

Therefore, Area $= w'(\text{cycle})$.

5.24 $\Delta S = C_p\ln(T_\text{f}/T_\text{h}) + C_p\ln(T_\text{f}/T_\text{c})$ [T_f: final temperature, 5.2.2]

$= C_p\ln(T_\text{f}^2/T_\text{h}T_\text{c})$. $T_\text{f} = \frac{1}{2}(T_\text{h} + T_\text{c})$ [Problem 5.6].

$C_p = [(500\,\text{g})/(63.6\,\text{g mol}^{-1})] \times (24.4\,\text{J K}^{-1}\,\text{mol}^{-1}) = 192\,\text{J K}^{-1}$.

$T_\text{f} = \frac{1}{2}(500 + 250)\,\text{K} = 375\,\text{K}$.

Therefore $\Delta S = (192\,\text{J K}^{-1}) \times \ln(375^2/500 \times 250) = \underline{22.6\,\text{J K}^{-1}}$.

5.25 $\Delta S_\text{m} = \Delta H_\text{m}/T_\text{f}$ [5.2.4] $= (1.90\,\text{kJ mol}^{-1})/(2000\,\text{K}) = \underline{0.95\,\text{J K}^{-1}\,\text{mol}^{-1}}$.

5.26 $\Delta S_\text{m} = \Delta H_\text{m}/T_\text{t}$ [5.2.4]

$= (1.19\,\text{kJ mol}^{-1})/(98.36\,\text{K}) = \underline{12.1\,\text{J K}^{-1}\,\text{mol}^{-1}}$.

$\Delta S_\text{m}^\text{univ} = \Delta S_\text{m}(\text{HCl}) + \Delta S_\text{m}(\text{copper}) = \underline{0}$.

$\Delta S_\text{m}(\text{copper}) = \Delta H_\text{m}/T_\text{t} = \underline{-12.1\,\text{J K}^{-1}\,\text{mol}^{-1}}$.

(The mol^{-1} refers to amount of substance of HCl.)

5.27 (a) $\text{Hg(l)} + \text{Cl}_2\text{(g)} \rightarrow \text{HgCl}_2\text{(s)}$

$\Delta_\text{r}S = (146.0\,\text{J K}^{-1}\,\text{mol}^{-1}) - (76.02\,\text{J K}^{-1}\,\text{mol}^{-1}) - (223.07\,\text{J K}^{-1}\,\text{mol}^{-1})$

$= \underline{-153.1\,\text{J K}^{-1}\,\text{mol}^{-1}}$.

(b) $\text{Zn(s)} + \text{CuSO}_4\text{(aq)} \rightarrow \text{Cu(s)} + \text{ZnSO}_4\text{(aq)}$, or $\text{Zn(s)} + \text{Cu}^{2+}\text{(aq)} \rightarrow \text{Cu(s)} + \text{Zn}^{2+}\text{(aq)}$

$\Delta_r S = [33.15 + (-112.1) - 41.63 - (-99.6)]\ \mathrm{J\,K^{-1}\,mol^{-1}} = \underline{-21.0\ \mathrm{J\,K^{-1}\,mol^{-1}}}.$

(c) sucrose + $12O_2(g) \rightarrow 12\,CO_2(g) + 11\,H_2O(l)$

$\Delta_r S = [12 \times (213.74) + 11 \times (69.91) - 360.2 - 12 \times (205.14)]\ \mathrm{J\,K^{-1}\,mol^{-1}}$

$= \underline{512.0\ \mathrm{J\,K^{-1}\,mol^{-1}}}.$

5.28 $\Delta_r G^\ominus = \Delta_r H^\ominus - T\Delta_r S^\ominus$ [5.3.6]

(a) $\Delta_r H^\ominus = -224.3\ \mathrm{kJ\,mol^{-1}}$ [Table 4.1]; $\Delta_r S^\ominus = -153\ \mathrm{J\,K^{-1}\,mol^{-1}}$.

$\Delta_r G^\ominus = (-224.3\ \mathrm{kJ\,mol^{-1}}) - (298.15\ \mathrm{K}) \times (-153.1\ \mathrm{J\,K^{-1}\,mol^{-1}})$

$= \underline{-178.7\ \mathrm{kJ\,mol^{-1}}}.$

(b) $\Delta_r H^\ominus = \Delta_f H^\ominus(Zn^{2+}, aq) - \Delta_f H^\ominus(Cu^{2+}, aq)$

$= (-153.89\ \mathrm{kJ\,mol^{-1}}) - (64.77\ \mathrm{kJ\,mol^{-1}})$ [Table 4.1]

$= -218.66\ \mathrm{kJ\,mol^{-1}}.$

$\Delta_r G^\ominus = (-218.66\ \mathrm{kJ\,mol^{-1}}) - (298.15\ \mathrm{K}) \times (-21.0\ \mathrm{J\,K^{-1}\,mol^{-1}})$

$= \underline{-212.4\ \mathrm{kJ\,mol^{-1}}}.$

(c) $\Delta_r H^\ominus = \Delta H_c^\ominus = -5645\ \mathrm{kJ\,mol^{-1}}$ [Table 4.2].

$\Delta_r G^\ominus = (-5645\ \mathrm{kJ\,mol^{-1}}) - (298.15\ \mathrm{K}) \times (512.0\ \mathrm{J\,K^{-1}\,mol^{-1}})$

$= \underline{-5798\ \mathrm{kJ\,mol^{-1}}}.$

5.29 (a) $H_2(g) + \frac{1}{2}O_2(g) \rightarrow H_2O(l)$

$\Delta_r H^\ominus = \Delta_f H^\ominus(H_2O, l) = \underline{-285.83\ \mathrm{kJ\,mol^{-1}}}.$

$\Delta_r S^\ominus = (69.91 - 130.69 - \frac{1}{2} \times 205.14)\ \mathrm{J\,K^{-1}\,mol^{-1}} = \underline{-163.35\ \mathrm{J\,K^{-1}\,mol^{-1}}}.$

$\Delta_r G^\ominus = \Delta_f G^\ominus(H_2O) = \underline{-237.13\ \mathrm{kJ\,mol^{-1}}}$ (spontaneous as written, under standard conditions).

(b) $3H_2(g) + C_6H_6(l) \rightarrow C_6H_{12}(l)$

$\Delta_r H^\ominus = \Delta_f H^\ominus(C_6H_{12}, l) - \Delta_f H^\ominus(C_6H_6, l) = \underline{-205.2\ \mathrm{kJ\,mol^{-1}}}.$

$\Delta_r S^\ominus = (204.3 - 173.3 - 3 \times 130.68)\ \mathrm{J\,K^{-1}\,mol^{-1}} = \underline{360.8\ \mathrm{J\,K^{-1}\,mol^{-1}}}.$

$\Delta_r G^\ominus = \Delta_f G^\ominus(C_6H_{12}, l) - \Delta_f G^\ominus(C_6H_6, l)$

$= 6.4\ \mathrm{kJ\,mol^{-1}} - 124.3\ \mathrm{kJ\,mol^{-1}}$

$= \underline{-117.9\ \mathrm{kJ\,mol^{-1}}}$ (spontaneous as written, under standard conditions).

(c) $CH_3CHO(g) + \frac{1}{2}O_2(g) \rightarrow CH_3COOH(l)$

$\Delta_r H^\ominus = \Delta_f H^\ominus(CH_3COOH, l) - \Delta_f H^\ominus(CH_3CHO, g) = -318.31\ \mathrm{kJ\,mol^{-1}}.$

$\Delta_r S^\ominus = (159.8 - 250.3 - \frac{1}{2} \times 205.14)\ \mathrm{J\,K^{-1}\,mol^{-1}}$

$= -193.1\ \mathrm{J\,K^{-1}\,mol^{-1}}.$

$\Delta_r G^\ominus = \Delta_f G^\ominus(CH_3COOH,l) - \Delta_f G^\ominus(CH_3CHO,g)$

$= -261.0\,kJ\,mol^{-1}$ (spontaneous as written, under standard conditions).

5.30 $\Delta_r G^\ominus = \Delta_r H^\ominus - T\Delta_r S^\ominus = 26.120\,kJ\,mol^{-1}$; $\Delta H^\ominus_m = 55.000\,kJ\,mol^{-1}$.

$\Delta S^\ominus_m = (55.000\,kJ\,mol^{-1} - 26.120\,kJ\,mol^{-1})/(298.15\,K)$

$= 96.864\,J\,K^{-1}\,mol^{-1}$.

$\Delta S^\ominus_m = 4S^\ominus_m(K^+, aq) + S^\ominus_m(Fe(CN)_6^{4-}, aq) + 3S^\ominus_m(H_2O,l)$

$- S^\ominus_m(K_4Fe(CN)_6.3H_2O,s)$

$S^\ominus_m(K^+, aq) = 102.5\,J\,K^{-1}\,mol^{-1}$, $S^\ominus_m(H_2O,l) = 69.91\,J\,K^{-1}\,mol^{-1}$,

$S^\ominus_m(K_4Fe(CN)_6.3H_2O,s) = 599.7\,J\,K^{-1}\,mol^{-1}$.

$S^\ominus_m(Fe(CN)_6^{4-}, aq) = (96.864 - 4 \times 102.5 - 3 \times 69.9 + 599.7)\,J\,K^{-1}\,mol^{-1}$

$= 76.9\,J\,K^{-1}\,mol^{-1}$.

5.31 Draw up the following Table:

T/K	10	20	30	40	50
$C_{p,m}/J\,K^{-1}\,mol^{-1}$	2.09	14.43	36.44	62.55	87.03
$(C_{p,m}/T)/\,J\,K^{-1}\,mol^{-1}$	0.209	0.722	1.215	1.564	1.741

T/K	60	70	80	90	100
$C_{p,m}/J\,K^{-1}\,mol^{-1}$	111.0	131.4	149.4	165.3	179.6
$(C_{p,m}/T)/J\,K^{-2}\,mol^{-1}$	1.850	1.877	1.868	1.837	1.796

T/K	110	120	130	140	150
$C_{p,m}/J\,K^{-1}\,mol^{-1}$	192.8	205.0	216.5	227.3	237.6
$(C_{p,m}/T)/J\,K^{-2}\,mol^{-1}$	1.753	1.708	1.665	1.624	1.584

T/K	160	170	180	190	200
$C_{p,m}/J\,K^{-1}\,mol^{-1}$	247.3	256.3	265.1	273.0	280.3
$(C_{p,m}/T)/J\,K^{-2}\,mol^{-1}$	1.546	1.508	1.473	1.437	1.402

Plot $(C_{p,\mathrm{m}}/T)$ against T, Fig. 5.3(a). Extrapolate to $T = 0$ using $C_{p,\mathrm{m}} = aT^3$ [Section 5.4] fitted to the point

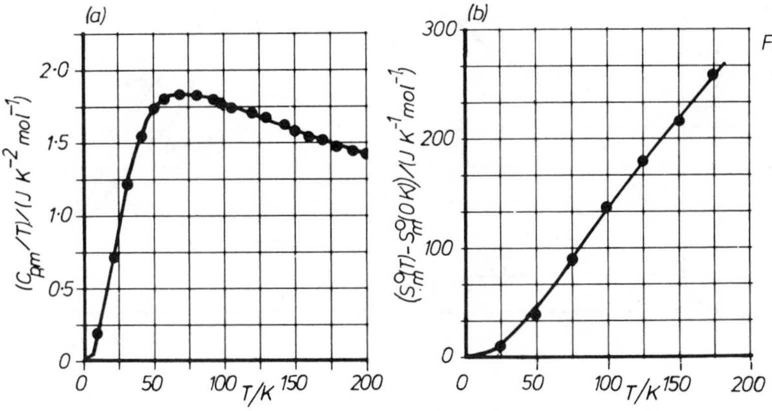

Fig 5.3

$(10\,\mathrm{K}, 2.09\,\mathrm{J\,K^{-1}\,mol^{-1}})$, which gives $a = 2.09 \times 10^{-3}\,\mathrm{J\,K^{-2}\,mol^{-1}}$. Determine the area under the graph up to each T [Section 5.4], and plot S_m against T, Fig. 5.3(b)

T/K	25	50	75	100
$(S_\mathrm{m} - S^\ominus_\mathrm{m})/\mathrm{J\,K^{-1}\,mol^{-1}}$	9.25	43.50	88.50	135.00

T/K	125	150	175	200
$(S_\mathrm{m} - S^\ominus_\mathrm{m})/\mathrm{J\,K^{-1}\,mol^{-1}}$	178.25	219.0	257.3	293.5

5.32 Plot $C_{p,\mathrm{m}}$ against T, Fig. 5.4(a), and evaluate the area. Then obtain

$H_\mathrm{m}(T) - H_\mathrm{m}(0) = \int_0^T C_{p,\mathrm{m}}\,\mathrm{d}T$. Draw up the following Table using

$G_\mathrm{m}(T) = H_\mathrm{m}(T) - TS_\mathrm{m}(T)$ so that $G_\mathrm{m}(T) - G_\mathrm{m}(0) = [H_\mathrm{m}(T) - H_\mathrm{m}(0)] - TS_\mathrm{m}(T)$

$$\Phi_0(T) = \frac{G_\mathrm{m}(T) - H_\mathrm{m}(0)}{T} = \frac{H_\mathrm{m}(T) - H_\mathrm{m}(0)}{T} - S_\mathrm{m}(T).$$

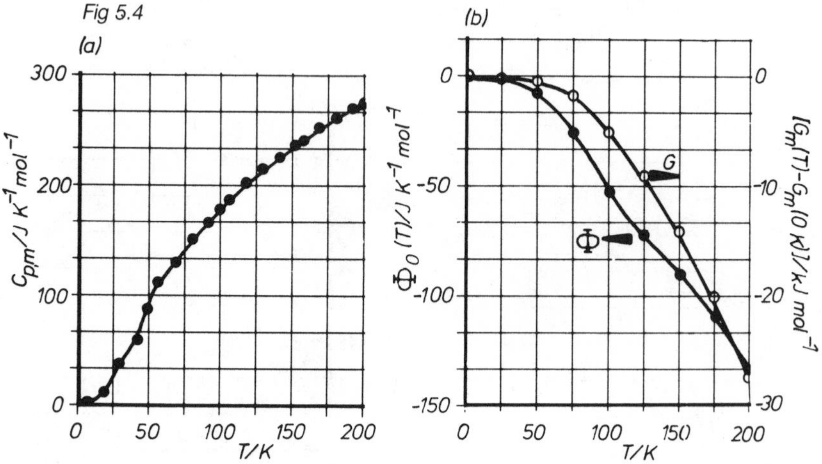

T/K	25	50	75	100
$[H_m(T)-H_m(0)]$/kJ mol^{-1} *	0.15	1.55	4.40	8.4
$S_m(T)$/J K^{-1} mol^{-1} †	9.25	43.5	88.5	135
$TS_m(T)$/kJ mol^{-1}	0.23	2.18	6.64	13.5
$[G_m(T)-G_m(0)]$/kJ mol^{-1}	−0.08	−0.63	−2.24	−5.10
$\Phi_0(T)$/J K^{-1} mol^{-1}	−3.2	−12.5	−29.9	−51.0

T/K	125	150	175	200
$[H_m(T)-H_m(0)]$/kJ mol^{-1} *	13.3	18.8	25.0	31.7
$S_m(T)$/J K^{-1} mol^{-1} †	178	219	257	294
$TS_m(T)$/kJ mol^{-1}	22.3	32.9	45.0	58.8
$[G_m(T)-G_m(0)]$/kJ mol^{-1}	−9.00	−14.1	−20.0	−27.1
$\Phi_0(T)$/J K^{-1} mol^{-1}	−72.0	−92.0	−114	−136

* From area under graph.
† From Problem 5.31. The last two lines of the Table are plotted in Fig. 5.4(b).

5.33 Draw up the following Table and proceed as in Problem 5.31.

T/K	14.14	16.33	20.03	31.15	44.08	64.81
$C_{p,\mathrm{m}}/\mathrm{J\,K^{-1}\,mol^{-1}}$	9.492	12.70	18.18	32.54	46.86	66.36
$(C_{p,\mathrm{m}}/T)/\mathrm{J\,K^{-2}\,mol^{-1}}$	0.671	0.778	0.908	1.045	1.063	1.024

T/K	100.90	140.86	183.59	225.10	262.99	298.06
$C_{p,\mathrm{m}}/\mathrm{J\,K^{-1}\,mol^{-1}}$	95.05	121.3	144.4	163.7	180.2	196.4
$(C_{p,\mathrm{m}}/T)\mathrm{J\,K^{-2}\,mol^{-1}}$	0.942	0.861	0.787	0.727	0.685	0.659

Fig 5.5

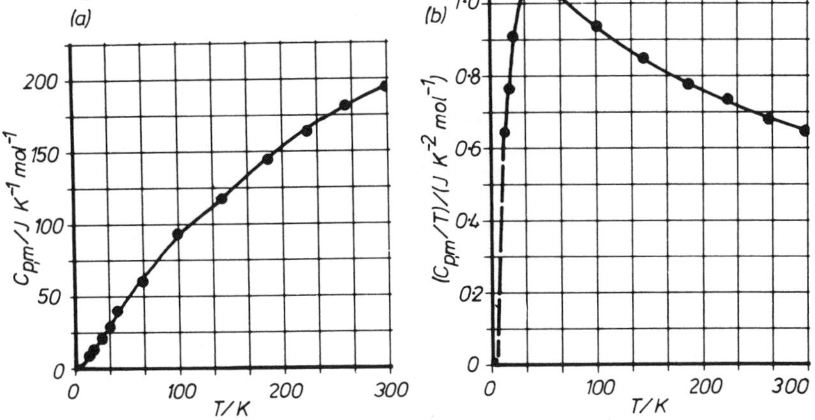

Plot $C_{p,\mathrm{m}}$ against T (Fig. 5.5(a)) and $C_{p,\mathrm{m}}/T$ against T (Fig. 5.5(b)), extrapolating to $T=0$ with $C_{p,\mathrm{m}}=aT^3$; fitting this to (14.14 K, 9.492 J K^{-1} mol^{-1}) gives $a = 3.36 \times 10^{-3}\,\mathrm{J\,K^{-2}\,mol^{-1}}$.

Then $\displaystyle\int_0^{298\mathrm{K}} C_{p,\mathrm{m}}\,\mathrm{d}T = 34.4\,\mathrm{kJ\,mol^{-1}}$,

so that $H^{\ominus}_{\mathrm{m}}(298\,\mathrm{K}) - H^{\ominus}_{\mathrm{m}}(0) = \underline{34.4\,\mathrm{kJ\,mol^{-1}}}$.

$$\int_0^{298\mathrm{K}} (C_{p,\mathrm{m}}/T)\,\mathrm{d}T = 243\,\mathrm{J\,K^{-1}\,mol^{-1}},$$

so that $S_{\mathrm{m}}^{\ominus}(298\ \mathrm{K}) - S_{\mathrm{m}}^{\ominus}(0) = \underline{243\ \mathrm{J\,K^{-1}\,mol^{-1}}}$.

$G_{\mathrm{m}}(298\ \mathrm{K}) - G_{\mathrm{m}}(0) = -38.0\ \mathrm{kJ\,mol^{-1}}$.

$\Phi_0(298\ \mathrm{K}) = (-38.0\ \mathrm{kJ\,mol^{-1}})/(298\ \mathrm{K}) = \underline{-128\ \mathrm{J\,K^{-1}\,mol^{-1}}}$.

6. The Second Law: the machinery

A6.1 $(\partial S/\partial V)_T = (\partial p/\partial T)_V = -(\partial V/\partial T)_p/(\partial V/\partial p)_T$

$= [V^{-1}(\partial V/\partial T)_p]/[V^{-1}(-\partial V/\partial p)_T] = \alpha/\kappa$ [Box 6.1, 3.2.9, 3.2.11]

$(\partial S/\partial p)_T = -(\partial V/\partial T)_p = \underline{-\alpha V}.$

A6.2 $(\partial p/\partial S)_V = -(\partial T/\partial V)_S = (\partial S/\partial V)_T/(\partial S/\partial T)_V = \underline{(\alpha/\kappa)/(C_V/T)}.$ [Box 6.1]

$(\partial V/\partial S)_p = (\partial T/\partial p)_S = -(\partial S/\partial p)_T/(\partial S/\partial T)_p = \underline{(\alpha V)/(C_p/T)}.$ [Problem A6.1]

A6.3 $\Delta S = -\partial\Delta G/\partial T$ [6.2.1] $= -\partial[-85.40 + 36.5(T/\text{K})]\,[\text{J}]/\partial(T/\text{K})$

$= \underline{-36.5\ \text{J}}.$

A6.4 $\Delta G = nRT\ln(p_f/p_i)$ [6.2.9] $= nRT\ln(V_i/V_f)$

$= (3.0 \times 10^{-3}\ \text{mol})(8.3\ \text{J K}^{-1}\ \text{mol}^{-1})(300\ \text{K})\ln(36\ \text{cm}^3/60\ \text{cm}^3) = \underline{-3.8\ \text{J}}.$

A6.5 $\Delta G = V\Delta p$ [6.2.7]; $\rho = \text{mass}/V = \text{mass}/(\Delta G/\Delta p)$

$\rho = (35 \times 10^{-3}\ \text{kg})(12 \times 10^3\ \text{J})^{-1}(3.0 \times 10^3\ \text{atm})(1.0 \times 10^5\ \text{Pa/atm}) = \underline{8.8 \times 10^2\ \text{kg m}^{-3}}.$

A6.6 $2CO(g) + O_2(g) \rightarrow 2CO_2(g)$

$\Delta_r G^\ominus(\mathcal{T}) = 2\Delta_f G^\ominus(\mathcal{T})[CO_2(g)] - 2\Delta_f G^\ominus \mathcal{T}[CO(g)]$ [5.4.4, Table 4.1.]

$= [2\ \text{mol}]\,[(-394.4\ \text{J mol}^{-1}) - (-137.2\ \text{J mol}^{-1})] = \underline{-514.4\ \text{kJ}}.$

$\Delta_r H^\ominus(\mathcal{T}) = 2\Delta_f H^\ominus(\mathcal{T})[CO_2(g)] - 2\Delta_f H^\ominus(\mathcal{T})[CO(g)]$ [4.1.4]

$= [2\ \text{mol}]\,[(-393.5\ \text{kJ mol}^{-1}) - (-110.5\ \text{kJ mol}^{-1})] = \underline{-566.0\ \text{kJ}}.$

$[\partial(\Delta_r G^\ominus/T)/\partial T]_p = -(\Delta_r H^\ominus)T^{-2} \approx -[\Delta_r H^\ominus(\mathcal{T})]T^{-2}$ [6.2.5]

$\Delta_r G^\ominus(375\ \text{K})/(375\ \text{K}) = \Delta_r G^\ominus(\mathcal{T})/\mathcal{T} + \Delta_r H^\ominus(\mathcal{T})(T^{-1} - \mathcal{T}^{-1})$

$= (-514.4\ \text{kJ})/(298\ \text{K}) + [-566.0\ \text{kJ}]\,[(375\ \text{K})^{-1} - (298\ \text{K})^{-1}]$

$= -1.336\ \text{kJ K}^{-1}.$

$\Delta_r G^\ominus(375\ \text{K}) = -(1.336\ \text{kJ K}^{-1})(375\ \text{K}) = \underline{-501.1\ \text{kJ}}.$

A6.7 $\Delta S = nR\ln(V_f/V_i) = nR\ln(p_i/p_f)$ [5.1.4].

$p_f = p_i\exp(-\Delta S/nR) = (3.50\ \text{atm})\exp[-(-25.0\ \text{J K}^{-1})(2.00\ \text{mol})^{-1}$

$\times (8.31\ \text{J K}^{-1}\ \text{mol}^{-1})^{-1}] = 15.8\ \text{atm}.$

$\Delta G = nRT\ln(p_f/p_i)$ [6.2.9] $= T(-\Delta S) = (330\ \text{K})(25.0\ \text{J K}^{-1})$

$= \underline{8.25 \times 10^3\ \text{J}}.$

A6.8 $f = (0.72)p = (0.72)(50\,\text{atm}) = 36\,\text{atm}$

$\mu - \mu^{\ominus} = RT\ln(f/p^{\ominus})$ [6.2.11] $= (8.3\,\text{J K}^{-1}\text{mol}^{-1})(200\,\text{K})\ln(36\,\text{atm}/1\,\text{atm})$

$= \underline{5.9 \times 10^3\,\text{J mol}^{-1}}.$

A6.9 $\Delta\mu = RT\ln(p_f/p_i)$ [6.2.10] $= (8.31\,\text{J K}^{-1}\text{mol}^{-1})(313\,\text{K})\ln(29.5\,\text{atm}/1.8\,\text{atm})$

$= \underline{7.27 \times 10^3\,\text{J mol}^{-1}}.$

A6.10 $B' = B/RT = (-81.7 \times 10^{-6}\,\text{m}^3\,\text{mol}^{-1})(8.31\,\text{J K}^{-1}\text{mol}^{-1})^{-1}(373\,\text{K})^{-1}$

$= \underline{-2.64 \times 10^{-8}\,\text{Pa}^{-1}}.$ [1.3.1, 1.3.2]

$f = p\exp(B'p)$ [Section 6.2(e)]

$f/p = \exp(B'p) = \exp[(-2.64 \times 10^{-8}\,\text{Pa}^{-1})(50.0\,\text{atm})(1.01 \times 10^5\,\text{Pa/atm})] = \underline{0.875}.$

6.1 (a) At constant volume, $dU = C_V dT$; $dS = dq_{\text{rev},V}/T = C_V dT/T$.
Therefore $(\partial U/\partial S)_V = C_V dT/(C_V dT/T) = \underline{T}$.
(b) Ensure constant entropy by considering a reversible, adiabatic change. Then
$dU_S = dw_{\text{rev}} = -p dV$; hence $(\partial U/\partial V)_S = \underline{-p}.$

6.2 There are two routes. Either use $H(p, S)$ a state function, $A(V, T)$ a state function and proceed as in Section 6.1(b).

$dH(p, S) = (\partial H/\partial p)_S\, dp + (\partial H/\partial S)_p dS = V dp + T dS$

[6.1.2, and $dH = dU + pdV + Vdp$]. Since dH is exact, $\underline{(\partial V/\partial S)_p = (\partial T/\partial p)_S}$ [Box 3.1].

$dA(V, T) = (\partial A/\partial V)_T dT + (\partial A/\partial T)_V dV = -SdT - pdV$ [6.1.1 and $dA = dU - TdS - SdT$]. dA is exact, hence $-(\partial S/\partial V)_T = -(\partial p/\partial T)_V$ or

$(\partial S/\partial V)_T = (\partial p/\partial T)_V$ as required.

Alternatively,

$(\partial S/\partial V)_T = (\partial S/\partial p)_T(\partial p/\partial V)_T = -(\partial V/\partial T)_p(\partial p/\partial V)_T$ [Box 3.1]

$= +1/(\partial T/\partial p)_V$ [chain relation, Box 3.1]

$= (\partial p/\partial T)_V$ [inversion, Box 3.1].

Similarly for $(\partial V/\partial S)_p$.

6.3 $(\partial S/\partial V)_T = (\partial p/\partial T)_V$ [above] $= [(\partial/\partial T)(nRT/V)]_V = nR/V$.
Therefore $dS = nRdV/V = nR\,d\ln V$; so that

$\underline{S = \text{const} + nR\ln V \text{ at const } T.}$

6.4 $dH = TdS + Vdp$ [6.1.1 and $H = U + pV$]

$= (\partial H/\partial S)_p dS + (\partial H/\partial p)_S dp$ [as $H = H(p, S)$].

Therefore $(\partial H/\partial S)_p = T$, $(\partial H/\partial p)_S = V$ [dH exact differential].

Also $(\partial H/\partial p)_T = (\partial H/\partial S)_p(\partial S/\partial p)_T + (\partial H/\partial p)_S$ [Relation 1, Box 3.1]

$= T(\partial S/\partial p)_T + V$ [above] $= \underline{-T(\partial V/\partial T)_p + V}$

[Maxwell relation, Box 6.1].

6.5 $(\partial H/\partial p)_T = -T(\partial V/\partial T)_p + V$ [above].

(a) $pV = nRT$, $V = nRT/p$, $(\partial V/\partial T)_p = nR/p$.

Therefore $(\partial H/\partial p)_T = -nRT/p + V = -V + V = 0$.

(b) $p = nRT/(V - nb) - an^2/V^2$ [Box 1.1], $(\partial V/\partial T)_p = 1/(\partial T/\partial V)_p$

$T = p(V - nb)/nR + an(V - nb)/RV^2$.

$(\partial T/\partial V)_p = p/nR + an/RV^2 - 2an(V - nb)/RV^3$.

$$\text{Therefore } (\partial H/\partial p)_T = \frac{-T}{p/nR + an/RV^2 - 2an(V - nb)/RV^3} + V$$

$$= \underline{\frac{nb - (2na/RT)\lambda^2}{1 - (2na/RTV)\lambda^2}, \lambda = 1 - nb/V.}$$

when $b/V_m \ll 1$, $\lambda^2 \approx 1$. Furthermore $2na/RTV = (2na/RT)(1/V)$

$\approx (2na/RT)(p/nRT) = 2pa/R^2T^2$.

$$\text{Therefore, } (\partial H/\partial p)_T \approx \frac{nb - (2na/RT)}{1 - (2pa/R^2T^2)}.$$ For argon,

$a = 1.345\ \text{dm}^6\,\text{atm}\,\text{mol}^{-2}$, $b = 3.219 \times 10^{-2}\ \text{dm}^3\,\text{mol}^{-1}$ [Table 1.3];

$T = 298\ \text{K}$, $p = 10\ \text{atm}$, $n = 1.0\ \text{mol}$.

$$2na/RT = \frac{2 \times (1.0\ \text{mol}) \times (1.345\ \text{dm}^6\,\text{atm}\,\text{mol}^{-2})}{(0.0821\ \text{dm}^3\,\text{atm}\,\text{K}^{-1}\,\text{mol}^{-1}) \times (298\ \text{K})} = 0.11\ \text{dm}^3.$$

$$2pa/R^2T^2 = \frac{2 \times (10\ \text{atm}) \times (1.345\ \text{dm}^6\,\text{atm}\,\text{mol}^{-2})}{(0.0821 \times 298\ \text{dm}^3\,\text{atm}\,\text{mol}^{-1})^2} = 0.045.$$

$$(\partial H/\partial p)_T \approx \frac{(3.22 \times 10^{-2} - 0.11)\text{dm}^3}{(1 - 0.045)} = -0.081\ \text{dm}^3 = \underline{-8.2\ \text{J}\,\text{atm}^{-1}}.$$

[$1\ \text{dm}^3 = 10^{-3}\ \text{m}^3 = 10^{-3}\ \text{N}\,\text{m}/\text{N}\,\text{m}^{-2}$

$= 10^{-3}\ \text{J}\,\text{atm}^{-1}(\text{atm}/\text{N}\,\text{m}^{-2})$ [$1\ \text{N}\,\text{m} = 1\text{J}$]

$= 10^{-6}\ \text{kJ atm}^{-1}(1.01325 \times 10^5)$ [end-paper 1]

$= 0.101325\ \text{kJ atm}^{-1}$.]

Therefore $(\partial H/\partial p)_T = -0.081 \times 0.101\ \text{kJ atm}^{-1} = \underline{-8.2\ \text{J atm}^{-1}}$.

$\delta H \approx (\partial H/\partial p)_T \delta p = (-8.2\ \text{J atm}^{-1}) \times (1\ \text{atm}) = \underline{-8.2\ \text{J.}}$

6.6 $(\partial U/\partial V)_T = T(\partial p/\partial T)_V - p$ [6.1.6]

$p = RT/V_m + RTB/V_m^2$ [given]

$(\partial p/\partial T)_V = R/V_m + RB/V_m^2 + (RT/V_m^2)(\partial B/\partial T)_V$

$\qquad = p/T + (RT/V_m^2)(\partial B/\partial T)_V$

$(\partial U/\partial V)_T = (RT^2/V_m^2)(\partial B/\partial T)_V \approx (RT^2/V_m^2)(\Delta B/\Delta T)_V$.

For $V_m \approx RT/p$ for $B \ll V_m$; $(\partial U/\partial V)_T \approx (p^2/R)(\Delta B/\Delta T)_V$.

$p =$ (a) 1 atm, (b) 10 atm, $\Delta T = 50\ \text{K}$,

$\Delta B = [-15.6 - (-28.0)]\ \text{cm}^3\ \text{mol}^{-1} = 12.4\ \text{cm}^3\ \text{mol}^{-1}$

$$(\partial U/\partial V)_T \approx \frac{(1\ \text{atm})^2 \times (12.4 \times 10^{-3}\ \text{dm}^3\ \text{mol}^{-1})}{(0.0821\ \text{dm}^3\ \text{atm mol}^{-1}) \times (50\ \text{K})} = 3.02 \times 10^{-3}\ \text{atm}$$

$\approx 3.02 \times 10^{-3}\ \text{N m}^{-2}(\text{atm/N m}^{-2}) = 3.02 \times 10^{-3} \times 1.013 \times 10^5\ \text{N m}^{-2}$

$= 306\ \text{N m}^{-2} = \underline{306\ \text{J m}^{-3}}$.

Since $(\partial U/\partial V)_T \propto p^2$, when $p = 10$ atm;

$(\partial U/\partial V)_T \approx 306 \times 10^2\ \text{J m}^{-3} = \underline{30.6\ \text{kJ m}^{-3}}$.

6.7 $C_V = (\partial U/\partial T)_V, C_p = (\partial H/\partial T)_p$.

$(\partial C_V/\partial V)_T = (\partial^2 U/\partial V \partial T) = (\partial^2 U/\partial V \partial T)$

$\qquad = (\partial/\partial T)(\partial U/\partial V)_T = 0\ [(\partial U/\partial V)_T = 0]$.

$(\partial C_V/\partial p)_T = (\partial/\partial T)(\partial U/\partial p)_T = (\partial/\partial T)(\partial U/\partial V)_T(\partial V/\partial p)_T = 0$.

$C_p = C_V + nR$; therefore $(\partial C_p/\partial X)_T = (\partial C_V/\partial X)_T$ for $X = p$ or V.

Hence $(\partial C_p/\partial V)_T = 0$ and $(\partial C_p/\partial p)_T = 0$ also. In general, C_V and C_p both depend on temperature (see Part 2).

6.8 $(\partial C_{V,m}/\partial V)_T = ((\partial/\partial V)(\partial U_m/\partial T)_V)_T = ((\partial/\partial T)(\partial U_m/\partial V)_T)_V$

$\qquad = (\partial/\partial T)\{(RT^2/V_m^2)(\partial B/\partial T)_V\}$ [Problem 6.6]

$\qquad = (2RT/V_m^2)(\partial B/\partial T)_V + (RT^2/V_m^2)(\partial^2 B/\partial T^2)_V$

$\qquad = \underline{(RT/V_m^2)[(\partial^2/\partial T^2)BT]_V}$.

$\partial(BT)/\partial T \approx \{(348\ \text{K}) \times (-7.14\ \text{cm}^3\ \text{mol}^{-1}) - 2(323\ \text{K}) \times (-11.06\ \text{cm}^3\ \text{mol}^{-1})$

$\qquad + (298\ \text{K}) \times (-15.49\ \text{cm}^3\ \text{mol}^{-1})\}/(25\ \text{K})^2 = 7.04 \times 10^{-2}\ \text{cm}^3\ \text{K}^{-1}\ \text{mol}^{-1}$.

$(\partial C_{V,\mathrm{m}}/\partial p)_T = (\partial C_{V,\mathrm{m}}/\partial V)_T(\partial V/\partial p)_T = (\partial C_{V,\mathrm{m}}/\partial V)_T/(\partial p/\partial V)_T.$

$(\partial p/\partial V)_T \approx -RT/V_\mathrm{m}^2 \approx -p/V.$

$$(\partial C_{V,\mathrm{m}}/\partial p)_T \approx (\partial C_{V,\mathrm{m}}/\partial V)_T(-V/p) \approx (-RT/V^2)\,(V/p)\,(\partial^2/\partial T^2)BT$$
$$\approx -(\partial^2(BT)/\partial T^2)_V$$
$$\approx -7.04 \times 10^{-2}\,\mathrm{cm^3\,K^{-1}\,mol^{-1}} = -7.04 \times 10^{-8}\,\mathrm{m^3\,K^{-1}\,mol^{-1}}.$$

Therefore, if $\delta p \approx -9\,\mathrm{atm} \mathrel{\widehat{=}} -9 \times 10^5\,\mathrm{N\,m^{-2}}$,

$$\delta C_{V,\mathrm{m}} \approx (-7 \times 10^{-8}\,\mathrm{m^3\,K^{-1}\,mol^{-1}}) \times (-9 \times 10^5\,\mathrm{N\,m^{-2}})$$
$$= 6 \times 10^{-2}\,\mathrm{N\,m\,K^{-1}\,mol^{-1}} = \underline{6 \times 10^{-2}\,\mathrm{J\,K^{-1}\,mol^{-1}}}.$$

6.9 $\mu_\mathrm{JT} = (\partial T/\partial p)_H$ [3.2.14], $C_p = (\partial H/\partial T)_p$ [2.3.7]

$\mu_\mathrm{JT}C_p = (\partial T/\partial p)_H(\partial H/\partial T)_p = -1/(\partial p/\partial H)_T$ [chain relation, Box 3.1]

$= -(\partial H/\partial p)_T$ [inversion, Box 3.1]

$= T(\partial V/\partial T)_p - V$ [equation of state, Problem 6.4].

$\alpha = (1/V)\,(\partial V/\partial T)_p$ [3.2.9]; hence $\underline{\mu_\mathrm{JT}C_p = V(\alpha T - 1)}$.

6.10 $\mu_\mathrm{J} = (\partial T/\partial V)_U, C_V = (\partial U/\partial T)_V$ [2.3.3]

$\mu_\mathrm{J}C_V = (\partial T/\partial V)_U(\partial U/\partial T)_V$

$= -1/(\partial V/\partial U)_T$ [chain relation, Box 3.1]

$= -(\partial U/\partial V)_T$ [inversion, Box 3.1]

$= p - T(\partial p/\partial T)_V$ [6.1.6].

$(\partial p/\partial T)_V = -(\partial V/\partial T)_p/(\partial V/\partial p)_T$ [chain relation]

$= \alpha V/\kappa V$ [$\kappa = -(1/V)\,(\partial V/\partial p)_T$, 3.2.11] $= \alpha/\kappa$.

Therefore $\underline{\mu_\mathrm{J}C_V = p - \alpha T/\kappa}$.

6.11 $(\partial U/\partial V)_T = T(\partial p/\partial T)_V - p$ [6.1.6]; $p = nRT/(V - nb) - n^2a/V^2$ [Box 1.1].

$(\partial p/\partial T)_V = nR/(V - nb)$;

$(\partial U/\partial V)_T = nRT/(V - nb) - p = n^2a/V^2 = \underline{a/V_\mathrm{m}^2}$.

$$\lim_{V_\mathrm{m}\to\infty} (\partial U/\partial V)_T = \underline{0}.$$

For argon, $a = 1.345\,\mathrm{dm^6\,atm\,mol^{-2}}$, $V_\mathrm{m} \approx RT/p$, $(\partial U/\partial V)_T \approx ap^2/R^2T^2$.

(a) $p = 1.0\,\mathrm{atm}$;

$$(\partial U/\partial V)_T \approx \frac{(1.345\,\mathrm{dm^6\,atm\,mol^{-2}}) \times (1.0\,\mathrm{atm})^2}{(0.0821\,\mathrm{dm^3\,atm\,K^{-1}\,mol^{-1}})^2 \times (298\,\mathrm{K})^2}$$

$= 2.3 \times 10^{-3}\,\text{atm} \approx (2.3 \times 10^{-3} \times 1.013 \times 10^{5})\,\text{J m}^{-3}$ [Problem 6.6]

$\approx \underline{0.23\,\text{kJ m}^{-3}}$.

(b) $p = 10\,\text{atm}$; $(\partial U/\partial V)_T \propto p^2$; $\underline{(\partial U/\partial V)_T \approx 23\,\text{kJ m}^{-3}}$.

6.12 $(\partial U/\partial V)_T = T(\partial p/\partial T)_V - p$ [6.1.6].

$p = \{nRT/(V - nb)\}\exp(-an/RTV)$ [Box 1.1].

$T(\partial p/\partial T)_V = \{nRT/(V-nb)\}\exp(-an/RTV)$

$+ (an/RTV) \times \{nRT/(V-nb)\}\exp(-an/RTV) = p + anp/RTV.$

Therefore $(\partial U/\partial V)_T = \underline{anp/RTV}$.

$p = p_r p_c = p_r a/4e^2b^2$, $V_m = V_r V_{c,m} = 2V_r b$.

$T = T_r T_c = T_r a/4bR$ [Box 1.1], $U = U_r(a/e^2 b)$ [given].

Therefore $(\partial U/\partial V)_T = (\partial U_r/\partial V_r)_T (a/2e^2b^2)$

$= ap/RTV_m$ [above] $= (ap_r/RT_r V_r)(p_c/T_c V_{m,c})$

$= (p_r/T_r V_r)(a/2e^2b^2)$.

Therefore $(\partial U_r/\partial V_r)_T = \underline{p_r/T_r V_r}$.

6.13 $\kappa_s = -(1/V)(\partial V/\partial p)_S$ (adiabatic, reversible implies $dS = 0$).

$pV^\gamma = \text{const.}$ for adiabatic, reversible change [3.3.9]; $p = \text{const.}/V^\gamma$.

$(\partial p/\partial V)_S = -\gamma\,\text{const}/V^{\gamma+1} = -\gamma p/V$.

$(\partial V/\partial p)_s = 1/(\partial p/\partial V)_S = -V/\gamma p$; $\kappa_S = -(1/V)(-V/\gamma p) = 1/\gamma p$.

Therefore $\underline{\gamma p \kappa_S = 1}$.

6.14 $dS = (\partial S/\partial T)_V dT + (\partial S/\partial V)_T dV$ [$S = S(V, T)$];

$TdS = T(\partial S/\partial T)_V dT + T(\partial S/\partial V)_T dV$.

(i) $(\partial S/\partial T)_V = (\partial S/\partial U)_V (\partial U/\partial T)_V = (1/T)C_V$ [6.1.3, 2.3.3].

(ii) $(\partial S/\partial V)_T = (\partial p/\partial T)_V$ [Maxwell relation, Box 6.1].

Therefore $\underline{TdS = C_V dT + T(\partial p/\partial T)_V dV}$.

For reversible, isothermal expansion $TdS = dq_{rev}$, $dT = 0$.

Therefore $dq_{rev} = T(\partial p/\partial T)_V dV = \{nRT/(V - nb)\}dV$ [Problem 6.11].

Therefore $q_{rev} = nRT \int_{V_i}^{V_f} \left(\dfrac{dV}{V - nb}\right) = \underline{nRT \ln\left(\dfrac{V_f - nb}{V_i - nb}\right)}$.

6.15 $dS = (\partial S/\partial T)_p\, dT + (\partial S/\partial p)_T dp$ [$S = S(p, T)$];

$TdS = T(\partial S/\partial T)_p dT + T(\partial S/\partial p)_T dp$.

(i) $(\partial S/\partial T)_p = (\partial S/\partial H)_p\,(\partial H/\partial T)_p$

$dH = dU + pdV + Vdp\ [H = U + pV] = TdS + Vdp\ [6.1.1]$

$\quad = (\partial H/\partial S)_p dS + (\partial H/\partial p)_S dp\ [H = H(p, S)]$.

Therefore $(\partial H/\partial S)_p = T$ [dH complete], $(\partial S/\partial H)_p = 1/T$ [inversion, Box 3.1].

$(\partial H/\partial T)_p = C_p$ [2.3.7]; $T(\partial S/\partial T)_p = C_p$.

$(\partial S/\partial p)_T = -(\partial V/\partial T)_p$ [Maxwell relation, Box 6.1].

Therefore $TdS = C_p dT - T(\partial V/\partial T)_p dp = \underline{C_p dT - \alpha TVdp}$

$[\alpha = (1/V)(\partial V/\partial T)_p, 3.2.9]$.

For reversible, isothermal compression $TdS = dq_{rev}$, $dT = 0$;

Therefore $dq_{rev} = -\alpha TVdp$.

$$q_{rev} = -T\int_{p_i}^{p_f} \alpha V dp = -\alpha T\int_{p_i}^{p_f} V dp \text{ if } \alpha = \text{const.}$$

For $V \approx$ const.,

$$q_{rev} \approx -\alpha TV\int_{p_i}^{p_f} dp = -\alpha TV(p_f - p_i) = \underline{-\alpha TV\Delta p.}$$

$\alpha = 1.82 \times 10^{-4}\,K^{-1}$, $T = 273\,K$, $V = 100\,cm^3 = 1.00 \times 10^{-4}\,m^3$,

$\Delta p = 1000\,atm = 1.013 \times 10^3 \times 10^5\,N\,m^{-2} = 1.013 \times 10^8\,N\,m^{-2}$.

$q_{rev} = -(1.82 \times 10^{-4}\,K^{-1}) \times (273\,K) \times (1.00 \times 10^{-4}\,m^3) \times (1.013 \times 10^8\,N\,m^{-2})$

$\quad = \underline{-0.50\,kJ.}$

6.16 $q_{rev} \approx -\alpha TV\Delta p$ [Problem 6.15] $= -(1.24 \times 10^{-3}\,K^{-1}) \times (298\,K)$

$\quad \times (100\,g/0.879\,g\,cm^{-3}) \times (4 \times 10^3 \times 1.013 \times 10^5\,N\,m^{-2})$

$\quad = \underline{-17.0\,kJ.}$

$$w_{rev} = -\int_{V_i}^{V_f} pdV = -\int_{p_i}^{p_f} p(\partial V/\partial p)_T\,dp = +\int_{p_i}^{p_f} \kappa pVdp$$

$$\approx +\kappa V\int_{p_i}^{p_f} pdp = +\tfrac{1}{2}\kappa V(p_f^2 - p_i^2)$$

$= \tfrac{1}{2} \times (9.6 \times 10^{-5}\,atm^{-1}) \times (1.14 \times 10^{-4}\,m^3) \times (4.00 \times 10^3\,atm)^2$

$= 87.6 \times 10^{-3}\,m^3\,atm = \underline{8.87\,kJ}$ [$1\,atm = 1.013 \times 10^5\,N\,m^{-2}$].

$\Delta U = w_{rev} + q_{rev} = +\,8.87\,kJ - 17.0\,kJ\,mol^{-1} = \underline{-8.1\,kJ.}$

6.17 $\delta G \approx V\delta p$ [6.2.7].

$V = 100\,\mathrm{cm^3}, \delta p = 99\,\mathrm{atm} = 99 \times 1.013 \times 10^5\,\mathrm{N\,m^{-2}}$.

$\delta G \approx (100 \times 10^{-6}\,\mathrm{m^3}) \times (99 \times 1.013 \times 10^5\,\mathrm{N\,m^{-2}}) = 1.00 \times 10^3\,\mathrm{N\,m} = \underline{1.0\,\mathrm{kJ}}$.

6.18 $\mathrm{d}G = (\partial G/\partial p)_T \mathrm{d}p = V\mathrm{d}p$ [6.2.2]

$(\partial V/\partial p)_T = -\kappa V$ [given]; $\mathrm{d}V/V = -\kappa \mathrm{d}p$ at const T.

$$\int_{V(p_\mathrm{i})}^{V(p)} \mathrm{d}V/V = -\kappa \int_{p_\mathrm{i}}^{p} \mathrm{d}p, \text{ or } \ln[V(p)/V(p_\mathrm{i})] = -\kappa(p - p_\mathrm{i}) \ [\kappa \approx \text{const.}].$$

Therefore $V(p) = V(p_\mathrm{i}) \exp[-\kappa(p - p_\mathrm{i})]$.

$\int \mathrm{d}G = V(p_\mathrm{i}) \int \exp[-\kappa(p - p_\mathrm{i})]\, \mathrm{d}p$, or

$$G(p_\mathrm{f}) - G(p_\mathrm{i}) = V(p_\mathrm{i}) \int_{p_\mathrm{i}}^{p_\mathrm{f}} \exp[-\kappa(p - p_\mathrm{i})]\, \mathrm{d}p$$

$$= V(p_\mathrm{i}) \{\exp[-\kappa(p_\mathrm{f} - p_\mathrm{i})] - 1\}/(-\kappa)$$

$$= \underline{(V(p_\mathrm{i})/\kappa)\{1 - \exp[-\kappa(p_\mathrm{f} - p_\mathrm{i})]\}}.$$

If $\kappa(p_\mathrm{f} - p_\mathrm{i}) \ll 1$, use $\mathrm{e}^{-x} \approx 1 - x + \dfrac{x^2}{2}$ and obtain

$$G(p_\mathrm{f}) \approx G(p_\mathrm{i}) + (V(p_\mathrm{i})/\kappa)\{\kappa(p_\mathrm{f} - p_\mathrm{i}) - \tfrac{1}{2}\kappa^2(p_\mathrm{f} - p_\mathrm{i})^2\}$$

$$\approx \underline{G(p_\mathrm{i}) + V\Delta p - \tfrac{1}{2}\kappa V(\Delta p)^2}.$$

6.19 $G_\mathrm{m}(p_\mathrm{f}) - G_\mathrm{m}(p_\mathrm{i}) \approx V_\mathrm{m}\Delta p - \frac{1}{2}\kappa V_\mathrm{m} \Delta p^2 = V_\mathrm{m}\Delta p\{1 - \frac{1}{2}\kappa\Delta p\}$

[Problem 6.18, $\kappa\Delta p \ll 1$].

$V_\mathrm{m} = (63.6\,\mathrm{g\,mol^{-1}})/(8.93\,\mathrm{g\,cm^{-3}}) = 7.12\,\mathrm{cm^3\,mol^{-1}}$;

$\kappa = 0.8 \times 10^{-6}\,\mathrm{atm^{-1}}$; $\Delta p =$ (a) 100 atm, (b) 10 000 atm.

[Check $\kappa\Delta p =$ (a) $0.8 \times 10^{-4} \ll 1$, (b) $0.8 \times 10^{-2} \ll 1$; therefore the approximation $\kappa\Delta p \ll 1$ is valid.]

(a) $\Delta G_\mathrm{m} \approx (7.12 \times 10^{-6}\,\mathrm{m^3\,mol^{-1}}) \times (100 \times 1.013 \times 10^5\,\mathrm{N\,m^{-2}})$

$\times \{1 - \frac{1}{2} \times (0.8 \times 10^{-6}\,\mathrm{atm^{-1}}) \times (100\,\mathrm{atm})\} = \underline{72\,\mathrm{J\,mol^{-1}}}$.

(b) $\Delta G_\mathrm{m} \approx (7.12 \times 10^{-6}\,\mathrm{m^3\,mol^{-1}}) \times (10^4 \times 1.013 \times 10^5\,\mathrm{N\,m^{-2}})$

$\times \{1 - \frac{1}{2} \times (0.8 \times 10^{-6}\,\mathrm{atm^{-1}}) \times (10^4\,\mathrm{atm})\} = \underline{7.2\,\mathrm{kJ\,mol^{-1}}}$.

If the block is assumed incompressible, $\Delta G_\mathrm{m} \approx V_\mathrm{m}\Delta p$, and so

(a) $\Delta G_\mathrm{m} \approx (7.12 \times 10^{-6}\,\mathrm{m^3\,mol^{-1}}) \times (1.013 \times 10^7\,\mathrm{N\,m^{-2}})$

$= \underline{72\,\mathrm{J\,mol^{-1}}}$.

(b) $\Delta G_\mathrm{m} \approx (7.12 \times 10^{-6}\,\mathrm{m^3\,mol^{-1}}) \times (1.013 \times 10^9\,\mathrm{N\,m^{-2}})$

$= \underline{7.2\,\mathrm{kJ\,mol^{-1}}}$.

6.20 $\Delta G_m \approx V_m \Delta p(1 - \frac{1}{2}\kappa\Delta p)$ [Problem 6.18, $(\kappa\Delta p)^2 \ll 1$].

$V_m = (18.02\ \mathrm{g\,mol^{-2}})/(0.997\ \mathrm{g\,cm^{-3}}) = 18.07\ \mathrm{cm^3\,mol^{-1}}$

$\kappa = 4.94 \times 10^{-5}\ \mathrm{atm^{-1}}$.

(a) $\Delta G_m \approx (18.07 \times 10^{-6}\ \mathrm{m^3\,mol^{-1}}) \times (1.0133 \times 10^7\ \mathrm{N\,m^{-2}})$

$\times \{1 - \frac{1}{2}(4.94 \times 10^{-5} \times 10^2)\} = \underline{183\ \mathrm{J\,mol^{-1}}}$.

(b) $\Delta G_m \approx (18.07 \times 10^{-6}\ \mathrm{m^3\,mol^{-1}}) \times (1.0133 \times 10^9\ \mathrm{N\,m^{-2}})$

$\times \{1 - \frac{1}{2}(4.94 \times 10^{-5} \times 10^4)\} = \underline{13.8\ \mathrm{kJ\,mol^{-1}}}$.

If the water is assumed incompressible the second term in {} is absent, and we find

(a) $\Delta G_m \approx \underline{183\ \mathrm{J\,mol^{-1}}}$ (b) $\Delta G_m \approx \underline{18.3\ \mathrm{kJ\,mol^{-1}}}$,

and the second value is significantly different from that calculated above.

6.21 $\{(\partial/\partial T)(\Delta G/T)\}_p = -\Delta H/T^2$ [6.2.5]; $\int \mathrm{d}\left(\frac{\Delta G}{T}\right) = -\int\left(\frac{\Delta H \mathrm{d}T}{T^2}\right)$.

(a) $\Delta G(T_f)/T_f - \Delta G(T_i)/T_i \approx -\Delta H(T_i)\left(\frac{1}{T_i} - \frac{1}{T_f}\right)$,

$$\Delta G(T_f) \approx \Delta G(T_i) + \left(\frac{T_f - T_i}{T_i}\right)\{\Delta G(T_i) - \Delta H(T_i)\}$$

$$\approx \underline{\tau\Delta G(T_i) + (1-\tau)\Delta H(T_i)},\ \tau = T_f/T_i.$$

(b) $\Delta H(T) = \Delta H(T_i) + (T - T_i)\Delta C_p$ [given].

$$\frac{\Delta G(T_f)}{T_f} - \frac{\Delta G(T_i)}{T_i} = -\int_{T_i}^{T_f}\left\{\frac{\Delta H(T_i)\mathrm{d}T}{T^2} + \frac{(T - T_i)\Delta C_p \mathrm{d}T}{T^2}\right\}$$

$$= -\left\{-\Delta H(T_i)\left(\frac{1}{T_f} - \frac{1}{T_i}\right) + \Delta C_p \ln\left(\frac{T_f}{T_i}\right) + T_i\Delta C_p\left(\frac{1}{T_f} - \frac{1}{T_i}\right)\right\}$$

$$= \{\Delta H(T_i) - T_i\Delta C_p\}\left(\frac{1}{T_f} - \frac{1}{T_i}\right) - \Delta C_p \ln\left(\frac{T_f}{T_i}\right).$$

Therefore $\Delta G(T_f) = (T_f/T_i)\Delta G(T_i) + \{\Delta H(T_i) - T_i\Delta C_p\}\left(1 - \frac{T_f}{T_i}\right) - T_f\Delta C_p \ln\left(\frac{T_f}{T_i}\right)$.

With $\tau = T_f/T_i$,

$\underline{\Delta G(T_f) = \tau\Delta G(T_i) + (1-\tau)\{\Delta H(T_i) - T_i\Delta C_p\} - T_f\Delta C_p \ln\tau.}$

6.22 $\Delta G_m^\ominus(\text{true}) - \Delta G_m^\ominus(\text{approx}) = \{(\tau - 1)T_i - T_f \ln\tau\}\Delta C_p$ [Problem 6.21].

$\Delta C_p = (75.3 - 28.8 - \frac{1}{2} \times 29.4)\,\mathrm{J\,K^{-1}\,mol^{-1}} = 31.8\,\mathrm{J\,K^{-1}\,mol^{-1}}$.

$\tau = T_f/T_i = 330/298 = 1.11$.

$$\Delta G_m^\ominus(\text{approx}) = \tau\Delta G^\ominus(T_i) + (1-\tau)\Delta H(T_i)$$
$$= 1.11 \times (-237.2\,\mathrm{kJ\,mol^{-1}}) - 0.11 \times (-285.8\,\mathrm{kJ\,mol^{-1}})$$
$$= \underline{-231.9\,\mathrm{kJ\,mol^{-1}}}.$$

$$\Delta G_m^\ominus(\text{true}) - \Delta G_m^\ominus(\text{approx}) = \{0.11 \times (298\,\mathrm{K}) - (330\,\mathrm{K})\ln 1.11\} \times (31.8\,\mathrm{J\,K^{-1}\,mol^{-1}})$$
$$= \underline{-52.8\,\mathrm{J\,mol^{-1}}}\ (0.02 \text{ per cent error}).$$

6.23 $\frac{1}{2}N_2 + \frac{3}{2}H_2 \rightarrow NH_3(g)$; $\Delta G_m^\ominus(298\,\mathrm{K}) = -31.0\,\mathrm{kJ\,mol^{-1}}$,
$\Delta H_m^\ominus(298\,\mathrm{K}) = -92.35\,\mathrm{kJ\,mol^{-1}}$.

$\Delta G_m^\ominus(T) \approx \tau\Delta G_m^\ominus(T_i) + (1-\tau)\Delta H_m^\ominus(T_i)$ [Problem 6.21].

(a) $T_f = 500\,\mathrm{K}$; $\tau = (500\,\mathrm{K})/(298\,\mathrm{K}) = 1.68$.

$$\Delta G_m^\ominus(500\,\mathrm{K}) \approx 1.68 \times (-31.0\,\mathrm{kJ\,mol^{-1}}) + (-0.68) \times (-92.38\,\mathrm{kJ\,mol^{-1}})$$
$$\approx \underline{10.7\,\mathrm{kJ\,mol^{-1}}}.$$

(b) $T_f = 1000\,\mathrm{K}$; $\tau = (1000\,\mathrm{K})/(298\,\mathrm{K}) = 3.36$

$$\Delta G_m^\ominus(1000\,\mathrm{K}) \approx 3.36 \times (-31.0\,\mathrm{kJ\,mol^{-1}})$$
$$+ (-2.36) \times (-92.38\,\mathrm{kJ\,mol^{-1}}) \approx \underline{114\,\mathrm{kJ\,mol^{-1}}}.$$

The reaction is therefore disfavored by a rise in temperature. The *complete* reaction from standard state to standard state (i.e. pure gases to pure ammonia) is not spontaneous ($\Delta G > 0$).

6.24 $w'_{e,\max} = -\Delta G$ [5.3.11] $\tau = (308\,\mathrm{K})/(298\,\mathrm{K}) = 1.03$.

$$\Delta G_m(35\,°\mathrm{C}) = 1.03\,\Delta G_m(298\,\mathrm{K}) + (1-1.03)\Delta H_m^\ominus \text{ [Problem 6.21]}$$
$$= (1.03) \times (-5797\,\mathrm{kJ\,mol^{-1}}) + (-0.03) \times (-5645\,\mathrm{kJ\,mol^{-1}})$$
$$= -5801\,\mathrm{kJ\,mol^{-1}}.$$

Therefore $\Delta G_m(35\,°\mathrm{C}) - \Delta G_m(25\,°\mathrm{C}) = (-5801\,\mathrm{kJ\,mol^{-1}}) - (-5797\,\mathrm{kJ\,mol^{-1}})$
$$= -5\,\mathrm{kJ\,mol^{-1}}.$$

Therefore, an extra amount $\underline{5\,\mathrm{kJ\,mol^{-1}}}$ of non-pV work may be obtained at 35 °C.

6.25 $G(p_f) - G(p_i) = nRT\ln(p_f/p_i)$ [6.2.9].

$\Delta G = (1.0\,\mathrm{mol}) \times (8.314\,\mathrm{J\,K^{-1}\,mol^{-1}}) \times (298\,\mathrm{K}) \times \ln(100\,\mathrm{atm}/1.0\,\mathrm{atm}) = \underline{11\,\mathrm{kJ}}.$

6.26 $\Delta G(\bar{p}) = G(0) + \int_0^{\bar{p}} V(\bar{p})\,\mathrm{d}\bar{p}$ [6.2.6].

$V(\bar{p}) = V_0 \exp(-\bar{p}/p^*)$, $\bar{p}$ is the excess pressure $p - p_i$.

$$G(\bar{p}) = G(0) + V_0 \int_0^{\bar{p}} \exp[-\bar{p}/p^*]\,\mathrm{d}\bar{p}$$

$$= \underline{G(p_i) + p^* V_0 \{1 - e^{-\bar{p}/p^*}\}}$$

Since $\exp\{-\bar{p}/p^*\} < 1$ if $\bar{p} > 0, G(\bar{p}) > G(0)$;

therefore $G(0) - G(\bar{p})$ is negative, and the natural direction of change is expansion.

6.27 $f = p \exp \int_0^p \left\{\dfrac{Z(p, T) - 1}{p}\right\} \mathrm{d}p$ [6.2.14].

Draw up the following Table; plot $(Z - 1)/p$ against p and determine the area, Fig. 6.1.

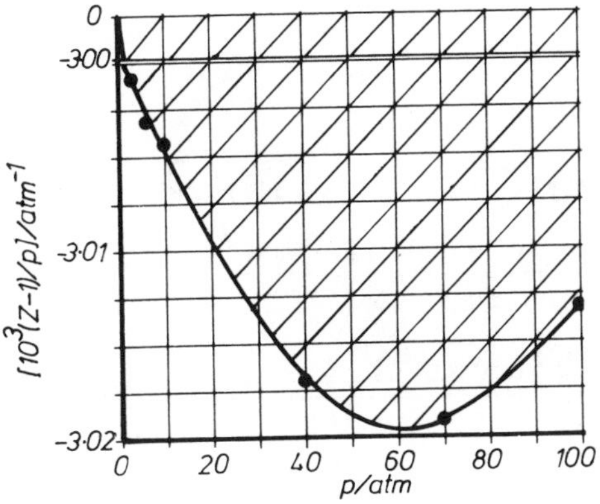

Fig 6·1

p/atm	1	4	7	10
Z	0.00701	0.98796	0.97880	0.96956
$\dfrac{(Z-1)/p}{\text{atm}^{-1}}$	-2.99×10^{-3}	-3.01×10^{-3}	-3.03×10^{-3}	-3.04×10^{-3}

p/atm	40	70	100
Z	0.8734	0.7764	0.6871
$\dfrac{(Z-1)/p}{\text{atm}^{-1}}$	-3.17×10^{-3}	-3.19×10^{-3}	-3.13×10^{-3}

From Fig. 6.1, $\int_0^{100\,\mathrm{atm}} \left(\frac{Z-1}{p}\right) \mathrm{d}p \approx -0.313$.

At 100 atm, $f \approx (100\text{ atm}) \exp(-0.313) = \underline{73.1\text{ atm.}}$

6.28 $f = p \exp \int_0^p \left(\frac{Z-1}{p}\right) \mathrm{d}p$ [6.2.14],

$Z = 1 + B/V_{\mathrm{m}} + CV_{\mathrm{m}}^2 + \ldots$ [1.3.2] $= 1 + B'p + C'p^2 + \ldots$ [1.3.1];
$B' = B/RT$, $C' = (C - B^2)/R^2T^2$ [Problem 1.27].

$$f = p \exp \int_0^p \left(\frac{B'p + C'p^2}{p}\right) \mathrm{d}p = p \exp \int_0^p (B' + C'p)\mathrm{d}p$$

$$= p \exp\{B'p + \tfrac{1}{2}C'p^2\}$$

$$= \underline{p \exp\{(Bp/RT) + [(C - B^2)/2R^2T^2]p^2\}}.$$

As $f = \gamma p$, $\underline{\ln \gamma = (B/RT)p + [(C - B^2)/2R^2T^2]p^2}$.

6.29 (a) 273 K, $B = -21.13\text{ cm}^3\text{ mol}^{-1}$, $C = 1054\text{ cm}^6\text{ mol}^{-2}$, $p = 1.00$ atm.

$$(B/RT)p = \frac{(-21.13 \times 10^{-3}\text{ dm}^3\text{ mol}^{-1}) \times (1.00\text{ atm})}{(0.0821\text{ dm}^3\text{ atm K}^{-1}\text{ mol}^{-1}) \times (273\text{ K})} = -9.43 \times 10^{-4};$$

$$\frac{(C - B^2)p^2}{2R^2T^2} = \frac{[(1.054 \times 10^{-3}\text{ dm}^6\text{ mol}^{-2}) - (-21.13 \times 10^{-3}\text{ dm}^3\text{ mol}^{-1})^2]\ (1.00\text{ atm})^2}{2 \times (0.0821 \times 273\text{ dm}^3\text{ atm mol}^{-1})^2}$$

$$= 6.05 \times 10^{-7};$$

$f = (1\text{ atm}) \times \exp\{-9.43 \times 10^{-4} + 6.05 \times 10^{-7}\} = \underline{0.9991\text{ atm.}}$

(b) 373 K, $B = -3.89\text{ cm}^3\text{ mol}^{-1}$, $C = 918\text{ cm}^6\text{ mol}^{-2}$, $p = 1.00$ atm.

$$(B/RT)p = \frac{(-3.89 \times 10^{-3}\text{ dm}^3\text{ mol}^{-1}) \times (1.00\text{ atm})}{(0.0821 \times 373\text{ dm}^3\text{ atm mol}^{-1})} = -1.27 \times 10^{-4};$$

$$\frac{(C - B^2)p^2}{2R^2T^2} = \frac{[(0.918 \times 10^{-3}\text{ dm}^6\text{ mol}^{-2}) - (-3.89 \times 10^{-3}\text{ dm}^3\text{ mol}^{-1})^2]\ (1.00\text{ atm})^2}{2 \times (0.0821 \times 373\text{ dm}^3\text{ atm mol}^{-1})^2}$$

$$= 4.81 \times 10^{-7};$$

$f = (1\text{ atm}) \times \exp\{-1.27 \times 10^{-4} + 0.05 \times 10^{-5}\}$
$= (1\text{ atm}) \exp(-1.27 \times 10^{-4}) = \underline{0.99999\text{ atm.}}$

6.30 $f = p \exp\{(Bp/RT) + [(C - B^2)/2R^2T^2]p^2\}$ [Problem 6.28].

At 273 K, using the data from the last problem (which was calculated for $p = 1.00$ atm),

$Bp/RT = (-9.43 \times 10^{-4}) \times (p/\text{atm});$

$(C - B^2)p^2/2R^2T^2 = (6.05 \times 10^{-7}) \times (p/\text{atm})^2.$

$f(p) = p\,\exp\{-9.43 \times 10^{-4}(p/\text{atm}) + 6.05 \times 10^{-7}(p/\text{atm})^2\} = p\gamma.$

Draw up the following Table $[\gamma = f/p]$

p/atm	1	3	10	30	100	300	1000
γ	0.9991	0.9972	0.9907	0.9726	0.9155	0.7958	0.7132
f/atm	0.9991	2.992	9.907	29.18	91.55	238.7	713.2

f against p is plotted in Fig. 6.2. $f = 1$ atm when $p = 1.00095$ atm (check by calculation).

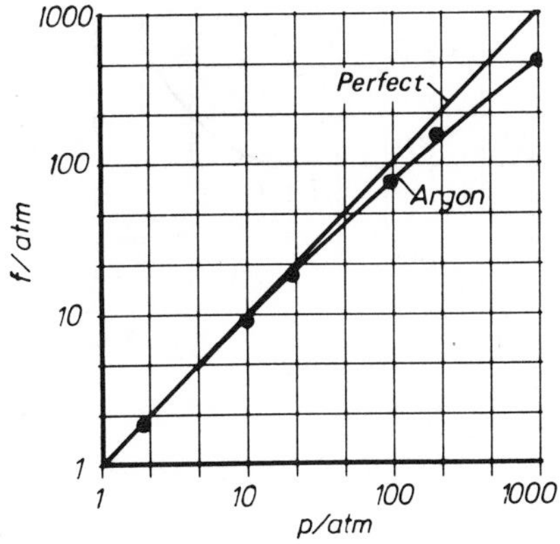

Fig 6·2

6.31 $f \approx p\,\exp(Bp/RT)$ [Problem 6.28, taking $(C - B^2/2R^2T^2)p^2 \ll Bp/RT$]; $B = -261\ \text{cm}^3\,\text{mol}^{-1} = -261 \times 10^{-3}\ \text{dm}^3\,\text{mol}^{-1}$.

$Bp/RT = (-261 \times 10^{-3}\ \text{dm}^3\,\text{mol}^{-1}) \times p/(0.0821 \times 298\ \text{dm}^3\,\text{atm}\,\text{mol}^{-1})$

$\qquad = -1.07 \times 10^{-2}(p/\text{atm}).$

(a) $p = 1$ atm; $f \approx (1\ \text{atm})\exp(-1.07 \times 10^{-2}) = \underline{0.989\ \text{atm.}}$

(b) $p = 100$ atm; $f \approx (100\ \text{atm})\exp(-1.07) = \underline{34.4\ \text{atm.}}$

6.32 $pV_m/RT = 1 + BT/V_m$ [given]

$(pV_m^2/RT) - V_m - BT = 0$ solves to $V_m = (RT/2p)\,[1 + \sqrt{(1 + 4pB/R)}]$,

$$f = p\,\exp\int_0^p \left(\frac{Z-1}{p}\right) \mathrm{d}p\ [6.2.14],\ Z = pV_m/RT.$$

$$(Z-1)/p=(pV_m/RT-1)/p=BT/pV_m=\frac{2(B/R)}{1+\surd[1+(4pB/R)]}.$$

$$\int_0^p\left(\frac{Z-1}{p}\right)\mathrm{d}p=2\left(\frac{B}{R}\right)\int_0^p\frac{\mathrm{d}p}{1+\surd[1+(4pB/R)]}=\int_2^a\left(\frac{a-1}{a}\right)\mathrm{d}a,$$

$[a=1+\surd(1+4pB/R)]$

$$=a-2-\ln(a/2),$$

$$=\surd(1+4pB/R)-1-\ln\tfrac{1}{2}[1+\surd(1+4pB/R)].$$

$$f=p\exp\{\surd(1+4pB/R)-1-\ln\tfrac{1}{2}[1+4pB/R]\}$$

$$=\frac{p\exp\{\surd(1+4pB/R)-1\}}{\tfrac{1}{2}\{1+\surd(1+4pB/R)\}}.$$

$\gamma=f/p$ is plotted against $4pB/R$ in Fig. 6.3.

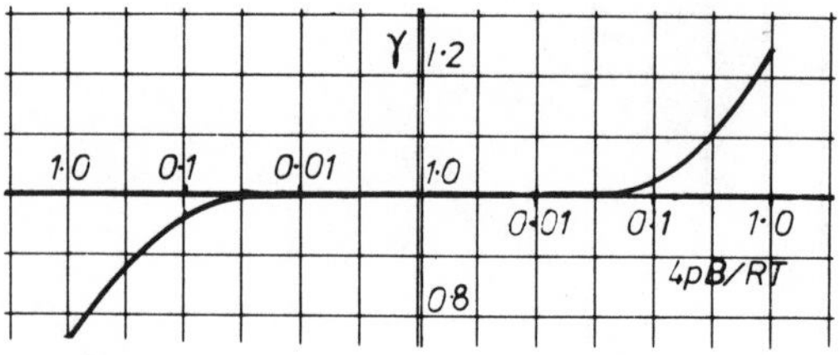

Fig 6·3

7. Changes of state: physical transformations of pure materials

A7.1 $\Delta S_m = \Delta V_m(dp/dT)$ [7.2.1] $= [(163.3 - 161.0) \times 10^{-6}\,m^3\,mol^{-1}]\,[(100 - 1) \times (1.013 \times 10^5\,Pa)]/[(351.26 - 350.75)K]$

$= \underline{45.23\,J\,K^{-1}\,mol^{-1}}$.

$\Delta H_{melt,m} = T_f \Delta S_{melt,m}$ [5.2.4] $= (350.75\,K)(45.23\,J\,K^{-1}\,mol^{-1})$

$= \underline{1.586 \times 10^4\,J\,mol^{-1}}$.

A7.2 $d(\ln p/\text{Torr})/d(T/K) = 2501.8(T/K)^{-2} = (\Delta H_{vap,m}/R)(T/K)^{-2}$ [7.2.4]

$\Delta H_{vap,m} = (8.314)(2501.8)\,J\,mol^{-1} = \underline{2.080 \times 10^4\,J\,mol^{-1}}$.

A7.3 $p = p^* \exp[(-\Delta H_{vap,m}/R)(T^{-1} - T^{*-1})]$ [7.2.5]

$T = [(T^*)^{-1} - (\Delta H_{vap,m}/R)^{-1} \ln(p/p^*)]^{-1}$

$= [(297.2\,K)^{-1} - (28.7 \times 10^3\,J\,mol^{-1}/8.31\,J\,K^{-1}\,mol^{-1})^{-1} \times \ln(500\,\text{Torr}/400\,\text{Torr})]^{-1}$

$= \underline{303.0\,K}$.

A7.4 $dp/dT = \Delta S_m/\Delta V_m = \Delta H_m/[T(\Delta V_m)]$ [7.2.1, 5.2.4]

$= (14.4 \times 10^3\,J\,mol^{-1})/[180\,K(14.5 - 0.1) \times 10^{-3}\,m^3\,mol^{-1})]$

$= \underline{5.56 \times 10^3\,Pa\,K^{-1}}$.

(dp/dT) [Clausius-Clapeyron, [7.2.4]] $= (\Delta H_{vap,m}/RT^2)p$

$= (14.4 \times 10^3\,J\,mol^{-1})(8.31\,J\,K^{-1}\,mol^{-1})^{-1}(180\,K)^{-2}(1.01 \times 10^5\,Pa)$

$= 5.40 \times 10^3\,Pa\,K^{-1}$.

% error $= [(5.56 - 5.40)/(5.56)]\,[100] = \underline{2.88\%}$.

A7.5 $(q_h/q_c)_{rev} = T_h/T_c$;

$T_c = T_h(q_c/q_h)_{rev} = (300\,K)(45\,kJ/67\,kJ) = \underline{201\,K}$. [Section 7.5(a)]

A7.6 $w = (q_c/T_c)(T_h - T_c)$ [7.5.1] $= (2.10\,kJ/80\,K)(200 - 80)K = \underline{3.15\,kJ}$.

A7.7 $w = \gamma\Delta\sigma$ [7.6.1] $= (7.20 \times 10^{-2}\,N\,m^{-1})(2500 - 150) \times 10^{-4}\,m^2$ [Table 7.1]

$= \underline{1.69 \times 10^{-2}\,J}$.

A7.8 $\gamma = (1/2)h\rho gr$ [7.6.7] $= (1/2)(1.20 \times 10^{-2}\,\text{m})(0.871 \times 10^{3}\,\text{kg m}^{-3})$

$$\times (9.81\,\text{m s}^{-2})(0.400 \times 10^{-3}\,\text{m})$$

$$= \underline{2.05 \times 10^{-2}\,\text{N m}^{-1}}.$$

A7.9 $r = (RT)^{-1}(2\gamma V_{\text{m}})\,[\ln(p_{\text{mist}}/p_{\text{bulk}})]^{-1}$ [7.6.5]

$$= (8.31\,\text{J K}^{-1}\,\text{mol}^{-1})^{-1}(293\,\text{K})^{-1}(2)(2.70 \times 10^{-2}\,\text{N m}^{-1})$$

$$\times (1.60 \times 10^{3}\,\text{kg m}^{-3})^{-1}(154 \times 10^{-3}\,\text{kg mol}^{-1})[\ln(87.95\,\text{Torr}/87.05\,\text{Torr})]^{-1}$$

$= \underline{2.08 \times 10^{-7}\,\text{m}.}$ [Table 7.1]

A7.10 $p_{\text{in}} = p_{\text{out}} + 2\gamma/r$ [7.6.3] $= (740\,\text{Torr})(133\,\text{Pa/Torr}) + (2)(5.7 \times 10^{-2}\,\text{N m}^{-1})$

$$\times (0.125 \times 10^{-3}\,\text{m})^{-1}$$

$$= \underline{9.93 \times 10^{4}\,\text{Pa}.}$$

7.1 $\Delta G_{\text{m}} = \Delta H_{\text{m}} - T\Delta S_{\text{m}}$ $[G = H - TS]$

$$= (1.8961\,\text{kJ mol}^{-1}) - (298.15\,\text{K}) \times (-3.2552\,\text{J K}^{-1}\,\text{mol}^{-1})$$

$$= 2.8666\,\text{kJ mol}^{-1}\ (\text{graphite} \rightarrow \text{diamond}).$$

The spontaneous direction is therefore $\underline{\text{diamond} \rightarrow \text{graphite}}$. For this reaction, $\Delta H_{\text{m}} = -1.8961\,\text{kJ mol}^{-1}$, and $\{(\partial/\partial T)(\Delta G_{\text{m}}/T)\}_p = -\Delta H_{\text{m}}/T^2$ [6.2.5] > 0 $[\Delta H_{\text{m}} < 0]$. The spontaneous reaction becomes less favored (in terms of the magnitude of K) by a rise in temperature (because $\Delta G_{\text{m}}/T$ rises towards and then through zero as T is increased).

7.2 $\Delta A(p) = \Delta G(p) - p\Delta V(p)$; $\Delta G(p_2) \approx \Delta G(p_1) + (p_2 - p_1)\Delta V(p_1)$ [6.2.7].
$\Delta A(p_2) = \Delta G(p_1) - p_2\Delta V(p_2) + (p_2 - p_1)\Delta V(p_1) \approx \Delta G(p_1) - p_1\Delta V(p_1) = \Delta A(p_1)$.
Therefore $\Delta A(p_2) \approx \Delta A(p_1)$, and ΔA is independent of pressure (at this level of approximation).

$$\Delta V_{\text{m}} = (12.01\,\text{g mol}^{-1}) \times \left(\frac{1}{3.52\,\text{g cm}^{-3}} - \frac{1}{2.27\,\text{g cm}^{-3}}\right) = -1.88\,\text{cm}^{3}\,\text{mol}^{-1}.$$

$\Delta A_{\text{m}} \approx 2.8666\,\text{kJ mol}^{-1}$ [Problem 7.1] $- (1.01325 \times 10^{5}\,\text{N m}^{-2})$

$$\times (-1.88 \times 10^{-6}\,\text{m}^{3}\,\text{mol}^{-1})$$

$$= \underline{2.8668\,\text{kJ mol}^{-1}}.$$

7.3 $(\partial\mu/\partial T)_p(\text{water}) - (\partial\mu/\partial T)_p(\text{ice}) = -S_{\text{m}}(\text{water}) + S_{\text{m}}(\text{ice})$ [7.1.1]

$= -\Delta S_{\text{m}}(\text{ice} \rightarrow \text{water}) = -\Delta H_{\text{m,fus}}/T_{\text{f}}$ [5.2.4]

$= -(6.008\,\text{kJ mol}^{-1})/(273.15\,\text{K})$ [Table 4.7] $= \underline{-22.00\,\text{J K}^{-1}\,\text{mol}^{-1}}.$

$(\partial\mu/\partial T)_p(\text{steam}) - (\partial\mu/\partial T)_p(\text{water}) = -S_{\text{m}}(\text{steam}) + S_{\text{m}}(\text{water})$ [7.1.1]

$= -\Delta S_m(\text{water} \rightarrow \text{steam}) = -\Delta H_{m,\text{vap}}/T_b$ [5.2.4]

$= -(40.66 \text{ kJ mol}^{-1})/(373.15 \text{ K})$ [Table 4.7] $= \underline{-109.0 \text{ J K}^{-1} \text{ mol}^{-1}}$.

7.4 $(\partial\mu/\partial p)_T(\text{water}) - (\partial\mu/\partial p)_T(\text{ice}) = V_m(\text{water}) - V_m(\text{ice})$ [7.1.2]

$$= (18.02 \text{ g mol}^{-1}) \times \left(\frac{1}{1.000 \text{ g cm}^{-3}} - \frac{1}{0.917 \text{ g cm}^{-3}}\right)$$

$= -1.63 \text{ cm}^3 \text{ mol}^{-1} = -1.63 \times 10^{-3} \text{ dm}^3 \text{ mol}^{-1}$.

$1 \text{ dm}^3 = 0.101325 \text{ kJ atm}^{-1}$ [Problem 6.5].

Therefore $(\partial\mu/\partial p)_T(\text{water}) - (\partial\mu/\partial p)_T(\text{ice}) = \underline{-1.65 \times 10^{-4} \text{ kJ mol}^{-1} \text{ atm}^{-1}}$.

$$V_m(\text{steam}) - V_m(\text{water}) = (18.02 \text{ g mol}^{-1}) \times \left(\frac{1}{0.598 \times 10^{-3} \text{ g cm}^{-3}} - \frac{1}{0.958 \text{ g cm}^{-3}}\right)$$

$= 30.1 \text{ dm}^3 \text{ mol}^{-1} = 3.04 \text{ kJ mol}^{-1} \text{ atm}^{-1}$.

Therefore $(\partial\mu/\partial p)_T(\text{steam}) - (\partial\mu/\partial p)_T(\text{water}) = \underline{3.04 \text{ kJ mol}^{-1} \text{ atm}^{-1}}$.

7.5 $\delta\mu \approx (\partial\mu/\partial T)_p \delta T = -S_m \delta T$ [7.1.1]

$\mu(\text{l}, -5\,^\circ\text{C}) - \mu(\text{s}, -5\,^\circ\text{C}) \approx \{\mu(\text{l}, 0\,^\circ\text{C}) + (5 \text{ K})S_m(\text{l})\} - \{\mu(\text{s}, 0\,^\circ\text{C}) + (5 \text{ K})S_m(\text{s})\}$

$= (5 \text{ K}) \times \{S_m(\text{l}) - S_m(\text{s})\}$ $[\mu(\text{l}, 0\,^\circ\text{C}) = \mu(\text{s}, 0\,^\circ\text{C})]$

$= (5 \text{ K}) \times \Delta S_m(\text{ice, water}) = (5 \text{ K}) \times (22.0 \text{ J K}^{-1} \text{ mol}^{-1})$ [Problem 7.3]

$= \underline{110 \text{ J mol}^{-1}}$. Since $\mu(\text{l}, -5\,^\circ\text{C}) > \mu(\text{s}, -5\,^\circ\text{C})$, there is a thermodynamic tendency to freeze.

7.6 $\delta\mu \approx (\partial\mu/\partial p)_T \delta p = V_m \delta p$ [7.1.2], $\delta\mu = (\partial\mu/\partial T)_p \delta T = -S_m \delta T$ [above];

$\mu(\text{g}, 95\,^\circ\text{C}) - \mu(\text{l}, 95\,^\circ\text{C}) \approx \{\mu(\text{g}, 100\,^\circ\text{C}) + (5 \text{ K})S_m(\text{g})\} - \{\mu(\text{l}, 100\,^\circ\text{C}) + (5 \text{ K})S_m(\text{l})\}$

$= (5 \text{ K}) \times \{S_m(\text{g}) - S_m(\text{l})\}$ $[\mu(\text{g}, 100\,^\circ\text{C}) = \mu(\text{l}, 100\,^\circ\text{C})]$

$= (5 \text{ K}) \times \Delta S_m(\text{l} \rightarrow \text{g}) = (5 \text{ K}) \times (109 \text{ J K}^{-1} \text{ mol}^{-1})$ [Problem 7.3]

$= \underline{0.55 \text{ kJ mol}^{-1}}$ (tendency to condense at 1 atm).

$\mu(\text{g}, 1.2 \text{ atm}) - \mu(\text{l}, 1.2 \text{ atm}) = (0.2 \text{ atm}) \times \Delta V_m$

$= (0.2 \text{ atm}) \times (3.04 \text{ kJ mol}^{-1} \text{ atm}^{-1})$ [Problem 7.4]

$= \underline{0.61 \text{ kJ mol}^{-1}}$ (tendency to condense at 100 °C).

7.7 $\delta\mu \approx (\partial\mu/\partial T)_p \delta T + (\partial\mu/\partial T)_T \delta p$;

$\delta\{\mu(\text{l}) - \mu(\text{s})\} = \{(\partial\mu/\partial T)_p(\text{l}) - (\partial\mu/\partial T)_p(\text{s})\}\delta T + \{(\partial\mu/\partial p)_T(\text{l}) - (\partial\mu/\partial p)_T(\text{s})\}\delta p$

$= -\Delta S_m(\text{s} \rightarrow \text{l})\delta T + \Delta V_m(\text{s} \rightarrow \text{l})\delta p$ [Problems 7.3, 7.4]. In order to maintain equilibrium $\mu(\text{l}) = \mu(\text{s})$; hence $\delta\{\mu(\text{l}) - \mu(\text{s})\} = 0$, and so

$\delta T = \{\Delta V_m(s \rightarrow 1)/\Delta S_m(s \rightarrow 1)\}\delta p$ [or from 7.2.1].

$\Delta V_m(s \rightarrow 1) = -1.63 \times 10^{-3}\,\mathrm{dm^3\,mol^{-1}} = -1.65 \times 10^{-4}\,\mathrm{kJ\,mol^{-1}\,atm^{-1}}$ [Problem 7.4];

$\Delta S_m(s \rightarrow 1) = 22.0 \times 10^{-3}\,\mathrm{kJ\,K^{-1}\,mol^{-1}}$ [Problem 7.3].

$$\delta T = -\frac{(1.65 \times 10^{-4}\,\mathrm{kJ\,mol^{-1}\,atm^{-1}}) \times (999\,\mathrm{atm})}{(22.0 \times 10^{-3}\,\mathrm{kJ\,K^{-1}\,mol^{-1}})} = -7.5\,\mathrm{K}.$$

Under 1000 atm, $T_f = (273.2 - 7.5)\mathrm{K} = \underline{265.7\,\mathrm{K}\,(-7.5\,°\mathrm{C})}$.

7.8 $\delta T = \{\Delta V_m(s \rightarrow 1)/\Delta S_m(s \rightarrow 1)\}\delta p$ [Problem 7.7].

$$\Delta V_m(s \rightarrow 1) = (78.115\,\mathrm{g\,mol^{-1}}) \times \left(\frac{1}{0.879\,\mathrm{g\,cm^{-3}}} - \frac{1}{0.891\,\mathrm{g\,cm^{-3}}}\right)$$

$= 1.197\,\mathrm{cm^3\,mol^{-1}} = 1.213 \times 10^{-4}\,\mathrm{kJ\,mol^{-1}\,atm^{-1}}$ [Problem 7.4].

$$\delta T = \frac{(1.213 \times 10^{-4}\,\mathrm{kJ\,mol^{-1}\,atm^{-1}}) \times (999\,\mathrm{atm})}{(10.59\,\mathrm{kJ\,mol^{-1}}/278.27\,\mathrm{K})} = 3.19\,\mathrm{K}.$$

Under 1000 atm, $T_f = (278.7 + 3.2)\mathrm{K} = \underline{281.9\,\mathrm{K}(8.7\,°\mathrm{C})}$.

7.9 $\mathrm{d}p/\mathrm{d}T = \Delta S_m/\Delta V_m = \Delta H_m/T_t\Delta V_m$ [7.2.1, 5.2.4] and so

$\delta T \approx (T_t\Delta V_m/\Delta H_m)\delta p$.

$T_t = 373\,\mathrm{K}$, $\Delta V_m = 30.1\,\mathrm{dm^3\,mol^{-1}} = 3.04\,\mathrm{kJ\,mol^{-1}\,atm^{-1}}$ [Problem 7.4];

$\Delta H_m = 40.7\,\mathrm{kJ\,mol^{-1}}$ [Table 4.7]; $\delta p = 10\,\mathrm{Torr} = (10/760)\,\mathrm{atm} = 0.13\,\mathrm{atm}$.

$$\delta T = \frac{(373\,\mathrm{K}) \times (3.04\,\mathrm{kJ\,mol^{-1}\,atm^{-1}}) \times (0.013\,\mathrm{atm})}{40.7\,\mathrm{kJ\,mol^{-1}}} = \underline{0.36\,\mathrm{K}}.$$

$T_b(770\,\mathrm{Torr}) = (373.2 + 0.4)\mathrm{K} = \underline{373.6\,\mathrm{K}\,(100.4\,°\mathrm{C})}$.

7.10 $\mathrm{d}H = C_p\mathrm{d}T + V\mathrm{d}p$; $\mathrm{d}\Delta H = \Delta C_p\mathrm{d}T + \Delta V\mathrm{d}p$; $\mathrm{d}p/\mathrm{d}T = \Delta H/T\Delta V$ [7.2.1]

$\mathrm{d}\Delta H = \{\Delta C_p + (\Delta H/T\Delta V)\Delta V\}\mathrm{d}T = \{\Delta C_p + \Delta H/T\}\mathrm{d}T$.

$T\mathrm{d}(\Delta H/T) = \mathrm{d}\Delta H - (\Delta H/T)\mathrm{d}T = \Delta C_p\mathrm{d}T$; $\underline{\mathrm{d}(\Delta H/T) = \Delta C_p\mathrm{d}\ln T}$.

$$\Delta H(T)/T = \Delta H(T^*)/T^* + \int_{T^*}^{T} \Delta C_p\,\mathrm{d}\ln T \approx \underline{\Delta H(T^*)/T^* + \Delta C_p\ln(T/T^*)}.$$

$\mathrm{d}p/\mathrm{d}T = (\Delta H/T)/\Delta V \approx (\Delta H_m/RT^2)p$ $[\Delta V \approx V_g \approx nRT/p]$, so that

$\mathrm{d}\ln p \approx (\Delta H_m/RT)\mathrm{d}T/T \approx \{\Delta H_m(T^*)/RT^*\}\mathrm{d}\ln T + (\Delta C_{p,m}/R)\ln(T/T^*)\mathrm{d}\ln T$.

$$\ln(p/p^*) \approx \{\Delta H_m(T^*)/RT^*\}\ln(T/T^*) + (\Delta C_{p,m}/R)\{\tfrac{1}{2}(\ln T)^2 - \tfrac{1}{2}(\ln T^*)^2 - (\ln T^*)\ln(T/T^*)\}$$

$$\approx \{\Delta H_m(T^*)/RT^*\}\ln(T/T^*) + (\Delta C_{p,m}/2R)(\ln T - \ln T^*)^2$$

$$\approx (\Delta H_m(T^*)/RT^*)\ln(T/T^*) + (\Delta C_{p,m}/2R)\{\ln(T/T^*)\}^2$$
$$\approx \{(\Delta H_m(T^*)/RT^*) + (\Delta C_{p,m}/2R)\ln(T/T^*)\}\ln(T/T^*)$$
$$\approx \ln(T/T^*)^a,\ a = (\Delta H_m/RT^*) + (\Delta C_p/2R)\ln(T/T^*).$$

Therefore, $\underline{p/p^* \approx (T/T^*)^a}$.

For water $\Delta H_m^*/RT^* = \dfrac{40.656\,\mathrm{kJ\,mol^{-1}}}{(8.3144\,\mathrm{J\,K^{-1}\,mol^{-1}}) \times (373.15\,\mathrm{K})} = 13.104.$

$$\Delta C_{p,m}/2R = \frac{(34.38 - 75.48)\,\mathrm{J\,K^{-1}\,mol^{-1}}}{2 \times (8.3144\,\mathrm{J\,K^{-1}\,mol^{-1}})} = -2.472.$$

$p^* = 1$ atm; $T^* = 373.15$ K. Draw up the following tables using $p/p^* = (T/373.15\,\mathrm{K})^{13.104-2.472\ln(T/373.15\,\mathrm{K})}$.

T/K	373.15	370	360	350	340
p/p^*	1.000	0.8947	0.6229	0.4277	0.2892

T/K	330	320	310	300
p/p^*	0.1925	0.1259	0.0809	0.0509

The points are plotted in Fig. 7.1.

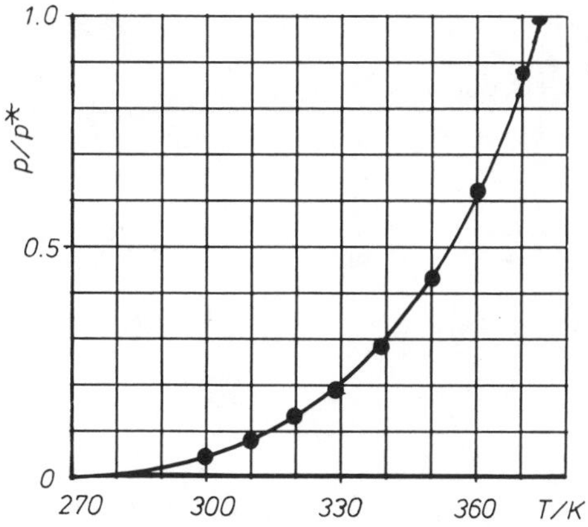

Fig 7.1

7.11 $\delta T \approx (T_t \Delta V_m / \Delta H_m)\delta p$ [Problem 7.9], $\delta p = \rho g h$ [hydrostatics].

$T_t = 234.3\,\text{K}$, $\Delta H_m = 2.292\,\text{kJ mol}^{-1}$, $\rho = 13.6\,\text{g cm}^{-3}$;

$\Delta V_m = 0.517\,\text{cm}^3\,\text{mol}^{-1}$, $g = 9.81\,\text{m s}^{-2}$, $h = 10\,\text{m}$.

$$\delta T = \frac{(234.3\,\text{K}) \times (0.517 \times 10^{-6}\,\text{m}^3\,\text{mol}^{-1}) \times (13.6 \times 10^3\,\text{kg m}^{-3}) \times (9.81\,\text{m s}^{-2}) \times (10\,\text{m})}{2.292 \times 10^3\,\text{J mol}^{-1}}$$

$= \underline{0.07\,\text{K}}$; hence $T_f = \underline{234.4\,\text{K}}$.

7.12 $n(\text{l}) = m/(M_m\,\text{g mol}^{-1})$, $n(\text{g}) = p(\text{g})V(\text{g})/RT$, $x(\text{l}) = \dfrac{n(\text{l})}{n(\text{l}) + n(\text{g})}$

$$p' = px(\text{l}) \quad [1.2.4]$$

$$= \frac{pn(\text{l})}{n(\text{l}) + n(\text{g})} = \frac{pm/M_m}{(m/M_m) + pV/RT}$$

$$= \frac{p[mRT/pVM_m]}{[mRT/pVM_m] + 1} = \frac{Apm}{1 + Am},$$

where $A = RT/M_m$.

7.13 $M_r = 154.2$, $T = 110\,^\circ\text{C} \mathrel{\hat{=}} 383\,\text{K}$, $V = 5.00\,\text{dm}^3$, 760 Torr, $m = 0.32\,\text{g}$

$$A = \frac{(0.0821\,\text{dm}^3\,\text{atm K}^{-1}\,\text{mol}^{-1}) \times (383\,\text{K})}{(154.2 \times 10^{-3}\,\text{kg mol}^{-1}) \times (5.00\,\text{dm}^3) \times (1.00\,\text{atm})} = 40.8\,\text{kg}^{-1}.$$

$$p' = \frac{(40.8\,\text{kg}^{-1}) \times (760\,\text{Torr}) \times (0.32 \times 10^{-3}\,\text{kg})}{1 + (40.8\,\text{kg}^{-1}) \times (0.32 \times 10^{-3}\,\text{kg})} = \underline{9.8\,\text{Torr.}}$$

7.14 $M_r = 154.2$, $T = 140\,^\circ\text{C} \mathrel{\hat{=}} 413\,\text{K}$, $V_g = 1.000\,\text{dm}^3$, $p = 760\,\text{Torr}$, $m = 243\,\text{mg}$.

$$A = \frac{(0.0821 \times 413\,\text{dm}^3\,\text{atm mol}^{-1})}{(154.2 \times 10^{-3}\,\text{kg mol}^{-1}) \times (1.000\,\text{dm}^3) \times (1.00\,\text{atm})} = 220\,\text{kg}^{-1}.$$

$$p' = \frac{(220\,\text{kg}^{-1}) \times (760\,\text{Torr}) \times (243 \times 10^{-6}\,\text{kg})}{1 + (220\,\text{kg}^{-1}) \times (243 \times 10^{-6}\,\text{kg})} = \underline{38.6\,\text{Torr.}}$$

In order to find ΔH_m use $\text{d}\ln p/\text{d}T = \Delta H_{\text{vap,m}}/RT^2$ [7.2.5].

$$\Delta H_{\text{vap,m}} \approx R\left\{\frac{\ln[p'(T_2)/p'(T_1)]}{(1/T_1) - (1/T_2)}\right\}$$

$\ln\{p(413\,\text{K})/p(383\,\text{K})\} = \ln\{38.6\,\text{Torr}/9.8\,\text{Torr}\} = 1.37$;

$1/T_1 - 1/T_2 = 1.897 \times 10^{-4}\,\mathrm{K}^{-1}$.

$\Delta H_{\mathrm{vap,m}} \approx (8.314\,\mathrm{J\,K^{-1}\,mol^{-1}}) \times 1.37/(1.897 \times 10^{-4}\,\mathrm{K^{-1}}) = \underline{60.0\,\mathrm{kJ\,mol^{-1}}}$.

In order to find boiling temperature, find T at which $p = 760$ Torr.

$$p = p^* \exp\left\{-\frac{\Delta H_{\mathrm{vap,m}}}{R}\left(\frac{1}{T} - \frac{1}{T^*}\right)\right\} \quad [7.2.5];$$

$$\frac{1}{T} = \left(\frac{R}{\Delta H_{\mathrm{vap,m}}}\right)\left\{\frac{\Delta H_{\mathrm{vap}}}{RT^*} - \ln(p/p^*)\right\} = \frac{1}{T^*} - \left(\frac{R}{\Delta H_{\mathrm{vap,m}}}\right) \times \ln(p/p^*).$$

$$\frac{1}{T_{\mathrm{b}}} = \frac{1}{413\,\mathrm{K}} - \left(\frac{8.314\,\mathrm{J\,K^{-1}\,mol^{-1}}}{60.0 \times 10^3\,\mathrm{J\,mol^{-1}}}\right) \ln\left(\frac{760\,\mathrm{Torr}}{38.6\,\mathrm{Torr}}\right) = 2.04 \times 10^{-3},$$

or $\underline{T_{\mathrm{b}} = 498\,\mathrm{K}}$.

7.15 At equilibrium $n(\mathrm{l}) = p(\mathrm{l})V/RT$; $q = -n(\mathrm{l})\Delta H_{\mathrm{vap,m}}$,

$\Delta T = q/C_p$; $\Delta H_{\mathrm{vap,m}} = 44.0\,\mathrm{kJ\,mol^{-1}}$ [Table 4.7],

$C_p = (75.5\,\mathrm{J\,K^{-1}\,mol^{-1}}) \times (250\,\mathrm{g}/18.02\,\mathrm{g\,mol^{-1}}) = 1.05\,\mathrm{kJ\,K^{-1}}$.

$$n(\mathrm{l}) = \frac{[(23.8/760)\,\mathrm{atm}] \times (50.0\,\mathrm{dm^3})}{(0.0821\,\mathrm{dm^3\,atm\,K^{-1}\,mol^{-1}}) \times (298\,\mathrm{K})} = 0.064\,\mathrm{mol}.$$

$q = -(0.064\,\mathrm{mol}) \times (44.0\,\mathrm{kJ\,mol^{-1}}) = -2.82\,\mathrm{kJ}$;

$\Delta T = (-2.82\,\mathrm{kJ})/(1.05\,\mathrm{kJ\,K^{-1}}) = 2.7\,\mathrm{K}$, or $T_{\mathrm{f}} \mathrel{\widehat{=}} 25\,°\mathrm{C} - 2.7\,°\mathrm{C} = \underline{22\,°\mathrm{C}}$.

7.16 $\mathrm{d}n/\mathrm{d}t = (1.2 \times 10^3\,\mathrm{W\,m^{-2}}) \times (50\,\mathrm{m^2})/(44.0 \times 10^3\,\mathrm{J\,mol^{-1}})$

$= 1.36\,\mathrm{mol\,s^{-1}}$ [$1\,\mathrm{W} = 1\,\mathrm{J\,s^{-1}}$].

Rate of evaporation is $(1.36\,\mathrm{mol\,s^{-1}}) \times (18.02\,\mathrm{g\,mol^{-1}}) = \underline{24\,\mathrm{g\,s^{-1}}, \text{ or } 86\,\mathrm{kg/hr}}$.

7.17 $n = pV/RT$; $M = nM_{\mathrm{m}}$, $V = 75\,\mathrm{m^3}$, $T = 298.15\,\mathrm{K}$.

$$n = \frac{(75 \times 10^3\,\mathrm{dm^3}) \times (p/\mathrm{Torr}) \times (\mathrm{Torr/atm}) \times (\mathrm{atm}/760\,\mathrm{Torr})}{(0.0821\,\mathrm{dm^3\,atm\,K^{-1}\,mol^{-1}}) \times (298.15\,\mathrm{K})}$$

$= (4.03\,\mathrm{mol}) \times (p/\mathrm{Torr})$ [$1\,\mathrm{atm} \mathrel{\widehat{=}} 760\,\mathrm{Torr}$].

(a) Water; $p = 24$ Torr, $M_{\mathrm{m}} = 18\,\mathrm{g\,mol^{-1}}$;

$n = (4.03\,\mathrm{mol}) \times (24) = 97\,\mathrm{mol}$; $M = (97\,\mathrm{mol}) \times (18\,\mathrm{g\,mol^{-1}}) = \underline{1.7\,\mathrm{kg}}$.

(b) Benzene; $p = 98$ Torr, $M_{\mathrm{m}} = 78\,\mathrm{g\,mol^{-1}}$, $n = (4.03\,\mathrm{mol}) \times 98 = 395\,\mathrm{mol}$;

$M = (395\,\mathrm{mol}) \times (78\,\mathrm{g\,mol^{-1}}) = \underline{30.8\,\mathrm{kg}}$.

(c) Mercury; $p = 1.7 \times 10^{-3}$ Torr, $M_{\mathrm{m}} = 201\,\mathrm{g\,mol^{-1}}$ (for atoms),

$n = (4.03\,\text{mol}) \times (1.7 \times 10^{-3}) = 6.9 \times 10^{-3}\,\text{mol}$;

$M = (6.9 \times 10^{-3}\,\text{mol}) \times (201\,\text{g mol}^{-1}) = \underline{1.4\,\text{g}}$.

7.18 Relative humidity = $[p(H_2O)/p] \times 100$ [definition; p is v.p. of water].
If relative humidity is 70%, $p(H_2O) = 0.70 \times 24\,\text{Torr} = \underline{17\,\text{Torr}}$.
Mass present = $(1.7\,\text{kg}) \times (0.70)$ [Problem 7.17a] = $\underline{1.2\,\text{kg}}$

7.19 T_b is the temperature for which $p(HNO_3) = 760\,\text{Torr}$.
$d(\ln p)/dT = \Delta H_{vap,m}/RT^2$ [7.2.4];

therefore $\ln p = \text{const} - \Delta H_{vap,m}/RT$ [assume ΔH independent of T]. Construct the following Table in order to plot $\ln p$ against $1/T$:

t/°C	0	20	40	50
p/Torr	14.4	47.9	133	208
T/K	273	293	313	323
$(1/T)$K	0.00366	0.00341	0.00319	0.00310
ln(p/Torr)	2.67	3.87	4.89	5.34

t/°C	70	80	90	100
p/Torr	467	670	937	1282
T/K	343	353	363	373
$(1/T)$K	0.00292	0.00283	0.00275	0.00268
ln(p/Torr)	6.15	6.51	6.84	7.16

ln(p/Torr) is plotted against $1/T$ in Fig. 7.2. The slope is −4546; hence
$-\Delta H_{vap,m}/R = -4546\,\text{K}$; hence

$\Delta H_{vap,m} = (4.60 \times 10^3\,\text{K}) \times (8.314\,\text{J K}^{-1}\text{mol}^{-1}) = \underline{38.2\,\text{kJ mol}^{-1}}$.

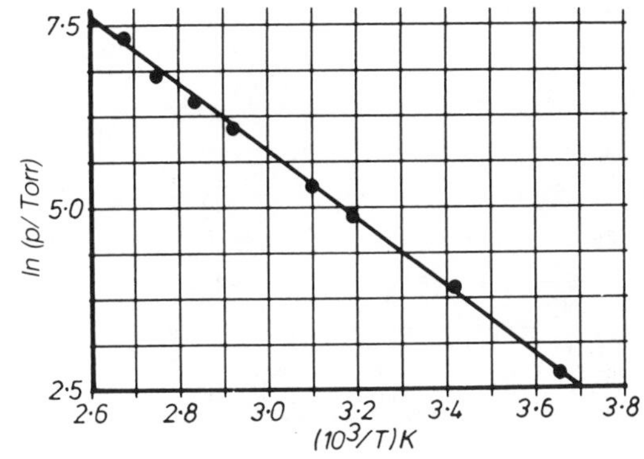

Fig 7.2

ln 760 = 6.63, a point reached when $1/T = 2.80 \times 10^{-3}\,K^{-1}$; therefore T_b = 357 K (84 °C). (Alternatively: Do a least squares fit of ln *p v.* $1/T$ using the procedure outlined in the Appendix; this avoids plotting the graph.)

7.20 Adopt the procedure of Problem 7.19, but note that T_b = 227.5 °C is obvious from the raw data.

t/°C	57.4	100.4	133.0
p/Torr	1.00	10.0	40.0
T/K	330.6	373.6	406.2
$(1/T)$K	3.02×10^{-3}	2.68×10^{-3}	2.46×10^{-3}
ln(p/Torr)	0.00	2.30	3.69

t/°C	157.3	203.5	227.5
p/Torr	100	400	760
T/K	430.5	476.7	500.7
$(1/T)$K	2.32×10^{-3}	2.10×10^{-3}	2.00×10^{-3}
ln(p/Torr)	4.61	5.99	6.63

ln(p/Torr) is plotted against $1/T$ in Fig. 7.3. The slope is -6.6×10^3; hence $-\Delta H_{vap,m}/R = -6.6 \times 10^3\,K$.

$\Delta H_{vap,m} = (6.6 \times 10^3 \text{ K})(8.314 \text{ J K}^{-1} \text{ mol}^{-1}) = \underline{55 \text{ kJ mol}^{-1}}.$

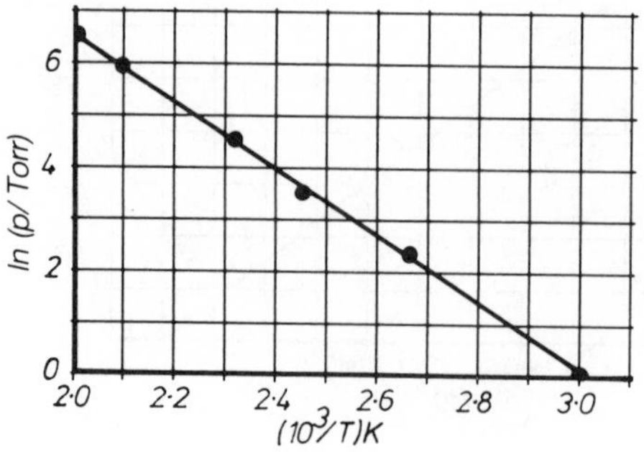

Fig 7·3

7.21 $p_{atmos}(h) = p_0 \exp(-M_m gh/RT)$ [Problem 1.31, parameters refer to the air].

$$p_{v.p.}(T) = p^* \exp - \left\{\frac{\Delta H_{vap,m}}{R}\left(\frac{1}{T} - \frac{1}{T^*}\right)\right\} \quad [7.2.5, \text{ parameters refer to the sample}].$$

Let $T^* = T_b$, the normal boiling point; then $p^* = 1$ atm. Let $T = T_h$, the b.p. at a height h. Take $p_0 = 1$ atm. The vapor pressure ($p_{v.p.}$) is equal to the ambient pressure when $p_{v.p.}(T) = p(h)$, and when this is so T in eqn (7.2.5) is at the b.p., T_h. Therefore, since $p_0 = p^*$, $p_{atmos}(h) = p(T)$ implies

$$\exp(-M_m gh/RT_{atmos}) = \exp\left\{-\frac{\Delta H_{vap,m}}{R}\left(\frac{1}{T_h} - \frac{1}{T_b}\right)\right\}.$$

It follows that $\dfrac{1}{T_h} = \dfrac{1}{T_b} + \dfrac{M_m gh}{T_{atmos}\Delta H_{vap,m}}$ [M_m is the molar mass of the *air*].

For water at 10 000 ft: $M_r = 29, g = 9.81 \text{ m s}^{-2}$,

$h = 10\,000 \text{ ft} \mathrel{\widehat{=}} 3.05 \text{ km}, T_b = 373 \text{ K}, T_{atmos} = 293 \text{ K}, \Delta H_{vap,m} = 40.7 \text{ kJ mol}^{-1}$.

$$\frac{1}{T_h} = \frac{1}{373 \text{ K}} + \frac{(29 \times 10^{-3} \text{ kg mol}^{-1}) \times (9.81 \text{ m s}^{-2}) \times (30.5 \times 10^3 \text{ m})}{(293 \text{ K}) \times (40.7 \times 10^3 \text{ J mol}^{-1})}$$

$$= \frac{1}{373 \text{ K}} + \frac{1}{1.38 \times 10^4 \text{ K}} = 2.75 \times 10^{-3} \text{ K}^{-1}, \text{ or } T_h = \underline{363 \text{ K}(90\,^\circ\text{C})}.$$

7.22 $\lg(p/\text{mmHg}) = b - 0.05223a/(T/\text{K})$ [given].

$\ln(p/\text{mmHg}) = \text{const.} - \Delta H_{vap,m}/RT$ [7.2.5].

(N.B., $\ln(p/\text{mmHg})$, $\ln(p/\text{N m}^{-2})$, $\ln(p/\text{atm})$ etc. could be used, the only change then being in the value of the constant. We have chosen to use $\ln(p/\text{mmHg})$.)

$$\lg(p/\text{mmHg}) = (1/2.303)\ln(p/\text{mmHg}) = \text{const.}' - (\Delta H_{\text{vap,m}}/2.303\,RT)$$
$$= \text{const.}' - (\Delta H_{\text{vap,m}}/2.303\,R) \times \{1/(T/\text{K})\text{K}\}.$$

$(\Delta H_{\text{vap,m}}/2.303\,R)/\text{K} = 0.05223a.$

Therefore $\Delta H_{\text{vap,m}} = (0.05223\,a\,\text{K}) \times 2.303\,R = 0.1203\,R \times (a\ \text{K}) = \underline{a\ \text{J mol}^{-1}}.$

For phosphorus $a = 63123$, $b = 9.6511$;

$\lg(p/\text{mmHg}) = 9.6511 - (0.05223) \times (63123)/(298) = -1.41;$

therefore $p = \underline{0.039\ \text{mmHg}}.$

$\Delta H_{\text{vap,m}} = \underline{63.1\ \text{kJ mol}^{-1}}.$

7.23 Vapor pressure of ice at -5 °C is 0.0039 atm [*Example* 7.3] = 3 Torr. Therefore the frost will sublime. A partial pressure of 3 Torr or more would ensure that the frost remained.

7.24 (a) Solid-liquid boundary:

$$p = p^* + (\Delta H_{\text{melt,m}}/\Delta V_{\text{melt,m}})\ln(T/T^*)\ [7.2.2].$$

(b) liquid-gas boundary:

$$p = p^* \exp\left\{-\frac{\Delta H_{\text{vap,m}}}{R}\left(\frac{1}{T} - \frac{1}{T^*}\right)\right\}\quad [7.2.5].$$

(c) gas-solid boundary:

$$p = p^* \exp\left\{-\frac{\Delta H_{\text{sub,m}}}{R}\left(\frac{1}{T} - \frac{1}{T^*}\right)\right\}\quad [7.2.6].$$

$\Delta H_{\text{melt,m}} = 10.6\ \text{kJ mol}^{-1}$, $\Delta H_{\text{vap,m}} = 30.8\ \text{kJ mol}^{-1}$,

$\Delta H_{\text{sub,m}} = \Delta H_{\text{melt,m}} + \Delta H_{\text{vap,m}} = 41.4\ \text{kJ mol}^{-1};$

$$\Delta V_{\text{melt,m}} = (78.12\ \text{g mol}^{-1}) \times \left(\frac{1}{0.899\ \text{g cm}^{-3}} - \frac{1}{0.91\ \text{g cm}^{-3}}\right)$$
$$= 1.05\ \text{cm}^3\ \text{mol}^{-1}.$$

(a) $$p = p^* + \left(\frac{10.6\ \text{kJ mol}^{-1}}{1.05 \times 10^{-6}\ \text{m}^3\ \text{mol}^{-1}}\right)\ln\left(\frac{T}{T^*}\right)$$

$$= p^* + (1.010 \times 10^{10}\ \text{N m}^{-2})\ln(T/T^*)\ [1\ \text{J} = 1\ \text{N m}]$$
$$= p^* + (9.96 \times 10^4\ \text{atm})\ln(T/T^*)\ [1\ \text{atm} \mathrel{\hat{=}} 1.0133 \times 10^5\ \text{N m}^{-2}]$$
$$= p^* + (7.57 \times 10^7\ \text{Torr})\ln(T/T^*)\ [1\ \text{atm} \mathrel{\hat{=}} 760\ \text{Torr}].$$

Draw up the following table based on $(p^*, T^*) = (36\ \text{Torr}, 5.50\ °\text{C})$.

t/°C	5.0	5.2	5.3	5.4
p/Torr	-1.36×10^5	-8.15×10^4	-5.43×10^4	-2.71×10^4

t/°C	5.5	5.6	5.7
p/Torr	36.0	2.72×10^4	5.43×10^4

These points are plotted in Fig. 7.4 as line a.

(b) $p = p^* \exp\left\{-(3705\ \text{K})\left(\frac{1}{T} - \frac{1}{T^*}\right)\right\}$. Draw up the following Table based on $(p^*, T^*) = (36\ \text{Torr}, 5.50\ °\text{C}\ [278.65\ \text{K}])$

t/°C	-10.0	-5.0	0	5.0	10.0	15.0
p/Torr	16.5	21.4	27.5	35.2	44.6	55.8

These are plotted in Fig. 7.4 as line b.

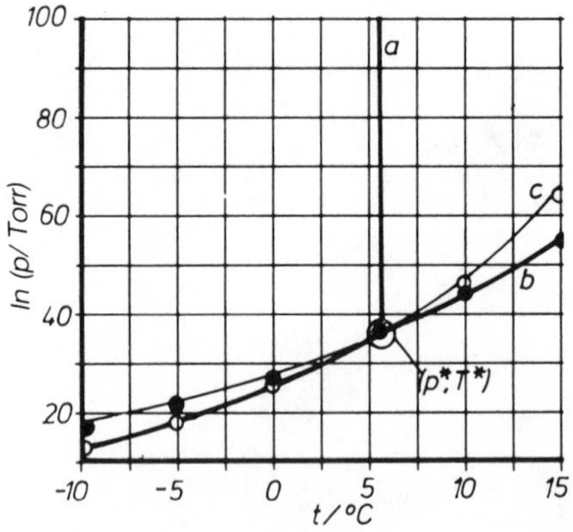

Fig 7·4

(c) $p = p^* \exp\left\{-(4979\ \text{K})\left(\frac{1}{T} - \frac{1}{T^*}\right)\right\}$. Draw up the following Table based on

$(p^*, T^*) = (36\ \text{Torr}, 5.50\ °\text{C})$

$t/°C$	−10.0	−5.0	0	5.0	10.0	15.0
p/Torr	12.6	17.9	25.1	34.9	47.8	64.9

These are plotted in Fig. 7.4 as line c.

7.25 Volume contracts as vapor is cooled from 400 K to 373 K. At 373 K the vapor condenses to a liquid (i.e. large contraction of volume at this temperature if 1 atm pressure maintained). Liquid cools with minor contraction of volume until 273 K, when the mass freezes. The direction of slope of the slope of the solid-liquid curve shows that the volume will then increase if 1 atm pressure maintained. Ice remains at 260 K. There will be a pause in the rate of cooling at 373 K (about 40 kJ mol^{-1} heat is released) and a pause at 273 K (about 6 kJ mol^{-1} of heat is released).

7.26 0.006 atm is the pressure of the triple point [Fig 7.6 of text]. Therefore, cooling from 400 K will cause the contraction of the vapor until 273.16 K is reached, when there will be a considerable contraction as solid ice is formed directly.

7.27 See Fig. 7.5. (a) The gas expands. (b) The gas contracts but remains gaseous

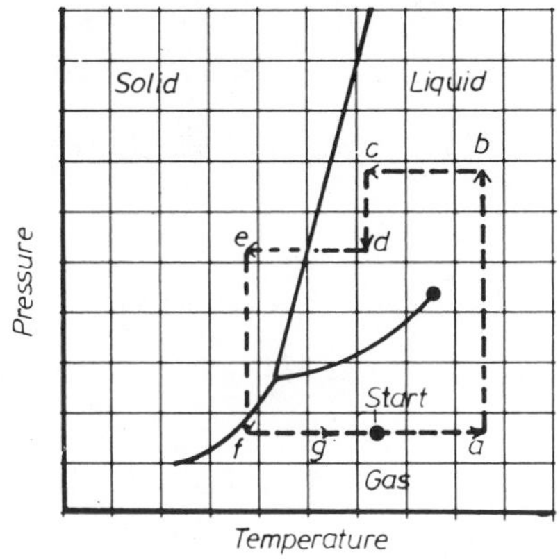

Fig 7·5

because 320 K is greater than the critical temperature [Table 1.2]. (c) The gas contracts and forms a liquid without discontinuity. (d) The volume increases as the liquid is decompressed. (e) The liquid cools, then freezes, contracting as it does so. (f) The solid expands slightly as the pressure is reduced, and sublimes when the pressure reaches about 5 atm. (g).The gas expands as it is heated to 298 K at constant pressure.

7.28 $c_0 = T_c/(T_h - T_c)$; $T_h = 293\ \text{K}$, $T_c =$ (a) 273 K, (b) 263 K.
$c_0 =$ (a) $273/20 = \underline{13.7}$, (b) $263/30 = \underline{8.8}$.

7.29 $c_0 = q_c/w_{rev}$ [Section 7.5(a)], $q_c = n\Delta H_{melt,m}$, $w_{min} = w_{rev} = q_c/c_0$
$= n\Delta H_{melt,m}/c_0$.
$\Delta H_{melt,m} = 6.01\ \text{kJ mol}^{-1}$, $n = (250\ \text{g})/(18.02\ \text{g mol}^{-1}) = 13.9\ \text{mol}$;
$c_0 = 13.7$ [Problem 7.28].
$w_{min} = (13.9\ \text{mol}) \times (6.01\ \text{kJ mol}^{-1})/(13.7) = \underline{6.10\ \text{kJ}}$.
This amount of work can be supplied in $(6.10 \times 10^3\ \text{J})/(100\ \text{J s}^{-1}) = 61\ \text{s}$, and so the minimum freezing time is $\underline{61\ \text{s}}$.

7.30 $c_0(T_c) = T_c/(T_h - T_c)$ [7.5.1], $dq_c = -C_p dT$.
$dw_{min}(T_c) = dq_c/c_0(T_c) = -C_p(T_c)dT_c/c_0(T_c)$.

$$w_{min} = -\int_{T_i}^{T_f} C_p(T_c)\left(\frac{T_h - T_c}{T_c}\right) dT_c \approx -C_p \int_{T_i}^{T_f}\left(\frac{T_h}{T_c} - 1\right) dT_c$$

$$\approx \underline{C_p\{(T_f - T_i) - T_h \ln(T_f/T_i)\}}.$$

7.31 $w_{min} = w_{min}(\text{cooling } T_i \rightarrow T_f = 273\ \text{K}) + w_{min}$ (freezing at 273 K);
$w_{min}(\text{cooling}) = C_p\{(T_f - T_i) - T_h \ln(T_f/T_i)\}$ [Problem 7.30]

$$= -(13.9\ \text{mol}) \times (75.5\ \text{J K}^{-1}\ \text{mol}^{-1})$$

$$\times \left\{20\ \text{K} + (293\ \text{K})\ln\left(\frac{273}{293}\right)\right\} \quad \text{[Table 4.7]} = 0.75\ \text{kJ}.$$

$w_{min}(\text{freezing}) = 6.10\ \text{kJ}$ [Problem 7.29].
$w_{min} = \underline{6.85\ \text{kJ}}$, which can be provided in $(6.85\ \text{kJ}/100\ \text{J s}^{-1}) = \underline{69\ \text{s}}$.
No extra work is required for cooling from 25 °C to 20 °C, as the process is spontaneous.

7.32 $c_0 = T_c/(T_h - T_c)$, $w_{min} = q/c_0 = nC_{p,m}\Delta T/c_0$.
$T_h = 1.20\ \text{K}$, $(T_c)_{mean} = \frac{1}{2}(1.10\ \text{K} + 0.10\ \text{K}) = 0.60\ \text{K}$.
$c_0 = (0.60\ \text{K})/(1.20\ \text{K} - 0.60\ \text{K}) = 1.00$.
$n = (1.0\ \text{g}/63.5\ \text{g mol}^{-1}) = 0.016\ \text{mol}$.
$w_{min} = (0.016\ \text{mol}) \times (3.9 \times 10^{-5}\ \text{J K}^{-1}\ \text{mol}^{-1}) \times (0.60\ \text{K})/1.00 = \underline{3.7 \times 10^{-7}\ \text{J}}$.

7.33 $$w_{min} = -\int_{T_i}^{T_f} C_p(T_c)\left(\frac{T_h - T_c}{T_c}\right) dT_c \quad \text{[Problem 7.30]}$$

$$= -n\int_{T_i}^{T_f}(AT_c^2 + B)(T_h - T_c)\mathrm{d}T_c$$

$$= n\{\tfrac{1}{4}A(T_f^4 - T_i^4) - \tfrac{1}{3}A(T_f^3 - T_i^3)T_h + \tfrac{1}{2}B(T_f^2 - T_i^2) - B(T_f - T_i)T_h\}.$$

$n = 0.016\,\mathrm{mol}, A = 4.82 \times 10^{-5}\,\mathrm{J\,K^{-4}\,mol^{-1}}, B = 6.88 \times 10^{-4}\,\mathrm{J\,K^{-2}\,mol^{-1}}$,

$T_h = 1.20\,\mathrm{K}, T_i = 1.10\,\mathrm{K}, T_f = 0.10\,\mathrm{K}$.

$w_{min} = (0.016\,\mathrm{mol}) \times (4.21 \times 10^{-4}\,\mathrm{J\,mol^{-1}}) = \underline{6.7 \times 10^{-6}\,\mathrm{J}}.$

7.34 $T_f = 10^{-6}\,\mathrm{K}$, remaining data as in Problem 7.32.

$w_{min} = (5.00 \times 10^{-4}\,\mathrm{J\,mol^{-1}}) \times (0.016\,\mathrm{mol}) = \underline{8.0 \times 10^{-6}\,\mathrm{J}}.$

A 1 μW refrigerator provides 10^{-6} J each s [1 W = 1 J s^{-1}];

therefore 8×10^{-6} J is provided in $\underline{8\ \mathrm{s}}$.

7.35 (a) No work need be done because the cooling is spontaneous.

(b) $c_o = T_c/(T_h - T_c)$; $T_h = 303\,\mathrm{K}$,

for $T_c \mathrel{\hat{=}} 22\,°\mathrm{C}$ (295 K), $c_o = 37$;

for $T_c \mathrel{\hat{=}} 26\,°\mathrm{C}$ (299 K), $c_o = 75$ (approx. mean value).

$w_{min} = nC_{p,m}\Delta T/c_o$.

$n = (75\,\mathrm{m^3}) \times (1.2 \times 10^{-3}\,\mathrm{g\,cm^{-3}})/(29\,\mathrm{g\,mol^{-1}}) = 3.1 \times 10^3\,\mathrm{mol}$.

Therefore, $w_{min} = (3.1 \times 10^3\,\mathrm{mol}) \times (29\,\mathrm{J\,K^{-1}\,mol^{-1}}) \times (8\,\mathrm{K})/75 = \underline{9.6\,\mathrm{kJ}}.$

7.36 $w_{min} = q_c/c_o$; $\mathrm{d}w_{min}/\mathrm{d}t = (\mathrm{d}q_c/\mathrm{d}t)/c_o$.

$c_o = T_c/(T_h - T_c) = 298/5 = 59.6$.

$\mathrm{d}q_c/\mathrm{d}t = 1$ kW (the rate of supply of energy as heat).

Therefore, the rate of doing work, $\mathrm{d}w_{min}/\mathrm{d}t = (1\,\mathrm{kW})/59.6 = \underline{17\,\mathrm{W}}.$

(Relatively small quantities of energy are needed to shift energy as heat: that is the basis of the heat pump.)

7.37 Radius of droplet: a;

surface area $= 4\pi a^2$, volume $= \frac{4}{3}\pi a^3$.

Radius of molecule: $r = 120 \times 10^{-12}\,\mathrm{m}$;

Area occupied by one molecule $= \pi r^2$,

Volume occupied by one molecule $= \frac{4}{3}\pi r^3$.

$$\frac{\text{Number on surface}}{\text{Total number in droplet}} = \frac{(4\pi a^2/\pi r^2)}{(\frac{4}{3}\pi a^3/\frac{4}{3}\pi r^3)} = \frac{4r}{a} = \frac{4.8 \times 10^{-10}\,\mathrm{m}}{a}.$$

(a) $a = 10^{-5}$ mm; ratio = $\underline{4.8 \times 10^{-2}}$ (1 in 21).

(b) $a = 10^{-2}$ mm; ratio = $\underline{4.8 \times 10^{-5}}$ (1 in 21 000),

(c) $a = 1.0$ mm; ratio = $\underline{4.8 \times 10^{-7}}$ (1 in 2.1 million).

7.38 $\Delta A = \gamma \Delta\sigma$ [7.6.2] Initial volume $V_i = M/\rho$; $M = 100$ g (given].
$\rho = 0.88$ g cm^{-3}. Volume of droplets $= N\frac{4}{3}\pi r^3 = M/\rho$, N = number of droplets; hence $N = 3M/4\pi\rho r^3$.

$$\left.\begin{array}{l}\text{Surface area of droplets} = 4\pi r^2 N = 3M/\rho r \\ \text{Surface area of initial sample} \approx 0\end{array}\right\} \Delta\sigma = 3M/\rho r.$$

$\Delta A = \gamma\Delta\sigma = 3M\gamma/\rho r$; $w = \gamma\Delta\sigma$ [7.6.1.].

$$\Delta A = \frac{3 \times (100\,\text{g}) \times (2.8 \times 10^{-2}\,\text{N m}^{-1})}{(0.88\,\text{g cm}^{-3}) \times (10^{-6}\,\text{m})} = 9.5 \times 10^{6}\,\text{N m}^{-2}\,\text{cm}^{3}$$

$$= 9.5\,\text{N m} = \underline{9.5\,\text{J}};\ w = \Delta A = \underline{9.5\,\text{J}}.$$

7.39 $p(\text{mist}) = p(\text{bulk}) \exp\{2\gamma V_m/rRT\}$ [7.6.5]

$V_m = M_m/\rho = (78.12\,\text{g mol}^{-1})/(0.88\,\text{g cm}^{-3}) = 89\,\text{cm}^3\,\text{mol}^{-1}$.

$$2\gamma V_m/RT = \frac{2 \times (2.8 \times 10^{-2}\,\text{N m}^{-1}) \times (89 \times 10^{-6}\,\text{m}^3\,\text{mol}^{-1})}{2.48 \times 10^{3}\,\text{J mol}^{-1}}$$

$$= 2.01 \times 10^{-9}\,\text{m}.$$

(a) $r = 10\,\mu\text{m} = 1.0 \times 10^{-5}$ m;

$p(\text{mist})/p(\text{bulk}) = \exp\{(2.01 \times 10^{-9}\,\text{m})/(1.0 \times 10^{-5}\,\text{m})\} = \exp(2.01 \times 10^{-4}) = \underline{1.0002}.$

(b) $r = 0.10\,\mu\text{m} = 1.0 \times 10^{-7}$ m;

$p(\text{mist})/p(\text{bulk}) = \exp(2.01 \times 10^{-2}) = \underline{1.020}.$

7.40 $M = nM_r\,\text{g mol}^{-1} = (pVM_r/RT)\,\text{g mol}^{-1}$ [Problem 7.17]

$p = 100$ Torr $\triangleq 0.13$ atm, $V \approx 10\,\text{dm}^3$, $T = 333$ K, $M_r = 100.2$

$$\text{Therefore, } M = \frac{(0.13\,\text{atm}) \times (10\,\text{dm}^3) \times (100.2\,\text{g mol}^{-1})}{(0.082\,\text{dm}^3\,\text{atm K}^{-1}\,\text{mol}^{-1}) \times (333\,\text{K})} = \underline{4.8\,\text{g}}.$$

$p(\text{mist}) = p(\text{bulk}) \exp\{2\gamma V_m/rRT\}$ [7.6.5].

Therefore M (mist) = M (bulk)$\exp\{2\gamma V_m/rRT\}$.

$\gamma \approx 2.8 \times 10^{-2}\,\text{N m}^{-1}$ [like benzene], $\rho(\text{l}) = 0.879\,\text{g cm}^{-3}$,

$V_m = (100.2\,\text{g mol}^{-1})/(0.879\,\text{g cm}^{-3}) = 114.0\,\text{cm}^3\,\text{mol}^{-1}$

$2\gamma V_m/rRT =$

$$\frac{2 \times (2.8 \times 10^{-2}\,\mathrm{N\,m^{-1}}) \times (114.0 \times 10^{-6}\,\mathrm{m^3\,mol^{-1}})}{(1.0 \times 10^{-7}\,\mathrm{m}) \times (8.314\,\mathrm{J\,K^{-1}\,mol^{-1}}) \times (333\,\mathrm{K})} = 0.023.$$

Therefore M (mist) $\approx$ (4.8 g)exp(0.023) = <u>4.9 g.</u>

7.41 $h = 2\gamma/\rho g r$ [7.6.7] (i) 20 °C.

$$h(20\,^\circ\mathrm{C}) = \left(\frac{2 \times (7.28 \times 10^{-2}\,\mathrm{N\,m^{-1}})}{(0.988 \times 10^{-3}\,\mathrm{kg\,m^{-3}}) \times (9.81\,\mathrm{m\,s^{-2}})}\right)\left(\frac{1}{r}\right) = \left(\frac{1.49 \times 10^{-5}\,\mathrm{m^2}}{r}\right).$$

(a) $r = 1.0\,\mathrm{mm}; h = \dfrac{1.49 \times 10^{-5}\,\mathrm{m^2}}{1.0 \times 10^{-3}\,\mathrm{m}} = 1.49 \times 10^{-2}\,\mathrm{m} = \underline{1.5\,\mathrm{cm.}}$

(b) $r = 0.10\,\mathrm{mm}; h = 15 \times 10^{-1}\,\mathrm{m} = \underline{15\,\mathrm{cm.}}$

$$h(100\,^\circ\mathrm{C}) = \frac{2 \times (5.80 \times 10^{-2}\,\mathrm{N\,m^{-1}})}{(0.958 \times 10^{3}\,\mathrm{kg\,m^{-3}}) \times (9.81\,\mathrm{m\,s^{-2}})}\left(\frac{1}{r}\right) = \left(\frac{1.23 \times 10^{-5}\,\mathrm{m^2}}{r}\right)$$

(a) $r = 1.0\,\mathrm{mm}; h = 1.2 \times 10^{-2}\,\mathrm{m} = \underline{1.2\,\mathrm{cm.}}$

(b) $r = 0.10\,\mathrm{mm}, h = 1.2 \times 10^{-1}\,\mathrm{m} = \underline{12\,\mathrm{cm.}}$

7.42 $h = 2\gamma/\rho g r$ [7.6.7]

$= 2 \times (2.189 \times 10^{-2}\,\mathrm{N\,m^{-1}})/[(0.780 \times 10^{3}\,\mathrm{kg\,m^{-3}})$
$\times (9.81\,\mathrm{m\,s^{-2}}) \times (0.10 \times 10^{-3}\,\mathrm{m})] = 0.058\,\mathrm{m}, \underline{5.8\,\mathrm{cm.}}$

Pressure = $2\gamma/r$ [Section 7.6(c)]

$= 2 \times (2.189 \times 10^{-2}\,\mathrm{N\,m^{-1}})/(0.10 \times 10^{-3}\,\mathrm{m})$
$= \underline{440\,\mathrm{N\,m^{-2}}}$ (0.0044 atm).

7.43 The surface is curved only in the radial direction, the circumferential direction being essentially flat, Fig. 7.6. Hence the pressure difference is γ/r instead of $2\gamma/r$, where $2r$ is the separation between rod and tube. Hence $h = \gamma/\rho g r$, $r = 0.0050$ cm.

Fig 7·6

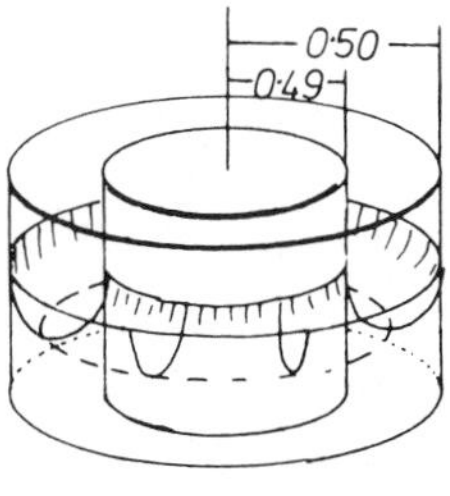

$$h = \frac{7.28 \times 10^{-2}\,\mathrm{N\,m^{-1}}}{(0.998 \times 10^{3}\,\mathrm{kg\,m^{-3}}) \times (9.81\,\mathrm{m\,s^{-2}}) \times (5.0 \times 10^{-5}\,\mathrm{m})}$$

$= \underline{0.15\,\mathrm{m} = 15\,\mathrm{cm}.}$

7.44 Regard the surface as spherical, but with a radius R that differs from the radius of the tube r, Fig. 7.7. From trigonometry and Fig. 7.7, $r/R = \sin(90° - \theta) = \cos\theta$. Therefore $R = r/\cos\theta$. Use this R in the Laplace equation for the pressure, $2\gamma/R$, and by repeating the argument in Section 7.6(c) arrive at $h = 2\gamma/\rho g R = \underline{2\gamma\cos\theta/\rho g r.}$

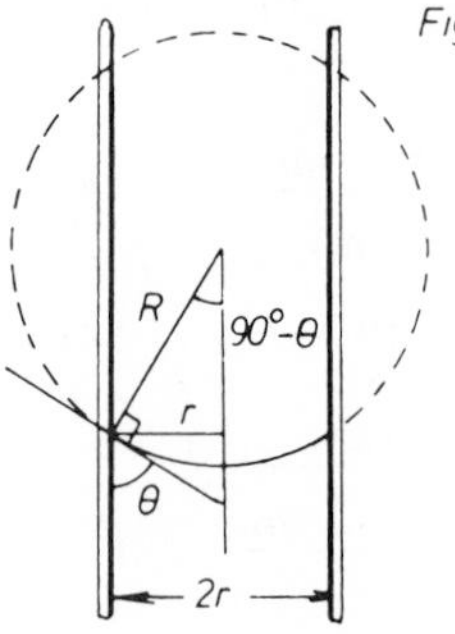

Fig 7·7

7.45 $\mathrm{d}\mu = -S\mathrm{d}T + \gamma\mathrm{d}\sigma + V\mathrm{d}p$

$\quad = V\mathrm{d}p + \gamma\mathrm{d}\sigma$ at $T = \text{const.}$

$(\partial V/\partial\sigma)_T = (\partial\gamma/\partial p)_{\sigma,T}$ [T = const; $\mathrm{d}\mu$ is exact; relation 4, Box 3.1].

For spherical droplets, $V = \frac{4}{3}\pi r^3$, $\sigma = 4\pi r^2$.

$\mathrm{d}V/\mathrm{d}\sigma = (\mathrm{d}V/\mathrm{d}r)(\mathrm{d}r/\mathrm{d}\sigma) = (\mathrm{d}V/\mathrm{d}r)/(\mathrm{d}\sigma/\mathrm{d}r) = 4\pi r^2/8\pi = \underline{r/2.}$

Therefore $(\partial\gamma/\partial p)_{\sigma,T} = r/2$, or $\mathrm{d}\gamma = \frac{1}{2}r\mathrm{d}p$ which integrates to

$\gamma = \frac{1}{2}r(p_{\text{in}} - p_{\text{out}})$; or $p_{\text{in}} - p_{\text{out}} = 2\gamma/r$, as required.

7.46 $(\mathrm{d}/\mathrm{d}t)mv = F$ [Newton] Both m and F depend on the time:

$m(t) = (\text{volume}) \times (\text{density}) = (\pi r^2\delta)\rho$.

$F(t) = 2 \times (\text{circumference}) \times (\text{surface tension})$

$\quad = 2 \times (2\pi r) \times \gamma = 4\pi r\gamma$.

$(\mathrm{d}/\mathrm{d}t)\,[\pi r^2\delta\rho v] = 4\pi r\gamma$, or $(\mathrm{d}/\mathrm{d}t)\,(r^2 v) = 4r\gamma/\rho\delta$.

Neglect acceleration; then $(\mathrm{d}/\mathrm{d}t)\,(r^2 v) \approx 2rv\mathrm{d}r/\mathrm{d}t = 2rv^2 = 4r\gamma/\rho\delta$, or $v \approx \surd(2\gamma/\delta\rho)$.

(a) $v \approx \surd\{2 \times (7.2 \times 10^{-2}\,\mathrm{N\,m^{-1}})/\delta \times (10^3\,\mathrm{kg\,m^{-3}})\} \approx 0.01\,\mathrm{m\,s^{-1}}/\surd(\delta/\mathrm{m})$.

For $\delta = 0.01$ mm, $v \approx (0.01\,\mathrm{m\,s^{-1}})/\surd 10^{-5} = \underline{4\,\mathrm{m\,s^{-1}}.}$

(b) $v \approx \sqrt{\{2 \times (2.6 \times 10^{-2}\,\mathrm{N\,m^{-1}})/\delta \times (10^{3}\,\mathrm{kg\,m^{-3}})\}} \approx 0.007\,\mathrm{m\,s^{-1}}/\sqrt{(\delta/\mathrm{m})}$.

For $\delta = 0.01$ mm, $v \approx 0.007\,\mathrm{m\,s^{-1}}/\sqrt{10^{-5}} = \underline{2\,\mathrm{m\,s^{-1}}}$.

8. Changes of state: physical transformations of simple mixtures

A8.1 $p_B/x_B = K_B$ [8.2.9]

$32.0\,\text{kPa}/0.005 = 6.40 \times 10^3\,\text{kPa}$; $76.9\,\text{kPa}/0.012 = 6.41 \times 10^3\,\text{kPa}$;

$121.8\,\text{kPa}/0.019 = 6.41 \times 10^3\,\text{kPa}$; $K_B = \underline{6.41 \times 10^3\,\text{kPa}}$.

A8.2 $\Delta H_{\text{vap,m}} = RT^2 \text{d}\ln p/\text{d}T$ [7.2.4] $= RT^2 \text{d}(\ln K)/\text{d}T = -R\, \text{d}(\ln K)/\text{d}(1/T)$

$= -(8.314\,\text{J K}^{-1}\,\text{mol}^{-1})(-1010\,\text{K}) = \underline{8.397 \times 10^3\,\text{J mol}^{-1}}$.

Change in state: HCl(solution) → HCl(g).

A8.3 $p_A = py_A$ and $p_B = py_B$ [Section 1.2(a)].

p_A/kPa	0	1.399	3.566	5.044	6.996	7.940	9.211	10.105
x_A	0	0.0898	0.2476	0.3577	0.5194	0.6036	0.7188	0.8019
y_A	0	0.0410	0.1154	0.1762	0.2772	0.3393	0.4450	0.5435

p_A/kPa	11.287	12.295
x_A	0.9105	1
y_A	0.7284	1

p_B/kPa	0	4.209	8.487	11.487	15.462	18.243	23.582	27.334
x_B	0	0.0895	0.1981	0.2812	0.3964	0.4806	0.6423	0.7524
y_B	0	0.2716	0.4565	0.5550	0.6607	0.7228	0.8238	0.8846

p_B/kPa	32.722	36.066
x_B	0.9102	1
y_B	0.9590	1

$K_A = p_A/x_A = 15.579\,\text{kPa}$ when $x_A = 0.0898$, [8.2.8]

$K_B = p_B/x_B = 47.028\,\text{kPa}$ when $x_B = 0.0895$.

See Fig. A8.1 for graphs of p_A v. x_A and p_B v. x_B.

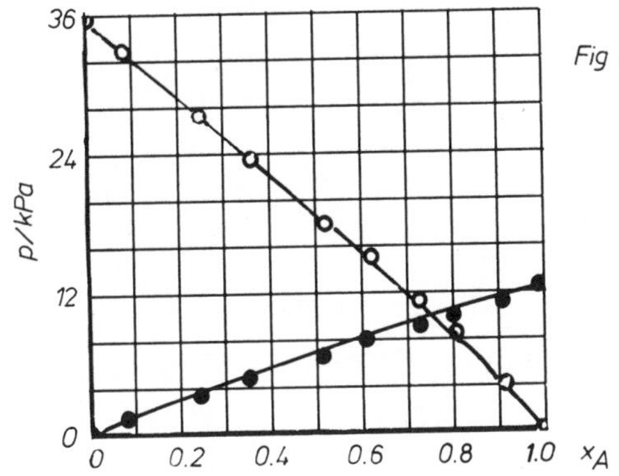

Fig A8.1

A8.4 $a_A = p_A/p_A^*$ [8.5.4]; $\gamma_A \doteq a_A/x_A$ [8.5.5]

a_A	0.1138	0.2900	0.4102	0.5690	0.6458	0.7492	0.8219	0.9180	1
γ_A	1.267	1.171	1.147	1.096	1.070	1.042	1.025	1.008	1
x_A	0.0898	0.2476	0.3577	0.5194	0.6036	0.7188	0.8019	0.9105	1

A8.5 $T^* - T = (RT^{*2}/\Delta H_{\text{melt,m}})x_B$ [8.3.3].

$T = 278.65\,\text{K} - (8.31\,\text{J K}^{-1}\,\text{mol}^{-1})(279\,\text{K})^2(9.84 \times 10^3\,\text{J mol}^{-1})^{-1}(1 - 0.905)$

$= 272.41\,\text{K}.$

A8.6 $\delta T = K_f m_B = K_f[(W_B/M_m)/(W_A/\text{kg})]$ [8.3.4, Table 8.2]

$M_m = (30\,\text{K kg mol}^{-1})(100\,\text{g})(0.750\,\text{kg})^{-1}(10.5\,\text{K})^{-1} = \underline{381\,\text{g mol}^{-1}}.$

A8.7 $\Pi V = n_B RT$ [8.3.10]; $n_B/V \approx m_B$ for dilute aqueous solutions.

$\delta T = K_f m_B$ [8.3.4] $= K_f(n_B/V) = K_f(\Pi/RT) = (1.86\,\text{K kg mol}^{-1})(120 \times 10^3\,\text{Pa})$

$\times (8.31\,\text{J K}^{-1}\,\text{mol}^{-1})^{-1}(300\,\text{K})^{-1}(10^{-3}\,\text{m}^3/\text{kg}) = 0.09\,\text{K}.$

$T = (273.15 - 0.09)\text{K} = \underline{273.06\,\text{K}}.$

A8.8 $p_A = 0.350\,p_t = (575\,\text{Torr})x_A$; $p_B = 0.650\,p_t = (390\,\text{Torr})(1 - x_A)$;

$0.350/0.650 = (575\,\text{Torr}/390\,\text{Torr})\,[x_A/(1 - x_A)]$ [8.2.7, Section 1.2(a)]

$x_A = 0.268$; $x_B = 1 - x_A = 0.732$; $p_t = (575\,\text{Torr})(0.268/0.350) = \underline{440\,\text{Torr}}.$

A8.9 $(\partial x_1/\partial n_1)_{n_2} = \{\partial\,[n_1(n_1 + n_2)^{-1}]/\partial n_1\}_{n_2} = x_2(n_1 + n_2)^{-1}$

$$\{\partial[(x_1)(1-x_1)]/\partial n_1\}_{n_2} = -x_1(\partial x_1/\partial n_1)_{n_2} + (1-x_1)(\partial x_1/\partial n_1)_{n_2}$$
$$= (n_1+n_2)^{-1}[-x_1x_2 + x_2^2].$$
$$(\partial G^{\mathrm{E}}/\partial n_1)_{n_2} = \{\partial[(n_1+n_2)(RTg_0)(x_1)(1-x_1)]/\partial n_1\}_{n_2}$$
$$= RTg_0\{(n_1+n_2)\partial[(x_1)(1-x_1)]/\partial n_1 + (x_1)(1-x_1)\}$$
$$= RTg_0\{-x_1x_2 + x_2^2 + x_1x_2\} = RTg_0 x_2^2.$$
$$\mu_1 = \mu_1^{\ominus} + RT\ln x_1 + RTg_0 x_2^2.$$

A8.10 $G^{\mathrm{E}} = (RT)(1/4)(3/4)[0.4857 - 0.1077(-1/2) + 0.0191(-1/2)^2] = 0.1021\,RT.$

$\Delta G_{\mathrm{mix}} = RT(n_{\mathrm{A}}\ln x_{\mathrm{A}} + n_{\mathrm{B}}\ln x_{\mathrm{B}}) + (n_{\mathrm{A}} + n_{\mathrm{B}})G^{\mathrm{E}}$ [8.2.1, Section 8.2(a)]

$= RT[(1)\ln(1/4) + (3)\ln(3/4) + (1+3)(0.1021)] = -1.841\,RT.$

8.1 $V_{\mathrm{A,m}} = (\partial V/\partial n_{\mathrm{A}})_{n_{\mathrm{B}}}$ [8.1.1]. For $n_{\mathrm{A}} = n_{\mathrm{NaCl}}$, $n_{\mathrm{B}} = n_{\mathrm{H_2O}}$

$V_{\mathrm{NaCl,m}} = (\partial V/\partial n_{\mathrm{NaCl}})_{n_{\mathrm{H_2O}}} = (\partial V/\partial m)_{n_{\mathrm{H_2O}}}$.

[More formally:

$V_{\mathrm{NaCl,m}} = (\partial V/\partial n_{\mathrm{NaCl}})_{n_{\mathrm{H_2O}}} = (\partial V/\partial n_{\mathrm{NaCl}}\mathrm{kg}^{-1})_{n_{\mathrm{H_2O}}}\mathrm{kg}^{-1}$

$= (\partial V/\partial m)_{n_{\mathrm{H_2O}}}\mathrm{kg}^{-1} = (\partial V/\partial[m/\mathrm{mol\,kg}^{-1}])_{n_{\mathrm{H_2O}}}\,\mathrm{kg}^{-1}/\mathrm{mol\,kg}^{-1}$

$= (\partial V/\partial m)_{n_{\mathrm{H_2O}}}\,\mathrm{mol}^{-1}$ with $m \equiv m/\mathrm{mol\,kg}^{-1}$.]

$V/\mathrm{cm}^3 = 1003 + 16.62\,m + 1.77\,m^{3/2} + 0.12\,\mathrm{m}^2$

$V_{\mathrm{NaCl,m}}/\mathrm{cm}^3 = [16.62 + \frac{3}{2}\times 1.77\,m^{1/2} + 2\times 0.12\,m]\,\mathrm{mol}^{-1}$

$= 17.5\,\mathrm{mol}^{-1}$ when $m = 0.1$, or $V_{\mathrm{NaCl,m}} = 17.5\,\mathrm{cm}^3\,\mathrm{mol}^{-1}$.

$V = n_{\mathrm{NaCl}}V_{\mathrm{NaCl,m}} + n_{\mathrm{H_2O}}V_{\mathrm{H_2O,m}}$ [8.1.2]. In the case of $m = 0.10\,\mathrm{mol\,kg}^{-1}$, the solution consists of $n_{\mathrm{NaCl}} = 0.10\,\mathrm{mol}$ in 1 kg of water, corresponding to $n_{\mathrm{H_2O}} = 55.49$ mol. Hence

$V = (0.10\,\mathrm{mol})\times(17.5\,\mathrm{cm}^3\,\mathrm{mol}^{-1}) + (55.49\,\mathrm{mol})\times V_{\mathrm{H_2O,m}}$

$= 1.75\,\mathrm{cm}^3 + (55.49\,\mathrm{mol})\times V_{\mathrm{H_2O,m}}$

$= [1003 + 16.62\times(0.1) + 1.77\times(0.1)^{3/2} + 0.12\times(0.1)^2]\,\mathrm{cm}^3$

$= 1004.7\,\mathrm{cm}^3$.

Therefore $V_{\mathrm{H_2O,m}} = (1004.7 - 1.75)\mathrm{cm}^3/55.49\,\mathrm{mol} = 18.1\,\mathrm{cm}^3\,\mathrm{mol}^{-1}$.

8.2 $V_{\mathrm{salt,m}} = (\partial V/\partial m)_{n(\mathrm{H_2O})}\,\mathrm{mol}^{-1}$ [Problem 8.1],

$(\partial V/\partial m) = (\partial/\partial m)[1001.21 + 34.69(m-0.07)^2]\,\mathrm{cm}^3 = 69.38\,(m-0.07)\,\mathrm{cm}^3$.

At $m = 0.05\,\mathrm{mol\,kg}^{-1}$:

$V_{\mathrm{salt,m}} = 69.38(0.05 - 0.07)\,\mathrm{cm}^3\,\mathrm{mol}^{-1} = -1.4\,\mathrm{cm}^3\,\mathrm{mol}^{-1}$.

$V = [1001.21 + 34.69\times 0.02^2]\,\mathrm{cm}^3 = 1001.20\,\mathrm{cm}^3$

$V_{\text{solv,m}} = \{1001.20\ \text{cm}^3 - (0.02\ \text{mol}) \times (-1.4\ \text{cm}^3\ \text{mol}^{-1})\}/(55.49\ \text{mol})$

$= \underline{18.0\ \text{cm}^3\ \text{mol}^{-1}}.$

8.3 Rework the derivation in Appendix 8.1 of the text with

$$w = \frac{M_B}{M_A + M_B},\ \rho = (M_A + M_B)/V,\ n_A = M_A/M_{A,m}:$$

$$\begin{aligned} V_{A,m} &= (\partial V/\partial n_A)_B = (\partial V/\partial M_A)_B M_{A,m} \\ &= (\partial/\partial M_A)\ [(M_A + M_B)/\rho]\,M_{A,m} \\ &= (M_{A,m}/\rho) + (M_A + M_B)M_{A,m}\,[(\partial/\partial M_A)(1/\rho)]. \end{aligned}$$

$$(\partial/\partial M_A)(1/\rho) = (\partial w/\partial M_A)(d/dw)(1/\rho) = -\left(\frac{w}{M_A + M_B}\right)(d/dw)(1/\rho).$$

Therefore, $V_{A,m} = (M_{A,m}/\rho) - \left(\dfrac{(M_A + M_B)M_{A,m}w}{M_A + M_B}\right)\dfrac{d}{dw}\left(\dfrac{1}{\rho}\right),$

or $\dfrac{1}{\rho} = (V_{A,m}/M_{A,m}) + \left(\dfrac{d}{dw}\dfrac{1}{\rho}\right)w$. Therefore, plot $1/\rho$ against w and extrapolate the tangent to $w = 0$ in order to obtain $V_{A,m}/M_{A,m}$ [as in Fig. 8.22 of the text]. Draw up the following Table

$100w$	2.162	10.98	20.80	30.00	39.2	51.68
$\rho/\text{g cm}^{-3}$	1.01	1.06	1.12	1.18	1.24	1.32
$(1/\rho)\,\text{g cm}^{-3}$	0.990	0.943	0.893	0.847	0.806	0.758

$100w$	62.64	71.57	82.33	93.40	99.60
$\rho/\text{g cm}^{-3}$	1.38	1.42	1.46	1.49	1.51
$(1/\rho)\,\text{g cm}^{-3}$	0.725	0.704	0.685	0.671	0.662

Plot $1/\rho$ against w as in Fig. 8.1 (a). Tangents have been drawn at four values of w, and $V_{A,m}/M_{A,m}$ read off from the intercepts at $w = 0$ and $V_{B,m}/M_{B,m}$ at $w = 1$. Since $A = H_2O$, $M_{A,m} = 18.02\ \text{g mol}^{-1}$, and $B = HNO_3$, $M_{B,m} = 63.02\ \text{g mol}^{-1}$, then form $V_{A,m}$ and $V_{B,m}$. Draw up the following Table.

$100w$	20	40	60	80	
$(V_{A,m}/M_{A,m})\,g\,cm^{-3}$	0.975	0.965	0.900	0.825	from intercepts at $w = 0$
$(V_{B,m}/M_{B,m})\,g\,cm^{-3}$	0.535	0.565	0.620	0.655	from intercepts at $w = 1$
$V_{A,m}/cm^3\,mol^{-1}$	17.6	17.4	16.2	14.9	from $M_{A,m} = 18.02\,g\,mol^{-1}$
$V_{B,m}/cm^3\,mol^{-1}$	33.7	35.6	39.1	41.3	from $M_{B,m} = 63.02\,g\,mol^{-1}$

Hence plot $V_{B,m}$ against w, Fig. 8.1(b).

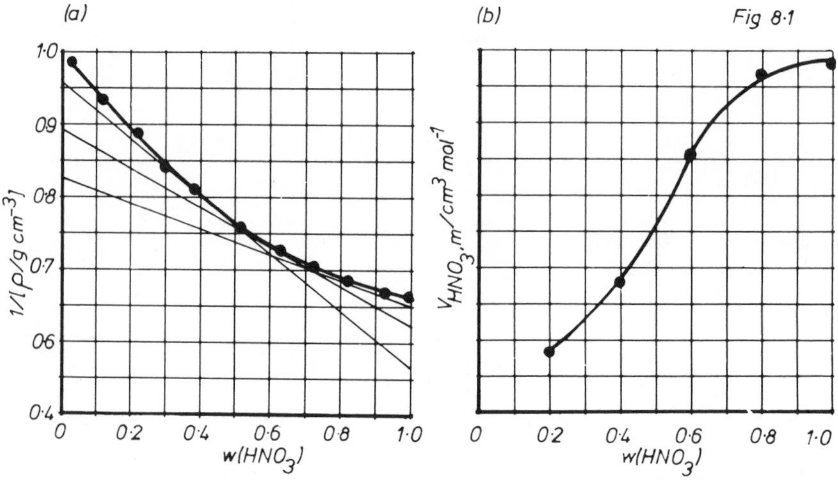

8.4 Use the same technique as in Problem 8.3. Although w is now replaced by the weight percentage the conversion is trivial '%' = $100\,w$. Draw up the following Table.

%	5	10	15	20
$\rho/g\,cm^{-3}$	1.051	1.107	1.167	1.230
$(1/\rho)\,g\,cm^{-3}$	0.951	0.903	0.857	0.813

Plot $1/\rho$ against %, Fig. 8.2; determine $V_{CuSO_4,m}/M_{CuSO_4,m}$ from the intercepts at % = 100. Within the precision of the plot, all four intercepts are coincident at 0.075, and so $V_{CuSO_4,m} = (0.075\,g^{-1}\,cm^3) \times (159.6\,g\,mol^{-1}) = \underline{12.0\,cm^3\,mol^{-1}}$.

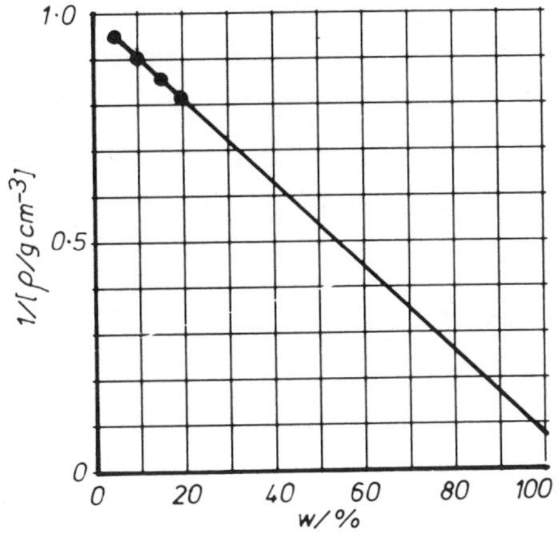

Fig 8·2

8.5 A: acetone; C: chloroform,

(i) $n_A M_{A,m} + n_C M_{C,m} = M\,[= 1.000\,\text{kg}]$.

$x_A = n_A/(n_A + n_C)$, or $(x_A - 1)n_A + x_A n_C = 0$, so that

(ii) $-x_C n_A + x_A n_C = 0$.

Solve (i) and (ii), to find

$n_A = (x_A/x_C)n_C$; $n_C = M/(x_A M_{A,m} + x_C M_{C,m})$.

$x_C = 0.4693$, so that $x_A = 1 - x_C = 0.5307$;

$M_{C,m} = 119.4\,\text{g mol}^{-1}$, $M_{A,m} = 58.08\,\text{g mol}^{-1}$.

$n_C = (0.4693 \times 1000\,\text{g})/[(0.5307 \times 58.08\,\text{g mol}^{-1}) + (0.4693 \times 119.4\,\text{g mol}^{-1})]$

$= 5.40\,\text{mol}$, $n_A = 6.11\,\text{mol}$.

$V = n_A V_{A,m} + n_C V_{C,m}$

$= (6.11\,\text{mol}) \times (74.166\,\text{cm}^3\,\text{mol}^{-1}) + (5.40\,\text{mol}) \times (80.235\,\text{cm}^3\,\text{mol}^{-1}) = \underline{886.4\,\text{cm}^3}$.

The volumes of the unmixed components are

$V_C = (5.40\,\text{mol}) \times (80.665\,\text{cm}^3\,\text{mol}^{-1}) = 435.6\,\text{cm}^3$

$V_A = (6.11\,\text{mol}) \times (73.993\,\text{cm}^3\,\text{mol}^{-1}) = 452.2\,\text{cm}^3$,

a total volume of $\underline{887.7\,\text{cm}^3}$. Therefore, there is a contraction of $1.3\,\text{cm}^3$ on mixing.

8.6 $n_E V_{E,m} + n_W V_{W,m} = V$. For 50:50 mixture by mass, $M_E = M_W$; implying

$n_E M_{E,m} = n_W M_{W,m}$ so that

$n_E V_{E,m} + n_E(M_{E,m}/M_{W,m})V_{W,m} = V$, $n_E = V/[V_{E,m} + (M_{E,m}/M_{W,m})V_{W,m}]$.

Furthermore, $x_E = n_E/(n_E + n_W) = 1/[1 + (M_{E,m}/M_{W,m})]$.

$M_{E,m}/M_{W,m} = (46.07\text{ g mol}^{-1})/(18.02\text{ g mol}^{-1}) = 2.557$; therefore

$x_E = 0.2811, x_W = 1 - x_E = 0.7189$. At this composition

$V_{E,m} = 56.0\text{ cm}^3\text{ mol}^{-1}$, $V_{W,m} = 17.5\text{ cm}^3\text{ mol}^{-1}$ [Fig. 8.1 of the text].

Therefore $n_E = (100\text{ cm}^3)/[(56.0\text{ cm}^3\text{ mol}^{-1}) + 2.556 \times (17.5\text{ cm}^3\text{ mol}^{-1})]$

$= \underline{0.993\text{ mol}}$, or $\underline{45.7\text{ g}}$, or $\underline{57.6\text{ cm}^3}$.

$n_W = 2.556 \times 0.993\text{ mol} = \underline{2.54\text{ mol}}$, or $\underline{45.7\text{ g}}$, or $\underline{45.7\text{ cm}^3}$.

$\Delta V \approx V_{E,m}\Delta n_E$ [Δn virtually infinitesimal]

$\approx (56.0\text{ cm}^3\text{ mol}^{-1}) \times (1/58)\text{mol}$ [$V_{E,m}(\text{pure}) = 58\text{ cm}^3\text{ mol}^{-1}$ and 1 cm^3 $\hat{=} (1/58)\text{mol}] \approx \underline{0.97\text{ cm}^3}$.

8.7 Proceed as in Appendix 8.1. Plot V_m against x_C; extrapolate the tangents, and obtain $V_{C,m}$ from the intercept at $x_C = 1$, $V_{A,m}$ from the intercept at $x_C = 0$. Fig. 8.3(a) enables us to construct the following table.

x_C	0.0	0.2	0.4	0.6	0.8	1.0	
$V_{A,m}/\text{cm}^3\text{ mol}^{-1}$	73.99	74.03	74.11	73.96	73.50	72.74	(a)
$V_{C,m}/\text{cm}^3\text{ mol}^{-1}$	80.85	80.53	80.31	80.37	80.60	80.66	(b)

(a) from intercept at $x_C = 0$ (b) from intercept at $x_C = 1$.

These points are plotted in Fig. 8.3(b).

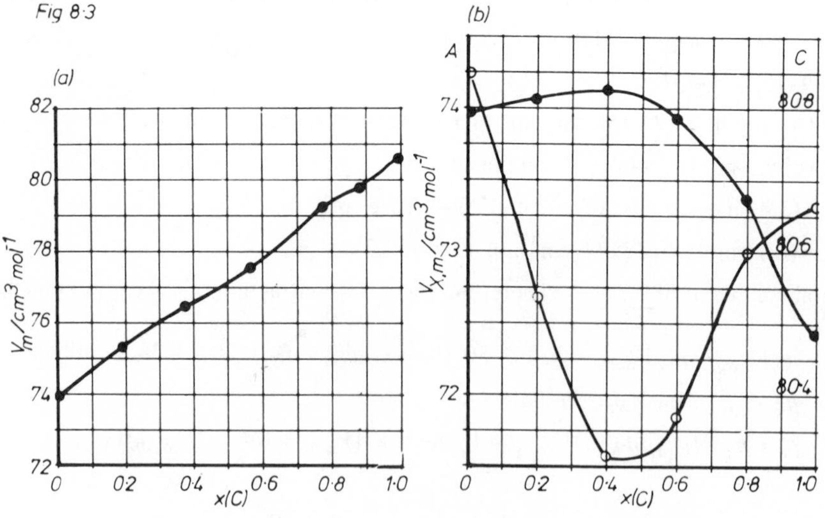

8.8 $V = n_A V_{A,m} + n_B V_{B,m}$ [8.1.2]

$dV = dn_A V_{A,m} + n_A dV_{A,m} + dn_B V_{B,m} + n_B dV_{B,m}$;

$dV = V_{A,m} dn_A + V_{B,m} dn_B$.

Therefore $\underline{n_A dV_{A,m} + n_B dV_{B,m} = 0.}$

Divide through by (a) $n_A + n_B$, (b) dx_B; then

$x_A(\partial V_{A,m}/\partial x_B) + x_B(\partial V_{B,m}/\partial x_B) = 0$;

therefore $(\partial V_{A,m}/\partial x_B)/(\partial V_{B,m}/\partial x_B) = -x_B/x_A = -1$

when $x_A = x_B = \frac{1}{2}$. Therefore, the slopes are equal but opposite at

$x_A = x_B = \frac{1}{2}$.

8.9 $x_A d\mu_A + x_B d\mu_B = 0$ [8.1.5]

Therefore $x_A(\partial\mu_A/\partial x_A)_{p,T} + x_B(\partial\mu_B/\partial x_A)_{p,T} = 0$,

and so $x_A(\partial\mu_A/\partial x_A)_{p,T} - x_B(\partial\mu_B/\partial x_B)_{p,T} = 0$ [as $dx_A = -dx_B$ since $x_A = 1 - x_B$],

or $(\partial\mu_A/\partial \ln x_A)_{p,T} = (\partial\mu_B/\partial \ln x_B)_{p,T}$ [$dx/x = d\ln x$].

Since $\mu_J = \mu_J^{\ominus} + RT \ln f_J$ [6.2.11];

$(\partial\mu_J/\partial \ln x_J)_{p,T} = RT(\partial \ln f_J/\partial \ln x_J)_{p,T}$.

Therefore $\underline{(\partial \ln f_A/\partial \ln x_A)_{p,T} = (\partial \ln f_B/\partial \ln x_B)_{p,T}}$.

Now replace f by p (for a perfect gas); then

$(\partial \ln p_A/\partial \ln x_A)_{p,T} = (\partial \ln p_B/\partial \ln x_B)_{p,T}$.

If A satisfies Raoult's law, $p_A = x_A p_A^*$, and then

$(\partial \ln p_A/\partial \ln x_A)_{p,T} = (x_A/p_A)(\partial p_A/\partial x_A)_{p,T} = (x_A/x_A p_A^*)p_A^* = 1$;

Therefore $(\partial \ln p_B/\partial \ln x_B)_{p,T} = 1$ [G–D–M equation].

This is satisfied if $p_B = x_B p_B^*$ [by integration]. Hence, if A obeys Raoult's law, so does B.

8.10 $n_A dV_{A,m} + n_B dV_{B,m} = 0$ [Problem 8.8], and so $(n_A/n_B)dV_{A,m} = -dV_{B,m}$.

$$V_{B,m}(x_A) - V_{B,m}(0) = -\int_{V_{A,m}(0)}^{V_{A,m}(x_A)} (n_A/n_B)dV_{A,m} = -\int_{V_{A,m}(0)}^{V_{A,m}(x_A)} \left(\frac{x_A dV_{A,m}}{1 - x_A}\right).$$

$$\text{Therefore } V_{B,m}(x_A, x_B) = V_{B,m}(0,1) - \int_{V_{A,m}(0,1)}^{V_{A,m}(x_A, x_B)} \left(\frac{x_A dV_{A,m}}{1 - x_A}\right).$$

Plot $x_A/(1 - x_A)$ against $V_{A,m}$ and evaluate the integral. For the present purposes we need to integrate up to $V_{A,m}(\frac{1}{2}, \frac{1}{2}) = 74.06\ \text{cm}^3\ \text{mol}^{-1}$ [Problem 8.7]. Use the data in Problem 8.7 to construct the following Table:

$V_{A,m}/cm^3\,mol^{-1}$	74.11	73.96	73.50	72.74
x_A	0.6	0.4	0.2	0
$x_A/(1-x_A)$	1.50	0.67	0.25	0

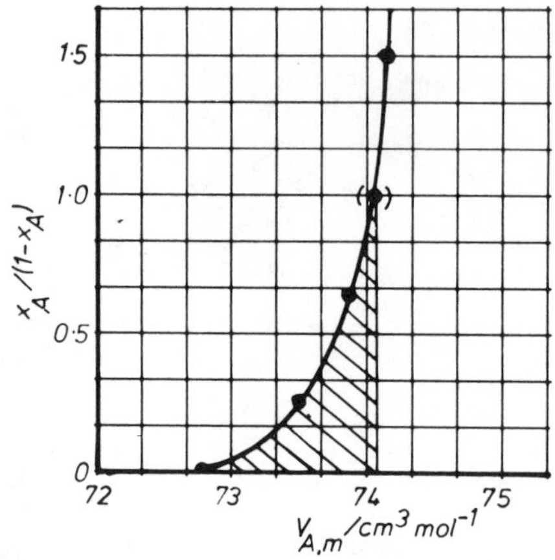

Fig 8·4

Draw Fig. 8.4. The area is 0.300, hence (identifying B as chloroform, and denoting it C):

$V_{C,m}(\frac{1}{2},\frac{1}{2}) = 80.66\ cm^3 - 0.30\ cm^3\,mol^{-1} = \underline{80.36\ cm^3\,mol^{-1}}.$

8.11 $\Delta G_{mix} = nRT\{x_A \ln x_A + x_B \ln x_B\}$ [8.2.1]; $x_A = x_B = \frac{1}{2}, n = pV/RT.$

$\Delta G_{mix} = pV \ln\frac{1}{2} = -(1.013 \times 10^5\ N\,m^{-2}) \times (5.0 \times 10^{-3}\ m^3) \ln 2 = \underline{-350\ J}.$

$\Delta S_{mix} = -(\Delta G_{mix}/T)$ [from 8.2.2] $= (+350\ J)/(298\ K) = \underline{1.2\ J\,K^{-1}}.$

8.12 (1) Expand nitrogen isothermally to 1 atm:

$G(N_2, 1\ atm) = G(N_2, 3\ atm) + n(N_2)RT \ln(1/3)$ [6.2.9].

(2) Allow components to mix:

$\Delta G_{mix} = nRT\{x(H_2) \ln x(H_2) + x(N_2) \ln x(N_2)\}$ [8.2.1]

$= nRT\{\frac{1}{4} \ln \frac{1}{4} + \frac{3}{4} \ln \frac{3}{4}\}$ $[x(H_2) = \frac{1}{4}, x(N_2) = \frac{3}{4}]$.

(3) Compress mixture back to initial volume (i.e. to $p = 2$ atm, the final pressure, since $p_f(N_2) = 1.5$ atm, $p_f(H_2) = 0.5$ atm): $G(\text{mixture}, 2\ atm) = G(\text{mixture}, 1\ atm) + nRT \ln 2$. Total change in Gibbs function:

$\Delta G = -n(N_2)RT\ln 3 + nRT\{\frac{1}{4}\ln\frac{1}{4} + \frac{3}{4}\ln\frac{3}{4}\} + nRT\ln 2.$

$n(N_2) = p_i(N_2)V_i/RT,\ n = p_f V_f/RT.$

Therefore $\Delta G = -p_i(N_2)V_i \times \ln 3 + p_f V_f\{\frac{1}{4}\ln\frac{1}{4} + \frac{3}{4}\ln\frac{3}{4} + \ln 2\}$

$p_i(N_2)V_i = 3 \times (1.013 \times 10^5\,\mathrm{N\,m^{-2}}) \times (2.5 \times 10^{-3}\,\mathrm{m^3}) = 760\,\mathrm{J}.$

$p_f V_f = 2 \times (1.013 \times 10^5\,\mathrm{N\,m^{-2}}) \times (5.0 \times 10^{-3}\,\mathrm{m^3}) = 1013\,\mathrm{J}.$

Therefore $\Delta G = -(760\,\mathrm{J})\ln 3 + (1013\,\mathrm{J})\{\frac{1}{4}\ln\frac{1}{4} + \frac{3}{4}\ln\frac{3}{4} + \ln 2\}$

$= (-830\,\mathrm{J}) + (130\,\mathrm{J}) = \underline{-700\,\mathrm{J}}.$

$\Delta S = -\Delta G/T$ [from 8.2.2, all contributions linear in T]

$= (700\,\mathrm{J})/(298\,\mathrm{K}) = \underline{2.4\,\mathrm{J\,K^{-1}}}.$

Perfect gases always mix spontaneously. Highly compressed real gases above their critical temperatures (so that, by definition, they are gases) may behave like immiscible liquids.

If the gases were the same, in this example there would be no Gibbs function or entropy of mixing. The ΔG would arise from the expansion from 3 atm to 2 atm of component A, and the compression of component B from 1 atm to 2 atm.

$\Delta G = n(A)RT\ln(2/3) + n(B)RT\ln(2/1)$ [6.2.9]

$= p_i(A)V_i\ln(2/3) + p_i(B)V_i\ln 2$

$= (760\,\mathrm{J})\ln(2/3) + (\frac{1}{3} \times 760\,\mathrm{J})\ln 2 = \underline{-133\,\mathrm{J}},$

using $V_i = 2.5\,\mathrm{dm^3}$, $p_i(A) = 3$ atm, $p_i(B) = 1$ atm.

8.13 $\Delta S_{mix} = -nR\sum_J x_J \ln x_J$ [8.2.2]

$\Delta S_{mix,m} = -R\{0.782\ln 0.782 + 0.209\ln 0.209 + 0.009\ln 0.009 + 0.0003\ln 0.0003\}$

$= 0.564R = \underline{4.69\,\mathrm{J\,K^{-1}\,mol^{-1}}}.$

8.14 $\Delta G_{mix} = nRT\sum_J x_J \ln x_J$ [8.2.1]

$\Delta S_{mix} = -nR\sum_J x_J \ln x_J$ [8.2.2]

$$\left.\begin{array}{l} n(\text{hex}) = (500\,\mathrm{g})/(86.178\,\mathrm{g\,mol^{-1}}) = 5.80\,\mathrm{mol} \\ n(\text{hep}) = (500\,\mathrm{g})/(100.20\,\mathrm{g\,mol^{-1}}) = 4.99\,\mathrm{mol} \end{array}\right\} n = 10.79\,\mathrm{mol}$$

$x(\text{hex}) = 5.80/10.79 = 0.538,\ x(\text{hep}) = 4.99/10.79 = 0.462.$

$\Delta G_{mix} = (10.79\,\mathrm{mol}) \times (2.48\,\mathrm{kJ\,mol^{-1}}) \times (0.537\ln 0.537 + 0.462\ln 0.462)$

$= \underline{-18.5\,\mathrm{kJ}}.$

$\Delta S_{mix} = (18.5 \times 10^3\,\mathrm{J})/(298\,\mathrm{K}) = \underline{62.0\,\mathrm{J\,K^{-1}}}.$

$\Delta H_{mix} = \underline{0}$ [8.2.3].

8.15 Find the condition for the maximum of $|\Delta G_{mix}|$. This is the maximum of $|x_A \ln x_A + x_B \ln x_B|$.

$$(d/dx_A)(x_A \ln x_A + x_B \ln x_B) = \ln x_A + x_A \left(\frac{d\ln x_A}{dx_A}\right) + \left(\frac{dx_B}{dx_A}\right) \ln x_B + x_B \left(\frac{d\ln x_B}{dx_A}\right) = 0.$$

$$\frac{d\ln x_A}{dx_A} = \frac{1}{x_A}, \frac{dx_B}{dx_A} = -1 \; [x_B = 1 - x_A], \frac{d\ln x_B}{dx_A} = -\frac{d\ln x_B}{dx_B} = -\frac{1}{x_B}.$$

Therefore $\ln x_A + 1 - \ln x_B - 1 = 0$, or $\ln x_A = \ln x_B$, and so $|\Delta G_{mix}|$ is a maximum when $x_A = x_B = 1 - x_A$; i.e. at $x_A = \frac{1}{2}$. Therefore (a) mix equal mole fractions, or (b) mix masses in the ratio of the RMMS, $M(\text{hex})/M(\text{hep}) = M_r(\text{hex})/M_r(\text{hep}) = 86.18/100.2 = \underline{0.860}$.

8.16 $p = Kx$ [8.2.9], $K = 1.25 \times 10^6$ Torr [Table 8.1];

$x = n(CO_2)/[n(CO_2) + n(H_2O)] \approx n(CO_2)/n(H_2O)$ so that

$n(CO_2) = n(H_2O)p(CO_2)/K = (1000\text{ g}/18.02\text{ g mol}^{-1}) \times (p/1.25 \times 10^6\text{ Torr})$

$= (4.44 \times 10^{-5}\text{ mol}) \times (p/\text{Torr})$ for 1 kg solvent (water).

(a) $p = 0.10\text{ atm} \triangleq 76\text{ Torr}$; $n(CO_2) = (4.44 \times 10^{-5}\text{ mol}) \times 76$

$= \underline{3.4 \times 10^{-3}\text{ mol.}}$ i.e. the solubility is $\underline{3.4\text{ mmol kg}^{-1}}$.

(b) $p = 1.0\text{ atm} \triangleq 760\text{ Torr}$; $n(CO_2) = \underline{3.4 \times 10^{-2}\text{ mol.}}$

I.e. the molality is $\underline{34\text{ mmol kg}^{-1}}$.

8.17 $K(N_2) = 6.51 \times 10^7$ Torr, $K(O_2) = 3.30 \times 10^7$ Torr;

$p(N_2) = 0.782 \times 760$ Torr, $p(O_2) = 0.209 \times 760$ Torr.

$n(N_2) \approx n(H_2O)p(N_2)/K(N_2)$; $n(H_2O) = (1000\text{ g})/(18.02\text{ g mol}^{-1}) = 55.5\text{mol}$.

$n(N_2) \approx (55.5\text{ mol}) \times (0.782 \times 760\text{ Torr})/(6.51 \times 10^7\text{ mmHg}) = 5.07 \times 10^{-4}$ mol.

$n(O_2) = (55.5\text{ mol}) \times (0.209 \times 760\text{ Torr})/(3.30 \times 10^7\text{ mmHg}) = 2.67 \times 10^{-4}$ mol.

These amounts correspond to 1 kg solvent; therefore, the molalities are $\underline{5 \times 10^{-4}\text{ mol kg}^{-1}}$ for nitrogen, and $3 \times 10^{-4}\text{ mol kg}^{-1}$ for oxygen.

8.18 Use Problem 8.16 with $p = 10$ atm: $n(CO_2) = 3.4 \times 10^{-1}$ mol. That is, the molaity is about $\underline{0.3\text{ mol kg}^{-1}}$ (a concentration of about 0.3 M).

8.19 Draw up the following Table.

$n(H_2O)$/mol	55.49	55.49	55.49	55.49
$n(CH_3Cl)$/mol	0.029	0.051	0.106	0.131
n(total)	55.52	55.54	55.60	55.62
$x(CH_3Cl)$	0.0005	0.0009	0.0019	0.0024
p/mmHg	205.2	363.2	756.1	945.9

Plot p against x, Fig. 8.5, and find a straight line. Since the slope is 3.94×10^5, and the intercept $p = 0$ at $x = 0$, the intercept at $x = 1$ is 3.94×10^5. Hence $K = 3.94 \times 10^5$ mmHg.

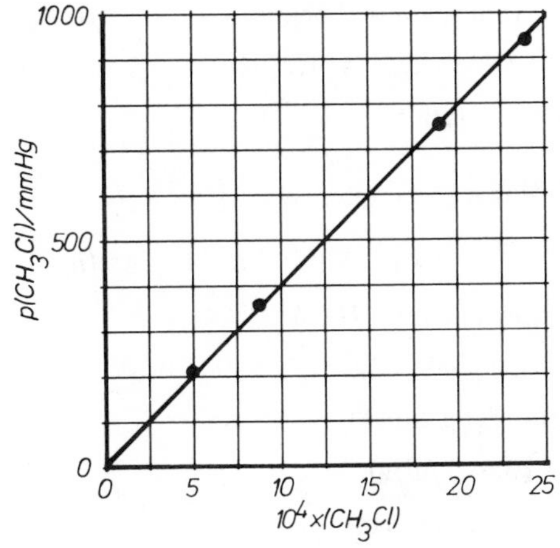

Fig 8·5

8.20 $p = p_A + p_B = x_A p_A^* + x_B p_B^*$ [8.4.2]. For boiling, $p = 0.5$ atm $\triangleq$ 380 mmHg. $p_A^* = 400$ mmHg, $p_B^* = 150$ mmHg.

Therefore solve $380 = 400\, x_A + 150(1 - x_A)$ [A: toluene]

Therefore, the mole fractions of the toluene/o-xylene mixture should be in the ratio 0.920:0.080 = 11.5:1.

The vapor composition is given by

$$y_A = \frac{x_A p_A^*}{p_B^* + (p_A^* - p_B^*)x_A} \text{ [8.4.3]} = \frac{0.920 \times 400}{150 + (400 - 150)0.920} = 0.968.$$

Therefore, the mole fractions in the vapor of toluene and o-xylene are in the ratio 0.968:0.032 = 30.3:1 (NB richer in toluene, the more volatile component).

8.21 $K_b = RT_b^{*2} M_{A,m}/\Delta H_{vap,m}$ [8.3.1];

$K_f = RT_f^{*2} M_{A,m}/\Delta H_{melt,m}$ [8.3.3]

$K_b = (8.314\,J\,K^{-1}\,mol^{-1}) \times (350\,K)^2 \times (153.8 \times 10^{-3}\,kg\,mol^{-1})/(30.0 \times 10^3\,J\,mol^{-1})$

$= 5.22\,K\,kg\,mol^{-1}$

$= \underline{5.22\,K/(mol\,kg^{-1})}.$

$K_f = (8.314\,J\,K^{-1}\,mol^{-1}) \times (250.3\,K)^2 \times (153.8 \times 10^{-3}\,kg\,mol^{-1})/(2.5 \times 10^3\,J\,mol^{-1})$

$= 32.0\,K\,kg\,mol^{-1} = \underline{32.0\,K/(mol\,kg^{-1})}.$

8.22 $K_f(\text{water}) = 1.86\,K/(mol\,kg^{-1})$, $\Delta T = K_f m_B$ [8.3.4]

$n_B = 2 \times (2\,g/58.44\,g\,mol^{-1}) = 0.068\,mol$ [$\times$ 2 because the NaCl ionizes into 2 ions]. Since 2 g is dissolved in 100 g water, $m_B = 0.68\,mol\,kg^{-1}$; therefore

$\Delta T = (0.68\,mol\,kg^{-1}) \times (1.86\,K/mol\,kg^{-1}) = 1.27\,K,$

and so the freezing point of the solution is $\underline{-1.3\,°C}$.

8.23 Let B denote benzene and A the solute.

$p_B = x_B p_B^*$ [8.2.7], $x_B = n_B/(n_A + n_B)$, and so $p_B = n_B p_B^*/(n_A + n_B)$.

Therefore $n_A = n_B(p_B^* - p_B)/p_B$, $n_A = M_A/M_{A,m}$.

$M_{A,m} = M_A p_B/n_B(p_B^* - p_B)$; $M_A = 19\,g$, $p_B^* = 400\,Torr$,

$p_B = 386\,Torr$, $n_B = (500\,g)/(78.1\,g\,mol^{-1}) = 6.40\,mol$.

$$\text{Therefore } M_{A,m} = \frac{(19\,g) \times (386\,mmHg)}{(6.40\,mol) \times (14\,mmHg)} = 82\,g\,mol^{-1}, \text{ and so } M_r = \underline{82}.$$

8.24 $\Delta T = K_f m_B$ [8.3.4], $K_f = 40\,K/mol\,kg^{-1}$.

$M_m\,[CF_3(CF_2)_3CF_3] = 288.1$; $M_m\,[CF_3(CF_2)_4CF_3] = 338.1$.

The amounts of substance corresponding to 1 g are

$n\,[CF_3(CF_2)_3CF_3] = 3.47 \times 10^{-3}\,mol$, $n\,[CF_3(CF_2)_4CF_3] = 2.96 \times 10^{-3}\,mol$.

The molalities of the two solutions formed from 1.0 g in 100 g solvent are therefore

$m\,[CF_3(CF_2)_3CF_3] = 0.0347\,mol\,kg^{-1}$, $m\,[CF_3(CF_2)_4CF_3] = 0.0296\,mol\,kg^{-1}$.

The freezing point depressions are therefore:

$\Delta T\,[CF_3(CF_2)_3CF_3] = (0.0347\,mol\,kg^{-1}) \times (40\,K/mol\,kg^{-1}) = 1.4\,K$;

$\Delta T\,[CF_3(CF_2)_4CF_3] = (0.0296\,mol\,kg^{-1}) \times (40\,K/mol\,kg^{-1}) = 1.2\,K$.

The temperature measurement must be able to distinguish between these two depressions, e.g. ±0.05 K.

8.25 $\ln x_A = -\Delta G_{\text{melt,m}}(T)/RT$ [Section 8.3(b)]

$$\mathrm{d}\ln x_A/\mathrm{d}T = -(1/R)\,(\mathrm{d}/\mathrm{d}T)\,[\Delta G_{\text{melt,m}}(T)/T]$$

$$= \Delta H_{\text{melt,m}}(T)/RT^2 \quad [G\text{–}H \text{ equation, 6.2.4}].$$

$$\int_1^{x_A} \mathrm{d}\ln x_A = \int_{T^*}^{T} \left\{\frac{\Delta H_{\text{melt,m}}(T)\,\mathrm{d}T}{RT^2}\right\}.$$

Take $\Delta H_{\text{melt,m}}(T) \approx \Delta H_{\text{melt,m}}(T^*)$; then

$$\ln x_A \Big|_1^{x_A} \approx \{\Delta H_{\text{melt,m}}(T^*)/R\} \int_{T^*}^{T} \left(\frac{\mathrm{d}T}{T^2}\right) = -\left\{\frac{\Delta H_{\text{melt,m}}(T^*)}{R}\right\}\left(\frac{1}{T}-\frac{1}{T^*}\right);$$

$$\ln x_A = \ln(1-x_B) \approx -x_B;$$

$$\text{therefore } x_B \approx \frac{\Delta H_{\text{melt,m}}(T^*)}{R}\left(\frac{1}{T}-\frac{1}{T^*}\right),$$

or $\Delta T = T^* - T \approx (RT^{*2}/\Delta H_{\text{melt,m}})x_B$, as before.

8.26 $\Delta H_{\text{melt,m}}(T) = \Delta H_{\text{melt,m}}(T^*) + \int_{T^*}^{T} \Delta C_{p,\text{m}}(T)\,\mathrm{d}T$ [4.1.6, p is constant]

with $\Delta C_{p,\text{m}}(T) = C_{p,\text{m}}(\text{l};T) - C_{p,\text{m}}(\text{s},T) \approx \Delta C_{p,\text{m}}(T^*)$, a constant.
Therefore $\Delta H_{\text{melt,m}}(T) \approx \Delta H_{\text{melt,m}}(T^*) + (T-T^*)\Delta C_{p,\text{m}}(T^*)$, and

$$\ln x_A = \int_{T^*}^{T} \{\Delta H_{\text{melt,m}}(T)/RT^2\}\mathrm{d}T$$

$$= \int_{T^*}^{T} \{\Delta H_{\text{melt,m}}(T^*) - T^*\Delta C_{p,\text{m}}(T^*)/RT^2\}\mathrm{d}T + \int_{T^*}^{T} \{\Delta C_{p,\text{m}}(T^*)/RT\}\mathrm{d}T$$

$$= \{\Delta H_{\text{melt,m}} - T^*\Delta C_{p,\text{m}}\}\frac{1}{R}\left(\frac{1}{T^*}-\frac{1}{T}\right) + (\Delta C_{p,\text{m}}/R)\ln(T/T^*)$$

with ΔH, ΔC relating to T^*. Write $\Delta T = T^* - T$, then

$$\ln x_A = -\left\{\frac{\Delta H_{\text{melt,m}} - T^*\Delta C_{p,\text{m}}}{RT^*}\right\}\left(\frac{\Delta T}{T}\right) + \left\{\frac{\Delta C_{p,\text{m}}}{R}\right\}\ln\left(1-\frac{\Delta T}{T^*}\right).$$

Use $\ln x_A = \ln(1-x_B) \approx -x_B$ and $\Delta T/T^* \ll 1$ to write

$$\Delta T/T = \Delta T/(T^*-\Delta T) = (\Delta T/T^*)/(1-\Delta T/T^*) \approx \Delta T/T^* + (\Delta T/T^{*2})$$

$\ln(1-\Delta T/T^*) \approx -\Delta T/T^* + (\Delta T/T^*)^2$.

Then $x_B \approx \left\{\dfrac{\Delta H_{\text{melt,m}} - T^*\Delta C_{p,\text{m}}}{RT^*}\right\}\left\{\dfrac{\Delta T}{T^*} + \left(\dfrac{\Delta T}{T^*}\right)^2\right\} + \left\{\dfrac{\Delta C_{p,\text{m}}}{R}\right\}\left\{\dfrac{\Delta T}{T^*} - \left(\dfrac{\Delta T}{T^*}\right)^2\right\}$

$$\approx \left\{\frac{\Delta H_{\text{melt,m}}}{RT^{*2}}\right\}\Delta T + \left\{\frac{\Delta H_{\text{melt,m}} - 2T^*\Delta C_{p,\text{m}}}{RT^{*3}}\right\}\Delta T^2 = a\Delta T + b\Delta T^2.$$

The solution of $b\Delta T^2 + a\Delta T - x_B = 0$ is

$$\Delta T = \left(\frac{1}{2b}\right)\{-a + \surd[a^2 + 4bx_B]\}\ [+\text{ root because } \Delta T = 0 \text{ when } x_B = 0]$$

$$= \left(\frac{a}{2b}\right)\{-1 + \surd[1 + 4bx_B/a^2]\} \approx \left(\frac{a}{2b}\right)\{-1 + 1 + 2bx_B/a^2\}$$

$\approx x_B/a = \{RT^{*2}/\Delta H_{\text{melt,m}}\}x_B$, as before.

Alternative 'exact' solution is obtained from

$b\Delta T^2 + a\Delta T + \ln x_A = 0$, or $\underline{\Delta T = (a/2b)\{-1 + \surd[1 - (4b/a^2)\ln x_A]\}}$.

With $\Delta H_{\text{melt,m}} = 6.01\ \text{kJ mol}^{-1}$, $\Delta C_{p,\text{m}} = 51.0\ \text{J K}^{-1}\ \text{mol}^{-1}$, $T^* = 273.15\ \text{K}$

$$a = \frac{\Delta H_{\text{melt,m}}}{RT^{*2}} = \frac{6.01\ \text{kJ mol}^{-1}}{(8.3144\ \text{J K}^{-1}\ \text{mol}^{-1}) \times (273.15\ \text{K})^2} = 9.69 \times 10^{-3}\ \text{K}^{-1}$$

$$b = \frac{\Delta H_{\text{melt,m}} - 2T^*\Delta C_{p,\text{m}}}{RT^{*3}} = \frac{[6.01 \times 10^3 - 2 \times (273.15) \times (51.0)]\ \text{J mol}^{-1}}{(8.3144\ \text{J K}^{-1}\ \text{mol}^{-1}) \times (273.15\ \text{K})^3}$$

$= -1.29 \times 10^{-4}\ \text{K}^{-2}$.

$a/2b = -37.6\ \text{K}$, $4b/a^2 = -5.50$.

Therefore, in the case of $x_B = 0.1$, the simple solution gives

$\Delta T \approx x_B/a = 0.1/(9.69 \times 10^{-3}\ \text{K}^{-1}) = 10.3\ \text{K}$,

while the more complete solution gives

$\Delta T \approx (37.6\ \text{K})\{1 - \surd[1 + 5.50 \ln x_A] \approx \underline{13.2\ \text{K.}}$

8.27 $n(\text{sucrose}) = (7.5\ \text{g})/(342.3\ \text{g mol}^{-1}) = 0.0219\ \text{mol}$;

$n(\text{water}) = (250\ \text{g})/(18.02\ \text{g mol}^{-1}) = 13.87\ \text{mol}$; $n(\text{total}) = 13.90\ \text{mol}$.

$x_B = 0.0219/13.90 = 0.0016$, $x_A = 0.9984$.

$\Delta T = (37.6)\{1 - \surd[1 + 5.50 \ln 0.9984]\}$ [last Problem] $= 0.17\ \text{K}$.

Therefore, the freezing point is $\underline{-0.17\ \text{K}}$.

8.28 $\Delta T = K_f m_s$ [8.3.4]. Let c denote the price of the salt per 100 kg. In order to achieve the same lowering of freezing point we require $m_A(\mathrm{NaCl}) = m_B(\mathrm{CaCl_2})$. But NaCl gives two ions, while $CaCl_2$, gives three. Therefore the amounts of substance of the salts must satisfy $n(\mathrm{NaCl}) = (3/2)n(\mathrm{CaCl_2})$. The masses must satisfy

$M(\mathrm{NaCl})/M_r(\mathrm{NaCl}) = (3/2)M(\mathrm{CaCl_2})/M_r(\mathrm{CaCl_2})$ or

$$M(\mathrm{NaCl})/M(\mathrm{CaCl_2}) = (3/2)M_r(\mathrm{NaCl})/M_r(\mathrm{CaCl_2}) = \frac{3 \times 58.44}{2 \times 110.98} = 0.79.$$

But $c(\mathrm{NaCl})/c(\mathrm{CaCl_2}) = 1.3$. Therefore $\mathrm{Cost(NaCl)/Cost(CaCl_2)} = 1.3 \times 0.79 = 1.03$.

Hence use $CaCl_2$.

8.29 $\Delta T_f = RT_f^2\, x_B/\Delta H_{\mathrm{melt,m}}$ [8.3.3];

$\Delta H_{\mathrm{melt,m}} = 11.4\,\mathrm{kJ\,mol^{-1}}$, $T_f = 290\,\mathrm{K}$, $M_r(\mathrm{AcOH}) = 60.05$ (1 kg $\widehat{=}$ 16.7 mol).

$$\Delta T_f = \{(8.314\,\mathrm{J\,K^{-1}\,mol^{-1}}) \times (290\,\mathrm{K})^2/(11.4\,\mathrm{kJ\,mol^{-1}})\}\,(m_B/16.7\,\mathrm{mol\,kg^{-1}})$$
$$= (3.67\,\mathrm{K/mol\,kg^{-1}})m_B$$

where m_B is the apparent molality of the solute. Write this as νm_B° where ν is the number of ions. Draw up the following Table.

$m^\circ(\mathrm{KF})/\mathrm{mol\,kg^{-1}}$	0.0015	0.037	0.077	0.295	0.602
$\Delta T_f/\mathrm{K}$	0.116	0.299	0.473	1.39	2.69
$m_B(\mathrm{KF})/\mathrm{mol\,kg^{-1}}$	0.0315	0.0814	0.129	0.378	0.734
ν	2.1	2.2	1.68	1.28	1.22

See original reference.

8.30 $m_B = \Delta T/K_f = (0.0703\,\mathrm{K})/(1.86\,\mathrm{K/mol\,kg^{-1}}) = 0.0378\,\mathrm{mol\,kg^{-1}}$. Since the solution is $0.0096\,\mathrm{mol\,kg^{-1}}$ in $Th(NO_3)_4$, the nitrate must dissociate into 0.0378/0.0096 = 4 ions. (More careful treatment of the data, see original reference, gives either 5 or 6.)

8.31 $$x_B = \exp\left\{\left(\frac{\Delta H_{\mathrm{melt,m}}}{R}\right)\left(\frac{1}{T^*} - \frac{1}{T}\right)\right\} \quad [8.3.5]$$

$$= \exp\left\{\frac{(5.2\,\mathrm{kJ\,mol^{-1}}) \times (-47.0\,\mathrm{K})}{(8.314\,\mathrm{J\,K^{-1}\,mol^{-1}}) \times (600\,\mathrm{K})^2}\right\} = \exp(-0.089) = \underline{0.92}.$$

$x_B = n(\mathrm{Pb})/[n(\mathrm{Pb}) + n(\mathrm{Bi})]$, so that $n(\mathrm{Pb}) = [x_B/(1 - x_B)]\,n(\mathrm{Bi})$.

For 1 kg Bi, $n(\mathrm{Bi}) = (10^3\,\mathrm{g})/(209\,\mathrm{g\,mol^{-1}}) = 4.8\,\mathrm{mol}$.

Therefore $n(\mathrm{Pb}) = (0.92/0.08)n(\mathrm{Bi}) = 55\,\mathrm{mol}$, or 11 kg(!)

8.32 $$x_\mathrm{B} = \exp\left\{\left(\frac{\Delta H_\mathrm{melt,m}}{R}\right)\left(\frac{1}{T^*} - \frac{1}{T}\right)\right\} \quad [8.3.5]$$

$$= \exp\left\{\left(\frac{28.87\,\mathrm{kJ\,mol^{-1}}}{8.314\,\mathrm{J\,K^{-1}\,mol^{-1}}}\right)\left(\frac{1}{490\,\mathrm{K}} - \frac{1}{298\,\mathrm{K}}\right)\right\}$$

$= \exp(-4.57) = 0.010$.

$n(\mathrm{anthr}) = (0.010/0.990) \times n(\mathrm{benzene}) = 0.011\,n(\mathrm{benzene})$.

1 kg benzene is an amount of substance $n(\mathrm{benzene}) = (1000\,\mathrm{g}/78.12\,\mathrm{g\,mol^{-1}})$ $= 12.8\,\mathrm{mol}$. Therefore $n(\mathrm{anthr}) = 0.13\,\mathrm{mol}$, or 24 g.

That is, 24 g anthracene will dissolve in 1 kg benzene at 25 °C if the solubility is ideal.

8.33 $\Pi = (n_\mathrm{B}/V)RT\,[8.3.10] = (M_\mathrm{B}/M_\mathrm{B,m}V)RT$

$= c_\mathrm{B}RT/M_\mathrm{B,m}$ where $c_\mathrm{B} = M_\mathrm{B}/V$.

$\Pi = \rho g h$ [hydrostatic pressure]; therefore $h = (RT/\rho g M_\mathrm{B,m})c_\mathrm{B}$.

Hence, plot h against c_B, identify the slope as $RT/\rho g M_\mathrm{B,m}$, and so find $M_\mathrm{B,m}$. Figure 8.6 shows the plot. We find slope = 0.29, so that

$RT/\rho g M_\mathrm{B,m} = 0.29\,\mathrm{cm/g\,dm^{-3}}$.

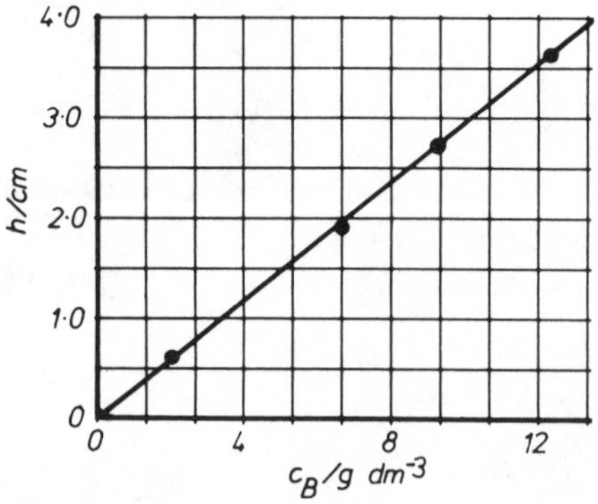

Fig 8·6

$$RT/\rho g = \frac{(8.314\,\mathrm{J\,K^{-1}\,mol^{-1}}) \times (298.15\,\mathrm{K})}{(1.004\,\mathrm{g\,cm^{-3}}) \times (9.81\,\mathrm{m\,s^{-2}})} = 251.8\,\mathrm{J\,g^{-1}\,cm^3\,m^{-1}\,s^2\,mol^{-1}}$$

$= 251.8\,\mathrm{kg\,m^2\,s^{-2}\,g^{-1}\,cm^3\,m^{-1}\,s^2\,mol^{-1}}$ [$\mathrm{J = kg\,m^2\,s^{-2}}$]

$= 251.8\,(\mathrm{kg/g})\,(\mathrm{m^4} \times 10^{-6})\,\mathrm{mol^{-1}}\ [\mathrm{cm^3} = 10^{-6}\,\mathrm{m^3}]$

$= 251.8 \times 10^{-3}\,\mathrm{m^4\,mol^{-1}}\ [\mathrm{kg/g} = 10^3]$.

$$M_{\mathrm{B,m}} = \frac{0.2518\,\mathrm{m^4\,mol^{-1}}}{0.29\,\mathrm{cm\,dm^3\,g^{-1}}} = \frac{0.2518}{0.29} \times 10^2 \times 10^3\,\mathrm{g\,mol^{-1}}$$

$= 87\,000\,\mathrm{g\,mol^{-1}}$. Therefore, the RMM is $\underline{87\,000.}$

8.34 Proceed as in Problem 8.33. The plot is shown in Fig. 8.7, and the slope has the value 1.78.

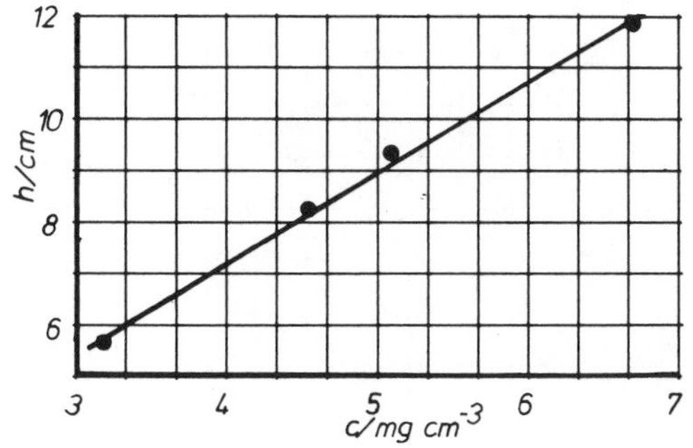

Fig 8·7

$RT/\rho g M_{\mathrm{B,m}} = 1.78\,\mathrm{cm/mg\,cm^{-3}} = 1.78\,\mathrm{cm^4\,mg^{-1}}$.

$$RT/\rho g = \frac{(8.314\,\mathrm{J\,K^{-1}\,mol^{-1}}) \times (293.15\,\mathrm{K})}{(1.000\,\mathrm{g\,cm^{-3}}) \times (9.81\,\mathrm{m\,s^{-2}})} = 0.249\,\mathrm{m^4\,mol^{-1}}.$$

$$M_{\mathrm{B,m}} = \frac{0.249\,\mathrm{m^4\,mol^{-1}}}{1.78\,\mathrm{cm^4\,mg^{-1}}} = 0.140\,(\mathrm{m^4/cm^4})\,(\mathrm{mg/g})\,\mathrm{g\,mol^{-1}}$$

$= 0.140 \times 10^8 \times 10^{-3}\,\mathrm{g\,mol^{-1}} = 14\,000\,\mathrm{g\,mol^{-1}}$.

Therefore, the RMM is $\underline{14\,000.}$

8.35 The data are plotted in Fig. 8.8.

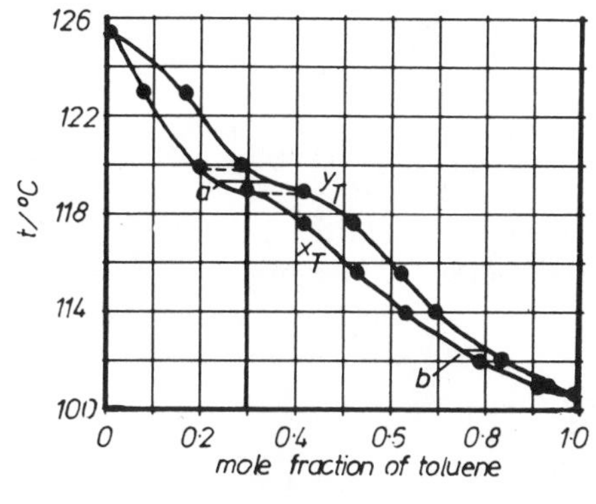

Fig 8·8

From the graph, the vapor in equilibrium with a liquid of composition (a) $x_T = 0.25$ has $y_T = 0.36$, (b) $x_T = 0.75$ has $y_T = 0.82$.

8.36. Raoult's law basis: $a = p/p^*$ [8.5.4], $a = \gamma x$ [8.5.5]; $\gamma = p/xp^*$.

Henry's law basis: $\gamma_B = p_B/K_B x_B$ [8.5.10 and 11].

Plot data and extrapolate low-concentration lines to find K. This is done in Fig. 8.9. We find $K_I = 465$ mmHg. Draw up the following Table.

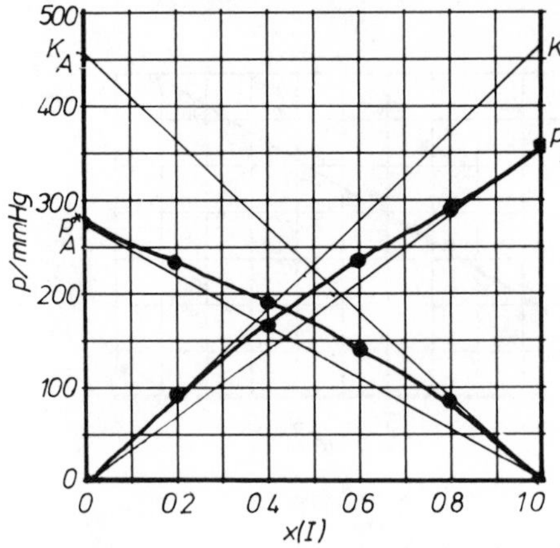

Fig 8·9

x_I	0	0.2	0.4	0.6	0.8	1.0	
p_I/mmHg	0	92	165	230	290	353($=p_I^*$)	
p_A/mmHg	280($=p_A^*$)	230	185	135	80	0	
$\gamma_I^{(R)}$	–	1.303	1.169	1.086	1.027	1.000	$[p_I/x_I p_I^*]$
$\gamma_A^{(R)}$	1.000	1.027	1.101	1.205	1.429	–	$[p_A/x_A p_A^*]$
$\gamma_I^{(H)}$	1.000	0.989	0.887	0.824	0.780	0.759	$[p_I/K_I x_I]$

8.37 Refer to Fig. 8.8. A liquid of composition $x_T = 0.3$ boils at 119 °C. The composition of the vapor (and hence the first drop of distillate) is obtained from the tie line: $y_T = 0.410$. Determine proportions from the lever rule [8.4.5] $n(\text{g})/n(\text{l}) = (z - x)/(y - z)$. Since at the b.pt. $z = x$, $n(\text{g})/n(\text{l}) = 0$, and there is only a trace of vapor. At 1 °C above the boiling temperature (120 °C), virtually the whole is vapor, with composition $y_T = 0.3$.

8.38 Figure 8.10 is a reproduction of Fig. 8.8. Start from $x_T = 0.3$ and draw a descending staircase until the point $y_T = 0.7$ is reached (this gives a condenstate with $x_T = 0.7$). From the diagram, we require 4 steps. Hence there are 4 theoretical plates.

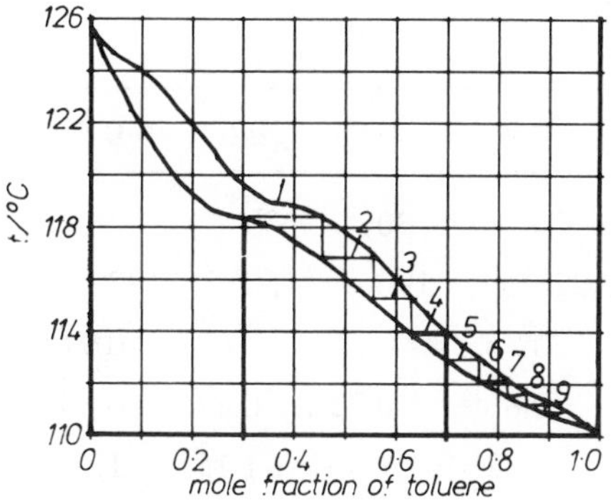

Fig 8·10

8.39 In order to reach a condensate with x_T not less than 0.9 it is necessary to reach a vapor with y_T not less than 0.9. Draw the descending staircase until this point is reached or passed. Figure. 8.10 shows that 5 further plates are required. Therefore at least a 9 plate column is required.

8.40 The plot of the data is shown in Fig. 8.11. The regions where the v.p. curves should approximate straight lines are denoted R, H for Raoult and Henry Law behavior respectively. A,B denote acetic acid and benzene.

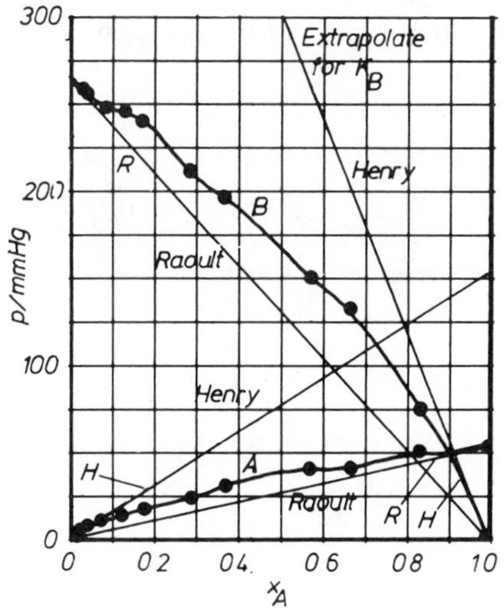

Fig 8·11

8.41 As in Problem 8.36 we require $\gamma_A^{(R)} = p_A/x_A p_A^*$, $\gamma_B^{(R)} = p_B/x_B p_B^*$, $\gamma_B^{(H)} = p_B/x_B K_B$. For the activities use $a^{(R)} = p/p^*$ and $a_B^{(H)} = p_B/K_B$. From Fig. 8.11 we have $p_A^* = 55$ mmHg, $p_B^* = 264$ mmHg, $K_B = 600$ mmHg. Draw up the following Table.

x_A	0	0.2	0.4	0.6	0.8	1.0	
p_A/mmHg	0	20	30	38	50	55($=p_A^*$)	
p_B/mmHg	264($=p_B^*$)	228	190	150	93	0	
$a_A^{(R)}$	0	0.36	0.55	0.69	0.91	1.00	[p_A/p_A^*]
$a_B^{(R)}$	1.00	0.86	0.72	0.57	0.35	0	[p_B/p_B^*]
$\gamma_A^{(R)}$	–	1.82	1.36	1.15	1.14	1.00	[$p_A/x_A p_A^*$]
$\gamma_B^{(R)}$	1.00	1.08	1.20	1.42	1.76	–	[$p_B/x_B p_B^*$]
$a_B^{(H)}$	0.44	0.38	0.32	0.25	0.16	0	[p_B/K_B]
$\gamma_B^{(H)}$	0.44	0.48	0.53	0.63	0.78	1.00	[$p_B/K_B x_B$]

8.42 $G_m^E = RT(x_A \ln \gamma_A + x_B \ln \gamma_B)$ [Section 8.2(d)] Draw up the following Table from the information in Problem 8.41 and $RT = 2.48$ kJ mol^{-1}:

x_A	0	0.2	0.4	0.6	0.8	1.0
$x_A \ln\gamma_A^{(R)}$	0	0.12	0.12	0.08	0.10	0
$x_B \ln\gamma_B^{(R)}$	0	0.06	0.11	0.14	0.11	0
G_m^E/kJ mol^{-1}	0	0.45	0.57	0.55	0.52	0

9. Equilibria: the general situation

A9.1

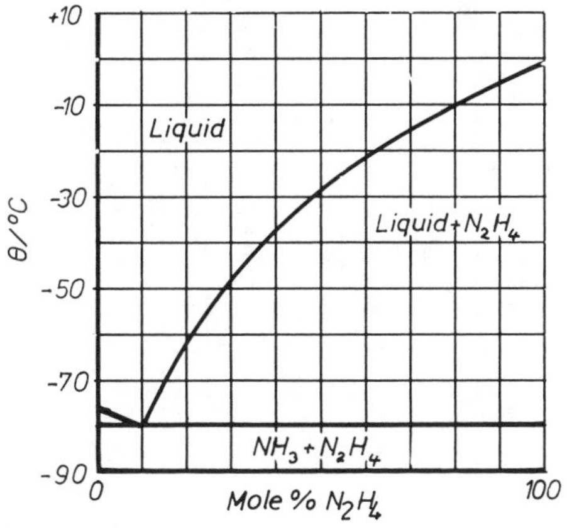

Fig A9.1

A9.2

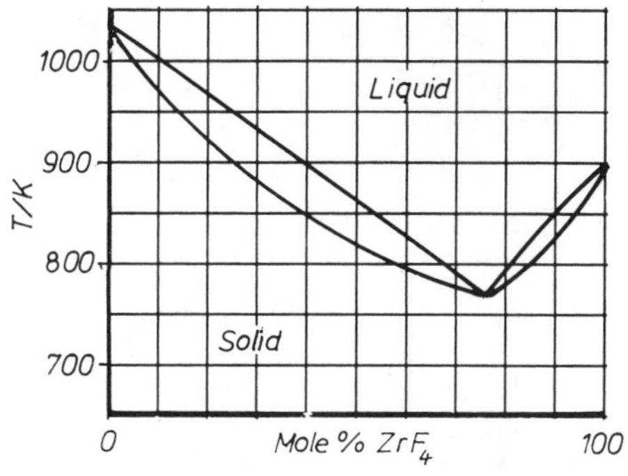

Fig A9.2

A solid solution which is 21 mol % ZrF_4 appears at 875 °C. The solid solution continues to form, and its ZrF_4 content increases until it reaches 40 mol % at 820 °C. At that temperature the liquid phase disappears.

A9.3

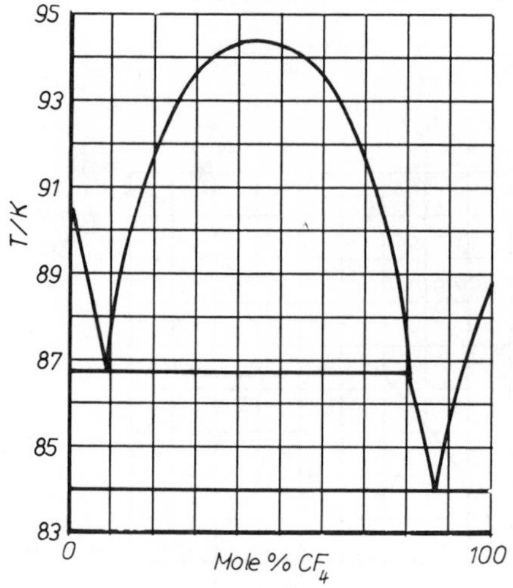

Fig A9.3

A9.4

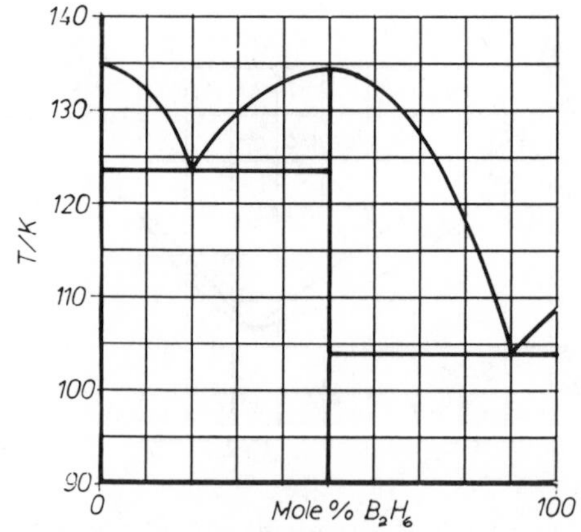

Fig A9.4

At 120 K, the solid compound beings to crystallize. The liquid becomes progressively richer in diborane until the liquid composition reaches 90 mol % at 104 K. At that point the liquid disappears as heat is withdrawn. Below 104 K, the system is a mixture of solid compound and solid diborane.

A9.5

Fig A9.5

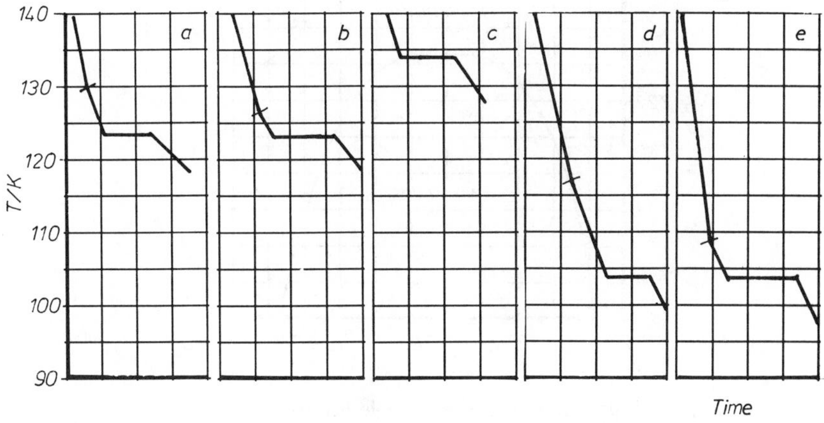

A9.6

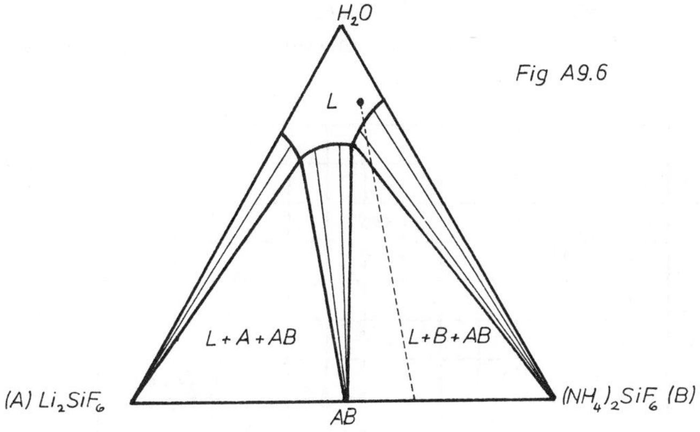

The composition points fall on the dotted line in Fig. 9.6. The first solid to appear is $(NH_4)_2SiF_6$. When the water content reaches 70.4 wt %, both $(NH_4)_2SiF_6$ and the double salt crystallize as more and more water is removed. The solution concentration remains fixed until the H_2O disappears.

A9.7

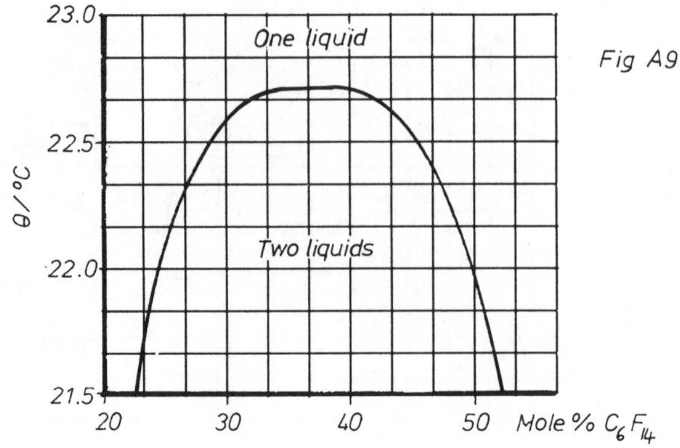

Fig A9.7

(a) For all compositions, the mixture is a single liquid phase.
(b) When the overall composition reaches 25 mol % C_6F_{14}, the mixture separates into two liquid phases, which are 25 and 48 mol % C_6F_{14}, respectively. The relative amounts of these phases change until the overall composition reaches 48 mol % C_6F_{14}. At all concentrations above that value, the mixture is a single liquid phase.

A9.8

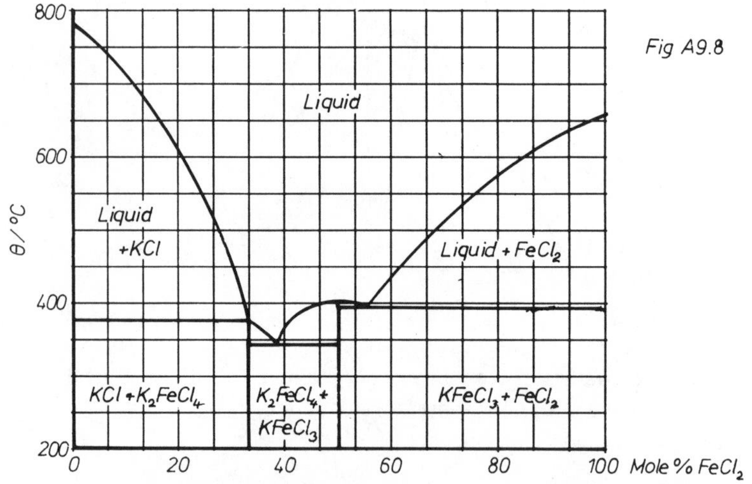

Fig A9.8

At 360 °C, K_2FeCl_4(s) appears. The solution becomes richer in $FeCl_2$ until the temperature reaches 351 °C, at which point $KFeCl_3$(s) also appears. Below 351 °C, the system is a mixture of K_2FeCl_4(s) and $KFeCl_3$(s).

A9.9

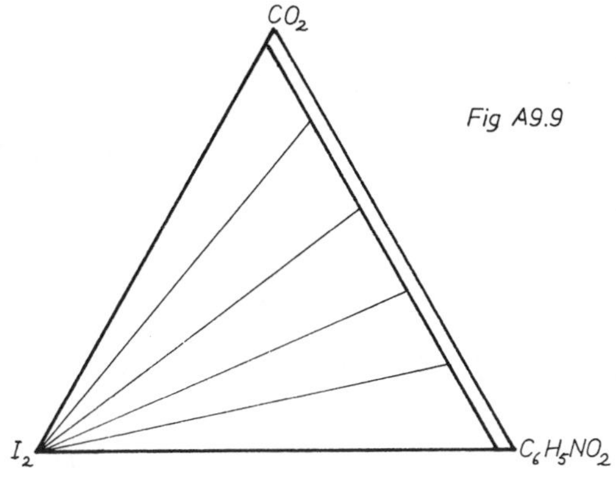

A9.10

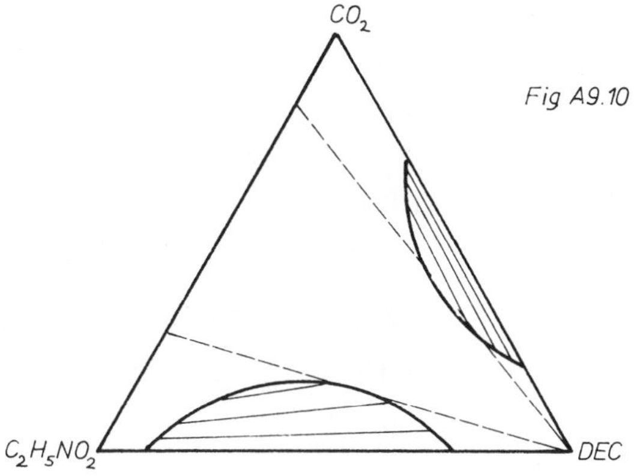

(b) Between 29 and 83 mol % $C_2H_5NO_2$.

9.1 $F = C - P + 2$. $C = 1$; at transition point $p = 3$(s,l,g) for melting and $p = 3$(l,l′,g) for the transition. $F = 1 - 3 + 2 = \underline{0}$ for both.

9.2 (a) Salt, water: $C = 2$,

(b) Na^+, H^+, $H_2PO_4^-$, HPO_4^{2-}, PO_4^{3-}, NaH_2PO_4, H_2O, OH^- (8 species).

There are 4 equilibria:

$NaH_2PO_4 \rightleftharpoons Na^+ + H_2PO_4^-$, $\quad H_2PO_4^- \rightleftharpoons H^+ + HPO_4^{2-}$

$HPO_4^{2-} \rightleftharpoons H^+ + PO_4^{3-}$, $\quad H^+ + OH^- \rightleftharpoons H_2O$.

There are two conditions for electrical neutrality: $[Na^+]$ = [phosphates] and $[H^+] = [OH^-]$ + [phosphate ions]. Hence the number of independent components is $8 - (4 + 2) = \underline{2}$.

(c) Al^{3+}, H^+, $AlCl_3$, $Al(OH)_3$, OH^-, Cl^-, H_2O, HCl (8 species).

There are 4 equilibria

$AlCl_3 + 3H_2O \rightleftharpoons Al(OH)_3 + 3HCl$, $\quad HCl \rightleftharpoons H^+ + Cl^-$

$AlCl_3 \rightleftharpoons Al^{3+} + 3Cl^-$, $\quad H_2O \rightleftharpoons H^+ + OH^-$.

There is one condition for electrical neutrality: $[H^+] + \frac{1}{3}[Al^{3+}] = [OH^-] + [Cl^-]$.

Hence $C = 8 - (4 + 1) = \underline{3}$.

9.3 Let substance A be in phases α and β which differ infinitesimally in temperature; i.e. $T(\beta) - T(\alpha) = dT$. Transfer an amount n of A from α to β.

$dG = n[\mu(\beta) - \mu(\alpha)] = -nS_m\,dT\,[d\mu = -S_m\,dT, 6.2.1]$;

hence $dG = 0$ only if $dT = 0$ (thermal equilibrium).

Likewise, let the phases differ infinitesimally in pressure; i.e. $p(\beta) - p(\alpha) = dp$.

$dG = n[\mu(\beta) - \mu(\alpha)] = nV_m\,dp\ [d\mu = V_m\,dp, 6.2.1]$;

hence $dG = 0$ only if $dp = 0$ (mechanical equilibrium).

9.4 $CuSO_4 \cdot 5H_2O \rightleftharpoons CuSO_4 + 5H_2O$.

We have to specify 'H_2O' for the gas phase and '$CuSO_4.5H_2O$' for the solid; $CuSO_4$ is fixed by the equilibrium [Section 9.1(c)]; hence $\underline{C = 2. P = 2}$ (solid, gas).

9.5 $NH_4Cl(s) \rightleftharpoons NH_3(g) + HCl(g)$; $\underline{C = 1}$ [Section 9.1(c)], $\underline{P = 2}$ (s.g).

If NH_3 is added before heating $\underline{C = 2}$ [NH_4Cl, NH_3 are now independent], $\underline{P = 2}$.

9.6 $\underline{C = 2}$ ($NaSO_4$, H_2O), $\underline{P = 3}$ (solid salt, liquid solution, vapor), $F = C - P + 2 = 2 - 3 + 2 = \underline{1}$. If the pressure is changed the temperature must change in order to maintain equilibrium.

9.7 $\underline{C = 2}$ ($NaSO_4$, H_2O), $\underline{P = 2}$ (liquid solution, vapor); $F = C - P + 2 = 2 - 2 + 2 = \underline{2}$. We are free to change the amount of dissolved salt and the pressure, but the temperature must then be changed to maintain equilibrium.

9.8 The data are plotted in Fig. 9.1.

9.9 From Fig. 9.1 (a) At $x(MgO) = 0.3$ solid and liquid are in equilibrium at $\underline{2150\ °C}$.

(b) From the tie-line at 2200 °C, the liquid composition is $y(MgO) = \underline{0.18}$ and the solid $x(MgO) = \underline{0.35}$. The proportions are given by the lever rule [8.4.5] liq:solid $= l_1/l_2 = 0.5/1.2 = \underline{0.42}$.

(c) Solidification begins at point c, corresponding to $\underline{2650\ °C}$.

9.10 $\Delta T \approx (RT^{*2}/\Delta H_{melt,m}(A))x_B$ [8.3.3].

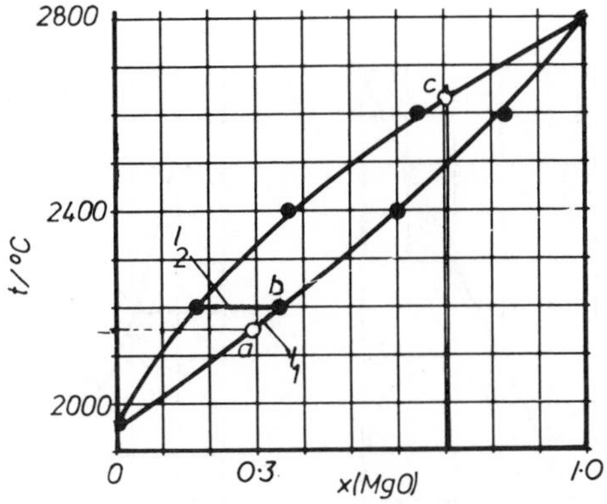

Fig 9.1

For Bi, $RT^{*2}/\Delta H_{\text{melt,m}} = \dfrac{(8.314\,\text{J K}^{-1}\,\text{mol}^{-1}) \times (544.5\,\text{K})^2}{10.88\,\text{kJ mol}^{-1}} = 227\,\text{K}.$

For Cd, $RT^{*2}/\Delta H_{\text{melt,m}} = \dfrac{(8.314\,\text{J K}^{-1}\,\text{mol}^{-1}) \times (594\,\text{K})^2}{6.07\,\text{kJ mol}^{-1}} = 483\,\text{K}.$

Construct the following Tables:

x(Cd)	01	0.2	0.3	0.4	
ΔT/K	22.7	45.4	68.1	90.8	[$\Delta T = (227\,\text{K})x(\text{Cd})$]
T_f/K	522	499	476	454	[$T_f = 544.5\,\text{K} - \Delta T$]

x(Bi)	0.1	0.2	0.3	0.4	
ΔT/K	48.3	96.6	145	193	[$\Delta T = (483\,\text{K})x(\text{Bi})$]
T_f/K	546	497	449	401	[$T_f = 594\,\text{K} - \Delta T$]

These figures are plotted in Fig. 9.2(a).

9.11 Refer to Fig. 9.2(a). Liquid at a cools without precipitation until a′ is reached (475 K). Solid Bi then precipitates, and liquid becomes richer in Cd. At a‴ (400 K) the composition is pure solid Bi + liquid of composition x(Bi) = 0.4. The whole mass then solidifies to solid Bi + solid Cd.

(a) At 460 K(a″) liquid/solid = 0.3/0.06 = $\underline{5}$ [lever rule].

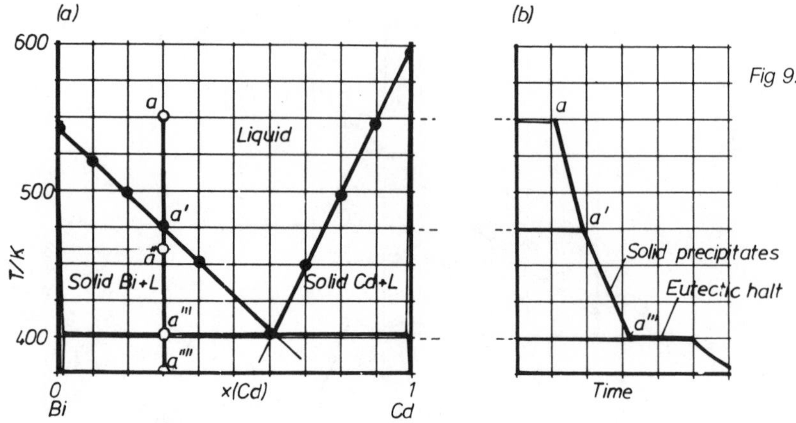

Fig 9.2

(b) At 350 K (a‴) there is no liquid. On rapid cooling, the solid would be a dispersal of Bi and Cd.

9.12 Refer to Section 9.3(c) and Fig. 9.2(a). Sketch the cooling curve in Fig. 9.2(b).

9.13 The data are plotted in Fig. 9.3. From the upper and lower extremes we find $T_{uc} = \underline{122\ °C}$, $T_{lc} = \underline{8\ °C}$ [Section 9.3(a)].

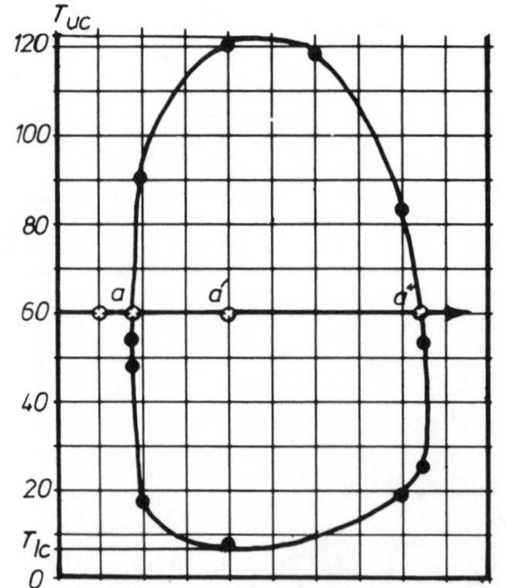

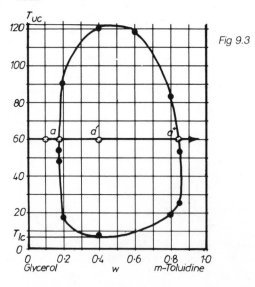

Fig 9.3

9.14 Refer to Fig. 9.3. Miscibility is complete up to point a. Therefore, before a, $P = 1, C = 2, F = 3(T, p, x)$. Two phases occur at a, corresponding to w(toluidine)

= 0.18. Then $P = 2, C = 2$ and $F = 2(p$ and x or $T)$. At the point a′ there are two phases of composition $w = 0.84$; they are present in the ratio (a″ − a′)/(a′ − a) = 0.44/0.22 = 2, with the former dominant. At a″ there are still two phases with compositions $w = 0.18$ and $w = 0.84$, but the former is present only as a trace. One more drop takes the system out of the two-phase region, and $P = 1, C = 2, F = 3$ again.

9.15 Refer to Fig. 9.8 in the text. At b_3 there are two phases, the compositions being $x_A = 0.18$ and $x_A = 0.70$ with abundances in the ratio 3.5 mm/28 mm = 0.13. Since $C = 2, P = 2$ we have $F = 2$ (e.g. p, x). On heating the phases merge and the single-phase region is encountered. Then $F = 3(p, T, x)$. The liquid comes into equilibrium with its vapor when the isopleth cuts the phase line. At this temperature, and for all points up to b_1, $C = 2, P = 2$, and so $F = 2$(e.g. p, x). The whole sample is vapor above b_1.

9.16 The phase diagram should be labeled as in Fig. 9.4(a).

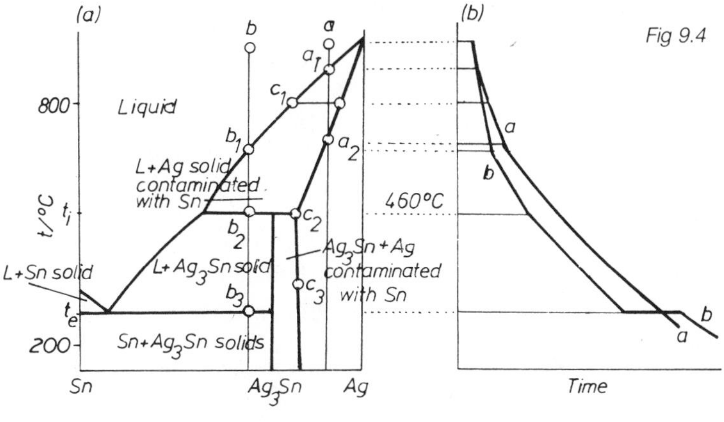

(a) Solid Ag with dissolved Sn begins to precipitate at a_1, and becomes completely solid at a_2.
(b) Solid Ag with dissolved Sn begins to precipitate at b_1 and the liquid becomes richer in Sn. The peritectic reaction occurs at b_2, and as cooling continues Ag_3Sn is precipitated and the liquid becomes richer in Sn. At b_3 it has its eutectic composition (e) and the system freezes without further change.

9.17 The incongruent melting point [Section 9.3(d)] is indicated on Fig. 9.4(a) ($t_i = 460$ °C). The composition of the eutectic is e($100\, w_e = 4$). It melts at $t_e = 215$ °C. The cooling curves are shown in Fig. 9.4(b). Note the eutectic halt in the isopleth (b).

9.18 Refer to Fig. 9.4(a). (a) The solubility of Ag in Sn at 800 °C is determined

by the point c_1 (for higher values of $w(Ag)$ a two-phase system occurs). c_1 corresponds to $100w(Ag) = 80$, $100w(Sn) = 20$; i.e. silver dissolves up to 80 per cent by mass.
(b) Ag_3Sn decomposes.
(c) The solubility of Ag_3Sn in Ag at 300 °C is given by point c_3.

9.19 The information has been used to construct Fig. 9.5(a). In $MgCu_2$ the weight percent of Mg is 100 [24.3/(24.31 + 127)] = 16, and in Mg_2Cu it is 100[48.6/(48.6 + 63.5)] = 43.

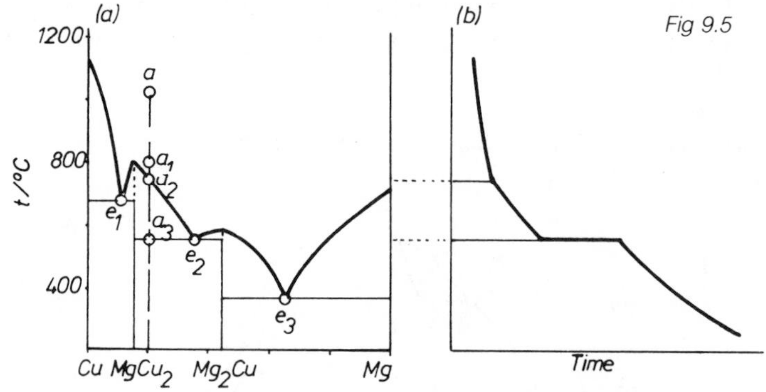

Fig 9.5

9.20 Refer to Fig. 9.5(a). Initial point is a_1, corresponding to a liquid, single-phase system. At a_2 (770 °C) $MgCu_2$ begins to precipitate and the liquid becomes richer in Mg, moving towards e_2. At a_3 there is solid $MgCu_2$ + liquid of composition e_2 (33 per cent weight Mg). This solution freezes without further change.

9.21 The cooling curve is sketched in Fig. 9.5(b).

9.22 The features are plotted in Fig. 9.6 [Section 9.4(a)]. For (d) we find the mole fractions corresponding to the stated weight percentages. Use $M_r(NaCl) = 58.4$, $M_r(H_2O) = 18.0$, $M_r(Na_2SO_4 . 10H_2O) = 322.2$. Therefore in 100 g sample, $n(NaCl) = 0.25 \times (100/58.4)$ mol = 0.43 mol, $n(H_2O) = 0.50 \times (100/18.0)$ mol = 2.8 mol, n(sulfate) = $0.25 \times (100/322.2)$ mol = 0.078 mol, corresponding to mole fractions 0.13, 0.85, and 0.02. This point is marked (d). In this calculation water is identified with B, hence the line labeled e is followed as water is added.

9.23 Refer to Fig. 9.7. From the properties of similar triangles (~ denotes similarity).

AA′C′ ~ AA″C″: a/c = a′/c′, implying a/a′ = c/c′.

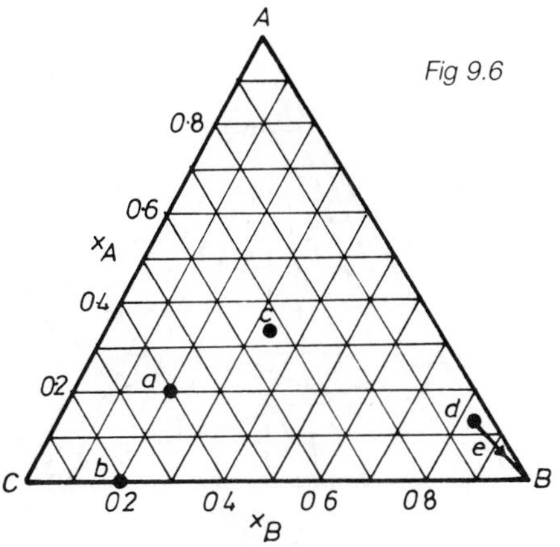

Fig 9.6

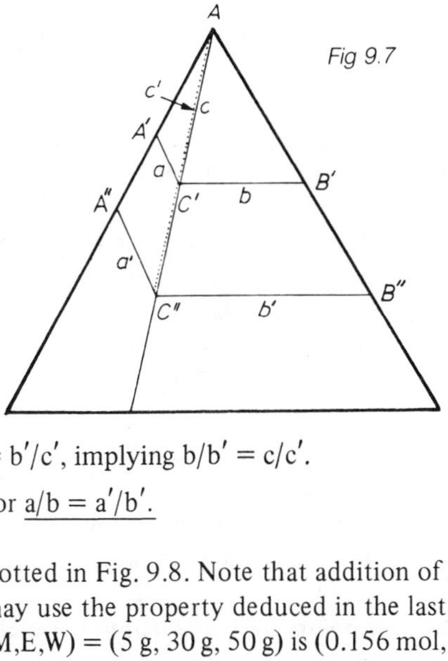

Fig 9.7

AB′C′ ~ AB″C″: b/c = b′/c′, implying b/b′ = c/c′.
Therefore a/a′ = b/b′, or <u>a/b = a′/b′.</u>

9.24 The points are plotted in Fig. 9.8. Note that addition of M preserves the E:W ratio, and so we may use the property deduced in the last problem.
Mole composition of (M,E,W) = (5 g, 30 g, 50 g) is (0.156 mol, 0.405 mol, 2.775 mol) since $M_r(M) = 32.04$, $M_r(E) = 74.12$, $M_r(W) = 18.02$. Therefore the mole fraction composition is (0.047, 0.121, 0.832). This is the point (a) in Fig. 9.8, in the <u>2-phase region</u>.
The line w–a corresponds to constant M:E ratio. When either of a_1 or a_2 is attained the single-phase region is reached. These correspond to the following compositions:
a_1: (0.02, 0.05, 0.93) in mole fractions. [Since n_E and n_M remain constant (at 0.156 mole and 0.405 mol).] This implies that $n_W \approx 7.3$ mol, or 131 g. Hence, <u>81 g water</u> must be added.

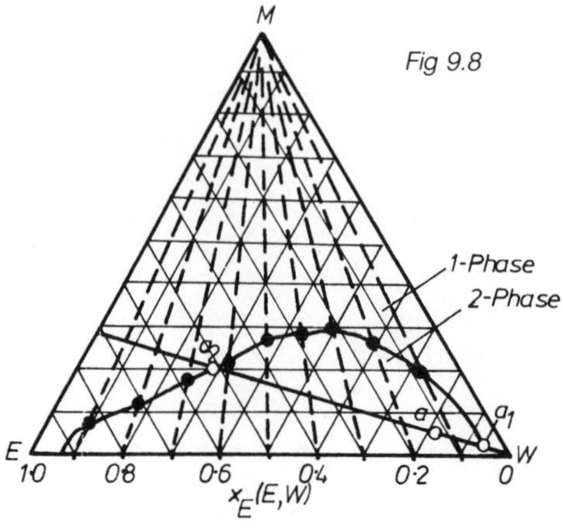

a_2: (0.195, 0.515, 0.290) in mole fractions. This likewise implies that $n_W \approx 0.23$ mol or 4.1 g. Hence the removal of 46 g of water will take the system into the single-phase region.

9.25 The composition (W,C,A) = (2.3 g, 9.2 g, 3.1 g) corresponds to (0.128 mol, 0.077 mol, 0.052 mol) because $M_r(W) = 18.02$, $M_r(C) = 119.4$, and $M_r(A) = 60.05$. In mole fractions this is (0.498, 0.300, 0.202).
Refer to Fig. 9.17 of the text. The point lies at q, the intersection of the broken line and the third tie-line. This is in the two-phase region. The two layers have compositions given by the points at the ends of the tie-lines namely (0.06, 0.82, 0.12) and (0.62, 0.16, 0.22) in mole fractions. Their relative abundances are given by the lever rule as 12 mm/45 mm = 0.27 (3.7:1).

9.26 Refer to Fig. 9.17 of the text. When water is added the composition moves along the line joining the point to the W apex. When $x(W) = 0.79$ the system enters the single-phase region. When acetic acid is added to the original mixture it becomes a single-phase system when $x(A) = 0.35$, the point a_3 in the diagram.

9.27 The positions of the four points are illustrated in the sketch in Fig. 9.9, which is a reproduction of Fig. 9.18 of the text.
(a) Two-phase system, solid $(NH_4)_2SO_4$ + liquid of composition a_1.
(b) Three-phase system; solid NH_4Cl, solid $(NH_4)_2SO_4$, and liquid of composition d.
(c) Single-phase system.
(d) Invariant point; system consists of the saturated solution of composition d.

9.28 Refer to Fig. 9.9. Solubilities are given by the compositions at which a binary system just fails to become two-phase. These are the points (a) s_1, corresponding to $x(NH_4Cl) = 0.26$ and (b) s_2, corresponding to $x((NH_4)_2SO_4)$

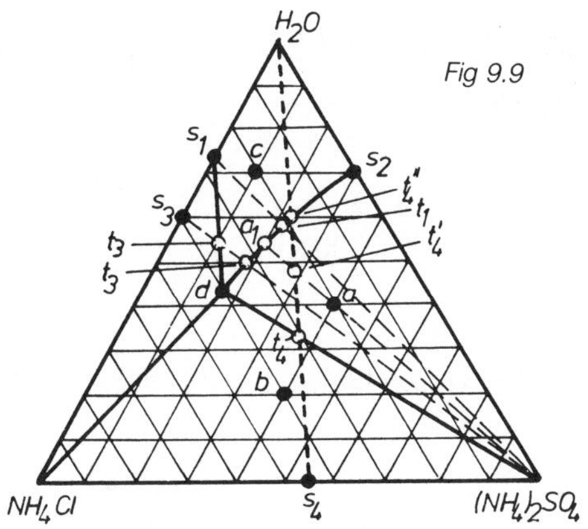

= 0.30. Convert to $\mathrm{mol\,kg^{-1}}$ and $\mathrm{g\,dm^{-3}}$ by taking $n(\mathrm{H_2O}) = (1\ \mathrm{kg}/18.02\ \mathrm{g\,mol^{-1}}) = 55.5\ \mathrm{mol}$, and noting that $M_r(\mathrm{NH_4Cl}) = 53.49$ and $M_r((\mathrm{NH_4})_2\mathrm{SO_4}) = 132.14$. Since $x(\mathrm{s}) = n(\mathrm{s})/[n(\mathrm{s}) + n(\mathrm{S})]$, $n(\mathrm{s}) = n(\mathrm{S})x_\mathrm{s}/[1 - x(\mathrm{s})]$. Therefore

(a) $n(\mathrm{NH_4Cl}) = 19.5$ mol, or 1.04 kg.

(b) $n((\mathrm{NH_4})_2\mathrm{SO_4}) = 23.8$ mol, or 3.14 kg.

Therefore the solubilities of the chloride and the sulfate are 19.5 $\mathrm{mol\,kg^{-1}}$ and 23.8 $\mathrm{mol\,kg^{-1}}$ respectively (approximately 1.0 $\mathrm{kg\,dm^{-3}}$ and 3.1 $\mathrm{kg\,dm^{-3}}$).

9.29 Refer to Fig. 9.9.

(a) Initially the system is at s_1. Addition of sulfate moves the system from s_1 towards t_1. The sulfate dissolves and the system remains single-phase until point t_1, when the sulfate ceases to dissolve, leaving a liquid of composition t_1 and excess solid sulfate.
(b) Initially the system is at, for example, s_3. There is saturated solution of composition s_1 and excess chloride. Addition of sulfate leads to a single-phase system when the composition reaches t_3 (common-ion effect). The sulfate continues to dissolve until t_3' is reached; after that the two-phase region is entered, and further sulfate remains undissolved.
(c) 25 g $\mathrm{NH_4Cl}$, 75 g $(\mathrm{NH_4})_2\mathrm{SO_4}$ corresponds to 0.47 mol, 0.57 mol, or the mole fractions 0.45, 0.55. This corresponds to this point s_4. Addition of water moves the system along the lines s_4, t_4. Three phases (solid chloride, solid sulfate, saturated solution d) occur until t_4 is passed. Then the two-phase region is reached. Present are solid sulfate, and a liquid that has a composition that migrates from d toward t_4''. For instance, when the overall composition is t_4', the liquid composition is a_1. At t_4'' the single-phase region is entered, and the solution from then on simply becomes progressively more dilute.

10. Changes of state: chemical reactions

A10.1 $\Delta_r G^{\ominus}(T) = -RT\ln K$ [10.1.15].

$\Delta_r G^{\ominus}(400\,\text{K}) = -(8.31\,\text{J K}^{-1}\,\text{mol}^{-1})(400\,\text{K})\ln 2.07 = \underline{-2.42 \times 10^3\,\text{J mol}^{-1}}.$

A10.2 $\Delta_r G^{\ominus}(T) = -RT\ln K$ [10.1. 15].

$K = \exp[-\Delta_r G^{\ominus}(T)/RT] = \exp[-(-3.67 \times 10^3\,\text{J mol}^{-1})(8.31\,\text{J K}^{-1}\,\text{mol}^{-1})^{-1}(400\,\text{K})^{-1}]$

$= \underline{3.02}.$

A10.3 $\Delta_r G^{\ominus}(T_2)/T_2 - \Delta_r G^{\ominus}(T_1)/T_1 = \Delta_r H^{\ominus}(T_2^{-1} - T_1^{-1})$. [5.3.6; ΔH, ΔS ind. of T]

$\Delta_r G^{\ominus}(T_2) = 0; -\Delta_r G^{\ominus}(1280)/1280\,\text{K} = \Delta_r H^{\ominus}(T_2^{-1} - 1/1280\,\text{K})$

$(-33 \times 10^3\,\text{J mol}^{-1}/1280\,\text{K}) = (224 \times 10^3\,\text{kJ mol}^{-1})(T_2^{-1} - 1/1280\,\text{K});$

$T_2 = \underline{1.3 \times 10^3\,\text{K}}.$

A10.4 $d(\ln K)/d(1/T) = -\Delta_r H^{\ominus}(T)/R$ [10.2.5]

$\Delta_r H^{\ominus}(T) = -R\ d(\ln K)/d(1/T) = -R[-1088 + 2(1.51 \times 10^5)(T/\text{K})^{-1}]$

$\Delta_r H^{\ominus}(400\,\text{K}) = -8.31[-1088 + (3.02 \times 10^5)(400)^{-1}]\,\text{J mol}^{-1} = \underline{2.27 \times 10^3\,\text{J mol}^{-1}}.$

$\Delta_r S^{\ominus}(T) = -(\partial \Delta_r G^{\ominus}/\partial T)_p$ [6.2.2] $= [\partial(RT\ln K)/\partial T]_p$

$= R[-1.04 - 1.51 \times 10^5 (T/\text{K})^{-2}]$

$\Delta_r S^{\ominus}(400\,\text{K}) = 8.31[-1.04 - (1.51 \times 10^5)(400)^{-2}]\,\text{J K}^{-1}\,\text{mol}^{-1} = \underline{-16.5\,\text{J K}^{-1}\,\text{mol}^{-1}}.$

A10.5 $p_b = p_t x_b = (600\,\text{Torr})[0.15/(0.15 + 0.30)] = 200\,\text{Torr}$ [1.2.4]

$p_i = p_t - p_b = (600 - 200)\,\text{Torr} = 400\,\text{Torr}.$

borneol(g) $\rightleftarrows$ isoborneol(g)

$\Delta_r G(503\,\text{K}) = \Delta_r G^{\ominus}(503\,\text{K}) + R(503\,\text{K})\ln(p_i/p_b)$ [10.1.3]

$\Delta_r G(503\,\text{K}) = 9.4 \times 10^3\,\text{J mol}^{-1} + (8.3\,\text{J K}^{-1}\,\text{mol}^{-1})(503\,\text{K})\ln(400/200)$

$= \underline{1.2 \times 10^4\,\text{J mol}^{-1}}.$

A10.6 α-U(s) + (3/2)H_2(g) $\rightleftharpoons$ β-UH_3(s)

$\Delta_f G^{\ominus}(500\,\text{K}) = -R(500\,\text{K})\ln K = -R(500\,\text{K})\ln p_{H_2}^{-3/2}$ [10.1.15; $f \to p$]

$= (3/2)(8.31\,\text{J K}^{-1}\,\text{mol}^{-1})(500\,\text{K})\ln[(1.04\,\text{Torr})(1.33 \times 10^{-3}\,\text{bar/Torr})]$

$= \underline{-4.10 \times 10^4\,\text{J mol}^{-1}}.$

A10.7 α-U(s) + (3/2)H_2(g) $\rightleftharpoons$ β-UH_3(s); $\ln K = \ln(p^{-3/2}) = -(3/2)\ln p$.

$\Delta_f H^{\ominus}(T) = RT^2 \mathrm{d}\ln K/\mathrm{d}T = -(3/2)RT^2 \mathrm{d}\ln p/\mathrm{d}T$. [10.2.4]

$\Delta_f H^{\ominus}(T) = -(3/2)R(T/\mathrm{K})^2 [+1.464 \times 10^4 (T/\mathrm{K})^{-2} - 5.65(T/\mathrm{K})^{-1}]$

$= -(3/2)R[1.464 \times 10^4 - 5.65(T/\mathrm{K})]$.

$\Delta_f C_p^{\ominus} = \{\partial \Delta_f H^{\ominus}(T)/\partial T\}_p = (3/2)R(5.65) = \underline{8.475\,R.}$

A10.8 $CaCl_2.NH_3$(s) $\rightleftharpoons$ NH_3(g) + $CaCl_2$(s)

$\Delta_r G^{\ominus}(400\,\mathrm{K}) = -R(400\,\mathrm{K})\ln p_{NH_3}$

$= -(8.314\,\mathrm{J\,K^{-1}\,mol^{-1}})(400\,\mathrm{K}) \times \ln[(12.8\,\mathrm{Torr})(1.33 \times 10^{-3}\,\mathrm{bar\,Torr^{-1}})]$

$= 1.354 \times 10^4\,\mathrm{J\,mol^{-1}}$

$T^{-1}\Delta_r G^{\ominus}(T) = (400\,\mathrm{K})^{-1}\Delta_r G^{\ominus}(400\,\mathrm{K}) + \Delta_r H^{\ominus}(T^{-1} - 400^{-1})$

$= (400\,\mathrm{K})^{-1}(1.354 \times 10^4\,\mathrm{J\,mol^{-1}}) + 7.815 \times 10^4\,\mathrm{J\,mol^{-1}} \times (T^{-1} - 400^{-1})$

$= T^{-1}(7.815 \times 10^4\,\mathrm{J\,mol^{-1}}) - 1.615 \times 10^2\,\mathrm{J\,mol^{-1}\,K^{-1}}$;

$\underline{\Delta_r G^{\ominus}(T) = [7.815 \times 10^4 - 161.5(T/\mathrm{K})]\,\mathrm{J\,mol^{-1}}.}$

A10.9 $K_x \propto p^{-\Delta\nu}$ [10.2.3]; (a) $\Delta\nu = 1$; $K_x(2\,\mathrm{atm})/K_x(1\,\mathrm{atm}) = 1/2$;

% change in $K_x = 100(\frac{1}{2} - 1) = -50$; (b) $\Delta\nu = 0$; $\underline{\text{no change}}$ in K_x with p.

A10.10 $K = x_i/x_b = (1 - x_b)/x_b$;

$0.106 = x_b^{-1} - 1$; $x_b = \underline{0.904.}$

10.1 Determine whether $\Delta_r G^{\ominus}$ is negative [Section 10.1(e)].

(a) $\Delta_r G^{\ominus}/\mathrm{kJ\,mol^{-1}} = (-202.87) - (-95.30 - 16.45) = -91.12$.

(b) $\Delta_r G^{\ominus}/\mathrm{kJ\,mol^{-1}} = 3(-856.64) - 2(-1582.3) = +594.7$.

(c) $\Delta_r G^{\ominus}/\mathrm{kJ\,mol^{-1}} = (-100.4) - (-33.56) = -66.8$.

(d) $\Delta_r G^{\ominus}/\mathrm{kJ\,mol^{-1}} = 2(-33.56) - (-166.9) = +99.8$.

(e) $\Delta_r G^{\ominus}/\mathrm{kJ\,mol^{-1}} = (-744.53) - [2(-120.35) + (-27.83)] = -476.00$.

Therefore, (a), (c), and (e) are spontaneous in the directions written under the conditions specified.

10.2 Use Section 10.2(c). $\Delta H_f^{\ominus}$ from Table 4.1.

(a) $\Delta H_m^{\ominus}/\mathrm{kJ\,mol^{-1}} = (-314.43) - (-46.11 - 92.31) = -176.01$.

(b) $\Delta H_m^{\ominus}/\mathrm{kJ\,mol^{-1}} = 3(-910.94) - 2(-1675.7) = +618.6$.

(c) $\Delta H_m^{\ominus}/\mathrm{kJ\,mol^{-1}} = (-100.0) - (-20.63) = -79.4$.

(d) $\Delta H_m^{\ominus}/\mathrm{kJ\,mol^{-1}} = 2(-20.63) - (-178.2) = +136.9$.

(e) $\Delta H_m^\ominus/\text{kJ mol}^{-1} = (-909.27) - [2(-187.78) + (-39.7)] = -494.0.$

a, c, and e are *exothermic*, and so a rise in temperature favors the *reactants*. b and d are *endothermic*, and so a rise in temperature favors the *products*.

10.3 $d\ln K/dT = \Delta_r H^\ominus(T)/RT^2$ [10.2.4].

$\int d\ln K = \int\{\Delta_r H^\ominus(T)/RT^2\}dT \approx \Delta_r H^\ominus \int dT(1/RT^2)$.

Therefore, $\ln\{K(T_2)/K(T_1)\} \approx \{\Delta_r H^\ominus/R\}\left(\dfrac{1}{T_1} - \dfrac{1}{T_2}\right) = (T_2 - T_1)\Delta_r H^\ominus/RT_1T_2$.

(a) $K(T_2) = 2K(T_1)$; $T_1 = 298\text{ K}$, $T_2 - T_1 = 10\text{ K}$.

$$\Delta_r H^\ominus \approx \{RT_1T_2/(T_2 - T_1)\}\ln 2 = \left(\frac{298 \times 308}{10}\right) \times (8.314\text{ J K}^{-1}\text{ mol}^{-1})\ln 2$$

$$= \underline{53\text{ kJ mol}^{-1}}.$$

(b) $K(T_2) = \frac{1}{2}K(T_1)$; $\ln K(T_2)/K(T_1) = -\ln 2$;

Therefore $\Delta_r H^\ominus = -\Delta_r H^\ominus(\text{a}) = \underline{-53\text{ kJ mol}^{-1}}$.

10.4 $\Delta_r G^\ominus = -RT\ln K$ [10.1.7].

$\Delta_r G^\ominus - \Delta_r G^{\ominus\prime} = -RT\ln(K/K') = -RT\ln 1.1 = \underline{-238\text{ J mol}^{-1}}$.

Percentage change: $100\left\{\dfrac{\Delta_r G^\ominus - \Delta_r G^{\ominus\prime}}{\Delta_r G^{\ominus\prime}}\right\} = \dfrac{100\ln(K/K')}{\ln K} = \underline{9.5/\ln K'}$.

10.5 $\Delta_r G^\ominus = -RT\ln K$ [10.1.17]

(a) $\frac{1}{2}N_2 + \frac{3}{2}H_2 \rightleftharpoons NH_3$; $\Delta_r G^\ominus = -16.5\text{ kJ mol}^{-1}$, $K = \{f_{NH_3}/f_{N_2}^{\frac{1}{2}}f_{H_2}^{\frac{3}{2}}\}$.

$K(\text{a}) = \exp\{-\Delta_r G^\ominus/RT\} = \exp\{(16.5\text{ kJ mol}^{-1})/(2.48\text{ kJ mol}^{-1})\} = \underline{775}$.

(b) $N_2 + 3H_2 \rightleftharpoons 2NH_3$,

$K = \{f_{NH_3}^2/f_{N_2}f_{H_2}^3\} = K^2(\text{a}) = \underline{6.0 \times 10^5}$.

(c) $NH_3 \rightleftharpoons \frac{1}{2}N_2 + \frac{3}{2}H_2$, $K = f_{H_2}^{\frac{3}{2}}f_{N_2}^{\frac{1}{2}}/f_{NH_3} = 1/K(\text{a}) = \underline{1.29 \times 10^{-3}}$.

10.6 $$\Delta_r G = \Delta_r G^\ominus + RT\ln\left\{\frac{[p(NH_3)/p^\ominus]}{[p(N_2)/p^\ominus]^{1/2}\,[p(H_2)/p^\ominus]^{3/2}}\right\}$$

$$= -16.5\text{ kJ mol}^{-1} + (2.48\text{ kJ mol}^{-1})\ln(4/\sqrt{3})$$

$$= \underline{-14\text{ kJ mol}^{-1}}.$$

10.7 $K = \exp\{-\Delta_r G^\ominus/RT\}$ [10.1.7].

$CO(g) + H_2(g) \rightleftharpoons H_2CO(l)$; $\Delta_r G^{\ominus\prime} = 28.95\text{ kJ mol}^{-1}$.

$H_2CO(l) \rightleftharpoons H_2CO(g), K'' = p/p^\ominus = \exp\{-\Delta_r G^{\ominus\prime\prime}/RT\}$;

$\Delta_r G^{\ominus\prime\prime} = -RT\ln(p/p^\ominus) = -(2.48\ \mathrm{kJ\ mol^{-1}}) \times \ln\{1500\ \mathrm{Torr}/760\ \mathrm{Torr}\}$

$= -1.69\ \mathrm{kJ\ mol^{-1}}$.

For $CO(g) + H_2(g) \rightleftharpoons H_2CO(g)$,

$\Delta_r G^\ominus = \Delta_r G^{\ominus\prime} + \Delta_r G^{\ominus\prime\prime} = 28.95\ \mathrm{kJ\ mol^{-1}} + (-1.69\ \mathrm{kJ\ mol^{-1}}) = 27.26\ \mathrm{kJ\ mol^{-1}}$,

$K = \exp\{-27.26/2.48\} = \underline{1.68 \times 10^{-5}}.$

10.8 $NH_4Cl(s) \rightleftharpoons NH_3(g) + HCl(g)$;

$p(NH_3) = p(HCl); p = p(NH_3) + p(HCl) = 2p(HCl)$.

(a) $K_p = [p(NH_3)/p^\ominus] \times [p(HCl)/p^\ominus] = [p(HCl)/p^\ominus]^2 = \frac{1}{4}[p/p^\ominus]^2$.

At 427 °C (700 K): $K_p(700\ \mathrm{K}) = \frac{1}{4} \times (608\ \mathrm{kPa}/101.3\ \mathrm{kPa})^2 = \underline{9.01}.$

At 459 °C (732 K): $K_p(732\ \mathrm{K}) = \frac{1}{4} \times (1115/101.3)^2 = \underline{30.3}.$

(b) $\Delta_r G^\ominus = -RT\ln K_p$ [10.1.7].

At 427 °C: $\Delta_r G^\ominus = -(8.314\ \mathrm{J\ K^{-1}\ mol^{-1}}) \times (700\ \mathrm{K}) \times \ln 9.01 = \underline{-12.8\ \mathrm{kJ\ mol^{-1}}}.$

(c) $\ln\{K(T_2)/K(T_1)\} \approx (T_2 - T_1)\Delta_r H^\ominus/RT_1T_2$ [10.2.6].

$\Delta_r H^\ominus \approx \{RT_1T_2/(T_2 - T_1)\}\ln\{K(T_2)/K(T_1)\}$

$$\approx \left\{\frac{(8.314\ \mathrm{J\ K^{-1}\ mol^{-1}}) \times 700\ \mathrm{K} \times 732\ \mathrm{K}}{32\ \mathrm{K}}\right\} \ln\left\{\frac{30.3}{9.01}\right\} = \underline{160\ \mathrm{kJ\ mol^{-1}}}.$$

(d) $$\Delta_r S^\ominus = \{\Delta_r H^\ominus - \Delta_r G^\ominus\}/T = \frac{\{160 - (-12.8)\}\ \mathrm{kJ\ mol^{-1}}}{700\ \mathrm{K}} = \underline{250\ \mathrm{J\ K^{-1}\ mol^{-1}}}.$$

10.9 $A_2 \rightleftharpoons 2A$.

Amount of substance of A_2 if all A were combined $= n$.

Amount actually present as $A_2 = (1 - \alpha)n$.

Amount present as $A = 2[n - (1 - \alpha)n] = 2\alpha n$.

Total amount of substance present $= n_{A_2} + n_A = (1 - \alpha)n + 2\alpha n = (1 + \alpha)n$.

$n = M/M_m(2CH_3CO_2H) = M/(120.1\ \mathrm{g\ mol^{-1}})$.

$x(A) = 2\alpha/(1 + \alpha); x(A_2) = (1 - \alpha)/(1 + \alpha)$.

$K = [p(A)/p^\ominus]^2/[p(A_2)/p^\ominus] = [x(A)p/p^\ominus]^2/[x(A_2)p/p^\ominus] = [x(A)^2/x(A_2)](p/p^\ominus)$

$= \{4\alpha^2/(1 - \alpha^2)\}(p/p^\ominus)$.

$pV = n_{total}RT = (1 + \alpha)nRT$, so that $\alpha = (pV/nRT) - 1$.

(a) $T = 437\ \mathrm{K}$, $V = 21.45\ \mathrm{cm^3}$, $p = 764.3\ \mathrm{Torr}\ (1.006\ \mathrm{atm})$, $M = 0.0519\ \mathrm{g}$.

$n = (0.0519\ \mathrm{g})/(120.1\ \mathrm{g\ mol^{-1}}) = 4.32 \times 10^{-4}\ \mathrm{mol}$.

$$pV/nRT = \frac{(1.006\,\text{atm}) \times (21.45 \times 10^{-3}\,\text{dm}^3)}{(4.32 \times 10^{-4}\,\text{mol}) \times (0.0821\,\text{dm}^3\,\text{atm}\,\text{K}^{-1}\,\text{mol}^{-1}) \times 437\,\text{K}} = 1.392,$$

$\alpha = 1.392 - 1 = 0.392$; hence $x(A_2) = \underline{0.44\ (44\%)}$ and $K = \underline{0.73}$.

(b) $T = 471\,\text{K}$, $V = 21.45\,\text{cm}^3$, $p = 764.3\,\text{Torr}\ (1.006\,\text{atm})$, $M = 0.038\,\text{g}$.

$n = (0.038\,\text{g})/(120.1\,\text{g}\,\text{mol}^{-1}) = 3.16 \times 10^{-4}\,\text{mol}$

$$pV/nRT = \frac{(1.006\,\text{atm}) \times (21.45 \times 10^{-3}\,\text{dm}^3)}{(3.16 \times 10^{-4}\,\text{mol}) \times (0.0821\,\text{dm}^3\,\text{atm}\,\text{K}^{-1}\,\text{mol}^{-1}) \times (471\,\text{K})} = 1.766,$$

$\alpha = 1.766 - 1 = 0.766$, hence $x(A_2) = \underline{0.13\ (13\%)}$ and $K = \underline{5.7}$.

$\Delta H^\ominus_m \approx \{RT_1T_2/(T_2 - T_1)\}\ln\{K(T_2)/K(T_1)\}$ [10.2.6]

$$\approx \left\{\frac{(8.3144\,\text{J}\,\text{K}^{-1}\,\text{mol}^{-1}) \times 437\,\text{K} \times 471\,\text{K}}{34\,\text{K}}\right\} \ln\left\{\frac{5.7}{0.73}\right\}$$

$= \underline{+100\,\text{kJ}\,(\text{mol dimer})^{-1}}$.

10.10 $K_{sp} = a(Ag^+)a(Cl^-)$; $AgCl(s) \rightleftharpoons Ag^+(aq) + Cl^-(aq)$.

$\Delta_r G^\ominus = \{77.11\,\text{kJ}\,\text{mol}^{-1} - 131.23\,\text{kJ}\,\text{mol}^{-1}\} - (-109.79\,\text{kJ}\,\text{mol}^{-1}) = 55.66\,\text{kJ}\,\text{mol}^{-1}$.

$K_{sp} = \exp\{-\Delta_r G^\ominus/RT\} = \exp\{-55.66/2.479\} = \underline{1.77 \times 10^{-10}}$.

$K_{sp} \approx [m(Ag^+)/m^\ominus]\ [m(Cl^-)/m^\ominus]$

$m(Ag^+) \approx (\sqrt{K_{sp}})\,\text{mol}\,\text{kg}^{-1} = 1.3 \times 10^{-5}\,\text{mol}\,\text{kg}^{-1}$.

The solubility of silver chloride in water at 25 °C is therefore approximately $\underline{1.3 \times 10^{-5}\,\text{mol}\,\text{kg}^{-1}}$.

10.11 $\Delta_r H^\ominus \approx \{RT_1T_2/(T_2 - T_1)\}\ln\{K(T_2)/K(T_1)\}$ [10.2.6]

$$\approx \left\{\frac{(8.314\,\text{J}\,\text{K}^{-1}\,\text{mol}^{-1}) \times 293.15\,\text{K} \times 303.15\,\text{K}}{10\,\text{K}}\right\} \ln\left\{\frac{1.45}{0.67}\right\}$$

$= \underline{57\,\text{kJ}\,\text{mol}^{-1}}$.

The maximum value of $\Delta H^\ominus_m$ is obtained when $K(T_1)$ is at the maximum of its range (1.46×10^{-14}) and $K(T_2)$ at the minimum of its (0.66×10^{-14}); then $\Delta_r H^\ominus \approx 59$ kJ mol^{-1}. The minimum value is obtained for $K(T_1)$ at its minimum (1.44×10^{-14}) and $K(T_2)$ at its maximum (0.68×10^{-14}); then $\Delta_r H^\ominus \approx 55\,\text{kJ}\,\text{mol}^{-1}$. Therefore, $\Delta_r H^\ominus = \underline{(57 \pm 2)\,\text{kJ}\,\text{mol}^{-1}}$.

10.12 $\Delta_r H^\ominus = -R\,\mathrm{d}\ln K/\mathrm{d}(1/T)$ [10.2.5];

$\lg s(H_2) = -5.39 - 768(\text{K}/T)$; $\ln s(H_2) = 2.303 \lg s(H_2)$.

$\Delta_r H^\ominus = -2.303R\,[\mathrm{d}/\mathrm{d}(1/T)]\ [-5.39 - 768(\text{K}/T)]$

$= 2.303\,R \times (768\,\text{K}) = \underline{14.7\,\text{kJ mol}^{-1}}.$

$\lg s(\text{CO}) = -5.98 - 980(\text{K}/T);$

$\Delta_r H^{\ominus} = -2.303 R \times (-980\,\text{K}) = \underline{18.8\,\text{kJ mol}^{-1}}.$

10.13 $CuSO_4.5H_2O(s) \rightleftharpoons 5H_2O(g) + CuSO_4(s); K_p = [p(H_2O/p^{\ominus}]^5.$

$\Delta_r G^{\ominus} = 5(-228.57\,\text{kJ mol}^{-1}) + (-661.8\,\text{kJ mol}^{-1}) - (-1879.7\,\text{kJ mol}^{-1})$

$= 75.05\,\text{kJ mol}^{-1}.$

$\Delta_r H^{\ominus} = 5(-241.82\,\text{kJ mol}^{-1}) + (-771.36\,\text{kJ mol}^{-1}) - (-2279.7\,\text{kJ mol}^{-1})$

$= 299.2\,\text{kJ mol}^{-1}.$

$K_p = \exp\{-\Delta_f G^{\ominus}/RT\} = \exp\{-75.05/2.479\} = 7.1 \times 10^{-14}$ at 298 K.

Therefore $p(H_2O) = (K_p)^{1/5}\, p^{\ominus} = \underline{2.3 \times 10^{-3}\,\text{bar}}$ at 298 K.

To find the higher temperatures required for (a) and (b), proceed as follows:

$\ln(K_2/K_1) = \{(T_2 - T_1)/RT_1T_2\}\Delta H_m^{\ominus}$ [10.2.6], so that

$$T_2 = \frac{T_1 \Delta_r H^{\ominus}}{\Delta_r H^{\ominus} - RT_1 \ln(K_2/K_1)} = \kappa T_1,\; 1/\kappa = 1 - \frac{5RT_1 \ln(p_2/p_1)}{\Delta_r H^{\ominus}}$$

$T_1 = 298.15\,\text{K}, \Delta_r H^{\ominus} = 299.2\,\text{kJ mol}^{-1}, p_1 = 2.3 \times 10^{-3}\,\text{bar}.$

$$5RT_1/\Delta H_m^{\ominus} = 5 \times \frac{8.3144\,\text{J K}^{-1}\,\text{mol}^{-1} \times 298.15\,\text{K}}{299.2 \times 10^3\,\text{J mol}^{-1}} = 4.14 \times 10^{-2}.$$

(a) $p_2 = 10\,\text{Torr} \mathrel{\widehat{=}} 0.013\,\text{bar};$

$1/\kappa = 1 - (4.15 \times 10^{-2})\ln(0.013/2.3 \times 10^{-3}) = 0.93; \kappa = 1.08.$

Therefore, $T_2 = 1.08 \times (298.15\,\text{K}) = \underline{32\,\text{K}}.$

(b) $p_2 = 1\,\text{atm} \approx 1\,\text{bar}$

$1/\kappa = 1 - (4.15 \times 10^{-2})\ln(1/2.3 \times 10^{-3}) = 0.75; \kappa = 1.3.$

Therefore, $T_2 = 1.3 \times (298.15\,\text{K}) = \underline{390\,\text{K}}.$

10.14	H_2	I_2	HI	
(1) Initial/mol	0.30	0.40	0.20	
(2) Stated change/mol	$-x$			
(3) Implied change/mol	$-x$	$-x$	$+2x$	$[H_2 + I_2 \rightleftharpoons 2HI]$
(4) Final composition/mol	$0.30 - x$	$0.40 - x$	$0.20 + 2x$	Total: 0.90
(5) Mole fraction	$\left(\frac{0.30 - x}{0.9}\right)$	$\left(\frac{0.40 - x}{0.9}\right)$	$\left(\frac{0.20 + 2x}{0.9}\right)$	

$$K_p = [p(\mathrm{HI})/p^{\ominus}]^2/[p(\mathrm{H_2})/p^{\ominus}][p(\mathrm{I_2})/p^{\ominus}]$$
$$= x(\mathrm{HI})^2/x(\mathrm{H_2})x(\mathrm{I_2})\ [p(\mathrm{J}) = x(\mathrm{J})p]$$
$$= \{(0.20 + 2x)^2/(0.30 - x)(0.40 - x)\} = 870\ [\text{given}].$$

Therefore $0.04 + 0.80x + 4x^2 = 870(0.12 - 0.7x + x^2)$, $866x^2 - 610x + 104 = 0$, $x = 0.29$, ($x = 0.42$ is excluded because $x \leqslant 0.30$).

The final composition is therefore: H_2:0.01 mol; I_2:0.11 mol; HI:0.78 mol.

10.15	H_2	I_2	HI	
(1)	a	b	c	
(2)	$-x$			
(3)	$-x$	$-x$	$+2x$	
(4)	$a-x$	$b-x$	$c+2x$	Total: $a+b+c$
(5)	$\left(\dfrac{a-x}{a+b+c}\right)$	$\left(\dfrac{b-x}{a+b+c}\right)$	$\left(\dfrac{c+2x}{a+b+c}\right)$	

$$K_p = (c + 2x)^2/(a - x)(b - x),$$
$$x = \frac{(a+b)K_p + 4c - \sqrt{\{[(a+b)K_p + 4c]^2 - 4(K_p - 4)(abK_p - c^2)\}}}{2(K_p - 4)}.$$

10.16	A	B	C	D	
(1)	1.0	2.0	0	1.0	
(2)			0.9		
(3)	−0.6	−0.3	0.9	0.6	$2A + B \rightarrow 3C + 2D$
(4)	0.4	1.7	0.9	1.6	total: 4.6
(5)	0.087	0.370	0.196	0.348	

$$K_x = x_C^3 x_D^2/x_A^2 x_B = 0.196^3 \times 0.348^2/0.087^2 \times 0.370 = \underline{0.33}.$$

10.17	N_2	H_2	NH_3	
Initially	n	$3n$	0	
Change	$-\zeta n$	$-3\zeta n$	$2\zeta n$	$0\leqslant\zeta\leqslant 1$; $N_2 + 3H_2 \rightarrow 2NH_3$
Final	$n(1-\zeta)$	$3n(1-\zeta)$	$2n\zeta$	Total: $2n(2-\zeta)$
Mole fraction	$\left(\dfrac{1-\zeta}{2(2-\zeta)}\right)$	$\left(\dfrac{3(1-\zeta)}{2(2-\zeta)}\right)$	$\left(\dfrac{\zeta}{2-\zeta}\right)$	

$$K_p = [p(\mathrm{NH})/p^\ominus]^2/[p(\mathrm{N_2})/p^\ominus]\ [p(\mathrm{H_2})/p^\ominus]^3$$

$$= \{x(\mathrm{NH_3})^2/x(\mathrm{N_2})x(\mathrm{H_2})^3\}\{1/(p/p^\ominus)^2\}$$

$$= \left\{\frac{\zeta^2}{(2-\zeta)^2}\cdot\frac{2(2-\zeta)}{(1-\zeta)}\cdot\frac{8(2-\zeta)^3}{27(1-\zeta)^3}\right\}\frac{1}{(p/p^\ominus)^2}$$

$$= \left\{\frac{16(2-\zeta)^2\zeta^2}{27(1-\zeta)^4}\right\}\frac{1}{(p/p^\ominus)^2}.$$

10.18 For K_p independent of pressure we require

$$\frac{(2-\zeta)^2\zeta^2}{(1-\zeta)^4} = a^2(p/p^\ominus)^2,\ a^2 \text{ a constant, } 27K_p/16.$$

$$(2-\zeta)\zeta/(1-\zeta)^2 = ap\,(p \equiv p/p^\ominus).$$

$$(1+ap)\zeta^2 - 2(1+ap)\zeta + ap = 0,\ \zeta = 1-\surd\left(\frac{1}{1+ap}\right)$$

by solving the quadratic equation and taking the negative root [because $\zeta \leqslant 1$]. But $a = \frac{3}{4}\surd(3K_p)$, and so

$$\zeta = 1 - \left\{\frac{1}{1+\frac{3}{4}\surd(3K_p p/p^\ominus)}\right\}^{1/2}.$$

10.19 From Problem 10.5, $K_p = 6.0 \times 10^5$. Therefore

$$\zeta_e = 1 - \left\{\frac{1}{1+1000\surd(p/p^\ominus)}\right\}^{1/2}.$$ Draw up the following Table:

$p/p^{\ominus}$	0.1	1.0	10.0	100	1000
ζ_e	0.94	0.97	0.98	0.99	0.99

These values are plotted in Fig. 10.1.

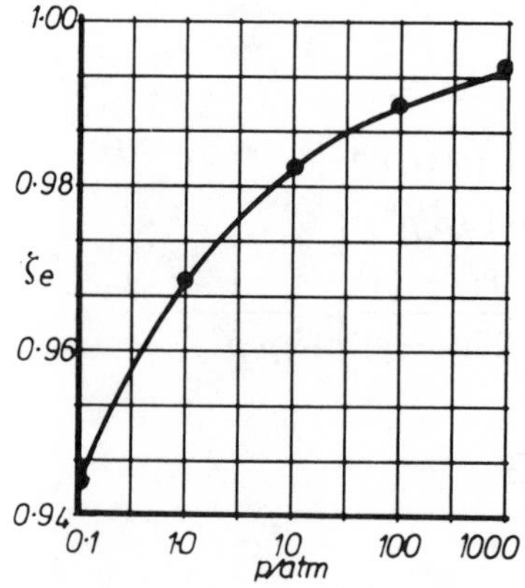

Fig 10.1

When $p = 500$ atm, $\zeta_e = 0.99$. The composition by mole fraction is then [Problem 10.17] $x(N_2) = 0.0033, x(H_2) = 0.0100, x(NH_3) = 0.99$.

10.20 K and $\ln K$ are plotted against t in Fig. 10.2. At $t = 20$ °C we find $K = 23\,300$.

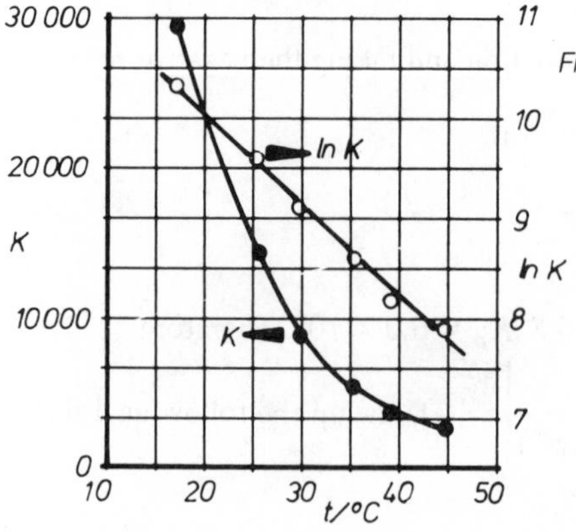

Fig 10.2

Therefore $\Delta_r G^\ominus = -RT\ln K$ [10.1.17] $= -(8.314\,\mathrm{J\,K^{-1}\,mol^{-1}}) \times (293.15\,\mathrm{K})$
$\times \ln 23\,300 = \underline{-24.5\,\mathrm{kJ\,mol^{-1}}}$.

$\Delta_r H^\ominus = RT^2\,\mathrm{d}\ln K/\mathrm{d}T$ [10.2.4]. From the graph, at $t = 20\,^\circ\mathrm{C}$ we have $\mathrm{d}\ln K/\mathrm{d}T = -0.926\,\mathrm{K^{-1}}$.

Therefore $\Delta_r H^\ominus = (8.314\,\mathrm{J\,K^{-1}\,mol^{-1}}) \times (293.15\,\mathrm{K})^2 \times (-0.0926\,\mathrm{K^{-1}})$
$= \underline{-66.1\,\mathrm{kJ\,mol^{-1}}}$.

$\Delta_r S^\ominus = (\Delta_r H^\ominus - \Delta_r G^\ominus)/T = \{-66.1\,\mathrm{kJ\,mol^{-1}} - (-24.5\,\mathrm{kJ\,mol^{-1}})\}/(293\,\mathrm{K})$
$= \underline{-142\,\mathrm{J\,K^{-1}\,mol^{-1}}}$.

10.21 $I_2 \rightleftharpoons 2I$. I_2 equilibrium amount: $n(1-\alpha)$, I equilibrium amount: $2n\alpha$.
$x(I_2) = (1-\alpha)/(1+\alpha)$; $x(I) = 2\alpha/(1+\alpha)$. $p(I_2) = x(I_2)p$, $p(I) = x(I)p$.
$K_p = p(I)^2/p(I_2) = x(I)^2 p/x(I_2) = 4\alpha^2 p/(1-\alpha^2)$; $p \equiv p/p^\ominus$.
If $p^\circ = nRT/V$, then $p = 2\alpha p^\circ + p^\circ(1-\alpha) = p^\circ(1+\alpha)$; and so $\alpha = (p - p^\circ)/p^\circ$. Draw up the following Table.

T/K	973	1073	1173
p/atm	0.06244	0.07500	0.09181
$10^4\,n/\mathrm{mol}\,I_2$	2.4709	2.4555	2.4366
p°/atm	0.05757	0.06309	0.06844
α	0.08459	0.1888	0.3415
K_p	1.800×10^{-3}	1.109×10^{-2}	4.848×10^{-2}

$\Delta H_\mathrm{m}^\ominus = RT^2\,(\mathrm{d}\ln K/\mathrm{d}T)$ [10.2.4] $\approx (8.314\,\mathrm{J\,K^{-1}\,mol^{-1}}) \times (1073\,\mathrm{K})^2$
$\times \{(-3.027) - (-6.320)\}/(200\,\mathrm{K}) \approx \underline{157.6\,\mathrm{kJ\,mol^{-1}}}$.

10.22 $2NO_2 \rightleftharpoons N_2O_4$; $K_p = [p(N_2O_4)/p^\ominus]/[p(NO_2)/p^\ominus]^2$
$\Delta_r G^\ominus = -RT\ln K_p$ [10.1.17], $\Delta_r H^\ominus = RT^2\,\mathrm{d}\ln K/\mathrm{d}T$ [10.2.4].
At 298 K: $K_p = [23/760]/[46/760]^2 = \underline{8.3}$.
$\Delta_r G^\ominus = -(2.48\,\mathrm{kJ\,mol^{-1}})\ln 8.3 = \underline{5.2\,\mathrm{kJ\,mol^{-1}}}$.
At 305 K: $K_p = [30/760]/[68/760]^2 = 4.9$;
$\mathrm{d}\ln K/\mathrm{d}T \approx (\ln 4.9 - \ln 8.3)/(7\,\mathrm{K}) = -0.075\,\mathrm{K^{-1}}$.

Therefore, $\Delta_r H^\ominus$ (298.15 K) $\approx$ (8.314 J K^{-1} mol^{-1}) $\times$ (298 K)^2 $\times$ (-0.075 K^{-1})

$= \underline{-55.6 \text{ kJ mol}^{-1}}$.

$\Delta_r S^\ominus$ (298 K) $\approx (\Delta_r H^\ominus - \Delta_r G^\ominus)/T$

$= [(-55.6 \text{ kJ mol}^{-1}) - (-5.2 \text{ kJ mol}^{-1})]/(298.15 \text{ K}) = \underline{-169 \text{ J K}^{-1} \text{ mol}^{-1}}$.

10.23 $K_p = p(N_2O_4)/[p(NO_2)]^2$ $[p \equiv p/\text{Torr}]$, $p = p(NO_2) + p(N_2O_4)$.

$K_p p(NO_2)^2 + p(NO_2) - p = 0$, so that $p(NO_2) = \{-1 + \sqrt{(1 + 4K_p p)}\}/2K_p$.

For equal absorptions (by NO_2) $l_1 p_1(NO_2) = l_2 p_2(NO_2)$, or $rp_1 = p_2$ $[r = l_1/l_2]$.

Therefore, $r\{\sqrt{(1 + 4K_p p_1)} - 1\} = \{\sqrt{(1 + 4K_p p_2)} - 1\}$.

$r\sqrt{(1 + 4K_p p_1)} = (r - 1) + \sqrt{(1 + 4K_p p_2)}$.

$r^2(1 + 4K_p p_1) = (r - 1)^2 + (1 + 4K_p p_2) + 2(r - 1)\sqrt{(1 + 4K_p p_2)}$,

$r - 1 + 2K_p(p_1 r^2 - p_2) = (r - 1)\sqrt{(1 + 4K_p p_2)}$,

$[r - 1 + 2K_p(p_1 r^2 - p_2)]^2 = (r - 1)^2(1 + 4K_p p_2)$,

$(p_1 r^2 - p_2)^2 K_p^2 + [(r - 1)(p_1 r^2 - p_2) - (r - 1)^2 p_2] K_p = 0$;

$$K_p = \frac{(p_1 r^2 - p_2)^2}{r(r - 1)(p_2 - p_1 r)}.$$

$r = l_1/l_2 = (395 \text{ mm})/(75 \text{ mm}) = 5.27$

$K_p = (27.8 p_1 - p_2)^2/[22.5(p_2 - 5.27 p_1)]$; $p \equiv p/\text{Torr}$.

Draw up the following Table.

Absorbance	p_1/Torr	p_2/Torr	K_p
0.05	1.00	5.47	110.8
0.10	2.10	12.00	102.5
0.15	3.15	18.65	103.0
		Mean:	105

10.24 $K_p = p(P)/p(A)^3$, $p \equiv p/\text{bar}$. $p(A) = x_A p^\circ(A)$, $p(P) = x_P p^\circ(P)$;

$p(A) + p(B) = p$.

Therefore $p = x_A p^\circ(A) + x_P p^\circ(P) = x_A p^\circ(A) + (1 - x_A)p^\circ(P)$, and so

$x_A = [p - p^\circ(P)]/[p^\circ(A) - p^\circ(P)]$.

It follows that $p(\mathrm{A}) = p^{\mathrm{o}}(\mathrm{A})\,[p - p^{\mathrm{o}}(\mathrm{P})]/[p^{\mathrm{o}}(\mathrm{A}) - p^{\mathrm{o}}(\mathrm{P})]$,

$p(\mathrm{P}) = p^{\mathrm{o}}(\mathrm{P})\,[p - p^{\mathrm{o}}(\mathrm{A})]/[p^{\mathrm{o}}(\mathrm{P}) - p^{\mathrm{o}}(\mathrm{A})]$,

$K_p = p^{\mathrm{o}}(\mathrm{P})\,[p^{\mathrm{o}}(\mathrm{A}) - p]\,[p^{\mathrm{o}}(\mathrm{A}) - p^{\mathrm{o}}(\mathrm{P})]^2/p^{\mathrm{o}}(\mathrm{A})^3\,[p - p^{\mathrm{o}}(\mathrm{P})]^3$.

For the saturated vapor pressure use

$\ln(p/\mathrm{kPa}) = \mathrm{const.} - \Delta H_{\mathrm{vap,m}}/RT$ [given].

$\Delta H_{\mathrm{vap,m}}(\mathrm{A}) = 25.6\ \mathrm{kJ\,mol^{-1}}$, $\Delta H_{\mathrm{vap,m}}(\mathrm{P}) = 41.5\ \mathrm{kJ\,mol^{-1}}$.

const(A) = 15.1, const(B) = 17.2, and so

$p^{\mathrm{o}}(\mathrm{A})/\mathrm{kPa} = 3.61 \times 10^6 \exp\{-3.08 \times 10^3/(T/\mathrm{K})\}$,

$p^{\mathrm{o}}(\mathrm{P})/\mathrm{kPa} = 2.95 \times 10^7 \exp\{-4.99 \times 10^3/(T/\mathrm{K})\}$.

Draw up the following Table.

$\theta/°\mathrm{C}$	20.0	22.0	26.0	28.0	30.0
T/K	293.2	295.2	299.2	301.2	303.2
$p^{\mathrm{o}}(\mathrm{A})/\mathrm{kPa}$	98.9	106.2	122.1	130.8	139.9
$p^{\mathrm{o}}(\mathrm{P})/\mathrm{kPa}$	1.20	1.34	1.69	1.88	2.10
p/kPa	23.9	27.3	36.5	42.6	49.9
$K_p \times 10^5$	7.59	5.55	2.73	1.82	1.20
$\ln K_p$	−9.49	−9.80	−10.51	−10.91	−11.33

$\theta/°\mathrm{C}$	32.0	34.0	36.0	38.0	40.0
T/K	305.2	307.2	309.2	311.2	313.2
$p^{\mathrm{o}}(\mathrm{A})/\mathrm{kPa}$	149.5	159.7	170.4	181.6	193.5
$p^{\mathrm{o}}(\mathrm{P})/\mathrm{kPa}$	2.34	2.60	2.89	3.21	3.55
p/kPa	56.9	65.1	74.3	85.0	96.2
$K_p \times 10^5$	0.865	0.610	0.433	0.301	0.216
$\ln K_p$	−11.66	−12.01	−12.35	−12.71	−13.05

$\ln K_p$ is plotted in Fig. 10.3.

$\Delta_{\mathrm{r}} H^{\ominus} = RT^2 \mathrm{d} \ln K_p/\mathrm{d}T$ [10.2.4]

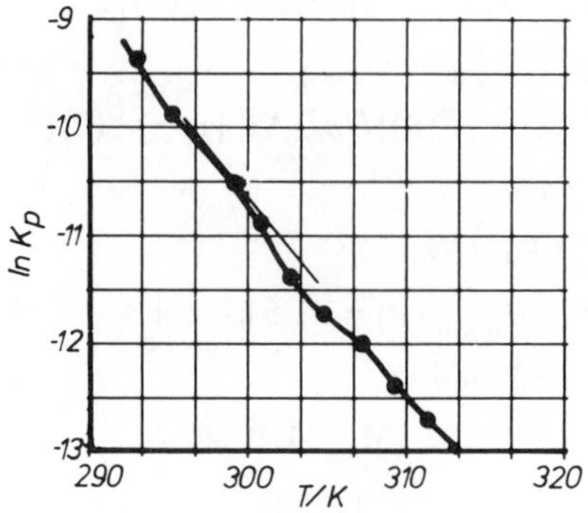

Fig 10.3

At 298 K, $d\ln K_p/dT = -0.185\ K^{-1}$,
therefore $\Delta_r H^\ominus = (8.314\ J\ K^{-1}\ mol^{-1}) \times (298.15\ K)^2 \times (-0.185\ K^{-1}) = \underline{-137\ kJ\ mol^{-1}}$.

10.25 $3A(g) \rightarrow A_3(g)$; $\Delta_r H^\ominus = -133.5\ kJ\ mol^{-1}$, $\Delta_r S^\ominus = -475.5\ J\ K^{-1}$.
$3A(l) \rightarrow 3A(g)$; $\Delta_r H^\ominus = 3 \times 25.6\ kJ\ mol^{-1} = 76.8\ kJ\ mol^{-1}$,
$\Delta_r S = 3 \times 25.6\ kJ\ mol^{-1}/294\ K = 261\ J\ K^{-1}\ mol^{-1}$.
$A_3(l) \rightarrow A_3(g)$; $\Delta_r H^\ominus = 41.5\ kJ\ mol^{-1}$.
$\Delta_r S = (41.5\ kJ\ mol^{-1})/398\ K = 104\ J\ K^{-1}\ mol^{-1}$.
$3A(l) \rightarrow A_3(l)$; $\Delta_r H^\ominus = 76.8\ kJ\ mol^{-1} - 133.5\ kJ\ mol^{-1} - 41.5\ kJ\ mol^{-1}$
$= \underline{-98.2\ kJ\ mol^{-1}}$.
$\Delta_r S = (261 - 457.5 - 104)\ J\ K^{-1}\ mol^{-1} = \underline{-301\ J\ K^{-1}\ mol^{-1}}$.
$\Delta_r G = -98.2\ kJ\ mol^{-1} - (298\ K) \times (-301\ J\ K^{-1}\ mol^{-1}) = -8.50\ kJ\ mol^{-1}$.
$K_p = \exp(8.50/2.48) = 30.8$.
$K_p(\text{gas})/K_p(\text{liquid}) = (3.2 \times 10^{-5})/(30.8) = \underline{1.04 \times 10^{-6}}$.

10.26 $K = K_p K_\gamma$ [10.1.18], $(\partial K/\partial p)_T = 0$ [10.2.1].
Therefore $(\partial K_p/\partial p)_T K_\gamma + (\partial K_\gamma/\partial p)_T K_p = 0$,
$(1/K_p)(\partial K_p/\partial p)_T + (1/K_\gamma)(\partial K_\gamma/\partial p)_T = 0$,
$\underline{(\partial \ln K_p/\partial p)_T = -(\partial \ln K_\gamma/\partial p)_T}$.
$I_2 + H_2 \rightleftharpoons 2HI$; $K = [f(HI)/p^\ominus]^2/[f(H_2)/p^\ominus]\ [f(I_2)/p^\ominus] = f(HI)^2/f(H_2)f(I_2)$.
$f(J) = p(J)\exp\{-p(J)a(J)/R^2T^2\} \equiv p(J)\gamma(J)$.
Therefore $K_\gamma = \gamma(HI)^2/\gamma(H_2)\gamma(I_2) = \exp\{-[2a(HI)p(HI) - a(H_2)p(H_2)$
$- a(I_2)p(I_2)]/R^2T^2\}$

$$= \exp\{-[2a(\mathrm{HI})x(\mathrm{HI}) - a(\mathrm{H_2})x(\mathrm{H_2}) - a(\mathrm{I_2})x(\mathrm{I_2})]\,p/R^2T^2\}.$$

$$(\partial \ln K_p/\partial p)_T = -(\partial/\partial p)\{-[2a(\mathrm{HI})x(\mathrm{HI}) - a(\mathrm{H_2})x(\mathrm{H_2}) - a(\mathrm{I_2})x(\mathrm{I_2})]\,p/R^2T^2\}$$
$$= \underline{\{2a(\mathrm{HI})x(\mathrm{HI}) - a(\mathrm{H_2})x(\mathrm{H_2}) - a(\mathrm{I_2})x(\mathrm{I_2})\}/R^2T^2}.$$

$a(\mathrm{HI}) \approx 6.2\ \mathrm{dm^6\,atm\,mol^{-2}}$, $a(\mathrm{H_2}) \approx 0.24\ \mathrm{dm^6\,atm\,mol^{-2}}$,

$a(\mathrm{I_2}) \approx 7.3\ \mathrm{dm^6\,atm\,mol^{-1}}$

$$(\partial \ln K_p/\partial p)_T \approx [12.4x(\mathrm{HI}) - 0.24x(\mathrm{H_2}) - 7.3x(\mathrm{I_2})] \times \frac{\mathrm{dm^6\,atm\,mol^{-2}}}{(0.0821\ \mathrm{dm^3\,atm\,K^{-1}\,mol^{-1}})^2\,T^2}$$

$$\approx [12.4x(\mathrm{HI}) - 0.24x(\mathrm{H_2}) - 7.3x(\mathrm{I_2})]\ (149\ \mathrm{K^2}/T^2)\,\mathrm{atm^{-1}}.$$

Suppose $x(\mathrm{HI}) \approx x(\mathrm{H_2}) \approx x(\mathrm{I_2}) \approx 1/3$, $(\partial \ln K_p/\partial p)_T \approx 1.6x(149\ \mathrm{K^2}/T^2)\,\mathrm{atm^{-1}}$.

Suppose $T \approx 298\ \mathrm{K}$, $(\partial \ln K_p/\partial p)_T \approx 2.7 \times 10^{-3}\,\mathrm{atm^{-1}}$.

Therefore $\delta \ln K_p \approx (\partial \ln K_p/\partial p)_T \delta p \approx (2.7 \times 10^{-3}\,\mathrm{atm^{-1}}) \times (50\ \mathrm{atm}) = 0.14$.

Therefore, $K_p(550\ \mathrm{atm}) \approx K_p(500\ \mathrm{atm})\ \mathrm{e}^{0.14} = 1.15\ K_p(500\ \mathrm{atm})$.

10.27 $w'_{\mathrm{e,max}} = -\Delta G$ [5.3.11], $q_p = \Delta H$

$$\Delta_r G^\ominus = \Delta_f G^\ominus(\mathrm{ZnSO_4,aq}) - \Delta_f G^\ominus(\mathrm{CuSO_4,aq}) = \Delta_f G^\ominus(\mathrm{Zn^{2+},aq}) - \Delta_f G^\ominus(\mathrm{Cu^{2+},aq})$$
$$= (-147.1\ \mathrm{kJ\,mol^{-1}}) - (65.5\ \mathrm{kJ\,mol^{-1}}) = -212.6\ \mathrm{kJ\,mol^{-1}}.$$

Maximum available electrical work: $\underline{212.6\ \mathrm{kJ\,mol^{-1}}}$ (done *by* system)

$$\Delta H_\mathrm{m}^\ominus = \Delta H_\mathrm{f}^\ominus(\mathrm{Zn^{2+},aq}) - \Delta H_\mathrm{f}^\ominus(\mathrm{Cu^{2+},aq}) = (-153.9\ \mathrm{kJ\,mol^{-1}}) - (64.8\ \mathrm{kJ\,mol^{-1}})$$
$$= -218.7\ \mathrm{kJ\,mol^{-1}}.$$

Maximum available heat output: $\underline{218.7\ \mathrm{kJ\,mol^{-1}}}$.

$$\Delta S_\mathrm{m}^\ominus = S^\ominus(\mathrm{Zn^{2+},aq}) - S^\ominus(\mathrm{Cu^{2+},aq}) = (-112.1\ \mathrm{J\,K^{-1}\,mol^{-1}}) - (-99.6\ \mathrm{J\,K^{-1}\,mol^{-1}})$$
$$= -12.5\ \mathrm{J\,K^{-1}\,mol^{-1}};$$

i.e. entropy has to be generated in the surroundings in order to overcome this negative change in the system's entropy. Therefore not the whole of the energy change is available to do work.

10.28 $\mathrm{C} + \mathrm{O_2(g)} \rightarrow \mathrm{CO_2(g)}$; $n(\mathrm{C}) = (100\ \mathrm{kg})/(12\ \mathrm{g\,mol^{-1}}) = 8.3 \times 10^3\ \mathrm{mol}$.

$w'_{\mathrm{e,max}} = -\Delta G$. For all materials supposed to be in their standard states

$\Delta G^\ominus = (8.3 \times 10^3\ \mathrm{mol}) \times \Delta G_\mathrm{m}^\ominus$; $\Delta G_\mathrm{m}^\ominus = \Delta G_\mathrm{f}^\ominus(\mathrm{CO_2}) = -393.5\ \mathrm{kJ\,mol^{-1}}$ [Table 4.1].

$w'_{\mathrm{e,max}} = -(8.3 \times 10^3\ \mathrm{mol}) \times (-393.5\ \mathrm{kJ\,mol^{-1}}) = \underline{3.3 \times 10^6\ \mathrm{kJ}}.$

$\Delta H_\mathrm{m}^\ominus = \Delta H_\mathrm{f}^\ominus(\mathrm{CO_2}) = -393.5\ \mathrm{kJ\,mol^{-1}}$ [Table 4.1].

$q_p = 3.3 \times 10^6\,\text{kJ}.$

$w'_o = c_o q_p,\ c_o = (T_h - T_c)/T_h$ [Section 5.2(e)].

$w'_o = [120\,\text{K}/423\,\text{K}]\ [3.3 \times 10^6\,\text{kJ}] = \underline{9.4 \times 10^5\,\text{kJ}}.$

10.29 $\Delta G = \Delta H - T\Delta S;\ \Delta H(T_2) = \Delta H(T_1) + \int_{T_1}^{T_2} \Delta C_p(T)\mathrm{d}T$ [4.1.6];

$\Delta S(T_2) = \Delta S(T_1) + \int_{T_1}^{T_2} [\Delta C_p(T)/T]\,\mathrm{d}T$ [5.2.1].

$$\Delta G(T_2) = \Delta H(T_2) - T_2\Delta S(T_2)$$

$$= \Delta H(T_1) + \int_{T_2}^{T_2} \Delta C_p(T)\mathrm{d}T - T_2\Delta S(T_1) - T_2 \int_{T_1}^{T_2} [\Delta C_p(T)/T]\,\mathrm{d}T$$

$$= \Delta G(T_1) + (T_1 - T_2) \times \Delta S(T_1) + \int_1^2 \Delta C_p(T)\ [1 - (T_2/T)]\,\mathrm{d}T.$$

$\Delta C_p(T) = \Delta a + \Delta bT + \Delta c/T^2,$

$$\int_1^2 \Delta C_p(T)\ [1 - (T_2/T)]\,\mathrm{d}T$$

$$= \Delta a\{(T_2 - T_1) - T_2\ln(T_2/T_1)\} + \Delta b\{\tfrac{1}{2}(T_2^2 - T_1^2) - T_2(T_2 - T_1)\}$$

$$+ \Delta c \left\{-\left(\frac{1}{T_2} - \frac{1}{T_1}\right) + \tfrac{1}{2}T_2\left(\frac{1}{T_2^2} - \frac{1}{T_1^2}\right)\right\}.$$

Therefore $\Delta G(T_2) = \Delta G(T_1) + (T_1 - T_2)\Delta S(T_1) + \alpha\Delta a + \beta\Delta b + \gamma\Delta c,$

$\alpha = T_2 - T_1 - T_2\ln(T_2/T_1),\ \beta = \tfrac{1}{2}(T_2^2 - T_1^2) - T_2(T_2 - T_1),$

$$\gamma = \left(\frac{1}{T_1} + \frac{1}{T_2}\right) + \tfrac{1}{2}T_2\left(\frac{1}{T_2^2} - \frac{1}{T_1^2}\right),$$

$\Delta S(T_1) = [\Delta H(T_1) - \Delta G(T_1)]/T_1.$

10.30 $H_2 + \tfrac{1}{2}O_2 \rightarrow H_2O(l);\ \Delta_f G^\ominus(298\,\text{K}) = -237.2\,\text{kJ mol}^{-1},$

$\Delta_f H^\ominus(298\,\text{K}) = -285.8\,\text{kJ mol}^{-1}.$

$\Delta_f S^\ominus(298\,\text{K}) = -163.3\,\text{J K}^{-1}\,\text{mol}^{-1}.$

$\Delta a = a(H_2O) - a(H_2) - \tfrac{1}{2}a(O_2) = [75.48 - 27.28 - 14.98]\,\text{J K}^{-1}\,\text{mol}^{-1}$

$= 33.22\,\text{J K}^{-1}\,\text{mol}^{-1};$

$\Delta b = b(H_2O) - b(H_2) - \frac{1}{2}b(O_2) = [0 - 3.26 \times 10^{-3} - 2.09 \times 10^{-3}]\ J\,K^{-2}\,mol^{-1}$
$= -5.35 \times 10^{-3}\,J\,K^{-2}\,mol^{-1}$;

$\Delta c = c(H_2O) - c(H_2) - \frac{1}{2}c(O_2) = [0 - 0.50 \times 10^5 + 0.83 \times 10^5]\ J\,K\,mol^{-1}$
$= 0.33 \times 10^5\,J\,K\,mol^{-1}$.

$T_1 = 298\,K, T_2 = 372\,K$.

$\alpha = 372\,K - 298\,K - (372\,K)\ln(372/298) = -8.5\,K$,

$\beta = [\frac{1}{2}(372^2 - 298^2) - 372(372 - 298)]\,K^2 = -2738\,K^2$,

$$\gamma = \left[\left(\frac{1}{298} - \frac{1}{372}\right) + \tfrac{1}{2} \times 372 \times \left(\frac{1}{372^2} - \frac{1}{298^2}\right)\right] K^{-1} = -8.288 \times 10^{-5}\,K^{-1}.$$

Therefore $\Delta G(372\,K) = -237.2\,kJ\,mol^{-1} + (-74\,K) \times (-163.0 \times 10^{-3}\,kJ\,K^{-1}\,mol^{-1})$
$+ (-8.5\,K) \times (33.22 \times 10^{-3}\,kJ\,K^{-1}\,mol^{-1})$
$+ (-2738\,K^2) \times (-5.35 \times 10^{-6}\,kJ\,K^{-2}\,mol^{-1})$
$+ (-8.29 \times 10^{-5}\,K^{-1}) \times (0.33 \times 10^2\,kJ\,K\,mol^{-1})$
$= \underline{-225.4\,kJ\,mol^{-1}}$.

10.31 $\Phi_0(T) = [G^\ominus_m(T) - H^\ominus_m(0)]/T, S(T) = [H(T) - G(T)]/T$.

$G^\ominus_m(T) = H^\ominus_m(0) + T\Phi_0$,

$S^\ominus_m(T) = [H^\ominus_m(T) - G^\ominus_m(T)]/T = [H^\ominus_m(T) - H^\ominus_m(0) - T\Phi_0]/T$
$= [H^\ominus_m(T) - H^\ominus_m(0)]/T - \Phi_0$.

10.32 $\Delta G^\ominus_m(T) = \Delta H^\ominus_m(0) + T\Delta\Phi_0 = \Delta G^\ominus_m(298\,K) + [T\Delta\Phi_0(T) - (298\,K)\Phi_0(298\,K)]$.

(a) $N_2 + 3H_2 \rightarrow 2NH_3$ at 1000 K.

$\Delta_r G^\ominus(298\,K) = -31.0\,kJ\,mol^{-1}$ [Table 4.1],

$\Delta\Phi_0(1000\,K) = 2 \times (-203.5\,J\,K^{-1}\,mol^{-1}) - (-197.9\,J\,K^{-1}\,mol^{-1})$
$- 3(-137.0\,J\,K^{-1}\,mol^{-1}) = 201.9\,J\,K^{-1}\,mol^{-1}$.

$\Delta\Phi_0(298\,K) = 2 \times (-159.0\,J\,K^{-1}\,mol^{-1}) - (-162.4\,J\,K^{-1}\,mol^{-1})$
$- 3(-102.2\,J\,K^{-1}\,mol^{-1}) = 151.0\,J\,K^{-1}\,mol^{-1}$.

Therefore $\Delta_r G^\ominus(1000\,K) = -31.0\,kJ\,mol^{-1} + (201.9\,kJ\,mol^{-1} - 45.0\,kJ\,mol^{-1})$
$= \underline{125.9\,kJ\,mol^{-1}}$.

(b) $H_2O + CO \rightarrow H_2 + CO_2$ at 500 K, 2000 K;

$\Delta_r G^\ominus(298\,K) = \Delta G^\ominus_f(CO_2) - \Delta G^\ominus_f(H_2O\,g) - \Delta G^\ominus_f(CO)$
$= [-394.4 - (-228.6) - (-137.2)]\ kJ\,mol^{-1}$ [Table 4.1]
$= -28.6\,kJ\,mol^{-1}$.

$\Delta\Phi_0(298\,\text{K})/\text{J K}^{-1}\,\text{mol}^{-1} = -182.3 - 102.2 + 155.5 + 168.4 = 39.4;$

$(298\,\text{K})\,\Delta\Phi_0(298\,\text{K}) = 11.7\,\text{kJ mol}^{-1}.$

$\Delta\Phi_0(500\,\text{K})/\text{J K}^{-1}\,\text{mol}^{-1} = -199.5 - 116.9 + 172.8 + 183.5 = 39.9;$

$(500\,\text{K})\Delta\Phi_0(500\,\text{K}) = 20.0\,\text{kJ mol}^{-1}.$

$\Delta\Phi_0(2000\,\text{K})/\text{J K}^{-1}\,\text{mol}^{-1} = -258.8 - 157.6 + 223.1 + 258.8 = 65.5;$

$(2000\,\text{K})\Delta\Phi_0(2000\,\text{K}) = 131\,\text{kJ mol}^{-1}.$

Therefore $\Delta_r G^\ominus(500\,\text{K})/\text{kJ mol}^{-1} = -28.6 + 20.0 - 11.7 = \underline{-20.3}$

$\Delta_r G^\ominus(2000\,\text{K})/\text{kJ mol}^{-1} = -28.6 + 131 - 11.7 = \underline{91}.$

10.33 $K_p = \exp\{-\Delta G_m^\ominus(T)/RT\}$ [10.1.17].

(a) $K_p = \exp\{-(125.9\,\text{kJ mol}^{-1})/(8.314\,\text{J K}^{-1}\,\text{mol}^{-1}) \times (1000\,\text{K})\}$

$= e^{-15.1} = \underline{2.7 \times 10^{-7}}.$

(b) $K_p(500\,\text{K}) = \exp\{-(-20.3\,\text{kJ mol}^{-1})/(8.314\,\text{J K}^{-1}\,\text{mol}^{-1}) \times (500\,\text{K})\}$

$= e^{+4.9} = \underline{130}.$

$K_p\,(2000\,\text{K}) = \exp\{-(25.2\,\text{kJ mol}^{-1})/(8.314\,\text{J K}^{-1}\,\text{mol}^{-1}) \times (2000\,\text{K})$

$= e^{-1.52} = \underline{0.22}.$

10.34 $\Phi = [G_m^\ominus(T) - H_m^\ominus(\mathcal{T})]/T$

$\Phi(\mathcal{T}) = [G_m^\ominus(\mathcal{T}) - H_m^\ominus(\mathcal{T})]/\mathcal{T} = -S_m^\ominus(\mathcal{T})$

$$\begin{aligned}\Phi &= [H_m^\ominus(T) - TS_m^\ominus(T) - H_m^\ominus(\mathcal{T})]/T \\ &= [H_m^\ominus(T) - H_m^\ominus(\mathcal{T})]/T - S_m^\ominus(T) \\ &= [H_m^\ominus(T) - H_m^\ominus(\mathcal{T})]/T - [S_m^\ominus(T) - S_m^\ominus(\mathcal{T})] - S_m^\ominus(\mathcal{T}) \\ &= \Phi(\mathcal{T}) + \frac{1}{T}\int_{\mathcal{T}}^{T} C_p(T')\,dT' - \int_{\mathcal{T}}^{T} [C_p(T')/T']\,dT' \\ &= \Phi(\mathcal{T}) + \int_{\mathcal{T}}^{T} C_p(T')\left(\frac{T'-T}{T'T}\right) dT'.\end{aligned}$$

$C_p(T') = a + bT' + cT'^{-2};$

$$\Delta\Phi(T) = \Delta\Phi(\mathcal{T}) + \Delta a\int_{\mathcal{T}}^{T}\left(\frac{T'-T}{T'T}\right)dT'$$

$$+ \Delta b\int_{\mathcal{T}}^{T}\left(\frac{T'-T}{T}\right) dT' + \Delta c\int_{\mathcal{T}}^{T}\left(\frac{T'-T}{T'^3 T}\right) dT'$$

$$= \Delta\Phi(\mathcal{T}) + A(T)\Delta a + B(T)\Delta b + C(T)\Delta c$$

$$A(T) = \frac{1}{T}\,(T - \mathcal{T}) - \ln(T/\mathcal{T}),$$

$$B(T) = \frac{1}{2T}\,(T^2 - \mathcal{T}^2) - (T - \mathcal{T})$$

$$C(T) = +\frac{1}{T}\left(\frac{1}{\mathcal{T}} - \frac{1}{T}\right) + \tfrac{1}{2}\left(\frac{1}{T^2} - \frac{1}{\mathcal{T}^2}\right).$$

11. Equilibrium electrochemistry: ions and electrodes

A11.1 $I = (1/2) \sum_j (m_j/m^\ominus) z_j^2$ [11.2.6] $= (1/2)[3(0.04)(+1)^2 + (0.04)(-3)^2$

$+ (0.03)(+1)^2 + (0.03)(-1)^2 + (0.05)(+1)^2 + (0.05)(-1)^2] = \underline{0.32}.$

A11.2 Let g_1 = mass of NaCl [RMM = 58.4].

Then $1.50 = [(g_1/58.4)/(800 - g_1)]\,10^3$; $g_1 = 64$ g. The NaCl solution contains $800 - 64 = 736$ g H_2O and 1.10 mol NaCl. The NaCl concentration in the final mixture is $1.10/(0.736 + 0.255) = 1.11$ mol kg^{-1}. Let g_2 = mass of Na_2SO_4 [RMM = 142]. Then $1.25 = [(g_2/142)/(300 - g_2)]\,10^3$; $g_2 = 45$ g. The Na_2SO_4 solution contains $300 - 45 = 255$ g H_2O and 0.317 mol Na_2SO_4. The Na_2SO_4 concentration in the final mixture is $0.317/(0.736 + 0.255)$ or 0.320 mol kg^{-1}.

$I = (1/2) \sum_j (m_j/m^\ominus) z_j^2 = (1/2)[1.11(+1)^2 + 1.11(-1)^2 + 2(0.320)(+1)^2$

$+ (0.320)(-2)^2] = \underline{2.07}.$

A11.3 Let g_1 = mass of KNO_3 [RMM = 101].

Then $0.15 = [(g_1/101)/(500 - g_1)]\,10^3$; $g_1 = 7.5$ g. The KNO_3 solution contains $500 - 8 = 492$ g H_2O and 0.074 mol KNO_3.

(a) Let g_2 = mass of $Ca(NO_3)_2$ [RMM = 164]

$I = (1/2) \sum_j (m_j/m^\ominus) z_j^2$ [11.2.6].

$0.25 = (1/2)[(0.15)(+1)^2 + (0.15)(-1)^2 + (g_2/164)(0.492)^{-1}(+2)^2$

$+ 2(g_2/164)(0.492)^{-1}(-1)^2]$; $\underline{g_2 = 2.7\text{ g}}.$

(b) Let g_3 = mass of NaCl [RMM = 58.4]

$0.25 = (1/2)[0.15)(+1)^2 + (0.15)(-1)^2 + (g_3/58.4)(0.492)^{-1}(+1)^2$

$+ (g_3/58.4)(0.492)^{-1}(-1)^2]$;

$\underline{g_3 = 2.9\text{ g}}$

A11.4 $a(Cl^-) = (\gamma_\pm)(2)(2.000) = (1.554)(2)(2.000) = \underline{6.216}.$

A11.5 Number of moles of electrolyte = (0.065)(5.00) = 0.325 mol

$w_e = (-1.04 \times 10^3\text{ J})/(0.325\text{ mol}) = \underline{-3.20 \times 10^3\text{ J mol}^{-1}}.$

$w_e = RT \ln \gamma_\pm^3$; $\gamma_\pm = \exp(w_e/3RT)$; [11.2.1]

$\gamma_\pm = \exp[(-3.20 \times 10^3\,\mathrm{J\,mol^{-1}})(3)^{-1}(8.31\,\mathrm{J\,K^{-1}\,mol^{-1}})^{-1}(298\,\mathrm{K})^{-1}]$
$= \underline{0.650.}$

A11.6 $I = (1/2)\sum_j (m_j/m^\ominus)z_j^2$ [11.2.6]
$= (1/2)[(0.100)(+2)^2 + 2(0.100)(-1)^2] = 0.300.$
$r_D^2 = \epsilon RT/2\rho e^2 I N_A^2 m^\ominus$ [11.2.8]; $\epsilon = 2r_D^2 \rho e^2 I N_A^2 m^\ominus/RT$
$= (2)(0.400 \times 10^{-9}\,\mathrm{m})^2(0.850 \times 10^3\,\mathrm{kg/m^3})(1.60 \times 10^{-19}\,\mathrm{C})^2(0.300)$
$\times (6.02 \times 10^{23}\,\mathrm{mol^{-1}})^2(1\,\mathrm{mol/kg})/(8.31\,\mathrm{J\,K^{-1}\,mol^{-1}})(298\,\mathrm{K})$
$= 3.06 \times 10^{-10}\,\mathrm{J^{-1}\,C^2\,m^{-1}}$
$\epsilon_r = \epsilon/\epsilon_0 = 3.06 \times 10^{-10}\,\mathrm{J^{-1}C^2m^{-1}}/8.85 \times 10^{-12}\,\mathrm{J^{-1}C^2m^{-1}} = \underline{34.6}$

A11.7 $I = (1/2)\sum_j (m_j/m^\ominus)z_j^2 = (1/2)[(0.50)(+3)^2 + 3(0.50)(-1)^2] = 3.00$ [11.2.6]
$\lg(\gamma_\pm)_{DLL} = -0.509\,|z_+z_-|\,I^{\frac{1}{2}}$ [11.2.11] $= -(0.509)(3)(3.00)^{\frac{1}{2}} = -2.65.$
$(\gamma_\pm)_{DLL} = 2.24 \times 10^{-3};$
% error $= (0.303 - 2.24 \times 10^{-3})(2.24 \times 10^{-3})^{-1}(100) = \underline{1.34 \times 10^4.}$

A11.8 $\lg\gamma_\pm = -0.509\,|z_+z_-|\,I^{\frac{1}{2}} + 0.509\,A^*\,|z_+z_-|\,I$ [11.2.14]
$|z_+z_-| = 1; A^* = (0.509 I)^{-1}[\lg\gamma_\pm + 0.509\,I^{\frac{1}{2}}].$
(a) $A^* = (0.509)^{-1}(0.005)^{-1}[\lg(0.930) + 0.509(0.005)^{\frac{1}{2}}] = \underline{1.75,}$
(b) $A^* = (0.509)^{-1}(0.010)^{-1}[\lg(0.907) + 0.509(0.010)^{\frac{1}{2}}] = \underline{1.67,}$
(c) $A^* = (0.509)^{-1}(0.020)^{-1}[\lg(0.879) + 0.509(0.020)^{\frac{1}{2}}] = \underline{1.57.}$

A11.9 $CaF_2(s) \rightleftharpoons Ca^{2+}(aq) + 2F^-(aq)$
$\Delta_r G^\ominus(T) = -RT \ln K_s = -(8.3\,\mathrm{J\,K^{-1}\,mol^{-1}})(298\,\mathrm{K})\ln(3.9 \times 10^{-11})$
$= 5.9 \times 10^4\,\mathrm{J\,mol^{-1}}.$
$5.9 \times 10^4\,\mathrm{J\,mol^{-1}} = \Delta_f G^\ominus(T, CaF_2(aq)) - \Delta_f G^\ominus(T, CaF_2(s))$ [5.4.4]
$= \Delta_f G^\ominus(T, CaF_2(aq)) - (-1.162 \times 10^6\,\mathrm{J\,mol^{-1}}).$
$\Delta_f G^\ominus(T, CaF_2(aq)) = \underline{-1.103 \times 10^6\,\mathrm{J\,mol^{-1}}.}$

A11.10 $a_{H^+}(0.020) = (0.879)(0.0200) = 0.0176.$
$a_{H^+}(0.005) = (0.930)(0.005) = 4.65 \times 10^{-3}$ [Problem A11.8]
$\Delta\phi(0.020\,\mathrm{mol/kg}) - \Delta\phi(0.005\,\mathrm{mol/kg})$
$= -(RT/F)\ln\,[f_{H_2}^{\frac{1}{2}}/a_{H^+}(0.020)] \times [f_{H_2}^{\frac{1}{2}}/a_{H^+}(0.005)]^{-1}$ [11.4.2]
$= -(0.0257\,\mathrm{V})\ln(4.65 \times 10^{-3}/0.0176) = \underline{3.42 \times 10^{-2}\,\mathrm{V}.}$

11.1 $I = \frac{1}{2}\sum_j (m_j/m^{\ominus})z_j^2$ [11.2.6].

Thus an amount of substance n_j is in 1 kg of solvent and $n_j/\text{mol} = m_j/\text{mol kg}^{-1}$. Equivalently, n_j is in a mass $1\text{ kg} + \sum_j n_j M_{j,\text{m}}$ of solution (because the mass of the solute is $n_j M_{j,\text{m}}$. Therefore, if the density of the solution is ρ, the amount n_j is in a volume $[1\text{ kg} + \sum_j n_j M_{j,\text{m}}]/\rho$ of solution. How many dm^3 is this? Write

$\rho = (\rho/\text{kg m}^{-3})\text{kg m}^{-3}$, for then the volume is $[1\text{ kg} + \sum_j n_j M_{j,\text{m}}]/[(\rho/\text{kg m}^{-3})\text{kg m}^{-3}]$

$$= [1 + (\sum_j n_j M_{j,\text{m}}/\text{kg})]\ \text{m}^3/(\rho/\text{kg m}^{-3})$$

$$= 1000\ [1 + \sum_j n_j M_{j,\text{m}}/\text{kg}]\ \text{dm}^3/(\rho/\text{kg m}^{-3}).$$

Therefore, the concentration is n_j divided by this volume:

$n_j(\rho_{\text{soln}}/\text{kg m}^{-3})/1000[1 + \sum_j n_j M_{j,\text{m}}/\text{kg}]$

$$c_j/\text{mol dm}^{-3} = \frac{(\rho_{\text{soln}}/\text{kg m}^{-3})}{1000[1 + \sum_j n_j M_{j,\text{m}}/\text{kg}]}\ m_j/\text{mol kg}^{-1}.$$

$$\rho/\text{kg m}^{-3} = (\rho/\text{g cm}^{-3})(\text{g cm}^{-3}/\text{kg m}^{-3}) = 1000(\rho/\text{g cm}^{-3}).$$

Therefore $c_j/\text{mol dm}^3 = \left(\dfrac{(\rho_{\text{soln}}/\text{g cm}^{-3})}{[1 + \sum_j n_j M_{j,\text{m}}/\text{kg}]}\right) m_j/m^{\ominus}$

and $I = \left\{\dfrac{[1 + \sum_j n_j M_{j,\text{m}}/\text{kg}]}{2(\rho_{\text{soln}}/\text{g cm}^{-3})}\right\} \sum_j (c_j/\text{M})z_j^2$.

For dilute solutions $\sum_j n_j M_{j,\text{m}}/\text{kg} \ll 1$ and $\rho_{\text{soln}} \approx \rho$, the solvent density.

Then $I \approx \{1/2(\rho/\text{g cm}^{-3})\}\sum_j (c_j/\text{M})z_j^2$.

11.2 $I = \frac{1}{2}\sum_j (m_j/m^{\ominus})z_j^2$ [11.2.6]. For M_aX_b, $m_+ = am$, $m_- = bm$ $[M_aX_b \rightarrow aM^{b+} + bX^{a-}]$.

$I = \frac{1}{2}(az_+^2 + bz_-^2)m/m^{\ominus}$

(a) $I(\text{KCl}) = \frac{1}{2}(z_+^2 + z_-^2)m/m^{\ominus} = m/m^{\ominus}$ $[|z_+| = |z_-| = 1]$.

(b) $I(\text{MgCl}_2) = \frac{1}{2}(z_+^2 + 2z_-^2)m/m^{\ominus} = 3m/m^{\ominus}$ $[|z_+| = |z_-| = 1]$.

(c) $I(\text{FeCl}_3) = \frac{1}{2}(z_+^2 + 3z_-^2)m/m^{\ominus} = 6m/m^{\ominus}$ $[|z_+| = 3, |z_-| = 1]$.

(d) $I(Al_2(SO_4)_3) = \frac{1}{2}(2z_+^2 + 3z_-^2)m/m^\ominus = 15m/m^\ominus$ $[|z_+| = 3, |z_-| = 2]$.

(e) $I(CuSO_4) = \frac{1}{2}(z_+^2 + z_-^2)m/m^\ominus = 4m/m^\ominus$ $[|z_+| = 2, |z_-| = 2]$.

11.3 $I = I(KCl) + I(CuSO_4)$ [11.2.6]

$= m(KCl)/m^\ominus + 4m(CuSO_4)/m^\ominus$ [Problem 11.2]

$= 0.1 + 4 \times 0.2 = \underline{0.9}.$

11.4 $n(KCl) = 5\,g/74.55\,g\,mol^{-1} = 0.067\,mol$; $m(KCl) = 0.67\,mol\,kg^{-1}$.
$n(FeCl_3) = 5\,g/162.2\,g\,mol^{-1} = 0.031\,mol$; $m(FeCl_3) = 0.31\,mol\,kg^{-1}$
$I = I(KCl) + I(FeCl_3) = m(KCl)/m^\ominus + 6m(FeCl_3)/m^\ominus$ [Problem 11.2]
$= 0.67 + 6 \times 0.31 = \underline{2.52}.$

11.5 $I(KCl) = m(KCl)/m^\ominus$, $I(CuSO_4) = 4m(CuSO_4)/m^\ominus$ [Problem 11.2].
For $I(KCl) = I(CuSO_4)$, $m(KCl) = 4m(CuSO_4)$.
Therefore $m(CuSO_4) = \underline{0.25\,mol\,kg^{-1}}$ for $m(KCl) = 1.0\,mol\,kg^{-1}$.

11.6 $M_pX_q \rightarrow pM + qX$; $\mu(M_pX_q) = p\mu(M) + q\mu(X)$.
$\mu = \mu^\ominus + RT\ln a$, and so $\mu(M_pX_q) = p\mu^\ominus(M) + q\mu^\ominus(X) + pRT\ln a(M) + qRT\ln a(X)$.
Write $a(M) = \gamma_+ m$, $a(X) = \gamma_- m$; then
$\mu(M_pX_q) = p\mu^\ominus(M) + pRT\ln m + q\mu^\ominus(X) + qRT\ln m + pRT\ln\gamma_+ + qRT\ln\gamma_-$.
With $\gamma_+^p\gamma_-^q = \gamma_\pm^{p+q}$, $p\ln\gamma_+ + q\ln\gamma_- = \ln\gamma_+^p\gamma_-^q = \ln\gamma_\pm^{p+q} = (p+q)\ln\gamma_\pm$,
and we can write
$\mu(M_pX_q) = p\{\mu^\ominus(M) + RT\ln m + RT\ln\gamma_\pm\} + q\{\mu^\ominus(X) + RT\ln m + RT\ln\gamma_\pm\}$
with the deviation from ideality distributed evenly. Thus, $a(M_pX_q) = a(M)^p a(X)^q$,
and using $a(M) = \gamma_\pm pm$, $a(X) = \gamma_\pm qm$, $a(M_pX_q) = \gamma_\pm^{p+q}p^pq^qm^{p+q}$.

11.7 Use the result derived in the last Problem; write $m \equiv m/m^\ominus$.
$a(KCl) = \underline{\gamma_\pm^2 m^2}$ $[p = 1, q = 1]$,
$a(MgCl_2) = \gamma_\pm^{1+2}\, 1^1 2^2 m^{1+2} = \underline{4\gamma_\pm^3 m^3}$ $[p = 1, q = 2]$,
$a(FeCl_3) = \gamma_\pm^{1+3}\, 1^1 3^3 m^{1+3} = \underline{27\gamma_\pm^4 m^4}$ $[p = 1, q = 3]$,
$a(CuSO_4) = \gamma_\pm^{1+1}\, 1^1 1^1 m^{1+1} = \underline{\gamma_\pm^2 m^2}$ $[p = 1, q = 1]$,
$a(Al_2(SO_4)_3) = \gamma_\pm^{2+3}\, 2^2 3^3 m^{2+3} = \underline{108\,\gamma_\pm^5 m^5}$ $[p = 2, q = 3]$.

11.8 $w_e = sRT\ln\gamma_\pm$ [11.2.1]. This is the work per mole of formula units, each giving rise to s ions.

(a) $w_e = 2RT \ln 0.679 = 2 \times 2.48\,\text{kJ mol}^{-1} \times \ln 0.679 = -1.92\,\text{kJ mol}^{-1}$.

Since $n \approx 2.00\,\text{dm}^3 \times 0.500\,\text{M} = 1.00\,\text{mol}$, $w_e = \underline{-1.92\,\text{kJ}}$.

(b) $w_e = 5RT \ln 0.014 = -53\,\text{kJ mol}^{-1}$, $n = 1.00\,\text{mol}$;

hence $w_e = \underline{-53\,\text{kJ}}$.

11.9 $F = q_1 q_2/4\pi\epsilon_0 r^2$ [Appendix 11.1]

$q_2(\text{shell}) = (4\pi r^2) \times (-e)/(1\,\text{cm}^2) = -4\pi e(r/\text{cm})^2; q_1 = e$.

$$F(r) = -\frac{4\pi e^2(r/\text{cm})^2}{4\pi\epsilon_0 r^2} = -e^2/(\epsilon_0\,\text{cm}^2)$$

$$= -(1.602 \times 10^{-19}\,\text{C})^2/(8.845 \times 10^{-12}\,\text{J}^{-1}\,\text{C}^2\,\text{m}^{-1}) \times (10^{-4}\,\text{m}^2)$$

$$= 3 \times 10^{-23}\,\text{J m}^{-1} = \underline{3 \times 10^{-23}\,\text{N}} \text{ for all distances.}$$

11.10 $F = -q_2(\text{d}/\text{d}r)\phi(r)$ [Appendix 11.1, $F = Eq$, $E = -\nabla\phi$].

$\phi(r) = (q_1/4\pi\epsilon_0)(1/r)\exp(-r/r_D)$ [11.2.4]

$F = -(q_1 q_2/4\pi\epsilon_0)\{-(1/r)^2 - (1/rr_D)\}\exp(-r/r_D)$

$= (q_1 q_2/4\pi\epsilon_0\epsilon_r)\{(1/r^2) + (1/rr_D)\}\exp(-r/r_D)$.

$q_2 = -4\pi e(r/\text{cm})^2, q_1 = e$ [Problem 11.9].

$F = -(4\pi e^2/4\pi\epsilon_0\,\text{cm}^2)\{1 + (r/r_D)\}e^{-r/r_D}$

$= -(e^2/\epsilon_0)\{1 + (r/r_D)\}(e^{-r/r_D}/10^{-4}\,\text{m}^2)$

$$= -\frac{(1.602 \times 10^{-19}\,\text{C})^2}{(8.854 \times 10^{-12}\,\text{J}^{-1}\,\text{C}^2\,\text{m}^{-1}) \times (10^{-4}\,\text{m}^2)}\left(1 + \frac{r}{r_D}\right)e^{-r/r_D}$$

$$= -(3 \times 10^{-23}\,\text{N}) \times \left(1 + \frac{r}{r_D}\right)e^{-r/r_D}$$

(a) $r_D = 10\,\text{cm}, r = 10\,\text{cm}; r/r_D = 1$;

$F = (-3 \times 10^{-23}\,\text{N}) \times (1 + 1)e^{-1} = \underline{-2 \times 10^{-23}\,\text{N}}$.

(b) $r_D = 10\,\text{cm}, r = 1\,\text{m}; r/r_D = 10$;

$F = (-3 \times 10^{-23}\,\text{N}) \times (1 + 10)e^{-10} = \underline{-1 \times 10^{-64}\,\text{N}}$.

(c) $r_D = 10\,\text{cm}, r = 1000\,\text{km}; r/r_D = 10^7$;

$F \propto \exp(-10^7) \approx \underline{0}$.

11.11 $r_D^2 = \epsilon RT/2\rho F^2 I m^\ominus$ [11.2.8]; $\epsilon = \epsilon_r\epsilon_0$; $\epsilon_r = 78, I = 3m/m^\ominus$ [Problem 11.2]

$= 0.0030$

$$= \frac{(8.854 \times 10^{-12}\,\mathrm{J^{-1}\,C^2\,m^{-1}}) \times 78 \times (8.314\,\mathrm{J\,K^{-1}\,mol^{-1}}) \times T}{2 \times (1.0 \times 10^3\,\mathrm{kg\,m^{-3}}) \times (9.648 \times 10^4\,\mathrm{C\,mol^{-1}})^2 \times (0.0030\,\mathrm{mol\,kg^{-1}})}$$

$= 1.03 \times 10^{-19}(T/\mathrm{K})\,\mathrm{m}^2$, or $r_\mathrm{D} = 3.2 \times 10^{-10}(T/\mathrm{K})^{\frac{1}{2}}\,\mathrm{m}$.

(a) $T = 298\,\mathrm{K}$; $r_\mathrm{D} = \underline{5.5\,\mathrm{nm}}$.

(b) $T = 273\,\mathrm{K}$; $r_\mathrm{D} = \underline{5.3\,\mathrm{nm}}$.

11.12 $r_\mathrm{D}^2 = \epsilon RT/2\rho F^2 I m^\ominus$.

$\epsilon = \epsilon_\mathrm{r}\epsilon_\mathrm{o}$, $\epsilon_\mathrm{r} = 22$, $T = 240\,\mathrm{K}$, $\rho = 0.69 \times 10^{-3}\,\mathrm{kg\,m^{-3}}$, $I = 3m/m^\ominus = 0.0030$.

$r_\mathrm{D}^2 =$

$$\frac{(8.854 \times 10^{-12}\,\mathrm{J^{-1}\,C^2\,m^{-1}}) \times 22 \times (8.314\,\mathrm{J\,K^{-1}\,mol^{-1}}) \times (240\,\mathrm{K})}{2 \times (0.69 \times 10^3\,\mathrm{kg\,m^{-3}}) \times (9.648 \times 10^4\,\mathrm{C\,mol^{-1}})^2 \times (0.0030\,\mathrm{mol\,kg^{-1}})}$$

$= 1.01 \times 10^{-17}\,\mathrm{m}^2$, so that $r_\mathrm{D} = \underline{3.2\,\mathrm{nm}}$.

11.13 $A = 1.825 \times 10^6\{(\rho/\mathrm{g\,cm^{-3}})/\epsilon_\mathrm{r}^3(T/\mathrm{K})^3\}^{\frac{1}{2}}$ [preceding 11.2.11]

$= 1.825 \times 10^6\{0.69/(22 \times 240)^3\}^{\frac{1}{2}} = \underline{-4.0.}$

Hence $\lg\gamma_\pm = -4.0|z_+z_-|I^{\frac{1}{2}}$.

11.14 $\lg\gamma_\pm = -0.509|z_+z_-|(I/\mathrm{mol\,kg^{-1}})^{\frac{1}{2}}$ [11.2.11]; $|z_+z_-| = 1$; $I = m$.

Draw up the following Table

$m/m^\ominus$	0.001	0.002	0.005	0.01	0.02
$I^{\frac{1}{2}}$	0.032	0.045	0.071	0.100	0.141
$\gamma_\pm$(calc)	0.964	0.949	0.920	0.889	0.847
$\gamma_\pm$(exp)	0.9649	0.9519	0.9275	0.9024	0.8712
$\lg\gamma_\pm$(exp)	−0.0155	−0.0214	−0.0327	−0.0446	−0.0599

The points are plotted against $\sqrt{I}$ in Fig. 11.1. Observe that the limiting slope of the experimental curve coincides with the calculated curve.

11.15 $\ln a_\mathrm{A} = -\Delta G_{\mathrm{melt,m}}/RT$ with $x_\mathrm{A} \to a_\mathrm{A}$ for real system.

$\mathrm{d}\ln a_\mathrm{A}/\mathrm{d}T = -(1/R)\,(\mathrm{d}/\mathrm{d}T)\,[\Delta G_{\mathrm{melt,m}}/T]$

$= \Delta H_{\mathrm{melt,m}}/RT^2$ [6.2.5].

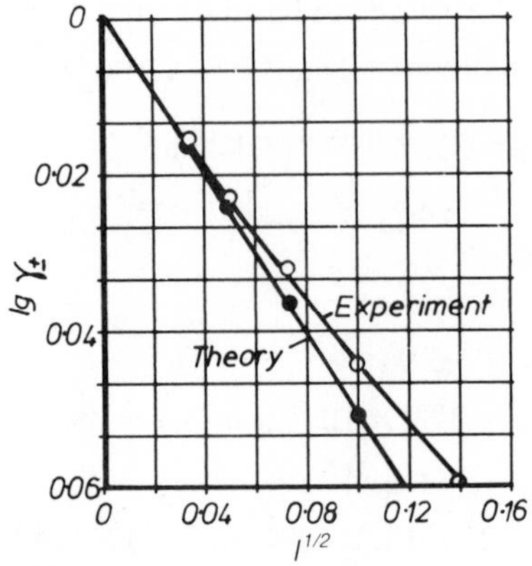

Fig 11·1

$dT = -d\delta T$ $[\delta T = T_f - T]$, and so

$d\ln a_A = -[\Delta H_{melt,m}/RT^2]\,d\delta T \approx -[\Delta H_{melt}(T_f)/RT_f^2]\,d\delta T.$

Write $K_f = RT_f^2 M_{A,m}/\Delta H_{melt,m}$, then

$\underline{d\ln a_A = -(M_{A,m}/K_f)\,d\delta T.}$

$n_A d\mu_A + n_B d\mu_B = 0$ [Gibbs-Duhem, 8.1.5],

$RT\{n_A d\ln a_A + n_B d\ln a_B\} = 0$ $[\mu = \mu^\ominus + RT\ln a]$,

and so $d\ln a_A = -(n_B/n_A)\,d\ln a_B$; therefore $d\ln a_B = (n_A M_{A,m}/n_B K_f)\,d\delta T$.

For a solution of molality m_B, $n_A = (1\,\text{kg}/M_{A,m}) = 1000\,\text{mol}/M_{A,r}$ and

$n_B = (m_B/\text{mol kg}^{-1})\text{mol}$. Therefore $n_A/n_B = 1000/M_{A,r}(m_B/\text{mol kg}^{-1})$.

Consequently $d\ln a_B = \left(\dfrac{1000\,\text{mol kg}^{-1}}{M_{A,r} m_B}\right)\left(\dfrac{M_{A,r}\,\text{g mol}^{-1}}{K_f}\right) d\delta T = (1/m_B K_f)\,d\delta T.$

11.16 $\phi = \delta T/2m_B K_f$ [given]

$\ln a_B = 2\ln\gamma_\pm + 2\ln m_B$ [Problem 11.6].

$d\ln\gamma_\pm + d\ln m_B = \tfrac{1}{2}d\ln a_B = (1/2m_B K_f)\,d\delta T$ [Problem 11.15].

$\ln\gamma_\pm = -A' m_B^{\frac{1}{2}}$ [11.2.11, 1,1-electrolyte; $A' = 2.303\,A$; $m_B \equiv m_B/m^\ominus$].

$d\ln\gamma_\pm = -\tfrac{1}{2}A' m_B^{-\frac{1}{2}}\,dm_B$; $d\ln m_B = m_B^{-1}\,dm_B$.

Therefore $(-\tfrac{1}{2}A' m_B^{-\frac{1}{2}} + m_B^{-1})\,dm_B = (1/2m_B K_f)\,d\delta T$,

$$\int_0^{m_B} [1 - \tfrac{1}{2}A' m_B^{\frac{1}{2}}]\,dm_B = \int_0^{\delta T} (1/2K_f)\,d\delta T.$$

$m_B - \tfrac{2}{3}\cdot\tfrac{1}{2}A' m_B^{3/2} = \delta T/2K_f$, or $1 - \tfrac{1}{3}A' m_B^{1/2} = \delta T/2m_B K_f = \phi$; hence

$\underline{\phi = 1 - \tfrac{1}{3}A' m_B^{1/2}}.$

11.17 $\phi = 1 - \frac{1}{3}A'(m_B/m^\ominus)^{1/2}$ [Problem 11.16, $m^\ominus = 1\ \mathrm{mol\,kg^{-1}}$] if D-H theory valid. Hence, plot $\phi = \delta T/2m_B K_f$ against $(m_B/m^\ominus)^{\frac{1}{2}}$ and expect a straight line, intercept 1, slope $-\frac{1}{3}A'$, in the limit of low concentrations.

$m/\mathrm{mol\,kg^{-1}}$	0.001	0.002	0.005	0.010	0.020
$(m/m^\ominus)^{\frac{1}{2}}$	0.032	0.045	0.071	0.100	0.141
$\delta T/\mathrm{K}$	3.696	7.376	18.36	36.43	72.54
ϕ	0.9946	0.9924	0.9880	0.9830	0.9760

These values are plotted in Fig. 11.2. They fall well as a straight line, confirming the Debye-Hückel law in the low concentration region.

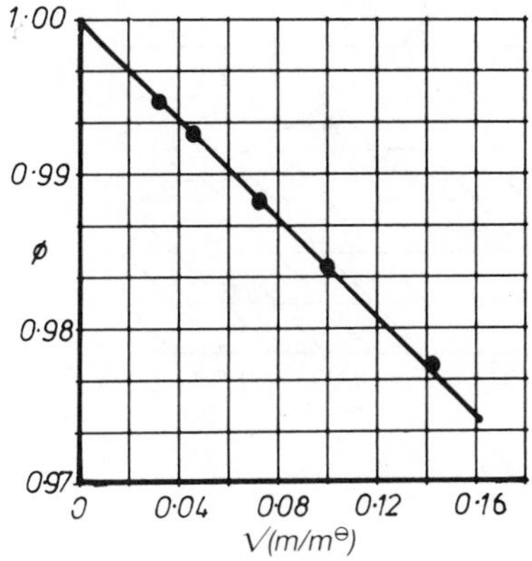

Fig 11·2

11.18 $\mathrm{d}\ln\gamma_\pm = -\mathrm{d}\ln m + (1/2mK_f)\mathrm{d}\delta T$ [Problem 11.16].
$\mathrm{d}\phi/\mathrm{d}m = (\mathrm{d}/\mathrm{d}m)(\delta T/2mK_f) = (\mathrm{d}\delta T/\mathrm{d}m)/2mK_f - \delta T/2m^2K_f$.
Therefore $\mathrm{d}\delta T/(2mK_f) = \mathrm{d}\phi + \delta T\mathrm{d}m/2m^2K_f = \mathrm{d}\phi + \phi\mathrm{d}m/m$,
hence $\mathrm{d}\ln\gamma_\pm = -\mathrm{d}m/m + \mathrm{d}\phi + \phi\mathrm{d}m/m = -(1-\phi)\mathrm{d}m/m + \mathrm{d}\phi$,

and so $\ln\gamma_\pm = \phi - 1 - \int_0^m \left(\frac{1-\phi}{m}\right)\mathrm{d}m$. $[\ln\gamma_\pm|_{m=1} = 0]$.

11.19 Draw up the following Table from the data and $\phi = \delta T/2m_B K_f$.

$m/\text{mol kg}^{-1}$	0.01	0.02	0.03	0.04	0.05
$\delta T/K$	0.0355	0.0697	0.0343	0.137	0.172
ϕ	0.955	0.938	0.925	0.922	0.926
$[(1-\phi)/m]\,\text{mol kg}^{-1}$	4.500	3.100	2.500	1.950	1.480

$(1-\phi)/m$ is plotted against m in Fig. 11.3. The value of $(1-\phi)/m$ approaches infinity as $m \to 0$, but we can be confident about the applicability of the D-H theory in this range and do the integral analytically up to $m = 0.01$.

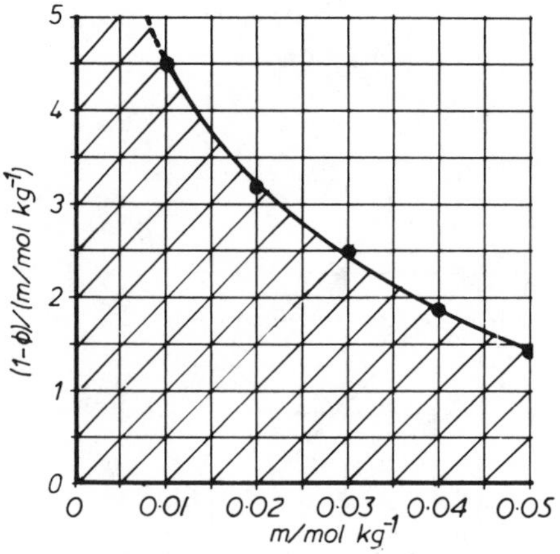

Fig 11·3

Thus $\int_0^m \left(\frac{1-\phi}{m}\right) dm = \frac{1}{3}A \int_0^m dm/\sqrt{m}$ [Problem 11.16] $= \frac{2}{3}A'\sqrt{m}$, with

$A' = 2.303 \times 0.509$. Therefore, up to $m = 0.01$, the value of the integral is 0.0781. Above that value proceed numerically. The value of the integral from 0.01 to 0.05 is 0.106; therefore the total integral up to $0.050\,\text{mol kg}^{-1}$ is 0.184. Hence

$\ln \gamma_\pm = 0.926 - 1 - 0.184 = -0.258$; $\gamma_\pm = \underline{0.77}$.

11.20 $K = a(\text{M}^+)a(\text{A}^-)/a(\text{MA}) = [c(\text{M}^+)c(\text{A}^-)/c(\text{MA})]\,\gamma_\pm^2/\gamma_{\text{MA}}$

$$= [(\alpha c)^2/(1-\alpha)c]\,(\gamma_\pm^2/\gamma_{\text{MA}}) = K_c\gamma_\pm^2/\gamma_{\text{MA}} \approx \gamma_\pm^2 K_c.$$

$\lg \gamma_\pm = -A\sqrt{(\alpha c)}$ [11.2.11; $c/\text{mol dm}^{-3} \approx m/\text{mol kg}^{-1}$].

$\lg K_c = \lg K + 2A\sqrt{(\alpha c)}$,

$K_c = (\alpha c)^2/(1-\alpha)c = \alpha^2 c/(1-\alpha)$. Plot $\lg K_c$ against $\sqrt{(\alpha c)}$, and hope to get a straight line. Draw up the following Table:

$10^3 c/\mathrm{M}$	0.0280	0.1114	0.2184
$\sqrt{(\alpha c)}$	3.89×10^{-3}	6.04×10^{-3}	7.36×10^{-3}
K_c	1.768×10^{-5}	1.779×10^{-5}	1.781×10^{-5}
$\lg K_c$	-4.753	-4.750	-4.749

$10^3 c/\mathrm{M}$	1.0283	2.414	5.9115
$\sqrt{(\alpha c)}$	1.13×10^{-2}	1.41×10^{-2}	1.79×10^{-2}
K_c	1.799×10^{-5}	1.809×10^{-5}	1.822×10^{-5}
$\lg K_c$	-4.745	-4.743	-4.739

$\lg K_c$ is plotted against $\sqrt{(\alpha c)}$ in Fig. 11.4, and a good straight line is obtained.

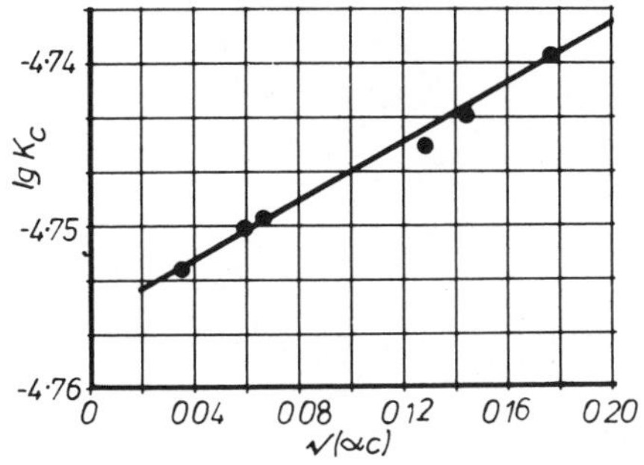

Fig 11·4

11.21 $K_a = a(H^+)a(A^-)/a(HA) = \gamma(H^+)\gamma(A^-)c(H^+)c(A^-)/c(HA)$

$$= \gamma(H^+)\gamma(A^-)K_a' = \gamma_\pm^2 K_a'.$$

Therefore $pK_a = -\lg K_a = -2\lg\gamma_\pm + pK_a'$.

$\lg\gamma_\pm = -A\sqrt{(m/m^\ominus)} \approx -A\sqrt{(c_\pm/\mathrm{M})}$ [11.2.11], and so

$pK_a \approx pK_a' + 2A\sqrt{c_\pm}$ $(c \equiv c/\mathrm{M})$ where $c_\pm$ is the concentration of ions.

$K'_a = c(H^+)c(A^-)/c(HA); c(H^+) \approx \surd[K'_a c(HA)] \approx \surd[K'_a c^o(HA)]$,

c^o (HA) is the concentration of acid added.

Therefore $pK'_a \approx pK_a - 2A\,[K'_a c^o(HA)]^{1/4} \approx pK_a - 2A\,[K_a c^o(HA)]^{1/4}$;

$pK'_a \approx 4.756 - 2 \times 0.509 \times [10^{-4.746} \times 0.1]^{\frac{1}{2}} = \underline{4.719.}$

11.22 $K_{sp} = a_+^p a_-^q = m_+^p m_-^q \gamma_-^p \gamma_-^q$ $(m \equiv m/m^\ominus)$; $M_pX_q \rightarrow pM + qX$

$\gamma_\pm^{p+q} = \gamma_+^p \gamma_-^q$ [Problem 11.6, 11.1.5], and $K_{sp} = m_+^p m_-^q \gamma_\pm^{p+q}$.

Let m denote the molality of dissolved salt; then $m_+ = pm$, $m_- = qm$.

Hence, $K_{sp} = p^p q^q m^{p+q}\ \gamma_\pm^{p+q}$.

For $\gamma_\pm \approx 1, K_{sp} \approx p^p q^q m^{p+q}$, or $K_{sp} \approx p^p q^q (c/M)^{p+q}$

[for $\rho \approx 1\ g\ cm^{-3}$, $c/M \approx m/mol\ kg^{-1}$].

(a) Ag Cl: $p = q = 1; c = 1.34 \times 10^{-5} M; K_{sp} = (1.34 \times 10^{-5})^2 = \underline{1.80 \times 10^{-10}}$.

(b) $BaSO_4$: $p = q = 1; c = 9.51 \times 10^{-4} M; K_{sp} = (9.51 \times 10^{-4})^2 = \underline{9.04 \times 10^{-7}}$.

11.23 $AgBr(s) \rightleftharpoons Ag^+(aq) + Br^-(aq); K_{sp} = a(Ag^+)a(Br^-)$.

$\Delta_r G^\ominus = (77.11\ kJ\ mol^{-1}) + (-103.96\ kJ\ mol^{-1}) - (-96.90\ kJ\ mol^{-1}) = 70.05\ kJ\ mol^{-1}$.

$K_{sp} = \exp\{-\Delta G^\ominus/RT\}$ [10.1.17]

$= \exp\{-(70.05\ kJ\ mol^{-1})/(2.48\ kJ\ mol^{-1})\} = 5.41 \times 10^{-13}$.

Suppose $a(Ag^+) \approx m(Ag^+)/m^\ominus; a(Br^-) \approx m(Br^-)/m^\ominus$; then $m(AgBr, aq)/m^\ominus = m(Ag^+)/m^\ominus = \surd K_{sp} = 7.4 \times 10^{-7}$' Therefore the solubility is $\underline{7.4 \times 10^{-7} mol\ kg^{-1}}$.

11.24 $MX \rightleftharpoons M^+ + X^-; K_{sp} \approx c(M^+)c(X^-)$ $[c \equiv c/mol\ dm^{-3}]$

$c(M^+) = c'_o, c(X^-) = c'_o + c, c(N^+) = c$.

$K_{sp} = \{c'^2_o + c'_o c\}$,

$c'^2_o + cc'_o - K_{sp} = 0$ solves to

$\underline{c'_o = \tfrac{1}{2}\{-c + \surd[c^2 + 4K_{sp}]\} \approx K_{sp}/c}$ when $4K_{sp}/c^2 \ll 1$.

11.25 $K_{sp} = a(M^+)a(X^-) = c(M^+)c(X^-)\gamma_\pm^2$

$= (c'^2_o + c'_o c)\gamma_\pm^2, \gamma_\pm = 10^{-A\surd c}$ [11.2.11]

Solve $c'^2_o + c'_o c - K_{sp}/\gamma_\pm^2 = 0$

to give $c'_o = \tfrac{1}{2}\{-c + [c^2 + 4K_{sp}/\gamma_\pm^2]^{\frac{1}{2}}\}$

$\approx K_{sp}/c\gamma_\pm^2$ when $4K_{sp}/c^2\gamma_\pm^2 \ll 1$.

$\underline{\text{Therefore, } c'_o = K_{sp} 10^{2A\surd c}/c.}$

11.26 $K_{sp} = 5.0 \times 10^{-13}$ [Problem 11.23]; $c(\mathrm{KBr}) = 0.01$ M.
$c'_0/\mathrm{M} \approx 5.0 \times 10^{-13}/(0.01\ \mathrm{M})$ [Problem 11.24] $= 5.0 \times 10^{-11}$.
Therefore $c'_0 = \underline{5.0 \times 10^{-11}\ \mathrm{M}}$.
Allowing for activity coefficients:

$$c'_0/\mathrm{M} \approx K_{sp} 10^{2A\sqrt{c}}/c \approx (4.99 \times 10^{-13}) \times 10^{2\times 0.509 \times 0.1}/0.01$$
$$= 6.3 \times 10^{-11}.$$

Hence $c'_0 \approx \underline{6.3 \times 10^{-11}\ \mathrm{M}}$.

11.27 $\mathrm{MX} \rightleftharpoons \mathrm{M}^+ + \mathrm{X}^-$, $K_{sp} = a(\mathrm{M}^+)a(\mathrm{X}^-)$.
$K_{sp} = m(\mathrm{M}^+)m(\mathrm{X}^-)\gamma_\pm^2$ $(m \equiv m/m^\ominus)$;
$m = (K_{sp}/\gamma_\pm^2)^{\frac{1}{2}} = K_{sp}^{\frac{1}{2}}/\gamma_\pm$.
$\gamma_\pm = 10^{-0.509\sqrt{c}}$ [11.2.11, $I \approx c/\mathrm{M}$; $c \to c/\mathrm{M}$];
$m = \sqrt{K_{sp}}\ 10^{0.509\sqrt{c}}$.
For $m \approx c$; $c \approx \underline{\sqrt{K_{sp}}\ 10^{0.509\sqrt{c}}}$.

11.28 (a) $c(\mathrm{AgCl}) \approx K_{sp}\ 10^{2A\sqrt{c}}/c$ [Problem 11.25, $c = c(\mathrm{KCl})/\mathrm{M}$].
$c(\mathrm{AgCl})/\mathrm{M} = (1.83 \times 10^{-10}) \times 10^{2\times 0.509 \times \sqrt{0.1}}/0.1 = \underline{3.8 \times 10^{-9}}$.
(b) $c(\mathrm{AgCl})/\mathrm{M} = (1.83 \times 10^{-10}) \times 10^{2\times 0.509 \times 0.1}/0.01 = \underline{2.3 \times 10^{-8}}$.
(c) $c(\mathrm{AgCl}) \approx K_{sp}^{\frac{1}{2}}\ 10^{0.509\sqrt{c}}$ [Problem 11.27]
$c(\mathrm{AgCl})/\mathrm{M} = (1.83 \times 10^{-10})^{\frac{1}{2}} \times 10^{0.509 \times 0.1} = \underline{1.5 \times 10^{-5}}$.

11.29 $K_{sp} = K'_{sp}K_\gamma = K'_{sp}\gamma_\pm^2$.
$\lg K_{sp} = \lg K'_{sp} + 2\lg\gamma_\pm = \lg K'_{sp} - 2A\sqrt{I}$ [11.211].
$K'_{sp} = [m'/m^\ominus]^2$;
$\lg[m'/m^\ominus] = \frac{1}{2}\lg K_{sp} + A\sqrt{I}(\mathrm{MgSO_4})$
$I(\mathrm{MgSO_4}) = 4m'/m^\ominus$ [11.2.6]; $\lg(m'/m^\ominus) = \frac{1}{2}\lg K_{sp} + 2A\sqrt{(m/m^\ominus)}$.
Draw up the following Table from the data:

$m/\mathrm{mol\,kg^{-1}}$	0.001	0.002	0.003
$\sqrt{(m/m^\ominus)}$	0.0316	0.0447	0.0548
$\lg(m'/m^\ominus)$	−4.843	−4.829	−4.811

$m/m^{\ominus}$	0.004	0.006	0.010
$\sqrt{(m/m^{\ominus})}$	0.0632	0.0775	0.100
$\lg(m'/m^{\ominus})$	−4.803	−4.796	−4.783

$\lg m'$ is plotted against $\sqrt{m}$ in Fig. 11.5. The graph is linear at low concentrations, and extrapolates to an intercept at −4.90, corresponding to $\frac{1}{2}\lg K_{sp} = -4.90$, or $K_{sp} = \underline{1.58 \times 10^{-10}}$.

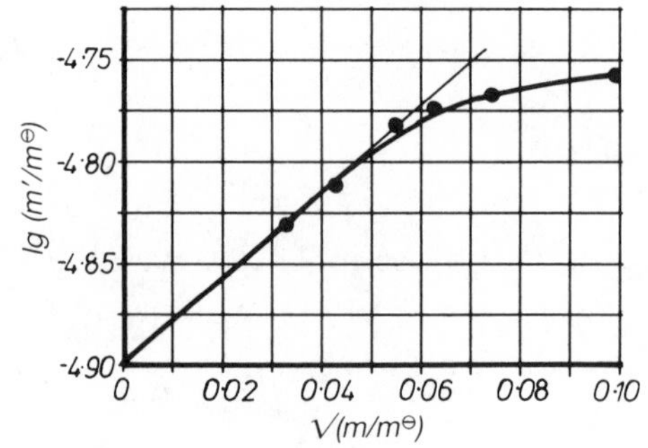

Fig 11·5

$\lg\gamma_{\pm} = \frac{1}{2}(\lg K_{sp} - \lg K'_{sp}) = \frac{1}{2}\lg(K_{sp}/K'_{sp})$.

At 0.004 mol kg^{-1}, $K'_{sp} = (1.575 \times 10^{-5})^2 = 2.481 \times 10^{-10}$.

Therefore $\lg\gamma_{\pm} = \frac{1}{2}\lg(1.58 \times 10^{-10}/2.48 \times 10^{-10}) = -0.0970$; $\underline{\gamma_{\pm} = 0.800}$.

11.30 $\bar{\mu}_i = \mu_i + z_i F\phi$ [11.3.1]

$\Delta\bar{\mu}(Cu^{2+}) = 2F\Delta\phi = 2 \times (9.648 \times 10^4\,C\,mol^{-1}) \times (2.0\,V) = \underline{390\,kJ\,mol^{-1}}$ [1 C V = 1 J].

For z_i negative, $z_i = -|z_i|$; $d\bar{\mu}_i = -|z_i|F d\phi < 0$ if $d\phi > 0$. Thus, ions move spontaneously in the direction of increasing ϕ.

11.31
$$\begin{aligned}\Delta\phi &= \Delta\phi^{\ominus} - (RT/F)\ln(f^{\frac{1}{2}}/a_{H^+}) \quad [11.4.2] \\ &= \Delta\phi^{\ominus} - (RT/F)\ln f^{\frac{1}{2}} + 2.303(RT/F)\lg a_{H^+} \\ &= \Delta\phi^{\ominus} - (RT/F)\ln f^{\frac{1}{2}} - (2.303RT/F)\mathrm{pH} \\ &= \text{const.} - (59.2\text{ mV})\mathrm{pH} \quad [\text{end-paper 1}].\end{aligned}$$

$\Delta\phi(\mathrm{pH}=14) - \Delta\phi(\mathrm{pH}=0) = -(14-0)(59.2\text{ mV}) = \underline{-0.83\text{ V}}$.

11.32 Proceed as in Section 11.4(a).

At equilibrium $\frac{1}{2}\bar{\mu}_{G_2,g} + z\bar{\mu}_{e^-} = \bar{\mu}_{G^{z-},soln}$

$\frac{1}{2}\mu^{\ominus}_{G_2} + \frac{1}{2}RT\ln f + z\mu^{\ominus}_{e^-} - zF\phi_M = \mu^{\ominus}_{G^{z-}} + RT\ln a - zF\phi_S$

$zF(\phi_M - \phi_S) = \frac{1}{2}\mu^{\ominus}_{G_2} + z\mu^{\ominus}_{e^-} - \mu^{\ominus}_{G^{z-}} + \frac{1}{2}RT\ln f - RT\ln a$

$zF\Delta\phi = zF\Delta\phi^{\ominus} + RT\ln(f^{\frac{1}{2}}/a)$

$\underline{\Delta\phi = \Delta\phi^{\ominus} + (RT/zF)\ln(f^{\frac{1}{2}}/a)}.$

$\Delta\phi$ increases as f increases. This is because the equilibrium is shifted towards G^{z-}: then e^- are withdrawn from the metal (so that ϕ increases) and G^{z-} added to the solution (so that ϕ decreases). Then, as $\Delta\phi = \phi_M - \phi_S$, the difference diverges, so that $\Delta\phi$ increases.

11.33 $\underbrace{2Sb(s) + 6OH^-(aq)}_{\text{Red}} \rightarrow \underbrace{Sb_2O_3(s) + 3H_2O(l)}_{\text{Ox}} + \underbrace{6e^-}_{\nu = 6}$

$\Delta\phi = \Delta\phi^{\ominus} + (RT/6F)\ln\{a_{Sb_2O_3}a^3_{H_2O}/a^2_{Sb}a^6_{OH^-}\}$ [11.4.3]

$= \Delta\phi^{\ominus} + (RT/6F)\ln\{1/a^6_{OH}\}$ $[a_{pure} = 1]$

$= \Delta\phi^{\ominus} - (RT/F)\ln a_{OH^-}$.

$a_{OH^-} = (m_{OH^-}/m^{\ominus})\gamma_{\pm}$; $\lg\gamma_{\pm} = -0.509\surd(m/\text{mol kg}^{-1})$ [11.2.11].

(a) $m_{OH^-} = 0.01\text{ mol kg}^{-1}$: $\lg\gamma_{\pm} = -0.0509$, $\gamma_{\pm} = 0.889$; $a_{OH^-} = 0.0089$.

(b) $m = 0.05\text{ mol kg}^{-1}$; $\lg\gamma_{\pm} = -0.114$, $\gamma_{\pm} = 0.770$; $a_{OH^-} = 0.0385$.

$\Delta\phi(0.05\text{ mol kg}^{-1}) - \Delta\phi(0.01\text{ mol kg}^{-1}) = -(RT/F)\{\ln 0.0385 - \ln 0.0089\}$

$= -(25.7\text{ mV})\ln(0.0385/0.0089)$

$= -38\text{ mV}$. $[RT/F = 25.7\text{ mV}]$.

11.34 $\underbrace{Cr_2O_7^{2-} + 14H^+(aq)}_{\text{Ox}} + \underbrace{6e^-}_{\nu = 6} \rightleftharpoons \underbrace{2Cr^{3+}(aq) + 7H_2O(l)}_{\text{Red}}.$

$\Delta\phi = \Delta\phi^{\ominus} + (RT/6F)\ln\{a_{Cr_2O_7^{2-}}a^{14}_{H^+}/a^2_{Cr^{3+}}a^7_{H_2O}\}$ [11.4.3]

$= \Delta\phi^{\ominus} + (RT/6F)\ln\{a_{Cr_2O_7^{2-}}a^{14}_{H^+}/a^2_{Cr^{3+}}\}$.

12. Equilibrium electrochemistry: electrochemical cells

A12.1 $Mn|MnCl_2(aq)|Cl_2(g)|Pt$; $Mn(s) \rightarrow Mn^{2+}(aq) + 2e^-$ [Box 12.1].
$Cl_2(g) + 2e^- \rightarrow 2Cl^-(aq)$; $E^\ominus(T) = E^\ominus_{Cl_2,Cl^-}(T) - E^\ominus_{Mn^{2+},Mn}(T)$ [Box 12.1].
$2.54\,V = 1.36\,V - E^\ominus_{Mn^{2+},Mn}(T)$; $E^\ominus_{Mn^{2+},Mn}(T) = (1.36 - 2.54)\,V = \underline{-1.18\,V.}$

A12.2 (a) $Zn(s) \rightarrow Zn^{2+}(aq) + 2e^-$; $2Ag^+(aq) + 2e^- \rightarrow 2Ag(s)$;
$Zn(s) + 2Ag^+(aq) \rightarrow Zn^{2+}(aq) + 2Ag(s)$.
(b) $Cd(s) \rightarrow Cd^{2+}(aq) + 2e^-$; $2H^+(aq) + 2e^- \rightarrow H_2(g)$;
$Cd(s) + 2H^+(aq) \rightarrow Cd^{2+}(aq) + H_2(g)$.
(c) $3Fe(CN)_6^{4-}(aq) \rightarrow 3Fe(CN)_6^{3-} + 3e^-$; $Cr^{3+}(aq) + 3e^- \rightarrow Cr(s)$;
$3Fe(CN)_6^{4-}(aq) + Cr^{3+}(aq) \rightarrow 3Fe(CN)_6^{3-} + Cr(s)$.
(d) $2Cl^-(aq) \rightarrow Cl_2(g) + 2e^-$; $Ag_2CrO_4(s) + 2e^- \rightarrow CrO_4^{2-}(aq) + 2Ag(s)$;
$Ag_2CrO_4(s) + 2Cl^-(aq) \rightarrow 2Ag(s) + Cl_2(g) + CrO_4^{2-}(aq)$

A12.3 $E^\ominus(T) = E^\ominus_{Tl^+,Tl}(T) - E^\ominus_{Hg^{2+},Hg}(T) = -0.34\,V - (0.86\,V) = -1.20\,V$
$E^\ominus_{Hg^{2+},Hg}(T) = (1/2)[E^\ominus_{Hg^{2+},Hg_2^{2+}}(T) + E^\ominus_{Hg_2^{2+},Hg}(T)]$.[Box 12.1].
$Hg(l) + 2Tl^+(aq) \rightarrow Hg^{2+}(aq) + 2Tl(s)$.
$E(T) = E^\ominus(T) - (RT/2F)\ln(a_{Hg^{2+}})/(a_{Tl^+})^2$ [12.1.6]
$= -1.20\,V - (1/2)(0.0257\,V)\ln(0.15/(0.93)^2 = \underline{-1.18\,V.}$

A12.4 (a) $E^\ominus(T) = -\Delta_r G^\ominus(T)/\nu F$ [12.3.1] $= -(-62.5 \times 10^3\,J)(2)^{-1}(9.65 \times 10^4 C)^{-1}$
$= \underline{0.324\,V}.$
(b) $E^\ominus(T) = E^\ominus_{Fe^{3+},Fe^{2+}}(T) - E^\ominus_{Ag_2CrO_4,CrO_4^{2-},Ag}(T)$, [Box 12.1]
$E^\ominus_{Ag_2CrO_4,CrO_4^{2-},Ag}(T) = (0.77 - 0.32)V = \underline{0.45\,V.}$

A12.5 $E^\ominus(T) = E^\ominus_{Cd^{2+},Cd}(T) - E^\ominus_{AgBr,Br^-,Ag}$ [Box 12.1] $= (-0.40 - 0.07)\,V$
$= \underline{-0.47\,V.}$
$2Ag(s) + 2Br^-(aq) + Cd^{2+}(aq) \rightarrow 2AgBr(s) + Cd(s)$
$\lg\gamma_{Br^-} = -0.509\,I^{\frac{1}{2}}$ [11.2.11] $= -0.509(0.050)^{\frac{1}{2}}$; $\gamma_{Br^-} = 0.769$
$a_{Br^-} = (0.769)(0.050) = 3.84 \times 10^{-2}$
$\lg\gamma_{Cd^{2+}} = -0.509(2)^2 I^{\frac{1}{2}} = -0.509(2)^2[1/2]^{\frac{1}{2}}[(0.010)(4) + (0.020)]^{\frac{1}{2}}$

$\gamma_{Cd^{2+}} = 0.444; a_{Cd^{2+}} = (0.444)(0.010) = 4.44 \times 10^{-3}$.

$E(\mathcal{T}) = E^{\ominus}(\mathcal{T}) - (R\mathcal{T}/2F)\ln(a_{Cd^{2+}})^{-1}(a_{Br^-})^{-2}$ [12.1.6]

$\quad = -0.47\,V - (1/2)(0.0257\,V)\ln(4.44 \times 10^{-3})^{-1}(3.84 \times 10^{-2})^{-2}$

$\quad = (-0.47 + 0.15)\,V = \underline{-0.32\,V}.$

A12.6 $2Ag(s) + Fe^{2+}(aq) \rightarrow 2Ag^{+}(aq) + Fe(s)$. [Box 12.1]

$E^{\ominus}(\mathcal{T}) = E^{\ominus}_{Fe^{2+},Fe}(\mathcal{T}) - E^{\ominus}_{Ag^{+},Ag}(\mathcal{T}) = (-0.44 - 0.80)\,V = \underline{-1.24}.$

$\Delta_r G^{\ominus}(\mathcal{T}) = 2\Delta_f G^{\ominus}(\mathcal{T}, Ag^{+}(aq)) - \Delta_f G^{\ominus}(\mathcal{T}, Fe^{2+}(aq))$ [5.4.4]

$\quad = [2(77.1) - (-78.9)]\,kJ\,mol^{-1} = \underline{233.1\,kJ\,mol^{-1}}.$

$\Delta_r H^{\ominus}(\mathcal{T}) = 2\Delta_f H^{\ominus}(\mathcal{T}, Ag^{+}(aq)) - \Delta_f H^{\ominus}(\mathcal{T}, Fe^{2+}(aq))$ [4.1.4]

$\quad = [2(105.6) - (-89.1)]\,kJ\,mol^{-1} = \underline{300.3\,kJ\,mol^{-1}}.$

$\partial(\Delta_r G^{\ominus}/T)/\partial(1/T) = \Delta_r H^{\ominus}$ [6.2.5] $\approx \underline{300.3\,kJ}.$

$\Delta_r G^{\ominus}(308.15\,K) = (308.15\,K)\{\Delta_r G^{\ominus}(\mathcal{T})/\mathcal{T} + (300.3\,kJ)(308.15^{-1} - \mathcal{T}^{-1})]$

$\quad = (308.15\,K)[233.1\,kJ\,mol^{-1}/298.15\,K$

$\quad + (300.3\,kJ\,mol^{-1})\{(308.15\,K)^{-1} - (298.15\,K)^{-1}\}$

$\quad = \underline{230.8\,kJ\,mol^{-1}}.$

$E^{\ominus}(308.15\,K) = -\Delta_r G^{\ominus}(308.15\,K)/2F$ [12.3.1]

$\quad = -(230.8 \times 10^{3}\,J)(2)^{-1} \times (9.648 \times 10^{4}\,C)^{-1}$

$\quad = \underline{-1.20\,V}.$

A12.7 (a) $Cu_3(PO_4)_2(s) \rightleftharpoons 3Cu^{2+}(aq) + 2PO_4^{3-}(aq)$ [Section 12.4(a)].

$K_s = a^3(Cu^{2+})a^2(PO_4^{3-}) = m^3(Cu^{2+})[(2/3)m(Cu^{2+})]^2 = (4/9)m^5(Cu^{2+})$

$m(Cu^{2+}) = (9/4)K_s^{1/5} = (9/4)(1.3 \times 10^{-37})^{1/5} = \underline{9.4 \times 10^{-8}}.$

(b) $H_2(g) + Cu^{2+}(aq) \rightarrow 2H^{+}(aq) + Cu(s)$ [Box 12.1]

$E^{\ominus}(\mathcal{T}) = E^{\ominus}_{Cu^{2+},Cu}(\mathcal{T}) = 0.34\,V$ [Table 12.1].

$E(\mathcal{T}) = E^{\ominus}(\mathcal{T}) - (R\mathcal{T}/2F)\ln[a^2(H^{+})a^{-1}(Cu^{2+})p^{-1}(H_2)]$ [12.1.6]

$\quad = 0.34\,V - (1/2)(0.0257\,V)\ln[(1.00)^2(9.4 \times 10^{-8})^{-1}(1.00)^{-1}]$

$\quad = \underline{0.13\,V}.$

A12.8 (a) $E^{\ominus}(\mathcal{T}) = E^{\ominus}_{Sn^{4+},Sn^{2+}}(\mathcal{T}) - E^{\ominus}_{Sn^{2+},Sn}(\mathcal{T}) = [+0.15 - (-0.14)]\,V$

$\quad = \underline{0.29\,V}.$ [Box 12.1, Table 12.1]

$K = \exp[-\Delta_r G^{\ominus}(\mathcal{T})/R\mathcal{T}] = \exp[\nu F E^{\ominus}(\mathcal{T})/R\mathcal{T}]$ [12.3.1]

$\quad = \exp[2(0.29\,V)(0.0257\,V)^{-1}] = \underline{2.0 \times 10^{9}}.$

(b) $E^{\ominus}(\mathcal{T}) = E^{\ominus}_{AgCl,Cl^-,Ag}(\mathcal{T}) - E^{\ominus}_{Sn^{2+},Sn}(\mathcal{T}) = [0.22 - (-0.14)]\,V = 0.36\,V$

$K = \exp[2(0.36\,\text{V})(0.0257\,\text{V})^{-1}] = \underline{1.3 \times 10^{12}}$.

(c) $E^{\ominus}(\mathcal{F}) = E^{\ominus}_{\text{Cu}^{2+},\text{Cu}} - E^{\ominus}_{\text{Ag}^+,\text{Ag}} = (0.34 - 0.80)\,\text{V} = -0.46\,\text{V}$

$K = \exp[2(-0.46\,\text{V})(0.0257\,\text{V})^{-1}] = \underline{2.8 \times 10^{-16}}$.

A12.9 (a) $-\lg K_a = pK_a$ [12.4.7] $= 9.31$; $\lg K_a = -9.31$; $K_a = \underline{4.90 \times 10^{-10}}$.

(b) $\text{pH} = (1/2)pK_a - (1/2)\lg A$ [12.4.11] $= (1/2)(9.31) - (1/2)\lg(0.25) = \underline{4.96}$.

(c) $\text{pH} = pK_a - \lg(A/S)$ [12.4.12] $= 9.31 - \lg(0.25/0.15) = \underline{9.09}$.

A12.10 $A = S$; $\lg(A/S) = 0$; $pK_a = \text{pH} = 5.40$ [12.4.12].

$-\lg K_a = 5.40$; $K_a = 3.98 \times 10^{-6}$,

$A = 0.60\,\text{mol}/2.50\,\text{dm}^3 = 0.24\,\text{M}$,

$\text{pH} = (1/2)pK_a - (1/2)\lg A = (1/2)(5.40) - (1/2\lg(0.24) = \underline{3.01}$.

12.1 Refer to Box 12.1

(a) $\text{Pt}|\text{H}_2(\text{g})|\text{HCl}(\text{aq})|\text{AgCl}|\text{Ag}$

Red_L: H_2, Ox_L: H^+; Red_R: $\text{Ag} + \text{Cl}^-$, Ox_R: AgCl

$H_2(\text{g}) + 2\text{AgCl}(\text{s}) \rightarrow 2\text{Ag}(\text{s}) + 2\text{HCl}(\text{aq})$ ($\nu = 2$).

L: $2\text{H}^+(\text{aq}) + 2\text{e}^- \rightarrow \text{H}_2(\text{g})$; R: $2\text{AgCl}(\text{s}) + 2\text{e}^- \rightarrow 2\text{Ag}(\text{s}) + 2\text{Cl}^-(\text{aq})$.

(b) $\text{Pt}|\text{FeCl}_2(\text{aq}), \text{FeCl}_3(\text{aq})||\text{SnCl}_4(\text{aq}), \text{SnCl}_2(\text{aq})|\text{Pt}$

Red_L: Fe^{2+}, Ox_L: Fe^{3+}; Red_R: Sn^{2+}, Ox_R: Sn^{4+}

$2\text{Fe}^{2+}(\text{aq}) + \text{Sn}^{4+}(\text{aq}) \rightarrow 2\text{Fe}^{3+}(\text{aq}) + \text{Sn}^{2+}(\text{aq})$, ($\nu = 2$)

L: $2\text{Fe}^{3+} + 2\text{e}^- \rightarrow 2\text{Fe}^{2+}$; R: $\text{Sn}^{4+} + 2\text{e}^- \rightarrow \text{Sn}^{2+}$.

(c) $\text{Cu}|\text{CuCl}_2(\text{aq})||\text{MnCl}_2(\text{aq}), \text{HCl}(\text{aq})|\text{MnO}_2(\text{s})|\text{Pt}$

Red_L: Cu, Ox_L: Cu^{2+}; Red_R: $\text{Mn}^{2+} + 2\text{H}_2\text{O}$, Ox_R: $\text{MnO}_2 + 4\text{H}^+$

$\text{Cu}(\text{s}) + \text{MnO}_2(\text{s}) + 4\text{H}^+(\text{aq}) \rightarrow \text{Mn}^{2+}(\text{aq}) + 2\text{H}_2\text{O}(\text{l}) + \text{Cu}^{2+}(\text{aq})$ ($\nu = 2$)

L: $\text{Cu}^{2+}(\text{aq}) + 2\text{e}^- \rightarrow \text{Cu}(\text{s})$, R: $\text{MnO}_2(\text{s}) + 4\text{H}^+ + 2\text{e}^- \rightarrow \text{Mn}^{2+}(\text{aq}) + 2\text{H}_2\text{O}(\text{l})$

(d) $\text{Ag}|\text{AgCl}|\text{HCl}(\text{aq})||\text{HBr}(\text{aq})|\text{AgBr}|\text{Ag}$

Red_L: $\text{Ag} + \text{Cl}^-$, Ox_L: AgCl; Red_R: $\text{Ag} + \text{Br}^-$, Ox_R: AgBr

$\text{Ag}(\text{s}) + \text{Cl}^-(\text{aq}) + \text{AgBr}(\text{s}) \rightarrow \text{Ag}(\text{s}) + \text{Br}^-(\text{aq}) + \text{AgCl}(\text{s})$

or: $\text{AgBr}(\text{s}) + \text{Cl}^-(\text{aq}) \rightarrow \text{AgCl}(\text{s}) + \text{Br}^-(\text{aq})$ ($\nu = 1$)

L: $\text{AgCl}(\text{s}) + \text{e}^- \rightarrow \text{Ag}(\text{s}) + \text{Cl}^-(\text{aq})$, R: $\text{AgBr}(\text{s}) + \text{e}^- \rightarrow \text{Ag}(\text{s}) + \text{Br}^-(\text{aq})$.

12.2 Refer to Box 12.1

(a) $\underset{\text{Red}_\text{L}}{\text{Zn}(\text{s})} + \underset{\text{Ox}_\text{R}}{\text{CuSO}_4(\text{aq})} \rightarrow \underset{\text{Ox}_\text{L}}{\text{ZnSO}_4(\text{aq})} + \underset{\text{Red}_\text{R}}{\text{Cu}(\text{s})}$

$Zn|ZnSO_4(aq)||CuSO_4(aq)|Cu$

(b) $AgCl(s) + \frac{1}{2}H_2(g) \rightarrow HCl(aq) + Ag(s)$

Ox_R Red_L Ox_L Red_R

$Pt|H_2|HCl(aq)|AgCl|Ag$

(c) Augment $H_2(g) + \frac{1}{2}O_2(g) \rightarrow H_2O(l)$ to

$H_2(g) + \underbrace{\tfrac{1}{2}O_2(g) + 2H^+(aq)} \rightarrow H_2O(l) + 2H^+(aq)$

Red_L Ox_R Red_R Ox_R

$Pt|H_2|H^+(aq), H_2O(l)|O_2|Pt$

or $Pt|H_2|HCl(aq)|O_2|Pt$.

(d) $Na(s) + H_2O(l) \rightarrow NaOH(aq) + \frac{1}{2}H_2(g)$

or: $Na(s) + H_2O(l) \rightarrow Na^+(aq) + \underbrace{OH^-(aq) + \tfrac{1}{2}H_2(g)}$

Red_L Ox_R Ox_L Red_R

$Na(s)|Na^+(aq), OH^-(aq), H_2O(l)|H_2|Pt$

or: $Na(s)|NaOH(aq)|H_2|Pt$.

To ensure a controllable reaction, dilute the Na into an amalgam and use

$Na|NaI(ethylamine)|Na, Hg|NaOH(aq)|H_2|Pt$.

(e) $H_2(g) + I_2(s) \rightarrow 2HI(aq) \rightarrow 2H^+(aq) + 2I^-(aq)$

Red_L Ox_R Ox_L Red_R

$Pt|H_2|H^+(aq), I^-(aq)|I_2(s)|Pt$

or: $Pt|H_2|HI(aq)|I_2(s)|Pt$.

12.3 For the cells in Problem 12.1:

$E^\ominus(a) = E^\ominus_{AgCl,Ag,Cl^-} - E^\ominus_{H^+,H_2} = E^\ominus_{AgCl,Ag,Cl^-} = 0.22\,V$ (Ag positive)

$E^\ominus(b) = E^\ominus_{Sn^{4+},Sn^{2+}} - E^\ominus_{Fe^{3+},Fe^{2+}} = 0.15\,V - 0.77\,V = -0.62\,V$ (Fe positive)

$E^\ominus(c) = E^\ominus_{MnO_2,H^+,Mn^{2+},H_2O} - E^\ominus_{Cu^{2+},Cu} = 1.23\,V - 0.34\,V = 0.89\,V$ (Mn positive)

$E^\ominus(d) = E^\ominus_{AgBr,Ag,Br^-} - E^\ominus_{AgCl,Ag,Cl^-} = 0.07\,V - 0.22\,V = -0.15\,V$ (AgCl positive).

For the cells in 12.2:

$E^\ominus(a) = E^\ominus_{Cu^{2+},Cu} - E^\ominus_{Zn^{2+},Zn} = 0.34\,V - (-0.76\,V) = 1.10\,V$ (Cu positive)

$E^\ominus(b) = E^\ominus_{AgCl,Ag,Cl^-} - E^\ominus_{H^+,H_2} = E^\ominus_{AgCl,Ag,Cl^-} = 0.22\,V$ (AgCl positive)

$E^\ominus(c) = E^\ominus_{O_2,H^+,H_2O} - E^\ominus_{H^+,H_2} = E^\ominus_{O_2,H^+,H_2O} = 1.23\,V$ (O_2 positive)

$E^\ominus(d) = E^\ominus_{H_2O,OH^-,H_2} - E^\ominus_{Na^+,Na} = -0.83\,V - (-2.71\,V) = 1.88\,V$ (H_2 positive)

$E^\ominus(e) = E^\ominus_{I_2,I^-} - E^\ominus_{H^+,H_2} = E^\ominus_{I_2,I^-} = 0.54\,V$ (I_2 positive)

12.4 $\Delta_r G^\ominus = -\nu F E^\ominus$ [12.3.1], $F = 9.648 \times 10^4\,\mathrm{C\,mol^{-1}}$

(a) $2Na + 2H_2O \rightarrow 2NaOH + H_2$, $E^\ominus = 1.88\,\mathrm{V}$ [Problem 12.3].

Therefore for the reaction as written ($\nu = 2$),

$\Delta_r G^\ominus = -2 \times (1.88\,\mathrm{V}) \times (9.6485 \times 10^4\,\mathrm{C\,mol^{-1}}) = \underline{-363\,\mathrm{kJ\,mol^{-1}}}$.

(b) $K + H_2O \rightarrow KOH + \frac{1}{2}H_2$: $\nu = 1$.

$$\left.\begin{array}{ll} \mathrm{R:}\ H_2O + e^- \rightarrow HO^- + \frac{1}{2}H_2 & E^\ominus = -0.83\,\mathrm{V} \\ \mathrm{L:}\ K^+ + e^- \rightarrow K & E^\ominus = -2.93\,\mathrm{V} \end{array}\right\} E^\ominus = 2.10\,\mathrm{V}$$

$\Delta_r G^\ominus = -(2.10\,\mathrm{V}) \times (9.6485 \times 10^4\,\mathrm{C\,mol^{-1}}) = \underline{-203\,\mathrm{V}}.$

(c) $K_2S_2O_8 + 2KI \rightarrow I_2 + 2K_2SO_4$; $\nu = 2$.

$$\left.\begin{array}{ll} \mathrm{R:}\ S_2O_8^{2-} + 2e^- \rightarrow 2SO_4^{2-} & E^\ominus = 2.05\,\mathrm{V} \\ \mathrm{L:}\ I_2 + 2e^- \rightarrow 2I^- & E^\ominus = 0.54\,\mathrm{V} \end{array}\right\} E^\ominus = 1.51\,\mathrm{V}.$$

$\Delta_r G^\ominus = -2 \times (1.51\,\mathrm{V}) \times (9.6485 \times 10^4\,\mathrm{C\,mol^{-1}}) = \underline{-291\,\mathrm{kJ\,mol^{-1}}}$.

(d) $Pb + ZnCO_3 \rightarrow PbCO_3 + Zn$; $\nu = 2$

$$\left.\begin{array}{ll} \mathrm{R:}\ Zn^{2+} + 2e^- \rightarrow Zn & E^\ominus = -0.76\,\mathrm{V} \\ \mathrm{L:}\ Pb^{2+} + 2e^- \rightarrow Pb & E^\ominus = -0.13\,\mathrm{V} \end{array}\right\} E^\ominus = -0.63\,\mathrm{V}$$

$\Delta_r G^\ominus = 2 \times (0.63\,\mathrm{V}) \times (9.6485 \times 10^4\,\mathrm{C\,mol^{-1}}) = 122\,\mathrm{kJ\,mol^{-1}}$.

12.5 $\ln K = \nu F E^\ominus / RT = \nu E^\ominus / 25.69\,\mathrm{mV}$ [Box 12.2]

(a) $Sn + CuSO_4 \rightleftharpoons Cu + SnSO_4$; $K = \dfrac{a(Cu)a(Sn^{2+})a(SO_4^{2-})}{a(Sn)a(Cu^{2+})a(SO_4^{2-})} = \dfrac{a(Sn^{2+})}{a(Cu^{2+})}$.

$$\left.\begin{array}{l} \mathrm{R:}\ Cu^{2+} + 2e^- \rightleftharpoons Cu;\ E^\ominus = 0.34\,\mathrm{V} \\ \mathrm{L:}\ Sn^{2+} + 2e^- \rightleftharpoons Sn;\ E^\ominus = -0.14\,\mathrm{V} \end{array}\right\} E_R^\ominus - E_L^\ominus = 0.48\,\mathrm{V},\ \nu = 2.$$

$\ln K = 2 \times 0.48\,\mathrm{V}/25.69\,\mathrm{mV} = 37$; $\underline{K = 1.2 \times 10^{16}}$.

(b) $2H_2(g) + O_2(g) \rightleftharpoons 2H_2O(l)$; $K = a^2(H_2O)/f^2(H_2)f(O_2)$.

$$\left.\begin{array}{ll} \mathrm{R:}\ 4H^+ + O_2 + 4e^- \rightleftharpoons 2H_2O;\ E^\ominus = 1.23\,\mathrm{V} & \\ \mathrm{L:}\ 4H^+ + 4e^- \rightarrow 2H_2; & E^\ominus = 0 \end{array}\right\} E_R^\ominus - E_L^\ominus = 1.23\,\mathrm{V},\ \nu = 4$$

$\ln K = 4 \times 1.23\,\mathrm{V}/25.69\,\mathrm{mV} = 192$; $\underline{K = 2.4 \times 10^{83}}$.

(c) $Cu^{2+} + Cu \rightleftharpoons 2Cu^+$; $K = a^2(Cu^+)/a(Cu^{2+})a(Cu) = a^2(Cu^+)/a(Cu^{2+})$.

$$\left.\begin{array}{l} \mathrm{R:}\ Cu^{2+} + e^- \rightleftharpoons Cu^+;\ E^\ominus = 0.16\,\mathrm{V} \\ \mathrm{L:}\ Cu^+ + e^- \rightleftharpoons Cu;\ \ E^\ominus = 0.52\,\mathrm{V} \end{array}\right\} E_R^\ominus - E_L^\ominus = -0.36\,\mathrm{V},\ \nu = 1$$

$\ln K = -0.36\,\mathrm{V}/25.69\,\mathrm{mV} = -14.0$; $\underline{K = 8.3 \times 10^{-7}}$.

12.6 $Zn|ZnSO_4(a_\pm = 1)||CuSO_4(a_\pm = 1)|Cu$

$Zn + CuSO_4 \rightleftharpoons Cu + ZnSO_4$ [Problem 12.2], $E^\ominus = 1.10\,\mathrm{V}$ [Problem 12.3].

(a) $E = E^\ominus = \underline{1.10\,\text{V}}\,[a_+ = 1$ implies standard states of half cells]

(b) $\Delta_r G^\ominus = -2 \times (1.10\,\text{V}) \times (9.64846 \times 10^4\,\text{C mol}^{-1}) = \underline{-212\,\text{kJ mol}^{-1}}$.

(c) $\ln K = 2 \times 1.10\,\text{V}/25.69\,\text{mV} = 85.6; K = \underline{1.5 \times 10^{37}}$.

(d) When the ion activities are at their equilibrium ratio K.

12.7 $Al\,|\,Al^{3+}(aq)\,||\,Sn^{2+}(aq), Sn^{4+}(aq)\,|\,Pt$

$\text{Red}_L: Al, \text{Ox}_L: Al^{3+}; \text{Red}_R: Sn^{2+}, \text{Ox}_R: Sn^{4+}$

$\tfrac{1}{3}Al(s) + \tfrac{1}{2}Sn^{4+}(aq) \rightarrow \tfrac{1}{3}Al^{3+}(Aq) + \tfrac{1}{2}Sn^{2+}(aq)$

or: $2Al(s) + 3Sn^{4+}(aq) \rightarrow 2Al^{3+}(aq) + 3Sn^{2+}(aq), \nu = 6$

$E = E^\ominus - (RT/6F)\ln Q\,[12.1.7]\,, Q = a^2_{Al^{3+}}a^3_{Sn^{2+}}/a^2_{Al}a^3_{Sn^{4+}}$

$E^\ominus = E^\ominus_{Sn^{4+},Sn^{2+}} - E^\ominus_{Al^{3+},Al} = 0.15\,\text{V} - (-1.66\,\text{V}) = 1.81\,\text{V}.$

(a) $Q = a^2_{Al^{3+}}a^3_{Sn^{2+}}/a^3_{Sn^{4+}} = 0.10^2 \times 0.10^3/0.10^3 = 0.010$

$E = 1.81\,\text{V} - (25.69\,\text{mV}/6)\ln 0.010 = \underline{1.83\,\text{V}}.$

when $a_{\text{ion}} = 1.0, E = E^\ominus = \underline{1.81\,\text{V}}.$

(b) $\Delta_r G^\ominus = -\nu F E^\ominus = -6 \times (9.6485 \times 10^4\,\text{C mol}^{-1}) \times (1.81\,\text{V}) = \underline{-1050\,\text{kJ mol}^{-1}}.$

(c) $\ln K = \nu F E^\ominus/RT = 6 \times 1.81\,\text{V}/25.69\,\text{mV} = 423; \underline{K = 10^{183}}.$

Since $E^\ominus > 0$, the Sn^{4+}, Sn^{2+} electrode is positive and electrons tend to flow towards it in an external circuit.

12.8 $Q \approx 0.010^2 \times 0.010^3/0.010^3\;\;[\gamma \approx 1] = 0.0010.$

$E = E^\ominus - (RT/6F)\ln Q$ [Problem 12.7]

$= 1.81\,\text{V} - (25.69\,\text{mV}/6)\ln 0.0010 = \underline{1.85\,\text{V}}.$

12.9 $Pb(s) + Hg_2SO_4(s) \rightarrow PbSO_4(s) + 2Hg(l), \nu = 2$

$\text{Red}_L: Pb, \text{Ox}_R: Hg_2SO_4(s) + SO_4^{2-}; \text{Red}_R: Hg, \text{Ox}_L: PbSO_4(s) + SO_4^{2-}$

$Pb\,|\,PbSO_4(s)\,|\,SO_4^{2-}(aq)\,||\,SO_4^{2-}(aq)\,|\,Hg_2SO_4(s)\,|\,Hg$

$E = E^\ominus + (RT/2F)\ln Q,$

$Q = a_{PbSO_4(s)}a_{SO_4^{2-}(aq)}a_{Hg(l)}/a_{Pb(s)}a_{Hg_2SO_4(s)}a_{SO_4^{2-}(aq)}$

$= a_{SO_4^{2-}(aq),L}/a_{SO_4^{2-}(aq),R}.$

When the solutions are saturated,

$K_{sp,Hg} = a_{Hg_2^{2+}}a_{SO_4^{2-}} = a^2_{SO_4^{2-}(aq),R}; \; a_{SO_4^{2-}(aq),R} = \sqrt{K_{sp,Hg_2SO_4}}$

Likewise, $a_{SO_4^{2-}(aq),L} = \sqrt{K_{sp,PbSO_4}}.$

$Q = \{K_{sp,PbSO_4}/K_{sp,Hg_2SO_4}\}^{\frac{1}{2}}$

$E = E^\ominus + (RT/2F)\ln Q = E^\ominus + (RT/4F)\ln\{K_{sp,PbSO_4}/K_{sp,Hg_2SO_4}\}$

$= E^\ominus + (25.69\,\text{mV}/4)\ln(2.43 \times 10^{-8}/1.46 \times 10^{-6})$

$= E^{\ominus} - 0.03\,\text{V}.$

$E^{\ominus} = E^{\ominus}_{Hg_2SO_4,Hg,SO_4^{2-}} - E^{\ominus}_{PbSO_4,SO_4^{2-}} = 0.62\,\text{V} - (-0.36\,\text{V})$ [Table 12.1]

$= 0.98\,\text{V}.$

Therefore, $E = 0.98\,\text{V} - 0.03\,\text{V} = \underline{0.95\,\text{V}}.$

12.10 $H_2|HCl(m_1)|HCl(m_2)|H_2$ [use 11.4.2]

R: $H^+(m_2) + e^- \rightleftharpoons \frac{1}{2}H_2; E = E^{\ominus} + (RT/F)\ln a(m_2), E^{\ominus} = 0$

L: $H^+(m_1) + e^- \rightleftharpoons \frac{1}{2}H_2; E = E^{\ominus} + (RT/F)\ln a(m_1), E^{\ominus} = 0.$

$E = E_R - E_L = (RT/F)\ln[a(m_2)/a(m_1)] = (25.7\,\text{mV})\ln(0.20 \times 0.790/0.10 \times 0.798)$

$= \underline{18\,\text{mV}}.$

Including the possibility of fugacity ($\approx$ pressure) differences:

$E = (RT/F)\ln[a(m_2)/a(m_1)] - (RT/2F)\ln(p_2/p_1)$[11.4.2]

$= 18\,\text{mV} - \frac{1}{2}(25.7\,\text{mV})\ln 10 = \underline{-12\,\text{mV}}.$

12.11 $H_2(g)|HCl(aq)|Hg_2Cl_2(s)|Hg(l)$

$Red_L: H_2, Ox_L: H^+; Red_R: Hg + Cl^-, Ox_R: Hg_2Cl_2$ [Box 12.1]

$H_2(g) + Hg_2Cl_2(s) \rightarrow 2Hg(l) + 2HCl(aq), \nu = 2$

$E = E^{\ominus} - (RT/2F)\ln Q$ [12.1.7], $E^{\ominus} = 0.27\,\text{V}$ [Table 12.1]

$Q = a_{H^+}a_{Cl^-}/f$ $[a_{Hg_2Cl_2} = a_{Hg} = 1;\ f \equiv f/p^{\ominus}]$

$= m^2\gamma_{\pm}^2/f$ $[a_{H^+}a_{Cl^-} = m^2\gamma_{\pm}^2]$ $= m^2\gamma_{\pm}^2/\gamma p$ $[p \equiv p/p^{\ominus}]$

$$\gamma = \exp\int_0^p\left(\frac{Z-1}{p}\right)dp\ [6.2.14] = \exp\int_0^p\{5.37 \times 10^{-4} + 3.5 \times 10^{-8}p\}dp$$

$= \exp\{5.37 \times 10^{-4}(p/p^{\ominus}) + \frac{1}{2}(3.5 \times 10^{-8})(p/p^{\ominus})^2\}.$

At 500 atm ($\approx 500\,p^{\ominus}$)

$\gamma = \exp\{5.37 \times 10^{-4} \times 500 + \frac{1}{2} \times 3.5 \times 10^{-8} \times 500^2\} = 1.31.$

Therefore,

$E = 0.27\,\text{V} - (25.69\,\text{mV}/2)\ln(m^4\gamma_{\pm}^4/\gamma p)$

$= 0.27\,\text{V} - (25.69\,\text{mV}/2)\ln\{0.10^4 \times 0.798^4/1.31 \times 500\}$

$= 0.27\,\text{V} - (-0.17\,\text{V}) = \underline{0.44\,\text{V}}.$

12.12 $H_2|HCl(aq)|Cl_2, H_2 + Cl_2 \rightleftharpoons 2HCl.$

$E = E^{\ominus} + (RT/F)\ln(f_{Cl_2}^{\frac{1}{2}}/a_{Cl^-}a_{H^+})\,[f_{H_2} \approx 1].$

$a_{Cl^-}a_{H^+} \approx (0.905 \times 0.01)^2 = 8.2 \times 10^{-5}$ [Table 11.2]

$E^{\ominus} = E^{\ominus}(Cl_2, Cl^-) - E^{\ominus}(H_2, H^+) = 1.36\,\text{V}$ [Table 12.1]

$E = 1.36\,\text{V} + (25.69\,\text{mV}/2)\ln f_{\text{Cl}_2} - (25.69\,\text{mV})\ln(8.2 \times 10^{-5})$

$\quad = 1.60\,\text{V} + (25.69\,\text{mV}/2)\ln f\ [f = f_{\text{Cl}_2}]$.

Therefore $\ln f = [E - 1.60\,\text{V}]/0.01284\,\text{V}$.

Draw up the following Table:

p/atm	1	50	100	
$\ln f$	0.03	3.26	3.51	
f/atm	1.03	26.1	33.5	
γ	1.03	0.52	0.34	$[\gamma = f/p]$

12.13 $H_2|HCl(aq)|AgCl, Ag$; $H_2 + 2AgCl \rightleftharpoons 2HCl + 2Ag$.

$E = E^{\ominus}(\text{Ag, AgCl}) - (RT/F)\ln a_{\text{H}^+}a_{\text{Cl}^-}$

$\quad \approx E^{\ominus}(\text{Ag, AgCl}) - (2RT/F)\ln(m_{\text{HCl}}/m^{\ominus})$

$\quad \approx \underline{E^{\ominus}(\text{Ag, AgCl}) + (2RT/F)\ln(1 + \kappa t)}$.

$(\partial E/\partial t) = (2RT/F)\ln(1 + \kappa t)/\partial t = \underline{(2\kappa RT/F)/(1 + \kappa t)}$.

12.14 $H_2 + \frac{1}{2}O_2 \rightleftharpoons H_2O$; $E^{\ominus} = 1.23\,\text{V}$ [Problem 12.5b].

$\Delta_r G^{\ominus} = 2 \times (1.23\,\text{V}) \times (9.6485 \times 10^4\,\text{C mol}^{-1})$ [12.3.1, $\nu = 2$]

$\quad = -237\,\text{kJ mol}^{-1}$;

$w'_{\text{e,m}} = -\Delta_r G^{\ominus}$ [5.3.11] $= 237\,\text{kJ mol}^{-1}$.

Therefore, maximum e.m.f. is $\underline{1.23\,\text{V}}$; and the maximum amount of electrical work available is $\underline{237\,\text{kJ}}$ per mole of hydrogen.

12.15 $C_4H_{10}(g) + \frac{13}{2}O_2(g) \rightarrow 4CO_2(g) + 5H_2O(l)$.

$\Delta H_c^{\ominus} = -2877\,\text{kJ mol}^{-1}$ [Table 4.2]

$\Delta_r G^{\ominus} = [4(-394.36) + 5(-237.13) - (-17.03)]\,\text{kJ mol}^{-1}$ [Table 4.1]

$\quad = -2746\,\text{kJ mol}^{-1}$.

$\Delta_r G^{\ominus} = \Delta_r A^{\ominus} + \Delta v_{\text{gas}}RT$; $\Delta v_{\text{gas}} = 4 - 1 - \frac{13}{2} = -3.5$.

$\Delta_r A^{\ominus} = [-2746 + 3.5 \times 2.48]\,\text{kJ mol}^{-1} = -2738\,\text{kJ mol}^{-1}$.

$|q|_p = |\Delta_r H^{\ominus}| = \underline{2877\,\text{kJ mol}^{-1}}$ [standard states].

$w'_{\text{max}} = -\Delta_r A^{\ominus}$ [5.3.9] $= \underline{2738\,\text{kJ mol}^{-1}}$.

$w'_{\text{e,max}} = -\Delta_r G^{\ominus}$ [5.3.11] $= \underline{2746\,\text{kJ mol}^{-1}}$.

12.16 $H_2|HCl(m)|AgCl, Ag$; $\frac{1}{2}H_2(g) + AgCl(s) \rightleftharpoons HCl(aq) + Ag(s)$.

$E = E^{\ominus} - (RT/F)\ln(a_{\text{H}^+}a_{\text{Cl}^-})$ [Problem 12.13]

$= E^{\ominus} - (RT/F)\ln m^2\gamma_{\pm}^2 \ (m \equiv m/m^{\ominus})$

$= E^{\ominus} - (2RT/F)\ln m - 2(2.303\ RT/F)\lg\gamma_{\pm}$

$= E^{\ominus} - (0.1183\ \mathrm{V})\lg m + (0.1183\ \mathrm{V}) \times (0.509)\sqrt{m} - (0.1183\ \mathrm{V}) \times Bm.$

Therefore $(E/V) + 0.1183 \lg m - 0.0602\sqrt{m} = (E^{\ominus}/\mathrm{V}) - 0.1183\,Bm.$

Hence, plot l.h.s. against m; then intercept $= E^{\ominus}/\mathrm{V}$, slope $= -0.1183\,B$.

12.17 Draw up the following Table:

$m/\mathrm{mol\ kg^{-1}}$	0.1238	0.02563	0.009138	0.005619	0.003215
$E/\mathrm{V} + 0.1183 \lg m - 0.0602\sqrt{m}$	0.2135	0.2204	0.2216	0.2218	0.2221

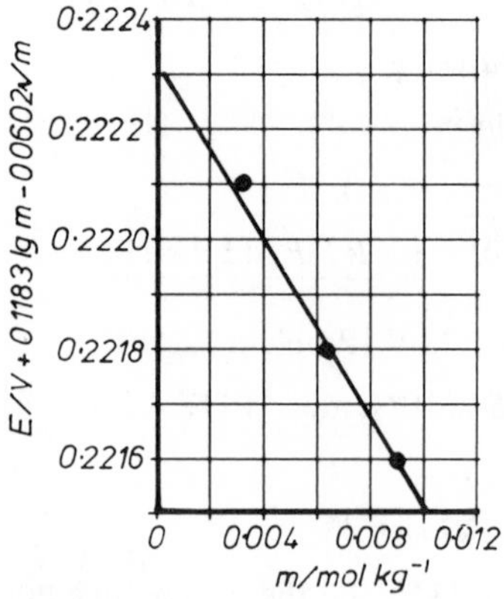

Fig 12·1

The last three points are plotted in Fig. 12.1.

The extrapolated intercept is 0.2223, and so

$E^{\ominus} = \underline{0.2223\ \mathrm{V}}$. Since $E^{\ominus}(H_2, H^+) = 0$, $E^{\ominus}(\mathrm{AgCl}, \mathrm{Cl}^-) = \underline{0.2223\ \mathrm{V}}$ also.

12.18 $E = E^{\ominus} - (2RT/F)\ln m - (2RT/F)\ln\gamma_{\pm}$ [Problem 12.16]

$\ln\gamma_{\pm} = [E^{\ominus} - E - (0.0514\ \mathrm{V})\ln m]/(0.0514\ \mathrm{V})$

$= [(0.2223\ \mathrm{V}) - (0.3524\ \mathrm{V}) - (0.0514\ \mathrm{V})\ln(0.100)]/(0.0514\ \mathrm{V})$

$= -0.2285,\ \gamma_{\pm} = 0.7957.$

(a) $a_{H^+} = m\gamma_{\pm}/m^{\ominus} = 0.7957 \times 0.100 = \underline{0.0796}$;

(b) $\gamma_{\pm} = \underline{0.7957}$

(c) $\mathrm{pH} = -\lg a_{H^+} = -\lg 0.0796 = \underline{1.10}.$

12.19 $\Delta_r G^{\ominus} = -\nu F E^{\ominus}$ [12.3.1], $\Delta_r S^{\ominus} = \nu F(\partial E^{\ominus}/\partial T)_m$ [12.3.4],

$\Delta_r H^\ominus = \Delta_r G^\ominus + T\Delta_r S^\ominus$ [12.3.5] ; $\nu = 1$.

$E^\ominus/\mathrm{V} = 0.23659 - 4.8564 \times 10^{-4}(\theta/°\mathrm{C}) - 3.4205 \times 10^{-6}(\theta/°\mathrm{C})^2$
$+ 5.869 \times 10^{-9}(\theta/°\mathrm{C})^3$,

$[\partial(E^\ominus/\mathrm{V})/\partial\theta] = -4.8564 \times 10^{-4} - 6.8410 \times 10^{-6}(\theta/°\mathrm{C}) + 1.7607 \times 10^{-8}(\theta/°\mathrm{C})^2$.

At 25 °C: $E^\ominus = 0.22240\,\mathrm{V}$, $\mathrm{d}E^\ominus/\mathrm{d}T = \mathrm{d}E^\ominus/\mathrm{d}\theta = -6.4566 \times 10^{-4}\,\mathrm{V\,K^{-1}}$.

$\Delta_r G^\ominus = -(9.64846 \times 10^4\,\mathrm{C\,mol^{-1}}) \times (0.22240\,\mathrm{V}) = \underline{-21.46\,\mathrm{kJ\,mol^{-1}}}$.

$\Delta_r S^\ominus = (9.64846 \times 10^4\,\mathrm{C\,mol^{-1}}) \times (-6.4566 \times 10^{-4}\,\mathrm{V\,K^{-1}}) = \underline{-62.30\,\mathrm{J\,K^{-1}\,mol^{-1}}}$.

$\Delta_r H^\ominus = (-21.46\,\mathrm{kJ\,mol^{-1}}) + (298.15\,\mathrm{K}) \times (-62.30\,\mathrm{J\,K^{-1}\,mol^{-1}})$
$= \underline{-40.03\,\mathrm{kJ\,mol^{-1}}}$.

$\tfrac{1}{2}H_2 + AgCl \rightleftharpoons Ag + HCl$.

$\Delta_r G^\ominus = \Delta_f G^\ominus(H^+) + \Delta_f G^\ominus(Cl^-) - \Delta_f G^\ominus(AgCl)$
$= \Delta_f G^\ominus(Cl^-) - \Delta_f G^\ominus(AgCl)$.

$\Delta_f G^\ominus(Cl^-) = \Delta_r G^\ominus + \Delta_f G^\ominus(AgCl) = (-21.46\,\mathrm{kJ\,mol^{-1}}) + (-109.79\,\mathrm{kJ\,mol^{-1}})$
$= \underline{-131.25\,\mathrm{kJ\,mol^{-1}}}$.

$S^\ominus(Cl^-) = \Delta_r S^\ominus + S^\ominus(AgCl) + \tfrac{1}{2}S^\ominus(H_2) - S^\ominus(Ag) = (-62.30\,\mathrm{J\,K^{-1}\,mol^{-1}})$
$+ (96.2\,\mathrm{J\,K^{-1}\,mol^{-1}}) + \tfrac{1}{2}(130.86\,\mathrm{J\,K^{-1}\,mol^{-1}}) - (42.55\,\mathrm{J\,K^{-1}\,mol^{-1}})$
$= \underline{56.78\,\mathrm{K^{-1}\,mol^{-1}}}$.

$\Delta_f H^\ominus(Cl^-) = \Delta_r H^\ominus + \Delta_f H^\ominus(AgCl) = (-40.03\,\mathrm{kJ\,mol^{-1}}) + (-127.07\,\mathrm{kJ\,mol^{-1}})$
$= \underline{-167.10\,\mathrm{J\,K^{-1}\,mol^{-1}}}$.

12.20 $H_2|HCl(aq)|AgCl|Ag$

$E = E^\ominus(AgCl, Cl^-) - (RT/F)\ln a_{Cl^-}a_{H^+}$
$= E^\ominus(AgCl, Cl^-) - 2(RT/F)\ln a_{H^+}$ $[a_{H^+} = a_{Cl^-}]$
$= 0.2223\,\mathrm{V} - 2 \times 2.303 \times (0.02569\,\mathrm{V})\lg a_{H^+}$
$= 0.2223\,\mathrm{V} + 0.1183\,\mathrm{V}\,\mathrm{pH}$,

$\mathrm{pH} = (E/\mathrm{V} - 0.2223)/0.1183 = (0.332 - 0.2223)/0.1183 = \underline{0.926}$.

12.21 $Ag|AgBr(aq)|AgBr(s)|Ag$

$\mathrm{Red_L}$: Ag, $\mathrm{Ox_L}$: Ag^+; $\mathrm{Red_R}$: $Ag + Br^-$, $\mathrm{Ox_R}$: AgBr [Box 12.1]

$Ag(s) + AgBr(s) \rightarrow Ag(s) + AgBr(aq)$, $\nu = 1$

or: $AgBr(s) \rightarrow AgBr(aq)$ $K_{sp} = \{a_{Ag^+}a_{Br^-}\}_{eq}$

$E = E^\ominus - (RT/F)\ln a_{Ag^+}a_{Br^-} = \underline{0}$ at equilibrium, when

$E^\ominus = (RT/F)\ln K_{sp}$.

12.22 $E^{\ominus} = (RT/F)\ln K_{sp}$ [Problem 12.21]

$K_{sp} = \exp[E^{\ominus}/(RT/F)] = \exp[-0.9509\ \text{V}/0.02569\ \text{V}]$

$= \exp(-37.01) = \underline{8.44 \times 10^{-17}}.$

$K_{sp} \approx (m/m^{\ominus})^2$, $m \approx \underline{9.19 \times 10^{-9}\ \text{mol kg}^{-1}}.$

12.23 $Ag|AgX|MX(m_1)|M_xHg$

Red_L: $Ag + X^-$, Ox_L: AgX; Red_R: M_xHg, Ox_R: M^+ [Box 12.1]

$Ag + X^- + M^+ \rightarrow AgX + M_xHg$, $\nu = 1$

$E = E^{\ominus} - (RT/F)\ln Q$, $Q = a_{AgX}a_{M_xHg}/a_{Ag}a_{X^-}a_{M^+}$

$Ag|AgX|MX(m_1)|M_xHg|MX(m_2)|AgX|Ag$

$E = \{E^{\ominus} - (RT/F)\ln Q\}_R - \{E^{\ominus} - (RT/F)\ln Q\}_L$

$= (RT/F)\ln\{Q_L/Q_R\}$

$= (RT/F)\ln\{(a_{M^+}a_{X^-})_L/(a_{M^+}a_{X^-})_R\}$

$= (2RT/F)\ln(m_1/m_2) + (2RT/F)\ln\{\gamma_\pm(1)/\gamma_\pm(2)\}.$

Take $m(2) = m_r$, the reference value, and write $m_1 = m$:

$E = (2RT/F)\{\ln(m/m_r) + \ln(\gamma_\pm/\gamma_r)\}.$

For $m = 0.914\ \text{mol kg}^{-1}$ the extended Debye-Hückel expression gives

$\lg\gamma_{\pm r} = -0.273$, or $\gamma_{\pm r} = 0.533$.

Therefore $\ln\gamma/\gamma_r = [E/(0.05139\ \text{V})] - \ln(m/m_r)$.

Draw up the following Table with $m_r = 0.0914\ \text{mol kg}^{-1}$, $\gamma_r = 0.533$.

$m/\text{mol kg}^{-1}$	0.0555	0.0914	0.1652	0.2171	1.040	1.350
E/V	−0.0220	0.0000	0.0263	0.0379	0.1156	0.1336
$\ln(\gamma/\gamma_r)$	0.0708	0.0000	−0.0801	−0.1276	−0.1823	−0.0929
γ	0.572	0.533	0.492	0.469	0.444	0.486

A more precise procedure is described in the original reference.

12.24 $H_2|HCl(aq)|Hg_2Cl_2|Hg$.

$E = E^{\ominus}(Hg_2Cl_2, Hg) - (RT/F)\ln a_{Cl^-}a_{H^+}$

$= E^{\ominus}(Hg_2Cl_2, Hg) - (2RT/F)\ln m - (2RT/F)\ln\gamma_\pm$

$= E^{\ominus}(Hg_2Cl_2, Hg) - (0.1183\ \text{V})\lg m + (0.1183\ \text{V})A\sqrt{m}$ [11.2.11],

$E + (0.1183\ \text{V})\lg m = E^\ominus(\text{Hg}_2\text{Cl}_2, \text{Hg}) + (0.1183\ \text{V})A\sqrt{m}.$

Plot $(E/\text{V}) + 0.1183 \lg m$ against $\sqrt{m}$; intercept at $m = 0$ is $E^\ominus/\text{V}$.

Draw up the following Table:

$100m/m^\ominus$	0.16077	0.30769	0.50403	0.76938	1.09474
$\sqrt{(m/m^\ominus)}$	0.04010	0.05547	0.087100	0.0771	0.10463
$(E/\text{V}) + 0.1183 \lg(m/m^\ominus)$	0.27029	0.27109	0.27186	0.27260	0.27337

These figures are plotted in Fig. 12.2 The intercept occurs at 0.26835; therefore $E^\ominus = 0.26835$ V. The least squares best fit (Appendix) gives an intercept of 0.26838 V and a coefficient of determination 0.99895.

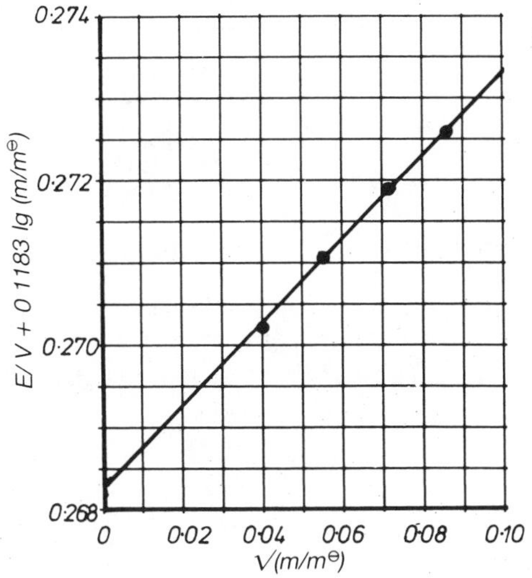

Fig 12·2

Form $\ln \gamma_\pm = (E^\ominus - E)/(2RT/F) - \ln(m/m^\ominus)$

$= \{0.26835 - (E/\text{V})\}/0.051\,38 - \ln(m/m^\ominus)$

and draw up the following Table:

$100m/m^\ominus$	0.160 77	0.307 69	0.504 03	0.769 38	1.094 74
$\ln \gamma_\pm$	−0.0375	−0.0531	−0.0680	−0.0824	−0.0975
$\gamma_\pm$	0.9632	0.9483	0.9342	0.9209	0.9071

12.25 $Pt|H_2|NaOH(aq), NaCl(aq)|AgCl|Ag$

$Red_L: H_2, Ox_L: H^+; Red_R: Ag + Cl^-, Ox_R: AgCl$

$H_2(g) + 2AgCl(s) \rightarrow 2Ag(s) + 2Cl^-(aq) + 2H^+(aq), \nu = 2$

$E = E^\ominus - (RT/F)\ln Q$

$Q = a_{H^+}a_{Ag}a_{Cl^-}/f^{\frac{1}{2}}a_{AgCl} = a_{H^+}a_{Cl^-}$

$= K_w a_{Cl^-}/a_{OH^-} = K_w \gamma m_{Cl^-}/\gamma_{OH^-}m_{OH^-}$

$= K_w m_{Cl^-}/m_{OH^-}.$

$E = E^\ominus - (RT/F)\ln K_w - (RT/F)\ln(m_{Cl^-}/m_{OH^-})$

$= E^\ominus + (2.303\, RT/F)pK_w - (RT/F)\ln(m_{Cl^-}/m_{OH^-})$

$= E^\ominus_{AgCl,Ag,Cl^-} + (2.303\, RT/F)pK_w - (RT/F)\ln(0.011\,25/0.0100)$

$pK_w = (E - E^\ominus_{AgCl,Ag,Cl^-})/(2.303\, RT/F) + (\ln 1.125)/2.303.$

Draw up the following Table:

$\theta/°C$	20.0	25.0	30.0
T/K	293.15	298.15	303.15
E/V	1.04774	1.04864	1.04942
$(2.303\, RT/F)/V$	0.05819	0.05918	0.06018
pK_w	14.23	14.01	13.8

$d\ln K_w/dT = \Delta_r H^\ominus/RT^2$ [10.2.4], K_w for $H_2O(l) \rightleftharpoons H^+(aq) + OH^-(aq)$

$\Delta_r H^\ominus = 2.303\, RT^2\, d\lg K/dT = -2.303\, RT^2 (dpK_w/dT);$

$dpK_w/dT \approx (13.79 - 14.23)/(10.0\,K) = -0.044\,K^{-1};$

$\Delta_r H^\ominus = -2.303 \times (8.314\,J\,K^{-1}\,mol^{-1}) \times (298.15\,K)^2 \times (-0.044\,K^{-1})$

$= \underline{74.9\,kJ\,mol^{-1}}.$

$\Delta_r G^\ominus = -RT\ln K_w = 2.303\, RT pK_w = \underline{80.0\,kJ\,mol^{-1}}.$

$\Delta_r S^\ominus = (\Delta_r H^\ominus - \Delta_r G^\ominus)/T = \underline{-17.1\,J\,K^{-1}\,mol^{-1}}.$

See the original reference for a careful analysis of the precise data.

12.26 $H_2|HCl(aq,urea)|AgCl|Ag.$

$E + (2RT/F)\ln(m/m^\ominus) = E^\ominus(AgCl,Ag) + (2 \times 2.303\, A) \times (RT/F)(m/m^\ominus)^{\frac{1}{2}}$

Plot l.h.s. against $\sqrt{m}$, Fig. 12.3, and extrapolate to $m = 0$ to obtain $E^\ominus$.

Construct the following Table:

$m/m^{\ominus}$	0.00558	0.01300	0.0192	0.0246	0.0349	0.0411
E/V	0.5616	0.5187	0.4999	0.4878	0.4708	0.4629
$\surd(m/m^{\ominus})$	0.0747	0.1140	0.1386	0.1568	0.1868	0.2027
$(E/\text{V}) + 0.0514 \ln m$	0.2950	0.2955	0.2968	0.2974	0.2983	0.2988

The intercept is at 0.2916, so that $E^{\ominus}(\text{AgCl,Cl}) = \underline{0.2916\text{ V}}$.

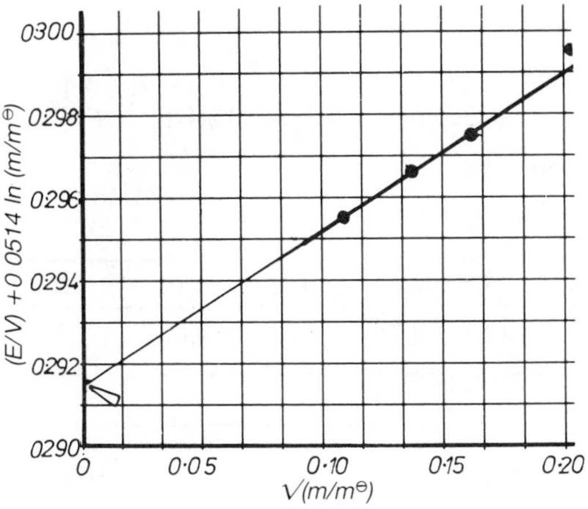

Fig 12·3

12.27 $A = 1.825 \times 10^6 \{(\rho/\text{g cm}^{-3})/\epsilon_r^3 (T/\text{K})^3\}^{\frac{1}{2}}$ [11.2.11]

$= 1.825 \times 10^6 \{1.0790/(91.76 \times 298.2)^3\}^{\frac{1}{2}} = \underline{0.419.}$

The slope of the graph in Problem 12.26 is $4.606\ (ART/F)/\text{V} = 0.1183\,A$. From the graph, the experimental slope is 0.0375, and so $A_{\text{exp}} = \underline{0.317}$.

12.28 (a) NH_4Cl; $\text{p}K_a = 9.25, S = 0.10, \lg S = -1.00$

$\text{pH} = \frac{1}{2} \times 9.25 + \frac{1}{2} \times 1.00$ [12.4.14] $= \underline{5.13}$.

(b) NaOAc; $\text{p}K_w = 14.00, \text{p}K_a = 4.76, S = 0.10, \lg S = -1.00$

$\text{pH} \approx \frac{1}{2}(14.00 + 4.76 - 1.00) = \underline{8.88}$ [12.4.13].

(c) NaOAc; $S = 1.0, \lg S = 0, \text{pH} \approx \frac{1}{2}(14.00 + 4.76) = \underline{9.38}$.

(d) AcOH: $\text{p}K_a = 4.75, A = 0.10$;

$\text{pH} \approx \frac{1}{2}\text{p}K_a - \frac{1}{2}\lg A$ [12.4.11] $= \frac{1}{2}[4.75 + 1.00] = 1.00] = \underline{2.88}$.

12.29 $\mathrm{pH} \approx \frac{1}{2}(\mathrm{p}K_\mathrm{w} + \mathrm{p}K_\mathrm{a} + \lg S)$ [12.4.13]; $\mathrm{p}K_\mathrm{a} = 3.86, S = 0.10$

$\mathrm{pH} \approx \frac{1}{2}(14.00 + 3.86 - 1.00) = \underline{8.43}.$

The pH of the end point has the value just calculated, that is $\underline{8.43}$ [Section 12.4(e)]..

12.30 Initially only salt is present, and so use 12.4.13:

$\mathrm{pH} = \frac{1}{2}\mathrm{p}K_\mathrm{a} + \frac{1}{2}\mathrm{p}K_\mathrm{w} + \frac{1}{2}\lg S, \lg S = -1.00$

$= \frac{1}{2}\{4.75 + 14.0 - 1.00\} = 8.88$ (a).

For $A \approx S$, use 12.4.12:

$\mathrm{pH} = \mathrm{p}K_\mathrm{a} - \lg(A/S) = 4.75 - \lg(A/0.10)$

$= 3.75 - \lg A$ (b).

When so much acid has been added that $A \gg S$, use 12.4.11

$\mathrm{pH} = \frac{1}{2}\mathrm{p}K_\mathrm{a} - \frac{1}{2}\lg A = 2.38 - \frac{1}{2}\lg A$ (c).

Draw up the following Table:

A	0	0.06	0.08	0.10	0.12	0.14	0.6	0.8	1.0
pH	888	4.97	4.85	4.75	4.67	4.60	2.49	2.43	2.33
	(a)			(b)				(c)	

These results are plotted in Fig. 12.4.

Since $\mathrm{p}K_\mathrm{a} = 9.14$, pH(buffer) $\approx \underline{9.14}$ [12.4.12, $A \approx S$]

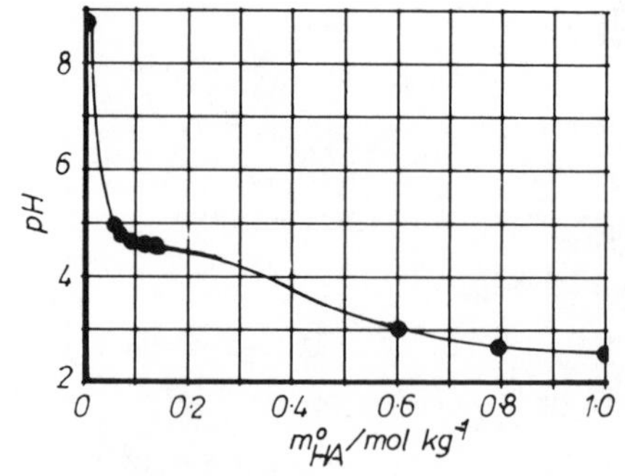

Fig 12·4

12.31 (a) For pH = 2.2 use disodium hydrogen phosphate + phosphoric acid, with $\mathrm{p}K_\mathrm{a} = 2.12$; hence pH(buffer) ≈ 2.12.

(b) For pH ≈ 7.0 use sodium dihydrogen phosphate + sodium hydrogen phosphate. with $\mathrm{p}K_\mathrm{a} = 7.2$; hence pH(buffer) ≈ 7.2.

12.32 $H = A/\{1 + (H/K_a)\} + K_w/H - S/\{1 + (K_a/H)\}$

$H^2(1 + H/K_a)(1 + K_a/H) = AH(1 + K_a/H) + K_w(1 + H/K_a)(1 + K_a/H) - SH(1 + H/K_a)$

$H^2(2 + H/K_a + K_a/H) = AH + AK_a + K_w(2 + H/K_a + K_a/H) - SH - SH^2/K_a$

$H^3/K_a + (2 + S/K_a)H^2 + (K_a - A - K_w/K_a + S)H - (2K_w + AK_a) - K_aK_w/H = 0$

$H^4 + (2K_a + S)H^3 + K_a(K_a - A + S - K_w/K_a)H^2 - K_a(2K_w + AK_a)H - K_a^2K_w = 0$

write $a_3 = 2K_a + S$

$a_2 = K_a(S - A + K_a - K_w/K_a)$

$a_1 = -2K_aK_w - AK_a^2$

$a_0 = -K_a^2K_w$

and solve

$H^4 + a_3H^3 + a_2H^2 + a_1H + a_0 = 0$

using the method described in Abramovitz and Stegun, Section 3.8.3.

12.33 $M + M'^{+} \rightarrow M^{+} + M'$ if $E(M'^{+}, M') > E(M^{+}, M)$ [Section 12.1(e)]

(a) $H_3O^+ + e^- \rightarrow H_2O + \frac{1}{2}H_2$;

$E = E^{\ominus} + (RT/F)\ln a_{H^+} = -(0.059\text{ V})\text{pH}$.

(b) $\frac{1}{4}O_2 + H^+ + e^- \rightarrow \frac{1}{2}H_2O$;

$E = E^{\ominus} + (RT/F)\ln a_{H^+} = 1.23\text{ V} - (0.059\text{ V})\text{pH}$.

(c) $\frac{1}{4}O_2 + \frac{1}{2}H_2O + e^- \rightarrow OH^-$,

$E = E^{\ominus} - (RT/F)\ln a_{OH^-} = (0.401\text{ V}) + (0.059\text{ V})\text{p(OH)}$

$= 0.401\text{ V} + (0.059\text{ V})(\text{p}K_w - \text{pH})$

$= 1.227\text{ V} - (0.059\text{ V})\text{pH}$.

$M^{+\nu} + \nu e^- \rightarrow M$

$E(M,M^+) \approx E^{\ominus}(M,M^+) + (RT/\nu F)\ln a_{M^+}$

$\approx E^{\ominus}(M,M^+) + (0.059\text{ V}/\nu)\lg a_{M^+} \approx E^{\ominus}(M,M^+) - (0.354\text{ V})/\nu$.

Decide whether $E(a, b, c) > E^{\ominus}(M^+,M) - (0.354\text{ V})/\nu$ in order to determine whether corrosion will proceed further. We need

(a) Al: $E^{\ominus} - (0.354\text{ V})/3 = -1.66\text{ V} - 0.118\text{ V} = -1.78\text{ V}$

(b) Cu: $E^{\ominus} - (0.354\text{ V})/2 = 0.34\text{ V} - 0.177\text{ V} = 0.16\text{ V}$

(c) Fe: $E^{\ominus} - (0.354\text{ V})/2 = -0.44\text{ V} - 0.177\text{ V} = -0.62\text{ V}$

(d) Pb: $E^{\ominus} - (0.354\text{ V})/2 = -0.13\text{ V} - 0.177\text{ V} = -0.31\text{ V}$

(e) Au: $E^{\ominus} - (0.354\text{ V})/3 = 1.40\text{ V} - 0.118\text{ V} = 1.28\text{ V}$.

(i) pH ≈ 6. $E(a) = -(0.059\text{ V}) \times 6 = -0.354\text{ V}$. This exceeds only Al and Fe, and so only these are thermodynamically disposed to corrode (but *rates* may be very slow).

$E(b) = 1.23\text{ V} - (0.059\text{ V}) \times 6 = 0.88\text{ V}$.

This exceeds all but Au and so all but Au will tend to corrode.

(ii) pH $\approx$ 8. E(c) $\approx$ 1.227 V − (0.059 V) × 8 = 0.76 V, which exceeds all but Au, and so all will tend to corrode.

(iii) pH $\approx$ 1.E(a) = −0.059 V, which exceeds all but Cu and Au, and so Pb is the only one that requires strong acid (apart from Cu, Au) to corrode by this process E(b) = 1.17 V, which exceeds all but Au, as in the pH $\approx$ 6 case.

(iv) pH $\approx$ 14. E(c) = 1.227 V − 14(0.059 V) = 0.40 V. This exceeds all but Au, as in the pH $\approx$ 8 case.

12.34 As in Problem 12.33, corrosion occurs significantly if $E_{OX} > -0.62$V [c]. The pH of the solution is 9.38 [Problem 12.28c]; therefore the potentials of the three oxidation reactions [Problem 12.34] are

E(a) = −0.55 V, E(b) = 0.68 V, E(c) = 0.67 V

All exceed − 0.617 V, and so corrosion will occur.

12.35 $\frac{1}{2}H_2(g) + (115)^+(aq) \rightarrow (115)(s) + H^+(aq)$

$\Delta_r H^\ominus = \Delta_r H\ [\frac{1}{2}H_2(g) \rightarrow H^+(aq)] - \Delta_r H\ [(115)(s) \rightarrow (115)^+(aq)]$

Construct the following Born–Haber cycles:

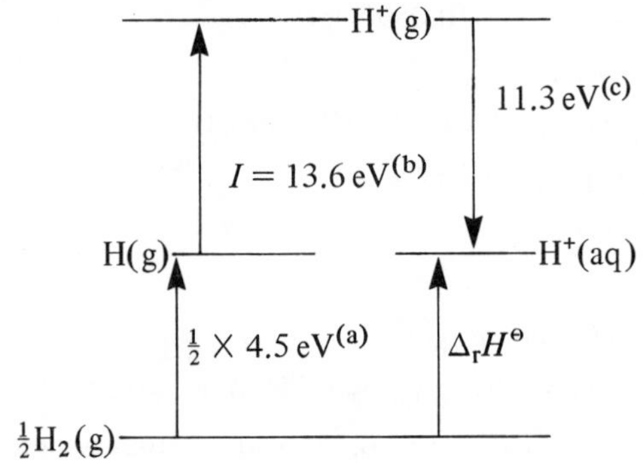

$\Delta_r H^\ominus$ = (13.6 eV + 2.2 eV − 11.3 eV) = 4.6 eV.

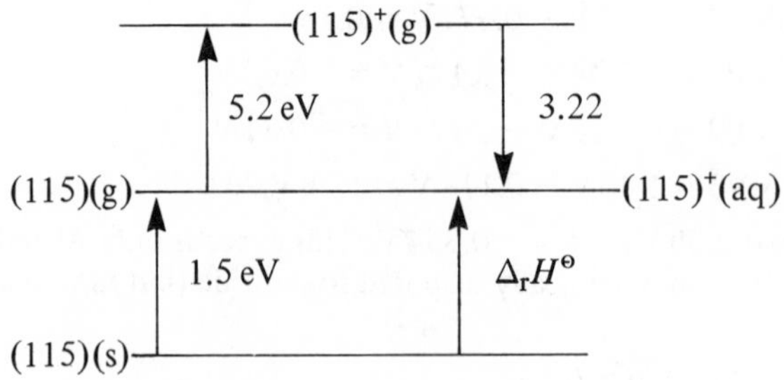

$\Delta_r H^\ominus = 1.5\,\text{eV} + 5.2\,\text{eV} - 3.22\,\text{eV} = 3.5\,\text{eV}$.

(a) Table 18.1, (b) Table 4.9, (c) Table 4.12.

$\Delta_r H^\ominus = 4.6\,\text{eV mol}^{-1} - 3.5\,\text{eV mol}^{-1} = 1.1\,\text{eV mol}^{-1}$.

$\Delta_r S^\ominus = \Delta S_m[\frac{1}{2}H_2(g) \rightarrow H^+(aq)] - \Delta S_m[(115)(s) \rightarrow (115)^+(aq)]$.

$\Delta_r S^\ominus[\frac{1}{2}H_2(g) \rightarrow H^+(aq)] = [0 - \frac{1}{2}(130.7\,\text{J K}^{-1}\,\text{mol}^{-1})] = -65.3\,\text{J K}^{-1}\,\text{mol}^{-1}$ [Table 4.1]

$= [(65.3\,\text{J K}^{-1}\,\text{mol}^{-1})/(96.5\,\text{kJ mol}^{-1})]\,\text{eV mol}^{-1}$

$= -6.8 \times 10^{-4}\,\text{eV K}^{-1}\,\text{mol}^{-1}$.

$\Delta_r S^\ominus[(115)(s) \rightarrow (115)^+(aq)] = [1.34 \times 10^{-3} - 0.69 \times 10^{-3}]\,\text{eV K}^{-1}\,\text{mol}^{-1}$

$= 6.5 \times 10^{-4}\,\text{eV K}^{-1}\,\text{mol}^{-1}$.

$\Delta_r S^\ominus = (6.8 \times 10^{-4} - 6.5 \times 10^{-4})\,\text{eV K}^{-1}\,\text{mol}^{-1} = 3 \times 10^{-5}\,\text{eV K}^{-1}\,\text{mol}^{-1}$.

$\Delta_r G^\ominus = \Delta_r H^\ominus - T\Delta_r S^\ominus = 1.1\,\text{eV mol}^{-1} - (298\,\text{K}) \times (3 \times 10^{-5}\,\text{eV K}^{-1}\,\text{mol}^{-1})$

$= 1.1\,\text{eV mol}^{-1}$.

$E^\ominus = -F\Delta_r G^\ominus = \underline{-1.1\,\text{V}}$ [$1.1\,\text{eV mol}^{-1} = 106\,\text{kJ mol}^{-1}$,

$(106\,\text{kJ mol}^{-1})/(9.65 \times 10^4\,\text{C mol}^{-1}) = 1.1\,\text{V}$].

PART 2: STRUCTURE

13. The microscopic world: quantum theory

A13.1 $M = \sigma T^4$; [Section 13.2(a)]

Power $= AM = (2.0\,\text{m} \times 3.0\,\text{m})(5.67 \times 10^{-8}\,\text{W m}^{-2}\,\text{K}^{-4})(1500\,\text{K})^4 = \underline{1.72 \times 10^6\,\text{W}}$.

A13.2 Power × time $= E = Nh\nu$ [Section 13.2(a)].

$$\nu = (\text{power} \times \text{time})/Nh = (0.72 \times 10^{-6}\,\text{W})(3.8 \times 10^{-3}\,\text{s})(8.0 \times 10^{7})^{-1} \times (6.63 \times 10^{-34}\,\text{J s})^{-1} = \underline{5.2 \times 10^{16}\,\text{Hz}}.$$

A13.3 $p = mv$ and $\lambda = h/p$ [13.2.8].

$$v = p/m = (h/\lambda)m^{-1} = (6.6 \times 10^{-34}\,\text{J s})(0.45 \times 10^{-9}\,\text{m})^{-1}(9.1 \times 10^{-31}\,\text{kg})^{-1} = \underline{1.6 \times 10^6\,\text{m s}^{-1}}.$$

A13.4 $p = h/\lambda$; [13.2.8]

(a) $p = (6.63 \times 10^{-34}\,\text{J s})(750 \times 10^{-9}\,\text{m})^{-1} = \underline{8.84 \times 10^{-28}\,\text{kg m s}^{-1}}$.

(b) $p = (6.63 \times 10^{-34}\,\text{J s})(70 \times 10^{-12}\,\text{m})^{-1} = \underline{9.5 \times 10^{-24}\,\text{kg m s}^{-1}}$.

(c) $p = (6.63 \times 10^{-34}\,\text{J s})(19\,\text{m})^{-1} = \underline{3.5 \times 10^{-35}\,\text{kg m s}^{-1}}$.

A13.5 $\frac{1}{2}mv^2 = h\nu - \Phi$ [13.2.6].

$$\lambda = c/\nu = ch[\Phi + \tfrac{1}{2}mv^2]^{-1}$$
$$= (3.00 \times 10^8\,\text{m s}^{-1})(6.63 \times 10^{-34}\,\text{J s})[3.44 \times 10^{-18}\,\text{J} + \tfrac{1}{2} \times (9.11 \times 10^{-31}\,\text{kg}) \times (1.03 \times 10^6\,\text{m/s})^2]^{-1} = 5.06 \times 10^{-8}\,\text{m, or } \underline{50.6\,\text{nm}}.$$

A13.6 $\delta\lambda = (h/m_e c)(1 - \cos\theta)$ [13.2.7].

$$\delta\lambda = (6.626 \times 10^{-34}\,\text{J s})(9.109 \times 10^{-31}\,\text{kg})^{-1}(2.998 \times 10^8\,\text{m s}^{-1})^{-1}(1 - 0.3420)$$
$$= 1.597 \times 10^{-12}\,\text{m or } 1.597\,\text{pm and } \lambda = 70.78\,\text{pm} + 1.60\,\text{pm} = \underline{72.38\,\text{pm}}.$$

A13.7 $p = mv = (1.67 \times 10^{-27}\,\text{kg})(4.50 \times 10^5\,\text{m/s}) = \underline{7.52 \times 10^{-22}\,\text{kg m s}^{-1}}$.

$\delta p = 10^{-4}p = \underline{7.52 \times 10^{-26}\,\text{kg m s}^{-1}}$.

$\delta q = h(4\pi\delta p)^{-1}$ [13.4.8]

$$= (6.63 \times 10^{-34}\,\text{J s})[4(3.14)(7.52 \times 10^{-26}\,\text{kg m s}^{-1})]^{-1} = \underline{7.02 \times 10^{-10}\,\text{m}}.$$

A13.8 $E = n^2h^2/8mL^2$ [14.1.9].

$L = (n^2h^2/8mE)^{\frac{1}{2}} = nh(8mE)^{-\frac{1}{2}} = 3(6.63 \times 10^{-34}\,\text{J s})(8)^{-\frac{1}{2}}(6.65 \times 10^{-27}\,\text{kg})^{-\frac{1}{2}} \times$
$\times (2.00 \times 10^{-24}\,\text{J})^{-\frac{1}{2}} = \underline{6.10 \times 10^{-9}\,\text{m}}.$

A13.9 $\psi_1 = (2/L)^{\frac{1}{2}} \sin(\pi x/L)$ [14.1.9].

Maximum value of $\psi_1 = (2/L)^{\frac{1}{2}}$;

$(\frac{1}{4})(2/L)^{\frac{1}{2}} = (2/L)^{\frac{1}{2}} \sin(\pi x/L)$, and $\sin(\pi x/L) = \frac{1}{4}$.

$x = (L/\pi)\arcsin(\frac{1}{4}) = (L/\pi)(0.253)$ or $(L/\pi) \times (\pi - 0.253) = \underline{8.05 \times 10^{-2}L}$ or $\underline{0.920\,L}$.

A13.10 $E_n = n^2h^2/8mL^2$ [14.1.9].

$E = (h^2/8mL^2)(5^2 - 4^2)$

$= (6.6 \times 10^{-34}\,\text{J s})^2(1.8)(3.3 \times 10^{-27}\,\text{kg})^{-1}(5.0 \times 10^{-9}\,\text{m})^{-2}(25 - 16) = \underline{5.9 \times 10^{-24}\,\text{J}}.$

13.1 $E = h\nu$ [Section 13.2(a)] $= hc/\lambda$.

$hc = (6.6262 \times 10^{-34}\,\text{J s}) \times (2.9979 \times 10^8\,\text{m s}^{-1}) = 1.986 \times 10^{-25}\,\text{J m}$.

$hcN_A = (1.986 \times 10^{-25}\,\text{J m}) \times (6.022 \times 10^{23}\,\text{mol}^{-1}) = 0.1196\,\text{J m mol}^{-1}$.

Draw up the following Table:

λ/nm	E/J	E/kJ mol^{-1}
600	3.31×10^{-19}	199
550	3.61×10^{-19}	218
400	4.97×10^{-19}	299
200	9.93×10^{-19}	598
$\lambda = 150$ pm	1.32×10^{-15}	79.8×10^4
$\lambda = 1$ cm	1.99×10^{-23}	0.012

13.2 $p = h/\lambda$ [Section 13.2(d)], $h = 6.626 \times 10^{-34}\,\text{J s}$.

If this momentum is acquired by the atom, its speed v is given by $mv = p$. Use $m = 1.008 \times (1.661 \times 10^{-27}\,\text{kg})$ [end-paper 3] $= 1.674 \times 10^{-27}\,\text{kg}$.

Draw up the following Table:

λ/nm	p/kg m s^{-1}	v/m s^{-1}
600	1.10×10^{-27}	0.66
550	1.20×10^{-27}	0.72
400	1.66×10^{-27}	0.99
200	3.31×10^{-27}	1.98
$\lambda = 150$ pm	4.42×10^{-24}	2640
$\lambda = 1$ cm	6.63×10^{-32}	3.96×10^{-5}

13.3 Energy of photon of 650 nm light is 3.055×10^{-19} J [$E = h\nu$]. Therefore, number of photons per second emitted by a 0.1 W [= 0.1 J s^{-1}] source is $(0.1\ \text{J s}^{-1})/(3.055 \times 10^{-19}\ \text{J}) = 3.27 \times 10^{17}\ \text{s}^{-1}$. The momentum of each photon is $1.019 \times 10^{-27}\ \text{kg m s}^{-1}$ [$p = h/\lambda$]. Therefore the change of momentum per second is $(1.019 \times 10^{-27}\ \text{kg m s}^{-1}) \times (3.27 \times 10^{17}\ \text{s}^{-1}) = 3.34 \times 10^{10}\ \text{kg m s}^{-2}$. This is equal to (acceleration) $\times$ (mass) [$\dot{p} = ma$]. Hence

$a = (3.34 \times 10^{-10}\ \text{kg m s}^{-2})/(5.0 \times 10^{-3}\ \text{kg}) = 6.68 \times 10^{-8}\ \text{m s}^{-2}$.

The final speed is $s = at$, and for $t = 10$ yr,

$s = (6.67 \times 10^{-8}\ \text{m s}^{-2}) \times (10 \times 3600 \times 24 \times 365.25\ \text{s}) = \underline{21\ \text{m s}^{-1}}$.

13.4 Photon energy $E = hc/\lambda = 3.61 \times 10^{-19}$ J [Problem 13.1], $1\ \text{W} = 1\ \text{J s}^{-1}$.

(a) $N = (1.0\ \text{J s}^{-1})/(3.61 \times 10^{-19}\ \text{J}) = \underline{2.8 \times 10^{18}\ \text{s}^{-1}}$.

(b) $N = (100\ \text{J s}^{-1})/(3.61 \times 10^{-19}\ \text{J}) = \underline{2.8 \times 10^{20}\ \text{s}^{-1}}$.

13.5 $\rho = (8\pi hc/\lambda^5)\left\{\dfrac{\exp(-hc/\lambda kT)}{1-\exp(-hc/\lambda kT)}\right\}$ $\quad \Delta\mathcal{U} \approx \rho\Delta\lambda$ [13.2.4],

$\Delta\lambda = 655\ \text{nm} - 650\ \text{nm} = 5\ \text{nm},\ \lambda \approx 652.5\ \text{nm}$

$hc/\lambda k = (1.439 \times 10^{-2}\ \text{m K})/\lambda$ [end-paper 1] $= 2.205 \times 10^4$ K

$$8\pi hc/\lambda^5 = 8\pi \times (6.626 \times 10^{-34}\ \text{J s}) \times (2.998 \times 10^8\ \text{m s}^{-1})/(652.5 \times 10^{-9}\ \text{m})^5$$
$$= 4.221 \times 10^7\ \text{J m}^{-4}.$$

$$\Delta\mathcal{U} = (4.221 \times 10^7\ \text{J m}^{-4}) \times (5 \times 10^{-9}\ \text{m}) \times \left\{\frac{\exp(-2.205 \times 10^4\ \text{K}/T)}{1-\exp(-2.205 \times 10^4\ \text{K}/T)}\right\}.$$

(a) $T = 298$ K (25 °C): $\Delta\mathcal{U} = (0.211\ \text{J m}^{-3}) \times (7.58 \times 10^{-33}) = \underline{1.6 \times 10^{-33}\ \text{J m}^{-3}}$.

(b) $T = 3273\,\text{K}$ (3000 °C): $\Delta\mathscr{U} = (0.211\,\text{J m}^{-3}) \times (1.191 \times 10^{-3}) = \underline{2.5 \times 10^{-4}\,\text{J m}^{-3}}$.

13.6 Find the wavelength corresponding to the maximum of ρ;
i.e. find λ for which $d\rho/d\lambda = 0$.
Use (13.2.4).

$$d\rho/d\lambda = \left(-\frac{5}{\lambda}\right)\left(\frac{8\pi hc}{\lambda^5}\right)\{\ldots\} + \left(\frac{hc}{\lambda^2 kT}\right)\left(\frac{8\pi hc}{\lambda^5}\right)\{\ldots\}$$

$$+ \left(\frac{hc}{\lambda^2 kT}\right)\left\{\frac{e^{-hc/\lambda kT}}{1 - e^{-hc/\lambda kT}}\right\}\left(\frac{8\pi hc}{\lambda^5}\right)\{\ldots\} = 0.$$

$$-5 + \left(\frac{hc}{\lambda kT}\right) + \left(\frac{hc}{\lambda kT}\right)\left\{\frac{\exp(-hc/\lambda kT)}{1 - \exp(-hc/\lambda kT)}\right\} = 0 \text{ at } \lambda = \lambda_{max}.$$

Therefore $-5 + 5\exp(-hc/\lambda_{max}kT) + (hc/\lambda_{max}kT) = 0$.
So long as $\lambda_{max}kT \ll hc$, $\exp(-hc/\lambda_{max}kT) \ll 1$;
therefore $-5 + hc/\lambda_{max}kT \approx 0$, or $\lambda_{max}T \approx \underline{hc/5k}$.

13.7 $\lambda_{max} = (hc/5k)(1/T)$ [Problem 13.6]. Hence, plot λ_{max} against $1/T$ and obtain $hc/5k$ for the slope, Fig. 13.1.

$\theta/°C$	1000	1500	2000
T/K	1273	1773	2273
$1/(T/K)$	7.86×10^{-4}	5.64×10^{-4}	4.40×10^{-4}
λ_{max}/nm	2180	1600	1240

$\theta/°C$	2500	3000	3500
T/K	2773	3273	3773
$1/(T/K)$	3.61×10^{-4}	3.06×10^{-4}	2.65×10^{-4}
λ_{max}/nm	1035	878	763

From graph, slope $= 2.83 \times 10^6$.
$hc/5k = 2.83 \times 10^6\,\text{nm}/(1/\text{K}) = 2.83 \times 10^{-3}\,\text{m K}$;

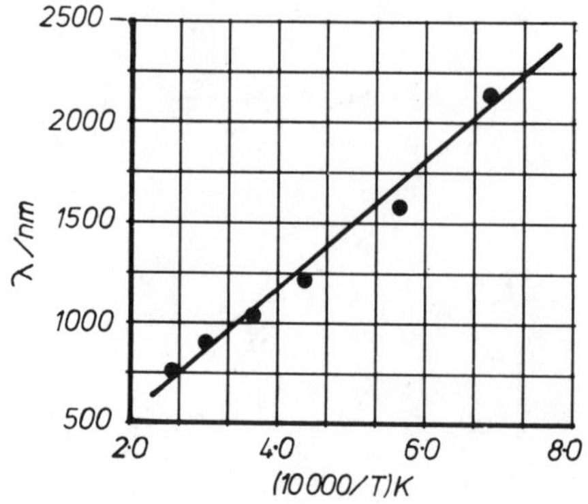

Fig 13·1

$$h = \frac{5 \times (1.38 \times 10^{-23}\,\mathrm{J\,K^{-1}}) \times (2.83 \times 10^{-3}\,\mathrm{m\,K})}{(2.998 \times 10^{8}\,\mathrm{m\,s^{-1}})} = \underline{6.51 \times 10^{-34}\,\mathrm{J\,s.}}$$

13.8 $T \approx hc/5k\lambda_{max}$, $hc/k = 1.439 \times 10^{-2}\,\mathrm{m\,K}$ [end-paper 1].

$\lambda_{max} = 480\,\mathrm{nm}$, $T \approx (1.439 \times 10^{-2}\,\mathrm{m\,K})/(5 \times 480 \times 10^{-9}\,\mathrm{m}) = \underline{6000\,\mathrm{K.}}$

13.10 $h\nu/k = (6.626 \times 10^{-34}\,\mathrm{J\,s}) \times (7.1 \times 10^{12}\,\mathrm{s^{-1}})/(1.381 \times 10^{-23}\,\mathrm{J\,K^{-1}}) = 341\,\mathrm{K}$.

$$C_{V,\mathrm{m}} = (24.9\,\mathrm{J\,K^{-1}\,mol^{-1}}) \times (341\,\mathrm{K}/T)^2 \times \left\{\frac{\exp(-341\,\mathrm{K}/T)}{[1 - \exp(-341\,\mathrm{K}/T)]^2}\right\} \quad [13.2.5].$$

(a) $T = 200\,\mathrm{K}$, $C_{V,\mathrm{m}} = \underline{19.7\,\mathrm{J\,K^{-1}\,mol^{-1}}}$.

(b) $T = 298\,\mathrm{K}$, $C_{V,\mathrm{m}} = \underline{22.4\,\mathrm{J\,K^{-1}\,mol^{-1}}}$.

(c) $T = 700\,\mathrm{K}$, $C_{V,\mathrm{m}} = \underline{24.4\,\mathrm{J\,K^{-1}\,mol^{-1}}}$.

Classical value: $C_{V,\mathrm{m}} = 3R = \underline{24.9\,\mathrm{J\,K^{-1}\,mol^{-1}}}$ at all temperatures.

13.11 $h\nu/k$ has the dimensions of temperature [Problem 13.10]. Therefore define $\theta_E = h\nu/k = (4.798 \times 10^{-11}\,\mathrm{s\,K})\nu$.

For $\nu = 7.1 \times 10^{12}\,\mathrm{Hz}$, $\theta_E = (4.798 \times 10^{-11}\,\mathrm{s\,K}) \times (7.1 \times 10^{12}\,\mathrm{s^{-1}}) = \underline{341\,\mathrm{K.}}$

13.12 $\frac{1}{2}mv^2 = h\nu - \Phi$ [13.2.6]

$$\Phi = 2.14\,\mathrm{eV} \mathrel{\hat{=}} 2.14 \times 1.602 \times 10^{-19}\,\mathrm{J}\ \text{[end-paper 1]} = 3.43 \times 10^{-19}\,\mathrm{J}.$$

(a) $\lambda = 700\,\mathrm{nm}$, $h\nu = hc/\lambda = 2.84 \times 10^{-19}\,\mathrm{J}$. As $h\nu < \Phi$, no ejection occurs.

(b) $\lambda = 300\,\mathrm{nm}$, $h\nu = hc/\lambda = 6.62 \times 10^{-19}\,\mathrm{J}$.

$\frac{1}{2}mv^2 = (6.62 \times 10^{-19}\,\mathrm{J}) - (3.43 \times 10^{-19}\,\mathrm{J}) = \underline{3.19 \times 10^{-19}\,\mathrm{J}, (1.99\,\mathrm{eV})}.$

$v = \sqrt{\{2 \times (3.19 \times 10^{-19}\,\text{J})/(9.11 \times 10^{-31}\,\text{kg})\}} = \underline{837\,\text{km s}^{-1}}$.

13.13 $\frac{1}{2}mv^2 = h\nu - I$, when the ionization energy I replaces the work function Φ.

$I = h\nu - \frac{1}{2}mv^2 = hc/\lambda - \frac{1}{2}mv^2 = 1.32 \times 10^{-15}\,\text{J} - \frac{1}{2} \times (9.1095 \times 10^{-31}\,\text{kg})$
$\times (2.14 \times 10^7\,\text{m s}^{-1})^2$ [Problem 13.1]
$= 1.11 \times 10^{-15}\,\text{J}$, 6930 eV [end-paper 1]. Therefore its binding energy was $\underline{6.93\,\text{eV}}$.

13.14 $\delta\lambda = (h/m_e c)(1 - \cos\theta)$ [13.2.7]; at $\theta = 90°$; $\delta\lambda = h/m_e c$.

$\delta\lambda = (6.626 \times 10^{-34}\,\text{J s})/(9.1095 \times 10^{-31}\,\text{kg}) \times (2.9979 \times 10^8\,\text{m s}^{-1})$.
$= 2.426 \times 10^{-12}\,\text{m}$, $\underline{2.426\,\text{pm}}$.

For a proton, $\delta\lambda = h/m_p c$,

$$\delta\lambda = (m_e/m_p) \times (2.426\,\text{pm}) = \left(\frac{9.1095 \times 10^{-31}}{1.6727 \times 10^{-27}}\right) \times (2.426\,\text{pm}) = \underline{1.321 \times 10^{-15}\,\text{m}}.$$

13.15 Refer to Fig. 13.2.

Energy conservation.

(1) $h\nu_i + m_e c^2 = h\nu_f + [p^2c^2 + m_e^2 c^4]^{\frac{1}{2}}$.

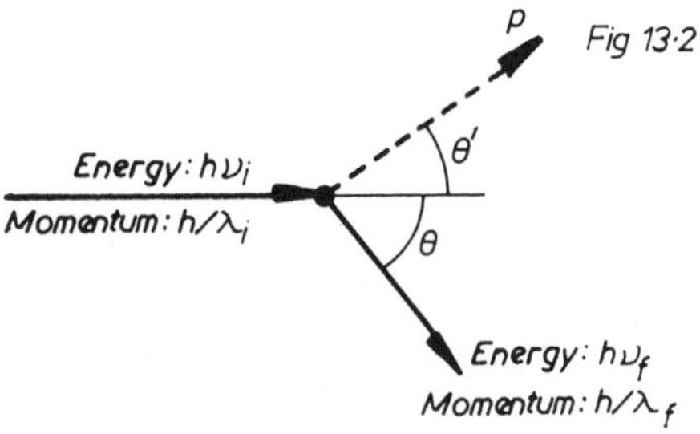

Fig 13·2

Momentum conservation.

(2) $h\nu_i/c = (h\nu_f/c)\cos\theta + p\cos\theta'$ (parallel)

(3) $0 = (h\nu_f/c)\sin\theta - p\sin\theta'$ (perpendicular).

From (2) and (3): $p^2\cos^2\theta' + p^2\sin^2\theta' = [(h\nu_i/c) - (h\nu_f/c)\cos\theta]^2 + [(h\nu_f/c)\sin\theta]^2$.

$p^2 = (h^2/c^2)\,[\nu_i^2 + \nu_f^2\cos^2\theta - 2\nu_i\nu_f\cos\theta + \nu_f^2\sin^2\theta]$
$= (h^2/c^2)\,[\nu_i^2 + \nu_f^2 - 2\nu_i\nu_f\cos\theta]$.

But from (1), $p^2c^2 = (h\nu_i + m_e c^2 - h\nu_f)^2 - m_e^2 c^4$;

therefore $\nu_i^2 + \nu_f^2 - 2\nu_i\nu_f\cos\theta = \nu_i^2 + \nu_f^2 + 2(m_e c^2/h)(\nu_i - \nu_f) - 2\nu_i\nu_f$,

or $2\nu_i\nu_f(1 - \cos\theta) = 2(m_e c^2/h)(\nu_i - \nu_f)$.

Therefore, $\dfrac{(\nu_i - \nu_f)}{\nu_i \nu_f} = \left(\dfrac{h}{m_e c^2}\right) \quad (1 - \cos\theta)$.

As $\dfrac{\nu_i - \nu_f}{\nu_i \nu_f} = \dfrac{1}{\nu_f} - \dfrac{1}{\nu_i} = (\lambda_f/c) - (\lambda_i/c)$,

$\underline{\lambda_f - \lambda_i = (h/m_e c)(1 - \cos\theta)}$.

13.16 $E = h\nu, \nu = 1/(\text{period})$;

(a) $E = (6.626 \times 10^{-34}\,\text{J s}) \times (1/10^{-15}\,\text{s}) = 6.626 \times 10^{-19}\,\text{J}, \underline{400\,\text{kJ mol}^{-1}}$.

(b) $E = (6.626 \times 10^{-34}\,\text{J s}) \times (1/10^{-14}\,\text{s}) = 6.626 \times 10^{-20}\,\text{J}, \underline{40\,\text{kJ mol}^{-1}}$.

(c) $E = (6.626 \times 10^{-34}\,\text{J s}) \times (1/1\,\text{s}) = 6.626 \times 10^{-34}\,\text{J}, 4 \times \underline{10^{-13}\,\text{kJ mol}^{-1}}$.

13.17 $\lambda = h/p = h/mv$ [13.2.8]

(a) $\lambda = (6.626 \times 10^{-34}\,\text{J s})/(1 \times 10^{-3}\,\text{kg}) \times (1 \times 10^{-2}\,\text{m s}^{-1}) = \underline{7 \times 10^{-29}\,\text{m}}$.

(b) $\lambda = (6.626 \times 10^{-34}\,\text{J s})/(1 \times 10^{-3}\,\text{kg}) \times (100 \times 10^{3}\,\text{m s}^{-1}) = 7 \times 10^{-36}\,\text{m}$.

(c) $\frac{1}{2}mv^2 \approx \frac{3}{2}kT$ [0.1.3], $v \approx \surd(3kT/m)$;

$\lambda \approx h/m\surd(3kT/m) = h/\surd(3kTm)$.

$m = 4.00 \times (1.66 \times 10^{-27}\,\text{kg})$ [end-paper 3] $= 6.64 \times 10^{-27}\,\text{kg}$.

$\lambda \approx (6.626 \times 10^{-34}\,\text{J s})/\surd[3 \times (6.64 \times 10^{-27}\,\text{kg}) \times (1.38 \times 10^{-23}\,\text{J K}^{-1}) \times (298\,\text{K})]$

$= 73 \times 10^{-12}\,\text{m}, \underline{73\,\text{pm}}$.

(d) $\frac{1}{2}mv^2 = e\Delta\phi;\ v = \surd(2e\Delta\phi/m)$

$\lambda = h/mv = h/\surd(2me\Delta\phi)$

$= (6.626 \times 10^{-34}\,\text{J s})/\surd[2 \times (9.1091 \times 10^{-31}\,\text{kg}) \times (1.6021 \times 10^{-19}\,\text{C}) \times \Delta\phi]$

$= (1.226 \times 10^{-9}\,\text{m})/\surd(\Delta\phi/\text{V})$ [J = C V]

$\Delta\phi = 100\,\text{V}, \lambda = (1.226 \times 10^{-9}\,\text{m})/\surd 100 = 1.23 \times 10^{-10}\,\text{m} = \underline{123\,\text{pm}}$.

$\Delta\phi = 1\,\text{kV}, \lambda = (1.226 \times 10^{-9}\,\text{m})/\surd 10^{3} = 4 \times 10^{-11}\,\text{m} = \underline{40\,\text{pm}}$.

$\Delta\phi = 100\,\text{kV}, \lambda = (1.226 \times 10^{-9}\,\text{m})/\surd 10^{5} = 4 \times 10^{-12}\,\text{m} = \underline{4\,\text{pm}}$.

13.18 $\delta p \delta q \geqslant \frac{1}{2}\hbar$ [13.4.8]; $\delta v = \delta p/m \geqslant \hbar/2m\delta q;\ \delta q \geqslant \hbar/2m\delta v$.

$\delta v \geqslant (1.0545 \times 10^{-34}\,\text{J s})/[2 \times (0.5\,\text{kg}) \times (10^{-6}\,\text{m})] = \underline{1 \times 10^{-28}\,\text{m s}^{-1}}$.

$\delta q \geqslant (1.0545 \times 10^{-34}\,\text{J s})/[2 \times (5 \times 10^{-3}\,\text{kg}) \times (10^{-5}\,\text{m s}^{-1})] = \underline{1 \times 10^{-27}\,\text{m}}$.

13.19 $\delta p \geqslant \hbar/2\delta q = (1.0545 \times 10^{-34}\,\text{J s})/[2 \times (10^{-10}\,\text{m})] = \underline{5 \times 10^{-25}\,\text{kg m s}^{-1}}$.

$\delta v = \delta p/m = (5 \times 10^{-25}\,\text{kg m s}^{-1})/(9.109 \times 10^{-31}\,\text{kg}) = \underline{5 \times 10^{5}\,\text{m s}^{-1}}$.

13.20 $\int \psi^* \psi \, d\tau = 1$ [13.3.7]; write $\psi = Nf$ and find N for the given f.

(a) $N^2 \int_0^L \sin^2(n\pi x/L)\,dx = \frac{1}{2}N^2 \int_0^L [1 - \cos(2n\pi x/L)]\,dx$

$= \frac{1}{2}N^2 [x - (L/2n\pi)\sin(2n\pi x/L)]_0^L = (L/2)N^2 = 1$, so that $\underline{N = \surd(2/L)}$.

(b) $N^2 \int_{-L}^{L} c^2\,dx = 2N^2c^2L = 1$, so that $\underline{N = 1/c\surd(2L)}$.

(c) $N^2 \int_0^\infty dr r^2 \int_0^\pi d\theta \sin\theta \int_0^{2\pi} d\phi e^{-2r/a_0}$ [Example 13.3]

$= N^2 \int_0^\infty r^2\, e^{-2r/a_0}\, dr \int_0^\pi d\theta \sin\theta \int_0^{2\pi} d\phi$

$= N^2(a_0^3/4)(2)(2\pi) = N^2 a_0^3 \pi$, so that $\underline{N = 1/\surd(\pi a_0^3)}$.

(d) $N^2 \int_0^\infty dr\, r^2 \int_0^\pi d\theta \sin\theta \int_0^{2\pi} d\phi r^2 \sin^2\theta \cos^2\phi\, e^{-r/a_0}$ $[x = r\sin\theta\cos\phi]$

$= N^2 \int_0^\infty r^4\, e^{-r/a_0}\, dr \int_0^\pi d\theta \sin^3\theta \int_0^{2\pi} d\phi \cos^2\phi$

$= N^2(4!a_0^5)(4/3)(\pi) = N^2 32\pi a_0^5$, so that $\underline{N = 1/\surd(32\pi a_0^5)}$.

$\left[\text{Use} \int_0^\pi d\theta \sin\theta \cos^n\theta = -\int_1^{-1} (d\cos\theta)\cos^n\theta = \int_{-1}^{1} x^n dx.\right]$

13.21 $\psi^2(x) = (2/L)\sin^2(\pi x/L), L = 10$ nm.
Probability of being between $x = a$ and $x = b$ is

$$P(a, b) = \int_a^b \psi^2(x)\,dx = (2/L)\int_a^b \sin^2(x\pi/L)\,dx$$

$$= [(x/L) - (1/2\pi)\sin(2\pi x/L)]_a^b.$$

(a) $a = 4.95$ nm, $b = 5.05$ nm, $L = 10$ nm:
$P = (0.10/10) - (1/2\pi)[\sin(2\pi \times 0.505) - \sin(2\pi \times 0.495)] = \underline{0.020\ (2\%)}$.

(b) $a = 1.95$ nm, $b = 2.05$ nm, $L = 10$ nm:
$P = 0.01 - (1/2\pi)[\sin(2\pi \times 0.205) - \sin(2\pi \times 0.195)] = \underline{0.007\ (0.7\%)}$.

(c) $a = 9.90$ nm, $b = 10.00$ nm, $L = 10$ nm:

$P = 0.01 - (1/2\pi)\ [\sin(2\pi) - \sin(2\pi \times 0.99)] = \underline{6.6 \times 10^{-6}.}$

(d) $P = \frac{1}{2}$ by symmetry.

(e) $a = L/3, b = 2L/3$

$P = \frac{1}{3} - (1/2\pi)\ [\sin(4\pi/3) - \sin(2\pi/3)] = \underline{0.61\ (61\%).}$

13.22 $\psi^2(r, \theta, \phi)\mathrm{d}\tau = (1/\pi a_0^3)\ \exp(-2r/a_0)\mathrm{d}\tau, a_0 = 53\ \mathrm{pm}$

$\mathrm{d}\tau \approx \frac{4}{3}\pi(1.0\ \mathrm{pm})^3 = 4.2\ \mathrm{pm}^3.$

(a) $r = 0;\ \psi^2 = 1/\pi a_0^3 = 1/(53^3\ \pi\ \mathrm{pm}^3).$

$P = (4.2\ \mathrm{pm}^3)/(53^3 \pi\ \mathrm{pm}^3) = \underline{9.0 \times 10^{-6}.}$

(b) $r = a_0$: $\psi^2 = \mathrm{e}^{-2}/\pi a_0^3.$

$P = 9.0 \times 10^{-6}\mathrm{e}^{-2} = \underline{1.2 \times 10^{-6}.}$

13.23 (a) $\psi = N(2 - r/a_0)\mathrm{e}^{-r/a_0}$

$$\int \psi^2 \mathrm{d}\tau = N^2 \int_0^\infty (2 - r/a_0)^2\ \mathrm{e}^{-r/a_0} r^2 \mathrm{d}r \int_0^\pi \sin\theta \mathrm{d}\theta \int_0^{2\pi} \mathrm{d}\phi$$

$$= N^2 \int_0^\infty (4r^2 - 4r^3/a_0 + r^4/a_0^2)\mathrm{e}^{-r/a_0}\mathrm{d}r \int_{-1}^{1} \mathrm{d}\cos\theta \int_0^{2\pi} \mathrm{d}\phi$$

$$= N^2\{4 \times 2a_0^3 - 4 \times 6a_0^4/a_0 + 24a_0^5/a_0^2\} \times 2 \times 2\pi$$

$$= 32\pi a_0^3 N^2;\ \text{hence}\ \underline{N = (1/32\pi a_0^3)^{\frac{1}{2}}.}$$

(b) $\psi = r \sin\theta\ \cos\phi \mathrm{e}^{-r/2a_0}$

$$\int \psi^2 \mathrm{d}\tau = N^2 \int_0^\infty r^4\,\mathrm{e}^{-r/a_0}\,\mathrm{d}r \int_0^\pi \sin^2\theta\ \sin\theta \mathrm{d}\theta \int_0^{2\pi} \cos^2\phi \mathrm{d}\phi$$

$$= N^2(4!a_0^5) \int_{-1}^{1} (1 - \cos^2\theta)\mathrm{d}\cos\theta \times \pi$$

$$= N^2(4!a_0^5)\ (2 - \tfrac{2}{3})\pi = 32\pi a_0^5 N^2;\ \text{hence}\ \underline{N = (1/32\pi a_0^5)^{\frac{1}{2}}.}$$

13.24 For ψ to be an eigenfunction of $\mathrm{d}/\mathrm{d}x$ we require $(\mathrm{d}/\mathrm{d}x)\psi = a\psi$. where a is a number (the eigenvalue) [13.4.3]

(a) $(\mathrm{d}/\mathrm{d}x)\ \mathrm{e}^{ikx} = ik\ \mathrm{e}^{ikx}$; yes, eigenvalue = $\underline{ik}$.

(b) $(\mathrm{d}/\mathrm{d}x)\ \cos kx = -k \sin kx$; no

(c) $(\mathrm{d}/\mathrm{d}x)\ k = 0$; yes, eigenvalue = $\underline{0}$.

(d) $(\mathrm{d}/\mathrm{d}x)\ kx = k = (1/x)kx$; no [$1/x$ is not a constant]

(e) $(\mathrm{d}/\mathrm{d}x)\ \mathrm{e}^{-\alpha x^2} = -2\alpha x\ \mathrm{e}^{-\alpha x^2}$; no [$-2\alpha x$ is not a constant].

13.25 (a) $(\mathrm{d}^2/\mathrm{d}x^2)\,\mathrm{e}^{ikx} = -k^2\,\mathrm{e}^{ikx}$; yes, eigenvalue $= \underline{-k^2}$.

(b) $(\mathrm{d}^2/\mathrm{d}x^2)\cos kx = -k^2\cos kx$; yes, eigenvalue $= \underline{-k^2}$.

(c) $(\mathrm{d}^2/\mathrm{d}x^2)\,k = 0$; yes; eigenvalue $= \underline{0}$.

(d) $(\mathrm{d}^2/\mathrm{d}x^2)\,kx = 0$; yes, eigenvalue $= \underline{0}$.

(e) $(\mathrm{d}^2/\mathrm{d}x^2)\,\mathrm{e}^{-\alpha x^2} = -2\alpha\mathrm{e}^{-\alpha x^2} + 4\alpha^2x^2\mathrm{e}^{-\alpha x^2}$; no.

So: (a), (b), (c), (d) are eigenfunctions of $\mathrm{d}^2/\mathrm{d}x^2$; (b), (d) are eigenfunctions of $\mathrm{d}^2/\mathrm{d}x^2$ but not of $\mathrm{d}/\mathrm{d}x$.

13.26 $\psi = \cos\chi\,\mathrm{e}^{ikx} + \sin\chi\,\mathrm{e}^{-ikx}$

(a) $P = \underline{\cos^2\chi}$ [Section 13.4(b)]

(b) $P = \underline{\sin^2\chi}$

(c) $\cos^2\chi = 0.90$; $\cos\chi = \pm 0.95$; $\sin^2\chi = 0.10$; $\sin\chi = \pm 0.32$.

Hence, $\psi = \underline{0.95\,\mathrm{e}^{ikx} \pm 0.32\,\mathrm{e}^{-ikx}}$ [overall sign irrelevant].

13.27 $\langle T\rangle = N^2\int \psi^*(\hat{p}^2/2m)\psi\,\mathrm{d}\tau$ [13.4.7]

$\hat{p}^2/2m = -(\hbar^2/2m)\mathrm{d}^2/\mathrm{d}x^2$ [13.4.5]

$$\begin{aligned}\hat{p}^2\psi &= -\hbar^2(\mathrm{d}^2/\mathrm{d}x^2)\{\cos\chi\,\mathrm{e}^{ikx} + \sin\chi\,\mathrm{e}^{-ikx}\} \quad [\psi \text{ not normalized}]\\ &= \hbar^2\{k^2\cos\chi\,\mathrm{e}^{ikx} + k^2\sin\chi\,\mathrm{e}^{-ikx}\}\\ &= k^2\hbar^2\{\cos\chi\,\mathrm{e}^{ikx} + \sin\chi\,\mathrm{e}^{-ikx}\} = k^2\hbar^2\psi\end{aligned}$$

$$\begin{aligned}\langle T\rangle &= \int\psi^*(\hat{p}^2/2m)\psi\,\mathrm{d}\tau\Big/\int\psi^*\psi\,\mathrm{d}\tau \quad [\text{now normalized}]\\ &= (k^2\hbar^2/2m)\int\psi^*\psi\,\mathrm{d}\tau\Big/\int\psi^*\psi\,\mathrm{d}\tau = \underline{k^2\hbar^2/2m}.\end{aligned}$$

13.28 $$\begin{aligned}\langle p_x\rangle &= \int_{-\infty}^{\infty}\psi^*(x)\,\hat{p}_x\psi(x)\mathrm{d}x \quad [13.4.7]\\ &= (\hbar/\mathrm{i})\int_{-\infty}^{\infty}\psi^*(x)(\mathrm{d}\psi/\mathrm{d}x)\mathrm{d}x \quad [13.4.5].\end{aligned}$$

(a) $\exp(ikx)$; $$\begin{aligned}\langle p_x\rangle &= (\hbar/\mathrm{i})\left\{\int_{-\infty}^{\infty}\mathrm{e}^{-ikx}(\mathrm{d}/\mathrm{d}x)\mathrm{e}^{ikx}\,\mathrm{d}x\right\}\Big/\left\{\int_{-\infty}^{\infty}\mathrm{e}^{-ikx}\,\mathrm{e}^{ikx}\,\mathrm{d}x\right\} \quad [\text{normalize}]\\ &= (\hbar/\mathrm{i})(ik)\left\{\int_{-\infty}^{\infty}\mathrm{e}^{-ikx}\times\mathrm{e}^{ikx}\mathrm{d}x\right\}\Big/\left\{\int_{-\infty}^{\infty}\mathrm{e}^{-ikx}\,\mathrm{e}^{ikx}\mathrm{d}x\right\} = \underline{\hbar k}.\end{aligned}$$

(b) $\cos kx$;

$$\langle p_x\rangle \propto (\hbar/\mathrm{i}) \int_{-\infty}^{\infty} \cos(kx)\,(\mathrm{d}/\mathrm{d}x)\,(\cos kx)\,\mathrm{d}x$$

$$= (\hbar/\mathrm{i})\,(-k) \int_{-\infty}^{\infty} \cos kx \sin kx\,\mathrm{d}x = \underline{0}.$$

(c) $\exp(-\alpha x^2)$;

$$\langle p_x\rangle \propto (\hbar/\mathrm{i}) \int_{-\infty}^{\infty} \mathrm{e}^{-\alpha x^2}\,(\mathrm{d}/\mathrm{d}x)\,\mathrm{e}^{-\alpha x^2}\,\mathrm{d}x$$

$$= -(2\alpha\hbar/\mathrm{i}) \int_{-\infty}^{\infty} x\,\mathrm{e}^{-2\alpha x^2}\,\mathrm{d}x = \underline{0}.$$

13.29 $\langle r\rangle = N^2 \int \psi^* r \psi\,\mathrm{d}\tau, \langle r^2\rangle = N^2 \int \psi^* r^2 \psi\,\mathrm{d}\tau$

(a) $\psi = (2 - r/a_0)\mathrm{e}^{-r/2a_0}; N = (1/32\pi a_0^3)^{\frac{1}{2}}$ [Problem 13.23]

$$\langle r\rangle = (1/32\pi a_0^3) \int_0^{\infty} r(2 - r/a_0)^2 r^2\,\mathrm{e}^{-r/a_0}\,\mathrm{d}r \times 4\pi$$

$$= (1/8a_0^3) \int_0^{\infty} (4r^3 - 4r^4/a_0 + r^5/a_0^2)\mathrm{e}^{-r/a_0}\,\mathrm{d}r$$

$$= (1/8a_0^3)\,\{4 \times 3!a_0^4 - 4 \times 4!a_0^4 + 5!a_0^4\} = \underline{6a_0.}$$

$$\langle r^2\rangle = (1/8a_0^3) \int_0^{\infty} (4r^4 - 4r^5/a_0 + r^6/a_0^2)\mathrm{e}^{-r/a_0}\,\mathrm{d}r$$

$$= (1/8a_0^3)\,\{4 \times 4! - 4 \times 5! + 6!]\,a_0^5 = \underline{42a_0^2}.$$

(b) $\psi = Nr \sin\theta \cos\phi\,\mathrm{e}^{-r/2a_0}; N = (1/32\pi a_0^5)^{\frac{1}{2}}$ [Problem 13.23]

$$\langle r\rangle = (1/32\pi a_0^5) \int_0^{\infty} r^5\,\mathrm{e}^{-r/a_0}\,\mathrm{d}r \times (4\pi/3)$$

$$= (1/24a_0^5)\,5!a_0^6 = \underline{5a_0.}$$

$$\langle r^2\rangle = (1/24a_0^5) \int_0^{\infty} r^6\,\mathrm{e}^{-r/a_0}\,\mathrm{d}r$$

$$= (1/24a_0^5)6!a_0^7 = \underline{30a_0^2}.$$

(c) $\psi = (1/\pi a_0^3)^{\frac{1}{2}}\mathrm{e}^{-r/a_0}$ [Problem 13.3]

$$\langle V \rangle = \int \psi^*(-e^2/4\pi\epsilon_0 r)\psi \mathrm{d}\tau$$

$$= -(e^2/4\pi\epsilon_0)(1/\pi a_0^3)\int_0^\infty (1/r)r^2 \mathrm{e}^{-2r/a_0}\mathrm{d}r \int_0^\pi \sin\theta \mathrm{d}\theta \int_0^{2\pi} \mathrm{d}\phi$$

$$= -(e^2/4\pi\epsilon_0)(4/a_0^3)\int_0^\infty r\mathrm{e}^{-2r/a_0}\mathrm{d}r$$

$$= -(e^2/4\pi\epsilon_0)(4/a_0^3)(a_0/2)^2 = \underline{-e^2/4\pi\epsilon_0 a_0}.$$

13.30 $\hat{x} = x$, $\hat{p}_x = (\hbar/\mathrm{i})(\partial/\partial x)$ [13.4.5]

$[\hat{x}, \hat{y}]\psi = [x, y]\psi = (xy - yx)\psi = 0$; therefore $[\hat{x}, \hat{y}] = 0$, and x, y not complementary

$[\hat{x}, \hat{x}]\psi = [x, x]\psi = (xx - xx)\psi = (x^2 - x^2)\psi = 0$;

therefore $\underline{[\hat{x}, \hat{x}]\psi = 0}$.

$[\hat{p}_x, \hat{p}_y]\psi = (\hbar/\mathrm{i})^2[(\partial/\partial x), (\partial/\partial y)]\psi = (\hbar/\mathrm{i})^2\{\partial^2/\partial x\partial y - \partial^2/\partial y\partial x\}\psi$,

$\partial^2\psi/\partial x\partial y = \partial^2\psi/\partial y\partial x$ [Box 3.1]; therefore $\underline{[\hat{p}_x, \hat{p}_y] = 0}$.

$$[\hat{x}, \hat{p}_x]\psi = (\hbar/\mathrm{i})[x, (\partial/\partial x)]\psi$$

$$= (\hbar/\mathrm{i})\{x(\partial/\partial x) - (\partial/\partial x)x\}\psi$$

$$= (\hbar/\mathrm{i})\left\{x\left(\frac{\partial\psi}{\partial x}\right) - \frac{\partial}{\partial x}(x\psi)\right\}$$

$$= (\hbar/\mathrm{i})\left\{x\left(\frac{\partial\psi}{\partial x}\right) - \psi - x\left(\frac{\partial\psi}{\partial x}\right)\right\} = \hbar\mathrm{i}\psi.$$

Therefore $\underline{[\hat{x}, \hat{p}_x] = \hbar\mathrm{i}}$, and x, p_x are complementary (dimensions J s)

$$[\hat{x}, \hat{p}_y]\psi = (\hbar/\mathrm{i})[x, (\partial/\partial y)]\psi$$

$$= (\hbar/\mathrm{i})\{x(\partial/\partial y) - (\partial/\partial y)x\}\psi = (\hbar/\mathrm{i})\left\{x\left(\frac{\partial\psi}{\partial y}\right) - \frac{\partial}{\partial y}(x\psi)\right\}$$

$$= (\hbar/\mathrm{i})\left\{x\left(\frac{\partial\psi}{\partial y}\right) - x\left(\frac{\partial\psi}{\partial y}\right)\right\} = 0.$$

Therefore $\underline{[\hat{x}, \hat{p}_y] = 0}$, and x, p_y are not complementary.

13.31 $[\hat{x}, \hat{p}_x] \neq 0$; therefore x, p_x cannot be determined simultaneously (to arbitrary precision).

$[\hat{y}, \hat{p}_x] = 0$ [as in Problem 13.31 for x, p_y]; therefore there is no constraint on the simultaneous determination of y and p_x.

$[\hat{x}, \hat{y}] = [\hat{x}, \hat{z}] = [\hat{y}, \hat{z}] = 0$ [as in Problem 13.30 for x, y]; therefore, the three coordinates of position may be specified simultaneously without constraint.

13.32 $\hat{l}_x = \hat{y}\hat{p}_z - \hat{z}\hat{p}_y = (\hbar/\mathrm{i})\{y(\partial/\partial z) - z(\partial/\partial y)\}$

$\hat{l}_y = \hat{z}\hat{p}_x - \hat{x}\hat{p}_z = (\hbar/\mathrm{i})\{z(\partial/\partial x) - x(\partial/\partial z)\}$

$\hat{l}_z = \hat{x}\hat{p}_y - \hat{y}\hat{p}_x = (\hbar/\mathrm{i})\{x(\partial/\partial y) - y(\partial/\partial x)\}$

$$[\hat{l}_x, \hat{l}_y]\,\psi = (\hbar/\mathrm{i})^2 \left[\left(y\frac{\partial}{\partial z} - z\frac{\partial}{\partial y}\right), \left(z\frac{\partial}{\partial x} - x\frac{\partial}{\partial z}\right)\right]\psi$$

$$= (\hbar/\mathrm{i})^2\{[y(\partial/\partial z) - z(\partial/\partial y)]\,[z(\partial/\partial x) - x(\partial/\partial z)] - [z(\partial/\partial x) - x(\partial/\partial z)]\,[y(\partial/\partial z) - z(\partial/\partial y)]\}\psi$$

$$= (\hbar/\mathrm{i})^2\{y(\partial/\partial z)z(\partial/\partial x) - y(\partial/\partial z)x(\partial/\partial z) - z(\partial/\partial y)z(\partial/\partial x) + z(\partial/\partial y)x(\partial/\partial z) - z(\partial/\partial x)y(\partial/\partial z) + z(\partial/\partial x)z(\partial/\partial y) + x(\partial/\partial z)y(\partial/\partial z) - x(\partial/\partial z)z(\partial/\partial y)\}\psi$$

$$= (\hbar/\mathrm{i})^2\{yz(\partial^2/\partial z\partial x) + y(\partial/\partial x) - yx(\partial^2/\partial z^2) - z^2(\partial^2/\partial y\partial x) + zx(\partial^2/\partial y\partial z) - zy(\partial^2/\partial x\partial z) + z^2(\partial^2/\partial x\partial y) + xy(\partial^2/\partial z^2) - x(\partial/\partial y) - xz(\partial^2/\partial z\partial y)\}\psi$$

$$= (\hbar/\mathrm{i})^2\{y(\partial/\partial x) - x(\partial/\partial y)\}\psi = -(\hbar/\mathrm{i})\hat{l}_z\psi = \mathrm{i}\hbar\hat{l}_z\psi.$$

Therefore $\underline{[\hat{l}_x, \hat{l}_y] = \mathrm{i}\hbar\hat{l}_z}$.

14. Quantum theory: techniques and applications

A14.1 $P = 1/(1+G)$

with $G = \{\exp([2m(V-E)(h/2\pi)^2]^{\frac{1}{2}}L) - \exp(-[2m(V-E)/(h/2\pi)^2]^{\frac{1}{2}}L)\}^2$
$\times \{4(E/V)[1-(E/V)]\}^{-1}$ [14.1.3].

$[L/(h/2\pi)][2m(V-E)]^{\frac{1}{2}} = (0.25 \times 10^{-9}\,\text{m})(2\pi)(6.6 \times 10^{-34}\,\text{J s})^{-1}$
$\times [(2)(9.1 \times 10^{-31}\,\text{kg})(2.0\,\text{V} - 0.9\,\text{V})(1.6 \times 10^{-19}\,\text{C})]^{\frac{1}{2}} = 1.3.$

$G = [\exp(1.3) - \exp(-1.3)]^2 [(4)(0.9/2.0)(1-0.9/2.0)]^{-1} = 12.$

$P = (1+G)^{-1} = 1/13 = \underline{7.7 \times 10^{-2}}.$

A14.2 $E = 3(3h^2/8mL^2) = 9h^2/8mL^2$. Hence $n_A^2 + n_B^2 + n_C^2 = 9$.

Possible values are $\underline{(1,2,2), (2,1,2), (2,2,1)}$ and the degeneracy is $\underline{3}$.

A14.3 $E = (\text{constant})/L^2$,

$(E_2 - E_1)/E_1 = [(0.9L)^{-2} - L^{-2}]/L^{-2} = (1-0.81)/0.81 = 0.24$, or $\underline{24\%}$.

A14.4 $E = (v+\frac{1}{2})(h/2\pi)\omega$ [14.2.4].

$E_0 = \frac{1}{2}(h/2\pi)\omega = \frac{1}{2}(h/2\pi)(k/m)^{\frac{1}{2}}$

$= (4\pi)^{-1}(6.63 \times 10^{-34}\,\text{J s})(155\,\text{N m}^{-1}/2.33 \times 10^{-26}\,\text{kg})^{\frac{1}{2}} = \underline{4.31 \times 10^{-21}\,\text{J}}.$

A14.5 $\Delta E = (h/2\pi)(k/m)^{\frac{1}{2}}(5\frac{1}{2} - 4\frac{1}{2})$. [Problem A14.4]

$k = m[(\Delta E)(2\pi)/h]^2 = (1.33 \times 10^{-25}\,\text{kg})[(4.82 \times 10^{-21}\,\text{J})(2\pi)/(6.63 \times 10^{-34}\,\text{J s})]^2$

$= \underline{277\,\text{N m}^{-1}}.$

A14.6 $\Delta E = (h/2\pi)(k/m)^{\frac{1}{2}} = hc/\lambda$ [Problem A14.4]

$\lambda = 2\pi c(k/m)^{-\frac{1}{2}} = 2\pi(3.00 \times 10^8\,\text{m s}^{-1})(855\,\text{N m}^{-1}/1.67 \times 10^{-27}\,\text{kg})^{-\frac{1}{2}}$

$= \underline{2.63 \times 10^{-6}\,\text{m}}.$

A14.7 $\lambda \propto m^{\frac{1}{2}}$, [Problem A14.6]

$\lambda = (2.63 \times 10^{-6}\,\text{m})(2)^{\frac{1}{2}} = 3.72 \times 10^{-6}\,\text{m}.$

$\Delta\lambda = (3.72 - 2.63)(10^{-6})\,\text{m} = \underline{1.09 \times 10^{-6}\,\text{m}}.$

A14.8 See Box 14.1. Let $\alpha \equiv [m\omega/(h/2\pi)]^{\frac{1}{2}}$

$\psi_1(y) = (\alpha/2\pi^{\frac{1}{2}})^{\frac{1}{2}}(2y)\exp(-\frac{1}{2}y^2)$. When $y = 0$ or $\underline{\pm\infty}$, $\psi_1(0) = 0$.

$\partial\psi_1/\partial y = (\psi_1/y) - \psi_1 y = \psi_1 y^{-1}(1-y^2) = 0$

$1 - y^2 = 0$ and $y = 1$ or -1, $\underline{y = 1}$ gives the maximum.

A14.9 $E = l(l+1)(h/2\pi)^2/2mR^2$. [14.3.23]

$R = [(l)(l+1)(h/2\pi)^2(2mE)^{-1}]^{\frac{1}{2}}$

$= [(2)(2+1)(6.63\times10^{-34}\,\text{J s})^2(2\pi)^{-2}(\tfrac{1}{2})(6.35\times10^{-26}\,\text{kg})^{-1}$

$\times(2.47\times10^{-23}\,\text{J})^{-1}]^{\frac{1}{2}} = 1.46\times10^{-10}\,\text{m}$, or $\underline{0.146\,\text{nm}}$.

A14.10 $J = [l(l+1)]^{\frac{1}{2}}(h/2\pi)$ [14.3.24]

$= [1(1+1)]^{\frac{1}{2}}(6.63\times10^{-34}\,\text{J s})(1/2\pi) = 1.49\times10^{-34}\,\text{J s}.$

$J_z = 0$ and $\pm(h/2\pi)$ [14.3.25]

$= \underline{0 \text{ and } \pm1.05\times10^{-34}\,\text{J s}}.$

14.1 $E_n = n^2h^2/8mL^2$ [14.1.9a]

$= n^2(6.626\times10^{-34}\,\text{J s})^2/[8\times(9.109\times10^{-31}\,\text{kg})\times(1.0\times10^{-9}\,\text{m})^2]$

$= (6.02\times10^{-20}\,\text{J})n^2$

$E_n = 36.3n^2\,\text{kJ mol}^{-1}$ $[N_AE_n]$

$= 0.376\,n^2\,\text{eV} \mathrel{\hat{=}} 3030\,n^2\,\text{kJ mol}^{-1} = \kappa n^2$ [end-paper 1].

(a) $E_2 - E_1 = \kappa(4-1) = 3\kappa = 1.8\times10^{-19}\,\text{J}$, $110\,\text{kJ mol}^{-1}$, $1.1\,\text{eV}$, $9100\,\text{cm}^{-1}$.

(b) $E_6 - E_5 = \kappa(36-25) = 11\kappa = 6.6\times10^{-19}\,\text{J}$, $400\,\text{kJ mol}^{-1}$, $41\,\text{eV}$, $33\,000\,\text{cm}^{-1}$.

14.2 $E_n = n^2h^2/8mL^2$ [14.1.9a];

$m = 32\times(1.661\times10^{-27}\,\text{kg}) = 5.3\times10^{-26}\,\text{kg}$ [end-paper 3].

$= n^2(6.626\times10^{-34}\,\text{J s})^2/8\times(5.3\times10^{-26}\,\text{kg})\times(0.05\,\text{m})^2$

$= 4.1\,n^2\times10^{-40}\,\text{J}.$

$E_2 - E_1 = (2^2-1^2)\times(4.1\times10^{-40}\,\text{J}) = 1.2\times10^{-39}\,\text{J}$, $\underline{7.5\times10^{-19}\,\text{kJ mol}^{-1}}$.

$4.1\,n^2\times10^{-40}\,\text{J} = \tfrac{1}{2}kT = \tfrac{1}{2}\times(1.381\times10^{-23}\,\text{J K}^{-1})\times(300\,\text{K}) = 2.07\times10^{-21}\,\text{J}$;

Therefore, $\underline{n = 2\times10^9}$.

$E_n - E_{n-1} = [n^2-(n-1)^2]\,(h^2/8mL^2) = (2n-1)(h^2/8mL^2)$

$\approx 2n(h^2/8mL^2)$ for $n \gg 1$.

Therefore, $E_n - E_{n-1} \approx (4\times10^9)\times(4.1\times10^{-40}\,\text{J}) = 1.6\times10^{-30}\,\text{J}$,

$\underline{9.6\times10^{-10}\,\text{kJ mol}^{-1}}$.

14.3 $-(\hbar^2/2m)(\partial^2/\partial x^2 + \partial^2/\partial y^2 + \partial^2/\partial z^2)\psi = E\psi$ [Box 13.1].

Try the solution $\psi(x, y, z) = X(x)Y(y)Z(z)$

$$-(\hbar^2/2m)\{YZ(\partial^2X/\partial x^2)+XZ(\partial^2Y/\partial y^2)+XY(\partial^2Z/\partial z^2)\}=EXYZ,$$
$$-(\hbar^2/2m)\{(\partial^2X/\partial x^2)/X+(\partial^2Y/\partial y^2)/Y+(\partial^2Z/\partial z^2)/Z\}=E.$$

$(\partial^2X/\partial x^2)/X$ depends only on x; therefore when x changes, only this term changes; but the sum of the three terms is a constant; therefore, this term alone is also a constant. Call it E^x.

Likewise for Y, Z.

$$-(\hbar^2/2m)(\partial^2X/\partial x^2)/X=E^x\text{, or }-(\hbar^2/2m)(\mathrm{d}^2X/\mathrm{d}x^2)=E^xX.$$

E^x, X require one quantum number, and likewise for Y, Z. The three constants must add up to E: $E^x_{n_1}+E^y_{n_2}+E^z_{n_3}=E_{n_1n_2n_3}$. Therefore, each dimension gives rise to an equation for a particle in a 1-dimensional box. Using [14.1.9]:

$$E_{n_1n_2n_3}=(h^2/8m)\{n_1^2/L_x^2+n_2^2/L_y^2+n_3^2/L_z^2\},$$
$$\psi_{n_1n_2n_3}=X_{n_1}Y_{n_2}Z_{n_3}$$
$$=\left(\frac{8}{L_xL_yL_z}\right)^{\frac{1}{2}}\sin\left(\frac{n_1\pi x}{L_x}\right)\sin\left(\frac{n_2\pi y}{L_y}\right)\sin\left(\frac{n_3\pi z}{L_z}\right).$$

For a cubic box, $L_x=L_y=L_z=L$

$$E_{n_1n_2n_3}=\underline{(h^2/8mL^2)\{n_1^2+n_2^2+n_3^2\}.}$$

14.4 $P=\int_{\text{barrier}}|\psi|^2\mathrm{d}\tau=\int_0^\infty|A|^2\,\mathrm{e}^{-2\kappa x}\mathrm{d}x$ [barrier at $x=0$]

$$=\underline{|A|^2/2\kappa.}$$

$$\langle x\rangle=\int_0^\infty\psi^*x\psi\mathrm{d}x=|A|^2\int_0^\infty x\,\mathrm{e}^{-2\kappa x}\mathrm{d}x$$
$$=|A|^2\{2!/(2\kappa)^2\}=|A|^2/2\kappa^2$$
$$=\underline{P/\kappa.}$$

14.5 Zone A: $\psi_A=A\mathrm{e}^{\mathrm{i}kx}+A'\mathrm{e}^{-\mathrm{i}kx}$, $k=\{2mE/\hbar^2\}^{\frac{1}{2}}$

Zone B: $\psi_B=B\mathrm{e}^{\kappa x}+B'\mathrm{e}^{-\kappa x}$, $\kappa=\{2m(V-E)/\hbar^2\}^{\frac{1}{2}}$

Zone C: $\psi_C=C\mathrm{e}^{\mathrm{i}k'x}+C'\mathrm{e}^{-\mathrm{i}k'x}$, $k'=\{2m(E-V')/\hbar^2\}^{\frac{1}{2}}$.

Boundary conditions:

$C'=0$ [no particles from right]

(i) $\psi_A(0)=\psi_B(0)$, (ii) $\psi'_A(0)=\psi'_B(0)$, (iii) $\psi_B(L)=\psi_C(L)$, (iv) $\psi'_B(L)=\psi'_C(L)$.

These imply

(i) $A+A'=B+B'$

(ii) $\mathrm{i}kA-\mathrm{i}kA'=\kappa B-\kappa B'$

(iii) $B\mathrm{e}^{\kappa L}+B'\mathrm{e}^{-\kappa L}=C\mathrm{e}^{\mathrm{i}k'L}$

(iv) $\kappa B\mathrm{e}^{\kappa L}-\kappa B'\mathrm{e}^{-\kappa L}=\mathrm{i}kC\mathrm{e}^{\mathrm{i}k'L}$

(i) and (ii) solve to

$A = \frac{1}{2}(1 + \kappa/\mathrm{i}k)B + \frac{1}{2}(1 - \kappa/\mathrm{i}k)B'$

(iii) and (iv) solve to

$B = \frac{1}{2}(1 + \mathrm{i}k'/\kappa)C\mathrm{e}^{\mathrm{i}k'L-\kappa L}$

$B' = \frac{1}{2}(1 - \mathrm{i}k'/\kappa)C\mathrm{e}^{\mathrm{i}k'L+\kappa L}$

Hence:

$$A = \tfrac{1}{4}(1 + \kappa/\mathrm{i}k)(1 + \mathrm{i}k'/\kappa)C\mathrm{e}^{\mathrm{i}k'L-\kappa L} + \tfrac{1}{4}(1 - \kappa/\mathrm{i}k)(1 - \mathrm{i}k'/\kappa)C\mathrm{e}^{\mathrm{i}k'L+\kappa L}$$
$$= \tfrac{1}{2}C\mathrm{e}^{\mathrm{i}k'L}\{(1 + \lambda)\cosh \kappa L - \mathrm{i}[(k'/\kappa) - (\kappa/k)]\sinh \kappa L\}\ [\lambda = k'/k]$$

$$|A/C|^2 = \tfrac{1}{4}\{(1 + \lambda)^2 \cosh^2 \kappa L + [(k'/\kappa) - (\kappa/k)]^2 \sinh^2 \kappa L\}$$
$$= \tfrac{1}{4}\{2\lambda + (1 + \lambda^2)\cosh^2 \kappa L + [\lambda^2(k/\kappa)^2 + (\kappa/k)^2]\sinh^2 \kappa L\}.$$

Hence, $P = |C/A|^2$

$$= 4/\{2\lambda + (1 + \lambda^2)\cosh^2 \kappa L + [\lambda^2(k/\kappa)^2 + (\kappa/k)^2]\sinh^2 \kappa L\}$$
$$= 4/\{(1 + \lambda)^2 + [1 + \lambda^2 + \lambda^2(k/\kappa)^2 + (\kappa/k)^2]\sinh^2 \kappa L]\},$$

and so $\underline{P = 1\Big/\left\{\left(\dfrac{1 + \lambda}{2}\right)^2 + G\right\}}$.

$$G = \tfrac{1}{4}\{1 + (\kappa/k)^2 + \lambda^2[1 + (k/\kappa)^2]\}\sinh^2 \kappa L$$
$$= \tfrac{1}{16}\{1 + (\kappa/k)^2 + \lambda^2[1 + (k/\kappa)^2]\}(\mathrm{e}^{\kappa L} - \mathrm{e}^{-\kappa L})^2$$

Note that $k^2/\kappa^2 = E/V - E = \epsilon/(1 - \epsilon)$, and so

$$G = \frac{1}{16}\left\{\left(\frac{1}{\epsilon}\right) + \lambda^2\left(\frac{1}{1-\epsilon}\right)\right\}(\mathrm{e}^{\kappa L} - \mathrm{e}^{-\kappa L})^2$$
$$\underline{= \frac{1 + (\lambda^2 - 1)\epsilon}{16\epsilon(1 - \epsilon)}(\mathrm{e}^{\kappa L} - \mathrm{e}^{-\kappa L})^2}$$

N.B. When $\lambda = 1$, this result is the same as (14.1.13) of the text.

14.6 As in *Example* 4.2:

Zone A: $\psi_{\mathrm{A}}(x) = A\mathrm{e}^{\mathrm{i}kx} + A'\mathrm{e}^{-\mathrm{i}kx}$, $k = (2mE/\hbar^2)^{\frac{1}{2}}$

Zone B: $\psi_{\mathrm{B}}(x) = B\mathrm{e}^{\mathrm{i}k'x} + B'\mathrm{e}^{-\mathrm{i}k'x}$, $k' = [2m(E - V)/\hbar^2]^{\frac{1}{2}}$

Zone C: $\psi_{\mathrm{C}}(x) = C\mathrm{e}^{\mathrm{i}kx} + C'\mathrm{e}^{-\mathrm{i}kx}$, $k = (2mE/\hbar^2)^{\frac{1}{2}}$.

Note the change in Zone B: when $E > V$, ψ oscillates.

$C' = 0$ [no projectiles from right]; $P = |C|^2/|A|^2$ [*Example* 4.2]

$\psi_{\mathrm{A}}(0) = \psi_{\mathrm{B}}(0)$, $\psi_{\mathrm{B}}(L) = \psi_{\mathrm{C}}(L)$ [ψ continuous]

$(\mathrm{d}\psi_{\mathrm{A}}/\mathrm{d}x)_0 = (\mathrm{d}\psi_{\mathrm{B}}/\mathrm{d}x)_0$, $(\mathrm{d}\psi_{\mathrm{B}}/\mathrm{d}x)_L = (\mathrm{d}\psi_{\mathrm{C}}/\mathrm{d}x)_L$ [$\mathrm{d}\psi/\mathrm{d}x$ continuous].

These imply:

$$A + A' = B + B', Be^{ik'L} + B'e^{-ik'L} = Ce^{ikL};$$

$$kA - kA' = k'B - k'B', k'Be^{ik'L} - k'B'e^{-ik'L} = kCe^{ikL}.$$

These solve to:

$$A = \tfrac{1}{2}\{[1 + (k'/k)]B + [1 - (k'/k)]B'\}$$

$$B = \tfrac{1}{2}[1 + (k/k')]Ce^{i(k-k')L}$$

$$B' = \tfrac{1}{2}[1 - (k/k')]Ce^{i(k+k')L},$$

which give A in terms of C. Then straightforward algebra leads (with $\lambda = V/E$) to

$$|A|^2/|C|^2 = 1 + \frac{\lambda^2[1 - \cos(2k'L)]}{8(1 - \lambda)} = 1 + \frac{\lambda^2 \sin^2 k'L}{4(1 - \lambda)}.$$

Therefore, $P = |C|^2/|A|^2 = \underline{1/(1 + G)}$

with $G = \dfrac{\lambda^2 \sin^2(k'L)}{4(1 - \lambda)} = \underline{\dfrac{(V/E)^2 \sin^2(k'L)}{4[1 - (V/E)]}}.$

When $V \to 0, G \to 0$ and $P \to 1$.

14.7 Use the calculation in Problem 14.6 with $V \to -V$ and P(reflection) = $1 - P$(transmission):

$$P = 1 - \frac{1}{1 + G} = \frac{G}{1 + G};$$

$$G = \frac{(V/E)^2 \sin^2\{[2m(E + V)/\hbar^2]^{\frac{1}{2}}L\}}{4[1 + (V/E)]}$$

Write $\lambda = E/V$; then

$$G = \underline{\frac{\sin^2\{[(2mV/\hbar^2)(1 + \lambda)]^{\frac{1}{2}}L\}}{4\lambda(1 + \lambda)}}.$$

$V = 5\text{ eV} \mathrel{\hat{=}} 8 \times 10^{-19}\text{ J}$ [end-paper 1]; $L = 0.1$ nm.

$(2mV/\hbar^2)^{\frac{1}{2}}L = 49.09$(proton), 69.42(deuteron).

Note that $P = 0$ when $G = 0$, which is when $(2mV/\hbar)^{\frac{1}{2}}L\ (1 + \lambda)^{\frac{1}{2}} = n\pi$, n an integer.

or $\lambda = (\hbar/2mV)(n\pi/L)^2 - 1$.

Find these values to simplify the plotting. Then find P for λ in the range 0 to 2. The results are drawn in Fig. 14.1.

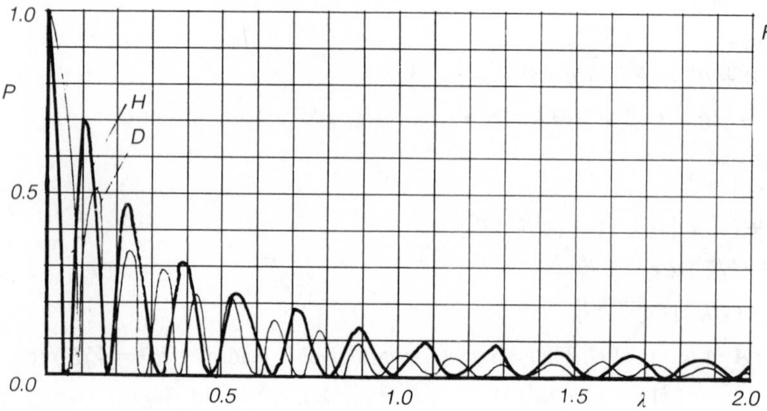

Fig 14.1

14.8 $\psi_0 = (1/\alpha\pi^{\frac{1}{2}})^{\frac{1}{2}} e^{-y^2/2}$, $\alpha^2 = \hbar/(mk)^{\frac{1}{2}}$, $y = x/\alpha$ [Box 14.1]

$\psi_0^2 = (1/\alpha\pi^{\frac{1}{2}})e^{-y^2}$.

For a proton, $\alpha^2 = (1.0545 \times 10^{-34}\,\text{J s})/\{(1.67 \times 10^{-27}\,\text{kg}) \times (500\,\text{N m}^{-1})\}^{\frac{1}{2}}$

$= 1.15 \times 10^{-22}\,\text{m}^2$

$1/\alpha\pi^{\frac{1}{2}} = 5.25 \times 10^{10}\,\text{m}^{-1}$

$\omega = (k/m)^{\frac{1}{2}} = 5.47 \times 10^{14}\,\text{s}^{-1}, E_0 = \frac{1}{2}\hbar\omega = 2.89 \times 10^{-20}\,\text{J}$.

For a deuteron, since $m \approx 2m_p$.

$\omega = (5.47 \times 10^{14}\,\text{s}^{-1})/\sqrt{2} = 3.87 \times 10^{14}\,\text{s}^{-1}$,

$\alpha^2 = (1.15 \times 10^{-22}/\sqrt{2})\text{m}^2 = 8.13 \times 10^{-23}\,\text{m}^2$,

$1/\alpha\pi^{\frac{1}{2}} = 6.25 \times 10^{10}\,\text{m}^{-1}$.

$E_0 = \frac{1}{2} \times (1.0545 \times 10^{-34}\,\text{J s}) \times (3.87 \times 10^{14}\,\text{s}^{-1}) = 2.04 \times 10^{-20}\,\text{J}$.

Plot the probability density $\psi_0^2(x)$.

In order to do so, draw up the following Table

x/pm	0	1	2	4	6	8
$\frac{1}{2}kx^2/\text{J} \times 10^{-20}$	0	0.025	0.100	0.40	0.90	1.6
$[\psi_0^2(x)/\text{pm}]_{\text{proton}}$	0.0525	0.0520	0.0507	0.0457	0.0384	0.0301
$[\psi_0^2(x)/\text{pm}]_{\text{deuteron}}$	0.0625	0.0617	0.0595	0.0513	0.0401	0.0284

x/pm	10	12	14	16	18	20
$\frac{1}{2}kx^2/\text{J} \times 10^{-20}$	2.5	3.6	4.9	6.4	8.1	10.0
$[\psi_0^2(x)/\text{pm}]_{\text{proton}}$	0.0221	0.0151	0.0096	0.0057	0.0036	0.0016
$[\psi_0^2(x)/\text{pm}]_{\text{deuteron}}$	0.0183	0.0106	0.0056	0.0027	0.0012	0.0005

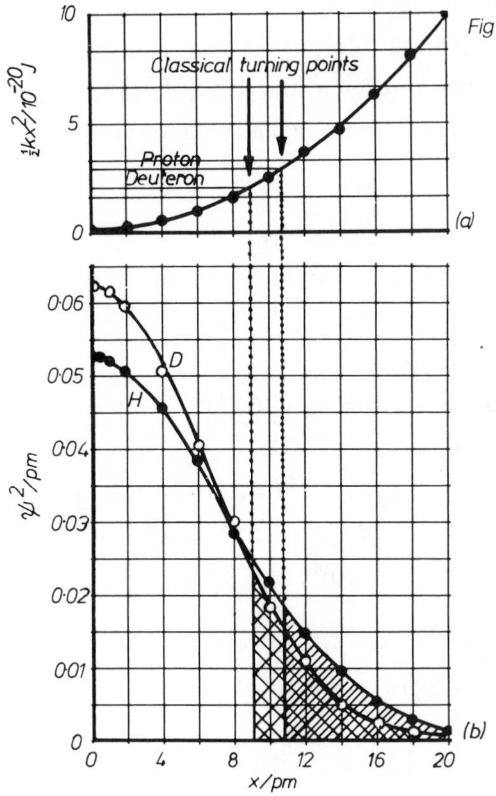

These points are plotted in Fig. 14.2. Note that the classical turning points are at $x_H = 10.7$ pm and $x_D = 9.0$ pm (where $E_0 = \frac{1}{2}kx^2$). Numerical integration of the areas beyond these points gives $p_H(x > 10.7\text{ pm}) = 0.073$, $p_D(x > 9.0\text{ pm}) = 0.075$. But don't forget the other end of the swing, which gives the same values. Hence the total probabilities of being found in the classically disallowed regions are

H : 0.146, D : 0.150

The difference between p_H and p_D is due to numerical error in the integration: the tunneling probabilities are analytically identical.

14.9 $-(\hbar^2/2m)\mathrm{d}^2\psi/\mathrm{d}x^2 + \frac{1}{2}kx^2\psi = E\psi$ [14.2.1].

$\psi = \exp(-gx^2)$, $\mathrm{d}\psi/\mathrm{d}x = -2gx\exp(-gx^2)$

$\mathrm{d}^2\psi/\mathrm{d}x^2 = -2g\exp(-gx^2) + 4g^2x^2\exp(-gx^2) = -2g\psi + 4g^2x^2\psi$,

$(\hbar^2 g/m)\psi - (2\hbar^2 g^2/m)x^2\psi + \frac{1}{2}kx^2\psi = E\psi$

$[(\hbar^2 g/m) - E]\psi + [\frac{1}{2}k - (2\hbar^2 g^2/m)]x^2\psi = 0.$

This is satisfied if $E = \hbar^2 g/m$ and $2\hbar^2 g^2 = \frac{1}{2}mk$, or $\underline{g = \frac{1}{2}\sqrt{(mk/\hbar^2)}}$.

Therefore, $E = \frac{1}{2}\hbar\sqrt{(k/m)} = \frac{1}{2}\hbar\omega$, on writing $\omega = \sqrt{(k/m)}$.

Since $E_v = (v + \frac{1}{2})\hbar\omega$ [14.2.4], the minimum excitation energy is $E_1 - E_0$ $= \hbar\omega = \underline{\hbar\sqrt{(k/m)}}$.

14.10 $\Delta E = \hbar\omega$ [14.2.5]; $\omega = \sqrt{(k/m)}$.

(a) $\omega = \sqrt{(g/l)}$ [classical physics] $= \sqrt{(9.81\ \mathrm{m\,s^{-2}}/1\ \mathrm{m})} = 3\ \mathrm{s^{-1}}$.

$\Delta E = (1.0545 \times 10^{-34}\ \mathrm{J\,s}) \times (3\ \mathrm{s^{-1}}) = \underline{3 \times 10^{-34}\ \mathrm{J}}$.

(b) $\nu \approx 5$ Hz, $\omega = 2\pi\nu$; $\omega = 30\ \mathrm{s^{-1}}$;

$\Delta E = (1.0545 \times 10^{-34}\ \mathrm{J\,s}) \times (3\ \mathrm{s^{-1}}) = \underline{30 \times 10^{-33}\ \mathrm{J}}$.

(c) $\omega = 2\pi \times (33 \times 10^3\ \mathrm{Hz}) = 2.1 \times 10^5\ \mathrm{s^{-1}}$;

$\Delta E = (1.0545 \times 10^{-34}\ \mathrm{J\,s}) \times (2.1 \times 10^5\ \mathrm{s^{-1}}) = \underline{2.2 \times 10^{-29}\ \mathrm{J}}$.

(d) $\omega = \sqrt{\{(1177\ \mathrm{N\,m^{-1}})/[\frac{1}{2} \times 16 \times (1.66 \times 10^{-27}\ \mathrm{kg})]\}} = 3.0 \times 10^{14}\ \mathrm{s^{-1}}$

$\Delta E = (1.0545 \times 10^{-34}\ \mathrm{J\,s}) \times (3.0 \times 10^{14}\ \mathrm{s^{-1}}) = 3.1 \times 10^{-20}\ \mathrm{J}$, $1600\ \mathrm{cm^{-1}}$ [end-paper 1].

14.11 $\omega = \sqrt{(k/m)}$; $k = m\omega^2$, $\omega = 2\pi\nu = 2\pi c/\lambda$.

$k = 4\pi^2 c^2 m/\lambda^2$, $1/\lambda = \tilde{\nu}$, $m = m_1 m_2/(m_1 + m_2)$.

$k = 4\pi^2 c^2 \tilde{\nu}^2\ m_1 m_2/(m_1 + m_2)$.

Draw up the following Table using $c = 2.9979 \times 10^8\ \mathrm{m\,s^{-1}}$ and the information on end-paper 3

	$^1H^{35}Cl$	$^1H^{80}Br$	$^1H^{127}I$	$^{12}C^{16}O$	$^{14}N^{16}O$
$\tilde{\nu}/m^{-1}$	298974	264972	23095_3	217021	190403
$m_1/\mathrm{kg} \times 10^{-27}$	1.6735	1.6735	1.6735	19.926	23.2521
$m_2/\mathrm{kg} \times 10^{-27}$	58.066	134.36	210.72	26.560	25.560
$k/\mathrm{N\,m^{-1}}$	515.9	411.8	314.2	1902	1595

Therefore, in orderof stiffness, CO > NO > HCl > HBr > HI.

14.12 $\langle T\rangle = \int \psi^* \hat{T}\psi \mathrm{d}\tau$ [13.4.7]

$\hat{T} = \hat{p}^2/2m$, $\hat{p} = (\hbar/\mathrm{i})\mathrm{d}/\mathrm{d}x$ [13.4.5];

$\hat{T} = -(\hbar^2/2m)\mathrm{d}^2/\mathrm{d}x^2 = -(\hbar^2/2\alpha^2 m)\mathrm{d}^2/\mathrm{d}y^2 = -\frac{1}{2}\hbar\omega\mathrm{d}^2/\mathrm{d}y^2.$

$\hat{T}\psi = -\frac{1}{2}\hbar\omega(\mathrm{d}^2\psi/\mathrm{d}y^2);\ \psi_v = N_v H_v \mathrm{e}^{-y^2/2}.$

$\mathrm{d}^2\psi/\mathrm{d}y^2 = N_v(\mathrm{d}^2/\mathrm{d}y^2)\{H_v \mathrm{e}^{-y^2/2}\}$

$\qquad = N_v\{H_v'' - 2yH_v' - H_v + y^2 H_v\}\mathrm{e}^{-y^2/2}.$

$H_v'' - 2yH_v' = -2vH_v$ [Box 14.1]

$y^2 H_v = y\{\frac{1}{2}H_{v+1} + vH_{v-1}\}$ [Box 14.1]

$\qquad = \frac{1}{2}\{\frac{1}{2}H_{v+2} + (v+1)H_v\} + v\{\frac{1}{2}H_v + (v-1)H_{v-2}\}$ [Box 14.1]

$\qquad = \frac{1}{4}H_{v+2} + v(v-1)H_{v-2} + (v+\frac{1}{2})H_v.$

$\mathrm{d}^2\psi/\mathrm{d}y^2 = N_v\{\frac{1}{4}H_{v+2} + v(v-1)H_{v-2} - (v+\frac{1}{2})H_v\}\mathrm{e}^{-y^2/2}$

$$\langle T\rangle = N_v^2(-\tfrac{1}{2}\hbar\omega)\int H_v\{\tfrac{1}{4}H_{v+2} + v(v-1)H_{v-2} - (v+\tfrac{1}{2})H_v\}\mathrm{e}^{-y^2}\,\mathrm{d}x$$

$$= \alpha N_v^2(-\tfrac{1}{2}\hbar\omega)\{0 + 0 - (v+\tfrac{1}{2})\pi^{\frac{1}{2}}2^v v!\} \text{ [Box 14.1]}$$

$$= \underline{\tfrac{1}{2}\hbar\omega(v+\tfrac{1}{2})}.\ [N_v^2 = 1/\alpha\pi^{\frac{1}{2}}2^v v!, \text{ Box 14.1}].$$

14.13 $\langle x^n\rangle = \alpha^n\langle y^n\rangle$ [Box 14.1]

$$= \alpha^n\int\psi y^n\psi\,\mathrm{d}x = \alpha^{n+1}\int\psi y^n\psi\mathrm{d}y \quad [x = \alpha y, \text{ Box 14.1}]$$

$\int\psi y^3\psi\mathrm{d}y = 0$ by symmetry.

Alternatively:

$y^2\psi = N_v y^3 H_v \mathrm{e}^{-y^2/2} = N_v y^2\{\frac{1}{2}H_{v+1} + vH_{v-1}\}\mathrm{e}^{-y^2/2}$

$\qquad = N_v y\{\frac{1}{2}[\frac{1}{2}H_{v+2} + (v+1)H_v] + v[\frac{1}{2}H_v + (v-1)H_{v-2}]\}\mathrm{e}^{-y^2/2}$

$\qquad = N_v y\{\frac{1}{4}H_{v+2} + (v+\frac{1}{2})H_v + v(v-1)H_{v-2}\}\mathrm{e}^{-y^2/2}$

$\qquad = N_v\{\frac{1}{4}[\frac{1}{2}H_{v+3} + (v+2)H_{v+1}] + (v+\frac{1}{2})[\frac{1}{2}H_{v+1} + vH_{v-1}]$

$\qquad\quad + v(v-1)[\frac{1}{2}H_{v-1} + (v-2)H_{v-3}]\}\mathrm{e}^{-y^2/2}.$

But $\int H_v H_{v'}\mathrm{e}^{-y^2}\mathrm{d}y = 0$ as $v' \neq v$; therefore $\langle y^3\rangle = 0$ and $\underline{\langle x^3\rangle = 0}$.

$$\langle x^4\rangle = \alpha^5\int\psi y^4\psi\mathrm{d}y$$

$y^4\psi = y(y^3\psi)$

$\qquad = yN_v\{\frac{1}{8}H_{v+3} + \frac{3}{4}(v+1)H_{v+1} + \frac{3}{2}v^2 H_{v-1} + v(v-1)(v-2)H_{v-3}\}\mathrm{e}^{-y^2/2}.$

Only yH_{v+1} and yH_{v-1} lead to H_v and contribute to the expectation value; therefore

$$\begin{aligned}y^4\psi &= \tfrac{3}{4}N_v y\{(v+1)H_{v+1} + 2v^2H_{v-1}\}e^{-y^2/2} + \\ &= \tfrac{3}{4}N_v\{(v+1)[\tfrac{1}{2}H_{v+2} + (v+1)H_v] + 2v^2[\tfrac{1}{2}H_v + (v-1)H_{v-2}]\}e^{-y^2/2} + \ldots \\ &= \tfrac{3}{4}N_v\{(v+1)^2H_v + v^2H_v\}e^{-y^2/2} + \ldots \\ &= \tfrac{3}{4}N_v(2v^2 + 2v + 1)H_v e^{-y^2/2} + \ldots\end{aligned}$$

$$\int \psi y^4 \psi \, dy = \tfrac{3}{4}N_v^2(2v^2 + 2v + 1)\int H_v^2 \, e^{-y^2} \, dy$$

$$= (3/4\alpha)(2v^2 + 2v + 1) \text{ [Box 14.1]}.$$

$$\langle x^4\rangle = \alpha^5 \times (3/4\alpha)(2v^2 + 2v + 1) = \underline{\tfrac{3}{4}(2v^2 + 2v + 1)\alpha^4}.$$

14.14 $\mu = \int \psi_{v'} x \psi_v \, dx = \alpha^2 \int \psi_{v'} y \psi_v \, dy \;\; [x = \alpha y]$

$y\psi_v = N_v\{\tfrac{1}{2}H_{v+1} + vH_{v-1}\}e^{-y^2/2}$ [Box 14.1]

$\mu = \alpha^2 N_{v'} N_v \int \{\tfrac{1}{2}H_{v'}H_{v+1} + vH_{v'}H_{v-1}\}e^{-y^2} \, dy = 0$ unless $\underline{v' = v \pm 1}$.

(a) $v' = v + 1$:

$$\mu = \tfrac{1}{2}\alpha^2 N_{v+1}N_v \int H_{v+1}^2 e^{-y^2} \, dy = \tfrac{1}{2}\alpha^2 N_{v+1}N_v \pi^{\frac{1}{2}} 2^{v+1}(v+1)!$$

$$= \underline{\alpha(1/2)^{\frac{1}{2}}(v+1)^{\frac{1}{2}}}.$$

(b) $v' = v - 1$:

$$\mu = v\alpha^2 N_{v-1}N_v \int H_{v-1}^2 e^{-y^2} \, dy = v\alpha^2 N_{v-1}N_v \pi^{\frac{1}{2}} 2^{v-1}(v-1)!$$

$$= \underline{\alpha(1/2)^{\frac{1}{2}} v^{\frac{1}{2}}}.$$

14.15 $V = -e^2/4\pi\epsilon_0 r = ax^b$ with $b = -1$ $[x \equiv r]$

Since $2\langle T\rangle = b\langle V\rangle$ [14.2.11],

$2\langle T\rangle = -\langle V\rangle$.

That is, $\underline{\langle T\rangle = -\tfrac{1}{2}\langle V\rangle}$.

14.16 $I = m_H R^2$; $E_{m_l} = m_l^2\hbar^2/2I$ [14.3.5]

$I = [1.0078 \times (1.6605 \times 10^{-27}\,\text{kg})] \times (160 \times 10^{-12}\,\text{m})^2 = 4.28 \times 10^{-47}\,\text{kg m}^2$

$$E_{m_l} = (1.30 \times 10^{-22}\,\text{J})m_l^2 \begin{cases} \triangleq (78.2 \times 10^{-3}\,\text{kJ mol}^{-1})m_l^2 \\ \triangleq (6.54\,\text{cm}^{-1})m_l^2 \text{ [end-paper 1]}. \end{cases}$$

Initially $m_l = 0$; after minimum excitation $m_l = \pm 1$. Hence minimum energy required is $\underline{78.23 \times 10^{-3}\,\text{kJ mol}^{-1}}$, or $\underline{6.54\,\text{cm}^{-1}}$. Minimum angular momentum (above zero) $= |\hbar m_l|$, $m_l = 1$; i.e. $\underline{1.055 \times 10^{-34}\,\text{J s}}$.

14.17 $\psi_{m_l} = (1/\surd(2\pi))\,e^{im\phi}$ [14.3.4].

(a) $m_l = 0$; $\psi = 1/\surd(2\pi)$. Therefore the H atom is uniformly distributed in a ring.

(b) $m_l = \pm 1$, $\psi_{m_l} = (1/\surd(2\pi))e^{\pm i\phi}$. If we know that the angular momentum is definitely $m_l = +1$, then $\psi = (1/\surd(2\pi))e^{+i\phi}$ if we knew it to be $m_l = -1$, then $\psi_{-1} = (1/\surd(2\pi))\,e^{-i\phi}$. Since in both cases $|\psi|^2 = (1/2\pi) \times e^{i\phi} \times e^{-i\phi} = 1/2\pi$, the hydrogen atom is also uniformly spread around the ring.

14.18 (a) $\hat{l}_z\,e^{i\phi} = (\hbar/i)(d/d\phi)e^{+i\phi} = \hbar e^{+i\phi}$; $\underline{l_z = +\hbar}$.

(b) $\hat{l}_z\,e^{-2i\phi} = (\hbar/i)(d/d\phi)e^{-2i\phi} = -2\hbar e^{-2i\phi}$; $\underline{l_z = -2\hbar}$.

(c) $$\langle l_z\rangle \propto \int_0^{2\pi} \cos\phi\,(\hbar/i)(d/d\phi)\cos\phi\,d\phi = \underline{0}.$$

$$\propto -(\hbar/i)\int_0^{2\pi} \cos\phi\,\sin\phi\,d\phi = \underline{0}.$$

(d) $$\langle l_z\rangle = N^2\int_0^{2\pi}(\cos\chi\,e^{i\phi} + \sin\chi\,e^{-i\phi})^*(\hbar/i)(d/d\phi)(\cos\chi\,e^{i\phi} + \sin\chi\,e^{-i\phi})d\phi$$

$$= (\hbar/i)\,N^2\int_0^{2\pi}(\cos\chi\,e^{-i\phi} + \sin\chi\,e^{i\phi})(i\cos\chi\,e^{i\phi} - i\sin\chi\,e^{-i\phi})d\phi$$

$$= \hbar N^2\int_0^{2\pi}\{\cos^2\chi - \sin^2\chi + \cos\chi\sin\chi\,(e^{2i\phi} - e^{-2i\phi})\}d\phi$$

$$= \hbar N^2(\cos^2\chi - \sin^2\chi) \times 2\pi = 2\pi\hbar N^2\cos 2\chi.$$

$$N^2\int_0^{2\pi}(\cos\chi\,e^{i\phi} + \sin\chi\,e^{-i\phi})^*(\cos\chi\,e^{i\phi} + \sin\chi\,e^{-i\phi})d\phi$$

$$= N^2\int_0^{2\pi}\{\cos^2\chi + \sin^2\chi + \cos\chi\sin\chi\,(e^{2i\phi} + e^{-2i\phi})\}d\phi$$

$$= 2\pi N^2(\cos^2\chi + \sin^2\chi) = 2\pi N^2 = 1; N^2 = 1/2\pi.$$

Hence, $\langle l_z\rangle = \underline{\hbar\cos 2\chi}$.

For the kinetic energy, use $\hat{T} = \hat{l}_z^2/2I = -(\hbar^2/2I)\mathrm{d}^2/\mathrm{d}\phi^2$

(a) $\hat{T}\mathrm{e}^{\mathrm{i}\phi} = -(\hbar^2/2I)\mathrm{i}^2\,\mathrm{e}^{\mathrm{i}\phi} = (\hbar^2/2I)\mathrm{e}^{\mathrm{i}\phi};\ T = \hbar^2/2I.$

(b) $\hat{T}\mathrm{e}^{-2\mathrm{i}\phi} = -(\hbar^2/2I)\,(2\mathrm{i})^2\,\mathrm{e}^{-2\mathrm{i}\phi} = (4\hbar^2/2I)\mathrm{e}^{-2\mathrm{i}\phi};\ T = \underline{4\hbar^2/2I.}$

(c) $\hat{T}\cos\phi = -(\hbar^2/2I)(-\cos\phi) = (\hbar^2/2I)\cos\phi;\ T = \underline{\hbar^2/2I.}$

(d) $\hat{T}\{\cos\chi\,\mathrm{e}^{\mathrm{i}\phi} + \sin\chi\,\mathrm{e}^{-\mathrm{i}\phi}\} = -(\hbar^2/2I)\,\{-\cos\chi\,\mathrm{e}^{\mathrm{i}\phi} - \sin\chi\,\mathrm{e}^{-\mathrm{i}\phi}\}$
$= (\hbar^2/2I)\,\{\cos\chi\,\mathrm{e}^{\mathrm{i}\phi} + \sin\chi\,\mathrm{e}^{-\mathrm{i}\phi}\};\ \underline{T = \hbar^2/2I.}$

14.19 $\psi = N\{a\mathrm{e}^{\mathrm{i}\phi} + b\mathrm{e}^{2\mathrm{i}\phi} + c\mathrm{e}^{3\mathrm{i}\phi}\}$

$$N^2\int_0^{2\pi}(a\mathrm{e}^{-\mathrm{i}\phi} + b\mathrm{e}^{-2\mathrm{i}\phi} + c\mathrm{e}^{-3\mathrm{i}\phi})(a\mathrm{e}^{\mathrm{i}\phi} + b\mathrm{e}^{2\mathrm{i}\phi} + c\mathrm{e}^{3\mathrm{i}\phi})\,\mathrm{d}\phi$$

$$= N^2\int_0^{2\pi}\{a^2 + b^2 + c^2 + \ldots\}\mathrm{d}\phi\ [\ldots \text{ integrate to zero}]$$

$= N^2 2\pi(a^2 + b^2 + c^2) = 1$; therefore $N^2 = 1/2\pi(a^2 + b^2 + c^2)$.

$$\langle l_z\rangle = (\hbar/\mathrm{i})N^2\int_0^{2\pi}\{a\mathrm{e}^{-\mathrm{i}\phi} + b\mathrm{e}^{-2\mathrm{i}\phi} + c\mathrm{e}^{-3\mathrm{i}\phi}\}\,(\mathrm{d}/\mathrm{d}\phi)\,\{a\mathrm{e}^{\mathrm{i}\phi} + b\mathrm{e}^{2\mathrm{i}\phi} + c\mathrm{e}^{3\mathrm{i}\phi}\}\mathrm{d}\phi$$

$$= \hbar N^2\int_0^{2\pi}\{a\mathrm{e}^{-\mathrm{i}\phi} + b\mathrm{e}^{-2\mathrm{i}\phi} + c\mathrm{e}^{-3\mathrm{i}\phi}\}\{a\mathrm{e}^{\mathrm{i}\phi} + 2b\mathrm{e}^{2\mathrm{i}\phi} + 3c\mathrm{e}^{3\mathrm{i}\phi}\}\mathrm{d}\phi$$

$= \hbar N^2 2\pi(a^2 + 2b^2 + 3c^2)$
$= \underline{\hbar(a^2 + 2b^2 + 3c^2)/(a^2 + b^2 + c^2).}$

$$\langle l_z^2\rangle = -\hbar^2 N^2\int_0^{2\pi}\{a\mathrm{e}^{-\mathrm{i}\phi} + b\mathrm{e}^{-2\mathrm{i}\phi} + c\mathrm{e}^{-3\mathrm{i}\phi}\}\,(\mathrm{d}^2/\mathrm{d}\phi^2)\,\{a\mathrm{e}^{\mathrm{i}\phi} + b\mathrm{e}^{2\mathrm{i}\phi} + c\mathrm{e}^{3\mathrm{i}\phi}\}\mathrm{d}\phi$$

$$= \hbar^2 N^2\int_0^{2\pi}\{a\mathrm{e}^{-\mathrm{i}\phi} + b\mathrm{e}^{-2\mathrm{i}\phi} + c\mathrm{e}^{-3\mathrm{i}\phi}\}\,\{a\mathrm{e}^{\mathrm{i}\phi} + 4b\mathrm{e}^{2\mathrm{i}\phi} + 9c\mathrm{e}^{3\mathrm{i}\phi}\}\mathrm{d}\phi$$

$= 2\pi\hbar^2 N^2(a^2 + 4b^2 + 9c^2)$
$= \hbar^2(a^2 + 4b^2 + 9c^2)/(a^2 + b^2 + c^2).$

$\langle T\rangle = \langle l_z^2\rangle/2I$
$= \underline{(\hbar^2/2I)\,(a^2 + 4b^2 + 9c^2)/(a^2 + b^2 + c^2).}$

$$\frac{\langle l_z^2\rangle - \langle l_z\rangle^2}{\hbar^2} = \frac{a^2 + 4b^2 + 9c^2}{a^2 + b^2 + c^2} - \left(\frac{a^2 + 2b^2 + 3c^2}{a^2 + b^2 + c^2}\right)^2$$

$$= (a^2b^2 + 4a^2c^2 + b^2c^2)/(a^2 + b^2 + c^2)^2$$

$\delta l_z = \underline{\hbar(a^2b^2 + 4a^2c^2 + b^2c^2)^{\frac{1}{2}}c/(a^2 + b^2 + c^2).}$

14.20 $E_l = l(l+1)\hbar^2/2I$ [14.3.22].

First four levels are

$E_0 = 0, E_1 = \hbar^2/I, E_2 = 3\hbar^2/I, E_3 = 6\hbar^2/I.$

Therefore the angular momenta are $\{l(l+1)\}^{\frac{1}{2}}\hbar$;

0	$2^{\frac{1}{2}}\hbar$	$6^{\frac{1}{2}}\hbar$	$12^{\frac{1}{2}}\hbar$

The numbers of states, $(2l+1)$, are

1	3	5	7

14.21 $E_J = J(J+1)\hbar^2/2I$ [14.3.22]; $I = [m_1 m_2/(m_1+m_2)]R^2$.

$m_1 = 1.6735 \times 10^{-27}\,\text{kg}, m_2 = 210.72 \times 10^{-27}\,\text{kg}$ [Problem 14.11]; $R = 160\,\text{pm}$.

$$I = \left(\frac{(1.6735 \times 10^{-27}\,\text{kg}) \times (210.72 \times 10^{-27}\,\text{kg})}{(1.6735 \times 10^{-27}\,\text{kg}) + (210.72 \times 10^{-27}\,\text{kg})}\right) \times (160 \times 10^{-12}\,\text{m})^2$$

$$= 4.2504 \times 10^{-47}\,\text{kg m}^2.$$

$$E_J = J(J+1)(1.0545 \times 10^{-34}\,\text{J s})^2/([2 \times (4.2504 \times 10^{-47}\,\text{kg m}^2)]$$

$$= (1.3083 \times 10^{-22}\,\text{J})J(J+1) \begin{cases} \triangleq (78.786 \times 10^{-3}\,\text{kJ mol}^{-1})J(J+1) \\ \triangleq (6.588\,\text{cm}^{-1})J(J+1). \end{cases}$$

The first four levels are

$$E_0 = \begin{cases} 0 \\ 0 \end{cases}, E_1 = \begin{cases} 0.158\,\text{kJ mol}^{-1} \\ 13.18\,\text{cm}^{-1} \end{cases}, E_2 = \begin{cases} 0.473\,\text{kJ mol}^{-1} \\ 39.5\,\text{cm}^{-1} \end{cases}, E_3 = \begin{cases} 0.945\,\text{kJ mol}^{-1} \\ 79.0\,\text{cm}^{-1} \end{cases}$$

14.22 $-(\hbar^2/2m)\nabla^2\psi + E\psi$ [14.3.12; $V = 0$]; $E_l = l(l+1)\hbar^2/2I$ [14.3.22],

$\nabla^2 = (\partial^2/\partial r^2) + (2/r)(\partial/\partial r) + (1/r^2)\Lambda^2$ [14.3.14],

$\Lambda^2 = (1/\sin\theta)^2(\partial^2/\partial\phi^2) + (\cos\theta/\sin\theta)(\partial/\partial\theta) + (\partial^2/\partial\theta^2).$

(a) $\psi_{0,0} = 1/2\pi^{\frac{1}{2}}$; $\nabla^2\psi_{0,0} = 0$ since $\psi_{0,0} = \text{const.}$, and so $E_{0,0} = 0$.

By [14.3.22]: $E_0 = 0$, which is consistent.

(b) $\psi_{1,0} = \frac{1}{2}(3/\pi)^{\frac{1}{2}}\cos\theta$

$$\nabla^2\psi_{1,0} = (1/r^2)\Lambda^2\psi_{1,0} = (1/r^2)\{(\cos\theta/\sin\theta)(\partial/\partial\theta) + (\partial^2/\partial\theta^2)\}\tfrac{1}{2}(3/\pi)^{\frac{1}{2}}\cos\theta$$

$$= \tfrac{1}{2}(3/\pi)^{\frac{1}{2}}(1/r^2)\{(\cos\theta/\sin\theta)(-\sin\theta) - \cos\theta\}$$

$$= -2(1/r^2)\tfrac{1}{2}(3/\pi)^{\frac{1}{2}}\cos\theta = -(2/r^2)\psi_{1,0}.$$

Therefore $E_1\psi_{1,0} = -(\hbar^2/2m)\nabla^2\psi_{1,0} = +2(\hbar^2/2mr^2)\psi_{1,0}$

$$= 2(\hbar^2/2I)\psi_{1,0}, \text{ and so } E_1 = 2(\hbar^2/2I).$$

By [14.3.22], $E_1 = 2(\hbar^2/2I)$, which is consistent.

(c) $\psi_{2,-1} = \frac{1}{2}(15/2\pi)^{\frac{1}{2}} \cos\theta \sin\theta \, e^{-i\phi}$

$$\nabla^2 \psi_{2,-1} = (1/r^2)\Lambda^2 \psi_{2,-1} = \tfrac{1}{2}(15/2\pi)^{\frac{1}{2}} (1/r^2) \{(1/\sin\theta)^2 (\partial^2/\partial\phi^2) + (\cos\theta/\sin\theta)(\partial/\partial\theta) + (\partial^2/\partial\theta^2)\} \cos\theta \sin\theta \, e^{-i\phi}$$

$$= \tfrac{1}{2}(15/2\pi)^{\frac{1}{2}} (1/r^2) \left\{ -\frac{\cos\theta\sin\theta \, e^{-i\phi}}{\sin^2\theta} + \left(\frac{\cos\theta}{\sin\theta}\right)(\cos^2\theta - \sin^2\theta)e^{-i\phi} - 4\cos\theta\sin\theta \, e^{-i\phi} \right\}$$

$$= \tfrac{1}{2}(15/2\pi)^{\frac{1}{2}} (1/r^2) \, e^{-i\phi} \cos\theta \sin\theta \left\{ -\frac{1}{\sin^2\theta} + \frac{\cos^2\theta}{\sin^2\theta} - 1 - 4 \right\}$$

$$= -6 \cdot \tfrac{1}{2}(15/2\pi)^{\frac{1}{2}} (1/r^2) \cos\theta \sin\theta \, e^{-i\phi}$$

$= -6\psi_{2,1}/r^2$, and so $E_2\psi_{2,-1} = -(\hbar^2/2m)\nabla^2\psi_{2,-1} = 6(\hbar^2/2mr^2)\psi_{2,-1}$, and so $E_2 = 6\hbar^2/2mr^2 = 6\hbar^2/2I$.

By [14.322], $E_2 = 6\hbar^2/2I$, which is consistent.

(d) $\psi_{3,3} = -\frac{1}{8}(35/\pi)^{\frac{1}{2}} \sin^3\theta \, e^{3i\phi}$

$$\nabla^2 \psi_{3,3} = -\tfrac{1}{8}(35/\pi)^{\frac{1}{2}} (1/r^2) \{(1/\sin\theta)^2 (\partial^2/\partial\phi^2) + (\cos\theta/\sin\theta)(\partial/\partial\theta) + (\partial^2/\partial\theta^2)\} \sin^3\theta \, e^{3i\phi}$$

$$= -\tfrac{1}{8}(35/\pi)^{\frac{1}{2}} (1/r^2) \times \left\{ \frac{-9\sin^3\theta e^{3i\phi}}{\sin^2\theta} + \left(\frac{\cos\theta}{\sin\theta}\right) 3\cos\theta\sin^2\theta \, e^{3i\phi} \right\} + [6\cos^2\theta\sin\theta - 3\sin^3\theta] \, e^{3i\phi}$$

$$= -\tfrac{1}{8}(35/\pi)^{\frac{1}{2}}(1/r^2)\sin^3\theta \, e^{3i\phi} \left\{ \frac{-9}{\sin^2\theta} + \frac{3\cos^2\theta}{\sin^2\theta} + \frac{6\cos^2\theta}{\sin^2\theta} - 3 \right\}$$

$$= +12(\tfrac{1}{8})(35\pi)^{\frac{1}{2}}(1/r^2)\sin^3\theta \, e^{3i\phi} = -12\psi_{3,3}/r^2.$$

Therefore, $E_3\psi_{3,3} = -(\hbar^2/2m)\nabla^2\psi_{3,3} = (12\hbar^2/2mr^2)\psi_{3,3}$, and so $E_3 = 12\hbar^2/2I$.

By [14.3.22], $E_3 = 12\hbar^2/2I$, which is consistent.

14.23 $\int_0^\pi d\theta \sin\theta \int_0^{2\pi} d\phi |\psi_{3,3}(\theta,\phi)|^2$

$$= \int_0^\pi d\theta\sin\theta \int_0^{2\pi} d\phi \left(\frac{1}{64}\right)\left(\frac{35}{\pi}\right) \sin^6\theta = \left(\frac{1}{64}\right)\left(\frac{35}{\pi}\right)(2\pi)\int_0^\pi d\theta \sin^7\theta.$$

$$\int_0^\pi d\theta \sin^7\theta = \int_0^\pi d\theta \sin\theta \sin^6\theta = \int_{-1}^{1} d\cos\theta(1-\cos^2\theta)^3$$

$$= \int_{-1}^{1} dx(1-3x^2+3x^4-x^6) = (x - x^3 + \tfrac{3}{5}x^5 - \tfrac{1}{7}x^7)\Big|_{-1}^{1} = 32/35.$$

Therefore $\int d\tau |\psi_{3,3}|^2 = \left(\frac{1}{64}\right) \cdot \left(\frac{35}{\pi}\right) \cdot (2\pi) \cdot \left(\frac{32}{35}\right) = 1$, as required.

14.24

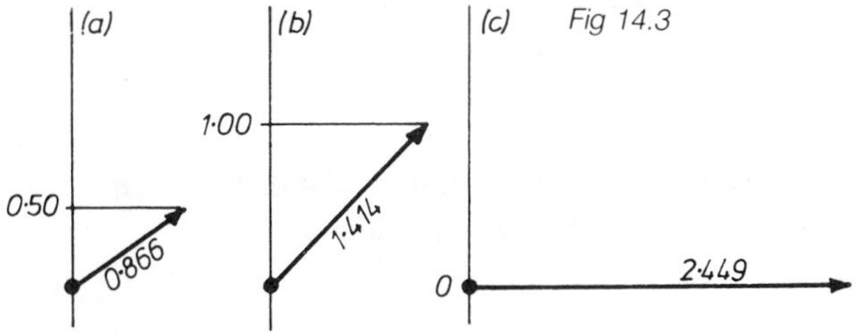

Fig 14.3

14.25 From the diagram, Fig. 14.4,

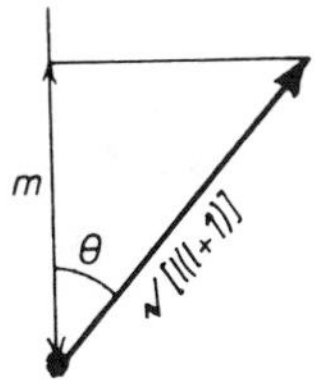

Fig 14.4

$\cos\theta = m_l / \sqrt{(l(l+1))}$;

$\theta = \arccos\{m_l/\sqrt{(l(l+1))}\}$, or $\theta = \arccos\{m_s/\sqrt{(s(s+1))}\}$.

For an α-electron, $m_s = +\frac{1}{2}, s = \frac{1}{2}$;

$\theta = \arccos(\frac{1}{2}/\sqrt{\frac{3}{4}}) = \arccos(1/\sqrt{3}) = \underline{54° 44'}$.

Minimum angle occurs for $m_l = l$.

$$\lim_{l\to\infty} \theta_{\min} = \lim_{l\to\infty} \arccos\left(\frac{l}{\sqrt{(l(l+1))}}\right) = \lim_{l\to\infty} \arccos\frac{l}{l} = \arccos 1 = 0.$$

14.26 Construct the 13(= $2l+1$) cones based on $\sqrt{(l(l+1))} = \sqrt{42} = 6.48$ and $m_l = 6, 5, \ldots -6$. These are drawn in Fig. 14.5. The electron with $m_l = 6$ will be

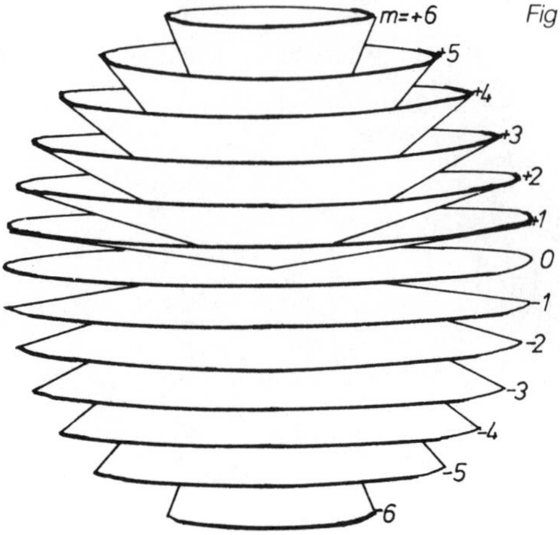

Fig 14.5

found most probably in the equatorial region, so will that with $m_l = -6$. The electron with $m_l = 0$ is predominantly in the vicinity of the poles.

15. Atomic structure and atomic spectra

A15.1 $\lambda^{-1} = R_H(\frac{1}{4} - n_2^{-2})$. [15.1.1]

$\lambda = R_H^{-1}[\frac{1}{4} - (\frac{1}{4})^2]^{-1} = (1.09677 \times 10^7\,\text{m}^{-1})^{-1}[\frac{1}{4} - (\frac{1}{4})^2]^{-1}$

$= 4.86276 \times 10^{-7}\,\text{m}$, or $\underline{486.276\ \text{nm}}$.

A15.2 $\lambda^{-1} = R_H(9^{-1} - n_2^{-2})$. [15.1.2]

$n_2 = [9^{-1} - (\lambda R_H)^{-1}]^{-\frac{1}{2}} = [9^{-1} - (\nu/cR_H)]^{-\frac{1}{2}}$

$= [9^{-1} - (2.7415 \times 10^{14}\,\text{Hz})(2.9979 \times 10^8\,\text{m/s})^{-1}(1.0968 \times 10^7\,\text{m}^{-1})^{-1}]^{-\frac{1}{2}}$

$= 6.0047$; that is, $\underline{n_2 = 6}$.

A15.3 $\lambda^{-1} = (486.1 \times 10^{-7}\,\text{cm})^{-1} = 20\,572\,\text{cm}^{-1}$.

Term $= 27\,414\,\text{cm}^{-1} - 20\,572\,\text{cm}^{-1} = \underline{6842\,\text{cm}^{-1}}$.

A15.4 $R_{20}(r) = (2a_0)^{-3/2}(2-\rho)\exp(-\rho/2)$ with $\rho = r/a_0$ [Box 15.1]

$\partial R_{20}/\partial r = a_0^{-1}\,\partial R_{20}/\partial\rho = 0$

$\partial R_{20}/\partial\rho = (2a_0)^{-3/2}\exp(-\rho/2)\,[(2-\rho)(-\frac{1}{2}) - 1] = 0$;

$\frac{1}{2}\rho - 1 = 1$ and $\rho = 4$. Hence $\underline{r = 4a_0}$ at the extreme.

$\partial^2 R_{20}/\partial\rho^2 = (2a_0)^{-3/2}\exp(-\rho/2)[(3/2) - (\rho/4)]$,

$[(3/2) - (\frac{1}{4})(4)] > 0$ at the extreme. Hence the extreme is a minimum.

$R_{20}(4a_0) = (2a_0)^{-3/2}(2-4)\exp(-4/2) \neq 0$ and the function is nonzero at the extreme.

A15.5 $R_{30}(r) = a_0^{-3/2}(1/9\sqrt{3})(6 - 6\rho + \rho^2)\exp(\rho/2)$ [Box 15.1]

with $\rho = 2r/3a_0$. When $6 - 6\rho + \rho^2 = 0$, $\rho = 3 \pm 3^{\frac{1}{2}} = 1.27$ and 4.73.

$r = (3/2)\rho a_0 = 1.91a_0$ and $7.10a_0 = (1.91)(52.9\,\text{pm}) = 101\,\text{pm}$

and $(7.10)(52.9\,\text{pm}) = \underline{376\,\text{pm}}$.

A15.6 $j = l + s$, with $s = \frac{1}{2}$, gives $l = 1$;

orbital angular momentum $= \{l(l+1)\}^{\frac{1}{2}}(h/2\pi)$

$= (2^{\frac{1}{2}})(6.63 \times 10^{-34}\,\text{J s})(\frac{1}{2})(3.14)^{-1} = \underline{1.49 \times 10^{-34}\,\text{J s}}$.

A15.7 D means $\underline{L = 2}$; 1 means $\underline{S = 0}$; 2 means $\underline{J = 2}$.

A15.8 For the ground state, probability density $\propto \exp(-2r/a_0)$ [Sec. 15.1(e)]
The maximum value of $\exp(-2r/a_0) = 1$. Hence, $0.50 = \exp(-2r/a_0)$;
$r_{50} = -(a_0/2)\ln(0.50) = (\frac{1}{2})(53 \text{ pm})(0.69) = \underline{18 \text{ pm}}$.

A15.9 $\text{RDF} = 4a_0^{-3}r^2\exp(-2r/a_0)$ with a maximum at $r = a_0$ [15.1.25]
(a) $4a_0^{-3}r_{50}^2\exp(-2r_{50}/a_0) = 0.50(4a_0^{-3}a_0^2\text{e}^{-2})$
$(r_{50}/a_0)\exp(-r_{50}/a_0) = (0.50)^{\frac{1}{2}}\text{e}^{-1} = 0.260$
Let $x \equiv r_{50}/a_0$. Then $x = 0.260\text{e}^x$. $x = \underline{2.079}$ by trial.
$r_{50} = 2.079(52.9 \text{ pm}) = \underline{110 \text{ pm}}$.
(b) Likewise, $x = 0.319\text{e}^x$; $x = 1.632$, $r_{95} = \underline{86.3 \text{ pm.}}$

A15.10 $E = \mu_B m_l B$ [15.3.6].
$m_l = E/\mu_B B = (2.23 \times 10^{-22} \text{ J})(9.27 \times 10^{-24} \text{ J T}^{-1})^{-1}(12 \text{ T})^{-1} = 2.00$.
Hence $m_l = 2$.

15.1 $1/\lambda = R\left(\dfrac{1}{n_1^2} - \dfrac{1}{n_2^2}\right)$ [15.1.2], $R = 109\,677 \text{ cm}^{-1}$.

Find n_1 from the value of λ_{max}, which arises from the transition $n_2 = n_1 + 1 \to n_1$:

$$1/\lambda_{max}R = \frac{1}{n_1^2} - \frac{1}{(n_1+1)^2} = \frac{2n_1+1}{n_1^2(n_1+1)^2}$$

$$\lambda_{max}R = \left\{\frac{n_1^2(n_1+1)^2}{(2n_1+1)}\right\}.$$

$\lambda_{max}R = (123\,368 \times 10^{-9} \text{ m}) \times (109\,677 \text{ cm}^{-1}) = 1.36(\text{m/cm}) = 136$.
Since $n_1 = 1, 2, 3, 4$ have been accounted for [Section 15.1], try $n_1 = 5, 6, \ldots$
With $n_1 = 6$ we get $n_1^2(n_1+1)^2/(2n_1+1) = 136$. Therefore the Humphreys series is
$\underline{n_2 \to n_1 = 6.}$ The transitions are given by

$$1/\lambda = (109\,677 \text{ cm}^{-1})\left(\frac{1}{6^2} - \frac{1}{n_2^2}\right), n_2 = 7, 8, 9\ldots$$

Thus the transitions are at 12 370 nm, 7503 nm, 5908 nm, 5129 nm, . . .
3908 ($n_2 = 15$), . . . converging to 3282 nm as $n_2 \to \infty$.

15.2 $\lambda_{max}R = n_1^2(n_1+1)^2/(2n_1+1)$ [Problem 15.1],
$= (656.46 \times 10^{-9} \text{ m}) \times (109\,677 \text{ cm}^{-1}) = 7.20$.
$n_1^2(n_1+1)^2/(2n_1+1) = 7.20$ for $n_1 = 2$. Therefore, the transitions are given by

$$1/\lambda = (109\,677\ \text{cm}^{-1})\left(\tfrac{1}{4} - \frac{1}{n_2^2}\right),\ n_2 = 3, 4, 5, 6, 7, \ldots$$

The next line has $n_2 = 7$;

$$1/\lambda = (109\,677\ \text{cm}^{-1})\left(\tfrac{1}{4} - \frac{1}{49}\right) = \underline{397.13\ \text{nm.}}$$

The energy required to ionize is obtained by letting $n_2 \to \infty$. Then
$1/\lambda_\infty = (109\,677\ \text{cm}^{-1})\,(\tfrac{1}{4} - 0) = 27\,419\ \text{cm}^{-1}$, or $\underline{3.40\ \text{eV}}$.
(NB This is the ionization energy of H in an excited state, that with $n = 2$.)

15.3 $1/\lambda = K\left(1 - \frac{1}{n^2}\right),\ n = 2, 3, 4, \ldots$ [as in 15.1.2].

$(1/\lambda)\Big/\left(1 - \frac{1}{n^2}\right) = K$, a constant, if the formula is appropriate.

Draw up the following Table

n	2	3	4
$(1/\lambda)/\text{cm}^{-1}$	740 747	877 924	925 933
$[(1/\lambda)/\left(1 - \frac{1}{n^2}\right)]/\text{cm}^{-1}$	987 663	987 665	987 662

Hence K is a constant, with the value $\underline{987\,663\ \text{cm}^{-1}}$.

15.4 $1/\lambda = K\left(\tfrac{1}{4} - \frac{1}{n^2}\right);\ n = 3, 4, 5, \ldots$

$$= (987\,663\ \text{cm}^{-1})\left(\tfrac{1}{4} - \frac{1}{n^2}\right) = \underline{137\,175\ \text{cm}^{-1},\ 185\,187\ \text{cm}^{-1}, \ldots}$$

15.5 $R_\text{H} = R_\infty/(1 + m_\text{e}/m_\text{H}), R_\text{D} = R_\infty/(1 + m_\text{e}/m_\text{D})$ [15.1.21]

$$1/\lambda_\text{H} = R_\text{H}\left(1 - \frac{1}{2^2}\right) = 0.75R_\text{H};\ 1/\lambda_\text{D} = 0.75R_\text{D}.$$

$R_\text{H}/R_\text{D} = (1/\lambda_\text{H})/(1/\lambda_\text{D}) = (82\,259.098\ \text{cm}^{-1})/(82\,281.476\ \text{cm}^{-1})$

$= 0.999\,728\,03 = (1 + m_e/m_D)/(1 + m_e/m_H)$.

$m_e/m_D = (0.999\,728\,03)\,(1 + m_e/m_H) - 1 = 0.999\,728\,03 \times (m_e/m_H) - 0.000\,271\,97$.

$$m_D = \frac{m_e}{0.999\,728\,03\,(m_e/m_H) - 0.000\,271\,97}$$

$$= \frac{9.109\,53 \times 10^{-31}\,\text{kg}}{\left(\dfrac{9.109\,53 \times 10^{-31}\,\text{kg}}{1.672\,65 \times 10^{-27}\,\text{kg}}\right) 0.997\,2803 - 0.000\,271\,97} = \underline{3.3594 \times 10^{-27}\,\text{kg}}.$$

15.6 $R_{Ps} = R_\infty/(1 + 1)$ [Problem 15.5] $= \frac{1}{2}R_\infty = 54\,869\,\text{cm}^{-1}$.

$$1/\lambda = (54\,869\,\text{cm}^{-1})\left(\tfrac{1}{4} - \frac{1}{n^2}\right), n = 3, 4, 5, \ldots$$

$$= \underline{7621\,\text{cm}^{-1}, 10\,288\,\text{cm}^{-1}, 11\,522\,\text{cm}^{-1}, \ldots}$$

Lyman series at $(54\,869\,\text{cm}^{-1})\left(1 - \dfrac{1}{n^2}\right)$, $n = 2, 3, \ldots$; energy to remove electron ($n = \infty$) is $54\,869\,\text{cm}^{-1}$. This is therefore the ionization energy of the ground state. Hence the binding energy is $54\,869\,\text{cm}^{-1}$, or $\underline{6.80\,\text{eV}}$.

15.7 Attractive Coulombic force $= Ze^2/4\pi\epsilon_0 r^2$ [electrostatics].

Repulsive, centrifugal force = (angular momentum)$^2/m_e r^3$ [classical physics].

Angular momentum $= n\hbar$, $n = 1, 2, \ldots$ [postulated]

Balance when $Ze^2/4\pi\epsilon_0 r^2 = n^2\hbar^2/m_e r^3$, or $r = 4\pi n^2\hbar^2\epsilon_0/Ze^2 m_e$.

Total energy = K.E. + P.E.

$$= (\text{angular momentum})^2/2I - Ze^2/4\pi\epsilon_0 r\ (I = \text{moment of inertia}, m_e r^2)$$

$$= \left(\frac{n^2\hbar^2}{2m_e r^2}\right) - \left(\frac{Ze^2}{4\pi\epsilon_0 r}\right) = \frac{n^2\hbar^2}{2m_e(4\pi n^2\hbar^2\epsilon_0/Ze^2 m_e)^2} - \left(\frac{Ze^2}{4\pi\epsilon_0}\right)\left(\frac{Ze^2 m_e}{4\pi n^2\hbar^2\epsilon_0}\right)$$

$$= -\frac{Z^2e^4 m_e}{32\pi^2\epsilon_0^2\hbar^2}\cdot\frac{1}{n^2} = -\frac{hcR_\infty}{n^2}\ [15.1.21].$$

15.8 (i) Trajectory defined, but this is impossible.
(ii) Angular momentum of a 3-dimensional system is given by $\sqrt{(l(l+1))}\hbar$, not by $n\hbar$. In the Bohr model the ground state possesses angular momentum ($n\hbar$, $n = 1$), but the actual atomic ground state has no angular momentum ($l = 0$). The distribution of the electron is quite different.

Distinguish experimentally between models by (i) showing that there is no angular momentum in the ground state (e.g. by examining magnetic properties), (ii) examining the electron distribution (e.g. by showing that the electron and nucleus do come into contact, Chapter 20).

15.9 $\psi_{1s} = (Z^3/\pi a_0^3)^{\frac{1}{2}} \exp(-Zr/a_0), a_0 = 53$ pm.

RDF: $P = 4\pi r^2 \psi_{1s}^2 = 4\pi r^2 (Z^3/\pi a_0^3)\exp(-2Zr/a_0)$. The most probable distance is the value of r for which the RDF is a maximum [Section 15.1(e)].

$(d/dr)P = 8\pi r(Z^3/\pi a_0^3)e^{-2Zr/a_0} - 8\pi(Z/a_0)r^2(Z^3/\pi a_0^3)e^{-2Zr/a_0} = 0$ at $r = r^*$.

Therefore $1 = Zr^*/a_0$, or $\underline{r^* = a_0/Z}$.

(a) $Z = 2; r^* = a_0/2 = \underline{26\text{ pm}}$,

(b) $Z = 9; r^* = a_0/9 = \underline{5.9\text{ pm}}$.

15.10 $r^* = a_0/Z$ [Problem 15.9] $= (53\text{ pm})/126 = \underline{0.42\text{ pm}}$.

15.11 Angular momentum $= \{l(l+1)\}^{\frac{1}{2}}\hbar$ [Box 14.2].

	s	p	d	f	g	...
Use the identification $l =$	0	1	2	3	4	...

(a) 1s: $l = 0$; (a.m.) $= 0$, N(radial nodes) $= 0$, N(ang. nodes) $= 0$.

(b) 3s: $l = 0$, (a.m.) $= 0$, N(radial) $= 2$, N(ang) $= 0$

(c) 3d: $l = 2$; (a.m.) $= \sqrt{(2.3)}\hbar = \sqrt{6}\,\hbar$, N(radial) $= 0$, N(ang) $= 2$.

(d) 2p: $l = 1$; (a.m.) $= \sqrt{2}\,\hbar$, N(radial) $= 0$, N(ang) $= 1$.

(e) 3p: $l = 1$; (a.m.) $= \sqrt{2}\,\hbar$, N(radial) $= 1$, N(ang) $= 1$.

In general: N(radial) $= n - l - 1$, N(ang) $= l$.

15.12 $\langle r\rangle_{2p} = \int_0^{\pi} r^2 R_{21}(r) r R_{21}(r)\,dr$, $\rho = 2Zr/na_0 = Zr/a_0$; $r = a_0\rho/Z$.

$$\langle r\rangle_{2p} = \left(\frac{Z}{a_0}\right)^3 \left(\frac{1}{2\sqrt{6}}\right)^3 \int_0^{\infty} r^3\rho^2 e^{-\rho}\,dr = \left(\frac{Z}{a_0}\right)^3 \left(\frac{1}{24}\right)\left(\frac{a_0}{Z}\right)^4 \times \int_0^{\infty} \rho^5 e^{-\rho}\,d\rho$$

[Box 15.1].

$$= \left(\frac{1}{24}\right)\left(\frac{a_0}{Z}\right) 5! \left[\int_0^{\infty} x^n e^{-x}dx = n!\right] = \underline{5a_0/Z}.$$

$$\langle r\rangle_{2s} = \int_0^{\infty} r^2 R_{20}(r) r R_{20}(r)\,dr$$

$$= \left(\frac{Z}{a_0}\right)^3 \cdot (\tfrac{1}{8}) \cdot \left(\frac{a_0}{Z}\right)^4 \times \int_0^\infty \rho^3(2-\rho)^2 e^{-\rho} d\rho$$

$$= (a_0/8Z) \int_0^\infty (4\rho^3 - 4\rho^4 + \rho^5) e^{-\rho} d\rho = (a_0/8Z)(4.3! - 4.4! + 5!) = 6a_0/Z.$$

Therefore $\langle r \rangle_{2p} < \langle r \rangle_{2s}$, and the 2p-electron is, an average, closer to the nucleus.

Calculate most probable distance of a 3s-electron by seeking the radius at which the RDF is a maximum. This can be done most easily graphically.

$\text{RDF} \propto 4\pi r^2 R_{30}^2(r) \propto r^2(6 - 6\rho + \rho^2)^2 e^{-\rho}$

$\propto \rho^2(6 - 6\rho + \rho^2)^2 e^{-\rho}$, $\rho = 2Zr/3a_0$ [Box 15.1].

Draw up the following Table

ρ	0	0.3	0.6	1.0	1.3	1.6	2.0	2.3	2.6	3.0
P	0	1.23	1.51	0.37	0.01	0.56	2.17	3.34	4.05	4.03

ρ	3.3	3.6	4.0	4.3	4.6	5.0	5.3	5.6	6.0	6.3
P	3.40	2.47	1.17	0.43	0.04	0.17	0.74	1.64	3.21	4.54

ρ	6.6	7.0	7.3	7.6	8.0	8.3	8.6	9.00	9.3	9.6
P	5.88	7.55	8.64	9.53	10.39	10.78	10.95	10.89	10.64	10.27

ρ	10.0	10.3	10.6	11.0	12.0	13.0	14.0
P	9.61	9.02	8.39	7.52	5.38	3.59	2.27

These points are plotted in Fig. 15.1. The principal maximum lies at $\rho = 8.8$; therefore $r^* = (3a_0/2) \times 8.8 = \underline{700 \text{ pm}}$.

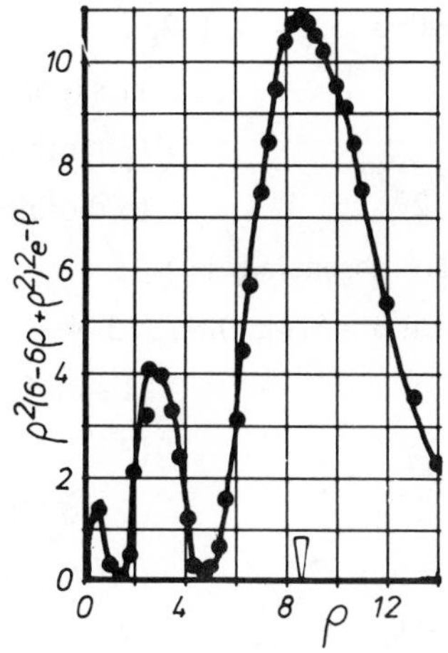

Fig 15.1

15.13 $\psi(r) \propto e^{-\rho/2} = e^{-Zr/a_0}$ [Box 15.1]; $a_0 = 4\pi\epsilon_0\hbar^2/me^2$.

$H = -(\hbar^2/2m)\nabla^2 - Ze^2/4\pi\epsilon_0 r$.

$\nabla^2\psi(r) = [(d^2/dr^2) + (2/r)(d/dr)]\,\psi(r)$ [15.1.7a; $\Lambda\psi = 0$]

$= [(d^2/dr^2) + (2/r)(d/dr)]\, e^{-Zr/a_0}$

$= [(Z/a_0)^2 - (2Z/ra_0)]\,e^{-Zr/a_0}$.

$H\psi = \{-(\hbar^2/2m)\,[(Z/a_0)^2 - (2Z/ra_0)] - (Ze^2/4\pi\epsilon_0 r)\}e^{-Zr/a_0}$

$= \{-(Z^2\hbar^2/2ma_0^2) + (\hbar^2 Z/mra_0) - Z\hbar^2/mra_0\}e^{-Zr/a_0}$

$= -(Z^2\hbar^2/2ma_0^2)\,e^{-Zr/a_0} = -(Z^2\hbar^2/2ma_0^2)\psi$.

Therefore $E_0 = -Z^2\hbar^2/2ma_0^2 = -Z^2me^4/32\pi^2\epsilon_0^2\hbar^2 = -Z^2R_H$ [as in 15.1.15].

In F^{8+}, $Z = 9$ and so $E_0 = -81R_H = -81R_H = -81 \times (13.6\,\text{eV}) = \underline{-1102\,\text{eV}}$.

15.14 The most probable point lies along the z-axis, and is where the radial function has its maximum value (that is where ψ^2 also has its maximum).

$R_{21}(r) \propto \rho e^{-\rho/2}$ [Box 15.1]. This has a maximum value when

$dR/dr = 0$, or $dR/d\rho = 0$ since $\rho = Zr/a_0$.

$dR/dr = (1 - \frac{1}{2}\rho)e^{-\rho/2} = 0$ when $\rho = 2$; therefore $r^* = 2a_0/Z$ and

the point of maximum probability of finding the electron lies at

$z = \pm 2a_0/Z = \underline{\pm 106\,\text{pm}}$.

15.15 $E_n = -R_H/n^2$ [15.1.15].

(a) $E = -R_H$ implies $n = 1$. When $n = 1, l = 0, m_l = 0$ [Section 15.1(c)], and so the level is <u>non-degenerate</u>.

(b) $E = -R_H/9$ implies $n = 3$. When $n = 3, l = 0, 1, 2$.

When $l = 0, m_l = 0$ (1 s-orbital)

When $l = 1, m_l = -1, 0, 1$ (3 p-orbitals)

When $l = 2, m_l = -2, -1, 0, 1, 2$ (5 d-orbitals).

That is $1 + 3 + 5 = 9$ states in all. The degeneracy is $\underline{9}$.

(c) $E = -R_H/25$ implies $n = 5$. When $n = 5, l = 0, 1, 2, 3, 4$.

When $l = 0, m_l = 0$ (1 s-orbital)

When $l = 1, m_l = -1, 0, 1$ (3 p-orbitals)

When $l = 2, m_l = -2, -1, 0, 1, 2$ (5 d-orbitals)

When $l = 3, m_l = -3, -2, -1, 0, 1, 2, 3$ (7 f-orbitals)

When $l = 4, m_l = -4, -3, -2, -1, 0, 1, 2, 3, 4$ (9 g-orbitals).

That is $1 + 3 + 5 + 7 + 9 = \underline{25}$ states in all. The degeneracy is $\underline{25}$.

[In general the degeneracy is n^2. We have ignored spin which, when taken into account (and in the absence of spin-orbit coupling) doubles the degeneracy (to $2n^2$).]

15.16 $\Delta l = \pm 1, \Delta n =$ any integer [Section 15.3(b)]

(a) $2s \rightarrow 1s, \Delta l = 0$; forbidden.

(b) $2p \rightarrow 1s, \Delta l = -1, \Delta n = -1$; allowed.

(c) $3d \rightarrow 2p, \Delta l = -1, \Delta n = -1$; allowed.

(d) $5d \rightarrow 3s, \Delta l = -2$; forbidden.

(e) $5p \rightarrow 3s, \Delta l = -1, \Delta n = -2$; allowed.

15.17 For a given l, there are $2l + 1$ values of m_l, and hence $2l + 1$ orbitals. Each one may be occupied by 2 electrons. Hence the maximum occupancy is $2(2l + 1)$.

(a) 1s: $l = 0; 2(2l + 1) = \underline{2}$. (b) 3p: $l = 1; 2(2l + 1) = \underline{6}$.

(c) 3d: $l = 2; 2(2l + 1) = \underline{10}$. (d) 6g: $l = 4; 2(2l + 1) = \underline{18}$.

15.18 Use the *Aufbau* principle [Section 15.2(a)] with the orbital energies $1s < 2s < 2p < 3s < 3p$.

H $1s^1$

He $1s^2$

Li $K2s^1; K \equiv 1s^2$

Be $K2s^2$

B $K2s^2 2p_x^1$

C $K2s^2 2p_x^1 2p_y^1$

N $K2s^2 2p_x^1 2p_y^1 2p_z^1$

O $K2s^2 2p_x^2 2p_y^1 2p_z^1$

F $K2s^2 2p_x^2 2p_y^2 2p_z^1$

Ne $K2s^2 2p_x^2 2p_y^2 2p_z^2 = K2s^2 2p^6 = KL; L \equiv 2s^2 2p^6$

Na $KL3s^1$

Mg $KL3s^2$

Al $KL3s^2 3p_x^1$

Si $KL3s^2 3p_x^1 3p_y^1$

P $KL3s^2 3p_x^1 3p_y^1 3p_z^1$

S $KL3s^2 3p_x^2 3p_y^1 3p_z^1$

Cl $KL3s^2 3p_x^2 3p_y^2 3p_z^1$

Ar $KL3s^2 3p_x^2 3p_y^2 3p_z^2 = KL3s^2 3p^6 = KLM; M \equiv 3s^2 3p^6$.

For the next period there is a similarity in energy between 4s, 4p, and 3d; hence the transition metals intervene as 3d is filled.

15.19 $(1/\lambda) = K\left(1 - \dfrac{1}{n^2}\right)$, $K = 987\,663\ \text{cm}^{-1}$ [Problem 15.3]; $E_n = -K/n^2$.

Maximum binding energy occurs with $n = 1, E_1 = -K$.

Therefore, ionization energy = $\underline{987\,663\ \text{cm}^{-1},\ 122.5\ \text{eV}}$.

15.20 Refer to Fig. 15.2. $E(1s^2 nd\ ^2D) = -K'/n^2$ [energies hydrogen-like].

Fig 15.2

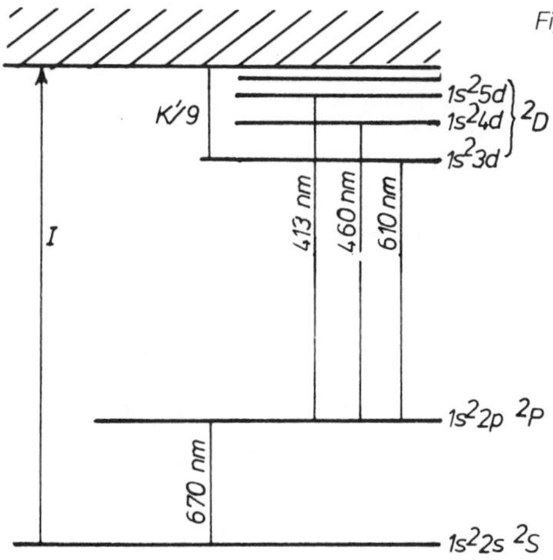

For the $^2D - ^2P$ transitions,

$1/\lambda = |E(1s^2 2p, ^2P)|/hc - K'/n^2$ [$\Delta E = h\nu$]

$|E(1s^2 2p, ^2P)|/hc = (1/\lambda) + K'/n^2$

$= (610.36 \times 10^{-7}\ \text{cm})^{-1} + K'/9$ (a)

$= (460.29 \times 10^{-7}\ \text{cm})^{-1} + K'/16$ (b)

$= (413.23 \times 10^{-7}\ \text{cm})^{-1} + K'/25$ (c)

(b) − (a): $(610.36 \times 10^{-7}\ \text{cm})^{-1} - (460.29 \times 10^{-7}\ \text{cm})^{-1} = K'/16 - K'/9$,

$K' = (5341.66\ \text{cm}^{-1})/(\frac{1}{9} - \frac{1}{16}) = 109\,886\ \text{cm}^{-1}$.

(a) − (c): $(610.36 \times 10^{-7}\ \text{cm})^{-1} - (413.23 \times 10^{-7}\ \text{cm})^{-1} = K'(\frac{1}{25} - \frac{1}{9})$,

$K' = 109\,910\ \text{cm}^{-1}$.

(b) − (c): $(460.29 \times 10^{-7}\ \text{cm})^{-1} - (413.23 \times 10^{-7}\ \text{cm})^{-1} = K'(\frac{1}{25} - \frac{1}{16})$,

$K' = 109\,963\ \text{cm}^{-1}$.

Average value: $K' = 109\,920\ \text{cm}^{-1}$.

The binding energy $E(1s^2 3d, ^2D) = -K'/9 = -12\,213\ \text{cm}^{-1}$.

The binding energy $E(1s^2 2p, ^2P) = (-610.36 \times 10^{-7}\ \text{cm})^{-1} + (12\,213\ \text{cm}^{-1})$

$= -28\,597\ \text{cm}^{-1}$.

The binding energy $E(1s^2 2s, ^2S) = (-670.78 \times 10^{-7}\ \text{cm})^{-1} + (-28\,597\ \text{cm}^{-1})$

$= -43\,505\ \text{cm}^{-1}$.

Therefore ionization energy: $I(1s^2 2s, ^2S) = \underline{43\,505\ \text{cm}^{-1},\ 5.39\ \text{eV}}$.

15.21 $h\nu = \frac{1}{2}m_e v^2 + I$

$\lambda = 58.4\ \text{nm} = 5.84 \times 10^{-6}\ \text{cm}$; $1/\lambda = 1.71 \times 10^5\ \text{cm}^{-1} \mathrel{\hat{=}} 21.2\ \text{eV}$ [end-paper 1].

$I = 21.2\ \text{eV} - \frac{1}{2}m_e v^2$.

(a) Kr, $\frac{1}{2}m_e v^2 = \frac{1}{2} \times (9.110 \times 10^{-31}\ \text{kg}) \times (1.59 \times 10^6\ \text{m s}^{-1})^2$

$= 1.15 \times 10^{-18}\ \text{J} \mathrel{\hat{=}} 7.19\ \text{eV}$.

Therefore $I = 21.2\ \text{eV} - 7.2\ \text{eV} = \underline{14.0\ \text{eV}}$.

(b) Rb, $\frac{1}{2}m_e v^2 = \frac{1}{2} \times (9.110 \times 10^{-31}\ \text{kg}) \times (2.45 \times 10^6\ \text{m s}^{-1})^2$

$= 2.73 \times 10^{-18}\ \text{J} \mathrel{\hat{=}} 17.1\ \text{eV}$.

Therefore $I = 21.2\ \text{eV} - 17.1\ \text{eV} = \underline{4.1\ \text{eV}}$.

15.22 $I_D/I_H = R_D/R_H = [1 + (m_e/m_H)]/[1 + (m_e/m_D)]$ [Problem 15.5]

$$= \frac{1 + (9.109\,53 \times 10^{-31}\ \text{kg})/(1.672\,65 \times 10^{-27}\ \text{kg})}{1 + (9.109\,53 \times 10^{-31}\ \text{kg})/(3.342\,95 \times 10^{-27}\ \text{kg})} = 1.000\,272.$$

Therefore $\underline{I_D = 1.000\,272\, I_H}$.

15.23 $l=3, s=\frac{1}{2}; j=l+s, l+s-1, \ldots |l-s|$ [15.3.1].

$|l-s| = 3-\frac{1}{2}=\frac{5}{2}; l+s=3+\frac{1}{2}=\frac{7}{2}$; therefore $j=\frac{7}{2},\frac{5}{2}$,

$$\text{Magnitude} = \sqrt{(j(j+1))}\hbar = \begin{cases} \sqrt{[\frac{7}{2}(\frac{9}{2})]}\,\hbar = \underline{\frac{3}{2}\sqrt{7}\,\hbar \text{ for } j=\frac{7}{2}} \\ \sqrt{[\frac{5}{2}(\frac{7}{2})]}\hbar = \underline{\frac{1}{2}\sqrt{35}\,\hbar \text{ for } j=\frac{5}{2}}. \end{cases}$$

15.24 $s=\frac{1}{2}, J_{\text{mol}}=20$.

$J_{\text{tot}} = J_{\text{mol}}+s, J_{\text{mol}}+s-1, \ldots, |J_{\text{mol}}-s|$ [15.3.1] $= \underline{41/2, 39/2}$

15.25 $J=j_1+j_2, j_1+j_2-1, \ldots |j_1-j_2|$ [15.2.1]

(a) $j_1=5, j_2=3; j_1+j_2=8; |j_1-j_2|=2$;

$\underline{J=8,7,6,5,4,3,2.}$

(b) $j_1=3, j_2=5; j_1+j_2=8; |j_1-j_2|=2$;

$\underline{J=8,7,6,5,4,3,2.}$

The magnitudes are given by $\hbar\sqrt{\{J(J+1)\}}$

15.26 The ground term is KLM4s^1 $^2S_{\frac{1}{2}}$; the excited term is KLM4p^1 ^2P. The latter has two levels $j=1+\frac{1}{2}, 1-\frac{1}{2}$ which are split by spin-orbit coupling [Section 15.3(a)]. Therefore ascribe the transitions to $^2P_{3/2} \rightarrow {}^2S_{1/2}$ and $^2P_{1/2} \rightarrow {}^2S_{1/2}$ (both of which are allowed). The splitting is equal to $3\lambda/2$ [*Example* 15.5], hence since

$(766.70 \times 10^{-7}\,\text{cm})^{-1} - (770.11 \times 10^{-7}\,\text{cm})^{-1} = 57.75\,\text{cm}^{-1}, \lambda = \underline{38.50\,\text{cm}^{-1}}$.

15.27 $S_{12}=s_1+s_2, s_1+s_2-1, \ldots |s_1-s_2|$ [15.2.1];

$S=S_{12}+s_3, S_{12}+s_3-1, \ldots |S_{12}-s_3|$.

(a) $s_1=\frac{1}{2}, s_2=\frac{1}{2}, \underline{S=1,0.}$

(b) $s_1=\frac{1}{2}, s_2=\frac{1}{2}, s_3=\frac{1}{2}; S_{12}=1,0$;

$$S = \left\{\begin{array}{l} 1+\frac{1}{2}, 1-\frac{1}{2}=\frac{3}{2},\frac{1}{2} \\ 0+\frac{1}{2}=\frac{1}{2} \end{array}\right\} \quad S=\frac{3}{2},\frac{1}{2},\frac{1}{2}.$$

(c) $s_1=\frac{1}{2}, s_2=\frac{1}{2}, s_3=\frac{1}{2}, s_4=\frac{1}{2}. S_{123}=\frac{3}{2},\frac{1}{2},\frac{1}{2}$;

$$S = \left\{\begin{array}{l} \frac{3}{2}+\frac{1}{2}, \frac{3}{2}+\frac{1}{2}-1 = 2,1 \\ \frac{1}{2}+\frac{1}{2}, \frac{1}{2}-\frac{1}{2} = 1,0 \\ \frac{1}{2}+\frac{1}{2}, \frac{1}{2}-\frac{1}{2} = 1,0 \end{array}\right\} \quad S=2,1,1,1,0,0.$$

The multiplicity is $2S+1$ in each case (so long as $S \leqslant L$); each repeated value represents a distinct state.

15.28 $J=L+S, L+S-1, \ldots |L-S|$ [15.3.4]; each J level has $2J+1$ states.

^{1}S: $L = 0, S = 0; J = 0$ i.e. $^1S_0$; $2J + 1 = 1$, 1 state.

^{2}P; $L = 1, S = \frac{1}{2}; J = \frac{3}{2}, \frac{1}{2}$ i.e. $^2P_{3/2}$, $^2P_{1/2}$ with 4, 2 states respectively.

^{3}P, $L = 1, S = 1; J = 2, 1, 0$ i.e. $^3P_2$, $^3P_1$, $^3P_0$ with 5, 3, 1 states respectively.

^{3}D; $L = 2, S = 1; J = 3, 2, 1$ i.e. $^3D_3$, $^3D_2$, $^3D_1$ with 7, 5, 3 states respectively.

^{2}D; $L = 2, S = \frac{1}{2}; J = \frac{5}{2}, \frac{3}{2}$ i.e. $^2D_{5/2}$, $^2D_{3/2}$ with 6, 4 states respectively.

^{1}D; $L = 2, S = 0; J = 2$ i.e. $^1D_2$ with 5 states.

^{4}D; $L = 2, S = \frac{3}{2}; J = \frac{7}{2}, \frac{5}{2}, \frac{3}{2}, \frac{1}{2}$ i.e. $^4D_{7/2}$, $^4D_{5/2}$, $^4D_{3/2}$, $^4D_{1/2}$ with 8, 6, 4, 2 states respectively.

15.29 $\Delta S = 0; \Delta L = \pm 1, 0; \Delta J = \pm 1, 0$ but $J = 0 \not\leftrightarrow J = 0$ [Section 15.3(b)]

^{1}S $\rightarrow$ none ($\Delta S = 0$; ^{1}S $\rightarrow$ ^{1}X; but ^{1}D involves $\Delta L = 2$).

^{2}P $\leftrightarrow$ ^{2}D: $^2P_{3/2} \leftrightarrow {}^2D_{5/2}, {}^2D_{3/2}$; $^2P_{1/2} \leftrightarrow {}^2D_{3/2}$.

^{3}P $\leftrightarrow$ ^{3}D: ($\Delta S = 0$, $\Delta L = 1$): $^3P_2 \leftrightarrow {}^3D_3, {}^3D_2, {}^3D_1$; $^3P_1 \leftrightarrow {}^3D_2, {}^3D_1$; $^3P_0 \leftrightarrow {}^3D_1$

by the ΔJ rule:

^{1}D $\rightarrow$ none, by the $\Delta S = 0$, $\Delta L = 0, \pm 1$ rule.

^{4}D $\rightarrow$ none, by the $\Delta S = 0$ rule.

15.30 (a) Li $1s^2 2s^1$ $S = \frac{1}{2}, L = 0; J = \frac{1}{2}$; $\underline{^2S_{1/2}}$ [Section 15.3(b)]

(b) Na$(1s^2 2s^2 2p^6)3p^1$ $S = \frac{1}{2}, L = 1; J = \frac{3}{2}, \frac{1}{2}$; $\underline{^2P_{3/2}, {}^2P_{1/2}}$.

(c) Sc(. . .)$3d^1$ $S = \frac{1}{2}, L = 2; J = \frac{5}{2}, \frac{3}{2}$; $\underline{^2D_{5/2}, {}^2D_{3/2}}$.

(d) Br(. . .)$4p^5 \equiv$ Br(. . .) $(4p^6)(4p)^{-1}$ [*Example* 15.7]. $S = \frac{1}{2}, L = 1; J = \frac{3}{2}, \frac{1}{2}$; $\underline{^2P_{3/2}, {}^2P_{1/2}}$.

15.31 $E(m_l) = \mu_B m_l B$ [15.3.6] $\mu_B = 0.467\ \text{cm}^{-1}\,\text{T}^{-1}$ [Section 15.3(c)]

$E(m_l + 1) - E(m_l) = \mu_B B = (0.467\ \text{cm}^{-1}\,\text{T}^{-1})B$.

$B = (1\ \text{cm}^{-1})/(0.467\ \text{cm}^{-1}\,\text{T}^{-1}) = \underline{2.14\ \text{T}}$ (21.4 kG).

16. Molecular structure

A16.1 $(1s\sigma)^2\ (1s\sigma^*)^2(2s\sigma)^2\ Li_2$ one bond [Section 16.2(d)], $(1s\sigma)^2(1s\sigma^*)^2(2s\sigma)^2(2s\sigma^*)^2\ Be_2$ no bond, $(1s\sigma)^2(1s\sigma^*)^2(2s\sigma)^2(2s\sigma^*)^2(2p\pi)^4\,C_2$ two bonds.

A16.2 $B_2\,(1s\sigma)^2(1s\sigma^*)^2(2s\sigma)^2(2s\sigma^*)^2(2p\pi)^2$ one bond [Section 16.2(d)], $C_2\,(1s\sigma)^2\,(1s\sigma^*)^2(2s\sigma)^2(2s\sigma^*)^2(2p\pi)^4$ two bonds.

Since more energy is required to break two bonds than to break one, C_2 has the greater bond dissociation energy.

A16.3 $2S+1=2$ and $S=\frac{1}{2}$. The symbol Σ means that the total orbital angular momentum is zero [Section 16.2(e)]. Hence the unpaired electron must be in a $2p\sigma_g$ orbital, and the configuration is:

$(1s\sigma_g)^2(1s\sigma_u^*)^2(2s\sigma_g)^2(2s\sigma_u^*)^2(2p\pi_u)^4(2p\sigma_g)^1$

A16.4 According to Hund's Rule, one $2p\pi_u$ electron and the $2p\sigma_g$ electron are unpaired. The total spin is 1, and the multiplicity is 3. The overall parity is $g \times u = u$ [Section 16.2(e)].

A16.5 The bond orders of NO and O_2 are 2.5 and 2 respectively. Hence NO should have the shorter internuclear distance. In NO, the distance is 115 pm, as contrasted with 121 pm in O_2 [Section 16.2(d)].

A16.6 Since the molecule has one unit of angular momentum and since one electron is in a σ-orbital, the other must be in a π-orbital. The relative stability of the molecule shows that the electrons are in bonding orbitals. Then the σ-orbital is g, and the π-orbital is u. The configuration is $(1s\sigma_g)^1(2p\pi_u)^1$ [Section 16.2(d)]

A16.7 $\int(3^{-\frac{1}{2}})^2(s+2^{\frac{1}{2}}p_x)^2\,d\tau = 3^{-1}[\int s^2\,d\tau + 2^{3/2}\int sp_x\,d\tau + 2\int p_x^2\,d\tau]$
$=3^{-1}[1+0+2(1)] = 1$, since s and p_x are normalized.

A16.8 $\psi_h = 4^{-1}(2\pi a_0^3)^{-\frac{1}{2}}\exp(-\rho/2)3^{-\frac{1}{2}}[(2-\rho)-2^{-\frac{1}{2}}\rho\sin\theta\cos\phi +$
$+\,3^{\frac{1}{2}}2^{-\frac{1}{2}}\rho\sin\theta\sin\phi]$. The two terms depending on θ and ϕ can be written $2^{-\frac{1}{2}}\rho\sin\theta(-\cos\phi+3^{\frac{1}{2}}\sin\phi)$. [Box 15.1].

The unit vector in the specified direction is $-\frac{1}{2}\mathbf{i}_x + (3^{\frac{1}{2}}/2)\mathbf{i}_y$. The projection of $\mathbf{r} = r\sin\theta\cos\phi\mathbf{i}_x + r\sin\theta\sin\phi\mathbf{i}_y + r\cos\theta\mathbf{i}_z$ on the unit vector is $\frac{1}{2}r\sin\theta[-\cos\phi + 3^{\frac{1}{2}}\sin\phi]$.

A16.9 $a^2 = \cos\theta/(\cos\theta - 1)$ [16.3.4] $= (\cos 92.2°)/[\cos 92.2° - 1]$
$= 0.0370$, or 3.7%.

$(a')^2 = (1 + \cos\theta)/(1 - \cos\theta)$ [16.3.5] $= (1 + \cos 92.2°)/(1 - \cos 92.2°)$
$= 0.926$, or 92.6%.

A16.10 $\psi_{2p_x} \propto \cos\phi$ and $\psi_{2p_y} \propto \sin\phi$

$\int_0^{2\pi} \cos\phi \sin\phi \, d\phi = 0$, since $\cos\phi \sin\phi \, d\phi = \frac{1}{2}d(\sin^2\phi)$.

16.1 $\psi_A = \cos(k_1 x)$ measuring x from A, $\psi_B = \cos[k_2(x - R)]$ measuring x from A.
$\psi = \psi_A + \cos(k_1 x) + \cos[k_2(x - R)]$
$= \cos(k_1 x) + \cos(k_2 R)\cos(k_2 x) + \sin(k_2 R)\sin(k_2 x)$
$[\cos(a - b) = \cos a \cos b + \sin a \sin b]$.

(a) $k_1 = k_2 = \pi/2R$: $\cos(k_2 R) = \cos(\pi/2) = 0$; $\sin(k_2 R) = \sin(\pi/2) = 1$.
$\psi(x) = \cos(x\pi/2R) + \sin(x\pi/2R)$.
For the mid'point, $x = R/2$.
$\psi(R/2) = \cos(\pi/4) + \sin(\pi/4) = \sqrt{2}[\cos(\pi/4) = \sin(\pi/4) = 1/\sqrt{2}]$
i.e. constructive interference.

(b) $k_1 = \pi/2R$, $k_2 = 3\pi/2R$; $\cos(k_2 R) = \cos(3\pi/2) = 0$, $\sin(k_2 R) = \sin(3\pi/2) = -1$.
$\psi(x) = \cos(x\pi/2R) - \sin(x\pi/2R)$.
For the mid-point, $x = R/2$:
$\psi(R/2) = \cos(\pi/4) - \sin(\pi/4) = 1/\sqrt{2} - 1/\sqrt{2} = 0$ i.e. destructive interference.

16.2 $\psi \approx 1s_A + 1s_B$ [16.1.4], $1s_A \propto e^{-r/a_0}$ ($r > 0$, and measured from the nucleus).
$\psi \propto e^{-|z|/a_0} + e^{-|z-R|/a_0}$ (with z measured from A along the axis towards B). Draw up the following Table, based on $a_0 = 52.9$ pm, $R = 106$ pm.

z/pm	−100	−80	−60	−40	−20	0	20	40
$\psi \propto$	0.17	0.25	0.37	0.53	0.78	1.13	0.88	0.76

z/pm	60	80	100	120	140	160	180	200
$\psi \propto$	0.74	0.83	1.04	0.87	0.60	0.41	0.28	0.19

This is plotted as ψ_+ in Fig. 16.1

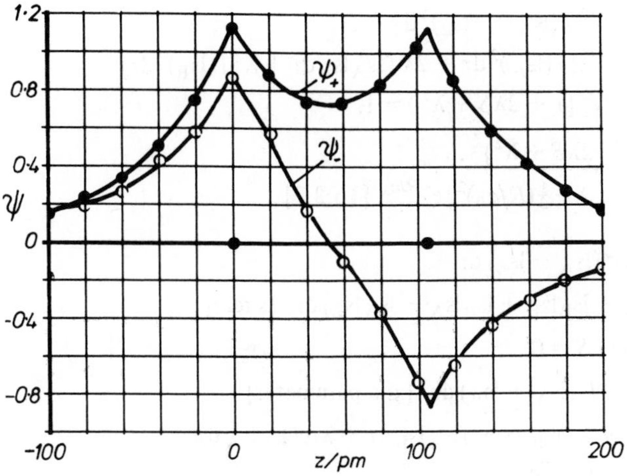

Fig 16.1

16.3 $\psi \approx 1s_A - 1s_B$ [Section 16.1(c)], $1s \propto e^{-r/a_0}$;

$\psi \propto e^{-|z|/a_0} - e^{-|z-R|/a_0}$ (with z measured from A towards B). Draw up the following Table, based on $a_0 = 52.9$ pm, $R = 106$ pm.

z/pm	−100	−80	−60	−40	−20	0	20	40
$\psi \propto$	0.13	0.19	0.28	0.41	0.59	0.87	0.49	0.18

z/pm	60	80	100	120	140	160	180	200
$\psi \propto$	−0.10	−0.39	−0.74	−0.66	−0.45	−0.31	−0.21	−0.15

This is also plotted in Fig. 16.1. Note that the two functions are not normalized.

15.4 Sketch the diagrams shown in Fig. 16.2.

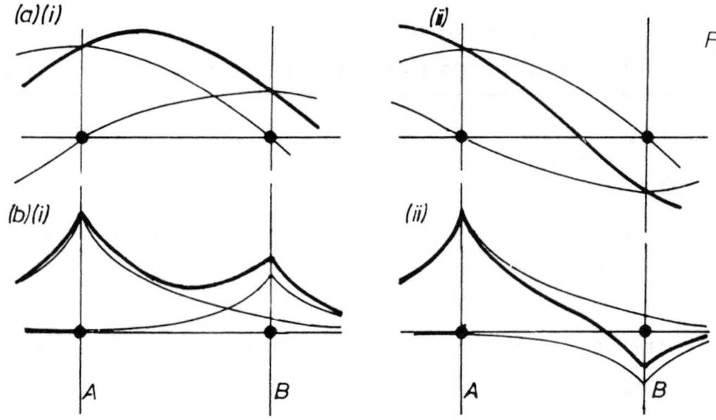

Fig 16.2

16.5 $\int\psi^*\psi\,d\tau = N^2\int(1s_A + \lambda 1s_B)^2\,d\tau$

$$= N^2\{\int(1s_A)^2\,d\tau + 2\lambda\int 1s_A 1s_B\,d\tau + \lambda^2\int(1s_B)^2\,d\tau\}$$

$$= N^2\{1 + 2\lambda S + \lambda^2\} = 1.$$

Hence, $\underline{N = 1/\{1 + 2\lambda S + \lambda^2\}^{\frac{1}{2}}}$,

with $S = \{1 + (R/a_0) + \frac{1}{3}(R/a_0)^2\}e^{-R/a_0}$ [16.2.2].

16.6 $\int(1s_A + 1s_B)^*(1s_A - 1s_B)\,d\tau$

$$= \int\{1s_A 1s_A - 1s_B 1s_B + 1s_B 1s_A - 1s_A 1s_B\}\,d\tau \quad [\text{s real}]$$

$$= 1 - 1 + S - S = 0.$$

$$\int(1s_A + \lambda 1s_B)(\mu 1s_A + 1s_B)\,d\tau \quad [\mu \text{ a parameter}]$$

$$= \mu\int 1s_A^2\,d\tau + \lambda\int 1s_B^2\,d\tau + \int 1s_A 1s_B\,d\tau + \lambda\mu\int 1s_B 1s_A\,d\tau$$

$$= \mu + \lambda + S + \lambda\mu S$$

$$= 0.$$

Hence, $\underline{\mu = -(\lambda + S)/(1 + \lambda S)}$.

16.7 The electron density is $N^2(1s_A \pm 1s_B)^2$. Draw up the following Table using the values of $1s_A \pm 1s_B$ calculated in Problems 16.2-3. Also calculate $\rho = N^2(1s_A^2 + 1s_B^2) = N^2\,[\exp(-2|z|/a_0) + \exp(-2|z - R|/a_0)]$ with $N^2 = 1/9.35 \times 10^5\,\text{pm}^3$ for the independent densities.

z/pm	−100	−80	−60	−40	−20	0	+20	+40
$\rho_+ \times 10^7/\text{pm}^{-3}$	0.19	0.42	0.92	1.89	4.10	8.61	5.22	3.89
$\rho_- \times 10^7/\text{pm}^{-3}$	0.44	0.93	2.03	4.34	9.00	19.6	6.21	0.84
$\rho \times 10^7/\text{pm}^{-3}$	0.25	0.53	1.13	2.40	5.11	10.9	5.44	3.24

z/pm	+60	+80	+100	+120	+140	+160	+180	+200
$\rho_+ \times 10^7/\text{pm}^{-3}$	3.69	4.64	7.29	5.10	2.43	1.13	0.53	0.24
$\rho_- \times 10^7/\text{pm}^{-3}$	0.26	3.93	14.2	11.3	5.23	2.48	1.14	0.58
$\rho \times 10^7/\text{pm}^{-3}$	2.99	4.52	8.77	6.41	3.01	1.41	0.66	0.31

where $\rho_+ = (1s_A + 1s_B)^2/(1218\,\text{pm})^{3/2})^2$, $\rho_- = (1s_A - 1s_B)^2/(622\,\text{pm}^{3/2})^2$, and $\rho = (1s_A{}^2 + 1s_B{}^2)/(9.35 \times 10^5\,\text{pm}^3)$. These points are plotted in Fig. 16.3.

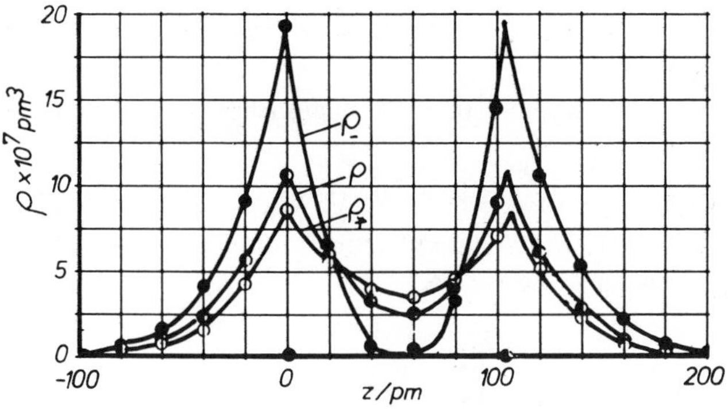

Fig 16.3

16.8 Form $\delta\rho_+ = \rho_+ - \rho$ and $\delta\rho = \rho_- - \rho$. Draw up the following Table based on the figures in Problem 16.7.

z/pm	−100	−80	−60	−40	−20	0	20	40
$\delta\rho_+ \times 10^7/\text{pm}^{-3}$	−0.06	−0.09	−0.11	−0.51	−1.01	−2.3	−0.22	+0.65
$\delta\rho_- \times 10^7/\text{pm}^{-3}$	0.19	0.40	0.90	1.94	3.89	8.7	0.77	−2.40

z/pm	60	80	100	120	140	160	180	200
$\delta\rho_+ \times 10^7/\text{pm}^{-3}$	+0.70	0.12	−1.48	−1.31	−0.58	−0.28	−0.13	−0.07
$\delta\rho_- \times 10^7/\text{pm}^{-3}$	−2.73	−0.59	5.4	4.9	2.22	1.07	0.48	0.27

These points are plotted in Fig. 16.4.

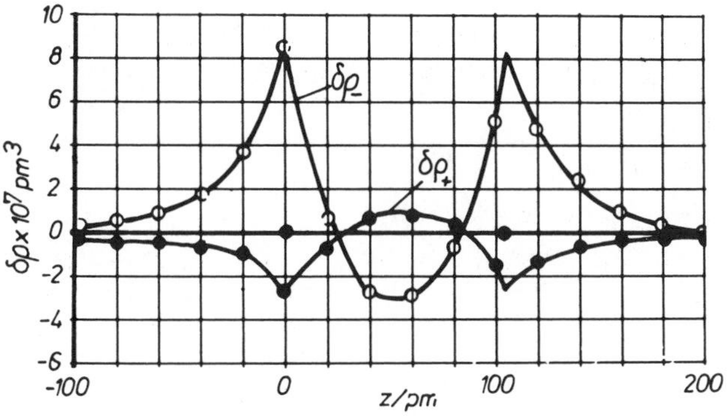

Fig 16.4

16.9 $dP = |\psi^*|^2 d\tau \approx |\psi^*|^2 \delta\tau$, $\delta\tau = 1\ \text{pm}^3$.

(a) From problem 16.7, $\psi_+^2(z=0) = \rho_+(z=0) = 8.6 \times 10^{-7}\text{pm}^{-3}$; therefore, the probability of finding the electron in the volume $\delta\tau$ at nucleus A is $(8.6 \times 10^{-7}\,\text{pm}^{-3}) \times (1\,\text{pm}^3) = \underline{8.6 \times 10^{-7}}$.

(b) By symmetry (or by taking $z = 106$ pm), the probability of finding the electron at nucleus B is also $\underline{8.6 \times 10^{-7}}$.

(c) $\psi_+^2(z = R/2) = 3.7 \times 10^{-7}\,\text{pm}^{-3}$ [Fig. 16.3]; $P = \underline{3.7 \times 10^{-7}}$.

(d) Evaluate $\psi_+ = (1s_A + 1s_B)/(1218\,\text{pm}^{3/2})$ at the appropriate point, which is $r_A = 22.4$ pm, $r_B = 86.6$ pm [see Fig. 16.5].

Fig 16.5

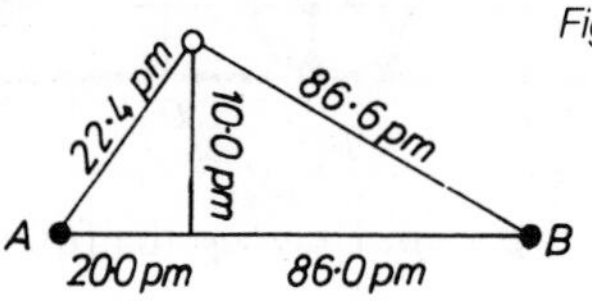

$$\psi_+ = (e^{-r_A/a_0} + e^{-r_B/a_0})/(1218\,\text{pm}^{3/2}) = (e^{-22.4/52.9} + e^{-86.6/52.9})/(1218\,\text{pm}^{3/2})$$
$$= (0.65 + 0.19)/(1218\,\text{pm}^{3/2}) = 6.97 \times 10^{-4}\,\text{pm}^{-3/2};$$

$\psi_+^2 = 4.9 \times 10^{-7}\,\text{pm}^{-3}$; $P = \underline{4.9 \times 10^{-7}}$.

16.10 (a) From Problem 16.7, $\psi_-^2(z = 0) = 19.6 \times 10^{-7}\,\text{pm}^{-3}$;

$P = (19.6 \times 10^{-7}\,\text{pm}^{-3}) \times (1\,\text{pm}^3) = \underline{2.0 \times 10^{-6}}$.

(b) By symmetry, $P = \underline{2.0 \times 10^{-6}}$.

(c) $\psi_-^2(z = R/2) = 0$; $P = \underline{0}$.

(d) Evaluate $\psi_- = (e^{-r_A/a_0} - e^{-r_B/a_0})/(6.22\,\text{pm}^{3/2})$ at the point $r_A = 22.4$ pm, $r_B = 86.6$ pm [Problem 16.9].

$\psi_- = (0.65 - 0.19)/(622\,\text{pm}^{3/2}) = 7.40 \times 10^{-4}\,\text{pm}^{-3/2}$

$\psi_-^2 = 5.47 \times 10^{-7}\,\text{pm}^{-3}$; $P = \underline{5.5 \times 10^{-7}}$.

16.11 $E - E_H = (e^2/4\pi\epsilon_0 R) - [V_1(R) + V_2(R)]/[1 + S(R)]$ with $E_H = -\frac{1}{2}\bar{R}_H$, $\bar{R}_H = me^4/16\pi^2\epsilon_0\hbar^2$ [15.1.2] $= 27.3$ eV. Draw up the following Table, basing it on the data in the question, and using

$$e^2/4\pi\epsilon_0 R = e^2/4\pi\epsilon_0 a_0(R/a_0)$$
$$= e^2/[4\pi\epsilon_0(4\pi\epsilon_0\hbar^2/m_e e^2)(R/a_0)]$$
$$= m_e e^4/[16\pi^2\epsilon_0^2\hbar^2(R/a_0)] = \bar{R}_H/(R/a_0), \text{ so that } (e^2/4\pi\epsilon_0 R)/\bar{R}_H = 1/(R/a_0).$$

R/a_0	0	1	2	3	4	∞
$(e^2/4\pi\epsilon_0 R)/\bar{R}_H$	∞	1	0.500	0.333	0.250	0
$(V_1 + V_2)/\bar{R}_H$	2.000	1.465	0.879	0.529	0.342	0
$(E - E_H)/\bar{R}_H$	∞	0.212	−0.054	−0.059	−0.038	0

The points are plotted in Fig. 16.6. The minimum occurs at $R/a_0 = 2.5$, so that $R = 2.5 \times 52.9$ pm = 130 pm. At that bond length $(E - E_H)/\bar{R}_H = -0.07$, and so $E - E_H = -0.07 \times 27.3$ eV = -1.91 eV. Hence (a) Dissociation energy = 1.9 eV, (b) Equilibrium bond length = 130 pm.

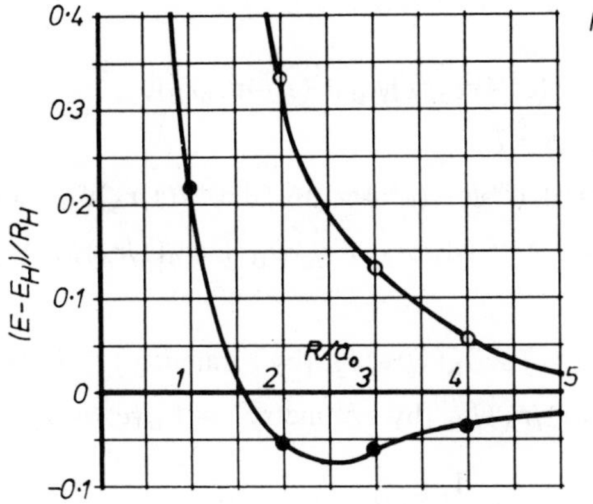

Fig 16.6

16.12 $E - E_H = (e^2/4\pi\epsilon_0 R) - [V_1(R) - V_2(R)]/[1 - S(R)]$.

Draw up the following Table

R/a_0	0	1	2	3	4	∞
$(e^2/4\pi\epsilon_0 R)/\bar{R}_H$	∞	1	0.500	0.333	0.250	0
$(V_1 - V_2)/\bar{R}_H$	0	−0.007	0.067	0.131	0.158	0
$(E - E_H)/\bar{R}_H$	∞	1.049	0.338	0.132	0.055	0

The points are also plotted in Fig. 16.6. V_2 drops off rapidly because it depends on the overlap of $1s_A$ and $1s_B$ [see Problem 16.14].

16.13 $\int \psi^2 d\tau = 1$; $\psi = N(\psi_A + \psi_B)$, $\psi_A = 1s_A$, $\psi_B = 1s_B$.

$$N^2 \int (\psi_A + \psi_B)^2 d\tau = N^2\{\int \psi_A^2 d\tau + \int \psi_B^2 d\tau + 2\int \psi_A \psi_B d\tau\}$$

$$= N^2\{1 + 1 + 2S\} = 1, \text{ where } S = \int \psi_A \psi_B d\tau.$$

$N = 1/\sqrt{[2(1+S)]}$.

$H = -(\hbar^2/2m)\nabla^2 - e^2/4\pi\epsilon_0 r_A - e^2/4\pi\epsilon_0 r_B + e^2/4\pi\epsilon_0 R$.

$H\psi = E\psi$, $\psi = N(\psi_A + \psi_B)$;

$$-(\hbar^2/2m)\nabla^2\psi - (e^2/4\pi\epsilon_0 r_A)\psi - (e^2/4\pi\epsilon_0 r_B)\psi + (e^2/4\pi\epsilon_0 R)\psi = E\psi.$$

Multiply by ψ^* and integrate:

$\int d\tau\psi^*\{(-\hbar^2/2m)\nabla^2 - (e^2/4\pi\epsilon_0 r_A) - (e^2/4\pi\epsilon_0 r_B) + (e^2/4\pi\epsilon_0 R)\}N(\psi_A + \psi_B)$
$= E\int d\tau\psi^*\psi = E.$

Since $-(\hbar^2/2m)\nabla^2\psi_A - (e^2/4\pi\epsilon_0 r_A)\psi_A = E_H\psi_A$,
and $(-\hbar^2/2m)\nabla^2\psi_B - (e^2/4\pi\epsilon_0 r_B)\psi_B = E_H\psi_B$,
the last equation becomes

$N\int d\tau\psi^*\{E_H\psi_A + E_H\psi_B - (e^2/4\pi\epsilon_0 r_A)\psi_B - (e^2/4\pi\epsilon_0 r_B)\psi_A$
$+ (e^2/4\pi\epsilon_0 R)(\psi_A + \psi_B)\} = E,$

$E_H\int d\tau\psi^*\psi + (e^2/4\pi\epsilon_0 R)\int d\tau\psi^*\psi - (e^2/4\pi\epsilon_0)N\int d\tau\psi^*\{(1/r_A)\psi_B + (1/r_B)\psi_A\} = E,$

$E_H + (e^2/4\pi\epsilon_0 R) - (e^2/4\pi\epsilon_0)N^2\int d\tau\{\psi_A(1/r_A)\psi_B + \psi_B(1/r_A)\psi_B + \psi_A(1/r_B)\psi_A$
$+ \psi_B(1/r_B)\psi_A\} = E.$

Then use $\int d\tau\psi_A(1/r_A)\psi_B = \int d\tau\psi_B(1/r_B)\psi_A$ [by symmetry] $= V_2/(e^2/4\pi\epsilon_0)$
$\int d\tau\psi_A(1/r_B)\psi_A = \int d\tau\psi_B(1/r_A)\psi_B$ [by symmetry] $= V_1/(e^2/4\pi\epsilon_0)$.

This gives $E_H + (e^2/4\pi\epsilon_0 R) - \dfrac{1}{(1+S)}(V_1 + V_2) = E,$

or $E = E_H - (V_1 + V_2)/(1 + S) + (e^2/4\pi\epsilon_0 R)$.

16.14 $S = \{1 + (R/a_0) + (R^2/3a_0^2)\}\exp(-R/a_0)$

Draw up the following Table.

R/a_0	0	1	2	3	4	5
S	1.000	0.858	0.586	0.349	0.189	0.097

R/a_0	6	7	8	9	10
S	0.047	0.022	0.010	0.005	0.002

These points are plotted in Fig. 16.7.

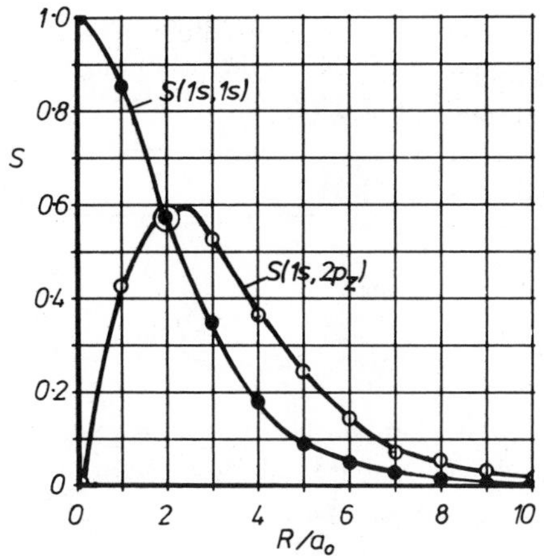

Fig 16.7

16.15 The s-orbital begins to spread into the region of negative amplitude of the p-orbital; when their centers coincide, the positive overlap cancels the negative.

$S = (R/2a_o)\{1 + (R/a_o) + (R^2/3a_o^2)\}\exp(-r/a_o)$

Draw up the following Table

R/a_o	0	1	2	3	4	5
S	0	0.429	0.588	0.523	0.379	0.241

R/a_o	6	7	8	9	10
S	0.141	0.078	0.041	0.021	0.010

These points are also plotted in Fig. 16.7. The maximum occurs at $R/a_o = 2.1$.

16.16 Use the building-up principle, after deciding on the number (n) of electrons to accommodate.

H_2^- $(n = 3)$: $(1s\sigma_g)^2(1s\sigma_u^*)^1$.

N_2 $(n = 14)$: $(1s\sigma_g)^2(1s\sigma_u^*)^2(2s\sigma_g)^2(2s\sigma_u^*)^2(2p\pi_u)^4(2p\sigma_g)^2$.

O_2 $(n = 16)$: $(1s\sigma_g)^2(1s\sigma_u^*)^2(2s\sigma_g)^2(2s\sigma_u^*)^2(2p\pi_u)^4(2p\sigma_g)^2(2p_x\pi_g^*)^1(2p_y\pi_g^*)^1$.

CO $(n = 14)$: $(1s\sigma)^2(1s\sigma^*)^2(2s\sigma)^2(2s\sigma^*)^2(2p\pi)^4(2p\sigma)^2$.

NO $(n = 15)$: $(1s\sigma)^2(1s\sigma^*)^2(2s\sigma)^2(2s\sigma^*)^2(2p\pi)^4(2p\sigma)^2(2p\pi^*).^1$

CN $(n = 13)$: $(1s\sigma)^2(1s\sigma^*)^2(2s\sigma)^2(2s\sigma^*)^2(2p\pi)^4(2p\sigma)^1$.

16.17 Decide whether the electron added or removed occupies a bonding or antibonding orbital. Draw up the following Table of the orbital involved. Refer to Fig. 16.12 of the text, and to Problem 16.16.

	N_2	NO	O_2	C_2	F_2	CN
(a) AB^-	$2p\pi^*$	$2p\pi^*$	$2p\pi^*$	$2p\sigma$	$2p\sigma^*$	$2p\sigma$
(b) AB^+	$2p\sigma$	$2p\pi^*$	$2p\pi^*$	$2p\pi$	$2p\pi^*$	$2p\sigma$

Therefore, C_2, CN are stabilized on formation of the negative ion [in each case a bonding electron is added], while NO, O_2, F_2, are stabilized on formation of the positive ion [in each case an antibonding electron is removed].

16.18 d-orbitals may form σ-orbitals ($d_{z^2} - d_{z^2}$), Fig. 16.8, π-orbitals ($d_{xz} - d_{xz}$, $d_{yz} - d_{yz}$), and δ-orbitals ($d_{xy} - d_{xy}$, $d_{x^2-y^2} - d_{x^2-y^2}$). The order of overlap is $\sigma > \pi > \delta$ and without much justification we take this to be the order of bond strengths. Two electrons may occupy the σ-orbital, 4 the two π-orbitals, and 4 the two δ-orbitals.

(a) $(d\sigma)^2$

(b) $(d\sigma)^2(d\pi)^4$

(c) $(d\sigma)^2(d\pi)^4(d\delta)^2$, ($d\delta^2$ will be $(d_{xy}\delta)^1(d_{x^2-y^2}\delta)^1$).

16.19 The same diagram as Fig. 16.12 of the text may be used. For CO insert 14 electrons; for XeF insert 15 electrons (the 1s, 2s, 2p, 3s, 3p, 3d, 4s, 4p, 4p electrons are too deep to worry about at this elementary level, so regard the configuration of Xe as . . . $(5s)^2(5p)^6$. (In real life, of course, the effect of the 4d-electrons and other inner and outer orbitals is significant.)

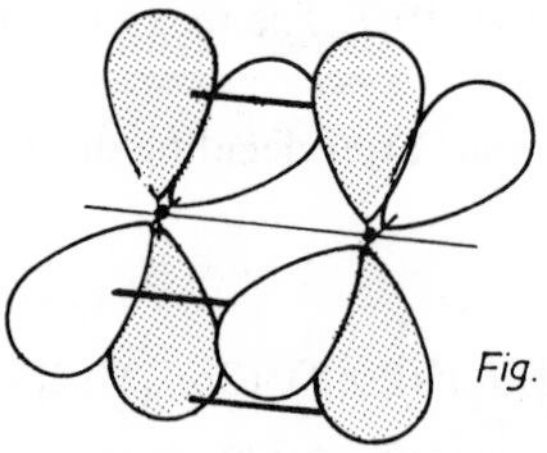

Fig. 16.8

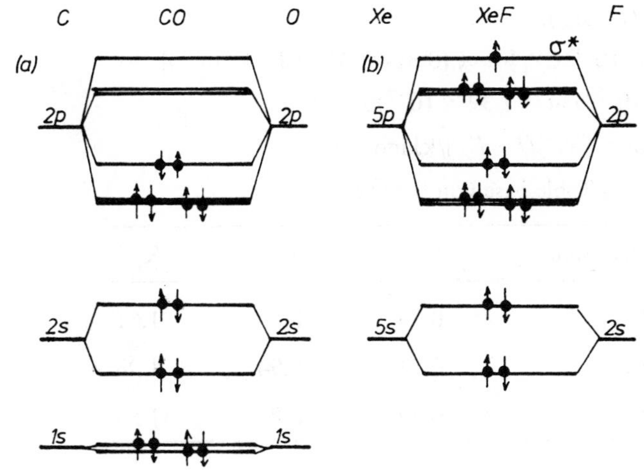

Fig 16.9

XeF^+ is likely to be more stable than XeF because a σ^*-electron is removed.

16.20 Refer to Fig. 16.13 of the text. (a) π^* is g, (b) g, u is inapplicable [no center of symmetry in NO], (c) δ is g [see diagram, Fig. 16.10 (a)], (d) δ^* is u [Fig. 16.10 (b)], (e) the orbitals are u, g, u, g(in order of increasing energy) [take into account the node in the plane of the ring of pπ-orbitals; center of symmetry lies at the center of the ring].

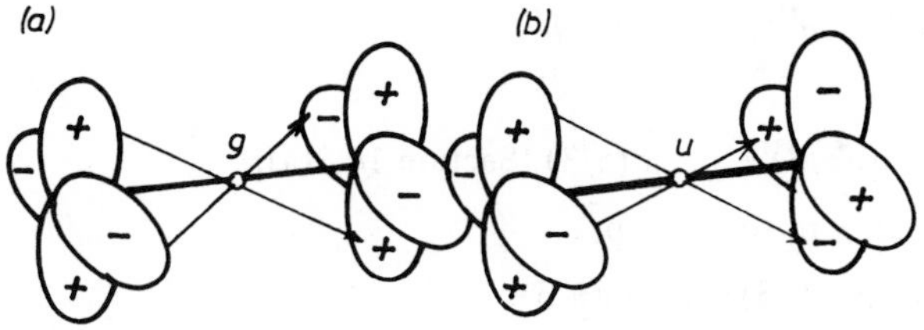

Fig 16.10

16.21 Coulombic energy between two ions separated by a distance R is $V(R) = -e^2/4\pi\epsilon_0 R = -(1.602 \times 10^{-19}\,\mathrm{C})^2/[4\pi \times (8.854 \times 10^{-12}\,\mathrm{J^{-1}\,C^2\,m^{-1}}) \times (294 \times 10^{-12}\,\mathrm{m})]$

$$= -7.85 \times 10^{-19}\,\mathrm{J}.$$

For 1 mol, the energy of separation is $(7.85 \times 10^{-19}\,\mathrm{J}) \times (6.022 \times 10^{23}\,\mathrm{mol^{-1}})$

$$= \underline{472\,\mathrm{kJ\,mol^{-1}}\ (4.89\,\mathrm{eV})}.$$

16.22 Energy required to form M^+: I (ionization energy)

Energy of formation of X^-: $-E_A$ (electron affinity)

Coulombic energy of attraction: $-e^2/4\pi\epsilon_0 R$.

The maximum distance apart at which ion formation will occur is therefore

$R_{max} = (e^2/4\pi\epsilon_0)/(I - E_A)$.

$e^2/4\pi\epsilon_0 = (1.602 \times 10^{-19}\,C)^2/[4\pi \times (8.854 \times 10^{-12}\,J^{-1}\,C^2\,m^{-1})]$

$= 2.31 \times 10^{-28}\,J\,m \mathrel{\hat{=}} 1.39 \times 10^{-7}\,kJ\,mol^{-1}\,m$.

Therefore $R_{max}/nm = 139/[(I - E_A)/kJ\,mol^{-1}]$.

Draw up the following Table based on the data.

R_{max}/nm	Li	Na	K
F	0.74	0.85	1.61
Cl	0.81	0.94	1.98
Br	0.72	0.83	1.53

16.23 Follow the argument in *Example* 16.4, with $\Phi = 2\pi/3$.

$$h = as + bp(\tfrac{1}{2}\Phi) = as + bp(\pi/3)$$

$$h' = a's + b'p\left(\tfrac{1}{2}\Phi + \frac{2\pi}{3}\right) = a's + b'p(\pi)$$

$$h'' = a''s + b''p(-\tfrac{1}{2}\Phi) = a''s + b''p(-\pi/3).$$

Normalization: $a^2 + b^2 = 1$, etc.

Equivalence: $a^2 = a'^2 = a''^2$; $b^2 = b'^2 = b''^2$.

Orthogonality:

Use $p(\pi/3) = p_x\cos(\pi/3) + p_y\sin(\pi/3)$ [Section 16.3(a)].

$p(\pi) = p_x\cos\pi + p_y\sin\pi = -p_x$.

$p(-\pi/3) = p_x\cos(\pi/3) - p_y\sin(\pi/3)$.

$$\int hh'\,d\tau = a^2 - b^2\cos(\pi/3) = a^2 - \tfrac{1}{2}b^2 = 0$$

$$\int h'h''\,d\tau = a^2 - b^2\cos(\pi/3) = a^2 - \tfrac{1}{2}b^2 = 0$$

$$\int hh''\,d\tau = a^2 + b^2\,[\cos^2(\pi/3) - \sin^2(\pi/3)] = a^2 - \tfrac{1}{2}b^2 = 0.$$

Therefore $a = b/\sqrt{2}$, and $a^2 + b^2 = 1$ gives $b = \sqrt{(2/3)}$:

$$h = (1/\sqrt{3})\{s + \sqrt{2}p(\pi/3)\}$$

$$h' = (1/\sqrt{3})\{s + \sqrt{2}p(\pi)\}$$

$$h'' = (1/\sqrt{3})\{s + \sqrt{2}p(-\pi/3)\}.$$

Each bond is therefore $s^{\frac{1}{3}}p^{\frac{2}{3}}$, or '$sp^2$', and there is a perpendicular lone pair of composition p_z^2.

The promotion is $2s^22p^3 \rightarrow (2s^{\frac{1}{3}}2p^{\frac{2}{3}})^3(p^2) = 2s2p^4$, requiring a promotion of <u>one</u> electron.

16.24 Mix the p_z-orbital into the three orbitals constructed in Problem 16.23:

$$h = as + bp, \quad p = p(\pi/3)\sin\Phi + p_z\cos\Phi$$
$$h' = as + bp', \quad p' = p(\pi)\sin\Phi + p_z\cos\Phi$$
$$h'' = as + bp'', \quad p'' = p(-\pi/3)\sin\Phi + p_z\cos\Phi$$
$$h''' = a's + b'p_z \quad \text{[lone pair orbital]}$$

Normalization: $a^2 + b^2 = a'^2 + b'^2 = 1$.

Orthogonality of h'', h''': $aa' + bb'\cos\Phi = 0$

Orthogonality of h, h': $a^2 - b^2\sin^2\Phi\cos(\pi/3) + b^2\cos^2\Phi = 0$.

Therefore $$a^2 = \frac{\sin^2\Phi - 2\cos^2\Phi}{3\sin^2\Phi} \quad [\cos(\pi/3) = 0.5].$$

Since $$\cos\Theta = \tfrac{1}{2}(3\cos^2\Phi - 1) \text{ [trigonometry]}$$

$$a^2 = \frac{\cos\Theta}{\cos\Theta - 1}, \qquad b^2 = 1 - a^2 = \frac{1}{1-\cos\Theta}.$$

Since $aa' + bb'\cos\Phi = 0$, $a^2a'^2 = b^2b'^2\cos^2\Phi$, and so

$$a'^2 = \frac{1 + 2\cos\Theta}{1-\cos\Theta}, \qquad b'^2 = 1 - a'^2 = \frac{3\cos\Theta}{\cos\Theta - 1}.$$

For bonds of composition $s^{a^2}p^{b^2}$(with one electron each) and a lone pair orbital $s^{a'^2}p^{b'^2}$ (with two electrons) the configuration is

$$(s^{a^2}p^{b^2})^3(s^{a'^2}p^{b'^2})^2 = s^{\{(2+\cos\Theta)/(1-\cos\Theta)\}}p^{3\{(1-\cos\Theta)/(1-\cos\Theta)\}}.$$

The promotion, $P(\Theta)$, from s^2p^3 to this configuration is therefore

$$P(\Theta) = 2 - \left\{\frac{2+\cos\Theta}{1-\cos\Theta}\right\} = \frac{3\cos\Theta}{\cos\Theta - 1}.$$

In the case of NH_3, with $\Theta = 106.7°$,

$$P(106.7°) = \frac{3\cos(106.7°)}{\cos(106.7°) - 1} = \underline{0.67},$$

or 67% of an electron is promoted from s to p.

16.25 CO_2: linear. Regard it as a σ-framework formed from sp-hybrids on the C and p_z on the two oxygens, plus a π-framework formed from $C(2p_x) - O(2p_x)$ and $C(2p_y) - O'(2p_y)$.

NO_2: bent. Regard it as isoelectronic with CO_2^-,

The extra electron is accommodated by the molecule bending, so as to give s-character to the lone 'half pair'.

NO_2^+: linear. Isoelectronic with CO_2.

NO_2^-: bent. One more electron than NO_2, so more bending influence.

SO_2: isoelectronic with NO_2^- if inner electrons disregarded; therefore bent.

H_2O: bent [Section 16.3].

H_2O^{2+}: linear [one pair removed].

16.26 Base your answer on NH_3, which is non-planar by virtue of the lone pair [Section 16.3].

NH_3: non-planar [as above].

NH_3^{2+}: planar [lone pair removed].

CH_3: planar, or slightly non-planar [isoelectronic with NH_3^+, which has only half a lone pair].

NO_3^-: planar [effectively isoelectronic with NH_3^{2+} if O^- is regarded as effectively isoelectronic with H].

CO_3^{2-}: planar [isoelectronic with NO_3^-]

16.27 For ethene construct Fig. 16.11(a) from CH_2 (sp^2, p_x).

For ethyne, construct Fig. 16.11(b) from CH(sp, p_x, p_y)

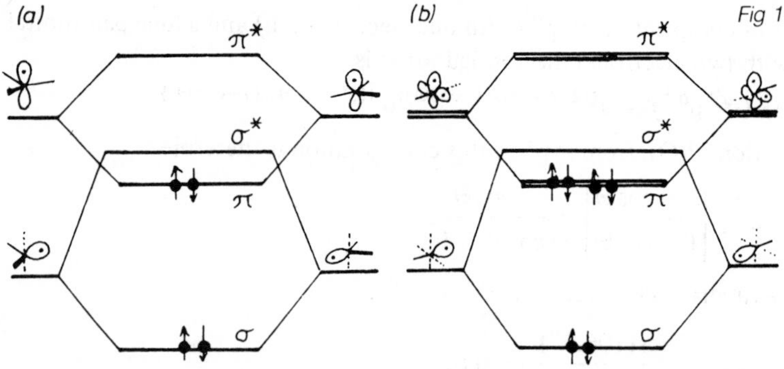

Fig 16.11

16.28 $\left.\begin{array}{l} E_n = n^2h^2/8m_eL^2; n = 1, 2, \ldots \\ \psi_n(x) = (2/L)^{\frac{1}{2}} \sin(n\pi x/L) \end{array}\right\}$ [14.1.9].

Pauli principle: only 2 electrons in each level.

Butadiene: 4 π-electrons

Therefore: 2 occupy ψ_1 (energy E_1), 2 occupy ψ_2 (energy E_2).

$\psi_1 = (2/L)^{\frac{1}{2}} \sin(\pi x/L)$, $\psi_2 = (2/L)^{\frac{1}{2}} \sin(2\pi x/L)$.

Hence the form of the orbitals is that shown in Fig. 16.12.

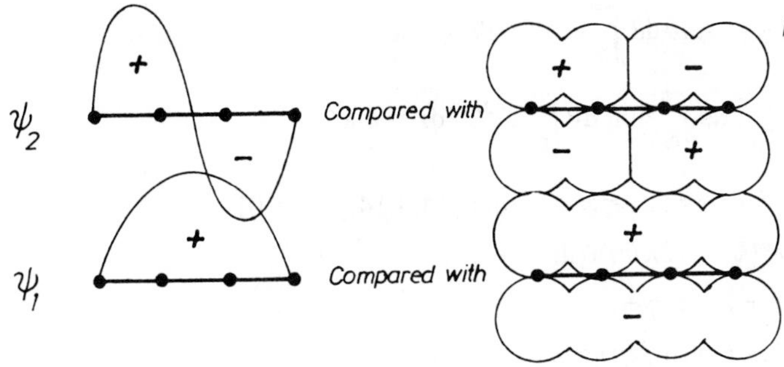

Fig 16.12

16.29 $\Delta E_{\min} = E_3 - E_2$

[ψ_3 is lowest unoccupied orbital (LUMO), ψ_2 is highest occupied orbital (HOMO)].

$\Delta E_{\min} = (h^2/8m_e L^2)(3^2 - 2^2) = 5(h^2/8m_e L^2)$.

16.30 For $CH_2 = CH - CH = CH - CH = CH - CH = CH_2$ there are 8π-electrons, and so the highest occupied orbital (HOMO) is ψ_4, and the lowest unoccupied orbital (LUMO) is ψ_5.

$\Delta E = E_5 - E_4 = (25 - 16)(h^2/8m_e L^2) = 9h^2/8m_e L^2$.

$L = 8R_{cc} = 1120$ pm

$\Delta E = 9 \times (6.626 \times 10^{-34}\,\text{J s})^2/[8 \times (9.110 \times 10^{-31}\,\text{kg}) \times (1.120 \times 10^{-9}\,\text{m})^2]$

$= \underline{4.3 \times 10^{-19}\,\text{J}}$ (2.7 eV).

$\Delta E = h\nu = hc/\lambda$.

$\lambda = hc/\Delta E = (6.26 \times 10^{-34}\,\text{J s}) \times (2.998 \times 10^8\,\text{m s}^{-1})/(4.3 \times 10^{-19}\,\text{J})$

$= 4.6 \times 10^{-7}$ m, 460 nm.

460 nm corresponds to blue light, and so the molecule is predicted to appear orange in white light. The uppermost filled orbital is $\psi_4 \propto \sin(4\pi x/L)$, Fig. 16.13.

Fig 16.13

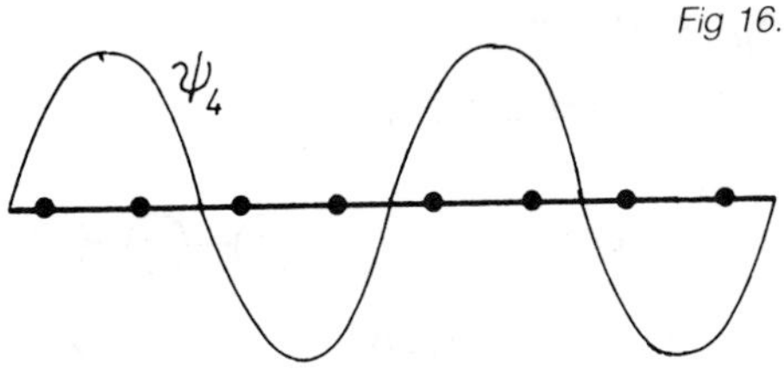

16.31 (a) $\psi = \mathrm{e}^{-kr}, H = -(\hbar^2/2\mu)\nabla^2 - \mathrm{e}^2/4\pi\epsilon_0 r$.

$$\int \psi^*\psi\,\mathrm{d}\tau = \int_0^{2\pi}\mathrm{d}\phi\int_0^{\pi}\sin\theta\,\mathrm{d}\theta\int_0^{\infty}\mathrm{e}^{-2kr}r^2\,\mathrm{d}r = \pi/k^3$$

$$\int \psi^*(1/r)\psi\,\mathrm{d}\tau = \int_0^{2\pi}\mathrm{d}\phi\int_0^{\pi}\sin\theta\,\mathrm{d}\theta\int_0^{\infty}\mathrm{e}^{-2kr}r\,\mathrm{d}r = \pi/k^2$$

$$\begin{aligned}\textstyle\int \psi^*\nabla^2\psi\,\mathrm{d}\tau &= \textstyle\int \psi^*\{(1/r)(\mathrm{d}^2/\mathrm{d}r^2)r\mathrm{e}^{-kr}\}\mathrm{d}\tau \quad [14.3.14, \Lambda\psi = 0]\\ &= \textstyle\int \psi^*\{k^2 - (2k/r)\}\psi\,\mathrm{d}\tau\\ &= \pi/k - 2\pi/k = -\pi/k.\end{aligned}$$

Therefore, $\int \psi^* H\psi\,\mathrm{d}\tau = (\hbar^2/2\mu)(\pi/k) - (e^2/4\pi\epsilon_0)(\pi/k^2)$.

$E = \{(\hbar^2/2\mu)(\pi/k) - (e^2/4\pi\epsilon_0)(\pi/k^2)\}/(\pi/k^3)$ [16.2.4]

$= (\hbar^2/2\mu)k^2 - (e^2/4\pi\epsilon_0)k$.

$\mathrm{d}E/\mathrm{d}k = 2(\hbar^2/2\mu)k - (e^2/4\pi\epsilon_0) = 0$ [16.2.5].

Hence, $k = e^2\mu/4\pi\epsilon_0\hbar^2$, and the optimum energy is

$E = \underline{-e^4\mu/32\pi^2\epsilon_0^2\hbar^2 = -hcR_{\mathrm{H}}}$.

(b) $\psi = \mathrm{e}^{-kr^2}, H = -(\hbar^2/2\mu)\nabla^2 - e^2/4\pi\epsilon_0 r$.

$$\int \psi^*\psi\,\mathrm{d}\tau = \int_0^{2\pi}\mathrm{d}\phi\int_0^{\pi}\sin\theta\,\mathrm{d}\theta\int_0^{\infty}\mathrm{e}^{-2kr^2}r^2\,\mathrm{d}r = (\pi/2)(\pi/2k^3)^{\frac{1}{2}}$$

$$\int \psi^*(1/r)\psi\,\mathrm{d}\tau = \int_0^{2\pi}\mathrm{d}\phi\int_0^{\pi}\sin\theta\,\mathrm{d}\theta\int_0^{\infty}\mathrm{e}^{-2kr}r\,\mathrm{d}r = \pi/k$$

$$\begin{aligned}\int \psi^*\nabla^2\psi\,\mathrm{d}\tau &= -2\int \psi^*(3k - 2k^2r^2)\psi\,\mathrm{d}\tau\\ &= -2\int_0^{2\pi}\mathrm{d}\phi\int_0^{\pi}\sin\theta\,\mathrm{d}\theta\int_0^{\infty}(3kr^2 - 2k^2r^4)\mathrm{e}^{-2kr^2}\,\mathrm{d}r\\ &= -8\pi\{(3k/8)(\pi/2k^3)^{\frac{1}{2}} - (3/16)k^2(\pi/2k^5)^{\frac{1}{2}}\}.\end{aligned}$$

$E = (3/2)(\hbar^2/\mu)k - [e^2/\epsilon_0(2\pi^3)^{\frac{1}{2}}]k^{\frac{1}{2}}$

$\mathrm{d}E/\mathrm{d}k = 0$ when $k = e^4\mu^2/18\pi^3\epsilon_0^2\hbar^4$.

Hence, $E = -e^4\mu/12\pi^3\epsilon_0^2\hbar^2 = \underline{-(8/3\pi)hcR_{\mathrm{H}}}$.

16.32 (a) $\psi = c_{\mathrm{A}}s_{\mathrm{A}} + c_{\mathrm{B}}s_{\mathrm{B}} + c_{\mathrm{C}}s_{\mathrm{C}}$

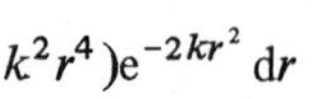

$$\det = \begin{vmatrix}\alpha - E & \beta & 0\\ \beta & \alpha - E & \beta\\ 0 & \beta & \alpha - E\end{vmatrix} = 0.$$

(b) $\psi = c_A s_A + c_B s_B + c_C s_C$

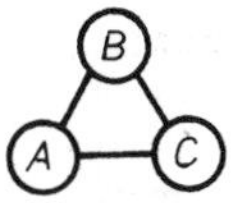

$$\det = \begin{vmatrix} \alpha - E & \beta & \beta \\ \beta & \alpha - E & \beta \\ \beta & \beta & \alpha - E \end{vmatrix} = 0.$$

[The symmetry adapted combinations for (a) are $a_1 = s_B$, $a_2 = s_A + s_C$, $a_3 = s_A - s_C$, which factorizes the determinant to quadratic and linear equations.]

16.33 (a) From the orbital energies [16.4.7] and Fig. 16.28 of the text:

Benzene$^-$: $a_{2u}^2 e_{1g}^4 e_{2u}^1$,

$E_\pi = 2(\alpha + 2\beta) + 4(\alpha + \beta) + (\alpha - \beta) = 7\alpha + 7\beta.$

(b) Benzene$^+$: $a_{2u}^2 e_{1g}^3$

$E_\pi = 2(\alpha + 2\beta) + 3(\alpha + \beta) = 5\alpha + 7\beta.$

16.34 Denote the orbitals H and F. Then the primitive valence bond structure is H(1)F(2). Allow for indistinguishability of electrons, and obtain

(a) $\psi^{\text{cov}} \approx$ H(1)F(2) + H(2)F(1) [16.6.1].

A purely ionic structure H^+F^- is F(1)F(2), and so

(b) $\psi^{\text{ion}} \approx$ F(1)F(2) [16.6.4].

(c) A resonance hybrid of H^+F^- and H–F is written

$\psi = c_1 \psi^{\text{cov}} + c_2 \psi^{\text{ion}}$, with $|c_1|^2 + |c_2|^2 = 1$.

Since $|c_1|^2 = 0.80$, $|c_2|^2 = 0.20$, $c_1 = 0.89$, $c_2 = 0.45$; therefore

$\psi = 0.89$ [H(1)F(2) + H(2)F(1)] + 0.45 [F(1)F(2)].

16.35 Base the answer on a theorem due to Rumer, that the complete set of linearly independent structures is obtained if the atoms are arranged in a circle, and all possible non-crossing bond interconnections are drawn.

For the π-structure of cyclobutadiene first draw

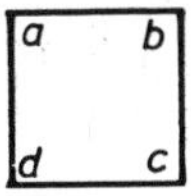

then the two Rumer structures

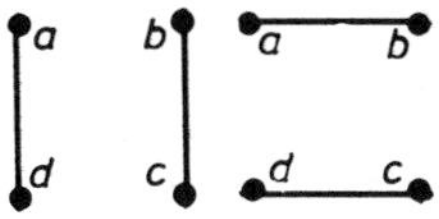

corresponding to

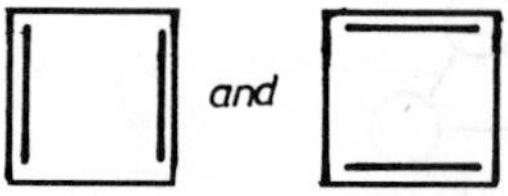

There are also the ionic structures, Fig. 16.14(a), and also doubly ionized structures Fig. 16.14(b), etc.

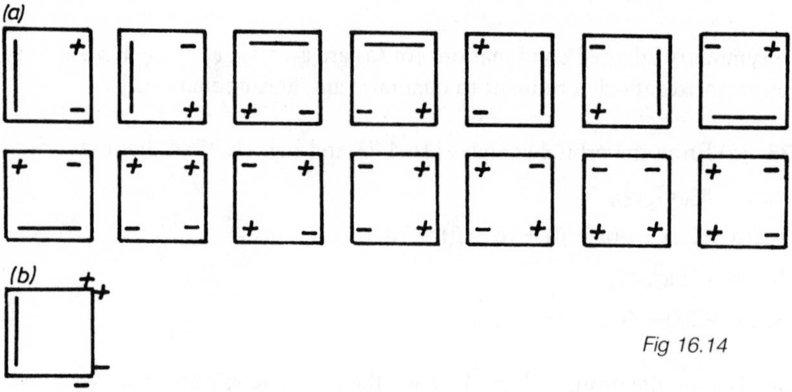

Fig 16.14

16.36 There are 1302 wavefunctions, 40 being wholly covalent, 1260 being singly polar. A selection involving only short bonds is shown in Fig. 16.15.

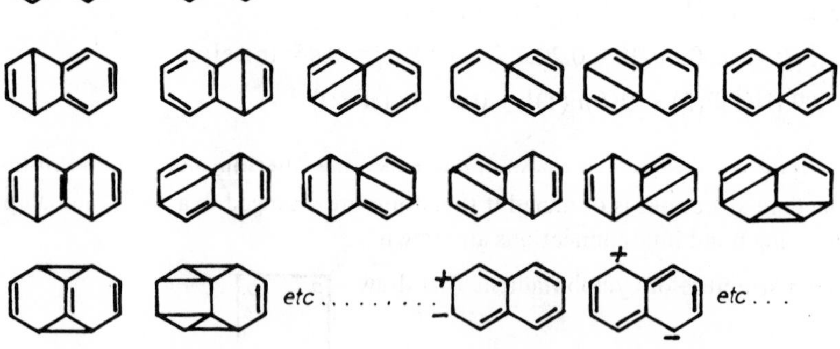

Fig 16.15

17. Symmetry: its description and consequences

A17.1 Four. The number of species of irreducible representations equals the number of classes [Section 17.2(c)].

A17.2 The elements are a C_3 axis and 3 vertical reflection planes. The atoms C and Cl lie on the C_3 axis. Each of the three reflection planes is defined by the positions of C, Cl, and a hydrogen atom [Section 17.1(a)].

A17.3 Only the symmetry groups C_n, C_{nv}, and C_s permit an electric dipole moment. Hence only pyridine, $C_2H_5NO_2$, and CH_3Cl may have moments [Section 17.1(c)].

A17.4

	E	$2C_4$	C_2	$2\sigma_v$	$2\sigma_d$
$f_3 = p_z$	1	1	1	1	1
$f_2 = z$	1	1	1	1	1
$f_2 f_3$	1	1	1	1	1
$f_1 = p_x$	2	0	−2	0	0
$f_1 f_2 f_3$	2	0	−2	0	0

The number of times A_1 appears $= (1/8)(2 + 0 - 2 + 0 + 0) = 0$. Hence the integral must vanish [Section 17.3(a)].

A17.5 [Section 17.3(c)]

	x			y			z		
A_1	1	1	1	1	1	1	1	1	1
	2	−1	0	2	−1	0	1	1	1
A_2	1	1	−1	1	1	−1	1	1	−1
	2	−1	0	2	−1	0	1	1	−1
	E			E			A_2.		

Since A_1 is not present, the transition electric dipole moment is zero.

A17.6 A_1 appears $(1/8)(5+2+1+6+2) = 2$ times, [*Example* 17.5]
A_2 appears $(1/8)(5+2+1-6-2) = 0$ times,
B_1 appears $(1/8)(5-2+1+6-2) = 1$ time,
B_2 appears $(1/8)(5-2+1-6+2) = 0$ times,
E appears $(1/8)(10+0-2+0+0) = 1$ time;

or $2A_1 + B_1 + E$.

The required orbitals are $p_z(A_1)$, $d_{x^2-y^2}(B_1)$, $d_{z^2}(A_1)$, and d_{xz}, d_{yz} (E).
The orbitals $d_{xy}(B_2)$ and (p_x, p_y)(E) cannot be used.

A17.7 Yes. The hybrids span A_1, B_1, and E. The A_1 orbitals, s and p_z, and the E orbitals, (p_x, p_y), have the appropriate symmetry for nonvanishing overlap [Section 17.3(b)].

A17.8 The elements of C_{4v} are E, C_4, C_2, σ_v, and σ_d.

Under E, $xy \to xy$ 1; under C_4, $x \to y, y \to -x, xy \to -xy$ -1;
under C_2, $x \to -x; y \to -y; xy \to xy$ 1; under σ_v, $x \to x, y \to -y$,
$xy \to -xy$ -1; under σ_d, $x \to -y; y \to -x; xy \to xy$ 1.
From the character table for C_{4v}, B_2 is 1, −1, 1, −1, 1.

A17.9 D_{2h} contains the element i. C_{3h} contains the elements C_3 and σ_h, equivalent to S_3. T_h contains the element i. T_d contains the element S_4 [Section 17.1].

A17.10

D_2 first → / second ↓	E	C_2	C_2'	C_2''
E	E	C_2	C_2'	C_2''
C_2	C_2	E	C_2''	C_2'
C_2'	C_2'	C_2''	E	C_2
C_2''	C_2''	C_2'	C_2	E

17.1 List the symmetry elements (the principal ones, not necessarily all the implied elements); then use Section 17.1(b).

Sphere: Rotations through any axis R_3;

Isosceles triangle: E, C_2, $2\sigma_v$; C_{2v}

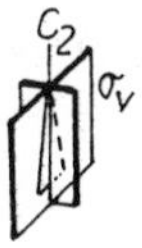

Equilateral triangle: $\underbrace{\underbrace{E, 2C_3, 3C_2}_{D_3}, \sigma_h, 3\sigma_v, 2S_3}_{D_{3h}}$;

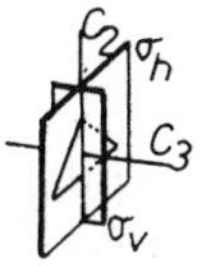

Unsharpened pencil (a uniform cylinder); E, C_∞, ∞C_2, σ_h; $D_{\infty h}$

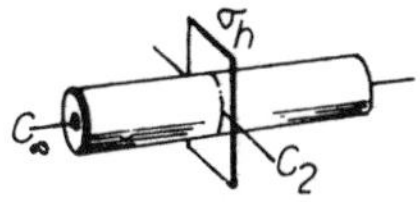

Sharpened pencil: E, C_∞, σ_v, $C_{\infty v}$

Three-bladed propellor: E, $2C_3$, $3C_2$; D_3

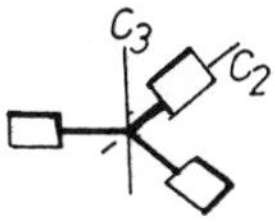

Snowflake: E, $2C_6$, $6C_2$, σ_h; D_{6h}

Table (a square plane on four legs); E, $2C_4$, $2\sigma_v$; C_{4v}

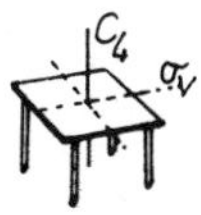

Yourself: E, σ_v (approximately); C_s

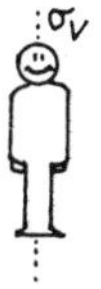

17.2 List the main symmetry elements (not necessarily the implied ones); then use Section 17.1(b) and Box 17.2.

NO_2: E, C_2, $2\sigma_v$; C_{2v}.

CH_3Cl: E, $2C_3$, $3\sigma_v$; C_{3v}.

CCl_3H: as for CH_3Cl; C_{3v}.

$CH_2 = CH_2$: E, C_2, $2C_2'$, σ_h; D_{2h}.

cis $CHCl = CHCl$: E, C_2, $2\sigma_v$; C_{2v}.

trans $CHCl = CHCl$: E, C_2, σ_h; C_{2h}.

naphthalene: E, C_2, $2C_2'$, σ_h; D_{3h}.

anthracene: E, C_2, $2C_2'$, σ_h; D_{2h}.

chlorobenzene: E, C_2, $2\sigma_v$; C_{2v}.

17.3 Staggered CH_3CH_3: $E, 2C_3, 3C_2, 3\sigma_d; \underline{D_{3d}}$ [Fig. 17.12 of the text].

cyclohexane(chair): $E, 2C_3, 3C_2, 3\sigma_d; \underline{D_{3d}}$.

B_2H_6: $E, C_2, 2C_2', \sigma_h; \underline{D_{2h}}$.

CO_2: $E, 2C_\infty, \infty C_2, \sigma_h; \underline{D_{\infty h}}$.

$Co(en)_3^{3+}$: $E, 2C_3, 3C_2; \underline{D_3}$.

S_8(crown): $E, 2C_4, C_2, 4C_2', 4\sigma_d, 2S_8$: $\underline{D_{4d}}$.

17.4 Base the answer on Fig. 17.1. Note that $R^2 = E$ for all the elements of this group, $ER = R$ always, $RR' = R'R$ for this group, $C_2\sigma_h = i$, $\sigma_h i = C_2$, $iC_2 = \sigma_h$.

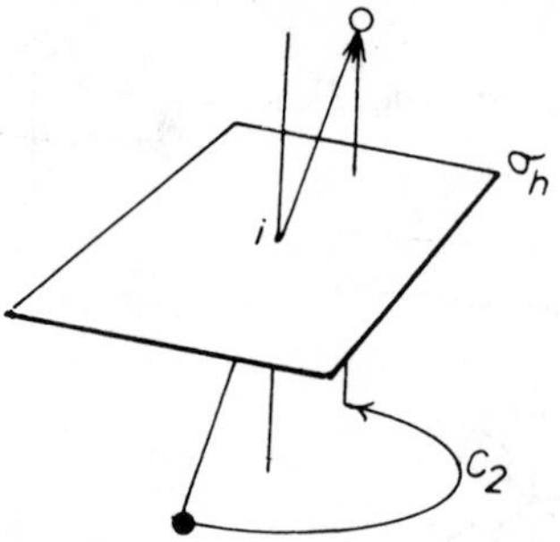

Fig 17.1

	E	C_2	σ_h	i
E	E	C_2	σ_h	i
C_2	C_2	E	i	σ_h
σ_h	σ_h	i	E	C_2
i	i	σ_h	C_2	E

trans CHCl=CHCl belongs to this group [Problem 17.2].

17.5 Consider Fig. 17.2; the effect of σ_h is to generate σ_hP from P, then the effect of C_2 on σ_hP is to generate the point $C_2\sigma_h$P. The same point may be generated by inversion from P, and so $C_2\sigma_h P = iP$ for all points P. Hence $C_2\sigma_h = i$, and i is a member of the group.

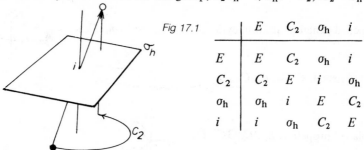

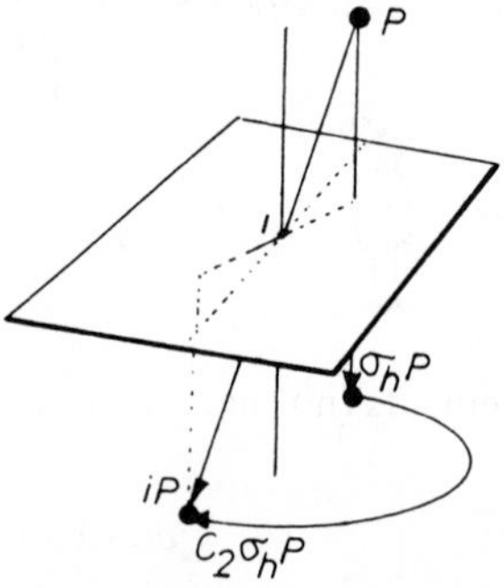

Fig 17.2

17.6 Only molecules belonging to the groups C_n, C_{nv}, C_s may have an electric dipole moment [Section 17.1(c)]. Therefore the molecules of Problems 17.2, 17.3 that may be polar are $NO_2(C_{2v})$, $CH_3Cl(C_{3v})$, $CCl_3H(C_{3v})$, *cis* CHCl=CHCl(C_{2v}), $C_6H_5Cl(C_{2v})$.

17.7 Only molecules lacking an S_n axis may be optically active [Section 17.1(c)]; note that $i \equiv S_2$, and C_{nh} groups all include S_n because they include C_n and σ_h [Section 17.1(c)]. Therefore, only $Co(en)_3^{3+}$ may be optically active, as D_3 does not include S_n. Note that $\sigma = S_1$, and so a mirror plane excludes activity.

17.8 Refer to Fig. 17.3 of the text. Place orbitals h_1, h_2 on the H-atoms, s, p_x, p_y, p_z on the O-atom. z is the C_2 axis, x lies perpendicular to σ_v', y lies perpendicular to σ_v. Draw up the following Table of the effects of the operations on the basis

	E	C	σ_v	σ_v'
h_1	h_1	h_2	h_2	h_1
h_2	h_2	h_1	h_1	h_2
s	s	s	s	s
p_x	p_x	$-p_x$	p_x	$-p_x$
p_y	p_y	$-p_y$	$-p_y$	p_y
p_z	p_z	p_z	p_z	p_z

Express the columns (headed by the operation R) in terms of the original basis according to (new) = (original)$D(R)$, where $D(R)$ is the 6 X 6 representative matrix of R [Section 16.2(a)]. Use the rules of matrix multiplication in Appendix 17.1.

(i) $E(h_1, h_2, s, p_x, p_y, p_z)$

$$= (h_1, h_2, s, p_x, p_y, p_z)\begin{pmatrix} 1 & 0 & 0 & 0 & 0 & 0 \\ 0 & 1 & 0 & 0 & 0 & 0 \\ 0 & 0 & 1 & 0 & 0 & 0 \\ 0 & 0 & 0 & 1 & 0 & 0 \\ 0 & 0 & 0 & 0 & 1 & 0 \\ 0 & 0 & 0 & 0 & 0 & 1 \end{pmatrix} \quad D(E)$$

(ii) $C_2(h_2\ h_1, s, -p_x, -p_y, p_z)$

$$= (h_1, h_2, s, p_x, p_y, p_z)\begin{pmatrix} 0 & 1 & 0 & 0 & 0 & 0 \\ 1 & 0 & 0 & 0 & 0 & 0 \\ 0 & 0 & 1 & 0 & 0 & 0 \\ 0 & 0 & 0 & -1 & 0 & 0 \\ 0 & 0 & 0 & 0 & -1 & 0 \\ 0 & 0 & 0 & 0 & 0 & 1 \end{pmatrix} \quad D(C_2)$$

(iii) $\sigma_v(h_2, h_1, s, p_x, -p_y, p_z)$

$$= (h_1, h_2, s, p_x, p_y, p_z)\begin{pmatrix} 0 & 1 & 0 & 0 & 0 & 0 \\ 1 & 0 & 0 & 0 & 0 & 0 \\ 0 & 0 & 1 & 0 & 0 & 0 \\ 0 & 0 & 0 & 1 & 0 & 0 \\ 0 & 0 & 0 & 0 & -1 & 0 \\ 0 & 0 & 0 & 0 & 0 & 1 \end{pmatrix} \quad D(\sigma_v)$$

(iv) $\sigma_v'(h_1, h_2, s, -p_x, p_y, p_z)$

$$= (h_1, h_2, s, p_x, p_y, p_z)\begin{pmatrix} 1 & 0 & 0 & 0 & 0 & 0 \\ 0 & 1 & 0 & 0 & 0 & 0 \\ 0 & 0 & 1 & 0 & 0 & 0 \\ 0 & 0 & 0 & -1 & 0 & 0 \\ 0 & 0 & 0 & 0 & 1 & 0 \\ 0 & 0 & 0 & 0 & 0 & 1 \end{pmatrix} \quad D(\sigma_v')$$

17.9 To show that $C_2\sigma_v = \sigma_v'$ is correctly represented: $D(C_2)D(\sigma_v) =$

$$\begin{pmatrix} 0 & 1 & 0 & 0 & 0 & 0 \\ 1 & 0 & 0 & 0 & 0 & 0 \\ 0 & 0 & 1 & 0 & 0 & 0 \\ 0 & 0 & 0 & -1 & 0 & 0 \\ 0 & 0 & 0 & 0 & -1 & 0 \\ 0 & 0 & 0 & 0 & 0 & 1 \end{pmatrix} \begin{pmatrix} 0 & 1 & 0 & 0 & 0 & 0 \\ 1 & 0 & 0 & 0 & 0 & 0 \\ 0 & 0 & 1 & 0 & 0 & 0 \\ 0 & 0 & 0 & 1 & 0 & 0 \\ 0 & 0 & 0 & 0 & -1 & 0 \\ 0 & 0 & 0 & 0 & 0 & 1 \end{pmatrix}$$

$$= \begin{pmatrix} 1 & 0 & 0 & 0 & 0 & 0 \\ 0 & 1 & 0 & 0 & 0 & 0 \\ 0 & 0 & 1 & 0 & 0 & 0 \\ 0 & 0 & 0 & -1 & 0 & 0 \\ 0 & 0 & 0 & 0 & 1 & 0 \\ 0 & 0 & 0 & 0 & 0 & 1 \end{pmatrix} = D(\sigma_v').$$

To show that $\sigma_v\sigma_v' = C_2$ is correctly represented: $D(\sigma_v)D(\sigma_v') =$

$$\begin{pmatrix} 0 & 1 & 0 & 0 & 0 & 0 \\ 1 & 0 & 0 & 0 & 0 & 0 \\ 0 & 0 & 1 & 0 & 0 & 0 \\ 0 & 0 & 0 & 1 & 0 & 0 \\ 0 & 0 & 0 & 0 & -1 & 0 \\ 0 & 0 & 0 & 0 & 0 & 1 \end{pmatrix} \begin{pmatrix} 1 & 0 & 0 & 0 & 0 & 0 \\ 0 & 1 & 0 & 0 & 0 & 0 \\ 0 & 0 & 1 & 0 & 0 & 0 \\ 0 & 0 & 0 & -1 & 0 & 0 \\ 0 & 0 & 0 & 0 & 1 & 0 \\ 0 & 0 & 0 & 0 & 0 & 1 \end{pmatrix}$$

$$= \begin{pmatrix} 0 & 1 & 0 & 0 & 0 & 0 \\ 1 & 0 & 0 & 0 & 0 & 0 \\ 0 & 0 & 1 & 0 & 0 & 0 \\ 0 & 0 & 0 & -1 & 0 & 0 \\ 0 & 0 & 0 & 0 & -1 & 0 \\ 0 & 0 & 0 & 0 & 0 & 1 \end{pmatrix} = D(C_2).$$

17.10 Rep 1.: $D(C_3)D(C_2) = 1 \times 1 = 1 = D(C_6)$ of Rep 1.

Rep 2.: $D(C_3)D(C_2) = 1 \times (-1) = -1 = D(C_6)$ of Rep 2.

Rep 1: The representation is either A_1 or A_2 [Character Table], and so $D(\sigma_v) = D(\sigma_d) = +1$ or $D(\sigma_v) = D(\sigma_d) = -1$ respectively.

Rep 2: the representation is either B_1 or B_2 [Character Table], and so $D(\sigma_v) = -D(\sigma_d) = 1$ or $D(\sigma_v) = -D(\sigma_d) = -1$ respectively.

17.11 Refer to the C_{2v} character table. The s-orbital spans A_1 (totally symmetric); the p-orbitals span $A_1(p_z)$, $B_1(p_x)$, $B_2(p_y)$. Therefore, no orbitals span A_2 and so $p_{x1} - p_{x2}$ is a *non-bonding* combination. In the case of sulfur, d-orbitals should be considered. d_{xy} (which transforms as xy [Section 17.3(b)]) is a basis for A_2, and so may have a non-vanishing overlap with $p_{x1} - p_{x2}$.

17.12 The electric dipole transition moment transforms as x, y, z according to the x, y, or z-polarization of the incident light. In C_{2v} x, y, z span B_1, B_2, A_1 respectively [Character Table]. Transitions are allowed if $\int d\tau \psi_f^* \mu \psi_i$ does not vanish [17.3.3]. ψ_i transforms as A_1 [given]. The integral vanishes unless $\Gamma_f \times \Gamma(\mu) \times \Gamma_i = \Gamma(\mu) \times A_1$ contains A_1 [Section 17.3(c)]. Note that $\Gamma(\mu) \times A_1 = \Gamma(\mu)$. $\Gamma_f \times \Gamma(\mu) = A_1$ if $\Gamma_f = \Gamma(\mu)$ in the case of C_{2v}. Therefore x-polarized light may case a transition to a B_1 state, y-polarized light to a B_2 state, and z-polarized light to an A_1 state.

17.13 $\Gamma_f \times \Gamma(\mu) \times \Gamma_i$ must contain A_1 [Section 17.3(c)]

$\Gamma_i = B_1$, $\Gamma(\mu) = \Gamma(\mu_y) = B_2$ [Character Table]

R	E	C_2	σ_v	σ_v'
B_2	1	−1	−1	1
B_1	1	−1	1	−1
$B_2 \times B_1$	1	1	−1	−1 $= A_2$

Hence the upper state is A_2 as $A_2 \times [B_2 \times B_1] = A_2 \times A_2 = A_1$.

17.14 (a) The symmetry group of benzene is D_{6h}, but we can draw conclusions by taking the smaller group C_{6v}. The components of μ transform as $E_1(x, y)$, $A_1(z)$. The ground state is A_1. Note that $E_1 \times A_1 = E_1$ and $A_1 \times A_1 = A_1$. Therefore, the upper state must be E_1 (since $E_1 \times E_1$ contains A_1) or A_1 (since $A_1 \times A_1 = A_1$).

(In D_{6h} μ spans $A_{2u}(z)$, $E_{1u}(x, y)$; the ground state is A_{1g}. Note that $A_{2u} \times A_{1g} = A_{2u}$, $E_{1u} \times A_{1g} = E_{1u}$. Furthermore, $A_{2u} \times A_{2u} = A_{1g}$ and $E_{1u} \times E_{1u} = A_{1g} + A_{2g} + E_{2g}$; therefore the upper state is either A_{2u} or E_{1u}in the D_{6h} classification.)

(b) Naphthalene belongs to C_{2v}. The ground state is A_1. Hence we come to the same conclusions as for NO_2 (Problem 17.11). The upper state reached by the transitions may be A_1 (z-polarization), $B_1(x)$, $B_2(y)$.

17.15 Use the technique specified in the *Comment* of *Example* 17.3.

Under E : All four orbitals are unchanged: $\chi = 4$

C_3: One orbital is unchanged $\chi = 1$

C_2: No orbitals are unchanged $\chi = 0$

S_4: No orbitals are unchanged $\chi = 0$

σ_d: Two orbitals are unchanged $\chi = 2$

The character set 4, 1, 0, 0, 2 spans $A_1 + T_2$. This decomposition is obtained either by inspection or using the technique specified in the *Comment* of *Example* 17.5.

It follows that the Hls-orbitals span A_1 and T_2 in the group T_d.

Inspection of the character table shows that s spans A_1 (totally symmetric, transforms as $r = (x^2 + y^2 + z^2)^{\frac{1}{2}}$) and p_x, p_y, p_z constitute a basis for T_2. Hence the s and p orbitals of the central carbon may form bonds with both bases.

In T_d the *d*-orbitals span E and T_2 (Character Table, final column) and so only the T_2 set (d_{xy}, d_{xz}, d_{yz}) may have a non-vanishing overlap, and so contribute to the bonding.

17.16 (a) C_{3v} symmetry. The Hls-orbitals now span the same irreducible representations as in NH_3, that is $A_1 + A_1 + E$ [Section 17.3(d)] ; there is an extra A_1 orbital because there is a fourth H-atom lying on the C_3 axis] . In C_{3v} the d-orbitals span $A_1 + E + E$ [C_{3v} Character Table, final columns] . Therefore, all five d-orbitals may contribute to the bonding.

(b) C_{2v} symmetry. The Hls-orbitals now span the same irreducible representations as in H_2O, but one of the 'H_2O' fragments is rotated by 90° with respect to the other. Therefore, whereas in H_2O the Hls-orbitals span $A_1 + B_2$ [$H_1 + H_2$; $H_1 - H_2$, see Problem 17.17] , in the distorted methane they span $A_1 + B_2 + A_1 + B_1$ [where the second A_1 is $H_3 + H_4$, B_1 is $H_3 - H_4$] . In C_{2v} the d-orbitals span $2A_1 + B_1 + B_2 + A_2$ [Character Table, final column] . Therefore, all except $d_{xy}(A_2)$ may take part in bonding.

17.17 Proceed as in Section 17.3(d). σ_v and σ_v' are defined in Fig. 17.3 of the text; x is perpendicular to σ_v', y to σ_v.

Original set:	H_1	H_2	O2s	O2p_x	O2p_y	O2p_z
under E	H_1	H_2	O2s	O2p_x	O2p_y	O2p_z
C_2	H_2	H_1	O2s	−O2p_x	−O2p_y	O2p_z
σ_v	H_2	H_1	O2s	O2p_x	−O2p_y	O2p_z
σ_v'	H_1	H_2	O2s	−O2p_x	O2p_y	O2p_z

For A_1 all characters are 1. Therefore steps (i) and (ii) in Section 17.3(d) yield

$2(H_1 + H_2)$	$2(H_1 + H_2)$	4O2s	0	0	4O2p_z

The order of the group is 4. Therefore, step (iii) yields

$\psi(A_1) = \frac{1}{2}(H_1 + H_2)$, $\psi(A_1) = $ O2s, $\psi(A_1) = $ O2p_z.

For A_2 the characters are 1, 1, − 1, − 1 and so step (i) gives

χ	H_1	H_2	O2s	O2p_x	O2p_y	O2p_z
$E(1)$	H_1	H_2	O2s	O2p_x	O2p_y	O2p_z
$C_2(1)$	H_2	H_1	O2s	−O2p_x	−O2p_y	O2p_z
$\sigma_v(-1)$	$-H_2$	$-H_1$	−O2s	−O2p_x	O2p_y	−O2p_z
$\sigma_v'(-1)$	$-H_1$	$-H_2$	−O2s	O2p_x	−O2p_y	−O2p_z
Step (ii):	0	0	0	0	0	0

Therefore, $\psi(A_2)$ is void. For B_1, where the characters are 1, − 1, 1, − 1, step (i) gives

χ	H_1	H_2	O2s	O2p_x	O2p_y	O2p_z
$E(1)$	H_1	H_2	O2s	O2p_x	O2p_y	O2p_z
$C_2(-1)$	$-H_2$	$-H_1$	−O2s	O2p_x	O2p_y	−O2p_z
$\sigma_v(-1)$	H_2	H_1	O2s	O2p_x	−O2p_y	O2p_z
$\sigma_v'(-1)$	$-H_1$	$-H_2$	−O2s	O2p_x	−O2p_y	−O2p_z
Step (ii)	0	0	0	4O2p_x	0	0

Therefore $\psi(B_1) = $ O2p_x.

For B_2, where the characters are 1, −1, −1, 1, step (i) gives

χ	H_1	H_2	O2s	$O2p_x$	$O2p_y$	$O2p_z$
$E(1)$	H_1	H_2	O2s	$O2p_x$	$O2p_y$	$O2p_z$
$C_2(-1)$	$-H_2$	$-H_1$	$-$O2s	$O2p_x$	$O2p_y$	$-O2p_z$
$\sigma_v(-1)$	$-H_2$	$-H_1$	$-$O2s	$-O2p_x$	$O2p_y$	$-O2p_z$
$\sigma_v'(1)$	H_1	H_1	O2s	$-O2p_x$	$O2p_y$	$O2p_z$
Step (ii)	$2(H_1-H_2)$	$2(H_2-H_1)$	0	0	$4O2p_y$	0

Therefore $\psi(B_2)=\frac{1}{2}(H_1-H_2)$, $\psi(B_2)=O2p_y$.
We may therefore form the linear combinations

$$\psi(A_1)=c_H(H_1+H_2)+c_{O1}\psi(O_{2s})+c_{O2}\psi(O_{2p_z})$$

$$\psi(B_1)=\psi(O_{2p_x})$$

$$\psi(B_2)=c_H'(H_1-H_2)+c_{O1}'\psi(O_{2p_y})$$

17.18 Refer to Problem 17.8. Calculate the characters by taking the sums of the diagonal elements:

$\chi(E)=6$ $\chi(C_2)=0$ $\chi(\sigma_v)=2$ $\chi(\sigma_{v'})=4$.

(a) All operations fall in different classes, so we should not necessarily expect equalities among the χs. (σ_v and $\sigma_{v'}$, although both reflections, are in different classes. This comes from the technical definition, that two elements R_1, R_2 are in the same class if and only if they can be related by $RR_1R^{-1}=R_2$, where R is some element of the group. σ_v and $\sigma_{v'}$ cannot be so related in C_{2v}.)

(b), (c) The characters (6, 0, 2, 4) can be expressed as $3A_1+B_1+2B_2$; hence the representation is reducible to these irreducible representations.

17.19 The simplest procedure is to work out the transformation properties by regarding each one as a product, and taking products of the irreducible representations. Transformation properties are listed in the Character Tables.

$f_{z^3}=z(5z^2-3r^2)f(r)$ $\quad f_{z(x^2-y^2)}=z(x^2-y^2)f(r)$

$f_{y^3}=y(5y^2-3r^2)f(r)$ $\quad f_{y(x^2-z^2)}=y(x^2-z^2)f(r)$

$f_{x^3}=x(5x^2-3r^2)f(r)$ $\quad f_{x(z^2-y^2)}=x(z^2-y^2)f(r)$

$f_{xyz}=xyzf(r)$.

(a) C_{2v}. x^2, y^2, z^2 are invariant under all operations of the group, and so f_{z^3} transforms as z (A_1), f_{y^3} as $y(B_2)$, f_{x^3} as $x(B_1)$, and likewise for $f_{z(x^2-y^2)}$ (A_1), $f_{y(x^2-y^2)}$ (B_2), and $f_{x(z^2-y^2)}(B_1)$. The remaining orbital, f_{xyz}, transforms as the product xyz, or $B_1\times B_2\times A_2=A_2$. That is,

$f \rightarrow \underline{2A_1 + A_2 + 2B_1 + 2B_2}$.

(b) C_{3v}. z transforms as A_1; hence f_{z^3} transforms as A_1. From the Character Table $(x^2 - y^2, xy)$ is a basis for E, and so f_{xyz} and $f_{z(x^2-y^2)}$ is a basis for $A_1 \times E = E$. The linear combinations $f_{y^3} + 5f_{y(x^2-z^2)} \propto y$ and $f_{x^3} + 5f_{x(z^2-y^2)} \propto x$ are a basis for E. Likewise, the two orthogonal combinations are another basis for E. That is,

$f \rightarrow \underline{A_1 + 3E}$.

(c) T_d. Make the inspired guess that the f-orbitals are a basis of dimension 3 + 3 + 1. Therefore, the decomposition is A + T + T. Is the A representation A_1 or A_2? The effect of S_4 discriminates. Under S_4 $x \rightarrow y$, $y \rightarrow -x$, $z \rightarrow -z$ and so $xyz \rightarrow y(-x)(-z) = xyz$. The character is 1, and so f_{xyz} spans A_1. Likewise $(x^3, y^3, z^3) \rightarrow (y^3, -x^3, -z^3)$, the trace of the corresponding matrix being $0 + 0 - 1 = -1$. Hence this trio spans T_1. Finally, $\{x(z^2 - y^2), y(z^2 - x^2), z(x^2 - y^2)\} \rightarrow \{y(z^2 - x^2), -x(z^2 - y^2), -z(y^2 - z^2)\}$, resulting in a trace equal to + 1, indicating T_2. Therefore, $f \rightarrow \underline{A_1 + T_1 + T_2}$.

(d) O_h. Anticipate an A + T + T decomposition. Since x, y, and z change sign under inversion, the representations are all u. Under S_4 $xyz \rightarrow xyz$ (as above), and so the representation is A_{2u} [Character Tables]. Under S_4 the (x^3, y^3, z^3) set change to $(y^3, -x^3, -z^3)$, as before, and the character is -1. This indicates T_{1u}. In the same way, the remaining three span T_{2u}. Hence,

$f \rightarrow \underline{A_{2u} + T_{1u} + T_{2u}}$

[NB The shapes of f-orbitals are shown in *J. Chem. Educ.* **62**, 207 (1985).]

17.20 The f-orbitals will break up into sets corresponding to the irreducible representations they span.

(a) T_d. $f \rightarrow T_1 + T_2 + A_1$; therefore there are two triply-degenerate sets (t_1 and t_2) and one non-degenerate (a_1).

(b) O_h. $f \rightarrow T_{1u} + T_{2u} + A_{2u}$; therefore there are also two triply-degenerate sets (t_{1u}, t_{2u}) and one non-degenerate set (a_{2u}).

17.21 (a) In T_d the transition moment transforms as T_2 [Character Table]. We require $\Gamma_f \times T_2 \times \Gamma_i$ to contain A_1 for a transition to be allowed.

(i) $\Gamma_i(d_{z^2}) = E$, $\Gamma_f(d_{xy}) = T_2$; $\Gamma_f \times T_2 \times \Gamma_i = T_2 \times T_2 \times E$.

As $T_2 \times E = \{6, 0, -2, 0, 0\}$, $T_2 \times T_2 \times E = \{18, 0, 2, 0, 0\}$.

Use the recipe in *Example* 17.5 to see if this contains A_1. This gives 1 as the number of times A_1 appears. Therefore the transition $d_{z^2} \rightarrow d_{xy}$ is not forbidden. [See the *Comment* in *Example* 17.7, which remarks that closer analysis of the problem shows that the transition *is* forbidden. 'Closer analysis' means dealing with the representatives themselves, and not just the characters.]

(ii) $\Gamma_i = \Gamma(d_{xy}) = T_2$, $\Gamma_f = \Gamma(f_{xyz}) = A_1$ [Problem 17.19].

$\Gamma_f \times T_2 \times \Gamma_i = A_1 \times T_2 \times T_2 = T_2 \times T_2 = A_1 + E + T_1 + T_2$.

Since the product contains A_1, the transition is allowed.

(b) In O_h the dipole moment transforms as T_{1u} [Character Table; u for a center of symmetry under which μ is antisymmetric].

(i) $\Gamma_i(d_{z^2}) = E_g$, $\Gamma_f(d_{xy}) = T_{2g}$. But $g \times g = g$, and $g \times u = u$; therefore the product $\Gamma_f \times T_{1u} \times \Gamma_i$ cannot transform as A_{1g}, and so the transition is forbidden.

(ii) $\Gamma_i(d_{xy}) = T_{2g}$, $\Gamma_f(f_{xyz}) = A_{2u}$ [Problem 17.19].

$$\Gamma_f \times T_{1u} \times \Gamma_i = A_{2u} \times T_{1u} \times T_{2g} = A_{2u} \times (A_{2u} + E_u + T_{1u} + T_{2u})$$
$$= A_{1g} + E_g + T_{2g} + T_{1g}.$$

The product contains A_{1g}, and so the transition is allowed.

17.22 $l_z = xp_y - yp_x$; find the effect of E, C_3^+, σ_v on l_z using Section 17.2(d).

$El_z = xp_y - yp_x = l_z$.

$\sigma_v l_z = (-x)p_y - y(-p_x) = -l_z$ [p_x transforms like x, p_y transforms like y].

$$C_3^+ l_z = (-\tfrac{1}{2}x + \tfrac{1}{2}\sqrt{3}\,y)(-\tfrac{1}{2}\sqrt{3}\,p_x - \tfrac{1}{2}p_y)$$
$$-(-\tfrac{1}{2}\sqrt{3}x - \tfrac{1}{2}y)(-\tfrac{1}{2}p_x + \tfrac{1}{2}\sqrt{3}\,p_y)$$
$$= \tfrac{1}{4}\sqrt{3}\,xp_x - \tfrac{1}{4}\sqrt{3}\,yp_y - \tfrac{3}{4}yp_x + \tfrac{1}{4}xp_y$$
$$- \tfrac{1}{4}\sqrt{3}\,xp_x + \tfrac{3}{4}xp_y - \tfrac{1}{4}yp_x + \tfrac{1}{4}\sqrt{3}\,yp_y$$
$$= xp_y - yp_x = l_z.$$

The representatives of E, σ_v, and C_3^+ are therefore all one-dimensional matrices with characters 1, − 1, 1 respectively. It follows that l_z is a basis for A_2 [C_{3v} Character Table].

17.23 Translations transform as x, y, z; rotations as R_x, R_y, R_z. Consult the Character Tables.

(a) C_{2v}: x, y, z transform as B_1, B_2, A_1 respectively.
R_x, R_y, R_z transform as B_2, B_1, A_2 respectively.

(b) C_{3v}: (x, y) span E, z transforms as A_1.
(R_x, R_y) span E, R_z transforms as A_2.

(c) C_{6v}: (x, y) span E_1, z transforms as A_1.
(R_x, R_y) span E_1, R_z transforms as A_2.

(d) O_h: (x, y, z) span T_{1u}.
(R_x, R_y, R_z) span T_{1g}.

17.24 The amount of mixing depends on integrals of the form $\int \psi_f^* \mu \psi_i \, d\tau$, where $\psi_i = s$, $\psi_f = p$, d, or f, and μ is the electric dipole moment (which transforms like x, y, or z). Decide whether the integral vanishes.

(a) O_h. s transforms as A_{1g}, μ transforms as T_{1u} [Character Table]. ψ_f must be u, because u $\times$ g $\times$ u = g. p, f-orbitals have u symmetry. Therefore, they must be considered.

(b) T_d. There is no center of inversion, and so the u, g classification is irrelevant. Therefore use p, d, and f-orbitals.

17.25 (a) The ground state of NO_2 has A_1 symmetry [Problem 17.12]. When the field is along *x, y, z* it transforms as B_2, B_1, A_2 respectively, and so it tends to mix in states that transform as $A_1 \times B_2 = B_2$, $A_1 \times B_1 = B_1$, $A_1 \times A_2 = A_2$ respectively [because in C_{2v} $\Gamma^2 = A_1$ for all Γ, and so, for example, $\Gamma \times A_1 \times B_2$ requires $\Gamma = B_2$ if the product is to contain A_1].

(b) The ground state is T_{2g}. In O_h the rotations transform as T_{1g}. Find Γ_f from the requirement that $\Gamma_f \times T_{1g} \times T_{2g}$ contains A_{1g}.

$T_{1g} \times T_{2g} = A_{2g} + E_g + T_{1g} + T_{2g}$.

Hence with Γ_f identified as A_{2g}, E_g, T_{1g}, and T_{2g} the overall product contains A_{1g}.

(c) The ground state is A_{1g}. Treat it as C_{6v}, so that the ground state simplifies to A_1. The effect of the field transforms as R_z, or A_2. Hence the state mixed in is Γ_f, such that $\Gamma_f \times A_2 \times A_1$ contains A_1. Since $A_2 \times A_1 = A_2$, and $A_2 \times A_2 = A_1$, $\Gamma_f = A_2$.

17.26 $I = \int_{-a}^{a} f_1 f_2 \, d\theta = \int_{-a}^{a} \sin\theta \cos\theta \, d\theta.$

Draw up the following Table:

	$\sin\theta$	$\cos\theta$
E	$\sin\theta$	$\cos\theta$
σ_h	$-\sin\theta$	$\cos\theta$

Clearly, $\sin\theta$ spans a representation with the characters 1, -1 (i.e. A″) while $\cos\theta$ spans one with characters 1, 1 (i.e. A′). Since $\sin\theta$ and $\cos\theta$ span different irreducible representations, the integral vanishes [Section 17.3(a)]. If the range of integration is not symmetrical, the reflection σ_h is not a symmetry element, and so the group C_s is irrelevant.

17.27 (a) xyz is antisymmetric under $z \to -z$ (or $x \to -x$, $y \to -y$), and so its integral along z (or x, or y) vanishes. Hence the volume integral vanishes.

(b) xyz transforms as A_1, and so the integral $\int xyz \, d\tau$ transforms as A_1, hence it need not vanish.

(c) xyz is antisymmetric under $z \to -z$, and so xyz cannot transform as A_{1g} in D_{6h}. Hence its integral must vanish.

17.28 Refer to Fig. 17.3.

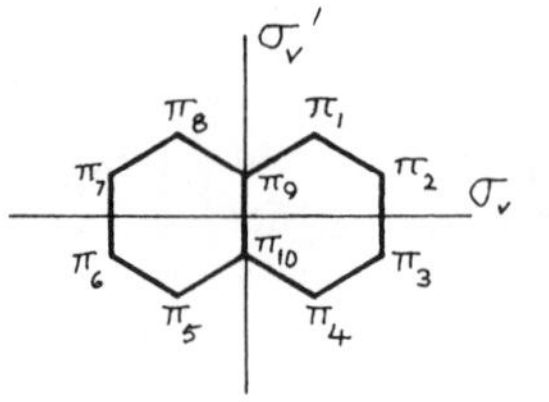

Fig 17.3

Draw up the following Table:

	π_1	π_2	π_3	π_4	π_5	π_6	π_7	π_8	π_9	π_{10}	χ
E	π_1	π_2	π_3	π_4	π_5	π_6	π_7	π_8	π_9	π_{10}	10
C_2	π_5	π_6	π_7	π_8	π_1	π_2	π_3	π_4	π_{10}	π_9	0
σ_v	π_4	π_3	π_2	π_1	π_8	π_7	π_6	π_5	π_{10}	π_9	0
σ_v'	π_8	π_7	π_6	π_5	π_4	π_3	π_2	π_1	π_9	π_{10}	2

[χ obtained from numbers of unchanged orbitals.] The character set {10, 0, 0, 2} decomposes as $3A_1 + 2A_2 + 2B_1 + 3B_2$. Form symmetry adapted contributions as explained in Section 17.3(d):

$\pi(A_1) = \pi_1 + \pi_4 + \pi_5 + \pi_8$ [from column 1]

$\pi(A_1) = \pi_2 + \pi_3 + \pi_6 + \pi_7$ [column 2]

$\pi(A_1) = \pi_9 + \pi_{10}$ [column 9]

$\pi(A_2) = \pi_1 + \pi_5 - \pi_4 - \pi_8$ [column 1]

$\pi(A_2) = \pi_2 + \pi_6 - \pi_3 - \pi_7$ [column 2]

$\pi(B_1) = \pi_1 - \pi_5 + \pi_4 - \pi_8$ [column 1]

$\pi(B_1) = \pi_2 - \pi_6 + \pi_3 - \pi_7$ [column 2]

$\pi(B_2) = \pi_1 - \pi_5 - \pi_4 + \pi_8$ [column 1]

$\pi(B_2) = \pi_2 - \pi_6 - \pi_3 + \pi_7$ [column 2]

$\pi(B_2) = \pi_9 - \pi_{10}$ [column 9]

17.29 Draw up the following Table

	N2s	N2p$_x$	N2p$_y$	N2p$_z$	O2p$_x$	O2p$_y$	O2p$_z$	O′2p$_x$	O′2p$_y$	O′2p$_z$	χ
E	N2s	N2p$_x$	N2p$_y$	N2p$_z$	O2p$_x$	O2p$_y$	O2p$_z$	O′2p$_x$	O′2p$_y$	O′2p$_z$	10
C_2	N2s	−N2p$_x$	−N2p$_y$	N2p$_z$	−O′2p$_x$	−O′2p$_y$	O′2p$_z$	−O2p$_x$	−O2p$_y$	O2p$_z$	0
σ_v	N2s	N2p$_x$	−N2p$_y$	N2p$_z$	O′2p$_x$	−O′2p$_y$	O′2p$_z$	O2p$_x$	−O2p$_y$	O2p$_z$	2
σ_v'	N2s	−N2p$_x$	N2p$_y$	N2p$_z$	−O2p$_x$	O2p$_y$	O2p$_z$	−O′2p$_x$	O′2p$_y$	O′2p$_z$	4

The character set {10, 0, 2, 4} decomposes into $4A_1 + 2B_1 + 3B_2 + A_2$. Form symmetry adapted linear combinations as described in Section 17.3(d):

$\psi(A_1) = N2s$ [column 1]
$\psi(A_1) = N2p_z$ [column 4]
$\psi(A_1) = O2p_z + O'2p_z$ [column 7]
$\psi(A_1) = O2p_y - O'2p_y$ [column 9]

$\psi(B_1) = N2p_x$ [column 2]
$\psi(B_1) = O2p_x + O'2p_y$ [column 5]

$\psi(B_2) = N2p_y$ [column 3]
$\psi(B_2) = O2p_y + O'2p_y$ [column 6]
$\psi(B_2) = O2p_z - O'2p_z$ [column 7]

$\psi(A_2) = O2p_x - O'2p_x$ [column 5]

17.30 H (the hamiltonian) transforms as A_1; therefore all integrals of the form $\int\psi' H\psi\,d\tau$ vanish unless ψ' and ψ belong to the same symmetry species [Section 17.3(a)]. The MOs constructed in the text span different irreps, and so the 6×6 secular determinant factorizes into $1 + 2 + 2 + 1$ dimensional determinants.

18. Determination of molecular structure: rotational and vibrational spectra

A18.1 $\mu^{-1} = m_1^{-1} + m_2^{-1}$ [18.3.2].

$^1H^{35}Cl$: $\mu = (1^{-1} + 35^{-1})^{-1}(1.66 \times 10^{-27}\,kg) = \underline{1.6 \times 10^{-27}\,kg}$;

^1H contributes the greater part.

$^2H^{35}Cl$: $\mu = (2^{-1} + 35^{-1})^{-1}(1.66 \times 10^{-27}\,kg) = \underline{3.1 \times 10^{-27}\,kg}$;

^2H contributes the greater part.

$^{133}Cs^{35}Cl$: $\mu = (133^{-1} + 35^{-1})^{-1}\,(1.66 \times 10^{-27}\,kg) = \underline{4.6 \times 10^{-26}\,kg}$;

^{35}Cl contributes the greater part.

A18.2 $I = m_1 m_2 (m_1 + m_2)^{-1} R^2$ [Box 18.1].

$$= (79)(81)(79 + 81)^{-1}(1.660 \times 10^{-27}\,kg)(0.228 \times 10^{-9}\,m)^2$$

$$= \underline{3.45 \times 10^{-45}\,kg\,m^2}.$$

A18.3 $I = h/(8\pi^2 cB)$ [18.2.3]

$$= (6.63 \times 10^{-34}\,J\,s)(1/8\pi^2)(3.0 \times 10^8\,m/s)^{-1}(11.42\,m^{-1})^{-1}$$

$$= \underline{2.45 \times 10^{-45}\,kg\,m^2}.$$

A18.4 In the transition, J changes from 0 to 2. Find B in Table 18.1.

$\tilde{\nu} = 2648.98\,cm^{-1} + (8.465\,cm^{-1})[(3)(4) - (2)(3)] = \underline{2598.19\,cm^{-1}}.$

A18.5 In this transition, v changes from 0 to 1, and J changes from 2 to 3. Use the data in Tables 18.1 and 18.2.

$\tilde{\nu} = 2648.98\,cm^{-1} + (8.465\,cm^{-1})\,[(3)(4) - (2)(3)] = \underline{2598.19\,cm^{-1}}.$

A18.6 $\mu_{35} = 23(35)/(23 + 35) = 13.9$, [18.3.2]

$\mu_{37} = 23(37)/(23 + 37) = 14.2.$

Since $\omega = (k/\mu)^{\frac{1}{2}}$, $|\Delta\omega/\omega| = \frac{1}{2}|\Delta\mu/\mu| = \frac{1}{2}(0.3)/(13.9) = \underline{1.1\,\%}.$

A18.7 $\omega = 2\pi\nu = 2\pi c\lambda^{-1} = 2\pi \times (2.998 \times 10^8\,m/s)(5.649 \times 10^4\,m^{-1})$

$$= \underline{1.064 \times 10^{14}\,s^{-1}}.$$

$k = \mu\omega^2 = (35/2)(1.66 \times 10^{-27}\,\text{kg})(1.065 \times 10^{14}\,\text{s}^{-1})^2 = \underline{330\,\text{N m}^{-1}}$ [14.2.4].

A18.8 For the first harmonics, $\Delta v = \pm 1$. The highest wavenumber (1 to 9) is $\tilde{\nu} - 2x_e\tilde{\nu} = 384.3 - 2(1.5) = 381.3\,\text{cm}^{-1}$. The second highest wavenumber (2 to 1) is $\tilde{\nu} - 4x_e\tilde{\nu} = 384.3 - 4(1.5) = \underline{378.3\,\text{cm}^{-1}}$ [18.3.14].

A18.9 Zero point energy $\hat{=} \frac{1}{2}(\omega - \frac{1}{2}\omega x_e)$ [18.3.6]

$$= 0.5(384.3 - 0.7) = \underline{191.8\,\text{cm}^{-1}}.$$

$D_e = D_0 + 191.8\,\text{cm}^{-1} = 2.153\,\text{eV}(8065.5\,\text{cm}^{-1}/\text{eV}) + 191.8\,\text{cm}^{-1}$ [18.3.14]

$= 1.756 \times 10^4\,\text{cm}^{-1}$, or $\underline{2.177\,\text{eV}}$.

A18.10 Use the character table for C_{2v} [*Example* 18.8]. The rotations are A_2, B_1, and B_2. The translations are A_1, B_1, and B_2. Hence the normal vibrations are $4A_1 + A_2 + 2B_1 + 2B_2$. A_1, B_1, and B_2 are infrared active, since they transform as do translations. All modes are Raman active, since they transform as quadratic forms.

18.1 Select those with permanent dipole moments [Section 18.1(b)]. They are HCl, CH_3Cl, CH_2Cl_2, H_2O, H_2O_2, NH_3, NH_4Cl (rotation occurs in the gas phase).

18.2 Select those in which a vibration may lead to a change of dipole moment [Section 18.1(b)]. They are HCl, CO_2, H_2O, CH_3CH_3, CH_4, CH_3Cl, N_3^-. (Take account of the possibility that a symmetrical molecule may bend, e.g. CO_2, and that individual bonds may stretch.)

18.3 Select those in which a rotation changes the polarizability of the molecule (i.e. molecules that have anisotropic polarizabilities) [Section 18.2(b)]. They are H_2, HCl, CH_3Cl, CH_2Cl_2, CH_3CH_3, H_2O.

18.4 Select those in which a vibration changes the polarizability of the molecule [Section 18.3(c)]. All are active.

18.5 $\lambda_{obs} = (1 + v/c)\lambda$ [Section 18.1(c)] ($v > 0$ for recession, $v < 0$ for approach).

50 m.p.h. $\hat{=}$ $(50 \times 1760 \times 36 \times 2.54 \times 10^{-2}\,\text{m})/(3600\,\text{s}) = 22.4\,\text{m s}^{-1}$;

$\lambda_{obs} = \{1 - (22.4\,\text{m s}^{-1})/(2.998 \times 10^8\,\text{m s}^{-1})\}(660\,\text{nm})$

$= 0.999\,999\,925 \times (660\,\text{nm})$.

$v = c\{(\lambda_0/\lambda) - 1\} = (2.998 \times 10^8\,\text{m s}^{-1}) \times \{(520\,\text{nm}/660\,\text{nm}) - 1\}$

$$= -6.36 \times 10^7\,\text{m s}^{-1} \hat{=} -1.42 \times 10^8\,\text{m.p.h.}$$

[Since $v \approx c$, the relativistic expression $\nu = \sqrt{\{[1 - (v/c)]/[1 + (v/c)]\}}\nu_0$ should really be used. This gives $-7.02 \times 10^7\,\text{m s}^{-}$.]

18.6 $v = c\{(\lambda_0/\lambda) - 1\}$ [Problem 18.5], $\Delta\lambda = 2(\lambda/c)(2kT\ln 2/m)^{\frac{1}{2}}$ [18.1.5].

$v = (2.998 \times 10^8\,\mathrm{m\,s^{-1}}) \times \{(706.5\,\mathrm{nm}/654.2\,\mathrm{nm}) - 1\}$

$= \underline{2.4 \times 10^4\,\mathrm{km\,s^{-1}}}$.

$T = (m/2k\ln 2)(c\Delta\lambda/2\lambda)^2$

$$= \left(\frac{48 \times 1.661 \times 10^{-27}\,\mathrm{kg}}{2 \times (1.381 \times 10^{-23}\,\mathrm{J\,K^{-1}})\ln 2}\right) \times \left(\frac{(2.998 \times 10^8\,\mathrm{m\,s^{-1}}) \times (61.8 \times 10^{-12}\,\mathrm{m})}{2 \times (654.2 \times 10^{-9}\,\mathrm{m})}\right)^2$$

$= (4.164 \times 10^{-3}\,\mathrm{kg\,J^{-1}\,K}) \times (2.005 \times 10^8\,\mathrm{m^2\,s^{-1}}) = \underline{8.4 \times 10^5\,\mathrm{K}}.$

18.7 $\Delta\lambda/\lambda = (2/c)(2kT\ln 2/m)^{\frac{1}{2}}$ [18.1.5]

$= \{2/(2.998 \times 10^8\,\mathrm{m\,s^{-1}})\}\{2 \times (1.381 \times 10^{-23}\,\mathrm{J\,K^{-1}}) \times (298\,\mathrm{K})\ln 2/m\}^{\frac{1}{2}}$

$= (5.04 \times 10^{-19})/(m/\mathrm{kg})^{\frac{1}{2}}$.

(a) $m(\mathrm{HCl}) \approx (35 + 1) \times (1.661 \times 10^{-27}\,\mathrm{kg}) = 6.0 \times 10^{-26}\,\mathrm{kg}$ [end-papers 3, 4]

$\Delta\lambda/\lambda = (5.04 \times 10^{-19})/(6.0 \times 10^{-26})^{\frac{1}{2}} = 2.1 \times 10^{-6}$.

$$\Delta\lambda/\lambda = (\lambda' - \lambda'')/\lambda = \nu\left(\frac{1}{\nu'} - \frac{1}{\nu''}\right) = \nu\Delta\nu/\nu'\nu'' \approx \Delta\nu/\nu = \Delta\tilde{\nu}/\tilde{\nu}.$$

$\Delta\nu(\text{Rotation}) \approx (2.1 \times 10^{-6})\nu \approx (2.1 \times 10^{-6})2Bc \approx (2.1 \times 10^{-6}) \times (10.6\,\mathrm{cm^{-1}})$

$\times\, 2 \times (2.998 \times 10^{10}\,\mathrm{cm\,s^{-1}})$ [Table 18.1]

$\approx 1.3 \times 10^6\,\mathrm{s^{-1}}$, or $\underline{1.3\,\mathrm{MHz}}$.

$\Delta\tilde{\nu}(\text{Vibration}) \approx (2.1 \times 10^{-6}) \times (2991\,\mathrm{cm^{-1}})$ [Table 18.1] $= \underline{0.006\,\mathrm{cm^{-1}}}$.

(b) $m(\mathrm{ICl}) \approx (127 + 35) \times (1.661 \times 10^{-27}\,\mathrm{kg}) = 2.69 \times 10^{-25}\,\mathrm{kg}$.

$\Delta\lambda/\lambda = (5.04 \times 10^{-19})/(2.69 \times 10^{-25})^{\frac{1}{2}} = 9.7 \times 10^{-7}$.

$\Delta\nu(\text{Rotation}) \approx (9.7 \times 10^{-7})B \approx (9.7 \times 10^{-7}) \times (0.114\,\mathrm{cm^{-1}})$

$\times\, (2.998 \times 10^{10}\,\mathrm{cm\,s^{-1}})$

$\approx 3.3 \times 10^3\,\mathrm{s^{-1}}$, or $\underline{3.3 \times 10^{-3}\,\mathrm{MHz}\ (3.3\,\mathrm{kHz})}$.

$\Delta\tilde{\nu}(\text{Vibration}) \approx (9.7 \times 10^{-7}) \times (384\,\mathrm{cm^{-1}}) = 3.7 \times 10^{-4}\,\mathrm{cm^{-1}}$.

18.8 $\tau \approx \hbar/\delta E$; $\delta E = h\delta\nu = hc\delta(1/\lambda) = hc\delta\tilde{\nu}$ ($\tilde{\nu}$ wavenumber).

$\tau \approx \hbar/hc\delta\tilde{\nu} = 1/2\pi c\delta\tilde{\nu}$; $\tau \approx \hbar/h\delta\nu = 1/2\pi\delta\nu$.

(a) $\delta\tilde{\nu} = 0.1\,\mathrm{cm^{-1}}$;

$\tau \approx 1/[2\pi \times (2.998 \times 10^{10}\,\mathrm{cm\,s^{-1}}) \times (0.1\,\mathrm{cm^{-1}})] = \underline{5 \times 10^{-11}\,\mathrm{s}}$.

(b) $\delta\tilde{\nu} = 1.0\,\mathrm{cm^{-1}}$; $\tau \approx 1/[2\pi \times (2.998 \times 10^{10}\,\mathrm{cm\,s^{-1}}) \times (1.0\,\mathrm{cm^{-1}})] = \underline{5 \times 10^{-12}\,\mathrm{s}}$.

(c) $\delta\nu = 100\,\mathrm{MHz}$; $\tau \approx 1/[2\pi \times (10^8\,\mathrm{s^{-1}})] = \underline{2 \times 10^{-9}\,\mathrm{s}}$.

18.9 $\delta\tilde{\nu} \approx 1/2\pi c\tau$ [Problem 18.8] $= (5 \times 10^{-12}\ \text{cm}^{-1})/(\tau/\text{s})$.

(a) $\tau \approx (1/10^{13})\text{s} = 10^{-13}\ \text{s}$;

$\delta\tilde{\nu} \approx 5 \times 10^{-12}\ \text{cm}^{-1})/10^{-13} = \underline{50\ \text{cm}^{-1}}$.

(b) $\tau \approx (10^2/10^{13})\text{s} = 10^{-11}\ \text{s}$;

$\delta\tilde{\nu} \approx (5 \times 10^{-12}\ \text{cm}^{-1})/10^{-11} = \underline{0.5\ \text{cm}^{-1}}$.

18.10 $\tau = 1/z = (kT/p)\,(\pi m/8kT)^{\frac{1}{2}}/\sqrt{2}\sigma$.

$$\text{For HCl, } \tau \approx \left\{\frac{1.381 \times 10^{-23}\ \text{J K}^{-1} \times 298\ \text{K}}{1.0133 \times 10^5\ \text{N m}^{-2}}\right\}$$

$$\times \left\{\frac{\pi \times 36 \times (1.661 \times 10^{-27}\ \text{kg})}{8 \times (1.381 \times 10^{-23}\ \text{J K}^{-1}) \times (298\ \text{K})}\right\}^{\frac{1}{2}} \left\{\frac{1}{\sqrt{2} \times (0.30 \times 10^{-18}\ \text{m}^2)}\right\}$$

$$\approx \underline{2 \times 10^{-10}\ \text{s}}.$$

$\delta\nu = 1/2\pi\tau$ [Problem 18.8] $= 1/(2\pi \times 2 \times 10^{-10}\ \text{s})$

$= 7 \times 10^8\ \text{s}^{-1} = \underline{700\ \text{MHz}}$.

$\delta\nu(\text{Doppler}) = 0.67\ \text{MHz}$ [Problem 18.7(a)].

$\delta\nu(\text{Collision}) \propto 1/\tau \propto p$.

Therefore the pressure must be reduced by a factor of (0.67 MHz)/(700 MHz) $= 1 \times 10^{-3}$ before Doppler broadening begins to dominate. Hence, the pressure must be reduced to 1×10^{-3} atm, or $\underline{0.8\ \text{Torr}}$.

18.11 $N(\text{upper})/N(\text{lower}) = \exp(-\Delta E/kT)$ [18.1.3] $= \exp(-hc\Delta\tilde{\nu}/kT)$

$$= \exp\left\{\frac{-(559.7\ \text{cm}^{-1}) \times (2.998 \times 10^{10}\ \text{cm s}^{-1}) \times (6.626 \times 10^{-34}\ \text{J s})}{(1.381 \times 10^{-23}\ \text{J K}^{-1})T}\right\}$$

$$= \exp\{-[805/(T/\text{K})]\}$$

(a) $T = 273\ \text{K}$, $N(\text{upper})/N(\text{lower}) = \exp(-805/273) = \underline{0.052}$.

(b) $T = 298\ \text{K}$, $N(\text{upper})/N(\text{lower}) = \exp(-805/298) = \underline{0.067}$.

(c) $T = 500\ \text{K}$, $N(\text{upper})/N(\text{lower}) = \exp(-805/500) = \underline{0.200}$.

18.12 $N_J \propto (2J+1)\exp\{-E_J/kT\}$ [18.1.2]

$= (2J+1) \times \exp\{-hcBJ(J+1)/kT\}$ [18.2.6].

For a maximum in N_J, find the value of $J = J^*$ for which $\mathrm{d}N_J/\mathrm{d}J = 0$.

$\mathrm{d}N_J/\mathrm{d}J \propto 2\exp\{-hcBJ(J+1)/kT\} - (2J+1)\,(hcB/kT)\,(2J+1)$

$\times \exp\{-hcBJ(J+1)/kT\}$

$2-(hcB/kT)(2J^*+1)^2 = 0$ for N_J a maximum.

$J^* = \frac{1}{2}\{\sqrt{(2kT/hcB)}-1\}$.

$kT/hc = 207.27\ \text{cm}^{-1}$ [end-paper 1]

$J^* = \frac{1}{2}\{\sqrt{[2\times 207.27\ \text{cm}^{-1})/(0.114\ \text{cm}^{-1})]}-1\} = 29.7$; i.e. $\underline{J^* \approx 30.}$

18.13 $N_J \propto (2J+1)^2 \exp\{-hcBJ(J+1)/kT\}$.

$\text{d}N_J/\text{d}J \propto 4(2J+1)\exp\{\ldots\}-(2J+1)(hcB/kT)(2J+1)^2\exp\{\ldots\} = 0$.

$4(2J+1)-(2J+1)^3(hcB/kT) = 0$ when $J = J^*$.

$J^* = \sqrt{(kT/hcB)}-\frac{1}{2}$.

$B(CH_4) = 5.24\ \text{cm}^{-1}$.

$kT/hcB = (207.2\ \text{cm}^{-1})/(5.24\ \text{cm}^{-1}) = 39.5$.

$J^* = \sqrt{39.5}-0.5 = 5.8$; therefore $\underline{J^* \approx 6.}$

For a given J there are $2J+1$ values of M_J, and $2J+1$ values of K. All these states have the same energy, and so the total degeneracy is $(2J+1)^2$.

18.14 $\mu = m_1m_2/(m_1+m_2)$ [18.3.2]; $I = \mu R^2$ [Box 18.1].

(a) $^1H^{35}Cl$; $m(^1H) = 1.0078 \times (1.660\,56\times 10^{-27}\ \text{kg}) = 1.6735\times 10^{-27}\ \text{kg}$ [end-paper 4].

$m(^{35}Cl) = 34.9688 \times (1.66056\times 10^{-27}\ \text{kg}) = 5.8068\times 10^{-26}\ \text{kg}$

$$\mu = \frac{(1.6735\times 10^{-27}\ \text{kg})\times(5.8068\times 10^{-26}\ \text{kg})}{(1.6735\times 10^{-27}\ \text{kg})+(5.8068\times 10^{-26}\ \text{kg})} = \underline{1.6266\times 10^{-27}\ \text{kg.}}$$

$I = (1.6266\times 10^{-27}\ \text{kg})\times(127.45\times 10^{-12}\ \text{m})^2 = \underline{2.6422\times 10^{-47}\ \text{kg m}^2.}$

(b) $^2H^{35}Cl$; $m(^2H) = 2.0141\times(1.6605\times 10^{-27}\ \text{kg}) = 3.3445\times 10^{-27}\ \text{kg}$.

$$\mu = \frac{(3.3445\times 10^{-27}\ \text{kg})\times(5.8068\times 10^{-26}\ \text{kg})}{(3.3445\times 10^{-27}\ \text{kg})+(5.8068\times 10^{-26}\ \text{kg})} = \underline{3.1622\times 10^{-27}\ \text{kg.}}$$

$I = (3.1622\times 10^{-27}\ \text{kg})\times(127.45\times 10^{-12}\ \text{m})^2 = \underline{5.1368\times 10^{-47}\ \text{kg m}^2.}$

(c) $^1H^{37}Cl$; $m(^{37}Cl) = 36.9651\times(1.6605\times 10^{-27}\ \text{kg}) = 6.1383\times 10^{-26}\ \text{kg}$

$$\mu = \frac{(1.6735\times 10^{-27}\ \text{kg})\times(6.1383\times 10^{-26}\ \text{kg})}{(1.6735\times 10^{-27}\ \text{kg})+(6.1383\times 10^{-26}\ \text{kg})} = \underline{1.6291\times 10^{-27}\ \text{kg.}}$$

$I = (1.6291\times 10^{-27}\ \text{kg})\times(127.45\times 10^{-12}\ \text{m})^2 = \underline{2.6462\times 10^{-47}\ \text{kg m}^2.}$

18.15 $E_{J+1} - E_J = 2hcB(J+1)$ [18.2.12]. Hence, lines occur at frequencies $2Bc$, $4Bc$, $6Bc$, . . . and their separation is $2Bc$, or $2B$ in wavenumbers.

$2Bc = 2 \times (298\ \text{GHz}) = \underline{596\ \text{GHz}}.$

$2B = (596 \times 10^{9}\ \text{s}^{-1})/(2.998 \times 10^{10}\ \text{cm s}^{-1}) = \underline{19.9\ \text{cm}^{-1}}.$

Lines occur at $19.9\ \text{cm}^{-1}$, $39.8\ \text{cm}^{-1}$, $59.7\ \text{cm}^{-1}$, . . . and hence at wavelengths 0.503 mm, 0.251 mm, 0.168 mm . . . and therefore with separations 0.252 mm, 0.083 mm, . . . , and hence with diminishing separation on the wavelength scale.

$hcB = \hbar^2/2I_\perp$ [18.2.3], $I_\perp = m_1R^2(1-\cos\theta) + (m_1m_2/m)R^2 \times (1+2\cos\theta)$ [Box 18.1].

$m_1 = 1.6735 \times 10^{-27}\ \text{kg}$ [Problem 18.14].

$m_2 = 14.0031 \times (1.6605 \times 10^{-27}\ \text{kg}) = 2.3252 \times 10^{-26}\ \text{kg}$ [end-paper 3].

$m = 3m_1 + m_2 = 2.8273 \times 10^{-26}\ \text{kg}$, $R = 101.4\ \text{pm}$.

$$I_\perp = (1.6735 \times 10^{-27}\ \text{kg}) \times (101.4 \times 10^{-12}\ \text{m})^2 \times \{1 - \cos(106°\ 47')\}$$
$$+ \left\{\frac{(1.6735 \times 10^{-27}\ \text{kg}) \times (2.3252 \times 10^{-26}\ \text{kg})}{2.8273 \times 10^{-26}\ \text{kg}}\right\}$$
$$\times (101.4 \times 10^{-12}\ \text{m})^2\{1 + 2\cos(106°\ 47')\}$$
$$= 2.8154 \times 10^{-47}\ \text{kg m}^2.$$

$hcB = (1.05459 \times 10^{-34}\ \text{J s})^2/[2 \times (2.8154 \times 10^{-47}\ \text{kg m}^2)] = 1.9751 \times 10^{-22}\ \text{J}.$

$B = (1.9751 \times 10^{-22}\ \text{J})/[(6.626\,18 \times 10^{-34}\ \text{J s}) \times (2.997\,93 \times 10^{10}\ \text{cm s}^{-1})]$

$= 9.94\ \text{cm}^{-1}$, in accord with $2B = 19.9\ \text{cm}^{-1}$ [above].

18.16 $I = mR^2$, $m = m(\text{C})m(\text{O})/[m(\text{C}) + m(\text{O})]$ [Box 18.1].

$m(^{12}\text{C}) = 12.0000 \times (1.6605 \times 10^{-27}\ \text{kg}) = 1.9926 \times 10^{-26}\ \text{kg}$ [end-paper 3].

$m(^{16}\text{O}) = 15.9949 \times (1.6605 \times 10^{-27}\ \text{kg}) = 2.6560 \times 10^{-26}\ \text{kg}.$

$\mu(^{12}\text{C}^{16}\text{O}) = m(^{12}\text{C})m(^{16}\text{O})/[m(^{12}\text{C}) + m(^{16}\text{O})] = 1.1385 \times 10^{-26}\ \text{kg};$

$I(^{12}\text{C}^{16}\text{O}) = (1.1385 \times 10^{-26}\ \text{kg}) \times (112.82 \times 10^{-12}\ \text{m})^2 = 1.4491 \times 10^{-46}\ \text{kg m}^2.$

$B = \hbar/4\pi cI = \underline{1.9318\ \text{cm}^{-1}}$; transitions at $\tilde{\nu} = 2B(J+1)$.

$m(^{13}\text{C}) = 13.0034 \times (1.6605 \times 10^{-27}\ \text{kg}) = 2.1592 \times 10^{-26}\ \text{kg}.$

$\mu(^{13}\text{C}^{16}\text{O}) = m(^{13}\text{C})m(^{16}\text{O})/[m(^{13}\text{C}) + m(^{16}\text{O})] = 1.1910 \times 10^{-26}\ \text{kg}.$

$I(^{13}\text{C}^{16}\text{O}) = (1.1910 \times 10^{-26}\ \text{kg}) \times (112.82 \times 10^{-12}\ \text{m})^2 = 1.5159 \times 10^{-46}\ \text{kg m}^2.$

$B(^{13}\text{C}^{16}\text{O}) = \underline{1.8466\ \text{cm}^{-1}}$; transitions at $\tilde{\nu} = 2B(J+1)$.

It follows [18.2.12], that the $^{12}\text{C}^{16}\text{O}$ spectrum has its (1 — 0) line at $3.8636\ \text{cm}^{-1}$ while the $^{13}\text{C}^{16}\text{O}$ spectrum has its at $3.6932\ \text{cm}^{-1}$. The equipment should be able to distinguish them, and therefore should have a resolution of at least $0.1\ \text{cm}^{-1}$.

18.17 The separations between neighboring lines are: 20.81, 20.60, 20.64, 20.52, 20.34, 20.37, 20.26 cm^{-1}. The average value is 20.51 cm^{-1}, which is equal to $2B$ [18.2.12].

$B = (20.51\ cm^{-1})/2 = 10.26\ cm^{-1}$.

$I = \hbar/4\pi cB$

$= (1.054\,59 \times 10^{-34}\ J\ s)/\{4\pi \times (2.997\,925 \times 10^{8}\ m\ s^{-1}) \times (10.26\ cm^{-1})\}$

$= \underline{2.728 \times 10^{-47}\ kg\ m^{2}}$.

$R = \sqrt{(I/\mu)}$ [Box 18.1], $\mu = 1.6266 \times 10^{-27}\ kg$ [Problem 18.14a].

$R = \sqrt{[(2.728 \times 10^{-47}\ kg\ m^{2})/(1.6266 \times 10^{-27}\ kg)]} = 1.295 \times 10^{-10}\ m$, $\underline{129.5\ pm}$.

(A more accurate value would be obtained by ascribing the variation of the separations to centrifugal distortion, and not taking a simple average.)

18.18 $B \propto 1/I \propto 1/\mu$;

$B(^{2}H^{35}Cl)/B(^{1}H^{35}Cl) = \mu(^{1}H^{35}Cl)/\mu(^{2}H^{35}Cl) = (1.6266 \times 10^{-27}\ kg)/(3.1622 \times 10^{-27}\ kg)$ [Problem 18.14] $= 0.5144$,

so that $B = 0.5144 \times 10.26\ cm^{-1} = 5.278\ cm^{-1}$. We expect lines at 10.56, 21.11, 31.67 cm^{-1} . . .

18.19 It is sensible to do Problems 18.35 and 18.36 first, and then to use the result $F_J = (\Delta E^{R}_{J-1} - \Delta E^{P}_{J+1})hc = 2B_0(2J+1)$.

Draw up the following Table:

HCl	$J=0$	1	2	3	4	5	6
$\Delta\tilde{\nu}^{R}_{J-1}/cm^{-1}$	–	2906.25	2925.92	2944.99	2963.35	2981.05	2998.05
$\Delta\tilde{\nu}^{P}_{J+1}/cm^{-1}$		2843.63	2821.59	2799.00	2775.77	2752.01	—
$F(J)/cm^{-1}$		62.62	104.33	145.99	187.58	229.04	—
$2B_0/cm^{-1}$	–	20.87	20.87	20.86	20.84	20.82	—

Hence, average $B_0 = 10.43\ cm^{-1}$.

DCl	$J=0$	1	2	3	4	5	6
$\Delta\tilde{\nu}^{R}_{J-1}/cm^{-1}$	–	2101.60	2111.94	2122.05	2131.91	2141.53	2150.93
$\Delta\tilde{\nu}^{P}_{J+1}cm^{-1}$		2069.24	2058.02	2046.58	2034.95	2023.12	–
$F(J)/cm^{-1}$		32.36	53.92	75.47	93.96	118.41	–
$2B_0/cm^{-1}$	–	10.79	10.78	10.78	10.77	10.76	

Hence, average $B_0 = 5.39\ \text{cm}^{-1}$.

$B = \hbar/4\pi cI, I = \mu R^2; R = \surd\{\hbar/4\pi c\mu B\}$.

$\mu(\text{HCl}) = 1.6266 \times 10^{-27}\,\text{kg}$ [Problem 18.14],.

$\mu(\text{DCl}) = 3.1622 \times 10^{-27}\,\text{kg}$ [Problem 18.14].

Hence, $R(\text{HCl}) = \underline{1.285 \times 10^{-10}\,\text{m}}$, $R(\text{DCl}) = \underline{1.282 \times 10^{-10}\,\text{m}}$.

In the original reference the effects of centrifugal distortion are taken into account.

18.20

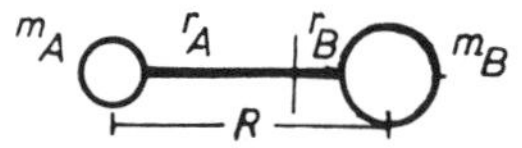

$r_A + r_B = R$. Center of mass at $m_A r_A = m_B r_B$.

Therefore $r_A = R/[1 + (m_A/m_B)]$, $r_B = R/[1 + (m_B/m_A)]$.

Moment of inertia $I = m_A r_A^2 + m_B r_B^2$ [definition]

$$= m_A R^2/[1 + (m_A/m_B)]^2 + m_B R^2/[1 + (m_B/m_A)]^2$$

$$= m_A m_B^2 R^2/(m_A + m_B)^2 + m_A^2 m_B R^2/(m_A + m_B).$$

$$= m_A m_B R^2/(m_A + m_B) = \mu R^2 \text{ if } \mu = m_A m_B/(m_A + m_B).$$

(a) $m_H = 1.0078 \times (1.6605 \times 10^{-27}\,\text{kg}) = 1.6735 \times 10^{-27}\,\text{kg}$

$\mu = m_H^2/2m_H = \frac{1}{2}m_H = 0.8367 \times 10^{-27}\,\text{kg}; R = 74.14\,\text{pm}$ [Table 18.1]

$I = (0.8367 \times 10^{-27}\,\text{kg}) \times (74.14 \times 10^{-12}\,\text{m})^2 = \underline{4.599 \times 10^{-48}\,\text{kg m}^2}.$

(b) $m_I = 126.9045 \times (1.66056 \times 10^{-27}\,\text{kg}) = 2.1073 \times 10^{-25}\,\text{kg}$,

$\mu = \frac{1}{2}m_I; R = 266.7\,\text{pm}$.

$I = \frac{1}{2} \times (2.1073 \times 10^{-25}\,\text{kg}) \times (266.7 \times 10^{-12}\,\text{pm})^2 = \underline{7.495 \times 10^{-45}\,\text{kg m}^2}.$

18.21 $B = \frac{1}{2}(13.10\,\text{cm}^{-1}) = 6.55\,\text{cm}^{-1}$

$B = \hbar/4\pi cI = \hbar/4\pi c\mu R^2; R = \surd\{\hbar/4\pi c\mu B\}$.

$$\mu(^1\text{H}^{127}\text{I}) = \frac{(1.0078 \times 126.9045) \times (1.6605 \times 10^{-27}\,\text{kg})}{1.0078 + 126.9045} = 1.6603 \times 10^{-27}\,\text{kg}.$$

$$R = \surd\{1.055 \times 10^{-34}\,\text{J s})/[4\pi \times (1.6603 \times 10^{-27}\,\text{kg}) \times (2.9979 \times 10^{10}\,\text{cm s}^{-1}) \times (6.55\,\text{cm}^{-1})]\}$$

$= 1.605 \times 10^{-10}\,\text{m}$, $\underline{160.5\,\text{pm}}$.

18.22 $\Delta\nu = 2cB(J + 1)$ [18.2.12].

$R = \surd\{\hbar/4\pi c\mu B\}$ [Problem 18.21]

$$\mu(\text{CuBr}) \approx \frac{63.55 \times 79.9 \times (1.66056 \times 10^{-27}\,\text{kg})}{63.55 + 79.9} = 5.88 \times 10^{-26}\,\text{kg}.$$

Draw up the following Table:

J	13	14	15	
$\Delta\nu$/MHz	84421.34	90449.25	96476.72	
B/cm^{-1}	0.10057	0.10057	0.10057	$[=\Delta\nu/2c(J+1)]$

$$R/\text{pm} = \sqrt{\{(1.055 \times 10^{-34}\,\text{J s})/[4\pi \times (5.88 \times 10^{-26}\,\text{kg}) \times (2.9979 \times 10^{10}\,\text{cm s}^{-1}) \times (0.1006\,\text{cm}^{-1})]\}}$$
$$= 2.176 \times 10^{-10}\,\text{m}, \underline{218\,\text{pm}}.$$

18.23 The separation between lines is $2Bc$, hence
$cB = 6.081\,45, 6.081\,41, 6.081\,22$ GHz, the mean being $6.081\,36$ GHz.

$$I = \hbar/4\pi cB$$
$$= (1.054\,59 \times 10^{-34}\,\text{J s})/[4\pi \times (6.081\,36 \times 10^{9}\,\text{s}^{-1})]$$
$$= \underline{1.379\,98 \times 10^{-45}\,\text{kg m}^2}.$$

That is, one piece of data comes from the experiment, but there are two independent bond lengths; hence we cannot find them from I alone.

17.24 From Box 18.1:

$$I(^{16}\text{O}^{12}\text{C}^{32}\text{S}) = \left(\frac{m(^{16}\text{O})m(^{32}\text{S})}{m(^{16}\text{O}^{12}\text{C}^{32}\text{S})}\right)(R+R')^2 + \frac{m(^{12}\text{C})\{m(^{16}\text{O})R^2 + m(^{32}\text{S})R'^2\}}{m(^{16}\text{O}^{12}\text{C}^{32}\text{S})}$$

$$I(^{16}\text{O}^{12}\text{C}^{34}\text{S}) = \left(\frac{m(^{16}\text{O})m(^{34}\text{S})}{m(^{16}\text{O}^{12}\text{C}^{34}\text{S})}\right)(R+R')^2 + \frac{m(^{12}\text{C})\{m(^{16}\text{O})R^2 + m(^{34}\text{S})R'^2\}}{m(^{16}\text{O}^{12}\text{C}^{34}\text{S})}$$

$m(^{16}\text{O}) = 15.9949 \times (1.6605 \times 10^{-27}\,\text{kg}) = 2.6560 \times 10^{-26}\,\text{kg}$
$m(^{12}\text{C}) = 12.0000 \times (1.6605 \times 10^{-27}\,\text{kg}) = 1.9926 \times 10^{-26}\,\text{kg}$
$m(^{32}\text{S}) = 31.9715 \times (1.6605 \times 10^{-27}\,\text{kg}) = 5.3089 \times 10^{-26}\,\text{kg}$
$m(^{34}\text{S}) = 33.9679 \times (1.6605 \times 10^{-27}\,\text{kg}) = 5.6404 \times 10^{-26}\,\text{kg}$
$m(^{16}\text{O}^{12}\text{C}^{32}\text{S}) = 9.9574 \times 10^{-26}\,\text{kg}$, $m(^{16}\text{O}^{12}\text{C}^{34}\text{S}) = 10.2890 \times 10^{-26}\,\text{kg}$
$I(^{16}\text{O}^{12}\text{C}^{34}\text{S}) = 1.379\,98 \times 10^{-45}\,\text{kg m}^2$ [Problem 18.23].

Obtain $I(^{16}\text{C}^{12}\text{C}^{34}\text{s})$ from the separation of the $1 \rightarrow 2$, $3 \rightarrow 4$ lines, which is $2Bc + 2Bc = 4Bc$;

$cB = 5.932\,52\,\text{GHz}$,

$I(^{16}\text{O}^{12}\text{C}^{34}\text{S}) = \hbar/4\pi cB = 1.414\,60 \times 10^{-45}\,\text{kg m}^2$.

Hence, the two equations above become

$$1.379\,98 \times 10^{-45}\,\text{m}^2 = (1.4161 \times 10^{-26})(R + R')^2 + 5.3150 \times 10^{-27} R^2 + 1.0624 \times 10^{-26} R'^2$$

$$1.414\,60 \times 10^{-45}\,\text{m}^2 = (1.4560 \times 10^{-26})(R + R')^2 + 5.1437 \times 10^{-27} R^2 + 1.0923 \times 10^{-26} R'^2$$

Now we have two simultaneous equations for the two unknowns R, R'. They are tedious to solve, but straightforward. The outcome is

$R = \underline{116.28\,\text{pm}}$, $R' = \underline{155.97\,\text{pm}}$.

18.25 For substitution of an atom lying on the axis the problem is solved if we can treat the case of a linear molecule. Let an atom of mass m lie at z from the center of mass, and another of mass m' lie at z' (the latter 'atom' may represent the remainder of the molecule). Then $mz = m'z'$ and $I = mz^2 + m'z'^2$. If the separation of the two atoms is R, we also have $z + z' = R$. Now let m be changed to $m + \delta m$, but remain in the same position. The center of mass is now determined by $(m + \delta m)\bar{z} = m'\bar{z}'$, but $\bar{z} + \bar{z}' = R$ still. The new moment of inertia is $I' = (m + \delta m)\bar{z}^2 + m'\bar{z}^2$. We now try to find an expression for $I' - I$. First, note that $z' = (m/m')z$; $z' = R - z$. Then also $\bar{z}' = [(m + \delta m)/m']\bar{z}$; $\bar{z} = R - \bar{z}'$.

$$\bar{z} = m'R/(m + m' + \delta m) = m'R/(M + \delta m) \; [M = m + m']$$
$$= [m'/(M + \delta m)]\,(Mz/m') = Mz/(M + \delta m).$$

$$I' - I = m'\bar{z}'^2 + (m + \delta m)\bar{z}^2 - m'z'^2 - mz^2$$
$$= \{(m + \delta m)^2 M^2/m'(M + \delta m)^2\}z^2 + \{(m + \delta m)M^2/(M + \delta m)^2\}z^2 - (m^2/m')z^2 - mz^2$$
$$= \{\delta m M/(M + \delta m)\}z^2, \text{ after some rearrangement.}$$

Put $\delta m = M' - M$, then $I' - I = \{(M' - M)M/M'\}z^2 = \bar{\mu}z^2$.

Now, $B = \hbar/4\pi cI$, $B' = \hbar/4\pi cI'$, and so

$$I' - I = (\hbar/4\pi c)\{(1/B') - (1/B)\} = (\hbar/4\pi c)(B - B')/BB' = \hbar\Delta B/4\pi cBB';$$

then $z^2 = \hbar\Delta B/4\pi cBB'\bar{\mu}$.

Now express the quantities as in the Problem:

$M = M_r\,\text{g mol}^{-1}/N_A$, and so $\bar{\mu} = \Delta M_r\,\text{g mol}^{-1}/N_A$, where

$\Delta M_r = (M_r' - M_r)M_r/M_r'$. Then

$$z^2 = (\hbar N_A/4\pi c)\,(\Delta B/BB'\Delta M_r\,\text{g mol}^{-1}).$$

$$(\hbar N_A/4\pi c \text{ g mol}^{-1}) = \frac{(6.022\,52 \times 10^{23}\text{ mol}^{-1}) \times (1.504\,59 \times 10^{-34}\text{ J s})}{4\pi \times (2.997\,925 \times 10^{8}\text{ m s}^{-1}) \times (\text{g mol}^{-1})}$$

$$= 1.685\,90 \times 10^{-17}\text{m} = (1.685\,90 \times 10^{-17}) \times (\text{pm})^2 \times (10^{24}\text{ m}^{-2})$$

$$= 1.685\,90 \times 10^{7}\text{pm}^2\text{ m}^{-1} = 1.685\,90 \times 10^{5}\text{ pm}^2\text{ cm}^{-1}.$$

$$(z/\text{pm})^2 = (1.685\,90 \times 10^5\text{ cm}^{-1}) \times (\Delta B/BB'\Delta M_r)$$

$$= 1.685\,90 \times 10^5 \times \frac{(\Delta B/\text{cm}^{-1})}{(B/\text{cm}^{-1}) \times (B'/\text{cm}^{-1})} \times \frac{1}{\Delta M_r}.$$

Alternatively, multiplying by c^2/c^2,

$$(z/\text{pm})^2 = (5.053\,80 \times 10^9)\frac{(c\Delta B/\text{MHz})}{(cB/\text{MHz}) \times (cB'/\text{MHz})}\cdot\frac{1}{\Delta M_r}.$$

The general case is discussed in the original reference (*Amer. J. Phys.* **21**, 17 (1953)).

18.26 $\Delta\nu(J) = 2(J+1)Bc.$

From the data (for $J = 10$)

(a) $cB(^{35}\text{Cl}^{126}\text{TeF}_5) = 30\,711.18\text{ MHz}/22 = 1395.96\text{ MHz}$

(b) $cB(^{35}\text{Cl}^{125}\text{TeF}_5) = 30\,713.24\text{ MHz}/22 = 1396.06\text{ MHz}$

(c) $cB(^{37}\text{Cl}^{126}\text{TeF}_5) = 29\,990.54\text{ MHz}/22 = 1363.21\text{ MHz}.$

$M_r(^{35}\text{Cl}^{126}\text{TeF}_5) = 34.9688 + 125.0331 + (5 \times 18.9984) = 254.9939.$

$M_r(^{35}\text{Cl}^{125}\text{TeF}_5) = 34.9688 + 124.0443 + (5 \times 18.9984) = 254.0051.$

$M_r(^{37}\text{Cl}^{126}\text{TeF}_5) = 36.9651 + 125.0331 + (5 \times 18.9984) = 256.9902.$

From (a), (b) $\Delta B/\text{MHz} = 0.10$, $\Delta M_r = 0.9850$

$z(\text{Te}) = \{5.053\,80 \times 10^9 \times 0.10/0.9850 \times 1535.559 \times 1535.662\}^{\frac{1}{2}}\text{ pm}$

$= \underline{(-)\ 15\text{ pm}}$ [Problem 18.25].

From (a), (c) $\Delta B/\text{MHz} = 32.75$, $\Delta M_r = 1.9808$

$z(\text{Cl}) = \{5.053\,80 \times 10^9 \times 32.75/1.9808 \times 1535.559 \times 1499.527\}^{\frac{1}{2}}\text{ pm} = \underline{191\text{ pm}}.$

Therefore $R(\text{Te}-\text{Cl}) = (191 + 15)\text{pm} = \underline{206\text{ pm}}.$

18.27 $E_{v,J} = (v + \frac{1}{2})\hbar\omega + hcBJ(J+1)$ [18.3.15]

O-branch: $\Delta v = 1, \Delta J = -2$ [Section 18.3(e)]; $\Delta E_J^{\text{O}} = \hbar\omega - 2hcB(2J-1)$

S-branch: $\Delta v = 1, \Delta J = +2$ [Section 18.3(e)]; $\Delta E_J^{\text{S}} = \hbar\omega + 2hcB(2J+3).$

The transition of maximum intensity corresponds, approximately, to the transition with the most probable value of J, i.e. J^* as given in Problem 18.12.

Peak-to-peak energy splitting is therefore

$\Delta E = \Delta E^{\mathrm{S}}_{J*} - \Delta E^{\mathrm{O}}_{J*} = 2hcB(2J* + 3) - [-2hcB(2J* - 1)] = 8hcB(J* + \frac{1}{2})$.

$J* = \frac{1}{2}\{\surd(2kT/hcB) - 1\}$[Problem 18.12];

$\Delta E = 4hcB(2kT/hcB)^{\frac{1}{2}} = \surd(32hcBkT)$.

$\Delta E = hc\delta\tilde{\nu}$ ($\tilde{\nu}$: wavenumber)

$\Delta\tilde{\nu} = \surd(32BkT/hc)$.

For application to the data, invert this relation to $B = hc(\Delta\tilde{\nu})^2/32kT$.

$$\mathrm{HgCl_2}: B = \left\{\frac{(6.626 \times 10^{-34}\ \mathrm{J\,s}) \times (2.9979 \times 10^{10}\ \mathrm{cm\,s^{-1}})}{32 \times (1.38066 \times 10^{-23}\ \mathrm{J\,K^{-1}}) \times (555\ \mathrm{K})}\right\} \times (23.8\ \mathrm{cm^{-1}})^2$$

$$= \left(\frac{0.04496\ \mathrm{cm}}{555}\right) \times (23.8\ \mathrm{cm^{-1}})^2 = \underline{0.0459\ \mathrm{cm^{-1}}}.$$

$$\mathrm{HgBr_2}: B = \left(\frac{0.04496\ \mathrm{cm}}{565}\right) \times (15.2\ \mathrm{cm^{-1}})^2 = \underline{0.0184\ \mathrm{cm^{-1}}}.$$

$$\mathrm{HgI_2}: B = \left(\frac{0.04496}{565}\right) \times (11.4\ \mathrm{cm^{-1}})^2 = \underline{0.0103\ \mathrm{cm^{-1}}}.$$

18.28 $\omega = \surd(k/\mu)$; $k = \mu\omega^2$; $\mu = m_1 m_2/(m_1 + m_2)$ [18.3.4].

$$\mu(\mathrm{HF}) = \left(\frac{1.0078 \times 18.99084}{1.0078 + 18.9984}\right) \times (1.6605 \times 10^{-27}\ \mathrm{kg}) = 1.5892 \times 10^{-27}\ \mathrm{kg}.$$

$$\mu(\mathrm{H^{35}Cl}) = \left(\frac{1.0078 \times 34.9688}{1.0078 + 34.9688}\right) \times (1.6605 \times 10^{-27}\ \mathrm{kg}) = 1.6266 \times 10^{-27}\ \mathrm{kg}.$$

$$\mu(\mathrm{H^{81}Br}) = \left(\frac{1.0078 \times 80.9163}{1.0078 + 80.9163}\right) \times (1.6605 \times 10^{-27}\ \mathrm{kg}) = 1.6529 \times 10^{-27}\ \mathrm{kg}.$$

$$\mu(\mathrm{H^{127}I}) = \left(\frac{1.0078 \times 126.9045}{1.0078 + 126.9045}\right) \times (1.6605 \times 10^{-27}\ \mathrm{kg}) = 1.6603 \times 10^{-27}\ \mathrm{kg}.$$

Form $k = \mu\omega^2$. Draw up the following Table using $\omega = 2\pi\nu = 2\pi c\tilde{\nu}$

	HF	HCl	HBr	HI
$\tilde{\nu}/\text{cm}^{-1}$	4141.3	2988.9	2649.7	2309.5
$\omega/\text{s}^{-1} \times 10^{14}$	7.8008	5.6300	4.9911	4.3503
$\mu/\text{kg} \times 10^{-27}$	1.5892	1.6266	1.6529	1.6603
$k/\text{N m}^{-1}$	967.1	515.6	411.8	314.2

18.29 Form $\tilde{\nu} = (\omega/2\pi c) = (1/2\pi c)\sqrt{(k/\mu)}$ with the appropriate values of μ and k.

$$\mu(^2\text{HF}) = \left(\frac{2.0141 \times 18.9984}{2.0141 + 18.9984}\right) \times (1.6605 \times 10^{-27}\ \text{kg}) = 3.0238 \times 10^{-27}\ \text{kg}.$$

$\mu(^2\text{H}^{35}\text{Cl}) = 3.1623 \times 10^{-27}$ kg
$\mu(^2\text{H}^{81}\text{Br}) = 3.2632 \times 10^{-27}$ kg
$\mu(^2\text{H}^{127}\text{I}) = 3.2992 \times 10^{-27}$ kg.

Draw up the following Table:

	^{2}HF	^{2}HCl	^{2}HBr	^{2}HI
$k/\text{N m}^{-1}$	967.1	515.6	411.8	314.2
$\mu/\text{kg} \times 10^{-27}$	3.0238	3.1623	3.2632	3.2922
$\omega/10^{14}\ \text{s}^{-1}$	5.6553	4.0379	3.5524	3.0893
$\tilde{\nu}/\text{cm}^{-1}$	3002.3	2143.7	1885.9	1640.1

18.30 $V(R) = D_e\{1 - \exp[-a(R - R_e)]^2$ [18.3.5].
$\tilde{\nu} = \omega/2\pi c = 936.8\ \text{cm}^{-1}; x\tilde{\nu} = 14.15\ \text{cm}^{-1}$.
$a = \omega(\mu/2D_e)^{\frac{1}{2}}; x = \hbar a^2/2\mu\omega$; therefore $D_e = \hbar\omega/4x = hc\tilde{\nu}/4x$.

$$\mu(\text{RbH}) = \left(\frac{1.008 \times 85.47}{1.008 + 85.47}\right) \times (1.6605 \times 10^{-27}\ \text{kg}) = 1.654 \times 10^{-27}\ \text{kg}.$$

$D_e/hc = \tilde{\nu}^2/4x\tilde{\nu} = (936.8\ \text{cm}^{-1})^2/(4 \times 14.15\ \text{cm}^{-1}) = 15\,505\ \text{cm}^{-1}$ (1.92 eV).
$a = 2\pi c\tilde{\nu}(\mu/2D_e)^{\frac{1}{2}} = 2\pi c\tilde{\nu}\{\mu/2(D_e/hc)hc\}^{\frac{1}{2}}$.
$= 2\pi \times (2.998 \times 10^{10}\ \text{cm s}^{-1}) \times (936.8\ \text{cm}^{-1})$

$$\times \sqrt{\left\{\frac{1.654 \times 10^{-27}\ \text{kg}}{2 \times (15\,505\ \text{cm}^{-1}) \times (6.626 \times 10^{-34}\ \text{J s}) \times (2.998 \times 10^{10}\ \text{cm s}^{-1})}\right\}}$$

$= 9.144 \times 10^9\ \text{m}^{-1}$.

$V(R)/D_e = \{1 - \exp[-(9.144 \times 10^9\ \text{m}^{-1})(R - R_e)]\}^2$,

$R_e = 236.7$ pm. Draw up the following Table, for R ranging from 50 pm to 800 pm.

R/pm	50	100	150	200	250	300	350
$V(R)/D_e$	20.4	6.20	1.46	0.159	0.0131	0.193	0.416

R/pm	400	450	500	550	600	700	800
$V(R)/D_e$	0.601	0.736	0.828	0.889	0.929	0.971	0.988

These points are plotted in Fig. 18.1 as the line labeled $J = 0$.

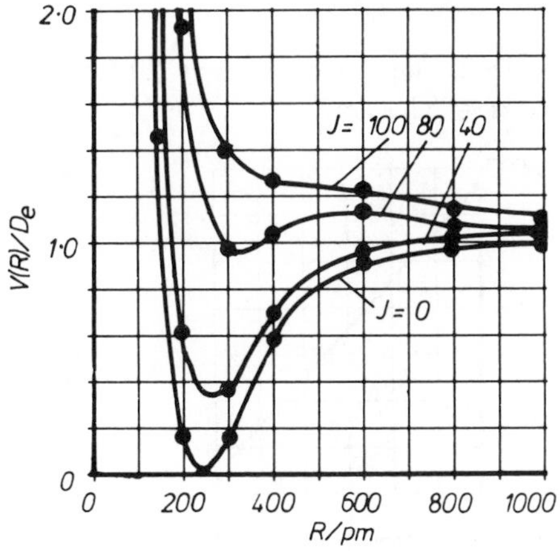

Fig 18.1

18.31 $V_J^*(R) = V(R) + hcB(R)J(J+1)$

$= V(R) + hcB(R_e)(R_e/R)^2 J(J+1)$, $hcB(R_e) = 3.020\ \text{cm}^{-1}$.

Draw up the following Table for $J = 40, 80, 100$ using $V(R)$ calculated in Problem 17.30.

R/pm	50	100	200	300	400	600	800	1000
R_e/R	4.73	2.37	1.18	0.79	0.59	0.39	0.30	0.24
V/D_e	20.4	6.20	0.159	0.193	0.601	0.929	0.988	1.000
V_{40}^*/D_e	27.5	7.99	0.606	0.392	0.713	0.979	1.016	1.016
V_{80}^*/D_e	48.7	13.3	1.93	0.979	1.043	1.13	1.099	1.069
V_{100}^*/D_e	64.5	17.2	2.91	1.42	1.29	1.24	1.16	1.11

These are also plotted in Fig. 18.1.

18.32 $E_v = (v + \frac{1}{2})\hbar\omega - (v + \frac{1}{2})^2\hbar\omega x$ [18.3.6]

$E_v/hc = (v + \frac{1}{2})\tilde{\nu} - (v + \frac{1}{2})^2 x\tilde{\nu}$

$(E_{v+1} - E_v)/hc = \tilde{\nu} - 2(v + 1)x\tilde{\nu} = (1 - 2x)\tilde{\nu} - 2vx\tilde{\nu}$.

Hence, plot $(E_{v+1} - E_v)/hc$ against v and determine $(1 - 2x)\tilde{\nu}$ from the intercept at $\tilde{\nu} = 0$ and $-2x\tilde{\nu}$ from the slope.

Draw up the following Table

v	0	1	2	3	4
E_v/hc	1481.86	4367.50	7149.04	9826.48	12399.8
$(E_{v+1} - E_v)/hc$	2885.64	2781.54	2677.44	2573.34	

The points are plotted in Fig. 18.2. The intercept lies at 2885.6 and the slope is $(-312.3/3) = -104.1$. Hence $x\tilde{\nu} = 52.1\ \text{cm}^{-1}$.

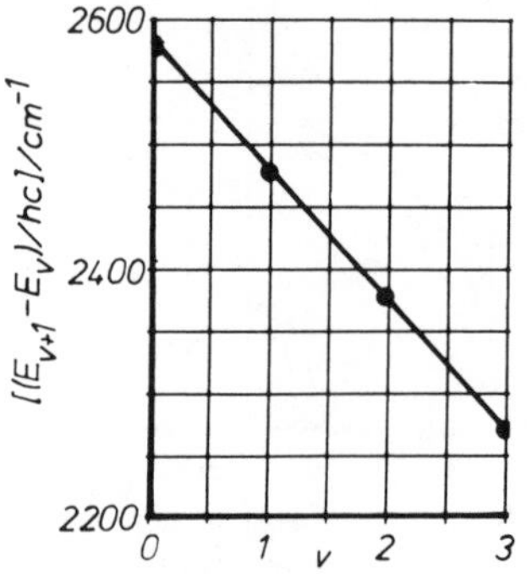

Fig 18.2

$\tilde{\nu} - 2x\tilde{\nu} = 2885.6\ \text{cm}^{-1}$, so that $\tilde{\nu} = (2885.6 + 104.2)\text{cm}^{-1} = 2989.8\ \text{cm}^{-1}$.

The dissociation energy may be obtained by assuming that the molecule is described by a Morse potential, then [Section 18.3(b)] $D_e = \tilde{\nu}^2/4x\tilde{\nu}$.

$D_e = (2989.8\ \text{cm}^{-1})^2/\ [4 \times (52.1\ \text{cm}^{-1})] = 42\,932\ \text{cm}^{-1}$, 5.32 eV.

The zero point energy level lies at

$E_0/hc = \frac{1}{2}\tilde{\nu} - \frac{1}{4}x\tilde{\nu} = 1481.9\ \text{cm}^{-1}$, or 0.18 eV.

Therefore, the dissociation energy is $(5.32 - 0.17)\text{eV} = \underline{5.14\ \text{eV}}$.

18.33 $\tilde{\nu}_v = (v + \frac{1}{2})\tilde{\nu} - (v + \frac{1}{2})^2 x\tilde{\nu}$

$\Delta\tilde{\nu}_v = \tilde{\nu}_{v+1} - \tilde{\nu}_v = \tilde{\nu} - 2(v + 1)x\tilde{\nu}$, $D_e = \tilde{\nu}/4x$ [Problem 18.32].

Draw up the following Table

v	0	1	2	3
$\tilde{\nu}_v/\text{cm}^{-1}$	142.81	427.31	710.31	991.81
$\Delta\tilde{\nu}_v/\text{cm}^{-1}$	284.50	283.00	281.50	

Draw Fig. 18.3. The intercept is at 28.60, hence $\tilde{\nu} = 286\ \text{cm}^{-1}$. The slope is -1.50, hence $x\tilde{\nu} = 0.75\ \text{cm}^{-1}$. It follows that $D_e = \tilde{\nu}^2/4x\tilde{\nu} = 27\,300\ \text{cm}^{-1}$, or 3.4 eV. The zero-point energy level is at $\underline{143\ \text{cm}^{-1}}$, and so $D_0 \approx \underline{3.4\ \text{eV}}$.

$$\text{Since } \mu = \left(\frac{22.99 \times 126.9}{22.99 + 126.9}\right) \times (1.6605 \times 10^{-27}\ \text{kg}) = 3.232 \times 10^{-26}\ \text{kg},$$

$$k = \mu\omega^2 = 4\pi^2c^2\mu\tilde{\nu}^2 = 4\pi^2 \times (2.9979 \times 10^{10}\ \text{cm}^{-1})^2 \times (3.232 \times 10^{-26}\ \text{kg}) \times (286\ \text{cm}^{-1})^2 = \underline{93.8\ \text{N m}^{-1}}.$$

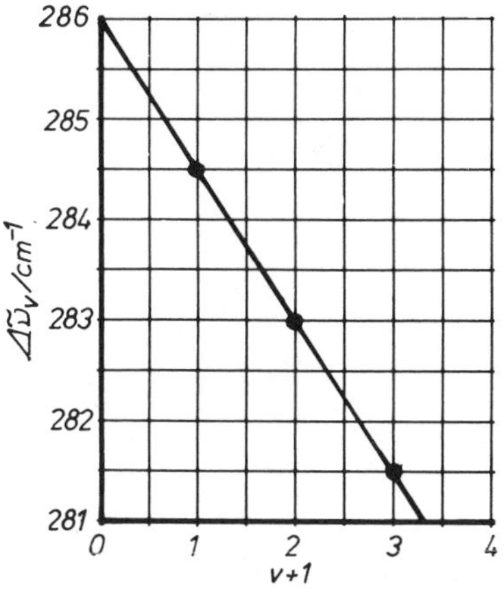

Fig 18.3

18.34 $D_0 = D_e - \tilde{\nu}'$, $\tilde{\nu}' = \frac{1}{2}\tilde{\nu} - \frac{1}{4}x\tilde{\nu}$ [18.3.14]

(a) HCl. $\tilde{\nu}' = 1344.8\ \text{cm}^{-1} - \frac{1}{4}(52.05\ \text{cm}^{-1}) = 1481.8\ \text{cm}^{-1}$, 0.184 eV.

$D_0 = 5.33\ \text{eV} - 0.18\ \text{eV} = \underline{5.15\ \text{eV}}$.

(b) DCl. $2\mu\omega x/\hbar = a^2$ [Section 18.3(b)], so that $\omega x \propto 1/\mu$ as a is constant.

$D_e = \tilde{\nu}/4x$ [Problem 18.32] $= \tilde{\nu}^2/4\tilde{\nu}x$.

D_e is the same for both potential curves, $\omega x \propto 1/\mu$; therefore $\tilde{\nu}^2 \propto 1/\mu$, implying $\tilde{\nu} \propto 1/\sqrt{\mu}$. Reduced masses were calculated in Problem 18.28 and 18.29.

$\tilde{\nu}(\text{DCl}) = \sqrt{\{\mu(\text{HCl})/\mu(\text{DCl})\}}\tilde{\nu}(\text{HCl}) = 0.7172 \times (2989.7\ \text{cm}^{-1}) = 2144.2\ \text{cm}^{-1}$.

$x\tilde{\nu}(\text{DCl}) = \{\mu(\text{HCl})/\mu(\text{DCl})\}x\tilde{\nu}(\text{HCl}) = 0.5144 \times (52.05\ \text{cm}^{-1}) = 26.77\ \text{cm}^{-1}$.

$\tilde{\nu}_0 = \frac{1}{2}(2144.2\ \text{cm}^{-1}) - \frac{1}{4}(26.77\ \text{cm}^{-1}) = 1065.4\ \text{cm}^{-1}, 0.13\ \text{eV}$.

$D_0 = 5.33\ \text{eV} - 0.13\ \text{eV} = \underline{5.20\ \text{eV}}$.

18.35 $E_{v,J} = (v + \frac{1}{2})\hbar\omega + hcB_vJ(J+1)$ [18.3.15, but with B depending on v]

$E_{v+1,J'} - E_{v,J} = \hbar\omega + hcB_{v+1}J'(J'+1) - hcB_vJ(J+1)$.

P-branch: $J' = J - 1$:

$\Delta E_J^{\text{P}}/hc = \tilde{\nu}_0 + B_{v+1}(J-1)J - B_vJ(J+1) = \underline{\tilde{\nu}_0 - (B_v + B_{v+1})J + (B_{v+1} - B_v)J^2}$.

Q-branch: $J' = J$:

$\Delta E_J^{\text{Q}}/hc = \tilde{\nu}_0 + B_{v+1}J(J+1) - B_vJ(J+1) = \tilde{\nu}_0 + \underline{(B_{v+1} - B_v)J(J+1)}$.

R-branch: $J' = J + 1$:

$$\Delta E_J^{\text{R}}/hc = \tilde{\nu}_0 + B_{v+1}(J+1)(J+2) - B_vJ(J+1)$$
$$= \underline{\tilde{\nu}_0 + 2B_{v+1} + (3B_{v+1} - B_v)J + (B_{v+1} - B_v)J^2}.$$

18.36 $(\Delta E_J^{\text{R}} - \Delta E_J^{\text{P}})/hc = 2B_{v+1} + (3B_{v+1} - B_v)J + (B_v + B_{v+1})J$ [Problem 18.35]

$$= 2B_{v+1} + 4B_{v+1}J = 2B_{v+1}(2J+1);$$

$B_{v+1} = \hbar^2/2I_{v+1},\ I_{v+1} = \mu R_{v+1}^2$.

$$(\Delta E_{J-1}^{\text{R}} - \Delta E_{J+1}^{\text{P}})/hc = \{2B_{v+1} + (3B_{v+1} - B_v)(J-1) + (B_{v+1} - B_v)(J-1)^2\}$$
$$- \{-(B_v + B_{v+1})(J+1) + (B_{v+1} - B_v)(J+1)^2\}$$
$$= 2B_v(2J+1);$$

$B_v = \hbar^2/2I_v,\ I_v = \mu R_v^2$.

Draw up the following Table:

	0	1	2	3	
$\Delta E_J^{\text{R}}/\text{cm}^{-1}$	2906.2	2925.9	2945.0	2963.3	
$\Delta E_J^{\text{P}}/\text{cm}^{-1}$		2865.1	2843.6	2821.6	
$(\Delta E_J^{\text{R}} - \Delta E_J^{\text{P}})/\text{cm}^{-1}$		60.80	101.4	141.7	$[\equiv \Delta]$
$(\Delta E_{J-1}^{\text{R}} - \Delta E_{J+1}^{\text{P}})/\text{cm}^{-2}$		62.60	104.3	–	$[\equiv \Delta']$
B_{v+1}/cm^{-1}		10.13	10.14	10.12	$[= \Delta/2(2J+1)]$
B_v/cm^{-1}		10.43	10.43	–	$[= \Delta'/2(2J+1)]$

Hence, since $v = 0$, $B_0 = 10.43\ \text{cm}^{-1}$, $B_1 = 10.13\ \text{cm}^{-1}$.

It follows that the bond lengths are given by

$R_v = \sqrt{\{\hbar/4\pi\mu c B_v\}}$ [Problem 18.21] with $\mu = 1.6266 \times 10^{-27}$ kg [Problem 18.14].

$$R_0 = \sqrt{\left\{\frac{1.054\,59 \times 10^{-34}\ \text{J s}}{4\pi \times (1.6266 \times 10^{-27}\ \text{kg}) \times (2.9979 \times 10^{10}\ \text{cm s}^{-1}) \times (10.43\ \text{cm}^{-1})}\right\}}$$

$= 4.148 \times 10^{-10}\ \text{m}/\sqrt{(10.43)} = 1.28 \times 10^{-10}\ \text{m} = \underline{128\ \text{pm}}.$

$R_1 = 4.148 \times 10^{10}\ \text{m}/\sqrt{(10.13)} = \underline{130\ \text{pm}}.$

For the force-constant, use

$\Delta E_0^{\text{R}} = \hbar\omega + 2B_{v+1}$ [Problem 18.35] with $v = 0$

$\tilde{\nu} = 2906.2\ \text{cm}^{-1} - 2 \times (10.13\ \text{cm}^{-1}) = 2885.9\ \text{cm}^{-1}.$

$\omega = 2\pi\tilde{\nu}c = 2\pi \times (2885.9\ \text{cm}^{-1}) \times (2.9979 \times 10^{10}\ \text{cm s}^{-1}) = 5.436 \times 10^{14}\ \text{s}^{-1}.$

$\omega = \sqrt{(k/\mu)};\ k = \mu\omega^2$:

$k = (1.6266 \times 10^{-27}\ \text{kg}) \times (5.436 \times 10^{14}\ \text{s}^{-1})^2 = 480.7\ \text{kg s}^{-2} = \underline{480.7\ \text{N m}^{-1}}.$

18.37 Separation of lines is $4B$ [Section 18.3(e)]

$B = (0.9752\ \text{cm}^{-1})/4 = 0.2438\ \text{cm}^{-1}.$

$R = \sqrt{(\hbar/4\pi\mu c B)}$ [Problem 18.21];

$$\mu = \frac{m(^{35}\text{Cl})m(^{35}\text{Cl})}{m(^{35}\text{Cl}) + m(^{35}\text{Cl})} = \tfrac{1}{2}m(^{35}\text{Cl}) = \tfrac{1}{2} \times (5.8096 \times 10^{-26}\ \text{kg})\ \text{[Problem 18.14]}.$$

$$R = \sqrt{\left\{\frac{1.054\,59 \times 10^{-34}\ \text{J s}}{4\pi \times \frac{1}{2} \times (5.8096 \times 10^{-26}\ \text{kg}) \times (2.9979 \times 10^{10}\ \text{cm s}^{-1}) \times (0.2438\ \text{cm}^{-1})}\right\}}$$

$= 1.9887 \times 10^{-10}\ \text{m},\ \underline{198.9\ \text{pm}}.$

18.38 Decide which modes correspond to (i) a changing polarizability, (ii) a changing dipole moment. Take note of the exclusion rule [Section 18.4(c)].

(a) Bent AB_2 molecule. All modes are Raman and infrared active.

(b) Linear AB_2 molecule (B – A – B). Refer to Fig. 18.18 of the text. ν_1 is symmetric and leads to no change in dipole; both ν_3 and ν_2 change the dipole from zero. So ν_1 is infrared inactive while ν_2 and ν_3 are infrared active. By the exclusion rule, ν_2 and ν_3 must be Raman inactive; ν_1 is active.

18.39 The molecule is centrosymmetric, and so the exclusion rule applies. The mode is infrared inactive [the symmetric mode leaves the zero dipole moment unchanged]; the mode may be Raman active (and is).

19. Determination of molecular structure: electronic spectroscopy

A19.1 $\lg(I_f/I_i) = -\epsilon c l$ [19.1.4] $= -(855\ \text{mol}^{-1}\ \text{dm}^3\ \text{cm}^{-1})(3.25 \times 10^{-3}\ \text{mol dm}^{-3})$
$\times\ (0.25\ \text{cm}) = -0.695.$

$I_f/I_i = 0.202$; hence the reduction is 79.8 %.

A19.2 $\alpha = -C^{-1}l^{-1}\ln(I_f/I_i)$ [19.1.3, C concentration]
$= -(6.75 \times 10^{-4}\ \text{mol dm}^{-3})^{-1}(0.35\ \text{cm})^{-1}\ln(0.655)$
$= 1.79 \times 10^3\ \text{M}^{-1}\ \text{cm}^{-1} = 1.79 \times 10^6\ \text{cm}^2\ \text{mol}^{-1}.$

A19.3 $C = -\alpha^{-1}l^{-1}\ln(I_f/I_i)$ [19.1.3, C concentration]
$= -(286\ \text{mol}^{-1}\ \text{dm}^3\ \text{cm}^{-1})^{-1}(0.65\ \text{cm})^{-1}\ln(0.535) = 3.36 \times 10^{-3}\ \text{M}.$

A19.4 $|\Delta I/I| = \alpha l|\delta C|$ [19.1.3]

$|\delta C| = (0.02)(275\ \text{mol}^{-1}\ \text{dm}^3\ \text{cm}^{-1})^{-1}(0.15\ \text{cm})^{-1} = 4.8 \times 10^{-4}\ \text{mol dm}^{-3}.$

A19.5 The absorption extends from $3.45 \times 10^4\ \text{cm}^{-1}$ to $4.35 \times 10^4\ \text{cm}^{-1}$; the range is $9000\ \text{cm}^{-1}$.

$\mathscr{A} = \int \epsilon\, d\nu = (1.21 \times 10^4\ \text{dm}^3\ \text{mol}^{-1}\ \text{cm}^{-1})(10^{-3}\ \text{m}^3\ \text{dm}^{-3})(100\ \text{cm m}^{-1})(9000/2\ \text{cm}^{-1})$
$\times\ (3.00 \times 10^{10}\ \text{cm s}^{-1}) = 1.63 \times 10^{17}\ \text{m}^2\ \text{s}^{-1}\ \text{mol}^{-1}$
$= 1.63 \times 10^{18}\ \text{M}^{-1}\ \text{cm}^{-1}\ \text{s}^{-1}.$ [19.1.5]

$f = 1.44 \times 10^{-19} \times 1.63 \times 10^{18} = 0.23.$ [19.1.6a]

A19.6 $f = (1.4095 \times 10^{42}\ \text{m}^{-2}\ \text{s C}^{-2})(35\,000\ \text{cm}^{-1})(3.00 \times 10^{10}\ \text{cm s}^{-1})$
$\times\ (2.65 \times 10^{-30}\ \text{C m})^2 = 0.0104.$ [19.1.8]

A19.7 0.91 and 0.75, strong; 2.9×10^{-2}, weak; 6.2×10^{-5} and 3.2×10^{-9}, forbidden [Section 19.1].

A19.8 Conjugation of double bonds in the diene causes the characteristic double bond absorption to be shifted to longer wavelengths. Hence the diene maximum is at 243 nm. The other peak is in the location typical for an isolated double bond. [Table 19.2]

A19.9 The weak absorption is typical of the C=O group. The strong absorptions of C=C and C=O typically about 180 nm have been shifted to longer wavelength, namely 213 nm, by conjugation of the C=C double bond with the double bond in C=O [Table 19.2].

A19.10 The difference in bond order shows that the internuclear distance in H_2^+ is greater than that in H_2. The change in nuclear separation and the shift in the potential energy curves reduces the Franck-Condon factor for the two ground vibrational states. It creates more favorable overlap of the H_2 ground vibrational state with an H_2^+ state having a nonzero vibrational quantum number [Section 19.3].

19.1 $\lg(I_f/I_i) = -\epsilon[J]l$ [19.1.4]; $\epsilon = -(1/[J]l)\lg(I_f/I_i)$.

Draw up the following Table based on $l = 0.20$ cm:

$[J]/M$	0.001	0.005	0.010	0.050	
I_f/I_i	0.814	0.356	0.127	3.0×10^{-5}	
$\epsilon/(M\ cm)^{-1}$	447	449	448	452	mean: 449

Hence, $\epsilon = 450\ M^{-1}\ cm^{-1}$.

19.2 $\epsilon = -(1/[J]l)\lg(I_f/I_i)$ [19.1.4] $= -\lg(0.48)/(0.010\ M) \times (0.20\ cm)$
$= 160\ M^{-1}\ cm^{-1}$.

19.3 $A = \epsilon[J]l$ [Section 19.1]

(a) $\epsilon[J] = (450\ M^{-1}\ cm^{-1}) \times [J] \times (0.20\ cm) = 90.0\,([J]/M)$

$[J]/M$	0.001	0.005	0.010	0.050
A	0.09	0.45	0.90	4.5

(b) $A = (160\ M^{-1}\ cm^{-1}) \times (0.010\ M) \times (0.20\ cm) = 0.32$.

18.4 $I_f/I_i = 10^{-\epsilon[J]l}$ [19.1.4] $\epsilon(\text{bromine}) = 450\ M^{-1}\ cm^{-1}$; $\epsilon(\text{benzene}) = 160\ M^{-1}\ cm^{-1}$.

(a) 0.010 M benzene.

(i) $l = 0.10$ cm; $I_f/I_i = 10^{-(160 cm^{-1} M^{-1}) \times (0.10 M) \times (0.10 cm)}$
$= 10^{-0.16} = 0.69$;

i.e. I_f is 69% of I_i.

(ii) $l = 10$ cm; $I_f/I_i = 10^{-160 \times 0.010 \times 10} = 10^{-16.0} = 1.0 \times 10^{-16}$, 1.0×10^{-14}%.

(b) 0.0010 M bromine.

(i) $l = 0.10$ cm; $I_f/I_i = 10^{-450 \times 0.0010 \times 0.10} = 10^{-0.045} = 0.90$ (90%).

(ii) $l = 10$ cm; $I_f/I_i = 10^{-450 \times 0.0010 \times 10} = 10^{-4.5} = 3.2 \times 10^{-5}$, 3.2×10^{-3}%

19.5 $I_f/I_i = 10^{-\epsilon[J]l}$ [19.1.4], $\epsilon = 6.2 \times 10^{-5}\,M^{-1}\,cm^{-1}$

$[J] = (1.00\,kg/18.02\,g\,mol^{-1})/dm^3 = 55.5\,mol\,dm^{-3} = 55.5\,M$.

$l = -(1/\epsilon[J])\lg(I_f/I_i)$

$= -\{1/(55.5\,mol\,dm^{-3}) \times (6.2 \times 10^{-5}\,M^{-1}\,cm^{-1})\} \times \lg(I_f/I_i) = -(290\,cm)\lg(I_f/I_i)$.

(a) $I_f/I_i = 0.50$; $l = -(290\,cm)\lg 0.50 = 88\,cm$.

(b) $I_f/I_i = 0.10$; $l = -(290\,cm)\lg 0.10 = 290\,cm$.

19.6 $\mathscr{A} = \int \epsilon(\nu)d\nu$ [19.1.5]

$\approx 2 \times (\frac{1}{2}\epsilon_{max}\Delta\nu)$ [Fig. 19.1] $= \epsilon_{max}\Delta\nu$.

Fig 19.1

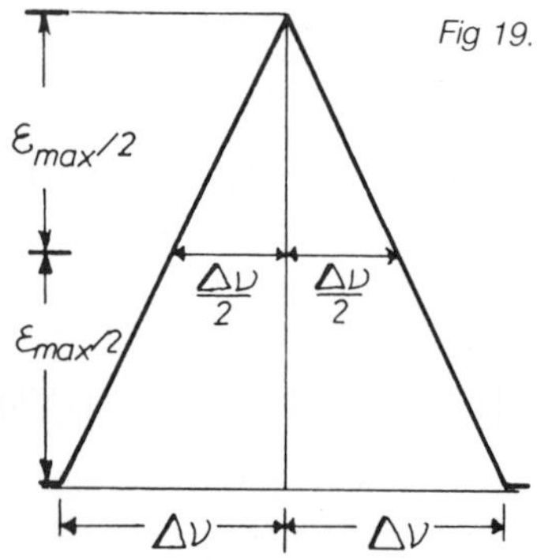

$\Delta\nu = (5000\,cm^{-1}) \times (2.998 \times 10^{10}\,cm\,s^{-1}) = 1.499 \times 10^{14}\,s^{-1}$

$\approx 1.5 \times 10^{14}\,s^{-1}$.

(a) $\mathscr{A} \approx (1 \times 10^4\,M^{-1}\,cm^{-1}) \times (1.5 \times 10^{14}\,s^{-1})$

$= 1.5 \times 10^{18}\,dm^3\,mol^{-1}\,cm^{-1}\,s^{-1} = 1.5 \times 10^{18}\,cm^2\,s^{-1}\,mmol^{-1}$.

(b) $\mathscr{A} \approx (5 \times 10^2\,M^{-1}\,cm^{-1}) \times (1.5 \times 10^{14}\,s^{-1})$

$= 7.5 \times 10^{16}\,dm^3\,mol^{-1}\,cm^{-1}\,s^{-1} = 7.5 \times 10^{16}\,cm^2\,s^{-1}\,mmol^{-1}$.

19.7 $f = (4m_e c\epsilon_0 \ln 10/N_A e^2)\mathscr{A}$ [19.1.6] $= 1.44 \times 10^{-19}(\mathscr{A}/cm^2\,s^{-1}\,mmol^{-1})$ [19.1.6a].

(a) $f = 1.44 \times 10^{-19} \times (1.5 \times 10^{18})$

$= \underline{0.22}$.

(b) $f = 1.44 \times 10^{-19} \times (7.5 \times 10^{16}) = \underline{0.011}$.

19.8 $\epsilon(\nu) = \epsilon_{max} \exp(-\nu^2/2\Gamma)$; $\nu = 0$ at center of band, Γ a constant.

$\epsilon(\nu) = \frac{1}{2}\epsilon_{max}$ when $\nu = \pm\nu_{\frac{1}{2}}$; $\nu_{\frac{1}{2}}^2 = 2\Gamma \ln 2$

Width at half-height: $\Delta\nu = 2\nu_{\frac{1}{2}} = 2\surd(2\Gamma \ln 2)$; $\Gamma = \Delta\nu^2/8 \ln 2$.

$$\mathscr{A} = \int \epsilon(\nu)\mathrm{d}\nu = \epsilon_{max} \int_{-\infty}^{\infty} \mathrm{e}^{-\nu^2/2\Gamma}\,\mathrm{d}\nu$$

$$= \epsilon_{max}\surd(2\pi\Gamma)\left[\int_{-\infty}^{\infty} \mathrm{e}^{-x^2}\,\mathrm{d}x = \surd\pi\right] = \epsilon_{max}\surd(2\pi\Delta\nu^2/8 \ln 2)$$

$$= [\tfrac{1}{2}\surd(\pi/\ln 2)]\,\epsilon_{max}\Delta\nu = 1.0645\,\epsilon_{max}\Delta\nu.$$

$\Delta\nu = c\Delta\tilde{\nu}$ [$\tilde{\nu}$; wavenumber] $\mathscr{A} = \underline{1.0645c\epsilon_{max}\Delta\tilde{\nu}}$.

19.9 From Fig. 19.26 of the text, $\epsilon_{max} \approx 9.5\ \mathrm{M^{-1}\,cm^{-1}}$, $\Delta\tilde{\nu}_{\frac{1}{2}} \approx 4760\ \mathrm{cm^{-1}}$

$\mathscr{A} = 1.0645 \times (2.998 \times 10^{10}\ \mathrm{cm\,s^{-1}}) \times (9.5\ \mathrm{dm^3\,mol^{-1}\,cm^{-1}}) \times (4760\ \mathrm{cm^{-1}})$

$= \underline{1.4 \times 10^{15}\ \mathrm{cm^2\,s^{-1}\,mmol^{-1}}}$.

$f = 1.44 \times 10^{-19} \times 1.4 \times 10^{15} \times 2.0 \times 10^{-4}$.

The area under the curve on the printed page is c. 1288 $\mathrm{mm^2}$; each $\mathrm{mm^2}$ corresponds to c. $(190.5\ \mathrm{cm^{-1}}) \times (0.189\ \mathrm{M^{-1}\,cm^{-1}})$; hence the value of the integral $\int\epsilon(\tilde{\nu})\mathrm{d}\tilde{\nu}$ is $4.64 \times 10^4\ \mathrm{M^{-1}\,cm^{-2}}$. The value of $\mathscr{A}$ is obtained from $c\int\epsilon(\tilde{\nu})\,\mathrm{d}\tilde{\nu}$ $= \underline{1.4 \times 10^{15}\ \mathrm{cm^2\,s^{-1}\,mmol^{-1}}}$, corresponding to $f = 2.0 \times 10^{-4}$. Since $f \ll 1$, the transition is forbidden [Section 19.1].

19.10 $\Delta\tilde{\nu}_{\frac{1}{2}} = \left(\dfrac{1}{\lambda'} - \dfrac{1}{\lambda''}\right)$, where λ', λ'' are the wavelengths at $\frac{1}{2}\epsilon_{max}$ on the short and long wavelength sides of the peak. From Fig. 19.2 of the text we can estimate the following values:

280 nm peak: $\lambda' \approx 260$ nm, $\lambda'' \approx 300$ nm;

$$\Delta\tilde{\nu}_{\frac{1}{2}} \approx \left(\frac{1}{260} - \frac{1}{300}\right) \times 10^9\ \mathrm{m^{-1}} = 5130\ \mathrm{cm^{-1}}.$$

$\epsilon_{max} \approx 11\ \mathrm{M^{-1}\,cm^{-1}}$.

$\mathscr{A} = 1.0645c\epsilon_{max}\,\Delta\tilde{\nu}$ [Problem 19.8] $= 1.0645 \times (2.998 \times 10^{10}\ \mathrm{cm\,s^{-1}})$

$\times (11\,\text{M}^{-1}\,\text{cm}^{-1}) \times (5130\,\text{cm}^{-1}) \approx 1.8 \times 10^{15}\,\text{cm}^2\,\text{s}^{-1}\,\text{mmol}^{-1}$.

$f = 1.44 \times 10^{-19} \times 1.8 \times 10^{15} = \underline{2.6 \times 10^{-4}}$.

430 nm peak: $\lambda' \approx 390\,\text{nm}$,

$$\lambda'' \approx 455\,\text{nm};\ \Delta\tilde{\nu}_{\frac{1}{2}} \approx \left(\frac{1}{390} - \frac{1}{455}\right) \times 10^9\,\text{m}^{-1} = 3660\,\text{cm}^{-1}.$$

$\epsilon_{max} \approx 18\,\text{M}^{-1}\,\text{cm}^{-1}$.

$\mathscr{A} = 1.0645 c\epsilon_{max}\Delta\tilde{\nu} \approx 2.1 \times 10^{15}\,\text{cm}^{-2}\,\text{s}^{-1}\,\text{mmol}^{-1}$.

$f \approx \underline{3 \times 10^{-4}}$.

For the conversion to a wavenumber scale, draw up the following Table:

λ/nm	250	260	270	280	290	300
$\tilde{\nu}$/1000 cm^{-1}	40	38.5	37.0	35.7	34.5	33.3
ϵ/M^{-1} cm^{-1}	3	4	6	10	11	8

λ/nm	310	320	330	340	350	360
$\tilde{\nu}$/1000 cm^{-1}	32.3	31.3	30.3	29.4	28.6	27.8
ϵ/M^{-1} cm^{-1}	5	3	1	1	1	3

λ/nm	360	370	380	390	400	410
$\tilde{\nu}$/1000 cm^{-1}	27.8	27.0	26.3	25.6	25.0	24.4
ϵ/M^{-1} cm^{-1}	3	5	8	11	14	17

λ/nm	420	430	440	450	460	470
$\tilde{\nu}$/1000 cm^{-1}	23.8	23.3	22.7	22.2	21.7	21.3
ϵ/M^{-1} cm^{-1}	17	16	16	14	1	0

These points are plotted in Fig. 19.2. The area under the 280 nm curve is 5.72×10^4 $M^{-1}\,cm^{-2}$, and that under the 430 nm curve is $6.8 \times 10^4\,M^{-1}\,cm^{-2}$. It follows that

$$\mathscr{A}\,(280\,\text{nm}) \approx (2.998 \times 10^{10}\,\text{cm s}^{-1}) \times (5.72 \times 10^4\,\text{M}^{-1}\,\text{cm}^{-2})$$
$$= 1.7 \times 10^{15}\,\text{cm}^2\,\text{s}^{-1}\,\text{mmol}^{-1},$$
$$\mathscr{A}\,(430\,\text{nm}) \approx (2.998 \times 10^{10}\,\text{cm s}^{-1}) \times (6.80 \times 10^4\,\text{M}^{-1}\,\text{cm}^{-2})$$
$$= 2.0 \times 10^{15}\,\text{cm}^2\,\text{mmol}^{-1};$$

$f(280\,\text{nm}) \approx \underline{2.5 \times 10^{-4}}$; $f(430\,\text{nm}) \approx \underline{2.9 \times 10^{-4}.}$

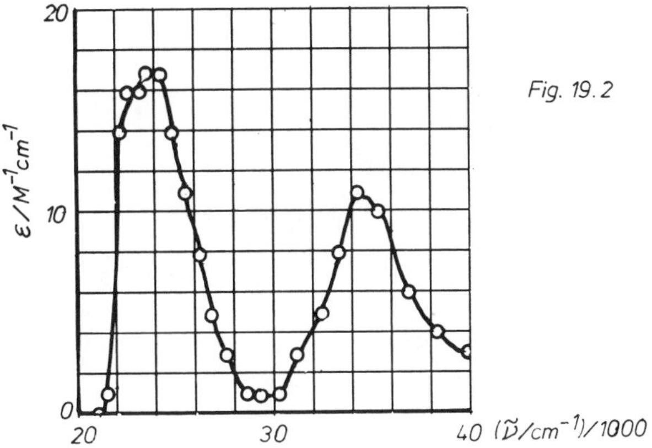

Fig. 19.2

For the final part, write $\nu = c/\lambda$, so that $d\nu = -c\,d\lambda/\lambda^2$. Then

$$\mathscr{A} = \int_0^\infty \epsilon(\lambda)\,(-c\,d\lambda/\lambda^2) = c\epsilon_{max}\int_0^\infty (1/\lambda^2)\exp\{-(\lambda-\lambda_o)^2/2\gamma\}d\lambda$$

where $\exp\{-(\lambda-\lambda_o)^2/2\gamma\}$ is the Gaussian curve centered on λ_o, with a width determined by λ_o. The integral may be evaluated numerically, or approximated by setting $\lambda^2 \approx \lambda_o^2$ and extending the lower limit to $-\infty$ (which introduces a negligible error for narrow lines). Then

$$\mathscr{A} \approx c\epsilon_{max}(1/\lambda_o^2)\int_{-\infty}^{\infty} \exp\{-(\lambda-\lambda_o)^2/2\gamma\}d\lambda$$

$$= c\epsilon_{max}(2\pi\gamma)^{\frac{1}{2}}/\lambda_o^2 \text{ with } \gamma = \Delta\lambda_{\frac{1}{2}}^2/8\ln 2 \text{ [as in Problem 19.8]}.$$

For the 280 nm peak, $\Delta\lambda_{\frac{1}{2}} \approx 60$ nm;

$\lambda_o \approx 280$ nm; $\epsilon_{max} \approx 11\,M^{-1}\,cm^{-1}$.

$\gamma = (60\,\text{nm})^2/8\ln 2 = 6.5 \times 10^{-16}\,\text{m}^2, \sqrt{(2\pi\gamma)} = 6.4 \times 10^{-8}\,\text{m};$

$\mathscr{A} \approx (2.998 \times 10^{10}\,\text{cm s}^{-1}) \times (11\,\text{M}^{-1}\,\text{cm}^{-1})$

$\times (6.4 \times 10^{-8}\,\text{m})/(280\,\text{nm})^2 \approx 2.7 \times 10^{15}\,\text{cm}^2\,\text{s}^{-1}\,\text{mmol}^{-1}$,

$f = \underline{3.9 \times 10^{-4}}$.

For the 430 nm peak, $\Delta\lambda_{\frac{1}{2}} \approx 65$ nm; $\lambda_0 \approx 430$ nm,

$\epsilon_{\text{max}} \approx 18\,\text{M}^{-1}\,\text{cm}^{-1}$;

$\gamma = (65\,\text{nm})^2/8\ln 2 = 7.6 \times 10^{-16}\,\text{m}^2, \sqrt{(2\pi\gamma)} = 6.9 \times 10^{-8}\,\text{m}$,

$\approx (2.998 \times 10^{10}\,\text{cm s}^{-1}) \times (18\,\text{M}^{-1}\,\text{cm}^{-1})$

$\times (6.9 \times 10^{-8}\,\text{m})/(430\,\text{nm})^2 \approx 2.0 \times 10^{15}\,\text{cm}^2\,\text{s}^{-1}\,\text{mmol}^{-1}$,

$f \approx \underline{2.9 \times 10^{-4}}$.

19.11 $\Delta\tilde{\nu}_{\frac{1}{2}} = \left(\dfrac{1}{\lambda'} - \dfrac{1}{\lambda''}\right)$ [Problem 19.10]; $\mathscr{A} \approx 1.0645 c\epsilon_{\text{max}}\Delta\tilde{\nu}_{\frac{1}{2}}$ [Problem 19.8].

$\lambda' \approx 267$ nm, $\lambda'' \approx 303$ nm; $\epsilon_{\text{max}} \approx 235\,\text{M}^{-1}\,\text{cm}^{-1}$ [from Fig. 19.27 of the text].

$$\Delta\tilde{\nu}_{\frac{1}{2}} \approx \left(\frac{1}{267} - \frac{1}{303}\right) \times 10^9\,\text{m}^{-1} = 4.45 \times 10^5\,\text{m}^{-1} = 4.45 \times 10^3\,\text{cm}^{-1}.$$

$\mathscr{A} \approx 1.0645 \times (2.998 \times 10^{10}\,\text{cm s}^{-1}) \times (235\,\text{M}^{-1}\,\text{cm}^{-1}) \times (4450\,\text{cm}^{-1})$

$\approx 3.3 \times 10^{16}\,\text{cm}^2\,\text{s}^{-1}\,\text{mmol}^{-1}$.

$f \approx 1.44 \times 10^{-19} \times 3.3 \times 10^{16} = \underline{4.8 \times 10^{-3}}$.

The transition appears to be weakly forbidden.

The transition dipole moment transforms as $A_1(z)$, $B_1(x)$, $B_2(y)$, [Problem 17.12]; hence excitations to A_1, B_1, and B_2 states are allowed.

19.12 $f = (8\pi^2/3)(m_e\nu/he^2)\,|\mu|^2$ [19.1.8].

$$\mu_x = -e\int_0^L \psi_n(x)x\psi_n(x)\,\text{d}x \text{ [19.1.7]}.$$

$\psi_n(x) = (2/L)^{\frac{1}{2}}\sin(n\pi x/L); E_n = n^2h^2/8m_eL^2$ [14.1.9].

$$\mu_x = -(2e/L)\int_0^L x\sin(n'\pi x/L)\sin(n\pi x/L)\,\text{d}x = (8eL/\pi^2)n(n+1)/(2n+1)^2,$$

for $n \to n+1$. For $n \to n+2$, $\mu_x = 0$.

$h\nu = E_{n+1} - E_n = (2n+1)(h^2/8m_eL^2)$.

$$f_{n\to n+1} = \left(\frac{8\pi^2}{3}\right)\left(\frac{m_e}{he^2}\right)\left(\frac{h}{8m_eL^2}\right)(2n+1)\left(\frac{8eL}{\pi^2}\right)^2\frac{n^2(n+1)^2}{(2n+1)^4}$$

$$= \left(\frac{64}{3\pi^2}\right)\left\{\frac{n^2(n+1)^2}{(2n+1)^3}\right\}.$$

$f_{n\to n+2} = 0.$

19.13 $\nu = (E_{n+1} - E_n)/h = (2n+1)(h/8m_eL^2), L \approx 22R_{cc}$,

$R_{cc} \approx 140$ pm [Problem 16.30]. Highest filled orbital has $n = 11$ [there are 22 π-electrons]; $2n + 1 = 23$:

$$\nu = 23h/8m_eL^2 = \frac{23 \times (6.626 \times 10^{-34}\,\text{J s})}{8 \times (9.110 \times 10^{-31}\,\text{kg}) \times (22 \times 140 \times 10^{-12}\,\text{m})^2}$$

$$= 2.2 \times 10^{14}\,\text{s}^{-1}.$$

$\tilde{\nu} = \nu/c = (2.2 \times 10^{14}\,\text{s}^{-1})/(2.998 \times 10^{10}\,\text{cm s}^{-1}) \approx 7400\,\text{cm}^{-1}$.

This suggests that carrots absorb in the infrared; which they do, but not for this reason. In order to get a carrot color, one needs absorption in the blue end of the spectrum.

$$f_{11\to 12} = (64/3\pi^2)\left\{\frac{11^2 12^2}{23^3}\right\} \text{ [Problem 19.12]} = 3.1$$

$$\mathscr{A} = (f/1.44 \times 10^{-19})\,\text{cm}^2\,\text{s}^{-1}\,\text{mmol}^{-1}$$
$$= 2.2 \times 10^{19}\,\text{cm}^2\,\text{s}^{-1}\,\text{mmol}^{-1}.$$

$$\epsilon_{max} \approx \mathscr{A}/\Delta\nu \approx \mathscr{A}/(1.5 \times 10^{14}\,\text{s}^{-1}) \text{ [Problem 19.6]}$$
$$\approx 1.4 \times 10^5\,\text{mol}^{-1}\,\text{dm}^3\,\text{cm}^{-1} = 1.4 \times 10^5\,\text{M}^{-1}\text{cm}^{-1}.$$

$l = -(1/[\text{J}]\,\epsilon)\lg(I_f/I_i)$ [19.1.4]; $I_f/I_i = \frac{1}{2}$.

$l = \lg 2/[(1\,\text{M}) \times (1.4 \times 10^5\,\text{M}^{-1}\,\text{cm}^{-1})] = 2 \times 10^{-6}$ cm

which is no more than a lick left on the plate. This shows the limitations of the FEMO method.

19.14 $f_{n\to n+1} = (64/3\pi^2)\{n^2(n+1)^2/(2n+1)^3\}$ [Problem 19.12].

The value of n depends on the number of bonds: every π-bond adds two π-electrons, and so n increases by 1. For large n, $f \propto n$. f for the lowest frequency transition therefore increases as the chain is lengthened. The energy of the transition is proportional to $(2n+1)/L^2$; but $n \propto L$, as just mentioned, and so the transition energy is proportional to $1/L$. Therefore, the transition moves towards the red as L is increased. Consequently the apparent color of the dye becomes bluer.

19.15 $\mu = -e\int \psi_{v'} x \psi_v \,d\tau$ [19.1.7]

From Problem 14.14:

$\mu_{1,0} = -e\int \psi_1 x \psi_0 \mathrm{d}\tau = -e\alpha(1/2)^{\frac{1}{2}}$

$= -e\alpha/2^{\frac{1}{2}} = -e\{\hbar/2(m_e k)^{\frac{1}{2}}\}^{\frac{1}{2}}$ [Box 14.1]

$f = (8\pi^2/3)(m_e\nu/he^2)\mu_{1,0}^2$ [19.1.8]

$= \frac{1}{2}(8\pi^2/3)(m_e\nu/he^2)e^2\hbar/(m_e k)^{\frac{1}{2}}$

$= (1/3)(m_e^{\frac{1}{2}}\omega/h)h/k^{\frac{1}{2}} = (1/3)\omega(m_e/k)^{\frac{1}{2}} = \underline{1/3}$ $[\omega = (k/m_e)^{\frac{1}{2}}]$.

19.16 $\mu = -eRS$ [given]; $S(R) = \{1 + (R/a_0) + \frac{1}{3}(R/a_0)^2\} \times \exp(-R/a_0)$ [Problem 16.14].

$f = (8\pi^2/3)(m_e\nu/he^2)\mu^2$ [19.1.8] $= (8\pi^2/3)(m_e\nu/h)R^2S^2$

$= (8\pi^2/3)(m_e\nu/h)a_0^2(R/a_0)^2S^2$.

Draw up the following Table

R/a_0	0	1	2	3	4
$f/(8\pi^2/3)(m_e\nu/h)a_0^2$	0	0.737	1.376	1.093	0.573

R/a_0	5	6	7	8
$f/(8\pi^2/3)(m_e\nu/h)a_0^2$	0.233	0.08	0.02	0.01

These points are plotted in Fig. 19.3.

The maximum of f occurs at the maximum of RS.

$(\mathrm{d}/\mathrm{d}R)RS = S + R(\mathrm{d}S/\mathrm{d}R)$

$= \{1 + (R/a_0) - \frac{1}{3}(R/a_0)^3\}\exp(-R/a_0) = 0$ at $R = R^*$.

That is, $1 + (R^*/a_0) - \frac{1}{3}(R^*/a_0)^3 = 0$.

Solve this numerically (e.g. by trying values close to $R/a_0 \approx 2.1$, see Fig. 19.3), or analytically [Abramowitz and Stegun, *Handbook of Mathematical Functions,* Section 3.8.2]: $R/a_0 = \underline{2.103\,80.}$

As $R \to 0$ the transition becomes $s \to s$, which is forbidden. As $R \to \infty$, the electron is confined to a single atom because its wavefunction does not extend to the other.

19.17 (a) Ethene belongs to D_{2h}; in this group translations (and hence μ) transform as $B_{1u}(z)$, $B_{2u}(y)$, $B_{3u}(x)$. The π-orbital is B_{1u} (like z); the π^* orbital B_{3g}. Since $B_{3g} \times$

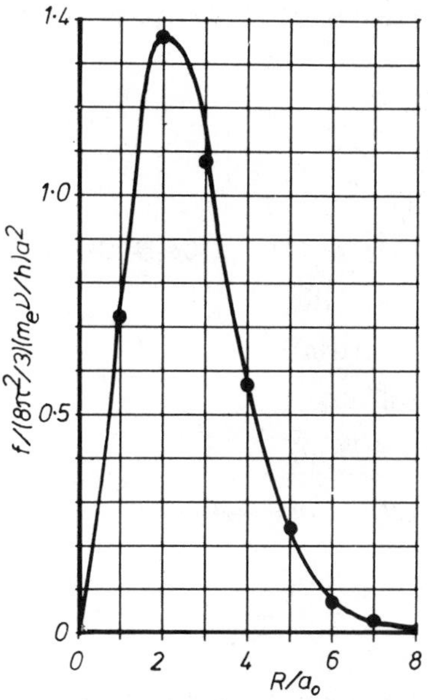

Fig 19.3

$B_{1u} = B_{2u}$ and $B_{2u} \times B_{2u} = A_{1g}$, the transition is allowed (with *y*-polarization).

(b) Regard the carbonyl group as locally C_{2v}. The transition moment has components transforming as A_1, B_1, B_2. The *n*-orbital is p_y (in the $>$CO plane), and hence transforms as B_2. The π^*-orbital is p_x (perpendicular to the plane), and hence transforms as B_1. $\Gamma_f \times \Gamma_i = B_1 \times B_2 = A_2$; but no component of μ transforms as A_2, and so the transition is forbidden.

19.18 Vibrational energy spacing of the *lower* state is determined by the spacing of the peaks of A [Section 19.4(a)]. From the spectrum $\tilde{\nu} \approx 1800\ cm^{-1}$ [the scale is about 1 cm $\widehat{=}$ 1175 cm^{-1}]. Nothing can be said about the spacing of the upper state levels (without a detailed analysis of the intensities).

19.19 The benzophenone does absorb in the 360 nm region, and after some vibrational decay is able to transfer its excitation energy to naphthalene. The latter then emits radiatively.

19.20 The fluorescence spectrum gives the vibrational splitting of the lower state. The wavelengths correspond to the wavenumbers 22 730, 24 390, 25 640, 27 030 cm^{-1}, indicating spacing of 1660, 1250, and 1390 cm^{-1}. The absorption spectrum spacing gives the separation of the vibrational levels in the upper state. The wavenumbers of the absorption peaks are 27 800, 29 000, 30 300, 32 800 cm^{-1}. The vibrational spacing is therefore 1200 cm^{-1}, 1300 cm^{-1}, 2500 cm^{-1}.

19.21 Absorbance $A = \epsilon[\mathrm{J}]l$ [Section 19.1]. When only HIn is present at a concentration C:

$A(\mathrm{HIn}) = \epsilon(\mathrm{HIn})\,[\mathrm{HIn}]_0 l = \epsilon(\mathrm{HIn})Cl.$

When all that HIn is present as In^-,

$A(\mathrm{In}^-) = \epsilon(\mathrm{In}^-)\,[\mathrm{In}^-]_0 l = \epsilon(\mathrm{In}^-)Cl.$

$A(\mathrm{mix}) = \epsilon(\mathrm{HIn})\,[\mathrm{HIn}]l + \epsilon(\mathrm{In}^-)\,[\mathrm{In}^-]l = (1-\alpha)C\epsilon(\mathrm{HIn})l + \alpha C\epsilon(\mathrm{In}^-)l,$

where α is the degree of dissociation of HIn.

$A(\mathrm{mix}) = C\epsilon(\mathrm{HIn})l + \alpha Cl\{\epsilon(\mathrm{In}^-) - \epsilon(\mathrm{HIn})\}$

$\quad = A(\mathrm{HIn}) + \alpha\{A(\mathrm{In}^-) - A(\mathrm{HIn})\}.$

$\alpha = \{A(\mathrm{mix}) - A(\mathrm{HIn})\}/\{A(\mathrm{In}^-) - A(\mathrm{HIn})\}.$

$K_{\mathrm{In}} = [\mathrm{H}^+]\,[\mathrm{In}^-]/[\mathrm{HIn}] = [\mathrm{H}^+]\,\alpha/(1-\alpha)$; therefore $[\mathrm{H}^+] = (1-\alpha)K_{\mathrm{In}}/\alpha$, and so

$\mathrm{pH} = \mathrm{p}K_{\mathrm{In}} - \lg\{(1-\alpha)/\alpha\},$

with α given by the expression above.

When $A(\mathrm{In}^-) = 0$ and $A(\mathrm{HIn}) = A$, $\alpha = 1 - A(\mathrm{mix})/A$, $(1-\alpha)/\alpha = 10^{\mathrm{p}K_{\mathrm{In}} - \mathrm{pH}}$.

$A(\mathrm{mix})/A = 1/\{1 + 10^{\mathrm{pH} - \mathrm{p}K_{\mathrm{In}}}\}.$

Draw up the following Table:

pH	1	2	3	3.5	4	4.5	5	6	7
$A(\mathrm{mix})/A$	1.00	0.90	0.91	0.76	0.50	0.24	0.09	0.01	0.001

These points are plotted in Fig. 19.4.

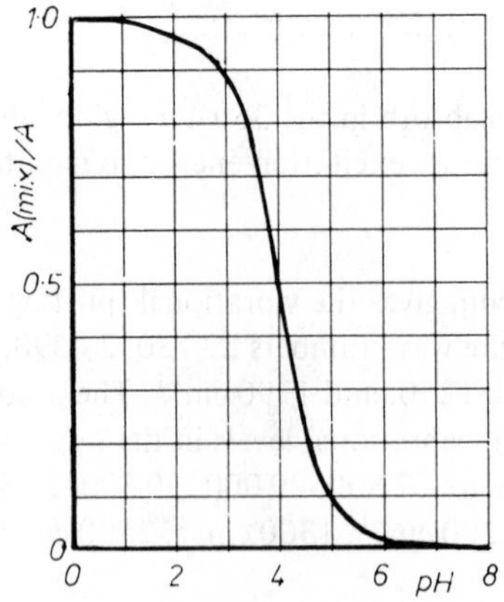

Fig 19.4

19.22 $A(\text{mix}) = A(\text{HIn}) + \alpha\{A(\text{In}^-) - A(\text{HIn})\}$ [Problem 19.21].

There will be some wavelength where $A(\text{In}^-) = A(\text{HIn})$; then $A(\text{mix})$ is independent of α. This is the isobestic point.

19.23 From the data, $\epsilon(\text{InH}) = 8.33 \times 10^3\,\text{M}^{-1}\,\text{cm}^{-1}$, $\epsilon(\text{In}^-) = 18.33 \times 10^3\,\text{M}^{-1}\,\text{cm}^{-1}$.

$A(\text{InH}) = (1-\alpha)Cl\epsilon(\text{InH}), A(\text{In}^-) = \alpha Cl\epsilon(\text{InH})$.

$A(\text{InH})/Cl$ and $A(\text{In}^-)/Cl$ are the effective molar absorption coefficients of the InH and In^-species; call these $E(\text{InH}), E(\text{In}^-)$.

Then $E(\text{InH}) = (1-\alpha)\epsilon(\text{InH}); E(\text{In}^-) = \alpha\epsilon(\text{In}^-)$.

Hence, draw up the following Table

pH	4	5	6	7	8	9	10	
	1	1	0.92	0.40	0.05	–	–	$1-\alpha = E(\text{InH})/\epsilon(\text{InH})$
hence α	0	0	0.08	0.50	0.95	–	–	
α	–	–	0.09	0.50	0.95	1.00	1.00	$\alpha = E(\text{In}^-)/\epsilon(\text{In}^-)$
average α	0	0	0.08	0.50	0.95	1.00	1.00	

Form pK_{In} from $pK_{\text{In}} = \text{pH} - \lg\{\alpha/(1-\alpha)\}$ [Problem 19.21]

and draw up the following Table:

pH	6.0	7.0	8.0	
pK_{In}	7.1	7.0	6.7	Average: 6.9.

19.24 Use the technique described in *Example* 18.6. Plot the differences $\Delta\tilde{\nu}_v$ against v. Fig. 19.5. The separation between neighboring lines vanishes at $v = 17$. Each square corresponds to $100\,\text{cm}^{-1}$. The area under the line is 68.0 squares, corresponding to $6800\,\text{cm}^{-1}$.

19.25 The ground state $\rightarrow {}^3\Sigma_u^-$ excitation energy (to $v = 0$) is $50\,062.6\,\text{cm}^{-1}$, or 6.21 eV. The ${}^3\Sigma_u^- \rightarrow \text{O} + \text{O}^*$ energy is 0.85 eV [Problem 19.24]. Hence $O_2 \rightarrow \text{O} + \text{O}^*$ is 7.06 eV. The $\text{O}^* \rightarrow \text{O}$ energy is $-190\,\text{kJ mol}^{-1}$, or -1.97 eV. Hence the $O_2 \rightarrow 2\text{O}$ energy is $7.06\,\text{eV} - 1.97\,\text{eV} = 5.09\,\text{eV}$.

19.26 Use the Clebsch-Gordan series [15.2.1] to compound the two resultant momenta; conserve angular momentum.

(a) O_2. $S = 1$; configuration of O is . . . $2p^4$, equivalent to . . . $(2p)^6(2p)^{-2}$; $S_1 = 1, S_2 = 0$ combine to $S = 1$; $S_1 = 1$, $S_2 = 1$ can combine to $S = 1$. Hence multiplicities $\underline{3 + 1,\ 3 + 3}$ may be expected.

(b) N_2. $S = 0$; Configuration of N is . . . $2p^3$. $S_1 = \frac{3}{2}, S_2 = \frac{3}{2}$ can combine to $S = 0$, $S_1 = \frac{1}{2}, S_2 = \frac{1}{2}$ can combine to $S = 0$. Hence multiplicities $\underline{4 + 4}$, $\underline{2 + 2}$ may be expected.

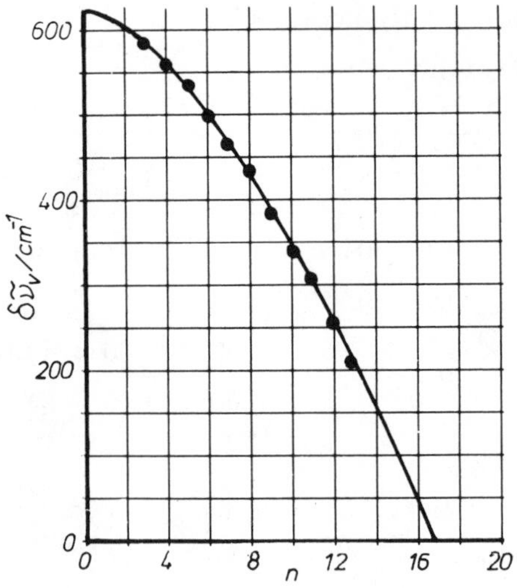

Fig 19.5

19.27

N_2: 5.6 eV line (binding energy: 15.6 eV): $2p\sigma_g$ electron

4.5 eV line (binding energy: 16.7 eV): $2p\pi_u$ electron

2.4 eV line (binding energy: 18.8 eV): $2s\sigma_u^*$ electron.

CO: 7.2 eV (b.e.: 14.0 eV): $2p\sigma$ electron

4.9 eV (b.e.: 16.3 eV): $2p\pi$ electron

1.7 eV (b.e.: 19.5 eV): $2s\sigma^*$ electron.

The spacing of the 4.5 eV N_2 lines is *c.* 0.24 eV, or *c.* 1940 cm^{-1}. The spacing of the 4.9 eV CO lines is *c.* 0.23 eV, or *c.* 1860 cm^{-1}. These are rough estimates from the illustrations of the separation of the vibrational levels of the N_2^+ and CO^+ ions in their relevant excited states.

19.28 Note that the configuration is $(2s\sigma^*)^2\,(2p\pi)^4\,(2p\sigma)^2\,(2p\pi^*)^1$; the data refer to the energy of the ejected electron, and so the ionization energies are 16.52 eV,

15.65 eV, and 9.21 eV. The 16.52 eV line refers to ionization of a 2pσ-electron, the 15.65 eV line (with its long vibrational progression) refers to ionization of a 2pπ-electron. The 9.21 eV line refers to the ionization of the least strongly attached electron, the one in 2pπ*.

19.29 0.41 eV corresponds to 3310 cm^{-1}, which is similar to the 3652 cm^{-1} of the non-ionized water. This suggests that the ejected electron comes from a non-bonding orbital.

19.30 0.125 eV corresponds to 1010 cm^{-1}, markedly less than the 1596 cm^{-1} of the bending mode. This suggests that the ejected electron tended to bond between the two hydrogens of the water molecule.

20. Determination of molecular structure: resonance techniques

A20.1 $m_I = 3/2, 1/2, -1/2, -3/2$. [Section 20.1]

$E_m = -g_I\mu_N m_I B$ [20.1.1] $= -(0.4289)(5.051 \times 10^{-27}\,\mathrm{J\,T^{-1}})(7.500\,\mathrm{T})m_I$

$= -1.625 \times 10^{-26} m_I\,\mathrm{J}; E_{3/2} = -E_{-3/2} = \underline{-2.437 \times 10^{-26}\,\mathrm{J}};$

$E_{1/2} = -E_{-1/2} = \underline{-8.124 \times 10^{-27}\,\mathrm{J}}.$

A20.2 $\Delta E = -g_I\mu_N B\Delta m_I$ [20.1.1].

$m_I = \pm 1$ for the lowest and highest energies

$|\Delta E| = (0.4036)(5.051 \times 10^{-27}\,\mathrm{J\,T^{-1}})(15.00\,\mathrm{T})(2) = \underline{6.116 \times 10^{-26}\,\mathrm{J}}.$

A20.3 $h\nu = g_I\mu_N B; B = h\nu g_I^{-1}\mu_N^{-1}$ [20.1.3].

$B = (6.626 \times 10^{-34}\,\mathrm{J\,s})(150.0 \times 10^6\,\mathrm{Hz})(5.586)^{-1}(5.051 \times 10^{-27}\,\mathrm{J\,T^{-1}})^{-1}$

$= \underline{3.523\,\mathrm{T}}.$

A20.4 $(2\pi\delta\nu)^{-1} = (2)^{-1}(3.14)^{-1}(90.0\,\mathrm{Hz})^{-1} = 1.77\,\mathrm{ms}$ [20.1.7].

Since 0.200 ms $\ll$ 1.77 ms, the lines will merge.

A20.5 $B = h\nu/(g_e\mu_B)$ [20.2.3]

$= (6.63 \times 10^{-34}\,\mathrm{J\,s})(3.00 \times 10^8\,\mathrm{m/s})(3.00 \times 10^{-2}\,\mathrm{m})^{-1}(3.10)^{-1}$

$\times (9.27 \times 10^{-24}\,\mathrm{J\,T^{-1}})^{-1} = \underline{0.231\,\mathrm{T}}.$

A20.6 $2I + 1 = 4$ and $I = \underline{3/2}$ [Section 20.2(c)].

A20.7 X^1H_2 has six sets (from X) of three lines (from two ^1H) or 18 lines. X^2H_2 has six sets of five lines (from two ^2H) or 30 lines [Section 20.2(c)].

A20.8 $\ln(N_\alpha/N_\beta) = -g_e\mu_B B/kT$ [0.1.2 and 20.2.3].

$T = -2.00(9.27 \times 10^{-24}\,\mathrm{J\,T^{-1}})(0.800)(1.38 \times 10^{-23}\,\mathrm{J\,K^{-1}})^{-1}[\ln(1/1.005)]^{-1}$

$= \underline{215\,\mathrm{K}}.$

A20.9 $v = \delta\nu c\nu^{-1}$ [*Example* 20.6] $= (30.5 \times 10^6\,\mathrm{s^{-1}})(26.8 \times 10^3\,\mathrm{eV})^{-1}$

$\times (8.07 \times 10^3\,\mathrm{cm^{-1}/eV})^{-1}$

$= 0.141\,\mathrm{cm\,s^{-1}}$, or $\underline{1.41\,\mathrm{mm\,s^{-1}}}$.

A20.10 Relative motion of sample and source detects a lowered frequency, and the sign of the shift is negative [Section 20.3(b)].

$\delta\nu = -\nu v c^{-1} = -(23.8 \times 10^3\,\text{eV})(8.07 \times 10^3\,\text{cm}^{-1}/\text{eV})(0.115\,\text{cm s}^{-1})$

$= \underline{-22.1\,\text{MHz.}}$ The tin is Sn(IV) [Section 20.3(c)].

20.1 $B = (h/g_I\mu_N)\nu$ [20.1.3]

$= \{(6.62618 \times 10^{-34}\,\text{J s})/(5.05082 \times 10^{-27}\,\text{J T}^{-1})\}\,(\nu/g_I)$

$= (1.3119 \times 10^{-7}\,\text{T s})\,(\nu/g_I)$.

Draw up the following Table with

(a) $\nu = 60\,\text{MHz}$, (b) $\nu = 300\,\text{MHz}$.

	^{1}H	^{2}H	^{13}C	^{14}N	^{19}F	^{31}P
g_I	5.5857	0.85745	1.4046	0.40356	5.2567	2.2634
B/T(a)	1.4	9.2	5.6	19.5	1.5	3.5
(b)	7.05	45.9	28.0	97.5	7.49	17.4

20.2 $(N_\alpha - N_\beta)/(N_\alpha + N_\beta) \approx g_I\,\mu_N B/2kT$ [20.1.4]

$= (5.5857 \times 5.05082 \times 10^{-27}\,\text{J T}^{-1})B/2 \times (1.38066 \times 10^{-23}\,\text{J K}^{-1})T$

$= 1.0217 \times 10^{-3}\,(B/\text{T})/(T/\text{K})$. [T in (B/T) is Tesla; T in (T/K) is temperature!].

Draw up the following Table with $T =$ (a) 4 K, (b) 300 K.

B/T	0.3	1.5	7.0
$\delta N/N$ (a)	7.7×10^{-5}	3.8×10^{-4}	1.8×10^{-3}
(b)	1.0×10^{-6}	5.1×10^{-6}	2.4×10^{-5}

20.3 $B = (h/g_I\mu_N)\nu$ [20.1.3]

$= (1.3119 \times 10^{-7}\,\text{T s}) \times (9 \times 10^9\,\text{Hz})/5.5854$ [Problem 20.1] $= 210\,\text{T}$.

$B = (h/g_e\mu_B)\nu = (0.71449 \times 10^{-10}\,\text{T s}^{-1}) \times (60 \times 10^6\,\text{Hz})/2 = 2.1 \times 10^{-3}\,\text{T}$.

Hence, use $\underline{210\,\text{T}}$ for proton NMR in an ESR spectrometer, and $\underline{2.1\,\text{mT}}$ for ESR in an NMR spectrometer.

20.4 $g_I = -3.8260$.

$B = (h/g_I\mu_N)\nu$ [20.1.3] $= (1.3119 \times 10^{-7}\,\mathrm{T\,s}) \times (60\,\mathrm{MHz})/3.8260 = \underline{2.06\,\mathrm{T}}$ (20.6 kG).
[The sign of g_I is irrelevant to the magnitude of B.]

$\delta N/N \approx g_I\mu_N B/2kT$ [20.1.4]

$$= -3.8260 \times (5.050\,82 \times 10^{-27}\,\mathrm{J\,T^{-1}}) \times (2.06\,\mathrm{T})/2 \times (1.381 \times 10^{-23}\,\mathrm{J\,K^{-1}}) \times (298.15\,\mathrm{K}) = \underline{-5 \times 10^{-6}}.$$

The $\beta(m = -\frac{1}{2})$ state lies lower, because $g_I < 0$ [20.1.1].

20.5 $B_{loc} = (1-\sigma)B$ [20.1.5]

$\delta B_{loc} = \delta\sigma B = (2.20 \times 10^{-6} - 9.80 \times 10^{-6})B = -7.60 \times 10^{-6}B$.

(a) $\delta B_{loc} = -7.60 \times 10^{-6} \times 1.5\,\mathrm{T} = \underline{-11\,\mu\mathrm{T}}.$

(b) $\delta B_{loc} = -7.60 \times 10^{-6} \times 7.0\,\mathrm{T} = \underline{-53\,\mu\mathrm{T}}.$

20.6 $\delta\nu = \nu\delta\sigma$ [Section 20.1(b)], $|\delta\sigma| = 7.60 \times 10^{-6}$.

(a) $\delta\nu = 7.60 \times 10^{-6} \times 60\,\mathrm{MHz} = \underline{460\,\mathrm{Hz}}.$

(b) $\delta\nu = 7.60 \times 10^{-6} \times 300\,\mathrm{MHz} = \underline{2.3\,\mathrm{kHz}}.$

20.7 See Fig. 20.1. On changing the frequency to 300 MHz the separation of the CH_3 and CHO peaks increases (by a factor of 5), the fine structure remains unchanged, and the intensity increases (because δN increases).

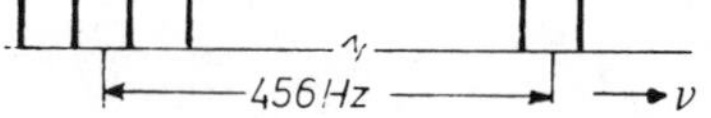

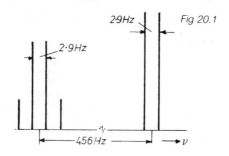

Fig 20.1

20.8 $|B_{nucl}| = g_I\mu_N(\mu_0/4\pi)(1/R^3)(1 - 3\cos^2\theta)m_I$ [20.1.6]

$$= g_I\mu_N(\mu_0/4\pi)(1/R^3) \text{ when } \theta = 0 \text{ and } m_I = -\tfrac{1}{2}.$$

$R = \{g_I\mu_N\mu_0/4\pi B_{nucl}\}^{1/3}$

$$= \left\{\frac{5.5857 \times (5.0508 \times 10^{-27}\,\mathrm{J\,T^{-1}}) \times (4\pi \times 10^{-7}\,\mathrm{T^2\,J^{-1}\,m^3})}{4\pi \times (0.715 \times 10^{-3}\,\mathrm{T})}\right\}^{1/3}$$

$$= \{3.946 \times 10^{-30}\,\mathrm{m^3}\}^{1/3}$$

$= \underline{1.58 \times 10^{-10}\,\text{m}\ (158\,\text{pm})}.$

20.9 $\langle B_{\text{nucl}}\rangle = g_I\mu_N(\mu_0/4\pi)(1/R^3)m_I \int_0^{\theta_{\max}} (1 - 3\cos^2\theta)\sin\theta\,\mathrm{d}\theta$

$$= -g_I\mu_N(\mu_0/4\pi)\,(1/R^3)m_I \int_1^{x_{\max}} (1 - 3x^2)\mathrm{d}x\ [x_{\max} = \cos\theta_{\max}]$$

$$= -g_I\mu_N(\mu_0/4\pi)\,(1/R^3)m_I\,\cos\theta_{\max}(1 - \cos^2\theta_{\max})$$

$$= -g_I\mu_N(\mu_0/4\pi)\,(1/R^3)m_I\,\cos\theta_{\max}\,\sin^2\theta_{\max}.$$

If $\theta_{\max} = \pi$, $\sin\theta_{\max} = 0$ and so $\langle B_{\text{nucl}}\rangle = 0$.

If $\theta_{\max} = 30°$, $\cos\theta_{\max}\,\sin^2\theta_{\max} = 0.217$.

$|\langle B_{\text{nucl}}\rangle| = 5.5857 \times (5.0508 \times 10^{-27}\,\text{J T}^{-1}) \times (10^{-7}\,\text{T}^2\,\text{J}^{-1}\,\text{m}^3)$

$\qquad \times (1/1.58 \times 10^{-10}\,\text{m})^3 \times \tfrac{1}{2} \times 0.217.$

$\qquad = 7.8 \times 10^{-5}\,\text{T}, \underline{78\,\mu\text{T}}.$

20.10 $\tau_J \approx 1/2\pi\delta\nu$ [20.1.7] $= 1/2\pi\nu\delta\sigma$.

$\tau_J \approx 1/2\pi \times (60 \times 10^6\,\text{Hz}) \times (5.2 \times 10^{-6} - 4.0 \times 10^{-6}) = 2.2 \times 10^{-3}\,\text{s}.$

The signals merge when the lifetime of each isomer is less than about 2 ms, corresponding to an interconversion rate of $\underline{500\,\text{s}^{-1}}$.

20.11 $\tau_J(280\,\text{K}) = 2.2$ ms [Problem 20.10].

$\tau_J(300\,\text{K}) = 1/2\pi \times (300 \times 10^6\,\text{Hz}) \times (1.2 \times 10^{-6}) = 4.4 \times 10^{-4}\,\text{s}.$

$$\tau_J = \tau_J^0 \exp(E_a/RT),\ \tau_J(T')/\tau_J(T) = \exp\left\{(E_a/R)\left(\frac{1}{T'} - \frac{1}{T}\right)\right\}.$$

$$E_a = R\left(\frac{1}{T'} - \frac{1}{T}\right)^{-1} \ln(\tau'/\tau)$$

$$= (8.314\,\text{J K}^{-1}\,\text{mol}^{-1}) \times \left(\frac{1}{300\,\text{K}} - \frac{1}{280\,\text{K}}\right)^{-1} \ln(4.4 \times 10^{-4}/2.2 \times 10^{-3})$$

$$= \underline{56\,\text{kJ mol}^{-1}}.$$

20.12 $J(\omega) \propto \text{re}\int_0^\infty \cos\omega_0 t\,\mathrm{e}^{-t/\tau + \mathrm{i}\omega t}\,\mathrm{d}t$

$$\propto \text{re}\int_0^\infty \{\mathrm{e}^{-t/\tau + \mathrm{i}(\omega+\omega_0)t} + \mathrm{e}^{-t/\tau + \mathrm{i}(\omega+\omega_0)t}\}\mathrm{d}t$$

$$\propto \text{re} \int_0^\infty \{e^{-[1/\tau - i(\omega+\omega_0)]t} + e^{-[1/\tau - i(\omega+\omega_0)]t}\} dt$$

$$\propto \text{re} \left\{ \frac{1}{1/\tau - i(\omega+\omega_0)} + \frac{1}{1/\tau - i(\omega-\omega_0)} \right\}$$

$$\propto \frac{1/\tau}{1/\tau^2 + (\omega+\omega_0)^2} + \frac{1/\tau}{1/\tau^2 + (\omega-\omega_0)^2}\,.$$

When $\omega \approx \omega_0$, only the second term is important; hence

$J(\omega) \propto \tau/\{1 + (\omega - \omega_0)^2\tau^2\}$,

which is a *Lorentzian function* centered on $\omega = \omega_0$, Fig. 20.2.

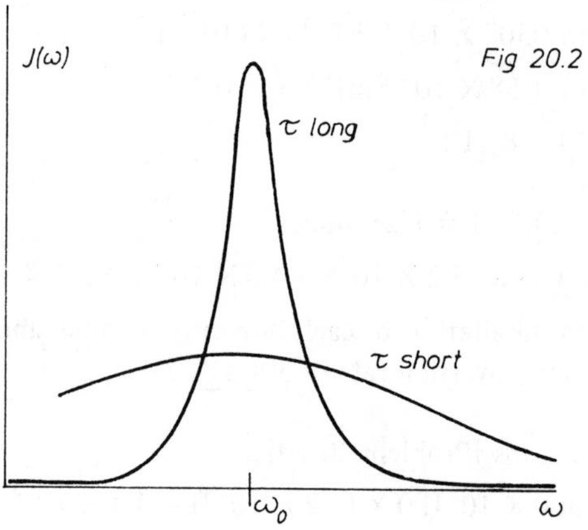

20.13 When $\omega \approx \omega_1, \omega_2$, use the result obtained in Problem 20.12, and write

$J(\omega) \propto A\tau/\{1 + (\omega_1 - \omega_0)^2\tau^2\} + B\tau/\{1 + (\omega_2 - \omega_0)^2\tau^2\}$,

which corresponds to the sum of two Lorentzians centered on ω_1 and ω_2, with relative intensities A and B respectively.

20.14 Form $G(t) = \sum_i A_i \cos \omega_i t e^{-t/\tau}$

where A_i are the relative intensities and ω_i the line centers, and plot $G(t)$ against t.

20.15 $h\nu = g\mu_B B$ [20.2.4] ; $\nu = c/\lambda$.

$B = hc/g\mu_B\lambda$

$= (6.626 \times 10^{-34}\,\text{J s}) \times (2.998 \times 10^8\,\text{m s}^{-1})/\{2 \times (9.274 \times 10^{-24}\,\text{J T}^{-1})$
$\times (8 \times 10^{-3}\,\text{m})\}$

$= \underline{1.3\,\text{T}, 13\,\text{kG}.}$

20.16 $n = 10^{10}/N_A = 10^{10}/(6.022 \times 10^{23}\,\text{mol}^{-1}) = 2 \times 10^{-14}\,\text{mol in }1\,\text{cm}^3$. Amount in dm^3 is therefore $2 \times 10^{-14} \times 10^3\,\text{mol} = 2 \times 10^{-11}\,\text{mol}$. Hence the spin concentration is $\underline{2 \times 10^{-11}\,\text{mol dm}^{-3}}$.

$$N_\beta - N_\alpha = (N_\beta + N_\alpha)\left\{\frac{1-\exp(-2\mu_B B/kT)}{1+\exp(-2\mu_B B/kT)}\right\} \quad [20.1.4]$$

$N_\alpha + N_\beta = 2.5 \times 10^{14}, B = 0.3\,\text{T}$ [typical X-band field, Section 20.21a]

$2\mu_B B/kT = 2 \times (0.3\,\text{T}) \times (9.27 \times 10^{-24}\,\text{J T}^{-1})/\{(1.38 \times 10^{-23}\,\text{J K}^{-1}) \times (298\,\text{K})\}$

$\qquad = 1.35 \times 10^{-3}$.

$\exp(-2\mu_B B/kT) = 0.998\,65$.

$N_\beta - N_\alpha \approx (2.5 \times 10^{14}) \times (6.75 \times 10^{-4}) = 1.7 \times 10^{11}$.

$(N_\beta - N_\alpha)/(N_\beta + N_\alpha) = \underline{6.8 \times 10^{-4}}$.

20.17 $$\frac{\delta N}{N} = \left\{\frac{1-\exp(-2\mu_B B/kT)}{1+\exp(-2\mu_B B/kT)}\right\} \quad [20.1.4].$$

$2\mu_B B/kT = 2 \times (0.3\,\text{T}) \times (9.274 \times 10^{-24}\,\text{J T}^{-1})/\{(1.381 \times 10^{-23}\,\text{J K}^{-1}) \times T\}$

$\qquad = 0.4029/(T/\text{K})$.

(a) $T = 4\,\text{K}, 2\mu_B B/kT = 0.1007, \delta N/N = \underline{0.05}$.

(b) $T = 300\,\text{K}, 2\mu_B B/kT = 0.0013, \delta N/N = \underline{0.0007}$.

20.18 $g = h\nu/\mu_B B$ [20.2.4]. We shall often need the value of h/μ_B:

$h/\mu_B = (6.626\,18 \times 10^{-34}\,\text{J s})/(9.274\,08 \times 10^{-24}\,\text{J T}^{-1}) = 7.144\,84 \times 10^{-11}\,\text{T s}$.

$g = (7.144\,84 \times 10^{-11}\,\text{T s}) \times (9.2231 \times 10^9\,\text{s}^{-1})/(329.12 \times 10^{-3}\,\text{T}) = \underline{2.00224.}$

20.19 $B = h\nu/g\mu_B$ [20.2.4].

(a) $B = (7.1448 \times 10^{-11}\,\text{T s}) \times (9.302 \times 10^9\,\text{s}^{-1})/(2.0025) = \underline{331.9\,\text{mT}}$ (3319 G)

(b) $B = (7.1448 \times 10^{-11}\,\text{T s}) \times (33.67 \times 10^9\,\text{s}^{-1})/(2.0025) = \underline{1.201\,\text{T}}$ (12.01 kG).

20.20 $\delta B = B_{\text{local}} - B = -\sigma B$ [Section 20.2(b)], $g = g_e(1-\sigma), g_e = 2.0023$.

$B = (g - g_e)B/g_e = (2.0102 - 2.0023)B/2.0023 = 3.9 \times 10^{-3}B$.

(a) $B = 3400\,\text{G}, \delta B = 3.9 \times 10^{-3} \times (3400\,\text{G}) = \underline{13\,\text{G}}$ (1.3 mT).

(b) $B = 12.3\,\text{kG}, \delta B = 3.9 \times 10^{-3} \times (12.3\,\text{kG}) = \underline{48\,\text{G}}$ (4.8 mT).

20.21 $g = h\nu/\mu_B B = (7.1448 \times 10^{-11}\,\text{T s}) \times (9.302 \times 10^9\,\text{s}^{-1})/B = 0.6646/(B/\text{T})$.

(a) $g = 0.6646/(333.64 \times 10^{-3}) = \underline{1.9920.}$

(b) $g = 0.6646/(331.94 \times 10^{-3}) = \underline{2.0022.}$

20.22 $a = B(2) - B(1)$ [20.2.6] $= 357.3\,\text{mT} - 306.6\,\text{mT} = \underline{50.7\,\text{mT}}$ (507 G).

20.23 $a = B(3) - B(2) = B(2) - B(1)$ [20.2.6]

$$\left.\begin{aligned} B(3) - B(2) &= 334.8\,\text{mT} - 332.5\,\text{mT} = 2.3\,\text{mT} \\ B(2) - B(1) &= 332.5\,\text{mT} - 330.2\,\text{mT} = 2.3\,\text{mT} \end{aligned}\right\} \; a = \underline{2.3\,\text{mT}.}$$

20.24 Use the center line to calculate g.

$g = h\nu/\mu_B B = (7.1148 \times 10^{-11}\,\text{T s}) \times (9.319 \times 10^9\,\text{s}^{-1})/(332.5\,\text{mT}) = \underline{2.0025.}$

The frequency corresponding to 1.0 mT and this g-value is

$\nu = g\mu_B B/h = 2.0025 \times (1.0 \times 10^{-3}\,\text{T})/(7.1448 \times 10^{-11}\,\text{T s}) = 2.803 \times 10^7\,\text{s}^{-1}$.

Therefore, a splitting constant of 2.3 mT may be expressed as $6.4 \times 10^7\,\text{s}^{-1}$, or $\underline{64\,\text{MHz}.}$

20.25 Center of spectrum: 332.5 mT

Proton 1: Splits the line into two with separation 2.0 mT and centered on the original line, hence the lines occur at 331.5 mT and 333.5 mT.

Proton 2: Splits the lines just mentioned into two, each separation being 2.6 mT and centered on the two lines; hence two lines occur at 331.5 mT ± 1.3 mT, and two at 333.5 mT ± 1.3 mT. The spectrum therefore consists of 4 lines of equal intensity, at the magnetic fields 330.2 mT, 332.2 mT, 332.8 mT, 334.8 mT.

20.26 $\tau_J \lesssim 1/2\pi\delta\nu$ [20.1.7]; $\delta\nu$ corresponds to the difference $|a(2) - a(1)|$ expressed as a frequency.

$|a(2) - a(1)| = 0.6\,\text{mT}$; use $1\,\text{mT} \approx 28\,\text{MHz}$ [Problem 20.24],

so that $\delta\nu \approx 0.6 \times 2.8 \times 10^7\,\text{s}^{-1} = 1.7 \times 10^7\,\text{s}^{-1}$.

$\tau_J \lesssim 1/2\pi(1.7 \times 10^7\,\text{s}^{-1}) = 9.4 \times 10^{-9}\,\text{s}$, corresponding to a conversion rate of $1/\tau_J = \underline{1.1 \times 10^8\,\text{s}^{-1}.}$

20.27 Construct Fig. 20.3(a) for CH_3 and Fig. 20.3(b) for CD_3.

20.28 Refer to Fig. 20.3. The width of the CH_3 spectrum is $3a_H$, or $\underline{0.69\,\text{mT}.}$ The width of the CD_3 spectrum is $6a_D$. The splittings are proportional to the nuclear g-values; hence

$a_D \approx (0.857\,45/5.5857)a_H = 0.1535a_H = 0.035\,\text{mT}$.

Overall width $= 6a_D = \underline{0.21\,\text{mT}.}$

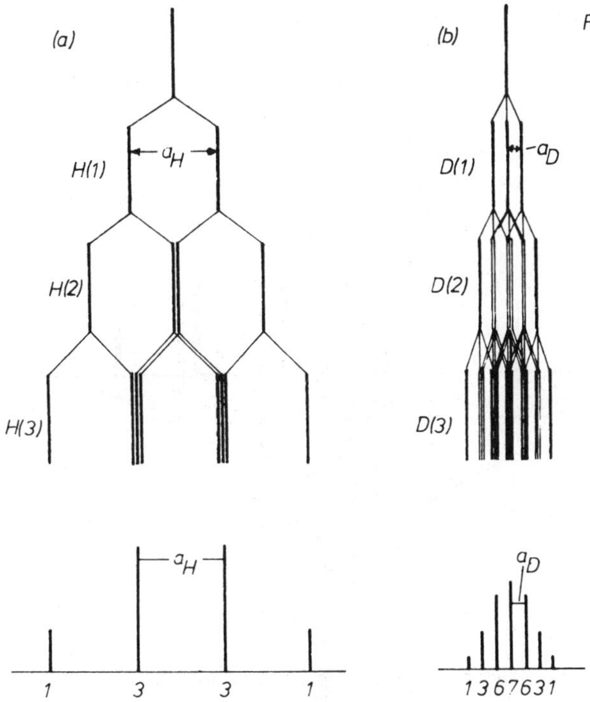

Fig 20.3

20.29 Construct the spectrum by taking account first of CH_3 splitting (which gives an initial 1:3:3:1 quartet) and then the splitting of each of these four lines into a 1:2:1 triplet by the CH_2 group. The construction is shown in Fig. 20.4.

On deuteration of the CH_2, four triplets are replaced by 1:2:3:2:1 quintets with a splitting smaller by a factor 0.1535 than the original portion CH_2 splitting; i.e. 0.034 mT.

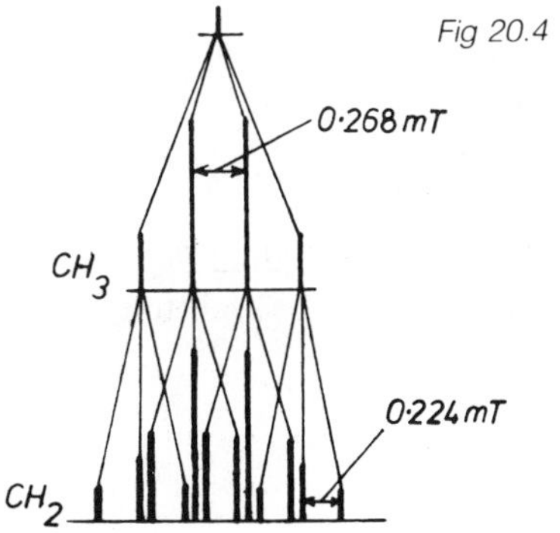

Fig 20.4

20.30 Construct the spectrum by taking account first of the two equivalent nitrogen splittings (into a 1:2:3:2:1 quintet), and then the splitting of each of these lines into a 1:4:6:4:1 quintet by the four equivalent protons. The resulting 25 line spectrum is shown in Fig. 20.5.

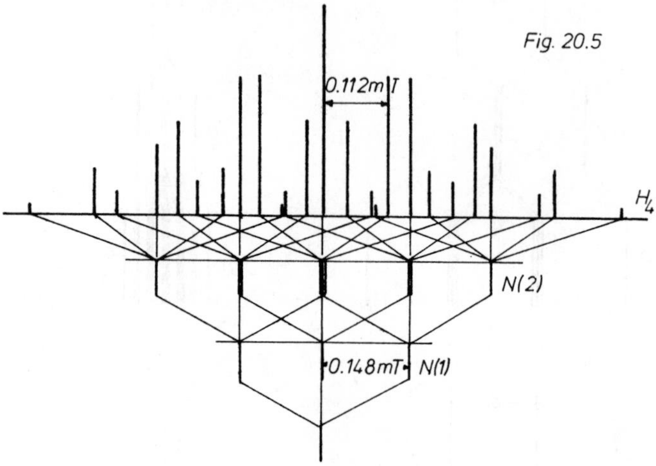

Fig. 20.5

20.31 $P(\text{N2s}) = (5.7\text{ mT})/(55.2\text{ mT}) = \underline{0.10}$ (10% of its time).

20.32 $P(\text{N2p}) = (1.3\text{ mT})/(3.4\text{ mT}) = \underline{0.38}$ (38% of its time).

20.33 $P(\text{N}) = P(\text{N2s}) + P(\text{N2p}) = \underline{0.48}$,

$P(\text{O}) = 1 - P(\text{N}) = \underline{0.52}$.

Hybridization ratio: $P(\text{N2p})/P(\text{N2s}) = 0.38/0.10 = \underline{3.8}$ ($sp^{3.8}$). The unparied electron therefore occupies an orbital resembling an sp^3 orbital on N, as in the discussion in Problem 16.24.

$a'^2 = (1 + \cos\Theta)/(1 - \cos\Theta)$ [16.3.5]

$b'^2 = 1 - a'^2 = -2\cos\Theta/(1 - \cos\Theta)$

$\lambda = b'^2/a'^2 = 2\cos\Theta/(1 + \cos\Theta)$; $\cos\Theta = -\lambda/(2 + \lambda)$.

Since $\lambda = 3.8$, $\cos\Theta = -0.66$; $\Theta = \underline{131°}$.

20.34 The (benzene)$^-$ h.f.s. is 0.375 mT [20.2.7], which is $\frac{1}{6} \times$ (2.25 mT). Therefore, unit electron spin density leads to a hyperfine splitting of 2.25 mT. Hence construct the following maps:

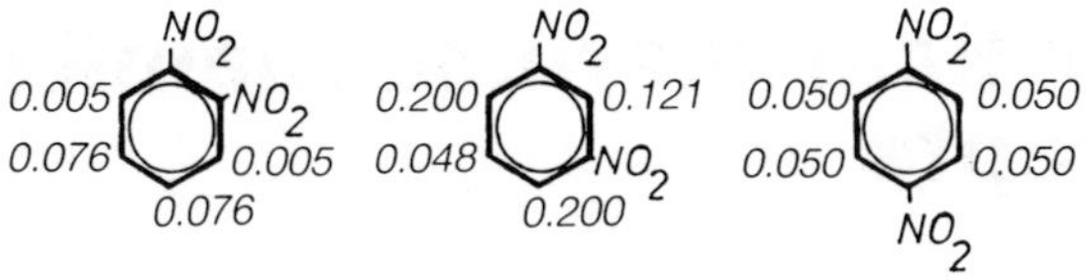

20.35 Use the (benzene)$^-$ value as in Problem 20.34.

20.36 Rotation about the bond modulates the h.f. coupling from 113.1 MHz to 11.2 MHz; use $\tau \lesssim 1/2\pi\delta\nu$ [20.1.7]. $\tau_J \lesssim 1/\{2\pi \times (113.1 - 11.2) \times 10^6\ \mathrm{s^{-1}}\}$ $= 1.6 \times 10^{-9}\ \mathrm{s}$. That is, at 115 K it rotates around the parallel axis so as to change from one orientation (113.1 MHz hyperfine coupling) to the other (11.2 MHz) in about $\underline{1.6 \times 10^{-9}\ \mathrm{s}}$.

20.37 Photon momentum $= h\nu/c = -$(atom momentum) $= mv$.

1 keV $= 1.602 \times 10^{-16}$ J [end-paper 1].

$v = h\nu/mc = 14.4 \times (1.602 \times 10^{-16}\ \mathrm{J})/m \times (2.998 \times 10^8\ \mathrm{m\,s^{-1}})$

$= (7.69 \times 10^{-24}\ \mathrm{m\,s^{-1}})/(m/\mathrm{kg})$.

(a) $m(^{57}\mathrm{Fe}) = 57 \times (1.661 \times 10^{-27}\ \mathrm{kg}) = 9.5 \times 10^{-26}\ \mathrm{kg}$;

$v = (7.69 \times 10^{-24}\ \mathrm{m\,s^{-1}})/(9.5 \times 10^{-26}) = \underline{80\ \mathrm{m\,s^{-1}}}$.

(b) $m(\text{crystal}) = 1.00 \times 10^{-4}\ \mathrm{kg}$;

$v = (7.69 \times 10^{-24}\ \mathrm{m\,s^{-1}})/10^{-4} = \underline{7.7 \times 10^{-20}\ \mathrm{m\,s^{-1}}}$.

$\delta\nu = \nu v/c$ [Section 20.3(a)] $= v(1.602 \times 10^{-16}\ \mathrm{J})/(6.626 \times 10^{-34}\ \mathrm{J\,s})$

$\times (2.998 \times 10^8\ \mathrm{m\,s^{-1}}) = (8.06 \times 10^8\ \mathrm{Hz}) \times (v/\mathrm{m\,s^{-1}})$.

(a) $\delta\nu = (8.06 \times 10^8\ \mathrm{Hz}) \times 80 = \underline{6.5 \times 10^{10}\ \mathrm{Hz}}$.

(b) $\delta\nu = \underline{6.2 \times 10^{-11}\ \mathrm{Hz}}$.

20.38 In $Na_4Fe(CN)_6$ the ^{57}Fe environment is octahedral and there is no quadrupole splitting [Section 20.3(c)]. In $Na_2Fe(CN)_5NO$ the environment is axially symmetrical, and the resonance is split into two [Section 20.3(c)].

20.39 Increasing ionic character reduces the amount of 6s character, and hence increases the magnitude of the isomer shift. Ionicity increases along the series AuI, AuBr, AuCl. See original reference.

21. Statistical thermodynamics: the concepts

A21.1 $q = (2\pi m/h^2\beta)^{3/2} V$. [21.1.15]

(a) $q = [2\pi \times (0.120\,\text{kg})(6.02 \times 10^{23})^{-1}(1.38 \times 10^{-23}\,\text{J/K})(300\,\text{K})]^{3/2}$
$\times (6.63 \times 10^{-34}\,\text{J s})^{-3}(2 \times 10^{-6}\,\text{m}^3) = \underline{2.58 \times 10^{27}}.$

(b) $q = 2.58 \times 10^{27}(400\,\text{K}/300\,\text{K})^{3/2} = \underline{3.97 \times 10^{27}}.$

A21.2 $4^{3/2}/2^{3/2} = \underline{2.83}.$ [21.1.15]

A21.3 $q = 3 + \exp(-3500\,\text{cm}^{-1} \times u) + 3\exp(-4700\,\text{cm}^{-1} \times u)$ [21.1.10]
where $u = hc/1900\,k = 1.439\,\text{cm K}/1900\,\text{K} = 7.573 \times 10^{-4}\,\text{cm}.$
$q = 3 + 0.0706 + (0.0285)(3) = \underline{3.156}.$

A21.4 $[U - U(0)]/N = q^{-1}[\epsilon_1\exp(-\epsilon_1\beta) + 3\epsilon_2\exp(-\epsilon_2\beta)]$
$= 1.986 \times 10^{-23}\,\text{J cm}(3.156)^{-1}[3500\,\text{cm}^{-1}\exp(-2.650) + 3(4700\,\text{cm}^{-1})\exp(-3.559)]$
$= 4.08 \times 10^{-21}\,\text{J} \,\hat{=}\, \underline{2.46\,\text{kJ mol}^{-1}}.$

A21.5 $10/90 = \exp(-540\,\text{cm}^{-1}u)$ and $u = 4.07 \times 10^{-3}\,\text{cm}$ [21.1.8]
$T = 1.439\,\text{cm K}/4.07 \times 10^{-3}\,\text{cm} = \underline{354\,\text{K}}.$

A21.6 $13! = 6\,227\,020\,800 \approx 6.227 \times 10^9$;
$\exp(13\ln 13 - 13) = 6.846 \times 10^8$;
$\exp[13.5\ln 13 - 13 + 0.5\ln(2\pi)] = 6.187 \times 10^9.$

A21.7 $S = nR\ln\{e^{5/2}(2\pi mkT/h^2)^{3/2}kT/p\}$ [21.3.10]
$= (1\,\text{mol}) \times (8.314\,\text{J K}^{-1}\text{mol}^{-1}) \times \ln\{e^{5/2}$
$\times (2\pi \times 20.18 \times 1.6606 \times 10^{-27}\,\text{kg})^{3/2}$
$\times (1.38 \times 10^{-23}\,\text{J K}^{-1} \times 298\,\text{K})^{5/2}/(6.626 \times 10^{-34}\,\text{J s})^3$
$\times (1.013 \times 10^5\,\text{N m}^{-2})\}$
$= (8.314\,\text{J K}^{-1}) \times 17.58 = \underline{146\,\text{J K}^{-1}}.$

A21.8 $\beta\epsilon = (1.44 \times 10^{-2}\,\text{m K})(7.32 \times 10^4\,\text{m}^{-1})/300\,\text{K} = 3.51.$ [21.2.4]
$q = (1 - \exp[-3.51])^{-1} = 1.03.$
$[U - U(0)]/T = nN_A q\epsilon[\exp(-\beta\epsilon)]/T$

$= (12.0\,\mathrm{J\,cm\,mol^{-1}})(732/\mathrm{cm})(\exp[-3.51])(1.03)(300\,\mathrm{K})^{-1}$

$= \underline{0.899\,\mathrm{J\,K^{-1}\,mol^{-1}}}.$

$R\ln q = (8.31\,\mathrm{J\,K^{-1}\,mol^{-1}})\ln(1.03) = 0.246\,\mathrm{J\,K^{-1}\,mol^{-1}},$

$S = 0.899 + 0.246 = \underline{1.14\,\mathrm{J\,K^{-1}\,mol^{-1}}}.$

A21.9 $S = nR\ln\{e^{5/2}(2\pi mkT/h^2)^{3/2}\,(kT/p)\}$. [21.3.11]

$m = (30.0)(1.66 \times 10^{-27}\,\mathrm{kg}) = 4.98 \times 10^{-26}\,\mathrm{kg}.$

$kT = (1.38 \times 10^{-23}\,\mathrm{J\,K^{-1}})(298\,\mathrm{K}) = 4.11 \times 10^{-21}\,\mathrm{J}.$

$2\pi mkT/h^2 = (2)(3.14)(4.98 \times 10^{-26}\,\mathrm{kg})(1.38 \times 10^{-23}\,\mathrm{J\,K^{-1}})(298\,\mathrm{K})$

$\times (6.63 \times 10^{-34}\,\mathrm{J\,s})^{-2} = 2.93 \times 10^{21}\,\mathrm{m^{-2}}.$

$S = (8.31\,\mathrm{J\,K^{-1}\,mol^{-1}})[(5/2) + (3/2)\ln(2.93 \times 10^{21}\,\mathrm{m^{-2}}) + \ln(4.11 \times 10^{-21}\,\mathrm{J})$

$- \ln(1.01 \times 10^5\,\mathrm{Pa})] = \underline{151\,\mathrm{J\,K^{-1}\,mol^{-1}}}.$

A21.10 $\epsilon/kT = (450\,\mathrm{cm^{-1}})(12.0\,\mathrm{J\,mol^{-1}/cm^{-1}})(8.31\,\mathrm{J\,K^{-1}\,mol^{-1}})^{-1}(300\,\mathrm{K})^{-1}$

$= 2.17.$

$q = 2 + 4\exp(-2.17) = \underline{2.46}.$

Equilibrium fraction at the higher energy $= 4\exp(-2.17)/2.46 = 0.186 \neq 0.30$.

21.1 $W = N!/n_1!n_2!\ldots$ [21.1.1]

$N = 5, n_1 = 5$ [all 5 molecules occupy the $j = 1$ level]

$W = 5!/5!0!0!\ldots = \underline{1}.$

21.2

ϵ_0	$\epsilon_0+\epsilon$	$\epsilon_0+2\epsilon$	$\epsilon_0+3\epsilon$	$\epsilon_0+4\epsilon$	$\epsilon_0+5\epsilon$	$W = N!/n_1!n_2!\ldots$	
4	0	0	0	0	1	5!/4!0!0!0!0!1!0! ...	= 5
3	1	0	0	1	0	5!/3!1!0!0!1!0! ...	= 20
3	0	1	1	0	0	5!/3!0!1!1!0!0! ...	= 20
2	2	0	1	0	0	5!/2!2!0!1!0!0! ...	= 30
2	1	2	0	0	0	5!/2!1!2!0!0! ...	= 30
1	3	1	0	0	0	5!/1!3!1!0!0! ...	= 20
0	5	0	0	0	0	5!/0!5!0!0! ...	= 1

The most probable configurations are {2, 2, 0, 1, 0, 0} and {2, 1, 2, 0, 0, 0} jointly.

21.3 See Table on next page.

ϵ_0	$\epsilon_0 + \epsilon$	$\epsilon_0 + 2\epsilon$	$\epsilon_0 + 3\epsilon$	$\epsilon_0 + 4\epsilon$	$\epsilon_0 + 5\epsilon$	$\epsilon_0 + 6\epsilon$	$\epsilon_0 + 7\epsilon$	$\epsilon_0 + 8\epsilon$	$\epsilon_0 + 9\epsilon$	W	
8	0	0	0	0	0	0	0	0	1	9!/8!	= 9
7	1	0	0	0	0	0	0	1	0	9!/7!	= 72
7	0	1	0	0	0	0	1	0	0	9!/7!	= 72
7	0	0	1	0	0	1	0	0	0	9!/7!	= 72
7	0	0	0	1	1	0	0	0	0	9!/7!	= 72
6	2	0	0	0	0	0	1	0	0	9!/6!2!	= 252
6	0	2	0	0	1	0	0	0	0	9!/6!2!	= 252
6	0	0	3	0	0	0	0	0	0	9!/6!3!	= 84
6	1	0	0	2	0	0	0	0	0	9!/6!2!	= 252
6	1	1	0	0	0	1	0	0	0	9!/6!	= 504
6	1	0	1	0	1	0	0	0	0	9!/6!	= 504
6	0	1	1	1	0	0	0	0	0	9!/6!	= 504
5	3	0	0	0	0	1	0	0	0	9!/5!3!	= 504
5	0	3	1	0	0	0	0	0	0	9!/5!3!	= 504
5	2	1	0	0	1	0	0	0	0	9!/5!2!	= 1512
5	2	0	1	1	0	0	0	0	0	9!/5!2!	= 1512
5	1	2	0	1	0	0	0	0	0	9!/5!2!	= 1512
5	1	1	2	0	0	0	0	0	0	9!/5!2!	= 1512
4	4	0	0	0	1	0	0	0	0	9!/4!4!	= 630
4	3	1	0	1	0	0	0	0	0	9!/4!3!	= 2520
4	3	0	2	0	0	0	0	0	0	9!/4!3!2!	= 1260
4	2	2	1	0	0	0	0	0	0	9!/4!2!2!	= 3780
3	5	0	0	1	0	0	0	0	0	9!/3!5!	= 504
3	4	1	1	0	0	0	0	0	0	9!/3!4!	= 2520
2	6	0	1	0	0	0	0	0	0	9!/2!6!	= 252
2	5	2	0	0	0	0	0	0	0	9!/2!5!2!	= 756
1	7	1	0	0	0	0	0	0	0	9!/7!	= 72
0	9	0	0	0	0	0	0	0	0	9!/9!	= 1

21.4 The weights are given in the final column of the Table on p. 306. The most probable configuration is {4, 2, 2, 1, 0, 0, 0, 0, 0, 0} with a weight of 3780. (The next most probable are the 'less exponential' forms {4, 3, 1, 0, 1, 0, 0, 0, 0, 0} and {3, 4, 1, 1, 0, 0, 0, 0, 0, 0}, both with weight 2520.)

21.5 $n_j^*/n_o^* = \exp[-\beta(\epsilon_o + j\epsilon)]/\exp[-\beta\epsilon_o]$ [21.1.9]

$= \exp(-\beta j\epsilon), \beta = 1/kT.$

$-\beta j\epsilon = \ln n_j^* - \ln n_o^*$, or $\ln n_j^* = \ln n_o^* - j\epsilon/kT.$

Therefore, a plot of $\ln n_j^*$ (or $\ln n_j^*/n_o^*$) against j should give a straight line with slope $-\epsilon/kT$. Draw up the following Table:

j	0	1	2	3
n_j^*	4	2	2	1
$\ln n_j^*$	1.39	0.69	0.69	0

These points are plotted in Fig. 21.1. The slope is -0.46. (In the thermodynamic limit one obtains a perfect straight line.) Since $\epsilon \mathrel{\hat=} 50\ \text{cm}^{-1}$, this slope corresponds to a temperature

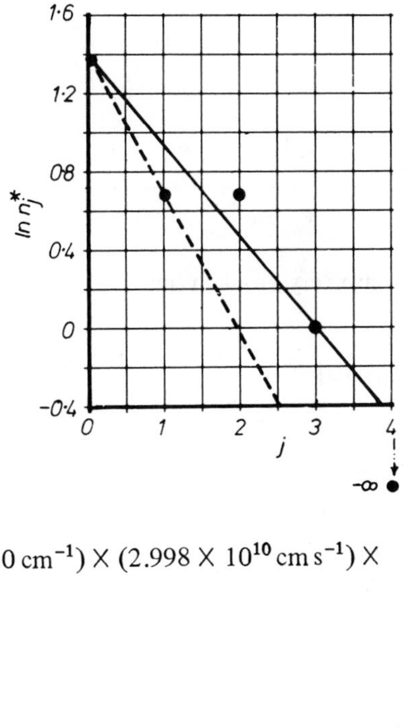

Fig 21.1

$T = hc\epsilon/0.46\,k = (50\ \text{cm}^{-1}) \times (2.998 \times 10^{10}\ \text{cm s}^{-1}) \times$

$\times$ (6.26 $\times$ 10^{-34} J s)/(0.46 $\times$ 1.381 $\times$ 10^{-23} J K^{-1})

= <u>156 K</u> $\approx$ <u>160 K</u>.

A better estimate (104 K) is found in Problem 21.6.

21.6 $U = -N \mathrm{d}\ln q/\mathrm{d}\beta$ [21.1.12 and $U(0) = 0$]; $q = 1/(1 - \mathrm{e}^{-\epsilon\beta})$ [21.1.13 and $\epsilon_0 = 0$].

$\mathrm{d}\ln q/\mathrm{d}\beta = (1/q)(\mathrm{d}q/\mathrm{d}\beta) = -\epsilon \mathrm{e}^{-\beta\epsilon}/(1 - \epsilon^{-\beta\epsilon})$.

$a\epsilon = U/N = -\mathrm{d}\ln q/\mathrm{d}\beta = \epsilon \mathrm{e}^{-\beta\epsilon}/(1 - \mathrm{e}^{-\beta\epsilon})$.

Therefore $a = \mathrm{e}^{-\beta\epsilon}/(1 - \mathrm{e}^{-\beta\epsilon})$; hence $\mathrm{e}^{-\beta\epsilon} = a/(1 + a)$, and so <u>$\beta = (1/\epsilon)\ln\{1 + (1/a)\}$</u>.

For $a = 1$, $\beta = 1/kT = (1/\epsilon)\ln 2$; and so $T = \epsilon/k \ln 2$.

For $\epsilon \mathrel{\widehat{=}} 50\ \mathrm{cm^{-1}} = 9.93 \times 10^{-22}$ J [endpaper 1],

$T = (993 \times 10^{-22}\ \mathrm{J})/(1.381 \times 10^{-23}\ \mathrm{J\,K^{-1}})\ln 2 =$ <u>104 K</u>.

$q = 1/(1 - \mathrm{e}^{-\beta\epsilon}) = 1/\{1 - a/(1 + a)\} =$ <u>$1 + a$</u>.

In the present case, $q = 2$.

21.7 Choose one of the weight 2520 distributions, and one of the weight 504 distributions. Draw up the following Table

	j	0	1	2	3	4
$W = 2520$	n_j	4	3	1	0	1
	$\ln n_j$	1.39	1.10	0	$-\infty$	0
$W = 504$	n_j	6	0	1	1	1
	$\ln n_j$	1.79	$-\infty$	0	0	0

Inspection confirms that these give very crooked lines.

21.8 $q = \sum_i \exp(-\beta\epsilon_i)$ [21.1.10]

$$= \sum_i \exp(-\beta\epsilon_0)\exp(-i\beta\epsilon) = \exp(-\beta\epsilon_0)/\{1 - \exp(-\beta\epsilon)\}.$$

Shift the origin so that $\epsilon_0 = 0$, then

$q = 1/\{1 - \exp(-\beta\epsilon)\}$. Note that when $T = 104\,\text{K}$, $kT/hc = 72.3\,\text{cm}^{-1}$.

$q(104\,\text{K}) = 1/\{1 - \exp(-50/723)\} = 2.00$

$q(100\,\text{K}) = 1/\{1 - \exp[-(50/72.3) \times (104/100]\} = 1.95$

$q(108\,\text{K}) = 1/\{1 - \exp[-(50/72.3) \times (104/108)]\} = 2.06.$

$\text{d}q/\text{d}\beta = (\text{d}/\text{d}\beta)\{1 - \exp(-\beta\epsilon)\}^{-1} = -\epsilon\exp(-\beta\epsilon)/\{1 - \exp(-\beta\epsilon)\}^2.$

For a numerical estimate use

$$\text{d}\ln q/\text{d}\beta = (1/q)(\text{d}q/\text{d}\beta) \approx (1/2.00)\left\{\frac{2.06 - 1.95}{(1/k)\left(\dfrac{1}{108\,\text{K}} - \dfrac{1}{100\,\text{K}}\right)}\right\}$$

$$\approx -1.03 \times 10^{-21}\,\text{J}.$$

Therefore $\epsilon_0 + a\epsilon = -\text{d}\ln q/\text{d}\beta \approx 1.03 \times 10^{-21}\,\text{J} \mathrel{\hat{=}} 52\,\text{cm}^{-1}$.

For an analytical result use

$$-\text{d}\ln q/\text{d}\beta = -(1/q)(\text{d}q/\text{d}\beta) = \epsilon\exp(-\beta\epsilon)/\{1 - \exp(-\beta\epsilon)\}.$$

$$= \frac{(50\,\text{cm}^{-1}) \times \exp(-50/72.3)}{1 - \exp(-50/72.3)} = 50\,\text{cm}^{-1}.$$

Therefore, the mean energy is $\epsilon_0 + 50\,\text{cm}^{-1}$. The slope corresponding to this temperature is marked on Fig. 21.1.

21.9 Decide on distinguishability [Section 21.2(b)].

(a) Yes; the atoms are intrinsically indistinguishable, and free to move.

(b) Yes; the same as in (a), but for molecules instead of atoms.

(c) No; the molecules are intrinsically indistinguishable, but trapped in a solid so that they can be labeled.

(d) Yes; as for (b).

(e) No; as for (c).

(f) Yes; the electrons are intrinsically indistinguishable, and mobile.

(g) The factor $N!$ applies only in the high temperature range; when this is inappropriate the correct Fermi–Dirac statistics have to be used. This is particularly important for an electron gas in a metal.

21.10 $q = (2\pi m/h^2\beta)^{3/2}V$ [21.1.15], $\beta = 1/kT$

$$= \left\{\frac{2\pi \times (6.64 \times 10^{-26}\,\text{kg}) \times (1.381 \times 10^{-23}\,\text{J K}^{-1}) \times T}{(6.626 \times 10^{-34}\,\text{J s})^2}\right\}^{3/2} \times (10^{-6}\,\text{m}^3)$$

$= 4.76 \times 10^{22}(T/\mathrm{K})^{3/2}$.

(a) $T = 100\,\mathrm{K}, q = \underline{4.76 \times 10^{25}}$.

(b) $T = 298\,\mathrm{K}, q = \underline{2.45 \times 10^{26}}$.

(c) $T = 10\,000\,\mathrm{K}, q = \underline{4.76 \times 10^{28}}$.

(d) $T = 0, q = \underline{1}$ [all molecules are in their lowest energy state].

21.11 $q_x = \sum_{n=1}^{\infty} \exp(-[n-1]^2 h^2\beta/8mX^2)$ [Section 21.1(e)], $q = q_x q_y q_z$.

The energy separation of neighboring levels is $(n+1)^2h^2/8mX^2 - n^2h^2/8mX^2 = (2n+1)h^2/8mX^2$, which is of the order of h^2/mX^2; the mean energy is of the order of kT, and so many levels are occupied if $h^2/mX^2kT \ll 1$. Explicit summation has to be used when this inequality is contravened.

For $q = 10 = 4.76 \times 10^{22}(T/\mathrm{K})^{3/2}$ [Problem 21.10].

$T = (10/4.76 \times 10^{22})^{2/3}\,\mathrm{K} = \underline{3.5 \times 10^{-15}\,\mathrm{K}}$.

At this temperature

$$h^2\beta/8mX^2 = (6.626 \times 10^{-34}\,\mathrm{J\,s})^2/\{8 \times (6.64 \times 10^{-26}\,\mathrm{kg}) \times (1.381 \times 10^{-23}\,\mathrm{J\,K^{-1}}) \times (3.5 \times 10^{-15}\,\mathrm{K}) \times (10^{-2}\,\mathrm{m})^2\} = 0.17.$$

Then $q_x = \sum_{n=1}^{\infty} \exp(-0.17[n-1]^2) = 1.00 + 0.84 + 0.51 + 0.22 + 0.07 + \ldots = 2.65$.

$q_y = q_z = q_x, \qquad q = q_x q_y q_z = (2.65)^3 = \underline{18.60}.$

21.12 $q = \sum_j \exp(-\beta\epsilon_j)$ [21.1.10].

At 298 K, $1/\beta hc = 207\,\mathrm{cm^{-1}}$; at 5000 K, $1/\beta hc = 3475\,\mathrm{cm^{-1}}$.

$$q(298\,\mathrm{K}) = 5 + 3\exp(-4751/207) + \exp(-4707/207) + 5\exp(-10\,559/207)$$
$$= 5 + 3.2 \times 10^{-10} + 1.3 \times 10^{-10} + 2.7 \times 10^{-22} = \underline{5.00}.$$

$$q(5000\,\mathrm{K}) = 5 + 3\exp(-4751/3475) + \exp(-4707/3475) + 5\exp(-10\,559/3475)$$
$$= 5.00 + 0.76 + 0.26 + 0.24 = \underline{6.25}.$$

21.13 $P_j = (1/q)\exp(-\epsilon_j\beta)$ [21.1.11]

$P_0 = 1/q =$ (a) $1/5.00 = 0.20$, (b) $1/6.25 = 0.16$.

But the ground level is 5-fold degenerate, and each of its states is occupied equally.

Therefore

(a) $P_0 = \underline{1.00}$, (b) $P_0 = 5 \times 0.16 = \underline{0.80}$.

$P_1 = \{\exp(-4751/207)\}/5.00 = 2.15 \times 10^{-11}$; but this level is 3-fold degenerate, and so

(a) $P_1 = 3 \times 2.15 \times 10^{-11} = \underline{6.5 \times 10^{-11}}$.

(b) $P_1 = 3 \times \{\exp(-4751/3475)\}/6.25 = \underline{0.12}$.

21.14 Measure energies from the lower state.

$$q = \sum_j \exp(-\beta\epsilon_j) = \sum_j \exp\{-(\beta hc)(\epsilon_j/hc)\}$$

$$= 2 + 2\exp\{-\beta hc \times (121.1\ \text{cm}^{-1})\}$$

$$\beta hc = hc/kT = \frac{(6.626 \times 10^{-34}\ \text{J s}) \times (2.998 \times 10^{10}\ \text{cm s}^{-1})}{(1.381 \times 10^{-23}\ \text{J K}^{-1})T}$$

$$= 1.438/(T/\text{K}).$$

$$q = 2 + 2\exp\{-174.4/(T/\text{K})\}.$$

This function is plotted in Fig. 21.2.

At 298 K, $q = 3.11$ and $P_0 = 1/q = 0.32$, $P_1 = \{\exp(-174.4/298)\}/q = 0.18$. But both levels are doubly degenerate, and so the population proportions at 298 K are $2 \times 0.32 = \underline{0.64}$ and $2 \times 0.18 = \underline{0.36}$ for the lower and upper levels respectively.

21.15 $U - U(0) = -N\partial \ln q/\partial\beta$ [21.1.12] $= -(N/q)\partial q/\partial\beta$

$$= -(N/q)(\partial/\partial\beta)\{2 + 2\exp(-\beta hc\tilde{\nu})\} \quad [\tilde{\nu} = 121.1\ \text{cm}^{-1}]$$

$$= -(N/q)\{-2hc\tilde{\nu}\exp(-\beta hc\tilde{\nu})\}$$

$$= \frac{Nhc\tilde{\nu}\exp(-\beta hc\tilde{\nu})}{1 + \exp(-\beta hc\tilde{\nu})}.$$

$$[U - U(0)]/Nhc = \frac{(121.1\ \text{cm}^{-1})\exp[-174.4/(T/\text{K})]}{1 + \exp[-174.4/(T/\text{K})]}$$

At $T = 298$ K

$$[U - U(0)]/Nhc = \frac{(121.1\ \text{cm}^{-1})\exp(-174.4/298)}{1 + \exp(-174.4/298)} = 43.3\ \text{cm}^{-1}.$$

Therefore, the molar internal energy is

$$U_m - U_m(0) = (43.3\ \text{cm}^{-1}) \times (6.26 \times 10^{-34}\ \text{J s}) \times (2.998 \times 10^{10}\ \text{cm s}^{-1})$$
$$\times (6.022 \times 10^{23}\ \text{mol}^{-1}) = \underline{0.518\ \text{kJ mol}^{-1}}.$$

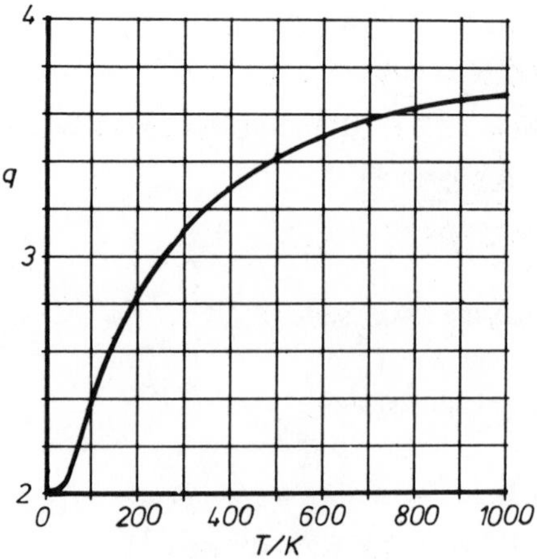

Fig 21.2

21.16 $q = \sum_j \exp(-\beta\epsilon_j)$ [21.1.10]

(a) 100 K, $1/\beta hc = 69.50\ \text{cm}^{-1}$ [endpaper 1].

$q = 1 + \exp(-213.30/69.50) + \exp(-425.39/69.50) + \exp(-636.27/69.50)$
$+ \exp(-845.93/69.50) + \exp(-1054.38/69.50) = \underline{1.049}.$

(b) 298.15 K, $1/\beta hc = 207.22\ \text{cm}^{-1}$ [endpaper 1].

$q = 1 + \exp(-213.30/207.22) + \exp(-425.39/207.22) + \exp(-636.27/207.22)$
$+ \exp(-845.93/207.22) + \exp(1054.38/207.22) = \underline{1.56}.$

21.17 $P_0 = 1/q =$ (a) $\underline{0.9535}$, (b) $\underline{0.6430}$.

$P_1 =$ (a) $\exp(-213.30/69.50)/1.0488 = \underline{0.0443}$
(b) $\exp(-213.30/207.22)/1.5553 = \underline{0.2298}$.

$P_2 =$ (a) $\exp(-425.39/69.50)/1.0488 = \underline{0.0021}$
(b) $\exp(-425.39/207.22)/1.5553 = \underline{0.0826}$.

21.18 $U - U(0) = N \sum_j \epsilon_j \exp(-\beta\epsilon_j)/q$

$[U - U(0)]/Nhc = \{0 + 213.30P_1 + 425.39P_2 + 636.27P_3 + 845.93P_4 +$
$+ 1054.38P_5\}\text{cm}^{-1}$

At 100 K, $P_1 = 0.0443, P_2 = 0.0021, P_3 = 1.01 \times 10^{-4}, P_4 = 4.95 \times 10^{-6}$,
$P_5 = 2.47 \times 10^{-7}$; $[U - U(0)]/Nhc = 10.41\ \text{cm}^{-1}$.

$U_m - U_m(0) = (10.41\ \text{cm}^{-1})N_A hc = \underline{125\ \text{J mol}^{-1}}.$

At 298 K, $P_1 = 0.2298, P_2 = 0.0826, P_3 = 0.0299, P_4 = 0.0109, P_5 = 0.0040;$

$[U - U(0)]/Nhc = 116.6\ \text{cm}^{-1}.$

$U_m - U_m(0) = (116.6\ \text{cm}^{-1})N_A hc = \underline{1.40\ \text{kJ mol}^{-1}}.$

21.19 $q = \sum_j \exp(-\beta\epsilon_j) = 1 + \exp(-2\mu_B B\beta)$, with energies measured from the lower spin state.

$-\partial \ln q/\partial\beta = -(1/q)(\partial/\partial\beta)\{1 + \exp(-2\mu_B B\beta)\} = (2\mu_B B/q)\exp(-2\mu_B B\beta),$

$$\langle\epsilon\rangle = -\partial \ln q/\partial\beta = \left\{\frac{2\mu_B B \exp(-2\mu_B B\beta)}{1 + \exp(-2\mu_B B\beta)}\right\}.$$

Write $x = 2\mu_B B\beta = 2\mu_B B/kT$, then $\langle\epsilon\rangle/2\mu_B B = e^{-x}/(1 + e^{-x})$. Therefore, by plotting the function on the right we get a 'universal' graph. The graph is plotted in Fig. 21.3. The relative populations are $P_0 = 1/q = 1/\{1 + e^{-x}\}, P_1 = e^{-x}/\{1 + e^{-x}\}, P_1/P_0 = e^{-x}$.

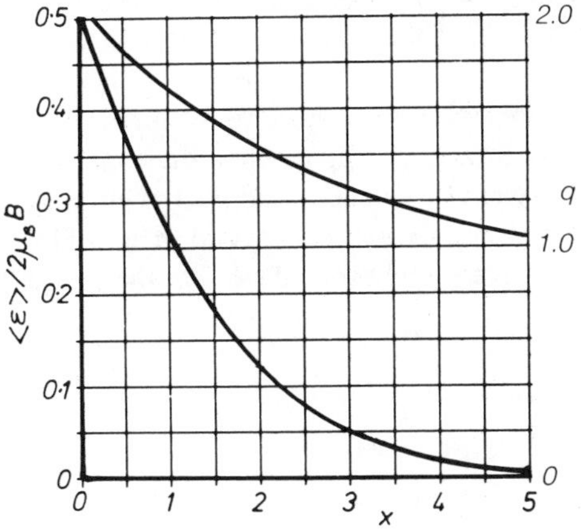

Fig 21.3

When $B = 300$ mT (3 kG), $x = 2 \times (9.274 \times 10^{-24}\ \text{J T}^{-1}) \times (0.3\ \text{T})/(1.381 \times 10^{-23}\ \text{J K}^{-1})T = 0.403/(T/\text{K})$.

(a) $T = 4$ K, $P_1/P_0 = e^{-0.101} = \underline{0.904}.$

(b) $T = 298$ K, $P_1/P_0 = e^{-0.001} = \underline{0.999}.$

21.20 $q = \sum_j \exp(-\beta\epsilon_j) = 1 + \exp(-x) + \exp(-2x), x = g_I\mu_N B\beta.$

$\partial q/\partial\beta = g_I\mu_N B(\partial q/\partial x) = g_I\mu_N B\{-e^{-x} - 2e^{-2x}\}.$

$\langle\epsilon\rangle = -(1/q)(\partial q/\partial\beta) = g_I\mu_N B(e^{-x} + 2e^{-2x})/(1 + e^{-x} + e^{-2x})$.

This refers to an energy zero for the lowest level; in order to take the central ($m_I = 0$) level as the energy zero, simply subtract the energy difference ($g_I\mu_N B$):

$$\langle\epsilon\rangle = g_I\mu_N B\{[(e^{-x} + 2e^{-2x})/(1 + e^{-x} + e^{-2x})] - 1\}$$
$$= -g_I\mu_N B\{(1 - e^{-2x})/(1 + e^{-x} + e^{-2x})\}.$$

For ^{14}N, $g_I = 0.403\,56$ [Table 20.1], $\mu_N = 5.051 \times 10^{-27}\,J\,T^{-1}$ [endpaper 1], and at 4 K, $\beta = 1/\{(1.381 \times 10^{-23}\,J\,K^{-1}) \times 4\,K\} = 1.810 \times 10^{22}\,J^{-1}$. Then $x = 0.403\,56 \times (5.051 \times 10^{-27}\,J\,T^{-1}) \times (1.810 \times 10^{22}\,J^{-1})B = 3.69 \times 10^{-5}(B/T)$. For $B = 1.4\,T$ (14 kG), $x = 3.69 \times 10^{-5} \times 1.4 = 5.17 \times 10^{-5}$; and so $q = 2.999\,85$.

21.21 $P_1/P_0 = \exp(-\epsilon\beta)$, where $\epsilon = E_1 - E_0$. Take E_0 as the energy of the lower state and E_1 as that of the upper. Then ϵ is positive. For $P_1 > P_0$ it is necessary for $\epsilon\beta$ to be negative, since then $\exp(-\epsilon\beta) > 1$. Therefore, as ϵ is positive, β must be negative for $P_1 > P_0$. Suppose β corresponds to a normal, thermal equilibrium population, such that $P_1/P_0 < 1$, as usual. Then suppose a new population distribution is created such that $P_1'/P_0' = P_0/P_1$ (i.e. the original population is inverted). Then the new (negative) temperature, β', is given by $P_1'/P_0' = \exp(-\beta'\epsilon) = P_0/P_1 = \{\exp(-\beta\epsilon)\}^{-1} = \exp(\beta\epsilon)$. As a consequence, $\beta' = -\beta$, and so $T' = -T$. Therefore the required temperatures are (a) $\underline{-298\,K}$, (b) $\underline{-10\,K}$, (c) $\underline{-0\,K}$. [Note the discontinuity in behavior across 0.]

21.22 Either when only two levels are occupied (or of interest), for their populations may be characterized by a single, negative, β; or, when the populations of the three levels are so arranged that they can be characterized by a single, negative β. It is always possible to do this, but the new populations correspond to actual inversion of the original only if the three levels are equally spaced (so that the central population remains unchanged).

21.23 $S/Nk = \{U - U(0)\}/NkT + \ln q$ [21.3.8; $Q = q^N$].

$$= a\beta\epsilon + \ln q \text{ [Problem 21.6]}$$
$$= a\ln\{1 + (1/a)\} + \ln\{1 + a\} \text{ [Problem 21.6]}$$
$$= (1 + a)\ln(1 + a) - a\ln a.$$

When the mean energy is $\epsilon_0 + \epsilon$, $a = 1$ [Problem 21.6], and so $S/Nk = \underline{2\ln 2}$.

21.24 $S = [U - U(0)]/T + k\ln Q$ [21.3.8]

$Q = q^N$ [No $N!$ because we are not interested in the translational contribution].

$S = [U - U(0)]/T + Nk\ln q$; $S_m = [U_m - U_m(0)]/T + R\ln q$.

$q(298\,K) = 5.00$, $q(5000\,K) = 6.25$ [Problem 21.12].

Evaluate $U - U(0)$ by direct summation:

$$U - U(0) = (N/q) \sum_j \epsilon_j e^{-\beta\epsilon_j}.$$

At 298 K:

$$[U_m - U_m(0)]/N_A hc = (1/5.00)\{0 + 3 \times (4751\ \text{cm}^{-1})\exp(-4751/207) + (4707\ \text{cm}^{-1})\exp(-4707/207) + \ldots\} = 4.32 \times 10^{-7}\ \text{cm}^{-1}.$$

$$U_m - U_m(0) = (4.32 \times 10^{-7}\ \text{cm}^{-1}) \times (6.022 \times 10^{23}\ \text{mol}^{-1}) \times (6.26 \times 10^{-34}\ \text{J s}) \times (2.998 \times 10^{10}\ \text{cm s}^{-1}) = 4.88 \times 10^{-6}\ \text{J mol}^{-1}.$$

$$[U_m - U_m(0)]/N_A hc = (1/6.25)\{0 + 3 \times (4751\ \text{cm}^{-1})\exp(-4751/3475) + (4707\ \text{cm}^{-1})\exp(-4707/3475) + 5 \times (10\,559\ \text{cm}^{-1})\exp(-10\,559/3475)\} = 1178\ \text{cm}^{-1}.$$

$$U_m - U_m(0) = (1178\ \text{cm}^{-1})N_A hc = 14.10\ \text{kJ mol}^{-1}.$$

It follows that $S_m(298\ \text{K}) = (4.88 \times 10^{-6}\ \text{J mol}^{-1})/(298\ \text{K}) + (8.314\ \text{J K}^{-1}\ \text{mol}^{-1})\ln 5.00$
$= \underline{13.38\ \text{J K}^{-1}\ \text{mol}^{-1}}$ (essentially $R \ln 5$).

$$S_m(5000\ \text{K}) = (14.10\ \text{kJ mol}^{-1})/(5000\ \text{K}) + (8.314\ \text{J K}^{-1}\ \text{mol}^{-1})\ln 6.25 = \underline{18.07\ \text{J K}^{-1}\ \text{mol}^{-1}}.$$

21.25 $q = 2 + 2\exp\{-174.4/(T/\text{K})\}$ [Problem 21.14]

$$U_m - U_m(0) = \frac{N_A hc(121.1\ \text{cm}^{-1})\exp\{-174.4/(T/\text{K})\}}{1 + \exp\{-174.4/(T/\text{K})\}} \quad \text{[Problem 21.15]}.$$

$(121.1\ \text{cm}^{-1})N_A hc = 1.449\ \text{kJ mol}^{-1}$

$S_m = [U_m - U_m(0)]/T + R\ln q$ [Problem 21.24].

(a) At 298 K, $q = 2 + 2\exp\{-174.4/298\} = 3.114$.

$$U_m - U_m(0) = \frac{(1.449\ \text{kJ mol}^{-1})\exp\{-174.4/298\}}{1 + \exp\{-174.4/298\}} = 0.518\ \text{kJ mol}^{-1};$$

$$S_m = (0.518\ \text{kJ mol}^{-1})/(298\ \text{K}) + (8.314\ \text{J K}^{-1}\ \text{mol}^{-1}) \times \ln 3.114 = \underline{11.2\ \text{J K}^{-1}\ \text{mol}^{-1}}.$$

(b) At 500 K, $q = 2 + 2\exp\{-174.4/500\} = 3.411$.

$$U_m - U_m(0) = \frac{(1.449\ \text{kJ mol}^{-1})\exp\{-174.4/500\}}{1 + \exp\{-174.4/500\}} = 0.599\ \text{kJ mol}^{-1};$$

$$S_m = (0.599\ \text{kJ mol}^{-1})/(500\ \text{K}) + (8.314\ \text{J K}^{-1}\ \text{mol}^{-1}) \times \ln 3.411 = \underline{11.4\ \text{J K}^{-1}\ \text{mol}^{-1}}.$$

21.26 $q(100\ \text{K}) = 1.049$, $q(298\ \text{K}) = 1.555$ [Problem 21.16]

$U_m - U_m(0) = 125\ \text{J mol}^{-1}$ at 100 K and $1400\ \text{J mol}^{-1}$ at 298 K [Problem 21.18].

$S_m = [U_m - U_m(0)]/T + R\ln q$ [Problem 21.24].

(a) $T = 100\,\text{K}$, $S_m = (125\,\text{J mol}^{-1})/(100\,\text{K}) + (8.314\,\text{J K}^{-1}\,\text{mol}^{-1})\ln 1.049$

$= \underline{1.65\,\text{J K}^{-1}\,\text{mol}^{-1}}$.

(b) $T = 298\,\text{K}$, $S_m = (1400\,\text{J mol}^{-1})/(298\,\text{K}) + (8.314\,\text{J K}^{-1}\,\text{mol}^{-1})\ln 1.555$

$= \underline{8.37\,\text{J K}^{-1}\,\text{mol}^{-1}}$.

21.27 $S_m = [U_m - U_m(0)]/T + R\ln q$; $q = 1 + \exp(-2\mu_B B\beta) = 1 + e^{-x}$,
$x = 2\mu_B B/kT$ [Problem 21.19]; $[U_m - U_m(0)] = 2\mu_B B N_A e^{-x}/(1 + e^{-x})$ [Problem 21.19].

$S_m = (2\mu_B B/T)N_A e^{-x}/(1 + e^{-x}) + R\ln\{1 + e^{-x}\}$

$= Rxe^{-x}/(1 + e^{-x}) + R\ln\{1 + e^{-x}\}$.

At low fields when $x \ll 1$, $e^{-x} \approx 1 - x + \frac{1}{2}x^2$, $\ln(1 + z) \approx z - \frac{1}{2}z^2$.

$S_m \approx Rx(1 - x)/(2 - x) + R\ln(2 - x + \frac{1}{2}x^2)$

$\approx \frac{1}{2}Rx(1 - x)(1 + \frac{1}{2}x) + R\ \ln 2 + R\ln(1 - \frac{1}{2}x + \frac{1}{4}x^2)$

$\approx \frac{1}{2}Rx(1 - \frac{1}{2}x) + R\ln 2 - \frac{1}{2}Rx + \frac{1}{4}Rx^2 - \frac{1}{8}Rx^2$

$\approx R\ln 2 - \frac{1}{8}Rx^2$, and $S_m \to R\ln 2$ as $T \to \infty$ (both states equally likely).

At high fields when $x \gg 1$, $1 + e^{-x} \approx 1$, $S_m \approx \frac{3}{2}Rxe^{-x}$ and $S_m \to 0$ as $T \to 0$ (only one state accessible).

21.28 $S(\text{initial}) = 0$.

$S(\text{final}) = nR\ln\{e^{\frac{5}{2}}kT/p\Lambda^3\}$ [21.3.11]

$\Delta S = S(\text{final}) - S(\text{initial}) = S(\text{final})$.

$$\Delta S_m = (8.314\,\text{J K}^{-1}\,\text{mol}^{-1})\ln\left\{e^{\frac{5}{2}}(2\pi)^{\frac{3}{2}} \times \frac{(1.381\times10^{-23}\,\text{J K}^{-1})\times 298\,\text{K})}{(1.013\times10^{5}\,\text{N m}^{-2})}\right.$$

$$\left.\times\left[\frac{(39.95\times1.6605\times10^{-27}\,\text{kg})\times(1.381\times10^{-23}\,\text{J K}^{-1})T}{(6.626\times10^{-34}\,\text{J s})^2}\right]^{3/2}\right\}$$

$= \underline{155\,\text{J K}^{-1}\,\text{mol}^{-1}}$ for $T = 298\,\text{K}$.

21.29 $S_m = R\ln\{e^{5/2}(2\pi m_e kT/h^2)^{3/2}V/nN_A\}$, $n = 1$ mol.

$$S_m = R\ln\{e^{5/2}(2\pi)^{3/2}\left[\frac{(9.105\times10^{-31}\,\text{kg})\times(1.381\times10^{-23}\,\text{J K}^{-1})}{(6.626\times10^{-34}\,\text{J s})^2}\right]^{3/2}$$

$$\times T^{3/2}V/(1\,\text{mol})\times(6.022\times10^{23}\,\text{mol}^{-1})\}$$

$= R\ln\{0.048\,83(T/\text{K})^{3/2}(V/\text{m}^3)\}$.

(a) $S_m = R\ln\{0.048\,83\times(298)^{3/2}\times10^{-2}\} = 0.921R = \underline{7.7\,\text{J K}^{-1}\,\text{mol}^{-1}}$.

(b) $S_m = R\ln\{0.048\,83 \times (5000)^{3/2} \times 10^{-2}\} = 5.15R = \underline{43\ \mathrm{J\,K^{-1}\,mol^{-1}}}$.

21.30 $S_m = R\ln\{e^{5/2}(2\pi mkT/h^2)^{3/2}(kT/p)\}$ [21.3.11] $= R\ln(A/p)$.

At constant temperature:

$S_m(p_f) - S_m(p_i) = R\ln(A/p_f) - R\ln(A/p_i) = \underline{R\ln(p_i/p_f)}$.

$S_m = R\ln\{e^{5/2}(2\pi mkT/h^2)^{3/2}\,V/nN_A\}$ [21.3.11] $= R\ln BT^{3/2}$.

At constant volume:

$S_m(T_f) - S_m(T_i) = R\ln BT_f^{3/2} - R\ln BT_i^{3/2} = R\ln(T_f^{3/2}/T_i^{3/2}) = (3/2)R\ln(T_f/T_i)$.

But $C_{V,m} = (3/2)R$, and so $\Delta S_m = \underline{C_{V,m}\ln(T_f/T_i)}$.

At constant pressure:

$\Delta S_m = R\ln(T_f^{5/2}/T_i^{5/2})$ [21.3.11] $= (5/2)R\ln(T_f/T_i)$

$= \underline{C_{p,m}\ln(T_f/T_i)}$ [as $C_{p,m} - C_{V,m} = R$].

22. Statistical thermodynamics: the machinery

A22.1 (a) 1 (b) 2 (c) 2 (d) 12. [Section 22.1(c)]

A22.2 $q^{R} = 2IkT(h/2\pi)^{-2}\sigma^{-1}$ [22.1.6]

$= (2)(7.99970)(1.6606 \times 10^{-27}\,\text{kg})(1.2075 \times 10^{-10}\,\text{m})^2$
$\times (1.3807 \times 10^{-23}\,\text{J K}^{-1})(300\,\text{K})(2\pi)^2(6.6262 \times 10^{-34}\,\text{J s})^{-2}(2)^{-1}$

$= \underline{72.114}.$

A22.3 $q^{R} = \sigma^{-1}(kT/hc)^{3/2}(\pi/ABC)^{1/2}$ [22.1.7]

$= (1)^{-1}[(373.15\,\text{K})(1.4388\,\text{cm K})^{-1}]^{3/2}(3.1416)^{1/2}$
$\times (3.1752\,\text{cm}^{-1})^{-1/2}(0.3951\,\text{cm}^{-1})^{-1/2}(0.3505\,\text{cm}^{-1})^{-1/2}$

$= \underline{1.116 \times 10^4}.$

A22.4 If $q^{V} = 1.001$, then $\tilde{\nu} = (kT/hc)\ln\{[1-(q^{V})^{-1}]^{-1}\}$ [22.1.8]
$\tilde{\nu} = (500/1.4388)\ln\{[1-(1.001)^{-1}]^{-1}\} = (500/1.4388)(6.9088)$
$= 2401\,\text{cm}^{-1}$. For $\tilde{\nu} \geqslant 2400\,\text{cm}^{-1}$, q^{V} may be considered unity with an error of 0.10% or less.

A22.5 $q^{R} = (kT)/(hcB\sigma) = (300\,\text{K}/1.4388\,\text{cm K})(0.3902\,\text{cm}^{-1})^{-1}(2)^{-1}$

$= 267.2$ [Box 22.1].

$(hc)/(kT) = 1.4388\,\text{cm K}/300\,\text{K} = 4.796 \times 10^{-3}\,\text{cm}.$

The values of $hc\tilde{\nu}/kT$ are 6.658, 3.201, 11.267.

$(q^{V})^{-1} = [1-\exp(-6.658)][1-\exp(-3.201)]^2[1-\exp(-11.267)]$

$= (0.9987)(0.9593)^2(1).$

$q^{V} = 1.088$ [Box 22.1].

Contribution to $G - G(0) = -nRT\ln(q^{i})$

$= -(8.314\,\text{J mol}^{-1}\,\text{K}^{-1})(300\text{K})\ln[(267.2)(1.088)]$

$= \underline{14.15\,\text{kJ mol}^{-1}}$. [Box 22.2]

A22.6 $q_{e} = 4 + 2\exp(-\beta\epsilon)$; [as in 22.1.10].
$\beta\epsilon = (881)(1.439)T^{-1} = 1268/T.$
$C_{V}^{e} = (N/kT^2)\{\partial[(\partial q^{e}/\partial\beta)/(q^{e})]/\partial\beta\}$ [22.3.9]

$= (N/kT^2)(8\epsilon^2)[\exp(-1268/T)]\,[4 + 2\exp(-1268/T)]^{-2}.$

At 500 K, $\beta\epsilon = 2.536$:

$C_V^e = (8.314\,\mathrm{J\,mol^{-1}\,K^{-1}})(8)(2.536)^2\exp(-2.536)[4 + 2\exp(-2.536)]^{-2}$

$= \underline{1.96\,\mathrm{J\,K^{-1}\,mol^{-1}}}.$

At 900 K, $\beta\epsilon = 1.408$:

$C_V^e = (8.314\,\mathrm{J\,mol^{-1}\,K^{-1}})(8)(1.408)^2\exp(-1.408)[4 + 2\exp(-1.408)]^{-2}$

$= \underline{1.60\,\mathrm{J\,K^{-1}\,mol^{-1}}}.$

A22.7 $q^e = 3 + 2\exp(-\beta\epsilon)$ [as in 22.1.10].

$\beta\epsilon \approx (1.4388\,\mathrm{cm\,K})(7918.1\,\mathrm{cm^{-1}})(400\,\mathrm{K})^{-1} = 28.48.$

$\exp(-28.48) = 4.279 \times 10^{-13}$; hence $q^e = 3$,

contribution to $G - G(0) = -nRT\ln(q^e) = -(8.31\,\mathrm{J\,mol^{-1}\,K^{-1}})(400\,\mathrm{K})\ln 3$

$= \underline{-3.65\,\mathrm{kJ\,mol^{-1}}}$ [22.2.8].

A22.8 The spin degeneracy of cobalt is $2S + 1 = 4$ and $q = 4$.

$S(\mathrm{spin}) = Nk\ln(q) = (8.31\,\mathrm{J\,K^{-1}\,mol^{-1}})\ln 4 = \underline{11.5\,\mathrm{J\,K^{-1}\,mol^{-1}}}$ [Section 22.3(c)].

A22.9 $C_V(\mathrm{trans}) = (3/2)R$ [22.3.11]; $C_V(\mathrm{rot}) = (3/2)R$ [Section 22.3(b)]

$C_V(\mathrm{vibr}) = [3(4) - 6]R = 6R$ [Section 22.3(b)].

$C_p(\mathrm{equipartition}) = 9R + R = 10R = 10(8.31\,\mathrm{J\,K^{-1}\,mol^{-1}}) = 83.1\,\mathrm{J\,K^{-1}\,mol^{-1}}.$

$C_p(\mathrm{experiment}) = 4.29R$, which shows that the heat capacity comes almost entirely from translation and rotation at 298 K. The vibrational modes of NH_3 are not excited to any great degree at this temperature.

A22.10 The product of the q^T terms is $[(2 \times 79)(2 \times 81)(79 + 81)^{-2}]^{3/2} \doteq 0.9998$, since q^T is proportional to $m^{3/2}$. Since q^R is proportional to μ/σ, the product of the q^R terms is $(2 \times 79)^{-1}(2 \times 81)^{-1}(79 + 81)^2(1)^2(2)^{-2} = 0.2500$. The vibrational wavenumbers are: $323.33\,\mathrm{cm^{-1}}$ for $^{79}Br^{81}Br$, $(80/79)^{1/2}(323.33) = 325.37\,\mathrm{cm^{-1}}$ for $^{79}Br^{79}Br$, and $(80/81)^{1/2}(323.33) = 321.33\,\mathrm{cm^{-1}}$ for $^{81}Br^{81}Br$. $hc/kT = 1.4388/300 = 0.004\,796$ cm. The corresponding values of $hc\tilde{\nu}/kT$ are 1.5507, 1.5605, and 1.5411. Hence the product of the vibrational terms $[1 - \exp(-hc\tilde{\nu}/kT)]^{-1}$ is:

$(1.2659)(1.2725)/(1.2692)^2 = \underline{1.0000}.$

$\beta\Delta E_0 = (1/2)(0.004\,796)(321.33 + 325.37 - 323.33 - 323.33)$

$= (1/2)(0.004\,796)(0.04) = 9.6 \times 10^{-5}.$

$\exp(-9.6 \times 10^{-5}) = 0.9999;$

$K_p = (0.9998)(0.2500)(1.0000)(0.9999) = \underline{0.2500}.$ [Section 22.3(d)].

22.1 $q^{\mathrm{R}} \approx kT/Bhc\sigma$ [Box 22.1] $= (0.6950/\sigma)(T/\mathrm{K})/(B/\mathrm{cm}^{-1})$

$B = 10.59\ \mathrm{cm}^{-1}$ [Table 18.1]; $\sigma = 1$.

$q^{\mathrm{R}} = (T/\mathrm{K})/15.24$.

(a) $T = 100\ \mathrm{K}$, $q^{\mathrm{R}} = \underline{6.56}$,

(b) $T = 298\ \mathrm{K}$, $q^{\mathrm{R}} = \underline{19.6}$,

(c) $T = 500\ \mathrm{K}$, $q^{\mathrm{R}} = \underline{32.8}$.

22.2 The transition wavenumbers are given by $B(J+1)(J+2) - BJ(J+1) = 2B(J+1)$; hence B may be found by dividing by $2(J+1)$. We find (in cm^{-1}) 10.60, 10.59, 10.59, 10.59, 10.593, 10.593, 10.594, 10.593, 10.593, . . . , and so take $B = 10.593\ \mathrm{cm}^{-1}$.

$$q^{\mathrm{R}} = \sum_{J=0}^{\infty} (2J+1)\exp(-\beta E_J) \text{ [22.1.4]}$$

$$= \sum_{J=0}^{\infty} (2J+1)\exp\{-B\beta J(J+1)\} = \sum_{J=0}^{\infty} (2J+1)\exp\{-(10.593\ \mathrm{cm}^{-1}) \times (hc/k)J(J+1)/T\}$$

$$= \sum_{J=0}^{\infty} (2J+1)\exp\{-15.241\,J(J+1)/(T/\mathrm{K})\}.$$

(a) $T = 100\ \mathrm{K}$, $q^{\mathrm{R}} = 1.0000 + 2.2118 + 2.0037 + 1.1241 + \ldots = \underline{6.9051}$.

(b) $T = 298\ \mathrm{K}$, $q^{\mathrm{R}} = 1.0000 + 2.7083 + 3.6787 + 3.7893 + \ldots = \underline{19.889}$.

22.3 $q^{\mathrm{R}} = 1.0270(1/\sigma)(T/\mathrm{K})^{3/2}/[(A/\mathrm{cm}^{-1})(B/\mathrm{cm}^{-1})(C/\mathrm{cm}^{-1})]^{\frac{1}{2}}$ [Box 22.1];

$\sigma = 2$, $T = 298\ \mathrm{K}$.

$q^{\mathrm{R}} = 1.0270 \times \frac{1}{2} \times (298)^{3/2}/(27.878 \times 14.509 \times 9.287)^{1/2} = \underline{43.10}$.

We require kT to be significantly larger than the largest rotational constant; that is, $kT \gg (27.9\ \mathrm{cm}^{-1})hc$, or $T \gg (27.9\ \mathrm{cm}^{-1}) \times (1.439\ \mathrm{cm\,K}) = 40\ \mathrm{K}$.

The highest temperature approximation therefore requires $\underline{T \gg 40\ \mathrm{K}}$.

22.4 $B = \hbar/4\pi cI$ [18.2.3], $I = (8/3)m_{\mathrm{H}}R^2$ [Box 17.1],

$q^{\mathrm{R}} = 1.0270(1/\sigma)(T/\mathrm{K})^{3/2}/(B/\mathrm{cm}^{-1})^{3/2}$ [Box 22.1, $A = B = C$];

$\sigma = 12$ [Section 22.1(c)]

$I = (8/3) \times (1.0078 \times 1.6605 \times 10^{-27}\ \mathrm{kg}) \times (109 \times 10^{-12}\ \mathrm{m})^2 = 5.302 \times 10^{-47}\ \mathrm{kg\,m}^2$.

$B = \hbar/4\pi cI = (1.054\,59 \times 10^{-34}\ \mathrm{J\,s})/[4\pi \times (2.9979 \times 10^{10}\ \mathrm{cm\,s}^{-1})$

$\times (5.302 \times 10^{-47}\,\mathrm{kg\,m^2})] = 5.2799\ \mathrm{cm^{-1}}$.

$q^{\mathrm{R}} = 1.0270 \times (1/12) \times (T/\mathrm{K})^{3/2}/(5.2799)^{3/2} = 7.054 \times 10^{-3} \times (T/\mathrm{K})^{3/2}$.

(a) $T = 298\ \mathrm{K}, q^{\mathrm{R}} = 7.054 \times 10^{-3} \times (298)^{3/2} = \underline{36.3}$,

(b) $T = 500\ \mathrm{K}, q^{\mathrm{R}} = 7.054 \times 10^{-3} \times (500)^{3/2} = \underline{78.9}$.

22.5 $q^{\mathrm{R}} = \sum_{JMK} \exp(-\beta E_J) = (1/\sigma)\sum_J (2J+1)^2 \exp\{-hcB\beta J(J+1)\}$

[Problem 18.13]

$$= (1/\sigma) \sum_J (2J+1)^2 \exp\{-(5.2799\ \mathrm{cm^{-1}})(hc/k)J(J+1)/T\}$$

[Problem 22.4]

$$= (1/\sigma)\sum_J (2J+1)^2 \exp\{-7.5966\,J(J+1)/(T/\mathrm{K})\}\ [hc/k \text{ on end-paper 1}].$$

At 298 K,

$q^{\mathrm{R}} = (1.0000 + 8.5526 + 21.4543 + 36.0863 + \ldots)/\sigma$

$= 439.2664/\sigma = \underline{36.6055}$.

At 500 K,

$q^{\mathrm{R}} = (1.0000 + 8.7306 + 22.8218 + 40.8335 + \ldots)/\sigma = 950.0591/\sigma = \underline{79.1716}$.

NB. These results are still approximate because the symmetry factor is a valid corrector only at high temperatures; in order to get exact values of q^{R} we should do a detailed analysis as to which rotational states are allowed by the Pauli principle.

22.6 $q^{\mathrm{T}} = q_x^{\mathrm{T}} q_y^{\mathrm{T}}, q_x^{\mathrm{T}} = (2\pi m X^2/h^2\beta)^{\frac{1}{2}}$ [Section 21.1(e)]

$q^{\mathrm{t}} = (2\pi m/h^2\beta)XY = (2\pi m/h^2\beta)\sigma, \sigma = XY$.

$U - U(0) = -(N/q)(\partial q/\partial\beta)_V = nRT$.

$S = [U - U(0)]/T + nR(\ln q - \ln nN_{\mathrm{A}} + 1)$ [Box 22.2]

$= nR + nR\ln(\mathrm{e}q/nN_{\mathrm{A}}) = nR\ln(\mathrm{e}^2 q/nN_{\mathrm{A}})$

$= nR\ln\{\mathrm{e}^2(2\pi m/h^2\beta)\sigma/nN_{\mathrm{A}}\}$.

$S_{\mathrm{m}}(3\mathrm{d}) = R\ln\{\mathrm{e}^{5/2}(2\pi m/h^2\beta)^{3/2}(V/nN_{\mathrm{A}})\}, n = 1\ \mathrm{mol}$ [21.3.10];

$S_{\mathrm{m}}(2\mathrm{d}) = R\ln\{\mathrm{e}^2(2\pi m/h^2\beta)(\sigma/nN_{\mathrm{A}})\}, n = 1\ \mathrm{mol}$.

$$\Delta S_{\mathrm{m}} = S_{\mathrm{m}}(2\mathrm{d}) - S_{\mathrm{m}}(3\mathrm{d}) = R\ln\left\{\frac{\mathrm{e}^2(2\pi m/h^2\beta)(\sigma/nN_{\mathrm{A}})}{\mathrm{e}^{5/2}(2\pi m/h^2\beta)^{3/2}(V/nN_{\mathrm{A}})}\right\}$$

$= \underline{R \ln\{(\sigma/V)(h^2\beta/2\pi m e)^{1/2}\}}.$

See also *J. Chem. Soc. Faraday* **1**, 1784 (1973), and Problem 22.8 for an application.

22.7 $S_m^R = [U_m - U_m(0)]/T + R \ln q^R$ [Box 22.2, internal modes]

$q^R = (\pi^{1/2}/\sigma)\,[(2I_A kT/\hbar^2)(2I_B kT/\hbar^2)(2I_C kT/\hbar^2)]^{1/2}$ [Box 22.1]

$= \{(\pi/\sigma^2) 8 I_A I_B I_C (kT/\hbar^2)^3\}^{1/2}$ [$\sigma = 12$, Section 22.1(c)]

$= \{(8\pi/144) \times (2.93 \times 10^{-45}\,\mathrm{kg\,m^2}) \times (1.46 \times 10^{-45}\,\mathrm{kg\,m^2})^2$

$\times\, [(1.381 \times 10^{-23}\,\mathrm{J\,K^{-1}}) \times (362\,\mathrm{K})/(1.05459 \times 10^{-34}\,\mathrm{J\,s})^2]^3\}^{1/2}$

$= 9950.$

$[U_m - U_m(0)]/T = \frac{3}{2}R$ [from q^R, or by equipartition].

$S_m^R = R\{\frac{3}{2} + \ln 9950\} = \underline{89\,\mathrm{J\,K^{-1}\,mol^{-1}}}.$

In two dimensions (rotation about one axis):

$$q^R = \sum_{m_l} \exp(-m_l^2\hbar^2/2I_A kT)\ [14.3.5 \text{ and } 21.1.9,\ m_l = 0, \pm 1, \pm 2, \ldots]$$

$$\approx (1/\sigma)\int_{-\infty}^{\infty} \exp(-m_l^2\hbar^2/2I_A kT)\,\mathrm{d}m_l$$

$$= (1/\sigma)(2I_A kT/\hbar^2)^{1/2}\int_{-\infty}^{\infty} \mathrm{e}^{-x^2}\,\mathrm{d}x$$

$$= (2\pi I_A kT/\hbar^2)^{1/2}(1/\sigma)\left[\int_{-\infty}^{\infty} \mathrm{e}^{-x^2}\,\mathrm{d}x = \sqrt{\pi}\right].$$

$$q^R = \left\{\frac{2\pi \times (2.93 \times 10^{-45}\,\mathrm{kg}) \times (1.381 \times 10^{-23}\,\mathrm{J\,K^{-1}}) \times (362\,\mathrm{K})}{(1.054\,59 \times 10^{-34}\,\mathrm{J\,s})^2}\right\}^{1/2}(1/\sigma)$$

$= 90.97/\sigma = 15.2$ [$\sigma = 6$ for such rotation].

$[U_m - U_m(0)]/T = \frac{1}{2}R$ [from q^R, or by equipartition in one mode].

$S_m^R(2\mathrm{d}) = R\{\frac{1}{2} + \ln 15.2\} = 26.8\,\mathrm{J\,K^{-1}\,mol^{-1}}.$

$\Delta S_m^R(3\mathrm{d} \to 2\mathrm{d}) = 27\,\mathrm{J\,K^{-1}\,mol^{-1}} - 89\,\mathrm{J\,K^{-1}\,mol^{-1}} = \underline{-62\,\mathrm{J\,K^{-1}\,mol^{-1}}}.$

22.8 $\Delta S_m^{\ominus T} = R \ln\{(\sigma^\ominus/V^\ominus)(h^2\beta/2\pi m e)^{1/2}\}$ [Problem 22.6]

$V^\ominus = (1\,\mathrm{mol})RT/(1\,\mathrm{atm}) = 8.207 \times 10^{-5}\,\mathrm{m^3}\,(T/\mathrm{K})$

$\sigma^\ominus = (1\,\mathrm{mol}) \times (4.08 \times 10^{-20}\,\mathrm{m^2}) \times (6.022 \times 10^{23}\,\mathrm{mol^{-1}}) \times (T/\mathrm{K})$

$= 2.457 \times 10^4\,\mathrm{m^2}\,(T/\mathrm{K}).$

[The standard state of the mobile 2-dimensional film is defined so that the average separation of adsorbed molecules at 273 K is the same as in the 3-dimensional gas at 273 K and 1 atm; see original reference.]

$\sigma^{\ominus}/V^{\ominus} = \{2.457 \times 10^4\ \mathrm{m^2}\ (T/\mathrm{K})\}/\{8.207 \times 10^{-5}\ \mathrm{m^3}\ (T/\mathrm{K})\} = 2.994 \times 10^8\ \mathrm{m^{-1}}$

$$(h^2\beta/2\pi m e)^{1/2} = \{(6.626 \times 10^{-34}\ \mathrm{J\,s})^2/[2\pi e(1.381 \times 10^{-23}\ \mathrm{J\,K^{-1}}) \times T \times M_r \times (1.660\,56 \times 10^{-27}\ \mathrm{kg})]\}^{1/2}$$
$$= 1.059 \times 10^{-9}\ m/\{(T/\mathrm{K})M_r\}^{1/2}$$

$$\Delta S_m^{\ominus T} = R \ln\left\{\frac{(2.994 \times 10^8\ \mathrm{m^{-1}}) \times (1.059 \times 10^{-9}\ \mathrm{m})}{[(T/\mathrm{K})M_r]^{1/2}}\right\}$$
$$= R \ln 0.317 - \tfrac{1}{2}R \ln\{(T/\mathrm{K})M_r\}$$
$$= -9.552\ \mathrm{J\,K^{-1}\,mol^{-1}} - \tfrac{1}{2}R \ln\{(T/\mathrm{K})M_r\}.$$

For $T = 362$ K, $M_r = 78.12$,

$\Delta S_m^{\ominus}$ (translation) $= -52.2\ \mathrm{J\,K^{-1}\,mol^{-1}}$.

The change of rotational entropy, if the molecule is able to rotate only about its 6-fold axis, is

$\Delta S_m^{\ominus}$ (rotation) $= -62\ \mathrm{J\,K^{-1}\,mol^{-1}}$ [Problem 22.7].

Hence the overall change of entropy is $\Delta S_m^{\ominus} = \underline{-114\ \mathrm{J\,K^{-1}\,mol^{-1}}}$, in agreement with the experimental value at low surface coverage, suggesting that the model of a mobile, single axis roation layer is appropriate (but rotation about some other axis may be involved, the data cannot distinguish between the axes).

At higher surface coverages the entropy change falls to $\Delta S_m^{\ominus} = -52\ \mathrm{J\,K^{-1}\,mol^{-1}}$, suggesting that rotation about all three axes is then possible, so that $\Delta S_m^{\ominus} = \Delta S_m^{\ominus}$(translation) $= -52\ \mathrm{J\,K^{-1}\,mol^{-1}}$. If the benzene were to be immobilized on the surface, $\Delta S_m^{\ominus}$(translation) $= -S_m^{\ominus}$(3d translation) $= -R \ln\{e^{5/2}(2\pi m/h^2\beta)^{3/2}(V^{\ominus}/nL)\}$ [Problem 22.6] $= 9.680\ \mathrm{J\,K^{-1}\,mol^{-1}} - R \ln\{M_r^{3/2}\,(T/\mathrm{K})^{5/2}\}$ [since $V^{\ominus} = RT/(1\ \mathrm{mol}) \times (1\ \mathrm{atm})$ and $n = 1$ mol]. Therefore, $\Delta S_m^{\ominus}$(translation) $= -167\ \mathrm{J\,K^{-1}\,mol^{-1}}$ at 362 K which is significantly larger than the largest experimental result.

22.9 (a) Two distinguishable orientations (NN′ and N′N); $\sigma = 2$.

(b) One orientation (NO and ON are distinct): $\sigma = 1$.

(c) Six orientations about the C_6 axis, and each one may be turned upside down about a C_2 axis; $\sigma = 12$.

(d) Three positions about each of the four CH axes; $\sigma = 12$.

(e) Three positions about the single CH axis; $\sigma = 3$.

Alternatively: identify the order of the rotational subgroup [Section 22.1(c)].

22.10 $q^{T\ominus}/N = 0.025\,61\,(T/\mathrm{K})^{5/2} M_r^{3/2}$ [Box 22.1]

$$= 0.02561 \times (298.15)^{5/2} \times (67.5)^{3/2} = 2.17 \times 10^7.$$

$q^{\mathrm{R}} = (\pi^{1/2}/\sigma)\{8I_{\mathrm{A}}I_{\mathrm{B}}I_{\mathrm{C}}(kT)^3/\hbar^6\}^{1/2}$ [Box 22.1].

Adapt the expressions in Box 18.1 to find the moments of inertia. For I_{A} the molecule is viewed from the side (parallel to the O—O distance) and it looks like a diatomic with bond length (149 pm) cos 59.25° = 76.2 pm and RMMs 32.0 and 35.5. Use the first expression in Box 18.1: $I_{\mathrm{A}} = (32.0 \times 35.5/67.5) \times (76.2\ \mathrm{pm})^2 \times (1.66056 \times 10^{-27}\ \mathrm{kg}) = 1.623 \times 10^{-46}\ \mathrm{kg\,m^2}$. For I_{C} the molecule is viewed along the C_2 axis, when it looks like a linear triatomic with $R = (149\ \mathrm{pm})\sin 59.25° = 128$ pm. Use the third expression in Box 18.1:

$$I_{\mathrm{C}} = 2 \times (16.0 \times 1.6605 \times 10^{-27}\ \mathrm{kg}) \times (128\ \mathrm{pm})^2 = 8.70 \times 10^{-46}\ \mathrm{kg\,m^2}.$$

For I_{B} use $\sum_i m_i R_i^2$; the center of mass is on the C_2 axis and at a distance (32.0/67.5) $\times$ (76.2 pm) = 36.12 pm from the Cl atom and therefore at $\surd[(128\ \mathrm{pm})^2 + (76.2\ \mathrm{pm} - 36.12\ \mathrm{pm})^2] = 134$ pm from each O atom. Hence $I_{\mathrm{B}} = [35.5 \times (36.12\ \mathrm{pm})^2 + 2 \times (16.0) \times 134\ \mathrm{pm})^2] \times (1.600\,56 \times 10^{-27}\ \mathrm{kg}) = 1.031 \times 10^{-45}\ \mathrm{kg\,m^2}$.

$$q^{\mathrm{R}} = (\pi^{1/2}/2)\{8 \times (1.623 \times 10^{-46}\ \mathrm{kg\,m^2}) \times (1.031 \times 10^{-45}\ \mathrm{kg\,m^2}) \times (8.70 \times 10^{-46}\ \mathrm{kg\,m^2}) \times [(1.3805 \times 10^{-23}\ \mathrm{J\,K^{-1}}) \times (298.15\ \mathrm{K})/(1.054\,59 \times 10^{-34}\ \mathrm{J\,s})^2]^3\}^{1/2} = 4816.$$

$q^{\mathrm{V}} = 1$ [no vibrations excited]. $\qquad q^{\mathrm{E}} = 2$ [doublet ground state].

$q^{\mathrm{T}\ominus}/N = q^{\mathrm{T}\ominus}/N)q^{\mathrm{R}}q^{\mathrm{V}}q^{\mathrm{E}} = (2.17 \times 10^7) \times (4816) \times 2 = 2.09 \times 10^{11}.$

$[U_{\mathrm{m}} - U_{\mathrm{m}}(0)]/T = \frac{3}{2}R + \frac{3}{2}R = 3R$ [equipartition].

$S_{\mathrm{m}} = [U_{\mathrm{m}} - U_{\mathrm{m}}(0)]/T + R[\ln(q/N) + 1]$ [Box 22.2].

$= R\{3 + 1 + \ln(2.09 \times 10^{11})\} = 30.07R = \underline{250\ \mathrm{J\,K^{-1}\,mol^{-1}}}.$

22.11 $K = \{q_{\mathrm{m}}^{\ominus}(\mathrm{CHD_3})q_{\mathrm{m}}^{\ominus}(\mathrm{DCl})/q_{\mathrm{m}}^{\ominus}(\mathrm{CD_4})q_{\mathrm{m}}^{\ominus}(\mathrm{HCl})\}e^{-\beta\Delta E_0}$ [22.3.21]

$q_{\mathrm{m}}^{\mathrm{T}\ominus}(\mathrm{CHD_3})/N_{\mathrm{A}} = 2.561 \times 10^{-2}(T/\mathrm{K})^{5/2}M_{\mathrm{r}}^{3/2}$ [Box 22.1]

$= 2.561 \times 10^{-2}(T/\mathrm{K})^{5/2} \times 19.06^{3/2} = 2.131 \times (T/\mathrm{K})^{5/2}$

$q_{\mathrm{m}}^{\mathrm{T}\ominus}(\mathrm{DCl})/N_{\mathrm{A}} = 5.872 \times (T/\mathrm{K})^{5/2}$

$q_{\mathrm{m}}^{\mathrm{T}\ominus}(\mathrm{CD_4})/N_{\mathrm{A}} = 2.303 \times (T/\mathrm{K})^{5/2}$

$q_{\mathrm{m}}^{\mathrm{T}\ominus}(\mathrm{HCl})/N_{\mathrm{A}} = 5.638 \times (T/\mathrm{K})^{5/2}$

$q^{\mathrm{R}}(\mathrm{CHD_3})/N_{\mathrm{A}} = (1.0270/3)(T/\mathrm{K})^{3/2}/(3.28 \times 3.28 \times 2.63)^{1/2}$ [Box 22.1]

$= 0.0644\,(T/\mathrm{K})^{3/2}$

$q^{\mathrm{R}}(\mathrm{DCl}) = 0.6950(T/\mathrm{K})/5.455 = 0.124(T/\mathrm{K})$

$q^{\mathrm{R}}(\mathrm{CD_4}) = (1.0270/12)(T/\mathrm{K})^{3/2}/(2.63)^{3/2} = 0.00669\,(T/\mathrm{K})^{3/2}$

$q^{R}(HCl) = 0.6950\,(T/K)/10.59 = 0.0656\,(T/K)$

$$K = \left(\frac{2.131 \times 5.872}{2.303 \times 5.638}\right) \times \left(\frac{0.0644 \times 0.1274}{0.00669 \times 0.0656}\right) \times \left\{\frac{q^{V}(CHD_3)q^{V}(DCl)}{q^{V}(CD_4)q^{V}(HCl)}\right\} e^{-\beta\Delta E_0}$$

$$= 18.00\,Qe^{-\beta\Delta E_0},$$

with Q the ratio of vibrational partition functions.

$$\Delta E_0/hc = \tfrac{1}{2}\{[2142 + 2(1291) + 3(1003) + 2(2993) + 2(1036) + 2145]$$
$$- [2109 + 2(1092) + 3(2259) + 3(996) + 2991]\}\,\mathrm{cm}^{-1}$$
$$= -1053\,\mathrm{cm}^{-1}\ \text{[differences of zero-point energies]}.$$

$$q^{V}(CHD_3) = \{1 - \exp[-3082/(T/K)]\}^{-1}\{1 - \exp[-1857/(T/K)]\}^{-2}$$
$$\{1 - \exp[-1491/(T/K)]\}^{-2}$$
$$\times \{1 - \exp[-1443/(T/K)]\}^{-3}\{1 - \exp[-4306/(T/K)]\}^{-1}$$

$[hc/k = 1.438\,78\ \mathrm{cm\,K.}]$.

$$q^{V}(DCl) = \{1 - \exp[-3086/(T/K)]\}^{-1}$$

$$q^{V}(DC_4) = \{1 - \exp[-3034/(T/K)]\}^{-1} \times \{1 - \exp[-1571/(T/K)]\}^{-2}$$
$$\times \{1 - \exp[-1491/(T/K)]\}^{-2}$$
$$\times \{1 - \exp[-1433/(T/K)]\}^{-3}\{1 - \exp[-3250/(T/K)]\}^{-3}.$$

$$q^{V}(HCl) = \{1 - \exp[-4303/(T/K)]\}^{-1}.$$

Collecting all the pieces leads to $K = 6.00 \times$

$$\left\{\frac{[1-E(3034)]\,[1-E(1572)]^2\,[1-E(1433)]^3\,[1-E(3250)]^3\,[1-E(4303)]}{[1-E(3082)]\,[1-E(1857)]^2\,[1-E(1443)]^3\,[1-E(4306)]\,[1-E(1491)]^2\,[1-E(3086)]}\right\}$$

$\times \exp\{+1515/(T/K)\}$ where $E(x) = \exp\{-x(T/K)\}$.

Draw up the following Table

T/K	500	1000	1500	2000	3000	4000	5000
K	22	6.1	4.5	4.0	3.7	3.6	3.5

22.12 $K = \{q^{\ominus}(HCl)/q^{\ominus}(DCl)\}\{q^{\ominus}(HDO)/q^{\ominus}(H_2O)\}\exp\{-\beta\Delta E_0\}$ [22.3.21].

$q^{\ominus}(HCl)/q^{\ominus}(DCl) = \{\Lambda(DCl)/\Lambda(HCl)\}^3\,\{q^{R}(HCl)/q^{R}(DCl)\}\{q^{V}(HCl)/q^{V}(DCl)\}$

$\{\Lambda(DCl)/\Lambda(HCl)\}^3 = \{M_r(HCl)/M_r(DCl)\}^{3/2}$ [Box 22.1] $= (36.46/37.46)^{3/2} = 0.960.$

$q^{R}(HCl)/q^{R}(DCl) = B(DCl)/B(HCl)$ [Box 22.1] $= 5.499/10.59 = 0.519.$

$\{\Lambda(H_2O)/\Lambda(HDO)\}^3 = \{M_r(HDO)/M_r(H_2O)\}^{3/2} = \{19.02/18.02\}^{3/2} = 1.084.$

$q^{R}(HDO)/q^{R}(H_2O) = 2\{A(H_2O)B(H_2O)C(H_2O)/A(HDO)B(HDO)C(HDO)\}^{1/2}$

$[\sigma = 2 \text{ for } H_2O] = 2\{27.88 \times 14.51 \times 9.29/23.38 \times 9.102 \times 6.417\}^{1/2} = 3.318.$

$$\Delta E_0/hc = \tfrac{1}{2}\{[2726.7 + 1402.2 + 3707.5 + 2991] - [3656.7 + 1594.8 + 3755.8 + 2145]\}\,\text{cm}^{-1} = -162\,\text{cm}^{-1}.$$

$\Delta E_0\beta = -162\,\text{cm}^{-1} \times (hc/k)/T = -233/(T/\text{K})$ [hc/k on end-paper 1]

$$K = 0.960 \times 0.519 \times 1.084 \times 3.318 \times \{q^V(\text{HCl})/q^V(\text{DCl})\}\{q^V(\text{HDO})/q^V(\text{H}_2\text{O})\} \times \exp(-\Delta E_0\beta)$$
$$= 1.792\,\{q^V(\text{HCl})/q^V(\text{DCl})\}\,\{q^V(\text{HDO})/q^V(\text{H}_2\text{O})\}\exp\{233/(T/\text{K})\}.$$

$$q^V(\text{HCl}) = \sum_{v=0}^{\infty} \exp\{-v\tilde{\nu}(\text{HCl})hc/kT\}$$

$$= \sum_v \exp\{-4303\,v/(T/\text{K})\}\,[hc/k = 1.4388\text{ cm K}, \tilde{\nu}(\text{HCl}) = 2991\text{ cm}^{-1}]$$

$$= \begin{cases} 1 + 0.0000 + \ldots = 1.000 \text{ at } 298\text{ K}, \\ 1 + 0.0046 + 0.000\,02 + \ldots = 1.005 \text{ at } 800\text{ K}. \end{cases}$$

$$q^V(\text{DCl}) = \sum_v \exp\{-3086v/(T/\text{K})\}$$
$$= \begin{cases} 1 + 0.0000 + \ldots = 1.000 \text{ at } 298\text{ K}, \\ 1 + 0.0211 + 0.0004 + \ldots = 1.022 \text{ at } 800\text{ K}. \end{cases}$$

$$q^V(\text{HDO}) = \{-\exp[-3923/(T/\text{K})]\}^{-1} \times \{1 - \exp[-2017/(T/\text{K})]\}^{-1} \times \{1 - \exp[-5334/(T/\text{K})]\}^{-1}$$

$$= \begin{cases} 1.001 \text{ at } 298\text{ K}, \\ 1.097 \text{ at } 800\text{ K}. \end{cases}$$

$$q^V(\text{HDO}) = \{1 - \exp[-5262/(T/\text{K})]\}^{-1}\{1 - \exp[-2295/(T/\text{K})]\}^{-1} \times \{1 - \exp[-5404/(T/\text{K})]\}^{-1}$$

$$= \begin{cases} 1.001 \text{ at } 298\text{ K}, \\ 1.063 \text{ at } 800\text{ K}. \end{cases}$$

(a) $K(298\text{ K}) = 1.792 \times \left(\dfrac{1.000}{1.000}\right) \times \left(\dfrac{1.001}{1.001}\right) \times \exp\{+233/298\} = \underline{3.917.}$

(b) $K(800\text{ K}) = 1.792 \times \left(\dfrac{1.005}{1.022}\right) \times \left(\dfrac{1.097}{1.063}\right) \times \exp\{+233/800\} = \underline{2.433.}$

22.13 $q_m^{T\ominus}/N_A = 2.561 \times 10^{-2}(T/K)^{5/2}M_r^{3/2}$ [Box 22.1]

$q_m^{T\ominus}(I_2)/N_A = 2.561 \times 10^{-2} \times 1000^{5/2} \times 253.8^{3/2} = 3.27 \times 10^9$.

$q_m^{T\ominus}(I)/N_A = 2.561 \times 10^{-2} \times 1000^{5/2} \times 126.9^{3/2} = 1.16 \times 10^9$.

$q^R(I_2) = (0.6950/2) \times 1000/0.0373$ [Box 22.1] $= 9316$.

$q^V(I_2) = 1/\{1 - \exp(-214.36/695)\}$ [Box 22.1] $= 3.77$

$q^E(I) = 4, q^E(I_2) = 1$.

$$K_p = \{q_m^\ominus(I)^2/q_m^\ominus(I_2)N_A\}e^{-\Delta E_0/RT} \; [22.3.21]$$
$$= \{[q_m^\ominus(I)/N_A]^2/[q_m^\ominus(I_2)/N_A]\}e^{-D_0/RT}$$
$$= \{(1.16 \times 10^9 \times 4)^2/(3.27 \times 10^9 \times 9316 \times 3.77)\}e^{-17.9}$$
$$= \underline{3.2 \times 10^{-3}}.$$

22.14 $q^E(I) = 4 + 2\exp(-7603/1390) = 4.008$ [$RT \,\hat{=}\, 1390\ \text{cm}^{-1}$ at 2000 K]. Let K_p be the true equilibrium constant at 2000 K and K'_p be the equilibrium constant at 2000 K calculated with neglect of the upper electronic states of the atoms. Then $K_p/K'_p = (4.008)^2/(4.000)^2 = \underline{1.004}$.

22.15 $q^E = \sum_{M_J} \exp\{-g\mu_B B\beta M_J\}, M_J = -\frac{3}{2}, -\frac{1}{2}, \frac{1}{2}, \frac{3}{2}, g = 4/3$.

Since $g\mu_B B\beta \ll 1$ for normal conditions,

$$q^E = \sum_{M_J}\{1 - g\mu_B B\beta m_J - \tfrac{1}{2}(g\mu_B B\beta M_J)^2 + \dots\}$$
$$= 4 + 0 - \tfrac{1}{2}(g\mu_B B\beta)^2\{(\tfrac{3}{2})^2 + (\tfrac{1}{2})^2 + (\tfrac{1}{2})^2 + (\tfrac{3}{2})^2\} + \dots$$
$$= 4 - (5/2)(g\mu_B B\beta)^2 + \dots = 4\{1 - (10/9)(\mu_B B\beta)^2 + \dots\}.$$

Therefore if K_p is the actual equilibrium constant, and K_p^0 is that calculated at zero field, from Problem 22.13, $K_p \approx \{1 - (10/9)(\mu_B B\beta)^2\}^2 K_p^0 \approx \{1 - (20/9)(\mu_B B\beta)^2\}K_p^0$.

For a 1% shift we require

$(20/9)(\mu_B B\beta)^2 \approx 0.01$, or $\mu_B B\beta \approx 0.067$;

hence

$$B \approx 0.067kT/\mu_B \approx 0.067 \times (1.381 \times 10^{-23}\ \text{J K}^{-1}) \times (1000\ \text{K})/(9.274 \times 10^{-24}\ \text{J T}^{-1})$$
$$\approx \underline{100\ \text{T}}.$$

22.16 $q = 1/\{1 - \exp(-\hbar\omega/kT)\}$ [Box 22.1] $= 1/\{1 - e^{-x}\}; x = \hbar\omega/kT = \hbar\omega\beta$.

$$U - U(0) = -N(\partial \ln q/\partial\beta) \; [\text{Box } 22.2] = -N(1/q)(\partial q/\partial\beta)_V$$
$$= -N(1 - e^{-x})(d/d\beta)(1 - e^{-x})^{-1} = N(1 - e^{-x})\hbar\omega e^{-x}(1 - e^{-x})^{-2}$$

$= \underline{N\hbar\omega e^{-x}/(1-e^{-x})}.$

$H - H(0) = U - U(0) = \underline{N\hbar\omega e^{-x}/(1-e^{-x})}.$

$S = [U - U(0)]/T + nR\ln q = Nkxe^{-x}/(1-e^{-x}) - Nk\ln(1-e^{-x})$

$= \underline{Nk\{xe^{-x}/(1-e^{-x}) - \ln(1-e^{-x})\}}.$

$A - A(0) = G - G(0) = -nRT\ln q = \underline{NkT\ln(1-e^{-x})}.$

Draw up the following Table

x	0.01	0.02	0.03	0.06	0.10	0.20
$[U-U(0)]/N\hbar\omega$	99.5	49.5	32.8	16.2	9.51	4.52
S/Nk	5.61	4.91	4.51	3.81	3.30	2.61
$[A-A(0)]/NkT$	−4.61	−3.92	−3.52	−2.84	−2.35	−1.71

x	0.30	0.60	1.0	2.0	3.0	6.0
$[U-U(0)]/N\hbar\omega$	2.86	1.22	0.58	0.16	0.05	0.002
S/Nk	2.21	1.53	1.04	0.46	0.21	0.02
$[A-A(0)]/NkT$	−1.35	−0.80	−0.46	−0.15	−0.05	−0.002

These are plotted in Fig. 22.1.

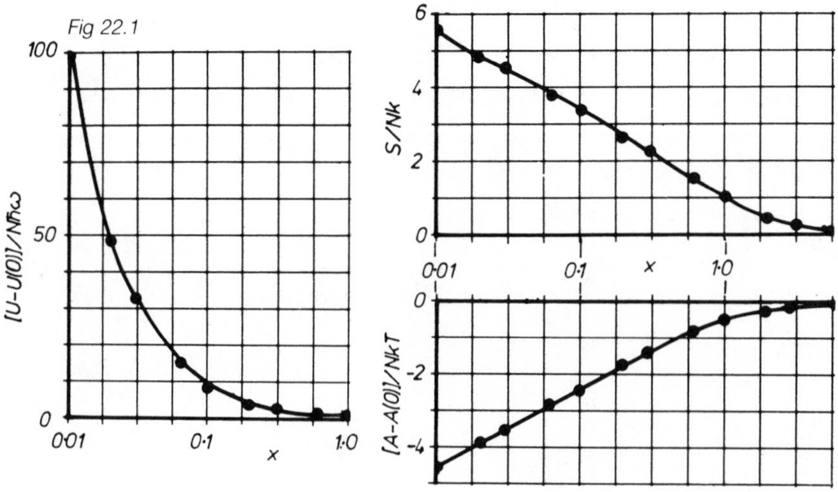

22.17 $\Phi_0^V = [G_m(T) - H_m(0)]/T = [G_m(T) - G_m(0)]/T = \underline{R\ln(1-e^{-x})}$.

22.18 For several modes j, $q = q_1 q_2 \ldots$, and so

$$\Phi_0^V(T) = R\sum_j \ln(1-e^{-x_j}),\ x_j = \hbar\omega_j\beta.$$

At 1000 K, $kT/hc = 695.03\ \text{cm}^{-1}$, and so

(a) NH_3: $x_1 = 3336.7/695.03 = 4.80, x_2 = 1.37, x_3 = 4.95, x_4 = 2.34$.

(b) CH_4: $x_1 = 4.19, x_2 = 2.21, x_3 = 4.34, x_4 = 1.88$.

(a) $\Phi_0^V = R\ln(1-e^{-4.80})(1-e^{-1.37})(1-e^{-4.95})^2(1-e^{-2.34})^2$

$= -0.518R = \underline{-4.31\ \text{J K}^{-1}\ \text{mol}^{-1}}$.

(b) $\Phi_0^V = R\ln(1-e^{-4.19})(1-e^{-2.21})^2(1-e^{-4.34})^3(1-e^{-1.88})^3$

$= -0.784R = \underline{-6.52\ \text{J K}^{-1}\ \text{mol}^{-1}}$.

22.19 $\Phi_0 = [G_m(T) - H_m(0)]/T = [G_m(T) - G_m(0)]/T$

$= -nR\ln(q_m^T/N_A) - nR\ln q^i = -nR\ln(q_m^T q^i/N_A)$ [Box 22.2].

(a) H_2: $(q_m^T/N_A)^\ominus = 0.02561 \times (1000)^{5/2} \times (2.01)^{3/2} = 2.31 \times 10^6$ [Box 22.1].

$q^R = \frac{1}{2} \times (0.6950) \times (1000)/(60.864) = 5.711$.

$q^V = 1/[1 - \exp(-4400.39/695.3)] = 1.002$.

$\Phi_0^\ominus = -R\ln 1.32 \times 10^7 = \underline{-136\ \text{J K}^{-1}\ \text{mol}^{-1}}$.

(b) Cl_2: $(q_m^T/N_A)^\ominus = 0.025\,61 \times (1000)^{5/2} \times (70.90)^{3/2} = 4.84 \times 10^8$.

$q^R = \frac{1}{2} \times (0.6950) \times (1000\ \text{K})/0.2441 = 1.424 \times 10^3$.

$q^V = 1/[1 - \exp(-559.71/695.3)] = 1.809$.

$\Phi_0^\ominus = -R\ln 1.24 \times 10^{12} = \underline{-232\ \text{J K}^{-1}\ \text{mol}^{-1}}$.

(c) NH_3: $(q_m^T/N_A)^\ominus = 0.02561 \times (1000)^{5/2} \times (17.03)^{3/2} = 5.69 \times 10^7$.

$q^R = \frac{1}{3} \times (1.0270) \times (1000)^{3/2}/(6.34 \times 9.98^2)^{1/2} = 431$.

$q^V = 1/(1-e^{-4.80})(1-e^{-1.37})(1-e^{-4.95})^2(1-e^{-2.34})^2 = 1.68$.

$\Phi_0^\ominus = -R\ln 4.12 \times 10^{10} = \underline{-203\ \text{J K}^{-1}\ \text{mol}^{-1}}$.

(d) N_2: $(q_m^T/N_A)^\ominus = 0.025\,61 \times (1000)^{5/2} \times (28.02)^{3/2} = 1.20 \times 10^8$.

$q^R = \frac{1}{3} \times (0.6950) \times (1000)/(1.9987) = 173.9$.

$q^V = 1/[1 - \exp(-2358.07/695.3)] = 1.035$.

$\Phi_0^\ominus = -R\ln 2.14 \times 10^{10} = \underline{-198\ \text{J K}^{-1}\ \text{mol}^{-1}}$.

(e) NO: $(q_m^T/N_A)^\ominus = 0.025\,61 \times (1000)^{5/2} \times (30.01)^{3/2} = 1.33 \times 10^8$

$q^R = (0.6950) \times (1000)/(1.7046) = 408$.

$q^{\mathrm{V}} = 1/[1 - \exp(-1904/695.3)] = 1.069.$

$q^{\mathrm{E}} = 2[1 + \exp(-121.1/695.3)] = 3.84$ [Problem 20.13].

$\Phi_0^{\ominus} = R \ln 2.14 \times 10^{11} = \underline{-217\ \mathrm{J\,K^{-1}\,mol^{-1}}}.$

22.20 $N_2 + 3H_2 \rightleftharpoons 2NH_3$; follow *Example* 10.5.

$\Delta_r\Phi_0 = \{2 \times (-203) - (-198) - 3(-136)\}\mathrm{J\,K^{-1}\,mol^{-1}}$

$\quad = 200\ \mathrm{J\,K^{-1}mol^{-1}}$ [Problem 22.19].

$\Delta_r H^{\ominus} = -92.2\ \mathrm{kJ\,mol^{-1}}$ [Example 10.5]

$\Delta_r H^{\ominus} - \Delta_r H^{\ominus}(0) = -14.24\ \mathrm{kJ\,mol^{-1}}$[Table 10.1, or else use Box 22.2 for a purely statistical thermodynamic calculation].

$$K = \exp\{-\Delta_r G^{\ominus}/RT\}$$

$$= \exp\{-\Delta_r\Phi_0^{\ominus}/R - \Delta_r H^{\ominus}/RT + [\Delta_r H^{\ominus} - \Delta_r H^{\ominus}(0)]/RT\}\ [10.1.13]$$

$$= \exp\{-(1/8.314\ \mathrm{J\,K^{-1}\,mol^{-1}})\,[200\ \mathrm{J\,K^{-1}mol^{-1}} - (92.2\ \mathrm{kJ\,mol^{-1}})/(1000\ \mathrm{K}) + (14.24\ \mathrm{kJ\,mol^{-1}})/1000\ \mathrm{K})]\} = \exp(-14.7) = \underline{4.1 \times 10^{-7}}.$$

22.21 $U - U(0) = -N(1/q)(\partial q/\partial\beta)_V$ [Box 22.2].

$$= N(1/q)\sum_j \epsilon_j \exp(-\beta\epsilon_j) = N(1/q)kTq^{\cdot} = \underline{nRT(q^{\cdot}/q)}.$$

$$S = [U - U(0)]/T + nR\,[\ln(q/N) + 1] = \underline{nR\{(q^{\cdot}/q) + \ln(eq/N)\}}.$$

$$C_V = (\partial U/\partial T)_V = (\mathrm{d}\beta/\mathrm{d}T)(\partial U/\partial\beta)_V$$

$$= -(1/kT^2)(\partial/\partial\beta)\{N(1/q)\sum_j \epsilon_j \exp(-\beta\epsilon_j)\}$$

$$= (N/kT^2)\left\{(1/q)\sum_j \epsilon_j^2 \exp(-\beta\epsilon_j) + (1/q^2)(\partial q/\partial\beta)\sum_j \epsilon_j \exp(-\beta\epsilon_j)\right\}$$

$$= (N/kT^2)\left\{(1/q)\sum_j \epsilon_j^2 \exp(-\beta\epsilon_j) - (1/q^2)\left[\sum_j \epsilon_j \exp(-\beta\epsilon_j)\right]^2\right\}$$

$$= (N/kT^2)\{(k^2T^2q^{\cdot\cdot}/q) - (1/q^2)k^2T^2(q^{\cdot})^2\}$$

$$= \underline{nR\{(q^{\cdot\cdot}/q) - (q^{\cdot}/q)^2\}}.$$

22.22 $U - U(0) = -(\partial \ln Q/\partial\beta)_V = -(\partial \ln Q_{\mathrm{int}}\,Q_{\mathrm{ext}}/\partial\beta)_V$

$$= -(\partial \ln(q_{\mathrm{int}}^N q_{\mathrm{ext}}^N/N!)/\partial\beta]_V = -\{\partial[\ln q_{\mathrm{int}}^N + \ln(q_{\mathrm{ext}}^N/N!)]/\partial\beta\}_V$$

$$= -(\partial \ln q_{\mathrm{int}}^N/\partial\beta)_V - (\partial \ln(q_{\mathrm{ext}}^N/N!)/\partial\beta)_V$$

$$= [U^{\mathrm{int}} - U^{\mathrm{int}}(0)] + [U^{\mathrm{ext}} - U^{\mathrm{ext}}(0)].$$

$$U^{\mathrm{int}} - U^{\mathrm{int}}(0) = -N(\partial \ln q_{\mathrm{int}}/\partial\beta)_V = \underline{nRT(q_{\mathrm{int}}^{\cdot}/q_{\mathrm{int}})}.$$

$$S = [U - U(0)]/T + k\ln Q = [U^{\text{int}} - U^{\text{int}}(0)]/T + [U^{\text{ext}} - U^{\text{ext}}(0)]/T$$
$$+ k\ln(q_{\text{int}}^N q_{\text{ext}}^N/N!)$$
$$= \{[U^{\text{int}} - U^{\text{int}}(0)]/T + k\ln q_{\text{int}}^N\} + \{[U^{\text{ext}} - U^{\text{ext}}(0)]/T$$
$$+ k\ln(q_{\text{ext}}^N/N!)]\} = S^{\text{int}} + S^{\text{ext}};$$

$$S^{\text{int}} = [U^{\text{int}} - U^{\text{int}}(0)]/T + Nk\ln q_{\text{int}}$$
$$= nR(\dot{q}_{\text{int}}/q_{\text{int}}) + nR\ln q_{\text{int}} = \underline{nR\{(q^{\cdot}/q)_{\text{int}} + \ln q_{\text{int}}\}}.$$
$$C_V = (\partial U/\partial T)_V = (\partial U^{\text{int}}/\partial T)_V + (\partial U^{\text{ext}}/\partial T)_V$$
$$C_V^{\text{int}} = (\partial U^{\text{int}}/\partial T)_V = \underline{nR\{(q^{\cdot\cdot}/q)_{\text{int}} - (q^{\cdot}/q)_{\text{int}}^2\}}.$$

22.23 At 5000 K, $kT/hc = 3475\ \text{cm}^{-1}$. Form the sums $q, q^{\cdot}, q^{\cdot\cdot}$:

$$q = \sum_j \exp(-\epsilon_j\beta) = 1 + \exp(-21\,850/3475) + 3\exp(-21\,870/3475) + \ldots = 1.0167.$$

$$q^{\cdot} = \sum_j (\epsilon_j/kT)\exp(-\epsilon_j\beta) = (hc/kT)\sum_j(\epsilon_j/hc)\exp(-\epsilon_j\beta)$$
$$= (1/3475\ \text{cm}^{-1})\{0 + (21\,850\ \text{cm}^{-1})\exp(-21\,850/3475)$$
$$+ 3(21\,870\ \text{cm}^{-1})\exp(-21\,870/3475) + \ldots\} = 0.1057.$$

$$q^{\cdot\cdot} = \sum_j (\epsilon_j/kT)^2\exp(-\epsilon_j\beta) = (hc/kT)^2\sum_j(\epsilon_j/hc)^2\exp(-\epsilon_j\beta)$$
$$= (1/3457\ \text{cm}^{-1})^2\{0 + (21\,850\ \text{cm}^{-1})^2 \times \exp(-21\,850/3475) + \ldots\} = 0.6719.$$

(a) $H_{\text{m}}^{\text{E}} - H_{\text{m}}^{\text{E}}(0) = U_{\text{m}}^{\text{E}} - U_{\text{m}}^{\text{E}}(0) = RT(\dot{q}^{\text{E}}/q^{\text{E}})$ [Problem 22.22]
$$= (8.314\ \text{J K}^{-1}\text{mol}^{-1}) \times (5000\ \text{K}) \times (0.1057/1.0167)$$
$$= \underline{4.322\ \text{kJ mol}^{-1}}.$$

(b) $\Phi_0^{\text{E}} = -R\ln q$ [Problem 22.17]
$$= -(8.314\ \text{J K}^{-1}\ \text{mol}^{-1})\ln 1.0167 = \underline{-0.138\ \text{J K}^{-1}\ \text{mol}^{-1}}.$$

$C_{V,\text{m}}^{\text{E}}(5000\ \text{K}) = R\{(q^{\cdot\cdot}/q)_{\text{E}} - (q^{\cdot}/q)_{\text{E}}^2\}$ [Problem 22.22]
$$= (8.314\ \text{J K}^{-1}\text{mol}^{-1}) \times \{(0.6719/1.0167) - (0.1057/1.0167)^2\}$$
$$= \underline{5.405\ \text{J K}^{-1}\text{mol}^{-1}}.$$

22.24 $\Phi_0^{\text{E}} = -R\ln q$ [Problem 22.17],

$$q = \sum_j \exp(-\beta\epsilon_j) = \sum_J (2J+1)\exp(-\beta E_J).$$

[A level J is $(2J+1)$-fold degenerate; and so the contribution of each level must be multiplied by $(2J+1)$.] Draw up the following Table:

T/K	1000	2000	3000	4000	5000
$(kT/hc)\text{cm}^{-1}$	695	1391	2085	2780	3475
q	2.000	2.000	2.002	2.014	2.053
$-\Phi_0^{\text{E}}/\text{J K}^{-1}\,\text{mol}^{-1}$	5.763	5.763	5.771	5.821	5.980

For C_V at 3000 K, see the next Problem.

22.25 $C_{V,\text{m}}^{\text{E}} = R\{(q^{\cdot\cdot}/q)_{\text{E}} - (q^{\cdot}/q)_{\text{E}}^2\}$ [Problem 22.22]

Draw up the following Table using the data in Problem 22.24.

T/K	1000	2000	3000	4000	5000
$(kT/hc)/\text{cm}^{-1}$	695	1391	2085	2780	3475
q	2.000	2.000	2.002	2.014	2.053
$q^{\cdot}$	3.69×10^{-9}	3.68×10^{-4}	1.46×10^{-2}	9.08×10^{-2}	0.289
$q^{\cdot\cdot}$	9.01×10^{-8}	4.50×10^{-3}	0.121	0.598	1.697
$C_{V,\text{m}}/R$	4.51×10^{-8}	2.25×10^{-3}	0.060	0.295	0.807

22.26 $\Phi_0^{\text{E}} = [G_\text{m}^\ominus - G_\text{m}^\ominus(0)]/T = -R\ln(q_\text{m}^\ominus/N_\text{A})$ [Box 22.2].

$\text{Na}_2 \rightleftharpoons 2\text{Na}$; $\Delta_\text{r}G^\ominus = -RT\ln K_p$.

$$-RT\ln K_p = 2G_{\text{Na,m}}^\ominus - G_{\text{Na}_2\text{,m}}^\ominus = 2T\Phi_{0,\text{Na}}^\ominus + 2G_{\text{Na,m}}^\ominus(0)$$
$$- T\Phi_{0,\text{Na}_2}^\ominus - G_{\text{Na}_2\text{,m}}^\ominus(0)$$
$$= T\{2\Phi_{0,\text{Na}}^\ominus - \Phi_{0,\text{Na}_2}^\ominus\} + D_\text{m}^\ominus\ [G(0) \to U(0)]$$
$$= -RT\ln\{(q_{\text{Na,m}}^\ominus/N_\text{A})^2/(q_{\text{Na}_2\text{,m}}^\ominus/N_\text{A})\} + D_\text{m}^\ominus.$$

Then $K_p = (q_{\text{Na,m}}^{\ominus 2}/q_{\text{Na}_2\text{,m}}N_\text{A})e^{-D_0/RT}$. Now follow *Example* 22.6:

$q_{\text{Na,m}}^{\text{T}\ominus}/N_\text{A} = 2.561 \times 10^{-2} \times 1163^{5/2} \times 22.99^{3/2}$ [Box 22.1] $= 1.30 \times 10^8$

$q_{\text{Na}_2\text{,m}}^{\text{T}\ominus}/N_\text{A} = 3.68 \times 10^8$

$q_{\text{Na}_2}^{\text{R}} = \frac{1}{2} \times 0.6950 \times 1163/0.1547 = 2612$

$q_{\text{Na}_2}^{\text{V}} = \{1 - \exp(-159/808)\}^{-1} = 5.598$

$q_{\text{Na}}^{\text{E}} = 2.00$ [Problem 22.24].

$$K_p = \{(1.30 \times 10^8 \times 2.00)^2/3.68 \times 10^8 \times 2612 \times 5.598\}e^{-D_0/RT}$$
$$= \underline{8.65}.$$

If the degree of dissociation is α_e, we have

$\alpha_e = \{K_p/(K_p + 4p^{\ominus})\}^{1/2}$ [10.2.2] $= \{8.65/(8.65 + 4.000)\}^{1/2}$

$= 0.827$ when $p = 1$ atm.

Hence, at equilibrium, the mole fractions are

$x(Na_2) = (1 - \alpha_e)/(1 + \alpha_e) = \underline{0.095}$,

$x(Na) = 2\alpha_e/(1 + \alpha_e) = \underline{0.905}$.

Determine the proportion of atoms by atomic absorption spectroscopy; the proportion of dimers by Raman spectroscopy.

22.27 $C_{V,m} = \frac{1}{2}R(3 + \nu_R^* + 2\nu_V^*)$ [22.3.14]

(a) $\nu_R^* = 2, \nu_V^* = 0$ (but probably contributes);

$C_{V,m} \gtrsim \frac{1}{2}R(3 + 2 + 0) = 5R/2 = \underline{21\ \text{J K}^{-1}\ \text{mol}^{-1}}$.

(b) $\nu_R^* = 2$ (but possibly less, because of quantum effects);

$C_{V,m} \approx \frac{1}{2}R(3 + 2 + 0) = 5R/2 = \underline{21\ \text{J K}^{-1}\ \text{mol}^{-1}}$.

(c) $\nu_R^* = 3, \nu_V^* = 0$;

$C_{V,m} = \frac{1}{2}R(3 + 3 + 0) = 3R = \underline{25\ \text{J K}^{-1}\text{mol}^{-1}}$.

(d) $\nu_R^* = 3, \nu_V^* = 0$; $C_{V,m} = 3R = \underline{25\ \text{J K}^{-1}\ \text{mol}^{-1}}$.

(e) $\nu_R^* = 3, \nu_V^* = 0$; $C_{V,m} = 3R = \underline{25\ \text{J K}^{-1}\ \text{mol}^{-1}}$.

(f) $\nu_R^* = 2, \nu_V^* = 0$; $C_{V,m} = 5R/2 = \underline{21\ \text{J K}^{-1}\ \text{mol}^{-1}}$.

22.28 $U - U(0) = N\hbar\omega e^{-x}/(1 - e^{-x})$ [$x = \hbar\omega\beta$, Problem 22.16]

$C_V = (\partial U/\partial T)_V = (d\beta/dT)(\partial U/\partial\beta)_V = -(1/kT^2)(\partial U/\partial\beta)_V$

$= -(N\hbar\omega/kT^2)\{-\hbar\omega e^{-x}/(1 - e^{-x}) - \hbar\omega e^{-2x}/(1 - e^{-x})^2\}$

$= (N\hbar^2\omega^2/kT^2)e^{-x}/(1 - e^{-x})^2 = Nkx^2 e^{-x}/(1 - e^{-x})^2$.

$C_{V,m}/R = \underline{x^2 e^{-x}/(1 - e^{-x})^2}$.

This function is plotted in Fig. 22.2

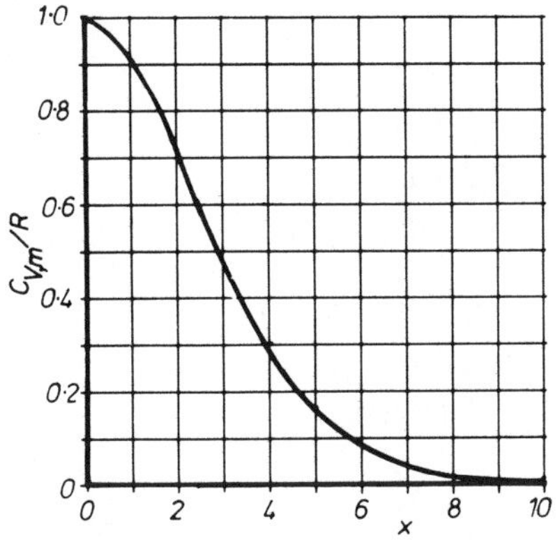

Fig 22.2

Use the data in Problem 22.18, and note the degeneracies (so that one vibrational frequency may contribute several times). Draw up Tables as below.

The translational and rotational contributions are $3R$ in each case [equipartition], and so the total heat capacities are

Ammonia (a) 298 K: $3.27\,R = \underline{27.2\ \mathrm{J\,K^{-1}\,mol^{-1}}}$,

(b) 500 K: $3.99\,R = \underline{33.2\ \mathrm{J\,K^{-1}\,mol^{-1}}}$.

Methane (a) 298 K: $3.28\,R = \underline{27.3\ \mathrm{J\,K^{-1}\,mol^{-1}}}$.

(b) 500 K: $4.58\,R = \underline{38.1\ \mathrm{J\,K^{-1}\,mol^{-1}}}$.

Ammonia

Mode	(a) 298 K		(b) 500 K	
$\tilde{\nu}$/cm	x	$C_{V,\mathrm{m}}/R$	x	$C_{V,\mathrm{m}}/R$
3336.7	16.12	2.6×10^{-5}	9.59	0.01
950.4	4.59	0.22	2.73	0.56
3443.8	16.64	1.6×10^{-5}	9.90	4.9×10^{-3}
3443.8	16.64	1.6×10^{-5}	9.90	4.9×10^{-3}
1626.8	7.86	0.02	4.67	0.21
1626.8	7.86	0.02	4.67	0.21
Total		0.27		0.99

Methane

Mode	(a) 298 K		(b) 500 K	
$\tilde{\nu}$/cm	x	$C_{V,\mathrm{m}}/R$	x	$C_{V,\mathrm{m}}/R$
2816.7	14.09	1.5×10^{-4}	8.34	0.02
1533.6	7.41	0.03	4.41	0.24
1533.6	7.41	0.03	4.41	0.24
3018.9	14.58	9.9×10^{-5}	8.68	0.01
3018.9	14.58	9.9×10^{-5}	8.68	0.01
3018.9	14.58	9.9×10^{-5}	8.68	0.01
1306.2	6.31	0.07	3.75	0.35
1306.2	6.31	0.07	3.75	0.35
1306.2	6.31	0.07	3.75	0.35
Total		0.28		1.58

22.29 $C_{V,\mathrm{m}}/R = x^2 e^{-x}/(1 - e^{-x})^2$ for each mode [Problem 22.28]. Draw up the following Table using $kT/hc = 207\ \mathrm{cm^{-1}}$ at 298 K and $348\ \mathrm{cm^{-1}}$ at 500 K.

$\tilde{\nu}/\mathrm{cm^{-1}}$	x(298 K)	x(500 K)	$C_{V,\mathrm{m}}$(298 K)/R	$C_{V,\mathrm{m}}$(500 K)/R
612	2.96	1.76	0.505	0.777
612	2.96	1.76	0.505	0.777
729	3.52	2.09	0.389	0.704
729	3.52	2.09	0.389	0.704
1974	9.54	5.67	0.007	0.112
3287	15.88	9.45	3.2×10^{-5}	0.007
3374	16.30	9.70	3.2×10^{-5}	0.006
Total			1.796	3.086

Therefore, at 298 K, $C^{\mathrm{V}}_{V,\mathrm{m}} = 1.796R$, and at 500 K, $C^{\mathrm{V}}_{V,\mathrm{m}} = 3.086R$. The rotational contribution is R and the translational $3R/2$ in each case. Hence, the total heat capacities are

(a) At 298 K: $C_{V,\mathrm{m}} = (1.796 + 1.000 + 1.500)R = 4.296R = \underline{35.72\ \mathrm{J\,K^{-1}\,mol^{-1}}}$.

(b) At 500 K: $C_{V,\mathrm{m}} = (3.086 + 1.000 + 1.500)R = 5.586R = \underline{46.44\ \mathrm{J\,K^{-1}\,mol^{-1}}}$.

22.30 $q = 1 + \exp(-\Delta/kT)$

$U - U(0) = N\Delta\exp(-\Delta/kT)/\{1 + \exp(-\Delta/kT)\} = N\Delta\exp(-\Delta\beta)/\{1 + \exp(-\Delta\beta)\}$

$C_{V,\mathrm{m}} = -(N/kT^2)(\partial U/\partial\beta)_V = N(\Delta^2/kT^2)e^{-\Delta\beta}/\{1 + e^{-\Delta\beta}\}^2$

$C_{V,\mathrm{m}}/R = \underline{x^2 e^{-x}/(1 + e^{-x})^2}$, $x = \Delta/kT$.

This function is plotted in Fig. 22.3. Note that $C_{V,\mathrm{m}} \to 0$ as $T \to 0$ and as $T \to \infty$.

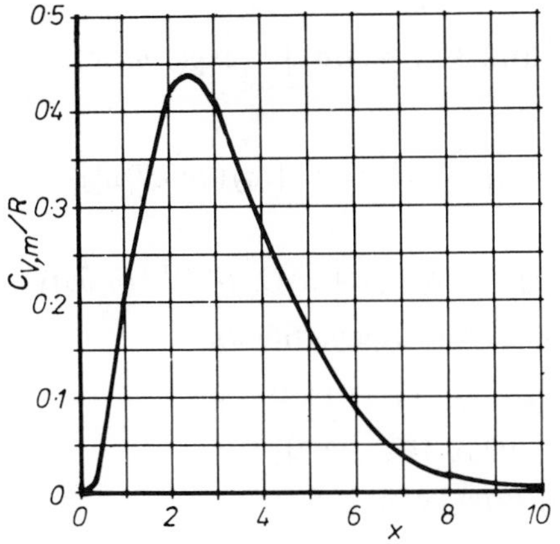

Fig 22.3

22.31 $C_{V,\mathrm{m}}/R = x^2 \mathrm{e}^{-x}/(1+\mathrm{e}^{-x})^2, x = \Delta\beta$ [Problem 22.31]

Draw up the following Table.

T/K	50	298	500
$(kT/hc)/\mathrm{cm}^{-1}$	34.8	207	348
$x = \Delta/kT$	3.46	0.585	0.348
$C_{V,\mathrm{m}}/R$	0.354	0.079	0.029
$C_{V,\mathrm{m}}/\mathrm{J\,K^{-1}\,mol^{-1}}$	2.94	0.654	0.244

Note that the double degeneracy of both levels does not affect the results (the 2s cancel in U) and that the electronic contribution to $C_{V,\mathrm{m}}$ decreases with temperature in this range.

22.32 $C^{\mathrm{E}}_{V,\mathrm{m}}/R = x^2 \mathrm{e}^{-x}/(1+\mathrm{e}^{-x})^2$ [Problem 22.31],

$x = \Delta\beta = 2\mu_{\mathrm{B}}B\beta$ [$\Delta = 2\mu_{\mathrm{B}}B$, [20.2.2]].

$$= \frac{2 \times (9.274 \times 10^{-24}\,\mathrm{J\,T^{-1}}) \times (5.0\,\mathrm{T})}{(1.381 \times 10^{-23}\,\mathrm{J\,K^{-1}})T} = 6.72/(T/\mathrm{K}).$$

(a) $T = 50\,\mathrm{K}, x = 6.72/50 = 0.134;\ C^{\mathrm{E}}_{V,\mathrm{m}} = 4.47 \times 10^{-3}\,R.$

Therefore, $C^{\mathrm{E}}_{V,\mathrm{m}} = \underline{3.72 \times 10^{-2}\,\mathrm{J\,K^{-1}\,mol^{-1}}}$.

(b) $T = 298\,\mathrm{K}, x = 6.72/298 = 2.26 \times 10^{-2};\ C^{\mathrm{E}}_{V,\mathrm{m}} = 1.27 \times 10^{-4} R.$

Therefore, $C^{\mathrm{E}}_{V,\mathrm{m}} = \underline{1.06 \times 10^{-3}\,\mathrm{J\,K^{-1}\,mol^{-1}}}$.

Since $C_{V,\mathrm{m}} \approx 3R \approx 25\,\mathrm{J\,K^{-1}\,mol^{-1}}$ these represent increases in the heat capacity of the order of 0.1 and 0.004% respectively.

22.33 $q = \sum_{m=-\infty}^{\infty} \exp(-m^2\hbar^2/2IkT) \approx (1/\sigma)\int_{-\infty}^{\infty} \exp(-m^2\hbar^2/2IkT)\mathrm{d}m$

$$\approx (1/\sigma)(2IkT/\hbar^2)^{1/2}\int_{-\infty}^{\infty} \mathrm{e}^{-x^2}\mathrm{d}x = (1/\sigma)(2\pi IkT/\hbar^2)^{\frac{1}{2}}.$$

$U - U(0) = -N(1/q)(\partial q/\partial\beta) = -N(1/q)(1/\sigma)(2\pi I/h^2)^{1/2}(\partial/\partial\beta)(1/\beta)^{1/2}$
$= N/2\beta = \frac{1}{2}kTN$ (or get by equipartition).

$C_{V,\mathrm{m}} = (\partial U_{\mathrm{m}}/\partial T)_V = \frac{1}{2}kN_{\mathrm{A}} = \frac{1}{2}R = \underline{4.16\,\mathrm{J\,K^{-1}\,mol^{-1}}}$.

$S_{\mathrm{m}} = [U_{\mathrm{m}} - U_{\mathrm{m}}(0)]/T + R\ln q$ [Box 22.2]

$= \frac{1}{2}R + R\ln\{(1/\sigma)(2\pi IkT/\hbar^2)^{1/2}\}.$

$\sigma = 3, I = 5.341 \times 10^{-47}\,\text{kg}\,\text{m}^2$;

$$(1/\sigma)(2\pi IkT/\hbar^2)^{1/2} = \tfrac{1}{3} \times \left\{\frac{2\pi \times (5.341 \times 10^{-47}\,\text{kg}\,\text{m}^2) \times (1.381 \times 10^{-23}\,\text{J}\,\text{K}^{-1})T}{(1.055 \times 10^{-34}\,\text{J}\,\text{s})^2}\right\}^{1/2}$$

$$= 0.215\,(T/\text{K})^{1/2}.$$

$S_m = R\{\tfrac{1}{2} + \ln[0.215(T/\text{K})^{1/2}]\} = R\{-1.037 + \tfrac{1}{2}\ln(T/\text{K})\}$

(Since $S_m > 0$, this is valid only for $T > 8$ K.)

When $T = 298$ K, $S_m = R\{-1.037 + \tfrac{1}{2}\ln 298\} = \underline{15.1\,\text{J}\,\text{K}^{-1}\,\text{mol}^{-1}}$.

22.34 $q = 1 + 5\exp(-\Delta\beta)$

$\Delta = E(J = 2) - E(J = 0) = 6hcB\ [E_J = hcBJ\,(J + 1)]$

$U - U(0) = N(1/q)5\Delta\exp(-\Delta\beta)$

$C_{V,m} = -(1/kT^2)(\partial U_m/\partial\beta) = (5R\Delta^2/k^2T^2)e^{-\Delta\beta}/(1 + 5e^{-\Delta\beta})^2$

$C_{V,m}/R = 5(6hcB/kT)^2 e^{-6hcB\beta}/(1 + 5e^{-6hcB\beta})^2$.

$hcB/k = (60.864\,\text{cm}^{-1})(hc/k) = 87.570\,\text{K}$.

$$C_{V,m}/R = \frac{1.3803 \times 10^6 \exp(-525.42\,\text{K}/T)}{(T/\text{K})^2\{1 + 5\exp(-525.42\,\text{K}/T)\}^2}.$$

Draw up the following Table

T/K	50	100	150	200	250
$C_{V,m}/R$	0.02	0.68	1.40	1.35	1.04

T/K	300	350	400	450	500
$C_{V,m}/R$	0.76	0.56	0.42	0.32	0.26

These values are plotted in Fig. 22.4.

22.35 $c_s = (\gamma RT/M_m)^{1/2}, \gamma = C_p/C_V = C_{p,m}/C_{V,m}, C_{p,m} = C_{V,m} + R$ [2.3.9].

(a) $C_{V,m} = \tfrac{1}{2}R(3 + \nu_R^* + 2\nu_V^*)$ [22.3.14] $= \tfrac{1}{2}R(3 + 2 + 0) = 5R/2$.

$C_{p,m} = 5R/2 + R = 7R/2$.

$\gamma = (7R/2)/(5R/2) = 7/5 = 1.40$,

$c_s = \underline{(1.40\,RT/M_m)^{1/2}}$.

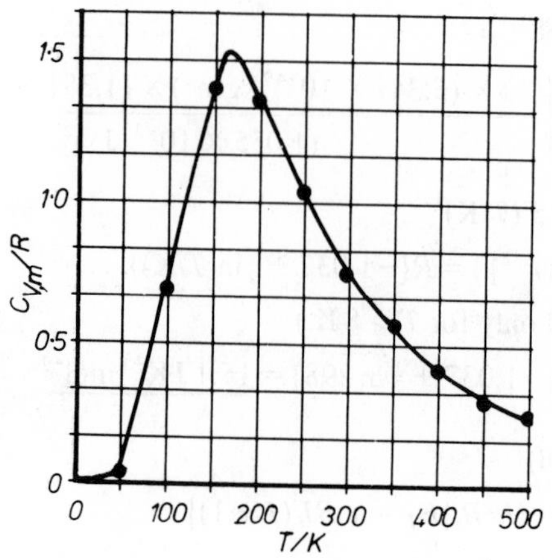

Fig 22.4

(b) $C_{V,\mathrm{m}} = 3R/2 + C^{\mathrm{R}}_{V,\mathrm{m}}(T)$

$C^{\mathrm{R}}_{V,\mathrm{m}} = 5R(6hcB/kT)^2 \mathrm{e}^{-6\,hcB\beta}/(1 + 5\mathrm{e}^{-6\,hcB\beta})^2$ [Problem 22.34].

$C_{p,\mathrm{m}} = 5R/2 + C^{\mathrm{R}}_{V,\mathrm{m}}(T)$.

$\gamma = \{5R/2 + C^{\mathrm{R}}_{V,\mathrm{m}}(T)\}/\{3R/2 + C^{\mathrm{R}}_{V,\mathrm{m}}(T)\}$.

$= (1 + a)/(\frac{3}{5} + \frac{2}{5}a),\ a = 2(6B/kT)^2 \mathrm{e}^{-6\,B\beta}/(1 + 5\mathrm{e}^{-6B\beta})^2$;

$c_{\mathrm{s}} = \underline{\{5(1 + a)RT/(3 + 5a)M_{\mathrm{m}}\}^{1/2}}$;

22.36 $c_{\mathrm{s}} = (1.40\,RT/M_{\mathrm{m}})^{1/2}$ [Problem 22.35(a)]

$M_{\mathrm{m}} \approx 29\ \mathrm{g\,mol^{-1}},\ T \approx 298\ \mathrm{K}$.

$c_{\mathrm{s}} \approx \{1.40 \times (2.48\ \mathrm{kJ\,mol^{-1}})/(29\ \mathrm{g\,mol^{-1}})\}^{1/2} = \underline{346\ \mathrm{m\,s^{-1}}}$.

22.37 $S_{\mathrm{m}} = R \ln p$ [Section 22.3(c), p is the number of possibilities].

(a) $S_{\mathrm{m}} = R \ln 3 = \underline{9.13\ \mathrm{J\,K^{-1}\,mol^{-1}}}$,

(b) $S_{\mathrm{m}} = R \ln 5 = \underline{13.4\ \mathrm{J\,K^{-1}\,mol^{-1}}}$,

(c) $S_{\mathrm{m}} = R \ln 6 = \underline{14.9\ \mathrm{J\,K^{-1}\,mol^{-1}}}$.

22.38 $n = 0$ and $n = 6$ both have $p = 1$ and so $S_{\mathrm{m}} = 0$.

$n = 1$ and $n = 5$ both have $p = 6$, and so $S_{\mathrm{m}} = \underline{14.9\ \mathrm{J\,K^{-1}\,mol^{-1}}}$.

$n = 2$ and $n = 4$ both have $p = 6$ for the *ortho* (1,2) and *meta* (1,3) forms, and so $S_{\mathrm{m}} = 14.9\ \mathrm{J\,K^{-1}\,mol^{-1}}$; but for the *para* (1,4) form, $p = 3$, and so $S_{\mathrm{m}} = \underline{9.13\ \mathrm{J\,K^{-1}\,mol^{-1}}}$.

$n = 3$ has $p = 6$ for the (1,2,3) and (1,2,4) forms, and so $S_{\mathrm{m}} = \underline{14.9\ \mathrm{J\,K^{-1}\,mol^{-1}}}$; but for the symmetrical (1,3,5) form, $p = 2$, and so $S_{\mathrm{m}} = \underline{5.8\ \mathrm{J\,K^{-1}\,mol^{-1}}}$.

22.39 $q_m^{T\ominus}/N_A = 0.025\,61 \times (298.15)^{5/2} \times (28.02)^{3/2}$ [Box 22.1] $= 5.830 \times 10^6$.

$q^R = \frac{1}{2} \times (0.6950) \times (298.15)/(1.9987) = 51.85$.

$q^V = 1/[1 - \exp(-2358/207.20)] = 1.000$.

$q^{T\ominus}q^Rq^V/N_A = 3.023 \times 10^8$.

$U_m - U_m(0) = \frac{3}{2}RT + RT = \frac{5}{2}RT$ [equipartition].

$S_m^\ominus = [U_m - U_m(0)]/T + R\{\ln(q_m^\ominus/N_A) + 1\}$ [Box 22.2],

$= \frac{5}{2}R + R\{\ln(3.023 \times 10^8) + 1\} = 23.03\,R = \underline{191.4\,\mathrm{J\,K^{-1}\,mol^{-1}}}$.

The discrepancy between this and the thermochemical value is negligible, implying that there is zero residual entropy in the crystal.

23. Determination of molecular structure: diffraction methods

A23.1 $\lambda = 2d\sin\theta = 2(99.3\text{ pm})\sin(20.85°) = \underline{70.7\text{ pm}}$. [23.2.1]

A23.2 $\sin\theta_1 = \lambda_1/(2d) = (154.051\text{ pm})(2)^{-1}(77.8\text{ pm})^{-1} = \underline{0.990\,05}$ [23.2.1].

$\sin\theta_2 = (154.433\text{ pm})(2)^{-1}(77.8\text{ pm})^{-1} = \underline{0.992\,50}$.

$\Delta\theta = 1.4482 - 1.4296 = 0.0186$ radian; separation $= (2)(5.74\text{ cm})(0.0186) = 0.21\text{ cm}$.

A23.3 $V = (651\text{ pm})^2(934\text{ pm}) = \underline{3.96 \times 10^{-28}\text{ m}^3}$.

A23.4 $d = Z(\text{RMM})(6.022 \times 10^{23})^{-1}/(abc)$

$Z = (3.9 \times 10^6\text{ g m}^{-3})[(633.8)(784.2)(515.5)(10^{-36}\text{ m}^3)](6.022 \times 10^{23})(154.77)^{-1}$

$= 3.9$.

Then $Z = 4$.

Density $= (4)(154.77)(6.022 \times 10^{23})^{-1}(633.8)^{-1}(784.2)^{-1}$

$\times (515.5)^{-1}(10^{36}) = 4.01 \times 10^6\text{ g m}^{-3}$, or $\underline{4.01\text{ g cm}^{-3}}$.

A23.5 $d = [(h/a)^2 + (k/b)^2 + (l/c)^2]^{-1/2}$

$= [(4/812)^2 + (1/947)^2 + (1/637)^2]^{-1/2} = \underline{190\text{ nm}}$.

A23.6 The plane cuts the axes at $a/5$, $b/2$, and $c/3$. The distances are: 240 pm, 606 pm, and 395 pm, respectively [Example 23.1].

A23.7 Since the reflection at 32.6° is (220), then $a = 8^{\frac{1}{2}}\lambda/2\sin\theta = 404$ pm.

$\theta/°$	$10^5(4\lambda^{-2}\sin^2\theta)/\text{pm}^2$	$h^2 + k^2 + l^2$	(hkl)	a/pm
19.4	1.86	3	(111)	401
22.5	2.47	4	(200)	402
32.6	4.90	8	(220)	404
39.4	6.80	11	(311)	402

The average value of a is $\underline{402\text{ pm}}$ [23.2.1].

A23.8 The four values of $hx + ky + lz$ are 0, 3/2, 3, and 7/2. The sum of the corresponding exponential terms is: $\exp(0) + \exp(3\pi i) + \exp(6\pi i) + \exp(7\pi i)$, which is $1 + (-1) + 1 + (-1) = 0$ [23.2.7].

A23.9 $E = p^2/2m = h^2/(2m\lambda^2)$ [13.2.8 and Section 23.5]

$= (6.62 \times 10^{-34}\,\text{J s})^2(2)^{-1}(1.67 \times 10^{-27}\,\text{kg})^{-1}(70 \times 10^{-12}\,\text{m})^{-2}$

$= \underline{2.68 \times 10^{-20}\,\text{J.}}$

A23.10 $E = p^2/2m = h^2/(2m\lambda^2)$ [13.2.8 and Section 23.6].

$V = E/(1.60 \times 10^{-19}\,\text{C})$

$= (6.62 \times 10^{-34}\,\text{J s})^2(2)^{-1}(9.11 \times 10^{-31}\,\text{kg})^{-1}(18 \times 10^{-12}\,\text{m})^{-2} \times (1.60 \times 10^{-19}\,\text{C})^{-1}$

$= \underline{4.64 \times 10^3\,\text{V}.}$

23.1 In the cubic system there are four 3-fold axes [Fig. 23.2 of text]. These are identified in Fig. 23.1. They have 3 × 2-fold axes, 4 × 3-fold axes, 3 planes of symmetry, and inversion symmetry; therefore, they belong to O_h ($m3m$).

Fig 23.1

23.2 There are four 3-fold axes, Fig. 23.2, hence the crystal belongs to the cubic system [Fig. 23.2 of text].

Fig 23.2

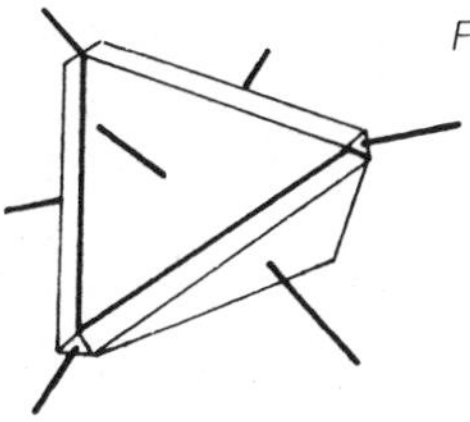

There are 4 × 3-fold axes, 3 × 2-fold axes, and 6 planes of symmetry; hence the class is T_d ($\bar{4}3m$).

23.3 If there is no axis of symmetry the system is triclinic [Fig. 23.8 of text]. The center of inversion implies the class $C_i(\bar{1})$.

23.4 Refer to Fig. 23.1 of text. The system is monoclinic.

23.5 The listing is $3C_4$, $4C_3$, $6C_2$, 3σ, i. This corresponds to the group of the regular octahedron and so the crystal is cubic, O_h ($m3m$).

23.6 In the opening sections of *The Origin of Species*, Darwin gives reasons why pigeons are good material for studies of evolution; one of the most cogent is that after you have finished the experiment you can eat the sample. One example of a face is illustrated in Fig. 23.3. From the illustration, $\tan\phi = 2/\sqrt{2} = \sqrt{2}$, hence $\phi = 54° 44'$.

Fig 23.3

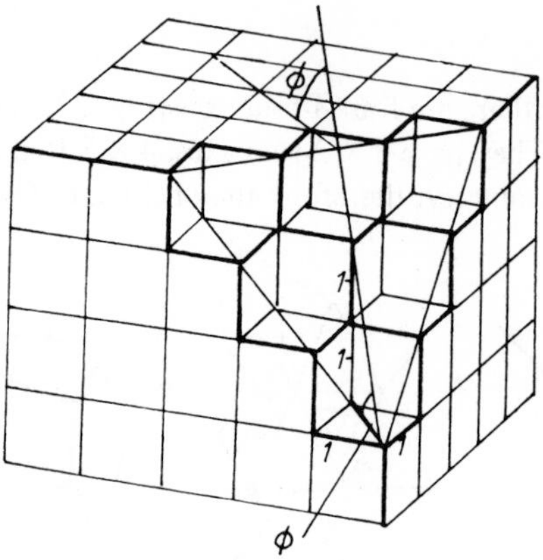

23.7 The points and planes are illustrated in Fig. 23.4(a)

Fig 23.4 (a)

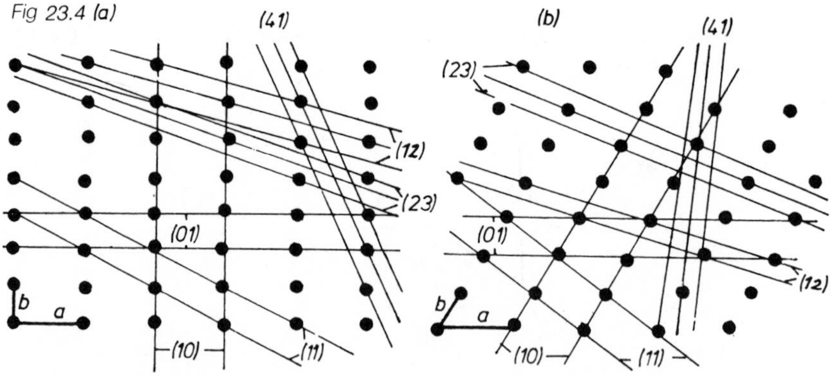

23.8 See Fig. 23.4(b).

23.9 Refer to Fig. 23.5(a).

$d = b \sin\alpha$, $\sin\alpha = a/(a^2 + b^2)^{1/2}$;

$d = ab/(a^2 + b^2)^{1/2}$.

(b) Refer to Fig. 23.5(b). $d = b \sin\alpha$

$a/\sin\alpha = c/\sin 60°$; $\sin\alpha = (a/c)\sin 60°$; $\sin 60° = \frac{1}{2}\sqrt{3}$

$c^2 = a^2 + b^2 - 2ab\cos 60° = a^2 + b^2 - ab$

$d = (ab/c)\sin 60° = \underline{(ab\sqrt{3})/2(a^2 + b^2 - ab)^{1/2}}$.

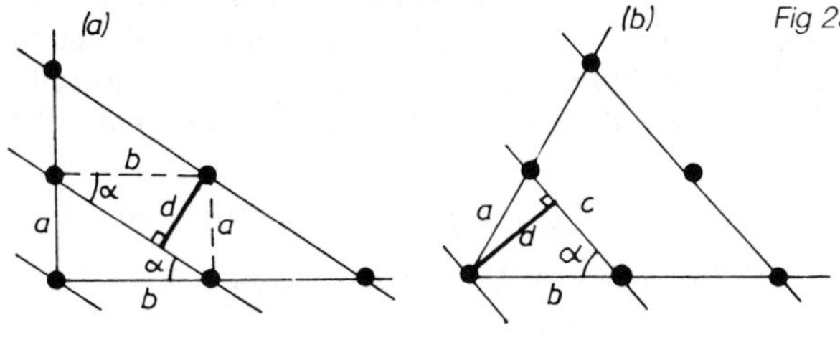

Fig 23.5

23.10 Refer to Section 23.1(c). Draw up the following Table.

Original	Reciprocal	Clear fractions	Miller
$(2a, 3b, c)$ or $(2, 3, 1)$	$(\frac{1}{2}, \frac{1}{3}, 1)$	$(3, 2, 6)$	(326)
(a, b, c) or $(1, 1, 1)$	$(1, 1, 1)$	$(1, 1, 1)$	(111)
$(6a, 3b, 3c)$ or $(6, 3, 3)$	$(\frac{1}{6}, \frac{1}{3}, \frac{1}{3})$	$(1, 2, 2)$	(122)
$(2a, -3b, -3c)$ or $(2, -3, -3)$	$(\frac{1}{2}, -\frac{1}{3}, -\frac{1}{3})$	$(3, -2, -2)$	$(3\bar{2}\bar{2})$

23.11 Refer to Section 23.1(c). The planes are drawn in Fig. 23.6(a) and (b) respectively.

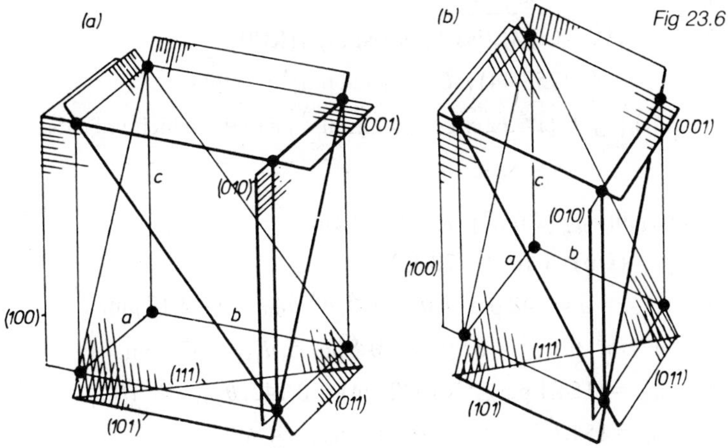

Fig 23.6

23.12 $d_{hkl} = a/(h^2 + k^2 + l^2)^{1/2}$ [23.1.1], $a = 432$ pm.

$d_{111} = (432\text{ pm})/\sqrt{3} = \underline{249\text{ pm}}$, $d_{211} = (432\text{ pm})/\sqrt{6} = \underline{176\text{ pm}}$,

$d_{100} = (432\text{ pm})/\sqrt{1} = \underline{432\text{ pm}}$.

23.13 $\lambda = 2a\sin\theta_{hkl}/\sqrt{(h^2 + k^2 + l^2)}$ [23.2.2] $= 2a\sin(6°0')/\sqrt{1} = 0.209\,a$.

Consider the unit cell shown in Fig. 23.7. Its total mass is $m = 4 \times (22.99 + 34.45) \times (1.660\,56 \times 10^{-27}\text{kg}) = 3.882 \times 10^{-25}\text{kg}$. [Each corner ion is shared by 8 cells, each edge ion by 4 cells, and each face ion by 2 cells, and so the unit cell contains four NaCl units.] The volume is a^3, hence $(3.882 \times 10^{-25}\text{kg})/a^3 = \rho = 2.17\text{ g cm}^{-3} = 2.17 \times 10^3\text{ kg m}^{-3}$.

$a = \{(3.882 \times 10^{-25}\text{kg})/(2.17 \times 10^3\text{ kg m}^{-3})\}^{1/3} = 5.63 \times 10^{-10}\text{m}$

$\lambda = 0.209 \times (2.82 \times 10^{-10}\text{m}) = 5.89 \times 10^{-11}\text{m} = \underline{58.9\text{ pm}}$.

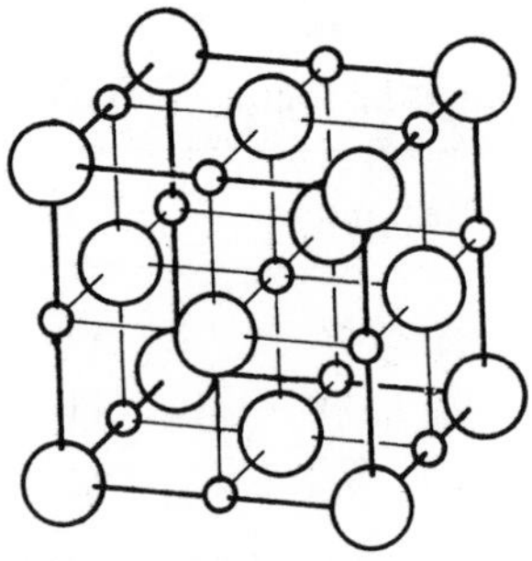

Fig. 23.7

23.14 $\lambda = 2a\sin\theta_{100}$ [23.2.2], $a = \lambda/2\sin\theta_{100}$

$a(\text{KCl})/a(\text{NaCl}) = \sin\theta_{100}(\text{NaCl})/\sin\theta_{100}(\text{KCl})$

$= \sin(6°0')/\sin(5°23') = 1.114$.

$a(\text{KCl}) = 1.114a(\text{NaCl}) = \underline{628\text{ pm}}$.

$\rho(\text{KCl})/\rho(\text{NaCl}) = \{M_r(\text{KCl})/M_r(\text{NaCl})\}\{a(\text{NaCl})/a(\text{KCl})\}^3$

$= \{74.55/58.44\}\{564\text{ pm}/628\text{ pm}\}^3 = 0.924$.

$\{\rho(\text{KCl})/\rho(\text{NaCl})\}_{\text{given}} = \{1.99\text{ g cm}^{-3}/2.17\text{ g cm}^{-3}\} = 0.92$, which indicates consistency.

23.15 $\lambda = 2d_{hkl}\sin\theta_{hkl}$ [23.2.2], $\lambda = 154.1$ pm

$1/d_{hkl}^2 = (h/a)^2 + (k/b)^2 + (l/c)^2$ [23.1.2]

$1/d_{100}^2 = 1/a^2$; $d_{100} = a = 542$ pm. $1/d_{010}^2 = 1/b^2$; $d_{010} = b = 917$ pm.

$1/d_{111}^2 = 1/a^2 + 1/b^2 + 1/c^2 = 6.997 \times 10^{-6}\text{ pm}^{-2}$; $d_{111} = 378$ pm.

$\sin\theta_{100} = \lambda/2d_{100} = (154.1\text{ pm})/2 \times (542\text{ pm}) = 0.142$; $\theta_{100} = \underline{8°10'}$.

$\sin\theta_{010} = \lambda/2d_{010} = 154.1/2 \times 917 = 0.084$; $\theta_{010} = \underline{4°49'}$.

$\sin\theta_{111} = \lambda/2d_{111} = 154.1/2 \times 378 = 0.204$; $\theta_{111} = \underline{11°46'}$.

23.16 Face centered cubic [systematic absences, Fig. 23.18 of the text and Section 23.2(b)].

23.17 $h + k + l =$ odd are absent, hence the cell is body-centered cubic [Fig. 23.18 of the text and Section 23.2(b)].

23.18 $d_{hkl} = a/(h^2 + k^2 + l^2)^{1/2}$ [23.1.1], $a = 564$ pm.

$d_{100} = a = \underline{564 \text{ pm}}$, $d_{111} = a/\sqrt{3} = \underline{326 \text{ pm}}$, $d_{012} = a/\sqrt{5} = \underline{252 \text{ pm}}$.

23.19 Consider, for simplicity, the 2-dimensional lattice and planes shown in Fig. 23.8. The (hk) planes cut the a and b axes at a/h and b/k. We have

$\sin \alpha = d/(a/h)$ and $\cos \alpha = d/(b/k)$

$d^2h^2/a^2 + d^2k^2/b^2 = \sin^2 \alpha + \cos^2 \alpha = 1.$

Therefore $h^2/a^2 + k^2/b^2 = 1/d^2$.

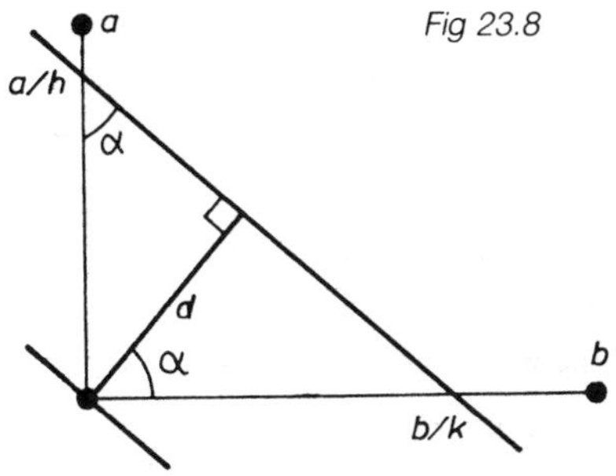

Fig 23.8

The argument extends by analogy (or by further trigonometry) to 3-dimensions to give $\underline{1/d_{hkl}^2 = h^2/a^2 + k^2/b^2 + l^2/c^2}$.

23.20 If the sides of the unit cell define the vectors **a**, **b**, **c**, then its volume is $V = \mathbf{a} \cdot \mathbf{b} \wedge \mathbf{c}$ [given]. Introduce an orthogonal set of vectors **i**, **j**, **k** so that

$$\mathbf{a} = a_x \mathbf{i} + a_y \mathbf{j} + a_z \mathbf{k}$$
$$\mathbf{b} = b_x \mathbf{i} + b_y \mathbf{j} + b_z \mathbf{k}$$
$$\mathbf{c} = c_x \mathbf{i} + c_y \mathbf{j} + c_z \mathbf{k}.$$

Then $V = \mathbf{a} \cdot \mathbf{b} \wedge \mathbf{c} = \begin{vmatrix} a_x & a_y & a_z \\ b_x & b_y & b_z \\ c_x & c_y & c_z \end{vmatrix}$

Therefore $V^2 = \begin{vmatrix} a_x & a_y & a_z \\ b_x & b_y & b_z \\ c_x & c_y & c_z \end{vmatrix} \times \begin{vmatrix} a_x & a_y & a_z \\ b_x & b_y & b_z \\ c_x & c_y & c_z \end{vmatrix}$

$$= \begin{vmatrix} a_x & a_y & a_z \\ b_x & b_y & b_z \\ c_x & c_y & c_z \end{vmatrix} \times \begin{vmatrix} a_x & b_x & c_x \\ a_y & b_y & c_y \\ a_z & b_z & c_z \end{vmatrix}$$

[interchange rows and columns; no change in value]

$$= \begin{vmatrix} a_xa_x + a_ya_y + a_za_z & a_xb_x + a_yb_y + a_zb_z & a_xc_x + a_yc_y + a_zc_z \\ b_xa_x + b_ya_y + b_za_z & b_xb_x + b_yb_y + b_zb_z & b_xc_x + b_yc_y + b_zc_z \\ c_xa_x + c_ya_y + c_za_z & c_xb_x + c_yb_y + c_zb_z & c_xc_x + c_yc_y + c_zc_z \end{vmatrix}$$

$$= \begin{vmatrix} \mathbf{a}\cdot\mathbf{a} & \mathbf{a}\cdot\mathbf{b} & \mathbf{a}\cdot\mathbf{c} \\ \mathbf{b}\cdot\mathbf{a} & \mathbf{b}\cdot\mathbf{b} & \mathbf{b}\cdot\mathbf{c} \\ \mathbf{c}\cdot\mathbf{a} & \mathbf{c}\cdot\mathbf{b} & \mathbf{c}\cdot\mathbf{c} \end{vmatrix}$$

Then use $\mathbf{a}\cdot\mathbf{a} = a^2$, $\mathbf{b}\cdot\mathbf{b} = b^2$, $\mathbf{c}\cdot\mathbf{c} = c^2$, $\mathbf{c} = c^2$, $\mathbf{a}\cdot\mathbf{b} = ab\cos\gamma$, $\mathbf{b}\cdot\mathbf{c} = bc\cos\alpha$, $\mathbf{c}\cdot\mathbf{a} = ac\cos\beta$, and expand the determinant:

$V^2 = a^2b^2c^2(1 - \cos^2\alpha - \cos^2\beta - \cos^2\gamma + 2\cos\alpha\cos\beta\cos\gamma)$

$\underline{V = abc(1 - \cos^2\alpha - \cos^2\beta - \cos^2\gamma + 2\cos\alpha\cos\beta\cos\gamma)^{1/2}}$.

23.21 For a monoclinic cell $\alpha = \gamma = 90°$,

$V = abc(1 - \cos^2\beta)^{1/2}$ [Problem 23.20] $= abc\sin\beta$.

$a = 1.377b$, $c = 1.436b$, $\beta = 122°49'$: $V = 1.377 \times 1.436\, b^3 \sin 122°49' = 1.662\, b^3$.

$\rho = 2 \times (12.8.18) \times (1.66056 \times 10^{-27}\,\text{kg})/1.662\, b^3$ [$M_r = 128.18$]

$= 1.152 \times 10^3\,\text{kg m}^{-3}$ [given].

$$b = \left\{\frac{2 \times (128.18) \times (1.660\,56 \times 10^{-27}\,\text{kg})}{1.662 \times (1.152 \times 10^3\,\text{kg m}^{-3})}\right\}^{1/3} = 6.058 \times 10^{-10}\,\text{m}.$$

$a = 1.377 \times 606\,\text{pm} = \underline{834\,\text{pm}}$, $b = \underline{606\,\text{pm}}$, $c = 1.436 \times 606\,\text{pm} = \underline{870\,\text{pm}}$.

23.22 $d_{111} = \lambda/2\sin\theta_{111}$ [23.2.2] $= (70.8\,\text{pm})/2\sin(8°44') = 233\,\text{pm}$.

$d_{111} = a/\sqrt{3}$ [23.1.1]; $a = (233\,\text{pm})\sqrt{3} = 404\,\text{pm}$.

$\rho = M_m/V_m = 2.601\,\text{g cm}^{-3} = 2.601 \times 10^6\,\text{g m}^{-3}$.

$M_m = 4 \times (25.94\,\text{g mol}^{-1}) = 103.8\,\text{g mol}^{-1}$ [4 LiF in a unit cell]. $V_m = a^3N_A$;

$N_A = M_m/\rho a^3 = (103.8\ \mathrm{g\,mol^{-1}})/(404 \times 10^{-12}\ \mathrm{m})^3 \times (2.601 \times 10^6\ \mathrm{g\,m^{-3}})$
$= \underline{6.05 \times 10^{23}\ \mathrm{mol^{-1}}}.$

23.23 (a) One atom at each of 8 corners; each one shared by 8 unit cells. Hence, $\underline{n = 1 \text{ per unit cell}}$.

(b) As in (a), but one more atom at the center. Hence, $n = \underline{2 \text{ per unit cell}}$.

(c) One atom at each of 8 corners, each shared by 8 unit cells; plus one atom on each of 6 faces, each shared by 2 unit cells. Hence, $n = 1 + 3 = \underline{4 \text{ per unit cell}}$.

(d) Refer to Fig. 23.9. There are 8 on the 8 corners, each shared by 8 unit cells; plus 6 on the faces, each shared by 2 unit cells; plus 4 inside the cell. Hence $n = 1 + 3 + 4 = \underline{8 \text{ per unit cell}}$.

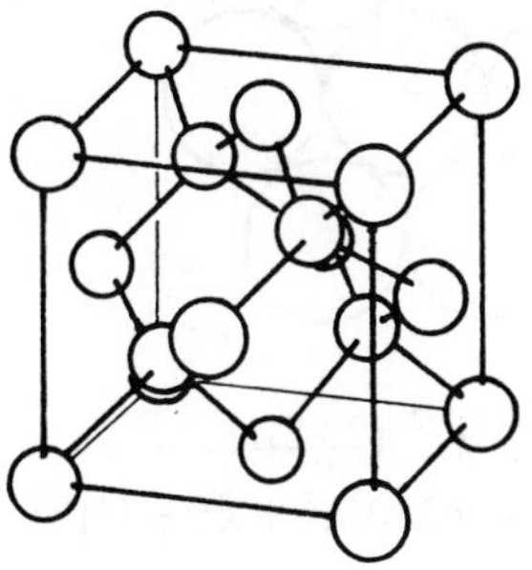
Fig 23.9

23.24 $f = NV_a/V_c$ where N is the number of atoms per unit cell, V_a their individual volumes, and V_c the volume of the unit cell. Refer to Fig. 23.10.

(a) $N = 1$ [Problem 23.23], $V_a = (4/3)\pi R^3$, $V_c = (2R)^3$;
$f = (4/3)\pi R^3/8R^3 = \pi/6 = \underline{0.5236}.$

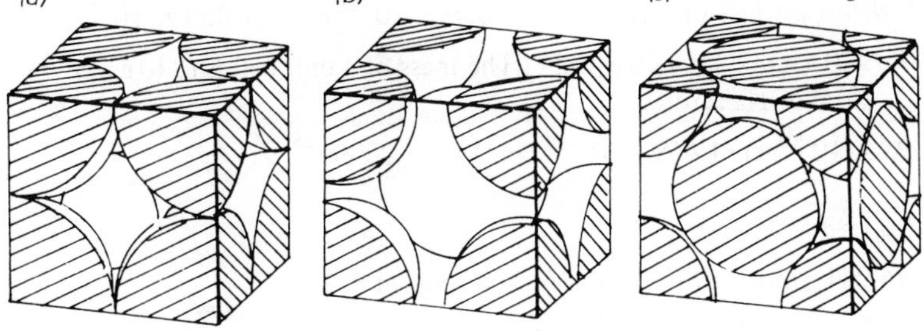

Fig 23.10

(b) $N = 2$ [Problem 23.23], $V_a = (4/3)\pi R^3$, $V_c = (4R/\sqrt{3})^3$ [body diagonal of $1 \times 1 \times 1$ unit cube is $\sqrt{3}$];
$f = 2(4/3)\pi R^3/(4R/\sqrt{3})^3 = \sqrt{3}(\pi/8) = \underline{0.6802}.$

(c) $N = 4$ [Problem 23.23], $V_a = (4/3)\pi R^3$, $V_c = (2\sqrt{2}R)^3$;

$f = 4(4/3)\pi R^3/(2\sqrt{2}R)^3 = \pi/3\sqrt{2} = \underline{0.7405}$.

Ship the oranges pakced in a f.c.c. lattice (or h.c.p., which has the same packing fraction).

23.25 Refer to Fig. 23.11 (see also Fig. 23.29 of the text). Area hatched is $(R\sqrt{3}) \times (2R) = 2R^2\sqrt{3}$. Number of cylinders per hatched area is 1. Area of each cylinder is πR^2. Convert to volumes by multiplying by L, the length of the cylinders.

$f = \pi R^2 L/2\sqrt{3}R^2 L = \pi/2\sqrt{3} = \underline{0.9069}$.

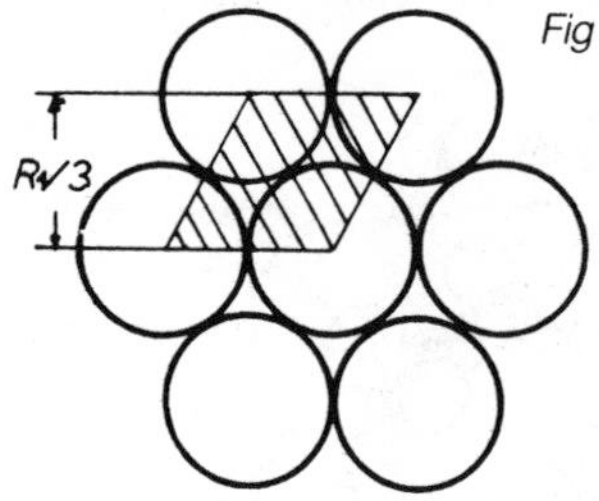

Fig 23.11

23.26 $\sin\theta_{hkl} = (\lambda/2a)(h^2 + k^2 + l^2)^{1/2}$ [23.2.1]

$\lambda = 154$ pm, $a = 334.5$ pm; $\sin\theta_{hkl} = 0.230(h^2 + k^2 + l^2)^{1/2}$.

hkl may range over all integral values [Fig. 23.18 of text], and so lines will occur at $\theta_{hkl} = 13°17'(100), 18°59'(110), 23°28'(111), 27°23'(200), 30°57'(210), \ldots$

$\rho = M_m/V_m = (210\ \text{g mol}^{-1})/(6.022 \times 10^{23}\ \text{mol}^{-1}) \times (334.5\ \text{pm})^3$

$= 9.32 \times 10^6\ \text{g m}^{-3} = \underline{9.32\ \text{g cm}^{-3}}$.

The radius of each atom is $\frac{1}{2}a = 167.3$ pm. In a f.c.c. lattice the diagonal would be $4 \times (167.3\ \text{pm}) = 669.0$ pm, and so the side is $(669.0\ \text{pm})/\sqrt{2} = 473.1$ pm. The volume is therefore $V = (473.1\ \text{pm})^3 = 1.059 \times 10^{-28}\ \text{m}^3 = 1.059 \times 10^{-22}\ \text{cm}^3$.

$M_m = 4 \times (210\ \text{g mol}^{-1}) = 840\ \text{g mol}^{-1}$. The mass of a unit cell is $(840\ \text{g mol}^{-1})/N_A = 1.395 \times 10^{-21}$ g. Therefore,

$\rho = (1.395 \times 10^{-21}\ \text{g})/(1.059 \times 10^{-22}\ \text{cm}^3) = \underline{13.2\ \text{g cm}^{-3}}$.

23.27 $d_{100} = a = 350$ pm.

$\rho = N \times (6.941\ \text{g mol}^{-1})/(350\ \text{pm})^3 N_A = 0.53\ \text{g cm}^{-3}$

$$N = \frac{(0.53 \times 10^6\ \text{g m}^{-3}) \times (350 \times 10^{-12}\ \text{m})^3 \times (6.022 \times 10^{23}\ \text{mol}^{-1})}{6.941\ \text{g mol}^{-1}} = 1.97.$$

f.c.c. has $N = 4$, b.c.c. has $N = 2$ [Problem 23.23];

hence Li is $\underline{\text{b.c.c.}}$

23.28 $\sin\theta_{hkl} = (\lambda/2a)(h^2 + k^2 + l^2)^{1/2}$ [23.2.1]. Systematic absences: (hkl) all even or all odd are the only permitted lines [Fig. 23.18 of text].

$(\lambda/2a) = 154\ \text{pm}/2 \times (361\ \text{pm}) = 0.213.$

$\theta_{hkl} = 21°41'(111), 25°15'(200), 37°06'(220), 45°02'(311), \ldots$ as in Fig. 23.18. of the text.

$\rho = 4 \times (63.55\ \text{g mol}^{-1})/(361\ \text{pm})^3 \times (6.022 \times 10^{23}\ \text{mol}^{-1}) = 8.97 \times 10^6\ \text{g m}^{-3}$
$= \underline{8.97\ \text{g cm}^{-3}}.$

23.29 $\theta(100\ \text{K}) = 22°2'25''$, $\theta(300\ \text{K}) = 21°57'59''$;

$\sin\theta(100\ \text{K}) = 0.375\,26$, $\sin\theta(300\ \text{K}) = 0.374\,06$,

$\sin\theta(300\ \text{K})/\sin\theta(100\ \text{K}) = 0.996\,81 = a(100\ \text{K})/a(300\ \text{K})$.

$a(100\ \text{K}) = 0.996\,81a(300\ \text{K})$.

$a(300\ \text{K}) = \lambda\sqrt{3}/2\sin\theta = \{(154.0562\ \text{pm})\sqrt{3}\}/2 \times 0.374\,06 = 356.67\ \text{pm}.$

$a(100\ \text{K}) = 0.996\,81 \times (356.67\ \text{pm}) = 355.53\ \text{pm}.$

$\delta a/a = (356.67\ \text{pm} - 355.53\ \text{pm})/(356.67\ \text{pm}) = 3.196 \times 10^{-3}.$

$\delta V/V = \{(356.67\ \text{pm})^3 - (355.53\ \text{pm})^3\}/\{356.67\ \text{pm}\}^3 = 0.009\,56.$

$\beta_{\text{vol}} = (1/V)(\delta V/\delta T) = 0.009\,56/(200\ \text{K}) = \underline{4.8 \times 10^{-5}\ \text{K}^{-1}}.$

$\beta_{\text{linear}} = (1/a)(\delta a/\delta T) = 3.196 \times 10^{-3}/(200\ \text{K}) = \underline{1.6 \times 10^{-5}\ \text{K}^{-1}}.$

23.30 Follow *Example* 23.3. Note that since $R = 28.7$ mm, $\theta/\text{deg} = (D/2R)(180/\pi) = D/\text{mm}$. Then proceed through the following sequence: (1) Convert from distance D to angle θ by $\theta/\text{deg} = D/\text{mm}$. (2) Calculate $\sin^2\theta$; (3) Find the common factor $A = \lambda^2/4a^2$ in $\sin^2\theta = (\lambda^2/4a^2)(h^2 + k^2 + l^2)$. (4) Index as $\sin^2\theta/A = h^2 + k^2 + l^2$. (5) Solve $A = \lambda^2/4a^2$ to find a. Draw up the following Table.

D/mm	14.5	20.6	25.4	29.6	33.4	37.1	44.0
θ/deg	14.5	20.6	25.4	29.6	33.4	37.1	44.0
$10^3 \sin^2\theta$	62.7	124	184	244	303	364	483
$\sin^2\theta/A$	1.03	2.03	3.02	4.00	4.97	5.97	7.92
(hkl)	(001)	(001)	(111)	(002)	(012)	(112)	(022)

D/mm	47.5	50.9	54.4	58.2	62.1	66.4	78.1
θ/deg	47.5	50.9	54.4	58.2	62.1	66.4	78.1
$10^3 \sin^2\theta$	544	602	661	722	781	840	957
$\sin^2\theta/A$	8.92	9.87	10.84	11.84	12.80	13.77	16.69
(hkl)	{(003), (122)}	(013)	(113)	(222)	(023)	(123)	(004)

with $A = 61.0 \times 10^{-3}$. Compare with Fig. 23.18 of the text: this shows that the lattice is primitive cubic.

$a = \lambda/2A^{1/2} = (154\,\text{pm})/2 \times (61.0 \times 10^{-3})^{1/2} = \underline{312\,\text{pm}}.$

23.31 Proceed as in Problem 23.30.

D/mm	18.9	22.1	31.9	38.3	40.4
θ/deg	18.9	22.1	31.9	38.3	40.4
$10^3 \sin^2\theta$	105	142	279	384	420
$\sin^2\theta/A$	3.00	4.06	7.97	10.97	12.00
(hkl)	(111)	(002)	(022)	(113)	(222)

D/mm	48.9	55.0	58.0	68.8	83.3
θ/deg	48.9	55.0	58.0	68.8	83.3
$10^3 \sin^2\theta$	568	671	719	869	986
$\sin^2\theta/A$	16.2	19.2	20.5	24.8	28.2
(hkl)	(004)	(133)	(024)	(224)	{(333), (511)}

with $A = 35.0 \times 10^{-3}$. Compare with Fig. 23.18 of the text; This shows that the lattice is face-centered cubic.

$a = \lambda/2A^{1/2} = (154\,\text{pm})/2 \times (35.0 \times 10^{-3})^{1/2} = \underline{412\,\text{pm}}.$

23.32 Measure the angles θ from the illustration, using 0.5 cm $\mathrel{\hat{=}}$ 10°. Then proceed as in Problem 23.30.

(a) D/cm	2.2	3.0	3.6	4.4	5.0	5.8	6.7	7.7
θ/deg	22	30	36	44	50	58	67	77
$10^3 \sin^2\theta$	140	250	345	482	587	719	847	949
$\sin^2\theta/A$	2.4	4.2	5.8	8.1	9.9	12.1	14.3	16.0
(hkl)	(011)	(002)	(112)	(022)	(013)	(222)	(123)	(004)

with $A = 0.0594$. Compare with Fig. 23.18 of the text: this shows that the lattice is body-centered cubic.

$a = \lambda/2A^{1/2} = (154\text{ pm})/2 \times (0.0594)^{1/2} = \underline{316\text{ pm}}$. Refer to Fig. 23.10(b):

$4R = \sqrt{3}a$; hence $R = 137$ pm.

(b) D/cm	2.1	2.5	3.7	4.5	4.7	5.9	6.7	7.2
θ/deg	21	25	37	45	47	59	67	72
$10^3 \sin^2\theta$	128	179	362	500	535	735	847	905
$\sin^2\theta/A$	2.8	3.9	8.0	11.0	11.8	16.2	18.6	19.9
(hkl)	(111)	(002)	(022)	(113)	(222)	(004)	(133)	(204)

with $A = 0.0455$. Compare with Fig. 22.10 of the text. This shows that the lattice is face-centered cubic.

$a = \lambda/2A^{1/2} = (154\text{ pm})/2 \times (0.0455)^{1/2} = \underline{361\text{ pm}}$. Refer to Fig. 23.10(c)

$4R = \sqrt{2}a$; $R = \underline{128\text{ pm}}$.

23.33 $d_{hkl} = (\lambda/2)/\sin\theta_{hkl}$ [23.2.2], $\lambda = 154$ pm.

$1/d_{hkl}^2 = (h/a)^2 + (k/b)^2 + (l/c)^2$ [23.1.2]

$d_{100} = a = (\lambda/2)/\sin\theta_{100} = (77\text{ pm})/\sin 7°25' = \underline{597\text{ pm}}$.

$d_{010} = b = (77\text{ pm})/\sin 3°28' = \underline{1270\text{ pm}}$.

$d_{001} = c = (77\text{ pm})/\sin 10°13' = \underline{434\text{ pm}}$.

$V(\text{cell}) = abc = 3.29 \times 10^{-28}\text{ m}^3$.

$\rho = NM_m/V_m = N \times (271.5\text{ g mol}^{-1})/(3.29 \times 10^{-28}\text{ m}^3) \times (6.022 \times 10^{23}\text{ mol}^{-1})$.

$= 1.37N \times 10^6\text{ g m}^{-3} = 1.37N\text{ g cm}^{-3}$.

But $\rho = 5.42\text{ g cm}^{-3}$, and so $N = 5.42/1.37 = 3.97$.

Hence, $N = 4$, and there are $\underline{4\ HgCl_2}$ per unit cell.

23.34 When a very narrow X-ray beam (with a spread of wavelengths) is directed on the center of a genuine pearl, all the crystallites are irradiated parallel to a trigonal axis and the result is a Laue photograph with sixfold symmetry. In a cultured pearl the narrow beam will have an arbitrary orientation with respect to the crystallite axes (of the central core) and an unsymmetrical Laue photograph will result. [See J. Bijvoet *et al.*, *X-ray analysis of crystals*, Butterworth, 1951.]

23.35 $F_{hkl} = \sum_i f_i \exp\{2\pi i(hx_i + ky_i + lz_i)\}$ [23.2.7]

$f_i = f/8$ [each atom shared by eight cells]

$$F_{hkl} = (f/8)\{1 + \exp(2\pi ih) + \exp(2\pi ik) + \exp(2\pi il) + \exp(2\pi i[h+k]) + \exp(2\pi i[h+l]) + \exp(2\pi i[k+l]) + \exp(2\pi i[h+k+l])\}.$$

$\exp(2\pi i) = 1$; h, k, l are integers; hence all terms are unity, and so $\underline{F_{hkl} = f}$.

23.36 $F_{hkl} = f_A + f_B \exp\{2\pi i \times \frac{1}{2} \times (h+k+l)\}$ [f_A arises as in Problem 23.35; there is one extra term in the sum for F_{hkl}, that due to the central atom b]

$F_{hkl} = f_A + f_B(\exp i\pi)^{h+k+l} = f_A + (-1)^{h+k+l} f_B$ [$e^{i\pi} = -1$].

(a) $f_A = f, f_B = 0$; $F_{hkl} = f$; no systematic absences.

(b) $f_B = \frac{1}{2} f_A$; $F_{hkl} = f_A[1 + \frac{1}{2}(-1)^{h+k+l}]$; when

$h + k + l$ is odd, $F_{hkl} = f_A[1 - \frac{1}{2}] = \frac{1}{2} f_A$ but when

$h + k + l$ is even, $F_{hkl} = f_A[1 + \frac{1}{2}] = \frac{3}{2} f_A$.

That is, there is an alternation of intensity ($I \propto F^2$) according to whether $h + k + l$ is odd or even.

(c) $f_A = f_B = f$; $F_{hkl} = f[1 + (-1)^{h+k+l}] = 0$ if $h + k + l$ odd.

Thus all $h + k + l =$ odd lines are missing [systematic absences, Fig. 23.18 of the text for b.c.c. unit cell].

23.37 Refer to *Example* 23.4

$F_{hkl} = 4(f_M + f_{Cl})$; h, k, l all even, M = K or Na

$F_{hkl} = 4(f_M - f_{Cl})$; h, k, l all odd.

The (311) line has h, k, l all odd and so $F = 4(f_M - f_{Cl})$.

The (222) line has h, k, l all even, and so $F = 4(f_M + f_{Cl})$; hence the former is weaker than the latter. For KCl, $f_K \approx f_{Cl}$ and the (311) line has vanishing intensity.

23.38 Draw points corresponding to the vectors joining all pairs of atoms, as in Fig. 23.22 of the text. Heavier atoms give more intense contributions than light atoms. Remember that there are two vectors connecting any pair of atoms, A → B and B ← A. Don't forget the zero vectors A — A for the center of the diagram. See Fig. 23.12.

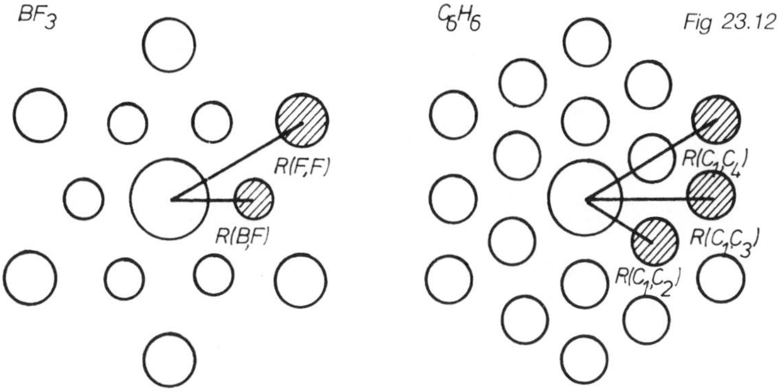

Fig 23.12

23.39 $\lambda = h/p$ [13.2.8] $= h/m_e v$.

$\frac{1}{2}m_e v^2 = e\Delta\phi$ [$\Delta\phi$: potential difference]; $v^2 = (2e/m_e)\Delta\phi$.

$\lambda = h/m_e(2e/m_e)^{\frac{1}{2}}\Delta\phi^{\frac{1}{2}} = (h^2/2m_e e\Delta\phi)^{\frac{1}{2}}$

$= \{(6.626 \times 10^{-34}\,\text{J s})^2/2 \times (9.1095 \times 10^{-31}\,\text{kg}) \times (1.602 \times 10^{-19}\,\text{C})\Delta\phi\}^{\frac{1}{2}}$

$= (1.226 \times 10^{-9}\,\text{m})/(\Delta\phi/\text{V})^{\frac{1}{2}}$.

(a) $\Delta\phi = 1\,\text{kV}$.

$\lambda = (1.226 \times 10^{-9}\,\text{m})/\sqrt{1000} = 3.88 \times 10^{-11}\,\text{m} = \underline{39\ \text{pm}}$.

(b) $\Delta\phi = 10\,\text{kV}$.

$\lambda = (1.226 \times 10^{-9}\,\text{m})/\sqrt{10^4} = 1.2 \times 10^{-11}\,\text{m} = \underline{12\ \text{pm}}$.

(c) $\Delta\phi = 40\,\text{kV}$.

$\lambda = (1.226 \times 10^{-9}\,\text{m})/\sqrt{(4 \times 10^4)} = 6.1 \times 10^{-12}\,\text{m} = \underline{6.1\ \text{pm}}$.

23.40 $\lambda = h/m_n v$ [13.2.8]; $v = h/m_n\lambda$

$v = (6.626 \times 10^{-34}\,\text{J s})/(1.675 \times 10^{-27}\,\text{kg}) \times (50 \times 10^{-12}\,\text{m}) = \underline{7.9\ \text{km s}^{-1}}$.

$\frac{1}{2}m_n v^2 = \frac{3}{2}kT$; $v = \sqrt{(3kT/m_n)}$

$\lambda = h/m_n v = \sqrt{(h^2/3m_n kT)}$

$= \{(6.626 \times 10^{-34}\,\text{J s})^2/3 \times (1.675 \times 10^{-27}\,\text{kg}) \times (1.381 \times 10^{-23}\,\text{J K}^{-1}) \times (300\,\text{K})\}^{\frac{1}{2}}$

$= 1.45 \times 10^{-10}\,\text{m} = \underline{145\ \text{pm}}$.

23.41 $I(\theta) = \sum_{ij} f_i f_j \sin(sR_{ij})/sR_{ij}$, $s = (4\pi/\lambda)\sin\frac{1}{2}\theta$ [23.5.2]

$$= 4 f_C f_{Cl} \sin(sR_{CCl})/sR_{CCl} + 6 f_{Cl} f_{Cl} \sin(sR_{ClCl})/sR_{ClCl}$$

$$= 4 \times 6 \times 17\{f^2 \sin(sR_{CCl}\} + 6 \times 17^2\{f^2 \sin[s(8/3)^{\frac{1}{2}} R_{CCl}]/s(8/3)^{\frac{1}{2}} R_{CCl}\}$$

$I/f^2 = 408\{\sin x/x\} + 1062\{\sin[(8/3)^{\frac{1}{2}} x]/x\}, x = sR_{CCl}$.

Draw up the following Table.

x	2.0	2.5	3.0	3.5	4.0	4.5	5.0	5.5	6.0
I/f^2	120	−247	−329	−204	−11.8	118	124	30.5	−83.8
x	6.5	7.0	7.5	8.0	8.5	9.0	9.5	10.0	10.5
I/f^2	−138	−99.3	6.6	114	159	119	18.4	−84	−134
x	11.0	11.5	12.0	12.5	13.0	13.5	14.0	14.5	15.0
I/f^2	−112	−37.5	41.9	82.8	69.6	20.0	−29.2	−46.4	−24.5
x	15.5	16.0	16.5	17.0	17.5	18.0	18.5	19.0	19.5
I/f^2	17.6	48.3	44.9	7.61	−40.9	−70.1	−61.2	−18.0	35.2
x	20.0	20.5	21.0	21.5	22.0	22.5	23.0	23.5	24.0
I/f^2	68.9	65.6	29.5	16.9	−47.5	−47.4	−21.5	11.0	28.7
x	24.5	25.0	25.5	26.0	26.5	27.0	27.5	28.0	28.5
I/f^2	22.2	−1.5	−24.1	−28.8	−11.0	18.7	41.2	41.3	17.3
x	29.0	29.5	30.0						
I/f^2	−17.8	−44.2	−47.3						

The function I/f^2 is plotted in Fig. 23.13.

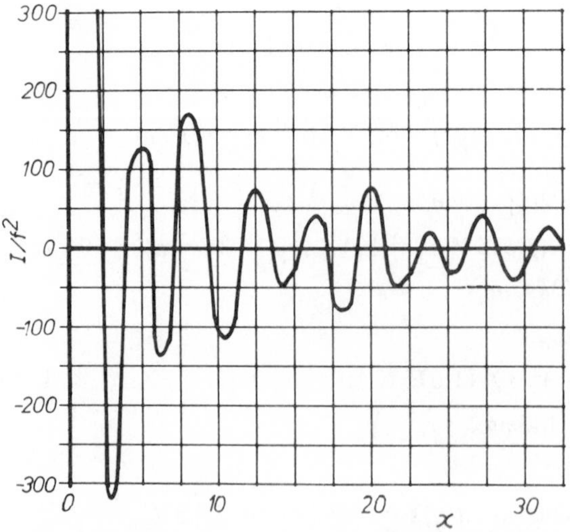

Fig 23.13

23.42 $\lambda = 12.26$ pm [Problem 23.39], $s = (4\pi/\lambda)\sin\frac{1}{2}\theta$, $x = sR_{\mathrm{CCl}}$.

Find x_{max} and x_{min} from Fig. 23.13 and find s_{max} and s_{min} from the data. Show that the ratio x/s gives a single value of R_{CCl} for all data.

Draw up the following Table:

	maxima			minima			
θ(expt.)	$3°\,10'$	$5°\,22'$	$7°\,54'$	$1°\,46'$	$4°\,6$	$6°\,10'$	$9°\,10'$
s/pm^{-1}	0.0284	0.0480	0.0706	0.0158	0.0367	0.0597	0.0819
x(calc.)	5.0	8.5	12.5	2.8	6.5	10.5	14.5
(x/s)/pm	176	177	177	177	177	176	177

Hence, $\underline{R_{\mathrm{CCl}} = 177\ \mathrm{pm}}$, and the experimental diffraction pattern is consistent with tetrahedral geometry.

24. The electric and magnetic properties of molecules

A24.1 $C = C_0\epsilon_r = (6.2\text{ pF})(35.5) = 220\text{ pF}$. [24.1.2]

A24.2 $\alpha + \mu^2/(3kT) = 3\epsilon_0 P_m/N_A$. [24.1.13a]

At 351.0 K, $\alpha + \mu^2[3(1.381 \times 10^{-23})(351.0\text{ K})]^{-1}$

$= (3)(8.854 \times 10^{-12})(70.62 \times 10^{-6}) \times (6.022 \times 10^{23})^{-1}$.

At 423.2 K, $\alpha + \mu^2[(3)(1.381 \times 10^{-23})(423.2\text{ K})]^{-1}$

$= (3)(8.854 \times 10^{-12})(62.47 \times 10^{-6}) \times (6.022 \times 10^{23})^{-1}$.

$\mu^2 = 3.062 \times 10^{-59}\text{ C}^2\text{ m}^2$; $\mu = 5.54 \times 10^{-30}\text{ C m}$, or $\underline{1.66\text{ D}}$.

$\alpha = \underline{1.01 \times 10^{-39}\text{ J}^{-1}\text{ C}^2\text{ m}^2}$.

A24.3 $P_m = (M_m/\rho)[(\epsilon_r - 1)/(\epsilon_r + 2)]$ [21.1.13b]

$27.18\text{ cm}^3 = (92.45\text{ g mol}^{-1})(1.89\text{ g cm}^{-3})^{-1}(\epsilon_r - 1)(\epsilon_r + 2)^{-1}$;

$\epsilon_r = \underline{4.75}$.

A24.4 Structure (1) should have a zero dipole moment. Hence structure (2), which has a nonzero moment, is more likely [Section 24.1(f)].

A24.5 The temperature dependent part of the polarization is proportional to $N\mu^2$ [24.1.11]. Since N becomes $N/2$ and since μ^2 becomes $4\mu^2$, the contribution to the polarization is doubled. The apparent moment of the dimer is $(2)^{\frac{1}{2}}\mu$.

A24.6 The dimers should have a zero dipole moment. The strong molecular interactions in the pure liquid probably break up the dimers and produce hydrogen bonded groups of molecules with a chainlike structure. In very dilute benzene solutions, the molecules should behave much like those in the gas and should tend to form planar dimers. Hence the relative permittivity should decrease as the dilution increases, [Section 24.1(c)].

A24.7 The molecule has 10 C–H, 2 C–C, and 2C–O bonds. They contribute

$10(1.65) + 2(1.20) + 2(1.41) = 21.72\text{ cm}^3\text{ mol}^{-1}$. [Example 24.4, Table 24.3]

$V_m = 74.12\text{ g mol}^{-1}/0.715\text{ g cm}^{-3} = 105.06\text{ cm}^3\text{ mol}^{-1}$.

$n_r = [105.06 + 2(21.72)]^{\frac{1}{2}}[105.06 - 21.72]^{-\frac{1}{2}} = \underline{1.34}$.

The experimental value is 1.354.

A24.8 $(n_r^2 - 1)/(n_r^2 + 2) = 0.400$ [24.1.14].

$3\epsilon_0 M_m \rho^{-1} N_A^{-1} = (3)(8.8542 \times 10^{-12}\,\mathrm{J^{-1}\,C^2\,m^{-1}})(267.8\,\mathrm{g\,mol^{-1}})(3.318\,\mathrm{g\,cm^{-3}})^{-1}$
$\times (6.022 \times 10^{23}\,\mathrm{mol^{-1}})^{-1}(10^{-6}\,\mathrm{m^3\,cm^{-3}}) = 3.560 \times 10^{-39}\,\mathrm{J^{-1}\,C^2\,m^2}$

$\alpha = (3.560 \times 10^{-39}\,\mathrm{J^{-1}\,C^2\,m^2})(0.400) = \underline{1.42 \times 10^{-39}\,\mathrm{J^{-1}\,C^2\,m^2}}.$

A24.9 $m = [4S(S+1)]^{\frac{1}{2}}$ Bohr magnetons [Section 24.6(b)].

$S(S+1) = (3.81)^2/4; S = 1.47$ [take positive root].

The spin of three unpaired electrons is 3/2.

A24.10 In the strong field case, the six electrons contributed by Co(III) fill the three t_{2g} orbitals. Since all the spins are paired, $K_3Co(CN)_6$ is diamagnetic. In the weak field case, two of the six electrons are paired. Hence K_3CoF_6 should have a spin-only moment derived from four unpaired electrons. Since $S = 2$, that moment is $[(4)(2)(2+1)]^{\frac{1}{2}}$ or 4.9 Bohr magnetons [Section 24.6(b)]. The observed value is slightly higher.

24.1 Refer to Fig. 4.9 of the text. Add individual moments vectorially.

(1) *p*-xylene. Resultant is zero; $\underline{\mu = 0.}$

(2) *o*-xylene. $\mu = (0.4\mathrm{D})\cos 30° + (0.4\mathrm{D})\cos 30° = \underline{0.7\ \mathrm{D}.}$

(3) *m*-xylene. $\mu = (0.4\mathrm{D})\cos 60° + (0.4\mathrm{D})\cos 60° = \underline{0.4\mathrm{D}.}$

The *p*-xylene value follows from the symmetry of the molecule and is independent of a detailed model.

24.2 $\mu(H_2O) = 2\mu(OH)\cos\frac{1}{2}\theta; \mu(OH) = (1.85\ \mathrm{D})/2\cos 52.3° = 1.51\ \mathrm{D}.$

$\mu(H_2O_2) = \underline{2(1.51\ \mathrm{D})\cos\frac{1}{2}\phi}$, directed perpendicular to the O-O bond.

$\phi = 2\arccos\{\mu(H_2O_2)/3.02\ \mathrm{D}\} = 2\arccos(2.12/3.00) = \underline{90.1°}$

24.3 The potential due to a charge q is $q/4\pi\epsilon_0 R$ [Appendix 11.1]. When the center of a dipole is at a distance R from any point, and directed towards it, a charge q is at a distance $R - \frac{1}{2}d$ and a charge $-q$ at $R + \frac{1}{2}d$. Hence the total potential at the point is

$$\phi = q/4\pi\epsilon_0(R - \tfrac{1}{2}d) - q/4\pi\epsilon_0(R + \tfrac{1}{2}d)$$
$$= (q/4\pi\epsilon_0 R)\left\{\left[\frac{1}{1-(d/2R)}\right] - \left[\frac{1}{1+(d/2R)}\right]\right\}$$
$$= (q/4\pi\epsilon_0 R)\{[1 + (d/2R) + \ldots] - [1 - (d/2R) + \ldots]\}$$
$$\approx (q/4\pi\epsilon_0 R)(2d/2R) = qd/4\pi\epsilon_0 R^2 = \mu/4\pi\epsilon_0 R^2.$$

The electric field is the negative gradient of the potential [Appendix 11.1], and so

$E = -\mathrm{d}\phi/\mathrm{d}R = 2\mu/4\pi\epsilon_0 R^3.$

For $\mu = 1.85\ \mathrm{D} = 1.85 \times (3.34 \times 10^{-39}\ \mathrm{C\,m})$ [endpaper 1],

$$E = 1.85 \times (3.34 \times 10^{-30}\ \mathrm{C\,m})/2\pi \times (8.854 \times 10^{-12}\ \mathrm{J^{-1}\,C^2\,m^{-1}}) \times R^3$$
$$= (1.11 \times 10^{-19}\ \mathrm{J\,C^{-1}\,m^{-2}})/R^3$$
$$= (1.11 \times 10^{-19}\ \mathrm{V\,m^{-1}})/(R/\mathrm{m})^3\ [1\ \mathrm{J} = 1\ \mathrm{V\,C}].$$

(a) $E = (1.11 \times 10^{-19}\ \mathrm{V\,m^{-1}})/(1.0 \times 10^{-9}) = \underline{1.1 \times 10^8\ \mathrm{V\,m^{-1}}}.$

(b) $E = (1.11 \times 10^{-19}\ \mathrm{V\,m^{-1}})/(3.0 \times 10^{-10})^3 = \underline{4.1 \times 10^9\ \mathrm{V\,m^{-1}}}.$

(c) $E = (1.11 \times 10^{-19}\ \mathrm{V\,m^{-1}})/(3.0 \times 10^{-8})^3 = \underline{4.1 \times 10^3\ \mathrm{V\,m^{-1}}}.$

The positive end of the dipole will adopt the position lying closer to the (negative) anion; the oxygen bears the negative end of the dipole.

24.4 A dipole μ making an angle θ to an external field E_{ex} has an energy

$$\mathscr{E} = -\mu E_{\mathrm{ex}}\cos\theta\ \text{[Section 24.1(b)]} = \begin{cases} -\mu E_{\mathrm{ex}}, & \theta = 0 \\ 0, & \theta = 90^\circ. \end{cases}$$

The energy of a (dipole, atom) pair is

$$\mathscr{E} = -(1/8\pi^2\epsilon_0^2)\alpha\mu^2/R^6$$

when the atom lies along the dipole's axis, and

$$\mathscr{E} = -(1/32\pi^2\epsilon_0^2)\alpha\mu^2/R^6$$

when it lies at right angles.

[$\mathscr{E} = -\tfrac{1}{2}\alpha\epsilon_0 E^2,\ \mathbf{E} = (1/4\pi\epsilon_0)(1/R^3)\{\mu - 3\mu\cdot\mathbf{RR}/R^2\}$

$$E^2 = \mathbf{E}\cdot\mathbf{E} = (1/4\pi\epsilon_0)^2(1/R^6)\{\mu\cdot\mu + 9(\mu\cdot\mathbf{R})^2\mathbf{R}\cdot\mathbf{R}/R^4 - 6\mu\cdot\mathbf{RR}\cdot\mu/R^2\}$$
$$= (1/4\pi\epsilon_0)^2(1/R^6)\{\mu^2 + 3(\mu\cdot\mathbf{R})^2/R^2\}$$

$$\mathscr{E} = -\tfrac{1}{2}\cdot(1/16\pi^2\epsilon_0^2)(1/R^6)\alpha\{\mu^2 + 3(\mu\cdot\mathbf{R})^2/R^2\}$$
$$= \begin{cases} -(1/32\pi^2\epsilon_0^2)(1/R^6)\alpha 4\mu^2 = -(1/8\pi^2\epsilon_0^2)\alpha\mu^2/R^6 \text{ for } \mathbf{R} \text{ parallel to } \mu \\ -(1/32\pi^2\epsilon_0^2)(1/R^6)\alpha\mu^2,\ \mathbf{R} \text{ perpendicular to } \mu. \end{cases}$$]

The change of energy on going from the initial (dipole parallel to E_{ex}, atom broadside on) to final (dipole perpendicular to E_{ex}, atom along axis) is therefore

$$\Delta\mathscr{E} = \{-(1/8\pi^2\epsilon_0^2)\alpha\mu^2/R^6\} - \{-\mu E_{\mathrm{ex}} - (1/32\pi^2\epsilon_0^2)\alpha\mu^2/R^6\}$$
$$= \mu E_{\mathrm{ex}} - (3/32\pi^2\epsilon_0^2)\alpha\mu^2/R^6.$$

This becomes negative (favorable) at the distance R^*, where

$(3/32\pi^2\epsilon_0^2)\alpha\mu^2/R^{*6} = \mu E_{ex}$, or $R^* = \{(3/32\pi^2\epsilon_0^2)\alpha\mu/E_{ex}\}^{1/6} = \{(3/8\pi\epsilon_0)\alpha'\mu/E_{ex}\}^{1/6}$.
Since $\alpha' = 1.66 \times 10^{-24}\,\text{cm}^3$ and $\mu = 1.84\,\text{D} \triangleq 6.17 \times 10^{-30}\,\text{C m}$, in a $1\,\text{kV m}^{-1}$ field

$$R^* = \left\{\frac{3 \times (1.66 \times 10^{-30}\,\text{m}^3) \times (6.17 \times 10^{-30}\,\text{C m})}{8\pi \times (8.854 \times 10^{-12}\,\text{J}^{-1}\,\text{C}^2\,\text{m}^{-1}) \times (10^3\,\text{V m}^{-1})}\right\}^{1/6}$$

$$= (1.38 \times 10^{-52}\,\text{J C}^{-1}\,\text{V}^{-1}\,\text{m}^6)^{1/6} = 2.27 \times 10^{-9}\,\text{m} = \underline{2.27\,\text{nm}}.$$

24.5 $\Delta = (\epsilon_r - 1)v$, where v is a relative specific volume taken to be unity at (273.15 K, 1 atm). Then at a temperature T, $v = (T/273.15\,\text{K})$. Note that $M_m/\rho = V_m$ and

$$V_m(T) = (T/273.15\,\text{K})V_m(273.15)$$
$$= (2.2413 \times 10^4\,\text{cm}^3\,\text{mol}^{-1})(T/273.15\,\text{K})$$
$$P_m = V_m\{(\epsilon_r - 1)/(\epsilon_r + 2)\}\ [24.1.13a]$$
$$= V_m(\Delta/v)/[3 + (\Delta/v)] = V_m\Delta/[3v + \Delta]$$
$$= \frac{(2.2413 \times 10^4\,\text{cm}^3\,\text{mol}^{-1})(T/273.15\,\text{K})\Delta}{3(T/273.15\,\text{K}) + \Delta}$$
$$= (N_A/3\epsilon_0)\{\alpha + \mu^2/3kT\}\ [24.1.13b].$$

Therefore, plot P_m against $(1/T)$, and obtain $N_A\alpha/3\epsilon_0 = 4\pi N_A\alpha'/3$ from the intercept and $N_A\mu^2/9\epsilon_0 k$ from the slope.

Draw up the following Table:

$\theta/°\text{C}$	0	100	200	300
T/K	273	373	473	573
$10^3/(T/\text{K})$	3.66	2.68	2.11	1.75
$10^3\Delta(\text{HCl})$	4.3	3.5	3.0	2.6
$P_m(\text{HCl})/\text{cm}^3\,\text{mol}^{-1}$	32.1	26.1	22.4	19.4
$10^3\Delta(\text{HBr})$	3.1	2.6	2.3	2.1
$P_m(\text{HBr})/\text{cm}^3\,\text{mol}^{-1}$	23.1	19.4	17.2	15.7
$10^3\Delta(\text{HI})$	2.3	2.2	2.1	2.1
$P_m(\text{HI})/\text{cm}^3\,\text{mol}^{-1}$	17.2	16.4	15.7	15.7

These points are plotted in Fig. 24.1.

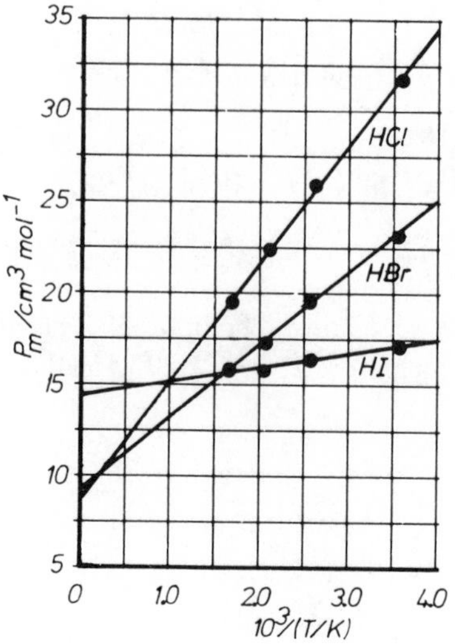

Fig 24.1

The intercepts and slopes are

	intercept	slope
HCl	8.9	6.4×10^3
HBr	9.3	3.8×10^3
HI	14.1	8.3×10^2

It follows that

$\alpha'(\text{HCl}) = (3/4\pi N_A)(8.9\ \text{cm}^3\,\text{mol}^{-1}) = \underline{3.5 \times 10^{-24}\ \text{cm}^3},$

$\alpha'(\text{HBr}) = (3/4\pi N_A)(9.3\ \text{cm}^3\,\text{mol}^{-1}) = \underline{3.7 \times 10^{-24}\ \text{cm}^3},$

$\alpha'(\text{HI}) = (3/4\pi N_A)(14.1\ \text{cm}^3\,\text{mol}^{-1}) = \underline{5.6 \times 10^{-24}\ \text{cm}^3}.$

$\mu = (\text{slope cm}^3\,\text{mol}^{-1}\,\text{K})^{1/2} \times (9\epsilon_0 k/N_A)^{1/2}.$

$$(9\epsilon_0 k/N_A)^{1/2} = \left\{\frac{9 \times (8.854 \times 10^{-12}\,\text{J}^{-1}\,\text{C}^2\,\text{m}^{-1}) \times (1.381 \times 10^{-23}\,\text{J K}^{-1})}{6.022 \times 10^{23}\,\text{mol}^{-1}}\right\}^{\frac{1}{2}}$$

$$= 4.275 \times 10^{-29}\,\text{C}(\text{mol/m K})^{1/2}$$

$\mu = 4.275 \times 10^{-29}\,\text{C}\ (\text{slope cm}^3\,\text{mol}^{-1}\,\text{K mol m}^{-1}\,\text{K}^{-1})^{1/2}$

$\quad = 4.275 \times 10^{-29}\,\text{C}\ (\text{slope } 10^{-6}\,\text{m}^2)^{1/2}$

$= (4.275 \times 10^{-32}\,\mathrm{C\,m}) \times (\mathrm{slope})^{1/2}$.

Convert to Debye using $1\,\mathrm{D} = 3.3356 \times 10^{-30}\,\mathrm{C\,m}$, then

$\mu = (1.282 \times 10^{-2}\,\mathrm{D}) \times (\mathrm{slope})^{1/2}$.

It follows that

$\mu(\mathrm{HCl}) = (1.282 \times 10^{-2}\,\mathrm{D}) \times (6.4 \times 10^{3})^{1/2} = \underline{1.03\,\mathrm{D}}$

$\mu(\mathrm{HBr}) = (1.282 \times 10^{-2}\,\mathrm{D}) \times (3.8 \times 10^{3})^{1/2} = \underline{0.80\,\mathrm{D}}$

$\mu(\mathrm{HI}) = (1.282 \times 10^{-2}\,\mathrm{D}) \times (8.3 \times 10^{2})^{1/2} = \underline{0.36\,\mathrm{D}}.$

24.6 $n_r = \{(V_m + 2R_m)/(V_m - R_m)\}^{1/2}$ [24.1.16]

$V_m = M_m/\rho = (18.02\,\mathrm{g\,mol^{-1}})/(1.00\,\mathrm{g\,cm^{-3}}) = 18.02\,\mathrm{cm^3\,mol^{-1}}$.

$R_m = 4\pi\alpha' N_A/3$ [24.1.15]

$= 4\pi(1.5 \times 10^{-24}\,\mathrm{cm^3}) \times (6.022 \times 10^{23}\,\mathrm{mol^{-1}})/3 = 3.8\,\mathrm{cm^3\,mol^{-1}}$.

$n_r = \{(18.02 + 7.6)/(18.02 - 3.8)\}^{1/2} = \underline{1.34}.$

Inaccurate local field correction, vibrational contribution.

24.7 $P_m = (M_m/\rho)\{(\epsilon_r - 1)/(\epsilon_r + 2)\}$ [24.1.13b].

$= 4\pi N_A\alpha'/3 + N_A\mu^2/9\epsilon_0 kT$ [24.1.13a].

Draw up the following Table using $M = 119.4\,\mathrm{g\,mol^{-1}}$:

$\theta/°\mathrm{C}$	−80	−70	−60	−40	−20	0	20
T/K	193	203	213	233	253	273	293
$10^3/(T/\mathrm{K})$	5.18	4.93	4.69	4.29	3.95	3.66	3.41
ϵ_r	3.1	3.1	7.0	6.5	6.0	5.5	5.0
$(\epsilon_r - 1)/(\epsilon_r + 2)$	0.41	0.41	0.67	0.65	0.63	0.60	0.57
$\rho/\mathrm{g\,cm^{-3}}$	1.65	1.64	1.64	1.61	1.57	1.53	1.50
$P_m/\mathrm{cm^3\,mol^{-1}}$	29.8	29.9	48.5	48.0	47.5	46.8	45.4

P_m is plotted against $1/T$ in Fig. 24.2. The intercept is at 30.00 and the slope 4.5×10^3. It follows that $\alpha' = 3 \times (30.0\,\mathrm{cm^3\,mol^{-1}})/4\pi(6.022 \times 10^{23}\,\mathrm{mol^{-1}}) = \underline{1.19 \times 10^{-23}\,\mathrm{cm^3}}$.

$\mu = (1.282 \times 10^{-2}\,\mathrm{D}) \times (\mathrm{slope})^{1/2}$ [Problem 24.5] $= (1.282 \times 10^{-2}\,\mathrm{D}) \times (4.5 \times 10^3)^{1/2}$

$= \underline{0.9\,\mathrm{D}}.$

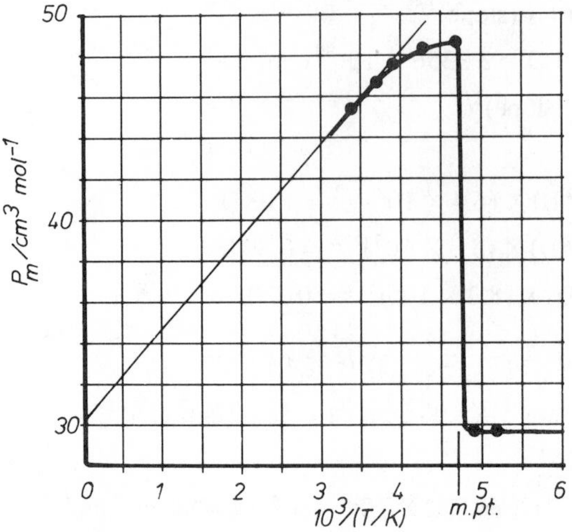

Fig 24.2

The sharp drop in the value of P_m occurs at the freezing point of chloroform (−63 °C), the dipole reorientation term is then frozen out. Note that P_m for the solid corresponds to the extrapolated, dipole free, value of P_m.

24.8 $P_m = (M_m/\rho)\{(\epsilon_r - 1)/(\epsilon_r + 2)\}$ [24.1.13b],

$= 4\pi N_A\alpha/3 + N_A\mu^2/9\epsilon_0 kT$ [24.1.13a].

The data have been corrected for variation of methanol density. Use the 20 °C value, 0.791 g cm^{-3}. Obtain μ and α' from the liquid range ($\theta > -95$ °C) results, but note that some molecular rotation occurs even below the freezing point (e.g. the −110 °C value of ϵ_r is close to the −80 °C value). Draw up the following Table using M_m = 32.0 g mol^{-1} and $P_m = (M_m/\rho)\{(\epsilon_r - 1)/(\epsilon_r + 2)\}$.

θ/°C	−80	−50	−20	0	20
T/K	193	223	253	273	293
$10^3/(T/\mathrm{K})$	5.18	4.48	3.95	3.66	3.41
ϵ_r	57	49	42	38	34
$(\epsilon_r - 1)/(\epsilon_r + 2)$	0.95	0.94	0.93	0.93	0.92
P_m/cm^3 mol^{-1}	38.5	38.1	37.4	37.7	37.2

P_m is plotted against $1/T$ in Fig. 24.3. The extrapolated intercept at $1/T = 0$ is 35.0 and the slope is 741 (from least squares analysis). It follows that

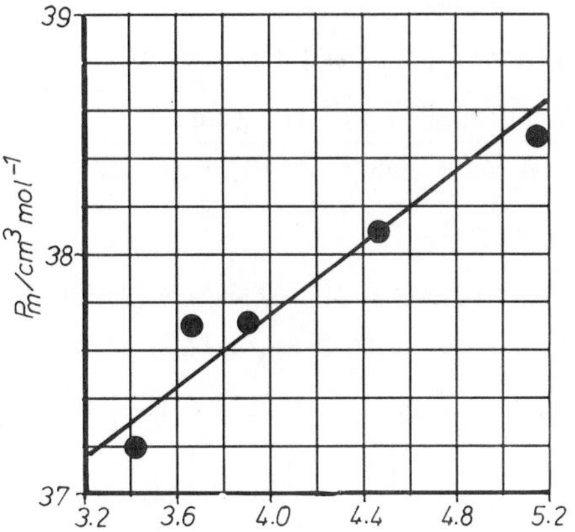

Fig 24.3

$\alpha' = 3 \times (35.0\,\text{cm}^3\,\text{mol}^{-1})/4\pi(6.022 \times 10^{23}\,\text{mol}^{-1}) = \underline{1.38 \times 10^{-23}\,\text{cm}^3}.$

$\mu = (1.282 \times 10^{-2}\,\text{D}) \times (\text{slope})^{1/2}$ [Problem 24.5]

$= (1.282 \times 10^{-2}\,\text{D}) \times \sqrt{741} = \underline{0.35\,\text{D}}.$

24.9 $(n_r^2 - 1)/(n_r^2 + 2) = N_A\rho\alpha/3\epsilon_0 M_m = 4\pi\alpha'\rho N_A/3M_m$ [24.1.4 and 24.1.15].

$\rho = M_m/V_m = M_m p/RT.$

$n_r^2 - 1 = (4\pi\alpha' p/3kT)(n_r^2 + 2)$, and so

$$n_r = \left\{\frac{1 + (8\pi\alpha' p/3kT)}{1 - (4\pi\alpha' p/3kT)}\right\}^{1/2} \approx \{(1 + 8\pi\alpha' p/3kT)(1 + 4\pi\alpha' p/3kT)\}^{1/2}$$

$$\approx \{1 + (12\pi\alpha' p/3kT)\}^{1/2} \approx 1 + (6\pi\alpha' p/3kT) = \underline{1 + (2\pi\alpha'/kT)p}.$$

For the inverse problem,

$\alpha' \approx (n_r - 1)(kT/2\pi p)$

or, better,

$\underline{\alpha' = (3kT/4\pi p)\{(n_r^2 - 1)/(n_r^2 + 2)\}}$ [from line 3 above].

24.10 The time-scale of the oscillations is about $1/(0.55\,\text{GHz}) = 2 \times 10^{-9}\,\text{s}$ for benzene and toluene, and $2.5 \times 10^{-9}\,\text{s}$ for the additional oscillations in toluene. Toluene has a permanent dipole moment, benzene does not. Both have dipole moments induced by fluctuations in the solvent. Both have anisotropic polarizabilities (so that the refractive index is modulated by molecular reorientation).

24.11 $(\epsilon_r - 1)/(\epsilon_r + 2) = (N_A\rho/3\epsilon_0 M_m)\{\alpha + \mu^2/3kT\} \equiv x$ [24.1.12].

Therefore $\epsilon_r = (1 + 2x)/(1 - x)$.

$\mu = 1.57\,\mathrm{D} \mathrel{\hat{=}} 5.24 \times 10^{-30}\,\mathrm{C\,m}$ [endpaper 1],

$\alpha = 4\pi\epsilon_0\alpha' = 1.37 \times 10^{-33}\,\mathrm{cm^3\,J^{-1}\,C^2\,m^{-1}}$; $\rho = 1.107\,\mathrm{g\,cm^{-3}}$.

$$N_A\rho/3\epsilon_0 M_m = \frac{(6.022 \times 10^{23}\,\mathrm{mol^{-1}}) \times (1.107\,\mathrm{g\,cm^{-3}})}{3 \times (8.854 \times 10^{-12}\,\mathrm{J^{-1}\,C^2\,m^{-1}}) \times (112.6\,\mathrm{g\,mol^{-1}})}$$

$$= 2.23 \times 10^{32}\,\mathrm{cm^{-3}\,J\,C^{-2}\,m}.$$

$\mu^2/3kT = (5.24 \times 10^{-30}\,\mathrm{C\,m})^2/3 \times (1.381 \times 10^{-23}\,\mathrm{J\,K^{-1}}) \times (298.15\,\mathrm{K})$

$= 2.22 \times 10^{-39}\,\mathrm{m^2\,J^{-1}\,C^2} = 2.22 \times 10^{-33}\,\mathrm{cm^3\,J^{-1}\,C^2\,m^{-1}}$.

$x = (2.23 \times 10^{32}\,\mathrm{cm^{-3}\,J\,C^{-2}\,m}) \times (1.37 \times 10^{-33} + 2.22 \times 10^{-33})\,\mathrm{cm^3\,J^{-1}\,C^2\,m^{-1}}$

$= 0.801$.

$\epsilon_r = (1 + 1.602)/(1 - 0.801) = \underline{13.1}.$

24.12 $n_r = \{(V_m + 2R_m)/(V_m - R_m)\}^{1/2}$ [24.1.16]; $R_m = 4\pi\alpha' N_A/3$ [24.1.15],

$V_m = M_m/\rho$, $M_m = 18.02\,\mathrm{g\,mol^{-1}}$, $\alpha' = 1.50 \times 10^{-24}\,\mathrm{cm^3}$.

$R_m = 4\pi(1.50 \times 10^{-24}\,\mathrm{cm^3}) \times (6.022 \times 10^{23}\,\mathrm{mol^{-1}})/3 = 3.78\,\mathrm{cm^3\,mol^{-1}}$.

Draw up the following Table.

$\theta/°\mathrm{C}$	0	20	40	60	80	100
$V_m/\mathrm{cm^3\,mol^{-1}}$	18.02	18.05	18.16	18.33	18.54	18.80
$(V_m + 2R_m)/\mathrm{cm^3\,mol^{-1}}$	25.58	25.61	25.72	25.89	26.10	26.36
$(V_m - R_m)/\mathrm{cm^3\,mol^{-1}}$	14.25	14.28	14.39	14.56	14.77	15.03
n_r	1.339	1.339	1.336	1.333	1.329	1.324

These points are plotted in Fig. 24.4.

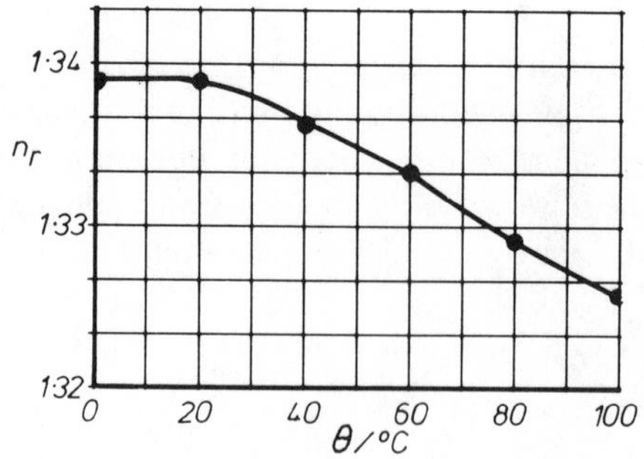

Fig 24.4 .

24.13 $n_r = \left\{ \dfrac{1 + (8\pi\alpha' p/3kT)}{1 - (4\pi\alpha' p/3kT)} \right\}^{1/2}$ [Problem 24.9],

$\alpha' = 1.50 \times 10^{-24}\,\mathrm{cm^3}$ [Problem 24.12].

$$4\pi\alpha' p/3kT = \frac{4\pi(1.50 \times 10^{-30}\,\mathrm{m^3}) \times (1.013 \times 10^5\,\mathrm{N\,m^{-2}})}{3 \times (1.381 \times 10^{-23}\,\mathrm{J\,K^{-1}}) \times (373.2\,\mathrm{K})} = 1.235 \times 10^{-4}.$$

$$n_r = \left\{ \frac{1 + 2.470 \times 10^{-4}}{1 - 1.235 \times 10^{-4}} \right\}^{1/2} = \underline{1.00019.}$$

$R_m(CaCl_2) = [1.19 + 2 \times (9.30)]\,\mathrm{cm^3\,mol^{-1}} = 19.8\,\mathrm{cm^3\,mol^{-1}}$;

$V_m(CaCl_2) = (111.0\,\mathrm{g\,mol^{-1}})/(2.15\,\mathrm{g\,cm^{-3}}) = 51.6\,\mathrm{cm^3\,mol^{-1}}$;

$$n_r = \left\{ \frac{V_m + 2R_m}{V_m - R_m} \right\}^{1/2} = \underline{1.69.}$$

$R_m(NaCl) = (0.46 + 9.30)\,\mathrm{cm^3\,mol^{-1}} = 9.80\,\mathrm{cm^3\,mol^{-1}}$;

$V_m(NaCl) = (58.4\,\mathrm{g\,mol^{-1}})/(2.163\,\mathrm{g\,cm^{-3}}) = 27.0\,\mathrm{cm^3\,mol^{-1}}$;

$n_r = \underline{1.65}$

$R_m(Ar) = 4.14\,\mathrm{cm^3\,mol^{-1}}$;

$V_m(Ar) = (39.95\,\mathrm{g\,mol^{-1}})/(1.42\,\mathrm{g\,cm^{-3}}) = 28.1\,\mathrm{cm^3\,mol^{-1}}$;

$n_r = \underline{1.23.}$

24.14 $P_m = (N_A/3\epsilon_0)\{\alpha + (\mu^2/3kT)\}$ [24.1.13a]. Therefore, plot P_m against $1/T$; intercept is $\alpha N_A/3\epsilon_0 = 4\pi\alpha' N_A/3$, slope $N_A\mu^2/9\epsilon_0 k$. Draw up the following Table.

T/K	292.2	309.0	333.0	387.0	413.0	446.0
$10^3/(T/\mathrm{K})$	3.42	3.24	3.00	2.58	2.42	2.24
$P_m/\mathrm{cm^3\,mol^{-1}}$	57.57	55.01	51.22	44.99	42.51	39.59

These points are plotted in Fig. 24.5. The extrapolated (least squares) intercept lies at 5.65, and so $(4\pi N_A/3)\alpha' = 5.65\,\mathrm{cm^3\,mol^{-1}}$; $\alpha' = 3(5.65\,\mathrm{cm^3\,mol^{-1}})/4\pi(6.022 \times 10^{23}\,\mathrm{mol^{-1}}) = \underline{2.24 \times 10^{-24}\,\mathrm{cm^3}.}$

The least squares slope is 1.52×10^4, and so

$N_A\mu^2/9\epsilon_0 k = 1.52 \times 10^4\,\mathrm{cm^3\,mol^{-1}\,K}$,

$\mu = \sqrt{\{(9\epsilon_0 k/N_A) \times (1.52 \times 10^4\,\mathrm{cm^3\,mol^{-1}\,K})\}}$

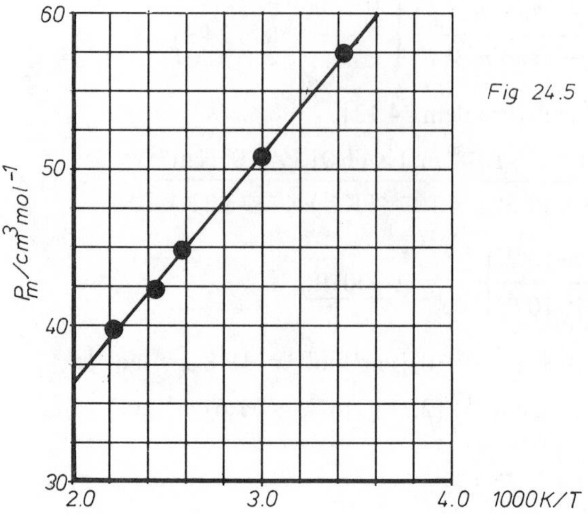

Fig 24.5

$$= \sqrt{\left\{\left(\frac{9 \times (8.854 \times 10^{-12}\,\mathrm{J^{-1}\,C^2\,m^{-2}}) \times (1.381 \times 10^{-23}\,\mathrm{J\,K^{-1}})}{6.022 \times 10^{23}\,\mathrm{mol^{-1}}}\right) \times (1.52 \times 10^{-2}\,\mathrm{m^3\,mol^{-1}\,K})\right\}}$$

$= \sqrt{\{(1.827 \times 10^{-57}) \times (1.52 \times 10^{-2})\}}\,\mathrm{C\,m} = 5.27 \times 10^{-30}\,\mathrm{C\,m}$, $\underline{1.58\ \mathrm{D}}$.

24.15 $P_m = 4\pi\alpha' N_A/3 = (M_m/\rho)(n_r^2 - 1)/(n_r^2 + 2)$ [24.1.14; $P_m = R_m$]
$= (RT/p)(n_r^2 - 1)/(n_r^2 + 2)$.

$n_r = 1.000\,379$, $(n_r^2 - 1)/(n_r^2 + 2) = 2.527 \times 10^{-4}$.

$RT/p = (8.314\,\mathrm{J\,K^{-1}\,mol^{-1}}) \times (273\,\mathrm{K})/(1.013\,25 \times 10^5\,\mathrm{N\,m^{-2}}) = 2.240 \times 10^4\,\mathrm{cm^3\,mol^{-1}}$.

$P_m = (2.527 \times 10^{-4}) \times (2.240 \times 10^4\,\mathrm{cm^3\,mol^{-1}}) = \underline{5.66\,\mathrm{cm^3\,mol^{-1}}}$.

P_m is independent of density, and so at 292 K P_m has the same value.

For a static measurement at 292 K,

$P_m(0) = (N_A/3\epsilon_0)\{4\pi\alpha' + (\mu^2/3kT)\} = 57.57\,\mathrm{cm^3\,mol^{-1}}$ [Problem 24.14].

The optical measurement gave $4\pi N_A\alpha'/3$; therefore

$\mu^2 N_A/9\epsilon_0 kT = P_m(0) - P_m(\text{optical}) = (57.57 - 5.66)\,\mathrm{cm^3\,mol^{-1}} = 51.91\,\mathrm{cm^3\,mol^{-1}}$.

Therefore $\mu^2 = (9\epsilon_0 kT/N_A) \times (51.91\,\mathrm{cm^3\,mol^{-1}})$
$= (1.827 \times 10^{-57} \times 292.2) \times (51.91 \times 10^{-6}\,\mathrm{C^2\,m^2})$
$= 2.771 \times 10^{-59}\,\mathrm{C^2\,m^2}$.

Consequently, $\mu = 5.264 \times 10^{-30}$ C m, $\underline{1.578\text{ D}}$.

In practice $\alpha(\omega)$ may differ sharply from $\alpha(0)$; but here the permanent dipole dominates, and so the error is not significant.

24.16 Consider a single molecule surrounded by $N-1(\approx N)$ others, in a container of volume V. The number of molecules in a spherical shell of thickness dR at a distance R is $(4\pi R^2 dR)(N/V)$. Therefore the interaction energy is

$$u = \int_d^{R_c} (4\pi R^2 dR)(N/V)(-C_6 R^6) = -4\pi(N/V)C_6 \int_d^{R_c} dR/R^4$$

where R_c is the radius of the vessel and d the molecular diameter (the distance of closest approach). Therefore,

$$u = (4\pi/3)(N/V)C_6 \left\{\frac{1}{R_c^3} - \frac{1}{d^3}\right\} \approx -(4\pi/3)C_6(N/V)/d^3$$

because $d \ll R_c$. The mutual pairwise interaction energy of all N molecules is $U = \frac{1}{2}Nu$ (the $\frac{1}{2}$ appears because each interaction must be counted only once; i.e. A with B, not A with B plus B with A).

$U = -(2\pi/3)(N^2/V)(C_6/d^3)$.

For a van der Waals gas, $(\partial U/\partial V)_T = n^2 a/V^2$ [*Example* 6.1], $n = N/N_A$. Therefore,

$a = (V^2/n^2)(\partial/\partial V)\{-(2\pi/3)(N^2/V)(C_6/d^3)\} = \underline{(2\pi/3)N_A^2(C_6/d^3)}$.

$$C_6 \approx -\left\{\frac{3I_1I_2}{2(I_1+I_2)}\right\} \alpha_1'\alpha_2' \;[24.2.3] = -3I\alpha'^2/4 \;[I_1 \approx I_2, \text{etc.}].$$

For argon $I = 1521$ kJ mol^{-1} [Table 4.9] $\triangleq 2.53 \times 10^{-18}$ J;

$\alpha' = 1.66 \times 10^{-24}$ cm^3 [Table 24.1] $= 1.66 \times 10^{-30}$ m^3.

$C_6 \approx 3 \times (2.53 \times 10^{-18}\text{ J}) \times (1.66 \times 10^{-30}\text{ m}^3)^2/4 = 5.2 \times 10^{-78}$ J m^6.

$a = (2\pi/3)N_A^2(C_6/d^3) = (2\pi/3) \times (6.022 \times 10^{23}\text{ mol}^{-1})^2 \times (5.2 \times 10^{-78}\text{ J m}^6)/(572\text{ pm})^3$

$= 0.021$ J m^3 mol^{-2} [$d \approx 2R_0, R_0$ from Table 23.2].

From Table 1.3, $a = 1.345$ dm^3 atm mol^{-2}

$= 1.345 \times (10^{-6}\text{ m}^6) \times (1.0133 \times 10^5\text{ N m}^{-2})\text{mol}^{-2}$

$= 0.14$ N m^4 mol^{-2} $= \underline{0.14\text{ J m}^3\text{ mol}^{-2}}$.

In order to obtain this value, select a smaller value of d (304 pm).

24.17 $B(T) = 2\pi N_A \int_0^\infty \{1 - e^{-V(R)/kT}\}R^2 dR$ [24.4.8]

$$= 2\pi N_A \int_0^d R^2 dR + 2\pi N_A \int_d^\infty \{1 - e^{+C_6/R^6 kT}\} R^2 dR$$

$$\approx \tfrac{2}{3}\pi N_A d^3 + 2\pi N_A \int_d^\infty (-C_6/R^6 kT) R^2 dR$$

$$= \tfrac{2}{3}\pi N_A d^3 - (2\pi N_A C_6/kT) \int_d^\infty dR/R^4$$

$$= \tfrac{2}{3}\pi N_A d^3 - (2\pi N_A C_6/3kTd^3) = \underline{\tfrac{2}{3}\pi N_A d^3 \{1 - (C_6/kTd^6)\}}.$$

24.18 $B = 2\pi N_A \int_0^\infty \{1 - e^{-V/kT}\} R^2 dR$ [24.4.8]

$$= 2\pi N_A \int_0^{\sigma_1} R^2 dR + 2\pi N_A \int_{\sigma_1}^{\sigma_2} \{1 - e^{\epsilon/kT}\} R^2 dR$$

$$= 2\pi N_A (\sigma_1^3/3) + 2\pi N_A \{1 - e^{\epsilon/kT}\} (\sigma_2^3 - \sigma_1^3)/3.$$

Suppose $\epsilon \ll kT$, then

$B = (2\pi/3) N_A \sigma_1^3 - (2\pi/3) N_A \epsilon(\sigma_2^3 - \sigma_1^3)/kT.$

For the van der Waals equation

$B = b - a/RT$ [1.4.4]

Hence, $\underline{b = (2\pi/3) N_A \sigma_1^3}$, $\underline{a = (2\pi/3) N_A^2 \epsilon(\sigma_2^3 - \sigma_1^3)}$.

24.19 Numerical integration, as in *Example* 24.4, leads to the following values

T/K	270	280	290	300	310	320 . . . 500	
B/cm^3 mol^{-1}	−22.3	−19.8	−17.6	−15.5	−13.5	−11.7	+7.04

24.20 $F = -dV/dR$ [Section 13.1].

$V = C_n/R^n - C_6/R^6$ [24.2.8],

$\underline{F = nC_n/R^{n+1} - 6C_6/R^7}.$

$F = 0$ when $nC_n/R^{n+1} = 6C_6/R^7$,

or $R^{n-6} = (n/6)C_n/C_6$, or $\underline{R = \{(n/6)C_n/C_6\}^{1/(n-6)}}.$

24.21 $C_6 \approx 3I\alpha'^2/4$ [Problem 24.16],
$B \approx (2\pi/3)N_A d^3\{1-(3I\alpha'^2/4kTd^6)\}$.
$\alpha' \approx 1.66 \times 10^{-24}\,\text{cm}^3$, $d \approx 572\,\text{pm}$, $I = 1520.6\,\text{kJ mol}^{-1} \mathrel{\hat{=}} 2.53 \times 10^{-18}\,\text{J}$.

$$3I\alpha'^2/4kTd^6 = \frac{3 \times (2.53 \times 10^{-18}\,\text{J}) \times (1.66 \times 10^{-24}\,\text{cm}^3)^2}{4 \times (1.381 \times 10^{-23}\,\text{J K}^{-1}) \times (298.15\,\text{K}) \times (572\,\text{pm})^6} = 0.0363.$$

$(2\pi/3)N_A d^3 = (2\pi/3) \times (6.022 \times 10^{23}\,\text{mol}^{-1}) \times (572\,\text{pm})^3 = 2.36 \times 10^{-4}\,\text{m}^3\,\text{mol}^{-1}$
Therefore, at 298 K, $B \approx (2.36 \times 10^{-4}\,\text{m}^3\,\text{mol}^{-1}) \times (1-0.0363) = \underline{230\,\text{cm}^3\,\text{mol}^{-1}}$.

24.22 $V_g(R) = -Gm_1m_2/R$ [Newtonian gravitational potential energy].
$V_e(R) = -C_6/R^6$ [attractive electrical potential energy].
Take $R \approx 572\,\text{pm}$, $C_6 = 1.02 \times 10^{-77}\,\text{J m}^6$ [Problem 24.16].
$V_e(572\,\text{pm}) = -(1.02 \times 10^{-77}\,\text{J m}^6)/(572 \times 10^{-12}\,\text{m})^6 = -2.91 \times 10^{-22}\,\text{J}$
$m_1 = m_2 = 40 \times (1.66 \times 10^{-27}\,\text{kg}) = 6.64 \times 10^{-26}\,\text{kg}$;
$V_g(572\,\text{pm}) = -(6.67 \times 10^{-11}\,\text{N m}^2\,\text{kg}^{-2}) \times (6.64 \times 10^{-26}\,\text{kg})^2/(572\,\text{pm})$
$= -5.14 \times 10^{-52}\,\text{J}$.
Hence, $V_g/V_e = 1.8 \times 10^{-30}$ at $R \approx 572\,\text{pm}$.

24.23 The number of molecules in the volume element $d\tau$ is $N(d\tau/V) = \mathcal{N}d\tau$. The energy of interaction of these molecules with one at a distance R is $V(R)\mathcal{N}d\tau$. The total interaction, taking account of the whole sample volume, is therefore

$$u = \int V(R)\mathcal{N}d\tau = \mathcal{N}\int V(R)d\tau \; [\mathcal{N} \text{ is uniform}].$$

The total interaction energy for a sample of N molecules is $\frac{1}{2}Nu$ (the $\frac{1}{2}$ in order to avoid double counting [Problem 24.16]), and so the cohesive energy density is

$$-U/V = -\tfrac{1}{2}Nu/V = -\tfrac{1}{2}\mathcal{N}u = -\tfrac{1}{2}\mathcal{N}^2\int V(R)d\tau.$$

For $V(R) = -C_6/R^6$ and $d\tau = 4\pi R^2\,dR$,

$$-U/V = 2\pi\mathcal{N}^2C_6\int_d^\infty dR/R^4 = (2\pi/3)\mathcal{N}^2C_6/d^3.$$

But $\mathcal{N} = N/V = nN_A/V = N_AM/M_mV = N_A\rho/M_m$ where M is the total sample mass and M_m the molar mass. Therefore,
$\underline{-U/V = (2\pi/3)(N_A\rho/M_m)^2(C_6/d^3)}$.

24.24 $\Delta H/V \approx (2\pi/3)(N_A\rho/M_m)^2(C_6/d^3)$.

Convert to molar enthalpy by multiplying by $V_m = M_m/\rho$;

$\Delta H_m \approx (2\pi/3)N_A^2(\rho/M_m)(C_6/d^3)$.

$C_6 \approx 3I\alpha'^2/4$.

$(4/3)\pi(d/2)^3 N_A \approx V_m$; therefore $d^3 \approx 6V_m/\pi N_A = 6M_m/\pi N_A\rho$.

$\Delta H_m \approx (2\pi/3)N_A^2(\rho/M_m)(3I\alpha'^2/4)(\pi N_A\rho/6M_m) = (\rho\pi/M_m)^2 N_A^3 I\alpha'^2/12$.

$\rho = 1.594\ \mathrm{g\,cm^{-3}}$, $\alpha' = 10.5 \times 10^{-24}\ \mathrm{cm^3}$, $M_m = 153.8\ \mathrm{g\,mol^{-1}}$, $I \approx 5\ \mathrm{eV} \mathrel{\hat=} 8 \times 10^{-19}\ \mathrm{J}$.

$$\Delta H_m \approx (6.022 \times 10^{23}\ \mathrm{mol^{-1}})^3 \times$$

$$\times \left\{\frac{1.594\pi\ \mathrm{g\,cm^{-3}}}{153.8\ \mathrm{g\,mol^{-1}}}\right\} \times \frac{(8.19 \times 10^{-19}\ \mathrm{J}) \times (1.05 \times 10^{-24}\ \mathrm{cm^3})^2}{12}$$

$$\approx \underline{1.8\ \mathrm{kJ\,mol^{-1}}}.$$

24.25 $U = -(2\pi/3)(N^2/V)(C_6/d^3)$; $(\partial U/\partial V)_T = n^2 a/V^2$, $n = N/N_A$.

$a = (2\pi/3)N_A^2(C_6/d^3)$ [Problem 24.16]

$b \approx (4/3)\pi(d/2)^3 N_A = (\pi/6)N_A d^3$.

$V_{m,c} = 3b = (\pi/2)N_A d^3$ [Box 1.1].

$p_c = a/27b^2$ [Box 1.1] $= (2\pi/3)N_A^2(C_6/d^3)/27(\pi/6)^2 N_A^2 d^6$

$= \underline{(8/9\pi)(C_6/d^9)}$.

$T_c = 8a/27Rb = (16\pi/3)N_A^2(C_6/d^3)/27R(\pi/6)N_A d^3$

$= \underline{(32/27)C_6/kd^6}$.

24.26 Refer to Fig. 24.6(a). The scattering angle is $\theta = 180° - 2\alpha$, if specular reflection occurs on collision (angle of impact equal to angle of departure from the suface). For an impact parameter $b \leqslant R_1 + R_2$, $\sin\alpha = b/(R_1 + R_2)$;

$$\theta = \begin{cases} 180° - 2\arcsin\{b/(R_1+R_2)\}, & b \leqslant R_1 + R_2, \\ 0 & b > R_1 + R_2. \end{cases}$$

This function is plotted in Fig. 24.6(b) (it could help you play a better game of billiards).

24.27
$$\theta(v) = \begin{cases} 180° - 2\arcsin\{b/[R_1 + R_2(v)]\}, & b \leqslant R_1 + R_2(v)\ \text{[Problem 24.26]} \\ 0 & b > R_1 + R_2(v). \end{cases}$$

$R_2(v) = R_2\exp(-v/v^*)$; $R_1 = \tfrac{1}{2}R_2$; $b = \tfrac{1}{2}R_2$.

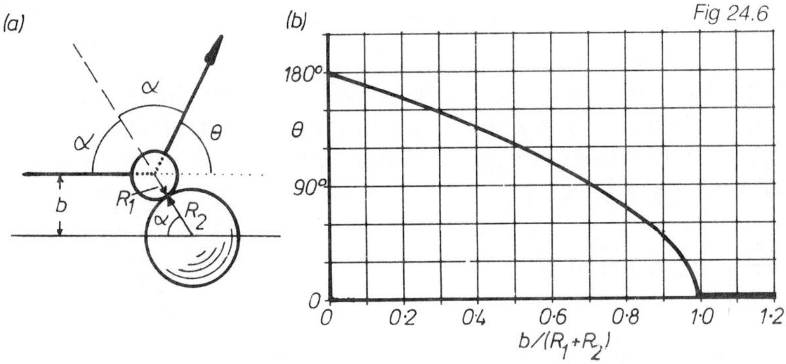

Fig 24.6

$$\theta(v) = 180° - 2\arcsin\left\{\frac{1}{1+2\exp(-v/v^*)}\right\},$$

[The restriction $b \leqslant R_1 + R_2(v)$ turns into $\frac{1}{2}R_2 \leqslant \frac{1}{2}R_2 + R_2\exp(-v/v^*)$, which is valid for all v.] This function is plotted in Fig. 24.7(a). The kinetic energy of approach is $E = \frac{1}{2}mv^2$, and so

$$\theta(E) = 180° - 2\arcsin\left\{\frac{1}{1+2\exp[-(2E/mv^{*2})^{1/2}]}\right\}$$

$$= 180° - 2\arcsin\left\{\frac{1}{1+2\exp[-(E/E^*)^{1/2}]}\right\}$$

where $E^* = \frac{1}{2}mv^{*2}$. This function is plotted in Fig. 24.7(b).

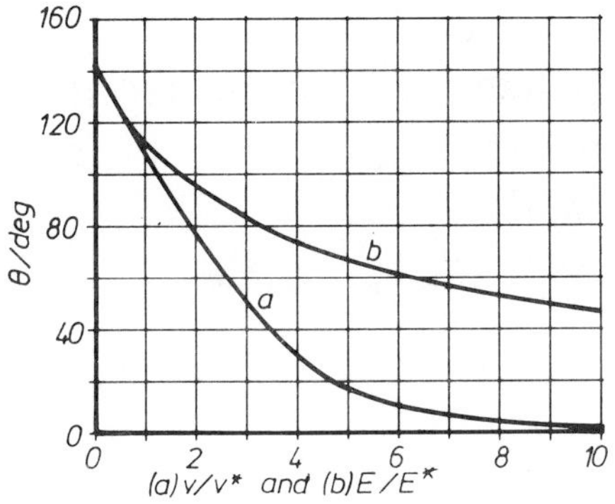

Fig 24.7

24.28 $\mathscr{M} = \frac{1}{2}\sum_i \left\{\frac{(z_i/z_-)}{\rho_{+i}} + \frac{(z_i/z_+)}{\rho_{-i}}\right\}$ [24.5.3]

$$\sum_i \left\{\frac{(z_i/z_-)}{\rho_{+i}}\right\} = 2\{1-\tfrac{1}{2}+\tfrac{1}{3}-\tfrac{1}{4}+\ldots\} = 2\ln 2.$$

[The leading factor of 2 arises because the ions occur on both sides of the one of interest; the cations are at $\rho = 2, 4, \ldots$ and for them $z_+/z_- = -1$; (the anions are at $\rho = 1, 3, \ldots$, and for them $z_+/z_- = 1$. We also use $\ln(1+z) = z - \tfrac{1}{2}z^2 + \tfrac{1}{3}z^3 - \ldots$, so that $\ln 2 = 1 - \tfrac{1}{2} + \tfrac{1}{3} - \ldots$.]

$$\sum_i \left\{\frac{z_i/z_+}{\rho_{-i}}\right\} = 2\ln 2 \text{ likewise.}$$

Therefore, $\mathcal{M} = \tfrac{1}{2}(2\ln 2 + 2\ln 2) = 2\ln 2 = \underline{1.386\,29\ldots}$

24.29 $(\partial U/\partial V)_T = T(\partial p/\partial T)_V - p$. At $T = 0$, $(\partial U/\partial V)_T = -p$.

$\kappa = -(1/V)(\partial V/\partial p)_T$ [3.2.11] $= -(1/V)/(\partial p/\partial V)_T$ [Box 3.1],

$(\partial p/\partial V)_T = (\partial/\partial V)(-\partial U/\partial V)_T = -(\partial^2 U/\partial V^2)_T$.

Therefore $\kappa = +(1/V)/(\partial^2 U/\partial V^2)_T$, or $\underline{1/\kappa = V(\partial^2 U/\partial V^2)_T}$.

$\partial U/\partial V = (\partial U/\partial R_0)(\mathrm{d}R_0/\mathrm{d}V)$; $V = cR_0^3$, $\mathrm{d}V/\mathrm{d}R_0 = 3cR_0^2$

$$\begin{aligned}\partial^2 U/\partial V^2 &= (\partial/\partial V)\{(\partial U/\partial R_0)(1/3cR_0^2)\}\\ &= (1/3cR_0^2)(\partial/\partial R_0)\{(\partial U/\partial R_0)(1/3cR_0^2)\}\\ &= (1/9c^2)(1/R_0^2)\{(\partial^2 U/\partial R_0^2)(1/R_0^2) - 2(\partial U/\partial R_0)(1/R_0^3)\}.\end{aligned}$$

$1/\kappa = cR_0^3(1/9c^2R_0^4)\{(\partial^2 U/\partial R_0^2) - (2/R_0)(\partial U/\partial R_0)\}$

$U = -(na\mathcal{M}/R_0)(1 - R^*/R_0)$ [24.5.7, $a = N_A e^2/4\pi\epsilon_0$]

$(\partial U/\partial R_0) = na\mathcal{M}\,\{(1/R_0^2) - (2R^*/R_0^3)\}$

$(\partial^2 U/\partial R_0^2) = -a\mathcal{M}\{(2/R_0^3) - (6R^*/R_0^4)\}$.

$$\begin{aligned}1/\kappa &= (na\mathcal{M}/9cR_0)\{-(2/R_0^3) + (6R^*/R_0^4) - (2/R_0^4) + (4R^*/R_0^4)\}\\ &= (2a\mathcal{M}/9cR_0^4)\,\{5(R^*/R_0) - 2\}\\ &= (2na\mathcal{M}/9R_0V)\{5(R^*/R_0) - 2\}.\end{aligned}$$

It follows that $\underline{R^* = \tfrac{2}{5}R_0 + (18\pi/5)\epsilon_0 R_0^2 V_m/\kappa N_A e^2 \mathcal{M}}$.

24.30

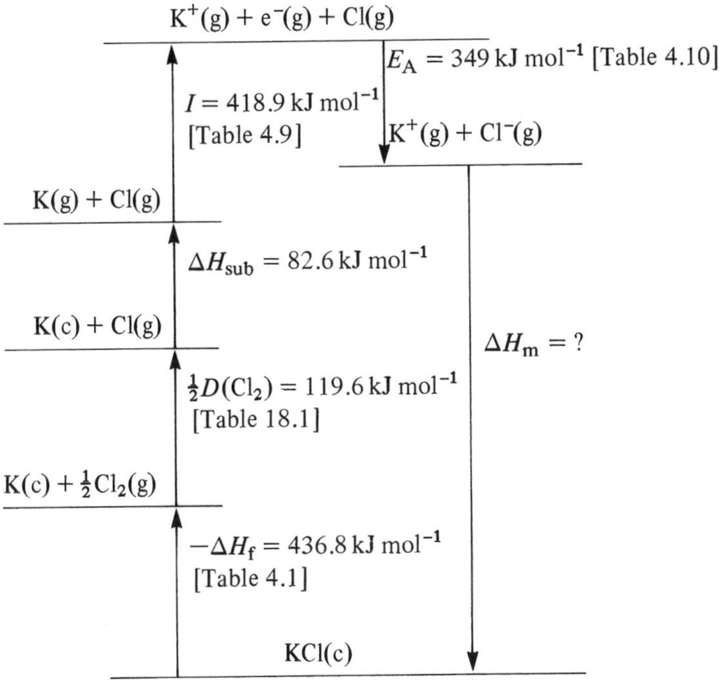

$$\Delta H_m/\text{kJ mol}^{-1} = -\{436.8 + 119.6 + 82.6 + 418.9 - 349\}$$
$$= \underline{-709.}$$

$U_m = -(N_A e^2 \mathscr{M}/4\pi\epsilon_0 R_0)\{1 - (R^*/R_0)\}$ [24.5.7];

$R^*/R_0 = \frac{2}{5} + (18\pi/5)\epsilon_0 R_0 V_m/\kappa N_A e^2 \mathscr{M}$ [Problem 24.29]

$\kappa = 1.1 \times 10^{-5}\ \text{atm}^{-1} = 1.1 \times 10^{-5}(\text{N m}^{-2})^{-1}\ (\text{N m}^{-2}/\text{atm})$

$= (1.1 \times 10^{-5}\ \text{N}^{-1}\ \text{m}^2)/1.013 \times 10^5 = 1.1 \times 10^{-10}\ \text{N}^{-1}\ \text{m}^2.$

$\mathscr{M} = 1.748$ [Table 24.6]; $R_0 = 138\ \text{pm} + 181\ \text{pm}$ [Table 23.1] $= 319\ \text{pm}.$

$V_m = M_m/\rho = (74.55\ \text{g mol}^{-1})/(1.984\ \text{g cm}^{-3}) = 37.58\ \text{cm}^3\ \text{mol}^{-1}.$

$$R^*/R_0 = \tfrac{2}{5} + \left\{\frac{(18\pi/5) \times (8.854 \times 10^{-12}\ \text{J}^{-1}\ \text{C}^2\ \text{m}^{-1}) \times (319 \times 10^{-12}\ \text{m}) \times (3.758 \times 10^{-5}\ \text{m}^3\ \text{mol}^{-1})}{(1.1 \times 10^{-10}\ \text{N}^{-1}\ \text{m}^2) \times (6.022 \times 10^{23}\ \text{mol}^{-1}) \times (1.602 \times 10^{-19}\ \text{C})^2 \times 1.748}\right\}$$

$= 0.804.$

$$U_m = -\left\{\frac{(6.022 \times 10^{23}\ \text{mol}^{-1}) \times (1.602 \times 10^{-19}\ \text{C})^2 \times 1.748}{4\pi \times (8.854 \times 10^{-12}\ \text{J}^{-1}\ \text{C}^2\ \text{m}^{-1}) \times (319 \times 10^{-12}\ \text{m})}\right\}$$

$\times \{1 - 0.804\} = -149\ \text{kJ mol}^{-1}.$

Therefore, $\Delta H_m = U_m - 2RT = \underline{-140\,\text{kJ mol}^{-1}}$.

24.31 $U_m = -(N_A e^2 \mathscr{M}/4\pi\epsilon_0 R_0)\{1-(R^*/R_0)\}$ [24.5.7].

$$N_A e^2/4\pi\epsilon_0 = \frac{(6.022\times 10^{23}\,\text{mol}^{-1})\times(1.602\times 10^{-19}\,\text{C})^2}{4\pi\times(8.854\times 10^{-12}\,\text{J}^{-1}\,\text{C}^2\,\text{m}^{-1})}$$

$$= 1.389\ 10^{-4}\,\text{J mol}^{-1}\,\text{m}.$$

$\mathscr{M} = 1.748$ [Table 23.5], $R_0 = 102\,\text{pm} + 133\,\text{pm} = 235\,\text{pm}$.

$$U_m = -\left\{\frac{(1.389\times 10^{-4}\,\text{J mol}^{-1}\,\text{m})\times 1.748}{235\times 10^{-12}\,\text{m}}\right\}\times\left\{1-\left(\frac{29}{235}\right)\right\}$$

$$= \underline{-910\,\text{kJ mol}^{-1}}.$$

24.32 $\mathscr{M} = 1.778$ [Table 24.6], $R_0 = 182\,\text{pm} + 181\,\text{pm} = 363\,\text{pm}$, $R^* = 40\,\text{pm}$.

$$U_m = -\left\{\frac{(1.389\times 10^{-4}\,\text{J mol}^{-1}\,\text{m})\times 1.778}{363\times 10^{-12}\,\text{m}}\right\}\times\left\{1-\frac{40}{363}\right\}$$

$$= \underline{-605\,\text{kJ mol}^{-1}}.$$

24.33 $\xi = -(e^2/6m_e)\langle r^2\rangle$.

$$\langle r^2\rangle = \int_0^\infty \psi^* r^2 \psi\,\text{d}\tau,\ \psi = (1/\pi a_0^3)^{1/2}\exp(-r/a_0)\ [15.1.24].$$

$$\langle r^2\rangle = 4\pi\int_0^\infty \psi^2 r^4\,\text{d}r\ [\text{d}\tau = 4\pi r^2\text{d}r] = (4/a_0^3)\int_0^\infty r^4\,\text{e}^{-2r/a_0}\text{d}r$$

$$= 3a_0^2\left[\int_0^\infty x^n\text{e}^{-ax}\text{d}x = n!/a^{n+1}\right].$$

$$\xi = -\frac{(1.6022\times 10^{-19}\,\text{C})^2\times 3\times(5.2918\times 10^{-11}\,\text{m})^2}{6\times(9.1095\times 10^{-31}\,\text{kg})} = \underline{-3.9456\times 10^{-29}\,\text{C}^2\,\text{m}^2\,\text{kg}^{-1}}.$$

$\kappa = \mathscr{N}\mu_0\xi$ [24.6.4] $= (N/V)\mu_0\xi = (\rho/m_H)\mu_0\xi$.

$\chi = \kappa/(\rho/\rho^\ominus) = (\rho/m_H)\mu_0\xi/(\rho/\text{kg m}^{-3}) = \{\mu_0\xi/(m_H/\text{kg})\}\text{m}^{-3}$

$$= -\frac{(4\pi\times 10^{-7}\,\text{J s}^2\,\text{C}^{-2}\,\text{m}^{-1})\times(3.9456\times 10^{-29}\,\text{C}^2\,\text{m}^2\,\text{kg}^{-1})\times\text{m}^{-3}}{1.008\times(1.6605\times 10^{-27})}$$

$$= \underline{-2.962\times 10^{-8}}.$$

24.34 $\chi = 6.3001 \times 10^{-3} S(S+1)/M_r(T/\text{K})$ [*Example* 24.6]

$= 6.3001 \times 10^{-3} \times \frac{3}{4}/1.008 \times 298.15 = \underline{1.572 \times 10^{-5}}.$

$\chi_{\text{total}} = \chi_{\text{para}} + \chi_{\text{dia}} = 1.572 \times 10^{-5} + (-2.9622 \times 10^{-8})$ [Problem 24.35]

$= \underline{1.569 \times 10^{-5}}.$

24.35 Only the upper level is magnetic, and has a magnetic moment $2\mu_B$. Let the proportion of molecules in the upper level be P, then

$P = e^{-hc\tilde{\nu}/kT}/\{1 + e^{-hc\tilde{\nu}/kT}\}$ [Problem 21.14]

with $\tilde{\nu} = 121.1\ \text{cm}^{-1}$. Adapt eqn (24.6.7) by replacing $S(S+1)\mu_B^2$ by $(4\mu_B)^2$ and the weighting factor P. Hence, from *Example* 24.6,

$\chi = (6.3001 \times 10^{-3}) \times 4P/M_r(T/\text{K}) = 8.40 \times 10^{-4} P/(T/\text{K})$ $[M_r = 30.01]$.

Since $hc\tilde{\nu}/k = (1.4388\ \text{cm K}) \times (121.1\ \text{cm}^{-1}) = 174.2\ \text{K}$ [endpaper 1],

$$\chi = \frac{\{8.40 \times 10^{-4}/(T/\text{K})\}e^{-174.2/(T/\text{K})}}{1 + e^{-174.2/(T/\text{K})}}.$$

This function is plotted in Fig. 24.8. At 25 °C, $\underline{\chi = 1.0 \times 10^{-6}}$.

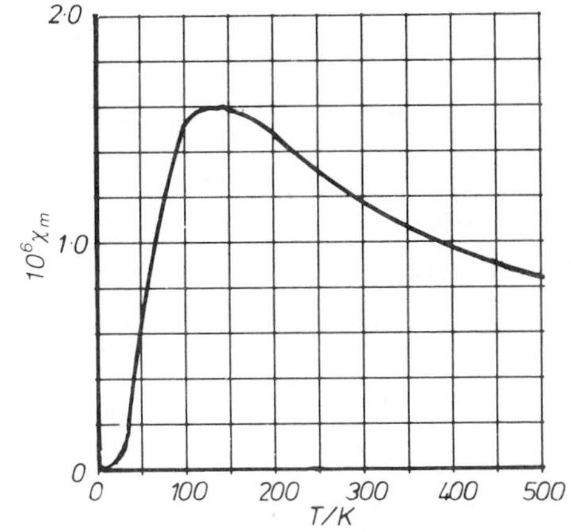

Fig 24.8

25. Macromolecules

A25.1 $\Pi/c = (RT/M_m)[1 + (Bc/M_m)]$ [25.1.2]

$c/\mathrm{g\,dm^{-3}}$	$\Pi c^{-1}/\mathrm{Pa\,g^{-1}\,dm^3}$	$\Delta(\Pi/c)/\Delta c$	$\Pi c^{-1} - 4.64c$
1.21	111		105
		4.64	
2.72	118		105
		4.66	
5.08	129		105
		4.61	
6.60	136		105
		avg = 4.64	avg = 105

$RTM_m^{-1} = 105\ \mathrm{Pa\,g^{-1}\,dm^3}$ [the intercept]

$M_m = (8.31\ \mathrm{J\,K^{-1}\,mol^{-1}})(293\ \mathrm{K})(1000\ \mathrm{dm^3\,m^{-3}})(105\ \mathrm{Pa\,g^{-1}\,dm^3})^{-1}$
$= \underline{2.32 \times 10^4\ \mathrm{g\,mol^{-1}}}.$

$RTBM_m^{-2} = 4.64\ \mathrm{Pa\,g^{-2}\,dm^6}$ [the slope of the fitted straight line]

$B = (4.64\ \mathrm{Pa\,g^{-2}\,dm^6})(2.32 \times 10^4\ \mathrm{g\,mol^{-1}})^2(8.31\ \mathrm{J\,K^{-1}\,mol^{-1}})^{-1}$
$\times (293\ \mathrm{K})^{-1}(1000\ \mathrm{dm^3\,m^{-3}})^{-1} = \underline{1.03 \times 10^3\ \mathrm{dm^3\,mol^{-1}}}.$

A25.2 Let u represent the moles of Cl^- in the first compartment.

$(0.1 + u)(u) = [(0.06 - u)/2]^2$ [Section 25.1(c), take positive root]

$u = 6.7 \times 10^{-3}$ mol: concentration $= \underline{6.7 \times 10^{-3}\ \mathrm{mol\,dm^{-3}}}.$

A25.3 Let u represent the moles of Na^+ which leave the first compartment.

$(0.030 + 0.010 - u)(0.010 - u) = (0.005 + u)^2$ [Section 25.1(c)]

$u = 6.25 \times 10^{-3}$ mol; $(Na^+)_1 = 0.034\ \mathrm{mol\,dm^{-3}}$.

$(Na^+)_2 = 0.011\ \mathrm{mol\,dm^{-3}}$.

Potential $= (RT/F)\ln(c_1/c_2) = (8.31\ \mathrm{J\,K^{-1}\,mol^{-1}})(300\ \mathrm{K})(9.65 \times 10^4\ \mathrm{C\,mol^{-1}})^{-1}$
$\times \ln(0.034/0.011) = \underline{29\ \mathrm{mV}}.$ [11.4.6]

A25.4 $\quad d(\ln c)/d(r^2) = M_m\omega^2(1-\rho\bar{v})/(2RT)$ [25.1.18]

$M_m = (729\ \text{cm}^{-2})(60\ \text{s/min})^2(2)(8.31\ \text{J mol}^{-1}\text{K}^{-1})(300\ \text{K})$

$\quad \times (5.00 \times 10^4\ \text{rev/min})^{-2}(2\pi)^{-2}[1-(0.997\ \text{g cm}^{-3})(0.61\ \text{cm}^3\text{g}^{-1})]^{-1}$

$\quad = \underline{3.39 \times 10^6\ \text{g mol}^{-1}}.$

A25.5 $\quad R_{rms} = N^{\frac{1}{2}}1$ [25.2.2] $= (700)^{\frac{1}{2}}(0.90\ \text{nm}) = \underline{23.8\ \text{nm}}.$

A25.6 $\quad R_g = N^{\frac{1}{2}}l(3^{-\frac{1}{2}})$ [25.2.4]

$N^{\frac{1}{2}} = (7.3 \times 10^{-9}\ \text{m})(1.732)(154 \times 10^{-12}\ \text{m})^{-1}; \underline{N = 6.74 \times 10^3}.$

A25.7 $\quad [\eta] = \lim[(\eta/\eta^*)-1]c^{-1}$ [25.1.22]

$c/\text{g dm}^{-3}$	$[(\eta/\eta^*)-1]c^{-1}/\text{dm}^3\text{g}^{-1}$
1.32	0.0731
2.89	0.0755
5.73	0.0771
9.17	0.0825

Extrapolation to $c = 0$ gives: $[\eta] = \underline{0.0715\ \text{dm}^3\text{g}^{-1}}.$

[Fig. A25.1]

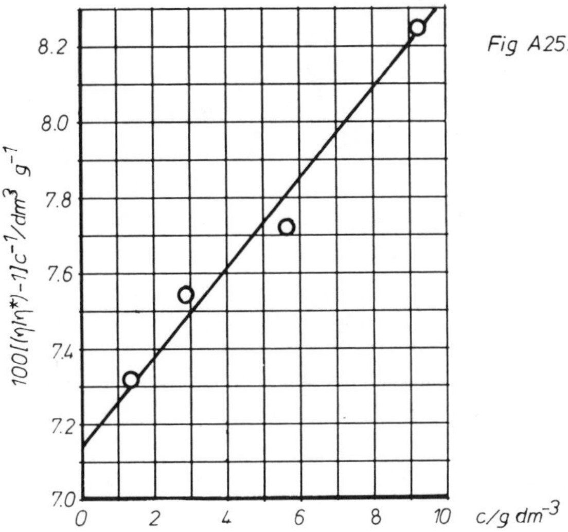

Fig A25.1

A25.8 $S = (dr/dt)/r\omega^2 = (d\ln r/dt)\omega^{-2}$ [25.1.14]

t/min	r/cm	ln(r/cm)
15.5	5.05	1.619
29.1	5.09	1.627
36.4	5.12	1.633
58.2	5.19	1.647

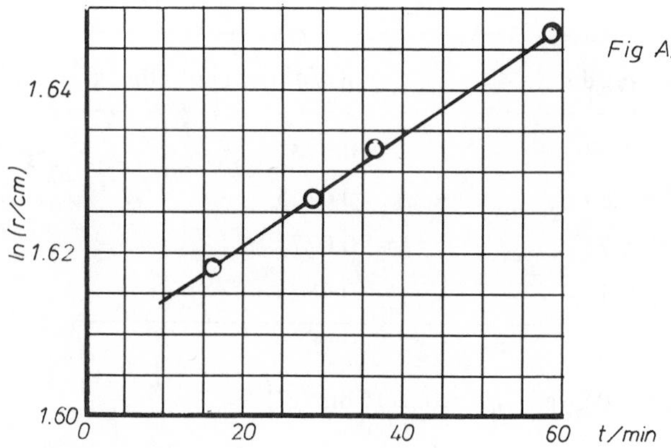

Fig A25.2

From the graph in Fig. A25.2,

$d(\ln r)/dt = 6.60 \times 10^{-4}\,\mathrm{min}^{-1}$,

$S = (6.60 \times 10^{-4}\,\mathrm{min}^{-1})(4.50 \times 10^4\,\mathrm{rev/min})^{-2}(2 \times 3.14\,\mathrm{rad/rev})^{-2}(60\,\mathrm{s/min})$

$= \underline{4.81 \times 10^{-13}\,\mathrm{s}}$.

A25.9 $M_m = SRT/bD$ [25.1.17]

$= (3.20 \times 10^{-13}\,\mathrm{s})(8.31\,\mathrm{J\,mol^{-1}\,K^{-1}})(293\,\mathrm{K})$

$\times\ [1 - (0.656\,\mathrm{cm^3\,g^{-1}})(1.06\,\mathrm{g\,cm^{-3}})]^{-1}(8.30 \times 10^{-11}\,\mathrm{m^2\,s^{-1}})]^{-1}$

$= \underline{3.1 \times 10^4\,\mathrm{g\,mol^{-1}}}$.

A25.10 (a) Number average RMM $= 100[(70/1.50 \times 10^4) + (30/3.00 \times 10^4)]^{-1}$

$= \underline{1.76 \times 10^4}$ [25.1.7].

(b) Mass average RMM $= 0.70(1.50 \times 10^4) + 0.30(3.00 \times 10^4) = \underline{1.95 \times 10^4}$ [25.1.23].

25.1 $\Pi/c_p = (RT/M_m)\{1 + (B/M_m)c_p\}$ [25.1.2].

$h/c_p = (RT/\rho g M_m) + (BRT/\rho g M_m^2)c_p$ [$\Pi = \rho g h$].

Plot h/c_p against c_p; obtain $RT/\rho g M_m$ from the intercept at $c_p = 0$.

Draw up the following Table:

c_p/mg cm^{-3}	3.2	4.8	5.7	6.88	7.94
h/cm	3.11	6.22	8.40	11.73	14.90
(h/c_p)/mg cm^{-4}	0.97	1.30	1.47	1.70	1.90

These points are plotted in Fig. 25.1.

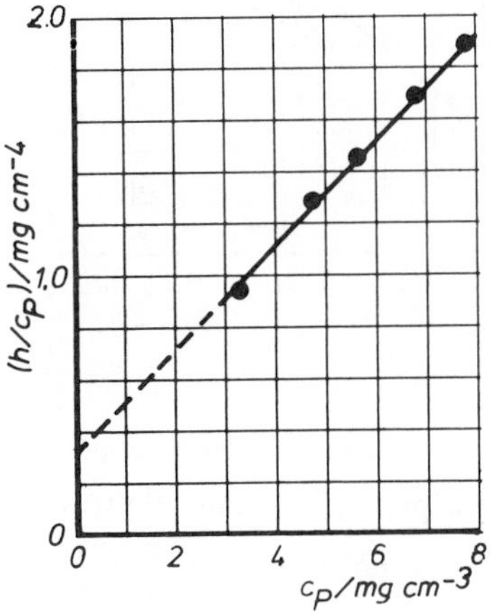

Fig 25.1

The intercept is at 0.33, and so $RT/\rho g M_m = 0.331\ \mathrm{cm^4\,mg^{-1}}$.

Therefore $M_m = RT/\rho g(\text{intercept})$

$$= \frac{(8.3144\ \mathrm{J\,K^{-1}\,mol^{-1}}) \times (298.15\ \mathrm{K})}{(0.867\ \mathrm{g\,cm^{-3}}) \times (9.81\ \mathrm{m\,s^{-2}}) \times (0.331\ \mathrm{cm^4\,mg^{-1}})}$$

$$= (880.5\ \mathrm{J\,mol^{-1}})/(\mathrm{g\,mg^{-1}\,m\,cm\,s^{-2}}) = 88.0\ \mathrm{kg\,mol^{-1}}.$$

Hence, $M_m = \underline{88\,000\ \mathrm{g\,mol^{-1}}}$ and $M_r = \underline{88\,000.}$

25.2 Use the same procedure as in Problem 25.1. Draw up the following Table:

$c_p/(g/100\ \text{cm}^3)$	0.200	0.400	0.600	0.800	1.00
h/cm	0.48	1.12	1.86	2.76	3.88
$(h/c_p)/(100\ \text{cm}^4\ \text{g}^{-1})$	2.4	2.80	3.10	3.45	3.88

These points are plotted in Fig. 25.2

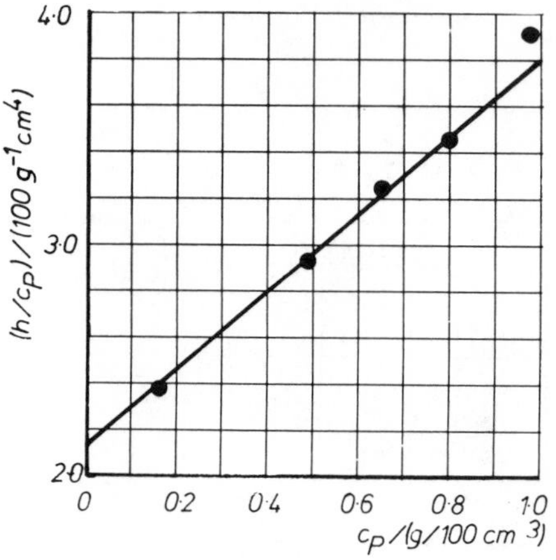

Fig 25.2

The intercept is at $(h/c_p)/(100\ \text{cm}^4\ \text{g}^{-1}) = 2.15$, corresponding to $h/c_p = 215\ \text{cm}^4\ \text{g}^{-1}$; consequently $M_m = RT/\rho g(\text{intercept}) = (2479\ \text{J mol}^{-1})/(0.798\ \text{g cm}^{-3})$

$$\times (9.81\ \text{m s}^{-2}) \times (215\ \text{cm}^4\ \text{g}^{-1})$$

$$= (1.47\ \text{J mol}^{-1})/(\text{m cm s}^{-2}) = 147\ \text{kg mol}^{-1}.$$

Therefore $\underline{M_m = 147\,000\ \text{g mol}^{-1}}$, $\underline{M_r = 147\,000.}$

The slope of the line is 1.63, and so

$$BRT/\rho g M_m^2 = 1.63 \times (100\ \text{cm}^4\ \text{g}^{-1})/(\text{g}\ 10^{-2}\ \text{cm}^{-3}) = 1.63 \times 10^4\ \text{cm}^7\ \text{g}^{-2}.$$

$$B = \frac{(1.63 \times 10^4\ \text{cm}^7\ \text{g}^{-2}) \times (0.798\ \text{g cm}^{-3}) \times (9.81\ \text{m s}^{-1}) \times (147\ \text{kg mol}^{-1})^2}{(8.3144\ \text{J K}^{-1}\ \text{mol}^{-1}) \times (298.15\ \text{K})}$$

$$= 1.11 \times 10^6\ (\text{cm}^4\ \text{g}^{-1}\ \text{m s}^{-2}\ \text{kg}^2\ \text{mol}^{-2})/(\text{kg m}^2\ \text{s}^{-2}\ \text{mol}^{-1})$$

$$= \underline{11\ \text{m}^3\ \text{mol}^{-1}}.$$

25.3 $\langle M_r\rangle_N = (1/N)(N_1 M_{r1} + N_2 M_{r2})$ [25.1.7] $= \frac{1}{2}(M_{r1} + M_{r2}) = \underline{70\,000.}$

$$\langle M_r \rangle_M = \frac{M_1 M_{r1} + M_2 M_{r2}}{M_1 + M_2} \; [25.1.23] = \frac{n_1 M_{m1} M_{r1} + n_2 M_{m2} M_{r2}}{n_1 M_{m1} + n_2 M_{m2}}$$

$$= \frac{M_{r1}^2 + M_{r2}^2}{M_{r1} + M_{r2}} \; [n_1 = n_2] = 70\,914 \approx \underline{71\,000.}$$

25.4 $dN_i \propto \exp\{-(M_{ri} - M_r)^2/2\Gamma\}dM_{ri}$.

Since $dN_i = K \int_0^\infty \exp\{-(M_{ri} - M_r)^2/2\Gamma\}dM_{ri} = N$,

put $x = (M_{ri} - M_r)/\sqrt{(2\Gamma)}$, so that $\sqrt{(2\Gamma)}dx = dM_{ri}$ and

$$N = K\sqrt{(2\Gamma)} \int_a^\infty e^{-x^2} \, dx \; [a = -M_r/\sqrt{(2\Gamma)}] \approx K\sqrt{(2\Gamma)} \int_0^\infty e^{-x^2} \, dx \; [a \approx 0]$$

$$= \{K\sqrt{(2\Gamma)}\}\tfrac{1}{2}\sqrt{\pi}; \text{ hence } K = (2/\Gamma\pi)^{\frac{1}{2}} N.$$

$$\langle M_r \rangle_N = (2/\Gamma\pi)^{\frac{1}{2}} \int_0^\infty M_{ri} \exp\{-(M_{ri} - M_r)^2/2\Gamma\}dM_{ri} \; [25.1.7, \text{continuous distribution}]$$

$$= (2/\Gamma\pi)^{\frac{1}{2}} (2\Gamma)^{\frac{1}{2}} (2\Gamma)^{\frac{1}{2}} \int_0^\infty dx \, (x + M_r/\sqrt{(2\Gamma)})e^{-x^2} \; [a \approx 0]$$

$$= (8\Gamma/\pi)^{\frac{1}{2}} \{\tfrac{1}{2} + (\pi/8\Gamma)^{\frac{1}{2}} M_r\} = \underline{M_r + (2\Gamma/\pi)^{\frac{1}{2}}}.$$

25.5 Centers cannot approach more closely than $2a$, hence the excluded volume is $\frac{4}{3}\pi(2a)^3 = 8(\frac{4}{3}\pi a^3) = 8v_{mol}$, where v_{mol} is the molecular volume.
Since $B = \frac{1}{2}N_A v_p$ [25.1.6],
$B(\text{b.s.v.}) = \frac{1}{2}N_A v_p = 4N_A v_{mol} = (16/3)\pi a^3 N_A$
$= (16/3)\pi \times (6.022 \times 10^{23} \text{ mol}^{-1}) \times (14.0 \times 10^{-9} \text{ m})^3 = \underline{28 \text{ m}^3 \text{ mol}^{-1}}$,
$B(\text{hem.}) = (16\pi/3) \times (6.022 \times 10^{23} \text{ mol}^{-1}) \times (3.2 \times 10^{-9} \text{ m})^3 = \underline{0.33 \text{ m}^3 \text{ mol}^{-1}}$.

25.6 $\Pi° = RT[P]$; $\Pi = RT[P] + BRT[P]^2$ [25.1.1].
$(\Pi - \Pi°)/\Pi° = BRT[P]^2/RT[P] = B[P]$.
$[P] = (1.0 \text{ g})/(100 \text{ cm}^3) \times M_m = (10^4 \text{ g})/(M_m \text{ m}^3)$.
For b.s.v., $[P] = (10^4 \text{ g})/(1.07 \times 10^7 \text{ g mol}^{-1} \text{ m}^3) = 9.35 \times 10^{-4} \text{ mol m}^{-3}$, and so $(\Pi - \Pi°)/\Pi° = (28 \text{ m}^3 \text{ mol}^{-1}) \times (9.35 \times 10^{-4} \text{ mol m}^{-3}) = 2.6 \times 10^{-2}$, or 2.6 percent. For hemoglobin, $[P] = (10^4 \text{ g})/(6.65 \times 10^4 \text{ g mol}^{-1} \text{ m}^3) = 0.15 \text{ mol m}^{-3}$, and so $(\Pi - \Pi°)/\Pi° = (0.15 \text{ mol m}^{-3}) \times (0.33 \text{ m}^3 \text{ mol}^{-1}) = 5.0 \times 10^{-2}$, 50 percent.

25.7 $B = \frac{1}{2}N_A v_p$ [25.1.6] $= 4N_A v_{mol}$ [Problem 25.5]

$= 4(4\pi/3)N_A R_e^3 = (16\pi/3)\gamma^3 N_A R_g^3.$

$R_g = N^{\frac{1}{2}}l/\sqrt{6}$ [25.2.3]; $B_{free} = (16\pi/3 \times 6^{3/2})\gamma^3 l^3 N^{3/2} N_A$

$= \underline{(4.22 \times 10^{23}\ \text{mol}^{-1})} \times \underline{(l\sqrt{N})^3}.$

For tetrahedral angles, multiply l by $\sqrt{2}$ [25.2.4], hence

$B_{tetr.} = (4.22 \times 10^{23}\ \text{mol}^{-1}) \times (l\sqrt{(2N)})^3 = \underline{(1.19 \times 10^{24}\ \text{mol}^{-1}) \times (l\sqrt{N})^3}.$

When $l = 154$ pm, $N = 4000$,

(a) $B_{free} = (4.22 \times 10^{23}\ \text{mol}^{-1}) \times (1.54 \times 10^{-10}\ \text{m})^3 \times (4000)^{3/2} = \underline{0.39\ \text{m}^3\ \text{mol}^{-1}}.$

(b) $B_{tetr.} = (1.19 \times 10^{23}\ \text{mol}^{-1}) \times (1.54 \times 10^{-10}\ \text{m})^3 \times (4000)^{3/2} = \underline{0.11\ \text{m}^3\ \text{mol}^{-1}}.$

25.8 For a chain with $M_r = 56\,000$, $N = M_r/14$ [$M_r(\text{CH}_2) = 14$].

$B = (1.19 \times 10^{24}\ \text{mol}^{-1}) \times (l\sqrt{N})^3$ [Problem 25.7, tetrahedral]

$= (1.19 \times 10^{24}\ \text{mol}^{-1}) \times (l\sqrt{M_r})^3/14^{3/2} = (2.27 \times 10^{22}\ \text{mol}^{-1}) \times (l\sqrt{M_r})^3.$

For $l = 154$ pm, $M_r = 56\,000$.

$B = (2.27 \times 10^{22}\ \text{mol}^{-1}) \times (1.54 \times 10^{-10}\ \text{m})^3 \times (56\,000)^{3/2} = \underline{1.10\ \text{m}^3\ \text{mol}^{-1}}.$

25.9 (a) $[\text{Na}^+]_L[\text{Cl}^-]_L = [\text{Na}^+]_R[\text{Cl}^-]_R$ [25.1.9],

(b) $[\text{Na}^+]_L = [\text{Cl}^-]_L + \nu[\text{P}]$ [25.1.10],

(c) $[\text{Na}^+]_R = [\text{Cl}^-]_R$ [25.1.10].

(d) $[\text{Na}^+]_L(-\nu[\text{P}] + [\text{Na}^+]_L) = [\text{Na}^+]_R^2$ [from a, b, c],

(e) $[\text{Cl}^-]_L([\text{Cl}^-]_L + \nu[\text{P}]) = [\text{Cl}^-]_R^2$ [from a, b, c].

$[\text{Na}^+]_R^2 - [\text{Na}^+]_L^2 = -\nu[\text{P}]\ [\text{Na}^+]_L$ [rearrange d],

$[\text{Na}^+]_R - [\text{Na}^+]_L = -\nu[\text{P}]\,[\text{Na}^+]_L/([\text{Na}^+]_R + [\text{Na}^+]_L)$

$= \underline{-\nu[\text{P}]\ [\text{Na}^+]_L/(2[\text{Cl}^-] + \nu\text{P})}$ [definition of $[\text{Cl}^-]$].

$[\text{Cl}^-]_R^2 - [\text{Cl}^-]_L^2 = \nu[\text{P}]\,[\text{Cl}^-]_L$ [rearrange e].

$[\text{Cl}^-]_R - [\text{Cl}^-]_L = \nu[\text{P}]\,[\text{Cl}^-]_L/([\text{Cl}^-]_R + [\text{Cl}^-]_L) = \underline{\nu[\text{P}]\,[\text{Cl}^-]_L/2[\text{Cl}^-]}.$

25.10

Left	Right
$\text{P}^{\nu-}$	0
M^+	M^+
X^{2-}	X^{2-}

(a) $[\text{M}^+]_L^2\,[\text{X}^{2-}]_L = [\text{M}^+]_R^2\,[\text{X}^{2-}]_R$ [equilibrium, $\gamma \approx 1$],

(b) $[M^+]_L = 2[X^{2-}]_L + \nu[P]$ [electrical neutrality on right].

(c) $[M^+]_R = 2[X^{2-}]_R$ [electrical neutrality on right].

Proceed as in Problem 25.9:

$$\left.\begin{aligned}&[M^+]_L^2\left(\tfrac{1}{2}[M^+]_L - \tfrac{1}{2}\nu[P]\right) = \tfrac{1}{2}[M^+]_R^3\\ &[X^{2-}]_L\left(2[X^{2-}]_L + \nu[P]\right)^2 = 4[X^{2-}]_R^3.\end{aligned}\right\}$$

$$\text{or}\ \left.\begin{aligned}&[M^+]_L^3 - \nu[M^+]_L^2[P] = [M^+]_R^3\\ &4[X^{2-}]_L^3 + 4\nu[X^{2-}]_L^2[P] + \nu^2[P]^2[X^{2-}]_L = 4[X^{2-}]_R^3.\end{aligned}\right\}$$

$$\left.\begin{aligned}&[M^+]_R^3 - [M^+]_L^3 = -\nu[M^+]_L^2[P]\\ &[X^{2-}]_R^3 - [X^{2-}]_L^3 = \nu[X^{2-}]_L^2[P] + \tfrac{1}{4}\nu^2[X^{2-}]_L[P]^2.\end{aligned}\right\}$$

$$[M^+]_R^3 - [M^+]_L^3 = ([M^+]_R - [M^+]_L)([M^+]_R^2 + [M^+]_R[M^+]_L + [M^+]_L^2).$$

Therefore, $[M^+]_R - [M^+]_L = \underline{-\nu[M^+]_L^2[P]/([M^+]_R^2 + [M^+]_R[M^+]_L + [M^+]_L^2)}$.

$$[X^{2-}]_R - [X^{2-}]_L = \frac{\nu[X^{2-}]_L[P]([X^{2-}]_L + \tfrac{1}{4}\nu[P])}{[X^{2-}]_R^2 + [X^{2-}]_R[X^{2-}]_L + [X^{2-}]_L^2}.$$

Note that $[M^+]_R^2 + [M^+]_R[M^+]_L + [M^+]_L^2 = \tfrac{1}{4}([M^+]_R - [M^+]_L)^2 + \tfrac{3}{4}([M^+]_R + [M^+]_L)^2$

$$= \tfrac{1}{4}([M^+]_R - [M^+]_L)^2 + \tfrac{3}{4}(2[X^{2-}] + \nu[P])^2$$

and $[X^{2-}]_R^2 + [X^{2-}]_R[X^{2-}]_L + [X^{2-}]_L^2 = \tfrac{1}{4}([X^{2-}]_R - [X^{2-}]_L)^2 + \tfrac{3}{4}([X^{2-}]_R + [X^{2-}]_L)^2$

$$= \tfrac{1}{4}([X^{2-}]_R - [X^{2-}]_L)^2 + 3[X^{2-}]^2$$

where $[X^{-2}] = \tfrac{1}{2}([X^{2-}]_R + [X^{2-}]_L)$, and so the expressions may be simplified further.

25.11 $[Na^+]_R^2 - [Na^+]_L^2 = -\nu[P][Na^+]_L$ [Problem 25.9]

$[Na^+]_L^2 - \nu[P][Na^+]_L - [Na^+]_R^2 = 0$,

$[Na^+]_L = \tfrac{1}{2}\{\nu[P] \pm \sqrt{[\nu^2[P]^2 + 4[Na^+]_R^2]}\}$,

$$[Na^+]_L/[Na^+]_R = (\nu[P]/2[Na^+]_R) \pm \{1 + (\nu[P]/2[Na^+]_R)^2\}^{\frac{1}{2}}$$

$$= x \pm (1 + x^2)^{\frac{1}{2}} \rightarrow \underline{x + (1 + x^2)^{\frac{1}{2}}}\ [\text{ratio} = 1 \text{ at } x = 0]$$

This function is plotted in Fig. 25.3.

25.12 $[Na^+]_L/[Na^+]_R = x + (1 + x^2)^{\frac{1}{2}}$ [Problem 25.11], $x = \nu[P]/2[Na^+]_R$

$[P] = (1\ g)/(100\ cm^3) \times (100\,000\ g\ mol^{-1}) = 10^{-7}\ mol\ cm^{-3}$.

$\nu[P]/2[Na^+]_R = 20 \times (10^{-7}\ mol\ cm^{-3})/2 \times (10^{-3}\ mol\ dm^{-3}) = 1.00$.

Therefore $[Na^+]_L/[Na^+]_R = 1 + \sqrt{2} = 2.41$, and $[Na^+]_L = \underline{0.002\,41\ mol\ dm^{-3}}$.

25.13 The equilibrium condition becomes

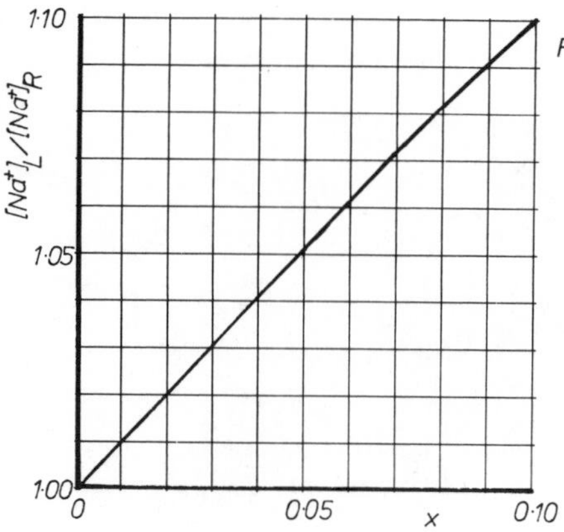

Fig 25.3

$\gamma_L^2 [Na^+]_L ([Na^+]_L - \nu[P]) = \gamma_R^2 [Na^+]_R^2,$

$[Na^+]_L^2 - \nu[P][Na^+]_L - (\gamma_R/\gamma_L)^2 [Na^+]_R = 0,$

$[Na^+]_L = \frac{1}{2}\{\nu[P] + \sqrt{[\nu^2[P]^2 + 4(\gamma_R/\gamma_L)^2 [Na^+]_R^2]}\},$

$[Na^+]_L/[Na^+]_R = x + [(\gamma_R/\gamma_L)^2 + x^2]^{\frac{1}{2}}, x = \nu[P]/2[Na^+]_R.$

$\gamma_R/\gamma_L = 10^{-A\sqrt{I_R}}/10^{-A\sqrt{I_L}}$ [11.2.11] $= 10^{-A([Na^+]_R^{\frac{1}{2}} - [Na^+]_L^{\frac{1}{2}})},$

and so $(\gamma_R/\gamma_L)^2 = 10^{-2A\delta}, \delta = [Na^+]_R^{\frac{1}{2}} - [Na^+]_L^{\frac{1}{2}}.$

For the preceding problem, $[Na^+]_R^{\frac{1}{2}} = \sqrt{10^{-3}} = 0.032$, $[Na^+]_L^{\frac{1}{2}} \approx 0.049$

and since $A \approx 0.509$ [11.2.11], $(\gamma_R/\gamma_L)^2 \approx 10^{0.017} = 1.041$.

Therefore $[Na^+]_L/[Na^+]_R \approx x + [1.041 + x^2]^{\frac{1}{2}} = 1.00 + \sqrt{2.041} = 2.43$,

and so $[Na^+]_L \approx 0.002\,43$ mol dm^{-3} in place of $0.002\,41$ mol dm^{-3}.

25.14 $\Pi = RT[P]\{1 + \nu^2[P]/(4[Cl^-] + \nu[P])\}$ [25.1.12]

$= RT[P]\{1 + \nu^2[P]/4[Cl^-](1 + \nu[P]/4[Cl^-])\}$

$\approx RT[P]\{1 + (\nu^2[P]/4[Cl^-]) - (\nu^3[P]^2/16[Cl^-]^2) + \ldots\}$

$[(1+x)^{-1} = 1 - x + \ldots]$

Therefore $B \approx \nu^2/4[Cl^-] = 400/4 \times (0.02$ mol dm$^{-3}) = \underline{5\text{ m}^3\text{ mol}^{-1}}$.

The excluded volume effect gives $B = \frac{1}{2}N_A v_p$ [25.1.6], and typical values [Problem 25.5] are larger than 5 m^3 mol^{-1}.

25.15 $F = m\omega^2 r$ [classical physics] $= 4\pi^2\nu^2 mr$ [$\omega = 2\pi\nu$] $= ma$ [Newton].

Therefore, a [acceleration] $= 4\pi^2\nu^2 r = 4\pi^2([8 \times 10^4/60]\text{ s}^{-1})^2 \times (6.0 \times 10^{-2}\text{ m})$

$= 4.21 \times 10^6\text{ m s}^{-2}.$

Since $g = 9.81$ m s^{-2}, $a = \underline{4.3 \times 10^5 g}$.

25.16 $\ln\{c(r_1)/c(r_2)\} = -\frac{1}{2}mb\omega^2(r_1^2 - r_2^2)/kT$ [25.1.18] $= 2\pi^2 mb\nu^2(r_2^2 - r_1^2)/kT$,

$$\nu^2 = kT\ln(c_1/c_2)/2\pi^2 mb(r_2^2 - r_1^2)$$

$$= RT\ln(c_1/c_2)/2\pi^2 M_m b(r_2^2 - r_1^2) \quad [m = M_m/N_A,\ N_A k = R]$$

$$= \frac{(2.48 \times 10^3\,\mathrm{J\,mol^{-1}})\ln 5}{2\pi^2 \times (10^5\,\mathrm{g\,mol^{-1}}) \times (1 - 0.75) \times (7^2 - 5^2) \times 10^{-4}\,\mathrm{m^2}} = 3370\,\mathrm{Hz^2}.$$

Therefore, $\nu = 58\,\mathrm{Hz} \mathrel{\hat{=}} \underline{3500\,\mathrm{r.p.m.}}$

25.17 Draw up the following Table

r/cm	5.0	5.1	5.2	5.3	5.4
$c/\mathrm{g\,dm^{-3}}$	0.536	0.284	0.148	0.077	0.039
$r^2/\mathrm{cm^2}$	25.0	26.0	27.0	28.1	29.2
$\ln(c/\mathrm{g\,dm^{-3}})$	−0.624	−1.259	−1.911	−2.564	−3.244

These points are plotted in Fig. 25.4. The slope is −0.62.

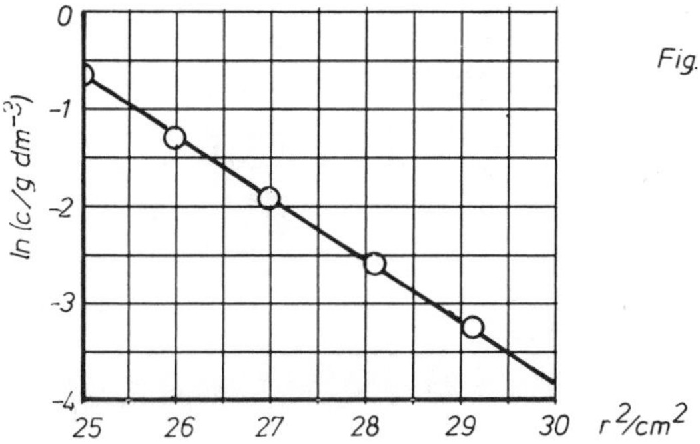

Fig. 25.4

It follows that $M_m(1 - \rho v)\omega^2/2RT = -0.62\,\mathrm{cm^{-2}} = -0.62 \times 10^4\,\mathrm{m^{-2}}$

$$M_m = \frac{(-0.62 \times 10^4\,\mathrm{m^{-2}}) \times 2 \times (2.48 \times 10^3\,\mathrm{J\,mol^{-1}})}{\{1 - (1.001\,\mathrm{g\,cm^{-3}}) \times (1.112\,\mathrm{cm^3\,g^{-1}})\} \times (2\pi \times 322\,\mathrm{s^{-1}})^2} = 66.4\,\mathrm{kg\,mol^{-1}}.$$

$= 66400\,\mathrm{g\,mol^{-1}}$. Therefore, $\underline{M_r = 66\,400.}$

25.18 $M_m = SRT/bD$ [25.1.17], $b = 1 - v_s\rho$.

$b = 1 - (0.998 \times 0.75) = 0.252.$

$$M_{\rm m} = \frac{(4.5 \times 10^{-13}\,{\rm s}) \times (8.3144 \times 293.15\,{\rm J\,mol^{-1}})}{0.252 \times (6.3 \times 10^{-11}\,{\rm m^2\,s^{-1}})} = \underline{69.1\,{\rm kg\,mol^{-1}}}.$$

Therefore $M_{\rm m} = \underline{69\,100\,{\rm g\,mol^{-1}}}$, $M_{\rm r} = \underline{69\,100.}$

25.19 $f = kT/D$ [25.1.16] $= 6\pi a\eta$ [Box 25.1].

$$a = kT/6\pi\eta D = \frac{(1.3807 \times 10^{-23}\,{\rm J\,K^{-1}}) \times (293.15\,{\rm K})}{6\pi \times (1.00 \times 10^{-3}\,{\rm kg\,m^{-1}\,s^{-1}}) \times (6.3 \times 10^{-11}\,{\rm m^2\,s^{-1}})} = 3.4 \times 10^{-9}\,{\rm m}.$$

Therefore, $a = \underline{3.4\,{\rm nm}}.$

25.20 $M_{\rm m} = SRT/bD$ [25.1.17], $b = 1 - v_{\rm s}\rho$.

$b = 1 - 1.0023 \times 0.734 = 0.264.$

$$M_{\rm m} = \frac{(5.01 \times 10^{-13}\,{\rm s}) \times (293.15\,{\rm K}) \times (8.314\,{\rm J\,K^{-1}\,mol^{-1}})}{0.264 \times (6.97 \times 10^{-11}\,{\rm m^2\,s^{-1}})} = 66.3\,{\rm kg\,mol^{-1}}.$$

$f = kT/D$ [25.1.16] $= (1.381 \times 10^{-23} \times 293.15\,{\rm kg\,m^2\,s^{-2}})/(6.97 \times 10^{-11}\,{\rm m^2\,s^{-1}})$
$= 5.81 \times 10^{-11}\,{\rm kg\,s^{-1}}.$

$V_{\rm m} = v_{\rm s}M_{\rm m} = (0.734\,{\rm cm^3\,g^{-1}}) \times (66.3 \times 10^3\,{\rm g\,mol^{-1}}) = 4.87 \times 10^4\,{\rm cm^3\,mol^{-1}}$
$= 4.87 \times 10^{-2}\,{\rm m^3\,mol^{-1}} \approx (4\pi/3)N_{\rm A}c^3.$

$c \approx (3V_{\rm m}/4\pi N_{\rm A})^{1/3} = \{3 \times (4.87 \times 10^{-2}\,{\rm m^3\,mol^{-1}})/4\pi \times (6.022 \times 10^{23}\,{\rm mol^{-1}})\}^{1/3}$
$\approx 2.68 \times 10^{-9}\,{\rm m}.$

$f_{\rm 0} = 6\pi a\eta$ [Box 25.1] $= 6\pi \times (2.68 \times 10^{-9}\,{\rm m}) \times (1.00 \times 10^{-3}\,{\rm kg\,m^{-1}\,s^{-1}})$
$= 5.05 \times 10^{-11}\,{\rm kg\,s^{-1}}.$

$f/f_{\rm 0} = 1.15 \mathrel{\hat{=}} a/b \approx 3.5$ [Box 25.1].

$v_{\rm mol} = (4\pi/3)c^3, c = (ab^2)^{1/3}$ [Box 25.1]

Therefore $ab^2 = (2.68 \times 10^{-9}\,{\rm m})^3 = 1.93 \times 10^{-26}\,{\rm m^3}$, and as $a \approx 3.5\,b$,

$\underline{b \approx 1.8\,{\rm nm}, a \approx 6.2\,{\rm nm}}.$

25.21 Draw up the following Table:

t/s	0	300	600	900	1200	1500	1800
r/cm	6.127	6.153	6.179	6.206	6.232	6.258	6.284
$10^5 s$/cm s^{-1}	–	8.67	8.67	9.00	8.67	8.67	8.67

Average drift speed $s = 8.67 \times 10^{-5}\,\text{cm s}^{-1}$.

$S = s/r\omega^2$ [25.1.14] $= (8.67 \times 10^{-5}\,\text{cm s}^{-1})/(6.127\,\text{cm}) \times (2\pi \times 50\,000/60\,\text{s}^{-1})^2$

$= \underline{5.16 \times 10^{-13}\,\text{s}}$.

$b = 1 - (0.728\,\text{cm}^3\,\text{g}^{-1}) \times (0.9981\,\text{g cm}^{-3}) = 0.273$.

$$M_{\text{m}} = SRT/bD \;[25.1.17] = \frac{(5.16 \times 10^{-13}\,\text{s}) \times (8.3144\,\text{J K}^{-1}\,\text{mol}^{-1}) \times (293.15\,\text{K})}{0.273 \times (7.62 \times 10^{-11}\,\text{m}^2\,\text{s}^{-1})}$$

$= 60.5\,\text{kg mol}^{-1} = \underline{60\,500\,\text{g mol}^{-1}}$.

25.22 $f = kT/D$ [25.1.16] $= (1.3807 \times 10^{-23}\,\text{J K}^{-1}) \times (293.15\,\text{K})/(7.62 \times 10^{-11}\,\text{m}^2\,\text{s}^{-1})$

$= 5.31 \times 10^{-11}\,\text{kg s}^{-1}$.

$c = (3V_{\text{m}}/4\pi N_{\text{A}})^{1/3}$ [Box 25.1].

$V_{\text{m}} = 0.728\,\text{cm}^3\,\text{g}^{-1} \times (60\,500\,\text{g mol}^{-1}) = 44\,044\,\text{cm}^3\,\text{mol}^{-1}$

$= 4.404 \times 10^{-2}\,\text{m}^3\,\text{mol}^{-1}$.

$c = \{3 \times (4.404 \times 10^{-2}\,\text{m}^3\,\text{mol}^{-1})/4\pi \times (6.022 \times 10^{23}\,\text{mol}^{-1})\}^{1/3} = 2.59\,\text{nm}$.

$f_{\text{o}} = 6\pi c\eta$ [Table 25.1] $= 6\pi \times (2.59 \times 10^{-9}\,\text{m}) \times (1.00 \times 10^{-3}\,\text{kg m}^{-1}\,\text{s}^{-1})$

$= 4.89 \times 10^{-11}\,\text{kg s}^{-1}$.

$f/f_{\text{o}} = 5.31/4.89 = 1.09$.

Therefore [Table 25.1], either oblate or prolate with $a/b \approx 2.8$.

25.23 $[\eta] = (8.3 \times 10^{-2}\,\text{cm}^3\,\text{g}^{-1}) \times M_{\text{r}}^{0.50}$ [Table 25.2],

$[\eta] = \lim_{c_{\text{p}} \to 0} \{(\eta/\eta^*) - 1]/c_{\text{p}}\}$ [25.1.20].

Draw up the following Table using $\eta^* = 0.647 \times 10^{-3}\,\text{kg m}^{-1}\,\text{s}^{-1}$.

$c_{\text{p}}/(\text{g}/100\,\text{cm}^3)$	0	0.2	0.4	0.6	0.8	1.0
$\eta/10^{-3}\,\text{kg m}^{-1}\,\text{s}^{-1}$	0.647	0.690	0.733	0.777	0.821	0.865
$(\eta/\eta^*) - 1$	0	0.066	0.133	0.201	0.269	0.337
$([(\eta/\eta^*) - 1]/c_{\text{p}})/100\,\text{cm}^3\,\text{g}^{-1}$	—	0.332	0.328	0.335	0.336	0.337

Plot the values as in Fig. 25.5

The limiting value at $c_{\text{p}} = 0$ is 0.329, and so

$[\eta] = 0.330 \times (100\,\text{cm}^3\,\text{g}^{-1}) = 33.0\,\text{cm}^3\,\text{g}^{-1}$.

Therefore $M_{\text{r}} = \{(33.0\,\text{cm}^3\,\text{g}^{-1})/(8.3 \times 10^{-2}\,\text{cm}^3\,\text{g}^{-1})\}^{2.00} = \underline{158\,000}$.

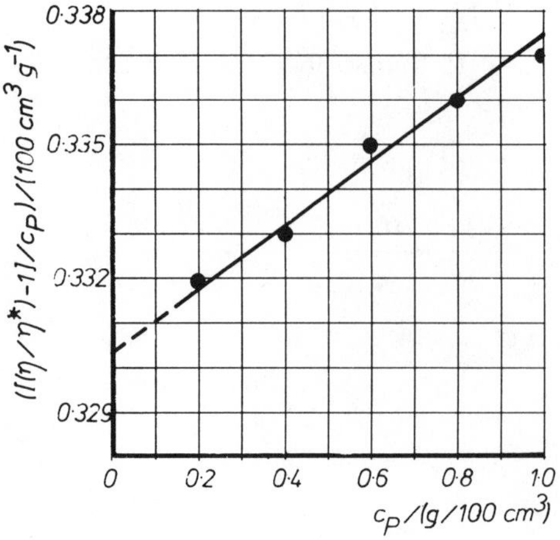

Fig 25.5

25.24 Refer to Fig. 25.6

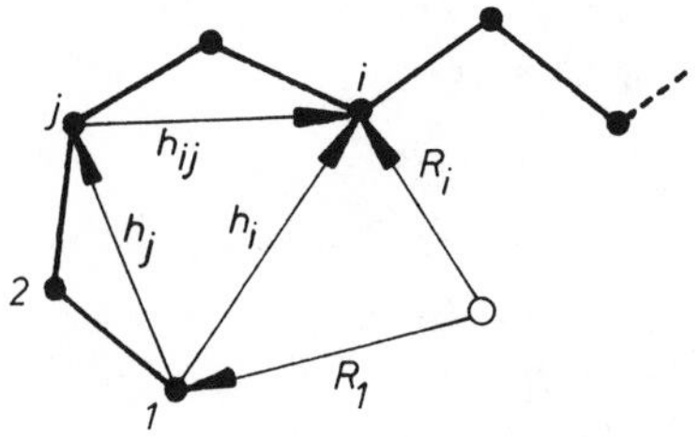

Fig 25.6

$\mathbf{R}_i = \mathbf{R}_1 + \mathbf{h}_i$

$\sum_i \mathbf{R}_i = 0$; and so $N\mathbf{R}_1 + \sum_i \mathbf{h}_i = 0$

Therefore $\mathbf{R}_1 = (-1/N) \sum_i \mathbf{h}_i$.

$R_1^2 = (1/N)^2 \sum_{ij} \mathbf{h}_i \cdot \mathbf{h}_j, \quad \mathbf{R}_1 \cdot \sum_i \mathbf{h}_i = (-1/N) \sum_{ij} \mathbf{h}_i \cdot \mathbf{h}_j.$

$R_g^2 = (1/N) \sum_i R_i^2$ [new definition]

$$= (1/N) \sum_i \left\{(\mathbf{R}_1 + \mathbf{h}_i).(\mathbf{R}_1 + \mathbf{h}_i)\right\} = (1/N) \left\{NR_1^2 + \sum_i h_i^2 + 2\mathbf{R}_1 \cdot \sum_i \mathbf{h}_i\right\}$$

$$=(1/N)\left\{\sum_i h_i^2-(1/N)\sum_{ij}\mathbf{h}_i\cdot\mathbf{h}_j\right\}.$$

$\mathbf{h}_i\cdot\mathbf{h}_j=\frac{1}{2}(h_i^2+h_j^2-h_{ij}^2)$ [cosine rule].

$$\text{Therefore } R_g^2=(1/N)\left\{\sum_i h_i^2+(1/2N)\sum_{ij}h_{ij}^2-\tfrac{1}{2}\sum_i h_i^2-\sum_j h_j^2\right\}$$

$$=(1/2N^2)\sum_{ij}h_{ij}^2\quad[=R_g^2,\text{eqn}(25.1.28)].$$

25.25 $R_{\text{rms}}^2=\int_0^\infty f(r)r^2\mathrm{d}r, f(r)=(a/\pi^{1/2})^3 4\pi r^2 \mathrm{e}^{-a^2r^2}, a^2=3/2Nl^2$ [25.2.1].

(a) $R_{\text{rms}}^2=4\pi(a/\pi^{1/2})^3\int_0^\infty r^4\mathrm{e}^{-a^2r^2}\,\mathrm{d}r=4\pi\left(\frac{a}{\pi^{1/2}}\right)^3\times\frac{3}{8}\left(\frac{\pi}{a^{10}}\right)^{1/2}=\frac{3}{2a^2}=\underline{Nl^2}.$

Therefore, $R_{\text{rms}}=\underline{l\sqrt{N}}.$

(b) $R_{\text{mean}}=\int_0^\infty f(r)r\mathrm{d}r=4\pi\left(\frac{a}{\pi^{1/2}}\right)^3\int_0^\infty r^3\mathrm{e}^{-a^2r^2}\,\mathrm{d}r=4\pi\left(\frac{a}{\pi^{1/2}}\right)^3\times\left(\frac{1}{2a^4}\right)=\frac{2}{a\sqrt{\pi}}$

$=\underline{l\sqrt{(8N/3\pi)}}.$

(c) $\mathrm{d}f/\mathrm{d}r=0$ at $r=R^*$.

$\mathrm{d}f/\mathrm{d}r=4\pi(a/\pi^{1/2})^3\{2r-2a^2r^3\}\mathrm{e}^{-a^2r^2}=0$ when $a^2r^2=1$.

Therefore $R^*=1/a=\underline{l\sqrt{(2N/3)}}.$

When $N=4000$ and $l=154$ pm, $R_{\text{rms}}=\underline{9.74\text{ nm}}$, $R_{\text{mean}}=\underline{8.97\text{ nm}}$, $R^*=\underline{7.95\text{ nm}}.$

25.26 A simple procedure is to generate numbers in the range 1 to 8, and to step N for 1 or 2, E for 3 or 4, S for 5 or 6, W for 7 or 8, all steps on a uniform grid. One such walk is shown in Fig. 25.7.

25.27 $R_g=(1/N)\sum_j R_j^2$ [Problem 25.24].

(a) Center of mass at center of sphere; therefore

$$R_g^2=\int_0^\infty 4\pi r^4\mathrm{d}r\Big/\int_0^\infty 4\pi r^2\mathrm{d}r\,[N\propto\text{volume}]=\tfrac{3}{5}a^2, R_g=\underline{a\sqrt{(3/5)}}.$$

(b) Center of mass at center of rod; therefore

$$R_g^2=2\int_0^{\frac{1}{2}l}r^2\mathrm{d}r\Big/2\int_0^{\frac{1}{2}l}\mathrm{d}r\ [\text{negligible width}]=l^2/12; R_g=l/\sqrt{12}.$$

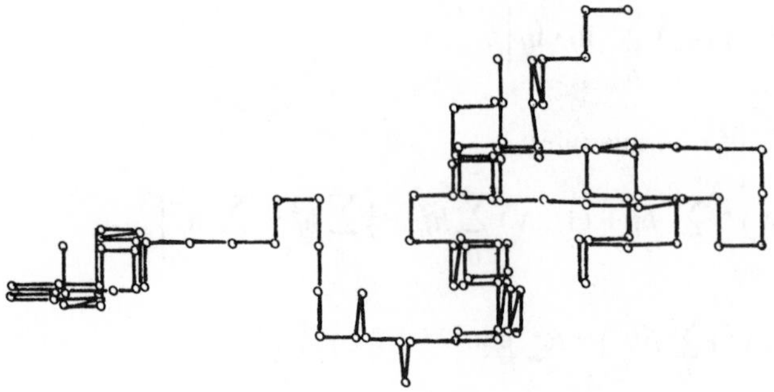

Fig 25.7

For a sphere, $a = (3V_m/4\pi N_A)^{1/3} = (3v_sM_m/4\pi N_A)^{1/3}$.

Therefore $R_g = (3/5)^{1/2}(3v_sM_m/4\pi N_A)^{1/3}$

and $R_g/\text{nm} = (3/5)^{1/2}\{3v_sM_r\,\text{g mol}^{-1}/4\pi N_A \times (10^{-9}\,\text{m})^3\}^{1/3}$

$= (3/5)^{1/2}\{(3v_sM_r\,\text{g m}^{-3})/4\pi \times (6.022 \times 10^{23}) \times 10^{-27}\}^{1/3}$

$= 0.0569 \times \{(v_s/\text{cm}^3\,\text{g}^{-1})M_r\}^{1/3}$.

When $M_r = 100\,000$ and $v_s = 0.750\,\text{cm}^3\,\text{g}^{-1}$,

$R_g/\text{nm} = 0.0569 \times \{0.750 \times 10^5\}^{1/3} = \underline{2.40}$.

For a rod, $v_{mol} = \pi a^2 l$, and so $R_g = v_{mol}/\pi a^2\sqrt{12} = v_{mol}M_m/\pi a^2 N_A\sqrt{12}$.

$$\text{Therefore, } R_g = \frac{(0.750\,\text{cm}^3\,\text{g}^{-1}) \times (10^5\,\text{g mol}^{-1})}{\pi \times (0.5 \times 10^{-7}\,\text{cm})^2 \times (6.022 \times 10^{23}\,\text{mol}^{-1}) \times \sqrt{12}} = 4.6 \times 10^{-6}\,\text{cm}$$

$$= 4.6 \times 10^{-8}\,\text{m} = \underline{46\,\text{nm}}.$$

25.28 Assume they are solid spheres, then

$R_g = (3/5)^{1/2}(3v_sM_m/4\pi N_A)^{1/3} = 0.0569 \times \{(v_s/\text{cm}^3\,\text{g}^{-1})M_r\}^{1/3}\,\text{nm}$. [Problem 25.27]

Draw up the following Table:

	M_r	$v_s/\text{cm}^3\,\text{g}^{-1}$	$(R_g/\text{nm})_{calc}$	$(R_g/\text{nm})_{expt}$
Serum albumin	66 000	0.752	2.09	2.98
BSV	10.6×10^6	0.741	11.3	12.0
DNA	4×10^6	0.556	7.43	117.0

Therefore, serum albumin and bushy stunt virus are probably spheres while DNA is not.

25.29 For a rigid rod, $R_g \propto l$ [Problem 25.27] $\propto M_r$, but for a random coil $R_g \propto \sqrt{N}$ [25.2.2], and as $N \propto M_r$ it follows that $R_g \propto M_r^{\frac{1}{2}}$. Therefore poly-$\gamma$-benzyl-L-glutamate is rod-like, while polystyrene in butanol is a random coil.

25.30 $P(\theta) = (1/N^2) \sum_{ij} \{\sin(sR_{ij})/(sR_{ij})\}, \quad s = (4\pi/\lambda)\sin\frac{1}{2}\theta$ [25.1.26].

There are N terms in the sums for which $R_{ij} = 0$, $2(N-1)$ terms for which $R_{ij} = l$, $2(N-2)$ for which $R_{ij} = 2l, \ldots$, and $2(N-k)$ for which $R_{ij} = kl$. Therefore,

$$P(\theta) = (1/N^2) \sum_{k=0}^{N-1} 2(N-k)\{\sin(skl)/(skl)\} - (1/N)$$

$$\approx (2/N)\int_0^{N-1} \frac{\sin(skl)}{skl}\,\mathrm{d}k - (2/N^2 sl)\int_0^{N-1} \sin(skl)\,\mathrm{d}k - (1/N).$$

Write $x = skl$, $\mathrm{d}k = \mathrm{d}x/sl$, $Nl = \mathcal{L}$(length of rod)

$$P(\theta) \approx (2/s\mathcal{L})\int_0^{(N-1)sl} \left(\frac{\sin x}{x}\right)\mathrm{d}x - (2/s^2\mathcal{L}^2)\int_0^{(N-1)sl} \sin x\,\mathrm{d}x - (1/N)$$

$$\approx (2/s\mathcal{L})\int_0^{(N-1)sl} \left(\frac{\sin x}{x}\right)\mathrm{d}x + (2/s^2\mathcal{L}^2)\{\cos(N-1)sl - 1\} - (1/N).$$

$\cos(N-1)sl = \{1 - 2\sin^2\frac{1}{2}(N-1)sl\}$.

Since the rod is long, $(N-1)sl \approx Nsl = s\mathcal{L}$, and $1/N \ll 1$. Therefore,

$$P(\theta) \approx (2/s\mathcal{L})\int_0^{s\mathcal{L}} \left(\frac{\sin x}{x}\right)\mathrm{d}x - \left\{\frac{\sin(\frac{1}{2}s\mathcal{L})}{\frac{1}{2}s\mathcal{L}}\right\}^2.$$

Introduce the sine integral $\mathrm{Si}(z) = \int_0^z \left(\frac{\sin x}{x}\right)\mathrm{d}x$, then

$$\underline{P(\theta) \approx (2/s\mathcal{L})\,\mathrm{Si}(s\mathcal{L}) - \{\sin(\tfrac{1}{2}s\mathcal{L})/(\tfrac{1}{2}s\mathcal{L})\}^2.}$$

25.31 $P(\theta) \approx (2/s\mathcal{L})\,\mathrm{Si}(s\mathcal{L}) - \{\sin(\frac{1}{2}s\mathcal{L})/(\frac{1}{2}s\mathcal{L})\}^2$ [Problem 25.30] and $s = (4\pi/\lambda)\sin\frac{1}{2}\theta$.

For $\mathcal{L} = \lambda$, $s\mathcal{L} = 4\pi\sin\frac{1}{2}\theta$

$P(\theta) \approx \mathrm{Si}(4\pi\sin\frac{1}{2}\theta)/(2\pi\sin\frac{1}{2}\theta) - \{\sin(2\pi\sin\frac{1}{2}\theta)/2\pi\sin\frac{1}{2}\theta\}^2$

Draw up the following Table (note that $\mathrm{Si}\,z \sim z$ as $z \to 0$).

θ	0	20	40	60	80
$4\pi \sin\frac{1}{2}\theta$	0	2.182	4.298	6.283	8.078
$\mathrm{Si}(4\pi \sin\frac{1}{2}\theta)$	0	1.69	1.70	1.42	1.59
$\sin(2\pi \sin\frac{1}{2}\theta)$	0	0.887	0.837	0.000	−0.782
$2\pi \sin\frac{1}{2}$	0	1.091	2.149	3.142	4.039
$P(\theta)$	1.000	0.888	0.639	0.452	0.356

θ	100	120	140	160	180
$4\pi \sin\frac{1}{2}\theta$	9.626	10.883	11.809	12.375	12.566
$\mathrm{Si}(4\pi \sin\frac{1}{2}\theta)$	1.67	1.58	1.53	1.50	1.49
$\sin(2\pi \sin\frac{1}{2}\theta)$	−0.782	−0.746	−0.370	−0.096	0.000
$2\pi \sin\frac{1}{2}\theta$	4.813	5.441	5.904	6.188	6.283
$P(\theta)$	0.304	0.272	0.255	0.242	0.237

These points are used to plot the graph in Fig. 25.8.

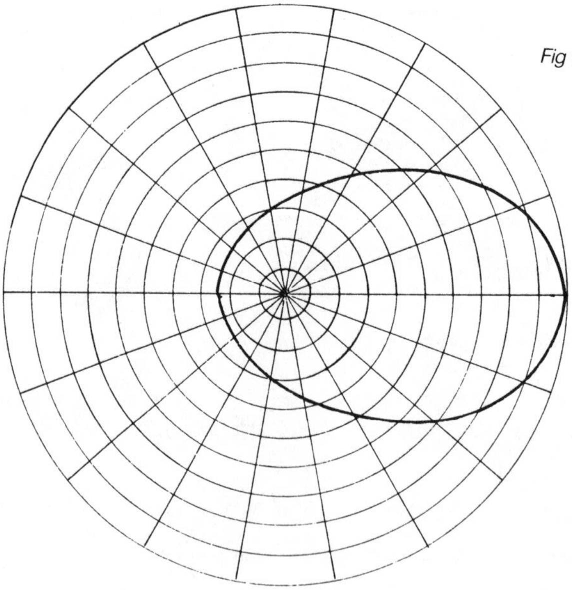

Fig 25.8

25.32 $\tau_{\text{rot}} = 4\pi a^3\eta/3kT$ [25.1.30]

$\eta(H_2O) = 0.8909 \times 10^{-3}\,\text{kg m}^{-1}\,\text{s}^{-1}$, $a(\text{S.A.}) \approx 3.0 \times 10^{-9}\,\text{m}$;

$$\tau_{\text{rot}} = \frac{4\pi \times (3.0 \times 10^{-9}\,\text{m})^3 \times (0.8909 \times 10^{-3}\,\text{kg m}^{-1}\,\text{s}^{-1})}{3 \times (1.3807 \times 10^{-23}\,\text{J K}^{-1}) \times (298.15\,\text{K})} = \underline{2.5 \times 10^{-8}\,\text{s}.}$$

$\eta(CCl_4) = 0.895 \times 10^{-3}\,\text{kg m}^{-1}\,\text{s}^{-1}, a(CCl_4) \approx 2.5 \times 10^{-10}\,\text{m}$;

$$\tau_{\text{rot}} = \frac{4\pi \times (2.5 \times 10^{-10}\,\text{m})^3 \times (0.895 \times 10^{-3}\,\text{kg m}^{-1}\,\text{s}^{-1})}{3 \times (1.3807 \times 10^{-23}\,\text{J K}^{-1}) \times (298.15\,\text{K})} = \underline{1.4 \times 10^{-11}\,\text{s}.}$$

25.33 $G = U - TS - tl$ [given],

$\mathrm{d}G = \mathrm{d}U - T\mathrm{d}S - S\mathrm{d}T - l\mathrm{d}t - t\mathrm{d}l$

$\quad = T\mathrm{d}S + t\mathrm{d}l - T\mathrm{d}S - S\mathrm{d}T - l\mathrm{d}t - t\mathrm{d}l = \underline{-S\mathrm{d}T - l\mathrm{d}t.}$

$A = U - TS = G + tl,$

$\mathrm{d}A = \mathrm{d}G + t\mathrm{d}l + l\mathrm{d}t = -S\mathrm{d}T - l\mathrm{d}t + t\mathrm{d}l + l\mathrm{d}t = \underline{-S\mathrm{d}T + t\mathrm{d}l.}$

Since $\mathrm{d}A$, $\mathrm{d}G$ are exact

$(\partial S/\partial l)_T = -(\partial t/\partial T)_l$ and $(\partial S/\partial t)_T = (\partial l/\partial T)_t$ [Box 3.1].

25.34 $\mathrm{d}U = T\mathrm{d}S + t\mathrm{d}l$ [Problem 25.33]

$(\partial U/\partial l)_T = T(\partial S/\partial l)_T + t$ [Box 3.1, Relation 1]

$\quad = \underline{-T(\partial t/\partial T)_l + t}$ [Problem 25.33].

25.35 $t = aT$ [$t \propto T$].

$(\partial t/\partial T)_l = a$; $(\partial U/\partial l)_T = t - T(\partial t/\partial T)_l = t - aT = 0$, and

so the internal energy is independent of length (T const.).

$(\partial S/\partial l)_T = -(\partial t/\partial T)_l$ [Problem 25.33] $= -a = -t/T$.

Therefore $t = \underline{-T(\partial S/\partial l)_T}$.

Extension reduces the disorder of the chains.

25.36 $f(s) = 1/(s^2 - 4) + 2/s^2 + \ln(1 - 4/s^2)$ [given].

Draw up the following Table:

s	4	5	6	7	8	9	10
$10^5 f(s)$	398	88.5	27.3	10.3	4.5	2.2	1.1

These points are plotted in Fig. 25.9.

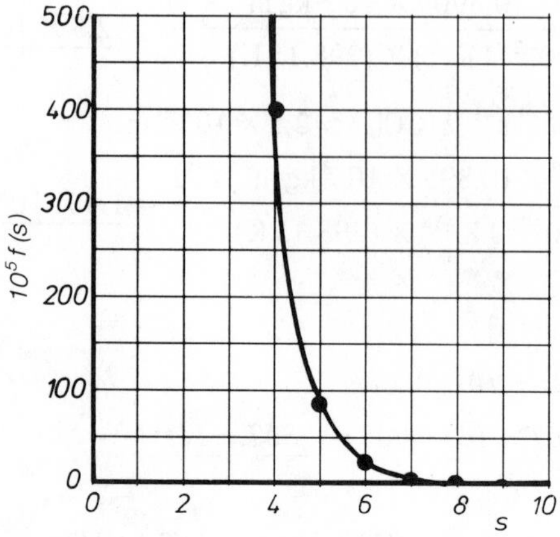

Fig 25.9

25.37 $\Gamma = -(c/RT)(\partial\gamma/\partial c)_T$ [25.4.7] $= -([A]/RT)(\partial\gamma/\partial[A])_T$.

Draw up the following Table using $\partial\gamma/\partial[A] \approx \Delta\gamma/\Delta[A]$:

$[A]/\text{mol dm}^{-3}$	0	0.10	0.20	0.30	0.40	0.50
$\gamma/\text{mN m}^{-1}$	72.8	70.2	67.7	65.1	62.8	59.8
$-(\partial\gamma/\partial[A])/\text{mN m}^{-1}\,\text{M}^{-1}$	—	26.0	25.0	26.0	23.0	30.0
$-[A](\partial\gamma/\partial[A])/\text{mN m}^{-1}$	—	2.60	5.00	7.80	9.20	15.0
$10^{10}\Gamma/\text{mol cm}^{-2}$	0	1.08	2.08	3.24	3.82	6.23

For the last line we have used

$\Gamma = -\{[A](\partial\gamma/\partial[A])_T/\text{mN m}^{-1}\}(\text{mN m}^{-1})/RT$

$= -\{[A]\ (\partial\gamma/\partial[A])_T/\text{mN m}^{-1}\}(10^{-3}\,\text{N m}^{-1})/(2412\,\text{J mol}^{-1})$

$= \{\text{line 4}\} \times (4.15 \times 10^{-7}\,\text{mol m}^{-2}) = \{\text{line 4}\} \times 4.15 \times 10^{-11}\,\text{mol cm}^{-2}$.

25.38 $\pi = RT\Gamma$ and $\pi = \gamma^* - \gamma$ [25.4.8].

Draw up the following Table using $\gamma^* = 72.8\,\text{mN m}^{-1}$ and $RT = 2412\,\text{J mol}^{-1}$.

$[A]/M$	0	0.10	0.20	0.30	0.40	0.50
$10^6\,\Gamma/\text{mol m}^{-2}$	0	1.08	2.08	3.24	3.82	6.23
$RT\Gamma/\text{mN m}^{-1}$	0	2.60	5.02	7.81	9.21	15.0
$(\gamma^* - \gamma)/\text{mN m}^{-1}$	0	2.6	5.1	7.7	10.0	13.0

The agreement is quite good.

25.39 $(\partial\gamma/\partial c)_T = -RT\Gamma/c$ [25.4.7].

Since $(\partial\gamma/\partial c)_T > 0$ [given], $\Gamma < 0$. Therefore the salt tends to avoid the surface.

25.40 $\Gamma = -(c/RT)(\partial\gamma/\partial c)_T$ [25.4.7].

$\gamma = \gamma^* + (c/\text{M})\Delta\gamma, (\partial\gamma/\partial c)_T = \Delta\gamma/\text{M}$.

$$\Gamma = -(c/RT)(\partial\gamma/\partial c)_T = -(c/RT)\Delta\gamma/\text{M}$$
$$= -(c/\text{M}) \times (\Delta\gamma/RT)$$
$$= -(c/\text{M}) \times (\Delta\gamma/\text{mN m}^{-1}) \times (10^{-3}\,\text{N m}^{-1}/RT)$$
$$= -(c/\text{M}) \times (\Delta\gamma/\text{mN m}^{-1}) \times (4.145 \times 10^{-7}\,\text{mol m}^{-2})$$
$$= -(4.145 \times 10^{-11}\,\text{mol cm}^{-2}) \times (c/\text{M}) \times (\Delta\gamma/\text{mN m}^{-1}).$$

Draw up the following Table with $c \approx 1$ M.

	KCl	NaCl	Na_2CO_3
$\Delta\gamma/\text{mN m}^{-1}$	1.4	1.64	2.7
$10^{11}\Gamma/\text{mol cm}^{-2}$	−5.80	−6.80	−11.2

PART 3: CHANGE

26. Molecules in motion: the kinetic theory of gases

A26.1 $\bar{c} = (8kT/\pi m)^{\frac{1}{2}}$ [26.1.10]

$= [(8)(1.38 \times 10^{-23}\,\mathrm{J\,K^{-1}})(650\,\mathrm{K})(\pi)^{-1}(131)^{-1}(1.66 \times 10^{-27}\,\mathrm{kg})^{-1}]^{\frac{1}{2}}$

$= \underline{324\,\mathrm{m\,s^{-1}}}.$

A26.2 $F(v) = 4\pi(m/2\pi kT)^{3/2}v^2 \exp(-mv^2/2kT)$, [26.1.9]

$m/(2kT) = (28.0)(1.66 \times 10^{-27}\,\mathrm{kg})(2)^{-1}(1.38 \times 10^{-23}\,\mathrm{J\,K^{-1}})^{-1}(500\,\mathrm{K})^{-1}$

$= 3.37 \times 10^{-6}\,\mathrm{m^{-2}\,s^2},$

$4\pi(m/2\pi kT)^{3/2} = 4(\pi)^{-\frac{1}{2}}(3.37 \times 10^{-6}\,\mathrm{m^{-2}\,s^2})^{3/2} = 1.40 \times 10^{-8}\,\mathrm{m^{-3}\,s^3}.$

$F(290\,\mathrm{m\,s^{-1}}) = (1.40 \times 10^{-8}\,\mathrm{m^{-3}\,s^3})(290\,\mathrm{m\,s^{-1}})^2 \exp[-(3.37 \times 10^{-6}\,\mathrm{m^{-2}\,s^2})$

$\times (290\,\mathrm{m\,s^{-1}})^2] = 8.87 \times 10^{-4}\,\mathrm{m^{-1}\,s},$

$F(300\,\mathrm{m\,s^{-1}}) = (1.40 \times 10^{-8}\,\mathrm{m^{-3}\,s^3})(300\,\mathrm{m\,s^{-1}})^2 \exp[-(3.37 \times 10^{-6}\,\mathrm{m^{-2}\,s^2})$

$\times (300\,\mathrm{m/s})^2] = 9.30 \times 10^{-4}\,\mathrm{m^{-1}\,s},$

mean $F = \underline{9.08 \times 10^{-4}\,\mathrm{m^{-1}\,s}}.$

Per cent in the specified range $= 100(9.08 \times 10^{-4}\,\mathrm{m^{-1}\,s})(10\,\mathrm{m\,s^{-1}}) = \underline{0.91\,\%}.$

A26.3 $Z_{\mathrm{W}} = p(2\pi mkT)^{-\frac{1}{2}}$ [26.2.9]

$= (90\,\mathrm{Pa})[(2\pi)(40)(1.7 \times 10^{-27}\,\mathrm{kg})(1.4 \times 10^{-23}\,\mathrm{J\,K^{-1}})(500\,\mathrm{K})]^{-\frac{1}{2}}$

$= 1.7 \times 10^{24}\,\mathrm{m^{-2}\,s^{-1}}.$

Number of collisions $= (1.7 \times 10^{24}\,\mathrm{m^{-2}\,s^{-1}})(2.5 \times 10^{-3}\,\mathrm{m})(3.0 \times 10^{-3}\,\mathrm{m})(15\,\mathrm{s})$

$= \underline{1.9 \times 10^{20}}.$

A26.4 $T = (2.00 \times 10^3\,\mathrm{Pa})(5.00 \times 10^{-3}\,\mathrm{m^3})(8.31\,\mathrm{J\,K^{-1}\,mol^{-1}})^{-1}(4.50 \times 10^{-3}\,\mathrm{mol})^{-1}$

$= \underline{267\,\mathrm{K}}.$ [1.1.1]

$d_{12} = (1/2)(d_1 + d_2) = (1/2)(\pi)^{-\frac{1}{2}}[(0.27)^{\frac{1}{2}} + (0.43)^{\frac{1}{2}}](10^{-9})\mathrm{m}$

$= \underline{0.332\,\mathrm{nm}}.$ [Table 26.2]

$\mu = (2.02)(28.0)(30.0)^{-1}(1.66 \times 10^{-27}\,\mathrm{kg}) = 3.13 \times 10^{-27}\,\mathrm{kg}.$

$8kT/\pi\mu = (8)(1.38 \times 10^{-23}\,\mathrm{J\,K^{-1}})(267\,\mathrm{K})(\pi)^{-1}(3.13 \times 10^{-27}\,\mathrm{kg})^{-1}$

$= 3.00 \times 10^6\,\mathrm{m^2\,s^{-2}}$

$Z_{12} = \pi d_{12}^2 (8kT/\pi\mu)^{\frac{1}{2}} (N_1 N_2/V^2)$ [26.2.5]

$= (3.14)(3.32 \times 10^{-10}\,\text{m})^2 (3.00 \times 10^6\,\text{m}^2\,\text{s}^{-2})^{\frac{1}{2}} (1.50 \times 10^{-3}\,\text{mol})$

$\times (3.00 \times 10^{-3}\,\text{mol})(6.02 \times 10^{23}\,\text{mol}^{-1})^2 (5.00 \times 10^{-3}\,\text{m}^3)^{-2}$

$= \underline{3.90 \times 10^{31}\,\text{m}^{-3}\,\text{s}^{-1}}.$

Number of collisions $= (3.90 \times 10^{31}\,\text{m}^{-3}\,\text{s}^{-1})(5.00 \times 10^{-3}\,\text{m}^3)(1.00 \times 10^{-3}\,\text{s})$

$= \underline{1.95 \times 10^{26}}.$

A26.5 $\sigma = 0.46\,\text{nm}^2$; $\lambda = (2^{\frac{1}{2}}\sigma)^{-1}(kT/p)$. [26.2.6]

$T = p\lambda 2^{\frac{1}{2}}\sigma/k$

$= (3.65 \times 10^3\,\text{Pa})(1.20 \times 10^{-6}\,\text{m})(1.41)(0.46 \times 10^{-18}\,\text{m}^2)(1.38 \times 10^{-23}\,\text{J K}^{-1})^{-1}$

$= 206$ K [Table 26.2].

A26.6 $\delta m = A_0 \tau p (2\pi kT/m)^{-\frac{1}{2}}$ [26.3.4]

$= (3.14)(1.25 \times 10^{-3}\,\text{m})^2 (7.20 \times 10^3\,\text{s})(0.835\,\text{Pa})$

$\times [(2\pi)(1.38 \times 10^{-23}\,\text{J K}^{-1})(400\,\text{K})(260)^{-1}(1.66 \times 10^{-27}\,\text{kg})^{-1}]^{-\frac{1}{2}}$

$= 1.04 \times 10^{-4}$ kg, or $\underline{104\,\text{mg}}.$

A26.7 $J_z(\text{energy}) = -\kappa\, dT/dz = -(1.63 \times 10^{-2}\,\text{J m}^{-1}\,\text{s}^{-1}\,\text{K}^{-1})(2.5\,\text{K m}^{-1})$

$= \underline{-0.041\,\text{J m}^{-2}\,\text{s}^{-1}}.$ [26.3.2, Table 26.3]

A26.8 $\kappa = (1/3)\bar{c}C_{V,\text{m}}(2^{\frac{1}{2}}\sigma N_A)^{-1} = 0.0465\,\text{J s}^{-1}\,\text{K}^{-1}\,\text{m}^{-1}$ [Table 26.3, 26.3.11]

$\bar{c} = [(8)(1.38 \times 10^{-23}\,\text{J K}^{-1})(273\,\text{K})(3.14)^{-1}(20.2)^{-1}(1.66 \times 10^{-27}\,\text{kg})^{-1}]^{\frac{1}{2}}$

$= 535\,\text{m s}^{-1}.$

$C_{V,\text{m}} = 3R/2 = (1.50)(8.31\,\text{J K}^{-1}\,\text{mol}^{-1}) = 12.5\,\text{J K}^{-1}\,\text{mol}^{-1}$

$\sigma = (0.0465\,\text{J m}^{-1}\,\text{s}^{-1}\,\text{K}^{-1})^{-1}(3)^{-1}(535\,\text{m s}^{-1})(12.5\,\text{J K}^{-1}\,\text{mol}^{-1})(2)^{-\frac{1}{2}}$

$\times (6.02 \times 10^{23}\,\text{mol}^{-1})^{-1} = 5.63 \times 10^{-20}\,\text{m}^2$, or $\underline{0.0563\,\text{nm}^2}.$

The tabulated value is $0.24\,\text{nm}^2$. [Table 26.2]

A26.9 $\eta = (1/3)(2)^{-\frac{1}{2}} m\bar{c}\sigma^{-1} = 298\,\mu\text{P}$. [Table 26.3, 26.3.13]

$\bar{c} = 535\,\text{m s}^{-1}$ (see solution for Problem A26.8).

$\sigma = (3^{-1})(2^{-\frac{1}{2}})(20.2 \times 1.66 \times 10^{-27}\,\text{kg})(535\,\text{m s}^{-1})(2.98 \times 10^{-5}\,\text{kg m}^{-1}\,\text{s}^{-1})^{-1}$

$= 1.42 \times 10^{-19}\,\text{m}^2$, or $\underline{0.142\,\text{nm}^2}.$

The tabulated value is $0.24\,\text{nm}^2$. [Table 26.2]

A26.10 $p_1^2 = p_2^2 + (dV/dt)(16)(l\eta p_0)(\pi r^4)^{-1}$ [26.3.14, Table 26.3]

$$= (10^5\,\text{Pa})^2 + (9.50 \times 10^2\,\text{m}^3)(3600\,\text{s})^{-1}(16)(8.50\,\text{m})$$
$$\times 1.76 \times 10^{-5}\,\text{kg m}^{-1}\,\text{s}^{-1})(10^5\,\text{Pa})(\pi)^{-1}(5.00 \times 10^{-3}\,\text{m})^{-4}$$
$$= (10^5\,\text{Pa})^2 + 3.22 \times 10^{10}\,\text{Pa}^2 = 4.22 \times 10^{10}\,\text{Pa}^2.$$

$p_1 = \underline{2.05 \times 10^5\,\text{Pa}}.$

26.1 $\lambda = kT/\sigma p\sqrt{2}$ [26.2.6]

$$= (1.381 \times 10^{-23}\,\text{J K}^{-1}) \times (298.15\,\text{K})/(0.43 \times 10^{-18}\,\text{m}^2)p\sqrt{2}$$
$$= (0.68 \times 10^{-2}\,\text{J m}^{-2})/p$$

(a) $p = 10\,\text{atm} \,\widehat{=}\, 1.013 \times 10^6\,\text{N m}^{-2}$.

$\lambda = (0.68 \times 10^{-2}\,\text{J m}^{-2})/(1.0133 \times 10^6\,\text{N m}^{-2})$

$= 0.67 \times 10^{-8}\,\text{J N}^{-1} = 0.67 \times 10^{-8}\,\text{m}$ [$1\,\text{J} = 1\,\text{N m}$] $= \underline{6.7\,\text{nm}}$.

(b) $p = 1.0\,\text{atm}$, $\lambda \propto 1/p$; therefore $\lambda = \underline{67\,\text{nm}}$,

(c) $p = 10^{-6}\,\text{atm}$, $\lambda = 67\,\text{nm} \times 10^6 = \underline{67\,\text{mm}}$.

26.2 $p = kT/\sigma\lambda\sqrt{2}$ [26.2.6], $\lambda \approx (1.0\,\text{dm}^3)^{1/3} = 1.0\,\text{dm}$.

$p = (1.381 \times 10^{-23}\,\text{J K}^{-1}) \times (298.15\,\text{K})/(0.36 \times 10^{-18}\,\text{m}^2) \times (0.10\,\text{m})\sqrt{2}$

$= 0.081\,\text{N m}^{-2}$

$\widehat{=} (0.081/1.013 \times 10^5)\text{atm}$ [end-paper 1] $= \underline{8.0 \times 10^{-7}\,\text{atm}}$.

26.3 $p = kT/\sigma\lambda\sqrt{2}$ [26.2.6], $\lambda \approx \sqrt{\sigma}$.

$p = (1.381 \times 10^{-23}\,\text{J K}^{-1}) \times (298.15\,\text{K})/(0.36 \times 10^{-18}\,\text{m}^2)^{3/2}\sqrt{2}$

$= 1.35 \times 10^7\,\text{N m}^{-2} \,\widehat{=}\, (1.35 \times 10^7/1.0133 \times 10^5)\text{atm} = \underline{130\,\text{atm}}$.

26.4 $\lambda = kT/\sigma p\sqrt{2}$ [26.2.6]

$$= (1.381 \times 10^{-23}\,\text{J K}^{-1}) \times (217\,\text{K})/(0.43 \times 10^{-18}\,\text{m}^2) \times (0.05 \times 1.0133$$
$$\times 10^5\,\text{N m}^{-2})\sqrt{2}$$
$$= \underline{9.7 \times 10^{-7}\,\text{m}, 970\,\text{nm}}.$$

26.5 $z = \sqrt{2}\sigma\bar{c}N/V$ [26.2.2], $N/V = nN_A/V = nN_Ap/nRT = p/kT$,

$\bar{c} = (8kT/\pi m)^{1/2}$ [26.1.10].

$z = (16kT/\pi m)^{1/2}\,\sigma p/kT = (16/\pi mkT)^{1/2}\,\sigma p$.

$m = 39.95 \times 1.660\,56 \times 10^{-27}\,\text{kg}$ [end-papers 3, 4] $= 6.63 \times 10^{-26}\,\text{kg}$,

$\sigma = 0.36\,\text{nm}^2$ [Problem 26.2].

$z = \{16/[\pi(6.63 \times 10^{-26}\,\text{kg}) \times (1.381 \times 10^{-23}\,\text{J K}^{-1}) \times (298.15\,\text{K})]\}^{1/2}$

$\times (0.36\,\text{nm}^2)p = (4.92 \times 10^4\,\text{s}^{-1}) \times (p/\text{N m}^{-2})$ [$1\,\text{J} = 1\,\text{N m}$].

$p/\mathrm{N\,m^{-2}} = (p/\mathrm{atm}) \times (\mathrm{atm/N\,m^{-2}}) = (p/\mathrm{atm}) \times (1.0133 \times 10^5)$.

$z = (4.92 \times 10^4\,\mathrm{s^{-1}}) \times (1.0133 \times 10^5) \times (p/\mathrm{atm})\mathrm{s^{-1}}$

$= (4.98 \times 10^9\,\mathrm{s^{-1}}) \times (p/\mathrm{atm}) \approx (5.0 \times 10^9\,\mathrm{s^{-1}}) \times (p/\mathrm{atm})$.

(a) $p = 10\,\mathrm{atm}$, $z = \underline{5 \times 10^{10}\,\mathrm{s^{-1}}}$,

(b) $p = 1\,\mathrm{atm}$, $z = \underline{5 \times 10^{9}\,\mathrm{s^{-1}}}$,

(c) $p = 10^{-6}\,\mathrm{atm}$, $z = \underline{5 \times 10^{3}\,\mathrm{s^{-1}}}$.

26.6 $Z_{AA} = \frac{1}{2}z(N/V)$ [26.2.3] $= zp/2kT$.

$p/2kT = (p/\mathrm{atm}) \times (1.0133 \times 10^5\,\mathrm{N\,m^{-2}})/2 \times (1.381 \times 10^{-23}\,\mathrm{J\,K^{-1}}) \times (298.15\,\mathrm{K})$

$= (1.230 \times 10^{25}\,\mathrm{m^{-3}}) \times (p/\mathrm{atm})$.

$Z_{AA} = (5.0 \times 10^9\,\mathrm{s^{-1}}) \times (p/\mathrm{atm}) \times (1.230 \times 10^{25}\,\mathrm{m^{-3}}) \times (p/\mathrm{atm})$ [Problem 26.5],

$= 6.2 \times 10^{34}\,(p/\mathrm{atm})^2\,\mathrm{s^{-1}\,m^{-3}}$.

Therefore, in 1 dm^3 the total collision frequency is

$Z_{AA} \times (1\,\mathrm{dm^3}) = 6.2 \times 10^{34} \times 10^{-3}(p/\mathrm{atm})^2 = 6 \times 10^{31}(p/\mathrm{atm})^2$

$$= \begin{cases} \text{(a) } \underline{6 \times 10^{33}} \text{ when } p = 10\,\mathrm{atm}, \\ \text{(b) } \underline{6 \times 10^{31}} \text{ when } p = 1\,\mathrm{atm}, \\ \text{(c) } \underline{6 \times 10^{19}} \text{ when } p = 10^{-6}\,\mathrm{atm}. \end{cases}$$

26.7 $z = (16/\pi mT)^{1/2}\sigma p$ [Problem 26.5]; $\sigma = 0.43\,\mathrm{nm^2}$,

$p = 0.05\,\mathrm{atm}$, $T = 217\,\mathrm{K}$ [Problem 26.4],

$m = 28.02 \times (1.660\,56 \times 10^{-27}\,\mathrm{kg}) = 4.65 \times 10^{-26}\,\mathrm{kg}$.

$z = \{16/\pi \times (4.65 \times 10^{-26}\,\mathrm{kg}) \times (1.381 \times 10^{-23}\,\mathrm{J\,K^{-1}}) \times (217\,\mathrm{K})\}^{1/2}$

$\times (0.43\,\mathrm{nm^2}) \times (0.05 \times 1.0133 \times 10^5\,\mathrm{N\,m^{-2}}) = \underline{4 \times 10^8\,\mathrm{s^{-1}}}$.

26.8 $Z_{AA} = \sigma(4kT/\pi m)^{1/2}(N/V)^2$ [26.2.4] $= \sigma(4kT/\pi m)^{1/2}(p/kT)^2$

$= \sigma(4/\pi k^3 T^3 m)^{1/2} p^2$.

$Z_{AB} = \sigma(8kT/\pi\mu)^{1/2}(NN'/V^2)$ [26.2.5] $= \sigma(8kT/\pi\mu)^{1/2}(p_A p_B/k^2T^2)$

$= \sigma(8/\pi\mu k^3 T^3)^{1/2} p_A p_B$, $\mu = m_A m_B/(m_A + m_B)$.

$\sigma(O_2) = \pi \times (357\,\mathrm{pm})^2 = 4.0 \times 10^{-19}\,\mathrm{m^2}$,

$\sigma(N_2, O_2) = \pi \times (178\,\mathrm{pm} + 185\,\mathrm{pm})^2 = 4.14 \times 10^{-19}\,\mathrm{m^2}$.

$m(O_2) = 32.00 \times (1.6605 \times 10^{-27}\,\mathrm{kg}) = 5.32 \times 10^{-26}\,\mathrm{kg}$,

$\mu(O_2, N_2) = (32.00 \times 28.02/60.02) \times (1.6605 \times 10^{-27}\,\mathrm{kg}) = 2.48 \times 10^{-26}\,\mathrm{kg}$.

$p(O_2) = 0.208\,\mathrm{atm}$ [*Example* 1.3] $\hat{=}\ 2.1 \times 10^4\,\mathrm{N\,m^{-2}}$ [end-paper 1],

$p(N_2) = 0.782\,\mathrm{atm}$ [*Example* 1.3] $\hat{=}\ 7.92 \times 10^4\,\mathrm{N\,m^{-2}}$.

$8/\pi k^3 T^3 = 8/\pi \times (1.381 \times 10^{-23}\,\mathrm{J\,K^{-1}})^3 \times (298.15\,\mathrm{K})^3 = 3.65 \times 10^{61}\,\mathrm{J^{-3}}$.

$$Z(\mathrm{O_2, O_2}) = (4.0 \times 10^{-19}\,\mathrm{m^2}) \times \left(\frac{1.83 \times 10^{61}\,\mathrm{J^{-3}}}{5.32 \times 10^{-26}\,\mathrm{kg}}\right)^{1/2} \times (2.12 \times 10^4\,\mathrm{N\,m^{-2}})^2$$

$$= 3.3 \times 10^{33}\,\mathrm{s^{-1}\,m^{-3}}.$$

Therefore, in a 1 $\mathrm{cm^3}$ sample, the number of $(\mathrm{O_2, O_2})$ collisions in one second is $(0.3 \times 10^{33}\,\mathrm{s^{-1}\,m^{-2}}) \times (1\,\mathrm{s}) \times (10^{-6}\,\mathrm{m^3}) = \underline{3 \times 10^{27}}$.

$$Z(\mathrm{O_2, N_2}) = (4.14 \times 10^{-19}\,\mathrm{m^2}) \times \left(\frac{3.65 \times 10^{61}\,\mathrm{J^{-3}}}{2.48 \times 10^{-26}\,\mathrm{kg}}\right)^{1/2} \times (2.12 \times 10^4\,\mathrm{N\,m^{-2}})$$

$$\times (7.92 \times 10^4\,\mathrm{N\,m^{-2}}) = 2.67 \times 10^{34}\,\mathrm{s^{-1}\,m^{-3}}.$$

Therefore, in a 1 $\mathrm{cm^3}$ sample, the number of $(\mathrm{O_2, N_2})$ collisions in 1 s is

$(2.67 \times 10^{34}\,\mathrm{s^{-1}\,m^{-3}}) \times (1\,\mathrm{s}) \times (10^{-6}\,\mathrm{m^3}) = \underline{3 \times 10^{28}}$.

26.9 $Z_{\mathrm{AA}} = \sigma(4/\pi k^3 T^3 m)^{1/2} p^2$ [Problem 26.8].

$m \approx 0.8m(\mathrm{N_2}) + 0.2m(\mathrm{O_2}) = (29 \times 1.66 \times 10^{-27}\,\mathrm{kg}) = 4.8 \times 10^{-26}\,\mathrm{kg}$;

$\sigma \approx 4.0 \times 10^{-19}\,\mathrm{m^2}$ [Problem 26.8]

$4/\pi k^3 T^3 = 1.83 \times 10^{61}\,\mathrm{J^{-3}}$ [Problem 26.8].

$$Z(\mathrm{Air, Air}) \approx (4.0 \times 10^{-19}\,\mathrm{m^2}) \times \left(\frac{1.83 \times 10^{61}\,\mathrm{J^{-3}}}{0.48 \times 10^{-26}\,\mathrm{kg}}\right)^{1/2}$$

$$\times \left(\frac{1.2\,\mathrm{Torr} \times 1.0133 \times 10^5\,\mathrm{N\,m^{-2}}}{760\,\mathrm{Torr}}\right)^2 = 2.0 \times 10^{29}\,\mathrm{s^{-1}\,m^{-3}}.$$

Therefore, in 1 $\mathrm{cm^3}$, the number of collisions per second is $\underline{2.0 \times 10^{23}}$.

26.10 $\bar{c} = (8kT/\pi m)^{1/2}$ [26.1.10].

$m = M_{\mathrm{m}}/N_{\mathrm{A}} = (M_{\mathrm{r}}\,\mathrm{g\,mol^{-1}})/N_{\mathrm{A}} = (10^{-3} M_{\mathrm{r}}\,\mathrm{kg\,mol^{-1}})/N_{\mathrm{A}}$.

$\bar{c} = (8RT/\pi M_{\mathrm{m}})^{1/2} = \{8 \times (8.3144\,\mathrm{J\,K^{-1}\,mol^{-1}})T/(10^{-3} M_{\mathrm{r}}\,\pi\,\mathrm{kg\,mol^{-1}})\}^{1/2}$

$= 145.5 \times \{(T/\mathrm{K^{-1}})/M_{\mathrm{r}}\}^{1/2}\,\mathrm{m\,s^{-1}}$.

Draw up the following Table using $M_{\mathrm{r}}(\mathrm{He}) = 4.0$, $M_{\mathrm{r}}(\mathrm{CH_4}) = 16.0$:

T/K	77	298	1000
$\bar{c}(\mathrm{He})/\mathrm{m\,s^{-1}}$	640	1260	2300
$\bar{c}(\mathrm{CH_4})/\mathrm{m\,s^{-1}}$	320	630	1150

26.11 $U_m = \frac{1}{2}mc^2N_A = \frac{1}{2}m(3kT/m)N_A$ [26.1.11] $= (3/2)RT$.
(Or by equipartition [Section 0.1(f)].)
At 300 K, $U_m = (3/2) \times (8.314\,\mathrm{J\,K^{-1}\,mol^{-1}}) \times (300\,\mathrm{K}) = \underline{3.7\,\mathrm{kJ\,mol^{-1}}}$,
for both species, independent of the pressure.

26.12 Time for neighboring slot to coincide with preceding slot is $(2°/360°)/\nu$. If an atom passes through, it must have a speed $(1\text{ cm})/\{(2°/360°)/\nu\} = 180\nu$ cm $= 180(\nu/\mathrm{Hz})\mathrm{cm\,s^{-1}}$ in the x-direction (parallel to the axis of rotation). Hence the distributions of v_x components of velocity are:

ν/Hz	20	40	80	100	200
$v_x/\mathrm{cm\,s^{-1}}$	3600	7200	14400	18000	36000
$I(40\,\mathrm{K})$	0.846	0.513	0.069	0.015	0.002
$I(100\,\mathrm{K})$	0.592	0.485	0.217	0.119	0.057

Theoretically, $f(v_x) = (m/2\pi kT)^{1/2}\exp\{-\frac{1}{2}mv_x^2/kT\}$ [26.1.8] and so, as $I \propto f$, $I \propto (1/T)^{1/2}\exp(-\frac{1}{2}mv_x^2/kT)$.
$m = 83.8 \times (1.660\,56 \times 10^{-27}\,\mathrm{kg}) = 1.39 \times 10^{-25}\,\mathrm{kg}$.

$$\tfrac{1}{2}mv_x^2/kT = \frac{(1.39 \times 10^{-25}\,\mathrm{kg}) \times (1.80\,\mathrm{m\,s^{-1}})^2 \times (\nu/\mathrm{Hz})^2}{2 \times (1.381 \times 10^{-23}\,\mathrm{J\,K^{-1}})T}$$

$$= 1.63 \times 10^{-2}\{(\nu/\mathrm{Hz})^2/(T/\mathrm{K})\}.$$

$I(T) \propto \{1/(T/\mathrm{K})\}^{1/2}\exp\{-1.63 \times 10^{-2}\{(\nu/\mathrm{Hz})^2/(T/\mathrm{K})\}\}$.
Draw up the following Table, the constant of proportionality obtained by fitting to the value for $T = 40$ K, $\nu = 80$ Hz.

ν/Hz	20	40	80	100	120
$I(40\,\mathrm{K})$	0.80	0.49	(0.069)	0.016	0.003
$I(100\,\mathrm{K})$	0.56	0.46	0.209	0.116	0.057

in fair agreement with the experimental data.

26.13 The probability of having a particular energy E is proportional to $\exp(-E/kT)$ [0.1.2]. Consider a one-dimensional system; then $E = \frac{1}{2}mv_x^2$. The probability of the molecule occurring in the velocity range dv_x around v_x, df_x, is therefore proportional to $\exp(-mv_x^2/2kT)dv_x$. Call the constant of proportionality K; then

$\int_{-\infty}^{\infty} K\exp(-mv_x^2/2kT)\mathrm{d}v_x = 1$. [The molecule must have some velocity between $v_x = -\infty$ and $v_x = +\infty$.]

$$K\int_{-\infty}^{\infty} \exp(-mv_x^2/2kT)\mathrm{d}v_x = (2kT/m)^{1/2}K\int_{-\infty}^{\infty} \mathrm{e}^{-x^2}\,\mathrm{d}x\,[x^2 = mv_x^2/2kT]$$

$$= (2kT/m)^{1/2}K\sqrt{\pi}.$$

Therefore, $K = (m/2\pi kT)^{1/2}$ and $\mathrm{d}f_x = (m/2\pi kT)^{1/2}\exp(-mv_x^2/2kT)$, which is eqn (26.1.8).

26.14 $\langle v_x\rangle_{\text{final}} = K\int_0^{\langle v_x\rangle_{\text{initial}}} v_x\mathrm{d}f_x$ [26.1.7, 26.1.8 with $f_x\mathrm{d}x = \mathrm{d}f_x$].

Find K from the requirement that

$K\int_0^{\langle v_x\rangle_{\text{initial}}} \mathrm{d}f_x = 1$. [The emergent molecules certainly have a velocity between 0 and $\langle v_x\rangle_{\text{initial}}$.] For simplicity, write $\langle v_x\rangle_{\text{initial}} = a$, then

$$K\int_0^a \mathrm{d}f_x = K(m/2\pi kT)^{1/2}\int_0^a \exp(-mv_x^2/2kT)\mathrm{d}v_x$$

$$= K(2kT/m)^{1/2}(m/2\pi kT)^{1/2}\int_0^b \mathrm{e}^{-x^2}\,\mathrm{d}x\,[b = (m/2kT)^{1/2}a]$$

$$= (K/\pi^{1/2})\int_0^b \mathrm{e}^{-x^2}\,\mathrm{d}x.$$

The *error function* is $\operatorname{erf} z \equiv (2/\sqrt{\pi})\int_0^z \mathrm{e}^{-x^2}\,\mathrm{d}x$ [Box 26.1].

Therefore, $K\int_0^a \mathrm{d}f_x = \tfrac{1}{2}K\operatorname{erf} b = 1$ [required].

Consequently, $K = 2/\operatorname{erf} b$.

The mean velocity in the emergent beam is $\langle v_x\rangle_{\text{final}} = (2/\operatorname{erf} b)\int_0^a v_x\mathrm{d}f_x$

$$= (2/\operatorname{erf} b)(m/2\pi kT)^{1/2}\int_0^a v_x\exp(-mv_x^2/2kT)\mathrm{d}v_x$$

$$= (2/\operatorname{erf} b)(m/2\pi kT)^{1/2}\int_0^a (-kT/m)(\mathrm{d}/\mathrm{d}v_x)\exp(-m_x^2/2kT)\mathrm{d}v_x$$

$$= -(2kT/\pi m)^{1/2}(1/\mathrm{erf}\, b)\exp(-mv_x^2/2kT)\Big|_0^a$$

$$= -(2kT/\pi m)^{1/2}(1/\mathrm{erf}\, b)\{\exp(-ma^2/2kT) - 1\}.$$

Now, $a = \langle v_x\rangle_{\text{initial}} = (2kT/\pi m)^{1/2}$. [Obtain this most quickly by using the expression for $\langle v_x\rangle_{\text{final}}$, but set $a = \infty$, implying erf $b = 1$.] It follows that $\exp(-ma^2/2kT) = \exp(-1/\pi)$ and erf $b = \mathrm{erf}(1/\sqrt{\pi})$.

Therefore, $\langle v_x\rangle_{\text{final}} = (2kT/\pi m)^{1/2}(1 - e^{-1/\pi})/\mathrm{erf}(1/\sqrt{\pi})$, and so

$\langle v_x\rangle_{\text{final}}/\langle v_x\rangle_{\text{initial}} = (1 - e^{-1/\pi})/\mathrm{erf}(1/\sqrt{\pi})$. From tables of the error function, $\mathrm{erf}(1/\sqrt{\pi}) = \mathrm{erf}(0.56) = 0.57$ and $\exp(-1/\pi) = 0.73$; therefore

$\langle v_x\rangle_{\text{final}}/\langle v_x\rangle_{\text{initial}} = \underline{0.47}.$

26.15 $\langle X\rangle = \sum_{i=1}^{z} (N_i/N)X_i$ [26.1.6], $N = 328$.

$$\langle v_x\rangle = (1/328)\{40 \times 50 + 62 \times 55 + \ldots + 2 \times 70 + 38 \times (-50) + 59 \times (-55) + \ldots 2 \times (-70)\}\ \text{m.p.h.} = \underline{18\ \text{m.p.h.}}$$

$$\langle |v_x|\rangle = (1/328)\{40 \times 50 + 62 \times 55 + \ldots + 2 \times 70 + 38 \times 50 + \ldots + 2 \times 70\}\text{m.p.h.}$$

$$= \underline{56\ \text{m.p.h.}}$$

$$\langle v_x^2\rangle = (1/328)\{40 \times 50^2 + 62 \times 55^2 + \ldots + 10 \times 65^2 \times 70^2\}(\text{m.p.h.})^2$$

$$= 3184\ (\text{m.p.h.})^2$$

$\sqrt{\langle v_x^2\rangle} = \underline{56\ \text{m.p.h.}}$ ($\sqrt{\langle v_x^2\rangle} \approx \langle |v_x|\rangle$ is coincidental.)

26.16 $\langle X\rangle = \sum_i (N_i/N)X_i$ [26.1.6], $N = 53$.

$\langle h\rangle = (1/53)\{(5'5'') + 2(5'6'') + 4(5'7'') + \ldots + 1(6'2'')\} = \underline{5'9\tfrac{1}{2}''}.$

$\langle h^2\rangle = (1/53)\{(5'5'')^2 + 2(5'6'')^2 + \ldots + (6'2'')^2\} = 33.54\ \text{ft}^2.$

$\sqrt{\langle h^2\rangle} = 5.79\ \text{ft} = \underline{5'9\tfrac{1}{2}''}.$

26.17 $F(v) = 4\pi(m/2\pi kT)^{3/2}v^2\exp(-mv^2/2kT)$ [26.1.9].

Proportion having a speed *less* than c is

$$\int_0^c F(v)\mathrm{d}v = 4\pi(m/2\pi kT)^{3/2}\int_0^c v^2\exp(-mv^2/2kT)\mathrm{d}v.$$

Write $a = m/2kT$, then

$$\int_0^c F(v)\mathrm{d}v = 4\pi(a/\pi)^{3/2}\int_0^c v^2 \mathrm{e}^{-av^2}\,\mathrm{d}v = -4\pi(a/\pi)^{3/2}(\mathrm{d}/\mathrm{d}a)\int_0^c \mathrm{e}^{-av^2}\,\mathrm{d}v$$

$$= -4\pi(a/\pi)^{3/2}(\mathrm{d}/\mathrm{d}a)(1/a)^{1/2}\int_0^{c\sqrt{a}} \mathrm{e}^{-x^2}\,\mathrm{d}x$$

$$= -4\pi(a/\pi)^{3/2}\left\{-\tfrac{1}{2}(1/a)^{3/2}\int_0^{c\sqrt{a}} \mathrm{e}^{-x^2}\,\mathrm{d}x\right.$$

$$\left.+(1/a)^{1/2}(\mathrm{d}/\mathrm{d}a)\int_0^{c\sqrt{a}} \mathrm{e}^{-x^2}\,\mathrm{d}x\right\}$$

$$\int_0^{c\sqrt{a}} \mathrm{e}^{-x^2}\,\mathrm{d}x = (\pi^{1/2}/2)\mathrm{erf}(c\sqrt{a})\ [\text{Box 26.1}].$$

$$(\mathrm{d}/\mathrm{d}a)\int_0^{c\sqrt{a}} \mathrm{e}^{-x^2}\,\mathrm{d}x = (\mathrm{d}c\sqrt{a}/\mathrm{d}a)\mathrm{e}^{-c^2a} = \tfrac{1}{2}(c/a^{1/2})\mathrm{e}^{-c^2a}\ \left[(\mathrm{d}/\mathrm{d}x)\int_0^x f(y)\mathrm{d}y = f(x)\right]$$

$$\int_0^c F(v)\mathrm{d}v = \mathrm{erf}(c\sqrt{a}) - (2/\pi^{1/2})(c\sqrt{a})\exp(-c^2a).$$

Now, $c = \sqrt{(3kT/m)}$ [26.1.11], and so $c\sqrt{a} = \sqrt{\{(3kT/m)(m/2kT)\}} = \sqrt{(3/2)}$.

Therefore, $\int_0^c F(v)\mathrm{d}v = \mathrm{erf}\sqrt{(3/2)} - \sqrt{(6/\pi)}\exp(-3/2) = 0.92 - 0.31 = \underline{0.61}.$

Therefore, 61 percent of the molecules have a speed less than the mean, and 39 percent have a speed greater than the root mean square value.

For the proportions in terms of the mean speed $\bar{c}$, replace c by $\bar{c} = (8kT/\pi m)^{1/2}$ [26.1.10] $= (8/3\pi)^{1/2}c$, so that $\bar{c}\sqrt{a} = 2/\sqrt{\pi}$. Then

$$\int_0^{\bar{c}} F(v)\mathrm{d}v = \mathrm{erfc}(\bar{c}\sqrt{a}) - (2/\pi^{1/2})(\bar{c}\sqrt{a})\exp(-\bar{c}^2 a)$$

$$= \mathrm{erfc}(2/\sqrt{\pi}) - (4/\pi)\exp(-4/\pi) = 0.889 - 0.356 = \underline{0.533.}$$

Therefore, 53 percent of the particles have a speed less than the mean, and 47 percent have a speed greater than the mean.

26.18 Consider a range of speeds $\mathrm{d}v$ around speeds c^* and nc^*; then

$$\frac{F(nc^*)}{F(c^*)} = \frac{(nc^*)^2\exp(-mn^2c^{*2}/2kT)}{c^{*2}\exp(-mc^{*2}/2kT)}\quad[26.1.9]$$

$$= n^2\exp\{-(n^2-1)mc^{*2}/2kT\}.$$

$c^* = (2kT/m)^{1/2}$ [26.1.12]; therefore, the ratio of probabilities is

$F(nc^*)/F(c^*) = n^2\exp(1-n^2)$.

$F(3c^*)/F(c^*) = 9\mathrm{e}^{-8} = \underline{3.02\times10^{-3}}$; $F(4c^*)/F(c^*) = 16\,\mathrm{e}^{-15} = \underline{4.9\times10^{-6}}$.

26.19 Work required in order to go from a radius R from the center of a planet of mass m_2 to infinity:

$$w = -\int_R^\infty (Gm_1m_2/R^2)\mathrm{d}R \text{ [Example 2.2] } = -Gm_1m_2/R.$$

Energy available: $E = \frac{1}{2}m_1v^2$. Therefore, minimum escape velocity is $\underline{v = \sqrt{(2Gm_2/R)}}$.
$G = 6.672 \times 10^{-11}\,\mathrm{N\,m^2\,kg^{-2}}$, $g = Gm_2/R^2$ [so that for small displacements $w = m_1gh$]

Therefore, $v = \sqrt{(2gR)}$.

(a) $v = \sqrt{\{2 \times (9.81\,\mathrm{m\,s^{-2}}) \times (6.37 \times 10^6\,\mathrm{m})\}} = \underline{11.2\,\mathrm{km\,s^{-1}}}$.

(b) $g(\text{Mars}) = Gm(\text{Mars})/R(\text{Mars})^2$
$= \{Gm(\text{Earth})/R(\text{Earth})^2\}\{R(\text{Earth})/R(\text{Mars})\}^2$
$\times \{m(\text{Mars})/m(\text{Earth})\} = g(\text{Earth}) \times \{6.37/3.38\}^2 \times \{0.108\}$
$= 0.38\,g(\text{Earth}) = 3.73\,\mathrm{m\,s^{-2}}$

$v = \sqrt{\{2 \times (3.73\,\mathrm{m\,s^{-2}}) \times (3.38 \times 10^6\,\mathrm{m})\}} = \underline{5.0\,\mathrm{km\,s^{-1}}}$.

$\bar{c} = (8kT/\pi m)^{1/2}$ [26.1.10], $T = \pi m\bar{c}^2/8k$;

$T = \pi M_\mathrm{m}\bar{c}^2/8R = \{4.72 \times 10^{-5}M_\mathrm{r}(\bar{c}/\mathrm{m\,s^{-1}})^2\}\mathrm{K}$ [$M_\mathrm{m} = M_\mathrm{r}\,\mathrm{g\,mol^{-1}}$].

Draw up the following Table using $M_\mathrm{r}(H_2) = 2.02$, $M_\mathrm{r}(\text{He}) = 4.00$, and $M_\mathrm{r}(O_2) = 32.00$.

T/K	H_2	He	O_2	
Earth	11,900	23,600	188,900	[$\bar{c} = 11.2\,\mathrm{km\,s^{-1}}$]
Mars	2,430	4,810	38,500	[$\bar{c} = 5.0\,\mathrm{km\,s^{-1}}$]

The proportion with speed greater than c_e, the escape speed, is

$$1 - \int_0^{c_\mathrm{e}} F(v)\mathrm{d}v = 1 - \operatorname{erf}(c_\mathrm{e}\sqrt{a}) + (2/\pi^{1/2})(c_\mathrm{e}\sqrt{a})\exp(-c_\mathrm{e}^2a) \text{ [Problem 26.17]}$$

with $a = m/2kT = M_\mathrm{m}/2RT$. Draw up the Tables shown on p. 406.

26.20 The rate of pressure change is

$\mathrm{d}p/\mathrm{d}t \propto -Z_\mathrm{w}A = -pA/\sqrt{(2\pi mkT)}$ [26.2.9]

where A is the area of the hole. Integrate this to

$p = p_0\exp\{-aAt/\sqrt{(2\pi kT)}\}$.

where a is the constant of proportionality in the expression for $\mathrm{d}p/\mathrm{d}t$ [see Problem 26.22 for its explicit form]. Therefore, the time for the pressure to drop from p_0 to p is

(a) $T = 240$ K		H_2	He	O_2
$a/\text{m}^{-2}\,\text{s}^2$		5.06×10^{-7}	1.00×10^{-6}	8.02×10^{-6}
$c_e\sqrt{a}$	Earth	7.97	11.2	31.7
	Mars	3.56	5.01	14.2
$1 - \text{erfc}(c_e\sqrt{a})$	Earth	1.8×10^{-29}	≈ 0	≈ 0
	Mars	4.8×10^{-7}	2.5×10^{-12}	≈ 0
$(c_e\sqrt{a})\exp(-c_e^2 a)$	Earth	2.06×10^{-27}	≈ 0	≈ 0
	Mars	1.12×10^{-5}	6.30×10^{-11}	≈ 0
Proportion	Earth	2.3×10^{-27}	≈ 0	≈ 0
	Mars	1.3×10^{-5}	7.4×10^{-11}	≈ 0

(b) $T = 1500$ K		H_2	He	O_2
$a/\text{m}^{-2}\,\text{s}^2$		8.10×10^{-8}	1.60×10^{-7}	1.28×10^{-6}
$c_e\sqrt{a}$	Earth	3.19	4.49	12.7
	Mars	1.42	2.00	5.66
$1 - \text{erf}(c_e\sqrt{a})$	Earth	6.4×10^{-6}	2.2×10^{-10}	≈ 0
	Mars	4.46×10^{-2}	4.70×10^{-3}	1.2×10^{-5}
$(c_e\sqrt{a})\exp(-c_e^2 a)$	Earth	1.21×10^{-4}	7.89×10^{-9}	≈ 0
	Mars	1.89×10^{-1}	3.66×10^{-2}	6.92×10^{-14}
Proportion	Earth	1.4×10^{-4}	9.1×10^{-9}	≈ 0
	Mars	0.26	0.046	7.9×10^{-14}

Solution 26.20 continued

$t = (2\pi mkT/A^2a^2)^{1/2}\ln(p_0/p) = (2\pi M_m RT/N_A^2A^2a^2)^{1/2}\ln(p_0/p)$.

Consequently, for two gases with RMMs M_r and M_r' for the same initial and final pressures $t/t' = \sqrt{(M_r/M_r')}$; and so $M_r' = M_r t'^2/t^2$.

Since $t' = 52$ s, $t = 42$ s, and $M_r = 28$, it follows that $M_r' = 28 \times (52/42)^2 = \underline{43}$.

26.21 $Z_W = p/\sqrt{(2\pi mkT)}$ [26.2.9]. Number of collisions per second $= AZ_W$, A the surface area of the filament.

$A = 2\pi(5\ \text{cm}) \times (0.1\ \text{mm}) = 3.14 \times 10^{-5}\ \text{m}^2$.

$$Z_W = \frac{(50\ \text{Torr}/760\ \text{Torr}) \times (1.013 \times 10^5\ \text{N m}^{-2})}{[2\pi \times (39.95 \times 1.660\,56 \times 10^{-27}\ \text{kg}) \times (1.381 \times 10^{-23}\ \text{J K}^{-1}) \times (1273\ \text{K})]^{1/2}}$$

$= 7.78 \times 10^{25}\ \text{s}^{-1}\ \text{m}^{-2}$.

Therefore, the collision frequency is

$(3.14 \times 10^{-5}\ \text{m}^2) \times (7.78 \times 10^{25}\ \text{s}^{-1}\ \text{m}^{-2}) = \underline{2.5 \times 10^{21}\ \text{s}^{-1}}$.

26.22 $p = nRT/V = nN_AkT/V = NkT/V$

$dp/dt = (dN/dt)(kT/V)$, $dN/dt = -Z_WA$, $Z_W = p/\sqrt{(2\pi mkT)}$ [26.2.9]

$dp/dt = -Z_WAkT/V = -pA(kT/V)/\sqrt{(2\pi mkT)} = -p(A/V)(kT/2\pi m)^{1/2}$.

Integrate this to $p = p_0 \exp\{-(tA/V)(kT/2\pi m)^{1/2}\}$ with the result that

$t = \{(V/A)(2\pi m/kT)^{1/2}\}\ln(p_0/p)$.

For $p_0 = 0.8$ atm, $p = 0.7$ atm, $M_r \approx 29$, $V = 3.0\ \text{m}^3$,

$A = \pi(0.1\ \text{mm})^2 = \pi \times 10^{-8}\ \text{m}^2$, $T = 298$ K.

$$t = (3.0\ \text{m}^3/\pi \times 10^{-8}\ \text{m}^2)\left\{\frac{2\pi \times (29 \times 1.660\,56 \times 10^{-27}\ \text{kg})}{(1.381 \times 10^{-23}\ \text{J K}^{-1}) \times (298\ \text{K})}\right\}^{1/2} \times \ln(0.8/0.7)$$

$= \underline{1.1 \times 10^5\ \text{s}\ (30\ \text{hours})}$.

26.23 $dN/dt = -Z_WA$, $Z_W = p/\sqrt{(2\pi mkT)}$ [26.2.9], where p is the (constant) vapor pressure of the solid. It follows that $\Delta N = -Z_WAt$ is the change in the number of molecules inside the container; and so the mass loss is

$\Delta m = (-\Delta N/N_A)M_m = Z_WAtM_m/N_A = pAtM_m/N_A\sqrt{(2\pi mkT)}$.

Therefore, as $M_m/N_A = m$, the molecular mass,

$\underline{p = (\Delta m/At)(2\pi kT/m)^{1/2}}$.

26.24 $T = 1273$ K, $t = 7200$ s, $\Delta m = 4.3 \times 10^{-8}$ kg,

$A = \pi \times (5 \times 10^{-4}\ \text{m})^2 = 7.85 \times 10^{-7}\ \text{m}^2$,

$m = 72.5 \times (1.6605 \times 10^{-27}\ \text{kg}) = 1.20 \times 10^{-25}$ kg.

$$p = \left\{\frac{4.3 \times 10^{-8}\ \text{kg}}{(7200\ \text{s}) \times (7.85 \times 10^{-7}\ \text{m}^2)}\right\} \times \left\{\frac{2\pi \times (1.381 \times 10^{-23}\ \text{J K}^{-1}) \times (1273\ \text{K})}{1.20 \times 10^{-25}\ \text{kg}}\right\}^{\frac{1}{2}}$$

$= 7.3 \times 10^{-3}\ \text{N m}^{-2} = \underline{7.3 \times 10^{-3}\ \text{Pa}}$.

26.25 $Z_w = p/\sqrt{(2\pi mkT)}$ [26.2.9, $M_r = 32$]

$$= \frac{(p/\text{atm}) \times (1.013 \times 10^5\ \text{N m}^{-2})}{[2\pi \times (32 \times 1.660\,56 \times 10^{-27}\,\text{kg}) \times (1.381 \times 10^{-23}\,\text{J K}^{-1}) \times (300\,\text{K})]^{1/2}}$$

$$= (2.72 \times 10^{-27}\,\text{s}^{-1}\,\text{m}^{-2}) \times (p/\text{atm}) = (2.72 \times 10^{23}\,\text{s}^{-1}\,\text{cm}^{-2}) \times (p/\text{atm}).$$

(a) $p = 1$ atm, $Z_w = \underline{2.7 \times 10^{23}\,\text{s}^{-1}\,\text{cm}^{-2}}$,

(b) $p = 10^{-6}$ atm, $Z_w = \underline{2.7 \times 10^{17}\,\text{s}^{-1}\,\text{cm}^{-2}}$,

(c) $p = 10^{-10}$ atm, $Z_w = \underline{2.7 \times 10^{13}\,\text{s}^{-1}\,\text{cm}^{-2}}$.

The nearest neighbor distance in titanium is 291 pm, and so the number of atoms per cm^2 is approximately 1.2×10^{15} (the precise value depends on the details of packing – h.c.p – and the type of surface involved). The number of collisions per exposed atom is therefore $Z_w/(1.2 \times 10^{15}\,\text{cm}^{-2})$.

(a) $p = 1$ atm, $Z_{\text{atom}} = \underline{2.3 \times 10^8\,\text{s}^{-1}}$,

(b) $p = 10^{-6}$ atm, $Z_{\text{atom}} = \underline{230\,\text{s}^{-1}}$,

(c) $p = 10^{-10}$ atm, $Z_{\text{atom}} = \underline{0.02\,\text{s}^{-1}}$.

26.26 $dN/dt = k_r[\text{Bk}] - Z_w A$, $Z_w = p/\sqrt{(2\pi mkT)}$ [26.2.9]

$[\text{Bk}] = [\text{Bk}]_o\,e^{-k_r t}$ [radioactive decay],

$p = nRT/V = NkT/V$.

$dp/dt = (kT/V)(dN/dt) = (kk_rT/V)\,[\text{Bk}]_o e^{-k_r t} - pA(kT/V)\sqrt{(2\pi mkT)}$.

Write $A' = (kk_rT/V)\,[\text{Bk}]_o$, $B = (A/V)(kT/2\pi m)^{1/2}$; then $dp/dt = A'e^{-k_r t} - Bp$.

Since at $t = 0$, $p = 0$, the solution is

$p(t) = [A'/(k_r - B)]\,\{\exp(-Bt) - \exp(-k_r t)\}$.

In the present problem,

$[\text{Bk}]/[\text{Bk}]_o = \frac{1}{2}$ when $t = 4.4$ hours; therefore

$k_r = [1/(4.4 \times 3600\,\text{s})]\ln 2 = 4.4 \times 10^{-5}\,\text{s}^{-1}$.

$[\text{Bk}]_o = (1.0 \times 10^{-3}\,\text{g}) \times (6.022 \times 10^{23}\,\text{mol}^{-1})/(244\,\text{g mol}^{-1}) = 2.5 \times 10^{18}$.

$A' = (1.381 \times 10^{-23}\,\text{J K}^{-1}) \times (4.4 \times 10^{-5}\,\text{s}^{-1}) \times (298\,\text{K}) \times (2.5 \times 10^{18})/(10^{-6}\,\text{m}^3)$

$= 0.45\,\text{N m}^{-2}\,\text{s}^{-1} = 0.45\,\text{Pa s}^{-1}$.

$A = \pi(2 \times 10^{-6}\,\text{m})^2 = 4\pi \times 10^{-12}\,\text{m}^2$.

$$B = \left(\frac{4\pi \times 10^{-12}\,\text{m}^2}{10^{-6}\,\text{m}^3}\right)\left\{\frac{(1.381 \times 10^{-23}\,\text{J K}^{-1}) \times (298\,\text{K})}{2\pi \times (4.0 \times 1.6605 \times 10^{-27}\,\text{kg})}\right\}^{1/2} = 3.9 \times 10^{-3}\,\text{s}^{-1}$$

$$p(t) = \left\{ \frac{0.45 \, \text{Pa s}^{-1}}{(4.4 \times 10^{-5} \text{s}^{-1}) - (3.9 \times 10^{-3} \text{s}^{-1})} \right\}$$

$$\times \{\exp[-3.9 \times 10^{-3} (t/s)] - \exp[-4.4 \times 10^{-5} (t/s)]\}$$

$$= 120 \, \text{Pa} \times \{\exp[-4.4 \times 10^{-5} (t/s)] - \exp[-3.9 \times 10^{-3} (t/s)]\}.$$

(a) $t = 1$ hour, 3600 s,

$p(t) = 120 \, \text{Pa} \times \{e^{-0.16} - e^{-14}\} = \underline{100 \, \text{Pa}}.$

(b) $t = 10$ hour, 36 000 s,

$p(t) = 120 \, \text{Pa} \times \{e^{-1.6} - e^{-140}\} = \underline{24 \, \text{Pa}}.$

26.27 $t = \{(V/A)(2\pi m/kT)^{1/2}\} \ln(p_0/p)$ [Problem 26.22].

$V = \frac{4}{3}\pi(5 \times 10^{-2}\text{m})^3 = 5.2 \times 10^{-4}\text{m}^3; A = \pi(3 \times 10^{-3}\text{m})^2 = 2.8 \times 10^{-5}\text{m}^2.$

$m = 18.02 \times (1.6605 \times 10^{-27}\text{kg}) = 2.99 \times 10^{-26}\text{kg}.$

$p_0/p = (1.0 \, \text{Torr})/(1.0 \times 10^{-5}\text{Torr}) = 1.0 \times 10^5.$

$$t = \left(\frac{5.2 \times 10^{-4}\text{m}^3}{2.8 \times 10^{-5}\text{m}^2}\right) \left\{ \frac{2\pi \times (2.99 \times 10^{-26}\text{kg})}{(1.381 \times 10^{-23}\text{J K}^{-1}) \times (300\text{K})} \right\}^{1/2} \times \ln 1.0 \times 10^5 = \underline{1.4 \, \text{s}.}$$

26.28 The atomic current is the number of atoms emerging from the slit per second, Z_wA.

$A = 1 \times 10^{-3}\text{cm}^2 = 1 \times 10^{-7}\text{m}^2,$

$Z_w = p/\sqrt{(2\pi mkT)}$ [26.2.9]

$$= \frac{(p/\text{kPa}) \times 10^3 \, \text{N m}^{-2}}{[2\pi M_r \times (1.660\,56 \times 10^{-27}\text{kg}) \times (1.381 \times 10^{-23}\text{J K}^{-1}) \times (380\text{K})]^{1/2}}$$

$= (1.35 \times 10^{26} \, \text{m}^{-2}\text{s}^{-1}) \times \{(p/\text{kPa})/M_r^{1/2}\}.$

(a) Cadmium, $p/\text{kPa} = 0.13 \times 10^{-3}, M_r = 112.4$;

$Z_wA = (10^{-7}\text{m}^2) \times (1.35 \times 10^{26} \, \text{m}^{-2}\text{s}^{-1}) \times (0.13 \times 10^{-3})/\sqrt{112.4} = \underline{1.7 \times 10^{14} \, \text{s}^{-1}.}$

(b) Mercury, $p/\text{kPa} = 152, M_r = 200.6$;

$Z_wA = (10^{-7}\text{m}^2) \times (1.35 \times 10^{26} \, \text{m}^{-2}\text{s}^{-1}) \times (152)/\sqrt{200.6} = \underline{1.4 \times 10^{20} \, \text{s}^{-1}.}$

26.29 $Z_{AA} = \sigma(4kT/\pi m)^{1/2} (N/V)^2$ [26.2.4] $= \sigma(4kT/\pi m)^{1/2}(p/kT)^2.$

$Z_{AB} = \sigma(8kT/\pi\mu)^{1/2}(p_Ap_B/k^2T^2)$ [26.2.5].

$\sigma(\text{H}_2) = 0.27 \, \text{nm}^2, \sigma(\text{I}_2) \approx 1.2 \, \text{nm}^2.$

$$Z(\text{H}_2, \text{H}_2) = (0.27 \times 10^{-18}\text{m}^2) \times \left\{ \frac{(4 \times 1.381 \times 10^{-23}\text{J K}^{-1}) \times (400\text{K})}{\pi \times (2.02 \times 1.6605 \times 10^{-27}\text{kg})} \right\}^{1/2}$$

$$\times \left\{ \frac{0.5 \times (1.0133 \times 10^{5}\,\mathrm{N\,m^{-2}})}{(1.381 \times 10^{-23}\,\mathrm{J\,K^{-1}}) \times (400\,\mathrm{K})} \right\}^{2} = \underline{3.3 \times 10^{34}\,\mathrm{m^{-3}\,s^{-1}}}.$$

$$Z(I_2, I_2) = \{M_r(H_2)/M_r(I_2)\}^{1/2}\{\sigma(I_2)/\sigma(H_2)\}Z(H_2, H_2)$$
$$= (2.02/254)^{1/2} \times (1.2/0.27) \times (3.3 \times 10^{34}\,\mathrm{m^{-3}\,s^{-1}})$$
$$= \underline{1.3 \times 10^{34}\,\mathrm{m^{-3}\,s^{-1}}}.$$

$$Z(H_2, I_2) = \{2M_r(H_2)/\mu_r\}^{1/2}\{\sigma(H_2, I_2)/\sigma(H_2, H_2)\}Z(H_2, H_2)$$
$$\mu_r = M_r(H_2)M_r(I_2)/\{M_r(H_2) + M_r(I_2)\} = 2.02 \times 254/\{2.02 + 254\} = 2.00.$$
$$\sigma(H_2, I_2) \approx \pi\{R(H_2) + R(I_2)\}^2$$
$$2R(H_2) \approx \{\sigma(H_2, H_2)/\pi\}^{1/2} = 2.9 \times 10^{-10}\,\mathrm{m},$$
$$2R(I_2) \approx \{\sigma(I_2, I_2)/\pi\}^{1/2} = 6.2 \times 10^{-10}\,\mathrm{m},$$
$$\sigma(H_2, I_2) \approx \tfrac{1}{4}\pi\{9.1 \times 10^{-10}\,\mathrm{m}\}^2 = 0.65\,\mathrm{nm}^2.$$
$$Z(H_2, I_2) = \{4.04/2.00\}^{1/2}\{0.65/0.27\} \times (3.29 \times 10^{34}\,\mathrm{m^{-3}\,s^{-1}})$$
$$= \underline{1.1 \times 10^{35}\,\mathrm{m^{-3}\,s^{-1}}}.$$

26.30 $\eta = \frac{1}{3}\lambda\bar{c}m\mathcal{N}$ [Box 26.2, simple kinetic theory result],

$\bar{c} = (8kT/\pi m)^{1/2}$ [26.1.10], $\lambda = kT/\sigma p\sqrt{2}$ [26.2.6], $\mathcal{N} = p/kT$ [$\mathcal{N} = N/V$].

$$\eta = \tfrac{1}{3}(kT/\sigma p\sqrt{2})(8kT/\pi m)^{1/2}m(p/kT) = \tfrac{2}{3}(kTm/\pi)^{1/2}/\sigma$$
$$= \tfrac{2}{3} \times \{(1.381 \times 10^{-23}\,\mathrm{J\,K^{-1}}) \times T \times (29 \times 1.660\,56 \times 10^{-27}\,\mathrm{kg})/\pi\}^{1/2}/(0.40 \times 10^{18}\,\mathrm{m^2})$$
$$= (7.67 \times 10^{-7}\,\mathrm{kg\,m^{-1}\,s^{-1}})\sqrt{(T/K)}.$$

(a) 273 K, $\eta = (7.67 \times 10^{-7}\,\mathrm{kg\,m^{-1}\,s^{-1}}) \times 16.5 = \underline{1.3 \times 10^{-5}\,\mathrm{kg\,m^{-1}\,s^{-1}}}$

(b) 298 K, $\eta = (7.67 \times 10^{-7}\,\mathrm{kg\,m^{-1}\,s^{-1}}) \times 17.3 = \underline{1.3 \times 10^{-5}\,\mathrm{kg\,m^{-1}\,s^{-1}}}.$

(c) 1000 K, $\eta = (7.67 \times 10^{-7}\,\mathrm{kg\,m^{-1}\,s^{-1}}) \times 31.6 = \underline{2.4 \times 10^{-5}\,\mathrm{kg\,m^{-1}\,s^{-1}}}.$

26.31 $\kappa = \bar{c}C_{V,\mathrm{m}}/3\sigma N_A\sqrt{2}$ [Box 26.2, simple kinetic theory result],

$\bar{c} = (8kT/\pi m)^{1/2}$ [26.1.10]; $\kappa = (4kT/\pi m)^{1/2}C_{V,\mathrm{m}}/3\sigma N_A$; $C_{V,\mathrm{m}} = \frac{3}{2}R$.

$$\kappa = (4kT/\pi m)^{1/2}(\tfrac{3}{2}R)/3\sigma N_A = (k^3T/\pi m)^{1/2}/\sigma$$
$$= \left\{ \frac{(1.3807 \times 10^{-23}\,\mathrm{J\,K^{-1}})^3 T}{\pi \times M_r \times (1.660\,56 \times 10^{-27}\,\mathrm{kg})} \right\}^{1/2} \Big/ \sigma$$
$$= (7.103 \times 10^{-4}\,\mathrm{J\,K^{-1}\,m^{-1}\,s^{-1}}) \times \{(T/K)^{1/2}/M_r^{1/2}(\sigma/\mathrm{nm}^2)\}.$$

(a) $M_r = 39.95$, $T = 300\,\mathrm{K}$, $\sigma = 0.36\,\mathrm{nm}^2$ [Table 26.2];

$$\kappa = (7.103 \times 10^{-4}\,\mathrm{J\,K^{-1}\,m^{-1}\,s^{-1}}) \times \{(300/39.95)^{1/2}/0.36\}$$
$$= \underline{5.4\,\mathrm{mJ\,K^{-1}\,m^{-1}\,s^{-1}}}.$$

(b) $M_r = 4.00$, $T = 300\,\mathrm{K}$, $\sigma = 0.21\,\mathrm{nm}^2$ [Table 26.2];

$\kappa = (7.103 \times 10^{-4}\,\mathrm{J\,K^{-1}\,m^{-1}}) \times \{(300/4.00)^{1/2}/0.21\}$

$= \underline{30\,\mathrm{mJ\,K^{-1}\,m^{-1}\,s^{-1}}}.$

$\mathrm{d}E/\mathrm{d}t = \kappa A(\mathrm{d}T/\mathrm{d}z)$, $A = 100\,\mathrm{cm}^2 = 1.00 \times 10^{-2}\,\mathrm{m}^2$,

$\mathrm{d}T/\mathrm{d}z = (310\,\mathrm{K} - 295\,\mathrm{K})/(10\,\mathrm{cm}) = 150\,\mathrm{K\,m^{-1}}$.

(a) Argon:

$\mathrm{d}E/\mathrm{d}t = (5.4 \times 10^{-3}\,\mathrm{J\,K^{-1}\,m^{-1}\,s^{-1}}) \times (1.00 \times 10^{-2}\,\mathrm{m}^2) \times 150\,\mathrm{K\,m^{-1}}) = \underline{8.1\,\mathrm{mJ\,s^{-1}}}.$

(b) Helium:

$\mathrm{d}E/\mathrm{d}t = (3 \times 10^{-2}\,\mathrm{J\,K^{-1}\,m^{-1}\,s^{-1}}) \times (1.00 \times 10^{-2}\,\mathrm{m}^2) \times (150\,\mathrm{K\,m^{-1}}) = \underline{40\,\mathrm{mJ\,s^{-1}}}.$

26.32 $\mathrm{d}V/\mathrm{d}t \propto 1/\eta$ [26.3.14]

$(\mathrm{d}V/\mathrm{d}t)_{CO_2}/(\mathrm{d}V/\mathrm{d}t)_{Ar} = \eta_{Ar}/\eta_{CO_2}$;

$(\mathrm{d}V/\mathrm{d}t)_{CO_2}/(\mathrm{d}V/\mathrm{d}t)_{Ar} = 83.55 = 1.5$.

$\eta_{CO_2} = \eta_{Ar}/1.5 = 208\,\mu\mathrm{P}/1.5 = 140\,\mu\mathrm{P}$.

$\eta = m\bar{c}/3\sigma\sqrt{2}$ [Box 26.2, simple kinetic theory]

$= m(8kT/\pi m)^{1/2}/3\sigma\sqrt{2}$ [26.1.10] $= (4kTm/9\pi)^{1/2}/\sigma$;

$\sigma = (4kTm/9\pi)^{1/2}/\eta$

$$= \frac{[4 \times (1.381 \times 10^{-23}\,\mathrm{J\,K^{-1}}) \times (298\,\mathrm{K}) \times (44 \times 1.6605 \times 10^{-27}\,\mathrm{kg})]^{1/2}}{3\pi^{1/2} \times (1.40 \times 10^{-5}\,\mathrm{kg\,m^{-1}\,s^{-1}})}$$

$= 4.7 \times 10^{-19}\,\mathrm{m}^2$.

$\sigma \approx \pi d^2$,

$d = (4.7 \times 10^{-19}\,\mathrm{m}^2/\pi)^{1/2} = \underline{390\,\mathrm{pm}}.$

26.33 $\kappa = (4kT/\pi m)^{1/2} C_{V,\mathrm{m}}/3\sigma N_A$ [Problem 26.31]

(a) $$\kappa = \left\{\frac{4 \times (1.381 \times 10^{-23}\,\mathrm{J\,K^{-1}}) \times (298\,\mathrm{K})}{\pi \times (39.95 \times 1.660\,56 \times 10^{-27}\,\mathrm{kg})}\right\}^{1/2}$$

$$\times \tfrac{1}{3} \times \left\{\frac{12.5\,\mathrm{J\,K^{-1}\,mol^{-1}}}{(0.36\,\mathrm{nm}^2) \times (6.022 \times 10^{23}\,\mathrm{mol^{-1}})}\right\} = \underline{5\,\mathrm{mJ\,K^{-1}\,m^{-1}\,s^{-1}}}.$$

(b) $$\kappa = \left\{\frac{4 \times (1.381 \times 10^{-23}\,\mathrm{J\,K^{-1}}) \times (298\,\mathrm{K})}{\pi \times (29 \times 1.660\,56 \times 10^{-27}\,\mathrm{kg})}\right\}^{1/2}$$

$$\times \tfrac{1}{3} \times \left\{\frac{21.0\,\mathrm{J\,K^{-1}\,mol^{-1}}}{(0.40\,\mathrm{nm}^2) \times (6.022 \times 10^{23}\,\mathrm{mol^{-1}})}\right\} = \underline{9.6\,\mathrm{mJ\,K^{-1}\,m^{-1}\,s^{-1}}}.$$

26.34 $\kappa(T_2)/\kappa(T_1) = (T_2/T_1)^{1/2} C_{V,m}(T_2)/C_{V,m}(T_1)$ [Problem 26.31].

$C_{V,m}(300\,\text{K}) \approx \frac{3}{2}R + R = \frac{5}{2}R$ [22.3.14]

$C_{V,m}(10\,\text{K}) \approx \frac{3}{2}R$ [Rotation not excited, Section 22.3(b)]

$\kappa(300\,\text{K})/\kappa(10\,\text{K}) = (\sqrt{30})(5/2)/(3/2) = \frac{5}{3}\sqrt{30} = \underline{9.1}.$

26.35 $\mathrm{d}E/\mathrm{d}t = \kappa A(\mathrm{d}T/\mathrm{d}z)$ [26.3.2]

$\kappa = 1 \times 10^{-2}\,\text{J m}^{-1}\,\text{s}^{-1}\,\text{K}^{-1}$ [Problem 26.33]; $A = 1\,\text{m}^2$.

$\mathrm{d}T/\mathrm{d}z = 35\,\text{K}/5\,\text{cm} = 7\,\text{K cm}^{-1} = 700\,\text{K m}^{-1}$.

$\mathrm{d}E/\mathrm{d}t = (1 \times 10^{-2}\,\text{J m}^{-1}\,\text{s}^{-1}\,\text{K}^{-1}) \times (1\,\text{m}^2) \times (700\,\text{K m}^{-1}) = \underline{7\,\text{J s}^{-1}}.$

A 7 W heater (or 7 W of an existing heater) is required to make good the loss.

26.36 $D = (4k^3T^3/9\pi m)^{1/2}/p\sigma$ [26.3.7]

$$= \left\{\frac{4 \times (1.381 \times 10^{-23}\,\text{J K}^{-1})^3 \times (298.15\,\text{K})^3}{9\pi \times (39.95 \times 1.660\,56 \times 10^{-27}\,\text{kg})}\right\}^{1/2}$$

$$\times \left\{\frac{1}{(1.013 \times 10^5\,\text{N m}^{-2}) \times (p/\text{atm}) \times (0.36\,\text{nm}^2)}\right\} = (1.06 \times 10^{-5}\,\text{m}^2\,\text{s}^{-1})/(p/\text{atm})$$

(a) $p = 10^{-6}\,\text{atm}$; $D = \underline{10\,\text{m}^2\,\text{s}^{-1}}$.

(b) $p = 10\,\text{atm}$; $D = \underline{1.1 \times 10^{-5}\,\text{m}^2\,\text{s}^{-1}}$.

(c) $p = 100\,\text{atm}$; $D = \underline{1.1 \times 10^{-7}\,\text{m}^2\,\text{s}^{-1}}$.

$J = -D\mathrm{d}\mathcal{N}/\mathrm{d}z$ [26.3.1], $\mathcal{N} = nN_A/V = p/kT$; therefore, $J = -(D/kT)\mathrm{d}p/\mathrm{d}z$.

For the present problem, $\mathrm{d}p/\mathrm{d}z = -0.1\,\text{atm cm}^{-1} = -1 \times 10^4\,\text{N m}^{-2}\,\text{cm}^{-1}$

$= -1 \times 10^6\,\text{N m}^{-3}$. Then, as $kT = 4.12 \times 10^{21}\,\text{J}$,

$J = (1 \times 10^6\,\text{N m}^{-3})D/(4.12 \times 10^{-21}\,\text{J}) = (2 \times 10^{26}\,D)\text{m}^{-4}$.

(a) $J = (2 \times 10^{26}\,\text{m}^{-4}) \times (10\,\text{m}^2\,\text{s}^{-1}) = \underline{2 \times 10^{27}\,\text{m}^{-2}\,\text{s}^{-1}}$

or $\underline{0.3\,\text{mol cm}^{-2}\,\text{s}^{-1}}$.

(b) $J = (2 \times 10^{26}\,\text{m}^{-4}) \times (1.1 \times 10^{-5}\,\text{m}^2\,\text{s}^{-1}) = \underline{2 \times 10^{21}\,\text{m}^{-2}\,\text{s}^{-1}}$,

or $\underline{3 \times 10^{-7}\,\text{mol cm}^{-2}\,\text{s}^{-1}}$.

(c) $J = (2 \times 10^{26}\,\text{m}^{-4}) \times (1.1 \times 10^{-7}\,\text{m}^2\,\text{s}^{-1}) = \underline{2 \times 10^{19}\,\text{m}^{-2}\,\text{s}^{-1}}$,

or $\underline{3 \times 10^{-9}\,\text{mol cm}^{-2}\,\text{s}^{-1}}$.

26.37 The rate of growth of the volume, $\mathrm{d}v/\mathrm{d}t$, is equal to the product of the collision frequency, Z_W, the surface area, A, and the volume added by each molecular collision, V_m/N_A. Therefore,

$dv/dt = sZ_w A V_m/N_A$.

For a spherical particle, $v = \frac{4}{3}\pi r^3$ and $A = 4\pi r^2$.

Therefore, $dv/dt = 4\pi r^2\, dr/dt = A\, dr/dt$.

Consequently $dr/dt = sZ_w V_m/N_A$.

$Z_w = p/\sqrt{(2\pi mkT)}$ [26.2.9] $= (kT/2\pi m)^{1/2}\mathcal{N}$; $\mathcal{N} = N/V = nN_A/V$,

$V_m = M_m/\rho$, $m = M_m/N_A$.

$dr/dt = s(kTN_A/2\pi M_m)^{1/2}\mathcal{N}M_m/\rho N_A = \underline{(s\mathcal{N}/N_A\rho)(M_m RT/2\pi)^{1/2}}$.

$\mathcal{N} \lesssim 3 \times 10^{15}\ \text{cm}^{-3} = 3 \times 10^{21}\ \text{m}^{-3}$, $M_m = 207\ \text{g mol}^{-1}$, $\rho \approx 11.5\ \text{g cm}^{-3}$, $T = 935\ \text{K}$, $s \approx 1$.

$$dr/dt \lesssim \left\{\frac{3 \times 10^{21}\ \text{m}^{-3}}{(6.022 \times 10^{23}\ \text{mol}^{-1}) \times (11.5 \times 10^{3}\ \text{kg m}^{-3})}\right\}$$

$$\times \left\{\frac{(207 \times 10^{-3}\ \text{kg mol}^{-1}) \times (8.314 \times \text{J K}^{-1}\ \text{mol}^{-1}) \times (935\ \text{K})}{2\pi}\right\}^{1/2}$$

$$= 7 \times 10^{-6}\ \text{m s}^{-1} = \underline{7 \times 10^{-4}\ \text{cm s}^{-1}}.$$

Therefore, in 0.5 ms, the growth in radius of the particle cannot exceed about $(7 \times 10^{-4}\ \text{cm s}^{-1}) \times (0.5 \times 10^{-3}\ \text{s}) = 4 \times 10^{-7}\ \text{cm}$, or $\underline{4\ \text{nm}}$.

27. Molecules in motion: ion transport and molecular diffusion

A27.1 $\rho = (\Lambda_m c)^{-1}$ [27.1.2, $\rho = 1/\kappa$] $= (135.5 \times 10^{-4}\,\mathrm{S\,m^2\,mol^{-1}})^{-1}$
$\times (53.5\,\mathrm{mol\,m^{-3}})^{-1}$
$= \underline{1.38\,\Omega\,\mathrm{m}}$.

A27.2 $\kappa = IR^{-1}A^{-1}$ [27.1.1] $= (2.75\,\mathrm{cm})(351\,\Omega)^{-1}(2.2\,\mathrm{cm})^{-2}$
$= \underline{1.62 \times 10^{-3}\,\mathrm{S\,cm^{-1}}}$.

A27.3 $\Lambda_m = \Lambda_m^0 - \mathscr{K}c^{\frac{1}{2}}$ [27.1.3]

$\Delta\Lambda_m = -\mathscr{K}\Delta(c^{\frac{1}{2}})$

$\Lambda_m^0 = \Lambda_m - [\Delta\Lambda_m/\Delta(c^{\frac{1}{2}})]c^{\frac{1}{2}}$

$= 109.9\,\mathrm{S\,cm^2\,mol^{-1}} - [(106.1 - 109.9)\mathrm{S\,cm^2\,mol^{-1}}]$
$\times (6.2 \times 10^{-3}\,\mathrm{mol\,dm^{-3}})^{\frac{1}{2}}[(0.0150)^{\frac{1}{2}} - (0.0062)^{\frac{1}{2}}]^{-1}(\mathrm{mol\,dm^{-3}})^{-\frac{1}{2}}$
$= \underline{116.7\,\mathrm{S\,cm^2\,mol^{-1}}}$.

A27.4 $\lambda_- = |z_-|u_-F$ [27.1.12b] $= (1)(6.85 \times 10^{-8}\,\mathrm{m^2\,s^{-1}\,V^{-1}})$
$\times (9.65 \times 10^4\,\mathrm{C\,mol^{-1}})$
$= \underline{6.61 \times 10^{-3}\,\mathrm{S\,m^2\,s^{-1}}}$.

A27.5 $s = uE$ [27.1.10] $= (7.92 \times 10^{-8}\,\mathrm{m^2\,s^{-1}\,V^{-1}})(35.0\,\mathrm{V})(8.00 \times 10^{-3}\,\mathrm{m})^{-1}$
$= \underline{3.47 \times 10^{-4}\,\mathrm{m\,s^{-1}}}$.

A27.6 $t_+ = u_+/(u_+ + u_-) = 4.01/(4.01 + 8.09) = \underline{0.331}$. [27.1.17, Table 27.2]

A27.7 $a = kT(6\pi\eta D)^{-1}$ [27.2.9]

$a = (1.4 \times 10^{-23}\,\mathrm{J\,K^{-1}})(2.9 \times 10^2\,\mathrm{K})(6\pi)^{-1}(1.0 \times 10^{-3}\,\mathrm{kg\,m^{-1}\,s^{-1}})^{-1}$
$\times (7.1 \times 10^{-11}\,\mathrm{m^2\,s^{-1}})^{-1} = 3.1 \times 10^{-9}\,\mathrm{m}$,

$M = (4/3)\pi a^3 N_A(\bar{V})^{-1} = (4\pi/3)(3.1 \times 10^{-9}\,\mathrm{m})^3(6.0 \times 10^{23}\,\mathrm{mol^{-1}})$
$\times (7.5 \times 10^{-4}\,\mathrm{m^3\,kg^{-1}})^{-1} = 99\,\mathrm{kg\,mol^{-1}}$,

RMM $= \underline{9.9 \times 10^4}$.

A27.8 $D = ukT/ez = uRT/Fz$ [27.2.5]

$= (7.40 \times 10^{-8}\,m^2\,s^{-1}\,V^{-1})(8.31\,J\,K^{-1}\,mol^{-1})(298\,K)(9.65 \times 10^4\,C\,mol^{-1})^{-1}(1)^{-1}$

$= \underline{1.90 \times 10^{-9}\,m^2\,s^{-1}}.$

A27.9 $a = kT(6\pi\eta D)^{-1}$ [27.2.9]

$= (1.4 \times 10^{-23}\,J\,K^{-1})(2.9 \times 10^2\,K)(6\pi)^{-1}(1.0 \times 10^{-3}\,kg\,m^{-1}\,s^{-1})^{-1} \times (4.0 \times 10^{-11}\,m^2\,s^{-1})^{-1}$

$= 5.5 \times 10^{-9}\,m$, or $\underline{5.5\,nm}$.

A27.10 $\tau = d^2(2D)^{-1}$ [27.3.12]

$= (5.00 \times 10^{-3}\,m)^2(1/2)(3.17 \times 10^{-9}\,m^2\,s^{-1})^{-1}$

$= \underline{3.94 \times 10^3\,s}.$

27.1 $\kappa = C/R$, $\Lambda_m = \kappa/c$ [27.1.2]

$\kappa(AcOH)/\kappa(KCl) = R(KCl)/R(AcOH)$.

$R(KCl) = 33.21\,\Omega$, $R(AcOH) = 300\,\Omega$.

$\kappa(AcOH) = (33.21\,\Omega/300\,\Omega) \times (1.1639 \times 10^{-2}\,S\,cm^{-1}) = 1.29 \times 10^{-3}\,S\,cm^{-1}$.

But $\kappa(AcOH)$ has a contribution of $7.6 \times 10^{-4}\,S\,cm^{-1}$ from the water; hence the conductivity due to the acetic acid is $(12.9 - 7.6) \times 10^{-4}\,S\,cm^{-1} = 5.3 \times 10^{-4}\,S\,cm^{-1}$.

$\Lambda_m = (5.3 \times 10^{-4}\,S\,cm^{-1})/(0.100\,mol\,dm^{-3})$

$= \underline{5.3\,S\,cm^2\,mol^{-1}}.$

27.2 $\kappa = C/R$, $\Lambda_m = \kappa/c$ [27.1.2]; $C = \kappa R = c\Lambda_m R$.

$C = (0.0200\,mol\,dm^{-3}) \times (138.3\,S\,cm^2\,mol^{-1}) \times (74.58\,\Omega)$

$= 206.3\,cm^2\,dm^{-3} = 206.3\,(cm^2/10^3\,cm^3) = \underline{0.2063\,cm^{-1}}, \underline{20.63\,m^{-1}}.$

27.3 $\Lambda_m = C/cR$ [Problem 27.2] $= \Lambda_m^o - \mathscr{K}\sqrt{c}$ [27.1.3].

Draw up the following Table, using $C = 0.2063\,cm^{-1}$ [Problem 27.2].

c/M	0.0005	0.001	0.005	0.010	0.020	0.050
$(c/M)^{1/2}$	0.0224	0.032	0.071	0.100	0.141	0.224
R/Ω	3314	1668	342.1	174.1	89.08	37.14
$\Lambda_m/S\,cm^2\,mol^{-1}$	124.5	123.7	120.6	118.5	115.8	111.1

Λ_m is plotted against $\sqrt{c}$ in Fig. 27.1. The limiting value is $\underline{\Lambda_m^o = 126\,S\,cm^2\,mol^{-1}}$. The slope is -76.5; hence $\mathscr{K} = \underline{76.5\,S\,cm^2\,mol^{-1}/M^{1/2}}$.

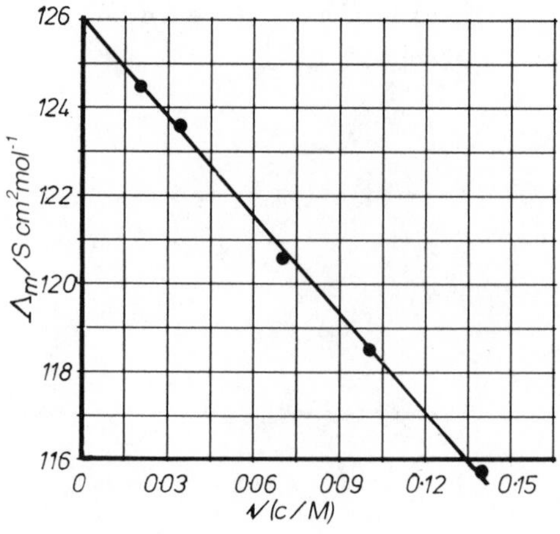

Fig 27.1

27.4 $\Lambda_m^o = \nu_+\lambda_+^o + \nu_+\lambda_-^o$ [27.1.4]

$\Lambda_m = \Lambda_m^o - \mathscr{K}\sqrt{c}$ [27.1.3], $\mathscr{K} = 76.5\ \mathrm{S\ cm^2\ mol^{-1}/M^{1/2}}$.

$\Lambda_m^o(\mathrm{NaI}) = (50.1 + 76.8)\ \mathrm{S\ cm^2\ mol^{-1}} = 126.9\ \mathrm{S\ cm^2\ mol^{-1}}$.

$\mathscr{K}\sqrt{c} = \{76.5\ \mathrm{S\ cm^2\ mol^{-1}/M^{1/2}}\} \times \{0.010\ \mathrm{M}\}^{1/2}$

$= 7.65\ \mathrm{S\ cm^2\ mol^{-1}}$.

(a) $\Lambda_m = 126.9\ \mathrm{S\ cm^2\ mol^{-1}} - 7.65\ \mathrm{S\ cm^2\ mol^{-1}}$

$= \underline{119.2\ \mathrm{S\ cm^2\ mol^{-1}}}$.

(b) $\kappa = c\Lambda_m$ [27.1.2] $= (0.010\ \mathrm{M}) \times (119.2\ \mathrm{S\ cm^2\ mol^{-1}})$

$= 1.192\ \mathrm{S\ cm^2\ dm^{-3}} = \underline{1.192 \times 10^{-3}\ \mathrm{S\ cm^{-1}}} = \underline{1.192\ \mathrm{mS\ cm^{-1}}}$.

(c) $R = c/\kappa = (0.2063\ \mathrm{cm^{-1}})/(1.192 \times 10^{-3}\ \mathrm{S\ cm^{-1}}) = \underline{173.1\ \Omega}$.

27.5 $\Lambda_m^o = \nu_+\lambda_+^o + \nu_-\lambda_-^o$ [27.1.4]

KCl: $\Lambda_m^o(\mathrm{KCl}) = \lambda_+^o(\mathrm{K^+}) + \lambda_-^o(\mathrm{Cl^-}) = 149.9\ \mathrm{S\ cm^2\ mol^{-1}}$,

KNO_3: $\Lambda_m^o(\mathrm{KNO_3}) = \lambda_+^o(\mathrm{K^+}) + \lambda_-^o(\mathrm{NO_3^-}) = 145.0\ \mathrm{S\ cm^2\ mol^{-1}}$,

$AgNO_3$: $\Lambda_m^o(\mathrm{AgNO_3}) = \lambda_+^o(\mathrm{Ag^+}) + \lambda_-^o(\mathrm{NO_3^-}) = 133.4\ \mathrm{S\ cm^2\ mol^{-1}}$,

AgCl: $\Lambda_m^o(\mathrm{AgCl}) = \lambda_+^o(\mathrm{Ag^+}) + \lambda_-^o(\mathrm{Cl^-}) = \Lambda_m^o(\mathrm{AgNO_3}) + \Lambda_m^o(\mathrm{KCl}) - \Lambda_m^o(\mathrm{KNO_3})$

$= (133.4 + 149.9 - 145.0)\ \mathrm{S\ cm^2\ mol^{-1}}$

$= \underline{138.3\ \mathrm{S\ cm^2\ mol^{-1}}}$.

27.6 $c = \kappa/\Lambda_m \approx \kappa/\Lambda_m^o$ [c small, conductivity of water allowed for in data.]

$= (1.887 \times 10^{-6}\ \mathrm{S\ cm^{-1}})/(138.3\ \mathrm{S\ cm^2\ mol^{-1}})$ [Problem 27.5]

$= 1.36 \times 10^{-8}\ \mathrm{mol\ cm^{-3}} = \underline{1.36 \times 10^{-5}\ \mathrm{M}}$.

$K_s \approx (1.36 \times 10^{-5})^2 = \underline{1.86 \times 10^{-10}}$ [activity coefficients ignored].
Correct for activities using $\gamma_\pm \approx 10^{-A\sqrt{c}}$ [11.2.11] ≈ 0.996. Hence $K_s = \gamma_\pm^2 \times (1.86 \times 10^{-10}) = 1.85 \times 10^{-10}$.

27.7 Conductivity of water allowed for in data.

$\Lambda_m^o(\text{AcONa}) = \lambda_+^o(\text{Na}^+) + \lambda_-^o(\text{AcO}^-) = 91.0\,\text{S cm}^2\,\text{mol}^{-1}$,

$\Lambda_m^o(\text{HCl}) = \lambda_+^o(\text{H}^+) + \lambda_-^o(\text{Cl}^-) = 425.0\,\text{S cm}^2\,\text{mol}^{-1}$,

$\Lambda_m^o(\text{NaCl}) = \lambda_+^o(\text{Na}^+) + \lambda_-^o(\text{Cl}^-) = 128.1\,\text{S cm}^2\,\text{mol}^{-1}$,

$\Lambda_m^o(\text{AcOH}) = \lambda_+^o(\text{H}^+) + \lambda_+^o(\text{AcO}^-) = \Lambda_m^o(\text{HCl}) + \Lambda_m^o(\text{AcONa}) - \Lambda_m^o(\text{NaCl})$

$= (425.0 + 91.0 - 128.1)\text{S cm}^2\,\text{mol}^{-1}$

$= \underline{387.9\,\text{S cm}^2\,\text{mol}^{-1}}$.

27.8 $\alpha = \Lambda_m/\Lambda_m^o$ [*Example* 27.3, AcOH fully ionized at infinite dilution].

$\Lambda_m = \kappa/c = C/cR$ [Problem 27.2; conductivity of water allowed for in data]

$= (0.2063\,\text{cm}^{-1})/[(0.020\,\text{M}) \times (888\,\Omega)]$

$= 1.16 \times 10^{-2}\,\text{S mol}^{-1}\,(\text{dm}^3/\text{cm}) = 11.6\,\text{S cm}^2\,\text{mol}^{-1}$.

$\alpha = (11.6\,\text{S cm}^2\,\text{mol}^{-1})/(387.9\,\text{S cm}^2\,\text{mol}^{-1})$ [Problem 27.7] $= 2.99 \times 10^{-2} = \underline{0.030}$.

27.9 $\text{pH} = \lg a_{\text{H}^+}$ [12.4.9] $= -\lg \gamma c_{\text{H}^+} = -\lg \gamma c\alpha;\ c \equiv c(\text{HA})/\text{M}$.

For $\gamma \approx 1$, $\text{pH} \approx -\lg \alpha c = -\lg(0.030 \times 0.020) = \underline{3.22}$.

For $c_{\text{H}^+} \approx 0.030 \times 0.020\,\text{M} = 6.0 \times 10^{-4}\,\text{M}$ we have

$\lg \gamma = -0.509\sqrt{I}$ [11.2.11] $\approx -0.509\sqrt{(6.0 \times 10^{-4})} = -0.012$.

$\text{pH} = -\lg \alpha c - \lg \gamma = 3.22 + 0.012 = \underline{3.23}$.

27.10 $1/\Lambda_m = 1/\Lambda_m^o + \Lambda_m c/K(\Lambda_m^o)^2$ [27.1.7]; use $\Lambda_m^o = \lambda_{\text{H}^+}^o + \lambda_{\text{Ac}^-}^o = 390.5\,\text{S cm}^2\,\text{mol}^{-1}$.
Draw up the following Table using $\Lambda_m = \kappa/c = C/cR$, $C = 0.2063\,\text{cm}^{-1}$ [Problem 27.2]

c/M	0.000 49	0.000 99	0.001 98	0.015 81	0.063 23	0.2529
$\Lambda_m/\text{S cm}^2\,\text{mol}^{-1}$	68.5	49.5	35.6	13.0	6.56	3.22
$10^5 c\Lambda_m/\text{S cm}^{-1}$	3.36	4.90	7.05	20.6	41.5	81.4
$100/(\Lambda_m/\text{S cm}^2\,\text{mol}^{-1})$	1.46	2.02	2.81	7.69	15.2	31.1

$10^2/\Lambda_m$ is plotted against $10^5 c\Delta_m$; a least squares fit gives an intercept equal to 0.352 and a slope 0.015 59. Since

$10^2\,\mathrm{S\,cm^2\,mol^{-1}}/\Lambda_m = 10^2\,\mathrm{S\,cm^2\,mol^{-1}}/\Lambda_m^o + 10^2\,\mathrm{S\,cm^2\,mol^{-1}}(1/K\Lambda_m^{o2})(10^5 c\Lambda_m/10^5\,\mathrm{S\,cm^{-1}})$

the slope of the plot is

Slope $= 10^2\,\mathrm{S^2\,cm\,mol^{-1}}/10^5 K\Lambda_m^{o2} = 10^{-3}\,\mathrm{S^2\,cm\,mol^{-1}}/K\Lambda_m^{o2} = 0.352.$

Hence, $K = 10^{-3}\,\mathrm{cm^{-3}\,mol^{-1}}/390.5^2 \times 0.352 = 1.86 \times 10^{-8}\,\mathrm{mol\,cm^{-3}}$

$= 1.86 \times 10^{-5}\,\mathrm{mol\,dm^{-3}}$, $\underline{\mathrm{p}K_a = 4.73}$.

27.11 $1/\Lambda_m = 1/\Lambda_m^o + \Lambda_m c/K\Lambda_m^{o2}$ [27.1.7], $\Lambda_m^o = 390.5\,\mathrm{S\,cm^2\,mol^{-1}}$ [Table 27.1]

$\Lambda_m^o = \Lambda_m + \Lambda_m^2 c/K\Lambda_m^o,$

$\Lambda_m^2 c/K\Lambda_m^o + \Lambda_m - \Lambda_m^o = 0,$

$\Lambda_m = (K/2c)\{-1 + [1 + 4c/K]^{1/2}\}\Lambda_m^o$

$= (1.91 \times 10^{-5}/2 \times 0.040)\{-1 + [1 + (4 \times 0.040/1.91 \times 10^{-5})]^{1/2}\}\Lambda_m^o$

$= 0.022\,\Lambda_m^o = \underline{8.59\,\mathrm{S\,cm^2\,mol^{-1}}}$.

$\kappa = c\Lambda_m = 0.040\,\mathrm{M} \times 8.59\,\mathrm{S\,cm^2\,mol^{-1}} = \underline{3.44 \times 10^{-4}\,\mathrm{S\,cm^{-1}}}$.

$R = C/\kappa = 0.2063\,\mathrm{cm^{-1}}/3.44 \times 10^{-4}\,\mathrm{S\,cm^{-1}} = \underline{600\,\Omega}$.

27.12 $\lambda_\pm = u_\pm|z_\pm|F$ [27.1.12], $u_\pm = \lambda_\pm/|z_\pm|F$

$u_+(\mathrm{Li^+}) = (38.7\,\mathrm{S\,cm^2\,mol^{-1}})/(9.648 \times 10^4\,\mathrm{C\,mol^{-1}})$

$= 4.01 \times 10^{-4}\,\mathrm{cm^2\,C^{-1}\,S} = \underline{4.01 \times 10^{-4}\,\mathrm{cm^2\,s^{-1}\,V^{-1}}}$

$[\mathrm{C\,\Omega = A\,s\,\Omega = V\,s;\ A\,\Omega = V}]$.

$u_+(\mathrm{Na^+}) = (50.1\,\mathrm{S\,cm^2\,mol^{-1}})/(9.648 \times 10^4\,\mathrm{C\,mol^{-1}})$

$= \underline{5.19 \times 10^{-4}\,\mathrm{cm^2\,s^{-1}\,V^{-1}}}$.

$u_+(\mathrm{K^+}) = (73.5\,\mathrm{S\,cm^2\,mol^{-1}})/(9.648 \times 10^4\,\mathrm{C\,mol^{-1}})$

$= \underline{7.62 \times 10^{-4}\,\mathrm{cm^2\,s^{-1}\,V^{-1}}}$.

27.13 $s = uE$ [27.1.10], $E = (10\,\mathrm{V})/(1.0\,\mathrm{cm}) = 10\,\mathrm{V\,cm^{-1}}$.

$s(\mathrm{Li^+}) = (4.01 \times 10^{-4}\,\mathrm{cm^2\,s^{-1}}) \times (10\,\mathrm{V\,cm^{-1}}) = \underline{4.0 \times 10^{-3}\,\mathrm{cm\,s^{-1}}}$,

$s(\mathrm{Na^+}) = (5.19 \times 10^{-4}\,\mathrm{cm^2\,s^{-1}\,V^{-1}}) \times (10\,\mathrm{V\,cm^{-1}}) = \underline{5.2 \times 10^{-3}\,\mathrm{cm\,s^{-1}}}$,

$s(\mathrm{K^+}) = (7.62 \times 10^{-4}\,\mathrm{cm^2\,s^{-1}\,V^{-1}}) \times (10\,\mathrm{V\,cm^{-1}}) = \underline{7.6 \times 10^{-3}\,\mathrm{cm\,s^{-1}}}$.

$t = d/s;\ d = 1\,\mathrm{cm}$.

$t(\mathrm{Li^+}) = (1.0\,\mathrm{cm})/(4.0 \times 10^{-3}\,\mathrm{cm\,s^{-1}}) = 250\,\mathrm{s} \approx \underline{4\,\mathrm{min}}$,

$t(\mathrm{Na^+}) = (1.0\,\mathrm{cm})/(5.2 \times 10^{-3}\,\mathrm{cm\,s^{-1}}) = 190\,\mathrm{s} \approx \underline{3\,\mathrm{min}}$,

$t(\mathrm{K^+}) = (1.0\,\mathrm{cm})/(7.6 \times 10^{-3}\,\mathrm{cm\,s^{-1}}) = 130\,\mathrm{s} \approx \underline{2\,\mathrm{min}}$.

For the distance moved during half a cycle, write $E = E_0 \sin(2\pi\nu t)$, then

$$d = \int_0^{1/2\nu} s(t)\mathrm{d}t = \int_0^{1/2\nu} uE\,\mathrm{d}t = uE_0 \int_0^{1/2\nu} \sin(2\pi\nu t)\mathrm{d}t = uE_0/\pi\nu.$$

Therefore, since $E_0 = 10\,\mathrm{V\,cm^{-1}}$ and $\nu = 1$ kHz,

$d = u \times (10\,\mathrm{V\,cm^{-1}})/(\pi \times 10^3\,\mathrm{Hz}) = 3.183 \times 10^{-3}(u\,\mathrm{V\,s\,cm^{-1}})$

or $d/\mathrm{cm} = 3.183 \times 10^{-3}(u/\mathrm{cm^2\,V^{-1}\,s^{-1}})$.

Therefore $d(\mathrm{Li^+}) = 3.183 \times 10^{-3} \times (4.0 \times 10^{-4}) = \underline{1.3 \times 10^{-6}\,\mathrm{cm}\ (43\ \mathrm{diameters})}$.

Likewise $d(\mathrm{Na^+}) = \underline{1.7 \times 10^{-6}\,\mathrm{cm}\ (55\ \mathrm{diameters})}$, $\underline{d(\mathrm{K^+}) = 2.4 \times 10^{-6}\,\mathrm{cm}}$ $\underline{(81\ \mathrm{diameters})}$.

27.14 The current I_i, carried by an ion i is proportional to its concentration, c_i, its mobility, u_i, and the magnitude of its charge, $|z_i|$. Therefore, denoting the constant of proportionality as A,

$I_i = Ac_i|z_i|u_i$.

The total current passing through the solution, I, is

$$I = A\sum_j c_j|z_j|u_j.$$

The fraction of current carried by i is therefore

$$t_i = I_i/I = Ac_i|z_i|u_i \Big/ A\sum_j c_j|z_j|u_j = c_i|z_i|u_i \Big/ \sum_j c_j|z_j|u_j.$$

If there are two cations in the mixture, then

$t'_+/t''_+ = c'_+|z'_+|u'_+/c''_+|z''_+|u''_+$.

If the cations have the same charge,

$\underline{t'_+/t''_+ = c'_+u'_+/c''_+u''_+}$.

27.15 $t(\mathrm{H^+}) = u(\mathrm{H^+})/[u(\mathrm{H^+}) + u(\mathrm{Cl^-})]$ [27.1.17]

$= 3.623 \times 10^{-3}/[3.623 \times 10^{-3} + 7.91 \times 10^{-4}] = \underline{0.82}$,

When NaCl is added,

$t(\mathrm{H^+}) = c(\mathrm{H^+})u(\mathrm{H^+})/[c(\mathrm{H^+})u(\mathrm{H^+}) + c(\mathrm{Na^+})u(\mathrm{Na^+}) + c(\mathrm{Cl^-})u(\mathrm{Cl^-})]$

$$= \frac{[10^{-3} \times (3.623 \times 10^{-3})]}{10^{-3} \times (3.623 \times 10^{-3}) + 1.0 \times (5.19 \times 10^{-4}) + [1.001 \times (7.91 \times 10^{-4})]}$$

$= 3.623 \times 10^{-6}/(1.31 \times 10^{-3}) = \underline{0.0028}$.

27.16 $t_+(It/z_+cF) = xA$ [27.1.20, $V = x \times A$; A area; x distance]

$I = 18.2\text{ mA}, z_+ = 1, c = 0.021\text{ M} = 21\text{ mol m}^{-3}$;

$A = \pi(2.073 \times 10^{-3}\text{ m})^2 = 1.35 \times 10^{-5}\text{ m}^2$

$t_+ = xAz_+cF/It$

$$= (x/t)\left\{\frac{(1.35 \times 10^{-5}\text{ m}^2) \times (21\text{ mol m}^{-3}) \times (9.65 \times 10^4\text{ C mol}^{-1})}{1.82 \times 10^{-2}\text{ A}}\right\}$$

$= 1.50 \times 10^3 (x/\text{m})/(t/\text{s})\ [\text{C} = \text{A s}] = 1.50\,(x/\text{mm})/(t/\text{s})$.

Draw up the following Table.

t/s	200	400	600	800	1000
x/mm	64	128	192	254	318
t_+	0.48	0.48	0.48	0.48	0.48
$t_- = 1 - t_+$	0.52	0.52	0.52	0.52	0.52

Hence, we conclude that $t_+ = \underline{0.48}$ and $t_- = \underline{0.52}$.

27.17 $t_+ = \lambda_\pm/\Lambda_m$ [27.1.18], $\lambda_\pm = u_\pm|z_\pm|F$ [27.1.12].

$u_\pm = \lambda_\pm/|z_\pm|F = t_\pm\Lambda_m/|z_\pm|F$.

$\Lambda_m = 149.9\text{ S cm}^2\text{ mol}^{-1}$ [Problem 27.5].

$u_+ = 0.48 \times (149.9\text{ S cm}^2\text{ mol}^{-1})/(9.65 \times 10^4\text{ C mol}^{-1})$

$= \underline{7.5 \times 10^{-4}\text{ cm}^2\text{ s}^{-1}\text{ V}^{-1}}$ $[\text{V} = \text{A}\,\Omega = \text{C}\,\Omega\,\text{s}^{-1}]$.

$\lambda_+ = t_+\Lambda_m = 0.48 \times (149.9\text{ S cm}^2\text{ mol}^{-1}) = \underline{72\text{ S cm}^2\text{ mol}^{-1}}$.

27.18 Consider the consequences of the passage of *IF* of electricity on the cell Ag. AgCl|HCl(c_1)||HCl(c_2)|AgCl, Ag.

On the right: 1 mol Cl^- generated, but t_-mol Cl^- migrate out across the junction. Therefore the net change in the amount of Cl^- is $(1 - t_-)$ mol $= t_+$mol. Furthermore, t_+mol H^+ migrate in from the left.

On the left: 1 mol Cl^- is lost (on formation of solid AgCl) but t_-mol flows in across the junction. The net change is $(-1 + t_-)$ mol $= -t_+$mol. Furthermore, t_+mol H^+ migrate out to the right.

The overall change in Gibbs function is therefore

$\Delta G = (t_+\text{ mol})\{\mu_{Cl^-}(c_2) + \mu_{H^+}(c_2)\} - (t_+\text{ mol})\{\mu_{Cl^-}(c_1) + \mu_{H^+}(c_1)\}$

$\Delta G_m = t_+\{\mu_{Cl^-}(c_2) + \mu_{H^+}(c_2) - \mu_{Cl^-}(c_1) - \mu_{H^+}(c_1)\}$

if the concentration dependence of t_+ is ignored. But $\mu = \mu^\ominus + RT\ln a$ [11.1.1] and $E = -\Delta G_m/F$ [12.3.1]. Therefore, denoting the e.m.f. with transference by E_t,

$$E_t = -(RT/F)t_+\ln\{a_{Cl^-}(2)a_{H^+}(2)/a_{Cl^-}(1)a_{H^+}(1)\}$$
$$= -2t_+(RT/F)\ln\{a(2)/a(1)\}$$

where a is the mean activity. Since in a cell without transference,

$E = -2(RT/F)\ln\{a(2)/a(1)\}$ [Section 12.1(f)] we find

$\underline{E_t = t_+E}$.

For electrodes reversible with respect to the cation, 1 mol M^+ is generated (or destroyed) and t_+ mol migrates out (or in), giving a net change of $\pm t_-$ mol. The remainder of the argument is analogous.

27.19 $t_+ = xA/(It/z_+cF)$ [27.1.20] $= xc(z_+AF/It)$; $I = 5.0\text{mA}$, $t = 2500\,\text{s}$.
$A = 1.35 \times 10^{-5}\,\text{m}^2$ [Problem 27.16].

$$z_+AF/It = \frac{(1.35 \times 10^{-5}\,\text{m}^2) \times (9.65 \times 10^4\,\text{C mol}^{-1})}{(5 \times 10^{-3}\,\text{A}) \times (2500\,\text{s})}$$

$$= 0.104\,\text{m}^2\,\text{mol}^{-1} = 0.104/\text{mm mol dm}^{-3}.$$

$t_+ = 0.104(x/\text{mm})(c/\text{mol dm}^{-3}) \approx 0.104(x/\text{mm})(m/\text{mol kg}^{-1})$.

(a) $t_+ = 0.104 \times 286.9 \times 0.013\,65 = 0.407$,

(b) $t_+ = 0.104 \times 92.03 \times 0.042\,55 = 0.407$.

Therefore $t(H^+) = \underline{0.407}$ and the mobility is not abnormal (for HI in water, $t(H^+) = 0.82$).

27.20 $R = C/\kappa$ $C = 2.063\,\text{cm}^{-1}$ [Problem 27.2]
$$= (0.2063\,\text{cm}^{-1})/(5.5 \times 10^{-8}\,\text{S cm}^{-1}) = 3.75 \times 10^6\,\Omega = \underline{3.75\,\text{M}\Omega}.$$

$$\Lambda_m = \kappa/c = (5.5 \times 10^{-8}\,\text{S cm}^{-1})/(55.5\,\text{mol dm}^{-3})$$
$$= 9.9 \times 10^{-10}\,\text{S cm}^{-1}\,\text{dm}^3\,\text{mol}^{-1} = 9.9 \times 10^{-7}\,\text{S cm}^2\,\text{mol}^{-1}.$$

$$\Lambda_m^\circ = \lambda(H^+) + \lambda(OH^-) = (349.8 + 197.6)\text{S cm}^2\,\text{mol}^{-1}$$
$$= 547.4\,\text{S cm}^2\,\text{mol}^{-1}.$$

$\alpha = \Lambda_m/\Lambda_m^\circ$ [Section 27.1(a)] $= 9.9 \times 10^{-7}/547.4 = 1.8 \times 10^{-9}$.

$$K_w = a(H^+)a(OH^-) \approx c(H^+)c(OH^-)/M^2$$
$$= \alpha^2\{c(H_2O)/M\}^2 = (1.8 \times 10^{-9})^2 \times (55.5)^2 = \underline{1.0 \times 10^{-14}}.$$

$pK_w = -\lg K_w = \underline{14.0}.$

$pH = -\lg a(H^+) = -\lg\sqrt{K_w} = -\tfrac{1}{2}\lg K_w = \underline{7.0}.$

27.21 $\Lambda_m = \Lambda_m^\circ - \mathscr{K}c^{1/2}$ [27.1.3] $= \Lambda_m^\circ - (A + B\Lambda_m^\circ)c^{1/2}$ [27.1.21].

$A = (z^2 eF^2/3\pi\eta)(2/\epsilon RT)^{1/2}$ [27.1.21]

$B = q(z^3 eF^2/24\pi\epsilon RT)(2/\pi\epsilon RT)^{1/2}$

$z = 1, \eta = 0.8904 \times 10^{-3}\,\mathrm{kg\,m^{-1}\,s^{-1}}$ [Table 24.5], $\epsilon_r = 78.54$ [Table 11.1]; hence

$\underline{A = 60.4\,\mathrm{S\,cm^2\,mol^{-1}/M^{1/2}}}$

$B = 4.12 \times 10^{-3}\,\mathrm{mol^{-1/2}\,m^{3/2}} = \underline{0.13/\mathrm{M}^{1/2}}$

$\Lambda_m^\circ = (50.11 + 76.34)\,\mathrm{S\,cm^2\,mol^{-1}} = 126.45\,\mathrm{S\,cm^2\,mol^{-1}}$

$\mathscr{K} = A + B\Lambda_m^\circ = \{60.4 + (0.13 \times 126.45)\}\,\mathrm{S\,cm^2\,mol^{-1}/M^{1/2}}$

$= \underline{76.8\,\mathrm{S\,cm^2\,mol^{-1}/M^{1/2}}}.$

(Problem 27.3 led to $\mathscr{K} = 76.5\,\mathrm{S\,cm^2\,mol^{-1}/M^{1/2}}$.)

27.22 $\mathscr{F} = -(RT/c)(\mathrm{d}c/\mathrm{d}x)$ [27.2.2]

$\mathrm{d}c/\mathrm{d}x = \{(0.05\,\mathrm{M}) - (0.10\,\mathrm{M})\}/(0.10\,\mathrm{m}) = -0.50\,\mathrm{M\,m^{-1}}.$

$RT = 2.48\,\mathrm{kJ\,mol^{-1}} = 2.48 \times 10^3\,\mathrm{J\,mol^{-1}} = 2.48 \times 10^3\,\mathrm{N\,m\,mol^{-1}}$

(a) $\mathscr{F} = -(2.48 \times 10^3\,\mathrm{N\,m\,mol^{-1}}) \times (-0.50\,\mathrm{M\,m^{-1}})/(0.10\,\mathrm{M})$

$= \underline{1.2 \times 10^4\,\mathrm{N\,mol^{-1}},\ 2.1 \times 10^{-20}\,\mathrm{N/molecule}}.$

(b) $\mathscr{F} = -(2.48 \times 10^3\,\mathrm{N\,m\,mol^{-1}}) \times (-0.50\,\mathrm{M\,m^{-1}})/(0.075\,\mathrm{M})$

$= \underline{1.7 \times 10^4\,\mathrm{N\,mol^{-1}},\ 2.8 \times 10^{-20}\,\mathrm{N/molecule}}.$

(c) $\mathscr{F} = -(2.48 \times 10^3\,\mathrm{N\,m\,mol^{-1}}) \times (-0.50\,\mathrm{M\,m^{-1}})/(0.05\,\mathrm{M})$

$= \underline{2.5 \times 10^4\,\mathrm{N\,mol^{-1}},\ 4.1 \times 10^{-20}\,\mathrm{N/molecule}}.$

27.23 $s = (D/kT)\mathscr{F}$ [27.2.3].

$D/kT = (5.2 \times 10^{-6}\,\mathrm{cm^2\,s^{-1}})/(1.381 \times 10^{-23}\,\mathrm{J\,K^{-1}}) \times (298.15\,\mathrm{K})$

$= 1.26 \times 10^{11}\,\mathrm{m^2\,s^{-1}\,J^{-1}} = 1.26 \times 10^{11}\,\mathrm{m\,s^{-1}\,N^{-1}}.$

(a) $s = (1.26 \times 10^{11}\,\mathrm{m\,s^{-1}\,N^{-1}}) \times (2.1 \times 10^{-20}\,\mathrm{N})$

$= 2.6 \times 10^{-9}\,\mathrm{m\,s^{-1}} = \underline{2.7\,\mathrm{nm\,s^{-1}}}.$

(b) $s = (1.26 \times 10^{11}\,\mathrm{m\,s^{-1}\,N^{-1}}) \times (2.8 \times 10^{-20}\,\mathrm{N}) = \underline{3.5\,\mathrm{nm\,s^{-1}}}.$

(c) $s = (1.26 \times 10^{11}\,\mathrm{m\,s^{-1}\,N^{-1}}) \times (4.1 \times 10^{-20}\,\mathrm{N}) = \underline{5.2\,\mathrm{nm\,s^{-1}}}.$

Monitor the concentration by refractive index, optical rotation, i.r. spectroscopy. The initial *flux* through a region is the same at every point because $\mathrm{d}c/\mathrm{d}x$ is a constant, except at the left boundary and at the right, open side, Fig. 27.2(a). The initial change is then as shown in Fig. 27.2(b). This initial distortion is then magnified as the time increases, and as $\mathrm{d}c/\mathrm{d}x$ is no longer constant anywhere, $\mathrm{d}c/\mathrm{d}t$ changes everywhere, Fig. 27.2(c). After a long while the concentration becomes virtually uniform, and sinks towards 0.075 M, Fig. 27.2(d).

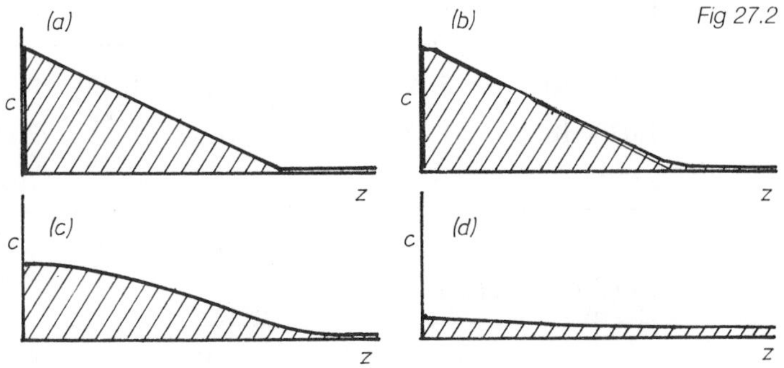

Fig 27.2

27.24 $D = kT/6\pi\eta a$ [27.2.9]

$a = kT/6\pi\eta D = (1.381 \times 10^{-23}\,\mathrm{J\,K^{-1}}) \times (298.15\,\mathrm{K})/6\pi \times (1.00 \times 10^{-3}\,\mathrm{kg\,m^{-1}\,s^{-1}})$
$\times (5.2 \times 10^{-10}\,\mathrm{m^2\,s^{-1}}) = 4.20 \times 10^{-10}\,\mathrm{m} = \underline{420\,\mathrm{pm}}.$

27.25 $\tau = d^2/2D$ [27.3.12]; $R(I_2) \approx 266$ pm; and so $d \approx 300$ pm.

$\tau \approx (300 \times 10^{-12}\,\mathrm{m})^2/2(2.13 \times 10^{-9}\,\mathrm{m^2\,s^{-1}}) = \underline{2.1 \times 10^{-11}\,\mathrm{s}}.$

27.26 $\bar{x} = (2Dt)^{1/2}$ [27.3.6]

(a) $\bar{x} = \sqrt{\{2 \times (2.13 \times 10^{-9}\,\mathrm{m^2\,s^{-1}}) \times (1\,\mathrm{s})\}} = \underline{6.5 \times 10^{-5}\,\mathrm{m}},$

(b) $\bar{x} = \sqrt{\{2 \times (5.2 \times 10^{-10}\,\mathrm{m^2\,s^{-1}}) \times (1\,\mathrm{s})\}} = \underline{3.2 \times 10^{-5}\,\mathrm{m}}.$

27.27 $t = \bar{x}^2/2D$ [27.3.6].

(a) $t(\text{iodine}) = (1.0 \times 10^{-3}\,\mathrm{m})^2/2 \times (2.13 \times 10^{-9}\,\mathrm{m^2\,s^{-1}}) = \underline{240\,\mathrm{s}}$ ($\approx$ 4 min).

$t(\text{sucrose}) = (1.0 \times 10^{-3}\,\mathrm{m})^2/2 \times (5.2 \times 10^{-10}\,\mathrm{m^2\,s^{-1}}) = \underline{960\,\mathrm{s}}$ ($\approx$ 16 min).

(b) $t(\text{iodine}) = (1.0 \times 10^{-2}\,\mathrm{m})^2/2 \times (2.13 \times 10^{-9}\,\mathrm{m^2\,s^{-1}}) = \underline{2.4 \times 10^4\,\mathrm{s}}$ ($\approx$ 7 hr).

$t(\text{sucrose}) = (1.0 \times 10^{-2}\,\mathrm{m})^2/2 \times (5.2 \times 10^{-10}\,\mathrm{m^2\,s^{-1}}) = \underline{9.6 \times 10^4\,\mathrm{s}}$ ($\approx$ 27 hr).

27.28 $D = ukT/ez$ [27.2.5], $a = ez/6\pi\eta u$ [27.2.8]

$kT/e = (1.381 \times 10^{-23}\,\mathrm{J\,K^{-1}}) \times (298.15\,\mathrm{K})/(1.602 \times 10^{-19}\,\mathrm{C}) = 2.57 \times 10^{-2}\,\mathrm{V}.$

$e/6\pi\eta = (1.602 \times 10^{-19}\,\mathrm{C})/6\pi \times (1.00 \times 10^{-3}\,\mathrm{kg\,m^{-1}\,s^{-1}})$
$= 8.50 \times 10^{-18}\,\mathrm{V^{-1}\,m^3\,s^{-1}}$ [$\mathrm{J = C\,V}$, $\mathrm{J = kg\,m^2\,s^{-2}}$].

$D/\mathrm{cm^2\,s^{-1}} = (2.57 \times 10^{-2}\,\mathrm{V})u/\mathrm{cm^2\,s^{-1}} = 2.57 \times 10^{-2}(u/\mathrm{cm^2\,s^{-1}\,V^{-1}}).$

$a/\mathrm{m} = (8.50 \times 10^{-18}\,\mathrm{V^{-1}\,m^2\,s^{-1}})/u = (8.50 \times 10^{-14}\,\mathrm{V^{-1}\,cm^2\,s^{-1}})/u;$

$a/\mathrm{pm} = 8.50 \times 10^{-2}/(u/\mathrm{cm^2\,s^{-1}\,V^{-1}}).$

Draw up the following Table using the data in Table 27.2.

	Li^+	Na^+	K^+	Rb^+
$u/cm^2\,s^{-1}\,V^{-1}$	4.01×10^{-4}	5.19×10^{-4}	7.62×10^{-4}	7.92×10^{-4}
D/cm^2	1.03×10^{-5}	1.33×10^{-5}	1.96×10^{-5}	2.04×10^{-5}
a/pm	212	164	112	107

27.29 The ionic radii [Table 23.1] are

	Li^+	Na^+	K^+	Rb^+
a_{ion}/pm	59	102	138	149

and so K^+ and Rb^+ have effective hydrodynamic radii that are smaller than their crystal radii. The effective hydrodynamic and ionic volumes of Li^+ and Na^+ are $(4/3)\pi a^3$, and so

(a) For Li^+: $\Delta v = (4/3)\pi(212^3 - 59^3) \times 10^{-36}\,m^3 = 3.9 \times 10^{-29}\,m^3$.

(b) For Na^+: $\Delta v = (4/3)\pi(164^3 - 102^3) \times 10^{-36}\,m^3 = 1.4 \times 10^{-29}\,m^3$.

The volume occupied by a single water molecule is approximately $(4/3)\pi(150\,pm)^3 = 1.4 \times 10^{-29}\,m^3$. Therefore Li^+ has about three firmly attached water molecules while Na^+ has only about one (according to these data).

27.30 $a = kT/6\pi\eta D$ [27.29]

$\eta = 0.972 \times 10^{-3}\,kg\,m^{-1}\,s^{-1}$ [Table 24.5] at 25 °C

$$a = \frac{(1.381 \times 10^{-23}\,J\,K^{-1}) \times (298.15\,K)}{6\pi \times (0.972 \times 10^{-3}\,kg\,m^{-1}\,s^{-1}) \times (2.89 \times 10^{-9}\,m^2\,s^{-1})}$$

$= 7.8 \times 10^{-11}\,m$, $\underline{78\text{ pm}}$.

The volume $(4\pi a^3/3)$ this corresponds to is $2.0 \times 10^{-30}\,m^3$, and hence the molar volume $(N_A v_{mol})$ is $1.2 \times 10^{-6}\,m^3\,mol^{-1}$, or $1.4 \times 10^{-3}\,dm^3\,mol^{-1}$.

Since $1/\tau \propto \exp(-E_a/RT)$ [activated process], and $D = d^2/2\tau$ [27.3.12], if d is independent of temperature we expect $D \propto \exp(-E_a/RT)$. Therefore

$$E_a = \left(\frac{RT_1T_2}{T_1 - T_2}\right) \ln\{D(T_2)/D(T_1)\}$$

$$= \left\{\frac{(8.314\,J\,K^{-1}\,mol^{-1}) \times (273\,K) \times (298\,K)}{25\,K}\right\} \times \ln\left\{\frac{2.89 \times 10^{-5}}{2.05 \times 10^{-5}}\right\}$$

$= 9.3\ \text{kJ mol}^{-1}$.

Hence, the activation energy for diffusion is about $\underline{9.3\ \text{kJ mol}^{-1}}$.

27.31 $\partial\mathcal{N}/\partial t = D\partial^2\mathcal{N}/\partial x^2$ [27.3.1]

$\mathcal{N} = (a/t^{1/2})\exp(-bx^2/t)$ [27.3.2], a, b constants,

$$\partial\mathcal{N}/\partial t = -\tfrac{1}{2}(a/t^{3/2})\exp(-bx^2/t) + (a/t^{1/2})(bx^2/t^2)\exp(-bx^2/t)$$
$$= -\tfrac{1}{2}\mathcal{N}/t + bx^2\mathcal{N}/t^2.$$
$$\partial\mathcal{N}/\partial x = (a/t^{1/2})(-2bx/t)\exp(-bx^2/t),$$
$$\partial^2\mathcal{N}/\partial x^2 = -(2b/t)(a/t^{1/2})\exp(-bx^2/t) + (a/t^{1/2})(2bx/t)^2\exp(-bx^2/t)$$
$$= -(2b/t)\mathcal{N} + (2bx/t)^2\mathcal{N} = -(1/2Dt)\mathcal{N} + (bx^2/Dt^2)\mathcal{N}[b = 1/4D]$$
$$= (\partial\mathcal{N}/\partial t)/D, \text{ as required.}$$

Initially the material is concentrated at $x = 0$. Note that $\mathcal{N}(x, t)$ is zero for all $x > 0$ when $t = 0$ because of the strong $\exp(-x^2/4Dt)$ factor $[e^{-\infty} = 0]$. When $x = 0$, $\exp(-x^2/4Dt)$ is unity. Confirm the correct behavior by noting that $\langle x\rangle = 0$ [27.3.4] and $\langle x^2\rangle = 0$ [27.3.6] at $t = 0$; hence all the material must be at $x = 0$ at $t = 0$.

27.32 $\mathcal{N}(x, t) = \{N_0/A(\pi Dt)^{1/2}\}\exp(-x^2/4Dt)$ [27.3.2]

$N_0 = (10\ \text{g}/342\ \text{g mol}^{-1})N_A = 1.76 \times 10^{22}$, $x = 5$ cm,

$A = 19.6\ \text{cm}^2$, $D = 5.2 \times 10^{-6}\ \text{cm}^2\text{s}^{-1}$ [Problem 27.23].

$$\mathcal{N}(5\ \text{cm}, t) = \frac{1.76 \times 10^{22}\exp[-25\ \text{cm}^2/4 \times (5.2 \times 10^{-6}\ \text{cm}^2\text{s}^{-1})t]}{(19.6\ \text{cm}^2) \times [\pi \times (5.2 \times 10^{-6}\ \text{cm}^2\text{s}^{-1})t]}$$
$$= (2.22 \times 10^{23}\ \text{cm}^{-3})\{1/(t/s)^{1/2}\}\exp\{-1.20 \times 10^6/(t/s)\}.$$

(a) $t = 10$ s;

$\mathcal{N} = (2.22 \times 10^{23}\ \text{cm}^{-3})\{1/10\}^{1/2}\exp\{-1.2 \times 10^5\} \approx \underline{0}$.

(b) $t = 1\ \text{yr} = 3.16 \times 10^7$ s;

$$= (2.22 \times 10^{23}\ \text{cm}^{-3})\{1/3.16 \times 10^7\}^{1/2}\exp\{-1.20 \times 10^6/3.16 \times 10^7\}$$
$$= \underline{3.80 \times 10^{19}\ \text{cm}^{-3},\ 3.80 \times 10^{22}\ \text{dm}^{-3},\ 0.06\ \text{M}}.$$

27.33 $P(x) = n!/\{[\tfrac{1}{2}(n+s)]!\,[\tfrac{1}{2}(n-s)]!2^n\}$ [27.A1.2], $s = x/d$.

$P(6d) = n!/\{[\tfrac{1}{2}(n+6)]!\,[\tfrac{1}{2}(n-6)]!2^n\}$.

(a) $n = 4$; $P(6d) = \underline{0}$ [$m! \equiv \infty$ for $m < 0$]

(b) $n = 6$; $P(6d) = 6!/\{6!0!2^6\} = 1/2^6$ [$0! \equiv 1$] $= 1/64 = \underline{0.016}$

(c) $n = 12$; $P(6d) = 12!/\{9!3!2^{12}\}$

$$= \frac{12.11.10}{3.2.2^{12}} = 55/2^{10} = \underline{0.054.}$$

27.34 Draw up the following Table based on $P(x)$ [27.A1.2] and the large n version [27.3.11].

n	4	6	8	10	20
$P(x)_{\text{exact}}$	0	0.016	0.0313	0.0439	0.0739
$P(x)_{\text{asymptotic}}$	0.004	0.0162	0.0297	0.0417	0.0725

n	30	40	60	100
$P(x)_{\text{exact}}$	0.0806	0.0807	0.0763	0.0666
$P(x)_{\text{asymptotic}}$	0.0799	0.0804	0.0763	0.0666

These points are plotted in Fig. 27.3. The discrepancy is no more than 0.1 percent when n exceeds 60.

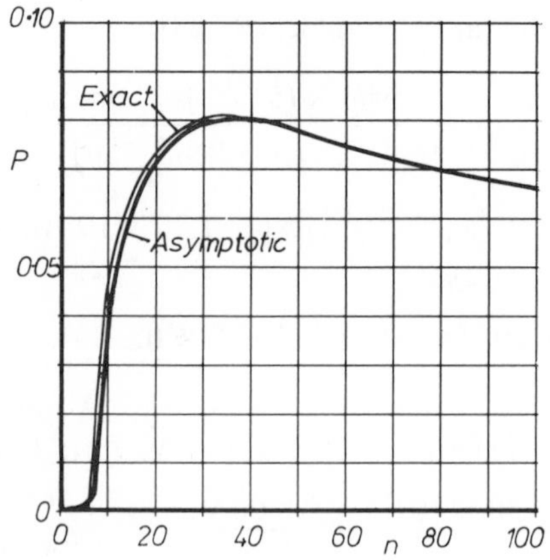

Fig 27.3

27.35 $\langle x^2 \rangle = 2Dt$ [27.3.6], $D = kT/6\pi\eta a$ [27.2.9].

$\eta = kT/6\pi Da = kTt/3\pi a\langle x^2 \rangle$

$$= \frac{(1.381 \times 10^{-23}\,\text{J K}^{-1}) \times (298.15\,\text{K})t}{3\pi \times (2.12 \times 10^{-7}\,\text{m})\langle x^2 \rangle} = (2.06 \times 10^{-15}\,\text{J m}^{-1})t/\langle x^2 \rangle,$$

$\eta/\text{kg m}^{-1}\text{s}^{-1} = 2.06 \times 10^{-11}(t/s)/(\langle x^2\rangle/\text{cm}^2)$

Draw up the following Table

t/s	30	60	90	120
$\langle x^2\rangle/\text{cm}$	88.2×10^{-8}	113.5×10^{-8}	128×10^{-8}	144×10^{-8}
$\eta/\text{kg m}^{-1}\text{s}^{-1}$	7.01×10^{-4}	1.09×10^{-3}	1.45×10^{-3}	1.72×10^{-3}

This gives a mean value of $\underline{1.2 \times 10^{-3}\,\text{kg m}^{-1}\text{s}^{-1}}$.

28. The rates of chemical reactions

A28.1 $d[A]/dt = -d[P]/dt = -k_1[A][B]$ [Section 28.2(e)]

$= -(3.67 \times 10^{-3}\,dm^3\,mol^{-1}\,s^{-1})(0.255\,mol)(0.605\,mol)$
$\times (1.70\,dm^3)^{-2} = \underline{-1.96 \times 10^{-4}\,mol\,dm^{-3}\,s^{-1}}.$

$d[B]/dt = -2(1.96 \times 10^{-4}) = \underline{-3.92 \times 10^{-4}\,mol\,dm^{-3}\,s^{-1}}.$

$d[P]/dt = -d[A]/dt$; $dn_B/dt = Vd[B]/dt = \underline{-6.7 \times 10^{-4}\,mol\,s^{-1}}.$

$\dot{\xi} = -dn_B/dt = \underline{3.4 \times 10^{-4}\,mol\,s^{-1}}.$

A28.2 $t_{\frac{1}{2}} = (k[A])^{-1}$ [28.2.22] $= (2.62 \times 10^{-3}\,dm^3\,mol^{-1}\,s^{-1})^{-1}(1.70\,mol\,dm^{-3})^{-1}$
$= \underline{225\,s}.$

A28.3 $[A]_2^{-1} - [A]_1^{-1} = k(t_2 - t_1)$ [28.2.16]

$t_2 - t_1 = (3.50 \times 10^{-4}\,dm^3\,mol^{-1}\,s^{-1})^{-1}[(0.0110\,mol\,dm^{-3})^{-1}$
$-(0.260\,mol\,dm^{-3})^{-1}] = \underline{2.49 \times 10^5\,s}.$

A28.4 $E_a = R(T_1^{-1} - T_2^{-1})^{-1}\ln(k_2/k_1)$ [28.3.4]

$= (8.31\,J\,mol^{-1})(303^{-1} - 323^{-1})^{-1}\ln(0.0138/0.00280)$

$= \underline{64.9\,kJ\,mol^{-1}}.$

$A = ke^{E_a/RT} = \underline{4.3 \times 10^8\,M^{-1}\,s^{-1}}.$

A28.5 The first step is rate determining. Hence: rate $= k_1[H_2O_2][M]$. The reaction is first order with respect to H_2O_2 and with respect to M^-. Overall, the reaction is second order [Section 28.3(d)].

A28.6 From the pre-equilibrium [Section 28.3(f)], $[A] = (k_1/2k_{-1})^{\frac{1}{2}}[A]^{\frac{1}{2}}$,
rate $= k_2[A][B] = k_2(k_1/2k_{-1})^{\frac{1}{2}}[A_2]^{\frac{1}{2}}[B]$.

A28.7 From the pre-equilibrium [Section 28.3(f)],

[two-base-pair helix] $= (k_1/k_{-1})[A][B]$;

rate of renaturation $= k_2(k_1/k_{-1})[A][B]$,

$\underline{k_{overall} = k_2(k_1/k_{-1})}.$

A28.8 Maximum rate $= k_1[E]_0$ [28.3.33].

$k_1[E]_0 = (\text{rate})(K_M + [S])/[S] = (1.15 \times 10^{-3}\,mol\,dm^{-3}\,s^{-1})(0.035 +$

$+ 0.110)(\text{mol dm}^{-3})(0.110 \text{ mol dm}^{-3})^{-1}$

$= \underline{1.52 \times 10^{-3} \text{ mol dm}^{-3} \text{ s}^{-1}}.$

A28.9 rate = (maximum rate)[S]/(K_M + [S]), [28.3.33]

$1/2 = [S]/(K_M + [S])$,

$[S] = K_M$.

A28.10 $k_{\text{eff}}^{-1} = (k_2 p)^{-1} + (k_{-2}/k_1 k_2)$ [28.3.40]

$(2.50 \times 10^{-4} \text{ s}^{-1})^{-1} = (1.30 \times 10^3 \text{ Pa})^{-1} k_2^{-1} + (k_{-2}/k_1 k_2)$

$(2.10 \times 10^{-5} \text{ s}^{-1})^{-1} = (12 \text{ Pa})^{-1} k_2^{-1} + (k_{-2}/k_1 k_2)$.

Solve these simultaneous equations for k_2.

$k_2 = \underline{1.89 \times 10^{-6} \text{ Pa}^{-1} \text{ s}^{-1}}.$

28.1 $d[J]/dt = (\nu_J/V)\dot{\xi}$ [28.2.4].

For A + 2B → 3C + D

$\nu_A = -1, \nu_B = -2, \nu_C = 3, \nu_D = 1$

$v_A = d[A]/dt = (-1/V)(1.0 \text{ mol s}^{-1}) = \underline{-1.0 \text{ M s}^{-1}}$ [$V = 1 \text{ dm}^3$]

$v_B = \underline{-2.0 \text{ M s}^{-1}}, \; v_C = \underline{+3.0 \text{ M s}^{-1}}, \; v_D = \underline{+1.0 \text{ M s}^{-1}}.$

28.2 $\dot{\xi} = (V/\nu_J) v_J$ [28.2.5]; $\nu_C = +2$

$= (1.0 \text{ dm}^3/2) \times (1.0 \text{ M s}^{-1}) = \underline{0.50 \text{ mol s}^{-1}}.$

$v_A = (-2/V) \times (0.50 \text{ mol s}^{-1})$ [28.2.4, $\nu_A = -2$] $= \underline{-1.0 \text{ M s}^{-1}}.$

$v_B = (-1/V)\dot{\xi} = \underline{-0.50 \text{ M s}^{-1}}.$

$v_D = (+3/V)\dot{\xi} = \underline{+1.5 \text{ M s}^{-1}}.$

28.3 $[\dot{\xi}] = \text{mol s}^{-1}$ $[[A][B]] = \text{mol}^2 \text{ dm}^{-6} = \text{M}^2$.

$[k] = [\dot{\xi}]/[[A][B]] = \text{mol s}^{-1}/\text{mol}^2 \text{ dm}^{-6} = \underline{\text{mol}^{-1} \text{ dm}^6 \text{ s}^{-1}}.$

$v_J = (\nu_J/V)\dot{\xi}$ [28.2.4]; $\nu_A = -1, \nu_C = +3$.

(a) $v_A = d[A]/dt = (-1/V)k[A][B] = \underline{-k'[A][B], k' = k/V}.$

(b) $v_C = d[C]/dt = (3/V)k[A][B] = \underline{k''[A][B], k'' = 3k/V}.$

28.4 $\dot{\xi} = (V/\nu_J)v_J, v_C = d[C]/dt, \nu_C = +2$.

$\dot{\xi} = (V/2)k[A][B][C] = \underline{k'[A][B][C], k' = kV/2}.$

$[k] = \text{M}^{-2} \text{ s}^{-1}$; $[k'] = (\text{mol}^{-2} \text{ dm}^6 \text{ s}^{-1}) \times \text{dm}^3 = \underline{\text{mol}^{-2} \text{ dm}^9 \text{ s}^{-1}}.$

28.5 $t_{1/2} = (1/k)\ln 2$ [28.2.22]

$= (1/4.8 \times 10^{-4} \text{ s}^{-1})\ln 2 = \underline{1.4 \times 10^3 \text{ s}}.$

$2N_2O_5(g) \rightarrow 4NO_2(g) + O_2(g)$;

$2N_2O_5 \rightarrow 4NO_2 + O_2$

$p(N_2O_5) = p_0(N_2O_5)\exp(-k_1 t)$ [28.2.14].

The pressure of N_2O_5 is therefore

$p(N_2O_5) = (500\,\text{Torr})\exp\{-4.8 \times 10^{-4}(t/\text{s})\}$.

(a) 10 s: $p(N_2O_5) = \underline{498\,\text{Torr}}$.

(b) 10 min, 600 s. $p(N_2O_5) = \underline{375\,\text{Torr}}$.

The total pressure is $p + 2(p_0 - p) + \frac{1}{2}(p_0 - p) = \frac{1}{2}(5p_0 - 3p)$,

where p is the N_2O_5 pressure. This gives

(a) 10 s, $p_{\text{total}} = \frac{1}{2}(5 \times 500 - 3 \times 498)\,\text{Torr} = \underline{503\,\text{Torr}}$

(b) 10 min: $p_{\text{total}} = \frac{1}{2}(5 \times 500 - 3 \times 375)\,\text{Torr} = \underline{688\,\text{Torr}}$.

28.6 $\mathrm{d}[\mathrm{A}]/\mathrm{d}t = k_n[\mathrm{A}]^n$. The dimensions of k_n must be such as to balance the units on both sides of this equation:

$[k_n]$ = [concentration or pressure]$^{1-n}$ [time]$^{-1}$.

Therefore, $[k_2]$ = [concentration or pressure]$^{-1}$ [time]$^{-1}$,

$[k_3]$ = [concentration or pressure]$^{-2}$ [time]$^{-1}$.

Consequently k_2 should be expressed in (a) $\underline{\text{M}^{-1}\,\text{s}^{-1}}$, (b) $\underline{\text{atm}^{-1}\,\text{s}^{-1}}$

and k_3 in (a) $\underline{\text{m}^{-2}\,\text{s}^{-1}}$, (b) $\underline{\text{atm}^{-2}\,\text{s}^{-1}}$.

28.7 $[^{14}\text{C}] = [^{14}\text{C}]_0\exp(-kt)$, $k = (1/t_{1/2})\ln 2$ [28.2.21]

$[^{14}\text{C}]/[^{14}\text{C}]_0 = \exp\{-(t/t_{1/2})\ln 2\}$.

$t = (t_{1/2}/\ln 2)\ln\{[^{14}\text{C}]_0/[^{14}\text{C}]\} = (5730\,\text{yr}/\ln 2) \times \ln(1/0.72) = \underline{2720\,\text{yr}}$.

28.8 $[^{90}\text{Sr}] = [^{90}\text{Sr}]_0\exp(-kt) = [^{90}\text{Sr}]_0\exp\{-(t/t_{1/2})\ln 2\}$ [Problem 28.7].

$(\ln 2)/t_{1/2} = 0.0247\,\text{yr}^{-1}$.

$m(^{90}\text{Sr}) = m_0(^{90}\text{Sr})\exp\{-(t/t_{1/2})\ln 2\} = (1.0\,\mu\text{g})\exp\{-0.0247(t/\text{yr})\}$.

(a) $m(^{90}\text{Sr}) = (1.0\,\mu\text{g})\exp\{-0.0247 \times 18\} = \underline{0.64\,\mu\text{g}}$,

(b) $m(^{90}\text{Sr}) = (1.0\,\mu\text{g})\exp\{-0.0247 \times 70\} = \underline{0.18\,\mu\text{g}}$.

28.9 $$kt = \left\{\frac{1}{[\mathrm{B}]_0 - [\mathrm{A}]_0}\right\} \ln \left\{\frac{[\mathrm{A}]_0([\mathrm{B}]_0 - x)}{([\mathrm{A}]_0 - x)\,[\mathrm{B}]_0}\right\} \quad [28.2.19]$$

$$\frac{[\mathrm{A}]_0\,([\mathrm{B}]_0 - x)}{([\mathrm{A}]_0 - x)\,[\mathrm{B}]_0} = \exp\{([\mathrm{B}]_0 - [\mathrm{A}]_0)kt\}$$

which solves to

$$x = \frac{[A]_o[B]_o\{\exp[([B]_o - [A]_o)kt] - 1\}}{[B]_o\exp[([B]_o - [A]_o)kt] - [A]_o}.$$

$k = 0.11\,M^{-1}\,s^{-1}$; $[A]_o = [NaOH]_o = 0.050\,M$,

$[B]_o = [AcOEt]_o = 0.100\,M$; $k([B]_o - [A_o]) = 5.5 \times 10^{-3}\,s^{-1}$.

$$x/M = \frac{(0.050 \times 0.100)\{\exp[5.5 \times 10^{-3}(t/s)] - 1\}}{0.100\exp[5.5 \times 10^{-3}(t/s)] - 0.050}$$

$$= \frac{0.100\{\exp[5.5 \times 10^{-3}(t/s)] - 1\}}{2\exp[5.5 \times 10^{-3}(t/s)] - 1}.$$

(a) $t = 10\,s$; $x/M = \dfrac{0.100(e^{0.055} - 1)}{2e^{0.055} - 1} = 5.1 \times 10^{-3}$;

$[NaOH] = (0.050 - 0.005)M = \underline{0.045\,M}$,

$[AcOEt] = (0.100 - 0.005)M = \underline{0.095\,M}$.

(b) $t = 10\,\text{min}, 600\,s$; $x/M = \dfrac{0.10(e^{3.3} - 1)}{(2\,e^{3.3} - 1)} = 0.049$.

$[NaOH] = (0.050 - 0.049)M = \underline{0.001\,M}$,

$[AcOEt] = (0.100 - 0.049)M = \underline{0.051\,M}$.

28.10 $2A + 3B \rightarrow P$, $dP/dt = k[A][B]$. Let the initial amounts of A, B, P be A_o, B_o, 0; then when an amount x of P is formed the amount of A changes to $A_o - 2x$ and the amount of B to $B_o - 3x$. Therefore

$dP/dt = dx/dt = k(A_o - 2x)(B_o - 3x)$; $x = 0$ at $t = 0$.

$$k\,dt = \frac{dx}{(A_o - 2x)(B_o - 3x)} = \left\{\frac{1}{3(A_o - 2x)} - \frac{1}{2(B_o - 3x)}\right\} \times \left\{\frac{dx}{2B_o - 3A_o}\right\}$$

$$= \left\{\frac{dx}{(x - \frac{1}{2}A_o)} - \frac{dx}{(x - \frac{1}{3}B_o)}\right\} \times \left\{\frac{1}{6(2B_o - 3A_o)}\right\}.$$

Integrate from 0 to t and from 0 to x:

$$kt = \left\{\frac{-1}{6(2B_o - 3A_o)}\right\} \ln \left\{\frac{x - \frac{1}{2}A_o}{x - \frac{1}{3}B_o}\right\}\Bigg|_0^x = \underline{\left\{\frac{-1}{6(2B_o - 3A_o)}\right\} \ln \left\{\frac{(2x - A_o)B_o}{A_o(3x - B_o)}\right\}}$$

28.11 $d[A]/dt = -k[A]^2[B]$, $2A + B \rightarrow P$.

Let $[P] = x$ at time t (at $t = 0, x = 0$); then $[A] = A_o - 2x$ and $[B] = B_o - x$.

Therefore

$d[A]/dt = -2dx/dt = -k(A_o - 2x)^2(B_o - x)$,

or $dx/dt = \frac{1}{2}k(A_o - 2x)^2(B_o - x)$.

In this special case, $B_o = \frac{1}{2}A_o$; consequently

$dx/dt = \frac{1}{2}k(A_o - 2x)^2(\frac{1}{2}A_o - x) = \frac{1}{4}k(A_o - 2x)^3$.

$$\tfrac{1}{4}kt = \int_0^x \frac{dx}{(A_o - 2x)^3} = \left\{\frac{1}{4(A_o - 2x)^2}\right\}\Bigg|_0^x$$

$$= \tfrac{1}{4}\left\{\left(\frac{1}{A_o - 2x}\right)^2 - \left(\frac{1}{A_o}\right)^2\right\}.$$

Therefore, $\underline{kt = 4x(A_o - x)/A_o^2(A_o - 2x)^2}$.

28.12 $dx/dt = \frac{1}{2}k(A_o - 2x)^2(B_o - x)$ [Problem 28.11]; $B_o = 2 \times (\frac{1}{2}A_o) = A_o$.
$dx/dt = \frac{1}{2}k(A_o - 2x)^2(A_o - x)$, ($x = 0$ at $t = 0$).

$$\tfrac{1}{2}kt = \int_0^x \left\{\frac{dx}{(A_o - 2x)^2(A_o - x)}\right\}.$$

Proceed by the method of partial fractions (here and for the general case too).

$$\frac{1}{(A_o - 2x)^2(A_o - x)} = \frac{\alpha}{(A_o - 2x)^2} + \frac{\beta}{(A_o - 2x)} + \frac{\gamma}{(A_o - x)};$$

$\alpha(A_o - x) + \beta(A_o - 2x)(A_o - x) + \gamma(A_o - 2x)^2 = 1$,

$(A_o\alpha + A_o^2\beta + A_o^2\gamma) - (\alpha + 3\beta A_o + 4\gamma A_o)x + (2\beta + 4\gamma)x^2 = 1$.

This is to be true for all x; therefore

$$\left.\begin{aligned} A_o\alpha + A_o^2\beta + A_o^2\gamma &= 1 \\ \alpha + 3\beta A_o + 4\gamma A_o &= 0 \\ 2\beta + 4\gamma &= 0 \end{aligned}\right\}$$

These solve to give $\alpha = 2/A_o$, $\beta = -2/A_o^2$, $\gamma = 1/A_o^2$.

Therefore,

$$\tfrac{1}{2}kt = \int_0^x \left\{\frac{(2/A_o)\,dx}{(A_o - 2x)^2} - \frac{(2/A_o^2)\,dx}{(A_o - 2x)} + \frac{(1/A_o^2)\,dx}{(A_o - x)}\right\}$$

$$= \left\{\frac{(1/A_o)}{(A_o - 2x)} + (1/A_o^2)\ln(A_o - 2x) - (1/A_o^2)\ln(A_o - x)\right\}\Bigg|_0^x$$

$$= \left\{\frac{2x}{A_0^2(A_0 - 2x)}\right\} + \frac{1}{A_0^2} \ln \left\{\frac{A_0 - 2x}{A_0 - x}\right\}$$

28.13 $kt = 4x(A_0 - x)/A_0^2(A_0 - 2x)^2$ [Problem 28.11]

$[A] = A_0 - 2x$, $[B] = B_0 - x$; $B_0 = \frac{1}{2}A_0$.

(a) $[A] = \frac{1}{2}A_0$ when $x = \frac{1}{4}A_0$; then

$kt_{1/2} = A_0(\frac{3}{4}A_0)/A_0^2(\frac{1}{2}A_0)^2 = 3/A_0^2$ so that $\underline{t_{1/2} = 3/kA_0^2}$.

(b) $[B] = \frac{1}{2}[B_0]$ when $x = \frac{1}{2}B_0 = \frac{1}{4}A_0$. Therefore $t_{1/2}$ is the same as in (a).

(c) The reaction is

$0 = -2A - B + P$, $\nu_A = -2$, $\nu_B = -1$.

Define ξ so that $\xi = 0$ initially and $\xi = 1$ finally. Write

$[B] = B_0(1 - \xi)$, then $[P] = B_0\xi$ and $[A] = A_0 - 2B_0\xi$.

$dA/dt = -2B_0\dot{\xi} = -kA^2B = -k(A_0 - 2B_0\xi)^2 B_0(1 - \xi)$.

Since $B_0 = \frac{1}{2}A_0$, $\dot{\xi} = \frac{1}{2}kA_0^2(1 - \xi)^3$.

$$\int_0^{\xi} \frac{d\xi}{(1 - \xi)^3} = \tfrac{1}{2}kA_0^2 t = \tfrac{1}{2}\left\{\left(\frac{1}{1 - \xi}\right)^2 - 1\right\} = \xi(2 - \xi)/2(1 - \xi)^2.$$

If $\xi = \frac{1}{2}$, $\frac{1}{2}kA_0^2 t_{1/2} = \frac{1}{2} \times \frac{3}{2}/2 \times \frac{1}{4} = 3/2$.

and so $\underline{t_{1/2} = 3/kA_0^2}$.

28.14 $dx/dt = k[A]^n$, $A \rightarrow P$

$$kt = \left(\frac{1}{n - 1}\right)\left\{\left(\frac{1}{A_0 - x}\right)^{n-1} - \left(\frac{1}{A_0}\right)^{n-1}\right\} \quad \text{[integration, or Box 28.1]}.$$

$x = A_0/2$ at $t = t_{1/2}$:

$$kt_{1/2} = \left(\frac{1}{n - 1}\right)\left\{\left(\frac{2}{A_0}\right)^{n-1} - \left(\frac{1}{A_0}\right)^{n-1}\right\} \underline{\propto 1/A_0^{n-1}}.$$

28.15 $$kt_{1/2} = \left(\frac{1}{n - 1}\right)\left\{\left(\frac{2}{A_0}\right)^{n-1} - \left(\frac{1}{A_0}\right)^{n-1}\right\} \quad [\text{Box 28.1}, x = \tfrac{1}{2}A_0]$$

$$kt_{3/4} = \left(\frac{1}{n - 1}\right)\left\{\left(\frac{4}{3A_0}\right)^{n-1} - \left(\frac{1}{A_0}\right)^{n-1}\right\} \quad [\text{Box 28.1}, x = \tfrac{1}{4}A_0]$$

$$t_{1/2}/t_{3/4} = \frac{2^{n-1} - 1}{(4/3)^{n-1} - 1}.$$

In the case $t_{1/2}/t_{1/4} = (2^{n-1} - 1)/(4^{n-1} - 1) = 1/(2^{n-1} + 1)$, and so $n = 1 + \ln(t_{1/4}/t_{1/2} - 1)/\ln 2$ is an explicit expression for n.

28.16 $[B]_\infty = \frac{1}{2}[A]_o$, hence $[A]_o = 0.624\,M$. For the reaction $2A \rightarrow B$, $[A] = [A]_o - 2[B]$; hence draw up the following Table.

t/s	0	600	1200	1800	2400
$[B]/M$	0	0.089	0.153	0.200	0.230
$[A]/M$	0.624	0.446	0.318	0.224	0.164

The data are plotted in Fig. 28.1(a). We find $t_{3/4} = 540\,s$, $t_{1/2} = 1230\,s$ implying $t_{1/2}/t_{3/4} = 2.3$.

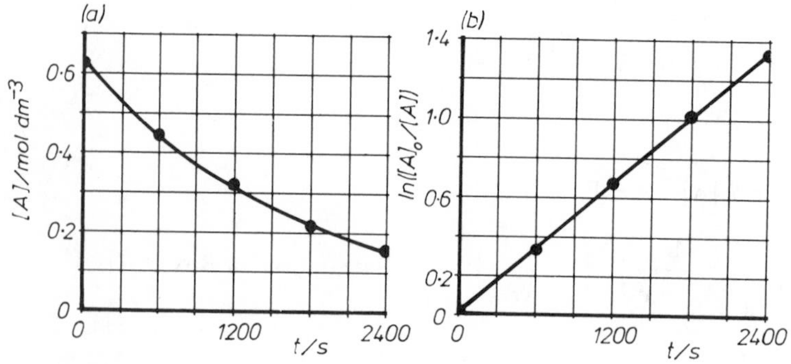

Fig 28.1

For a first-order reaction, $t_{1/2}/t_{3/4} = 2.4$ [Problem 28.15, or $kt_{1/2} = \ln(A_o/\frac{1}{2}A_o)$, $kt_{3/4} = \ln(A_o/\frac{3}{4}A_o)$].

For a second-order reaction, $t_{1/2}/t_{3/4} = 3.0$ [Problem 28.15]. Therefore, the reaction is first order. Confirm by plotting data accordingly:

$\ln\{[A]_o/[A]\} = kt$ [28.2.13].

Plot l.h.s. against t. Draw up the following Table:

t/s	0	600	1200	1800	2400
$\ln\{[\mathrm{A}]_0/[\mathrm{A}]\}$	0	0.34	0.67	1.02	1.34

These points are plotted in Fig. 28.1(b). The points lie in a straight line, confirming first-order kinetics. Since the slope is 5.6×10^{-4} we conclude that $\underline{k = 5.6 \times 10^{-4}\,\mathrm{s}^{-1}}$.

28.17 Inspection of the data suggests that the production of water is increasing like $1 - \mathrm{e}^{-kt}$; compare the data for [B] in Problem 28.16. Test for first-order behavior as follows. Denote the reaction $\mathrm{A} \rightarrow \mathrm{B} + \mathrm{C}$, where B is the water. For a first-order reaction with this stoichiometry,

$$\mathrm{d}[\mathrm{B}]/\mathrm{d}t = k[\mathrm{A}] = k\{[\mathrm{A}]_0 - [\mathrm{B}]\}$$

$$[\mathrm{B}] = [\mathrm{A}]_0\{1 - \mathrm{e}^{-kt}\} = [\mathrm{B}]_\infty\{1 - \mathrm{e}^{-kt}\}$$

where $[\mathrm{B}]_\infty$ is the amount (e.g. volume) of water when all the initial compound has decomposed, It follows that

$$\mathrm{e}^{-kt} = \{[\mathrm{B}]_\infty - [\mathrm{B}]\}/[\mathrm{B}]_\infty, \text{ or } \ln\left\{\frac{[\mathrm{B}]_\infty}{[\mathrm{B}]_\infty - [\mathrm{B}]}\right\} = kt.$$

Draw up the following Table:

t/s	30	60	90	120	150
$\{V(\infty)/[V(\infty) - V]\}$	2.0	3.3	5.0	6.7	10.0
$\ln\{V(\infty)/[V(\infty) - V]\}$	0.69	1.20	1.61	1.90	2.30

These points are plotted in Fig. 28.2(a). They fall on a straight line, confirming first-order kinetics. The slope is 1.3×10^{-2}, and so $\underline{k = 1.4 \times 10^{-2}\,\mathrm{s}^{-1}}$. The C_4H_6 is probably reactive under the conditions of the experiment.

28.18 $k = A\exp(-E_\mathrm{a}/RT)$ [28.3.4, assuming first-order process also activated]. Then $\ln k = \ln A - E_\mathrm{a}/RT$, and so plot $\ln k$ against $1/T$. Draw up the following Table:

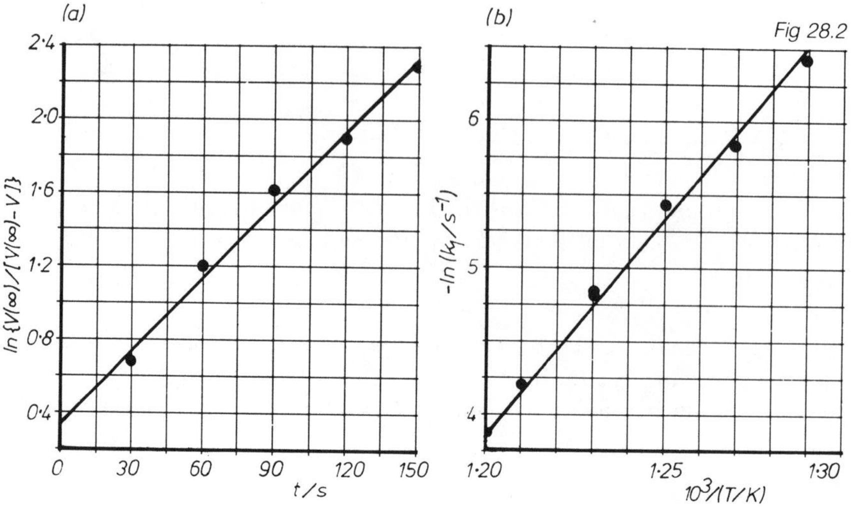

T/K	773.5	786	797.5	810	810	824	834
$10^3/(T/\mathrm{K})$	1.29	1.27	1.25	1.23	1.23	1.21	1.20
$k/10^{-3}\,\mathrm{s}^{-1}$	1.63	2.95	4.19	8.13	8.19	14.9	22.2
$-\ln(k/\mathrm{s}^{-1})$	6.42	5.83	5.48	4.81	4.80	4.21	3.81

These points are plotted in Fig. 28.2(b). The slope of the line is 2.9×10^4, implying $E_a = (2.9 \times 10^4\,\mathrm{K})R = \underline{240\,\mathrm{kJ\,mol^{-1}}}$. The extrapolated intercept lies at $-\ln(k/\mathrm{s}^{-1}) = -30$, implying $A = \mathrm{e}^{30}\,\mathrm{s}^{-1} = \underline{1.1 \times 10^{13}\,\mathrm{s}^{-1}}$.

28.19 If the reaction is first-order the pressure, p, of cyclopropane should obey $p/p_0 = \mathrm{e}^{-kt}$ [28.2.14]. Then $(1/t)\ln(p_0/p)$ should be a constant and equal to k. Test this by drawing up the following Table:

p_0/Torr	200	200	400
t/s	100	200	100
p/Torr	186	173	373
$[1/(t/\mathrm{s})]\ln(p_0/p)$	7.3×10^{-4}	7.3×10^{-4}	7.0×10^{-4}

p_0/Torr	400	600	600
t/s	200	100	200
p/Torr	347	559	520
$[1/(t/\mathrm{s})]\ln(p_0/p)$	7.1×10^{-4}	7.1×10^{-4}	7.2×10^{-4}

These are virtually constant, and so the reaction has first-order kinetics (in this pressure range) with $k = 7.2 \times 10^{-4}\,\mathrm{s}^{-1}$.

28.20 $2\mathrm{A} \rightarrow \mathrm{B},\ \mathrm{d}[\mathrm{A}]/\mathrm{d}t = -k[\mathrm{A}]^2$.

$[\mathrm{A}] = \mathrm{A_0}/(1 + kt\mathrm{A_0})$ [28.2.17, $\mathrm{A_0} \equiv [\mathrm{A}]_0$].

$[\mathrm{B}] = \mathrm{B_0} + \frac{1}{2}(\mathrm{A_0} - [\mathrm{A}]) = \frac{1}{2}(\mathrm{A_0} - [\mathrm{A}])$ [$\mathrm{B_0} = 0$].

In terms of pressures:

$p_\mathrm{A} = p_0/(1 + ktp_0),\ p_\mathrm{B} = \frac{1}{2}(p_0 - p_\mathrm{A})$.

Total pressure: $p = p_\mathrm{A} + p_\mathrm{B} = \frac{1}{2}(p_0 + p_\mathrm{A})$

$$p = \tfrac{1}{2}p_0\left\{1 + \left(\frac{1}{1 + ktp_0}\right)\right\} = \tfrac{1}{2}p_0\left\{\frac{2 + ktp_0}{1 + ktp_0}\right\},$$

$$p/p_0 = \left\{\frac{1 + \frac{1}{2}x}{1 + x}\right\},\ x = p_0 kt.$$

This function is plotted in Fig. 28.3. The final value of the pressure is $\frac{1}{2}p_0$; half way to this pressure corresponds to $p = \frac{3}{4}p_0$. The time to attain this pressure is given by

$$\tfrac{3}{4} = \left\{\frac{1 + \frac{1}{2}x}{1 + x}\right\},\ \text{or } x = 1.\ \text{Therefore, } t = 1/p_0 k.$$

The total pressure may be expressed in terms of the advancement ξ [$\xi = \xi/\mathrm{mol}$] as $p = p_0(1 - \xi) + \frac{1}{2}p_0\xi = p_0(1 - \frac{1}{2}\xi)$. Therefore $p/p_0 = 1 - \frac{1}{2}\xi$. When $p/p_0 = \frac{3}{4}$, $\xi = \frac{1}{2}$.

28.21 Test whether the reaction is second order by examining the fit of the data to

$$p/p_0 = \left\{\frac{1 + \frac{1}{2}x}{1 + x}\right\},\ x = p_0 kt\ \text{[Problem 28.20]}.$$

Rearrange to $p_0 kt = \left\{\dfrac{1 - (p/p_0)}{(p/p_0) - \frac{1}{2}}\right\}$. Draw up the following Table, based on

$p_0 = 400$ Torr [$t = 0$ value]:

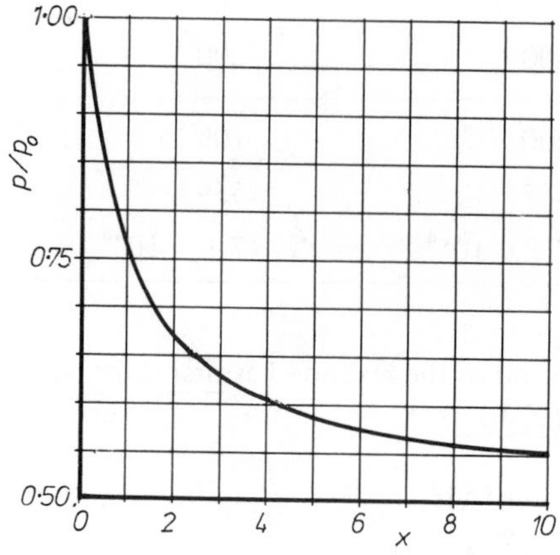

Fig 28.3

t/s	0	100	200	300	400
p/Torr	400	322	288	268	256
p/p_0	1	0.805	0.720	0.670	0.640
r.h.s.	0	0.639	1.273	1.941	2.571

These points are plotted in Fig. 28.4. They fall on a good straight line, confirming that the reaction is second-order. The slope is 6.4×10^{-3}, and so $p_0 k = 6.4 \times 10^{-3}\,\mathrm{s}^{-1}$. Since $p_0 = 400$ Torr, this implies that $k = 1.6 \times 10^{-5}\,\mathrm{Torr}^{-1}\,\mathrm{s}^{-1}$. (If the reaction rate law had been written $d[B]/dt = k'[A]^2$ we would have found $k' = 8.1 \times 10^{-6}\,\mathrm{Torr}^{-1}\,\mathrm{s}^{-1}$.)

28.22 ${}^{239}_{92}\mathrm{U} \xrightarrow{t_{1/2}} {}^{239}_{93}\mathrm{Np} \xrightarrow{t'_{1/2}} {}^{239}_{94}\mathrm{Pu}$, $t_{1/2} = 23.5$ min, $t'_{1/2} = 2.35$ day [Section 28.3(d)]; $[\mathrm{U}]/[\mathrm{U}]_0 = e^{-kt}$ [28.3.14a],

$$[\mathrm{Np}]/[\mathrm{U}]_0 = \left(\frac{k}{k'-k}\right)(e^{-kt} - e^{-k't}) \text{ [28.3.14b]},$$

$$[\mathrm{Pu}]/[\mathrm{U}]_0 = 1 + \left(\frac{1}{k-k'}\right)(k'e^{-kt} - ke^{-k't}) \text{ [28.3.14c]}.$$

$k = (1/t_{1/2})\ln 2$ [28.2.21] $= 2.95 \times 10^{-2}\,\mathrm{min}^{-1}$; $k' = (1/t'_{1/2})\ln 2 = 0.295\,\mathrm{day}^{-1}$.

Draw up the following Tables:

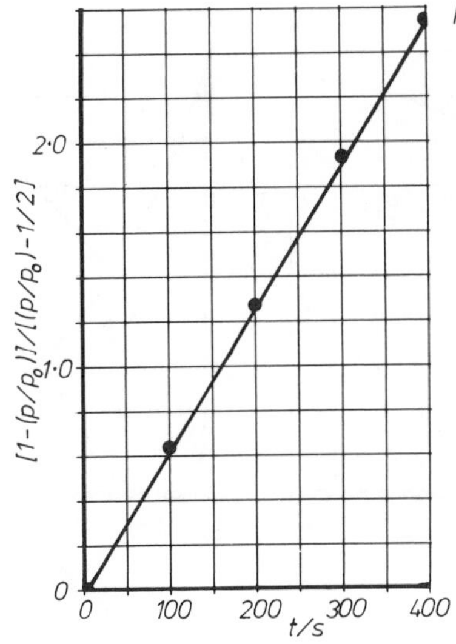

t/min	0	20	40	60	80	100
$[U]/[U]_o$	1.00	0.55	0.31	0.17	0.09	0.05
$[Np]/[U]_o$	0	0.44	0.69	0.82	0.90	0.93
$[Pu]/[U]_o$	0	1.00×10^{-3}	3.4×10^{-3}	6.5×10^{-3}	0.0100	0.0138

t/day	0	2	4	6	8	10
$[U]/[U]_o$	1.00	0.00	0.00	0.00	0.00	0.00
$[Np]/[U]_o$	0	0.56	0.31	0.17	0.095	0.05
$[Pu]/[U]_o$	0	0.44	0.69	0.83	0.905	0.95

These points are plotted in Fig. 28.5(a) and (b).

28.23 $A + B \rightarrow P$, $d[P]/dt = k[A]^m [B]^n$.

$\Delta[P] \approx k[A]^m [B]^n \Delta t$. Therefore, since $\Delta[P] = [P]_t - [P]_o = [P]_t$,

$[P]/[A] = k[A]^{m-1} [B]^n \Delta t$.

(a) [chloropropane]/[propene] independent of [propene] implies $m = 1$.

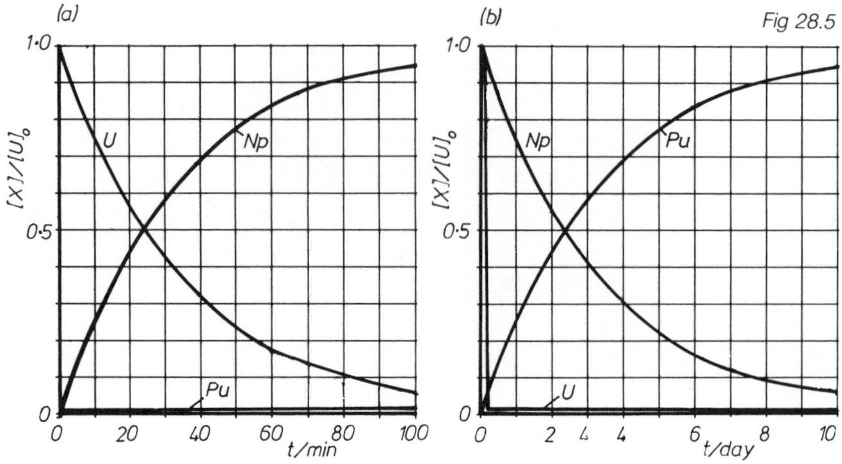

(b) [chloropropane] / [HCl], at $\Delta t = 100\,\text{hr}$, gives the ratio 0.05:0.03:0.01, or 5:3:1 for $p(\text{HCl})$ in the ratio 10:7.5:5.0. This ratio is 100:56:25≈5:3:1 when the pressures are squared. Hence we conclude that $m = 3$ when A is identified as HCl. Therefore the rate law is

$$\mathrm{d}[\text{chloropropane}]/\mathrm{d}t = k[\text{HCl}]^3[\text{propene}];$$

that is, 3rd order in HCl, 1st-order in propene.

28.24 $2\text{HCl} \rightleftharpoons (\text{HCl})_2, K_1$; therefore $[(\text{HCl})_2] = K_1[\text{HCl}]^2$.

$CH_3CH{=}CH_2 + HCl \rightleftharpoons \text{complex}, K_2$; therefore, $[(\text{complex})] = K_2[\text{HCl}][CH_3CH{=}CH_2]$.

$(\text{HCl})_2 + \text{complex} \rightarrow CH_3CHClCH_3 + 2\text{HCl}, k$

$$\begin{aligned}\mathrm{d}[CH_3CHClCH_3]/\mathrm{d}t &= k\,[(\text{HCl})_2]\,[(\text{complex})]\\ &= kK_1[\text{HCl}]^2K_2[\text{HCl}][CH_3CH{=}CH_2]\\ &= k_{\text{eff}}[\text{HCl}]^3[CH_3CH{=}CH_2],\ k_{\text{eff}} = kK_1K_2.\end{aligned}$$

Use i.r. spectroscopy to search for $(\text{HCl})_2$.

28.25 $k_{\text{eff}} = A\mathrm{e}^{-E_a/RT}$ [28.3.4].

$$k_{\text{eff}}(292\,\text{K})/k_{\text{eff}}(343\,\text{K}) = \exp\left\{-(E_a/R)\left[\left(\frac{1}{292\,\text{K}}\right) - \left(\frac{1}{343\,\text{K}}\right)\right]\right\} = 3;$$

$$E_a = R\left(\frac{1}{343\,\text{K}} - \frac{1}{292\,\text{K}}\right)^{-1}\ln 3 = \underline{-20\,\text{kJ mol}^{-1}},$$

$k_{\text{eff}} = kK_1K_2$ [Problem 28.24]

$\ln k_{\text{eff}} = \ln k + \ln K_1 + \ln K_2,$

$E_a = -R\{\text{d}\ln k_{\text{eff}}/\text{d}(1/T)\}$ [28.3.6]

$= E_a' + \Delta_r U_1^\ominus + \Delta_r U_2^\ominus$ [28.3.7] $= E_a' + 2RT + \Delta_r H_1^\ominus + \Delta_r H_2^\ominus.$

$E_a' = E_a - 2RT - \Delta_r H_1^\ominus - \Delta_r H_2^\ominus$

$= \{-18 - 5 + 14 + 14\}\,\text{kJ mol}^{-1} = \underline{+5\,\text{kJ mol}^{-1}}.$

28.26 $\ln k = \ln A - E_a/RT$ [28.3.3];

$E_a = \left(\frac{1}{T_2} - \frac{1}{T_1}\right)^{-1} R\ln\{k(T_1)/k(T_2)\}$. Draw up the following Table:

T_1/K	300.3	300.3	341.2
T_2/K	341.2	392.2	392.2
$k(T_1)/\text{M}^{-1}\,\text{s}^{-1}$	1.44×10^7	1.44×10^7	3.03×10^7
$k(T_2)/\text{M}^{-1}\,\text{s}^{-1}$	3.03×10^7	6.9×10^7	6.9×10^7
$E_a/\text{kJ mol}^{-1}$	15.5	16.7	18.0

The mean is $\underline{16.7\,\text{kJ mol}^{-1}}$.

For A, use $A = k\exp(E_a/RT)$. Draw up the following Table:

T/K	300.3	341.2	392.2
$k/\text{M}^{-1}\,\text{s}^{-1}$	1.44×10^7	3.03×10^7	6.9×10^7
E_a/RT	6.69	5.89	5.12
$A/\text{M}^{-1}\,\text{s}^{-1}$	1.16×10^{10}	1.10×10^{10}	1.16×10^{10}

The means is $\underline{1.14 \times 10^{10}\,\text{M}^{-1}\,\text{s}^{-1}}$.

28.27 $\ln(k/\text{M}^{-1}\,\text{s}^{-1}) = \ln(A/\text{M}^{-1}\,\text{s}^{-1}) - E_a/RT.$

Draw up the following Table:

$\theta/°C$	0	10	15	25	34.5
T/K	273	283	288	298	308
$10^3/(T/K)$	3.66	3.53	3.47	3.36	3.25
$\ln(k/M^{-1}\,s^{-1})$	−10.65	−9.60	−9.19	−8.24	−7.44

These points are plotted in Fig. 28.6. The slope is 7900, implying $E_a = 7.9 \times 10^3 R$ $= \underline{66\,kJ\,mol^{-1}}$. The intercept lies at −18.3, implying $A/M^{-1}\,s^{-1} = e^{18.3}$ $= 8.7 \times 10^7$. Therefore, $A = \underline{8.7 \times 10^7\,M^{-1}\,s^{-1}}$.

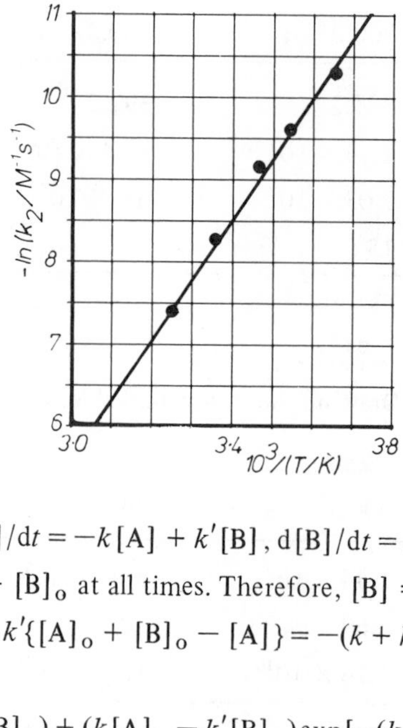

Fig 28.6

28.28 $A \rightleftharpoons B$; $d[A]/dt = -k[A] + k'[B]$, $d[B]/dt = k'[B] + k[A]$.

$[A] + [B] = [A]_o + [B]_o$ at all times. Therefore, $[B] = [A]_o + [B]_o - [A]$,

$d[A]/dt = -k[A] + k'\{[A]_o + [B]_o - [A]\} = -(k + k')[A] + k'\{[A]_o + [B]_o\}$.

The solution is:

$$[A] = \left\{\frac{k'([A]_o + [B]_o) + (k[A]_o - k'[B]_o)\exp[-(k + k')t]}{k + k'}\right\}.$$

The final composition is obtained by setting $t = \infty$.

Then $[A]_\infty = \{k'/(k + k')\}\{[A]_o + [B]_o\}$,

$[B]_\infty = [A]_o + [B]_o - [A]_\infty = \{k/(k + k')\}\{[A]_o + [B]_o\}$.

Note that $[B]_\infty/[A]_\infty = k/k'$.

28.29 $1/k_{eff} = 1/k_a[M] + k_a'/k_a k_b$ [28.3.40], or $1/k_{eff} = 1/k_a p + k_a'/k_a k_b$.

Expect a straight line when $1/k_{eff}$ is plotted against $1/p$. Draw up the following Table:

p/Torr	84.1	11.0	2.89	0.569	0.120	0.067
$1/(p/\text{Torr})$	0.012	0.091	0.346	1.76	8.33	14.9
$10^{-4}/(k_{eff}/s^{-1})$	0.336	0.448	0.649	1.17	2.55	3.30

These points are plotted in Fig. 28.7. There are marked deviations from a straight line at low pressures, indicating that the Lindemann theory is deficient.

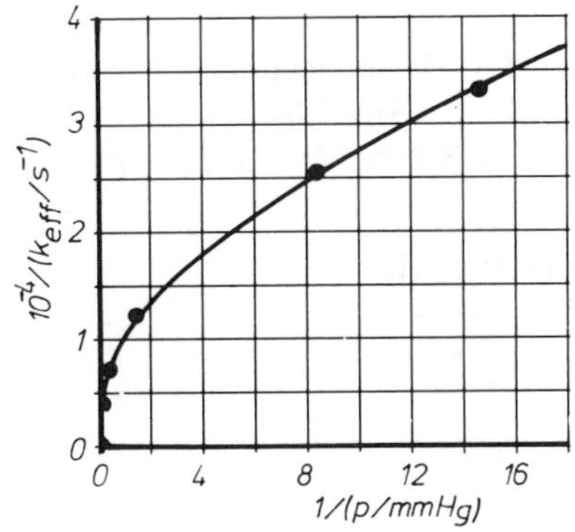

Fig 28.7

28.30 $NH_2OH + OH^- \rightarrow NH_2O^- + H_2O$; $NH_2O^- + O_2 \rightarrow$ products.

$-d[(NH_2OH)]/dt = k_{obs}[(NH_2OH)][O_2]$ (k_{obs} is the effective first-order rate constant for NH_2OH),

$-d[(NH_2OH)]/dt = k[NH_2O^-][O_2]$,

$k_{obs}[(NH_2OH)][O_2] = k[NH_2O^-][O_2]$ and $[(NH_2OH)] = [NH_2OH] + [NH_2O^-]$.

Therefore, $k_{obs}[NH_2OH] = (k - k_{obs})[NH_2O^-]$.

$1/k_{obs} = 1/k + [NH_2OH]/k[NH_2O^-] = 1/k + [H^+]/kK_bK_w$.

$[K_b = [NH_2O^-]/[NH_2OH][OH^-], K_w = [OH^-][H^+]$; all $[x]$ to be interpreted as $[x]/M]$.

$$K_bK_w = \frac{[NH_2O^-][H^+][OH^-]}{[NH_2OH][OH^-]} = \frac{[NH_2O^-][H^+]}{[NH_2OH]} = K_a.$$

Therefore, $\underline{1/k_{obs} = 1/k + [H^+]/kK_a}$. Hence, plotting $1/k_{obs}$ against $[H^+]$ should give a straight line, with slope $1/kK_a$ and intercept $1/k$.

28.31 $1/k_{obs} = 1/k + [H^+]/kK_a$ [Problem 28.30]

$$= 1/k + K_w/kK_a[OH^-] \;[K_w = [H^+][OH^-]].$$

Draw up the following Table, using $f = k_{obs}/k$ [Problem 28.31], with k determined below.

$[OH^-]/M$	0.50	1.00	1.6	2.4
$1/([OH^-]/M)$	2.00	1.00	0.63	0.42
$10^{-3}/(k_{obs}/s^{-1})$	4.65	3.53	3.01	2.83
f	0.51	0.66	0.77	0.82

These points are plotted in Fig. 28.8. The intercept is at 2.35×10^3, implying that $k = (2.35 \times 10^3)^{-1}\,s^{-1} = 4.3 \times 10^{-4}\,s^{-1}$. The slope is 1.15×10^3, implying $K_w/kK_a = 1.15 \times 10^3 (s^{-1})^{-1} = 1.15 \times 10^3\,s$. Therefore, as $k = 4.3 \times 10^{-4}\,s^{-1}$ and $K_w = 10^{-14}$, we have

$$K_a = 10^{-14}/(4.3 \times 10^{-4}\,s^{-1}) \times (1.15 \times 10^3\,s)$$

$$= 2.0 \times 10^{-14}, \text{ and so } pK_a = 13.7.$$

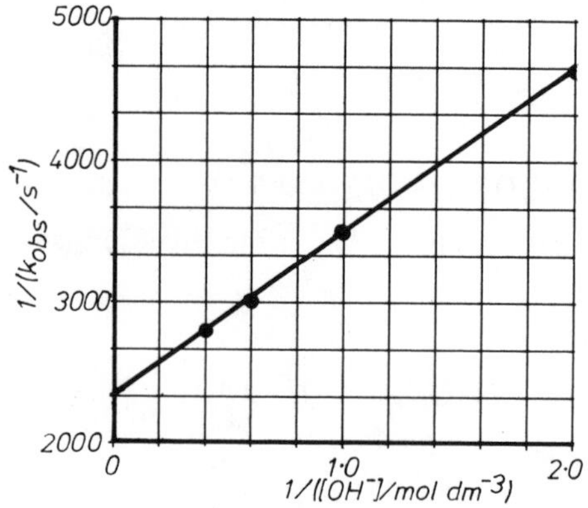

Fig 28.8

28.32 $d[P]/dt = k_1[E]_o[S]/(K_M + [S])$ [28.3.33]

$1/(d[P]/dt) = 1/k_1[E]_o + K_M/k_1[E]_o[S]$.

Draw up the following Table:

[S]/M	0.050	0.017	0.010	0.005	0.002
1/([S]/M)	20.0	58.8	100	200	500
(d[P]/dt)/mm^3 min^{-1}	16.6	12.4	10.1	6.6	3.3
1/(d[P]/dt)/mm^3 min^{-1}	0.0602	0.0806	0.0990	0.152	0.303

These points are plotted in Fig. 28.9.

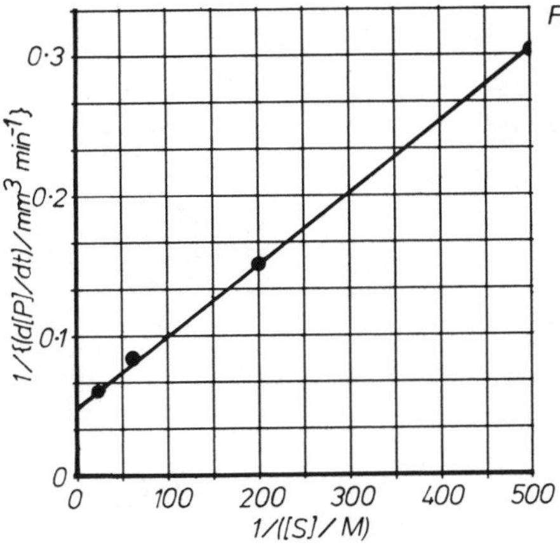

Fig 28.9

The intercept lies at 0.050, which implies that $1/k_1[E]_o = 0.050\,mm^{-3}\,min$. The slope is 5.06×10^{-4}, which implies that $K_M/k_1[E]_o = 5.06 \times 10^{-4}\,mm^{-3}\,min\,mol\,dm^{-3}$. Therefore $K_M = (5.06 \times 10^{-4}\,mm^{-3}\,min\,mol\,dm^{-3})/(0.050\,mm^{-3}\,min) = \underline{0.010\,M}$.

29. The kinetics of complex reactions

A29.1 The initiation step is step (1). Steps (3–7) are chain propagation steps. Steps (2 and 8) are chain termination steps [Section 29.1(a)].

A29.2 $\mathrm{d}[\mathrm{Cr(CO)_5}]/\mathrm{d}t = I - k_2[\mathrm{Cr(CO)_5}][\mathrm{CO}] - k_3[\mathrm{Cr(CO)_5}][\mathrm{M}]$

$+ k_4[\mathrm{Cr(CO)_5M}] = 0$ [Section 29.1(a)]

$[\mathrm{Cr(CO)_5}] = (I + k_4[\mathrm{Cr(CO)_5M}])/(k_2[\mathrm{CO}] + k_3[\mathrm{M}])$;

$\mathrm{d}[\mathrm{Cr(CO)_5M}]/\mathrm{d}t = k_3[\mathrm{Cr(CO)_5}][\mathrm{M}] - k_4[\mathrm{Cr(CO)_5M}]$

$= \{k_3 I - k_2 k_4[\mathrm{Cr(CO)_5M}][\mathrm{CO}]\}(k_2[\mathrm{CO}] + k_3[\mathrm{M}])^{-1}$;

$f = k_2 k_4[\mathrm{CO}](k_2[\mathrm{CO}] + k_3[\mathrm{M}])^{-1}$ if $k_3 I \ll k_2 k_4[\mathrm{CO}][\mathrm{Cr(CO)_5M}]$;

$\underline{f^{-1} = (k_4)^{-1} + k_3(k_2 k_4[\mathrm{CO}])^{-1}[\mathrm{M}]}$.

A29.3 $\mathrm{d}[\mathrm{R}]/\mathrm{d}t = 2k_1[\mathrm{R_2}] - k_2[\mathrm{R}][\mathrm{R_2}] + k_3[\mathrm{R'}] - 2k_4[\mathrm{R}]^2$ [Section 29.1(a)]

$\mathrm{d}[\mathrm{R'}]/\mathrm{d}t = k_2[\mathrm{R}][\mathrm{R_2}] - k_3[\mathrm{R'}]$.

If the steady state approximation is used for these rate equations,

$[\mathrm{R}] = (k_1 k_4^{-1}[\mathrm{R_2}])^{\frac{1}{2}}$;

$\mathrm{d}[\mathrm{R_2}]/\mathrm{d}t = -k_1[\mathrm{R_2}] - k_2[\mathrm{R_2}][\mathrm{R}] = \underline{-k_1[\mathrm{R_2}] - k_2(k_1/k_4)^{\frac{1}{2}}[\mathrm{R_2}]^{3/2}}$.

A29.4 At 700 K, $282\ \mathrm{Pa} \leqslant p \leqslant 2.24 \times 10^3\ \mathrm{Pa}$ [Section 29.1(c)].

At 800 K, $141\ \mathrm{Pa} \leqslant p \leqslant 8.91 \times 10^3\ \mathrm{Pa}$; at 900 K, $112\ \mathrm{Pa} \leqslant p$.

A29.5 Number of photons absorbed = Φ^{-1} (number of molecules which react) [29.2.1]

$= (2.10 \times 10^2\ \mathrm{mol\ einstein^{-1}})^{-1}(1.14 \times 10^{-3}\ \mathrm{mol})(6.02 \times 10^{23}\ \mathrm{einstein^{-1}})$

$= \underline{3.27 \times 10^{18}}$.

A29.6 Number of einsteins from the source =

$(100\ \mathrm{J\ s^{-1}})(45 \times 60\ \mathrm{s})(490 \times 10^{-9}\ \mathrm{m})(1.99 \times 10^{-25}\ \mathrm{J\ m})^{-1} \times (6.02 \times 10^{23}\ \mathrm{einstein^{-1}})^{-1}$

$= 1.10$ einstein.

Number of einsteins absorbed = 0.60(1.10) = 0.660.

$\Phi = 0.344\ \mathrm{mol}/0.660\ \mathrm{einstein} = \underline{0.521\ \mathrm{mol\ einstein^{-1}}}$.

A29.7 $\mathrm{d}[\mathrm{A^-}]/\mathrm{d}t = k_1[\mathrm{AH}][\mathrm{B}] - k_2[\mathrm{A^-}][\mathrm{BH^+}] - k_3[\mathrm{A^-}][\mathrm{A}]$ [Section 29.3(a)]

$[A^-] = k_1[AH][B](k_2[BH^+] + k_3[A])^{-1}$

$\underline{d[product]/dt = k_1k_3[A][AH][B](k_2[BH^+] + k_3[A])^{-1}.}$

A29.8 $d[AH]/dt = k_3[HAH^+][B] = k_3(k_1/k_2)[HA][H^+][B]$ [Section 29.3(a)]

$K_i = [H^+][B]/[HB^+]$; $d[AH]/dt = k_3(k_1/k_2)K_i[HA][HB^+]$.

A29.9 $K_{eq} = k_1/k_2$ [Section 29.5(c)].

$k_1 = (4.0 \times 10^{10}\,dm^3\,mol^{-1}\,s^{-1})(1.8 \times 10^{-5}\,mol\,dm^{-3}) = 7.2 \times 10^5\,s^{-1}$.

$\tau^{-1} = k_1 + k_2([NH_4^+] + [OH^-])$

$= 7.2 \times 10^5\,s^{-1} + (4.0 \times 10^{10}\,dm^3\,mol^{-1}\,s^{-1})(2)(1.8 \times 10^{-5}\,mol\,dm^{-3})^{\frac{1}{2}}$

$\times (0.15\,mol\,dm^{-3})^{\frac{1}{2}} = 1.3 \times 10^8\,s^{-1}$.

$\tau = \underline{7.7\,ns.}$

A29.10 $\tau^{-1} = k_1 + k_2([B] + [C])$ [*Example* 29.4]

$(3 \times 10^{-6}\,s)^{-1} = k_1 + (2)(2.0 \times 10^{-4}\,mol\,dm^{-3})k_2$.

$K_{eq} = k_1/k_2$; $k_1 = 2.0 \times 10^{-16}\,k_2$.

$k_2 = (3 \times 10^{-6})^{-1}[(2.0 \times 10^{-16}) + (4.0 \times 10^{-4})]^{-1} = \underline{8.3 \times 10^8\,dm^3\,mol^{-1}\,s^{-1}.}$

$k_1 = (2.0 \times 10^{-16}\,mol\,dm^{-3})(8.3 \times 10^8\,dm^3\,mol^{-1}\,s^{-1}) = \underline{1.66 \times 10^{-7}\,s^{-1}.}$

29.1 (a) Initiation [radicals formed, Section 29.1(a)]

(b) Propagation [new radicals formed]

(c) Propagation [new radicals formed]

(d) Termination [non-radical product formed].

$d[AH]/dt = -k_a[AH] - k_c[A\cdot][B\cdot]$

(i) $d[A\cdot]/dt = k_a[AH] - k_b[A\cdot] + k_c[AH][B\cdot] - k_d[A\cdot][B\cdot] \approx 0$

(ii) $d[B\cdot]/dt = k_b[A\cdot] - k_c[AH][B\cdot] - k_d[A\cdot][B\cdot] \approx 0$.

(i) + (ii): $[A\cdot][B\cdot] = (k_a/2k_d)[AH]$,

(i) − (iii): $[A\cdot] = (1/2k_b)\{k_a + 2k_c[B]\}[AH]$.

Solve for $[A\cdot]$: $[A\cdot] = k[AH]$, $k = (k_a/4k_b)\{1 + \surd[1 + 4k_bk_c/k_ak_d]\}$.

Then $[B\cdot] = k_a[AH]/2k_d[A] = k_a/2kk_d$.

Hence, $d[AH]/dt = -k_a[AH] - (k_ak_c/2kk_d)[AH] = k_{eff}[AH]$,

with $k_{eff} = k_a + k_ak_c/2kk_d$.

29.2 $CH_3CH_3 \rightarrow 2CH_3$, k_a.

$CH_3 + CH_3CH_3 \rightarrow CH_4 + CH_3CH_2$, k_b.

$CH_3CH_2 \rightarrow CH_2{:}CH_2 + H$, k_c.

$H + CH_3CH_3 \rightarrow H_2 + CH_3CH_2, k_d.$

$H + CH_3CH_2 \rightarrow CH_3CH_3, k_e$

$$d[CH_3CH_3]/dt = -k_a[CH_3CH_3] - k_b[CH_3][CH_3CH_3] - k_d[CH_3CH_3][H] + k_e[CH_3CH_2][H].$$

$d[CH_3]/dt = 2k_a[CH_3CH_3] - k_b[CH_3CH_3][CH_3] = 0$ implying $[CH_3] = 2k_a/k_b$.

$$d[CH_3CH_2]/dt = k_b[CH_3][CH_3CH_3] - k_c[CH_3CH_2] + k_d[CH_3CH_3][H] - k_e[CH_3CH_2][H] = 0.$$

$$d[H]/dt = k_c[CH_3CH_2] - k_d[CH_3CH_3][H] - k_e[CH_3CH_2][H] = 0.$$

These three equations give:

$[H] = k_c/\{k_e + k_d[CH_3CH_3]/[CH_3CH_2]\}$

$[CH_3CH_2]^2 - (k_a/k_c)[CH_3CH_3][CH_3CH_2] - (k_ak_d/k_ck_e) \times [CH_3CH_3]^2 = 0$

or $[CH_3CH_2] = [CH_3CH_3]\{(k_a/2k_c) + \sqrt{[(k_a/2k_c)^2 + (k_ak_d/k_c/k_e)]}\}$, implying

$[H] = k_c/\{k_e + k_d/[(k_a/2k_c) + \sqrt{\{(k_a/2k_c)^2 + (k_ak_d/k_ck_e)\}}]\}$.

If k_d is small in the sense that only the lowest order of k_a should be retained,

$[CH_3CH_2] \approx [CH_3CH_3](k_ak_d/k_ck_e)^{1/2}$,

$[H] \approx k_c/\{k_e + k_d(k_ck_e/k_ak_d)^{1/2}\} \approx (k_ak_c/k_dk_e)^{1/2}$.

Then $-d[CH_3CH_3]/dt = k_a[CH_3CH_3] + k_b(2k_a/k_b)[CH_3CH_3]$
$+ k_d(k_ak_c/k_dk_e)^{1/2}[CH_3CH_3] - k_e(k_ak_d/k_ck_e)^{1/2} \times (k_ak_c/k_dk_e)^{1/2}[CH_3CH_3]$
$= \{2k_a + (k_ak_ck_d/k_e)^{1/2}\}[CH_3CH_3] \approx (k_ak_ck_d/k_e)^{1/2}[CH_3CH_3]$ to lowest order in k_a. Hence the reaction displays first-order kinetics when k_a is small in the sense $k_ak_d/k_ck_e \gg (k_a/2k_c)^2$. Different orders may arise if the reaction is sensitized so that k_a is effectively increased.

29.3 $CH_3CHO \rightarrow CH_3 + CHO, k_a.$

$CH_3 + CH_3CHO \rightarrow CH_4 + CH_2CHO, k_b.$

$CH_2CHO \rightarrow CO + CH_3, k_e.$

$CH_3 + CH_3 \rightarrow CH_3CH_3, k_d.$

$d[CH_4]/dt = k_b[CH_3][CH_3CHO].$

$d[CH_3CHO]/dt = -k_a[CH_3CHO] - k_b[CH_3CHO][CH_3].$

$d[CH_3]/dt = k_a[CH_3CHO] - k_b[CH_3CHO][CH_3] + k_c[CH_2CHO] - 2k_d[CH_3]^2 = 0.$

$d[CH_2CHO]/dt = k_b[CH_3][CH_3CHO] - k_c[CH_2CHO] = 0.$

Adding the last two equations gives

$k_a[CH_3CHO] - 2k_d[CH_3]^2 = 0,$

or $[CH_3] = (k_a/2k_d)^{1/2}\ [CH_3CHO]^{1/2}$.

Therefore, $d[CH_4]/dt = k_b(k_a/2k_d)^{1/2}\ [CH_3CHO]^{3/2}$.

$d[CH_3CHO]/dt = -k_a[CH_3CHO] - k_b(k_a/2k_d)^{1/2}[CH_3CHO]^{3/2}$.

Note that to lowest order in k_a,

$d[CH_3CHO]/dt \approx -k_b(k_a/2k_d)^{1/2}\ [CH_3CHO]^{3/2}$, a $\frac{3}{2}$-order reaction.

29.4 $Cl_2 \rightleftharpoons 2Cl\ \ k_a, k_a'$: $[Cl]^2/[Cl_2] = K = k_a/k_a'$

$Cl + CO \rightleftharpoons COCl\ k_b, k_b'$: $[COCl]/[CO][Cl] = K' = k_b/k_b'$

$COCl + Cl_2 \rightarrow COCl_2 + Cl, k_c$.

$$\begin{aligned} d[COCl_2]/dt &= k_c[COCl][Cl_2] \\ &= k_cK'[CO][Cl][Cl_2] \\ &= k_cK'[CO]K^{\frac{1}{2}}[Cl_2]^{\frac{1}{2}}[Cl_2] \\ &= k_{eff}[CO][Cl_2]^{3/2},\ k_{eff} = k_cK'K^{\frac{1}{2}}. \end{aligned}$$

$[CO] = a - x$, $[Cl_2] = a - x$, $[COCl_2] = x$,

$dx/dt = k_{eff}(a-x)^{5/2}$

$$\int_0^x \frac{dx}{(a-x)^{5/2}} = k_{eff}t;\ k_{eff}t = \tfrac{2}{3}(a-x)^{-3/2}\Big|_0^x$$

$$3k_{eff}t/2 = \left(\frac{1}{a-x}\right)^{3/2} - \left(\frac{1}{a}\right)^{3/2}.$$

29.5 (i) $d[COCl_2]/dt = k_c[COCl][Cl_2]$

(ii) $d[COCl]/dt = k_b[Cl][CO] - k_b'[COCl] - k_c[COCl][Cl_2] = 0$

(iii) $d[Cl]/dt = 2k_a[Cl_2] - 2k_a'[Cl]^2 - k_b[Cl][CO] + k_b'[COCl]$
$+ k_c[COCl][Cl_2] = 0$,

From (ii): $[COCl] = k_b[Cl][CO]/(k_b' + k_c[Cl_2])$ (iv)

Then (iii) becomes $k_a[Cl_2] - k_a'[Cl]^2 = 0$,

so that $[Cl] = K^{1/2}[Cl_2]^{1/2}, K = k_a/k_a'$.

Then substitution into (iv), and that into (i) gives the rate law

$d[COCl_2]/dt = k_cK'K^{1/2}[CO][Cl_2]^{3/2}/\{1 + (k_c/k_b')[Cl_2]\}$, with $K' = k_b/k_b'$.

29.6 Write $a = [COCl_2], b = [Cl_2], c = [CO]$
$x = [COCl], y = [Cl]$
and replace the differential equations in Problem 29.5 by the coupled finite difference equations

(i) $a(t_{i+1}) = a(t_i) + k_c x(t_i) b(t_i) \Delta t$

(ii) $x(t_{i+1}) = x(t_i) + k_b y(t_i) c(t_i) - k_b' x(t_i) - k_c x(t_i) b(t_i)$

(iii) $y(t_{i+1}) = y(t_i) + 2k_a b(t_i) - 2k_a' y(t_i)^2 - k_b y(t_i) c(t_i) + k_b' x(t_i) + k_c x(t_i) b(t_i)$,

and iterate the solutions.

29.7 Proceed as in Section 29.1(b). $d[M\cdot]/dt = k_i f[I]$ [initiation]
$d[R]/dt = -2k_t[R]^2$ [termination]
$d[R]/dt = k_i f[I] - 2k_t[R]^2 = 0$ [steady state];
hence, $[R] = \{k_i f[I]/2k_t\}^{1/2}$.
Rate of propagation:
$d[M]/dt = -k_p[R][M] = \underline{-k_p\{k_i f/2k_t\}^{1/2}[M][I]^{1/2}}$.
$\chi = k_p\{k_i f/2k_t\}^{1/2}[M][I]^{1/2}/k_i f[I]$ [29.1.9]
$= \underline{\{k_p/(2fk_t k_i)^{1/2}\}[M][I]^{-1/2}}$.

29.8 $d[M]/dt = k_i[M][I]$ [initiation]
$d[R]/dt = -2k_t^0(1 + a[M])[R]^2$ [termination]
$d[M]/dt = -k_p^0(1 + b[M])[R][M]$ [propagation].
Steady state:
$d[R]/dt = k_i[M][I] - 2k_t^0(1 + a[M])[R]^2 = 0$,
$[R] = \{k_i[M][I]/2k_t^0(1 + a[M])\}^{1/2}$
$d[M]/dt = -k_p^0(1 + b[M])[M]\{k_i[M][I]/2k_t^0(1 + a[M])\}^{1/2}$

$$= \underline{-\{k_p^0(k_i/2k_t^0)^{1/2}\left\{\frac{1 + b[M]}{(1 + a[M])^{1/2}}\right\}[I]^{1/2}[M]^{3/2}}.$$

29.9 $d[A]/dt = -k[A]^3$ [given]
$2kt = 1/[A]_0^2 - 1/[A]^2$,
hence $[A] = [A]_0/(1 - 2[A]_0^2 kt)^{1/2}$.
$p = ([A]_0 - [A])/[A]_0$ [29.1.11]
$= \underline{1 - 1/(1 - 2[A]_0^2 kt)^{1/2}}$.

29.10 $\langle M\rangle_M = M_{\text{mon}}(1+p)/(1-p)$ [*Example* 29.1]

$1/(1-p) = 1 + kt[\text{A}]_{\text{o}}$, $1 + p = (1 + 2kt[\text{A}]_{\text{o}})/(1 + kt[\text{A}]_{\text{o}})$

$\underline{\langle M\rangle_M = M_{\text{mon}}(1 + 2kt[\text{A}]_{\text{o}}).}$

Hence, $\langle M\rangle_M$ grows linearly with time (until the supply of monomer is terminated).

29.11 $\langle M\rangle_N = M_{\text{mon}}/(1-p)$ [Exercise of *Example* 29.1]

$= \underline{M_{\text{mon}}(1 + kt[\text{A}]_{\text{o}}).}$

$\langle M\rangle_N/\langle M\rangle_M = (1 + kt[\text{A}]_{\text{o}})/(1 + 2kt[\text{A}]_{\text{o}})$

For $2kt[\text{A}]_{\text{o}} \ll 1$, $\langle M\rangle_N/\langle M\rangle_M \approx 1 - kt[\text{A}]_{\text{o}}$

For $kt[\text{A}]_{\text{o}} \gg 1$, $\langle M\rangle_N/\langle M\rangle_M \approx \frac{1}{2}$.

29.12 $\langle M_{\text{r}}\rangle_N = M_{\text{mon}}/(1-p)$ [*Example* 29.1]

$\langle M_{\text{r}}^2\rangle_N = M_{\text{mon}}^2 \sum_n n^2 P_n$ [$M_{\text{r}} = nM_{\text{mon}}$, probability P_n]

$$= M_{\text{mon}}^2(1-p)\sum_n n^2 p^{n-1} \quad [29.1.13]$$

$$= M_{\text{mon}}^2(1-p)(\text{d}/\text{d}p)p(\text{d}/\text{d}p)\sum_n p^n$$

$$= M_{\text{mon}}^2(1-p)(\text{d}/\text{d}p)p(\text{d}/\text{d}p)(1-p)^{-1}$$

$$= M_{\text{mon}}^2(1+p)/(1-p)^2.$$

$\langle M_{\text{r}}^2\rangle_N - \langle M_{\text{r}}\rangle_N^2 = M_{\text{mon}}^2\{(1+p)/(1-p)^2 - 1/(1-p)^2\}$

$= pM_{\text{mon}}^2/(1-p)^2.$

Hence, $\underline{\delta M_{\text{r}} = p^{1/2}M_{\text{mon}}/(1-p)}$

The time dependence is given by combining this relation with

$1/(1-p) = 1 + kt[\text{A}]_{\text{o}}$ [29.1.12]

$\underline{\delta M_{\text{r}} = M_{\text{mon}}\{kt[\text{A}]_{\text{o}} + k^2t^2[\text{A}]_{\text{o}}^2\}^{1/2}.}$

29.13 $\langle M_{\text{r}}^3\rangle_N = M_{\text{mon}}^3 \sum_n n^3 P_n$ [$M_{\text{r}} = nM_{\text{mon}}$]

$$= M_{\text{mon}}^3(1-p)\sum_n n^3 p^{n-1} \quad [29.1.13]$$

$$= M_{\text{mon}}^3(1-p)(\text{d}/\text{d}p)\sum_n n^2 p^n$$

$$= M_{\text{mon}}^3(1-p)(\text{d}/\text{d}p)p(\text{d}/\text{d}p)p(\text{d}/\text{d}p)\sum_n p^n$$

$$= M_{\text{mon}}^3(1-p)(\mathrm{d}/\mathrm{d}p)p(\mathrm{d}/\mathrm{d}p)p(\mathrm{d}/\mathrm{d}p)(1-p)^{-1}$$
$$= M_{\text{mon}}^3(1+4p+p^2)/(1-p)^3.$$

$\langle M_r^3\rangle_N = M_{\text{mon}}^2(1+p)/(1-p)^2$ [Problem 29.12]

$\underline{\langle M_r^3\rangle_N/\langle M_r^2\rangle_N = M_{\text{mon}}(1+4p+p^2)/(1-p^2)}.$

Then, since $\chi = 1/(1-p)$ [29.1.14], and $p = 1 - 1/\chi$,

$\underline{\langle M_r^3\rangle_N/\langle M_r^2\rangle_N = M_{\text{mon}}(6\chi^2 - 6\chi + 1)/(2\chi - 1)}.$

29.14 (i) $\mathrm{d}[\mathrm{H}]/\mathrm{d}t = k_b[\mathrm{H_2}][\mathrm{OH}] - k_c[\mathrm{O_2}][\mathrm{H}\cdot] + k_d[\mathrm{H_2}][\mathrm{O}] - k_e[\mathrm{H}\cdot] = 0$

(ii) $\mathrm{d}[\mathrm{O}]/\mathrm{d}t = k_c[\mathrm{O_2}][\mathrm{H}\cdot] - k_d[\mathrm{H_2}][\mathrm{O}] = 0$

(iii) $\mathrm{d}[\mathrm{OH}]/\mathrm{d}t = r_a - k_b[\mathrm{H_2}][\mathrm{OH}] + k_c[\mathrm{O_2}][\mathrm{H}\cdot] + k_d[\mathrm{H_2}][\mathrm{O}] = 0$.

From (ii): $[\mathrm{O}] = (k_c/k_d)[\mathrm{O_2}][\mathrm{H}\cdot]/[\mathrm{H_2}]$.

From (i) + (iii): $r_a + 2k_d[\mathrm{H_2}][\mathrm{O}] - k_e[\mathrm{H}\cdot] = 0$,

hence $r_a + 2k_c[\mathrm{H_2}][\mathrm{O_2}][\mathrm{H}\cdot]/[\mathrm{H_2}] - k_e[\mathrm{H}\cdot] = 0$,

so that $\underline{[\mathrm{H}\cdot] = r_a/(k_e - 2k_c[\mathrm{O_2}])}$,

and $[\mathrm{H}\cdot] \to \infty$ if $2k_c[\mathrm{O_2}] \to k_e$.

29.15 $UO_2^{2+} + h\nu \to (UO_2^{2+})^*$

$(UO_2^{2+})^* + (COOH)_2 \to UO_2^{2+} + H_2O + CO_2 + CO$.

$2MnO_4^- + 5(CO_2H)_2 + 6H^+ \to 10CO_2 + 8H_2O + 2Mn^{2+}$,

or $2KMnO_4 + 5(CO_2H)_2 + 6HCl \to 10CO_2 + 8H_2O + 2MnCl_2 + 2KCl$.

17.0 cm^3 of 0.212 M $KMnO_4$ is equivalent to

$(5/2) \times (17.0\ \mathrm{cm^3}) \times (0.212\ \mathrm{M}) = 9.01 \times 10^3$ mol oxalic acid.

The initial sample contained 5.232 g oxalic acid, or $(5.232\ \mathrm{g}/90.04\ \mathrm{g\,mol^{-1}}) = 5.81 \times 10^{-2}$ mol. Therefore $5.81 \times 10^{-2}\ \mathrm{mol} - 9.01 \times 10^{-3}\ \mathrm{mol} = 4.91 \times 10^{-2}$ mol of acid has been destroyed. A quantum efficiency of 0.53 implies that the amount of photons absorbed must have been $(4.91 \times 10^{-2}\ \mathrm{mol})/0.53 = 9.3 \times 10^{-2}$ mol. Since the exposure was for 300 s, the rate of incidence of photons was $(9.3 \times 10^{-2}\ \mathrm{mol})/300\ \mathrm{s} = 3.1 \times 10^{-4}\ \mathrm{mol\,s^{-1}}$. Since 1 mol of photons is 1 einstein, the incident rate is $\underline{3.1 \times 10^{-4}\ \text{einstein s}^{-1}}$ or $3.1 \times 10^{-4} N_A$ photons per second; that is, $\underline{1.9 \times 10^{20}\ \mathrm{s^{-1}}}$.

29.16 $\mathrm{M} + h\nu_i \to \mathrm{M}^*, I_a$.

$\mathrm{M}^* + \mathrm{Q} \to \mathrm{M} + \mathrm{Q}, k_q$.

$\mathrm{M}^* \to \mathrm{M} + h\nu_f, k_f$.

$\mathrm{d}[\mathrm{M}^*]/\mathrm{d}t = I_a - k_f[\mathrm{M}^*] - k_q[\mathrm{Q}][\mathrm{M}^*] \approx 0$, which implies that

$[\mathrm{M}^*] = I_a/\{k_f + k_q[\mathrm{Q}]\}$.

$I_f = k_f[M^*] = k_f I_a/\{k_f + k_q[Q]\}$, hence $\underline{1/I_f = 1/I_a + k_q[Q]/k_f I_a}$.

If the exciting light is extinguished $[M^*]$, and hence I_f, decays as $\exp(-k_f t)$ in the absence of a quencher. Therefore measure k_f and unravel k_q from the slope of the $1/I_f$ against $[Q]$ graph (slope $= k_q/k_f I_a$, intercept $1/I_a$).

29.17 $1/I_f = 1/I_a + k_q[Q]/k_f I_a$ [Problem 29.16].

Draw up the following Table.

$[Q]/M$	0.001	0.005	0.010
$1/I_f$	2.4	4.0	6.3

These points are plotted in Fig. 29.1. The intercept lies at 2.0, and so $I_a = 1/2.0 = 0.50$. The slope is 430, and so $k_q/k_f I_a = 430\,M^{-1}$. Since $I_a = 0.50$,

$$k_q = (215\,M^{-1})k_f = (215\,M^{-1}) \times (1/t_{1/2})\ln 2 \quad [27.2.10]$$
$$= (215\,M^{-1}) \times (1/2.9 \times 10^{-7}\,s)\ln 2 = \underline{5.1 \times 10^8\,M^{-1}\,s^{-1}}.$$

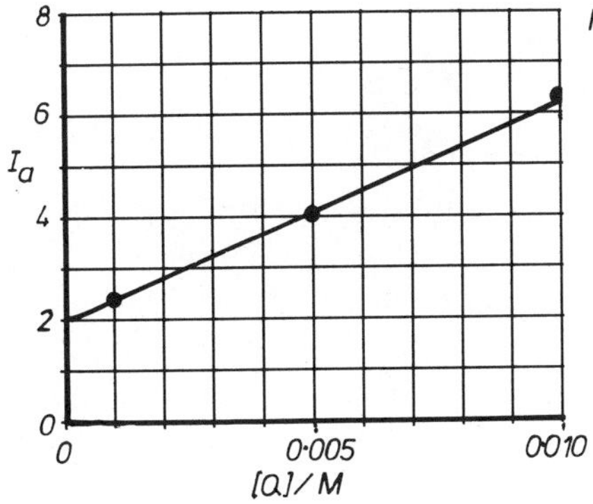

Fig 29.1

29.18 $A \rightarrow 2R, I_a$.

$A + R \rightarrow R + B, k_p$.

$R + R \rightarrow R_2, k_t$.

$d[A]/dt = -I_a - k_p[A][R]$; $d[R]/dt = 2I_a - 2k_t[R]^2 = 0$.

The latter implies that $[R] = (I_a/k_t)^{1/2}$, and so

$d[A]/dt = -I_a - k_p(I_a/k_t)^{1/2}\,[A]$

$d[B]/dt = k_p[A][R] = k_p(I_a/k_t)^{1/2}\,[A]$.

Therefore, only the combination $k_p/k_t^{1/2}$ may be determined if the reaction attains a steady state.

29.19 $Cl_2 + h\nu \rightarrow 2Cl$, I_a,

$Cl + CHCl_3 \rightarrow CCl_3 + HCl$ k_a,

$CCl_3 + Cl_2 \rightarrow CCl_4 + Cl$, k_b,

$2CCl_3 + Cl_2 \rightarrow 2CCl_4$, k_c.

(i) $d[CCl_4]/dt = 2k_c[CCl_3]^2[Cl_2] + k_b[CCl_3][Cl_2]$.

(ii) $d[CCl_3]/dt = k_a[Cl][CHCl_3] - k_b[CCl_3][Cl_2] - 2k_c[CCl_3]^2[Cl_2] = 0$.

(iii) $d[Cl]/dt = 2I_a - k_a[Cl][CHCl_3] + k_b[CCl_3][Cl_2] = 0$.

(iv) $d[Cl_2]/dt = -I_a - k_b[CCl_3][Cl_2] - k_c[CCl_3]^2[Cl_2]$.

Therefore, $I_a = k_c[CCl_3]^2[Cl_2]$ [(ii) + (iii)], implying $[CCl_3] = (1/k_c)^{1/2}(I_a/[Cl_2])^{1/2}$

Using (i) leads to

$d[CCl_4]/dt = 2I_a + k_b(1/k_c)^{1/2}I_a^{1/2}[Cl_2]^{1/2}$.

At high chlorine pressures, and for slow initiation (in the sense that the lowest powers of I_a dominate), the second term dominates the first, and so $d[CCl_4]/dt = k_b(1/k_c)^{1/2}I_a^{1/2}[Cl_2]^{1/2} = k_{1/2}I_a^{1/2}[Cl_2]^{1/2}$ with $k_{1/2} = k_b(1/k_c)^{1/2}$. It seems to be necessary to suppose that Cl + Cl recombination (which requires a third body) is unimportant.

29.20 $A \rightarrow B$, $d[B]/dt = I_a$; $B \rightarrow A$, $d[B]/dt = -k[B]^2$.

In the photostationary state, $I_a - k[B]^2 = 0$. $[B] = (I_a/k)^{1/2} \propto \underline{[A]^{1/2}}$.

The illumination may increase the rate of the forward reaction without affecting the reverse reaction. Hence, the position of equilibrium may be shifted towards products.

29.21 $A + h\nu \rightarrow A^*, I_a$;

$A^* + A \rightarrow A_2, k$;

$A^* \rightarrow A + h\nu_f, k_f; I_f = k_f[A^*]$.

$\Phi = (-d[A]/dt)/I_a$.

$d[A]/dt = -I_a - k[A^*][A] + k_f[A^*]$.

$d[A^*]/dt = I_a - k[A^*][A] - k_f[A^*] \approx 0$.

$[A^*] \approx I_a/(k_f + k[A])$;

therefore $d[A]/dt \approx -I_a + (k_f - k[A])I_a/(k_f + k[A])$

$\approx -2kI_a[A]/(k_f + k[A])$.

Consequently, $\underline{\Phi \approx 2k[A]/(k_f + k[A])}$.

If $k[A] \ll k_f$; $\Phi \approx 2(k/k_f)[A]$, and the efficiency is determined by the availability of A in the vicinity of A*. If $k[A] \gg k_f$, $\Phi \approx 2$, and the rate is determined by the excitation step because there is plenty of A to react to form A_2 (which implies the removal of two A species).

29.22 $d[P]/dt = k[A]^2[P]$.

$[A] = [A]_0 - x$, $[P] = [P]_0 + x$, $d[P]/dt = dx/dt$,

$dx/dt = k([A]_0 - x)^2([P]_0 + x)$,

$$kt = \int_0^x dx/([A]_0 - x)^2([P]_0 + x);$$

solve this by partial fractions:

$$\frac{1}{([A]_0 - x)^2([P]_0 + x)} = \frac{\alpha}{([A]_0 - x)^2} + \frac{\beta}{[A]_0 - x} + \frac{\gamma}{[P]_0 + x}$$

$$= \frac{\alpha([P]_0 + x) + \beta([A]_0 - x)([P]_0 + x) + \gamma([A]_0 - x)^2}{([A]_0 - x)^2([P]_0 + x)}$$

$$\left.\begin{aligned} &\alpha[P]_0 + \beta[A]_0[P]_0 + \gamma[A]_0^2 = 1, \\ &\alpha + ([A]_0 - [P]_0)\beta - 2\gamma[A]_0 = 0, \\ &-\beta + \gamma = 0. \end{aligned}\right\}$$

These solve to

$\alpha = 1/([A]_0 + [P]_0)$, $\beta = \gamma = \alpha/([A]_0 + [P]_0)$.

Therefore,

$$kt = \left(\frac{1}{[A]_0 + [P]_0}\right)\int_0^x dx\left\{\left(\frac{1}{[A]_0 - x}\right)^2 + \left(\frac{1}{[A]_0 + [P]_0}\right)\left(\frac{1}{[A]_0 - x} + \frac{1}{[P]_0 + x}\right)\right\}$$

$$= \left(\frac{1}{[A]_0 + [P]_0}\right)\left\{\left(\frac{1}{[A]_0 - x} - \frac{1}{[A]_0}\right) + \left(\frac{1}{[A]_0 + [P]_0}\right) \times \left[\ln\left(\frac{[A]_0}{[A]_0 - x}\right) + \ln\left(\frac{[P]_0 + x}{[P]_0}\right)\right]\right\}$$

$$= \left(\frac{1}{[A]_0 + [P]_0}\right)\left\{\frac{x}{[A]_0([A]_0 - x)} + \left(\frac{1}{[A]_0 + [P]_0}\right)\ln\left(\frac{[A]_0([P]_0 + x)}{([A]_0 - x)[P]_0}\right)\right\}.$$

Therefore, with $y = x/[A]_0$ and $p = [P]_0/[A]_0$,

$[A]_0([A]_0 + [P]_0)kt = \underline{y/(1 - y) + \{1/(1 + p)\}\ln\{(p + y)/(1 - y)p\}}.$

29.23 $d[P]/dt = k[A][P]^2$

$dx/dt = k([A]_0 - x)([P]_0 + x)^2$, $x = [P] - [P]_0$

$$kt = \int_0^x \mathrm{d}x/([\mathrm{A}]_o - x)([\mathrm{P}]_o + x)^2.$$

Integrate by partial fractions [Problem 29.22]

$$kt = \left(\frac{1}{[\mathrm{A}]_o + [\mathrm{P}]_o}\right)\int_0^x \mathrm{d}x \left\{\left(\frac{1}{[\mathrm{P}]_o + x}\right)^2 + \left(\frac{1}{[\mathrm{A}]_o + [\mathrm{P}]_o}\right) \times \right.$$

$$\left. \times \left[\left(\frac{1}{[\mathrm{P}]_o + x}\right) + \left(\frac{1}{[\mathrm{A}]_o - x}\right)\right]\right\}$$

$$= \left(\frac{1}{[\mathrm{A}]_o + [\mathrm{P}]_o}\right)\left\{\left(\frac{1}{[\mathrm{P}]_o} - \frac{1}{[\mathrm{P}]_o + x}\right) + \left(\frac{1}{[\mathrm{A}]_o + [\mathrm{P}]_o}\right) \times \right.$$

$$\left. \times \left[\ln\left(\frac{[\mathrm{P}]_o + x}{[\mathrm{P}]_o}\right) + \ln\left(\frac{[\mathrm{A}]_o}{[\mathrm{A}]_o - x}\right)\right]\right\}$$

$$= \left(\frac{1}{[\mathrm{A}]_o + [\mathrm{P}]_o}\right)\left\{\frac{x}{[\mathrm{P}]_o([\mathrm{P}]_o + x)} + \left(\frac{1}{[\mathrm{A}]_o + [\mathrm{P}]_o}\right)\ln\left(\frac{([\mathrm{P}]_o + x)[\mathrm{A}]_o}{[\mathrm{P}]_o([\mathrm{A}]_o - x)}\right)\right\}.$$

$$[\mathrm{A}]_o([\mathrm{A}]_o + [\mathrm{P}]_o)kt = \underline{y/p(p+y) + \{1/(1+p)\}\ln\{(p+y)/(1-y)p\}}$$

with $y = x/[\mathrm{A}]_o$ and $p = [\mathrm{P}]_o/[\mathrm{A}]_o$.

29.24 (a) $v_\mathrm{P} = k[\mathrm{A}]^2[\mathrm{P}]$.

$$\mathrm{d}v_\mathrm{P}/\mathrm{d}t = 2k[\mathrm{A}](\mathrm{d}[\mathrm{A}]/\mathrm{d}t)[\mathrm{P}] + k[\mathrm{A}]^2\mathrm{d}[\mathrm{P}]/\mathrm{d}t$$

$$= -2k[\mathrm{A}][\mathrm{P}]v_\mathrm{P} + k[\mathrm{A}]^2 v_\mathrm{P} \ [v_\mathrm{A} = -v_\mathrm{P}]$$

$$= k[\mathrm{A}]([\mathrm{A}] - 2[\mathrm{P}])v_\mathrm{P}$$

$$= 0 \text{ when } [\mathrm{A}] = 2[\mathrm{P}].$$

That is, the rate is a maximum when $[\mathrm{A}]_o - x = 2[\mathrm{P}]_o + 2x$, which implies that $x = \frac{1}{3}([\mathrm{A}]_o - 2[\mathrm{P}]_o)$, or $y = \frac{1}{3}(1 - 2p)$. On substituting this into the solution in Problem 29.22, we find

$$[\mathrm{A}]_o([\mathrm{A}]_o + [\mathrm{P}]_o)kt_{max} = \{1/(1+p)\}\{\tfrac{1}{2}(1-2p) + \ln(1/2p)\},$$

or $([\mathrm{A}]_o + [\mathrm{P}]_o)^2 kt_{max} = \underline{\tfrac{1}{2} - p + \ln(1/2p)}$.

(b) $v_\mathrm{P} = k[\mathrm{A}][\mathrm{P}]^2$.

$$\mathrm{d}v_\mathrm{P}/\mathrm{d}t = 2k[\mathrm{A}][\mathrm{P}]\mathrm{d}[\mathrm{P}]/\mathrm{d}t + k(\mathrm{d}[\mathrm{A}]/\mathrm{d}t)[\mathrm{P}]^2$$

$$= 2k[\mathrm{A}][\mathrm{P}]v_\mathrm{P} - k[\mathrm{P}]^2 v_\mathrm{P}$$

$$= k[\mathrm{P}](2[\mathrm{A}] - [\mathrm{P}])v_\mathrm{P}.$$

$$= 0 \text{ when } [\mathrm{A}] = \tfrac{1}{2}[\mathrm{P}].$$

That is, the rate is a maximum when $2[\mathrm{A}]_o - 2x = [\mathrm{P}]_o + x$, which implies that $x = \frac{1}{3}(2[\mathrm{A}]_o - [\mathrm{P}]_o)$, or $y = \frac{1}{3}(2 - p)$. On substituting this into the solution in

Problem 29.23 we find

$[A]_o([A]_o + [P]_o)kt_{max} = (2-p)/2p(1+p) + \{1/(1+p)\}\ln(2/p)$,

or $([A]_o + [P]_o)^2 kt_{max} = \underline{(2-p)/2p + \ln(2/p)}$.

29.25 Write the differential equations for [X] and [Y]:

(i) $d[X]/dt = k_a[A][X] - k_b[X][Y]$

(ii) $d[Y]/dt = k_b[X][Y] - k_c[Y]$.

Express these as finite difference equations:

(i) $X(t_{i+1}) = X(t_i) + k_a[A]X(t_i)\Delta t - k_b X(t_i)Y(t_i)\Delta t$

(ii) $Y(t_{i+1}) = Y(t_i) - k_c Y(t_i)\Delta t + k_b X(t_i)Y(t_i)\Delta t$.

and iterate for different values of [A], X(0), Y(0).

29.26 For the steady state

(i) $d[X]/dt = k_a[A][X] - k_b[X][Y] = 0$

(ii) $d[Y]/dt = k_b[X][Y] - k_c[Y] = 0$,

which solve to

(ii) $k_b[X] = k_c$,

(i) $k_a[A] = k_b[Y]$;

hence $\underline{[X] = k_c/k_b}$, $\underline{[Y] = k_a[A]/k_b}$.

29.27 (i) $d[X]/dt = k_a[A] + k_b[X]^2[Y] - k_c[B][X] - k_d[X]$

(ii) $d[Y]/dt = -k_b[X]^2[Y] + k_c[B][X]$ [29.4.2].

Express these as finite difference equations, and iterate:

(i) $X(t_{i+1}) = X(t_i) + \{k_a[A] + k_b X^2(t_i)Y(t_i) - k_c[B]X(t_i) - k_d[X]\}\Delta t$

(ii) $Y(t_{i+1}) = Y(t_i) + \{k_c[B]X(t_i) - k_b X^2(t_i)Y(t_i)\}\Delta t$.

See Fig. 29.9 of the text.

29.28 (i) $d[X]/dt = k_a[A][Y] - k_b[X][Y] + k_c[B][X] - 2k_d[X]^2$

(ii) $d[Y]/dt = -k_a[A][Y] - k_b[X][Y] + k_e[Z]$ [29.4.3]

Express these as finite differences equations, and iterate:

(i) $X(t_{i+1}) = X(t_i) + \{k_a[A]Y(t_i) - k_b X(t_i)Y(t_i) + k_c[B]X(t_i) - 2k_d X^2(t_i)\}\Delta t$,

(ii) $Y(t_{i+1}) = Y(t_i) + \{k_e[Z] - k_a[A]Y(t_i) - k_b X(t_i)Y(t_i)\}\Delta t$.

29.29 $H + NO_2 \rightarrow OH + NO$, $k = 2.9 \times 10^{10}\,M^{-1}\,s^{-1}$,

$OH + OH \rightarrow H_2O + O$, $k' = 1.55 \times 10^{9}\,M^{-1}\,s^{-1}$,

$O + OH \rightarrow O_2 + H$, $k'' = 1.1 \times 10^{10}\,M^{-1}\,s^{-1}$.

$[H]_o = 4.5 \times 10^{-10}\,mol\,cm^{-3}$, $[NO_2]_o = 5.6 \times 10^{-10}\,mol\,cm^{-3}$.

$d[O]/dt = k'[OH]^2 - k''[O][OH]$

$d[O_2]/dt = k''[O][OH]$

$d[OH]/dt = k[H][NO_2] - 2k'[OH]^2 - k''[O][OH]$

$d[NO_2]/dt = -k[H][NO_2]$

$d[H]/dt = k''[O][OH] - k[H][NO_2]$.

These equations serve to show how even a simple sequence of reactions leads to a complicated set of non-linear differential equations. Since we are interested in the time behavior of the composition we may not invoke the steady-state assumption. The only thing left is to use a computer, and to integrate the equations numerically. The outcome of this is the set of curves shown in Fig. 29.2 (they have been sketched from the original reference). The similarity to an A→B→C scheme should be noticed (and expected); and the general features can be analyzed quite simply in terms of the underlying reactions.

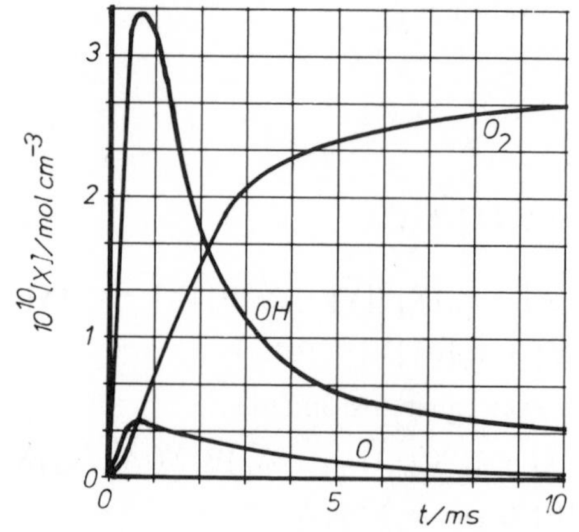

Fig 29.2

29.30 $O + Cl_2 \rightarrow ClO + Cl$. $p(Cl_2) \approx$ constant [Cl_2 at high pressure]; therefore the reaction is probably pseudo-first-order and $[O]/[O]_o = \exp(-k't)$. Therefore

$\ln [O]_o/[O] = k't = k[Cl_2]t = k[Cl_2](d/v)$,

where $k' = k[Cl_2] \approx$ constant and d is the distance along the tube.

Draw up the following Table:

d/cm	0	2	4	6	8	10	12	14	16	18
$\ln\{[O]_o/[O]\}$	0.27	0.31	0.34	0.38	0.45	0.46	0.50	0.55	0.56	0.60

These points are plotted in Fig. 29.3. The slope is 0.0189, and so $k[\mathrm{Cl_2}]/v = 0.0189\ \mathrm{cm^{-1}}$.

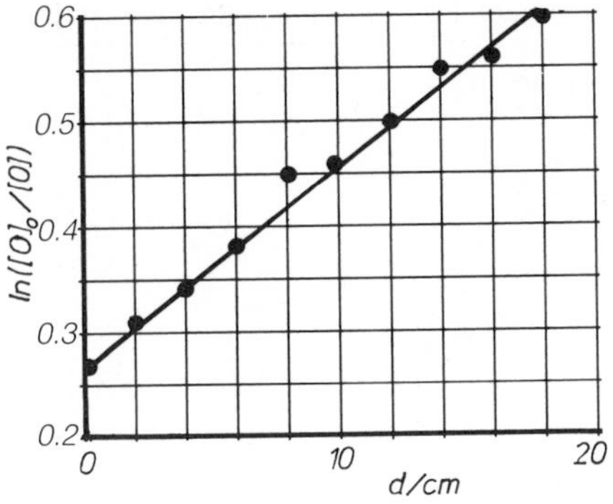

Fig 29.3

$$k = (0.0189\ \mathrm{cm^{-1}})v/[\mathrm{Cl_2}]$$

$$= \frac{(0.0189\ \mathrm{cm^{-1}}) \times (6.66 \times 10^2\ \mathrm{cm\ s^{-1}})}{2.54 \times 10^{-7}\ \mathrm{mol\ dm^{-3}}} = 5.0 \times 10^7\ \mathrm{M^{-1}\ s^{-1}}.$$

[There is also a very fast $\mathrm{O + ClO \rightarrow Cl + O_2}$ reaction, and so the answer given is actually *twice* the correct value.]

29.31 $\mathrm{A \rightleftharpoons B + C}$.

$\mathrm{A \rightarrow B + C}$; $\mathrm{d[A]}/\mathrm{d}t = -k_1[\mathrm{A}]$,

$\mathrm{B + C \rightarrow A}$, $\mathrm{d[A]}/\mathrm{d}t = k_2[\mathrm{B}][\mathrm{C}]$.

At equilibrium $k_1[\mathrm{A}]_\mathrm{e} = k_2[\mathrm{B}]_\mathrm{e}[\mathrm{C}]_\mathrm{e}$, $k_1'[\mathrm{A}]_\mathrm{e}' = k_2'[\mathrm{B}]_\mathrm{e}'[\mathrm{C}]_\mathrm{e}'$ under two sets of conditions. Let the primed set be the initial set of conditions. Then, when the unprimed conditions are suddenly attained,

$\mathrm{d[A]}/\mathrm{d}t = -k_1[\mathrm{A}] + k_2[\mathrm{B}][\mathrm{C}]$ with initial conditions $[\mathrm{A}]_\mathrm{e}'$, $[\mathrm{B}]_\mathrm{e}'$, $[\mathrm{C}]_\mathrm{e}'$.

Write $[\mathrm{A}] = x + [\mathrm{A}]_\mathrm{e}$. Then $[\mathrm{B}] = -x + [\mathrm{B}]_\mathrm{e}$, $[\mathrm{C}] = -x + [\mathrm{C}]_\mathrm{e}$ since every A that decays (or is formed) increases (or decreases) B and C by one each. Therefore

$$\mathrm{d[A]}/\mathrm{d}t = \mathrm{d}x/\mathrm{d}t = -k_1\{x + [\mathrm{A}]_\mathrm{e}\} + k_2\{-x + [\mathrm{B}]_\mathrm{e}\}\{-x + [\mathrm{C}]_\mathrm{e}\}$$

$$= -k_1x - k_1[\mathrm{A}]_\mathrm{e} - xk_2[\mathrm{C}]_\mathrm{e} - xk_2[\mathrm{B}]_\mathrm{e} + k_2x^2 + k_2[\mathrm{B}]_\mathrm{e}[\mathrm{C}]_\mathrm{e}.$$

Since $k_1[\mathrm{A}]_\mathrm{e} = k_2[\mathrm{B}]_\mathrm{e}[\mathrm{C}]_\mathrm{e}$ the second and sixth terms cancel, and so

$$\mathrm{d}x/\mathrm{d}t = -(k_1 + k_2[\mathrm{B}]_\mathrm{e} + k_2[\mathrm{C}]_\mathrm{e})x + k_2x^2.$$

For small jumps x^2 is negligible, and so

$$\mathrm{d}x/\mathrm{d}t = -(k_1 + k_2[\mathrm{B}]_\mathrm{e} + k_2[\mathrm{C}]_\mathrm{e})x,$$

$x = x_0\{\exp -(k_1 + k_2[\mathrm{B}]_e + k_2[\mathrm{C}]_e)t\}$.

Since $x_0 = [\mathrm{A}]_0 - [\mathrm{A}]_e = [\mathrm{A}]'_e - [\mathrm{A}]_e$,

$[\mathrm{A}] - [\mathrm{A}]_e = \{[\mathrm{A}]'_e - [\mathrm{A}]_e\}e^{-t/\tau}$ where $\underline{1/\tau = k_1 + k_2[\mathrm{B}]_e + k_2[\mathrm{C}]_e}$.

30. Molecular reaction dynamics

A30.1 $\sigma^* N_A(8kT/\pi\mu)^{\frac{1}{2}} = 3.72 \times 10^{12}\,dm^3\,mol^{-1}\,min^{-1}(60\,s/min)^{-1}$

$\times (10\,dm/m)^{-3} = 6.20 \times 10^7\,m^3\,mol^{-1}\,s^{-1}.$

$\mu = (116)^{-1}(100)(16) = 13.8$

$8kT/\pi\mu = 8(1.38 \times 10^{-23}\,J\,K^{-1})(298\,K)(\pi)^{-1}(13.8)^{-1}(1.66 \times 10^{-27}\,kg)^{-1}$

$= 4.57 \times 10^5\,m^2\,s^{-2}.$

$\sigma^* = (6.20 \times 10^7\,m^3\,mol^{-1}\,s^{-1})(4.57 \times 10^5\,m^2\,s^{-2})^{-\frac{1}{2}}(6.02 \times 10^{23}\,mol^{-1})^{-1}$

$= 1.52 \times 10^{-19}\,m^2$, or $\underline{0.152\,nm^2.}$ [30.1.7]

A30.2 $P = \sigma^*/\sigma$ [30.1.8] $= 9.2 \times 10^{-22}\,m^2\,[0.5(0.95 + 0.65) \times 10^{-18}\,m^2]^{-1}$

$= \underline{1.2 \times 10^{-3}.}$

A30.3 $d[P]/dt = k_2[A][B].$

$k_2 = 4(R_A + R_B)(RT)(6\eta)^{-1}(R_A^{-1} + R_B^{-1})$ [30.2.8] $= 4(0.294 + 0.825)(10^{-9}\,m)$

$\times (8.31\,J\,K^{-1}\,mol^{-1})(313\,K)(6)^{-1}(2.37 \times 10^{-3}\,kg\,m^{-1}\,s^{-1})^{-1}$

$\times (0.294^{-1} + 0.825^{-1})(10^9\,m^{-1}) = 3.78 \times 10^6\,mol^{-1}\,m^3\,s^{-1}$

$= \underline{3.78 \times 10^9\,mol^{-1}\,dm^3\,s^{-1}.}$

$d[P]/dt = (3.78 \times 10^9\,dm^3\,mol^{-1}\,s^{-1})(0.150)(0.330)\,mol^2\,dm^{-6}$

$= 1.87 \times 10^8\,mol\,dm^{-3}\,s^{-1}.$

A30.4 $k_2 = P(8RT/3\eta), P = 0.19$ [30.2.9].

$k_2 = (0.193)(8)(8.31\,J\,K^{-1}\,mol^{-1})(303\,K)(3)^{-1}(3.70 \times 10^{-3}\,kg\,m^{-1}\,s^{-1})^{-1}$

$= 3.50 \times 10^5\,m^3\,mol^{-1}\,s^{-1}$, or $\underline{3.5 \times 10^8\,dm^3\,mol^{-1}\,s^{-1}.}$

A30.5 $E_a/R = 8681\,K; E_a = (8681\,K)(8.314\,J\,K^{-1}\,mol^{-1}) = 72.17\,kJ\,mol^{-1}.$

$2.05 \times 10^{13} = ekTh^{-1}\exp(\Delta S^{\neq}/R)$. [Section 30.3(d)]

$1 + \Delta S^{\neq}/8.31\,J\,K^{-1}\,mol^{-1} = \ln[(2.05 \times 10^{13})(6.62 \times 10^{-34}\,J\,s)(1.38 \times 10^{-23}\,J\,K^{-1})^{-1}$

$\times (303\,K)^{-1}] = 1.18;$

$\Delta S^{\neq} = 0.18(8.3\,J\,K^{-1}\,mol^{-1}) = \underline{1.5\,J\,K^{-1}\,mol^{-1}.}$

A30.6 $\Delta H^{\neq} = E_a - RT = R[(E_a/R) - T] = [8.314\,J\,K^{-1}\,mol^{-1}][(9134 - 303)K]$

$= \underline{73.42\,kJ\,mol^{-1}.}$ [Section 30.3(d)]

$\Delta G^{\neq} = \Delta H^{\neq} - T\Delta S^{\neq} = 73.42\,\text{kJ mol}^{-1} - (303\,\text{K})(31.7 \times 10^{-3})\,\text{kJ K}^{-1}\,\text{mol}^{-1}$
$= \underline{63.81\,\text{kJ mol}^{-1}}.$

A30.7 $p^{\ominus}k_r = e^2 kTh^{-1}\exp(\Delta S^{\neq}/R)\exp(-E_a/RT)$ [30.3.22, using $[X] = n_X p_X/RT$ and $dp_A/dt = -k_r p_A p_B$, so that $k_r = k_{eff}/RT$]

$2 + \Delta S^{\neq}/R = (E_a/RT) + \ln(hp^{\ominus}k_r/kT)$
$= (58.6 \times 10^3\,\text{J mol}^{-1})(8.31\,\text{J K}^{-1}\,\text{mol}^{-1})^{-1}(338\,\text{K})^{-1}$
$+ \ln[(6.626 \times 10^{-34}\,\text{J s}) \times (10^5\,\text{N m}^{-2}) \times (7.84 \times 10^{-6}\,\text{N}^{-2}\,\text{m}^2\,\text{s}^{-1})/ (1.381 \times 10^{-23}\,\text{J K}^{-1}) \times (338\,\text{K})]$
$= 20.9 - 29.8 = -8.9$

$\Delta S^{\neq} = (8.31\,\text{J K}^{-1}\,\text{mol}^{-1})(-10.9) = \underline{-90.6\,\text{J K}^{-1}\,\text{mol}^{-1}}.$

A30.8 $\lg(k) = \lg(k^{\circ}) + 1.02 z_A z_B I^{\frac{1}{2}}$ [30.3.28].
$\lg(k^{\circ}) = \lg(12.2) - 1.02(-1)(+1)(0.0525)^{\frac{1}{2}} = 1.32;$
$k^{\circ} = \underline{20.9\,\text{dm}^6\,\text{mol}^{-2}\,\text{min}^{-1}}.$

A30.9 Figure A30.1 shows that $\lg(k_r)$ is a linear function of I. This result suggests that $\lg(\gamma)$ is proportional to I for neutral molecules.
From the graph, $\lg(k_r^{\circ}/\text{M}^{-1}\,\text{min}^{-1}) = -0.18;$
hence $k_r^{\circ} = \underline{0.66\,\text{M}^{-1}\,\text{min}^{-1}}.$

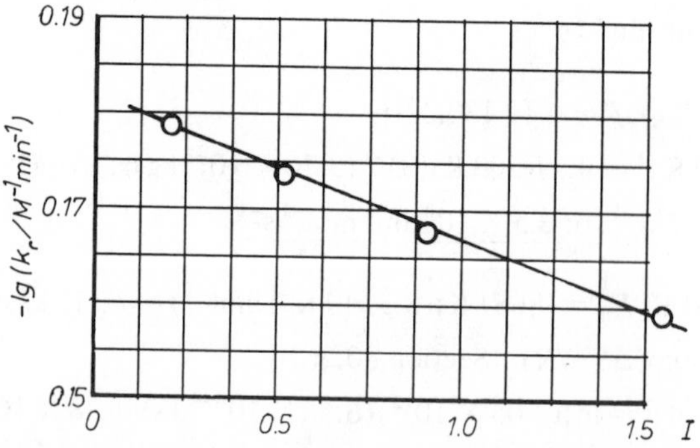

Fig A30.1

A30.10 $K_a = [H^+][A^-][HA]^{-1}(\gamma_{H^+}\gamma_{A^-})(\gamma_{HA})^{-1}$ [30.3.25].
$\lg[H^+] = \lg(K_a) + \lg([HA]/[A^-]) + 2AI^{\frac{1}{2}}.$
$\lg(\text{rate}) = \lg(k_r[B]) + \lg[H^+]$
Since $\lg[H^+]$ is linear in $I^{\frac{1}{2}}$, $\lg(\text{rate})$ should be linear in $I^{\frac{1}{2}}$.

30.1 $z = 2^{\frac{1}{2}}\sigma\bar{c}p/kT$ [26.2.2], $\bar{c} = (8kT/\pi m)^{\frac{1}{2}}$ [26.1.10]
$z = 4\sigma p(1/\pi mkT)^{1/2}$, $\sigma = \pi d^2 \approx 4\pi R^2$ $[d = 2R]$.

$Z_{AA} = \sigma(4kT/\pi m)^{1/2}(N/V)^2$ [26.2.4] $= \sigma(4kT/\pi m)^{1/2}(p/kT)^2$.

$$z = \frac{16\pi R^2(1.0133 \times 10^5\,\mathrm{N\,m^{-2}})}{[\pi \times M_r \times (1.660\,56 \times 10^{-27}\,\mathrm{kg}) \times (1.3807 \times 10^{-23}\,\mathrm{J\,K^{-1}}) \times (298.15\,\mathrm{K})]^{1/2}}$$

$$= \{1.099 \times 10^6 (R/\mathrm{pm})^2/M_r^{1/2}\}\mathrm{s^{-1}}.$$

$$Z_{AA} = 4\pi R^2 \left\{\frac{4 \times (1.3807 \times 10^{-23}\,\mathrm{J\,K^{-1}}) \times (298.15\,\mathrm{K})}{\pi(1.660\,56 \times 10^{-27}\,\mathrm{kg}) \times M_r}\right\}^{1/2}$$

$$\times \left\{\frac{1.0133 \times 10^5\,\mathrm{N\,m^{-2}}}{(1.3807 \times 10^{-23}\,\mathrm{J\,K^{-1}}) \times (298.15\,\mathrm{K})}\right\}^2$$

$$= \{1.353 \times 10^{31}(R/\mathrm{pm})^2/M_r^{1/2}\}\mathrm{s^{-1}\,m^{-3}}.$$

(a) Ammonia. $R = 190$ pm, $M_r = 17$;

$z = \{1.099 \times 10^6 \times (190)^2/17^{1/2}\}\mathrm{s^{-1}} = \underline{9.6 \times 10^9\,\mathrm{s^{-1}}}.$

$Z_{AA} = \{1.353 \times 10^{31} \times (190)^2/17^{1/2}\}\mathrm{s^{-1}\,m^{-3}}$

$= 1.2 \times 10^{35}\,\mathrm{s^{-1}\,m^{-3}} = \underline{1.2 \times 10^{29}\,\mathrm{s^{-1}\,cm^{-3}}}.$

(b) Carbon monoxide. $R = 180$ pm, $M_r = 28$;

$z = \{1.099 \times 10^6 \times (180)^2/28^{1/2}\}\mathrm{s^{-1}} = \underline{6.7 \times 10^9\,\mathrm{s^{-1}}}.$

$Z_{AA} = \{1.35 \times 10^{31} \times (180)^2/28^{1/2}\}\mathrm{s^{-1}\,m^{-3}} = \underline{8.3 \times 10^{28}\,\mathrm{s^{-1}\,cm^{-3}}}.$

For the percentage increases at constant volume, use

$\mathrm{d}z/\mathrm{d}T = \sqrt{2}\sigma(N/V)\mathrm{d}\bar{c}/\mathrm{d}T$, $\mathrm{d}\bar{c}/\mathrm{d}T = \bar{c}/2T$ or $\mathrm{d}z/\mathrm{d}T = z/2T$.

Therefore $100(\delta z/z) = 100(\mathrm{d}z/\mathrm{d}T)\delta T/z = 50(\delta T/T)$;

likewise, $\mathrm{d}Z/\mathrm{d}T = Z/2T$ so that $100(\delta Z/Z) = 50(\delta T/T)$.

Since $\delta T/T = (10\,\mathrm{K})/(298\,\mathrm{K}) = 0.034$, the increases in both z and Z are $\underline{1.7\%}$.

30.2 $\mathrm{d}N(E) = K\mathrm{e}^{-\beta E}\,\mathrm{d}E$ [given; K to be found].

$$N = \int_0^\infty \mathrm{d}N(E) = K\int_0^\infty \mathrm{e}^{-\beta E}\,\mathrm{d}E = K/\beta. \text{ Therefore}$$

$K = N\beta = \underline{N/kT}$ [N is the total number of molecules].

$$P(E \geqslant E_a) = (1/N)\int_{E_a}^\infty K\mathrm{e}^{-\beta E}\,\mathrm{d}E = (K/N\beta)\exp(-\beta E_a) = \underline{\exp(-\beta E_a)}.$$

Note that $\exp(-\beta E)$ gives the proportion with energy E as well as the proportion with at least that energy.

If the density of states is proportional to E^n,

$dN(E) = KE^n e^{-\beta E}$ and $K = N\beta^{n+1}/n!$.

This leads to

$$P(E \geqslant E_a) = \int_{E_a}^{\infty} KE^n e^{-\beta E} dE = e^{-\beta E_a} \sum_{k=0}^{n} \{(\beta E_a)^{n-k}/(n-k)!\}.$$

For $n = 1, P(E \geqslant E_a) = (1 + \beta E_a)e^{-\beta E_a}$.

30.3 For a uniform density of states, $P(E > E_a) = \exp(-E_a/kT)$ [Problem 30.2] $= \exp(-E_a/RT)$, when E_a is expressed as a molar quantity. Draw up the following Table, using $R = 8.314\ \mathrm{J\,K^{-1}\,mol^{-1}}$.

$P(E > E_a)$		200 K	300 K	500 K	1000 K
E_a	10 kJ mol^{-1}	2.44×10^{-3}	1.81×10^{-2}	9.02×10^{-2}	3.00×10^{-1}
	1000 kJ mol^{-1}	7.62×10^{-27}	3.87×10^{-18}	3.57×10^{-11}	5.98×10^{-6}

For a linearly increasing density of states,

$P(E > E_a)$		200 K	300 K	500 K	1000 K
E_a	10 kJ mol^{-1}	1.71×10^{-2}	9.07×10^{-2}	3.07×10^{-1}	6.61×10^{-1}
	100 kJ mol^{-1}	4.66×10^{-25}	1.59×10^{-16}	8.94×10^{-10}	7.79×10^{-5}

30.4 The percentage increase is approximately

$100(1/P)(dP/dT)\delta T = 100(d\ln P/dT)\delta T = 100(d/dT)(-E_a/RT)\delta T = 100E_a\delta T/RT^2$.

Draw up the following Table, using $\delta T = 10$ K for the uniform density of states.

$100E_a\delta T/RT^2$		200 K	300 K	500 K	1000 K
E_a	10 kJ mol^{-1}	30.1	13.4	4.8	1.2
	100 kJ mol^{-1}	301	134	48	12

The entries are percentages.

30.5 $2A \rightarrow A_2, -d[A]/dt = k[A]^2$.

$d[A]/dt = \{d(N/V)/dt\}/N_A$ $[[A] = n/V = N/N_A V]$;

$d(N/V)/dt = -2Z_{AA} \exp(-E_a/RT)$ [2A removed on each successful collision].

Therefore

$$-d[A]/dt = (2/N_A)Z_{AA} \exp(-E_a/RT)$$
$$= (2/N_A)\sigma^*(4kT/\pi m)^{1/2}(N/V)^2 \exp(-E_a/RT)$$
$$= 4\sigma^*(kT/\pi m)^{1/2} N_A [A]^2 \exp(-E_a/RT) = k[A]^2.$$

Therefore, $k = 4\sigma^*(kT/\pi m)^{1/2} N_A \exp(-E_a/RT) = A \exp(-E_a/RT)$,

and so $A = 4\sigma^*(kT/\pi m)^{1/2} N_A$.

$$4(kT/\pi m)^{1/2} N_A = 4 \times \left\{\frac{(1.381 \times 10^{-23}\,\mathrm{J\,K^{-1}}) \times (298.15\,\mathrm{K})}{\pi \times (15 \times 1.660\,56 \times 10^{-27}\,\mathrm{kg})}\right\}^{1/2}$$
$$\times (6.022 \times 10^{23}\,\mathrm{mol^{-1}}) = 5.52 \times 10^{26}\,\mathrm{mol^{-1}\,m\,s^{-1}}.$$

(a) Since $A_{expt} = 2.4 \times 10^{10}\,\mathrm{M^{-1}\,s^{-1}}$.

$\sigma^* = A_{expt}/4(kT/\pi m)^{1/2} N_A = (2.4 \times 10^7\,\mathrm{m^3\,mol^{-1}\,s^{-1}})/(5.52 \times 10^{26}\,\mathrm{mol^{-1}\,m\,s^{-1}})$

$= \underline{4.3 \times 10^{-20}\,\mathrm{m^2}}$.

(b) The C-H bond length is 154 pm, and so $\sigma \approx \pi \times (308\,\mathrm{pm})^2 = 3.0 \times 10^{-19}\,\mathrm{m^2}$.

Hence, $P = \sigma^*/\sigma$ [Section 30.1(b)] $= (4.3 \times 10^{-20}\,\mathrm{m^2})/(3.0 \times 10^{-19}\,\mathrm{m^2}) = \underline{0.14}$.

30.6 $A_{expt} = 1.14 \times 10^{10}\,\mathrm{M^{-1}\,s^{-1}}$ [Problem 28.26]

$= \sigma^* N_A(8kT/\pi\mu)^{1/2}$ [30.1.5] so that $\sigma^* = A_{expt}/N_A(8kT/\pi\mu)^{1/2}$.

$1/\mu = 1/m(\mathrm{O}) + 1/m(\mathrm{benzene})$,

$\mu = \{16 \times 78/(16 + 78)\} \times (1.6605 \times 10^{-27}\,\mathrm{kg}) = 2.20 \times 10^{-26}\,\mathrm{kg}$.

$$N_A(8kT/\pi\mu)^{1/2} = (6.022 \times 10^{23}\,\mathrm{mol^{-1}}) \times \left\{\frac{8 \times (1.381 \times 10^{-23}\,\mathrm{J\,K^{-1}}) \times (340\,\mathrm{K})}{\pi \times (2.20 \times 10^{-26}\,\mathrm{kg})}\right\}^{1/2}$$
$$= 4.44 \times 10^{26}\,\mathrm{mol^{-1}\,m^{-1}\,s^{-1}}.$$

$\sigma^* = (1.14 \times 10^7\,\mathrm{m^3\,mol^{-1}\,s^{-1}})/(4.44 \times 10^{26}\,\mathrm{mol^{-1}\,m^{-1}\,s^{-1}})$

$= \underline{2.6 \times 10^{-20}\,\mathrm{m^2} = 0.026\,\mathrm{nm^2}}$.

$R(\mathrm{O}) \approx 78$ pm, $R(\mathrm{benzene}) \approx 265$ pm; therefore

$\sigma \approx \pi(78\,\mathrm{pm} + 265\,\mathrm{pm})^2 = 3.7 \times 10^{-19}\,\mathrm{m^2}$. Consequently,

$P = \sigma^*/\sigma$ [Section 30.1(b)] $= 2.6 \times 10^{-20}/3.7 \times 10^{-19} = \underline{0.07}$.

30.7 Draw up the following Table as the basis for an Arrhenius plot [28.3.3]:

T/K	600	700	800	1000
$10^3/(T/\mathrm{K})$	1.67	1.43	1.25	1.00
$k/\mathrm{cm^3\,mol^{-1}\,s^{-1}}$	4.6×10^2	9.7×10^3	1.3×10^5	3.1×10^6
$\ln(k/\mathrm{cm^3\,mol^{-1}\,s^{-1}})$	6.13	9.18	11.8	15.0

These points are plotted in Fig. 30.1. The least squares intercept at $1/T = 0$ is at 28.3, which implies that $A/\mathrm{cm^3\,mol^{-1}\,s^{-1}} = e^{28.3} = 2.0 \times 10^{12}$.

$\sigma^* = A_{\mathrm{expt}}/4(kT/\pi m)^{1/2}N_A$ [Problem 30.5]. Use $T \approx 750\,\mathrm{K}, M_r(NO_2) = 46$.

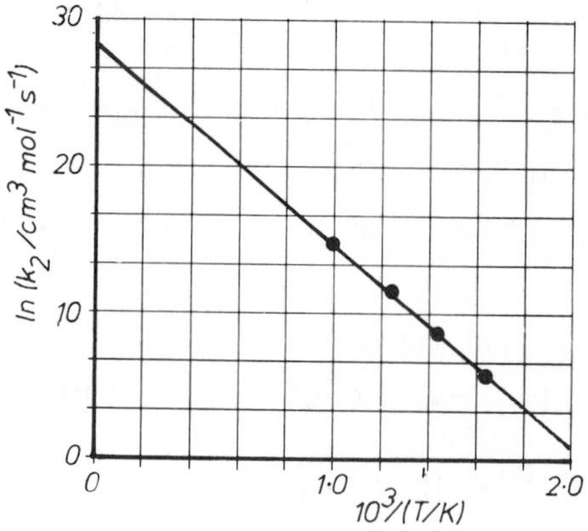

Fig 30.1

$$4(kT/\pi m)^{1/2}N_A = 4 \times (6.022 \times 10^{23}\,\mathrm{mol^{-1}}) \times \left\{\frac{(1.381 \times 10^{-23}\,\mathrm{J\,K^{-1}}) \times (750\,\mathrm{K})}{\pi \times 46 \times (1.660\,56 \times 10^{-27}\,\mathrm{kg})}\right\}^{1/2}$$

$$= \underline{5.00 \times 10^{26}\,\mathrm{mol^{-1}\,m\,s^{-1}}}.$$

Therefore, $\sigma^* = (2.0 \times 10^{12}\,\mathrm{cm^3\,mol^{-1}\,s^{-1}})/(5.00 \times 10^{26}\,\mathrm{mol^{-1}\,m\,s^{-1}}) = \underline{4.0 \times 10^{21}\,\mathrm{m^2}}$.

Use $\sigma \approx 0.60\,\mathrm{nm^2}$, then $P = (4.0 \times 10^{-21}\,\mathrm{m^2})/(0.60 \times 10^{-18}\,\mathrm{m^2}) = \underline{0.007}$.

30.8 k will have its maximum value for $E_a = 0$ and $P = 1$ (or more), for then every collision is successful.

$k_{\max} = 4\sigma(kT/\pi m)^{1/2}N_A$ [30.1.5, $\mu = m/2$]

$4(kT/\pi m)^{1/2}N_A = 5.52 \times 10^{26}\,\mathrm{mol^{-1}\,m\,s^{-1}}$ [$T = 198$ K, Problem 30.5].

$\sigma \approx \pi(380\,\mathrm{pm})^2 = 4.5 \times 10^{-19}\,\mathrm{m^2}$.

Therefore, $k_{\max} \approx (4.5 \times 10^{-19}\,\mathrm{m^2}) \times (5.52 \times 10^{26}\,\mathrm{mol^{-1}\,m\,s^{-1}})$

$$= 2.5 \times 10^8\,\mathrm{m^3\,mol^{-1}\,s^{-1}} = \underline{2.5 \times 10^{11}\,\mathrm{M^{-1}\,s^{-1}}}.$$

30.9 $d[C_2H_6]/dt = k[CH_3]^2$; $k = 2.5 \times 10^{11} M^{-1} s^{-1}$ [Problem 30.8]

$[CH_3] = [CH_3]_0 - 2[C_2H_6]$, and so $d[CH_3]/dt = -2d[C_2H_6]/dt = -2k[CH_3]^2$.

$1/[CH_3] - 1/[CH_3]_0 = 2kt$.

For 90 percent recombination, $[CH_3] = 0.1[CH_3]_0$, and so $2kt = 9/[CH_3]_0$.

$$[CH_3]_0 = 0.1 \times 2 \times [C_2H_6]_0 = 0.2 \times (p/RT)$$
$$= 0.2 \times (1.013 \times 10^5 N m^{-2})/(2.48 \times 10^3 J mol^{-1})$$
$$= 8.17 mol m^{-3} = 8.17 \times 10^{-3} M.$$

Therefore, $t = 4.5/(2.5 \times 10^{11} M^{-1} s^{-1}) \times (8.17 \times 10^{-3} M) = \underline{22 ns}$.

30.10 $k_d = 8RT/3\eta$ [30.2.9] $= 8 \times (2.4789 kJ mol^{-1})/3\eta$

$$= (6.610 \times 10^3/\eta) J mol^{-1}$$
$$= \{6.610 \times 10^3/(\eta/kg m^{-1} s^{-1})\}(J/kg m^{-1} s^{-1}) mol^{-1}$$

$[J/kg m^{-1} s^{-1} = kg m^2 s^{-2}/kg m^{-1} s^{-1} = m^3 s^{-1} = 10^3 dm^3 s^{-1}]$.

$$k_d = (6.610 \times 10^6 dm^3 mol^{-1} s^{-1})/(\eta/kg m^{-1} s^{-1})$$
$$= (6.610 \times 10^9 M^{-1} s^{-1})/(\eta/cP)$$ [conversion defined in *Example* 26.6]

(a) <u>Water</u>; $\eta = 1.00 \times 10^{-3} kg m^{-1} s^{-1}$.

$k_d = (6.610 \times 10^6 M^{-1} s^{-1})/1.00 \times 10^{-3} = \underline{6.6 \times 10^9 M^{-1} s^{-1}}$.

(b) <u>n-pentane</u>; $\eta = 0.22 \times 10^{-3} kg m^{-1} s^{-1}$.

$k_d = (6.610 \times 10^6 M^{-1} s^{-1})/0.22 \times 10^{-3} = \underline{3.0 \times 10^{10} M^{-1} s^{-1}}$.

(c) <u>n-decylbenzene</u>; $\eta = 3.36 \times 10^{-3} kg m^{-1} s^{-1}$.

$k_d = (6.610 \times 10^6 M^{-1} s^{-1})/3.36 \times 10^{-3} = \underline{2.0 \times 10^9 M^{-1} s^{-1}}$.

30.11 $\partial[J]^*/\partial t = k[J]e^{-kt} + (\partial[J]/\partial t)e^{-kt} - k[J]e^{-kt}$

$$= (\partial[J]/\partial t)e^{-kt}.$$

$$\partial^2[J]^*/\partial x^2 = k\int_0^t (\partial^2[J]/\partial x^2)e^{-kt}dt + (\partial^2[J]/\partial x^2)e^{-kt}.$$

Then, since $D\partial^2[J]/\partial x^2 = \partial[J]/\partial t$ [30.2.13, $k = 0$],

$$D\partial^2[J]^*/\partial x^2 = k\int_0^t (\partial[J]/\partial t)e^{-kt}dt + (\partial[J]/\partial t)e^{-kt}$$

$$= k\int_0^t (\partial[J]^*/\partial t)dt + \partial[J]^*/\partial t \text{ [line 1]}$$

$$= k[J]^* + \partial[J]^*/\partial t,$$

which rearranges to eqn (30.2.13).

When $t = 0$, $[\mathrm{J}]^* = [\mathrm{J}]$ [30.2.14 with $t = 0$], and so the same initial conditions are satisfied. (The same boundary conditions are also satisfied.)

30.12 Simpson's rule is specified in *Example* 24.4. Write

$z^2 = kx^2/4D, \tau = kt, j = (A/n_o)(\pi D/k)^{1/2}[\mathrm{J}]^*$,

$$\text{then } j = \int_0^{\tau} \tau^{-1/2} e^{-(z^2/\tau+\tau)} d\tau + \tau^{-1/2} e^{-(z^2/\tau+\tau)},$$

which should be evaluated.

30.13 $q_m^{\ominus T}/N_A = 2.561 \times 10^{-2}(T/\mathrm{K})^{5/2} M_r^{3/2}$ [Box 22.1].

For $T \approx 300\,\mathrm{K}, M_r \approx 50, q_m^{\ominus T}/N_A \approx \underline{1.4 \times 10^7.}$

$q^R_{\text{non-linear}} = (1.0270/\sigma)(T/\mathrm{K})^{3/2}/(ABC/\mathrm{cm}^{-3})^{1/2}$ [Box 22.1]

For $T \approx 300\,\mathrm{K}, A \approx B \approx C \approx 2\,\mathrm{cm}^{-1}, \sigma \approx 2, q^R_{\mathrm{nl}} \approx \underline{900}.$

$q^R_{\text{linear}} = (0.6950/\sigma)(T/\mathrm{K})/(B/\mathrm{cm}^{-1})$ [Box 22.1].

For $T \approx 300\,\mathrm{K}, B \approx 1\,\mathrm{cm}^{-1}, \sigma \approx 1, q^R_{\mathrm{l}} \approx \underline{200.}$

$q^V \approx \underline{1},\ q^E \approx \underline{1}$ [Box 22.1].

For the second part:

$k_{\mathrm{eff}} = \kappa(kT/h)K$ [30.3.11]

$K = (RT/p^{\ominus})\bar{K}_p$ [30.3.10b]

$\quad = (RT/p^{\ominus})\{N_A \bar{q}^{\ominus}_{\mathrm{C,m}}/q^{\ominus}_{\mathrm{A,m}} q^{\ominus}_{\mathrm{B,m}}\} e^{-\Delta E_0^{\neq}/RT}$ [30.3.10c].

$q^{\ominus}_{\mathrm{A,m}}/N_A = q^{\ominus T}_{\mathrm{A,m}}/N_A \approx 1.4 \times 10^7$ [above]

$q^{\ominus}_{\mathrm{B,m}}/N_A = q^{\ominus T}_{\mathrm{B,m}}/N_A \approx 1.4 \times 10^7$ [above]

$\bar{q}^{\ominus}_{\mathrm{C,m}}/N_A = (q^{\ominus T}_{\mathrm{C,m}}/N_A) q^R_{\mathrm{l}} \approx 2^{3/2} \times 1.4 \times 10^7 \times 200$

[$2^{3/2}$ as $m_C = 2m_A + m_B \approx 2m_A$, and $q \propto m^{3/2}$]

$$K = (RT/p^{\ominus})\left\{\frac{2^{3/2} \times 1.4 \times 10^7 \times 200}{(1.4 \times 10^7)^2}\right\} e^{-\Delta E_0^{\neq}/RT}$$

$\quad = (RT/p^{\ominus}) \times 4.2 \times 10^{-5} \times e^{-\Delta E_0^{\neq}/RT}.$

Since $RT/p^{\ominus} = 2.5 \times 10^{-2}\,\mathrm{m^3\,mol^{-1}}$,

$K \approx (1.05 \times 10^{-6}\,\mathrm{m^3\,mol^{-1}}) e^{-\Delta E_0^{\neq}/RT}.$

Hence $A \approx (kT/h) \times (1.05 \times 10^{-6}\,\mathrm{m^3\,mol^{-1}})$

$\quad \approx (6.2 \times 10^{12}\,\mathrm{s^{-1}}) \times (1.05 \times 10^{-6}\,\mathrm{m^3\,mol^{-1}})$

$\quad \approx 6.5 \times 10^6\,\mathrm{m^3\,mol^{-1}\,s^{-1}} = \underline{6.5 \times 10^9\,\mathrm{M^{-1}\,s^{-1}}.}$

30.14 For all species non-linear

$q^{\ominus}_{A,m}/N_A \approx 1.4 \times 10^7 \times 900 = 1.3 \times 10^{10}$

$q^{\ominus}_{B,m}/N_A \approx 1.4 \times 10^7 \times 900 = 1.3 \times 10^{10}$

$q^{\ominus}_{C,m}/N_A \approx 2^{3/2} \times 1.4 \times 10^7 \times 900 = 3.6 \times 10^{10}$

$K = (RT/p^{\ominus})\{3.6 \times 10^{10}/(1.3 \times 10^{10})^2\}e^{-\Delta E_0^{\neq}/RT}$

$\quad = 2.1 \times 10^{-10}(RT/p^{\ominus})e^{-\Delta E_0^{\neq}/RT}.$

Therefore $k(\text{true})/k(\text{simple}) = 2.1 \times 10^{-10}/4.2 \times 10^{-5}$ [Problem 30.13]

$= 5 \times 10^{-6}.$

Hence $\underline{P \approx 5 \times 10^{-6}}$.

30.15 If cleavage of a CD or CH bond is involved in the rate-determining step, use

$$k_2(\text{D})/k_2(\text{H}) = \exp\left\{\tfrac{1}{2}(\hbar k_f^{1/2}/kT)\left[\left(\frac{1}{\mu_{CD}}\right)^{1/2} - \left(\frac{1}{\mu_{CH}}\right)^{1/2}\right]\right\} \quad [30.3.16].$$

$\mu_{CD} = \{12 \times 2/(12+2)\} \times (1.6605 \times 10^{-27}\,\text{kg}) = 2.8 \times 10^{-27}\,\text{kg},$

$\mu_{CH} = \{12 \times 1/(12+1)\} \times (1.6605 \times 10^{-27}\,\text{kg}) = 1.5 \times 10^{-27}\,\text{kg},$

$k_f \approx 450\,\text{N m}^{-1}.$

$$k_2(\text{D})/k_2(\text{H}) = \exp\left\{\tfrac{1}{2}\left[\frac{(1.054 \times 10^{-34}\,\text{J s}) \times (450\,\text{N m}^{-1})^{1/2}}{(1.381 \times 10^{-23}\,\text{J K}^{-1}) \times (298\,\text{K})}\right]\right.$$

$$\left.\times\left[\left(\frac{10^{27}}{2.8\,\text{kg}}\right)^{1/2} - \left(\frac{10^{27}}{1.5\,\text{kg}}\right)^{1/2}\right]\right\} = e^{-1.88} = 0.15 = 1/6.6.$$

That is, $k_2(\text{D}) \approx k_2(\text{H})/7$, in reasonable accord with the observed ratio of 4.3.

30.16 $\mu_{CT} = \{12 \times 3/(12+3)\} \times (1.6605 \times 10^{-27}\,\text{kg}) = 40 \times 10^{-27}\,\text{kg},$

$\mu_{CO(16)} = \{12 \times 16/(12+16)\} \times (1.6605 \times 10^{-27}\,\text{kg}) = 1.14 \times 10^{-26}\,\text{kg},$

$\mu_{CO(18)} = \{12 \times 18/(12+18)\} \times (1.6605 \times 10^{-27}\,\text{kg}) = 1.20 \times 10^{-26}\,\text{kg}.$

(a) $\tfrac{1}{2}(\hbar k_f^{1/2}/kT)\,[(1/\mu_{CT})^{1/2} - (1/\mu_{CH})^{1/2}]$

$$= \tfrac{1}{2} \times \left\{\frac{(1.054 \times 10^{-34}\,\text{J s}) \times (450\,\text{N m}^{-1})^{1/2}}{(1.381 \times 10^{-23}\,\text{J K}^{-1}) \times (298.15\,\text{K})}\right\}$$

$$\times\left\{\left(\frac{10^{27}}{4.0\,\text{kg}}\right)^{1/2} - \left(\frac{10^{27}}{1.5\,\text{kg}}\right)^{1/2}\right\} = -2.7.$$

Therefore, $k_2(\text{T})/k_2(\text{H}) = e^{-2.7} = \underline{1/15}.$

(b) $\frac{1}{2}(\hbar_f^{1/2}/kT)\,[(1/\mu_{CO(18)})^{1/2} - (1/\mu_{CO(16)})^{1/2}]$

$$= \tfrac{1}{2} \times \left\{ \frac{(1.054 \times 10^{-34}\,\mathrm{J\,s}) \times (1750\,\mathrm{N\,m^{-1}})^{1/2}}{(1.381 \times 10^{-23}\,\mathrm{J\,K^{-1}}) \times (298\,\mathrm{K})} \right\}$$

$$\times \left\{ \left(\frac{10^{26}}{1.2\,\mathrm{kg}}\right)^{1/2} - \left(\frac{10^{26}}{1.1\,\mathrm{kg}}\right)^{1/2} \right\} = -0.12.$$

Therefore, $k_2(\mathrm{CO}(18))/k_2(\mathrm{CO}(16)) = \mathrm{e}^{-0.12} = 0.89 = \underline{1/1.1}$.

In order to discover whether raising the temperature enhances the effect, determine the sign of $(\mathrm{d}/\mathrm{d}T)\,\{k_2(x')/k_2(x)\}$.

$$(\mathrm{d}/\mathrm{d}T)\,\{k_2(x')/k_2(x)\} = -\tfrac{1}{2}(\hbar k_f^{1/2}/kT^2)\left[\left(\frac{1}{\mu_{x'}}\right)^{1/2} - \left(\frac{1}{\mu_x}\right)^{1/2}\right] \exp\{\ldots\}$$

$$= -\tfrac{1}{2}(\hbar k_f^{1/2}/kT^2)\left[\left(\frac{1}{\mu_{x'}}\right)^{1/2} - \left(\frac{1}{\mu_x}\right)^{1/2}\right] \{k_2(x')/k_2(x)\}.$$

This is >0 if $\mu_{x'} > \mu_x$. But if $\mu_{x'} > \mu_x$, $k_2(x')/k_2(x) < 1$; and so the rise in temperature increases this ratio towards unity, and so tends to eliminate the effect. The same is true if $\mu_{x'} < \mu_x$. In all cases the isotope effect is reduced by a rise in temperature.

30.17 The structure of the activated complex is shown in Fig. 30.2a. The moments of inertia are as follows:

$I_A = 2m_D \times (44\,\mathrm{pm})^2 = 1.3 \times 10^{-47}\,\mathrm{kg\,m^2}$

$I_B = m_H(68\,\mathrm{pm})^2 + 2m_D(17\,\mathrm{pm})^2 = 9.6 \times 10^{-48}\,\mathrm{kg\,m^2}$

$I_C = m_H(68\,\mathrm{pm})^2 + 2m_D(48\,\mathrm{pm})^2 = 2.3 \times 10^{-47}\,\mathrm{kg\,m^2}$.

The rotational constants are therefore

$A = \hbar/4\pi c I_A = (1.054 \times 10^{-34}\,\mathrm{J\,s})/4\pi(2.998 \times 10^{10}\,\mathrm{cm\,s^{-1}})I_A$

$\quad = (2.8 \times 10^{-46}\,\mathrm{cm^{-1}})/(I_A/\mathrm{kg\,m^2}) = 22\,\mathrm{cm^{-1}}$.

$B = (2.8 \times 10^{-46}\,\mathrm{cm^{-1}})/(9.6 \times 10^{-48}) = 29\,\mathrm{cm^{-1}}$,

$C = (2.8 \times 10^{-46}\,\mathrm{cm^{-1}})/(2.3 \times 10^{-47}) = 12\,\mathrm{cm^{-1}}$.

Since $I(D_2) = 2m_D(37\,\mathrm{pm})^2 = 9.1 \times 10^{-48}\,\mathrm{kg\,m^2}$ we also have $B(D_2) = (2.8 \times 10^{-46}\,\mathrm{cm^{-1}})/(9.1 \times 10^{-48}) = 31\,\mathrm{cm^{-1}}$. Then, from Box 22.1, $q^{\ddagger}_{rot} = 1.027 \times (1/2) \times (400)^{3/2}/(22 \times 29 \times 12)^{1/2} = 47$,

$q_{rot}(D_2) = 0.695 \times (1/2) \times 400/31 = 4.5$.

Vibrational partition functions are $q_{vib} = 1/\{1 - \exp(-\hbar\omega/kT)\}$ for each mode. Use $kT/hc \approx 280\,\mathrm{cm^{-1}}$ at 400 K, then $q_{vib} \approx 1/\{1 - \exp(-3.6)\} = 1.03$. The complex has $3N - 6 = 3\,[N = 3]$ modes, but one is the reaction mode, and so $q^{\ddagger}_{vib} \approx (1.03)^2 \approx 1.06$. For D_2 itself $q_{vib} \approx 1$. The translational partition functions are

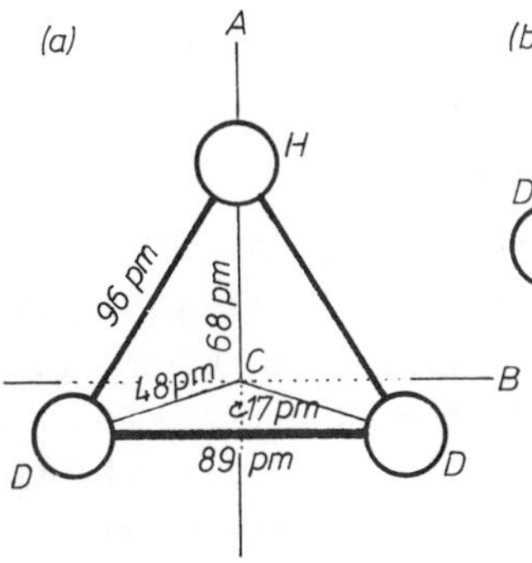

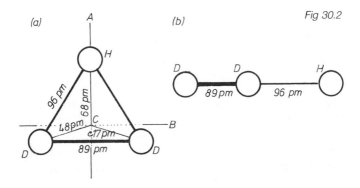

Fig 30.2

H: $q_m^{\ominus T}/N_A = 2.561 \times 10^{-2} \times 400^{5/2} \times 1.01^{3/2} = 8.3 \times 10^4$ [Box 22.1],

D_2: $q_m^{\ominus T}/N_A = 2.3 \times 10^5$,

Complex: $q_m^{\ominus T}/N_A = 4.3 \times 10^5$.

The electronic partition functions are

$q_e(H) = 2$ [doublet ground state], $q_e(D_2) = 1$,

$q_e^{\ddagger} = 2$ [odd number of electrons, presumably a doublet].

$A = \kappa(kT/h)(RT/p^{\ominus})N_A \bar{q}_m^{\ddagger\ominus}/q_{A,m}^{\ominus} q_{B,m}^{\ominus}$.

$kT/h = \{(1.381 \times 10^{-23}\,J\,K^{-1}) \times (400\,K)/(6.626 \times 10^{-34}\,J\,s)\} = 8.34 \times 10^{12}\,s^{-1}$,

$RT/p^{\ominus} = 3.28 \times 10^{-2}\,m^3\,mol^{-1}$.

$$A = \frac{(8.34 \times 10^{12}\,s^{-1}) \times (3.28 \times 10\,dm^3\,mol^{-1}) \times (4.3 \times 10^5) \times (47) \times (1.06) \times 2}{(8.3 \times 10^4) \times (2.3 \times 10^5) \times (4.5) \times (1.03) \times 2}$$

$= 6.6 \times 10^{10}\,M^{-1}\,s^{-1}$.

$k \approx A\exp(-E_a/RT) = (6.6 \times 10^{10}\,M\,s^{-1})\exp(-10.52)$

$= \underline{1.8 \times 10^6\,M^{-1}\,s^{-1}}$.

(The experimental value is $4 \times 10^5\,M^{-1}\,s^{-1}$.)

30.18 The structure of the activated complex is show in Fig. 30.2(b). The moment of inertia is as follows [Box 18.1]:

$I = (m_H m_D/m)(96\,pm + 89\,pm)^2 + (m_D/m)[m_H(96\,pm)^2 + m_D(89\,pm)^2]$

$= 3.9 \times 10^{-47}\,kg\,m^2$,

$B = (2.8 \times 10^{-46}\,cm^{-1})/(3.9 \times 10^{-47})$ [Problem 30.18] $= 7.1\,cm^{-1}$.

$q_{rot} = 0.6952 \times 400/7.1$ [Box 22.1, $\sigma = 1$] $= 39$.

Since $3N - 5 = 4$, there are 4 vibrational modes in the complex, and so, counting one as the reaction coordinate, $q^{\ddagger}_{vib} = (1.03)^3 = 1.09$. All other contributions are as in Problem 30.18, which gave $A_{(30.18)}$. Therefore:

$A \approx A_{(30.18)} \times (39/47) \times (1.09/1.06) = 0.85A$

Therefore, $k = 0.85 \times (1.8 \times 10^6\,M^{-1}\,s^{-1}) = \underline{1.5 \times 10^6\,M^{-1}\,s^{-1}}$.

30.19 Consider the following models (in order of complexity). (1) Collinear attack, varying R(HD) and R(DD) independently. (2) Broadside attack, varying $R(H\text{-}D_2)$ and R(DD) independently. (3) Attack at some angle θ to the D-D axis; once again varying bond-lengths independently. At this level of simplicity, you have to modify only the rotational partition functions in order to go between the various models.

30.20 $\Delta S^{\ominus}_m = R \ln\{hAp^{\ominus}/N_A(ekT)^2\}$ [30.3.23b]

$= R \ln\{7.8119 \times 10^{-11}) \times (A/M^{-1}\,s^{-1})/(T/K)^2\}$ [*Example* 30.4].

$A = \sigma N_A(8kT/\pi\mu)^{1/2}$ [30.1.5] $= \sigma(8N_A RT/\pi\mu)^{1/2} = \sigma(8N_A RT/\pi\mu m_u)^{1/2}$

where μ_r is the relative reduced mass $M_{A,r}M_{B,r}/(M_{A,r} + M_{B,r})$ and

$m_u = 1.660\,56 \times 10^{-27}$ kg [end-paper 1].

$$A = \sigma \times \left\{\frac{8 \times (6.022\,05 \times 10^{23}\,mol^{-1}) \times (8.314\,41\,J\,K^{-1}\,mol^{-1}) \times T}{\pi \times \mu_r \times (1.660\,56 \times 10^{-27}\,kg)}\right\}^{1/2}$$

$= \sigma \times (8.7626 \times 10^{25}\,mol^{-1}\,m\,s^{-1}) \times \{(T/K)/\mu_r\}^{1/2}$

$= (8.7626 \times 10^{10}\,M^{-1}\,s^{-1}) \times (\sigma/nm^2) \times \{(T/K)/\mu_r\}^{1/2}$.

Therefore, $\Delta S^{\ddagger}_m = R \ln\{(7.8119 \times 10^{-11}) \times (8.7626 \times 10^{10})$

$\times\ [(\sigma/nm^2)/(T/K)^{3/2}\mu_r^{1/2}]\}$

$= R \ln\{6.845(\sigma/nm^2)/(T/K)^{3/2}\mu_r^{1/2}\}$.

For $\sigma \approx 0.4\,nm^2$, $T \approx 300$ K, $M_{A,r} \approx M_{B,r} \approx 50$(so that $\mu_r \approx 25$),

$\Delta S^{\ddagger}_m \approx R \ln\{6.845 \times 0.40/300^{3/2} \times 25^{1/2}\}$

$\approx R \ln(1.054 \times 10^{-4}) = \underline{-76\,J\,K^{-1}\,mol^{-1}}$.

30.21 $\Delta S^{\ddagger}_m = R \ln\{(7.8119 \times 10^{-11}) \times (A/M^{-1}\,s^{-1})/(T/K)^2\}$ [*Example* 30.4].

(a) $A = 6.6 \times 10^{10}\,M^{-1}\,s^{-1}$ [Problem 30.17],

$\Delta S^{\ddagger}_m = R \ln\{(7.8119 \times 10^{-11}) \times (6.6 \times 10^{10})/(400)^2\} = \underline{-86\,J\,K^{-1}\,mol^{-1}}$.

(b) $A = 0.85 \times 6.6 \times 10^{10}\,M^{-1}\,s^{-1} = 5.6 \times 10^{10}\,M^{-1}\,s^{-1}$,

$\Delta S^{\ddagger}_m = R \ln(2.7 \times 10^{-5}) = \underline{-87\,J\,K^{-1}\,mol^{-1}}$.

30.22 $q^{\ddagger} = q^{\ddagger}_{vib,z}q^{\ddagger}_{vib,x}$ [y is the direction of diffusion]

$q = q_{vib,x}q_{vib,y}q_{vib,z}$ [for the atom at the bottom of the well]. For classical vibration,

$q_{\text{vib}} \approx kT/h\nu$ [Box 22.1, $h\nu \ll kT$]. The rate of diffusion is essentially the rate of change of concentration at a particular region of the surface, $-\text{d}[x]/\text{d}t$. This is also equal to $[x]^{\ddagger}\nu$, by the arguments in Section 30.3(b), and as $K^{\ddagger} = [x]^{\ddagger}/[x]$ we arrive at $-\text{d}[x]/\text{d}t = \nu[x]K^{\ddagger} = k_1[x]$. Therefore, $k_1 = \nu K^{\ddagger} = \nu(kT/h\nu)(q^{\ddagger}/q)\exp(-\beta\Delta E)$ where $q^{\ddagger}$ and q are the (vibrational) partition functions at the top and foot of the well respectively. Therefore,

$$k_1 = (kT/h)\{q^{\ddagger}_{\text{vib},z}q^{\ddagger}_{\text{vib},y}/q_{\text{vib},z}q_{\text{vib},y}q_{\text{vib},x}\} \times \exp(-\beta\Delta E)$$
$$\approx (kT/h)\{(kT/h\nu^{\ddagger})^2/(kT/h\nu)^3\}\exp(-\beta\Delta E) = \underline{(\nu^3/\nu^{\ddagger 2})\exp(-\beta\Delta E).}$$

(a) If $\nu^{\ddagger} = \nu$, $k_1 = \nu\exp(-\beta\Delta E)$;

$k_1 = (10^{11}\ \text{Hz})\exp\{-60\ \text{kJ mol}^{-1}/(8.314\ \text{J K}^{-1}\ \text{mol}^{-1}) \times (500\ \text{K})\} = 5.4 \times 10^4\ \text{s}^{-1}$.

But $D = d^2/2\tau$ [Box 27.1] $= \frac{1}{2}d^2k_1 = \frac{1}{2} \times (316\ \text{pm})^2 \times (5.4 \times 10^4\ \text{s}^{-1})$

$= 2.7 \times 10^{-15}\ \text{m}^2\ \text{s}^{-1} = \underline{2.7 \times 10^{-11}\ \text{cm}^2\ \text{s}^{-1}.}$

(b) If $\nu^{\ddagger} = \frac{1}{2}\nu$, $k_1 = 4\nu\exp(-\beta\Delta E) = 2.2 \times 10^5\ \text{s}^{-1}$.

Therefore, $D = 4 \times 2.7 \times 10^{-11}\ \text{cm}^2\ \text{s}^{-1} = \underline{1.1 \times 10^{-10}\ \text{cm}^2\ \text{s}^{-1}.}$

30.23 $k_1 = (kT/h)(q^{\ddagger}/q)\exp(-\beta\Delta E)$ [Problem 30.22]

$q^{\ddagger} = q^{\ddagger}_{\text{vib},z}q^{\ddagger}_{\text{vib},y}q_{\text{rot}} \approx (kT/h\nu^{\ddagger})^2 q_{\text{rot}}$.

$q_{\text{rot}} \approx (1.027/\sigma) \times (T/\text{K})^{3/2}/(B/\text{cm}^{-1})^{3/2}$ [Box 22.1, $A = B = C$] ≈ 80,

$q = q_{\text{vib},z}q_{\text{vib},y}q_{\text{vib},x} \approx (kT/h\nu)^3$.

Therefore, $k_1 \approx 80(\nu^3/\nu^{\ddagger 2})\exp(-\beta\Delta E) \approx 80 \times 5.4 \times 10^4\ \text{s}^{-1} = 4 \times 10^6\ \text{s}^{-1}$.

Consequently, $D \approx 80 \times (2.7 \times 10^{-11}\ \text{cm}^2\ \text{s}^{-1}) = \underline{2 \times 10^{-9}\ \text{cm}^2\ \text{s}^{-1}}$ if $\nu^{\ddagger} = \nu$, and $\underline{8 \times 10^{-9}\ \text{cm}^2\ \text{s}^{-1}}$ if $\nu^{\ddagger} = \frac{1}{2}\nu$.

30.24 $k_{\text{eff}} = \kappa(kT/h)\exp(-\Delta G^{\ddagger}_{\text{m}}/RT)$ [30.3.18], $k_{\text{eff}} \approx 1.0 \times 10^8\ \text{Hz}$, $T = 115\ \text{K}$;

$$\Delta G^{\ddagger}_{\text{m}} \approx -RT\ln(hk_{\text{eff}}/kT)$$
$$= -(8.314\ \text{J K}^{-1}\ \text{mol}^{-1}) \times (115\ \text{K}) \times \ln\left\{\frac{(6.626 \times 10^{-34}\ \text{J s}) \times (1.0 \times 10^8\ \text{s}^{-1})}{(1.381 \times 10^{-23}\ \text{J K}^{-1}) \times (115\ \text{K})}\right\}$$
$$= \underline{9.6\ \text{kJ mol}^{-1}.}$$

30.25 $\Delta S^{\ddagger}_{\text{m}} = R\ln\{(7.8119 \times 10^{-11}) \times (A/\text{M}^{-1}\ \text{s}^{-1})/(T/\text{K})^2\}$ [*Example* 30.4]

$= R\ln\{(7.8119 \times 10^{-11}) \times (4.6 \times 10^{12})/(298.15)^2\}$

$= \underline{-46\ \text{J K}^{-1}\ \text{mol}^{-1}.}$

$\Delta H^{\ddagger}_{\text{m}} = E_{\text{a}} - 2RT$ [30.3.21] $= 10\ \text{kJ mol}^{-1} - 2 \times (2.48\ \text{kJ mol}^{-1}) = \underline{5\ \text{kJ mol}^{-1}.}$

$\Delta G^{\ddagger}_{\text{m}} = \Delta H^{\ddagger}_{\text{m}} - T\Delta S^{\ddagger}_{\text{m}} = 5\ \text{kJ mol}^{-1} - (298.15\ \text{K}) \times (-46\ \text{J K}^{-1}\ \text{mol}^{-1})$

$= \underline{19\ \text{kJ mol}^{-1}.}$

30.26 Draw up the following Table as the basis of an Arrhenius plot:

$\theta/°C$	-24.82	-20.73	-17.02	-13.00	-8.95
T/K	248.33	252.42	256.13	260.15	264.20
$10^3/(T/K)$	4.027	3.962	3.904	3.844	3.785
$\ln(k/s^{-1})$	-9.01	-8.37	-7.73	-7.07	-6.55

These points are plotted in Fig. 30.3. They fall on the line $-\ln(k/s^{-1}) = 6.0 + \{[10^3/(T/K)] - 3.74\}10.91$ or $\ln(k/s^{-1}) = -6.0 - 10.91 \times 10^3\{1/T/K) - 3.74 \times 10^{-3}\}$ and so the intercept (at $1/T = 0$) is $+34.8$ and the slope -10.91×10^3. The former implies that $\ln(A/s^{-1}) = 34.8$, or $A = 1.3 \times 10^{15}\,s^{-1}$.

The slope implies

$E_a/R = 10.91 \times 10^3\,K$, or $E_a = 90.7\,kJ\,mol^{-1}$.

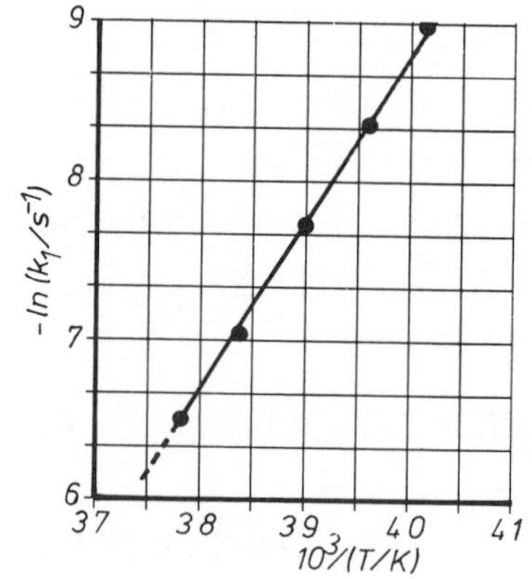

Fig 30.3

In solution $\Delta H_m^\ddagger = E_a - RT$ [footnote to 30.2.21]. Therefore, in the present case, $\Delta H_m^\ddagger = 90.7\,kJ\,mol^{-1} - 2.48\,kJ\,mol^{-1} = 88.2\,kJ\,mol^{-1}$.

For a first-order process, $\Delta S_m^\ddagger = R\ln(hA/ekT)$ [adapt eqns (30.3.20)-(30.3.23), with $k_{eff} = (kT/h)e^{-\Delta G^\ddagger/RT}$]. Therefore, for $T = 253\,K$ ($-20\,°C$),

$\Delta S_m^\ddagger = R\{\ln(1.3 \times 10^{15}\,s^{-1}/6.212 \times 10^{12}\,s^{-1}) - 1\} = 5.34\,R$

$= 44\,J\,K^{-1}\,mol^{-1}$.

$\Delta G_m^\ddagger = \Delta H_m^\ddagger - T\Delta S_m^\ddagger = 88.2\,kJ\,mol^{-1} - (253\,K) \times (44\,J\,K^{-1}\,mol^{-1})$

$= 77\,kJ\,mol^{-1}$.

30.27 The work required to bring two ions from infinity to a separation $R^{\ddagger}$ in a medium of relative permittivity ϵ_r is

$w = z'z'' e^2/4\pi\epsilon_0\epsilon_r R^{\ddagger}$ [Appendix 11.1].

This electrical work is a contribution to the Gibbs function, and so

$\Delta\bar{G}_m^{\ddagger} = \Delta G_m^{\ddagger} + z'z''N_A e^2/4\pi\epsilon_0\epsilon_r R^{\ddagger}$.

Since $k_{eff} \propto \exp(-\Delta G_m^{\ddagger}/RT)$ [30.3.18], the effect of ionic charge is to change k_{eff} to $\bar{k}_{eff}$, where

$\bar{k}_{eff} = k_{eff}\exp(-z'z''N_A e^2/4\pi\epsilon_0\epsilon_r R^{\ddagger}RT) = k_{eff}\exp(-z'z''e^2/4\pi\epsilon_0\epsilon_r R^{\ddagger}kT)$.

$\ln\bar{k}_{eff} = \ln k_{eff} - z'z''e^2/4\pi\epsilon_0\epsilon_r R^{\ddagger}kT$.

If z' and z'' have the same sign, $\bar{k}_{eff} < k_{eff}$; if opposite then $\bar{k}_{eff} > k_{eff}$ because the formation of the complex is favored. Note that the higher the value of ϵ_r, the smaller the effect of ionic charge.

30.28 $\ln\bar{k}_{eff} = \ln k_{eff} - z'z''B/\epsilon_r$ [Problem 30.27] with $B = e^2/4\pi\epsilon_0 R^{\ddagger}kT$. Therefore, plot $\ln\bar{k}_{eff}$ or $\lg\bar{k}_{eff}$, against $1/\epsilon_r$ and get straight lines of slope proportional to $z'z''$ if the model is correct. Draw up the following Tables:

(a) Bromophenol blue, $z'z'' = (-1)\times(-2) = 2$.

ϵ_r	60	65	70	75	79
$10^3/\epsilon_r$	16.7	15.4	14.3	13.3	12.7
$\lg\bar{k}_{eff}$	−0.987	0.201	0.751	1.172	1.401

(b) Azodicarbonate, $z'z'' = (-2)\times(+1) = -2$

ϵ_r	27	35	45	55	65	79
$10^3/\epsilon_r$	37.0	28.6	22.2	18.2	15.4	12.7
$\lg\bar{k}_{eff}$	12.95	12.22	11.58	11.14	10.73	10.34

These points are plotted in Fig. 30.4.

The lines are reasonably straight and have the signs appropriate to the model of the activated complex; that is, (a) negative and (b) positive.

30.29 $\lg k = \lg k^{\circ} + 2Az_A z_B I^{1/2}$ [30.3.28],

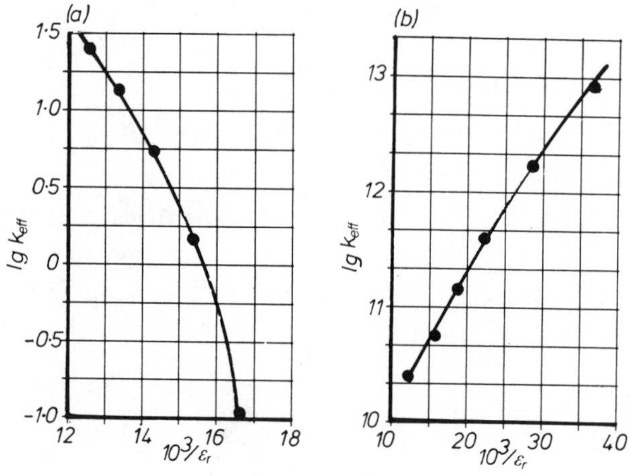

Fig 30.4

$A = 0.509$ [11.2.11]. Since $|z_A| = 1$, plot $\lg k$ against $\sqrt{I}$ and determine z_B from the slope. Draw up the following Table:

I	0.0025	0.0037	0.0045	0.0065	0.0085
$\sqrt{I}$	0.050	0.061	0.0067	0.081	0.092
$\lg(k/\mathrm{M}^{-1}\,\mathrm{s}^{-1})$	0.021	0.049	0.064	0.072	0.100

These points are plotted in Fig. 30.5. The slope of the limiting line is 2.4. Since this slope is equal to $2Az_Az_B = 1.018\,z_Az_B$, we have $z_Az_B = 2.4$. But $|z_A| = 1$, and so $|z_B| = 2$. Furthermore, z_A and z_B have the same sign because $z_Az_B > 0$. (The data refer to I^- and persulfate.)

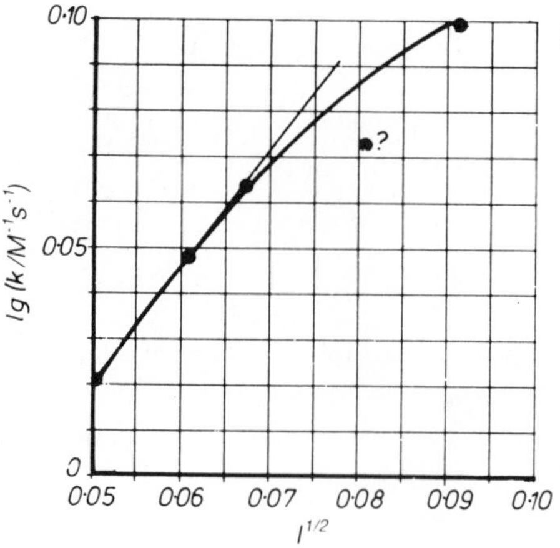

Fig 30.5

30.30 The change in intensity in the beam, dI, is proportional to the number of scatterers per unit volume, $\mathcal{N}_s$, the intensity of the beam, I, and the length of the infinitesimal slab, dl. The constant of proportionality is *defined* as the collision cross-section, σ. Therefore,

$dI = -\sigma \mathcal{N}_s I dl$, or $d \ln I = -\sigma \mathcal{N}_s dl$.

If the incident intensity (at $l = 0$) is I_0, the emergent intensity, I, is obtained by integrating this expression:

$\ln(I/I_0) = -\sigma \mathcal{N}_s l$, or $\underline{I = I_0 \exp(-\sigma \mathcal{N}_s l)}$.

30.31 $\ln(I/I_0) = -\sigma \mathcal{N}_s l$ [Problem 30.30]

$\sigma(CH_2F_2)/\sigma(Ar) = \ln 0.6/\ln 0.9 = \underline{5}$.

CH_2F_2 is a polar molecule, Ar is not; CsCl is polar and is more strongly scattered by the polar CH_2F_2.

30.32 $\sigma^*/\sigma \approx \{e^2/4\pi\epsilon_0 d[I(M) - E_A(X_2)]\}^2$ [30.1.8] with $d \approx R(M) + R(X_2)$.

Taking $\sigma \approx \pi d^2$ gives

$\sigma^* \approx \pi \times \{e^2/4\pi\epsilon_0 [I(M) - E_A(X_2)]\}^2 = (6.5\ \text{nm}^2)/[(I - E_A)/\text{eV}]^2$.

σ^* is predicted to increase as $I(M) - E_A(X_2)$ decreases.

The data let us construct the following Table.

σ^*/nm^2	Cl_2	Br_2	I_2
Na	0.45	0.42	0.56
K	0.72	0.68	0.97
Rb	0.77	0.72	1.05
Cs	0.97	0.90	1.34

All values of σ^* are less than the experimental values, but the values show the correct trend down columns. The dependence on E_A, across the Table, is not so good, reflecting the doubt about which values of E_A to use. Can you find better values of E_A?

31. Processes at solid surfaces

A31.1 Rate $= \pi r^2 p(2\pi mkT)^{-1/2}$ [31.1.1].

$p = (4.5 \times 10^{20}\,\mathrm{s^{-1}})(\pi)^{-1/2}(7.5 \times 10^{-4}\,\mathrm{m})^{-2}(2)^{1/2}(40 \times 10^{-3}\,\mathrm{kg\,mol^{-1}})^{1/2}$
$\quad \times (6.0 \times 10^{23}\,\mathrm{mol^{-1}})^{-1}(8.3\,\mathrm{J\,K^{-1}\,mol^{-1}})^{1/2}(4.5 \times 10^2\,\mathrm{K})^{1/2} = 13\,\mathrm{kPa}.$

A31.2 The average area associated with a Cu atom is $(1/2)(3.61 \times 10^{-10}\,\mathrm{m})^2$ or $6.5 \times 10^{-20}\,\mathrm{m^2}$;

$Z = p(2\pi mkT)^{-1/2}$ [31.1.1] $= (35\,\mathrm{Pa})(2\pi)^{1/2}(4.0 \times 10^{-3}\,\mathrm{kg\,mol^{-1}})^{-1/2}$
$\quad \times (8.3\,\mathrm{J\,K^{-1}\,mol^{-1}})^{-1/2}(6.0 \times 10^{23}\,\mathrm{mol^{-1}})(80\,\mathrm{K})^{-1/2}$
$\quad = 5.2 \times 10^{24}\,\mathrm{s^{-1}\,m^{-2}}.$

rate per Cu $= (5.2 \times 10^{24}\,\mathrm{s^{-1}\,m^{-2}})(6.5 \times 10^{-20}\,\mathrm{m^2}) = \underline{3.4 \times 10^5\,\mathrm{s^{-1}}}.$

A31.3 Chemisorption. The enthalpy of physisorption is about one-tenth of the observed value [Section 31.2(b)].

$\tau = (10^{-14}\,\mathrm{s})\exp(E_a/RT)$
$\quad = (10^{-14}\,\mathrm{s})\exp[(1.20 \times 10^5\,\mathrm{J\,mol^{-1}})(8.31\,\mathrm{J\,K^{-1}\,mol^{-1}})^{-1}(400\,\mathrm{K})^{-1}]$
$\quad = \underline{48\,\mathrm{s}}.$

A31.4 (a) $0.15 = 0.85\,\mathrm{kPa^{-1}}\,p[1 + (0.85\,\mathrm{kPa^{-1}})p]^{-1}$ [31.3.3];

$p = \underline{0.21\,\mathrm{kPa}}.$

(b) $0.95 = (0.85\,\mathrm{kPa^{-1}})\,p[1 + (0.85\,\mathrm{kPa^{-1}})p]^{-1}$;

$p = \underline{22\,\mathrm{kPa}}.$

A31.5 $w_1/w_2 = \theta_1/\theta_2 = p_1(1 + Kp_2)[(1 + Kp_1)(p_2)]^{-1}$ [31.3.3];

$0.44\,\mathrm{mg}/0.19\,\mathrm{mg} = (26.0\,\mathrm{kPa}/3.0\,\mathrm{kPa})[1 + (3.0\,\mathrm{kPa})K]\;[1 + (3.0\,\mathrm{kPa})K]^{-1}.$

$K = 0.186\,\mathrm{kPa^{-1}}; Kp_1 = 4.84; \theta_1 = 4.84/5.84 = \underline{82.9\,\%},$

$Kp_2 = 0.558; \theta_2 = 0.558/1.56 = \underline{35.8\,\%}.$

A31.6 $\ln(p) = A - \Delta H/RT$, [*Example* 31.3].

$\ln(p_2/p_1) = -(\Delta H/R)(T_2^{-1} - T_1^{-1}).$

$\ln(p_2/12\,\mathrm{kPa}) = (-1.02 \times 10^4\,\mathrm{J\,mol^{-1}}/8.31\,\mathrm{J\,mol^{-1}\,K^{-1}})[(313\,\mathrm{K})^{-1} - (298\,\mathrm{K})^{-1}]$
$\quad = 0.197.$

$p_2 = (12\,\mathrm{kPa})\exp(0.197) = \underline{14\,\mathrm{kPa}}.$

A31.7 On gold, $\theta \approx 1$; rate $= k_r\theta \approx$ constant, i.e. order $= \underline{0}$ [Section 31.4(a)].
On platinum. $\theta \approx Kp$; rate $= k_r\theta \approx k_r Kp$; i.e., order $= \underline{1}$.

31.1 $Z_w/\text{cm}^{-2}\,\text{s}^{-1} \approx 2.03 \times 10^{21}(p/\text{Torr})/\sqrt{M_r}$ [31.1.2].

(a) $M_r = 2$;

(i) $Z_w \approx \{(2.03 \times 10^{21}) \times (1/\sqrt{2})\}\,\text{cm}^{-2}\,\text{s}^{-1} = \underline{1.4 \times 10^{21}\,\text{cm}^{-2}\,\text{s}^{-1}}$.

(ii) $Z_w = \underline{1.4 \times 10^{14}\,\text{cm}^{-2}\,\text{s}^{-1}}$.

(b) $M_r = 44.1$;

(i) $Z_w \approx \{(2.03 \times 10^{21}) \times (1)/\sqrt{44.1}\}\,\text{cm}^{-2}\,\text{s}^{-1} = \underline{3.1 \times 10^{20}\,\text{cm}^{-2}\,\text{s}^{-1}}$.

(ii) $Z_w = \underline{3.1 \times 10^{13}\,\text{cm}^{-2}\,\text{s}^{-1}}$.

31.2 Refer to Fig. 31.1. The (100) and (110) faces expose 2 atoms, the (111) exposes 4. The areas of the faces of each cell are (a) $(352\,\text{pm})^2 = 1.24 \times 10^{-15}\,\text{cm}^2$, (b) $\sqrt{2} \times (352\,\text{pm})^2 = 1.75 \times 10^{-15}\,\text{cm}^2$, (c) $\sqrt{3} \times (352\,\text{pm})^2 = 2.15 \times 10^{-15}\,\text{cm}^2$. The number of atoms exposed per cm^2 is therefore

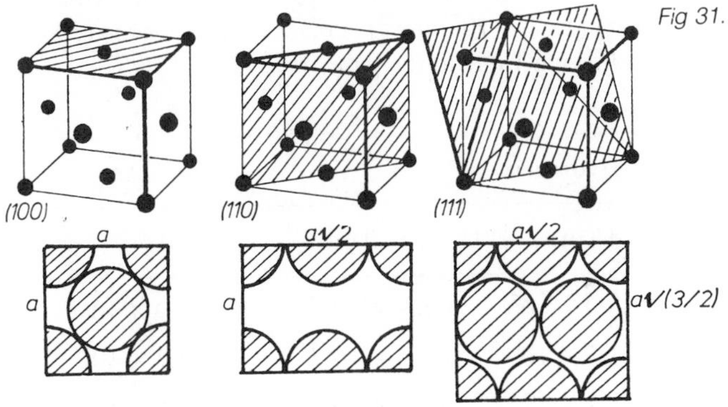

Fig 31.1

(a) $2/(1.24 \times 10^{-15}\,\text{cm}^2) = \underline{1.61 \times 10^{15}\,\text{cm}^{-2}}$,

(b) $2/(1.75 \times 10^{-15}\,\text{cm}^2) = \underline{1.14 \times 10^{15}\,\text{cm}^{-2}}$,

(c) $4/(2.15 \times 10^{-15}\,\text{cm}^2) = \underline{1.86 \times 10^{15}\,\text{cm}^{-2}}$.

31.3 Refer to Fig. 31.2. The (100) face exposes 1 atom per unit cell, the (110) and (111) faces expose 2 (approximately). The areas of the three types of faces are (a) $(316\,\text{pm})^2 = 9.99 \times 10^{-16}\,\text{cm}^2$, (b) $\sqrt{2}(316\,\text{pm})^2 = 1.41 \times 10^{-15}\,\text{cm}^2$, (c) $\sqrt{3}(316\,\text{pm})^2 = 1.73 \times 10^{-15}\,\text{cm}^2$. The numbers of atoms exposed are therefore

(a) $1/(9.99 \times 10^{-16}\,\text{cm}^2) = \underline{1.00 \times 10^{15}\,\text{cm}^{-2}}$,

(b) $2/(1.41 \times 10^{-15}\,\text{cm}^2) = \underline{1.41 \times 10^{15}\,\text{cm}^{-2}}$,

Fig 31.2

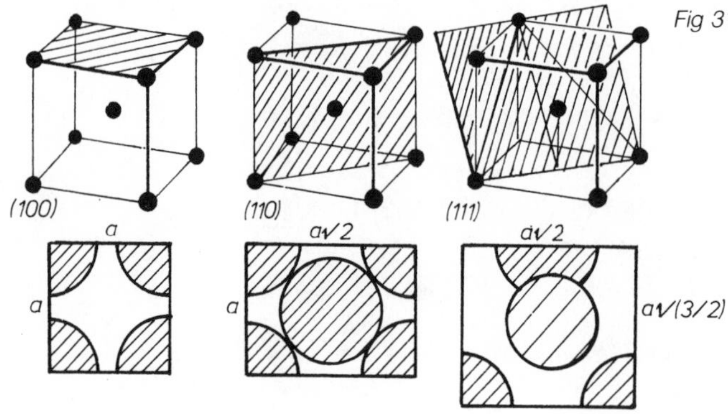

(c) $2/(1.73 \times 10^{-15}\,\text{cm}^2) = \underline{1.16 \times 10^{15}\,\text{cm}^{-2}}$.
The average number exposed is $\frac{1}{2}(1.00 + 1.4) \times 10^{15}\,\text{cm}^{-2} = \underline{1.20 \times 10^{15}\,\text{cm}^{-2}}$.

31.4 When the collision frequency is $1.44 \times 10^{21}\,\text{cm}^{-2}\,\text{s}^{-1}$ the frequency per atom is $(1.44 \times 10^{21}\,\text{cm}^{-2}\,\text{s}^{-1})/(1.61 \times 10^{15}\,\text{cm}^{-2}) = 8.9 \times 10^{5}\,\text{s}^{-1}$ for the (100) faces of nickel. Draw up the following Table in the same way:

	Hydrogen		Propane	
$Z/\text{atom}^{-1}\,\text{s}^{-1}$	1 Torr	10^{-7} Torr	1 Torr	10^{-7} Torr
Ni(100)	8.9×10^{5}	8.9×10^{-2}	1.9×10^{5}	1.9×10^{-2}
(110)	1.3×10^{6}	1.3×10^{-1}	2.7×10^{5}	2.7×10^{-2}
(111)	7.7×10^{5}	7.7×10^{-2}	1.6×10^{5}	1.6×10^{-2}
W(100)	1.4×10^{6}	1.4×10^{-1}	3.1×10^{5}	3.1×10^{-2}
(110)	1.0×10^{6}	1.0×10^{-1}	2.2×10^{5}	2.2×10^{-2}
(111)	1.2×10^{6}	1.2×10^{-1}	2.6×10^{5}	2.6×10^{-2}

31.5 $\tau \approx \tau_0 \exp(E_a/RT)$ [Section 31.2(e)] $= (10^{-13}\,\text{s})\exp(E_a/2.48\,\text{kJ mol}^{-1})$.
(a) $E_a = 15\,\text{kJ mol}^{-1}$, $\tau = (10^{-13}\,\text{s})e^{6.05} = \underline{4.2 \times 10^{-11}\,\text{s}}$,
(b) $E_a = 150\,\text{kJ mol}^{-1}$, $\tau = (10^{-13}\,\text{s})e^{60.5} = \underline{1.9 \times 10^{13}\,\text{s}\ (600\,000\ \text{yrs})}$.

31.6 At 1000 K, $RT = 8.31\,\text{kJ mol}^{-1}$; therefore, $\tau = (10^{-13}\,\text{s})\exp(E_a/8.31\,\text{kJ mol}^{-1})$.

(a) $E_a = 15\,\text{kJ mol}^{-1}$, $\tau = (10^{-13}\,\text{s})e^{1.81} = \underline{6.1 \times 10^{-13}\,\text{s}}$,

(b) $E_a = 150\,\text{kJ mol}^{-1}$, $\tau = (10^{-13}\,\text{s})e^{18.1} = \underline{7.3 \times 10^{-6}\,\text{s}}$,

31.7 Deuteration has two effects: it changes the vibrational frequency in the well, and hence changes τ_0. It also changes the zero-point energy, and hence it changes E_a.

$1/\tau_0 = \nu = (1/2\pi)\sqrt{(k/m)}$; that is, $\tau_0 \propto \sqrt{m}$. Therefore, $\tau_{0D} \approx \underline{\tau_{0H}\sqrt{2}}$.

The zero-point energies are $\frac{1}{2}h\nu_H$ and $\frac{1}{2}h\nu_D$; therefore

$$E_{aD} = E_{aH} + \tfrac{1}{2}h\nu_H - \tfrac{1}{2}h\nu_D = E_{aH} + \tfrac{1}{2}h\nu_H\left(1 - \frac{1}{\sqrt{2}}\right) = E_{aH} + 0.15\,h\nu_H.$$

Since $\nu_H = 10^{13}\,\text{s}^{-1}$, $h\nu_H N_A = 4.0\,\text{kJ mol}^{-1}$; consequently $E_{aD} = E_{aH} + 0.6\,\text{kJ mol}^{-1}$.

Therefore,

$\tau_D = \sqrt{2}\tau_{0H}\exp(E_{aH}/RT)\exp(0.6\,\text{kJ mol}^{-1}/RT) = 1.41\,\tau_H\exp(0.6\,\text{kJ mol}^{-1}/RT)$.

At 298 K, $\underline{\tau_D/\tau_H = 1.80}$, and at 1000 K, $\underline{\tau_D/\tau_H = 1.52}$.

31.8 $\tau(T) = \tau_0\exp(E_a/RT)$ [Section 31.2(e)]

$$E_a = \left(\frac{1}{T} - \frac{1}{T'}\right)^{-1} R\ln\{\tau(T)/\tau(T')\}$$

$$= \left(\frac{1}{2548\,\text{K}} - \frac{1}{2362\,\text{K}}\right)^{-1} \times (8.314\,\text{J K}^{-1}\text{mol}^{-1}) \times \ln(0.36/3.49) = \underline{610\,\text{kJ mol}^{-1}}.$$

$\tau_0 = (3.49\,\text{s})\exp\{-610\,\text{kJ mol}^{-1})/(8.314\,\text{J K}^{-1}\text{mol}^{-1}) \times (2362\,\text{K})\} = \underline{1.1 \times 10^{-13}\,\text{s}}.$

31.9 $$E_a = \left(\frac{1}{T} - \frac{1}{T'}\right)^{-1} R\ln\{\tau(T)/\tau(T')\}\ \text{[Problem 31.8]}.$$

$\tau(1000\,\text{K})/\tau(600\,\text{K}) \approx 1/1.35 = 0.74$.

$$E_a = \left(\frac{1}{1000\,\text{K}} - \frac{1}{600\,\text{K}}\right)^{-1} R\ln 0.74 = \underline{3.7\,\text{kJ mol}^{-1}}.$$

31.10 Refer to Fig. 31.3. Evaluate the sum of $\pm 1/r_i$, where r_i is the distance from the ion of interest to the ion i, taking the + sign for ions of like charge and the − sign for ions of opposite charge. The array has been divided up into five zones. Zones B and D can be summed analytically [Problem 24.29], the result being $-\ln 2 = -0.69$.

The summation on the other zones, each of which gives the same result, is tedious because of the very slow convergence of the sum. Unless you make a very clever choice of the sequence of ions (grouping them so that their contributions almost cancel) you will find the value 0.259 for a 10 × 10 array, 0.273 for a 20 × 20 array, 0.283 for a 50 × 50 array, and 0.286 for a 100 × 100 array (10^4 ions, 10^4 calculations). By the time you get to 200 × 200 you find 0.289, in good agreement with the analytical value, 0.289 2597 . . .

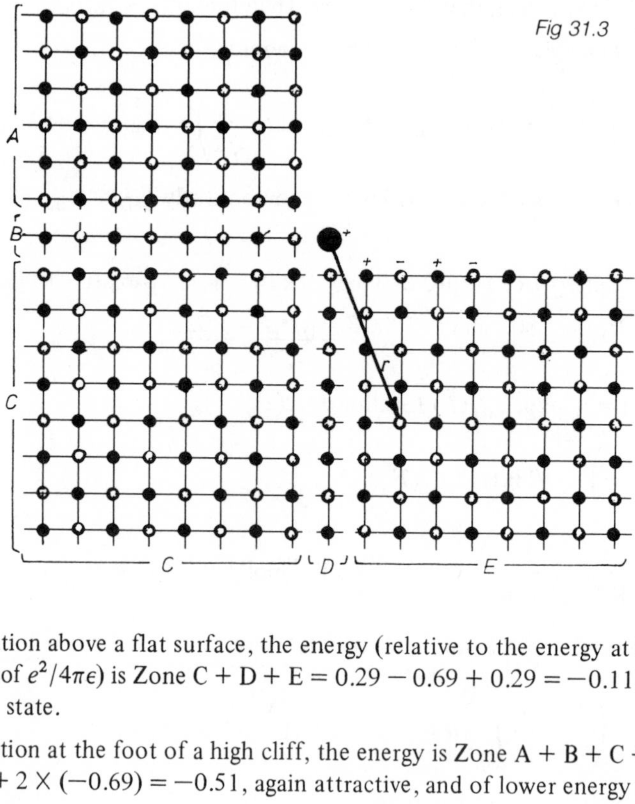

Fig 31.3

(a) For a cation above a flat surface, the energy (relative to the energy at infinity, and in units of $e^2/4\pi\epsilon$) is Zone C + D + E = 0.29 − 0.69 + 0.29 = −0.11, implying an attractive state.

(b) For a cation at the foot of a high cliff, the energy is Zone A + B + C + D + E = 3 × 0.29 + 2 × (−0.69) = −0.51, again attractive, and of lower energy than case (a).

31.11 $\theta = Kp/(1 + Kp)$ [31.3.3], $1/\theta = 1 + 1/Kp$.

Write $\theta = V_a/V_a^o$, then $V_a^o/V = 1 + 1/Kp$. Therefore, $p/V_a = p/V_a^o + 1/KV_a^o$, and a plot of p/V_a against p should give a straight line with slope $1/V_a^o$ and intercept $1/KV_a^o$. Rearrange the isotherm into $\theta = Kp(1 - \theta)$, then $\ln(\theta/p) = \ln K + \ln(1 - \theta)$ $\approx \ln K - \theta$ if $\theta \ll 1$. Therefore, a plot of $\ln(\theta/p)$ against θ should be a straight line of slope -1 for $\theta \ll 1$.

Since $\theta = V_a/V_a^o$, the last expression may also be written $\ln(V_a/p) \approx \ln(KV_a^o) - (V_a/V_a^o)$ and so a plot of $\ln(V_a/p)$ against V_a should give a straight line of slope $-1/V_a^o$.

31.12 Draw up the following Table.

p/Torr	0.19	0.97	1.90	4.05	7.50	11.95
(p/V_a)/(Torr/cm^3)	4.52	5.95	8.60	12.6	18.3	25.4

p/V_a is plotted against p in Fig. 31.4. The low pressure points fall on a straight line with intercept 4.0 and slope 2.1. It follows that $1/V_a^o = 2.1\ \text{Torr cm}^{-3}/\text{Torr} = 2.1\ \text{cm}^{-3}$, or $V_a^o = 0.48\ \text{cm}^3$ and $1/KV_a^o = 4.0\ \text{Torr cm}^{-3}$. Therefore, $K = 1/(4.0\ \text{Torr cm}^{-3}) \times (0.48\ \text{cm}^3) = \underline{0.52\ \text{Torr}^{-1}}$.

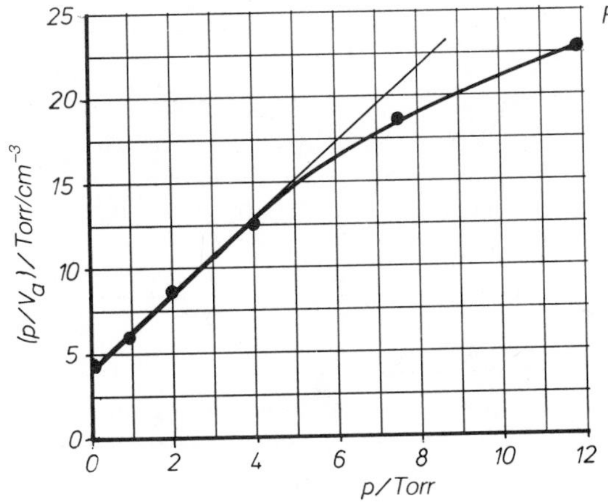

Fig 31.4

31.13 (a) For adsorption without dissociation $\theta = Kp/(1 + Kp)$ [31.3.3] and $p/V_a = p/V_a^o + 1/KV_a^o$ [Problem 31.11].

(b) For adsorption with dissociation into $O + O_2$, $\theta \approx (Kp)^{1/2}/[1 + (Kp)^{1/2}]$ [31.3.4; but this is only an approximation because it is based on the assumption that any bimolecular collision on the surface leads to O_3, but $O + O$ could not; can you improve the calculation? The simple justification for this approach is to suppose that $\frac{1}{3}$ of all possible collisions are between O and O_2; then $\frac{1}{3}$ is incorporated into k_d.]. Then

$1/\theta = 1 + 1/(Kp)^{1/2}$ and so $p^{1/2}/V_a = p^{1/2}/V_a^o + 1/K^{1/2}V_a^o$, and a plot of $p^{1/2}/V_a$ against $p^{1/2}$ should give a straight line.

(c) For adsorption with dissociation into O + O + O. $\theta = (Kp)^{1/3}/[1 + (Kp)^{1/3}]$ [by the same argument as in Section 31.3(a)] and so $p^{1/3}/V_a = p^{1/3}/V_a^o + 1/K^{1/3}V_a^o$ and a plot of $p^{1/3}/V_a$ against $p^{1/3}$ should give a straight line.

31.14 $z/(1-z)V = 1/cV_{mon} + (c-1)z/cV_{mon}$, $z = p/p^*$ [31.3.14]. Draw up the following Tables:

(a) 0 °C							
p/Torr	105	282	492	594	620	755	798
z	0.0326	0.0875	0.1527	0.1844	0.1924	0.2343	0.2477
$10^3\{z/(1-z)(V/cm^3)\}$	3.035	7.103	12.10	14.13	15.37	17.69	19.95

(b) 18.6 °C				
p/Torr	39.5	62.7	108	219
z	0.0064	0.0102	0.0176	0.0356
$10^3\{z/(1-z)(V/cm^3)\}$	0.700	1.051	1.739	3.267

p/Torr	466	555	601	765
z	0.0758	0.0903	0.0978	0.1244
$10^3\{z/(1-z)(V/cm^3)\}$	6.358	7.577	8.09	10.08

The points are plotted in Fig. 31.5(a). Analyse the data by a least squares procedure. The intercepts are at (a) 0.466, (b) 0.303, and so

(a) $1/cV_{mon} = 0.466 \times 10^{-3}\, cm^{-3}$, (b) $1/cV_{mon} = 0.303 \times 10^{-3}\, cm^{-3}$.

The slopes of the lines are (a) 76.10, (b) 79.54, and so

(a) $(c-1)/cV_{mon} = 76.10 \times 10^{-3}\, cm^{-3}$, (b) $(c-1)/cV_{mon} = 79.54 \times 10^{-3}\, cm^{-3}$.

Solving the equation gives $c - 1 =$ (a) 163.3, (b) 262.5, and so $c =$ (a) 164.3.

(b) 263.5, and V_{mon} = (a) 13.1 cm^3, (b) 12.5 cm^3.

31.15 $V_a = c_1 p^{1/c_2}$ [given]; therefore $\ln V_a = \ln c_1 + (1/c_2)\ln p$. The Langmuir isotherm leads to $p/V_a = p/V_a^\circ + 1/KV_a^\circ$ [Problem 31.11]. Therefore plot (a) $\ln V_a$ against $\ln p$ and (b) p/V_a against p, and assess which gives the straighter line. Draw up the following Table:

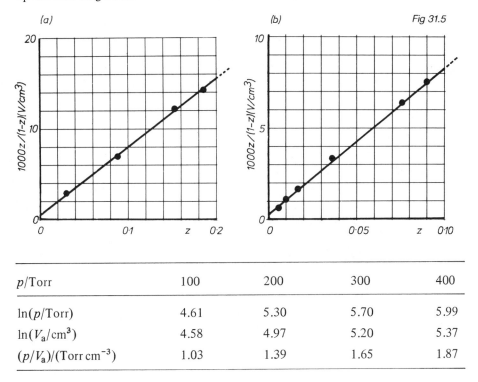

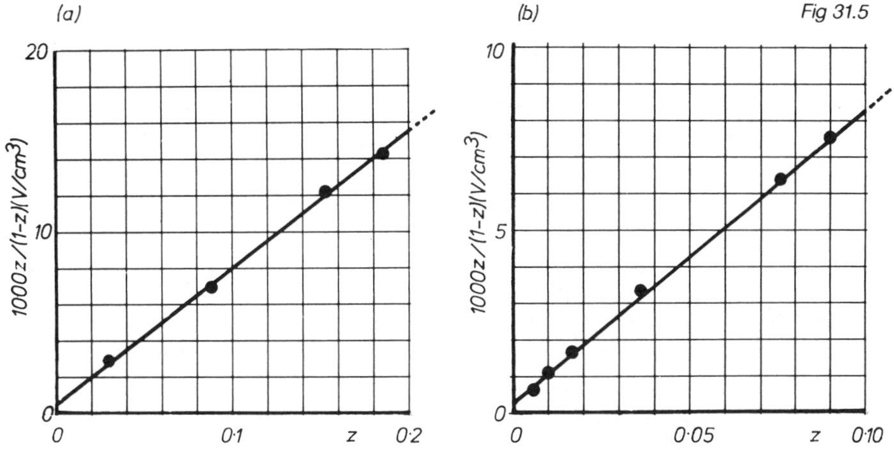

p/Torr	100	200	300	400
$\ln(p/\text{Torr})$	4.61	5.30	5.70	5.99
$\ln(V_a/\text{cm}^3)$	4.58	4.97	5.20	5.37
$(p/V_a)/(\text{Torr cm}^{-3})$	1.03	1.39	1.65	1.87

These points are plotted in Fig. 31.6 (a) and (b). The Freundlich isotherm gives a significantly better straight line. The coefficients of determination (Appendix) are 0.9870 for the Langmuir plot and 0.9999 for the Freundlich.

31.16 Repeat the analysis of the preceding Problem. Draw up the following Table:

p/Torr	100	200	300	400	500	600
$\ln(p/\text{Torr})$	4.61	5.30	5.70	5.99	6.21	6.40
$\ln(V_a/\text{cm}^3)$	−2.04	−1.90	−1.80	−1.82	−1.74	−1.71
$(p/V_a)/(\text{Torr cm}^{-3})$	769	1330	1850	2410	2860	3330

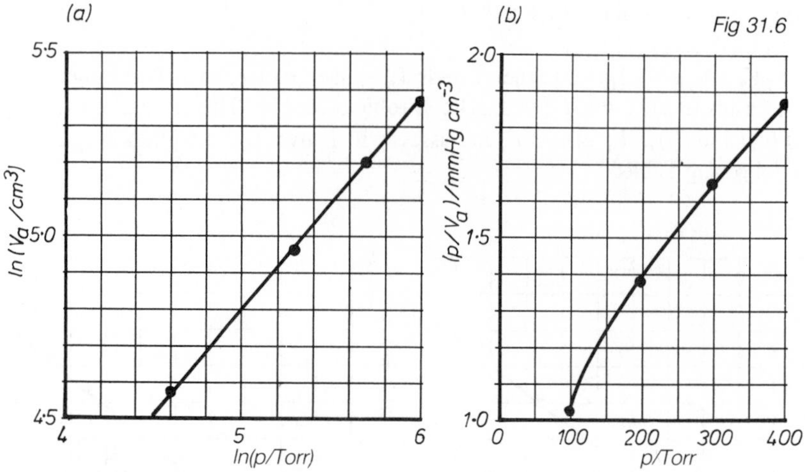

These points are plotted in Fig. 31.7. The Langmuir plot (b) gives a better straight line (correlation coefficient 0.9983, the Freundlich plot, (a), gives 0.9517). From the Langmuir plot we find an intercept at 297 and a slope of 5.1. It follows [Problem 31.11] that $1/V_a^o = 5.1\ \text{cm}^{-3}$, so that $V_a^o = 0.196\ \text{cm}^3$.

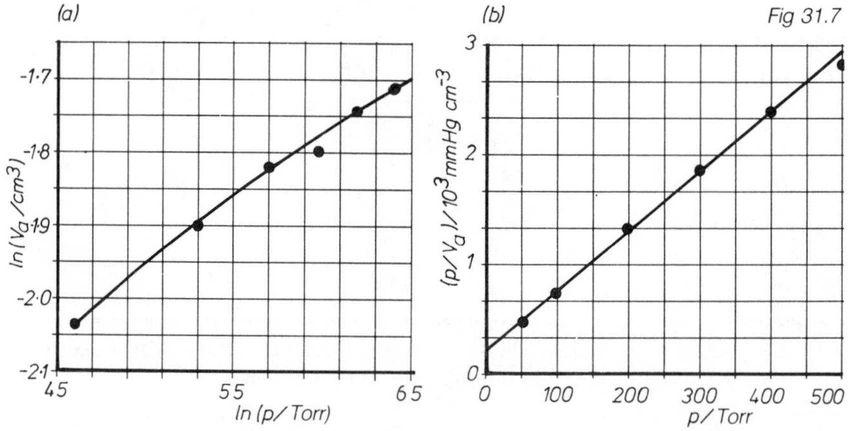

Furthermore, $1/KV_a^o = 297\ \text{Torr cm}^{-3}$; therefore $K = 1/(297\ \text{Torr cm}^{-3}) \times (0.196\ \text{cm}^3) = \underline{0.0172\ \text{Torr}^{-1}}$. Since $V_a^o = 0.196\ \text{cm}^3$ (at standard temperature and pressure), the number of molecules adsorbed is

$$N = pV_a^o/kT = \frac{(1.013 \times 10^5\ \text{N m}^{-2}) \times (1.96 \times 10^{-7}\ \text{m}^3)}{(1.381 \times 10^{-23}\ \text{J K}^{-1}) \times (298\ \text{K})} = 4.8 \times 10^{18}.$$

Since the total area of the sample is $6.2 \times 10^3\,cm^2 = 6.2 \times 10^{17}\,nm^2$, the area occupied by each molecule is $(6.2 \times 10^{17}\,nm^2)/(4.8 \times 10^{18}) = \underline{0.13\,nm^2}$.

31.17 $V_a = \theta V_a^o = KpV_a^o/(1 + Kp)$ [data in Problem 31.16]

$$= \frac{(0.0172\,Torr^{-1}) \times (760\,Torr) \times (0.196\,cm^3)}{1 + (0.0172\,Torr^{-1}) \times (760\,Torr)} = \underline{0.19\,cm^3}.$$

31.18 Draw up the following Table

p/Torr	100	200	300	400	500	600
$(p/V_a)/(\mathrm{Torr\,cm^{-3}})$	5.59	6.06	6.38	6.58	6.64	6.57

These points are plotted in Fig. 31.8. They result in a significantly curved graph, and (except possibly at pressures lower than 300 Torr) the Langmuir isotherm does not describe the adsorption behavior.

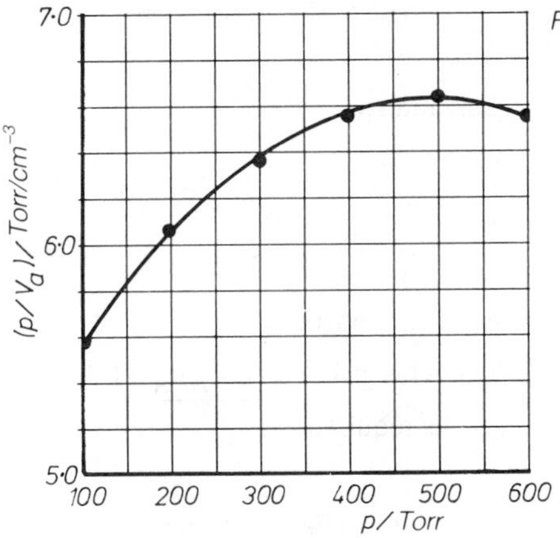

Fig 31.8

31.19 Follow the procedure in Problem 31.14. Draw up the following Table.

p/Torr	100	200	300	400	500	600
z	0.067	0.133	0.200	0.267	0.333	0.400
$10^3\{z/(1-z)(V/\mathrm{cm^3})\}$	4.01	4.66	5.32	5.98	6.64	7.30

The points are plotted in Fig. 31.9, and fall on a good straight line.

The intercept is at 3.33×10^{-3}, and so $1/cV_{mon} = 3.33 \times 10^{-3}\,cm^{-3}$. The slope is 9.93, and so $(c-1)/cV_{mon} = 9.93 \times 10^{-3}\,cm^{-3}$. Therefore $c - 1 = 2.98$, so that $c = 3.98$ and $V_{mon} = 75.4\,cm^3$.

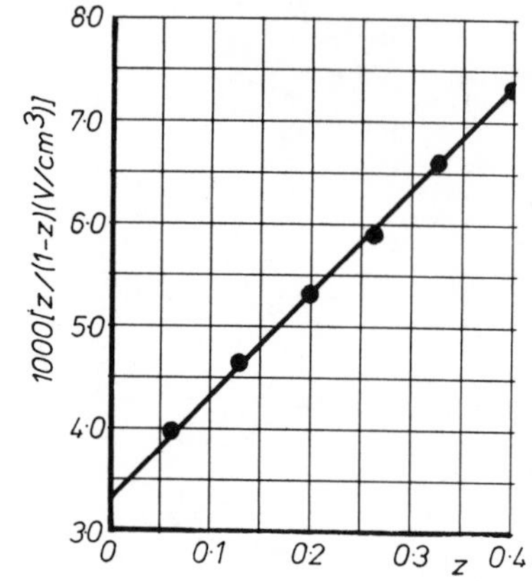

Fig 31.9

31.20 Rate of adsorption of A $= k_{aA}p_A N(1 - \theta_A - \theta_B)$.

Rate of desorption of A $= k_{dA}N\theta_A$.

At equilibrium, the rates are equal, and so

$k_{aA}p_A N(1 - \theta_A - \theta_B) = k_{dA}N\theta_A$.

Similarly for B:

$k_{aB}p_B N(1 - \theta_A - \theta_B) = k_{dB}N\theta_B$.

Solve this pair of simultaneous equations writing

$K_A = k_{aA}/k_{dA}$ and $K_B = k_{aB}/k_{dB}$. This gives $\theta_A = K_A p_A/(1 + K_A p_A + K_B p_B)$, $\theta_B = K_B p_B/(1 + K_A p_A + K_B p_B)$ as required.

31.21 $-dp_A/dt = kK_A K_B p_A p_B/(1 + K_A p_A + K_B p_B)^2$.

$p_A = p - x$, $p_B = p - x$ [$p_A(0) = p_B(0) = p$, A + B → products].

$A \mathrel{\hat=} kK_A K_B$, $B \mathrel{\hat=} 1 + (K_A + K_B)p = 1 + Kp$, $K = K_A + K_B$.

$dx/dt = A(p - x)^2/(B - Kx)^2$,

$$\int_0^t A\,dt = \int_0^x \frac{B^2 dx}{(p-x)^2} - \int_0^x \frac{2BKx dx}{(p-x)^2} + \int_0^x \frac{K^2x^2 dx}{(p-x)^2}.$$

$$\int_0^x \frac{dx}{(p-x)^2} = \frac{1}{p-x}, \quad \int_0^x \frac{x\,dx}{(p-x)^2} = \frac{x}{p-x} - \ln\left(\frac{p}{p-x}\right),$$

$$\int_0^x \frac{x^2 dx}{(p-x)^2} = \frac{x^2-2p^2}{x-p} + 2p\ln(x-p).$$

$$At = B^2\left\{\left(\frac{1}{p-x}\right) - \frac{1}{p}\right\} - 2BK\left\{\left(\frac{x}{p-x}\right) - \ln\left(\frac{p}{p-x}\right)\right\} + K^2\left\{\left(\frac{x^2-2p^2}{x-p}\right) - 2p + 2p\ln\left(\frac{p-x}{p}\right)\right\}$$

$$= \left(\frac{1}{p}\right)\left(\frac{x}{p-x}\right) + K^2x + 2K\ln\{p/(p-x)\}.$$

For $p = 1, K_A \approx K_B \approx 1, K \approx 2, A \approx k$, then

$kt = x/(1-x) + 4x - 4\ln(1-x)$.

This function is plotted in Fig. 31.10

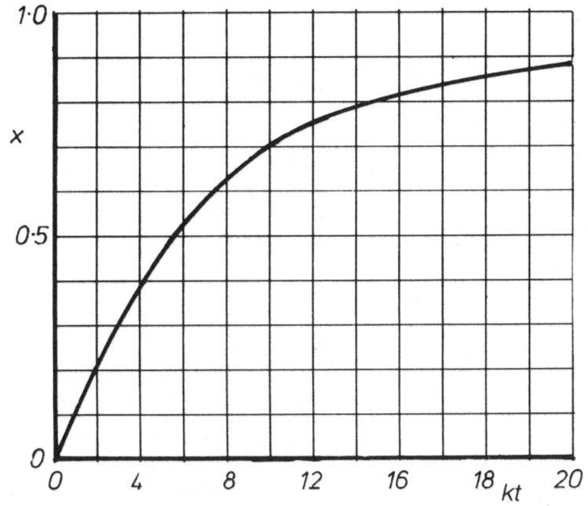

Fig 31.10

31.22 $\theta(\mathrm{F}) = (Kp_{\mathrm{F}})^{1/2}/[1+(Kp_{\mathrm{F}})^{1/2}]$ [31.3.4].

$\theta(\text{butadiene}) = c_1 p_{\mathrm{B}}^{1/2}$ $[\theta = V_a/V_a^{\circ} \propto p^{1/c_2}$, Problem 31.15$]$.

Reaction rate $= k'\theta(\mathrm{F})\theta(\mathrm{B}) = k'c_1K^{1/2}p_{\mathrm{F}}^{1/2}p_{\mathrm{B}}^{1/2}[1+(Kp_{\mathrm{F}})^{1/2}]$. Write $k = k'c_1K^{1/2}$,

then reaction rate $= kp_{\mathrm{F}}^{1/2}p_{\mathrm{B}}^{1/2}/[1+(Kp_{\mathrm{F}})^{1/2}]$.

When $(kp_{\mathrm{F}})^{1/2} \gg 1$, rate $\approx (k/K^{1/2})p_{\mathrm{B}}^{1/2}$, independent of p_{F}.

31.23 $\theta(T_1) = K(T_1)p(T_1)/[1 + K(T_1)p(T_1)]$ [31.3.3],
$\theta(T_2) = k(T_2)p(T_2)/[1 + K(T_2)p(T_2)]$.
$\theta(T_1) = \theta(T_2)$ implies
$K(T_1)p(T_1)/[1 + K(T_1)p(T_1)] = K(T_2)p(T_2)/[1 + k(T_2)p(T_2)]$
or $K(T_1)p(T_1) = K(T_2)p(T_2)$.
$\Delta_{ad}H^\ominus = RT^2(\partial \ln K/\partial T)_\theta$ [31.3.5].

$$\mathrm{d}\ln K/\mathrm{d}T \approx \frac{\ln K(T_2) - \ln K(T_1)}{T_2 - T_1} = \frac{\ln[K(T_2)/K(T_1)]}{T_2 - T_1} = \frac{\ln[p(T_1)/p(T_2)]}{T_2 - T_1}.$$

Therefore, $\Delta_{ad}H^\ominus \approx \{RT^2/(T_2 - T_1)\}\ln\{p(T_1)/p(T_2)\}$.
$T \approx \frac{1}{2}(T_1 + T_2) = 220\,\mathrm{K}, T_2 - T_1 = 60\,\mathrm{K}$.

$$\Delta H_m^\ominus \approx \left\{\frac{(8.314\,\mathrm{J\,K^{-1}\,mol^{-1}}) \times (220\,\mathrm{K})^2}{60\,\mathrm{K}}\right\} \ln\{4.8/32\} = \underline{-13\,\mathrm{kJ\,mol^{-1}}}.$$

31.24 The desorption time for a given volume is proportional to τ, the lifetime of the adsorbed species [Section 31.2(e)]. Therefore, as $\tau \propto \exp(E_a/RT)$ [31.2.2]

$$E_a = \left(\frac{1}{T} - \frac{1}{T'}\right)^{-1} R\ln\{\tau(T)/\tau(T')\}.$$

Evaluate E_a for two temperature ranges:

$$E_a = \left(\frac{1}{1856\,\mathrm{K}} - \frac{1}{1978\,\mathrm{K}}\right)^{-1} R\ln(27/2) = 650\,\mathrm{kJ\,mol^{-1}},$$

$$E_a = \left(\frac{1}{1978\,\mathrm{K}} - \frac{1}{2070\,\mathrm{K}}\right)^{-1} R\ln(2/0.3) = 700\,\mathrm{kJ\,mol^{-1}}.$$

To one significant figure, these conform to $\underline{E_a = 700\,\mathrm{kJ\,mol^{-1}}}$. At 1856 K,
$\tau = \tau_0 \exp\{(700\,\mathrm{kJ\,mol^{-1}})/(8.314\,\mathrm{J\,K^{-1}\,mol^{-1}}) \times (1856\,\mathrm{K})\} = \tau_0 \times (5.03 \times 10^{19})$.
Since t, the time for desorption of the stated volume, is proportional to τ, we have $t(1856\,\mathrm{K}) = K\tau = K\tau_0 \times 5.03 \times 10^{19}$.

Therefore, $K\tau_0 = 27\,\mathrm{min}/5.03 \times 10^{19} = 5.4 \times 10^{-19}\,\mathrm{min}$.

Consequently, at 298 K,

$t(298\,\mathrm{K}) = (5.4 \times 10^{-19}\,\mathrm{min})\exp(700\,\mathrm{kJ\,mol^{-1}}/2.48\,\mathrm{kJ\,mol^{-1}}) = \underline{2 \times 10^{104}\,\mathrm{min}}$, which is just about forever.

At 3000 K,

$t(3000\,\text{K}) = (5.4 \times 10^{-19}\,\text{min})\exp(700\,\text{kJ mol}^{-1}/24.9\,\text{kJ mol}^{-1})$

$= \underline{8 \times 10^{-7}\,\text{min}, 50\,\mu\text{s}}.$

31.25 The rate of reaction appears to be independent of the pressure of ammonia, and so the reaction is zeroth-order. Check this by writing

$-\mathrm{d}p(\text{NH}_3)/\mathrm{d}t = k$ [zeroth-order rate law], $p_0(\text{NH}_3) - p(\text{NH}_3) = kt.$

Therefore, $\Delta p/t$ should be constant.

(i) $\Delta p/t = (8\,\text{kPa})/(500\,\text{s}) = 16\,\text{Pa s}^{-1}$,

(ii) $\Delta p/t = (15\,\text{kPa})/(1000\,\text{s}) = 15\,\text{Pa s}^{-1}$.

These two values are essentially the same, and so we conclude that the reaction is zeroth-order, and $k = \underline{16\,\text{Pa s}^{-1}}$. Zeroth-order kinetics occur when the gas pressure is so high that the same amount of adsorbed species is always present whatever the pressure (i.e. essentially constant surface coverage even though p varies).

31.26 $\theta = Kp/(1 + Kp)$ [31.3.3]. This rearranges to $Kp(1 - \theta) = \theta$. For a strongly adsorbed species, $\theta \approx 1$. Therefore, the fraction of uncovered sites, $1 - \theta$, is approximately $\underline{1 - \theta \approx 1/Kp}$.

$-\mathrm{d}p(\text{NH}_3)/\mathrm{d}t = k_c p(\text{NH}_3)(1 - \theta)$. [The reaction rate is proportional to the pressure of ammonia and the fraction of sites left uncovered by the strongly adsorbed hydrogen in the product.] $(1 - \theta) \approx 1/Kp(\text{H}_2)$ [above, H_2 adsorbs strongly].

$\underline{-\mathrm{d}p(\text{NH}_3)/\mathrm{d}t = (k_c/K)p(\text{NH}_3)/p(\text{H}_2)}.$

31.27 $p(\text{H}_2) = \tfrac{3}{2}\{p_0(\text{NH}_3) - p(\text{NH}_3)\}$, $[\text{NH}_3 \rightarrow \tfrac{1}{2}\text{N}_2 + \tfrac{3}{2}\text{H}_2]$.

Write $p(\text{NH}_3) = p$, $p_0(\text{NH}_3) = p_0$. Then

$-\mathrm{d}p/\mathrm{d}t = k_c p/(p_0 - p)$ [Problem 31.26], where $k_c = \tfrac{2}{3}k_c'/K$.

This integrates as follows

$$\int_{p_0}^{p} (1 - p_0/p)\mathrm{d}p = k_c \int_0^t \mathrm{d}t, \text{ or } (p - p_0)/t = k_c + (p_0/t)\ln(p/p_0).$$

On writing $F(t) = (p_0/t)\ln(p/p_0)$, $G(t) = (p - p_0)/t$, we have $G(t) = k_c + F(t)$, and a plot of $G(t)$ against $F(t)$ should give a straight line with intercept k_c. Alternatively, the difference $G(t) - F(t)$ should be a constant, k_c. Draw up the following Table:

t/s	0	30	60	100
p/Torr	100	88	84	80
$G(t)$/Torr s^{-1}	–	−0.40	−0.27	−0.20
$F(t)$/Torr s^{-1}	–	−0.43	−0.29	−0.22
$[G(t)-F(t)]$/Torr s^{-1}	–	0.03	0.02	0.02

t/s	160	200	250
p/Torr	77	74	72
$G(t)$/Torr s^{-1}	−0.14	−0.13	−0.11
$F(t)$/Torr s^{-1}	−0.16	−0.15	−0.13
$[G(t)-F(t)]$/Torr s^{-1}	0.02	0.02	0.02

That is, the data fit the rate law, and we conclude that $k_c = \underline{0.02\ \text{Torr s}^{-1}}$.

31.28 $-\mathrm{d}p/\mathrm{d}t = k_c p(1-\theta)$ [Problem 31.2.6], $\theta = Kp'/(1+Kp')$ [31.3.3, p' is the pressure of the product gas].

Therefore: $\underline{-\mathrm{d}p/\mathrm{d}t = k_c p/(1+Kp')}$. For the reaction $\mathrm{A} \rightarrow \mathrm{B} + \mathrm{C}$, $p' = p_\mathrm{B} = p_\mathrm{o} - p$ [p is the pressure of A]. Then $-\mathrm{d}p/\mathrm{d}t = k_c p/(1 + Kp_\mathrm{o} - Kp)$ and

$$\int_{p_\mathrm{o}}^{p} [K - (1+Kp_\mathrm{o})/p]\,\mathrm{d}p = \int_0^t k_c \mathrm{d}t.$$

Therefore, $K(p-p_\mathrm{o}) - (1+Kp_\mathrm{o})\ln(p/p_\mathrm{o}) = k_c t$. On writing $F(t) = (p_\mathrm{o}/t)\ln(p/p_\mathrm{o})$ and $G(t) = (p-p_\mathrm{o})/t$. This becomes

$KG(t) - \{(1+Kp_\mathrm{o})/p_\mathrm{o}\}F(t) = k_\mathrm{c}$

or $G(t) = (k_\mathrm{c}/K) + \{(1+Kp_\mathrm{o})/Kp_\mathrm{o}\}F(t)$,

and so by plotting $G(t)$ against $F(t)$ we should get k_c/K from the intercept at $F(t) = 0$ and $1 + (1/Kp_\mathrm{o})$ from the slope.

31.29 Draw up the following Table:

t/s	0	315	750	1400
p/Torr	95	85	75	65
$F(t)$/Torr s^{-1}	–	−0.034	−0.030	−0.026
$G(t)$/Torr s^{-1}	–	−0.032	−0.027	−0.021

t/s	2250	3450	5150
p/Torr	55	45	35
$F(t)$/Torr s^{-1}	−0.023	−0.021	−0.018
$G(t)$/Torr s^{-1}	−0.018	−0.014	−0.012

These points are plotted in Fig. 31.11. The intercept lies at 0.013, and so $k_c/K = 0.013$ Torr s^{-1}.

The slope is 1.32, and so $(1 + Kp_0)/Kp_0 = 1.32$. Therefore $Kp_0 = 3.13$; and as $p_0 = 95$ Torr, $K = 0.033$ Torr^{-1}. Combining this with $k_c/K = 0.013$ Torr s^{-1} leads to $k_c = 4.3 \times 10^{-4}\,s^{-1}$.

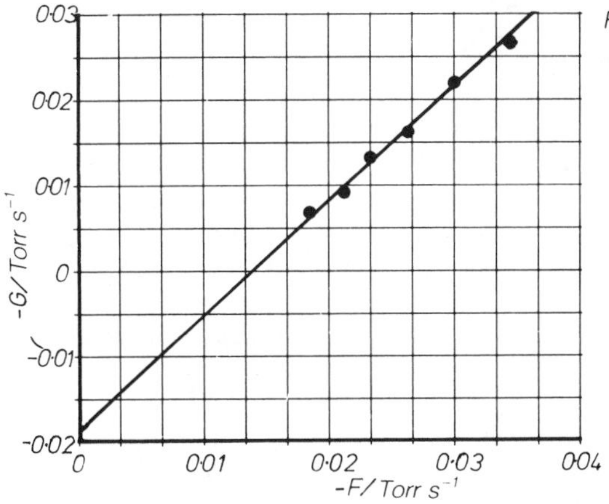

Fig 31.11

31.30 Refer to Fig. 31.12. Let the number density of atoms in the solid be $\mathcal{N}$. Then the number in the annulus between radii r and $r + \mathrm{d}r$ and thickness dz at a depth z is $2\pi\mathcal{N}r\mathrm{d}r\mathrm{d}z$. The interaction energy of these atoms and the adsorbate atom at a height R above the surface is

$$dU = -2\pi\mathcal{N} r\,dr\,dz\, C_6/\{(R+z)^2+r^2\}^3$$

if the individual atoms interact as $-C_6/d^6$ $[d^2 = (R+z)^2 + r^2]$. The total interaction energy of the atom with the (semi)infinite slab of uniform density is therefore

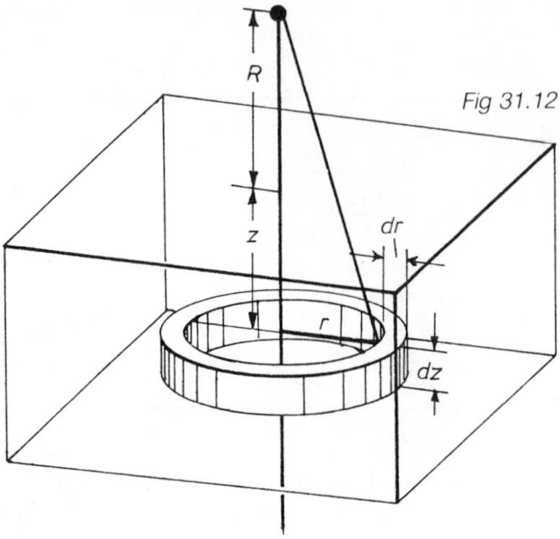

Fig 31.12

$$U = -2\pi\mathcal{N} C_6 \int_0^\infty dr \int_0^\infty dz\, r\{(R+z)^2 + r^2\}^{-3}.$$

$$\int_0^\infty \frac{r\,dr}{(a^2+r^2)^3} = \tfrac{1}{2}\int_0^\infty \frac{dr^2}{(a^2+r^2)^3} = \tfrac{1}{2}\int_0^\infty \frac{dx}{(a^2+x)^3} = \frac{1}{4a^4}$$

$$U = -(\pi/2)\mathcal{N} C_6 \int_0^\infty \frac{dz}{(R+z)^4} = \underline{-\pi\mathcal{N} C_6/6R^3}.$$

This confirms that $U \propto 1/R^3$. [A shorter way is to proceed by a dimensional argument, but we need the full form of U for the next Problem.]

31.31 $V(R) = 4\epsilon\{(\sigma/R)^{12} - (\sigma/R)^6\}$ [24.2.9] $= C_{12}/R^{12} - C_6/R^6$ [24.2.8]. Follow the procedure in Problem 31.30 for the R^{-12} term:

$$U = 2\pi\mathcal{N} C_{12} \int_0^\infty dr \int_0^\infty dz r\{(R+z)^2 + r^2\}^{-6} - \pi\mathcal{N} C_6/6R^3$$

$$= 2\pi\mathcal{N} C_{12} \int_0^\infty dz(1/10)(R+z)^{-10} - \pi\mathcal{N} C_6/6R^3$$

$$= 2\pi\mathcal{N} C_{11}/90R^9 - \pi\mathcal{N} C_6/6R^3 = 8\pi\epsilon\sigma^3\mathcal{N}\{(1/90)(\sigma/R)^9 - (1/12)(\sigma/R)^3\}.$$

For the equilibrium position, find R for which $dU/dR = 0$.

$dU/dR = 8\pi\epsilon\sigma^3\mathcal{N}\{(-1/10)(\sigma^9/R^{10}) + (1/4)(\sigma^3/R^4)\} = 0.$

Therefore $\sigma^9/10R^{10} = \sigma^3/4R^4$, or $R = (2/5)^{1/6}\sigma = \underline{0.858\sigma}.$

For $\sigma \approx 342$ pm [Table 24.4], $R \approx \underline{294 \text{ pm}}.$

31.32 $\theta = c_1 p_A^{1/c_2}$ [31.3.17]. Adapt this to adsorption from a liquid by noting that $w_s \propto \theta$ and replacing p_A by [A], the concentration of the solute. Then $w_s = c_1[A]^{1/c}$, or $\lg w_s = \lg c_1 + (1/c_2)\lg [A]$.

Draw up the following Table:

[A]/M	0.05	0.10	0.50	1.0	1.5
lg([A]/M)	−1.30	−1.00	−0.30	−0.00	0.18
$\lg(w_s/g)$	−1.40	−1.22	−0.92	−0.80	−0.72

These points are plotted in Fig. 31.13(a). They fall on a reasonably straight line with slope 0.42 and intercept −0.80. Therefore $c_2 = 1/0.42 = \underline{2.4}$ and $c_1 = \underline{0.16}$. [The units of c_1 are bizarre: $c_1 = 0.16 \text{ g mol}^{-0.42} \text{ dm}^{1.36}$].

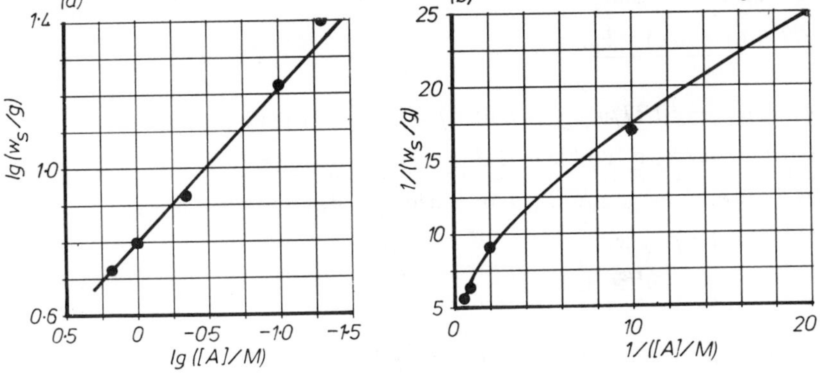

Fig 31.13

The adaptation of the Langmuir isotherm to the present case is $w_s = K[A]/(1 + K[A])$. In order to test this, write $1/w_s = 1 + 1/K[A]$.

Draw up the following Table:

[A]/M	0.05	0.10	0.50	1.0	1.5
1/([A]/M)	20	10	2.0	1.0	0.67
$1/(w_s/g)$	25	17	8.3	6.3	5.3

These points are plotted in Fig. 31.13(b). The plot is not such a good straight line, when fitted by eye, but the coefficients of determination are (a) 0.9491 and (b) 0.9865.

31.33 A general change in the Gibbs function for a 1-component system is

$\mathrm{d}G = -S\mathrm{d}T + V\mathrm{d}p + \gamma\mathrm{d}\sigma + \mu\mathrm{d}n$ [Section 25.4].

Let $G = G(g) + G(\sigma)$, $n = n(g) + n(\sigma)$; then

$\mathrm{d}G(g) = -S(g)\mathrm{d}T + V(g)\mathrm{d}p + \mu(g)\mathrm{d}n(g)$,

$\mathrm{d}G(\sigma) = -S(\sigma)\mathrm{d}T + \gamma\mathrm{d}\sigma + \mu(\sigma)\mathrm{d}n(\sigma)$.

At equilibrium $\mu(\sigma) = \mu(g) = \mu$. At constant temperature, $\mathrm{d}G(\sigma) = \gamma\mathrm{d}\sigma + \mu\mathrm{d}n(\sigma)$. Since $\mathrm{d}G$ is an exact differential this integrates to $G(\sigma) = \gamma\sigma + \mu n(\sigma)$. Therefore, $\mathrm{d}G(\sigma) = \sigma\mathrm{d}\gamma + \gamma\mathrm{d}\sigma + \mu\mathrm{d}n(\sigma) + n(\sigma)\mathrm{d}\mu$. But, since $\mathrm{d}G(\sigma) = \gamma\mathrm{d}\sigma + \mu\mathrm{d}n(\sigma)$, we conclude that $\sigma\mathrm{d}\gamma + n(\sigma)\mathrm{d}\mu = 0$. Since $\mathrm{d}\mu = RT\mathrm{d}\ln p = -(\sigma/RT)(\mathrm{d}\gamma/\mathrm{d}\ln p) = n(\sigma)$. Express $n(\sigma)$ as a volume absorbed V_a, $n(\sigma) = p^\ominus V_a/RT^\ominus$, and $\mathrm{d}\gamma$ as a kind of chemical potential $\mathrm{d}\mu'$ through $\mathrm{d}\mu' = (RT^\ominus/p^\ominus)\mathrm{d}\gamma$, evaluated at some standard temperature and pressure, then

$\underline{-(\sigma/RT)(\mathrm{d}\mu'/\mathrm{d}\ln p) = V_a}$.

31.34 $\mathrm{d}\mu' = -c_2(RT/\sigma)\mathrm{d}V_a$, $\mathrm{d}\mu'/\mathrm{d}\ln p = -c_2(RT/\sigma)\mathrm{d}V_a/\mathrm{d}\ln p$,

$\mathrm{d}\mu'/\mathrm{d}\ln p = -RTV_a/\sigma$ [Problem 31.33]. Therefore,

$-c_2(RT/\sigma)\mathrm{d}V_a/\mathrm{d}\ln p = -RTV_a/\sigma$, or $c_2\mathrm{d}\ln V_a = \mathrm{d}\ln p$ [$\mathrm{d}x/x = \mathrm{d}\ln x$],

or $\mathrm{d}\ln V_a^{c_2} = \mathrm{d}\ln p$. Therefore

$V_a^{c_2} \propto p$, or $\underline{V_a = c_1 p^{1/c_2}}$ [31.3.17].

31.35 $\theta = Kp/(1 + Kp)$ [31.3.3], $\theta = V_a/V_a^o$.

$p = \theta/K(1-\theta) = V_a/K(V_a^o - V_a)$.

$\mathrm{d}p/\mathrm{d}V_a = 1/K(V_a^o - V_a) + V_a/K(V_a^o - V_a)^2 = V_a^o/K(V_a^o - V_a)^2$.

$$\begin{aligned}\mathrm{d}\mu' &= -(RT/\sigma)V_a\mathrm{d}\ln p = -(RT/p\sigma)V_a\mathrm{d}p\\ &= -(RT/\sigma)\{K(V_a^o - V_a)/V_a\}V_a\{V_a^o/K(V_a^o - V_a)^2\}\mathrm{d}V_a\\ &= -(RT/\sigma)V_a^o\mathrm{d}V_a/(V_a^o - V_a).\end{aligned}$$

Therefore we have the several alternative forms

$$\mathrm{d}\mu' = -\left\{\frac{(RT/\sigma)V_\mathrm{a}^\mathrm{o}}{V_\mathrm{a}^\mathrm{o} - V_\mathrm{a}}\right\}\mathrm{d}V_\mathrm{a} = -\left\{\frac{(RT/\sigma)}{1-\theta}\right\}\mathrm{d}V_\mathrm{a}$$

$$= -\left\{\frac{(RTV_\mathrm{a}^\mathrm{o}/\sigma)}{1-\theta}\right\}\mathrm{d}\theta = (RTV_\mathrm{a}^\mathrm{o}/\sigma)\,\mathrm{d}\ln(1-\theta).$$

32. Dynamic electrochemistry

A32.1 $\ln j = \ln j_0 + (1-\alpha)\eta F/RT$ [32.1.10a].

$\ln(j_2/j_1) = (1-\alpha)(\eta_2 - \eta_1)F/RT.$

$\ln(75/55) = (1-0.39)(\eta_2 - 125\ \text{mV})/(25.7\ \text{mV}).$

$\eta_2 = 125\ \text{mV} + 13\ \text{mV} = \underline{138\ \text{mV}}.$

A32.2 $j_0 = j\exp[(\alpha-1)\eta F/RT]$ [32.1.10a]

$= (55.0\ \text{mA cm}^{-2})\exp[(0.39-1)(125\ \text{mV})/(25.7\ \text{mV})]$

$= \underline{2.83\ \text{mA cm}^{-2}}.$

A32.3 $j_L = (zFD/\delta)c$ [32.2.8]

$zFD_+ = RT\lambda_+/zF = (8.31\ \text{J K}^{-1}\text{mol}^{-1})(298\ \text{K})(+1)^{-1}(9.65\times10^4\ \text{C mol}^{-1})^{-1}$
$\times (61.9\times10^{-4}\ \text{S m}^2\text{mol}^{-1})$

$= 1.59\times10^{-4}\ \text{A m}^2\text{mol}^{-1};$

$j_L = (1.59\times10^{-4}\ \text{A m}^2\text{mol}^{-1})(2.50\ \text{mol m}^{-3})(4.00\times10^{-4}\ \text{m})^{-1}$

$= \underline{0.994\ \text{A m}^{-2}}.$

32.1 $j = j_0\{\exp([1-\alpha]\eta F/RT) - \exp(-\alpha\eta F/RT)\}$ [32.1.7],

$j/j_0 = \exp(\eta F/2RT) - \exp(-\eta F/2RT)$ $[\alpha = \frac{1}{2}]$

$= 2\sinh(\eta F/2RT)$ $[\sinh x \equiv \frac{1}{2}(e^x - e^{-x})]$.

$2RT/F = 51.4\ \text{mV}$ [endpaper 1, $T = 298$ K]. The function $j/j_0 = 2\sinh\{(\eta/51.4\ \text{mV})\}$ is plotted in Fig. 32.1.

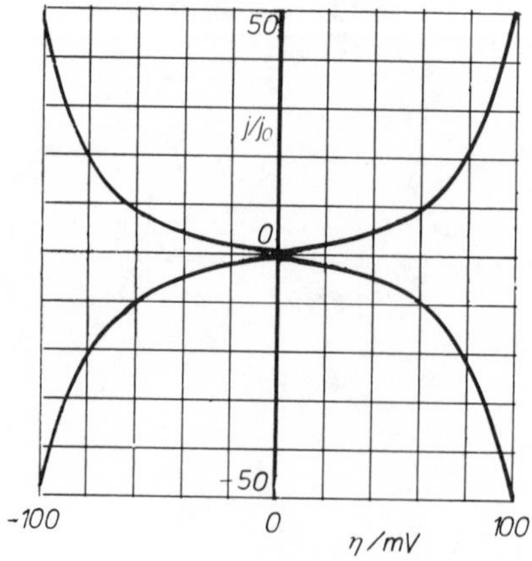

Fig 32.1

32.2 $j = 2j_0 \sinh(\eta/51.4\,\text{mV})$ [Problem 32.1] $= (1.58\,\text{mA cm}^{-2}) \sinh(\eta/51.4\,\text{mV})$.

(a) $\eta = 10\,\text{mV}$;

$j = (1.58\,\text{mA cm}^{-2}) \sinh(10/51.4) = \underline{0.31\,\text{mA cm}^{-2}}$ $[\sinh x = \frac{1}{2}(e^x - e^{-x})]$.

(b) $\eta = 100\,\text{mV}$;

$j = (1.58\,\text{mA cm}^{-2}) \sinh(100/51.4) = \underline{5.41\,\text{mA cm}^{-2}}$.

(c) $\eta = -5.0\,\text{V}$;

$j = (1.58\,\text{mA cm}^{-2}) \sinh(-5000/51.4) = \underline{-1.39 \times 10^{42}\,\text{mA cm}^{-1}\,(!)}$.

32.3 $I = jS$ [S is the area of the electrode] $= 2j_0 S \sinh(\eta/51.4\,\text{mV})$

$= 2 \times (2.5\,\text{mA cm}^{-2}) \times (1\,\text{cm}^2) \sinh(\eta/51.4\,\text{mV})$

$= (5.0\,\text{mA}) \sinh\{(E - E^{\ominus})/51.4\,\text{mV}\}$.

[The equilibrium e.m.f., E_e, is equal to $E^{\ominus}$ when $a = 1$.]

Draw up the following Table based on $E^{\ominus} = 771\,\text{mV}$.

E/mV	500	600	700	771	800	900	1000
$\lvert I\rvert$/mA	487	69.5	9.32	0	2.97	30.6	215

32.4 $E_e(Fe^{2+}, Fe^{3+}) = E^{\ominus}(Fe^{2+}, Fe^{3+}) + (RT/F)\ln\{a(Fe^{3+})/a(Fe^{2+})\}$ [11.4.5].

$E_e/\text{mV} = 771 + 25.7 \ln\{a(Fe^{3+})/a(Fe^{2+})\}$,

$\eta = \Delta\phi - \Delta\phi_e$ [32.1.5],

$\eta/\text{mV} = 1000 - \{771 + 25.7 \ln(a^{3+}/a^{2+})\} = 229 - 25.7 \ln(a^{3+}/a^{2+})$.

$I = 2j_0 S \sinh(\eta/51.4\,\text{mV})$ [Problem 32.3]

$= (5.0\,\text{mA}) \sinh\{4.46 - 0.50 \ln(a^{3+}/a^{2+})\}$.

Draw up the following Table:

$a(Fe^{3+})/a(Fe^{2+})$	0.1	0.3	0.6	1.0	3.0	6.0	10.0
$\lvert I\rvert$/mA	684	395	278	215	124	88	68.0

The current drops to zero when $4.46 = 0.50 \ln(a^{3+}/a^{2+})$, which is at $a^{3+}/a^{2+} = 7480$, for then $E_e = 1.00\,\text{V}$.

32.5 For a large overpotential (to be checked for consistency later),

$j \approx j_e \exp(-\eta F/2RT)$ [32.1.10, $\alpha \approx \frac{1}{2}$, $\eta < 0$].

$I = jS = 20\,\text{mA}$, $S = 1\,\text{cm}^2$ [Problem 32.3].

$\eta = (2RT/F)\ln(j/j_0)$

$= (51.4\,\text{mV})\ln(20\,\text{mA cm}^{-2}/2.5\,\text{mA cm}^{-2}) = \underline{110\,\text{mV}}.$

Note that $|\eta F/2RT| = 110\,\text{mV}/51.4\,\text{mV} = 2.1$, and $e^x \approx 8 \gg e^{-x} \approx 0.12$, and so the approximation is consistent (just).

32.6 The current density of electrons is j_0/e, because each one carries a charge of magnitude e. Therefore,

$J = j_0/(1.602 \times 10^{-19}\,\text{C})$.

(a) $Pt|H_2|H^+$; $j_0 = 7.9 \times 10^{-4}\,\text{A cm}^{-2}$ [Table 32.1];

$J = (7.9 \times 10^{-4}\,\text{A cm}^{-2})/(1.602 \times 10^{-19}\,\text{C}) = \underline{4.9 \times 10^{15}\,\text{cm}^{-2}\,\text{s}^{-1}}.$

(b) $Pt|Fe^{3+}, Fe^{2+}$; $j_0 = 2.5 \times 10^{-3}\,\text{A cm}^{-2}$ [Table 32.1];

$J = (2.5 \times 10^{-3}\,\text{A cm}^{-2})/(1.602 \times 10^{-19}\,\text{C}) = \underline{1.6 \times 10^{16}\,\text{cm}^{-2}\,\text{s}^{-1}}.$

(c) $Pb|H_2|H^+$; $j_0 = 5.0 \times 10^{-12}\,\text{A cm}^{-1}$;

$J = (5.0 \times 10^{-12}\,\text{A cm}^{-2})/(1.602 \times 10^{-19}\,\text{C}) = \underline{3.1 \times 10^{7}\,\text{cm}^{-2}\,\text{s}^{-1}}.$

32.7 There are approximately $1\,\text{cm}^2/(280\,\text{pm})^2 = 1.3 \times 10^{15}$ atoms in each square centimeter of surface. The numbers of electrons per second per atom in the three cases dealt with in the last Problem (taking Pb to be similar to Pt) are therefore $\underline{3.8, 12, \text{and } 2.4 \times 10^{-8}}$. (The last corresponds to less than one event a year.)

32.8 $\eta = (RT/F)j/j_0$ [32.1.9]

$|I| = |\{Sj_0F/RT\}|\,|\eta|$.

An ohmic conductor behaves as $|I| = |\Delta\phi|/|R_\Omega|$, and so the resistance may be identified as

$R_\Omega = RT/Sj_0F$

$= (2.4789\,\text{kJ mol}^{-1})/[(1\,\text{cm}^2) \times (9.6485 \times 10^4\,\text{C mol}^{-1})\,j_0]$

$= (2.57 \times 10^{-2}\,\Omega)/(j_0/\text{A cm}^{-2})$ [$\Omega = \text{VA}^{-1} = \text{J C}^{-1}\text{A}^{-1}$].

Therefore,

(a) $Pt|H_2|H^+$; $j_0 = 7.9 \times 10^{-4}\,\text{A cm}^{-2}$.

$R_\Omega = (2.57 \times 10^{-2}\,\Omega)/(7.90 \times 10^{-4}) = \underline{33\,\Omega}.$

(b) $Hg|H_2|H^+$; $j_0 = 0.79 \times 10^{-12}\,\text{A cm}^{-2}$,

$R_\Omega = (2.57 \times 10^{-2}\,\Omega)/(0.79 \times 10^{-12}) = \underline{3.3 \times 10^{10}\,\Omega}.$

32.9 $j = j_0\{\exp([1-\alpha]\eta F/RT) - \exp(-\alpha\eta F/RT)\}$ [32.1.7]

$$= j_0\{1 + ([1-\alpha]\eta F/RT) + \tfrac{1}{2}([1-\alpha]\eta F/RT)^2 - \ldots - 1 - (-\alpha\eta F/RT) - \tfrac{1}{2}(-\alpha\eta F/RT)^2 - \ldots\}$$

$$= j_0\{\eta F/RT + \tfrac{1}{2}(\eta F/RT)^2(1-2\alpha) + \ldots\}.$$

$$\langle j\rangle = j_0\{(F/RT)\langle\eta\rangle + \tfrac{1}{2}(1-2\alpha)(F/RT)^2\langle\eta^2\rangle + \ldots\}.$$

$$\langle\eta\rangle = 0 \quad \left[\left(\frac{\omega}{2\pi}\right)\int_0^{2\pi/\omega} \cos\omega t\, dt = 0, 2\pi/\omega \text{ is the period}\right],$$

$$\langle\eta^2\rangle = \tfrac{1}{2}\eta_0^2 \quad \left[\left(\frac{\omega}{2\pi}\right)\int_0^{2\pi/\omega} \cos^2\omega t = \tfrac{1}{2}\right].$$

Therefore $\langle j\rangle = \tfrac{1}{4}(1-2\alpha)(F/RT)^2 j_0\eta_0^2$.

Note that $\langle j\rangle = 0$ when $\alpha = \tfrac{1}{2}$, as stated.

32.10 $\langle I\rangle = \tfrac{1}{4}S(1-2\alpha)(F/RT)^2 j_0\eta_0^2$ [Problem 32.9]

$$= \tfrac{1}{4} \times (1\ \text{cm}^2) \times (1-0.76) \times (1/0.0257\ \text{V})^2 \times (7.90 \times 10^{-4}\ \text{A cm}^{-2}) \times (10\ \text{mV})^2 = 7.2\ \mu\text{A}.$$

32.11 Let η oscillate between η_+ and η_- around a mean value η_0, then if η_- is large and positive,

$j \approx j_0 \exp\{(1-\alpha)\eta F/RT\}$ [32.1.10a] $= j_0\exp\{\eta F/2RT\}$ $[\alpha = \tfrac{1}{2}]$.

η behaves as in Fig. 32.2(a). Therefore j is a chain of increasing and decreasing exponentials $j = j_0\exp\{(\eta_- + \gamma t)F/2RT\} \propto e^{t/\tau}$ during the increasing phase of η, and $j = j_0\exp\{(\eta_+ - \gamma t)F/2RT\} \propto e^{-t/\tau}$ during the decreasing phase, Fig. 32.2(b), with $\tau = 2RT/\gamma F$, γ some constant.

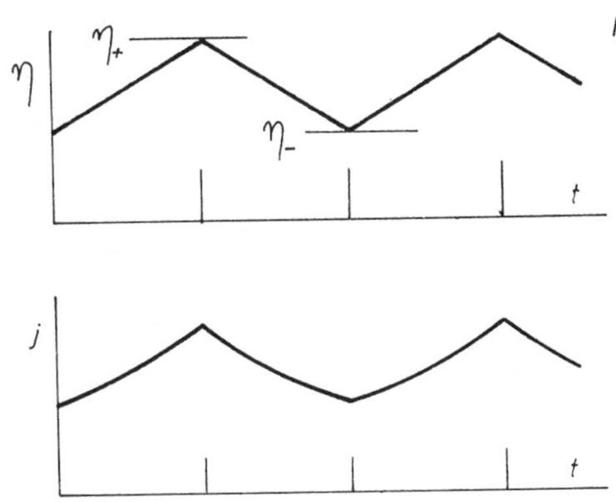

Fig 32.2

32.12 $\ln j = \ln j_0 + (1-\alpha)\eta F/RT$ [32.1.10a].

Draw up the following Table:

η/mV	50	100	150	200	250
$\ln(j^+/\text{mA cm}^{-2})$	0.98	2.19	3.40	4.61	5.81

These points are plotted in Fig. 32.3. The intercept is at -0.25, and so $j_0/\text{mA cm}^{-2} = e^{-0.25} = \underline{0.78}$. The slope is 0.0243, and so $(1-\alpha)F/RT = 0.0243\ \text{mV}^{-1}$. It follows that $1-\alpha = 0.62$, and so $\alpha = \underline{0.38}$.

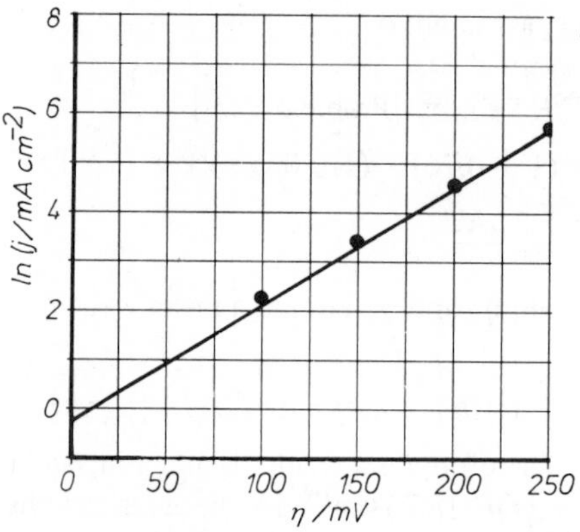

Fig 32.3

32.13 If η is large but negative

$j \approx -j_0 \exp(-\alpha\eta F/RT) = -(0.78\ \text{mA cm}^{-2})\exp(-0.38\eta/25.7\ \text{mV})$
$= \underline{-(0.78\ \text{mA cm}^{-2})\exp\{-0.015(\eta/\text{mV})\}}, \eta < 0.$

31.14 For deposition of cations a significant net current towards the electrode is necessary.

In the case of copper and zinc, we have $E_e(\text{Cu}) \approx 0.34$ V and $E_e(\text{Zn}) \approx -0.76$ V. Therefore deposition of copper occurs when E falls below 0.34 V (this is $\Delta\phi(\text{M, S})$ in the vicinity of the cathode), and continues until the copper is exhausted to the point that the limiting current density is attained. Then a further drop in potential difference, no longer compensated by a flow of copper ions, brings E below -0.76 V, when zinc is deposited.

32.15 Take activity coefficients as about unity; then the deposition of copper and zinc will occur when $E < E_e \approx E^\ominus$. This is also the condition for the first exponential in the Butler-Volmer equation [32.1.7] to dominate the second. Therefore the minimum potential differences are 0.34 V and −0.76 V respectively. When the concentrations are 0.01 M we have [Problem 32.14], $E_e = E^\ominus + (RT/2F)\ln 0.01 = E^\ominus - 0.06\text{ V}$ and so the deposition potentials for copper and zinc become (0.34 − 0.06)V = 0.28 V and (−0.76 − 0.06)V = −0.82 V respectively.

32.16 Hydrogen evolution occurs significantly (with a current density of 1 mA cm^{-2}, which is 6.2×10^{15} electrons $cm^{-2}\,s^{-1}$, which is 1.0×10^{-8} mol $cm^{-2}\,s^{-1}$, and which is about $10^{-4}\,cm^3\,cm^{-2}\,s^{-1}$, or about 1 cm^3 gas per hour per cm^2 of electrode surface) when the overpotential is − 1V. Since $E_e = E^\ominus + (RT/F)\ln a_{H^+}$ [11.4.3] $= -(59\text{ mV})\text{pH}$, this rate of evolution occurs when the potential difference at the electrode is about − 1.06 V ≈ − 1 V (when pH ≈ 1). But both $Ag^+ (E^\ominus = 0.80\text{ V})$ and $Cd^{2+} (E^\ominus = -0.44\text{ V})$ have more positive deposition potentials [for $a(M^+) \approx 1$] and so deposit first.

32.17 Zinc will deposit from a solution of unit activity when the potential difference drops below −0.76 V. The proton current towards the zinc electrode is then

$$j(H^+) = (5 \times 10^{-11}\text{ A cm}^{-2}) \times \exp(76\text{ mV}/51.4\text{ mV})$$
$$= 1.4 \times 10^{-4}\text{ A cm}^{-2} = 0.14\text{ mA cm}^{-2}.$$

This is a negligible evolution of hydrogen [Problem 32.6], and so zinc may be deposited from the solution.

32.18 Use the same argument as in the last Problem: the proton current toward the platinum electrode when zinc starts to deposit is

$$j(H^+) = (0.79\text{ mA cm}^{-2}) \times \exp(76\text{ mV}/51.4\text{ mV}) = 2.2 \times 10^3\text{ A cm}^{-2},$$

and so there will be massive hydrogen evolution before the zinc deposition potential is attained.

32.19 Since $E^\ominus(Mg, Mg^{2+}) = -2.37$ V [Table 12.1], magnesium deposition will occur when the potential difference drops to this value (if the Mg^{2+} ions are at unit activity). The hydrogen ion current is then

$$j(H^+) = (5 \times 10^{-11}\text{ A cm}^{-2})\exp(2370/51.4) = 5.3 \times 10^9\text{ A cm}^{-2},$$

which is a lot of hydrogen ($10^6\,dm^3\,cm^{-2}\,s^{-1}$), and so magnesium will not be plated out.

32.20 $j = (zcFD/\delta)\{1 - \exp(F\eta^c/RT)\}$ [32.2.7] $= j_L\{1 - \exp(F\eta^c/RT)\}$ as $j_L = (zFD/\delta)c$ [32.2.8]. The form of this expression is shown in Fig. 32.4 [η_c is negative].

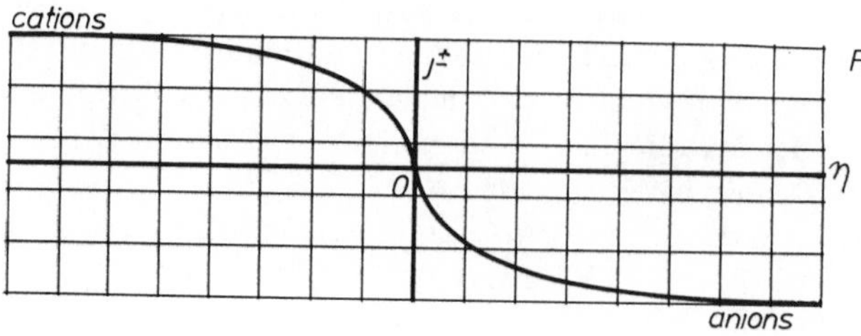

Fig 32.4

For an anion current, change the sign of η^c, so that the flow of anions approaches its limiting value as η^c becomes more positive, Fig. 32.4.

32.21 $j_L = (FD/\delta)c$ [32.2.8].

$\delta = \{FDc_X/j_L\} = (9.65 \times 10^4\,C\,mol^{-1}) \times (1.14 \times 10^{-9}\,m^2\,s^{-1})$
$\times (6.6 \times 10^{-1}\,mol\,m^{-3})/(28.9 \times 10^{-2}\,A\,m^{-2}) = 2.5 \times 10^{-4}\,m = \underline{0.25\,mm}.$

32.22 $j_L = (zFD/\delta)c$ [32.2.8], $D = (RT/z^2F^2)\lambda_+$ [Box 27.1].

$j_L = (zF/\delta)(RT/z^2F^2)\lambda_+ c = \underline{(RT/zF)(\lambda_+/\delta)c}.$

32.23 $j_L = (RT/zF)(\lambda_+/\delta)c$ [Problem 32.22]. Draw up the following Table using $j_L = I/S$, $S = 40\,cm^2$.

$c(Fe^{2+})/M$	0.250	0.125	0.063	0.031
$j_L/mA\,cm^2$	5.38	2.68	1.23	0.58

These points are plotted in Fig. 32.5. They fall as a good straight line with slope 22.3. It follows that $(RT/zF)(\lambda_+/\delta) = 22.3\,mA\,cm^{-2}/M = 0.223\,A\,m\,mol^{-1}$.

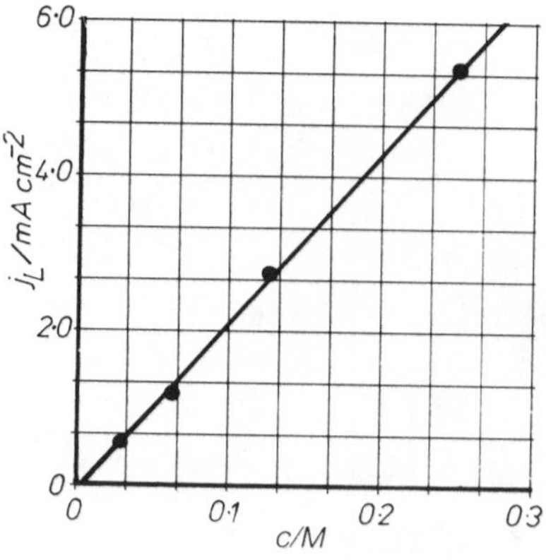

Fig 32.5

$(RT/zF)\lambda_+ = \frac{1}{2} \times (0.0257\ \text{V}) \times (40\ \text{S cm}^2\ \text{mol}^{-1}) = 0.514\ \text{V S cm}^2\ \text{mol}^{-1}$
$= 0.514 \times 10^{-4}\ \text{A m}^2\ \text{mol}^{-1}$.

Therefore, $\delta = (0.514 \times 10^{-4}\ \text{A m}^2\ \text{mol}^{-1})/(0.223\ \text{A m mol}^{-1}) = 2.3 \times 10^{-4}\ \text{m}$
$= \underline{0.23\ \text{mm}}$.

Use refractive index, spectroscopic, or ellipsometric measurements for independent determinations of λ.

32.24 $E_e(\text{M}, \text{M}^{z+}) = E^\ominus(\text{M}, \text{M}^{z+}) + (RT/z_+F)\ln a(\text{M}^{z+})$ [11.4.3].

Deposition occurs when E falls to $E_e(\text{M}, \text{M}^{z+})$. Simultaneous deposition will therefore occur when $E_e(\text{Sn}, \text{Sn}^{2+}) = E_e(\text{Pb}, \text{Pb}^{2+})$. This condition requires

$E^\ominus(\text{Sn}, \text{Sn}^{3+}) + (RT/2F)\ln a(\text{Sn}^{2+}) = E^\ominus(\text{Pb}, \text{Pb}^{2+}) + (RT/2F)\ln a(\text{Pb}^{2+})$

or $\ln\{a(\text{Sn}^{2+})/a(\text{Pb}^{2+})\} = (2F/RT)\{E^\ominus(\text{Pb}, \text{Pb}^{2+}) - E^\ominus(\text{Sn}, \text{Sn}^{2+})\}$
$= (2/0.0257\ \text{V})\{-0.126\ \text{V} - (-0.136\ \text{V})\} = 0.78$.

That is, $a(\text{Sn}^{2+})/a(\text{Pb}^{2+}) \approx \underline{2.2}$.

32.25 The values of $E^\ominus(\text{M}, \text{M}^+)$ are far apart, and so simultaneous deposition of the simple ions is unexpected. But the deposition potential is E_e, not $E^\ominus$, and so if the activities of the ions are modified, the values of E_e may be brought into coincidence. This may be achieved by adding a complexing agent (CN^-), which has a different stability constant for each metal ion.

32.26 The cell is described in Section 32.4(b).

R.H.E.: $\text{Cd(OH)}_2 + 2\text{e}^- \rightarrow \text{Cd} + 2\text{OH}^-, E^\ominus = -0.81\ \text{V}$.

L.H.E.: $\text{NiOOH} + \text{e}^- + \text{H}_2\text{O} \rightarrow \text{Ni(OH)}_2 + \text{OH}^-, E^\ominus = 0.49\ \text{V}$.

[Values taken from Table 12.1.] Therefore, the e.m.f. of the cell is $-0.81\ \text{V} - 0.49\ \text{V} = \underline{-1.30\ \text{V}}$, with Cd as the right-hand electrode. This is the maximum potential difference of the cell, when it is working reversibly. If the cell is working reversibly, yet is producing 100 mA, the power it produces is

$P = IE_e$ [32.3.6] $= (100 \times 10^{-3}\ \text{A}) \times (1.3\ \text{V}) = \underline{0.13\ \text{W}}$.

32.27 $E^\ominus = -\Delta_r G^\ominus/\nu F$ [12.3.1.], when species are in their standard states.

(a) $\text{H}_2 + \frac{1}{2}\text{O}_2 \rightleftharpoons \text{H}_2\text{O}, \Delta_r G^\ominus = -237.1\ \text{kJ mol}^{-1}$ [Table 4.1].

This reaction corresponds to the transfer of two electrons. Therefore

$E^\ominus = -(-237.1\ \text{kJ mol}^{-1})/2 \times (9.648 \times 10^4\ \text{C mol}^{-1}) = \underline{1.23\ \text{V}}$.

(b) $\text{CH}_4 + 2\text{O}_2 \rightleftharpoons \text{CO}_2 + 2\text{H}_2\text{O}$;

$\Delta_r G^\ominus = 2\Delta_f G^\ominus(\text{H}_2\text{O}) + \Delta_f G^\ominus(\text{CO}_2) - \Delta_f G^\ominus(\text{CH}_4)$
$= \{2(-237.1) + (-394.4) - (-50.7)\}\ \text{kJ mol}^{-1} = -817.9\ \text{kJ mol}^{-1}$.

As written, the reaction corresponds to the transfer of eight electrons. It follows that, for the species in their standard states,

$E^{\ominus} = -(-817.9\,\text{kJ mol}^{-1})/(8 \times 9.648 \times 10^4\,\text{C mol}^{-1}) = \underline{1.06\,\text{V}}.$

32.28 $E = E_e - IR_s - (2RT/zF)\ln f(I)$ [32.3.5a],

$f(I) = (I^2/A^2 j_0 j_0')/\{(1 - I/Aj_L)^{1/2}(1 - I/Aj_L')^{1/2}\}.$

$j_L = (zFD/\delta)c$ [32.2.8] $= (RT/zF)(\lambda_+/\delta)c$ [*Example* 32.3].

$R_s = l/\kappa A$ [27.1.1, A is actually the cross-section of the cell, but we shall suppose that the electrodes form opposite walls, and so their individual areas are the same as the cross-section]; $\kappa = \Lambda_m c$ [27.1.2]. Therefore $R_s = l/c\Lambda_m A$ [$\Lambda_m = \lambda_+ + \lambda_-$].

Therefore,

$E = E_e - (Il/cA\Lambda_m) - (2RT/zF)\ln f(I).$

$f(I) = (I^2/A^2 j_0 j_0')/\{[1 - (I/Aa\lambda_+)]^{1/2}[1 - (I/Aa'\lambda_+')]^{1/2}\}$

where $a = (RT/zF)(\lambda_+/\delta)c$

and $a' = (RT/z'F)(\lambda_+'/\delta')c'$.

32.29 $\text{Zn}|\text{ZnSO}_4(\text{aq})||\text{CuSO}_4(\text{aq})|\text{Cu}$

$l = 5\,\text{cm}, A = 5\,\text{cm}^2, c(\text{M}^+) = c(\text{M}'^+) = 1\,\text{M},$

$z = z' = 2, \lambda_+ = 107\,\text{S cm}^2\,\text{mol}^{-1}$ [Table 27.1], $\lambda_+' = 106\,\text{S cm}^2\,\text{mol}^{-1}$ [Table 27.1];

use $\lambda_+ \approx \lambda_+' = 107\,\text{S cm}^2\,\text{mol}^{-1}$.

$\Lambda_m \approx (107 + 160)\text{S cm}^2\,\text{mol}^{-1} = 267\,\text{S cm}^2\,\text{mol}^{-1}$ for both salt solutions,

$\lambda \approx 0.25\,\text{mm}$ [Problem 32.21]. $j_0 \approx 1\,\text{mA cm}^{-2} \approx j_0'^{+}$.

$E^{\ominus}[a \approx 1] = E^{\ominus}(\text{Cu}, \text{Cu}^{2+}) - E^{\ominus}(\text{Zn}, \text{Zn}^{2+}) = 0.34\,\text{V} - (-0.76\,\text{V}) = 1.10\,\text{V}.$

$R_s = (5\,\text{cm})/[(1\,\text{M}) \times (267\,\text{S cm}^2\,\text{mol}^{-1}) \times (5\,\text{cm}^2)] = 4\,\Omega.$

$j_L \approx j_L^+ = \tfrac{1}{2}(0.0257\,\text{V}) \times (107\,\text{S cm}^2\,\text{mol}^{-1}) \times (1\,\text{M})/(0.25\,\text{mm})$

$= 5.5 \times 10^{-2}\,\text{S V cm}^{-2} = 5.5 \times 10^{-2}\,\text{A cm}^{-2}.$

$$E/\text{V} = 1.100 - 3.8(I/\text{A}) - 0.0257\ln\left\{\frac{(I/5 \times 10^{-3}\,\text{A})^2}{1 - 3.6(I/\text{A})}\right\}$$

$$= 1.100 - 3.8(I/\text{A}) - 0.0257\ln\left\{\frac{4 \times 10^4(I/\text{A})^2}{1 - 3.6(I/\text{A})}\right\}$$

The function is plotted in Fig. 32.6.

32.30 $P = IE$ [32.3.6].

$$P/\text{W} = 1.100\,(I/\text{A}) - 3.8\,(I/\text{A})^2 - 0.0257(I/\text{A})\ln\left\{\frac{4 \times 10^4\,(I/\text{A})^2}{1 - 3.6(I/\text{A})}\right\} \quad \text{[Problem 32.29]}.$$

This function is also plotted in Fig. 32.6. Maximum power is delivered at about 120 mA and 0.6 V and is about 60 mW.

32.31 $E = E_e - (4RT/zF)\ln\{I/A\surd(j_0 j_0')\} - IR_s$ [32.3.5]
$P = IE = IE_e - aI\ln(I/I_0) - I^2R_s$, where $a = 4RT/zF$, $I_0 = A\surd(j_0 j_0')$.

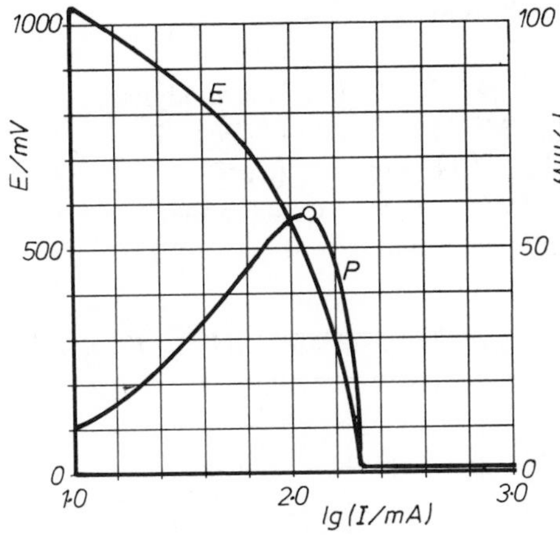

Fig 32.6

For a maximum, $dP/dI = 0$; therefore $E_e - a\ln(I/I_0) - a - 2IR_s = 0$, or
$\ln(I/I_0) = \{(E_e/a) - 1\} - 2IR_s/a$ for a maximum of P.

This is of the form

$\ln(I/I_0) = c_1 - c_2 I$

where $c_1 = E_e/a - 1 = (zE_eF/4RT) - 1$

and $c_2 = 2R_s/a = zFR_s/2RT$. For the present Problem use the data in Problem 32.29.

Then

$I_0 = A\surd(j_0 j_0') = 5\ \text{cm}^2 \times (1\ \text{mA cm}^{-2}) = 5\ \text{mA}$,

$c_1 = [2 \times (1.10\ \text{V})/(4 \times 0.0257\ \text{V})] - 1 = 20.40$

$c_2 = 2 \times (3.8\ \Omega)/[2 \times (0.0257\ \text{V})] = 148\ \Omega\ \text{V}^{-1} = 148\ \text{A}^{-1}$.

That is, $\ln(0.20I/\text{mA}) = 20.40 - 0.148(I/\text{mA})$.

Draw up the following Table.

I/mA	115	116	117	118	120
$\ln(0.20I/\text{mA})$	3.14	3.14	3.15	3.16	3.18
$20.40 - 0.148(I/\text{mA})$	3.38	3.23	3.08	2.94	2.64

The two sets of points are plotted in Fig. 32.7. The lines intersect at $I = 116.5$ mA, which therefore corresponds to the current at which maximum power is delivered The power at this current is

$$P = (116.5\ \text{mA}) \times (1.10\ \text{V}) - (0.0514\ \text{V}) \times (116.5\ \text{mA}) \ln(116.5/5) - (116.5\ \text{mA})^2 \times (3.8\ \Omega) = \underline{57.7\ \text{mW}}.$$

The point (116.5 mA, 57.7 mW) is marked on Fig. 32.7.

32.32 The reaction $M + M'^{+} \rightarrow M^{+} + M'$ has a thermodynamic tendency to proceed as written if $E_e(M'^{+}, M') > E_e(M^{+}, M)$. We have $E^{\ominus}(Fe^{2+}, Fe) = -0.44$ V and $E^{\ominus}(Cu^{2+}, Cu) = 0.34$ V [Table 12.1], and so $E^{\ominus}(Cu^{2+}, Cu) > E^{\ominus}(Fe^{2+}, Fe)$. Therefore, the reaction $Fe + Cu^{2+} \rightarrow Fe^{2+} + Cu$ has a thermodynamic tendency to proceed, and the iron components will corrode.

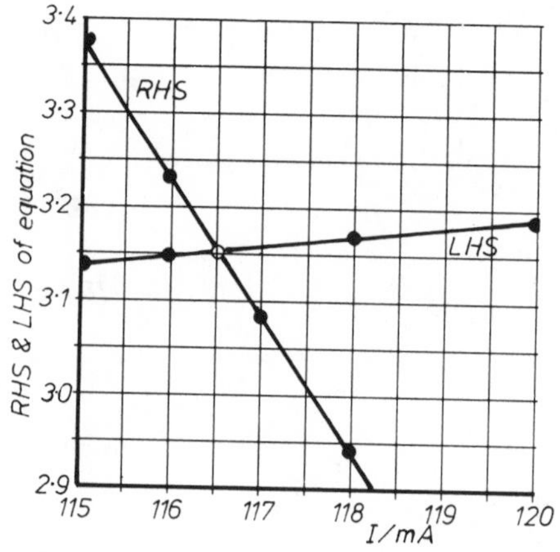

Fig 32.7

32.33 $2H_2O + O_2 + 4e^- \rightleftharpoons 4OH^-, E^{\ominus} = 0.40$ V.

$E_e = E^{\ominus} - (RT/F)\ln a(OH^-)$ [11.4.5].

But $a(OH^-)a(H^+) = K_w$, and so

$$E_e = \{E^{\ominus} - (RT/F)\ln K_w\} + (RT/F)\ln a(H^+)$$
$$= \underline{E^{\ominus} + (2.303RT/F)pK_w - (2.303RT/F)\text{pH}}$$

The exchange current density for H^+ on metals (e.g. iron) is typically of the order of 10^{-6} A cm^{-2}, whereas that for oxygen evolution is more typically 10^{-14} A cm^{-2}. Therefore the hydrogen reaction is kinetically favored.

32.34 (a) $E(H_2, H^+) = -(0.059\ \text{V})\text{pH} = -7 \times (0.059\ \text{V}) = -0.41$ V.

(b) $E(O_2, H^+) = (1.23\ \text{V}) - (0.059\ \text{V})\text{pH} = 0.82$ V.

$E(M, M^+) = E^\ominus(M, M^+) + (0.059\ V/z_+)\lg 10^{-6} = E^\ominus(M, M^+) - (0.35\ V/z_+)$.
Corrosion will tend to occur if $E(a)$ or $E(b) > E(M, M^+)$. Consult Table 12.1 for standard electrode potentials.

(a) Fe: $E^\ominus(Fe, Fe^{2+}) = -0.44\ V, z_+ = 2$
$E(Fe, Fe^{2+}) = -0.44\ V - 0.18\ V = -0.62\ V < E(\text{a and b})$.

(b) Cu; $E^\ominus(Cu, Cu^+) = 0.52\ V - 0.35\ V = 0.17\ V \begin{cases} > E(a) \\ < E(b). \end{cases}$

$E(Cu, Cu^{2+}) = 0.4\ V - 0.18\ V = 0.16\ V \begin{cases} > E(a) \\ < E(b). \end{cases}$

(c) Pb: $E^\ominus(Pb, Pb^{2+}) = -0.13\ V$,

$E(Pb, Pb^{2+}) = -0.13\ V - 0.18\ V = -0.31\ V \begin{cases} > E(a) \\ < E(b). \end{cases}$

(d) Al: $E^\ominus(Al, Al^{3+}) = -1.66\ V$,
$E(Al, Al^{3+}) = -1.66\ V - 0.12\ V = -1.78\ V < E(a)$ and $E(b)$.

(e) Ag: $E^\ominus(Ag, Ag^+) = 0.80\ V$.

$E(Ag, Ag^+) = 0.80\ V - 0.35\ V = 0.45\ V \begin{cases} > E(a) \\ < E(b). \end{cases}$

(f) Cr: $E^\ominus(Cr, Cr^{3+}) = -0.74\ V$,
$E(Cr, Cr^{3+}) = -0.74\ V - 0.12\ V = -0.86\ V < E(a)$ and $E(b)$.

(g) Co: $E^\ominus(Co, Co^{2+}) = -0.28\ V$,
$E(Co, Co^{2+}) = -0.28\ V - 0.15\ V = -0.43\ V < E(a)$ and $E(b)$.

Therefore, the metals having a thermodynamic tendency to corrode in moist conditions at pH = 7 are Fe, Al, Co, Cr if oxygen is absent, but if oxygen is present, all seven elements have such a tendency.

32.35 $I_{corr} = \bar{A}\bar{j}_0\ e^{FE/4RT}$ [32.4.3].
$\bar{A} = 0.25\ cm^2,\ \bar{j}_0 = 10^{-6}\ A\ cm^{-2},\ z \approx 1$
$E = -0.62\ V - (-0.94\ V)$ [Problem 32.34] $= 0.32\ V$.
$I_{corr} \approx (0.25 \times 10^{-6}\ A) \times e^{0.32/4 \times 0.0257}$
$\approx 6 \times 10^{-6}\ A$, $\underline{6\ \mu A}$.

APPENDIX: Linear regression

Very often in the solutions to the Problems, and in real life, it is necessary to draw the 'best straight line' through a set of points. The fitting can be done either by eye or better, by a simple recipe. We seek the constants a and b in the expression $y = a + bx$ that give closest agreement with the experimental points. The technique is called linear regression by the method of least squares. The recipe is as follows.

(1) Let (x_i, y_i) be the pairs of data points, i running from 1 to N.

(2) Form $\langle x\rangle = (1/N)\sum_i x_i$, $\langle y\rangle = (1/N)\sum_i y_i$

$$\langle xy\rangle = (1/N)\sum_i x_i y_i,$$

$$\langle x^2\rangle = (1/N)\sum_i x_i^2,\ \langle y^2\rangle = (1/N)\sum_i y_i^2.$$

(3) Then $a = \langle y\rangle - b\langle x\rangle$

$$b = \left\{\frac{\langle xy\rangle - \langle x\rangle\langle y\rangle}{\langle x^2\rangle - \langle x\rangle^2}\right\}.$$

(4) The quality of the fit is assessed by the coefficient of determination, r^2, where

$$r^2 = \left\{\frac{[\langle xy\rangle - \langle x\rangle\langle y\rangle]^2}{[\langle x^2\rangle - \langle x\rangle^2]\ [\langle y^2\rangle - \langle y\rangle^2]}\right\}.$$

The closer r^2 is to 1, the better the fit.